The Excel 5 SUPER BOOK

REFERENCE CARD

Super Keys

COMMAND	KEYS
Open new workbook	Ctrl+N
Open	Ctrl+O
Save	Ctrl+S
Save As	F12
Print	Ctrl+P
Cancel	Esc
Repeat	F4
Undo	Ctrl+Z
Cut	Ctrl+X
Copy	Ctrl+C
Paste	Ctrl+V
Fill down	Ctrl+D
Fill right	Ctrl+R
Clear contents of cell(s)	Delete
Add or remove bold	Ctrl+B
Add or remove italic	Ctrl+I
Add or remove strikethrough	Ctrl+5
Find	Ctrl+F
Replace	Ctrl+H
Find next	Shift+F4
Find previous	Ctrl+Shift+F4
Go to	F5
Exit Excel	Alt+F4

Navigating Worksheets

ACTION	KEYS
Move down one screen	Page Down
Move up one screen	Page Up
Move right one screen	Alt+Page Down
Move left one screen	Alt+Page Up
Move to next sheet in workbook	Ctrl+Page Down
Move to previous sheet in workbook	Ctrl+Page Up
Move one cell in any direction	Arrow key
Move up to the edge of current data region	Ctrl+up arrow
Move down to the edge of current data region	Ctrl+down arrow
Move left to the edge of current data region	Ctrl+left arrow
Move right to the edge of current data region	Ctrl+right arrow
Move among unlocked cells in protected worksheet	Tab
Move to beginning of row	Home
Move to beginning of the worksheet	Ctrl+Home
Move to last cell of worksheet	Ctrl+End
Move down through worksheet	Enter
Move up through worksheet	Shift+Enter
Move right through worksheet	Tab
Move left through worksheet	Shift+Tab

Function Keys

COMMAND	KEYS
Help	F1
Context-sensitive Help	Shift+F1
Activate formula bar	F2
Display Info window	Ctrl+F2
Note	Shift+F2
Display Paste Name dialog box	F3
Define	Ctrl+F3
Display Function Wizard	Shift+F3
Create	Ctrl+Shift+F3
Convert reference	F4
Close window	Ctrl+F4
Repeat last action	Shift+F4
Close Excel	Alt+F4
Go to command	F5
Restore window size	Ctrl+F5
Next pane	F6
Next window	Ctrl+F6
Previous pane	Shift+F6
Previous window	Ctrl+Shift+F6
Check spelling	F7

COMMAND	KEYS
Move	Ctrl+F7
Turn Extend mode on or off	F8
Size	Ctrl+F8
Turn Add mode on or off	Shift+F8
Calculate all sheets in all open workbooks	F9
Minimize the workbook	Ctrl+F9
Calculate the active sheet	Shift+F9
Activate menu bar if transition Navigation Keys check box is selected	F10
Maximize the workbook	Ctrl+F10
Activate shortcut menu	Shift+F10
Insert new chart sheet	F11
Insert new Excel 4.0 macro sheet	Ctrl+F11
Insert new worksheet	Shift+F11
Save As	F12
Open	Ctrl+F12
Save	Shift+F12
Print	Ctrl+Shift+F12

Navigating Worksheets

ACTION	KEYS
Extend cell selection by one cell	Shift+arrow key
Extend selection to beginning of row	Shift+Home
Extend selection to end of row	Shift+End
Extend selection to beginning of worksheet	Ctrl+Shift+Home
Extend selection to end of worksheet	Ctrl+Shift+End
Extend selection down one screen	Shift+Page Down
Extend selection up one screen	Shift+Page Up
Select entire row	Shift+Spacebar
Select entire column	Ctrl+Spacebar
Select entire worksheet	Ctrl+A
Return selection to active cell	Shift+Backspace

What Makes This Book SUPER

The Projects Workshop contains projects that can be used as templates or that can teach you how to strengthen future projects of your own.

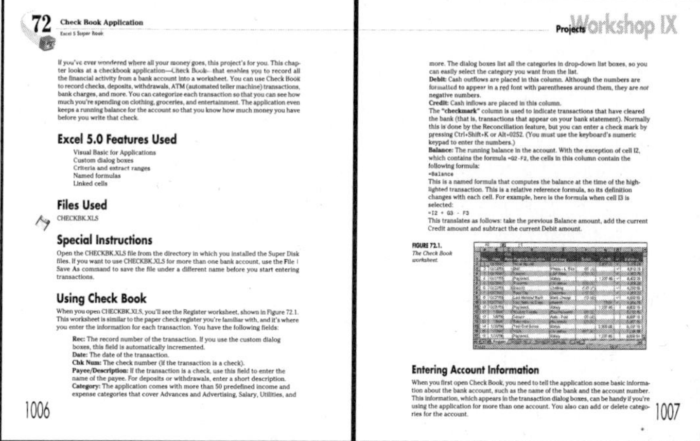

72 **Check Book Application**

Excel 5 Super Book

If you've ever wondered where all your money goes, this project's for you. This chapter looks at a checkbook application—Check Book—that enables you to record all the financial activity from a bank account into a worksheet. You can use Check Book to record checks, deposits, withdrawals, ATM (automated teller machine) transactions, bank charges, and more. You can categorize each transaction so that you can see how much you're spending on clothing, groceries, and entertainment. The application even keeps a running balance for the account so that you know how much money you have before you write that check.

Excel 5.0 Features Used

Visual Basic for Applications
Custom dialog boxes
Criteria and extract ranges
Named formulas
Linked cells

Files Used

CHECKBK.XLS

Special Instructions

Open the CHECKBK.XLS file from the directory in which you installed the Super Disk files. If you want to use CHECKBK.XLS for more than one bank account, use the File | Save As command to save the file under a different name before you start entering transactions.

Using Check Book

When you open CHECKBK.XLS, you'll see the Register worksheet, shown in Figure 72.1. This worksheet is similar to the paper check register you're familiar with, and it's where you enter the information for each transaction. You have the following fields:

Rec: The record number of the transaction. If you use the custom dialog boxes, this field is automatically incremented.
Date: The date of the transaction.
Chk Num: The check number (if the transaction is a check).
Payee/Description: If the transaction is a check, use this field to enter the name of the payee. For deposits or withdrawals, enter a short description.
Category: The application comes with more than 50 predefined income and expense categories that cover Advances and Advertising, Salary, Utilities, and

1006

Projects Workshop IX

more. The dialog boxes list all the categories in drop-down list boxes, so you can easily select the category you want from the list.
Debit: Cash outflows are placed in this column. Although the numbers are formatted to appear in a red font with parentheses around them, they are *not* negative numbers.
Credit: Cash inflows are placed in this column.
The **"checkmark"** column is used to indicate transactions that have cleared the bank (that is, transactions that appear on your bank statement). Normally this is done by the Reconciliation feature, but you can enter a check mark by pressing Ctrl+Shift+K or Alt+0252. (You must use the keyboard's numeric keypad to enter the numbers.)
Balance: The running balance in the account. With the exception of cell I2, which contains the formula `=G2-F2`, the cells in this column contain the following formula:
`=Balance`
This is a named formula that computes the balance at the time of the highlighted transaction. This is a relative reference formula, so its definition changes with each cell. For example, here is the formula when cell I3 is selected:
`=I2 + G3 - F3`
This translates as follows: take the previous Balance amount, add the current Credit amount and subtract the current Debit amount.

FIGURE 72.1. *The Check Book worksheet.*

Entering Account Information

When you first open Check Book, you need to tell the application some basic information about the bank account, such as the name of the bank and the account number. This information, which appears in the transaction dialog boxes, can be handy if you're using the application for more than one account. You also can add or delete categories for the account.

1007

What's on the Super Disk

The Baarns Utilities, Version 1: This top-rated program is a collection of tools designed to increase your Excel productivity. These utilities make your everyday Excel activities easier and give you power-user status without the power-user learning curve.

Super Projects

Included are templates for valuable projects, including

- Backing up worksheets within Excel
- Creating an icon for an open workbook
- Managing your finances
- Forecasting business performance
- Planning a trip
- Recording checkbook activity
- Tracking customer information
- Playing the Game of Life, Excel style

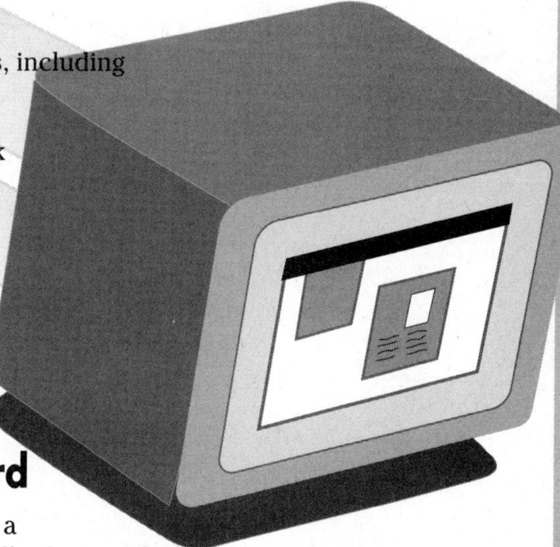

The Command Reference Card

The tear-out card in the front of this book is a convenient reference that lists many of Excel's shortcut keys.

EXCEL 5 SUPER BOOK

EXCEL 5 SUPER BOOK

Paul McFedries

SAMS PUBLISHING
A Division of Prentice Hall Computer Publishing
201 West 103rd Street, Indianapolis, Indiana 46290

Dedicated…

To Toronto Blue Jay outfielder Joe Carter. Thanks, Joe, for giving me and a few million of my closest friends the greatest thrill we've ever known.

FIRST EDITION

International Standard Book Number: 0-672-30385-X

Library of Congress Catalog Card Number: 93-85115

96 95 94 93 4 3 2 1

Interpretation of the printing code: the rightmost double-digit number is the year of the book's printing; the rightmost single-digit, the number of the book's printing. For example, a printing code of 93-1 shows that the first printing of the book occurred in 1993.

Composed in Cheltenham, Futura, Helvetica, and MCPdigital by Prentice Hall Computer Publishing

Printed in the United States of America

Trademarks

PUBLISHER
Richard K. Swadley

ASSOCIATE PUBLISHER
Jordan Gold

ACQUISITIONS MANAGER
Stacy Hiquet

MANAGING EDITOR
Cindy Morrow

ACQUISITIONS EDITOR
Gregg Bushyeager

DEVELOPMENT EDITOR
Rosemarie Graham

PRODUCTION EDITOR
Gayle L. Johnson

COPY EDITORS
Kristi Hart
Mary Inderstrodt

EDITORIAL COORDINATOR
Bill Whitmer

EDITORIAL ASSISTANTS
Sharon Cox
Lynette Quinn

TECHNICAL REVIEWER
Bradley D. Hiquet

SOFTWARE DEVELOPMENT SPECIALIST
Keith Davenport

MARKETING MANAGER
Greg Wiegand

BOOK AND COVER DESIGNER
Michele Laseau

DIRECTOR OF PRODUCTION AND MANUFACTURING
Jeff Valler

IMPRINT MANAGER
Kelli Widdifield

PRODUCTION ANALYST
Mary Beth Wakefield

PROOFREADING/INDEXING COORDINATOR
Joelynn Gifford

GRAPHICS IMAGE SPECIALISTS
Tim Montgomery
Dennis Sheehan
Sue VandeWalle

PRODUCTION
Nick Anderson
Ayrika Byrant
Laurie Casey
Lisa Daugherty
Rich Evers
Brook Farling
Kim Hannel
Stephanie McComb
Jamie Milazzo
Shelly Palma
Angela Pozdol Judy
Linda Quigley
Ryan Rader
Tonya R. Simpson
Tina Trettin
Suzanne Tully
Dennis Wesner
Alyssa Yesh

INDEXERS
Jennifer Eberhardt
Joy Dean Lee
John Sleeva
Suzanne Snyder

Overview

Workshop IV Databases and Lists

Workshop V Data Analysis

Workshop VI Excel 4.0 Macro Language

Workshop VII Visual Basic for Applications

Overview

Workshop VIII Advanced Topics

Workshop IX Projects

Contents

Workshop II Publishing and Printing

Workshop VI Excel 4.0 Macro Language

Workshop IX Projects

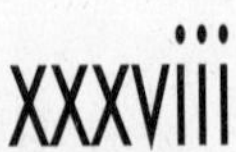

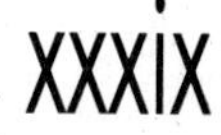

Acknowledgments

When I write books for Sams, putting together the acknowledgments is always the easiest part of the project, and one that I always look forward to. That's because the people I deal with in the Sams editorial department produce consistently excellent work that is a pleasure to behold.

For this project, everything began many moons ago when Acquisitions Editor Gregg Bushyeager asked me to take on the entire book for the new edition (I worked with three other authors in the first edition). Thanks, Gregg, and good luck in your new endeavors.

My main contact throughout this project has been Development Editor Rosemarie Graham. I'd like to thank Rosemarie for shepherding the book expertly through the editorial process, for her insightful comments concerning the structure of the book, and for not getting mad at me when I nagged her about when the next beta was shipping.

I want to give an extra big thank-you to Production Editor Gayle Johnson. Gayle's unflagging energy, keen eye, and calm-in-the-eye-of-the-storm demeanor played no small part in making this a decidedly better book.

The unsung heroes (or, in this case, heroines) of the publishing world are the Copy Editors who toil without fanfare and glory while they dot the i's and cross the t's of sloppy authors. For this book, Kristi Hart and Mary Inderstrodt did an outstanding job of whipping my prose into shape. Thanks to both of you for making me look good.

I'd also like to thank my friends in the Excel Beta Technical Support group and those on the Excel CompuServe forum. Believe me, they bailed me out of many a sticky wicket!

About the Author

Paul McFedries has worked with computers since 1975. After spending many years in the business world, McFedries quit the rat race to start his own computer consulting firm specializing in spreadsheet and database applications. McFedries also is a freelance writer with more than a dozen books to his credit, including the Sams Publishing books *DOS for the Guru Wanna-Be* and *Excel 4 Super Book* (as a coauthor). McFedries lives in Toronto, but he is open to offers of accommodation in a warmer clime.

Introduction

Before Windows 3.0 was introduced in 1990, Windows languished in the PC never-never land of good ideas whose time had not come. Its clunky interface and not-ready-for-prime-time features ensured it would remain a mere curiosity in a world in love with the DOS command line.

Sharing this software oblivion was Excel, one of the first major packages that took full advantage of the Windows environment. Originally ported from a highly successful Macintosh version, the first couple of releases of Excel waited patiently in the wings while its DOS peers (especially Lotus 1-2-3) took their bows on center stage.

When Microsoft introduced Windows 3.0 in the spring of 1990, the reaction from computer users everywhere was nothing short of overwhelming. Millions of people seeking increased productivity and an easy-to-use interface (not to mention a great game of Solitaire) followed Microsoft's vision of the PC environment of the future.

Excel, too, soon released its own version 3.0, and it rode Windows' coattails to the top of the Windows spreadsheet charts. People from all walks of life suddenly discovered that spreadsheets didn't have to be ugly and unintuitive. Why, it almost made number-crunching a pleasure (almost). Then, when version 4.0 shipped a couple of years later, it was a case of the best getting better. Everyone wondered what Excel could possibly do for an encore.

Welcome to Version 5.0

With the release of Excel 5.0, Microsoft's software designers have proven that they still have plenty of tricks up their sleeves. Although Excel 5.0 isn't a radical redesign (if it ain't broke, etc.), a fistful of new and improved features will please everyone from spreadsheet novices to power users. Here's a summary of just a few of these new toys:

A new workbook metaphor: Workbooks incorporate multiple sheets (worksheets, charts, macro sheets) into a single file. 5.0 has no contents page. Instead, you access each sheet simply by clicking on "tabs" at the bottom of the screen.

True 3-D capabilities: You can use the new workbook model to construct true 3-D references that act on multiple worksheets. You can even *spear* data. This means that data and formatting you add to one worksheet are automatically applied to other selected worksheets in the workbook.

Improved menu system: If the previous versions of Excel had an Achilles' heel, it was that its menu system didn't always make sense. For example, you had to look at the Formula menu to discover options such as **G**oto, **F**ind, and R**e**place. 5.0 features a revamped menu tree that makes much more sense. And if it still doesn't suit the way you work, you can create your own custom menu system using the Menu Editor.

Tabbed dialog boxes: Another problem with earlier Excel versions was that you often had to run a gauntlet of dialog boxes to find the feature you wanted. (This is a problem shared by many Windows products, including Windows itself!) Version 5.0 fixes this problem by moving some features onto submenus and using new *tabbed dialog boxes* for the rest. These dialog boxes include tabs that represent different, but related, options. For example, when you're formatting a range, the Format Cells dialog box has one tab for numeric formats, another for alignments, another for fonts, and so on.

More and better toolbars: Version 5.0 has more toolbars that do a better job of grouping related features. Best of all, these toolbars are highly customizable. You can move the buttons, delete them, add new ones, create entire new toolbars, and even design your own button faces.

More Wizards: Microsoft's Wizards are tools that take you through complex operations step-by-step. The ChartWizard and CrosstabWizard in version 4.0 were so successful that Microsoft decided to add a few more Wizards to 5.0. The FunctionWizard helps you build complex functions, the TextImport-Wizard makes the previously unreliable and tedious chore of importing text files a breeze, and the TipWizard "watches" how you use Excel and suggests more efficient methods.

Pivot tables: Excel 4.0's crosstab tables were a powerful way of summarizing data, but they suffered from an inherent rigidity. Viewing your table from a different perspective required almost as much work as setting up the table in the first place. 5.0's new pivot tables solve this problem. Not only do they make summary tables easy to create (using the PivotTable Wizard), but customizing the view also is a simple task. You simply drag "fields" from one part of the table to another.

Lists: Microsoft has incorporated many improvements to lists (what used to be called *databases*). These include an AutoFilter that enables you to filter data simply by selecting items from drop-down boxes right on the worksheet, a Subtotal feature that can add automatic subtotals to the data (for sums, averages, and more), and an improved Sort command that makes sorting faster and easier.

Microsoft Query: If you need to work with external databases, the new Microsoft Query program replaces Q+E. This program enables you to open and work with database files from many different formats. Its simple drag-and-drop interface makes it a breeze to get the data you need and import it into an Excel worksheet.

Worksheet dialog box controls: You can add dialog box controls directly to worksheets in 5.0. For example, you could add a spinner to increment and decrement numbers in a cell. For cells that require `TRUE` or `FALSE` entries, you could add check boxes.

OLE 2.0 support: Version 5.0 supports the OLE (Object Linking and Embedding) 2.0 standard. This enables you, among other things, to edit objects from OLE 2.0 *in-place*—that is, you stay in Excel, but the toolbars and menus change to that of the other application.

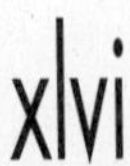

Visual Basic for Applications: Although Excel still includes its own macro language, Visual Basic for Applications is the macro programming environment of the future. It's a full-featured language that you can use for everything from the simplest macros to full-blown applications. Its debugging tools and its integrated dialog box sheets that enable you to create dialog boxes simply by "drawing" them on-screen make it the preferred choice for macro mavens.

What You Should Know Before Reading This Book

My goal in writing *Excel 5 Super Book* is to give you complete coverage of Excel. This means that I turn over every Excel stone, from basic tasks such as entering and editing data to more complex operations such as auditing a worksheet. However, I stick to the credo that it's better to learn only what you need to know, not everything there is to know.

To that end, you won't find many long-winded theoretical discussions or excruciatingly detailed instructions. Instead, I generally get to the point quickly so you can do what you have to do and then get on with your life.

One of the ways I keep the chapters uncluttered is to make a few assumptions about what you know and don't know:

- I assume you have knowledge of rudimentary computer concepts such as files and directories.
- I assume you're familiar with Windows and that you know how to launch applications and use applets such as Notepad and Control Panel.
- I assume you're comfortable with the basic Windows interface. This book doesn't tell you how to work with things such as pulldown menus, dialog boxes (although I do include some basics about Excel 5.0's new tabbed dialog boxes), and the Excel Help system.
- I assume you can operate peripherals attached to your computer, such as the keyboard, mouse, printer, and modem.
- I assume you have installed Excel and are ready to dive in at a moment's notice.
- I don't assume you have any prior knowledge of either Excel or spreadsheets in general. However, I do assume you're a quick study, so there's not a lot of hand-holding in the early chapters.
- I assume you have a brain and are willing to use it.

How This Book is Organized

To help you find the information you need, *Excel 5 Super Book* is divided into nine *Workshops* that group related tasks. The next few sections offer a summary of each Workshop.

Basic Skills Workshop

The Basic Skills Workshop takes you on a quick tour of some of Excel's fundamentals. You'll learn how to enter data, how to save and open workbooks, how to work with ranges, and how to use formulas and functions.

Publishing and Printing Workshop

The Publishing and Printing Workshop leads you through all of Excel's extensive publishing and printing features. You'll learn how to format cells, create your own styles, spell-check your worksheets, print reports, and more.

Graphics Workshop

The Graphics Workshop gives you an in-depth tour of Excel's charting and graphics features. The first part of the workshop includes chapters on creating and formatting charts, working with 3-D charts, and using chart overlays. The second part covers topics such as drawing lines and shapes, formatting graphic objects, and creating slide shows.

Databases and Lists Workshop

The Databases and Lists Workshop introduces you to Excel lists and external databases. You'll learn basic skills such as creating and sorting a list, using a data form, and filtering list records. This Workshop also covers more advanced skills including subtotals, list functions, querying external databases, and working with pivot tables.

Data Analysis Workshop

The Data Analysis Workshop shows you how to get the most out of Excel's impressive array of analytic features. The first chapter covers basic analysis techniques such as what-if, iteration, and trend analysis. The rest of the Workshop covers Excel's powerful analytical tools: Analysis Toolpack, Goal Seek, Solver, and Scenario Manager.

Excel 4.0 Macro Language Workshop

The Excel 4.0 Macro Workshop takes a close look at Excel's powerful macro language. The first few chapters show you the basics of command macros, function macros, and

macro programming. Subsequent chapters cover communicating with the user; debugging macros; creating custom menus, toolbars, and dialog boxes; and more.

Visual Basic for Applications Workshop

The Visual Basic for Applications Workshop introduces you to Excel's new macro programming language. First, you learn how to record simple Visual Basic macros, then I show you how to add your own code to make your programs more powerful and more flexible. You'll also learn how to build custom dialog boxes, menus, and toolbars; how to make Visual Basic respond to events; how to debug your macros; and more.

Advanced Topics Workshop

The Advanced Topics Workshop rounds out your Excel education with coverage of Excel's power features. You'll learn advanced techniques for ranges, formulas, and functions, as well as how to protect your data. Other chapters discuss such power tools as templates, outlines, and linking, as well as using dialog box controls on worksheets. The last three chapters show you how to exchange data with other applications (including Lotus 1-2-3) and how to customize Excel to suit the way you work.

Projects Workshop

An example is worth a thousand pages of theory. After all, it's one thing to be told how something works, and quite another to actually see it working. In this spirit, the Projects Workshop offers eight examples of Excel 5 in action. Each application offers various combinations of worksheets, charts, and macros to create a practical working model you can use yourself. Each chapter explains the project in detail, so you learn not only how to use the application, but also what's going on "behind the scenes." The files for each project are on the Super Disk that comes with this book, so you can follow along and even make your own modifications.

About the Super Disk

This book comes with a *Super Disk* that includes the following files:

- All the files used in the Projects Workshop.
- Miscellaneous files from examples used in this book.
- A full-featured, working version of the Baarns Utilities, an impressive collection of Excel utilities designed to make Excel more powerful and easier to use.

The disk icon tells you that the file being discussed is available on the Super Disk.

Special Features of This Book

Excel 5 Super Book is designed to give you the information you need without making you wade through ponderous explanations and interminable technical background. To make your life easier, this book includes various features and conventions that help you get the most out of the book and Excel itself.

Procedures: Throughout the book, each Excel task is summarized step-by-step in Procedures. These Procedures are numbered, and you'll find a convenient summary of the Procedure titles in the index.

Things you type: Whenever I suggest that you type something, what you type appears in a `monospace` font.

Commands: I use the following style and convention for Excel menu commands: **F**ile | **O**pen. This means that you pull down the **F**ile menu and select the **O**pen command.

Dialog box controls: The names of dialog box controls have bold accelerator keys: **C**lose.

Functions: Excel worksheet and macro functions appear in capital letters and are followed by parentheses: `SUM()`. When I list the arguments you can use with a function, *required* arguments appear in ***bold italic monospace*** type, and *optional* arguments appear in *italic monospace* type: `CELL(`***`info_type`***`,`*`reference`*`)`.

Visual Basic keywords: Keywords reserved in the Visual Basic language are printed in monospace type: `Range`.

This book also uses the following boxes to draw your attention to important (or merely interesting) information.

> **SUPER NOTE**
>
> The Note box presents asides that give you more information about the topic under discussion. These tidbits provide extra insights that give you a better understanding of the task at hand. In many cases, they refer you to other sections of the book for more information.

> **SUPER TIP**
>
> The Tip box tells you about Excel methods that are easier, faster, or more efficient than the standard methods.

SUPER

CAUTION

The all-important Caution box tells you about potential accidents waiting to happen. There are always ways to mess things up when you're working with computers. These boxes help you avoid at least some of the pitfalls.

SUPER

UPGRADE NOTE

In case you've upgraded to Excel 5 from an earlier version of Excel, the Upgrade Note box tells you about features that are new to Excel 5.

Workshop I

Basic Skills

Chapter 1

Entering and Editing Worksheet Data

A spreadsheet is only as useful—and as accurate—as the data it contains. Even a small mistake can render your results meaningless. Therefore, Rule Number One of good spreadsheet style is to enter your data carefully.

This chapter shows you the basics of entering and editing data in Excel worksheets. The more familiar you are with these basics, the less likely you are to make mistakes.

Excel's Data Types

Worksheet cells can hold three kinds of data: text, numbers, and formulas:

- Text entries usually are labels such as *August Sales* or *Territory* that make a worksheet easier to read, but they also can be text/number combinations for items such as phone numbers and account codes.
- The numbers you enter into a cell can be dollar values, weights, interest rates, or any other numerical quantity.
- A formula is a calculation involving two or more values, such as =2*5 or =A1+A2+A3. I discuss formulas in more detail in Chapter 5, "Building Formulas."

Entering Data

Worksheets have 16,384 rows (numbered from 1 to 16384) and 256 columns (labeled from A to IV). The intersection of each row and column is called a *cell,* and you use these cells to enter data.

Entering data in a worksheet cell is straightforward. All you do is move the active cell to the cell you want to use and then start typing. Your entry appears in both the cell and the *formula bar*—the horizontal strip below the toolbars (see Figure 1.1). You'll also see an *insertion point*—a blinking vertical bar—inside the cell; this marker shows you where the character or number you type will appear.

NOTE

The *active cell* is surrounded by a heavy border, and it has a small black rectangle in the bottom-right corner (see Figure 1.1).

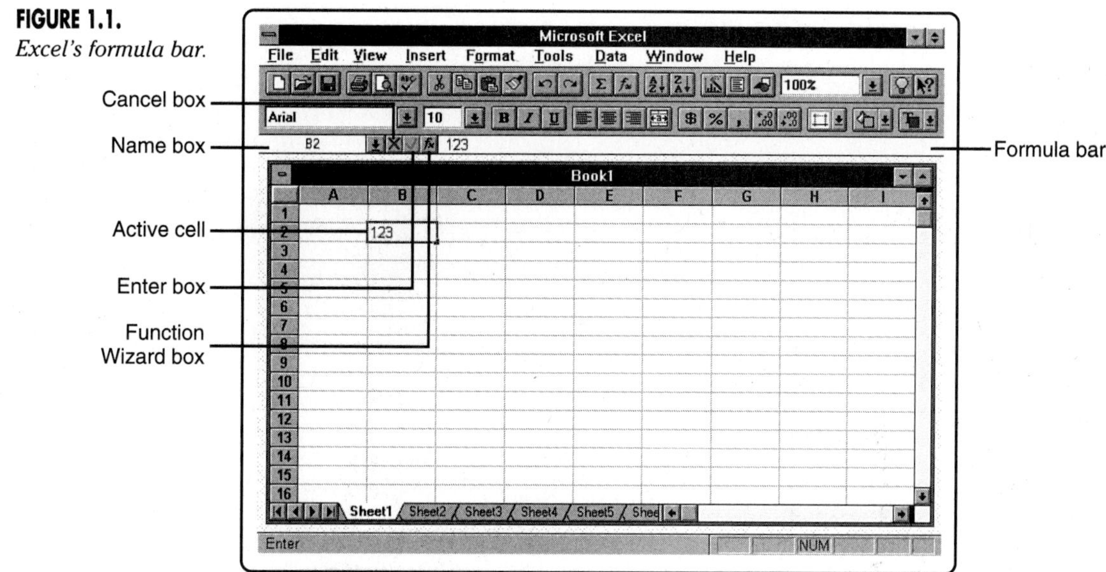

FIGURE 1.1.
Excel's formula bar.

Besides displaying what you type, the formula bar also shows you the following information:

Name box: Displays the address or name of the selected cell. If you're new to spreadsheets, a cell's *address* is a combination of its column letter and row number. For example, cell B2 is at the intersection of column B and row 2.

Enter box: This box appears only when you're entering data. You click on it to accept your data. You also can accept an entry by pressing Enter.

Cancel box: This box also appears only when you're entering data. You click on it to cancel data entry. If you don't have a mouse, you can cancel data entry by pressing the Esc key.

Function Wizard box: This box makes it easy to add Excel's built-in functions to your cell entries. See Chapter 6, "Working with Functions," to learn more about Excel's functions.

SUPER TIP

When entering numbers or text, you can accept your entry by pressing any of the arrow keys or by clicking on another cell. The active cell moves either in the direction of the arrow or to the selected cell. This is handy if you have, for example, a lengthy column of data to type in. This tip doesn't work for formulas because Excel assumes that you're trying to select a cell reference for the formula (see Chapter 4, "Working with Ranges").

Entering Text

In Excel, text entries can include any combination of letters, symbols, numbers, and spaces. Although text sometimes is used as data, you'll find that you mostly use text to describe the contents of your worksheets. This is very important, because even a modest-sized spreadsheet can become a confusing jumble of numbers without some kind of guideline to keep things straight. Text entries can be up to 255 characters long, but in general you shouldn't use anything too fancy or elaborate; a simple phrase such as *Monthly Expenses* or *Payment Date* usually will suffice.

Excel uses the property of *data type coercion* to determine the data type of a cell entry. For example, Excel automatically treats any cell that contains only numbers as a numeric type, but if the cell has at least one letter or symbol, Excel treats it as text. You can use this property to force Excel to interpret a number as a text entry by simply preceding the number with a single quote (').

SUPER NOTE

Not all symbols force Excel to interpret an entry as text. The exceptions are the forward slash (/), used in dates, the colon (:), used in times, and the following symbols:

```
. , + - ( ) $ %
```

The section in this chapter titled "Entering Numbers" tells you how these symbols affect numeric entries.

SUPER TIP

How can you tell whether a number in a cell is a text or numeric entry? One way is to look at how Excel aligns the data in the cell. Text entries are automatically aligned on the left, and numeric entries are aligned on the right.

SUPER TIP

Some zip codes begin with a zero. If you try to enter these as numbers, Excel strips off the leading zero. To avoid this, enter zip codes as text (that is, preceded by a single quote). This isn't a problem for the new zip codes (the ones that have the form 12345-0001), because the dash tells Excel that this is a text entry. Alternatively, you can set up a special numeric format for zip codes. See Chapter 7, "Formatting Numbers, Dates, and Times," for details.

Using Other Characters

In Excel, your text entries are not restricted to the letters, numbers, and symbols on your keyboard. With Windows' ANSI character set, you have access to all kinds of useful characters. To see this in action, select a cell, hold down the Alt key, and then type 0165 using the number keys on the keyboard's numeric keypad. (These entries won't work if you try to use the number keys across the top of the keyboard.) When you release Alt, the symbol for the Japanese yen appears. Table 1.1 lists a few other commonly used symbols and their Alt+*key* equivalents. (See Appendix B, "The Windows ANSI Character Set," for the complete set.)

Table 1.1. Some symbols from the Windows ANSI character set.

Symbol	*Press Alt+*
¢	0162
£	0163
©	0169
®	0174
¼	0188
½	0189
¾	0190
×	0215
÷	0247

Entering Numbers

Numbers are what worksheets are all about. You add them, subtract them, take their average, or perform any number of mathematical operations on them.

SUPER NOTE

If you enter a number and Excel displays ######## in the cell, it means that the number is too big to fit in the cell. See Chapter 10, "Working with Columns and Rows," to learn how to adjust column widths.

According to Excel's data type coercion, a cell entry that contains only numbers is considered a numeric data type. However, Excel also recognizes that you're entering a number if you start the entry with a decimal point (.), a plus sign (+), a minus sign (–), or a dollar sign ($). Here are some other rules for entering numbers:

- You can enter percentages by following the number with a percent sign (%). Excel displays both the number and the percent sign in the cell, but it stores the number as a decimal. For example, an entry such as 15% is stored as 0.15.
- You can use scientific notation when entering numbers. For example, to enter the number 3,879,000,000, you could type `3.88E+09`.
- You can use parentheses to indicate a negative number. If you make an entry such as (125), Excel assumes you mean negative 125.
- You can use commas to separate thousands, but you must make sure that each comma appears in the appropriate place. Excel will interpret an entry such as 12,34 as text.
- If you want to enter a fraction, you need to type an integer, a space, and then the fraction (`5 1/8`, for example). This is true even if you're entering only the fractional part. In this case, you would need to type a zero, a space, and then the fraction, or Excel would interpret the entry as a date. For example, `0 1/8` is the fraction one-eighth, but `1/8` is January 8th.

For more information on number formatting, see Chapter 7, "Formatting Numbers, Dates, and Times."

> **SUPER CAUTION**
>
> A common source of errors in worksheets is to mistakenly enter a lowercase L (l) instead of a one (1) or an uppercase O instead of a zero (0). Watch for these errors when you enter your data.

Entering Dates and Times

Excel uses *serial numbers* to represent specific dates and times. To compute a date serial number, Excel uses December 31, 1899 as an arbitrary starting point and then counts the number of days that have passed since then. For example, the date serial number for January 1, 1900 is 1; January 2, 1900 is 2; and so on. Table 1.2 displays some sample date serial numbers.

Table 1.2. Examples of date serial numbers.

Serial Number	*Date*
366	December 31, 1900
16,229	June 6, 1944
34,334	December 31, 1993

To compute a time serial number, Excel expresses time as a decimal fraction of the 24-hour day to get a number between 0 and 1. The starting point, midnight, is given the value 0, and noon—halfway through the day—has a serial number of 0.5. Table 1.3 displays some sample time serial numbers.

Table 1.3. Examples of time serial numbers.

Serial Number	*Time*
0.25	6:00:00 a.m.
0.375	9:00:00 a.m.
0.70833	5:00:00 p.m.
.99999	11:59:59 p.m.

You can combine the two types of serial numbers. For example, 34,334.5 represents noon on December 31, 1993.

The advantage of using serial numbers in this way is that it makes calculations involving dates and times very easy. Because a date or a time is really just a number, any mathematical operation you can perform on a number also can be performed on a date. This is invaluable for worksheets that track delivery times, monitor the aging of accounts receivable or accounts payable invoices, calculate invoice discount dates, and so on.

Although it's true that serial numbers make it easier for the computer to manipulate dates and times, it's not the best format for humans to comprehend. For example, the number 25,404.95555 is meaningless, but the moment it represents (July 20, 1969 at 10:56 p.m. EDT) is one of the great moments in history (Neil Armstrong setting foot on the moon). Fortunately, Excel takes care of the conversion between these formats, so you never have to worry about it. To enter a date or a time, use any of the formats outlined in Table 1.4.

Table 1.4. Excel date and time formats.

Format	*Example*
m/d/yy	8/23/94
d–mmm–yy	23–Aug–94
d–mmm	23–Aug (Excel assumes the current year)
mmm–yy	Aug–93 (Excel assumes the first day of the month)
h:mm:ss AM/PM	10:35:10 p.m.
h:mm AM/PM	10:35 p.m.
h:mm:ss	22:35:10
h:mm	22:35
m/d/y h:mm	8/23/94 22:35

SUPER TIP

Here are a couple of shortcuts that will enable you to enter dates and times quickly. To enter the current date in a cell, press Ctrl+; (semicolon). To enter the current time, press Ctrl+: (colon).

Table 1.4 represents Excel's built-in formats, but these are not set in stone. You're free to mix and match these formats as long as you observe the following rules:

- You can use either a forward slash (/) or a hyphen (–) as a date separator. Always use a colon (:) as a time separator.
- You can combine any date and time format as long as you separate them with a space.
- You can enter date and time values using either uppercase or lowercase letters. Excel automatically adjusts the capitalization to its standard format.
- To display times using the 12-hour clock, include either AM (or just A) or PM (or just P). If you leave these off, Excel will use the 24-hour clock.

For more information on formatting dates and times, see Chapter 7, "Formatting Numbers, Dates, and Times."

Tips for Easier Data Entry

Data entry is the unglamorous side of worksheets, but it's a necessary chore. To make life easier, this section presents a few tips designed to ease your data-entry burden.

Moving After Entering Data

I mentioned earlier that you can confirm your data and move to the next cell at the same time by pressing one of the arrow keys. This works fine, but many people still prefer to press the Enter key, either out of habit or because it's a bigger target to aim for. Normally, Excel moves the active cell down one row after you press Enter. If you're entering a column of numbers and Excel doesn't move down one row after you press Enter, you need to activate this feature. To do this, first select the **T**ools | **O**ptions command to display the Options dialog box. Select the Edit tab to display Excel's editing options (see Figure 1.2). Next, activate the **M**ove Selection after Enter check box and click on OK or press Enter. Excel now will move the cell pointer down each time you press Enter to confirm your data.

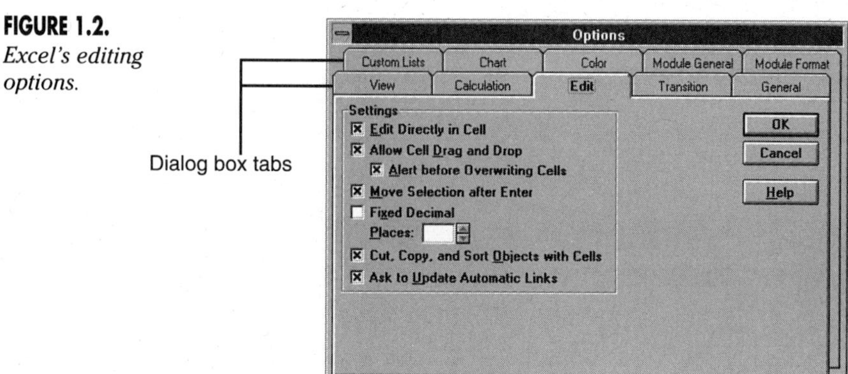

FIGURE 1.2.
Excel's editing options.

SUPER UPGRADE NOTE

Tabbed dialog boxes are a new feature in Excel 5.0 that you might not be familiar with. Each of the tabs at the top of the dialog box represents a related group of controls. (For example, the Edit tab in the Options dialog box holds all of Excel's editing options.) To select a tab, either click on it or hold down the Ctrl key and use the arrow keys to move through the tabs.

Faster Numeric Keypad Entries

If you like to use the keyboard's numeric keypad to enter numbers, you can set things up so that Excel automatically inserts a decimal point. Select the Tools | Options command, then select the Edit tab in the Options dialog box. Activate the Fixed Decimal check box in the Options dialog box (see Figure 1.2) and use the Places edit box to enter the number of decimal places you want to use. Click on OK or press Enter to put the option into effect.

To enter a number such as 1234.56, you just type `123456` and press Enter. Excel automatically inserts the decimal point. If you need to override the automatic decimal, just type the decimal in the appropriate spot as you enter the number.

Copying and Moving Cells

If you need to make a copy of a cell, you could just retype it, but Excel's Copy command is much easier. All you do is select the cell you want to copy and then choose Edit | Copy. Next, select the cell that will receive the copy, then select Edit | Paste. Excel enters the data in the new cell. If you need to make other copies, just select the appropriate cells and choose Edit | Paste.

If you need to *move* a cell to a different location, the procedure is slightly different. Select the cell you want to move and choose **Edit** | **Cut**. Select the new destination and choose **Edit** | **Paste**. Excel moves the data to the new location.

SUPER TIP

For faster copying and moving, use the following shortcut keys: Ctrl+C for Copy, Ctrl+X for Cut, and Ctrl+V for Paste. Also, if you're going to paste your cut or copied cell only once, you can just press Enter instead of selecting **Edit** | **Paste**.

SUPER TIP

If you want the active cell to have the same data as the cell directly above it, just press Ctrl+" (quotation marks) and press Enter to make a quick copy.

For more information on the Cut, Copy, and Paste commands, see Chapter 4, "Working with Ranges."

Excel's Navigation Keys

Data entry goes much faster if you can navigate your worksheets quickly. Table 1.5 lists the most commonly used navigation keys.

Table 1.5. Excel's worksheet navigation keys.

Key	*Action*
Arrow keys	Moves left, right, up, or down one cell
Home	Moves to the beginning of the row
Page Up	Moves up one screen
Page Down	Moves down one screen
Ctrl+Home	Moves to the beginning of the worksheet
Ctrl+End	Moves to the bottom-right corner of the worksheet
Ctrl+arrow keys	Moves in the direction of the arrow to the next nonblank cell if the current cell is blank, or to the last nonblank cell if the current cell is nonblank

SUPER TIP

The approximate mouse equivalent of the Ctrl+arrow keys combination is to position the mouse pointer on an edge of the cell (the pointer changes to an arrow) and then double-click. If you're on a blank cell, Excel moves to the last blank cell before any data. If you're on a nonblank cell, Excel moves to the last nonblank cell. The direction Excel moves depends on which edge you double-click. For example, double-clicking on the right edge moves the active cell to the right.

Finding Data

If you need to find a particular piece of data, you could scroll through the worksheet, but Excel has a Find feature that is both faster and more accurate. Procedure 1.1 shows you how to use it.

PROCEDURE 1.1. USING EXCEL'S FIND FEATURE.

1. Select **E**dit | **F**ind. Excel displays the Find dialog box, as shown in Figure 1.3.

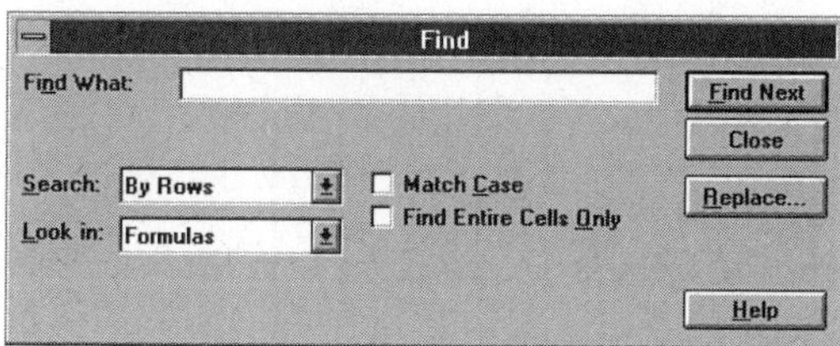

FIGURE 1.3.
Use the Find dialog box to search for worksheet data.

2. Enter what you want to search for in the Fi**n**d What edit box.
3. In the **S**earch drop-down list, select By Rows to search across the worksheet rows starting from the current cell, or select By Columns to search through the worksheet columns.
4. Tell Excel what types of cells to search through by selecting either Formulas, Values, or Notes from the **L**ook in drop-down list.
5. For a case-sensitive search, activate the Match **C**ase check box.
6. If you want your search text to match the entire cell's contents, select the Find Entire Cells **O**nly check box.
7. Select **F**ind Next to search forward (that is, down columns and from left to right). To search backward (up columns and from right to left), hold down the Shift key and click on **F**ind Next.

SUPER TIP

To display the Find dialog box quickly, press Ctrl+F. When you exit the Find dialog box, you can find the next match by pressing Shift+F4. To find the previous match, press Ctrl+Shift+F4.

Instead of searching for exact matches, you can use *wildcards* to substitute for one or more characters. Use the question mark (?) to replace a single character and the asterisk (*) to replace a group of characters. For example, entering `??st` in the **Find** What edit box will match all four-letter words that end with *st* (such as *east* and *west*). The search text $*.95 will find all dollar amounts that end with 95 cents.

SUPER NOTE

If you want to search for an expression that includes either ? or *, precede that character with a tilde (~). For example, to find 24.95*1.07, you would enter `24.95~*1.07` in the **Find** What text box.

Replacing Data

If you need to make global changes to a worksheet (such as changing all labels with *Exp.* to *Expenses*), Excel's Replace feature makes it easy. Procedure 1.2 outlines the steps.

PROCEDURE 1.2. USING EXCEL'S REPLACE FEATURE.

1. Select the **Edit** | Replace command. Excel displays the Replace dialog box, shown in Figure 1.4.

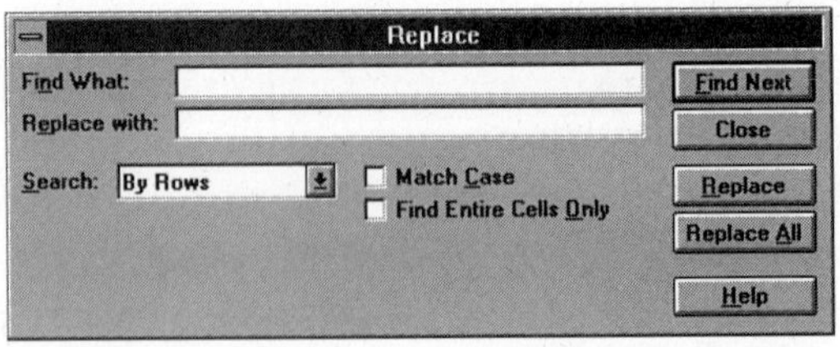

FIGURE 1.4.
Use the Replace dialog box to search for and replace worksheet data.

2. Enter what you want to replace in the Find What edit box.
3. Enter the replacement text in the Replace with edit box.
4. Select any other options you want to use (see Procedure 1.1 for details).
5. To replace every instance of the text in the Find What box, click on the Replace All button. To replace only selected matches, choose Find Next and, when you find a match you want to replace, click on the Replace button.

SUPER TIP

To display the Replace dialog box quickly, press Ctrl+H.

Editing Cell Contents

If you make a mistake when entering data, or you want to update the contents of a cell, you need to edit the cell to get the correct value. One option you have is just to select the cell and begin typing the new data. This overwrites the previous contents with whatever you type. Often, however, you need to change only a single character or value, so retyping the entire cell would be wasteful. Instead, you can modify the contents of a cell without erasing everything in the cell. To edit a cell, follow the steps inProcedure 1.3.

PROCEDURE 1.3. EDITING A WORKSHEET CELL.

1. Select the cell you want to edit. The cell contents appear in the formula bar's text box.
2. Double-click on the cell or press F2. The insertion point appears inside the cell at the end of the entry.
3. Use the mouse and keyboard actions described in Table 1.6 to edit the contents of the cell.
4. Confirm your changes by clicking on the Enter box or by pressing Enter. To cancel the procedure without saving your changes, click on Cancel or press the Esc key.

Table 1.6. Mouse and keyboard editing actions.

Action	*Result*
Press left or right arrow or click one character to the left or right	Moves the cursor left or right one character
Press Home or End or click at the beginning or end of the entry	Moves the cursor to the beginning or end of the entry
Press Ctrl+left arrow or Ctrl+right arrow or click on the character	Moves the cursor left or right one word
Click to the left of the first character and drag to the last character, or hold down Shift and press left or right arrow	Selects characters
Press Backspace	Deletes the character to the left of the cursor or deletes highlighted characters
Press Delete	Deletes characters to the right of the cursor or deletes highlighted characters
Press Insert	Toggles between insert mode and overstrike mode

Clearing a Cell's Contents

If you no longer need the contents of a cell, you can clear it by following the steps in Procedure 1.4.

PROCEDURE 1.4. CLEARING THE CONTENTS OF A CELL.

1. Select the cell you want to clear.
2. Choose **E**dit | Cle**a**r. A submenu of Clear commands appears.
3. Select **C**ontents to clear only the cell's contents, **F**ormats to clear the formatting, and **N**otes to clear the cell's notes. (See Chapter 15, "Adding Comments with Text Boxes and Notes," to learn about cell notes.) To clear everything, select **A**ll.

SUPER TIP

To clear a cell's contents quickly, press the Delete key. You also can right-click on the cell and select the Clear Contents command from the shortcut menu.

SUPER CAUTION

Some people like to "clear" the contents of a cell by highlighting the cell and entering a space. Unfortunately, these cells are not empty at all: they contain a text entry consisting of a single space. This uses up memory, it can cause problems when you navigate with the End key, and it can cause macros to behave strangely. Always use the method just mentioned when you clear the contents of a cell.

Using the Undo Feature

Because nobody's perfect, occasionally you'll make a mistake when you edit or erase your worksheet data. Fortunately, Excel comes with an Undo feature that enables you to recover from your mistakes.

Every time you make a change to your worksheet, Excel keeps a record of that change in memory. Undo works by examining this record and reversing the change to restore the worksheet to its previous state. It's important to remember that only your most recent change is stored in memory. If you make a mistake and then make further changes to the worksheet, you won't be able to undo the error.

To use Undo, simply select the **U**ndo command from the **E**dit menu. The actual name of the command depends on the operation you're trying to reverse. For example, if you accidentally clear a cell, the **U**ndo command is called **U**ndo Clear.

SUPER TIP

Press Ctrl+Z to activate Undo without accessing a menu.

Click on this tool in the Standard toolbar to undo your most recent action.

Using the Repeat Feature

If you need to repeat a command or a dialog box selection, you often don't have to go through all of the original steps. Excel's Repeat feature enables you to redo an action quickly.

To use Repeat, select the **R**epeat command from the **E**dit menu. As with **U**ndo, the actual name of the command depends on the operation you've just completed. For example, if you've just cleared a cell, the Repeat command is called **R**epeat Clear.

> **SUPER TIP**
>
> Press F4 to activate Repeat without accessing a menu.

Click on this tool in the Utility toolbar to repeat your most recent action.

Chapter

2

Workbook Basics

Now that you know how to enter data into a worksheet, you need to know how to save your workbooks for posterity. This chapter shows you how, as well as covering other basics, such as opening and closing a worksheet, starting a new workbook, and deleting a workbook.

About Excel 5.0's New Workbooks

Imagine reading a book that contains your company's sales information. It would show reports such as sales by region, sales by sales rep, sales by product, and so on. It would make sense if each page of the book represented a particular month. Page one could be January sales, page two could be February sales, and so on. By placing labeled tabs on each page, you could easily find, for example, sales by region for April. The last page of the book could show the totals for the year. You can extend this idea to include a second book showing monthly expenses, and a third book—the profit and loss book—which combines information from the other two volumes.

This is how Excel 5.0's files are organized. Each file is called a *workbook,* and each workbook contains one or more *sheets*. Each sheet can be a worksheet, chart, Visual Basic module, or Excel 4.0 macro sheet. As in the previous example, you could assign a sheet for each month of the year and record your information for the month on that sheet, whether it's sales, expenses, or something else. For easy reference, each page is given a tab at the bottom of the screen in which you can enter a label such as *January Sales* or *May Budget* (see Figure 2.1).

FIGURE 2.1.
Excel 5.0 files use a new workbook format.

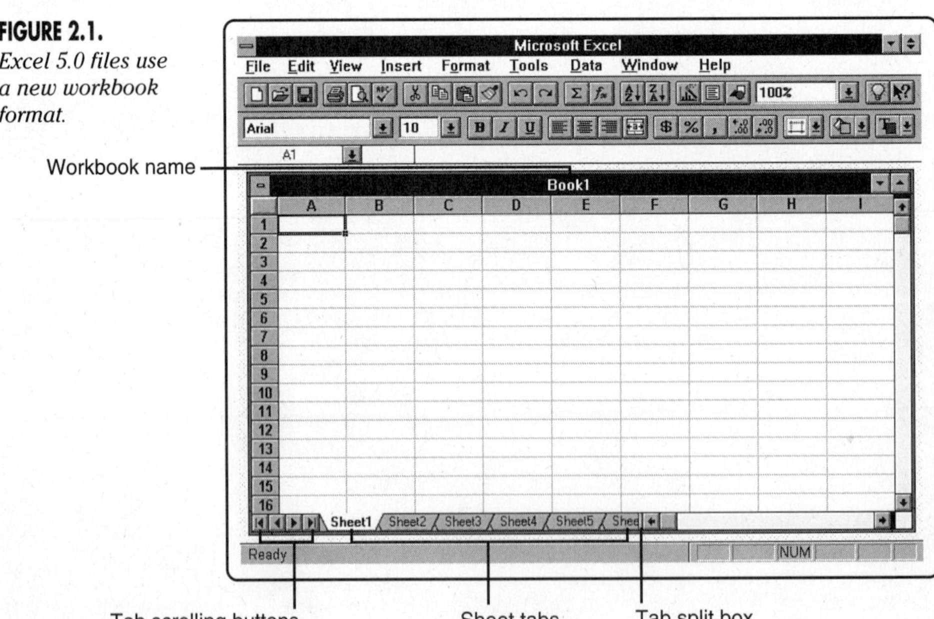

SUPER NOTE

If you have a workbook that doesn't display tabs, select the **Tools | Options** command. Then select the View tab in the Options dialog box and activate the Sheet Tabs check box.

Working with Workbook Sheets

When you start Excel, it displays a default workbook named Book1. This workbook contains 16 sheets labeled Sheet1 through Sheet16. You can use this file as the starting point for your new workbooks. You can add data to any sheet, insert new sheets, delete ones you don't need, supply your own names for the sheet tabs, and more. This section covers the basics of working with workbook sheets.

Navigating a Workbook

The first order of business is to learn how to move among the different sheets in a workbook. This is most easily accomplished with the mouse, and you can use either of the following techniques:

- If you can see the tab of the sheet you want, click on the tab.
- To scroll through the tabs, use the tab scrolling buttons, as described in Table 2.1.

Table 2.1. Excel's tab scrolling buttons.

Button to Click On	*Result*
⏮	Moves to the first tab in the workbook.
◀	Moves to the previous tab. Hold down Shift to move several tabs at a time.
▶	Moves to the next tab. Hold down Shift to move several tabs at a time.
⏭	Moves to the last tab in the workbook.

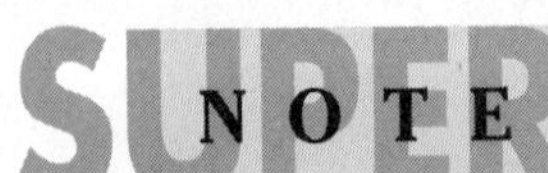

SUPER NOTE

If you would like to see more sheet tabs, drag the tab split box (see Figure 2.1) to the right.

You also can use the keyboard to navigate the sheet tabs, as described in Table 2.2.

Table 2.2. Using the keyboard to navigate workbook tabs.

Key Combination	*Action*
Ctrl+Page Up	Moves to the next sheet on the left
Ctrl+Page Down	Moves to the next sheet on the right

Selecting Multiple Workbook Sheets

Although you'll mostly be working with workbook sheets one at a time, it's possible to select multiple sheets. This is handy if you want to insert or delete several sheets at once, but the real advantage is that selecting multiple sheets enables you to enter data into the same cells on multiple sheets (see the next section for details).

To select multiple sheets, you can use any of the following techniques:

- To select adjacent sheets, click on the tab of the first sheet, hold down the Shift key, and click on the tab of the last sheet.
- To select noncontiguous sheets, hold down the Ctrl key and click on the tab of each sheet you want to include in the group.
- To select all the sheets in a workbook, right-click on any sheet tab and click on the Select All Sheets command.

When you've selected your sheets, each tab is highlighted and [Group] appears in the workbook title bar. To ungroup the sheets, click on a tab that isn't in the group or right-click on one of the group's tabs and select the Ungroup Sheets command from the shortcut menu.

Entering and Editing Data in a Group

One of the handiest features of worksheet groups is that you can enter and edit data in all the sheets at once. Procedure 2.1 shows you how.

PROCEDURE 2.1. ENTERING AND EDITING DATA IN A GROUP.

1. Select the group of sheets you want to work with.
2. In one of the sheets, select the cell you want to use.
3. Enter or edit the data in the cell.
4. Press Enter or click on the Enter box. Excel adds the data to the same cell in every sheet in the group.

Renaming a Workbook Sheet

The default sheet names (Sheet1, Sheet2, and so on) aren't very descriptive. To use your own names, follow the steps in Procedure 2.2.

PROCEDURE 2.2. RENAMING A WORKBOOK SHEET.

1. Select the sheet you want to rename.
2. Select the F**o**rmat | S**h**eet | **R**ename command. Excel displays the Rename Sheet dialog box, shown in Figure 2.2.

> **SUPER TIP**
>
> To display the Rename Sheet dialog box quickly, either double-click on the sheet tab or right-click on the tab and select the **R**ename command.

FIGURE 2.2.
Use the Rename Sheet dialog box to rename a workbook sheet.

3. Enter the new name in the **N**ame edit box. The name can be up to 31 characters long (including spaces), but it can't be enclosed in square brackets ([Budget], for example) and it can't include any of the following characters:

   : \ / ? *

4. Click on OK or press Enter. Excel changes the sheet tab to reflect your new name.

Moving or Copying a Workbook Sheet

You can rearrange you workbook sheets by moving them or copying them to a different location. Procedure 2.3 gives you the details.

PROCEDURE 2.3. MOVING OR COPYING A WORKBOOK SHEET.

1. Select the sheet you want to move or copy.
2. Select the Edit | Move or Copy Sheet command. Excel displays the Move or Copy dialog box, as shown in Figure 2.3.

> **SUPER TIP**
>
> To display the Move or Copy dialog box quickly, right-click on the sheet's tab and select the Move or Copy command.

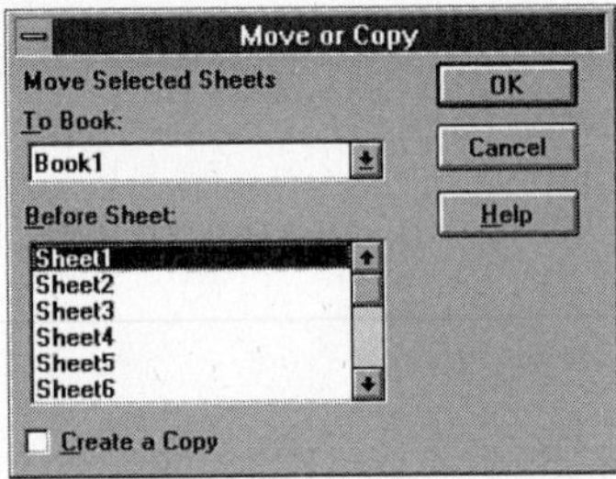

FIGURE 2.3.
Use the Move or Copy dialog box to move or copy a workbook sheet.

3. If you want to move or copy the sheet to a different workbook, select the one you want from the To Book drop-down list. If you want to use a new workbook, select the (new book) option.
4. Use the Before Sheet list to select a destination for the sheet.
5. If you want to copy the sheet instead of moving it, activate the Create a Copy check box.
6. Click on OK or press Enter. Excel moves or copies the sheet.

> **SUPER TIP**
>
> You also can move or copy a sheet by dragging the sheet tab with the mouse. As you drag, an arrow appears over the sheet tabs to tell you where the sheet will be placed. A normal drag moves the sheet. To make a copy, hold down the Ctrl key while dragging.

Inserting a New Workbook Sheet

You get 16 sheets in the default workbook, but you're free to add as many as you like (the only restriction is the amount of free memory on your system). When you add a sheet, Excel inserts it before the active sheet. For example, if the active sheet is Sheet3, the new sheet will be added between Sheet2 and Sheet3. Follow the steps in Procedure 2.4 to insert a new sheet in a workbook.

SUPER NOTE

You can tell Excel to use a different number of sheets in the default workbook. See Chapter 66, "Customizing Excel's Options and Workspace."

PROCEDURE 2.4. INSERTING A NEW WORKBOOK SHEET.

1. Select the sheet before which you want the new sheet to appear. If you want to insert several sheets, select the number of sheets you want to insert. For example, to insert two sheets before Sheet2, select Sheet2 and Sheet3.
2. Select the **I**nsert | **W**orksheet command. Excel inserts the sheet (or sheets) in the workbook.

SUPER TIP

You can insert a new worksheet by pressing either Shift+F11 or Alt+Shift+F1 or by right-clicking on a Sheet tab and selecting Insert from the shortcut menu that appears.

Deleting a Workbook Sheet

If you have sheets you no longer need, you can delete them to save disk space and memory. Procedure 2.5 outlines the necessary steps.

PROCEDURE 2.5. DELETING A WORKBOOK SHEET.

1. Select the sheet you want to delete.
2. Select the **E**dit | De**l**ete Sheet command. Excel asks if you're sure you want to delete the sheet.

SUPER TIP

You also can delete a sheet by right-clicking on the sheet tab and selecting the Delete command.

3. Click on OK or press Enter to delete the sheet.

Saving a Workbook

To enable you to work with a workbook, Excel copies it into your computer's random access memory (RAM). This makes things much faster (memory chips operate blindingly fast compared to hard disks) but inherently more dangerous, because the contents of memory are purged whenever you turn off your computer. This means that a program crash or power failure could wipe out all your work in the blink of an eye.

To be safe, you should regularly save a copy of your work to the relatively secure confines of your hard disk. Happily, saving a file in Excel is only a couple mouse clicks or keystrokes away. Procedure 2.6 shows you how.

SUPER CAUTION

Here are some guidelines you can follow to help determine how often you should save your work:

- After making major structural changes to a workbook (such as copying or moving a chunk of data or formatting a large section)
- After every few cells during data entry
- Whenever you're about to leave your desk for more than a few minutes
- Every five or ten minutes

PROCEDURE 2.6. SAVING A WORKBOOK.

1. Select the **File** | **S**ave command. If you're saving a new workbook, the Save As dialog box appears, shown in Figure 2.4. If you're saving an existing workbook, Excel saves your changes. Watch the status bar for the progress of the save.

TIP

The shortcut key for the Save command is Ctrl+S.

Click on this tool in the Standard toolbar to save a workbook.

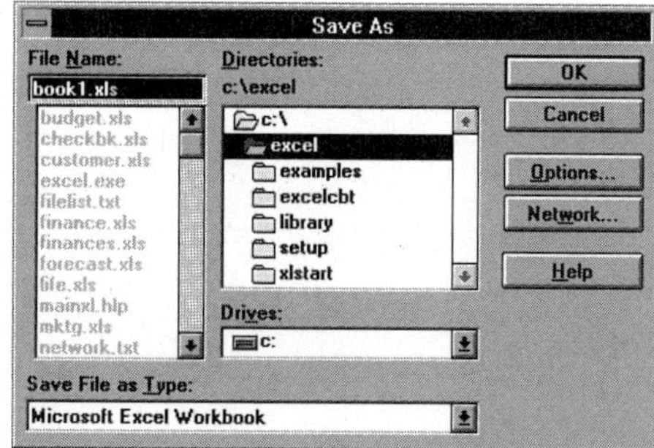

FIGURE 2.4.
The Save As dialog box appears when you're saving a new workbook.

2. Use the File **N**ame edit box to enter the name you want to use for the file. (Excel automatically adds its default .XLS extension, so you don't need to include it.)

SUPER NOTE

Try to save your files with names that will help you to remember the contents of the file. A name such as Sales_92 is much more descriptive than something such as Book1. The only restriction you face is that you must use legal DOS filenames. This means that each name must be no more than eight characters long and can't include spaces or any of the following characters:

```
+ = / [ ] " : ; , . ? * \ < > ¦
```

3. If you would like to save the file on a different drive, select the drive from the Dri**v**es drop-down list. If you choose a floppy drive, be sure to insert a disk before continuing.
4. To save the file in a different directory, select the directory from the **D**irectories list box.
5. Click on OK or press Enter. Excel displays the Summary Info dialog box.
6. Enter the summary information for the workbook (this is optional).

SUPER NOTE

You can change one of Excel's default options to avoid being prompted for summary information. See Chapter 66, "Customizing Excel's Options and Workspace."

7. Click on OK or press Enter.

Saving a File Under a Different Name

One of the fundamental axioms of computer productivity is "Don't reinvent the wheel." If you have a nicely formatted spreadsheet that works properly, and you need something similar, don't start from scratch. Instead, use Excel's Save As command to make a copy of the existing workbook under a different name. Follow the steps in Procedure 2.7.

PROCEDURE 2.7. SAVING A WORKBOOK UNDER A DIFFERENT NAME.

1. Open the workbook you want to save under a different name. (See the next section for details on opening a workbook.)
2. Select the **F**ile | Save **A**s command. Excel displays the Save As dialog box.
3. Fill in the Save As dialog box as described in Procedure 2.6.
4. Click on OK or press Enter. Excel closes the original file, makes a copy, and then opens the new file.

> **SUPER TIP**
>
> Press either F12 or Alt+F2 to activate the Save As command quickly.

Opening a File

When you start Excel, the program automatically displays a new blank workbook called Book1. You have the option of using this workbook or opening an existing one. Procedure 2.8 leads you through the steps necessary to open an existing workbook.

PROCEDURE 2.8. OPENING AN EXISTING WORKBOOK.

1. Select the **F**ile | **O**pen command. The Open dialog box appears, shown in Figure 2.5.

> **SUPER TIP**
>
> The shortcut key for the Open command is Ctrl+O.

Click on this tool in the Standard toolbar to display the Open dialog box.

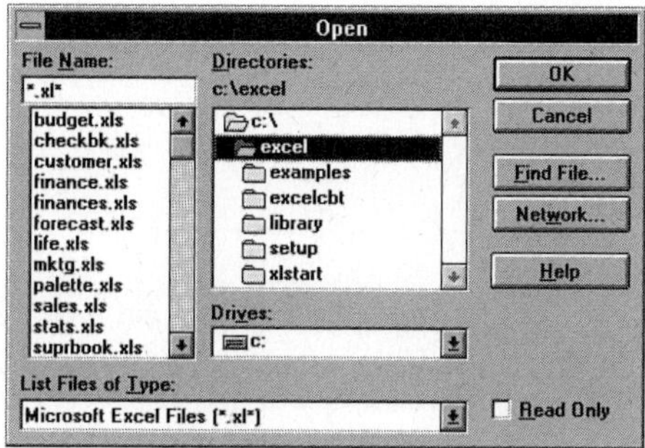

FIGURE 2.5.
Use the Open dialog box to open an existing workbook.

2. If the file exists on a different drive, select the drive from the Drives drop-down list. For floppy drives, make sure you place a disk in the drive before doing this.
3. If necessary, use the Directories list box to select the appropriate directory for the file.
4. Select the file from the File Name list box.
5. Click on OK or press Enter. Excel opens the file.

Tips for Opening Files

The next few sections outline a few tips and methods for opening files in Excel.

Opening Multiple Workbooks

If you regularly work with multiple workbooks, you don't need to run a separate Open command for each file. Instead, Excel enables you to choose multiple files from the Open dialog box. There are two methods you can use:

- If the files are listed together in the File Name box, click on the first file you need, hold down the Shift key, and click on the last file you need. Using the keyboard, highlight the first file, hold down the Shift key, and use the down arrow key to highlight the other files.
- If the files aren't listed together, click on the first file you need, hold down the Ctrl key, and click on the other files. Using the keyboard, highlight the first

file, press Shift+F8, and then for the other files, highlight each one and press the Spacebar.

SUPER NOTE

For more information about working with multiple workbooks, see Chapter 13, "Changing the Workbook View."

Opening a Workbook Automatically When You Start Excel

If you have a workbook you use all the time, you can have Excel open it for you automatically. There are two methods you can use: adding the file to the XLSTART directory or adjusting Excel's program item properties in Program Manager.

Using the XLSTART Directory

XLSTART is a subdirectory of your main Excel directory. Any workbooks in this directory are opened automatically by Excel every time you start the program. To open a specific workbook each time you start Excel, save the file in the XLSTART directory or move it there using Windows' File Manager.

SUPER NOTE

Excel enables you to specify a different startup directory. See Chapter 66, "Customizing Excel's Options and Workspace," for details.

Altering Excel's Program Item Properties

The other way to open a workbook automatically is to change the properties of Excel's program item in Program Manager. Procedure 2.9 lists the appropriate steps.

PROCEDURE 2.9. ALTERING EXCEL'S PROGRAM ITEM PROPERTIES.

1. Switch to Program Manager and highlight the Microsoft Excel icon.
2. Select **F**ile | **P**roperties or press Alt+Enter. The Program Item Properties dialog box appears (see Figure 2.6).
3. You should see something like this in the **C**ommand Line text box: `C:\EXCEL\EXCEL.EXE`. Add a space after this text and enter the name of the workbook file. Be sure to include the full path name—that is, the drive, directory, filename, and extension.
4. Click on OK or press Enter.

FIGURE 2.6.
The Program Item Properties dialog box.

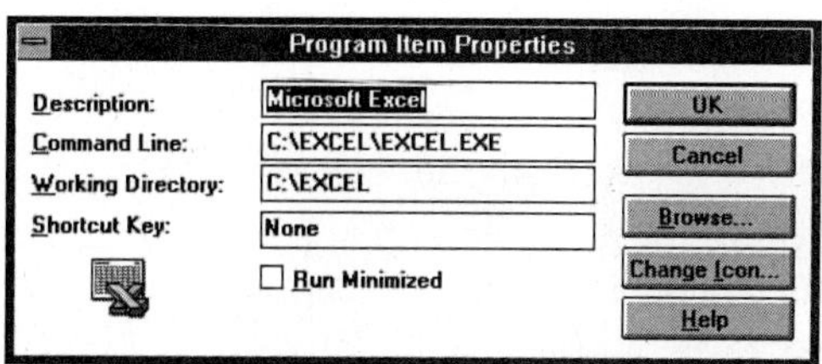

SUPER TIP

You also can create separate Program Manager icons for individual Excel workbooks. See Chapter 68, "Using DDE to Create Icons for Excel Workbooks," for details.

Starting Excel Without Book1

Many people never use the blank Book1 workbook that Excel automatically opens on startup. To avoid the hassle of closing the workbook every time, you can tell Excel not to display it. Just follow the steps in Procedure 2.9 that tell you how to alter Excel's program item properties and, in the **Command Line** text box, add the `/E` parameter.

SUPER TIP

If you prefer, you can create your own startup sheet, or you can have Excel open the template you specify. To learn how, see Chapter 62, "Working with Templates and Outlines."

Opening a New Workbook

To open a new workbook, just follow the steps outlined in Procedure 2.10.

PROCEDURE 2.10. OPENING A NEW WORKBOOK.

1. Select the **File** | **New** command. Excel displays the New dialog box.

To start a new workbook quickly, press either Alt+Shift+F1 or Shift+F11.

Click on this tool in the Standard toolbar to open a new workbook.

2. Select Workbook from the **N**ew list.
3. Click on OK or press Enter. Excel displays a fresh workbook with the name Book*n*; *n* means that this file is the *n*th new workbook you've opened in this work session.

Using Excel's Find File Feature

Excel 5.0 offers a new Find File command that enables you to search for files on your hard disk. Once you've found them, you can view their contents, open them, delete them, or even print them. To start Find File, select the **F**ile | F**i**nd File command. Excel displays the Find File dialog box, shown in Figure 2.7.

SUPER NOTE

Excel has many toolbars other than the Standard and Formatting toolbars you normally see. To display any of the other toolbars, select the **V**iew | **T**oolbars command, activate one or more check boxes in the **T**oolbars list, and click on OK. You also can view a toolbar by right-clicking on a displayed toolbar and selecting the one you want from the shortcut menu that appears.

Click on this tool in the Workgroup toolbar to open a new workbook.

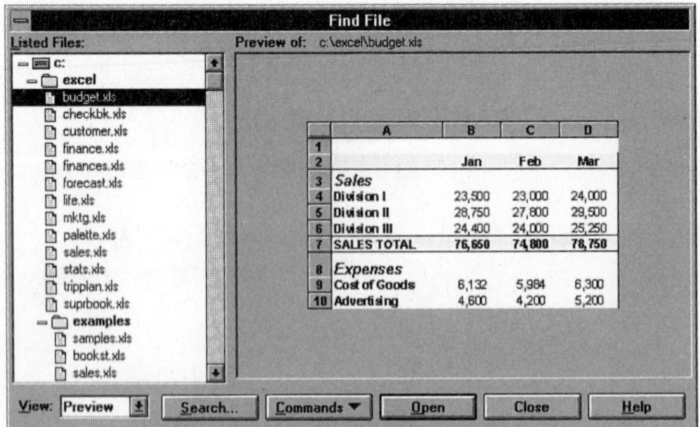

FIGURE 2.7.
The Find File dialog box enables you to search for files on your hard disk.

The Find File dialog box contains the following features:

Listed Files: Displays the current drive and directory and the files contained in that directory.

Preview of: Shows a preview of the file highlighted in the Listed Files box. Use the View list to display different information in this area.

View: This drop-down list determines what you see to the right of the Listed Files box. You can select Preview (the default), File Info (to see things such as the file size, author, and date), or Summary (to see the file summary).

Search: Enables you to search your system for files. See the next section for more information.

Commands: The options in this pop-up list enable you to work with the highlighted files.

Searching for Files

Find File includes a powerful Search feature that enables you to look for files anywhere on your system. Procedure 2.11 shows you how to use Search.

PROCEDURE 2.11. SEARCHING FOR FILES WITH FIND FILE.

1. In the Find File dialog box, click on the Search button. Excel displays the Search dialog box, shown in Figure 2.8.

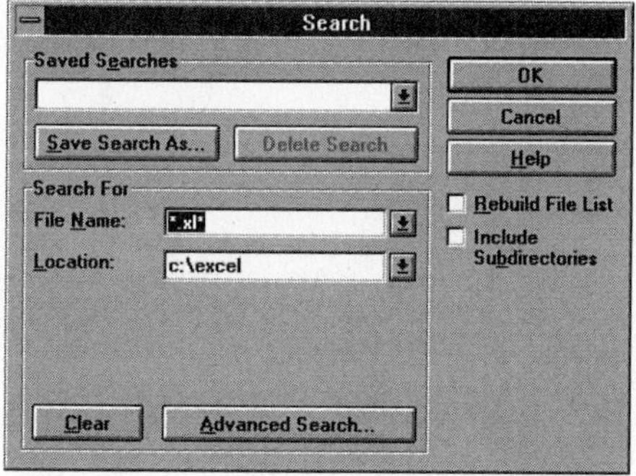

FIGURE 2.8.
The Search dialog box.

2. In the File Name drop-down list, enter a file specification or select one from the list.
3. Use the Location drop-down list to specify the drive and directory you want to search.
4. If you want to include any subdirectories in the search, activate the Include Subdirectories check box.

5. If you think you'll be using these options regularly, you can save the search. Select the Save Search As button and enter a name for the search in the dialog box that appears. To use a saved search, select one from the Saved Searches list.
6. Click on OK or press Enter. Excel searches for the files and displays the results in the Find File dialog box.

> **SUPER NOTE**
>
> The Search dialog box also includes an Advanced Search button that enables you to search by location, summary information, or timestamp.

Copying a File

The Find File dialog box enables you to copy any of the displayed files. To do this, follow the steps in Procedure 2.12.

PROCEDURE 2.12. COPYING A FILE IN THE FIND FILE DIALOG BOX.

1. Highlight the file or files you want to copy. (To highlight multiple files, see the instructions in the section of this chapter titled "Opening Multiple Workbooks.")
2. Select the Commands pop-up list and select the Copy command. The Copy dialog box appears.
3. Select the drive and directory where you want the file copied.

> **SUPER TIP**
>
> If the directory you want to use doesn't exist, click on the New button in the Copy dialog box and enter the new directory name in the Create Directory dialog box that appears.

4. Click on OK or press Enter. Excel copies the file to the directory you selected.

Deleting a File

To delete a file from the Find File dialog box, follow the steps in Procedure 2.13.

PROCEDURE 2.13. DELETING A FILE IN THE FIND FILE DIALOG BOX.

1. Highlight the file or files you want to delete.

2. Select the **C**ommands pop-up list and select the **D**elete command. Excel asks you to confirm the deletion.
3. Select **Y**es to delete the file.

Closing a Workbook

Each open workbook uses some of your system's precious memory. The larger the file, the more memory it uses. To conserve your system's resources, you should close any workbooks you've finished working with. Follow the steps in Procedure 2.14 to close a workbook.

PROCEDURE 2.14. CLOSING A WORKBOOK.

1. Switch to the workbook you want to close. (See Chapter 13, "Changing the Workbook View," to learn how to navigate among multiple open workbooks.)
2. Select the **F**ile | **C**lose command. If you made changes to the workbook, Excel asks whether you want to save your changes.
3. To save your changes, click on **Y**es or press Enter. If you're saving a new workbook, Excel displays the Save As dialog box. To close the workbook without saving changes, click on **N**o.
4. If necessary, fill in the Save As dialog box as described in Procedure 2.6.

SUPER TIP

To close a workbook quickly, press Ctrl+F4 or double-click on the workbook's Control-menu box.

If you have several workbooks open and you want to close them all, hold down the Shift key and select the **F**ile | **C**lose All command. Excel closes each file in turn and, if needed, prompts you to save any changes you've made to the files.

Chapter

3

Getting Started with Ranges

For small worksheets, working with individual cells usually doesn't present a problem. However, as your worksheets get larger, you'll find that performing operations cell by cell wastes both time and energy. To overcome this, Excel enables you to work with multiple cells (a cell range) in a single operation. You can then move, copy, delete, or format the range as a whole. Excel even enables you to enter data in a range. This chapter gets you started by showing you how to select and name ranges. See Chapter 4, "Working with Ranges," for more information.

Learning About Ranges

A *range* is defined as any group of related cells. A range can be as small as a single cell or as large as the entire spreadsheet. Most ranges are rectangular groups of adjacent cells, but Excel enables you to create ranges with noncontiguous cells. Rectangular ranges, like individual cells, have an address that is given in terms of *range coordinates.* Range coordinates have the form *UL:LR* where *UL* is the address of the cell in the upper-left corner of the range and *LR* is the address of the cell in the lower-right corner of the range.

Figure 3.1 shows some sample ranges and their coordinate addresses. Although Figure 3.1 shows several ranges, in practice you can highlight only one range at a time. It's possible, however, to designate many ranges on a single spreadsheet by using range names. See the section in this chapter titled "Using Range Names."

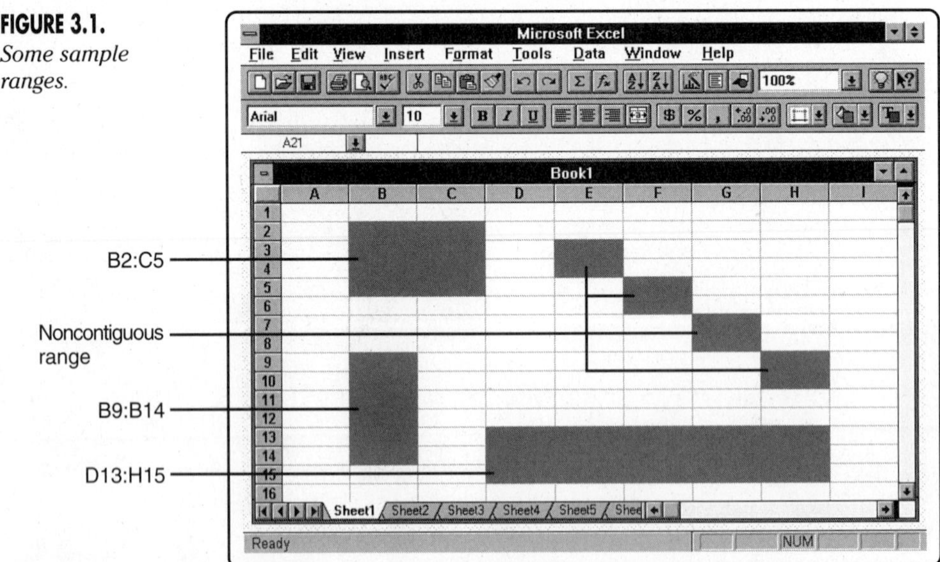

FIGURE 3.1.
Some sample ranges.

Ranges speed up your work by enabling you to perform operations or define functions on many cells at once instead of on one cell at a time. For example, suppose you wanted to copy a large section of a worksheet to another file. When you work with individual cells, you might have to perform the copy procedure dozens of times. However, by creating a range that covers the entire section, you could copy a range with a single copy command.

Similarly, suppose you wanted to know the average of a column of numbers running from B1 to B50. You could enter all 50 numbers as arguments in the `AVERAGE` function, but typing `=AVERAGE(B1:B50)` is decidedly quicker.

Now that you've seen the advantages of working with ranges, it's time to learn how to use them. I'll begin with the most basic operation: selecting a range.

Selecting a Range

There are three situations in which you'll select a cell range:

- In a dialog box field that requires a range input
- While entering a function argument
- Before selecting a command that uses a range input

In a dialog box field or function argument, the most straightforward way to select a range is to simply enter the range coordinates. Just type the address of the upper-left cell (called the *anchor cell*), followed by a colon, and then the address of the lower-right cell. To use this method, you either have to be able to see the range you want to select, or you have to know the range coordinates you want in advance. Because often this is not the case, most people don't type the range coordinates directly; instead, they select ranges using either the mouse or the keyboard.

Selecting a Range with the Mouse

Although you can use either the mouse or the keyboard to select a range, you'll find that the mouse makes the job much easier. The following sections take you through several methods you can use to select a range with the mouse.

Selecting a Contiguous Range with the Mouse

A rectangular, contiguous grouping of cells is the most common type of range. To use the mouse to select such a range, follow the steps outlined in Procedure 3.1.

PROCEDURE 3.1. SELECTING A CONTIGUOUS RANGE WITH THE MOUSE.

1. Point the mouse at the upper-left cell of the range (the anchor), then press and hold down the left mouse button.

2. With the left mouse button still pressed, drag the mouse pointer to the lower-right cell of the range. The cell selector remains around the anchor cell, and Excel highlights the other cells in the range in reverse video. The formula bar's Name box shows the number of rows and columns you've selected, as shown in Figure 3.2.

FIGURE 3.2.
As you select a range, the Name box shows the number of rows and columns you've selected.

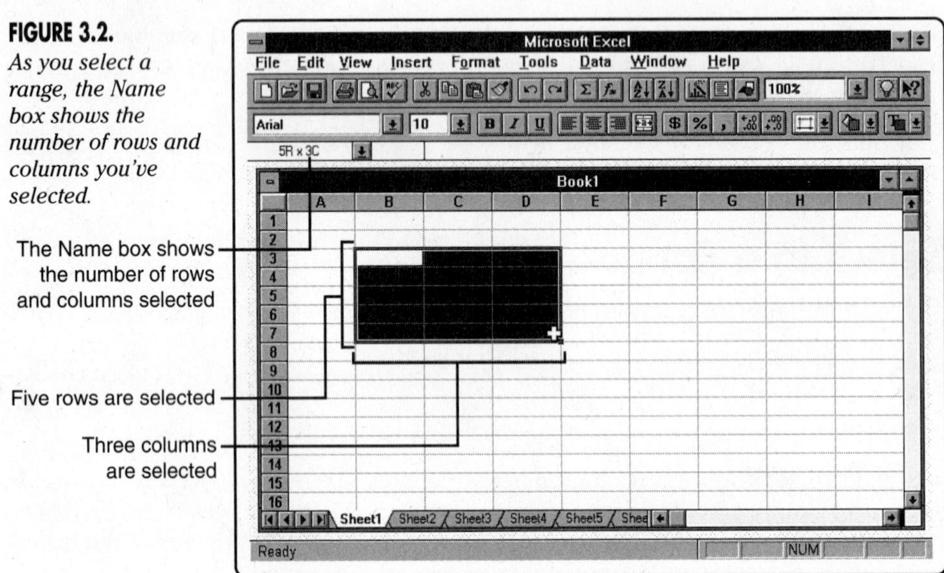

3. Release the mouse button. The cells remain selected to show the range you've defined.

> **SUPER TIP**
>
> Sometimes you select the wrong lower-right corner and your range ends up either too big or too small. If this happens, you don't have to start over. Hold down the Shift key and click on the correct lower-right cell. The range adjusts automatically.

Selecting a Row or Column with the Mouse

Using the worksheet row and column headings, you can quickly select a range that is an entire row or column. For a row, click on the row's heading. For a column, click on the column's heading. If you need to select adjacent rows or columns, just drag the mouse pointer across the appropriate headings.

Selecting a Range in Extend Mode with the Mouse

An alternative method uses the mouse with the F8 key to select a rectangular, contiguous range. You can do this by following the steps in Procedure 3.2.

PROCEDURE 3.2. SELECTING A RANGE IN EXTEND MODE WITH THE MOUSE.

1. Click on the upper-left cell of the range.
2. Press F8. Excel enters Extend mode (you'll see EXT in the status bar).
3. Click on the lower-right cell of the range. Excel selects the entire range.
4. Press F8 to turn off Extend mode.

SUPER TIP

After selecting a large range, you'll often no longer see the active cell because you've scrolled it off the screen. If you need to see the active cell before continuing, you can either use the scroll bars to bring it into view or press Ctrl+Backspace.

Selecting a Noncontiguous Range with the Mouse

The secret to defining a noncontiguous range is to hold down the Ctrl key while selecting the cells. Procedure 3.3 gives you the details.

SUPER CAUTION

Be careful when selecting cells with this method. Once you've selected a cell, the only way to deselect it is by starting over.

PROCEDURE 3.3. SELECTING A NONCONTIGUOUS RANGE USING THE MOUSE.

1. Select the first cell or the first rectangular range you want to include in the noncontiguous range. If you're selecting a rectangular range, you can use any of the methods described previously.
2. Press and hold down the Ctrl key.
3. Select the other cells or rectangular ranges you want to include in the noncontiguous range. For subsequent rectangular ranges, you can't use Procedure 3.2 (Extend mode).
4. When you've finished selecting cells, release the Ctrl key.

SUPER CAUTION

Always press and hold down the Ctrl key *after* you've selected your first cell or range. Otherwise, Excel includes the currently selected cell or range as part of the noncontiguous range. This could create a circular reference in a function if you were defining the range as an argument.

Selecting Cell Ranges with the Keyboard

If you don't have a mouse, you can use the keyboard to select a cell range. In fact, you have three methods to choose from.

Selecting a Range in Extend Mode with the Keyboard

In Excel, F8 is called the Extend key because it's used to extend a range selection. Procedure 3.4 shows how it works.

PROCEDURE 3.4. SELECTING A RANGE IN EXTEND MODE WITH THE KEYBOARD.

1. Select the upper-left cell of the range (this is the anchor cell).
2. Press F8. Excel enters Extend mode, and EXT appears in the status bar.
3. Use Excel's navigation keys (described in Chapter 1, "Entering and Editing Worksheet Data") to extend the selection. The anchor cell remains in position and the other cells appear in reverse video.
4. Press F8 to turn off Extend mode.

SUPER TIP

To adjust the size of the selected range, press F8 again and use the navigation keys to move the selection.

Selecting a Row or a Column with the Keyboard

Selecting a row or column using the keyboard is easy. Just select a cell in the row or column you want and then press either Ctrl+Spacebar to select the current column or Shift+Spacebar to select the current row.

Selecting a Noncontiguous Range with the Keyboard

If you need to select a noncontiguous range with the keyboard, follow the steps in Procedure 3.5.

PROCEDURE 3.5. SELECTING A NONCONTIGUOUS RANGE WITH THE KEYBOARD.

1. Select the first cell or range you want to include in the noncontiguous range.
2. Press Shift+F8 to enter Add mode. (ADD appears in the status line.)
3. Select the next cell or range you want to include in the noncontiguous range.
4. Repeat steps 2 and 3 to complete the range.

Working with 3-D Ranges

A *3-D range* is a range selected on multiple sheets. This is a powerful concept because it means that you can select a range on two or more sheets and then enter data, apply formatting, or give a command, and the operation will affect all the ranges at once.

To create a 3-D range, you first need to group the worksheets you want to work with (see Chapter 2, "Workbook Basics," for details). Then select the range you want to work with using any of the methods outlined earlier in this chapter.

Using Range Names

Although ranges enable you to work efficiently with large groups of cells, there are some disadvantages to using ranges:

- You can't work with more than one range at a time. Each time you want to use a range, you have to redefine its coordinates.
- Range notation is unintuitive; to know what a function such as `SUM(E6:E10)` is adding, you have to look at the range itself.
- A slight mistake in defining a range can lead to disastrous results, especially when you're erasing a range.

You can overcome these problems by using range names. You can assign names of up to 255 characters to any single cell or range on your spreadsheet. To include the range in a formula or range command, you simply use the name instead of selecting the range or typing in its coordinates. You can create as many range names as you like, and you can even assign multiple names to the same range.

Range names also make your formulas intuitive and easy to read. For example, by assigning the name *AugustSales* to a range such as E6:E10, the purpose of a function such as `=SUM(AugustSales)` becomes immediately clear.

Range names also increase the accuracy of your range operations because you don't have to specify range coordinates. In addition to overcoming the problems mentioned earlier, range names also add several advantages:

- Names are easier to remember than range coordinates.
- Names don't change when you move a range to another part of the worksheet.

- Named ranges adjust automatically whenever you insert or delete rows or columns within the range. (See Chapter 4, "Working with Ranges," to learn how to insert and delete rows and columns.)
- Names make it easier to navigate a worksheet. You can use the Go To command (again, see Chapter 4) to jump to a named range quickly.
- You can use worksheet labels to create range names quickly.

Defining a Range Name

Besides having a maximum length of 255 characters, range names must also follow these guidelines:

- The name must begin with either a letter or the underscore character (_). For the rest of the name, you can use any combination of characters, numbers, or symbols, except spaces. For multiple-word names, separate the words by using the underscore character or by mixing case (for example, *CostOfGoods*). Excel doesn't distinguish between uppercase and lowercase letters in range names.
- Don't use cell addresses or any of the operator symbols (such as + – * / < > &), because these could cause confusion if you use the name in a formula.
- To make typing easier, try to keep your names as short as possible while still retaining their meaning. `TotalProfit93` is faster to type than `Total_Profit_For_Fiscal_Year_93`, and it's certainly clearer than something such as `TotPft93`.

Follow the steps in Procedure 3.6 to define a range name.

PROCEDURE 3.6. DEFINING A RANGE NAME.

1. Select the range you want to name.
2. Select the **I**nsert | **N**ame | **D**efine command. The Define Name dialog box appears, shown in Figure 3.3.

> **SUPER TIP**
>
> Press Ctrl+F3 to quickly open the Define Name dialog box.

3. Enter the range name in the Names in **W**orkbook edit box.

FIGURE 3.3.
Use the Define Name dialog box to define a name for the selected range.

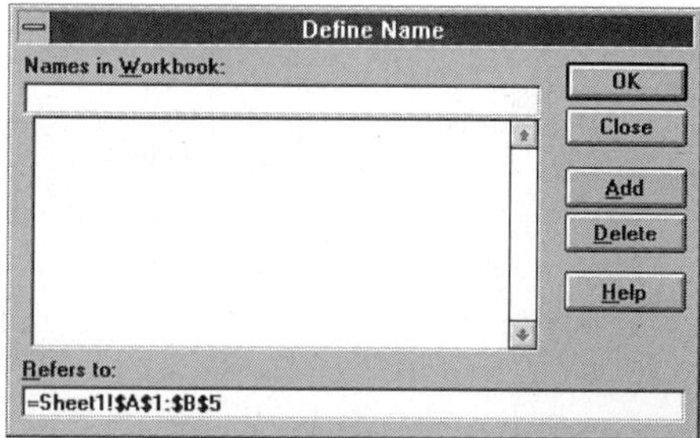

SUPER TIP

To speed up future error-checking, always enter at least the first letter of a range name in uppercase when defining it. Then, when you use the range name later in a formula, type it entirely in lowercase. Normally, Excel converts the name to the case you used when you first defined it. If not, Excel can't find the name. In this case, you might have made a mistake entering the name in the formula.

4. If the range displayed in the **R**efers to box is incorrect, you can use one of two methods to change it:
   - Type in the correct range address (be sure to begin it with an equals sign).
   - Move the cursor into the **R**efers to box and then use the mouse or keyboard to select a new range on the worksheet.

SUPER TIP

If you need move around inside the **R**efers to box with the arrow keys, press F2 to put Excel into Edit mode. If you don't, Excel assumes you're trying to select a cell on the worksheet.

5. Click on **A**dd. Excel adds the name to the Names in **W**orkbook list.
6. Repeat steps 3-5 for any other ranges you want to name.
7. When you're done, click on the Close button to return to the worksheet.

SUPER NOTE

As soon as you've defined a range name, the name appears in the formula bar's Name box whenever you select the range.

SUPER NOTE

Range names are available to all the sheets in a workbook. This means, for example, that a formula in Sheet1 can refer to a named range in Sheet16 simply by using the name directly. If the named range exists in a different workbook, you have to precede the name with the name of the file. For example, if the MORTGAGE.XLS workbook contained a range named `Rate`, you would refer to this range in a different workbook, like this:

```
MORTGAGE.XLS!Rate
```

Working with the Name Box

The Name box in Excel 5.0's formula bar gives you some extra features that help make it easier to work with range names:

- As soon as you've defined a name, it appears in the Name box whenever you select the range.
- The Name box doubles as a drop-down list. To select a named range quickly, drop the list down and select the name you want. Excel moves to the range and selects the cells.
- You also can use the Name box as an easy way to define a range name. Just select the range and click inside the Name box to display the insertion point. Enter the name you want to use and then press Enter. Excel defines the new name automatically.

Using Worksheet Text to Define Names

When you select the **I**nsert | **N**ame | **D**efine command, Excel sometimes suggests a name for the selected range. For example, Figure 3.4 shows that Excel has suggested the name *Advertising* for the range C6:E6. As you can see, *Advertising* is the row heading of the selected range, so Excel has used an adjacent text entry to make an educated guess about what you'll want to use as a name.

FIGURE 3.4.
Excel uses adjacent text to guess at the range name you want to use.

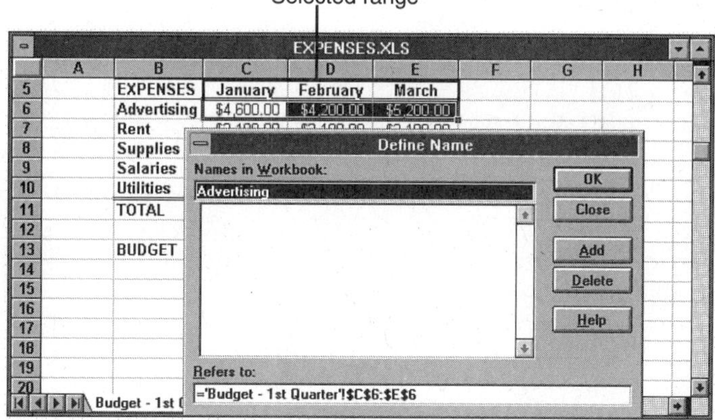

Instead of waiting for Excel to guess, you can tell the program explicitly to use adjacent text as a range name. Procedure 3.7 shows you the appropriate steps.

PROCEDURE 3.7. DEFINING RANGE NAMES FROM WORKSHEET TEXT.

1. Select the range of cells you want to name, including the appropriate text cells that you want to use as the range names (see Figure 3.5).

FIGURE 3.5.
Include the text you want to use as names when you select the range.

EXPENSES.XLS

	A	B	C	D	E	F	G	H
1	Expense Budget Calculation - 1st Quarter							
2								
3		INCREASE	1.09					
4								
5		EXPENSES	January	February	March			
6		Advertising	$4,600.00	$4,200.00	$5,200.00			
7		Rent	$2,100.00	$2,100.00	$2,100.00			
8		Supplies	$1,300.00	$1,200.00	$1,400.00			
9		Salaries	$16,000.00	$16,000.00	$16,500.00			
10		Utilities	$500.00	$600.00	$600.00			
11		TOTAL	$24,500.00	$24,100.00	$25,800.00			
12								
13		BUDGET	$26,705.00	$26,269.00	$28,122.00			
14								
15								

Budget - 1st Quarter / Budget - 2nd Quarter / Bud

2. Select the **I**nsert | **N**ame | **C**reate command. Excel displays the Create Names dialog box, shown in Figure 3.6.

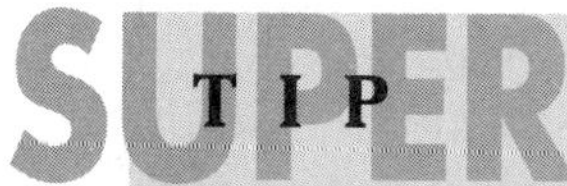

SUPER TIP

The shortcut key for the Create Names dialog box is Ctrl+Shift+F3.

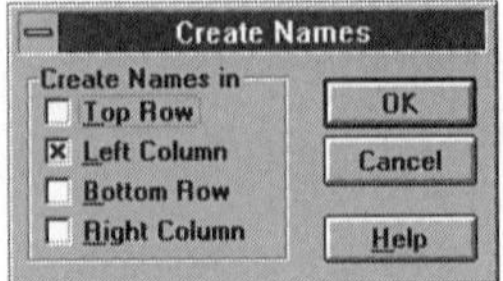

FIGURE 3.6.
Use the Create Names dialog box to specify the location of the text to use as range names.

3. Tell Excel the location of the text for the range names by selecting the appropriate check box.
4. Click on OK or press Enter.

> **SUPER NOTE**
>
> If the text you want to use as a range name contains any illegal characters (such as a space), Excel replaces them with an underscore character (_).

When naming ranges from text, you're not restricted to working with just columns or rows. You can select ranges that include both row *and* column headings, and Excel will happily assign names to each row and column. For example, in Figure 3.7, the Create Names dialog box appears with both the **T**op Row and **L**eft Column check boxes activated.

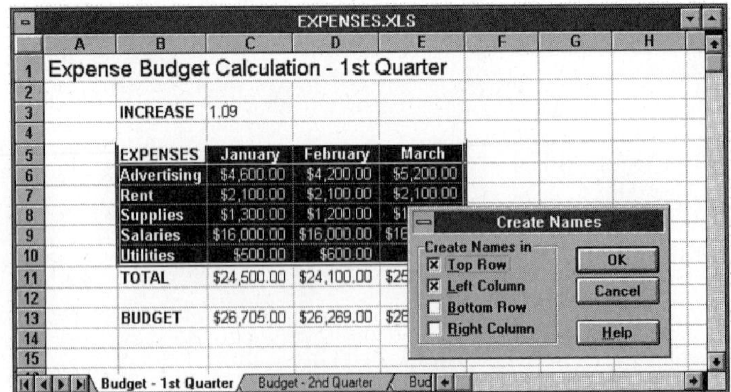

FIGURE 3.7.
Excel creates names for rows and columns at the same time.

SUPER NOTE

When you define names for the rows and columns in a range, you can refer to each cell as the intersection of two ranges. For example, in Figure 3.7, cell C7 would be *January Rent*. See Chapter 60, "Advanced Range Topics," for more information about the intersection operator.

Naming Constants

One of the best ways to make your worksheets comprehensible is to define names for any constant value. For example, if your worksheet uses an interest rate variable in several formulas, you could define a constant named *Rate* and use the name in your formulas to make them more readable. There are two ways to do this:

- Set aside an area of your worksheet for constants and name the individual cells (see Figure 3.8).

FIGURE 3.8.
Grouping formula constants and naming them makes worksheets easy to read.

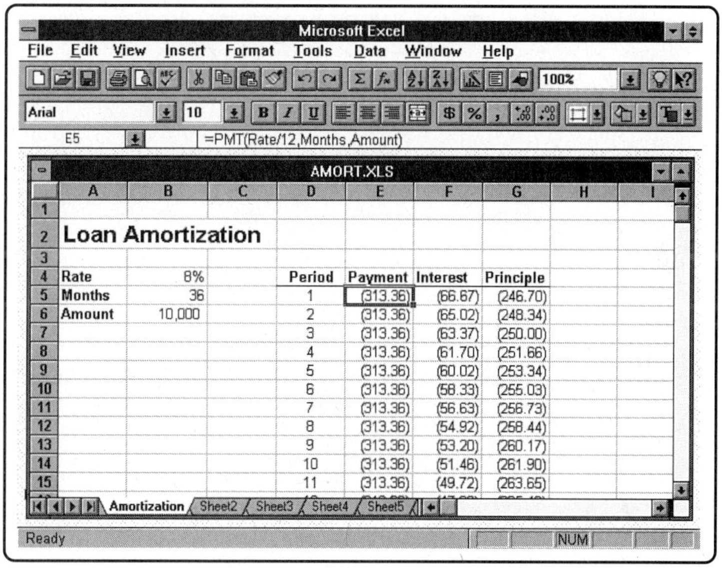

- If you don't want to clutter a worksheet, you can name constants without entering them in the worksheet. Just select the **I**nsert | **N**ame | **D**efine command, enter a name for the constant in the Names in **W**orkbook edit box, and enter an equals sign (=) and the constant's value in the **R**efers to text box. Figure 3.9 shows an example.

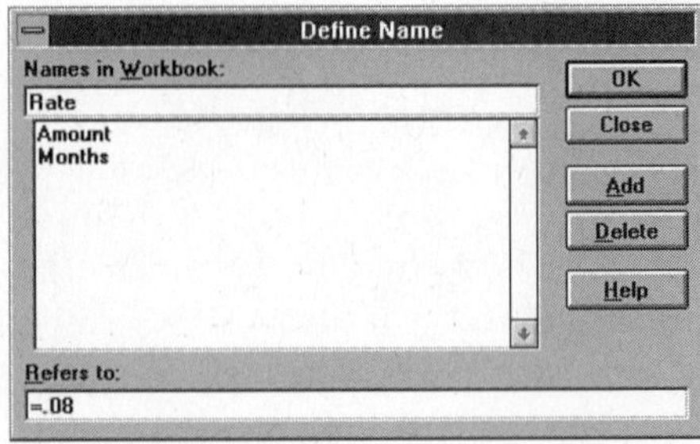

FIGURE 3.9.
You can create and name constants in the Define Name dialog box.

Pasting a List of Range Names in a Worksheet

If you need to document a worksheet for others to read (or figure out the worksheet yourself a few months from now), you can paste a list of the worksheet's range names. This list includes the name and the range it represents (or the value it represents, if the name refers to a constant). Follow the steps in Procedure 3.8 to paste a list of range names.

PROCEDURE 3.8. PASTING A LIST OF RANGE NAMES.

1. Move the cell pointer to an empty area of the worksheet that is large enough to accept the list without overwriting any other data.
2. Select the **I**nsert | **N**ame | **P**aste command. Excel displays the Paste Name dialog box.

> **SUPER TIP**
>
> You also can press F3 to display the Paste Name dialog box.

3. Select the Paste **L**ist button. Excel pastes the worksheet's names and ranges.

Changing a Range Name

If you need to change the name of one or more ranges, you can use one of two methods:

- If you've changed some row or column labels, just redefine the range names based on the new text and delete the old names (as described in the next section).
- Select the **I**nsert | **N**ame | **D**efine command, highlight the name you want to change in the Names in **W**orkbook list, make your changes in the edit box, and click on the **A**dd button.

Deleting a Range Name

If you no longer need a range name, you should delete the name from the worksheet to avoid cluttering the name list. Procedure 3.9 outlines the necessary steps.

PROCEDURE 3.9. DELETING A RANGE NAME.

1. Select the **I**nsert | **N**ame | **D**efine command to display the Define Name dialog box.
2. In the Names in **W**orkbook list, select the name you want to delete.
3. Select **D**elete. Excel deletes the name from the list.
4. Repeat steps 2 and 3 for any other names you want to delete.
5. When you're done, click on OK or press Enter.

Chapter

4

Working with Ranges

Once you've selected a range (and, optionally, given it a name), you need to do something with it. What can you do with a range? Well, perhaps a better question is what *can't* you do with a range. You'll find that most Excel tasks you perform will involve a range in one form or another. In this chapter, I show you some of the most common range chores, including copying, moving, and clearing ranges, inserting and deleting rows and columns, entering data in a range, and using the fill handle.

Copying a Range

As I mentioned in Chapter 2, "Workbook Basics," the quickest way to become productive with Excel is to avoid reinventing your worksheets. If you have a formula that works, or a piece of formatting that you've put a lot of effort into, don't start from scratch to create something similar. Instead, make a copy and then adjust the copy as necessary.

Thankfully, Excel offers all kinds of ways to make copies of your worksheet ranges. Most of these methods involve the Copy command, but I'll begin by showing you the very handy drag-and-drop method.

Using Drag-and-Drop to Copy a Range

If you have a mouse, you can use it to copy a range by selecting the range and then dragging it to the appropriate destination. There are no menus to maneuver and no risks of accidentally overwriting data because you can see exactly where the copied range will go. Procedure 4.1 shows you how to copy a range.

PROCEDURE 4.1. USING DRAG-AND-DROP TO COPY A RANGE.

1. Select the range you want to copy.
2. Hold down the Ctrl key.
3. Move the mouse pointer over any edge of the selection. You'll know you've positioned the mouse pointer correctly when it changes to an arrow with a plus sign (+).
4. With Ctrl still held down, begin dragging the mouse pointer to the destination range. Excel displays a gray outline that shows you the border of the copy.
5. When you've positioned the range border properly in the destination area, release the mouse button and then the Ctrl key (in that order). Excel pastes a copy of the original range.

SUPER NOTE

If you can't get drag-and-drop to work, you need to turn it on. Select the **T**ools | **O**ptions command, select the Edit tab, and activate the Allow Cell **D**rag and Drop check box.

Using the Copy Command

In Chapter 1, "Entering and Editing Data," you learned how to use Excel's Copy command to copy a single cell. Now that you know how to select a range, it's simple to extend the Copy operation to include multiple cells. You just need to remember that you can treat a range of cells as a unit; therefore, you can work with a range as though it were an individual cell.

SUPER CAUTION

Before copying a range, look at the destination area and make sure you won't be overwriting any nonblank cells. Remember that you can use the Undo command if you accidentally destroy some data. If you want to insert the range among some existing cells, see the section in this chapter titled "Inserting a Copy of a Range."

Follow the steps in Procedure 4.2 to copy a range using the Copy command.

PROCEDURE 4.2. COPYING A RANGE WITH THE COPY COMMAND.

1. Select the range you want to copy.
2. Select the **E**dit | **C**opy command. Excel copies the contents of the range to the Clipboard and displays a moving border around the range.
3. Select the upper-left cell of the destination range.
4. Select the **E**dit | **P**aste command. Excel pastes the range from the Clipboard to your destination.

SUPER NOTE

The Clipboard is a temporary storage location for the most recently cut or copied item.

Copying Shortcuts

Because copying a range is one of the most common worksheet tasks, Excel gives you several shortcut methods to help you get the job done quickly. Here's a summary:

- Toolbar method:

   Click on this tool in the Standard toolbar to copy the contents of the selected range to the Clipboard.

   Click on this tool in the Standard toolbar to paste the contents of the Clipboard into the destination range.
- Shortcut keys method: Press Ctrl+C to copy the selected range and Ctrl+V to paste it. If you're going to paste the copied range only once, you can just press Enter instead of selecting **E**dit | **P**aste.
- Shortcut menu method: Click on the right mouse button inside a selected range or cell to display the Range shortcut menu. Then select **C**opy or **P**aste as needed.

Making Multiple Copies of a Range

If you need to make multiple copies of a range, you can execute a separate Paste command for each destination, but Excel offers an easier way. Procedure 4.3 outlines the steps.

PROCEDURE 4.3. MAKING MULTIPLE COPIES OF A RANGE.

1. Select the range you want to copy.
2. Copy the range using any of the methods described previously.
3. Select the upper-left cell for each destination range (see Figure 4.1). The cells you select can be contiguous or noncontiguous. (See Chapter 3, "Getting Started with Ranges," to learn how to select noncontiguous cells.)

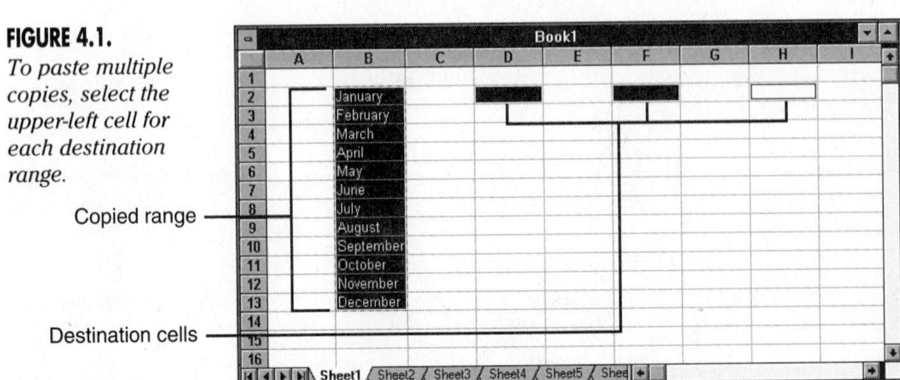

FIGURE 4.1.
To paste multiple copies, select the upper-left cell for each destination range.

4. Select the **Edit | Paste** command. Excel pastes the range from the Clipboard to each destination, as shown in Figure 4.2.

FIGURE 4.2.
When you execute the Paste command, Excel copies the range to each destination.

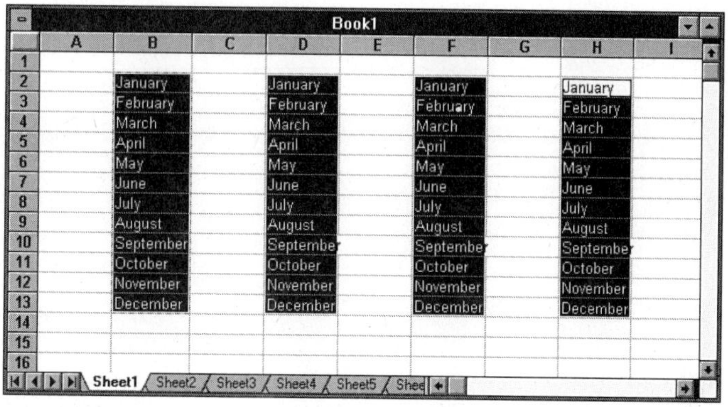

Inserting a Copy of a Range

If you don't want a pasted range to overwrite existing cells, you can tell Excel to *insert* the range. In this case, Excel moves the existing cells out of harm's way before pasting the range from the Clipboard. (As you'll see, you have control over where Excel moves the existing cells.) Follow the steps in Procedure 4.4 to insert a copy of a range.

PROCEDURE 4.4. INSERTING A COPY OF A RANGE.

1. Select the range you want to copy.
2. Use any of the methods described earlier in this chapter to copy the range to the Clipboard.
3. Select the upper-left cell of the destination range.
4. Select the **Insert | Copied Cells** command. Excel displays the Insert Paste dialog box to enable you to choose where to move the existing cells that would otherwise be overwritten (see Figure 4.3).

SUPER TIP

You also can insert a copied range by right-clicking on the destination cell and selecting the Insert Copied Cells command from the shortcut menu.

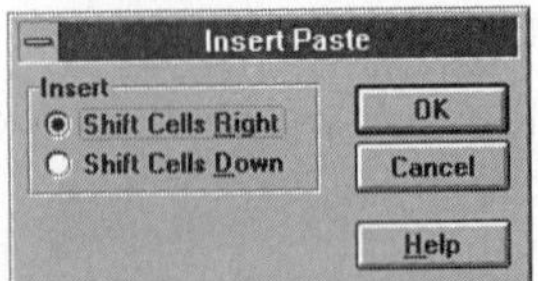

FIGURE 4.3.
Use the Insert Paste dialog box to tell Excel which direction to move the existing cells.

5. Select Shift Cells **R**ight to move the cells to the right or Shift Cells **D**own to move them down.
6. Click on OK or press Enter. Excel shifts the existing cells and then pastes the range from the Clipboard.

SUPER NOTE

To learn about more advanced range-copying techniques, such as copying only specific cell attributes and transposing rows and columns, see Chapter 60, "Advanced Range Topics."

Moving a Range

Moving a range is very similar to copying a range, except that, as with moving individual cells, the source range is deleted. You also have the choice of using drag-and-drop or the menu commands.

Using Drag-and-Drop to Move a Range

The drag-and-drop method for moving a range is identical to the one you learned for copying a range, except that you don't have to hold down the Ctrl key. Follow the steps in Procedure 4.5.

PROCEDURE 4.5. USING DRAG-AND-DROP TO MOVE A RANGE.

1. Select the range you want to move.
2. Move the mouse pointer over any edge of the selection until you see the pointer change to an arrow.
3. Drag the mouse pointer to the destination range. Excel displays a gray outline that shows the border of the copy.
4. When you've positioned the range border properly in the destination area, release the mouse button.
5. If your moved range will paste over any nonblank cells, Excel asks whether you want to overwrite them. Click on OK to continue. Otherwise, Excel deletes the original range and pastes it in the destination.

Using the Menu Commands to Move a Range

To move a range with the menu commands, you need to cut the range to the Clipboard and then paste it. Procedure 4.6 details the steps involved.

SUPER CAUTION

As with copying, you need to be careful when moving ranges so that you don't write over any existing data. If necessary, you can always insert the range using the **I**nsert | Cut C**e**lls command. If you do make a mistake, be sure to select the **E**dit | **U**ndo command right away.

PROCEDURE 4.6. MOVING A RANGE WITH THE MENU COMMANDS.

1. Select the range you want to move.
2. Select the **E**dit | Cu**t** command. Excel cuts the contents of the range to the Clipboard and displays a moving border around the range.
3. Select the upper-left cell of the destination range.
4. Select the **E**dit | **P**aste command. Excel pastes the range from the Clipboard to your destination.

SUPER TIP

For faster range moving, press Ctrl+X instead of selecting the **E**dit | Cu**t** command, or right-click on the source range and select the Cu**t** command from the Range shortcut menu.

Inserting and Deleting a Range

When you begin a worksheet, you use up rows and columns sequentially as you add data and formulas. Invariably, however, you'll need to go back and add some values or labels that you forgot or that you need for another part of the worksheet. When this happens, you need to insert ranges into your spreadsheet to make room for your new information. Conversely, you often have to remove old or unnecessary data from a spreadsheet, which requires you to delete ranges. The next couple of sections describe methods for inserting and deleting ranges in Excel.

Inserting an Entire Row or Column

The easiest way to insert a range into a worksheet is to insert an entire row or column. Procedure 4.7 shows you how.

PROCEDURE 4.7. INSERTING AN ENTIRE ROW OR COLUMN.

1. Select the row or column before which you want to insert the new row or column. If you want to insert multiple rows or columns, select the appropriate number of rows or columns, as shown in Figure 4.4.

FIGURE 4.4.
I've selected two rows at the point where I want to insert two new rows.

QTLYSUMM.XLS

	A	B	C	D	E	F	G	H	I	J
1										
2		Quarterly Expenses					Quarterly Sales			
3										
4		January	February	March			January	February	March	
5	Advertising	13,800	12,600	15,600		East	48,550	44,600	50,200	
6	Freight	8,700	8,250	9,100		West	42,100	40,900	43,750	
7	Rent	6,300	6,300	6,300		Midwest	38,500	37,800	40,050	
8	Supplies	3,900	3,600	4,200		South	43,750	41,400	45,650	
9	Salaries	48,000	48,000	49,500		TOTAL	172,900	164,700	179,650	
10	Travel	8,400	7,200	9,000						
11	Vehicles	1,500	1,800	1,800						
12	TOTAL	90,600	87,750	95,500						
13										
14										
15										

1st Quarter / 2nd Quarter / 3rd Quarter / 4th Quarter

2. If you're inserting rows, select the **Insert | Rows** command. Excel shifts the selected rows down, as shown in Figure 4.5. If you're inserting columns, select the **Insert | Columns** command. Excel shifts the selected columns to the right.

FIGURE 4.5.
When you insert rows, Excel shifts the existing cells down.

QTLYSUMM.XLS

	A	B	C	D	E	F	G	H	I	J
1										
2		Quarterly Expenses					Quarterly Sales			
3										
4		January	February	March			January	February	March	
5	Advertising	13,800	12,600	15,600		East	48,550	44,600	50,200	
6	Freight	8,700	8,250	9,100		West	42,100	40,900	43,750	
7	Rent	6,300	6,300	6,300		Midwest	38,500	37,800	40,050	
8	Supplies	3,900	3,600	4,200		South	43,750	41,400	45,650	
9	Salaries	48,000	48,000	49,500		TOTAL	172,900	164,700	179,650	
10	Travel	8,400	7,200	9,000						
11										
12										
13	Vehicles	1,500	1,800	1,800						
14	TOTAL	90,600	87,750	95,500						
15										

1st Quarter / 2nd Quarter / 3rd Quarter / 4th Quarter

SUPER TIP

As soon as you've selected a row or column, press Ctrl+plus sign (+) to insert a row or column quickly. You also can select Insert from the shortcut menu.

Inserting a Cell or Range

In some worksheets, you might need to insert only a single cell or a range of cells so as not to disturb the arrangement of surrounding data. For example, suppose you wanted to add a Repair line between Rent and Supplies in the Quarterly Expenses table in Figure 4.6. You wouldn't want to add an entire row because it would create a gap in the Quarterly Sales table. Instead, you could simply insert a range that covers just the area you need. Follow the steps in Procedure 4.8 to see how this is done.

QTLYSUMM.XLS

	A	B	C	D	E	F	G	H	I	J
1										
2	Quarterly Expenses					Quarterly Sales				
3										
4		January	February	March			January	February	March	
5	Advertising	13,800	12,600	15,600		East	48,550	44,600	50,200	
6	Freight	8,700	8,250	9,100		West	42,100	40,900	43,750	
7	Rent	6,300	6,300	6,300		Midwest	38,500	37,800	40,050	
8	Supplies	3,900	3,600	4,200		South	43,750	41,400	45,650	
9	Salaries	48,000	48,000	49,500		TOTAL	172,900	164,700	179,650	
10	Travel	8,400	7,200	9,000						
11	Vehicles	1,500	1,800	1,800						
12	TOTAL	90,600	87,750	95,500						
13										
14										
15										

1st Quarter / 2nd Quarter / 3rd Quarter / 4th Quarte

FIGURE 4.6.
When you insert cells in the Quarterly Expenses table, you don't want to disturb the Quarterly Sales table.

PROCEDURE 4.8. INSERTING A CELL OR RANGE.

1. Select the range where you want the new range to appear. In the Quarterly Expenses example, you would select the range A8:D8 (see Figure 4.6).
2. Select the **I**nsert | C**e**lls command. Excel displays the Insert dialog box.
3. Select either Shift Cells **R**ight or Shift Cells **D**own, as appropriate.
4. Click on OK or press Enter. Excel inserts the range (see Figure 4.7).

QTLYSUMM.XLS

	A	B	C	D	E	F	G	H	I	J
1										
2	Quarterly Expenses					Quarterly Sales				
3										
4		January	February	March			January	February	March	
5	Advertising	13,800	12,600	15,600		East	48,550	44,600	50,200	
6	Freight	8,700	8,250	9,100		West	42,100	40,900	43,750	
7	Rent	6,300	6,300	6,300		Midwest	38,500	37,800	40,050	
8						South	43,750	41,400	45,650	
9	Supplies	3,900	3,600	4,200		TOTAL	172,900	164,700	179,650	
10	Salaries	48,000	48,000	49,500						
11	Travel	8,400	7,200	9,000						
12	Vehicles	1,500	1,800	1,800						
13	TOTAL	90,600	87,750	95,500						
14										
15										

1st Quarter / 2nd Quarter / 3rd Quarter / 4th Quarte

FIGURE 4.7.
Excel has shifted the existing cells down to create room for the new range.

Deleting an Entire Row or Column

Deleting a row or column is similar to inserting. In this case, however, you need to exercise a little more caution because a hasty deletion can have disastrous effects on your worksheet. (However, you can select the **Edit | Undo** command if you make any mistakes.)

Procedure 4.9 shows you how to delete a row or column.

PROCEDURE 4.9. DELETING AN ENTIRE ROW OR COLUMN.

1. Select the row or column you want to delete.

> **SUPER TIP**
>
> Press Ctrl+Spacebar to select an entire column or Shift+Spacebar to select an entire row.

2. Select the **Edit | Delete** command. Excel deletes the row or column and shifts the remaining data appropriately.

> **SUPER TIP**
>
> Press Ctrl+minus sign (–) to quickly delete a row or column. You also can select Delete from the shortcut menu.

Deleting a Cell or Range

If you need to delete only one cell or a range to avoid deleting surrounding data, follow the steps Procedure 4.10.

PROCEDURE 4.10. DELETING A CELL OR RANGE.

1. Select the cell or range you want to delete.
2. Select the **E**dit | **D**elete command. Excel displays the Delete dialog box.
3. Select either Shift Cells **L**eft or Shift Cells **U**p, as appropriate.
4. Click on OK or press Enter. Excel deletes the range.

Clearing a Range

As you've seen, deleting a range actually removes the cells from the worksheet. What if you want the cells to remain, but you want their contents or formats cleared? For that, you can use Excel's Clear command, as described in Procedure 4.11.

PROCEDURE 4.11. CLEARING A RANGE.

1. Select the range you want to clear.
2. Select the **E**dit | Cle**a**r command. Excel displays a submenu of Clear commands.
3. Select either **A**ll, **F**ormats, **C**ontents, or **N**otes, as appropriate.
4. Click on OK or press Enter.

SUPER TIP

To quickly delete the contents of a range, press Delete. You also can select Clear Contents from the Range shortcut menu.

Using Excel's Go To Command

The Go To command enables you to leap quickly and accurately around a worksheet. If you like, you can enter just cell references in the Go To dialog box, but its real power is evident when you use it to jump to (and simultaneously select) range names. Procedure 4.12 outlines how you use the Go To feature.

PROCEDURE 4.12. USING THE GO TO COMMAND.

1. Select the **E**dit | **G**o To command. Excel displays the Go To dialog box.
2. Select a range name from the **G**o To list, or type in a cell reference or range name in the **R**eference text box.
3. Click on OK or press Enter. Excel selects the range or cell.

SUPER TIP

Press F5 to quickly activate the Go To command.

SUPER TIP

After selecting a range with Go To, you can return to your previous location by selecting **E**dit | **G**o To and then selecting OK without changing anything in the **R**eference area.

Data Entry in a Range

If you know in advance the range you'll be using for data entry, you can save yourself some time and keystrokes by selecting the range before you begin. As you enter your data in each cell, use the keys listed in Table 4.1 to navigate the range.

Table 4.1. Navigation keys for a selected range.

Key	*Result*
Enter	Moves down one row
Shift+Enter	Moves up one row
Tab	Moves right one column
Shift+Tab	Moves left one column
Ctrl+. (period)	Moves from corner to corner in the range
Ctrl+Alt+right arrow	Moves to the next range in a noncontiguous selection
Ctrl+Alt+left arrow	Moves to the previous range in a noncontiguous selection

The advantage of this technique is that the active cell never leaves the range. For example, if you press Enter after adding data to a cell in the last row of the range, the active cell moves back to the top row and over one column.

Filling a Range

If you need to fill in a range with a particular value or formula, Excel gives you two methods:

- Select the range you want to fill, type the value or formula, and press Ctrl+Enter. Excel fills the entire range with whatever you entered in the formula bar.
- Enter the initial value or formula, select the range you want to fill (including the initial cell), and select the **E**dit | F**i**ll command. Then select the appropriate command from the submenu that appears. For example, if you're filling a range down from the initial cell, select the **D**own command. If multiple sheets are selected, use the **E**dit | F**i**ll | **A**cross Worksheets command to fill the range in each worksheet.

SUPER TIP

Press Ctrl+R to select the **E**dit | F**i**ll | **R**ight command or Ctrl+D to select the **E**dit | F**i**ll | **D**own command.

Using the Fill Handle

The *fill handle* is the small black square in the bottom-right corner of the active cell or range. This handy little tool can do many useful things, including creating a series of text or numeric values and filling, clearing, inserting, and deleting ranges. The next few sections show you how to use the fill handle to perform each of these operations.

Creating Text and Numeric Series

Worksheets often use text series (such as January, February, March or Sunday, Monday, Tuesday) and numeric series (such as 1, 3, 5 or 1993, 1994, 1995). Rather than entering these series by hand, you can use the fill handle to create them automatically. Procedure 4.13 covers the details.

PROCEDURE 4.13. CREATING A SERIES WITH THE FILL HANDLE.

1. For a text series, select the first cell of the range you want to use and enter the initial value. For a numeric series, enter the first two values and then select both cells.

2. Position the mouse pointer over the fill handle. The pointer changes to a plus sign (+).
3. Drag the mouse pointer until the gray border encompasses the range you want to fill. If you're not sure where to stop, look at the formula bar's Name box, which shows you the series value of the last selected cell.
4. Release the mouse button. Excel fills in the range with the series.

Figure 4.8 shows several series created with the fill handle (the bold cells are the initial fill values). Notice, in particular, that Excel increments any text value with a numeric component (such as Quarter 1).

FILLS.XLS

	A	B	C	D	E	F	G
1	Series Created with the Fill Handle						
2							
3	**1**	**1-Jan**	**Sunday**	**9:00**	**1st Value**	**Quarter 1**	**Customer 1001**
4	**3**	**8-Jan**	Monday	10:00	2nd Value	Quarter 2	**Name:**
5	5	15-Jan	Tuesday	11:00	3rd Value	Quarter 3	Customer 1002
6	7	22-Jan	Wednesday	12:00	4th Value	Quarter 4	Name:
7	9	29-Jan	Thursday	13:00	5th Value	Quarter 1	Customer 1003
8	11	5-Feb	Friday	14:00	6th Value	Quarter 2	Name:
9	13	12-Feb	Saturday	15:00	7th Value	Quarter 3	Customer 1004
10	15	19-Feb	Sunday	16:00	8th Value	Quarter 4	Name:
11	17	26-Feb	Monday	17:00	9th Value	Quarter 1	Customer 1005
12	19	5-Mar	Tuesday	18:00	10th Value	Quarter 2	Name:
13	21	12-Mar	Wednesday	19:00	11th Value	Quarter 3	Customer 1006
14	23	19-Mar	Thursday	20:00	12th Value	Quarter 4	Name:
15	25	26-Mar	Friday	21:00	13th Value	Quarter 1	Customer 1007
16	27	2-Apr	Saturday	22:00	14th Value	Quarter 2	Name:
17	29	9-Apr	Sunday	23:00	15th Value	Quarter 3	Customer 1008

Sheet1 / Sheet2 / Sheet3 / Sheet4 / Sheet5 / Shee

FIGURE 4.8.
Some sample series created with the fill handle. Bold entries are the initial fill values.

Here are a few guidelines to keep in mind when using the fill handle to create series:

- Dragging the handle down or to the right increments the values. Dragging it up or to the left decrements the values.
- The fill handle recognizes standard abbreviations such as Jan and Sun.
- To vary the series interval for a text series, enter the first two values of the series and then select both of them before dragging. For example, entering `1st` and `3rd` would produce the series `1st, 3rd, 5th,` and so on.
- If you use three or more numbers as the initial values for the fill handle series, Excel creates a "best-fit" or "trend" line. To learn more about using Excel for trend analysis, see Chapter 35, "Basic Analytic Methods."

SUPER NOTE

Excel 5.0 enables you to create custom AutoFill series. See Chapter 66, "Customizing Excel's Options and Workspace," to learn more.

Filling a Range

You can use the fill handle to fill a range with a value or formula. Just enter your initial values or formulas, select them, and then drag the fill handle over the destination range (assuming that the data you're copying won't create a series). When you release the mouse button, Excel fills the range.

Clearing a Range

To clear the values and formulas in a range with the fill handle, you can use either of two techniques:

- If you want to clear only the values and formulas in a range, just drag the fill handle into the range and over the cells you want to clear. Excel grays out the cells as you select them. When you release the mouse button, Excel clears the cell's values and formulas.
- If you want to clear everything from the range (values, formulas, formats, and notes), hold down the Ctrl key. Next, drag the fill handle into the range and over each cell you want to clear. Excel clears the cells when you release the mouse button.

Inserting a Row or Column

You can use the fill handle to quickly insert entire rows and columns. Begin by selecting the row or column where you want to perform the insertion. You'll see that the first cell in the row or column contains the fill handle. Next, hold down the Shift key and drag the fill handle in the direction that you want to insert the rows or columns. The number of rows or columns you drag across determines the number of rows or columns that gets inserted. When you release the mouse button and the Shift key, Excel performs the insertion.

Inserting a Range

If you need to insert only a range, select the range in which you want the insertion to occur, hold down the Shift key, and drag the fill handle over the area where you want the new range inserted. When you release the mouse button and the Shift key, Excel inserts the range.

Creating a Series

You also can use the Excel's Series command to fill in a range of values. Follow the steps outlined in Procedure 4.14.

PROCEDURE 4.14. CREATING A SERIES.

1. Select the first cell you want to use for the series and enter the starting value. If you want to create a series out of a particular pattern (such as 2,4,6,...), fill in enough cells to define the pattern.
2. Select the entire range you want to fill.
3. Select the **E**dit | F**i**ll | **S**eries command. Excel displays the Series dialog box, shown in Figure 4.9.

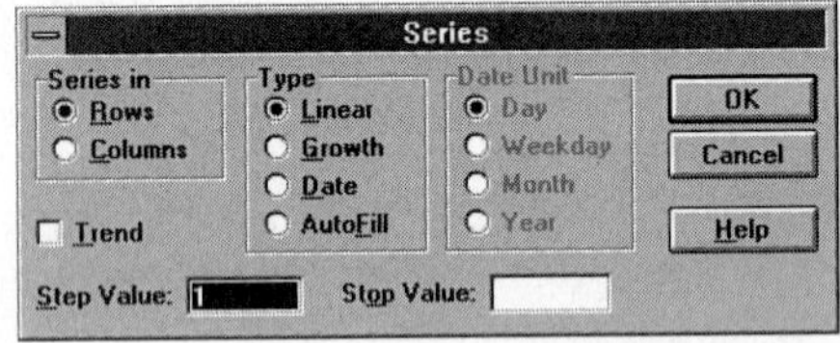

FIGURE 4.9.
Use the Series dialog box to define the series you want to create.

4. In the Series in group, select **R**ows to create the series in rows starting from the active cell, or **C**olumns to create the series in columns.
5. Use the Type group to enter the type of series you want. You have the following options:

Linear	The next series value is found by adding the step value (see step 7) to the previous value in the series.
Growth	The next series value is found by multiplying the previous value by the step value.
Date	Creates a series of dates based on the option you select in the Date Unit group (D**a**y, **W**eekday, **M**onth, or **Y**ear).
Auto**F**ill	This option works much like the fill handle does. You can use it to extend a numeric pattern or a text series (for example, Qtr1, Qtr2, Qtr3).

6. If you want to extend a series trend, activate the **T**rend check box. (See Chapter 35, "Basic Analytic Methods," for a discussion of trend analysis.) This option is available only if you selected a **L**inear or **G**rowth series type.
7. If you selected a **L**inear, **G**rowth, or **D**ate series type, enter a number in the **S**tep Value box. This number is what Excel uses to increment each value in the series.
8. To place a limit on the series, enter the appropriate number in the St**o**p Value box.
9. Click on OK or press Enter. Excel fills in the series and returns you to the worksheet.

Figure 4.10 shows some sample column series. The Growth series stops at cell C14 (value 128) because the next term in the series (256) is greater than the stop value of 250. The Day series fills the range with every second date (because the step value is 2). The Weekday series is slightly different; the dates are sequential, but weekends are skipped.

FIGURE 4.10.

Some sample column series generated with the Series command.

SERIES.XLS

	A	B	C	D	E	F	G	H
1	Series Created with the Series Command							
3	Series Type:	Linear	Growth	Date (Day)	Date (Weekday)	Date (Month)		
4	Step Value:	5	2	2	1	6		
5	Stop Value:	-	250					
7		0	1	1/1/94	1/1/94	1/1/94		
8		5	2	1/3/94	1/3/94	7/1/94		
9		10	4	1/5/94	1/4/94	1/1/95		
10		15	8	1/7/94	1/5/94	7/1/95		
11		20	16	1/9/94	1/6/94	1/1/96		
12		25	32	1/11/94	1/7/94	7/1/96		
13		30	64	1/13/94	1/10/94	1/1/97		
14		35	128	1/15/94	1/11/94	7/1/97		
15		40		1/17/94	1/12/94	1/1/98		
16		45		1/19/94	1/13/94	7/1/98		

Sheet1 / Sheet2 / Sheet3 / Sheet4 / Sheet5 / Shee

Chapter

5

Building Formulas

A worksheet is merely a collection of numbers and text until you define some kind of relationship among the various entries. You do this by creating *formulas* that perform calculations and produce results. This chapter takes you through some formula basics and then shows you how to build your own formulas.

Understanding Formula Basics

Most worksheets are created to provide answers to specific questions: What is the company's profit? Are expenses over or under budget and by how much? What is the future value of an investment? You can answer these questions, and an infinite variety of others, by using Excel formulas.

In the simplest case, you could enter something such as =2+3 into a cell (go ahead and try it). The answer, 5, appears in the cell immediately. You supplied an equals sign (=) to tell Excel you're entering a formula (and not just a constant), a couple of *values* (the numbers 2 and 3), and an *operator* (the plus sign). This is the basic structure of all Excel formulas. By combining any number of values and operators with the equals sign, you can create formulas that are as complex as your needs.

Procedure 5.1 outlines the basic steps in building a formula.

PROCEDURE 5.1. BUILDING A FORMULA.

1. Select the cell you want to use for the formula.
2. Type an equals sign (=).
3. Enter a value, cell reference, range, range name, or function name.

SUPER NOTE

When entering a cell reference or range in a formula, you could just type in the cell address or range coordinates, but it's often faster and more accurate to select them with your mouse. Just click on the cell or select the range (using any of the mouse techniques you learned in Chapter 3, "Getting Started with Ranges"). The address or range coordinates appear automatically in the formula at the insertion point.

SUPER TIP

If you need to enter a range name in a formula, select the name from the formula bar's Name box.

4. Enter an operator (such as + or *).

5. Repeat steps 3 and 4 until the formula is complete.
6. Click on the Enter box or press Enter to accept the formula.

If you want the active cell to have the same formula as the cell directly above it, press Ctrl+' (apostrophe) to make a quick copy.

Excel divides formulas into four groups: arithmetic, comparison, text, and reference. Each group has its own set of operators, and you use each group in different ways. In the next few sections, I'll show you how to use each type of formula.

Using Arithmetic Formulas

Arithmetic formulas are by far the most common type of formula. They combine numbers, cell addresses, and function results with mathematical operators to perform calculations. I've summarized the mathematical operators used in arithmetic formulas in Table 5.1.

Table 5.1. The arithmetic operators.

Operator	*Name*	*Example*	*Result*
+	Addition	=10+5	15
–	Subtraction	=10–5	5
–	Negation	=–10	–10
*	Multiplication	=10*5	50
/	Division	=10/5	2
%	Percentage	=10%	0.1
^	Exponentiation	=10^5	10000

Most of these are straightforward, but the exponentiation operator may require further explanation. The formula =x^y means that the value *x* is raised to the power *y*. For example, =3^2 produces the result 9 (that is, 3*3=9). Similarly, =2^4 produces 16 (that is, 2*2*2*2=16).

Using Comparison Formulas

A *comparison formula* is a statement that compares two or more numbers, text strings, cell contents, or function results. If the statement is true, the result of the formula is given the logical value TRUE (which is equivalent to 1). If the statement is false, the formula returns the logical value FALSE (which is equivalent to 0). Table 5.2 summarizes the operators you can use in logical formulas.

Table 5.2. Comparison formula operators.

Operator	*Name*	*Example*	*Result*
=	Equal to	=10=5	FALSE
>	Greater than	=10>5	TRUE
<	Less than	=10<5	FALSE
>=	Greater than or equal to	="a">="b"	FALSE
<=	Less than or equal to	="a"<="b"	TRUE
<>	Not equal to	="a"<>"b"	TRUE

There are many uses for comparison formulas. For example, you could determine whether or not to pay a salesperson a bonus by using a comparison formula to compare their actual sales with a predetermined quota. If the sales are greater than the quota, the rep is awarded the bonus. You also can monitor credit collection. For example, if the amount a customer owes is more than 150 days past due, you might send the invoice to a collection agency.

Using Text Formulas

So far, I've discussed formulas that calculate or make comparisons and return values. A *text formula* is a formula that returns text. Text formulas use the ampersand (&) operator to work with text cells, text strings enclosed in quotation marks, and text function results.

One way to use text formulas is to concatenate text strings. For example, if you enter the formula ="soft"&"ware" into a cell, Excel displays software. Note that the quotation marks and ampersand are not shown in the result. I show you other uses for text formulas in Chapter 6, "Working with Functions."

Using Reference Formulas

The reference operators combine two cell references or ranges to create a single joint reference. I discuss reference formulas in detail in Chapter 60, "Advanced Range Topics." For now, Table 5.3 summarizes the available operators.

Table 5.3. Reference formula operators.

Operator	*Name*	*Description*
: (colon)	Range	Produces a range from two cell references (for example, A1:C5)
(space)	Intersection	Produces a range that is the intersection of two ranges
, (comma)	Union	Produces a range that is the union of two ranges

Understanding Operator Precedence

You'll often use simple formulas that contain just two values and a single operator. In practice, however, most formulas you use will have a number of values and operators. In these more complex expressions, the order in which the calculations are performed becomes crucial. For example, consider the formula =3+5^2. If you calculate from left to right, the answer you get is 64 (3+5 equals 8 and 8^2 equals 64). However, if you perform the exponentiation first and then the addition, the result is 28 (5^2 equals 25 and 3+25 equals 28). As you can see, a single formula can produce multiple answers depending on the order in which you perform the calculations.

To control this problem, Excel evaluates a formula according to a predefined *order of precedence*. This order of precedence enables Excel to calculate a formula unambiguously by determining which part of the formula it calculates first, which part second, and so on.

The Order of Precedence

The order of precedence that Excel uses is determined by the various formula operators I outlined earlier. Table 5.4 summarizes the complete order of precedence used by Excel.

Table 5.4. The Excel order of precedence.

Operator	*Operation*	*Order of Precedence*
:	Range	1st
Space	Intersection	2nd
,	Union	3rd

continues

Table 5.4. continued

Operator	*Operation*	*Order of Precedence*
–	Negation	4th
%	Percentage	5th
^	Exponentiation	6th
* and /	Multiplication and division	7th
+ and –	Addition and subtraction	8th
&	Concatenation	9th
= < > <= >= <>	Comparison	10th

From this table, you can see that Excel performs exponentiation before addition. Therefore, the correct answer for the formula =3+5^2, given previously, is 28. Notice, as well, that some operators in Table 5.4 have the same order of precedence (for example, multiplication and division). This means that it doesn't matter which order these operators are evaluated. For example, consider the formula =5*10/2. If you perform the multiplication first, the answer you get is 25 (5*10 equals 50, and 50/2 equals 25). If you perform the division first, you also get an answer of 25 (10/2 equals 5, and 5*5 equals 25). By convention, Excel evaluates operators with the same order of precedence from left to right.

Controlling the Order of Precedence

There are times when you want to override the order of precedence. For example, suppose you want to create a formula that calculates the pre-tax cost of an item. If you bought something for $10.65, including 7 percent sales tax, and you wanted to find the cost of the item less the tax, you would use the formula =10.65/1.07, which gives you the correct answer of $9.95. In general, the formula is

```
               Total Cost
Pre-tax cost = ----------
               1 + Tax Rate
```

Figure 5.1 shows how you might implement such a formula. Cell B5 displays the `Total Cost` variable, and cell B6 displays the `Tax Rate` variable. Given these parameters, your first instinct might be to use the formula =B5/1+B6 to calculate the original cost. This formula is shown in cell E9, and the result is given in cell D9.

As you can see, this answer is incorrect. What happened? Well, according to the rules of precedence, Excel performs division before addition, so the value in B5 first is divided by 1 and then is added to the value in B6. To get the correct answer, you have to override the order of precedence so that the addition 1+B6 is performed first.

You do this by surrounding that part of the formula with parentheses, as shown in cell E10. When this is done, you get the correct answer (cell D10).

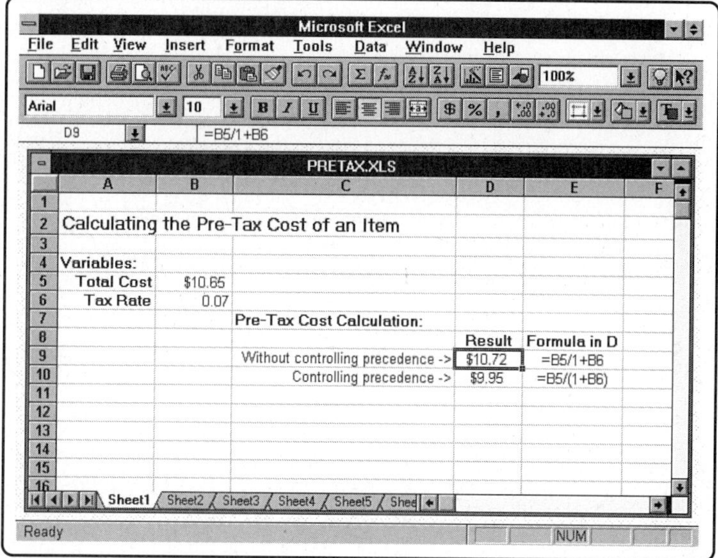

FIGURE 5.1.
Controlling the order of precedence.

In general, you can use parentheses to control the order that Excel uses to calculate formulas. Terms inside parentheses are always calculated first; terms outside parentheses are calculated sequentially (according to the order of precedence). To gain even more control over your formulas, you can place parentheses inside one another; this is called *nesting* parentheses. Excel always evaluates the innermost set of parentheses first. Following are some sample formulas:

Formula	*1st Step*	*2nd Step*	*3rd Step*	*Result*
3^(15/5)*2-5	3^3*2-5	27*2-5	54-5	49
3^((15/5)*2-5)	3^(3*2-5)	3^(6-5)	3^1	3
3^(15/(5*2-5))	3^(15/(10-5))	3^(15/5)	3^3	27

Notice that the order of precedence rules also hold within parentheses. For example, in the expression (5*2-5), the term 5*2 is calculated before 5 is subtracted.

Using parentheses to determine the order of calculations enables you to gain full control over Excel formulas. This way, you can make sure that the answer given by a formula is the one *you* want.

SUPER CAUTION

One of the most common mistakes when using parentheses in formulas is to forget to close a parenthetic term with a right parenthesis. If you do this, Excel generates a `Parentheses do not match` message. To make sure you've closed each parenthetic term, count all the left and right parentheses. If these totals don't match, you know you've left out a parenthesis.

Controlling Worksheet Calculation

Excel always calculates a formula when you confirm its entry, and the program normally recalculates existing formulas automatically whenever their data changes. This behavior is fine for small worksheets, but it can slow you down if you have a complex model that takes several seconds or even several *minutes* to recalculate.

To turn off automatic recalculation, follow the steps in Procedure 5.2.

PROCEDURE 5.2. CONTROLLING WORKSHEET CALCULATIONS.

1. Select the **T**ools | **O**ptions command. The Options dialog box appears.
2. Select the Calculation tab to display the Calculation options (see Figure 5.2).

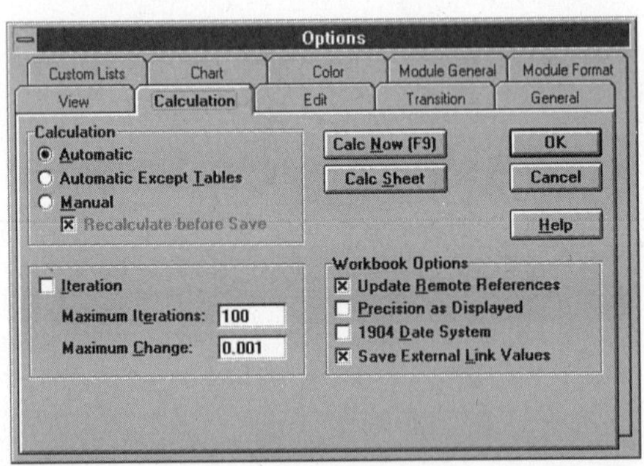

FIGURE 5.2.
Select the Calculation tab in the Options dialog box to control worksheet calculations.

3. To disable automatic recalculation, select the **M**anual option. If you would prefer to leave automatic calculation on except for data tables, select the Automatic Except **T**ables option.
4. If you chose **M**anual, you also can decide not to recalculate before saving the worksheet. Just turn off the Recalc**u**late before Save check box.

5. Click on OK or press Enter.

With manual calculation turned on, you'll see a Calculate message appear in the status bar whenever your worksheet data changes and your formula results need to be updated. When you want to recalculate, select **T**ools | **O**ptions and choose one of the following from the Calculation tab:

- Click on the Calc **N**ow button to recalculate every open worksheet.
- Click on the Calc **S**heet button to recalculate only the active worksheet.

SUPER TIP

You can quickly recalculate the open worksheets by pressing F9. If you want to calculate only the active worksheet, press Shift+F9.

If you want to recalculate only part of your worksheet while manual calculation is turned on, you have two options:

- To recalculate a single formula, select the cell containing the formula, activate the formula bar, and then confirm the cell (by pressing Enter or clicking on the Enter button).
- To recalculate a range, select the range, select the **E**dit | R**e**place command, and enter an equals sign (=) in both the Fi**n**d What and Re**p**lace With boxes. (Make sure that the Find Entire Cells **O**nly check box is deactivated.) When you select Replace **A**ll, Excel "replaces" the equals sign in each formula with another equals sign. This doesn't change anything, but it forces Excel to recalculate each formula.

Copying and Moving Formulas

In Chapter 4, "Working with Ranges," you learned how to copy and move ranges. The techniques for copying and moving ranges that contain formulas are identical, but the results are not as straightforward. For an example, see Figure 5.3, which shows a list of expense data for a company. The formula in cell C11 totals the January expenses. Excel's worksheet will calculate a new expense budget number for 1994 as a percentage increase of the actual 1993 total. Cell C3 displays the INCREASE variable (in this case, the increase being used is 9 percent). The formula that calculates the 1994 BUDGET number (cell C13 for the month of January) multiplies the 1993 TOTAL by the INCREASE (that is, =C11*C3).

The next step is to calculate the 1993 TOTAL expenses and the 1994 BUDGET figure for February. You could just type in each new formula, but you learned in the previous chapter that you can copy a cell much more quickly. Figure 5.4 shows the results when you copy the contents of cell C11 into cell D11. As you can see, Excel adjusts each term in the formula so only the February expenses are totaled. How did Excel know to do this? To answer this question, you need to know about Excel's *relative reference format*.

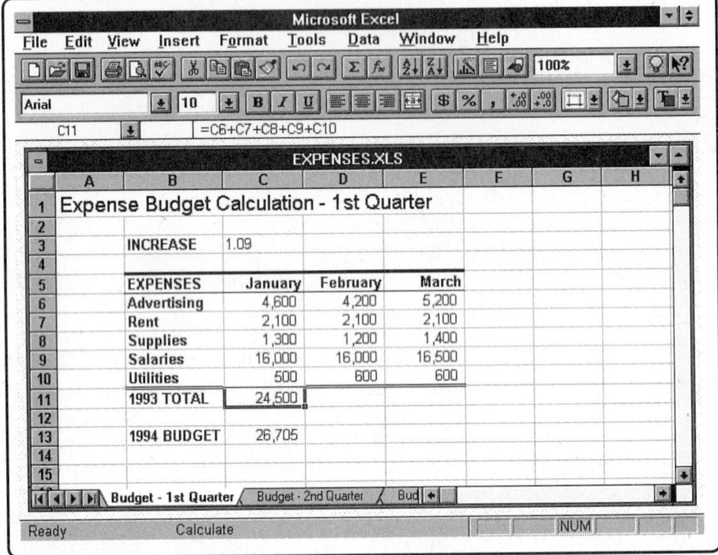

FIGURE 5.3.
A budget expenses worksheet.

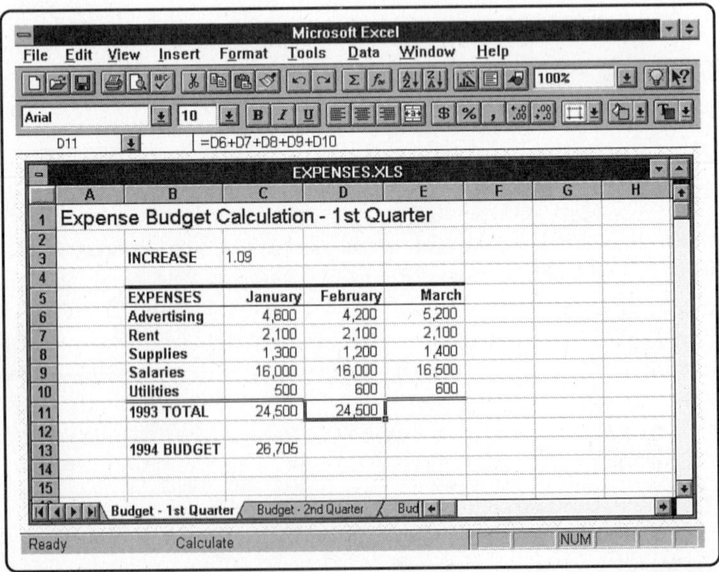

FIGURE 5.4.
When you copy the January 1993 TOTAL formula to February, Excel automatically adjusts the cell references.

Understanding Relative Reference Format

When you use a cell reference in a formula, Excel looks at the cell address relative to the location of the formula. For example, suppose you have the formula =A1*2 in cell A2. To Excel, this formula says, "Multiply the contents of the cell one row above this one by 2." This is called the *relative reference format*, and it's the default format for Excel. This means that if you copy this formula to cell A5, the relative reference is still "Multiply the contents of the cell one row above this one by 2," but the formula changes to =A4*2, because A4 is one row above A5.

Figure 5.4 shows why this format is useful. You had to copy only the formula in cell C11 to cell D11 and, thanks to relative referencing, everything comes out perfectly. To get the expense total for March, recopy the formula into cell E11. You'll find that this way of handling copy operations will save you incredible amounts of time when building your worksheet applications.

However, you need to exercise some care when copying or moving formulas. Return to the budget expense worksheet and try copying the 1994 BUDGET formula in cell C13 to cell D13. Figure 5.5 shows that the result is 0! What happened? The formula bar shows the problem: the new formula is =D11*D3. Cell D11 is the February 1993 TOTAL, and that's fine, but instead of the INCREASE cell (C3), the formula refers to a blank cell (D3). Excel treats blank cells as 0, so the answer is 0. The problem is the relative reference format. When the formula was copied, Excel assumed that the new formula should refer to cell D3. To see how you can correct this, you need to learn about another format: the *absolute reference format.*

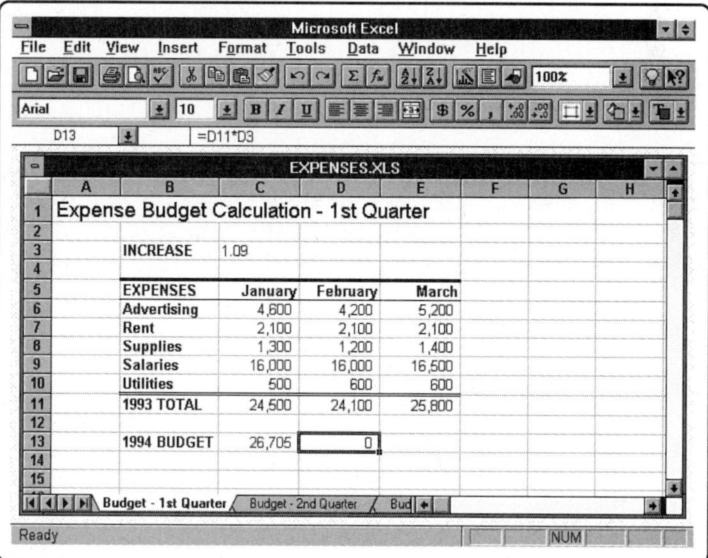

FIGURE 5.5.
Copying the January 1993 BUDGET formula to February creates a problem.

NOTE

The relative reference format problem doesn't occur when you move a formula. When you move a formula, Excel assumes you want to keep the same cell references.

Understanding Absolute Reference Format

When you refer to a cell in a formula using the absolute reference format, Excel uses the physical address of the cell. You tell the program that you want to use an absolute reference by placing dollar signs ($) before the row and column of the cell address. To return to the example in the preceding section, Excel interprets the formula =$A$1*2 as "Multiply the contents of cell A1 by 2." No matter where you copy or move this formula, the cell reference doesn't change. The cell address is said to be *anchored.*

To fix the budget expense worksheet, you need to anchor the INCREASE variable. To do this, change the October 1994 BUDGET formula in cell C13 to read =C11*$C$3. Once you've made this change, try copying the formula again to the February 1994 BUDGET column. You should get the proper value this time.

SUPER CAUTION

Most range names refer to absolute cell references. This means that when you copy a formula that uses a range name, the copied formula will use the same range name as the original, which might produce errors in your worksheet.

You also should know that you can enter a cell reference using a mixed reference format. In this format, you anchor either the cell's row (by placing the dollar sign in front of the row address only—for example, B$6) or its column (by placing the dollar sign in front of the column address only—for example, $B6).

SUPER TIP

You can quickly change the reference format of a cell address by using the F4 key. When editing a formula, place the cursor to the left of the cell address and keep pressing F4. Excel cycles through the various formats.

Copying a Formula Without Adjusting Relative References

If you need to copy a formula, but you don't want the formula's relative references to change, you can use three methods:

- If you want to copy the formula to the cell below it, just select the cell and press Ctrl+' (apostrophe).
- Activate the formula bar and use the mouse or keyboard to highlight the entire formula. Next, copy the formula to the Clipboard (by selecting **E**dit | **C**opy or by pressing Ctrl+C), then press the Esc key to deactivate the formula bar. Finally, select the cell in which you want the copy to appear and paste the formula there.
- Activate the formula bar and type an apostrophe (') at the beginning of the formula to convert it to text. Confirm the edit, copy the cell, paste it, and delete the apostrophe.

Displaying Worksheet Formulas

By default, Excel displays the results of a formula, rather than the formula itself, in cells. If you need to see a formula, you can simply choose the appropriate cell and look at the formula bar. However, there will be times when you'll want to see all the formulas in a worksheet (such as when you're troubleshooting your work). To do this, follow the steps in Procedure 5.3.

PROCEDURE 5.3. DISPLAYING WORKSHEET FORMULAS.

1. Select the **T**ools | **O**ptions command. The Options dialog box appears.
2. Select the View tab.
3. Activate the Fo**r**mulas check box.
4. Click on OK or press Enter. Excel displays the worksheet formulas.

SUPER TIP

Press Ctrl+` (backquote) to toggle a worksheet between values and formulas.

SUPER NOTE

For more information about troubleshooting formulas, see Chapter 61, "Advanced Formulas and Functions."

Converting a Formula to a Value

If a cell contains a formula whose value will never change, you can convert the formula to that value. This frees up memory for your worksheet because values use much less memory than formulas do. For example, you might have formulas in part of your worksheet that use values from a previous fiscal year. Because these numbers aren't likely to change, you can safely convert the formulas to their values. To do this, follow the steps in Procedure 5.4.

PROCEDURE 5.4. CONVERTING A FORMULA TO A VALUE.

1. Select the cell containing the formula you want to convert.
2. Double-click on the cell or press F2 to activate in-cell editing.
3. Press F9. The formula changes to its value.
4. Press Enter or click on the Enter box. Excel changes the cell to the value.

You'll often need to use the result of a formula in several places. If a formula is in cell C5, for example, you can enter `=C5` in every cell that you want to use the result. This is the best method if you think the formula result might change, because if it does, Excel updates the other cells automatically. However, if you're sure the result won't change, you can copy only the value of the formula into the other cells. Follow Procedure 5.5 to do this.

PROCEDURE 5.5. COPYING A FORMULA'S VALUE TO OTHER CELLS.

1. Select the cell that contains the formula.
2. Copy the cell.
3. Select the cell or cells to which you want to copy the value.
4. Select the **E**dit | Paste **S**pecial command. The Paste Special dialog box appears.
5. Activate the **V**alues option button in the Paste box.
6. Click on OK or press Enter. Excel pastes the cell's value to each cell you selected.

Working with Array Formulas

Many worksheets have rectangular ranges containing formulas that are identical except for the formula's cell references. For example, in the EXPENSE.XLS worksheet shown in Figure 5.6, the 1994 BUDGET figures are calculated with three formulas: C11*$C$4 (for January), D11*$C$4 (for February), and E11*$C$4 (for March). These formulas are identical except for the 1993 TOTAL cells used in each calculation (cells C11, D11, and E11—that is, the range C11:E11).

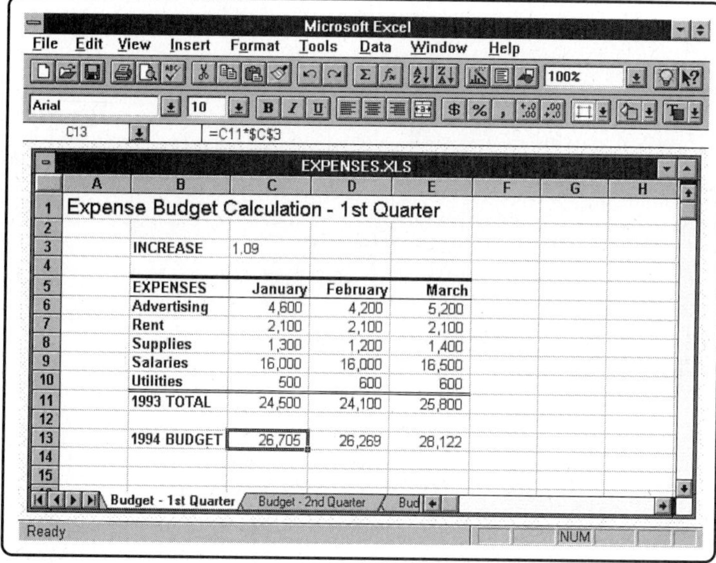

FIGURE 5.6.
The 1994 BUDGET calculations use three nearly identical formulas.

You could save some memory (as well as data entry time) by replacing all those formulas with a single *array formula*. Instead of using individual cell references, an array formula uses a range as data. This range tells Excel where to apply the formula; therefore, only the one formula needs to be stored in memory. Figure 5.7 shows the single array formula that replaces the three original calculations. You'll notice two things about this formula:

- The original individual cell references have been replaced by the range C11:E11.
- The formula is surrounded by braces ({ }). This identifies the formula as an array formula. (When you enter array formulas, you never need to enter these braces yourself. Excel adds them automatically, as you'll see in Procedure 5.6.)

Follow the steps in Procedure 5.6 to enter an array formula.

PROCEDURE 5.6. ENTERING AN ARRAY FORMULA.

1. Select the range you want to use for the array formula.
2. Enter the formula. Instead of entering individual cell references as variables, enter the appropriate range coordinates (or select the range using the mouse).
3. When your formula is complete, create the array by pressing Ctrl+Shift+Enter. Excel puts braces around the formula.

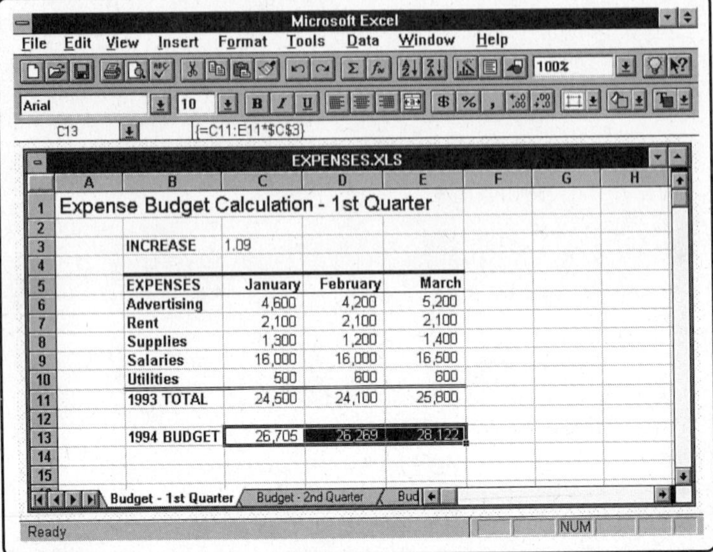

FIGURE 5.7.
The three formulas replaced by a single array formula.

SUPER NOTE

For more detailed information on arrays, see Chapter 60, "Advanced Range Topics."

Chapter

6

Working with Functions

This chapter introduces you to Excel's built-in functions. You'll learn what the functions are, what they can do, and how to use them. We'll also take a quick tour through each of Excel's nine function categories.

About Excel's Functions

Functions are formulas that have been predefined by Excel. They're designed to take you beyond the basic arithmetic and text formulas you've seen so far. They do this in three ways:

- Functions make simple but cumbersome formulas easier to use. For example, suppose you want to add a list of 100 numbers in a column starting at cell A1 and finishing at cell A100. Even if you wanted to, you wouldn't be able to enter 100 separate additions in a cell because you would run out of room (recall that cells are limited to 255 characters). Luckily, there's an alternative: the `SUM()` function. With this function, you'd simply enter `=SUM(A1:A100)`.
- Functions enable you to include complex mathematical expressions in your worksheets that otherwise would be impossible to construct using simple arithmetic operators. For example, determining a mortgage payment given the principal, interest, and term is a complicated matter at best, but Excel's `PMT()` function does it without breaking a sweat.
- Functions enable you to include data in your applications that you couldn't access otherwise. For example, the `INFO()` function can tell you how much memory is available on your system, what operating system you're using, what version number it is, and more.

As you can see, functions are a powerful addition to your worksheet-building arsenal. With the proper use of these tools, there is no practical limit to the kinds of applications you can create.

The Structure of a Function

Every function has the same basic form:

```
FUNCTION(argument1, argument2, ...)
```

The function begins with the function name (`SUM` or `PMT`, for example), which is followed by a list of *arguments* separated by commas and enclosed in parentheses. The arguments are the function's inputs—the data it uses to perform its calculations.

For example, the `FV()` function determines the future value of a regular investment based on three required arguments (and two optional ones I'll ignore for now; see the section in this chapter titled "Financial Functions"):

FV(***rate***,***nper***,***pmt***)

rate	The fixed rate of interest over the term of the investment.
nper	The number of deposits over the term of the investment.
pmt	The amount you'll deposit each time.

SUPER NOTE

Throughout this book, when I introduce a new function, I show the argument syntax and then describe each argument (as I just did with the `FV()` function). In the syntax line, I show the function's required arguments in ***`bold italic monospace`*** type and the optional arguments in *`regular italic monospace`* type.

After processing these inputs, `FV()` returns the total value of the investment at the end of the term. Figure 6.1 shows a simple future-value calculator that uses this function. (In case you're wondering, the `FV()` function returns a negative value—indicated by the brackets in cell C7—because Excel treats any money you have to pay as a negative number.)

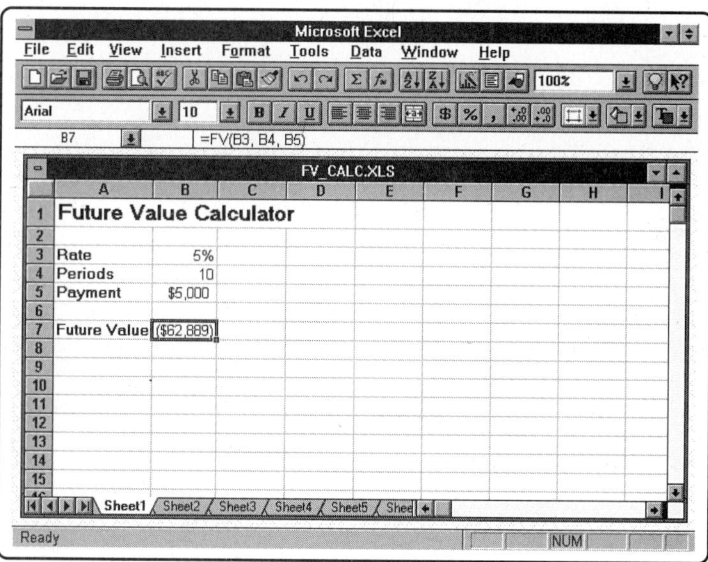

FIGURE 6.1.
The `FV()` function in action.

Entering Functions

You enter functions as you do any other data, but you have to follow these rules:

- You can enter the function name in either uppercase or lowercase letters. Excel always converts function names to uppercase.

- Always enclose function arguments in parentheses.
- Always separate multiple arguments with commas. (You might want to add a space after each comma to make the functions more readable.)
- You can use a function as an argument for another function. This is called *nesting* functions. For example, the function `AVERAGE(SUM(A1:A10), SUM(B1:B15))` sums two columns of numbers and returns the average of the two sums.

Using the Function Wizard

Although normally you'll type in your functions, there might be times when you can't remember the spelling of a function or the arguments it takes. To help you, Excel 5.0 provides a tool called the Function Wizard. It enables you to select the function you want from a list and prompts you to enter the appropriate arguments. Procedure 6.1 shows you how the Function Wizard works.

PROCEDURE 6.1. USING THE FUNCTION WIZARD.

1. To start a formula with a function, click on the Function Wizard tool in the Standard toolbar. Excel activates the formula bar, enters an equals sign and the most recently used function in the cell, and displays the Function Wizard - Step 1 of 2 dialog box, shown in Figure 6.2.

   If the Standard toolbar isn't displayed, you can activate the Function Wizard by clicking on the Function Wizard box in the formula bar.

Click on the Function Wizard tool in the Standard toolbar to start the Function Wizard.

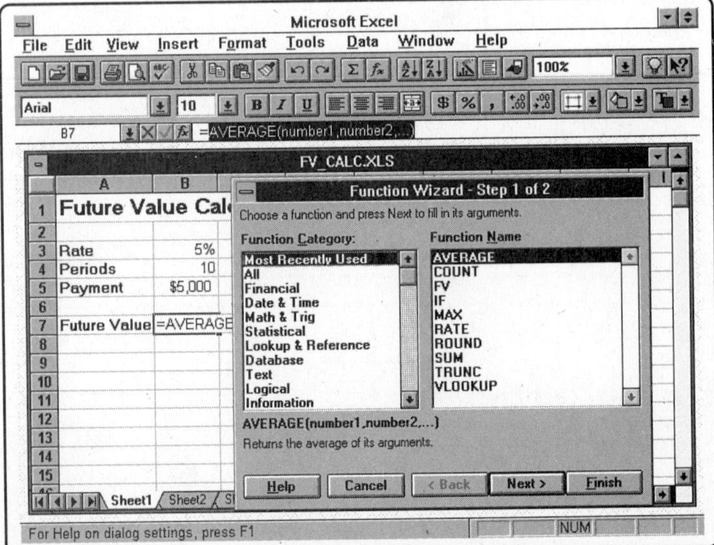

FIGURE 6.2.
Use the first Function Wizard dialog box to select a function.

SUPER TIP

To skip Step 1 of the Function Wizard, enter the name of the function in the cell and then either click on the Function Wizard button or press Ctrl+A.

2. In the Function **C**ategory list, select the type of function you need. If you're not sure, select All.
3. Select the function you want to use from the Function **N**ame list.
4. If you don't want to paste the function's arguments, click on the **F**inish button to return to the worksheet. Otherwise, click on the Next > button. Excel displays the Function Wizard - Step 2 of 2 dialog box, shown in Figure 6.3.

FIGURE 6.3.
Use the second Function Wizard dialog box to enter values for the function's arguments.

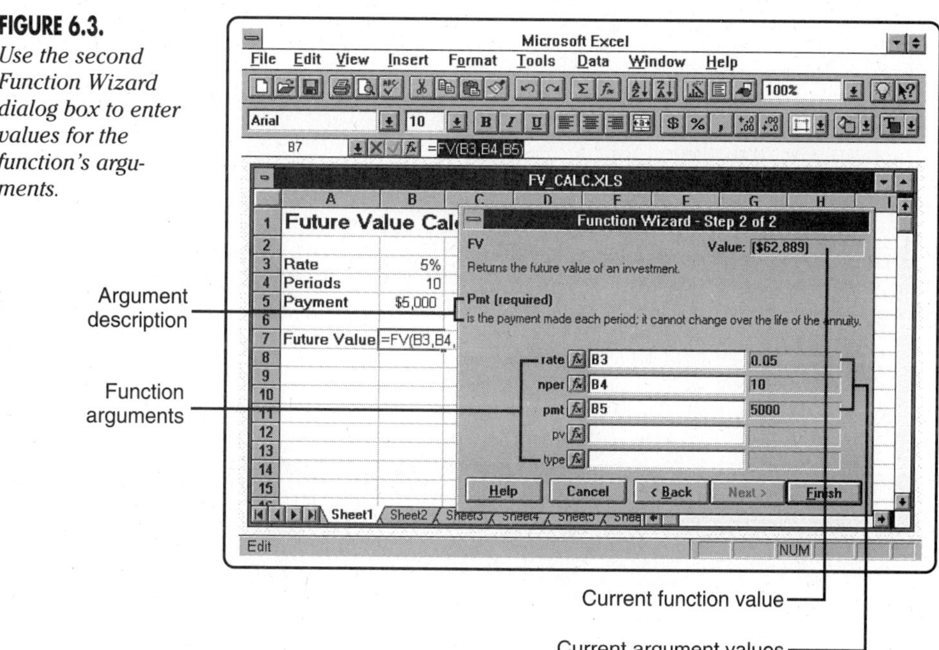

5. For each required argument and each optional argument you want to use, enter a value in the appropriate edit box.
6. When you're done, click on **F**inish. Excel pastes the function and its arguments into the cell.

Using Excel's Functions

Excel has a number of function categories, including the following:

- Database and list
- Date and time
- Financial
- Information
- Logical
- Lookup and reference
- Math and trigonometry
- Statistical
- Text

SUPER NOTE

Many Excel functions are available only by loading the Analysis Toolpack add-in macro. See Chapter 36, "Working with the Analysis Toolpack," for more information.

The following sections give you a brief overview of each function category, along with some examples.

SUPER NOTE

If you can't find what you need among Excel's built-in functions, you can create your own. See either Chapter 41, "Creating Function Macros," to learn how to create functions with the Excel 4.0 macro language, or Chapter 50, "Getting Started with Visual Basic," to learn how to create functions with Visual Basic for Applications.

SUPER NOTE

Some of the following sections contain tables of frequently used functions. Just to reiterate, ***`bold italic monospace`*** arguments are required by the function and *`regular italic monospace`* arguments are optional.

Database and List Functions

Excel's database and list functions help you analyze database information. They return values such as the maximum and minimum quantities in a field, the average of a field, and more. I won't discuss these functions in detail here, because I've devoted an entire chapter to them (see Chapter 32, "Summarizing List Data").

Date and Time Functions

The date and time functions enable you to convert dates and times to serial numbers and perform operations on those numbers. This is useful for such things as accounts receivable aging, project scheduling, and time management applications. Table 6.1 lists a few of the most commonly used date and time functions.

Table 6.1. Common date and time functions.

Function	*Description*
`DATE(`***year***`,`***month***`,`***day***`)`	Returns the serial number of a date
`DATEVALUE(`***date_text***`)`	Converts a date from text to a serial number
`DAY(`***serial_number***`)`	Converts a serial number to a day of the month
`HOUR(`***serial_number***`)`	Converts a serial number to an hour
`MINUTE(`***serial_number***`)`	Converts a serial number to a minute
`MONTH(`***serial_number***`)`	Converts a serial number to a month number (January = 1)
`NOW()`	Returns the serial number of the current date and time
`SECOND(`***serial_number***`)`	Converts a serial number to a second
`TIME(`***hour***`,`***minute***`,`***second***`)`	Returns the serial number of a time
`TIMEVALUE(`***time_text***`)`	Converts a time from text to a serial number
`TODAY()`	Returns the serial number of the current date
`WEEKDAY(`***serial_number***`)`	Converts a serial number to a day of the week (Sunday = 1)
`YEAR(`***serial_number***`)`	Converts a serial number to a year

Figure 6.4 shows an accounts receivable database. For each invoice, the due date is calculated by simply adding 30 to the invoice date. Column E uses the `TODAY()` function to calculate the number of days each invoice is past due.

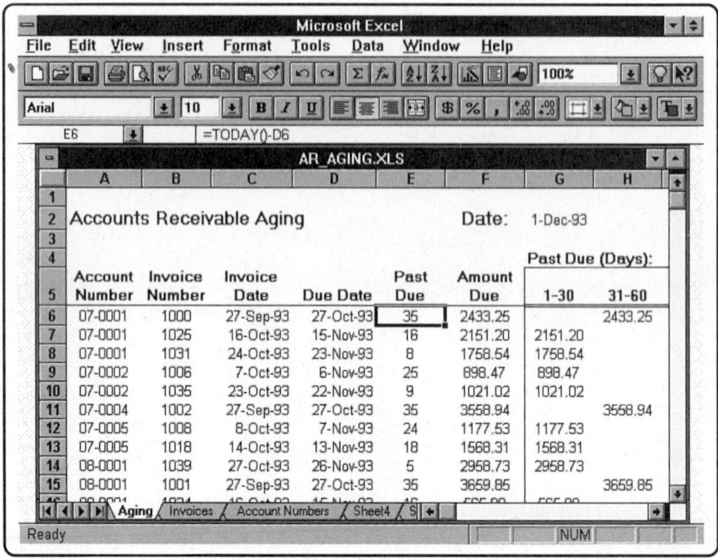

FIGURE 6.4. *This worksheet uses the* `TODAY()` *function to calculate the number of days an invoice is past due.*

Financial Functions

Excel's financial functions offer you powerful tools for building applications that manage both business and personal finances. You can use these functions to calculate such things as the internal rate of return of an investment, the future value of an annuity, or the yearly depreciation of an asset.

Although Excel has dozens of financial functions that use many different arguments, the following list covers those you'll use most frequently:

rate The fixed rate of interest over the term of the loan or investment.

nper The number of payments or deposit periods over the term of the loan or investment.

pmt The periodic payment or deposit.

pv The present value of the loan (the principal) or the initial deposit in an investment.

fv The future value of the loan or investment.

type The type of payment or deposit. Use 0 (the default) for end-of-period payments or deposits and 1 for beginning-of-period payments or deposits.

For most financial functions, the following rules apply:

- The underlying unit of both the interest rate and the period must be the same. For example, if the ***rate*** is the annual interest rate, you must express ***nper*** in years. Similarly, if you have a monthly interest rate, you must express ***nper*** in months.

- You enter money you receive as a positive quantity, and you enter money you pay as a negative quantity. For example, you always enter the loan principal as a positive number because it's money you receive from the bank.
- The ***nper*** argument should always be a positive integer quantity.

Table 6.2 lists a few common financial functions.

Table 6.2. Common financial functions.

Function	*Description*
`DB(`***cost***`,`***salvage***`,`***life***`,`***period***`,`*month*`)`	Returns the depreciation of an asset over a specified period using the fixed-declining balance method
`DDB(`***cost***`,`***salvage***`,`***life***`,`***period***`,`*factor*`)`	Returns the depreciation of an asset over a specified period using the double-declining balance method
`FV(`***rate***`,`***nper***`,`***pmt***`,`*pv*`,`*type*`)`	Returns the future value of an investment or loan
`IPMT(`***rate***`,`***per***`,`***nper***`,`***pv***`,`*fv*`,`*type*`)`	Returns the interest payment for a specified period of a loan
`IRR(`***values***`,`*guess*`)`	Returns the internal rate of return for a series of cash flows
`MIRR(`***values***`,`***finance_rate***`,`***reinvest_rate***`)`	Returns the modified internal rate of return for a series of periodic cash flows
`NPER(`***rate***`,`***pmt***`,`***pv***`,`*fv*`,`*type*`)`	Returns the number of periods for an investment or loan
`NPV(`***rate***`,`***value1***`,`*value2...*`)`	Returns the net present value of an investment based on a series of cash flows and a discount rate
`PMT(`***rate***`,`***nper***`,`***pv***`,`*fv*`,`*type*`)`	Returns the periodic payment for a loan or investment
`PPMT(`***rate***`,`***per***`,`***nper***`,`***pv***`,`*fv*`,`*type*`)`	Returns the principal payment for a specified period of a loan
`PV(`***rate***`,`***nper***`,`***pmt***`,`*fv*`,`*type*`)`	Returns the present value of an investment

continues

Table 6.2. continued

Function	*Description*
`RATE(`***`nper`***`,`***`pmt`***`,`***`pv`***`,`*`fv`*`,`*`type`*`,`*`guess`*`)`	Returns the periodic interest rate for a loan or investment
`SLN(`***`cost`***`,`***`salvage`***`,`***`life`***`)`	Returns the straight-line depreciation of an asset over one period
`SYD(`***`cost`***`,`***`salvage`***`,`***`life`***`,`***`per`***`)`	Returns sum-of-years digits depreciation of an asset over a specified period

Figure 6.5 shows a loan amortization schedule. The Amount, Rate, and Term variables represent the ***pv***, ***rate***, and ***nper*** arguments, respectively. Column E shows the monthly payment, column F the monthly interest, and column G the monthly principal. (Column D, the Period, is used by the `PPMT()` and `IPMT()` functions.) In the `PMT()` function, notice how I divided the annual interest rate by 12 ($B$4/12) to get the monthly rate, and how I multiplied the term by 12 ($B$5*12) to get the number of months in the loan. This enables me to determine the monthly payment.

FIGURE 6.5.
A loan amortization schedule built with the functions `PMT()`, `PPMT()`, and `IPMT()`.

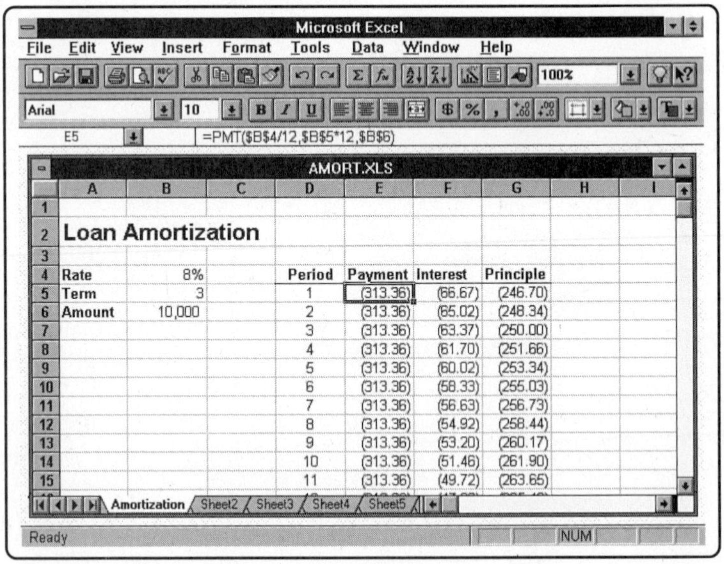
Microsoft Excel
File Edit View Insert Format Tools Data Window Help
Arial
10
100%
E5
=PMT($B$4/12,$B$5*12,$B$6)
AMORT.XLS
Loan Amortization
Rate 8%
Term 3
Amount 10,000
Period Payment Interest Principle
1 (313.36) (66.67) (246.70)
2 (313.36) (65.02) (248.34)
3 (313.36) (63.37) (250.00)
4 (313.36) (61.70) (251.66)
5 (313.36) (60.02) (253.34)
6 (313.36) (58.33) (255.03)
7 (313.36) (56.63) (256.73)
8 (313.36) (54.92) (258.44)
9 (313.36) (53.20) (260.17)
10 (313.36) (51.46) (261.90)
11 (313.36) (49.72) (263.65)
Amortization
Sheet2
Sheet3
Sheet4
Sheet5
Ready
NUM

Information Functions

Information functions return data concerning cells, worksheets, and formula results. They're mostly used in macros to test for particular conditions, such as which version of Excel the user has. Table 6.3 lists all the information functions.

Table 6.3. Excel's information functions.

Function	*Description*
`CELL(`***`info_type`***`,`*`reference`*`)`	Returns information about various cell attributes, including formatting, contents, and location
`ERROR.TYPE(`***`error_val`***`)`	Returns a number corresponding to an error type
`INFO(`***`type_text`***`)`	Returns information about the operating system and environment
`ISBLANK(`***`value`***`)`	Returns `TRUE` if the value is blank
`ISERR(`***`value`***`)`	Returns `TRUE` if the value is any error value except `#NA`
`ISERROR(`***`value`***`)`	Returns `TRUE` if the value is any error value
`ISLOGICAL(`***`value`***`)`	Returns `TRUE` if the value is a logical value
`ISNA(`***`value`***`)`	Returns `TRUE` if the value is the `#NA` error value
`ISNONTEXT(`***`value`***`)`	Returns `TRUE` if the value is not text
`ISNUMBER(`***`value`***`)`	Returns `TRUE` if the value is a number
`ISREF(`***`value`***`)`	Returns `TRUE` if the value is a reference
`ISTEXT(`***`value`***`)`	Returns `TRUE` if the value is text
`N(`***`value`***`)`	Returns the value converted to a number
`NA()`	Returns the error value `#NA`
`TYPE(`***`value`***`)`	Returns a number that indicates the data type of the value

`CELL()` is one of the most useful information functions. The ***`info_type`*** argument is a string value that represents the information you want to know about a particular cell. Some sample attributes are "address," "row," "col," and "contents." Figure 6.6 illustrates how to use the `CELL()` function. The "type" attribute used in row 11 tells you whether the cell contains a value (v), a label (l), or a blank (b). The "width" attribute tells you the width of the cell's column.

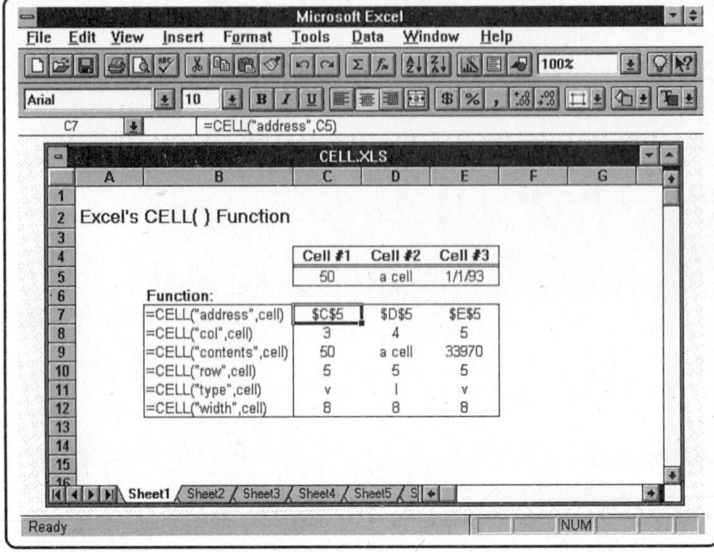

FIGURE 6.6.
Some examples of the CELL( ) function.

Logical Functions

You can use the logical functions to create decision-making formulas. You can test whether a certain condition exists within your spreadsheet and have the program take specific actions based on the result. For example, you can test cell contents to see whether they're numbers or labels, or you can test formula results for errors. Table 6.4 summarizes some of the logical functions.

Table 6.4. Excel's logical functions.

Function	*Description*
AND(***logical1***,*logical2,...*)	Returns TRUE if all the arguments are TRUE
FALSE()	Returns FALSE
IF(***logical_test***,*true_expr*,*false_expr*)	Performs a logical test and returns a value based on the result
NOT(***logical***)	Reverses the logical value of the argument
OR(***logical1***,*logical2,...*)	Returns TRUE if any argument is TRUE
TRUE()	Returns TRUE

Let's examine one of the most powerful logical functions: `IF()`. As you can see from Table 6.4, this function takes the form `IF(`***`logical_test`***`,`*`true_expr`*`,`*`false_expr`*`)` where ***`logical_test`*** is the logical expression to be tested. The argument *`true_expr`* is the value returned if ***`logical_test`*** is true, and *`false_expr`* is the value returned if ***`logical_test`*** is false. For example, consider the function `IF(A1>=1000,"It's big!","It's not!")`. The logical expression `A1>=1000` is used as the test. If this proves to be true, the function returns the string `It's big!`; if the condition is false, the function returns `It's not!`.

Figure 6.7 returns to the accounts receivable aging report. The idea of the report is to arrange past-due invoices according to the number of days they're past due. If an invoice is between 1 and 30 days past due, the invoice amount should appear in the 1-30 column. If it's between 31 and 60 days past due, the amount should appear in the 31-60 days column, and so on.

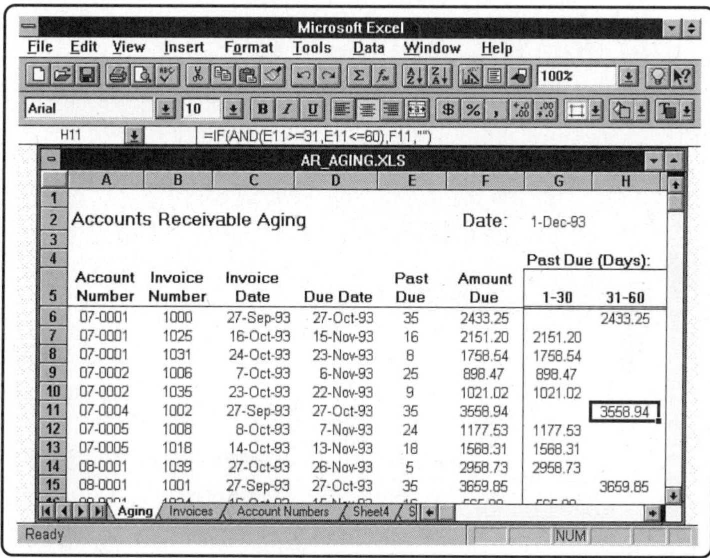

Accounts Receivable Aging — Date: 1-Dec-93

Account Number	Invoice Number	Invoice Date	Due Date	Past Due	Amount Due	Past Due (Days): 1-30	31-60
07-0001	1000	27-Sep-93	27-Oct-93	35	2433.25		2433.25
07-0001	1025	16-Oct-93	15-Nov-93	16	2151.20	2151.20	
07-0001	1031	24-Oct-93	23-Nov-93	8	1758.54	1758.54	
07-0002	1006	7-Oct-93	6-Nov-93	25	898.47	898.47	
07-0002	1035	23-Oct-93	22-Nov-93	9	1021.02	1021.02	
07-0004	1002	27-Sep-93	27-Oct-93	35	3558.94		3558.94
07-0005	1008	8-Oct-93	7-Nov-93	24	1177.53	1177.53	
07-0005	1018	14-Oct-93	13-Nov-93	18	1568.31	1568.31	
08-0001	1039	27-Oct-93	26-Nov-93	5	2958.73	2958.73	
08-0001	1001	27-Sep-93	27-Oct-93	35	3659.85		3659.85

FIGURE 6.7.
Using `IF()` and `AND()` to arrange past-due invoices.

The function shown in cell H11 accomplishes this. The logical test analyzes the figure in the Past Due column (column E). The expression `AND(E11 >= 31, E11 <= 60)` tests for past-due figures between 31 and 60 days. If this is true, the function displays the amount due (from column F). Otherwise, the function displays a blank. Similar functions are used for the cells in the 1-30 days column.

Lookup and Reference Functions

The lookup functions (such as `LOOKUP()`, `MATCH()`, and `INDEX()`) are powerful tools that enable you to retrieve values from tables. I'll postpone a discussion of these functions until Chapter 61, "Advanced Formulas and Functions."

The reference functions are useful for determining cell contents and obtaining information about ranges. Table 6.5 lists some of the available reference functions.

Table 6.5. Some reference functions.

Function	*Description*
AREAS(***reference***)	Returns the number of areas in a reference
COLUMN(*reference*)	Returns the column number of a reference
COLUMNS(***array***)	Returns the number of columns in an array
ROW(*reference*)	Returns the row number of a reference
ROWS(***array***)	Returns the number of rows in an array

Math and Trigonometric Functions

The math functions perform tasks such as calculating square roots and logarithms and generating random numbers. The trigonometric functions take an angle argument and calculate values such as its sine, cosine, and arctangent. Excel has dozens of math functions. Table 6.6 lists a few of the most common.

Table 6.6. Common math functions.

Function	*Description*
ABS(***number***)	Returns the absolute value of a number
CEILING(***number***,***significance***)	Rounds a number up to the nearest integer
EXP(***number***)	Returns *e* raised to the power of a number
EVEN(***number***)	Rounds a number up to the nearest even integer
FLOOR(***number***,***significance***)	Rounds a number down to the nearest integer
INT(***number***)	Rounds a number down to the nearest integer
LN(***number***)	Returns the natural logarithm of a number
MOD(***number***,***divisor***)	Returns the remainder of a number after dividing
ODD(***number***)	Rounds a number up to the nearest odd integer

Function	*Description*
`PI()`	Returns the value pi
`RAND()`	Returns a random number between 0 and 1
`ROUND(`***`number`***`,`***`num_digits`***`)`	Rounds a number to a specified number of digits
`SQRT(`***`number`***`)`	Returns the positive square root of a number
`SUM(`***`number1`***`,`*`number2`*`,...)`	Returns the sum of the arguments
`TRUNC(`***`number`***`,`*`num_digits`*`)`	Truncates a number to an integer

Rounding Functions

To demonstrate the mathematical functions, let's look at the differences between Excel's seven rounding functions: `ROUND()`, `CEILING()`, `FLOOR()`, `EVEN()`, `ODD()`, `INT()`, and `TRUNC()`.

The most common rounding function is `ROUND()`, which takes two arguments, ***`number`*** and ***`num_digits`***. ***`num_digits`*** specifies the number of digits you want ***`number`*** rounded to, as follows:

- If ***`num_digits`*** is greater than 0, Excel rounds ***`number`*** to ***`num_digits`*** decimal places.
- If ***`num_digits`*** is 0, Excel rounds ***`number`*** to the nearest integer.
- If ***`num_digits`*** is less than 0, Excel rounds ***`number`*** to ***`num_digits`*** to the left of the decimal point.

Table 6.7 demonstrates the effect of the ***`num_digits`*** argument on the results of the `ROUND()` function. Here, ***`number`*** is 1234.5678.

Table 6.7. The `ROUND()` function.

`num_digits`	*Result*
3	1234.568
2	1234.57
1	1234.6
0	1235
–1	1230
–2	1200
–3	1000

The CEILING() and FLOOR() functions take two arguments, ***number*** and ***significance***. These functions round the value given by ***number*** to a multiple of the value given by ***significance***. The difference is that CEILING() rounds *away* from zero and FLOOR() rounds *toward* zero. For example, CEILING(1.56,0.1) returns 1.6 and CEILING(-2.33,-0.5) returns –2.5. Similarly, FLOOR(1.56,0.1) returns 1.5 and FLOOR(-2.33,-0.5) returns –2.0.

SUPER CAUTION

For the CEILING() and FLOOR() functions, both arguments must have the same sign or they'll return the error value #NUM!. Also, if you enter a 0 for the second argument of the FLOOR() function, you'll get the error #DIV/0!.

The EVEN() and ODD() functions round a single numeric argument away from zero. EVEN() rounds the number to the next even number and ODD() rounds it to the next odd number. For example, EVEN(14.2) returns 16 and EVEN(-23) returns –24. Similarly, ODD(58.1) returns 59 and ODD(-6) returns –7.

The INT() and TRUNC() functions are similar in that you can use both to convert a value to its integer portion. For example, INT(6.75) returns 6 and TRUNC(3.6) returns 3. However, these functions have two major differences that you should keep in mind:

- For negative values, INT() returns the next number *away* from zero. For example, INT(-3.42) returns –4. If you just want to lop off the decimal part, you need to use TRUNC() instead.
- TRUNC() can take a second argument—*num_digits*—that you can use to specify the number of decimal places to leave on. For example, TRUNC(123.456,2) returns 123.45.

SUPER NOTE

As if these rounding functions weren't enough, the Analysis Toolpack add-in macro supplies another one: MROUND(***number***,***multiple***). This handy function rounds ***number*** to the nearest multiple of the value given by ***multiple***. See Chapter 36, "Working with the Analysis Toolpack," for details.

Using the AutoSum Feature

The Standard toolbar includes the AutoSum button, which will sum a row or column of numbers automatically. Procedure 6.2 shows you the steps to follow.

Click on the AutoSum button in the Standard toolbar to sum a range automatically.

PROCEDURE 6.2. USING THE AUTOSUM BUTTON.

1. If you're summing a column, select the cell immediately below the values. For a row, select the cell immediately to the right of the values.
2. Click on the AutoSum button. Excel enters a `SUM()` function that uses the range of numbers as an argument.

TIP

You also can run the AutoSum feature by pressing Alt+= (equals sign).

3. Adjust the range coordinates, if necessary.
4. Press Enter or click on the Enter button to confirm the cell.

Statistical Functions

The statistical functions calculate all the standard statistical measures such as average, maximum, minimum, and standard deviation. For most of the statistical functions, you supply a list of values (called a *sample* or *population*). You can enter individual values or cells, or you can specify a range. Table 6.8 lists a few of the statistical functions.

Table 6.8. Common statistical functions.

Function	*Description*
`AVERAGE(`***number1***`,`*number2*`,...)`	Returns the average
`COUNT(`***value1***`,`*value2*`,...)`	Counts the numbers in the argument list
`COUNTA(`***value1***`,`*value2*`,...)`	Counts the values in the argument list
`MAX(`***number1***`,`*number2*`,...)`	Returns the maximum value
`MEDIAN(`***number1***`,`*number2*`,...)`	Returns the median value
`MIN(`***number1***`,`*number2*`,...)`	Returns the minimum value

continues

Table 6.8. continued

Function	*Description*
`MODE(`***number1***`,`*number2*`,...)`	Returns the most common value
`RANK(`***number***`,`***ref***`,`*order*`)`	Returns the rank of a number in a list
`STDEV(`***number1***`,`*number2*`,...)`	Returns the standard deviation based on a sample
`STDEVP(`***number1***`,`*number2*`,...)`	Returns the standard deviation based on an entire population
`VAR(`***number1***`,`*number2*`,...)`	Returns the variance based on a sample
`VARP(`***number1***`,`*number2*`,...)`	Returns the variance based on an entire population

Figure 6.8 illustrates the use of several statistical functions.

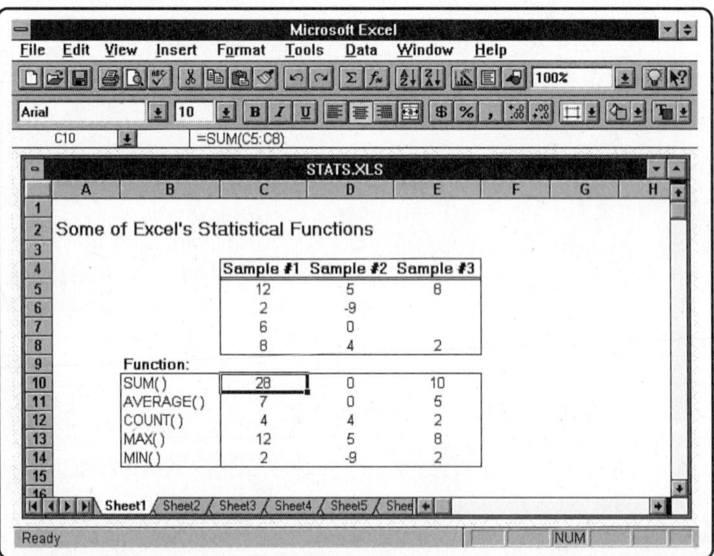

FIGURE 6.8.
Examples of statistical functions.

Text Functions

Excel's text functions enable you to manipulate text strings and labels. With these functions, you can convert numbers to strings, change lowercase letters to uppercase (and vice versa), compare two strings, and more. Table 6.9 summarizes several of the most useful text functions.

Table 6.9. Some text functions.

Function	*Description*
`CHAR(`***number***`)`	Returns the character that corresponds to the code number
`EXACT(`***text1***`,`***text2***`)`	Compares two strings to see whether they are identical
`LEFT(`***text***`,`*num_chars*`)`	Returns the leftmost characters from a string
`LEN(`***text***`)`	Returns the length of a string
`LOWER(`***text***`)`	Converts text to lowercase
`MID(`***text***`,`***start_num***`,`***num_chars***`)`	Returns a specified number of characters from a string
`PROPER(`***text***`)`	Converts text to proper case (first letter of each word capitalized)
`RIGHT(`***text***`,`*num_chars*`)`	Returns the rightmost characters from a string
`T(`***value***`)`	Converts a value to text
`TEXT(`***value***`,`***format***`)`	Formats a number and converts it to text
`TRIM(`***text***`)`	Removes excess spaces from a string
`UPPER(`***text***`)`	Converts text to uppercase

Figure 6.9 demonstrates several of the text functions.

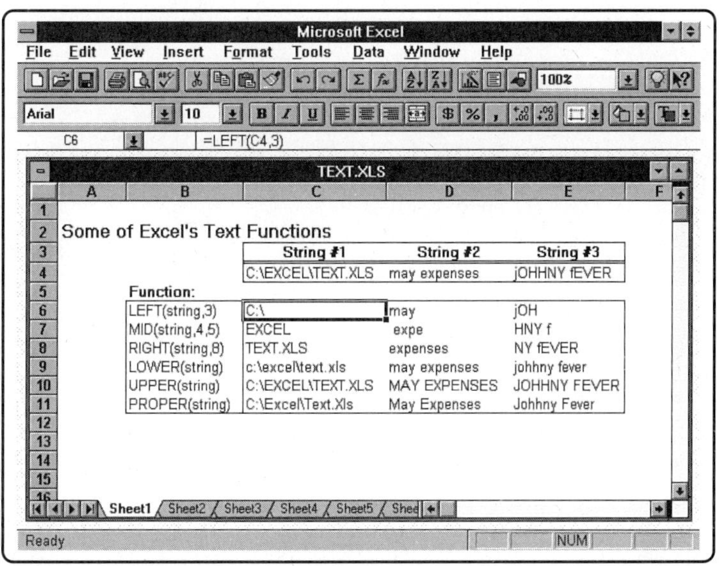

FIGURE 6.9.
Examples of text functions.

Publishing and Printing

Chapter

7

Formatting Numbers, Dates, and Times

One of the best ways to improve the readability of your worksheets is to display your data in a format that is logical, consistent, and straightforward. Formatting currency amounts with leading dollar signs, percentages with trailing percent signs, and large numbers with commas are a few of the ways you can improve your spreadsheet style.

This chapter shows you how to format numbers, dates, and times using Excel's built-in formatting options. You'll also learn how to create your own formats to gain maximum control over the appearance of your data.

Numeric Display Formats

When you enter numbers in a worksheet, Excel removes any leading or trailing zeros. For example, if you enter 0123.4500, Excel displays 123.45. The exception to this rule occurs when you enter a number that is wider than the cell. In this case, Excel tailors the number to fit in the cell by either rounding off some decimal places or by using scientific notation. A number such as 123.45678 is displayed as 123.4568, and 123456789 is displayed as 1.23+08. In both cases, the number is changed for display purposes only; Excel still retains the original number internally.

When you create a worksheet, each cell uses this format, known as the *general* number format, by default. If you want your numbers to appear differently, you can choose from the seven other built-in numeric formats supplied by Excel. Table 7.1 lists these formats, along with some examples.

Table 7.1. Excel's built-in numeric formats.

Format	*1234.5*	*–1234.5*	*.4375*
General	1234.5	–1234.5	0.4375
0	1235	–1235	0
0.00	1234.50	–1234.50	0.44
#,##0	1,235	–1,235	0
#,##0.00	1,234.50	–1,234.50	0.44
$#,##0_);($#,##0)	$1,235	($1,235)	$0
$#,##0_);[Red] ($#,##0)	$1,235	($1,235)*	$0
$#,##0.00_); ($#,##0.00)	$1,234.50	($1,234.50)	$0.44
$#,##0.00_);[Red] ($#,##0.00)	$1,234.50	($1,234.50)*	$0.44
0%	123450%	–123450%	44%
0.00%	123450.00%	–123450.00%	43.75%

Format	1234.5	–1234.5	.4375
0.00E+00	1.23E+03	–1.23E+03	4.38E_01
# ?/?	1234 1/2	–1234 1/2	4/9
# ??/??	1234 1/2	–1234 1/2	7/16

*This format displays negative numbers in red.

These built-in formats use special symbols (for example, #, 0, and ?) to create *format codes* that define how each format treats your numbers. You can use these symbols to create your own custom formats. See the section in this chapter titled "Customizing Numeric Formats."

Changing Numeric Formats

The quickest way to format numbers is to specify the format as you enter your data. For example, if you begin a dollar amount with a dollar sign ($), Excel automatically formats the number as currency. Similarly, if you type a percent sign (%) after a number, Excel automatically formats the number as a percentage. The following are some more examples of this technique. Note that you can enter a negative value using either the negative sign (–) or parentheses (( )).

Number Entered	Number Displayed	Format Used
$1234.567	$1,234.57	Currency
($1234.5)	($1,234.50)	Currency
10%	10%	Percentage
123E+02	1.23E+04	Scientific
5 3/4	5 3/4	Fraction
0 3/4	3/4	Fraction
3/4	4–Mar	Date

SUPER NOTE

Excel interprets a simple fraction such as 3/4 as a date (March 4th, in this case). Always include a leading zero, followed by a space, if you want to enter a simple fraction from the formula bar.

Specifying the numeric format as you enter a number is fast and efficient because Excel guesses the format you want to use. Unfortunately, Excel sometimes guesses wrong (for example, interpreting a simple fraction as a date). In any case, you don't have access to all the available formats (for example, displaying negative dollar amounts in red). To overcome these limitations, you can select your numeric formats from the Number tab in the Format Cells dialog box (see Figure 7.1). This dialog box is divided into four sections:

Category — This list box contains the various categories of numeric formats, such as Currency and Percentage.

Format Codes — This list box displays the formats associated with each category.

Code — This edit box displays the currently selected format. It can be edited when you want to create your own custom formats.

Sample — This information line shows you what the contents of the active cell will look like using the currently selected format.

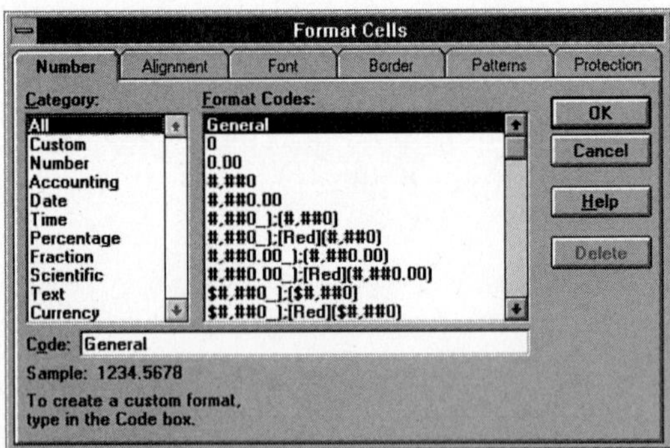

FIGURE 7.1.
The Format Cells dialog box.

To open the Format Cells dialog box and select a format, follow the steps in Procedure 7.1.

PROCEDURE 7.1. SELECTING A NUMERIC FORMAT.

1. Select the cell or range of cells to which you want the new format to apply.
2. Select Format | Cells. The Format Cells dialog box appears.

> **SUPER TIP**
>
> To open the Format Cells dialog box quickly, either press Ctrl+1 or right-click on the cell or range and then select the Format Cells command from the shortcut menu.

3. Select the Number tab.
4. Select a format category from the **C**ategory list box. The listing of format codes changes to reflect the category you choose.
5. Select the numeric format from the **F**ormat Codes list box. The currently highlighted format appears in the C**o**de edit box. The Sample information box shows a sample of the format applied to the current cell's contents.
6. Click on OK or press Enter. Excel returns you to the worksheet with the new formatting applied.

As an alternative to the Format Cells dialog box, Excel offers several keyboard shortcuts for setting the numeric format. Select the cell or range you want to format and use one of the key combinations listed in Table 7.2.

Table 7.2. Shortcut keys for selecting numeric formats.

Shortcut Key	*Format*
Ctrl+~	General
Ctrl+!	#,##0.00
Ctrl+$	$#,##0.00_);($#,##0.00)
Ctrl+%	0%
Ctrl+^	0.00E+00

If you have a mouse, you can use the tools in the Standard toolbar as another method of selecting numeric formats. Here are the four available tools:

Click on the Currency Style tool to apply the $#,###0.00_); [Red]($#,##0.00) format.

Click on the Comma Style tool to apply the #,##0.00 format.

Click on the Percent Style tool to apply the 0% format.

Click on the Increase Decimal tool to increase the number of decimal places in the current format. Hold down the Shift key and click on this tool to decrease the number of decimal places.

Customizing Numeric Formats

You have much control over how your numbers are displayed, but the built-in numeric formats have their limitations. For example, no built-in format enables you to display a different currency symbol (the British pound—£, for example) or display a zip code with a leading zero (01234, for example). To overcome these limitations, you need to create your own custom numeric formats. You can do this either by editing an existing format or by entering your own from scratch. The formatting syntax and symbols are explained in detail later in this section. To customize a numeric format, select the cell or range you want to format and follow Procedure 7.2.

PROCEDURE 7.2. CUSTOMIZING A NUMERIC FORMAT.

1. Display the Number tab in the Format Cells dialog box using one of the methods outlined in the preceding section.
2. Select the format category that's appropriate for your custom format. The formats associated with the category appear in the **F**ormat Codes list box.
3. If you're editing an existing format, highlight it in the **F**ormat Codes list box. The format appears in the C**o**de edit box. If you're creating a format from scratch, skip to step 4.
4. Click on the C**o**de edit box or press the Tab key. A blinking cursor appears in the C**o**de edit box.
5. Edit the displayed format code or enter your own format from scratch.
6. Click on OK or press Enter. Excel returns you to the worksheet with the custom format applied.

Excel stores each new format definition in the Custom category. If you edited an existing format, the original format is left intact, and the new format is added to the list. You can select the custom formats the same way you select the built-in formats. To use your custom format in other workbooks, you need to copy a cell containing the format to that workbook. See Chapter 12, "Working with Cell Formats," to learn about copying and moving cell formats.

Every Excel numeric format, whether it's built-in or customized, has the following syntax:

positive format;negative format;zero format;text format

The four parts, separated by semicolons, determine how various numbers are presented. The first part defines how a positive number is displayed, the second part defines how a negative number is displayed, the third part defines how zero is displayed, and the fourth part defines how text is displayed. If you leave out one or more of these parts (recall that the built-in formats use only one or two parts), numbers are controlled as follows:

Parts Used	*Format Syntax*
Three	positive format;negative format;zero format
Two	positive and zero format; negative format
One	positive, negative, and zero format

Table 7.3 lists the special symbols you use to define each of these parts.

Table 7.3. Numeric formatting symbols.

Symbol	*Description*
General	Displays the number with the General format.
#	Holds a place for a digit and displays the digit exactly as typed. Displays nothing if no number is entered.
0	Holds a place for a digit and displays the digit exactly as typed. Displays zero if no number is entered.
?	Holds a place for a digit and displays the digit exactly as typed. Displays a space if no number is entered.
. (period)	Sets the location of the decimal point.
, (comma)	Sets the location of thousands. Marks only the location of the first thousand.
%	Multiplies the number by 100 (for display only) and adds the percent (%) character.
E+ e+ E– e–	Displays the number in scientific format. E– and e– place a minus sign in the exponent; E+ and e+ place a plus sign in the exponent.
/ (slash)	Sets the location of the fraction separator.
$ ( ) : – + space	Displays the character.
*	Repeats the character immediately following the symbol until the cell is full. Doesn't replace other symbols or numbers.
_ (underscore)	Inserts a blank space the width of the character following the symbol.
\ (backslash)	Inserts the character following the symbol.
"*text*"	Inserts text within the quotation marks.
@	Holds a place for text.
[*Color*]	Displays the cell contents in the specified color. See Chapter 11, "Using Color in Worksheets."
[*condition value*]	Uses conditional statements to specify when the format is to be used.

Figure 7.2 shows some sample custom formats. The format in Example 1 always displays four decimal places. Example 2 shows how you can reduce a large number to a smaller, more readable one by using the thousands separator; each comma represents three zeros (although Excel uses the original number in calculations). Use the format in Example 3 when you don't want to display any leading or trailing zeros. Example 4 shows a four-part format. In Example 5, the British pound sign (£) is used in place of the dollar sign. To enter the pound sign, press Alt+0163 on the keyboard's numeric keypad. (This won't work if you use the numbers along the top of the keyboard.) Table 7.4 shows some common ANSI characters you can use. (See Appendix B, "The Windows ANSI Character Set," for the complete ANSI character set.)

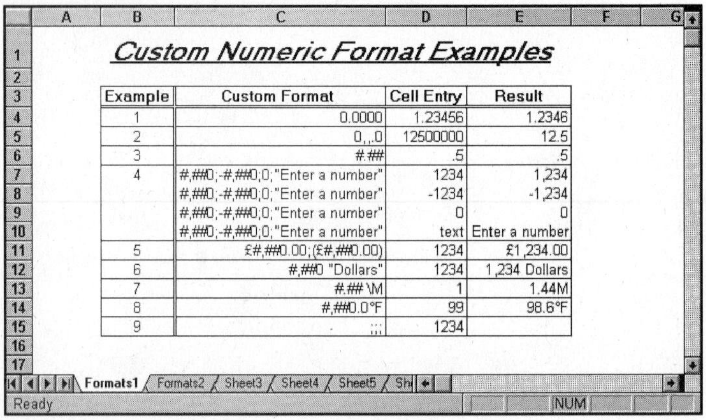

FIGURE 7.2.
Sample custom numeric formats.

Custom Numeric Format Examples

Example	Custom Format	Cell Entry	Result
1	0.0000	1.23456	1.2346
2	0,,.0	12500000	12.5
3	#.##	.5	.5
4	#,##0;-#,##0;0;"Enter a number"	1234	1,234
	#,##0;-#,##0;0;"Enter a number"	-1234	-1,234
	#,##0;-#,##0;0;"Enter a number"	0	0
	#,##0;-#,##0;0;"Enter a number"	text	Enter a number
5	£#,##0.00;(£#,##0.00)	1234	£1,234.00
6	#,##0 "Dollars"	1234	1,234 Dollars
7	#.## \M	1	1.44M
8	#,##0.0°F	99	98.6°F
9	;;;	1234	

Formats1 / Formats2 / Sheet3 / Sheet4 / Sheet5 / Sh
Ready NUM

Table 7.4. ANSI character key combinations.

Key Combination	*ANSI Character*
Alt+0163	£
Alt+0162	¢
Alt+0165	¥
Alt+0169	©
Alt+0174	®
Alt+0176	°

Example 6 adds the text string "Dollars" to the format. In Example 7, an M is appended to any number, which is useful if your spreadsheet units are in megabytes. Example 8 uses the degree symbol (°) to display temperatures. Finally, the three semicolons used in Example 9 result in no number being displayed.

The formats used in Figure 7.2 were all designed to work with numbers or dollar values. You can create numeric formats for other types of entries, such as telephone numbers, account numbers, and zip codes. Figure 7.3 shows some examples of these types of formats.

FIGURE 7.3.
Other types of numeric formats.

Other Numeric Format Examples

Type	Custom Format	Cell Entry	Result
Phone Number	(###)000-0000	1234567890	(123)456-7890
	(###)000-0000	4567890	()456-7890
Social Security No.	000-00-0000	123456789	123-45-6789
Zip Code	00000	12345	12345
	00000	1234	01234
	00000-0000	123456789	12345-6789
Account Number	"Acct"\# 00-0000;;;"Don't enter dash"	123456	Acct# 12-3456
	"Acct"\# 00-0000;;;"Don't enter dash"	12-3456	Don't enter dash
Dot Trailer	#*.	1234	1235................
	;;;@*.	March	March..............
Dot Leader	;;;*.@	March	..............March
Stock Prices	+?? ?/?;[Red]-?? /?	13	12.75

Hiding Zeros

Worksheets look less cluttered and are easier to read if you hide unnecessary zeros. Excel enables you to hide zeros either throughout the entire worksheet or only in selected cells.

To hide all zeros, select **T**ools | **O**ptions, click on the View tab in Options dialog box, and deactivate the **Z**ero Values check box.

To hide zeros in selected cells, create a custom format that uses the following format syntax:

positive format;negative format;

The extra semicolon at the end acts as a placeholder for the zero format. Because there is no definition for a zero value, nothing is displayed. For example, the format $#,##0.00_);($#,##0.00); displays standard dollar values, but it leaves the cell blank if it contains zero.

SUPER TIP

If your worksheet contains only integers (no fractions or decimal places), you can use the format #,### to hide zeros.

Using Condition Values

The action of the formats you've seen so far have depended on whether the cell contents were positive, negative, zero, or text. Although this is fine for most applications, there are times when you need to format a cell based on different conditions. For example, you might want only specific numbers, or numbers within a certain range, to take on a particular format. You can achieve this by using the [*condition value*] format symbol. With this symbol, you set up conditional statements using the logical operators =, <, >, <=, >=, and <>, and the appropriate numbers. You then assign these conditions to each part of your format definition.

For example, suppose you have a worksheet where the data must be within the range –1,000 and 1,000. To flag numbers outside this range, you'd set up the following format:

```
[>=1000]"Error: Value>=1,000";[<=-1000]"Error: Value<=-1,000";0.00
```

The first part defines the format for numbers greater than or equal to 1,000 (an error message). The second part defines the format for numbers less than or equal to –1,000 (also an error message). The third part defines the format for all other numbers (0.00).

Date and Time Display Formats

If you include dates or times in your worksheets, you need to make sure that they're presented in a readable, unambiguous format. For example, most people would interpret the date 8/5/94 as August 5, 1994. However, there are countries where this date would mean May 8, 1994. Similarly, if you use the time 2:45, do you mean a.m. or p.m.? To avoid these kinds of problems, you can use Excel's built-in date and time formats, listed in Table 7.5.

Table 7.5. Excel's date and time formats.

Format	*Display*
m/d/yy	8/23/94
d–mmm–yy	23–Aug–94
d–mmm	23–Aug
mmm–yy	Aug–94
h:mm AM/PM	3:10 p.m.
h:mm:ss AM/PM	3:10:45 p.m.
h:mm	15:10
h:mm:ss	15:10:45

Format	*Display*
mm:ss	10:45
mm:ss.0	10:45.7
[h]:mm:ss	0:15:22
m/d/yy h:mm	8/23/94 15:10

You use the same methods you used for numeric formats to select date and time formats. In particular, you can specify the date and time format as you input your data. For example, entering `Jan-94` automatically formats the cell with the mmm-yy format. Also, you can use the following shortcut keys:

Shortcut Key	*Format*
Ctrl+#	d–mmm–yy
Ctrl+@	h:mm AM/PM
Ctrl+;	Current date (m/d/yy)
Ctrl+:	Current time (h:mm AM/PM)

SUPER TIP

Excel for the Macintosh uses a different date system than Excel for Windows. If you share files between these environments, you need to use Macintosh dates in your Excel for Windows worksheets to maintain the correct dates when you move from one system to another. Select **T**ools | **O**ptions, click on the Calculation tab, and check the 1904 **D**ate System check box.

Customizing Date and Time Formats

Although the built-in date and time formats are fine for most applications, you might need to create your own custom formats. For example, you might want to display the full month name ("August" instead of "Aug") or even the day of the week. Custom date and time formats generally are simpler to create than custom numeric formats. There are fewer formatting symbols, and you usually don't need to specify different formats for different conditions. Table 7.6 lists the date and time formatting symbols.

Table 7.6. The date and time formatting symbols.

Symbol	*Description*
Date Formats	
d	Day number without a leading zero (1 to 31)
dd	Day number with a leading zero (01 to 31)
ddd	Three-letter day abbreviation (Mon, for example)
dddd	Full day name (Monday, for example)
m	Month number without a leading zero (1 to 12)
mm	Month number with a leading zero (01 to 12)
mmm	Three-letter month abbreviation (Aug, for example)
mmmm	Full month name (August, for example)
yy	Two-digit year (00 to 99)
yyyy	Full year (1900 to 2078)
Time Formats	
h	Hour without a leading zero (0 to 24)
hh	Hour with a leading zero (00 to 24)
m	Minute without a leading zero (0 to 59)
mm	Minute with a leading zero (00 to 59)
s	Second without a leading zero (0 to 59)
ss	Second with a leading zero (00 to 59)
AM/PM, am/pm, A/P	Displays the time using a 12-hour clock
/ : . –	Symbols used to separate parts of dates or times
[COLOR]	Displays the date or time in the color specified
[*condition value*]	Uses conditional statements to specify when the format is to be used

Figure 7.4 shows some examples of custom date and time formats.

Deleting Custom Formats

The best way to become familiar with custom formats is try your own experiments. Just remember, however, that Excel stores each format you try. If you find that your format lists are getting too long or that they are cluttered with unused formats, you can delete formats by following the steps outlined in Procedure 7.3.

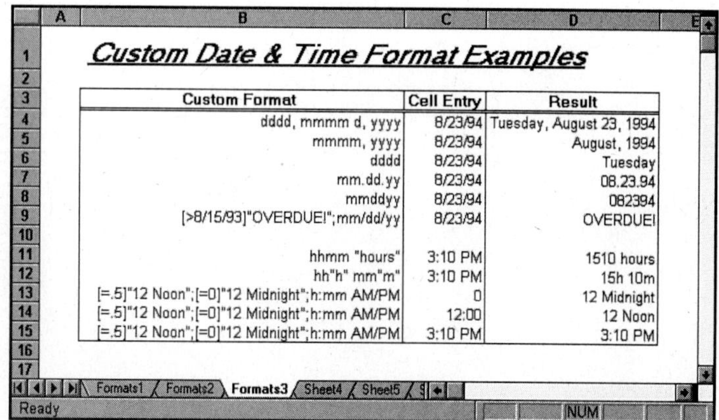

Custom Date & Time Format Examples

Custom Format	Cell Entry	Result
dddd, mmmm d, yyyy	8/23/94	Tuesday, August 23, 1994
mmmm, yyyy	8/23/94	August, 1994
dddd	8/23/94	Tuesday
mm.dd.yy	8/23/94	08.23.94
mmddyy	8/23/94	082394
[>8/15/93]"OVERDUE!";mm/dd/yy	8/23/94	OVERDUE!
hhmm "hours"	3:10 PM	1510 hours
hh"h" mm"m"	3:10 PM	15h 10m
[=.5]"12 Noon";[=0]"12 Midnight";h:mm AM/PM	0	12 Midnight
[=.5]"12 Noon";[=0]"12 Midnight";h:mm AM/PM	12:00	12 Noon
[=.5]"12 Noon";[=0]"12 Midnight";h:mm AM/PM	3:10 PM	3:10 PM

FIGURE 7.4.
Sample custom date and time formats.

PROCEDURE 7.3. DELETING CUSTOM FORMATS.

1. Choose Format | Cells, then select the Number tab in the Options dialog box.
2. Select the format category that contains the format you want to delete.
3. Highlight the format in the Format Codes list box.
4. Click on the Delete button. Excel removes the format from the list.
5. To delete other formats, repeat steps 2-4.
6. Click on OK or press Enter. Excel returns you to the spreadsheet.

SUPER NOTE

You can't delete built-in formats.

Chapter

8

Working with Fonts

Chapter 7 showed you how to format worksheet numbers, dates, and times. You learned that assigning appropriate formats to these numbers can greatly enhance the readability of your data. But no matter how skillfully you've applied your formatting, a worksheet full of numbers will still cause the eyes of your audience to glaze over very quickly. The next step in creating a presentation-quality report is to surround your numbers with attractive labels and headings.

This chapter teaches you about Excel's extensive font capabilities. You'll learn about the various font attributes and how to apply them to your worksheets. Throughout this chapter, the emphasis is on selecting fonts that improve the impact and effectiveness of your worksheets.

Learning About Fonts

The characters you enter into your Excel worksheets have several attributes: the typeface, the type size, and the type style. Taken all together, these attributes define the character's *font.*

The first of these attributes, the *typeface,* refers to a distinctive graphic design of letters and numbers. Typefaces differ according to the shape and thickness of characters, as well as a number of other stylistic features. As Figure 8.1 shows, typefaces can be very different.

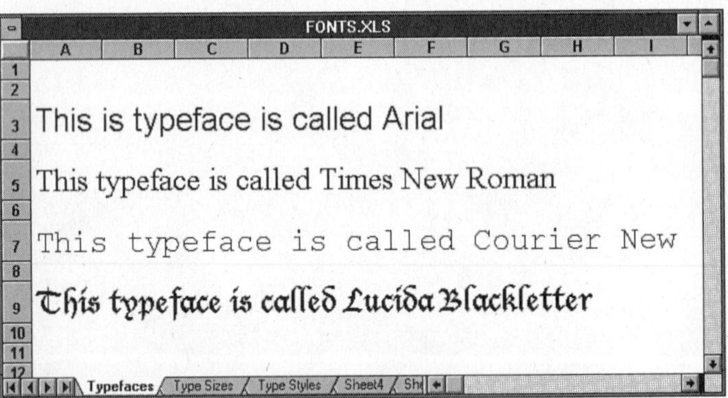

FIGURE 8.1. *Some sample typefaces.*

All typefaces are classified as either *serif, sans serif,* or *decorative.* A serif typeface contains fine cross strokes, or "feet," at the end of each main character stroke. For example, look at the capital T in the Times New Roman typeface in Figure 8.1. A sans serif typeface, such as the Arial example in Figure 8.1, doesn't contain these cross strokes. Decorative typefaces, such as the Lucida Blackletter in Figure 8.1, have unique designs that are used for special effects. Here are some general rules for selecting worksheet typefaces:

- Use sans serif typefaces for numbers, headings, and titles. Sans serif characters tend to be wider and cleaner-looking than their serif counterparts, which is helpful when you're displaying numbers or brief but large text entries. (A sans serif typeface—Arial—is the default typeface used by Excel.)
- Use serif typefaces for lengthy sections of text. The elegant serif design makes smaller characters easy to read.
- When choosing a typeface for a report, take your audience into consideration. If you're presenting to a business group, you should use more conservative typefaces such as Bookman or Helvetica-Narrow. In more relaxed settings, you can try Avant Garde or even (in small doses) a calligraphic font such as Lucida Calligraphy.
- Try to limit yourself to two typefaces (at most) in a single worksheet. Using more makes your reports look jumbled and confusing. It's much more effective to vary type size and style within a single typeface than to use many different typefaces.

SUPER NOTE

The number of typefaces you have available depends on the printer you use and whether you have a printer font cartridge or a font management program installed on your computer. The TrueType software built into Windows 3.1 is an example of a font management program.

The next font attribute is the size of the typeface. Type size, the measure of the height of a font, is measured in points. There are 72 points in an inch, so selecting a type size of 72 gives you letters approximately one inch high. (Technically, type size is measured from the highest point of a tall letter such as *h* to the lowest point of a descending letter such as *y*.) Figure 8.2 shows some sample type sizes.

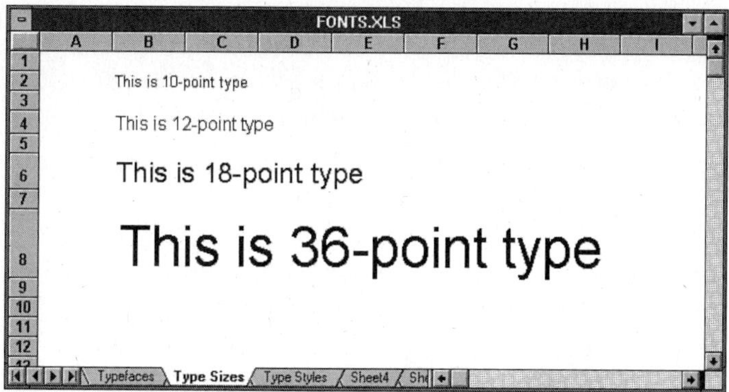

FIGURE 8.2.
Some sample type sizes.

Use different type sizes in your worksheets to differentiate titles and headings from data:

- Use 24- or even 36-point type for worksheet titles, but remember that your title must fit on a single page. If your report has a subtitle, use a type size that's slightly smaller than the one used in the main title. For example, if your title is in 24-point type, make the subtitle 18-point type.
- Column and row labels look good in 12- or 14-point type, but, again, watch the size. If your labels are too large, you'll have to widen your columns accordingly.
- For most reports, the standard 10-point type is fine for your data, although you'll probably have to switch to a larger type (such as 12-point) if you plan to present your work on a slide or overhead.

The *type style* of a font refers to attributes such as regular, bold, and italic. Figure 8.3 shows examples of each of these attributes.

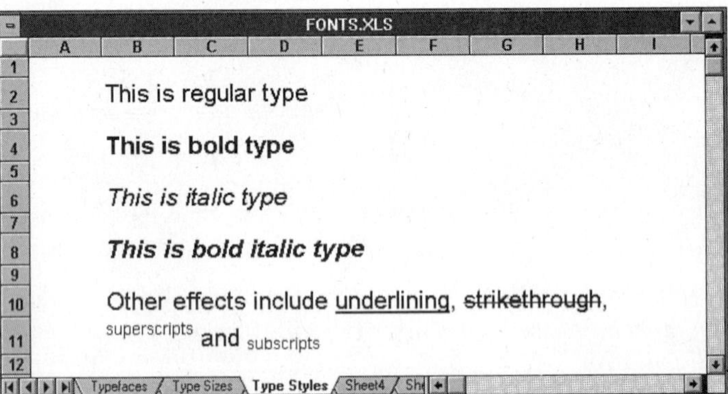

FIGURE 8.3.
Some type style attributes.

Use any of these type styles to make sections of your worksheet stand out. Bold often is used for worksheet titles, and headings often are displayed as both bold and italic. In general, however, you should use these styles sparingly, because overuse diminishes their impact. Other type styles (often called type *effects*) include underlining, strikethrough, superscript, and subscript.

Figure 8.4 shows an Excel spreadsheet that implements many of the features described in this chapter. As you can see, fonts are a powerful way to improve your worksheet design. The next section shows you how to implement fonts in Excel.

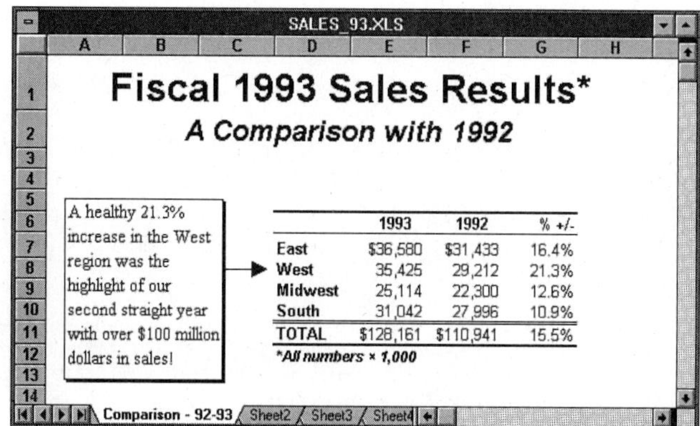

FIGURE 8.4.
Using fonts effectively can greatly improve the look of your worksheets.

Using Fonts

With Excel, you can use up to 256 different fonts on a single worksheet, although, in practice, a presentation-quality report should use only a few fonts. (Remember that a font is a specific combination of typeface, size, and style. This means that 10-point Arial is a different font than 24-point Arial Bold.)

You can set all the font attributes from the Font tab in the Format Cells dialog box, shown in Figure 8.5. This tab is divided into eight areas:

Font	This is a list of available typefaces (the terms *font* and *typeface* often are used interchangeably). Excel shows printer fonts with a printer graphic beside them, and TrueType fonts (the ones that come with Windows 3.1) have the double-T TrueType logo beside them.
Font Style	This is a list of font styles available for the highlighted typeface.
Size	This list box displays the available type sizes for the highlighted typeface.
Underline	This is a list of underlining options.
Color	This drop-down list box enables you to select a font color. See Chapter 11, “Using Color in Worksheets,” for a discussion of color.
Normal Font	Activate this check box to select Excel’s default font. See Chapter 12, “Working with Cell Formats,” to learn how to change the default font.
Effects	Use this section to choose the Strikethrough, Superscript, or Subscript font effects.
Preview	This section shows you how your font selections look.

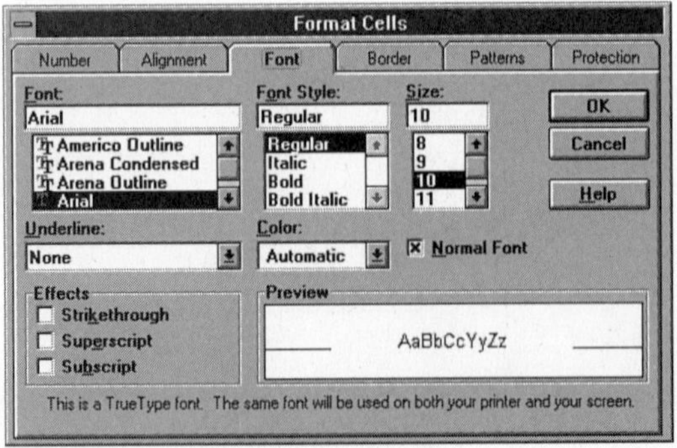

FIGURE 8.5.
The Font dialog box.

To select a font using the Font dialog box, follow the steps in Procedure 8.1.

PROCEDURE 8.1. SELECTING A FONT.

1. Select a cell, a range, or a group of characters inside a cell.

> **SUPER NOTE**
>
> To select characters inside a cell, press F2 or double-click on the cell to activate in-cell editing. Then use the mouse or the keyboard to highlight the characters you want to format. Note that you can format individual cell characters only if the cell contains text. The characters in formulas and numbers all use the same formatting.

2. Select the F**o**rmat | C**e**lls command, then select the Font tab in the Format Cells dialog box.
3. Select a typeface from the **F**ont list box. Excel displays the selected typeface in the Preview area.
4. Select a font style from the F**o**nt Style list box.
5. Select a type size from the **S**ize list box.
6. Select any other font options you want to use.
7. Click on OK or press Enter. Excel returns you to the worksheet and formats the cells with the font you chose.

Selecting Fonts with the Formatting Toolbar

Besides using the Font tab, you can set many of the font attributes using the Formatting toolbar, which contains the following font tools:

Arial

Use the Font drop-down list box to select a typeface.

10

Use the Font Size drop-down list box to select a font size.

B

Click on the Bold tool to apply the bold font style.

I

Click on the Italic tool to apply the italic font style.

U

Click on the Underline tool to apply the underline font style.

Selecting Font Attributes with Shortcut Keys

If you don't have a mouse or if you prefer to use the keyboard, Excel provides a number of keyboard shortcuts you can use to select font attributes. Table 8.1 lists these shortcut key combinations.

Table 8.1. Shortcut keys for selecting font attributes.

Shortcut Keys	*Result*
Ctrl+2 or Ctrl+B	Toggles the bold style on or off
Ctrl+3 or Ctrl+I	Toggles the italic style on or off
Ctrl+4 or Ctrl+U	Toggles the underline effect on or off
Ctrl+5	Toggles the strikethrough effect on or off

Chapter

9

Formatting Other Cell Attributes

This chapter teaches you about other cell attributes, such as cell borders and patterns, and the alignment within cells and across ranges.

Aligning Cell Contents

When you place data in an unformatted cell, Excel aligns text entries with the left edge of the cell, numbers and dates with the right edge of the cell, and error and logical values in the center of the cell. This is the default General alignment scheme. Although this format is useful for distinguishing text entries from numerical ones, it tends to make a worksheet look messy and poorly organized. To remedy this, Excel enables you to apply a number of alignment options.

You set alignment attributes using the Alignment tab of the Format Cells dialog box, shown in Figure 9.1. This tab is divided into four areas: Horizontal, Vertical, Orientation, and Wrap Text. The Horizontal section contains the following options (see Figure 9.2 for an example of each option):

General	Uses the default alignment settings.
Left	Left-aligns the cell contents.
Center	Centers the cell contents.
Right	Right-aligns the cell contents.
Fill	Repeats the contents of the cell until the cell is filled.
Justify	Aligns the cell contents with the left and right edges of the cell. For text entries longer than the cell width, the cell height is increased to accommodate the text.
Center across	Centers the cell contents across the selected selection range.

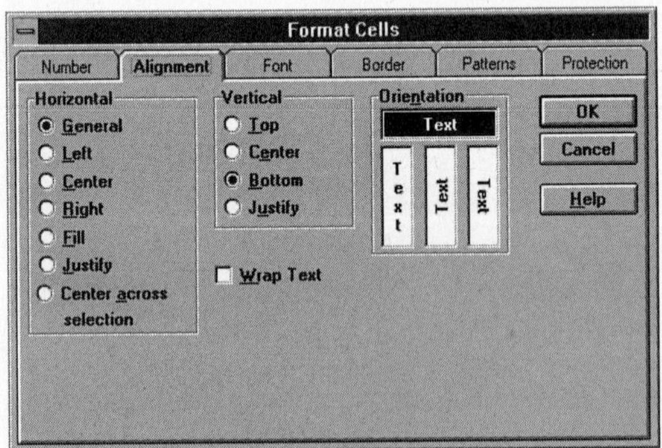

FIGURE 9.1.
The Alignment tab.

FIGURE 9.2.
The horizontal alignment options.

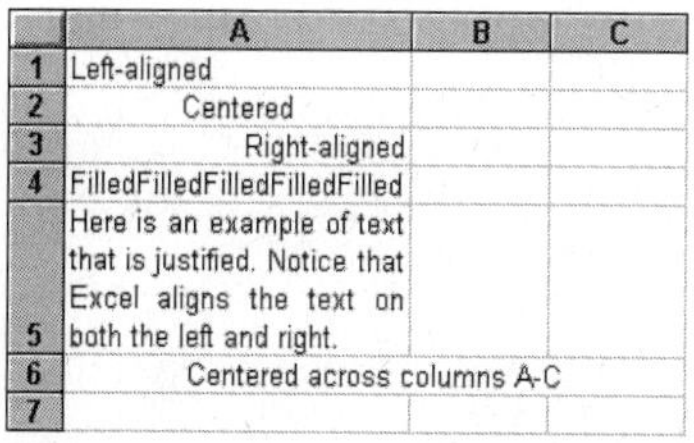

	A	B	C
1	Left-aligned		
2	Centered		
3	Right-aligned		
4	FilledFilledFilledFilledFilled		
5	Here is an example of text that is justified. Notice that Excel aligns the text on both the left and right.		
6	Centered across columns A-C		
7			

Click on this tool in the Formatting toolbar to left-align cell contents.

Click on this tool in the Formatting toolbar to center cell contents across the selection.

Click on this tool in the Standard toolbar to right-align cell contents.

Click on this tool in the Standard toolbar to center a cell across the selection.

If you increase the height of a row (as explained in Chapter 10, "Working with Columns and Rows"), the Vertical section of the Alignment tab enables you to position cell entries vertically using the following options (see Figure 9.3 for an example of each option except Justify):

Top	Aligns the cell contents with the top of the cell
Center	Aligns the cell contents with the center of the cell
Bottom	Aligns the cell contents with the bottom of the cell
Justify	Justifies the cell contents vertically

FIGURE 9.3.
The vertical alignment options.

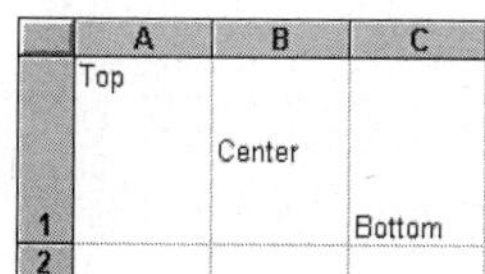

	A	B	C
1	Top	Center	Bottom
2			

The Orientation section of the Alignment tab enables you to orient your cell entries in four ways: left-to-right (normal), vertically, sideways with characters running from bottom to top, and sideways with characters running from top to bottom (although this doesn't necessarily mean the top and bottom of the cell boundaries). Figure 9.4 shows an example of each option.

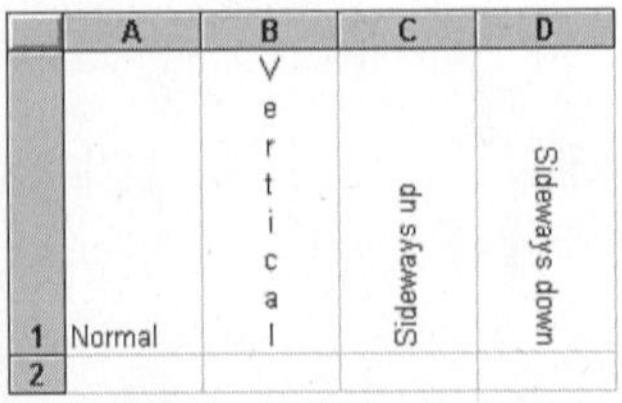

FIGURE 9.4.
The orientation alignment options.

	A	B	C	D
1	Normal	Vertical	Sideways up	Sideways down
2				

SUPER NOTE

If you choose either the vertical or sideways orientation with a long text entry, you have to adjust the height of the cell to see all the text. See Chapter 10, "Working with Columns and Rows," for instructions on adjusting row height.

The final option in the Alignment tab is the **W**rap Text check box, which enables you to wrap long cell entries so that they're displayed on multiple lines in a single cell (see Figure 9.5). You can left-align, center, right-align, or justify wrapped entries.

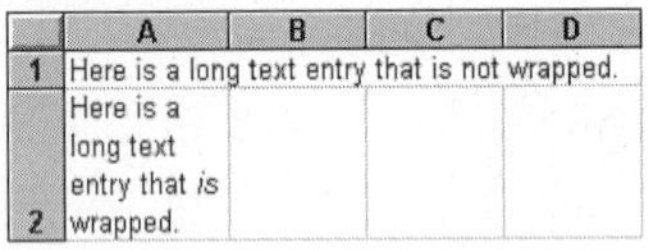

FIGURE 9.5.
The Word Wrap alignment option.

	A	B	C	D
1	Here is a long text entry that is not wrapped.			
2	Here is a long text entry that *is* wrapped.			

SUPER TIP

You can enter carriage returns and tabs in your wrapped cells. To enter a carriage return, position the cursor in the cell and press Alt+Enter. To enter a tab, press Ctrl+Alt+Tab.

Procedure 9.1 shows you how to select alignment attributes using the Alignment dialog box.

PROCEDURE 9.1. SELECTING ALIGNMENT ATTRIBUTES USING THE ALIGNMENT DIALOG BOX.

1. Select the cell or range that you want to align.
2. Select F**o**rmat | C**e**lls and then select the Alignment tab in the Format Cells dialog box.
3. Select your alignment choices as described earlier.

4. Click on OK or press Enter. Excel returns you to the worksheet with the new alignment activated.

Working with Cell Borders

Excel enables you to place borders of various weights and patterns around your worksheet cells. This is useful for enclosing different parts of the worksheet, defining data entry areas, and marking totals. You apply cell borders using the Border tab of the Format Cells dialog box, shown in Figure 9.6. This tab is divided into three sections: Border, Style, and Color (see Chapter 11, "Using Color in Worksheets").

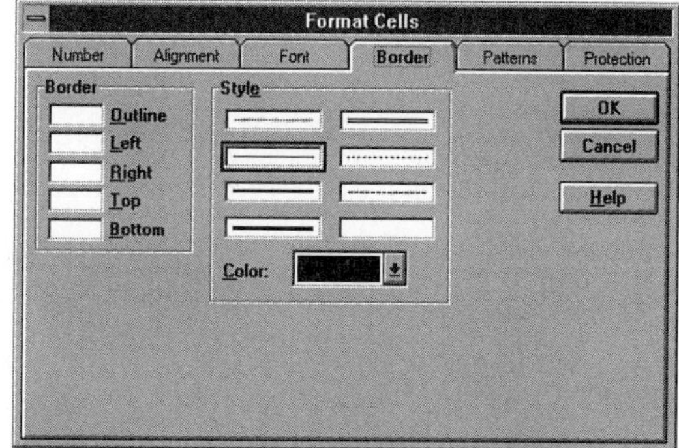

FIGURE 9.6.
The Border tab in the Format Cells dialog box.

SUPER TIP

To see your borders better, turn off the worksheet gridlines. Choose Tools | Options, select the View tab, and deactivate the Gridlines check box.

The Border section contains five options:

Outline	Applies the currently selected border style to the outer edges of the selected range
Left	Applies the currently selected border style to the left edge of each cell in the selected range
Right	Applies the currently selected border style to the right edge of each cell in the selected range
Top	Applies the currently selected border style to the top edge of each cell in the selected range
Bottom	Applies the currently selected border style to the bottom edge of each cell in the selected range

SUPER TIP

Press Ctrl+& (ampersand) to put an outline border around the selected cells. Press Ctrl+_ (underscore) to remove all borders from the selected cells.

The Style section contains the eight border styles you can use. Figure 9.7 demonstrates each of these styles.

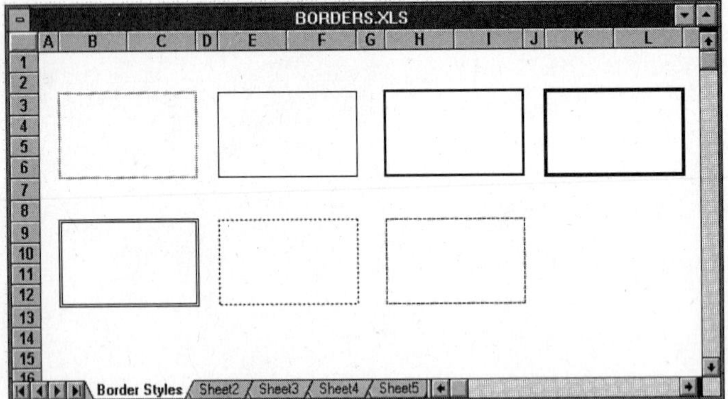

FIGURE 9.7.
Excel's border styles.

Follow Procedure 9.2 to apply a border to a cell or range.

PROCEDURE 9.2. APPLYING A BORDER TO A CELL OR RANGE.

1. Select the cell or range to be bordered.
2. Select Format | Cells, then select the Border tab in the Format Cells dialog box.
3. Select the border location from the Border section of the dialog box. Excel displays a sample of the currently selected border style beside the Border option.
4. Select a different border style if necessary. When you select a style, a sample appears in the box to the left of the selected Border option.
5. Click on OK or press Enter. Excel returns you to the worksheet with the borders applied.

Figure 9.8 shows how you can use cell borders to create an invoice form. In a business document such as this, your borders should be strictly functional. You should avoid the merely decorative, and, as in Figure 9.8, you should make your borders serve a purpose, whether it's marking a data area or separating parts of the form.

FIGURE 9.8.
Using cell borders to create an invoice form.

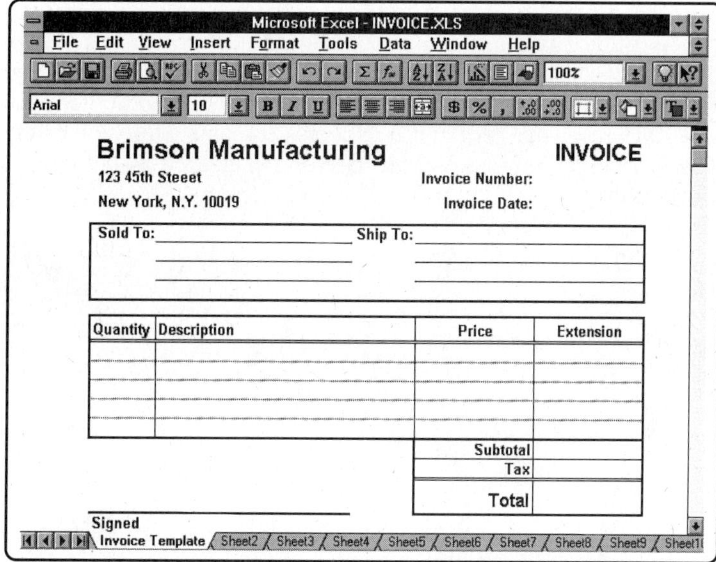

Using the Borders Tear-Off Tool

Excel 5.0's toolbars include a few tear-off tools that can make your formatting chores easier. The Borders tool in the Formatting toolbar is an example:

The Borders tool from the Formatting toolbar.

You can use a tear-off tool in one of two ways:

- As a drop-down list. Click on the arrow to display a box of formatting options. In the Borders tool, for example, the box displays a dozen common border combinations.
- As a floating toolbar. If you position the mouse pointer anywhere inside the dropped-down box, hold down the left mouse button, then drag the pointer outside the box, the box "tears off" from the toolbar. When you release the mouse button, Excel displays the box as a floating toolbar. This makes it easy to make selections when you're doing a lot of formatting.

Working with Cell Patterns

One of the most effective ways to make an area of your worksheet stand out is to apply a pattern or shading to the cells. By shading titles, headings, and important results, you give your reports a polished, professional appearance.

Excel 5.0 offers 18 different patterns, as shown in Figure 9.9. You apply these patterns by using the Patterns tab in the Format Cells dialog box, shown in Figure 9.10. This dialog box is divided into three areas. The **P**attern drop-down list box contains the 18 cell patterns and the foreground color. The **C**olor box sets the background color. (See Chapter 11, "Using Color in Worksheets," for instructions on using these color options.) The Sample area shows how the currently selected pattern options will appear on the worksheet.

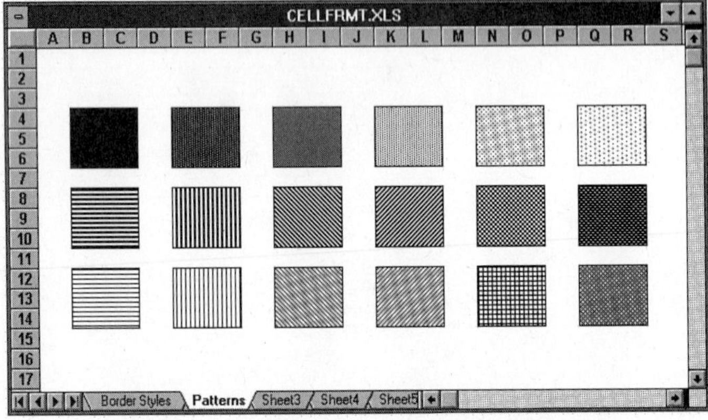

FIGURE 9.9.
Excel offers 18 different cell patterns.

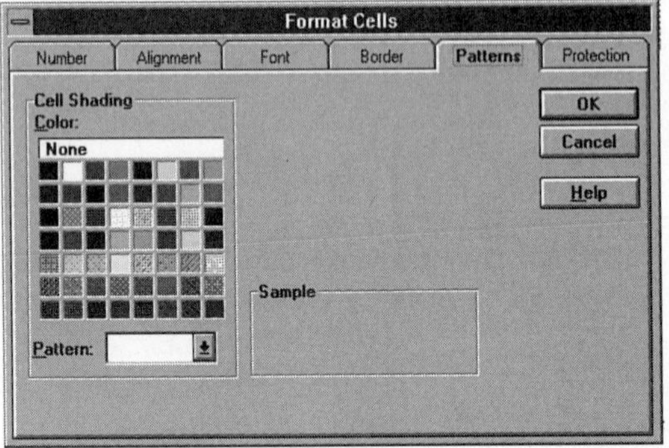

FIGURE 9.10.
The Patterns tab in the Cell Formats dialog box.

To apply a pattern to a cell or a range of cells, select F**o**rmat | C**e**lls, select the Patterns tab in the Cell Formats dialog box, then select your pattern from the **P**attern list. When you click on OK or press Enter, Excel returns you to the worksheet with the patterns applied.

Figure 9.11 shows the Brimson Manufacturing invoice with some shading effects. Figure 9.12 shows another application of cell patterns. In this example, patterns are used to create a time line (also known as a Gantt chart) for a project management application. Each project task is listed on the left, and the bars show where each task starts and ends. You can use different cell patterns to represent tasks not yet started, tasks partially completed, tasks fully completed, and tasks delayed.

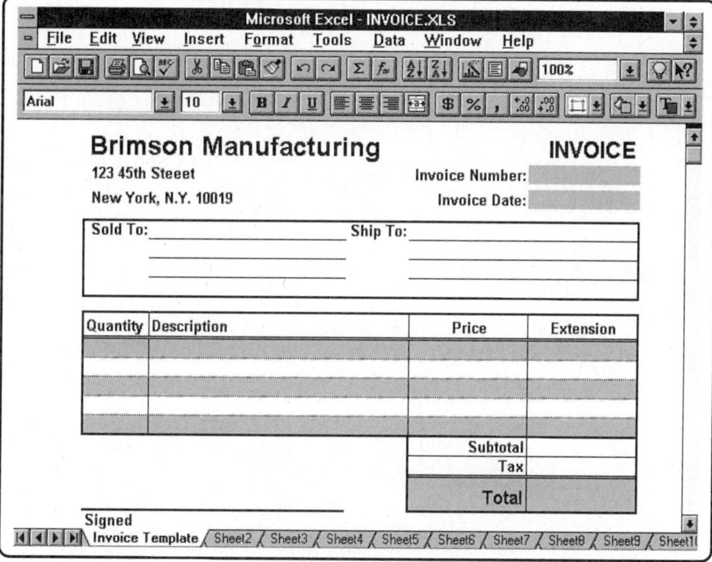

FIGURE 9.11.
The Brimson Manufacturing invoice with shading effects.

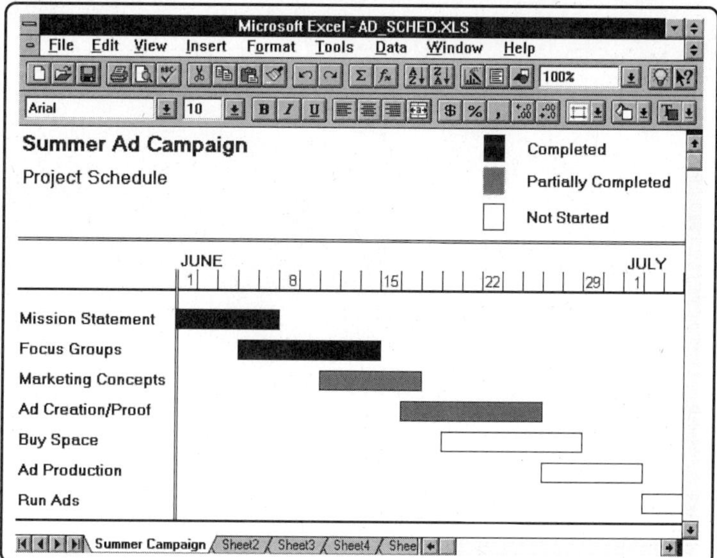

FIGURE 9.12.
Using cell patterns to create a Gantt chart.

Chapter

10

Working with Columns and Rows

An easy way to improve the appearance of your worksheet is to manipulate its rows and columns. This chapter teaches you how to adjust column widths and row heights. It also explains how to hide and unhide entire rows and columns, gridlines, and headings.

Adjusting Column Widths

You can use column width adjustments to improve the appearance of your worksheet in a number of different ways:

- When you're faced with a truncated text entry or a number that Excel shows as ######, you can enlarge the column so that the entry will be displayed in full.
- If your worksheet contains many numbers, you can widen the columns to spread the numbers out and make the worksheet less cluttered.
- You can make your columns smaller so that the entire worksheet fits on-screen or on a single printed page.
- You can adjust the column width so that the entire worksheet creates a grid for a time-line chart. An example of this is shown in Chapter 9, "Formatting Other Cell Attributes." See Figure 9.12.

SUPER TIP

If you have a column of numbers in which one number (such as a date) is wider than the column and appears as ######, you don't need to widen the column to accommodate the number. Instead, use the TEXT() function to display the number as text. This allows the number to flow into the next column (provided, of course, that the next column is empty). For details, see the Function Reference that comes with Excel.

Excel measures column width in characters. When you create a new worksheet, each column uses a standard width of 8.43 characters. The actual column width you see on-screen depends on the width of the default font. For example, the standard column width with 10-point Arial (7 pixels per character unit) is only half the size of the standard width with 20-point Arial (14 pixels per character unit). (For instructions on how to change the default font, see Chapter 12, "Working with Cell Formats.") You can use any of the following four methods to adjust your column widths:

- Enter a specific column width.
- Use the mouse to set the column width.
- Set the standard width of all columns.
- Have Excel set the width automatically with the AutoFit feature.

Method One: Entering a Specific Column Width

Excel enables you to set column widths as short as 0 characters or as long as 255 characters. To enter a column width, follow the steps in Procedure 10.1.

PROCEDURE 10.1. ENTERING A COLUMN WIDTH.

1. Select at least one cell in each column that you want to adjust.
2. Select Format | Column | Width. Excel displays the Column Width dialog box. The Column Width edit box shows the width of the selected columns. (This box will be blank if you've chosen columns with varying widths.)

> **SUPER TIP**
>
> To quickly open the Column Width dialog box, right-click on the column header and then choose Column Width from the shortcut menu.

3. Enter the desired width in the Column Width edit box.
4. Click on OK or press Enter. Excel sets the column width and returns you to the worksheet.

When entering column widths, you can use an integer or a decimal number. However, if you enter a width such as 10.1 and call up the Column Width dialog box for the same column, you'll notice that the Column Width edit box actually says 10.14. What happened is that Excel adjusted the column width to the nearest pixel. For 10-point Arial (Excel's default font), a character unit has 7 pixels, or roughly 0.143 characters per pixel. This means that Excel will round a column width of 10.1 to 10.14. Similarly, a width of 9.35 is rounded down to 9.29.

Method Two: Using the Mouse to Set the Column Width

You can bypass the Column Width dialog box by using the mouse to drag a column to the width you want. Procedure 10.2 lists the steps you need to follow to do this.

PROCEDURE 10.2. USING THE MOUSE TO SET THE COLUMN WIDTH.

1. Move the mouse pointer to the column header area and position the pointer at the right edge of the column you want to adjust. The mouse pointer changes to the shape shown in Figure 10.1.
2. Press and hold down the left mouse button. The formula bar's Name box displays the current column width, and the column's right gridline turns into a dashed line (see Figure 10.1).

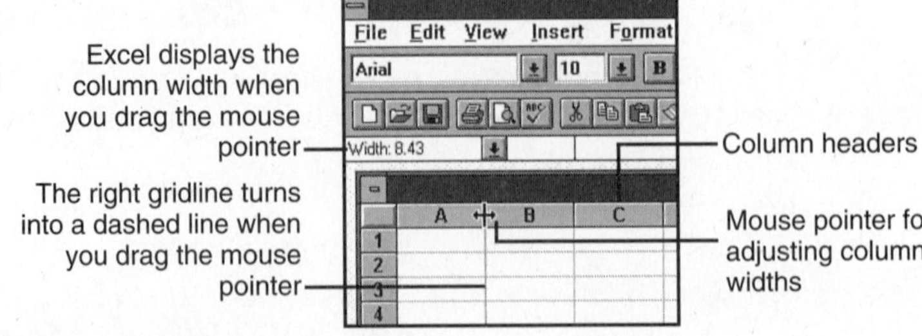

FIGURE 10.1.
You can use the mouse to adjust the column width.

3. Drag the pointer left or right to the desired width. As you move the pointer, the formula bar displays the new width.
4. Release the mouse button. Excel adjusts the column width accordingly.

You can use this technique to set the width of several columns at once. For every column you want to adjust, select the entire column and then perform the preceding steps on any one column. Excel applies the new width to each selected column.

Method Three: Setting the Standard Width for All the Columns

Using Excel's standard font, the standard column width is 8.43. You can change this by following the steps in Procedure 10.3.

PROCEDURE 10.3. SETTING THE STANDARD COLUMN WIDTH.

1. Select the Format | Column | Standard Width command. Excel displays the Standard Width dialog box.
2. Enter the desired width in the Standard Column Width edit box.
3. Click on OK or press Enter. Excel applies the new column width to all the columns in the worksheet (except those not using the standard width).

Method Four: Using Excel's AutoFit Feature

If you have a long column of entries of varying widths, it might take you a few tries to get the optimum column width. To avoid guesswork, you can have Excel set the width automatically using the AutoFit feature. When you use this feature, Excel examines the column's contents and sets the width slightly larger than the longest entry. Follow Procedure 10.4 to set the column width using AutoFit.

PROCEDURE 10.4. SETTING THE COLUMN WIDTH USING AUTOFIT.

1. Select each column you want to adjust.
2. Select Format | Column | AutoFit Selection. Excel adjusts the columns to their optimal width and returns you to the worksheet.

SUPER TIP

To quickly set the AutoFit width, position the mouse pointer at the right edge of the column header and double-click.

Adjusting Row Height

You can set the height of your worksheet rows by using techniques similar to those used for adjusting column widths. Excel normally adjusts row heights automatically to accommodate the tallest font in a row. However, you can make your own height adjustments to give your worksheet more breathing room or to reduce the amount of space taken up by unused rows.

SUPER CAUTION

When reducing a row height, always keep the height larger than the tallest font to avoid cutting off the tops of any characters.

Excel measures row height in *points*—the same units used for type size. When you create a new worksheet, Excel assigns a standard row height of 12.75 points, which is high enough to accommodate the default 10-point Arial font. If you were to change the default font to 20-point Arial, each row height would increase accordingly. (See Chapter 12, "Working with Cell Formats," for instructions on changing the default font.)

You can use any of these three methods to adjust row heights:

- Enter a specific row height.
- Use the mouse to set the row height.
- Have Excel set the height automatically using the AutoFit feature.

Method One: Entering a Specific Row Height

Excel enables you to set row heights as small as 0 points or as large as 409 points. To enter a row height, follow the steps in Procedure 10.5.

PROCEDURE 10.5. ENTERING A ROW HEIGHT.

1. Select at least one cell in each row you want to adjust.
2. Select the F**o**rmat | **R**ow | H**e**ight command. Excel displays the Row Height dialog box. The **R**ow Height edit box shows the height of the selected rows. (This box will be blank if you've chosen rows with varying heights.)

SUPER TIP

To quickly open the Row Height dialog box, right-click on the row header and then choose Row Height from the shortcut menu.

3. Enter the height you want in the **R**ow Height edit box.
4. Click on OK or press Enter. Excel sets the row height and returns you to the worksheet.

Method Two: Using the Mouse to Set the Row Height

You can bypass the **R**ow Height dialog box by using the mouse to drag a row to the height you want. Follow Procedure 10.6 to do this.

PROCEDURE 10.6. USING THE MOUSE TO SET THE ROW HEIGHT.

1. Move the mouse pointer to the row header area and position the pointer at the bottom edge of the row you want to adjust. The mouse pointer changes to the shape shown in Figure 10.2.

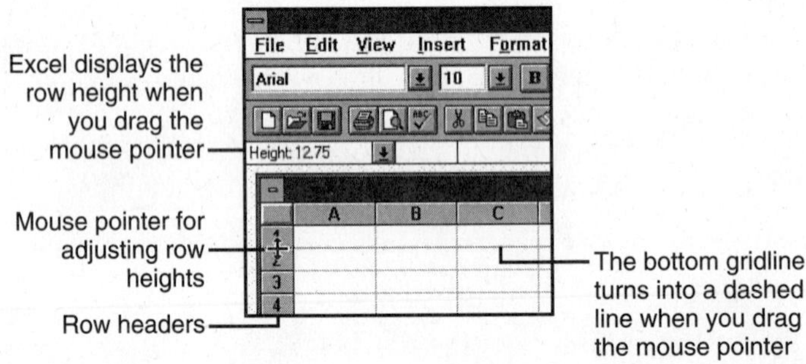

FIGURE 10.2.
You can use the mouse to adjust the row height.

2. Press and hold down the left mouse button. The formula bar displays the current row height, and the row's bottom gridline turns into a dashed line (see Figure 10.2).
3. Drag the pointer up or down to reach the desired height. As you move the pointer, the formula bar displays the new height.
4. Release the mouse button. Excel adjusts the row height accordingly.

You can use this technique to set the height of several rows at once. For every row you want to adjust, select the entire row and then perform the preceding steps on any one row. Excel applies the new height to each row.

Method Three: Using Excel's AutoFit Feature

If you've made several font changes and height adjustments to a long row of entries, you might need to try several times to set an optimum row height. To avoid guesswork, you can use Excel's AutoFit feature to set the height automatically to the best fit. Procedure 10.7 shows you how it's done.

PROCEDURE 10.7. SETTING THE ROW HEIGHT WITH AUTOFIT.

1. Select each row you want to adjust.
2. Select F**o**rmat | **R**ow | **A**utoFit. Excel adjusts the rows to their optimal height and returns you to the worksheet.

SUPER TIP

To quickly set the AutoFit height, position the mouse pointer at the bottom edge of the row header and double-click.

Hiding Columns and Rows

Your worksheets might contain confidential information (such as payroll figures) or unimportant information (such as the period numbers used when calculating interest payments). In either case, you can hide the appropriate columns or rows when showing your worksheet to others. The data remains intact but isn't displayed onscreen. The next two sections show you how to hide and unhide columns and rows.

Hiding and Unhiding Columns

When you hide a column, you set the column width to 0. Procedure 10.8 shows you the necessary steps.

PROCEDURE 10.8. HIDING COLUMNS.

1. Select at least one cell in each column you want to hide.
2. Select F**o**rmat | **C**olumn | **H**ide. Excel hides the column and returns you to the worksheet.

SUPER TIP

A quick way to hide columns is to select a cell from each column and press Ctrl+0 (zero). You also can right-click on the column header and then choose **H**ide from the shortcut menu.

SUPER TIP

To hide a column with the mouse, position the pointer on the right edge of the column header, click the left button, and drag the pointer to the left, past the left edge of the column header.

When you hide a column, the column letter no longer appears in the headers. For example, Figure 10.3 shows a worksheet with confidential payroll information in columns C, D, and E. Figure 10.4 shows the same worksheet with these columns hidden and their letters missing from the column headers. Despite this, you still can refer to cells in the hidden columns in formulas and searches.

FIGURE 10.3.

Columns C, D, and E contain confidential information.

PAYROLL.XLS

	A	B	C	D	E	F	G
1							
2			Salary	Commission	Total	Region Totals	
3		*Eastern Reps:*					
4		Willie Odlum	$56,000	$15,000	$71,000		
5		Bill Kimmo	$58,000	$14,000	$72,000		
6		Karen Hammond	$62,000	$18,000	$80,000		
7			$176,000	$47,000	$223,000	$223,000	
8		*Western Reps:*					
9		Vince Durbin	$58,000	$14,000	$72,000		
10		Sharon Severn	$56,000	$15,000	$71,000		
11		Beth Dodgson	$58,000	$16,000	$74,000		
12			$172,000	$45,000	$217,000	$217,000	
13		*Region Totals*	$348,000	$92,000	$440,000	$440,000	
14							

Sheet1 / Sheet2 / Sheet3 / Sheet4 / Sheet5 / She

FIGURE 10.4.

The same worksheet with columns C, D, and E hidden.

PAYROLL.XLS

	A	B	F	G	H	I	J	K
1								
2			Region Totals					
3		*Eastern Reps:*						
4		Willie Odlum						
5		Bill Kimmo						
6		Karen Hammond						
7			$223,000					
8		*Western Reps:*						
9		Vince Durbin						
10		Sharon Severn						
11		Beth Dodgson						
12			$217,000					
13		*Region Totals*	$440,000					
14								

Sheet1 / Sheet2 / Sheet3 / Sheet4 / Sheet5 / She

To unhide a range of columns, follow Procedure 10.9.

PROCEDURE 10.9. UNHIDING A RANGE OF COLUMNS.

1. Select at least one cell from each column on either side of the hidden columns. For example, to unhide columns C, D, and E, select a cell in columns B and F.
2. Choose F**o**rmat | **C**olumn | **U**nhide. Excel unhides the columns.

SUPER TIP

A quick way to unhide columns is to select a cell on each side of the hidden columns and then either press Ctrl+) or right-click on the selection and choose Unhide from the shortcut menu.

If you have just one column hidden, you can use Procedure 10.9 to unhide it. However, if you want to unhide a single column out of a *group* of hidden columns (for example, column C out of columns C, D, and E), use Procedure 10.10.

PROCEDURE 10.10. UNHIDING A SINGLE COLUMN.

1. Choose the **E**dit | **G**o To command. Excel displays the Go To dialog box.
2. Enter a cell address in the column you want to unhide. For example, to unhide column C, enter `C1`.
3. Click on OK or press Enter. Excel moves to the cell address.
4. Choose F**o**rmat | **C**olumn | **U**nhide. Excel unhides the column and returns you to the worksheet.

Hiding and Unhiding Rows

Hiding rows is similar to hiding columns. Follow the steps in Procedure 10.11.

PROCEDURE 10.11. HIDING ROWS.

1. Select at least one cell in every row you want to hide.
2. Choose F**o**rmat | **R**ow | **H**ide. Excel returns you to the worksheet with the rows hidden.

SUPER TIP

A quick way to hide columns is to select a cell from each row and press Ctrl+9. You also can right-click on the row header and then choose **H**ide from the shortcut menu.

SUPER TIP

To hide a row with the mouse, position the pointer on the bottom edge of the row header and drag the pointer up *past* the top edge of the row header.

As with columns, when you hide a row, the row letter no longer appears in the headers. However, you still can refer to cells in the hidden rows in formulas and searches.

To unhide a range of rows, use the steps shown in Procedure 10.12.

PROCEDURE 10.12. UNHIDING A RANGE OF ROWS.

1. Select at least one cell from each row on either side of the hidden rows. For example, to unhide rows 3, 4, and 5, select a cell in rows 2 and 6.
2. Choose F**o**rmat | **R**ow | **U**nhide. Excel unhides the rows and returns you to the worksheet.

SUPER TIP

A quick way to unhide rows is to select a cell from each row on either side of the hidden rows and press Ctrl+(. You also can right-click on the selected rows and choose **U**nhide from the shortcut menu.

If you have just one row hidden, use Procedure 10.12 to unhide it. However, if you want to unhide a single row out of a *group* of hidden rows (for example, row 3 out of rows 3, 4, and 5), use Procedure 10.13.

PROCEDURE 10.13. UNHIDING A SINGLE ROW.

1. Choose the **E**dit | **G**o To command. Excel displays the Go To dialog box.
2. Enter a cell address in the row you want to unhide. For example, to unhide row 3, enter A3.
3. Click on OK or press Enter. Excel moves to the cell address.
4. Choose F**o**rmat | **R**ow | **U**nhide. Excel unhides the rows and returns you to the worksheet.

Hiding Gridlines and Headers

Excel enables you to hide both your worksheet gridlines and the row and column headers. This is useful for displaying your worksheet to others on-screen or on an overhead, or for a data entry application. Removing gridlines also helps your cell border and shading effects show up better.

Procedure 10.14 shows you how to remove your worksheet gridlines and headers.

PROCEDURE 10.14. HIDING WORKSHEET GRIDLINES AND HEADERS.

1. Select the **T**ools | **O**ptions command and, in the Options dialog box that appears, select the View tab.
2. To remove gridlines, deactivate the **G**ridlines check box.
3. To remove the headers, deactivate the Row and Column H**e**aders check box.
4. Click on OK or press Enter. Excel returns you to the worksheet with your chosen display options in effect.

To restore gridlines or row and column headers, repeat the preceding steps and activate the appropriate check boxes.

Chapter

11

Using Color in Worksheets

The previous chapters in this Workshop have shown you how to turn a plain, unformatted worksheet into an attractive, professional-quality report. The final touch involves adding just the right amount of color to your presentation. With colors, you can emphasize important results, shape the layout of your page, and add subtle psychological effects.

If you don't have access to a color printer, you can use color in your worksheets for on-screen presentations or to convert worksheets and charts to overheads or slides using an offsite graphics service.

Excel has extensive color capabilities. This chapter shows you how to add color to your cell contents, borders, and backgrounds using Excel's default 56-color palette.

Excel's Color Palette

When applying colors to your worksheet elements, Excel enables you to choose from a palette of 56 colors. Figure 11.1 shows the default palette. Later in this chapter, you'll learn how to customize this palette with your own colors.

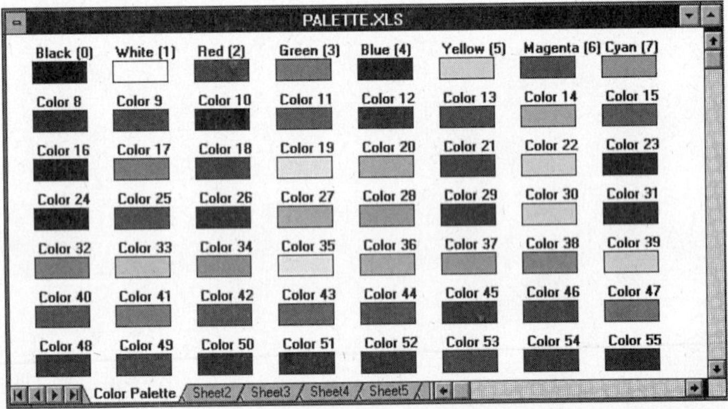

FIGURE 11.1.
Excel's 56-color palette.

SUPER NOTE

The palette colors on your system appear differently, depending on whether you're using a 16- or 256-color video driver. The 256-color driver shows the palette as solid colors (as shown in Figure 11.1), and the 16-color driver shows colors 16 through 55 as patterns.

PALETTE.XLS is available on the Super Disk.

Assigning Colors to Cell Contents

You can use any of the palette colors to format individual cell entries. Colors make worksheet titles and headings stand out and also emphasize interesting results. You can use two methods to change the color of cell contents:

- Assign font colors
- Use color symbols in custom numeric and date formats

Assigning a Font Color

To apply a font color to a cell's contents, follow the steps in Procedure 11.1.

PROCEDURE 11.1. ASSIGNING A FONT COLOR TO A CELL'S CONTENTS.

1. Select the cell or range of cells you want to format.
2. Choose the Format | Cells command and select the Font tab in the Format Cells dialog box.
3. Select a color from the Color drop-down list. The font in the Preview box changes color to match your selection.
4. Click on OK or press Enter. Excel returns you to the worksheet with the color applied.

You also can use the Font Color tear-off tool in the Formatting toolbar to assign a color to a cell's contents.

Assigning a Color Using Numeric Formats

You can gain even more control over the coloring of cell entries by using numeric formats. Recall the following currency formats from Chapter 7, "Formatting Numbers, Dates, and Times":

```
$#,##0_);[RED]($#,##0)
$#,##0.00_);[RED]($#,##0.00)
```

In each example, the second part of the format applies the color red to any negative amount. By creating your own custom formats, you can apply a color to any number or range of numbers. Table 11.1 lists the 9 color symbols you can use in your custom numeric color formats.

Table 11.1. The color symbols to use in numeric formats.

Symbol	*Color*
[BLACK]	Black
[WHITE]	White

continues

Table 11.1. continued

Symbol	*Color*
[RED]	Red
[GREEN]	Green
[BLUE]	Blue
[YELLOW]	Yellow
[MAGENTA]	Magenta
[CYAN]	Cyan
[COLOR *n*]	A color from the color palette, where *n* is a number between 0 and 55 (see Figure 11.1)

The following format displays positive numbers in blue, negative numbers in red, zero values in green, and text in magenta:

```
[BLUE]0.00;[RED]-0.00;[GREEN]0;[MAGENTA]
```

You can add condition values to your formats to handle just about any situation. For example, if you have an accounts receivable worksheet that contains a column showing the number of days that invoices are past due, use the format `[>90][MAGENTA]###;###` to display numbers over 90 in magenta.

Assigning Colors to Borders and Patterns

In Chapter 9, "Formatting Other Cell Attributes," you learned that using cell borders and patterns can make your worksheets appear more organized and dynamic. You can extend these advantages by applying colors to your borders and cell patterns. Procedure 11.2 shows you how.

PROCEDURE 11.2. ASSIGNING COLORS TO BORDERS AND PATTERNS.

1. Select the cell or range of cells you want to format.
2. Choose the Format | Cells command to display the Format Cells dialog box.
3. To apply a border color, select the Border tab and choose the color you want from the Color drop-down list.
4. To apply a pattern color, first select the Patterns tab.
5. To apply a background color, choose one of the boxes in the Color section. To apply a foreground color, choose a color from the Pattern drop-down list.
6. Click on OK or press Enter. Excel returns you to the worksheet with the color applied.

You also can use the Color tear-off tool in the Formatting toolbar to assign a background color to a cell pattern.

By mixing the pattern and its foreground and background colors, you can create different shades of any palette color. Figure 11.2 shows an example of this. Here, in each of the Result columns, the foreground color used is Dark Cyan. In the first six columns, the background color is black, and the pattern varies from solid to the widely spaced dots of the pattern on the left. As you can see, the original color becomes progressively darker. In the last five columns, the background color is switched to white. In this case, as you move through the dot patterns, the original color becomes lighter. With this simple trick, you get an additional 10 colors for every palette color.

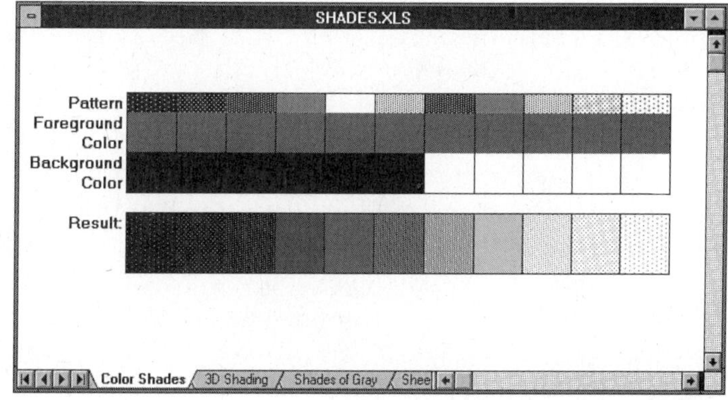

FIGURE 11.2.
Use the dot patterns with dark or light background colors to produce shades of the foreground color.

Creating 3-D Effects

You can use contrasting border and pattern colors to achieve impressive 3-D effects in your worksheets. Begin by coloring each cell in the worksheet with a neutral color (not too dark, not too light) such as gray. (Depending on which color you use, you might have to make most of your cell contents bold to make them show up properly.) With 3-D effects, you can format an area to look as though it's raised up from the worksheet or depressed into the worksheet. To create a raised effect, follow the steps in Procedure 11.3.

PROCEDURE 11.3. CREATING A RAISED 3-D EFFECT.

1. Select the top row of cells in the range. In the Border tab of the Format Cells dialog box, add a border to the **T**op and select white from the **C**olor list.
2. Select the left column of cells in the range. In the Border tab, add a border to the **L**eft and select white from the **C**olor list.

> **SUPER NOTE**
>
> When you perform this procedure, you'll notice that some of the Border boxes are grayed. This is normal. It means that only some of the selected cells have the border applied.

3. Select the bottom row of cells in the range. In the Border tab, add a border to the **B**ottom and select black from the **C**olor list.
4. Select the right column of cells in the range. In the Border tab, add a border to the **R**ight and select black from the **C**olor list.

Procedure 11.4 outlines the steps to follow to create a pressed effect.

PROCEDURE 11.4. CREATING A PRESSED 3-D EFFECT.

1. Select the top row of cells in the range. In the Border tab of the Format Cells dialog box, add a border to the **T**op and select black from the **C**olor list.
2. Select the left column of cells in the range. In the Border tab, add a border to the **L**eft and select black from the **C**olor list.
3. Select the bottom row of cells in the range. In the Border tab, add a border to the **B**ottom and select white from the **C**olor list.
4. Select the right column of cells in the range. In the Border tab, add a border to the **R**ight and select white from the **C**olor list.

Figure 11.3 shows a worksheet formatted with 3-D effects.

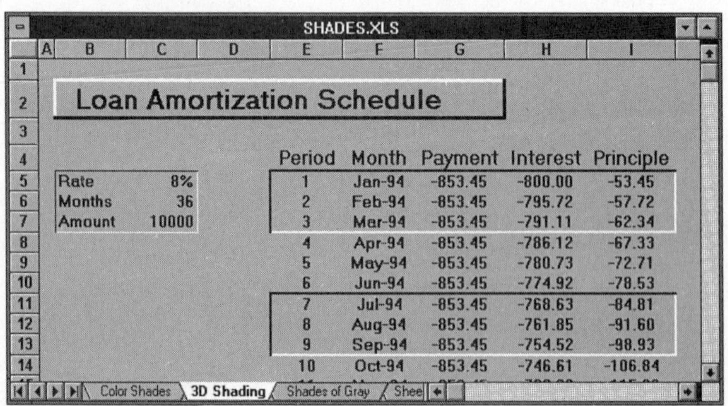

SHADES.XLS
Loan Amortization Schedule
Rate 8%
Months 36
Amount 10000
Period Month Payment Interest Principle
1 Jan-94 -853.45 -800.00 -53.45
2 Feb-94 -853.45 -795.72 -57.72
3 Mar-94 -853.45 -791.11 -62.34
4 Apr-94 -853.45 -786.12 -67.33
5 May-94 -853.45 -780.73 -72.71
6 Jun-94 -853.45 -774.92 -78.53
7 Jul-94 -853.45 -768.63 -84.81
8 Aug-94 -853.45 -761.85 -91.60
9 Sep-94 -853.45 -754.52 -98.93
10 Oct-94 -853.45 -746.61 -106.84
Color Shades
3D Shading
Shades of Gray

FIGURE 11.3. *You can use borders and shading to create 3-D effects.*

Assigning Colors to Gridlines

You can change the color of your worksheet gridlines. Procedure 11.5 lists the appropriate steps.

PROCEDURE 11.5. ASSIGNING COLORS TO WORKSHEET GRIDLINES.

1. Select **T**ools | **O**ptions and then select the View tab from the Options dialog box.
2. Select a color from the **C**olor drop-down list under the **G**ridlines check box.
3. Click on OK or press Enter. Excel returns you to the worksheet with the new color applied.

Customizing the Color Palette

As you've seen in this chapter, you use the Excel color palette throughout the program. The 56 default colors are usually fine for most applications, and you may never need another color. However, if a particular shade would be just right for your presentation, Excel enables you to customize the color palette.

SUPER TIP

If you use your corporate colors in presentations, you can create a custom palette containing several hues and shades of your company's colors.

You customize your own colors using the Color Picker dialog box (see Figure 11.4). You can use one of two methods to select a color. The first method utilizes the fact that you can create any color in the spectrum by mixing the three primary colors: red, green, and blue. The Color Picker dialog box enables you to enter specific numbers between 0 and 255 for each of these colors. A lower number means the color is less intense, and a higher number means the color is more intense.

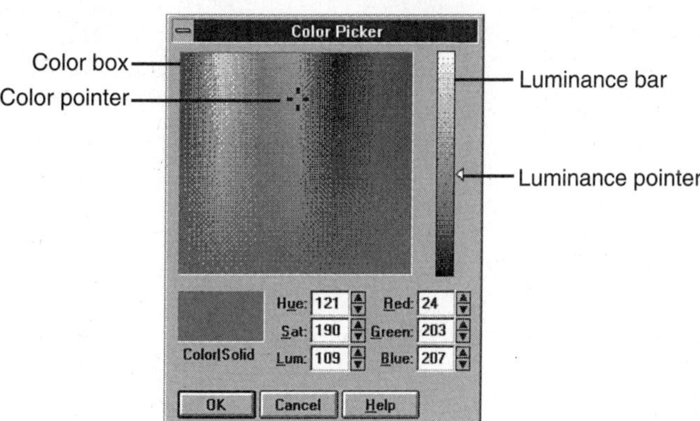

FIGURE 11.4.
The Color Picker dialog box.

To give you some idea of how this works, Table 11.2 lists the first eight colors of the default palette and their respective red, green, and blue numbers.

Table 11.2. The red, green, and blue numbers for eight default palette colors.

Color	*Red*	*Green*	*Blue*
Black	0	0	0
White	255	255	255
Red	255	0	0
Green	0	255	0
Blue	0	0	255
Yellow	255	255	0
Magenta	255	0	255
Cyan	0	255	255

SUPER NOTE

Whenever the **R**ed, **G**reen, and **B**lue values are equal, you get a gray-scale color. Lower numbers produce darker grays, and higher numbers produce lighter grays.

The second method for selecting colors involves setting three different attributes: hue, saturation, and luminance.

Hue: This number (which is more or less equivalent to the term *color*) measures the position on the color spectrum. Lower numbers indicate a position near the red end, and higher numbers move through the yellow, green, blue, and violet parts of the spectrum. As you increase the hue, the color pointer moves from left to right.

Saturation: This number is a measure of the purity of a given hue. A saturation setting of 240 means that the hue is a pure color. Lower numbers indicate that more gray is mixed with the hue until, at 0, the color becomes part of the gray-scale. As you increase the saturation, the color pointer moves toward the top of the color palette.

Luminance: This number is a measure of the brightness of a color. Lower numbers are darker, and higher numbers are brighter. The luminance bar to the right of the color palette shows the luminance scale for the selected color. As you increase the luminance, the slider moves toward the top of the bar.

Follow Procedure 11.6 to create a custom palette.

PROCEDURE 11.6. CREATING A CUSTOM COLOR PALETTE.

1. Choose **T**ools | **O**ptions and then select the Color tab from the Options dialog box. The Color tab displays all 56 colors in the Excel palette.
2. Select a color from the color palette.

> **SUPER TIP**
>
> If you need to reset the palette to the default colors, select the **R**eset button.

3. Select **M**odify. The Color Picker dialog box appears with the selected color's numbers displayed.
4. To select a new color, enter the appropriate values in the text boxes. You also can use the mouse to move the color pointer in the color box and move the slider up or down the luminance bar.

> **SUPER TIP**
>
> You can quickly select a custom color by clicking on a color in the Color Picker dialog's color palette. To set the luminance, click on the appropriate area in the luminance bar or drag the slider.

5. (Optional) The Color | Solid box shows the selected color on the left and the nearest solid color on the right (if you're using a 16-color video driver). If you want to use the solid color, double-click on it.
6. Click on OK or press Enter. Excel returns you to the Color tab.
7. Repeat steps 2-6 to customize other colors in the palette.
8. When you finish, click on OK or press Enter. Excel returns you to the worksheet with the new palette.

SUPER NOTE

To use your new colors in custom numeric formats, refer to the palette number. For example, if you replace black in the default palette, refer to the new color as [COLOR 1] in your format definitions.

Copying Custom Color Palettes

You can copy custom color palettes created in other workbooks by following the steps in Procedure 11.7.

PROCEDURE 11.7. COPYING A CUSTOM COLOR PALETTE TO ANOTHER WORKBOOK.

1. Open the workbook that contains the custom color palette.
2. Activate the worksheet from which you want to receive the copy of the custom palette.
3. Choose the Tools | Options command and select the Color tab in the Options dialog box.
4. In the Copy Colors from drop-down list, select the workbook that contains the custom colors you want to copy. The Color tab displays the color palette from the selected workbook.
5. Click on OK or press Enter. Excel copies the color palette into the current workbook.

SUPER NOTE

Save color schemes that you use frequently (such as your company's colors or the colors of major clients) in their own workbooks. You then can copy the colors into your current worksheet whenever you need them.

Using Color Effectively

Now you know how to apply colors to your Excel worksheets, but that's only half the battle. Colors that are poorly matched or improperly applied can make a presentation look worse, not better. This section examines a few basics for effectively using colors in your worksheets.

With so many colors available, the temptation is to go overboard and use a dozen different hues on each page. However, using too many colors can confuse your audience and even cause eye fatigue. Try to stick to three or four colors at most. If you must use more, try to use different shades of three or four hues.

Before finalizing your color scheme, you need to make sure that the colors you've selected work well together. For example, blue and black are often difficult to distinguish and green/red combinations clash. Other color combinations to avoid are red/blue, green/blue, and brown/black. On the other hand, color combinations such as red/yellow, gray/red, and blue/yellow go well together, as do contrasting shades of the same color, such as black and gray.

SUPER NOTE

Another good reason to avoid using too much green and red in your worksheets is that approximately eight percent of the male population suffers from red-green color blindness.

When selecting colors, think about the psychological impact that your scheme will have on your audience. Studies have shown that "cool" colors such as blue and gray evoke a sense of dependability and trust. Use these colors for business meetings. For presentations that require a little more excitement, "warm" colors such as red, yellow, and orange can evoke a festive, fun atmosphere. For a safe, comfortable ambiance, try using brown and yellow. For an environmental touch, use green and brown.

After you've settled on a color scheme, use it consistently throughout your presentation. Charts, clip art, and slides should all use the same colors.

Chapter

12

Working with Cell Formats

Excel contains powerful formatting features that can make your worksheets look their best. The problem is that you can end up spending more time working on the appearance of a spreadsheet than on the actual data. To remedy this, Excel offers a number of features that make your cell formatting faster and more efficient.

This chapter shows you how to display cell format information, copy and move existing formats, define format styles, and use Excel's handy AutoFormat and Format Painter features.

SUPER TIP

Worksheet templates and start-up sheets give you easy access to your formats. See Chapter 62, "Working with Templates and Outlines," for information about working with Excel templates.

Displaying Cell Format Information

With so many formatting options available, it's easy to lose track of which cells are formatted with which options. To help, Excel provides an Info window that can show you the attributes of any cell. To use the Info window to learn about a cell's formatting, follow the steps in Procedure 12.1.

PROCEDURE 12.1. DISPLAYING FORMATTING OPTIONS WITH THE INFO WINDOW.

1. Move to the cell you want to use.
2. Select the **T**ools | **O**ptions command and then select the View tab in the Options dialog box.
3. Activate the Info **W**indow check box.
4. Click on OK or press Enter. Excel displays the Info window and the Info window menu bar.
5. Select the **I**nfo | Forma**t** command. Excel displays the cell format information in the Info window.

SUPER TIP

To quickly display the Info window, select the cell you want and press Ctrl+F2.

Figure 12.1 shows an Info window displaying the format options of cell I5 from the 3D Shading worksheet.

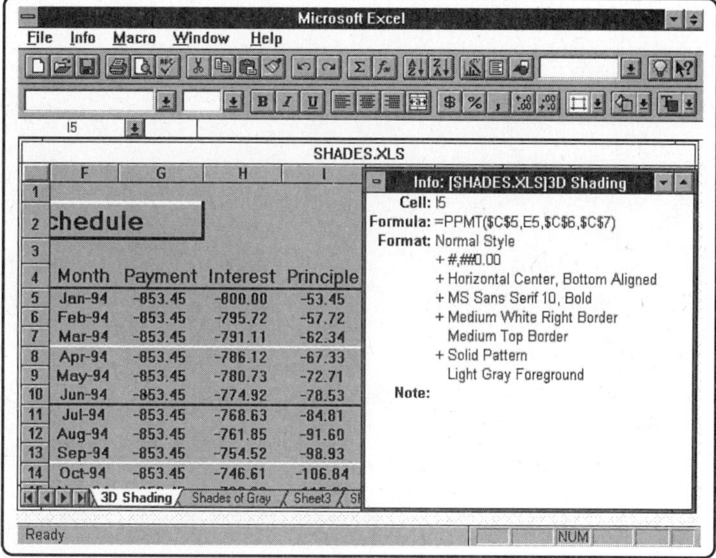

FIGURE 12.1.
The Info window displaying cell formats.

Copying Cell Formats

As soon as you've formatted a cell the way you want it, you can use the same format in other parts of your worksheet by copying the entire cell. When you copy a cell, Excel pastes both the cell contents and the cell format to the new location.

However, if you want to copy only the formatting and not the contents, Excel gives you two methods:

- Using Paste Special to paste formats.
- Using the Format Painter to apply existing formats to a selected range.

Copying Formats with Paste Special

To copy only formats to a destination, use the Paste Special command, as described in Procedure 12.2.

PROCEDURE 12.2. COPYING CELL FORMATS WITH PASTE SPECIAL.

1. Select the cell or range you want to copy.
2. Choose the **E**dit | **C**opy command.
3. Select the destination range.
4. Choose the **E**dit | Paste **S**pecial command. Excel displays the Paste Special dialog box.
5. In the Paste section, select Forma**t**s.

6. Click on OK or press Enter. Excel copies only the formats from the original cells.

Copying Cell Formats with the Format Painter

Excel 5.0 features a new Format Painter tool that enables you to easily apply an existing format to a selected range. Procedure 12.3 shows you how it's done.

PROCEDURE 12.3. COPYING CELL FORMATS WITH FORMAT PAINTER.

1. Select the cell or range that contains the format you want to copy (see Figure 12.2).

PAINTER.XLS

	A	B	C	D	E
1					
2	Formatting to copy:	Bold	$123.45	Shaded/Bordered	Centered
3					
4					
5	Destination range:	Sample text	123.456	Sample text	Sample text
6		Sample text	123.456	Sample text	Sample text
7		Sample text	123.456	Sample text	Sample text
8		Sample text	123.456	Sample text	Sample text
9		Sample text	123.456	Sample text	Sample text
10		Sample text	123.456	Sample text	Sample text
11		Sample text	123.456	Sample text	Sample text
12		Sample text	123.456	Sample text	Sample text

Sheet1 / Sheet2 / Sheet3 / Sheet4 / Sheet5

FIGURE 12.2. *Select the range containing the format you want to copy.*

2. Click on the Format Painter tool in the Standard toolbar. A small paintbrush appears beside the mouse pointer, as shown in Figure 12.3.

The Format Painter tool.

PAINTER.XLS

	A	B	C	D	E
1					
2	Formatting to copy:	Bold	$123.45	Shaded/Bordered	Centered
3					
4					
5	Destination range:	Sample text	123.456	Sample text	Sample text
6		Sample text	123.456	Sample text	Sample text
7		Sample text	123.456	Sample text	Sample text
8		Sample text	123.456	Sample text	Sample text
9		Sample text	123.456	Sample text	Sample text
10		Sample text	123.456	Sample text	Sample text
11		Sample text	123.456	Sample text	Sample text
12		Sample text	123.456	Sample text	Sample text

Sheet1 / Sheet2 / Sheet3 / Sheet4 / Sheet5

FIGURE 12.3. *Select the Format Painter tool and then drag the mouse pointer over the range where you want to copy the format.*

3. Drag the mouse pointer over the range to which you want to copy the format (see Figure 12.3).
4. Release the mouse button. Excel copies the format from the original range into the destination range, as shown in Figure 12.4.

FIGURE 12.4.
When you release the button, Excel pastes the original format into the destination range.

PAINTER.XLS

	A	B	C	D	E	F
1						
2	Formatting to copy:	Bold	$123.45	Shaded/Bordered	Centered	
3						
4						
5	Destination range:	Sample text	$123.46	Sample text	Sample text	
6		Sample text	$123.46	Sample text	Sample text	
7		Sample text	$123.46	Sample text	Sample text	
8		Sample text	$123.46	Sample text	Sample text	
9		Sample text	$123.46	Sample text	Sample text	
10		Sample text	$123.46	Sample text	Sample text	
11		Sample text	$123.46	Sample text	Sample text	
12		Sample text	$123.46	Sample text	Sample text	
13						
14						
15						
16						

Sheet1 / Sheet2 / Sheet3 / Sheet4 / Sheet5 / She

Clearing Cell Formats

Clearing only the format in a cell (and leaving the contents intact) is easy, as you'll see in Procedure 12.4.

PROCEDURE 12.4. CLEARING CELL FORMATS.

1. Select the cell or range with the formats you want to clear.
2. Select the **E**dit | Cle**a**r | **F**ormats command. Excel clears the cell format.

Working with Styles

Depending on the options you choose, formatting a single cell or range can take dozens of mouse clicks or keystrokes. If you plan to use a specific formatting combination repeatedly, don't reinvent the wheel each time. Using Excel's Style feature, you can summarize any combination of formatting options under a single style name.

Styles also save time if you need to reformat your document. Normally, you would have to select every cell containing the format you want to change (including blank cells) and then make the adjustment. With styles, you just redefine the style, and Excel updates all the associated cells automatically.

A style can contain many of the formatting features you've learned about in this Workshop, including fonts, alignment, borders, patterns, and number, date, and time formats. Excel comes with several built-in styles: Comma, Comma [0], Currency, Currency [0], Percent, and Normal. Normal is the default style for the entire workbook.

Applying a Style

Procedure 12.5 shows you how to apply a style.

PROCEDURE 12.5. APPLYING A STYLE.

1. Select the cell or range you want to format.
2. Select the Format | Style command. Excel displays the Style dialog box, shown in Figure 12.5.

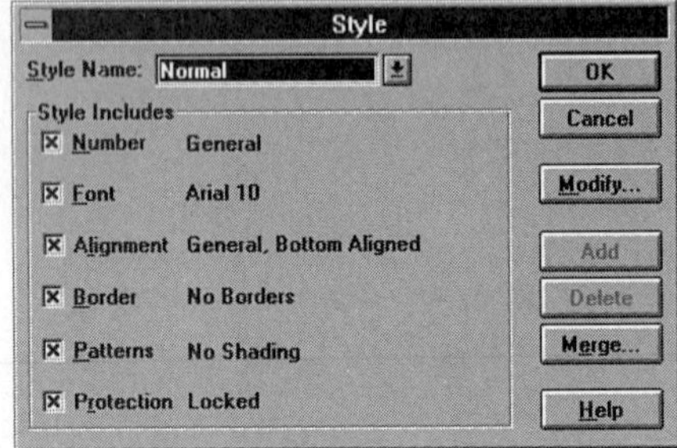

FIGURE 12.5.
The Style dialog box.

3. Select the style you want from the Style Name drop-down list. A description of the formatting options included in the selected style appears in the Style Includes group.
4. If you don't want to use some part of the style, deactivate the appropriate check box in the Style Includes group.
5. Click on OK or press Enter. Excel applies the style to the selected cells.

When you apply a style to a cell, Excel overwrites the cell's existing format. Similarly, if you apply a style first and then format the cell, the new formatting overwrites the style. In both cases, however, only defined attributes change. For example, if you apply the Percent style to a cell already formatted as left-aligned, the alignment doesn't change.

Creating a Style

Besides using the built-in styles supplied by Excel, you can define your own styles to suit your needs. Any style you create appears in the Style Name list for that workbook. Excel provides three ways to define styles:

- By example
- By definition
- By merging styles from another document

SUPER NOTE

It's a good idea to create a style for frequently used sections of your worksheet. For example, a Heading style would contain attributes of your worksheet headings, and a Title style would contain your worksheet title format.

Creating a Style by Example

If you have a cell that contains a format combination you want to use as a style, you can tell Excel to define a new style based on the cell format. This is called the *style by example* method. Procedure 12.6 outlines the steps for this method.

PROCEDURE 12.6. CREATING A STYLE BY EXAMPLE.

1. Select the cell that contains the format combination you want to turn into a style.
2. Select the Format | Style command to display the Style dialog box.
3. Type the new style name in the Style Name edit box.
4. Click on OK or press Enter. Excel creates the new style.

You can select multiple cells to use as an example. In this case, Excel assigns only formats that the cells have in common. For example, suppose you have a cell that's left-aligned with a border and another that's left-aligned without a border. If you select both cells to use as your example, Excel defines the new style as left-aligned only.

Creating a Style by Definition

The second method for creating a style involves setting the specific format options using the Style dialog box. This is called the *style by definition* method. Follow Procedure 12.7 to create a style by definition.

PROCEDURE 12.7. CREATING A STYLE BY DEFINITION.

1. Select the Format | Style command to display the Style dialog box.
2. Enter the new style name in the Style Name edit box.
3. Click on the Modify button. Excel displays the Format Cells dialog box.
4. Use the tabs in the Format Cells dialog box to select your style options. When you're done, click on OK or press Enter to return to the Style dialog box.
5. To accept the new style, click on the Add button.

6. To create more styles, repeat steps 2-4. Otherwise, you can either apply the new style to the selected cells by clicking on OK or pressing Enter, or you can exit the dialog without applying the style by clicking on Close.

Merging Styles from Another Document

The third method for creating styles involves copying the existing styles from another document into the current workbook. This is called *merging* styles. This method is useful if you have other workbooks in which you've already defined several styles. Instead of defining them again in the current workbook, you simply copy them. Before proceeding, you need to open the workbook containing the styles, and the workbook receiving the styles must be the active window. Procedure 12.8 shows you how to merge styles.

PROCEDURE 12.8. MERGING STYLES FROM ANOTHER DOCUMENT.

1. Select the **F**ormat | **S**tyle command to display the Style dialog box.
2. Click on the **M**erge button. The Merge Styles dialog box appears with a list of the currently open workbooks.
3. Select the workbook with the styles you want to copy.
4. Click on OK or press Enter. Excel copies the styles from the file and returns you to the Style dialog box.
5. To apply a new style, select it from the **S**tyle Name list box and then click on OK or press Enter. Otherwise, click on Close.

SUPER CAUTION

If the receiving workbook contains any styles with the same name as styles being merged, Excel displays a warning box. Click on **Y**es to overwrite the existing styles or **N**o to merge all styles except those with the same name.

SUPER NOTE

If you have a number of styles you use frequently, create a workbook to store the styles. To use these styles in the current workbook, just merge them from the styles workbook.

Redefining a Style

As you can see, styles can save time when you have to apply many formats to a worksheet. Styles also can save time by making it easier to reformat your documents. If you've used styles to format a worksheet, just redefine the style, and Excel automatically updates every cell containing the style to match the new style definition. You also can redefine any of Excel's built-in styles, including the Normal style, which is the default used for all cells in any new worksheet. You can redefine styles in two ways:

- By example
- By definition

Redefining a Style by Example

You can use the style by example method to redefine an existing style. Follow the steps in Procedure 12.9.

PROCEDURE 12.9. REDEFINING A STYLE BY EXAMPLE.

1. Select a cell that contains the format you want to use to redefine the style.
2. Select the Format | Style command to display the Style dialog box.
3. In the Style Name edit box, type the name of the style you want to redefine. (You need to type the name, not merely select it from the list.)
4. Click on OK or press Enter. Excel redefines the style and updates all the workbook cells that use the style.

Redefining a Style by Definition

You can use the style by definition method to redefine an existing style. Procedure 12.10 lists the required steps.

PROCEDURE 12.10. REDEFINING A STYLE BY DEFINITION.

1. Select the Format | Style command to display the Style dialog box.
2. Select the style that you want to redefine from the Style Name list.
3. Click on the Modify button to display the Format Cells dialog box.
4. Make your changes to the style attributes and then click on OK or press Enter to return to the Style dialog box.
5. Click on OK or press Enter. Excel redefines the style.

Deleting a Style

To keep your style lists to a minimum, you should delete any styles you no longer use. When you delete a style, any associated cells revert to the Normal style. (Any other formatting options you added on top of the style remain in effect, however.) Follow the steps in Procedure 12.11 to delete a style from a worksheet.

PROCEDURE 12.11. DELETING A STYLE.

1. Select the Format | Style command to display the Style dialog box.
2. Select the style that you want to delete from the Style Name list box.
3. Click on the Delete button. Excel deletes the style and converts every cell in the workbook that uses the style to Normal.
4. Repeat steps 2 and 3 to delete other styles.
5. Click on OK or press Enter.

SUPER NOTE

You can't delete the Normal style.

Using the AutoFormat Feature

Excel offers a feature that enables you to easily format any worksheet range. This feature, called *AutoFormat*, can automatically apply certain predefined format combinations to create attractive, professional-quality tables and lists.

There are 17 predefined AutoFormat combinations. Each one uses selected format options to display numbers, fonts, borders, and patterns and to set cell alignment, column width, and row height. AutoFormat doesn't just apply a single format combination to each cell. Instead, it applies separate formatting for row and column headings, data, and summary lines (for example, subtotals and totals). If you have formatting that you want left intact, you can tell Excel to leave out the appropriate format options from the automatic format. For example, if you've already set up your font options, you can exclude the font formats from the AutoFormat table.

SUPER CAUTION

You can't apply an AutoFormat to a single cell or to a noncontiguous range. If you try, Excel displays an error box. You can, however, select a single cell if it's within a range. Excel will detect the range automatically.

Procedure 12.12 lists the basic steps to follow to use the AutoFormat feature.

PROCEDURE 12.12. USING EXCEL'S AUTOFORMAT FEATURE.

1. Select the range you want to format.
2. Select the **Format** | **AutoFormat** command. Excel displays the AutoFormat dialog box, as shown in Figure 12.6.

FIGURE 12.6.
The AutoFormat dialog box.

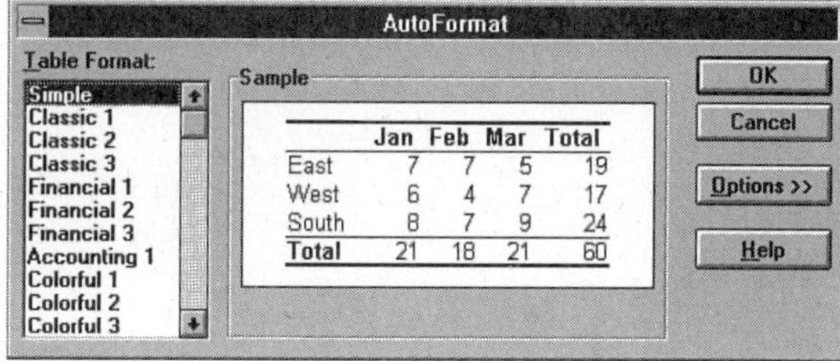

3. Select a format combination from the **T**able Format list box. An example of each format appears in the Sample box.
4. To exclude formatting, click on the **O**ptions button and, in the Formats to Apply section that appears, uncheck the format types you want to exclude. The displayed example adjusts accordingly.
5. Click on OK or press Enter. Excel applies the formatting to the range you selected.

When using the AutoFormat feature, keep the following points in mind:

- AutoFormat usually assumes that the top row and the left column in your range contain the range headings. To avoid improper formatting, be sure to include your headings when you select the range.
- Each table format uses the typeface defined in the Normal font. To use a different typeface in all your AutoFormat tables, change the Normal font to the typeface you want.
- The Classic table formats are designed to be used in any worksheet to make your data more readable. Headings and totals are separated with borders or shading.
- The Financial table formats can be used in any worksheet that contains currency values. Initial data values and totals are formatted as currency.
- The Colorful table formats are suitable for on-screen or slide presentations or for reports produced on a color printer.
- The List table formats can be used with lists and databases. Shading and borders are used to make the data more readable.
- The 3D Effects table formats give your worksheets a professional-quality appearance suitable for any presentation.

Chapter

13

Changing the Workbook View

When you work with large and complex workbooks, only a small part of the total document fits into a single window. The result is that you spend a lot of time scrolling through your workbook and jumping back and forth between data areas. What you need is a way to simultaneously view separate parts of a workbook.

This chapter shows you how to do just that. With Excel, you can view a single workbook in multiple windows, split a single window into multiple panes, and even view the same workbook with different formatting and display options.

Displaying Multiple Workbook Windows

As a user of the Windows environment, you know what an advantage it is to have multiple applications running in their own windows. Most Windows applications take this concept a step farther by enabling you to open multiple documents in their own windows. However, Excel goes one better by enabling you to open multiple windows for the *same* document.

When you open a second window on a workbook, you're not opening a new file; you're viewing the same file twice. You can navigate independently in each window; therefore, you can display different parts of a workbook at the same time. Excel even enables you to change the workbook display for every window.

SUPER NOTE

You can change a value in one part of the workbook and watch its effect in another part. This is invaluable for "what-if" analysis. See Chapter 35, "Basic Analytic Methods," for more information on what-if analysis.

Opening a New Workbook Window

To open another window for the current workbook, select the **W**indow | **N**ew Window command. When Excel opens a new window, it changes the names appearing in the workbook title bar. Excel appends :1 to the title of the original window, and it appends :2 to the title of the second window. Figure 13.1 shows an example using the SALES_93.XLS workbook. Notice that the original window now has the title SALES_93.XLS:1, and the new window has the title SALES_93.XLS:2.

The number of windows you can open for a workbook is limited by your computer's memory. Any window you open can be moved and sized to suit your taste. Because each window is a view of the same workbook, any editing or formatting changes you make in one window are automatically reflected in all the other windows.

FIGURE 13.1.
Two windows containing the same workbook.

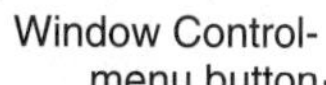

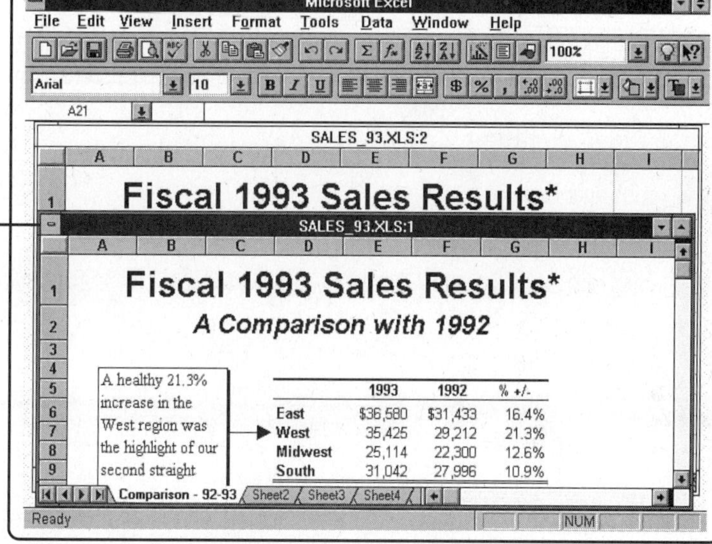

SUPER NOTE

You can use multiple windows to make data entry easier. Open one window for the data entry area and then use other windows to display a list of data codes (for example, part numbers or general ledger accounts).

Navigating Workbook Windows

Once you've opened two or more windows, you'll need to switch between them. Use any of the following techniques to navigate among workbook windows:

- Click on any visible part of a window to activate it.
- Pull down the **W**indow menu and select one of the windows listed at the bottom of the menu. Excel displays a check mark beside the currently active window.
- Press Ctrl+Tab to move to the next window. Press Ctrl+Shift+Tab to move to the previous window.
- Pull down the window's Control menu by clicking on the window's Control menu button or by pressing Alt+– (hyphen). Select the Ne**x**t Window command.

Setting Window Display Options

One of the most useful aspects of multiple workbook windows is that you can set different display options (such as showing gridlines or row and column headers) in each window. For example, you could troubleshoot formula errors by displaying formulas in one window and results in another (see Figure 13.2).

SUPER TIP

To quickly toggle the display between formulas and results, press Ctrl+ ' (backquote).

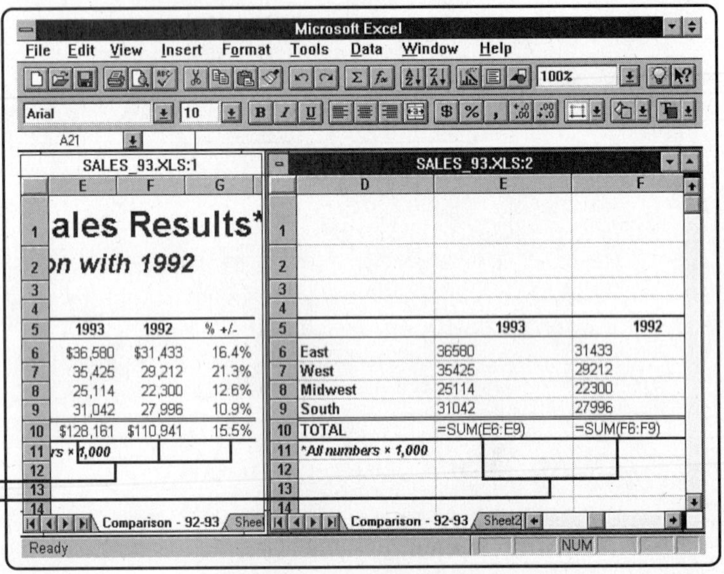

FIGURE 13.2. *You can set different display options in each workbook window, such as displaying formulas in one window and results in another.*

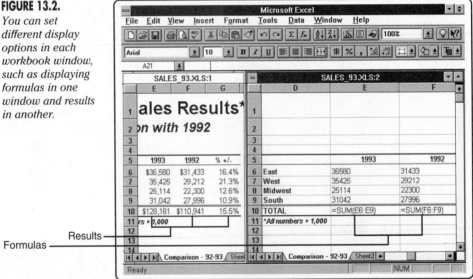

Follow the steps in Procedure 13.1 to set display options for a window.

PROCEDURE 13.1. SETTING DISPLAY OPTIONS FOR A WINDOW.

1. Activate the window in which you want to change the display.
2. Select the **T**ools | **O**ptions command and then select the View tab in the Options dialog box.
3. Use the controls in the Window Options group to set up the window the way you want.
4. Click on OK or press Enter. Excel returns you to the window with the new options in effect.

Arranging Workbook Windows

One of the problems with having several windows open at once is that they tend to get in each other's way. In most cases, it's preferable to give each window its own portion of the work area. Even though you can move and size windows yourself, you may prefer to have Excel handle this for you. You use the Arrange Windows dialog box, shown in Figure 13.3, to do this. The Arrange section contains the following options:

Tiled	Divides the work area into rectangles of approximately equal size (called *tiles*) and assigns each open window to a tile
Horizontal	Divides the work area into horizontal strips of equal size and assigns each open window to a strip
Vertical	Divides the work area into vertical strips of equal size and assigns each open window to a strip
Cascade	Arranges the windows so they overlap each other and so you can see each window's title bar

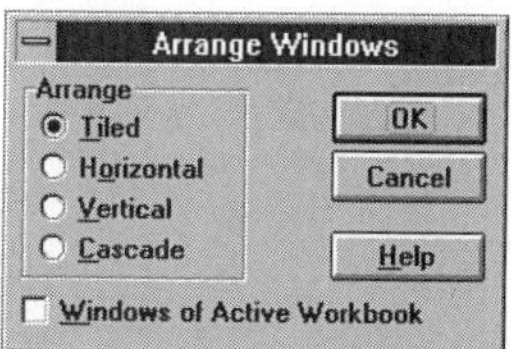

FIGURE 13.3.
The Arrange Windows dialog box.

If you have other workbooks open at the same time, and you want to arrange only the current workbook windows, activate the Windows of Active Workbook check box in the Arrange Windows dialog box. This tells Excel to apply the selected Arrange option to the current workbook windows only.

If you don't want to include a window in an arrangement, activate the window and select the Window | Hide command. Excel removes the window from the screen, but the window remains open in memory. To view the window again, select Window | Unhide and select the window from the Unhide dialog box that appears.

Closing a Workbook Window

If you find your work area getting cluttered with open windows, you can close a window by following the steps in Procedure 13.2.

PROCEDURE 13.2. CLOSING A WORKBOOK WINDOW.

1. Select the window you want to close.
2. Activate the window Control menu by clicking on the Control-menu box or by pressing Alt+– (hyphen).
3. Click on Close. Excel closes the window.

> **SUPER NOTE**
>
> To close a window quickly, double-click on the Control menu button or press Ctrl+F4.

When you close a workbook, Excel remembers the current window sizes and positions. The next time you open the workbook, Excel arranges the windows in their previous positions. If you don't want Excel to save the window information, you need to close any unwanted windows.

Displaying Multiple Worksheet Panes

Another way to simultaneously view different parts of a large worksheet is to use Excel's Split feature. You can use Split to divide a worksheet into two or four *panes* in which each pane displays a different area of the sheet. The panes scroll simultaneously horizontally and vertically. You also can freeze the panes to keep a worksheet area in view at all times.

Splitting a Worksheet into Panes

Depending on the type of split you want, you can use one of the following two methods to split your worksheets:

- Use the **W**indow | **S**plit command to split the worksheet into four panes at the selected cell. (Later, you can adjust the split to two panes if you like.)
- Use the horizontal or vertical split boxes to split the worksheet into two panes at a position you specify (horizontally or vertically, respectively).

Using the Split Command

When you use the Split command, Excel splits the worksheet into four *panes* at the currently selected cell. How do you know which cell to select? Look at Figure 13.4, which shows a sheet called Amortization in the LOAN.XLS workbook in which cell C6 is selected. When the worksheet is split using this method, the results are as shown in Figure 13.5. Notice that Excel places the *horizontal split bar* on the top edge of the selected cell's row and the *vertical split bar* on the left edge of the selected cell's column. This is convenient because now the loan variables are in the upper-left pane, the periods and months are in the lower-left pane, the title and column headings are in the upper-right pane, and the loan data is in the lower-right pane. The panes are synchronized so that as you move down through the loan data, the period and month values also move down.

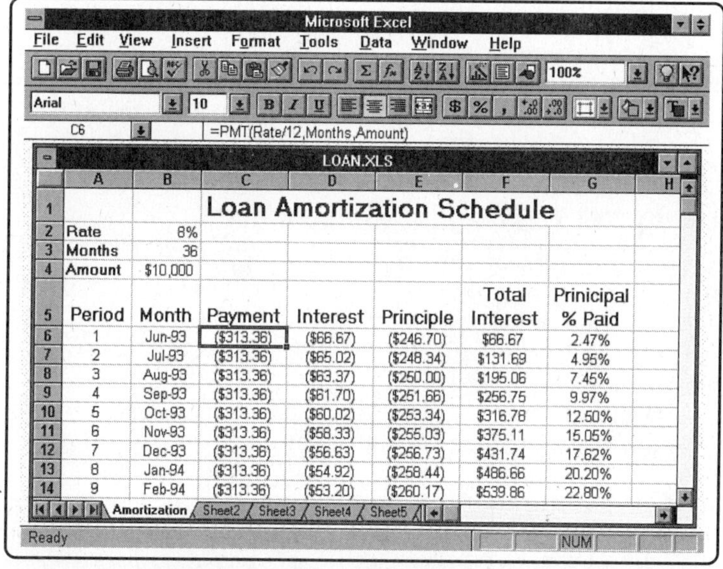

FIGURE 13.4.
The Amortization worksheet workbook before splitting.

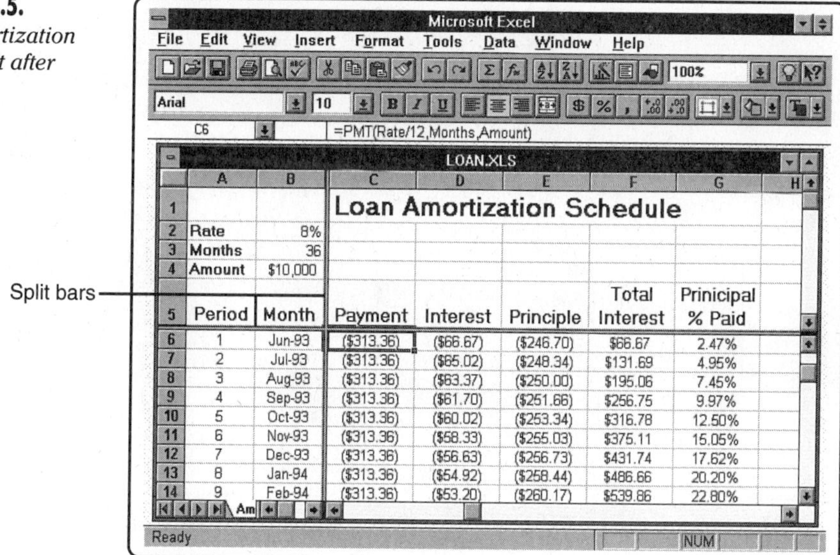

FIGURE 13.5.
The Amortization worksheet after splitting.

Procedure 13.3 outlines the steps involved in splitting the worksheet.

PROCEDURE 13.3. SPLITTING A WORKSHEET WITH THE SPLIT COMMAND.

1. Select the cell in which you want the worksheet to be split.

2. Select the **W**indow | **S**plit command. Excel displays split bars at the cell location.
3. If the split isn't where you want it, you can adjust it by dragging the appropriate split bar. Alternatively, you can select the **W**indow | Remove **S**plit command and try again.

Using the Window Split Boxes

Using the mouse, you can use the horizontal and vertical split boxes to create a two-pane split. The horizontal split box is the black area located between the vertical scrollbar's up arrow and the window's Maximize button (see Figure 13.6). The vertical split box is the black area between the horizontal scrollbar's left arrow and the window's border (see Figure 13.6).

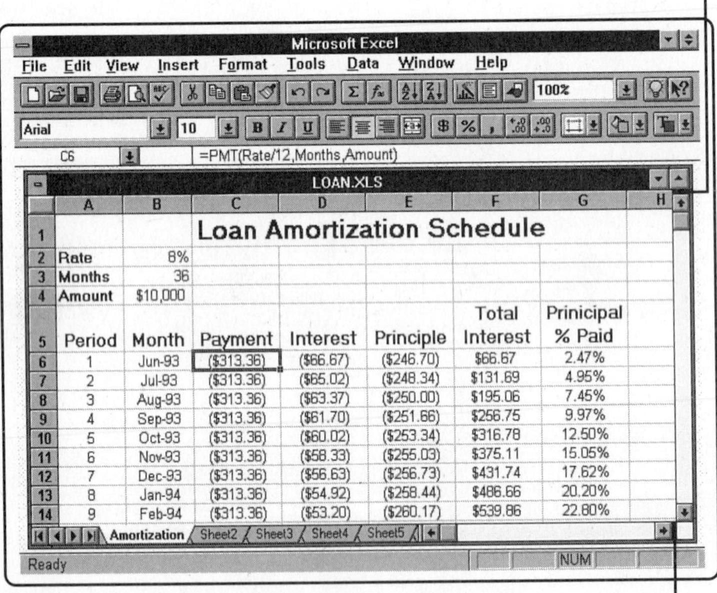

FIGURE 13.6.
You can use the split boxes to split a worksheet.

Follow the steps in Procedure 13.4 to split a worksheet using the split boxes.

PROCEDURE 13.4. SPLITTING A WORKSHEET WITH THE SPLIT BOXES.

1. Position the mouse pointer on the split box you want. The pointer changes to a two-sided arrow.
2. Press and hold the left mouse button. Excel displays a light gray bar to indicate the current split position.

3. Drag the pointer to the desired split location.
4. Release the mouse button. Excel splits the worksheet at the selected location. The split box moves to the split location.

SUPER TIP

To remove the split, drag the split box back to its original location or select the **W**indow | Remove **S**plit command.

Freezing Worksheet Titles

One of the problems with viewing multiple panes is that the work area can get confusing when some of the panes contain the same cells. For example, Figure 13.7 shows the Amortization worksheet split into four panes, each of which contains cell C8 in its upper-left corner. Clearly, such a display is meaningless. To prevent this from happening, you can freeze your panes so that areas displaying worksheet titles or column headings remain in place.

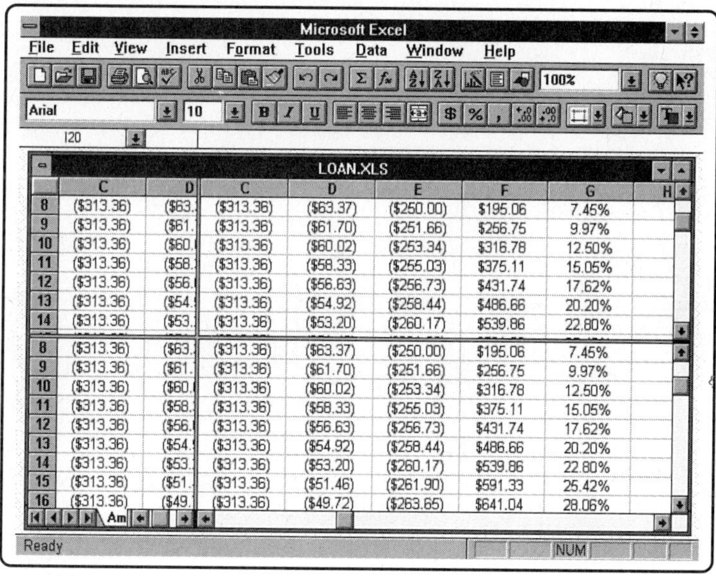

FIGURE 13.7.
Split worksheets often can become confusing.

The required steps are listed in Procedure 13.5.

PROCEDURE 13.5. FREEZING WORKSHEET PANES.

1. Split the worksheet and arrange each pane with the desired information (titles, headings, and so on).
2. Select the **W**indow | **F**reeze Panes command. Excel replaces the thick gray split bars with thin black freeze bars.

Figure 13.8 shows the Amortization worksheet with frozen panes. In this case, the panes were frozen from the split position shown in Figure 13.5. In this example, the frozen panes provide the following advantages:

- No matter where you move up or down in the worksheet, the column headings and loan variables remain visible.
- As you move up or down in the worksheet, the values in the bottom panes remain synchronized.
- No matter where you move left or right in the worksheet, the period and month values remain visible.
- As you move left or right in the worksheet, the values in the two right panes remain synchronized.

FIGURE 13.8.
The Amortization worksheet with frozen panes.

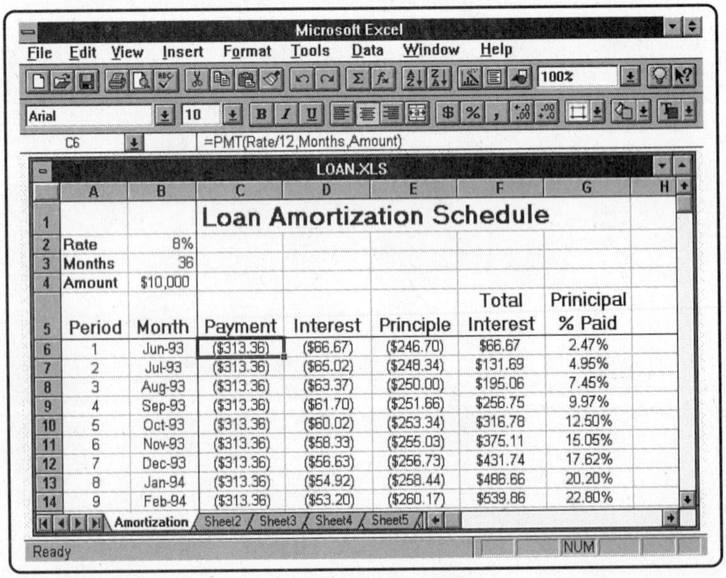

SUPER TIP

To unfreeze panes without removing the splits, select the **W**indow | Un**f**reeze Panes command. To unfreeze panes *and* remove the splits, select the **W**indow | Remove **S**plit command.

Zooming In and Out

So far, you've seen a number of methods for viewing your workbooks. Most of these techniques help you work easily with large spreadsheets by enabling you to simultaneously view different parts of the document. Even though this is very valuable, what you often need is the capability to see the big picture, because even the largest window can display only a few dozen cells at most. Excel offers a Zoom feature that enables you to see your workbooks with various degrees of *magnification*.

With Zoom, a magnification value of 100 percent represents the normal workbook view. If you select a lower magnification, Zoom scales each cell smaller by the amount you specify and therefore displays more cells in the window. For example, if you choose the 50 percent magnification, the workbook cells become smaller by half. If you choose a higher magnification, Zoom scales each cell larger. All your data and formatting options remain intact, and you can make changes to the workbook at any magnification.

Follow the steps in Procedure 13.6 to use the Zoom feature.

PROCEDURE 13.6. ZOOMING A WORKBOOK.

1. Select the **V**iew | **Z**oom command. Excel displays the Zoom dialog box, shown in Figure 13.9.

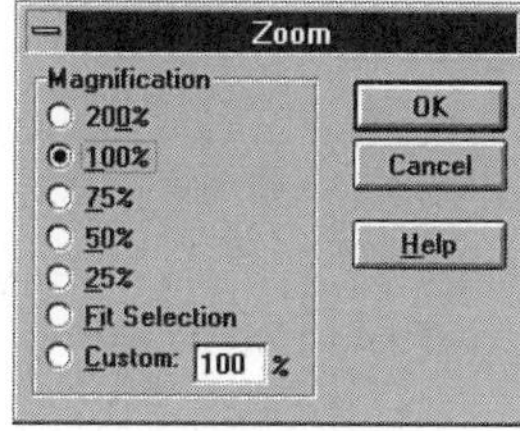

FIGURE 13.9.
The Zoom dialog box.

2. Select the option you want from the Magnification group. The **F**it Selection option scales the workbook so the selected range fits inside the window. The **C**ustom option enables you to enter your own magnification (enter a number between 10 and 400).

3. Click on OK or press Enter. Excel adjusts the Zoom magnification and redisplays the workbook.

You also can use the Zoom tool in the Standard toolbar to select a magnification.

SUPER TIP

Another way to see more of a workbook is to select the **View | Full** Screen command. Excel removes the following items to enable you to see the maximum amount of workbook real estate: the title bars from the main Excel window and the workbook window, the toolbars, the formula bar, and the status bar. To revert to the normal view, either select **View | Full** Screen again or click on the button in the Full Screen toolbar.

Displaying Multiple Workbook Views

Displaying the same file in multiple windows or panes is a great way to manage large workbooks. Unfortunately, managing the windows can be time-consuming. You have to open each window, scroll to the worksheet area you want, set your display options, size the window, and position it where you can see it. Of course, you could save your window configurations with the workbook, and Excel will reinstate them every time you open the file. However, you might not want all those windows active all the time. The solution is to create different views of your workbooks.

A *view* is a specific workbook configuration that can include the window size and position, panes and frozen titles, zoom magnification, selected cells, display options, row heights and column widths (including hidden rows and columns), and print settings. Once you've saved a view, you can conveniently recall it any time from a list of views.

SUPER TIP

The first view you create should be of your worksheet in its basic configuration (give it the name "Normal"). This way, you can always revert to this configuration from your other views.

Creating a View

You use Excel's View Manager to create workbook views. Procedure 13.7 shows the steps to follow.

PROCEDURE 13.7. CREATING A WORKBOOK VIEW.

1. Set up your workbook (or one of your workbook windows) with the view configuration you want.
2. Select the **V**iew | **V**iew Manager command. Excel displays the View Manager dialog box.
3. Click on the **A**dd button. Excel displays the Add View dialog box.
4. Enter a name for the view in the **N**ame edit box. The name must begin with a letter.
5. In the View Includes section, select the extra settings you want to include in the view.
6. Click on OK or press Enter. Excel saves the view and returns you to the workbook.

SUPER NOTE

If you use macro buttons in a workbook, group them together and create a view that shows the buttons in a window. This way, you can display the buttons only when you need them, and they will remain in view no matter where you are in your workbook.

Displaying a View

One of the main advantages to views is that you can display them only when you need them. Excel makes displaying views easy. Procedure 13.8 lists the steps to follow.

PROCEDURE 13.8. DISPLAYING A WORKBOOK VIEW.

1. Select the **V**iew | **V**iew Manager command to display the View Manager dialog box.
2. Use the **V**iews list to highlight the view you want to use.
3. Click on the **S**how button. Excel displays the view.

Deleting a View

To delete a workbook view, follow Procedure 13.9.

PROCEDURE 13.9. DELETING A WORKBOOK VIEW.

1. Select the **V**iew | **V**iew Manager command to display the View Manager dialog box.
2. Use the **V**iews list to highlight the view you want to delete.
3. Click on the **D**elete button. Excel deletes the view.
4. Repeat steps 2 and 3 to delete other views.
5. Click on Close to return to the workbook.

Chapter

14

Spell-Checking the Worksheet

One of the easiest ways to lose face in a presentation is to display a worksheet that contains spelling mistakes. No matter how professionally organized and formatted your report appears, a simple spelling error will stick out like a sore thumb. However, mistakes will happen, especially when your presentation includes a large number of complicated documents. To help you catch those errors, Excel includes a spell-checking utility.

This chapter shows you how to use the spell checker to check your entire worksheet, a range, or even a single word. You'll also learn how to augment Excel's dictionary with your own custom dictionary.

Spell-Checking a Range

When you invoke the Spelling command, Excel compares each word in your selected range with those in its standard dictionary. If Excel doesn't find the word, it displays the Spelling dialog box, shown in Figure 14.1.

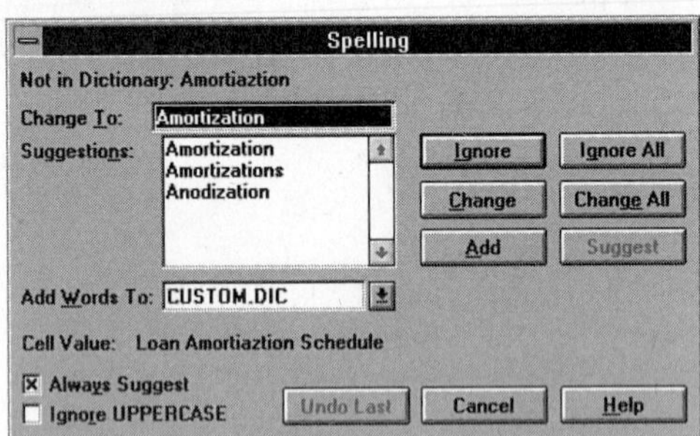

FIGURE 14.1.
The Spelling dialog box.

The Spelling dialog box contains the following elements:

Not in Dictionary — This information box displays a word that Excel can't find (that is, the *unknown word*).

Change To — Select this edit box to see the word that Excel has determined is closest to the unknown word. If you turn off the Always Suggest option, Excel displays the unknown word. In either case, you can enter your own correction in this box.

Suggestions — This list box displays the words that Excel has determined are close to the unknown word. No suggestions appear if you turn off the Always Suggest option.

Ignore — Click on this button if you want to skip an instance of a word.

Ignore All — Click on this button if you want to skip all instances of a word.

Change	Click on this button if you want to change the unknown word to the word displayed in the Change To box.
Change All	Click on this button if you want to change all instances of the unknown word to the word displayed in the Change To box.
Add	Click on this button if you want to add the unknown word to the dictionary shown in the Add Words To box.
Suggest	Click on this button to have Excel suggest corrections. This button is active only when you turn off the Always Suggest option.
Add Words To	Select this box to see the current custom dictionary. See the section in this chapter titled "Using Custom Dictionaries."
Ignore UPPERCASE	Select this option to have Excel skip uppercase versions of words that are found in the dictionary in lowercase. This option is off by default.
Always Suggest	Select this option to have Excel make suggestions for every unknown word. This option is on by default.
Undo Last	Reverses the last change.
Cell Value	Select this information box to see the full contents of the cell containing the unknown word.

If you don't select a range for the spell check, Excel checks the entire worksheet including cell notes, embedded charts, macro buttons, headers, and footers. Follow the steps in Procedure 14.1 to spell-check a range or worksheet.

PROCEDURE 14.1. SPELL-CHECKING A RANGE OR WORKSHEET.

1. Select the range you want to check. (To check the entire worksheet, leave only the current cell selected.)

> **SUPER TIP**
>
> If you're spell-checking your entire worksheet, make cell A1 active before invoking the Spelling command. This prevents Excel from asking whether you would like to continue checking at the beginning of the sheet.

2. Select the Tools | Spelling command. If Excel finds a word that isn't in any open dictionary, the Spelling dialog box appears. If you have the Always Suggest option turned on, Excel usually suggests a new word.

Click on this tool in the Standard toolbar to start the spell check.

SUPER TIP

You also can start the spell check by pressing F7.

3. Click on the appropriate command button. For example, to continue the spell check, click on the Ignore button.
4. If you're checking the entire worksheet and you began from a cell that wasn't at the beginning of the sheet, when Excel reaches the bottom, it asks whether you want to continue the check from the beginning (see Figure 14.2). Click on Yes to continue or No to end the spell check.

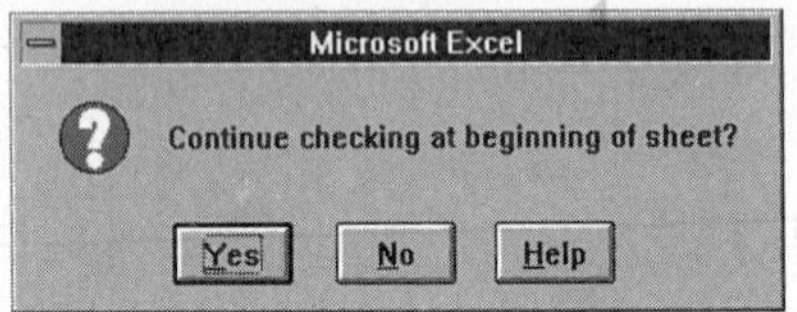

FIGURE 14.2.
Excel asks whether you want to continue the spell check at the beginning of the sheet.

5. When Excel finishes checking the entire range or worksheet, it displays a message to that effect. Click on OK or press Enter to return to the worksheet.

Spell-Checking a Single Word

Excel can check the spelling of a single word in a cell or in an edit box or macro button. Procedure 14.2 outlines the steps to follow.

PROCEDURE 14.2. SPELL-CHECKING A SINGLE WORD.

1. Select a cell and activate it by pressing F2 or by double-clicking on it.
2. Highlight the word you want to check.
3. Select the Tools | Spelling command. If Excel can't find the word in any open dictionary, it displays the Spelling dialog box.
4. Select the appropriate options from the dialog box.
5. If Excel determines that the word is spelled correctly, it displays the message shown in Figure 14.3. If Excel doesn't find the word, after you make your choice in the Spelling dialog box Excel tells you that the check is complete. In either case, click on OK or press Enter to return to the worksheet.

FIGURE 14.3.
Excel displays this message if the word is spelled correctly.

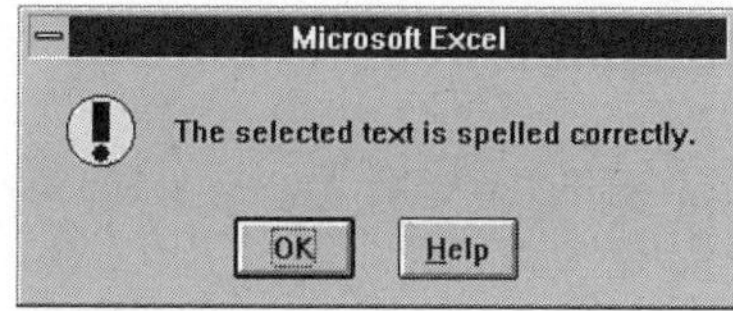

Using Custom Dictionaries

Although the dictionary Excel uses to check spelling is extensive, it obviously can't include every word in the English language. You'll find that Excel often flags names of people or companies, as well as unusual technical terms. To account for this, you can use custom dictionaries to hold words that you use frequently but that Excel doesn't recognize. The default custom dictionary is called CUSTOM.DIC. You can add your words to this dictionary or create your own dictionary. To create a custom dictionary, follow the steps in Procedure 14.3.

PROCEDURE 14.3. CREATING A CUSTOM DICTIONARY.

1. Select the **T**ools | **S**pelling command to display the Spelling dialog box. (I'm assuming that there is at least one word in the worksheet that the Spelling feature won't recognize. If there isn't, the Spelling dialog box won't appear.)
2. In the Add **W**ords To edit box, enter the name for the new dictionary. (You don't need to add the extension .DIC to the dictionary name; Excel does this for you.)
3. Press Enter. Excel asks whether you want to create a new dictionary (see Figure 14.4).

FIGURE 14.4.
Excel asks you to confirm that you want to create the dictionary.

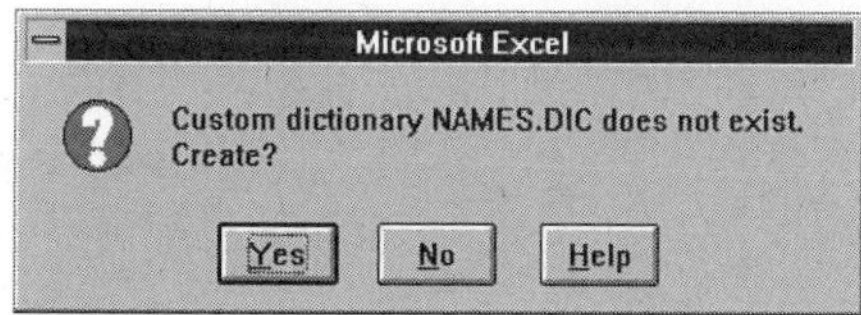

4. Click on **Y**es to create the dictionary.
5. You can continue with the spell check or cancel to return to the worksheet.

You can create as many different dictionaries as you need. For example, you could have a dictionary for technical terms used in your industry, another for employee or customer names, and another for common abbreviations. However, keep in mind that you can use only one custom dictionary at a time.

Chapter

15

Adding Comments with Text Boxes and Notes

This Workshop has shown you many techniques for making your worksheets clearer and more readable. However, a well-organized worksheet can be difficult to read if you use formulas and calculations that are obscure to other users. Because you can't always be there to explain your work, Excel enables you to add comments to your documents in the form of *text boxes, text notes,* and *sound notes*. You use text boxes to add explanatory remarks that sit "on top" of the worksheet. You use text notes to attach comments to individual cells. If your computer has a sound card, you can record sound notes and attach them to a cell. This chapter shows you how to work with all three kinds of objects.

Working with Text Boxes

Many people like to add handwritten comments directly to their printed worksheets or on sticky notes. For a more professional look, or for times when you're presenting your work on-screen or on a slide, add an Excel text box to your worksheet. A text box is a block of text that sits on the worksheet. The text box is a graphic "object," so you can position, size, edit, and format it independently of the worksheet cells. (For more information on Excel's graphic objects, especially on object properties and formatting, see the appropriate chapters in the Graphics Workshop.)

Adding a Text Box

To create a text box, follow the steps in Procedure 15.1.

PROCEDURE 15.1. ADDING A TEXT BOX.

1. Click on the Text box tool in the Standard toolbar. (If you want to create more than one text box, double-click on the tool.) The regular mouse pointer changes to a crosshair pointer.

The Text box tool from the Standard toolbar.

2. Position the pointer where you want the top-left corner of the text box to be.
3. Press and hold down the left mouse button.
4. Drag the mouse pointer to where you want the bottom-right corner of the text box to be. As you drag the pointer, Excel draws an outline of the box.
5. Release the mouse button. If you're drawing only one box, Excel places a blinking insertion point cursor in the upper-left corner of the box. If you double-clicked the Text box tool, but you want to draw only a single box, skip to step 7.
6. If you're creating more boxes, repeat steps 2-5. When you've finished, click on the first box in which you want to enter text.

7. Type your text in the box. The text automatically wraps and scrolls within the box.
8. To add text to another box, click on the box (or press the Tab key to move to the next box) and enter the text you want.
9. When you're finished, click on an empty area of the worksheet or press the Esc key.

SUPER TIP

To make the text box a square, hold down Shift while dragging the pointer. To align the text box with the worksheet gridlines, hold down the Alt key while dragging the pointer.

SUPER NOTE

Use text boxes for short explanations or to point out key worksheet results. For longer, more technical comments, attach a text note or a sound note to a cell (see the appropriate sections later in this chapter).

Making Text Box Adjustments

Once you've added a text box to a worksheet, you're free to edit the text contained in the box and to make adjustments to the size, shape, and position of the box. (For information on other formatting options such as alignment, fonts, and shading, see Chapter 27, "Editing Graphic Objects.")

To edit the contents of a text box, follow the steps in Procedure 15.2.

PROCEDURE 15.2. EDITING THE CONTENTS OF A TEXT BOX.

1. Click on the text box you want to edit.
2. Click inside the text box to position the cursor for inserting text, or highlight the text you want to change.
3. Edit the text using the same techniques you learned for editing cell contents.
4. When you're finished, click outside the box or press the Esc key.

SUPER CAUTION

If you click only once on the text box and then begin typing, Excel replaces the entire contents of the box with your typing. If this happens, immediately select the **Edit | Undo Typing** command or press Ctrl+Z.

SUPER TIP

When editing a text box, press Enter to start a new line. To enter a tab, press Ctrl+Tab.

To adjust the position of a text box, follow Procedure 15.3.

PROCEDURE 15.3. MOVING A TEXT BOX.

1. Click on the text box and hold down the left mouse button.
2. Drag the text box to the desired location. The box border changes to a dotted line as you drag the pointer.
3. Release the mouse button. Excel drops the box in the new location.

You can adjust the size of any text box to suit your needs. You size a text box by using *sizing handles*. These handles appear whenever you select a text box. Excel displays eight handles for each box—one on each side of the box and one in each corner. You adjust the box size by dragging these handles with the mouse pointer. Procedure 15.4 shows the steps to follow.

PROCEDURE 15.4. ADJUSTING THE SIZE OF A TEXT BOX.

1. Click on the text box you want to adjust. Excel changes the box border into a thicker, broken line and displays the sizing handles, as shown in Figure 15.1.
2. Position the mouse pointer over a handle. The pointer changes to the shape shown in Figure 15.1.
3. Press and hold down the left mouse button. The pointer changes to a crosshair.
4. Drag the handle to the desired location. As you drag the mouse pointer, Excel displays the new border as a dashed line.
5. Release the mouse button. Excel adjusts the size of the text box.
6. To adjust other parts of the box, repeat steps 2-5.

FIGURE 15.1.
You can change the size of your text boxes.

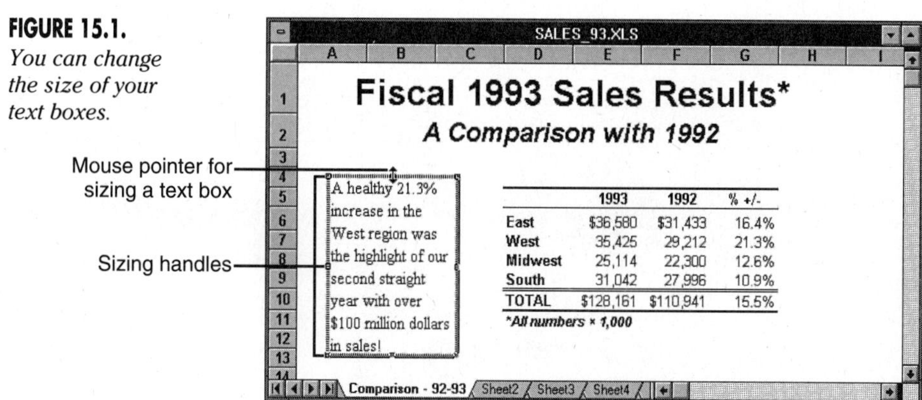

SUPER NOTE

Use text boxes to show others your worksheet formulas. To enter a formula in a text box, select the cell and highlight the formula in the cell. Then select **Edit** | **Copy**. Position the cursor inside the text box and select **Edit** | **Paste** to enter the formula into the box.

Attaching an Arrow to a Text Box

Many of your text boxes will refer to specific worksheet cells or ranges. For added clarity, you can attach an arrow to the text box so that it points at the appropriate cell or range. Procedure 15.5 shows you how to attach a text box arrow.

PROCEDURE 15.5. ATTACHING AN ARROW TO A TEXT BOX.

1. Click on the Arrow tool in the Drawing toolbar. To draw more than one arrow, double-click on the tool. The mouse pointer changes to a crosshair.

The Arrow tool from the Drawing toolbar.

2. Position the crosshair pointer where you want the arrow to start. For a text box, you usually start the arrow at the edge of the box nearest the cell that you want to single out.
3. Press and hold down the left mouse button.
4. Drag the pointer to where you want the arrow to point. Excel draws a line as you drag the mouse pointer.
5. Release the mouse button. Excel adds an arrowhead to the line.

6. If you're drawing other arrows, repeat steps 2-5. When you're finished, click on an empty part of the worksheet or press Esc.

SUPER NOTE

You can adjust the style and weight of both the arrow line and the arrowhead. See Chapter 27, "Editing Graphic Objects."

Figure 15.2 shows a worksheet with a text box and an attached arrow. To move or adjust the size of an arrow, use the same techniques you used for text boxes. Note that the resizing pointer is displayed as a crosshair pointer, not as an arrow.

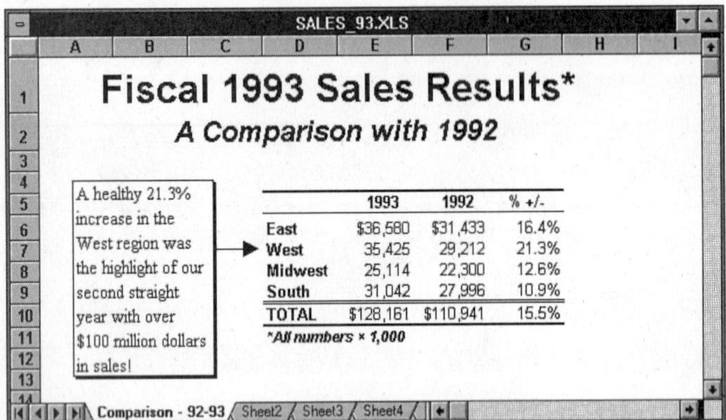

FIGURE 15.2.
You can attach arrows to your text boxes.

Deleting a Text Box or Arrow

If your worksheet contains a text box or arrow that you no longer need, you can delete the object by following the steps in Procedure 15.6.

PROCEDURE 15.6. DELETING A TEXT BOX OR ARROW.

1. Click on the text box or arrow. Excel displays the object's sizing handles.
2. Select the Edit | Cut command or press Delete. Excel removes the text box or arrow from the worksheet.

SUPER TIP

In some cases, you might prefer to hide text boxes and arrows instead of deleting them. To do this, select the Tools | Options command and then select the View tab in the Options dialog box. In the Objects group, select Hide All.

Working with Text Notes

If you don't want to display comments on your worksheet, you can attach text notes to specific cells. These notes remain hidden and can be viewed only within the Cell Note dialog box. A note indicator marks each cell that contains a note.

SUPER NOTE

You can print your worksheet notes separately. To learn how to print notes, see Chapter 16, "Printing a Workbook."

A text note is similar to a footnote in a book or report. A text note can be as long as you like; therefore, you can use it for a lengthy explanation of your worksheet assumptions—without interfering with the appearance of the document. You also can use text notes for technical explanations, analyses of worksheet results, or just your name.

SUPER NOTE

For audited worksheets, enter the name of the person who created the worksheet, the auditor, and the date of the last revision in a text note. Use a consistent cell for the note, such as A1. Be sure to protect each worksheet so that no unauthorized revisions can be made. For more information on protecting worksheets, see Chapter 63, "Other Advanced Workbook Topics."

Adding a Text Note

You can add text notes to individual worksheet cells. Procedure 15.7 gives you the details.

PROCEDURE 15.7. ADDING A TEXT NOTE TO A CELL.

1. Select the cell to which you want to add the note.
2. Select the **I**nsert | N**o**te command. Excel displays the Cell Note dialog box, shown in Figure 15.3.

FIGURE 15.3.
The Cell Note dialog box.

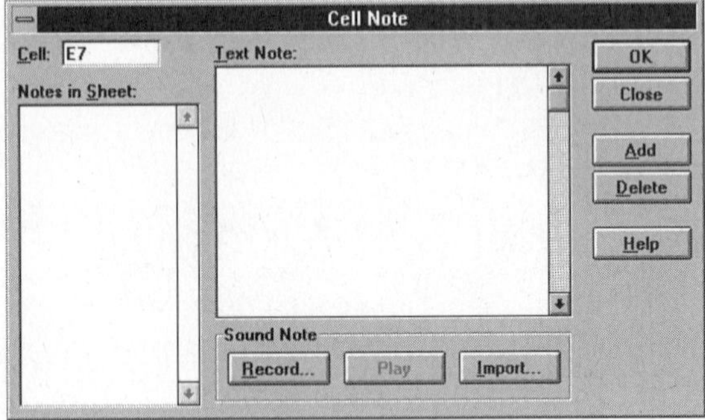

3. Enter the note in the Text Note box.
4. Click on the Add button. Excel displays the cell address and the first few characters of the note in the Notes in Sheet list box.
5. To add a note to another cell, enter the cell address in the Cell box (or use the arrow keys to select a cell) and repeat steps 3 and 4.
6. Click on OK or press Enter. Excel returns you to the worksheet.

When you add a text note to a cell, a small red square (called a *note indicator*) appears in the upper-right corner of the cell.

SUPER TIP

You can turn off the note indicators if you're presenting your worksheet on-screen. Select the Tools | Options command. Then select the View tab and deactivate the Note Indicator check box.

Viewing a Text Note

To view a text note, follow the steps in Procedure 15.8.

PROCEDURE 15.8. VIEWING A TEXT NOTE.

1. Select the cell containing the note.
2. Select the Insert | Note command to display the Cell Note dialog box. The note attached to the selected cell appears in the Text Note box.
3. All the worksheet text notes appear in the Notes in Sheet list box (see Figure 15.4). Select an item from this list to display another note.
4. Click on Close to return to the worksheet.

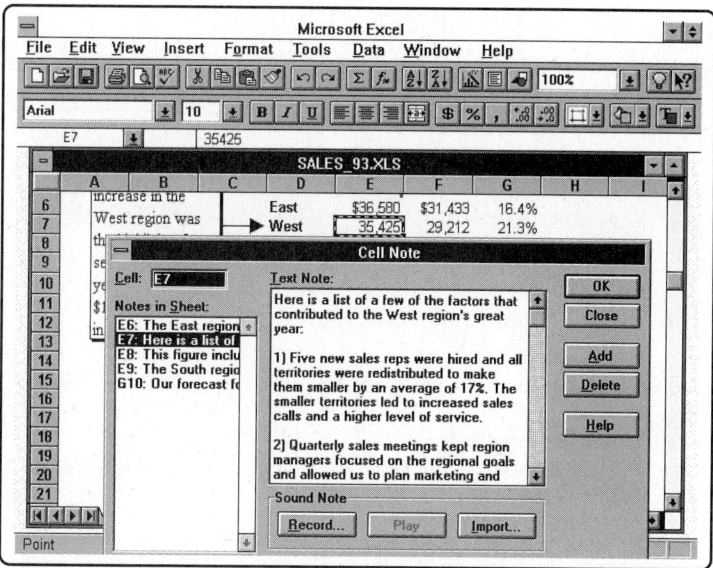

FIGURE 15.4.
Select the text note you want to view from the Cell Note dialog box.

SUPER TIP

To quickly view a cell note, select a cell and press Shift+F2.

SUPER TIP

When entering or editing a text note, press Enter to start a new line.

Use the preceding procedure to edit your text notes. After you've selected a note, use the same editing methods you use in the formula bar.

SUPER TIP

If you're not sure which cell contains the note you want, use the **Edit | Find** command to search for a word or phrase from the note. In the Find dialog box, enter the word or phrase in the **Find What** box and select Notes from the **Look in** drop-down list.

Copying a Text Note

If you need to copy a text note to another cell, follow Procedure 15.9.

PROCEDURE 15.9. COPYING A TEXT NOTE.

1. Select the Insert | Note command to display the Cell Note dialog box.
2. Select the note you want to copy from the Notes in Sheet list box.
3. In the Cell box, enter the address of the cell to which you want to copy the note.
4. Click on OK or press Enter. Excel copies the note to the new cell.

SUPER TIP

You also can copy a text note using the cut-and-paste method. Select the cell containing the note and choose Edit | Copy. Select the destination cell and choose Edit | Paste Special. In the Paste Special dialog box, activate Notes and then click on OK.

Deleting a Text Note

If your worksheet contains notes that you no longer need, you can delete them by selecting the cell and running the Edit | Clear | Notes command. If you're in the Cell Note dialog box, you also can delete a cell note by following the steps in Procedure 15.10.

PROCEDURE 15.10. DELETING A TEXT NOTE FROM THE CELL NOTE DIALOG BOX.

1. Select the note you want to delete from the Notes in Sheet list box.
2. Click on the Delete button. Excel displays a message warning you that the note will be permanently deleted.
3. Click on OK or press Enter. Excel returns you to the Cell Note dialog box with the note removed from the cell.
4. Click on Close to return to the worksheet.

To delete all the notes in a worksheet, follow Procedure 15.11.

PROCEDURE 15.11. DELETING ALL THE TEXT NOTES IN A WORKSHEET.

1. Run the Edit | Go To command to display the Go To dialog box.
2. Click on the Special button. Excel displays the Go To Special dialog box.
3. Activate the Notes option.

4. Click on OK or press Enter. Excel selects all cells in the worksheet that contain notes.

SUPER TIP

You also can select all the cells with text notes by pressing Ctrl+? (question mark).

5. Select the **E**dit | Cle**a**r | **N**otes command. Excel clears all the notes.

Working with Sound Notes

Text notes can convey information, but they lack the nuances and subtleties of the human voice. To really get your point across, you can record messages and insert them as a note in a cell. This section shows you how to work with sound notes in your worksheets.

SUPER NOTE

To make voice recordings, you need a sound card with a microphone jack and either Windows 3.0 with Multimedia Extensions 1.0 or Windows 3.1.

Recording a Sound Note

To record a sound note, follow the steps in Procedure 15.12.

PROCEDURE 15.12. RECORDING A SOUND NOTE.

1. Select the cell in which you want add the sound note.
2. Select the **I**nsert | No**t**e command to display the Cell Note dialog box.
3. In the Sound Note group, click on the **R**ecord button. Excel displays the Record dialog box, shown in Figure 15.5.

FIGURE 15.5.
Use the Record dialog box to record sound notes.

4. Click on the **R**ecord button and speak your message into the microphone. Your notes can be up to two minutes long. If you need to stop the recording temporarily, click on the P**a**use button.
5. When you've finished, click on the **S**top button.
6. To play back the message, click on the **P**lay button.
7. When you're done, click on OK or press Enter to return to the Cell Note dialog box.
8. Click on OK or press Enter to return to the worksheet. Excel places a cell note indicator in the top-right corner of the cell.

Playing a Sound Note

To play a sound note, follow the steps outlined in Procedure 15.13. (Again, you must have the appropriate hardware and software to play a sound note.)

PROCEDURE 15.13. PLAYING A SOUND NOTE.

1. Select the **I**nsert | No**t**e command to display the Cell Note dialog box.
2. In the Notes in **S**heet list, highlight the cell containing the sound note you want to hear. (A sound note appears as an asterisk beside the cell address.)
3. Click on the **P**lay button.

Erasing a Sound Note

If you want to rerecord a sound note, you need to erase the old one by following the steps in Procedure 15.14.

PROCEDURE 15.14. ERASING A SOUND NOTE.

1. Select the **I**nsert | No**t**e command to display the Cell Note dialog box.
2. In the Notes in **S**heet list, highlight the cell containing the sound note you want to erase.
3. Click on the **E**rase button. Excel erases the recording.

Chapter 16

Printing a Workbook

After you set up your workbook, you can print it for all to see. This chapter guides you through the basics of Excel's printing features. You'll learn how to select page setup options, define a print area, preview the print job, and produce hard copy.

Selecting Page Setup Options

Before printing, you need to decide how you want your worksheet pages to appear. This includes deciding the paper orientation (landscape or portrait) and the size of your margins. To do this, select the **File** | Page Setup command. You'll see the Page Setup dialog box, shown in Figure 16.1. The next few sections explain most of the options in this dialog box. When you're finished choosing your options, click on OK or press Enter to return to the document.

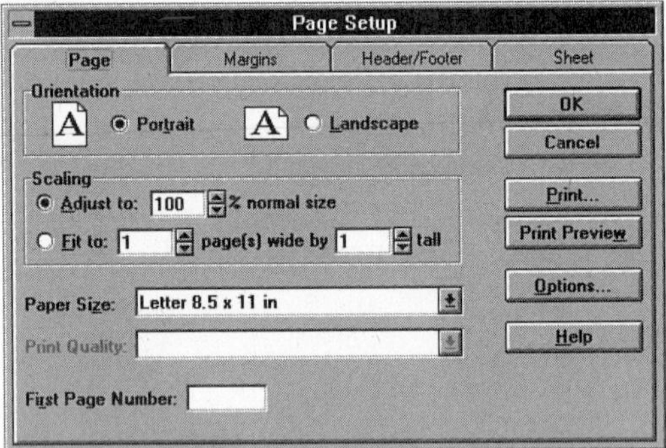

FIGURE 16.1.
Use the Page Setup dialog box to control the look of your printed worksheet pages.

> **SUPER NOTE**
> To learn how to set up headers and footers, and how to scale your worksheets, see Chapter 17, "Advanced Print Operations."

Changing the Page Orientation

The *page orientation* determines how Excel lays out the worksheet data on the page. The Page tab in the Page Setup dialog box gives you two options:

Portrait — Prints along the short side of the page (this is the normal page orientation). Assuming Excel's default margin sizes of 0.75 inches on the left and right and 1 inch on the top and bottom, and the default 8.5-inch by 11-inch letter-size paper setting, this orientation gives you a print area that is 7 inches wide and 9 inches high on each page.

Landscape	Prints along the long side of the page. With the default margins on letter-size paper, this orientation gives you a page print area 9.5 inches wide and 6.5 inches high.

SUPER NOTE

If the document you're printing is part of a larger report, you might want to start your page numbers at a number other than 1. To do this, enter the appropriate number in the Page tab's First Page Number edit box.

Selecting a Different Paper Size

Use the Page tab's Paper Size drop-down list to select a different paper size for your printout. The options in this list include standard letter size (8 1/2 x 11) and legal size (8 1/2 x 14). Depending on the currently selected printer, you might see other sizes too. Make sure that the size you select matches the paper loaded in the printer.

Setting Page Margins

The *page margins* are the blank areas that surround the printed text on a page. By default, Excel decrees the left and right margins to be 0.75 inches and the top and bottom margins to be 1 inch, but you can override that if you like. Why would you want to do such a thing? Here are a few good reasons:

- If someone else is going to be making notes on the page, it helps to include bigger margins (to give that person more room to write).
- Smaller margins all around mean that you get more text on a page. On a long worksheet, this could save you a few pages when you print.
- If you have a worksheet that won't quite fit on a page, you could decrease the appropriate margins enough to fit the extra lines onto a single page. (You should read Chapter 17, "Advanced Print Operations," to learn some other ways to squeeze more data on a page.)

To adjust the margins, select the Margins tab in the Page Setup dialog box (see Figure 16.2). You can then select the following options:

Margins	The **T**op, **B**ottom, **L**eft, and **R**ight edit boxes enable you to enter your new margin values.
From Edge	These options control how far the headers and footers appear from the edge of the page. Use He**a**der to set the distance from the top of the page to the top of the header. Use **F**ooter to set the distance from the bottom of the page to the bottom of the footer.

Center on Page — These options tell Excel to center the printout between the margins. Activate the Horizontally check box to center between the left and right margins; activate the Vertically check box to center between the top and bottom margins.

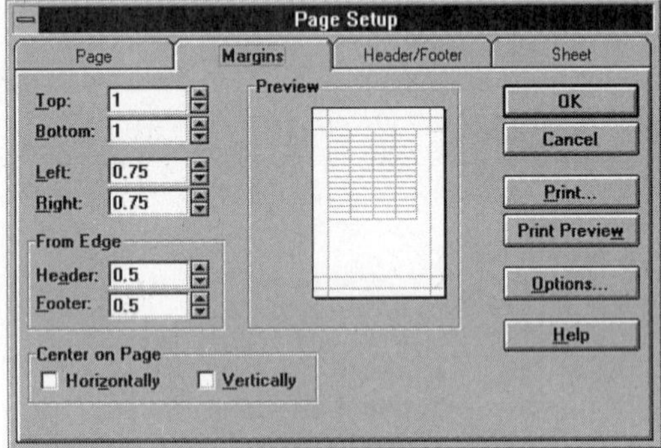

FIGURE 16.2.
The Margins tab in the Page Setup dialog box.

SUPER CAUTION

If you plan to print a sheet on a laser printer, remember that most lasers can't print anything that is closer than one-quarter inch or so to the edge of the page.

Adjusting the Appearance of Each Page

The Sheet tab in the Page Setup dialog box gives you several options that affect the look of your printed pages (see Figure 16.3).

Gridlines — Excel normally prints the worksheet gridlines (unless you've turned off the gridlines with the Tools | Options command). If you prefer not to see the gridlines, deactivate the Gridlines check box.

Notes — If your workbook contains cell notes, activate this check box to print the notes with the workbook.

Draft Quality — For faster (but lower-quality) printing, activate this check box. Excel speeds up printing by suppressing some graphics and gridlines in the printout.

Black & White	If you've added any color formatting to your cells or charts, most printers print these colors as patterns. If this isn't the look you want, activate this check box to tell Excel to print these colors as shades of gray or, in the case of text, as black and white.
Row and Column Headings	If you're printing the worksheet as documentation, you'll probably want to print the row and columns headings too. (This is especially true if you display the document's formulas before printing.) You can do this by activating this check box.
Page Order	When you're printing a range that is larger than a single page, Excel works its way down through the range when printing the pages. It then jumps back to the top of the range, moves over to the next group of columns, and works down again. If you prefer to print across the range first, and then down through the rows, activate the Across then Down option button.

Figure 16.3 shows the Sheet tab in the Page Setup dialog box.

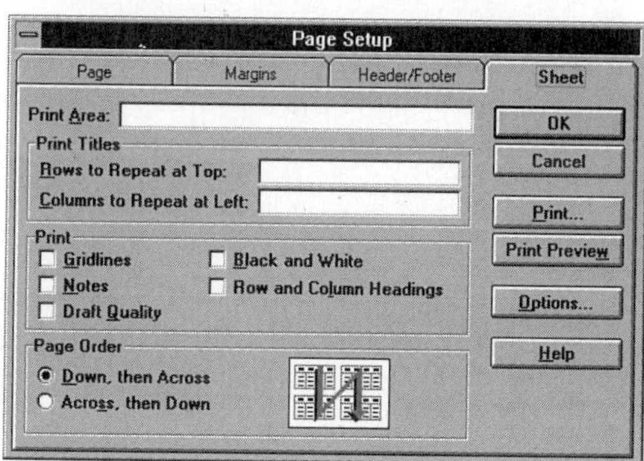

FIGURE 16.3.
The Sheet tab in the Page Setup dialog box.

Defining a Print Area

Once you have your pages laid out the way you want, you need to decide how much of the worksheet you want to print. By default, Excel prints the entire document, but you can print only a part of the sheet by specifying a *print area*. A print area is a special range that defines the cells you want to print. To set it up, follow the steps in Procedure 16.1.

PROCEDURE 16.1. SETTING UP A PRINT AREA.

1. Select the File | Page Setup command and then select the Sheet tab in the Page Setup dialog box.
2. In the Print Area edit box, type in the range you want to print or use the mouse or the keyboard to select the range on the worksheet. You can enter as many ranges as you need.
3. Click on OK or press Enter. Excel displays a dotted line around the range to mark the print area and names the range Print_Area.

Removing a Print Area

If you no longer need a print area, you can remove it with any of the following methods:

- Define a different print area.
- Select the Insert | Name | Define command and delete the Print_Area name.
- Select the File | Page Setup command and delete the reference from the Print Area edit box.

Defining Titles to Print on Every Page

If your printout extends for more than a single page, your row and column titles normally print only on the first page. This can make the subsequent pages confusing and difficult to read. To get around this problem, you can tell Excel to print the appropriate row and column headings on every page. If you select one or more rows, they'll print at the top of each page; if you select one or more columns, they'll print on the left of each page. Follow the steps in Procedure 16.2 to define the titles you want to print on every page.

PROCEDURE 16.2. DEFINING TITLES TO PRINT ON EVERY PAGE.

1. Select the File | Page Setup command and then select the Sheet tab in the Page Setup dialog box.
2. In the Rows to Repeat at Top edit box, type in the range for the column headings that you want to appear at the top of each page. You also can select the range on the worksheet using the mouse or the keyboard.
3. In the Columns to Repeat at Left edit box, type in the range for the row headings that you want to appear at the left of each page. You also can use the mouse or the keyboard to select the range on the worksheet.
4. Click on OK or press Enter. Excel defines the name Print_Titles for the ranges you entered.

Removing Print Titles

To turn off print titles, do either of the following:

- Select the **I**nsert | **N**ame | **D**efine command and delete the Print_Titles name.
- Select the **F**ile | Page Se**t**up command and then delete the references from the **R**ows to Repeat at Top and **C**olumns to Repeat at Left edit boxes.

Previewing the Printout

You can't see page elements such as margins, headers, and footers in Excel's normal screen display. Because these features play such a large part in determining the look of your printouts, Excel offers a Print Preview feature. This feature, by showing you a scaled down, full-page version of your worksheet pages, enables you to get the "big picture." You can see the effect of each of the page layout and print options you've selected. You also have easy access to the Page Setup dialog box, where you can make changes and immediately see the effect on the printout. Print Preview also enables you to adjust your margins visually using the mouse. You also can print from the preview screen.

To see the preview screen, select the **F**ile | Print Pre**v**iew command. You'll see a screen similar to the one shown in Figure 16.4.

Click on this tool in the Standard toolbar to display the Print Preview screen.

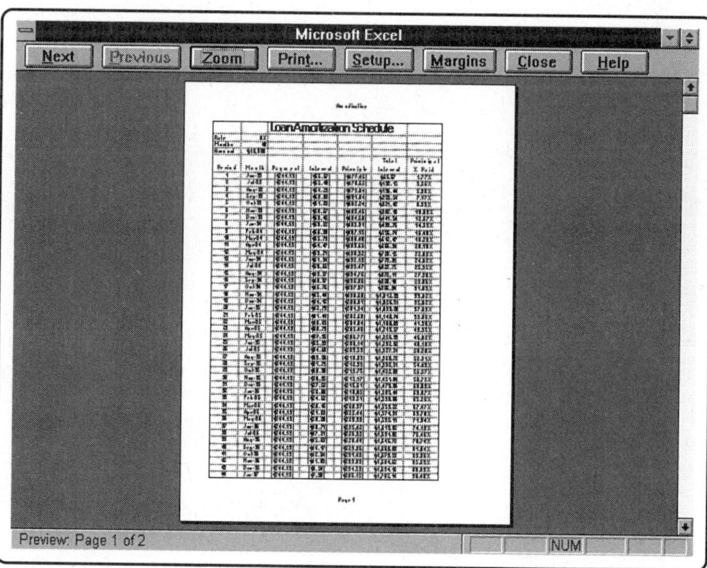

FIGURE 16.4.
Excel's Print Preview screen.

Changing the Print Preview Magnification

When you start Print Preview, Excel displays the first page of the printout full size. To toggle between full size and actual size (that is, the actual size of the printed page), you can do the following:

- Click on the **Z**oom button. To return to the full page view, select **Z**oom again.
- Move the mouse pointer to the page so that the pointer changes to a magnifying glass. Position the pointer over the area you want to zoom and then click. To return to the full page view, click on the worksheet.

Navigating the Print Preview Pages

When you're working with the Print Preview pages full size, you can display other pages in your printout by clicking on the **N**ext and **P**revious buttons. You also can use the keys listed in Table 16.1.

Table 16.1. Navigating Print Preview in full-size mode.

Key	*Result*
Down arrow	Moves to the next page
Up arrow	Moves to the previous page
End	Moves to the last page
Home	Moves to the first page

When you're viewing a page actual size, use the scrollbars to move around the page using the mouse. With the keyboard, use the keys listed in Table 16.2.

Table 16.2. Navigating Print Preview in actual-size mode.

Key	*Result*
Arrow key	Moves left, right, down, or up
Ctrl+right arrow or End	Moves to the right side of the page
Ctrl+left arrow or Home	Moves to the left side of the page
Ctrl+down arrow	Moves to the bottom of the page
Ctrl+up arrow	Moves to the top of the page
Ctrl+End	Moves to the bottom-right corner of the page
Ctrl+Home	Moves to the top-left corner of the page

Adjusting Page Margins and Column Widths in Print Preview

One of the big advantages of Print Preview is that it enables you to change your page margins and column widths easily. If you click on the **M**argins button, Excel displays margin and column *handles* at the top of the screen and indicates the margins with dotted lines (see Figure 16.5). By dragging the handles, you can change the margins and columns visually.

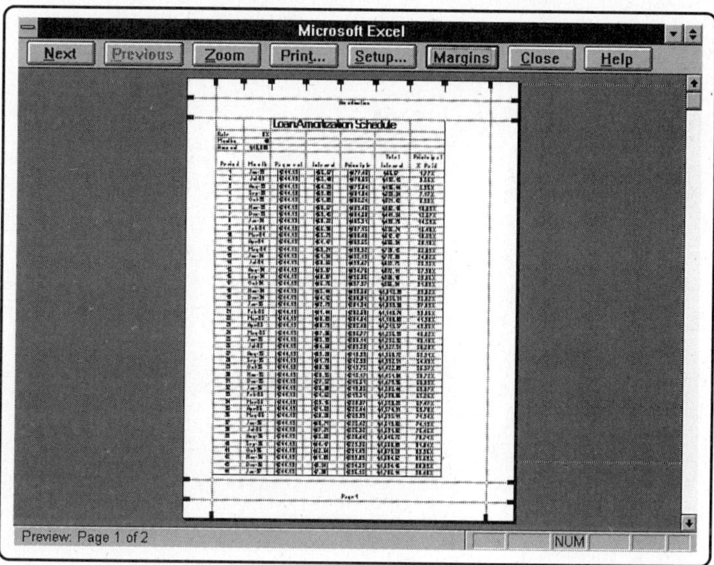

FIGURE 16.5.
In Print Preview, click on the Margins button to change the page margins and column widths by dragging the handles that appear at the top of the screen.

Follow the steps in Procedure 16.3 to adjust your page margins or column widths.

PROCEDURE 16.3. ADJUSTING PAGE MARGINS AND COLUMN WIDTHS IN PRINT PREVIEW.

1. In the Print Preview screen, click on the **M**argins button.
2. Position the mouse pointer over the handle of the margin or column you want to adjust. The pointer changes to a two-sided arrow with a line through it, and Excel displays the current margin size or column width in the status bar.
3. Drag the handle to the new location.
4. Repeat steps 2 and 3 for the other margins or columns you want to adjust.

Other Print Preview Buttons

The Print Preview screen also includes three other buttons:

- **Print** — This button displays the Print dialog box. I'll explain the various options in this dialog box in the next section.
- **Setup** — This button displays the Page Setup dialog box (discussed earlier in this chapter). If you change any Page Setup options, Excel shows you the effect of the new settings when you return to Print Preview.
- **Close** — Click on this button to exit Print Preview and return to the worksheet.

Printing a Worksheet

After setting up your pages, defining your print area and print titles, and previewing the output, you're ready to start printing. Before you do, though, make sure your printer is turned on and ready to receive output (it should be online, have enough paper, and so on). Then select the **File | Print** command. Excel displays the Print dialog box, shown in Figure 16.6.

FIGURE 16.6.
Use the Print dialog box to specify your print options.

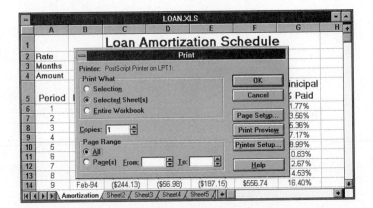

Here's a rundown on the various options available in the Print dialog box:

- **Print What** — Use these option buttons to determine how much of the workbook you want to print. Selection prints the selected range, Selected Sheet(s) prints the current sheet group, and Entire Workbook prints everything.
- **Copies** — Use this spinner to enter the number of copies you want Excel to print.

Page Range	Use this option to select the number of pages to print. Select **A**ll to print everything and Pa**g**e(s) to print a range of pages (which you specify with the **F**rom and **T**o spinners).
Page Set**u**p	Click on this button to display the Page Setup dialog box (described earlier).
Print Previe**w**	Activate this check box to see a preview of the document before it's printed.
P**r**inter	Select this option to choose a different printer.

Procedure 16.4 gives you the complete rundown of the steps involved in printing an Excel workbook.

PROCEDURE 16.4. PRINTING AN EXCEL WORKBOOK.

1. Make sure your printer is turned on and is online.
2. Activate the document you want to print.
3. Select the **F**ile | Page Se**t**up command and enter your page layout options.
4. If you don't want to print the entire document, use the Sheet tab's Print **A**rea box to select the range you want to print.
5. If you want row or column titles to appear on every page, use the Sheet tab's **R**ows to Repeat at Top and **C**olumns to Repeat at Left edit boxes to select them.
6. Click on OK or press Enter to return to the worksheet.
7. Select the **F**ile | **P**rint command to display the Print dialog box.

SUPER TIP

You also can display the Print dialog box by pressing Ctrl+P.

8. Enter your print options.
9. Click on OK or press Enter to print the document.

Click on this tool in the Standard toolbar to print the workbook without displaying the Print dialog box.

Chapter 17

Advanced Print Operations

This chapter explains how to get the most out of your printer with Excel. You'll learn how to select different printers, adjust page breaks, add headers and footers to your document, and much more.

Selecting a Printer

If you have access to more than one printer, or if you have a printer with multiple modes (such as a LaserJet printer with a PostScript cartridge installed), you'll need to use the Windows Control Panel to install a *driver* for each printer. After you install a printer driver (see your Windows documentation for details), you can select the printer you want to use with Excel by following the steps in Procedure 17.1.

PROCEDURE 17.1. SELECTING A PRINTER.

1. Select the **File** | **Print** command. Excel displays the Print dialog box.
2. Click on the P**r**inter Setup button. Excel displays the Printer Setup dialog box, shown in Figure 17.1.

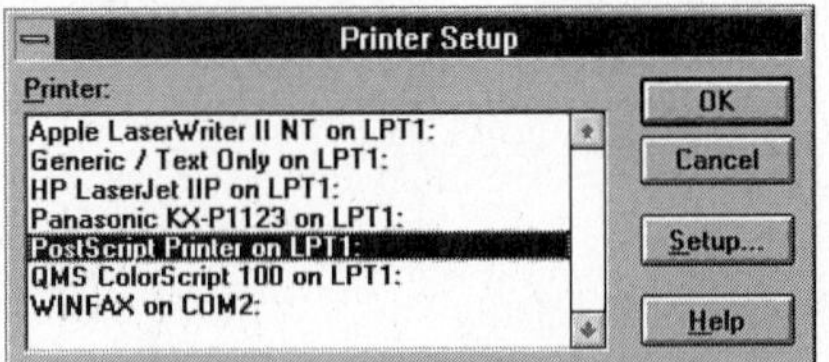

FIGURE 17.1.
The Printer Setup dialog box.

3. Use the **P**rinter list to highlight the printer you want to use.
4. (Optional) Click on the **S**etup button to modify the printer's options.
5. Click on OK or press Enter. Your selection becomes Excel's default printer (in all work sessions) until you specify another default.

SUPER CAUTION

If you choose the **S**etup button for the new printer, any adjustments you make to the printer options will affect *all* documents in *all* your Windows applications. To change settings for individual worksheets only, use the **File** | Page Set**u**p command.

Adjusting Page Breaks

Excel breaks up large worksheets into pages in which the size of each page is a function of the paper size, the default font, and the margin settings in the Page Setup dialog box. Using these parameters, Excel sets automatic page breaks to delineate the print area for each page. Although you can't adjust automatic page breaks, you can override them using manual page breaks. This enables you to control which data is printed on each page.

SUPER TIP

To see Excel's automatic page breaks before printing, select the **T**ools | **O**ptions command and then select the View tab. Activate the A**u**tomatic Page Breaks option.

Before setting a manual page break, you need to position the cell pointer correctly. Figure 17.2 uses the BREAKS.XLS workbook to illustrate the correct cell positions. In the Both Breaks worksheet, the cell pointer is on cell C10. Inserting a manual page break here creates a horizontal break above the cell and a vertical break to the left of the cell. In the Horizontal Break worksheet, the break is inserted with the cell pointer in the first column (cell A5). Here, Excel inserts only a horizontal page break above the cell. In the Vertical Break worksheet, the break is inserted with the cell pointer in the first row (cell C1). In this case, Excel inserts only a vertical page break to the left of the cell.

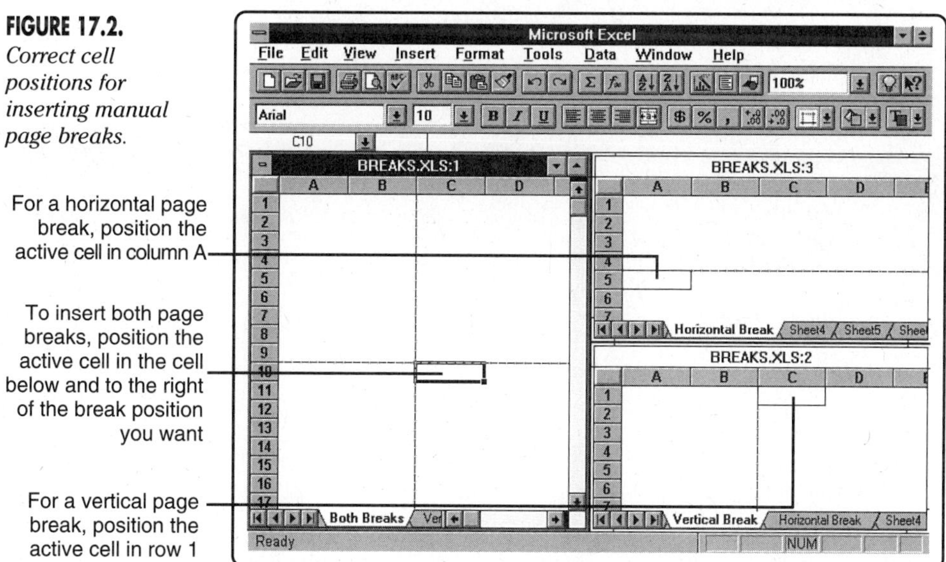
For a horizontal page break, position the active cell in column A
To insert both page breaks, position the active cell in the cell below and to the right of the break position you want
For a vertical page break, position the active cell in row 1
Microsoft Excel
File Edit View Insert Format Tools Data Window Help
BREAKS.XLS:1
BREAKS.XLS:3
BREAKS.XLS:2
Both Breaks
Horizontal Break
Vertical Break
Ready

FIGURE 17.2. *Correct cell positions for inserting manual page breaks.*

SUPER TIP

You can see page breaks easily if you turn off the worksheet gridlines. Select the Tools | Options command and then select the View tab. Deactivate the Gridlines check box.

Follow the steps in Procedure 17.2 to insert a manual page break.

PROCEDURE 17.2. INSERTING A MANUAL PAGE BREAK.

1. Position the cell pointer appropriately for the break you want.
2. Select the Insert | Page Break command. Excel inserts the page break at the cell you selected.

To remove manual page breaks, move to any cell immediately below a horizontal page break or immediately to the right of a vertical page break. Then select the Insert | Remove Page Break command.

SUPER NOTE

Automatic and manual page breaks appear as dashed lines on your worksheet. You can tell the two kinds of page breaks apart by noting that automatic page breaks use smaller dashes with more space between each dash.

Fitting More Data on a Page

When you print a worksheet, you often end up with a couple rows or columns that can't fit on a page. These are printed on a separate page, which usually is inconvenient and unattractive. This section examines several techniques you can use to fit more information on a page.

Adjusting the Normal Font

A worksheet's default column width and row height are functions of the *font* defined in the Normal style. In general, the smaller the type size of the Normal font, the more rows and columns will fit on a single printed page. For example, 10-point Arial prints 51 standard-height rows on a single page (assuming that you're using 8 1/2-inch by 11-inch paper). However, if you reduce the Normal type size to 8 points, a single page will print 58 standard-height rows. Similarly, using a narrower font will increase the number of columns printed per page. For example, 10-point Arial prints nine standard-width columns per page, but this increases to 12 standard-width columns if you use 10-point Helvetica Narrow.

SUPER NOTE

For instructions on adjusting the Normal style, see Chapter 12, "Working with Cell Formats."

Setting Smaller Margins

Because margins determine the amount of space surrounding your printed data, reducing margin size means more room on each page for printing. For example, reducing all four margins (right, left, top, and bottom) to 0.25 inches increases the number of columns printed from 9 to 11 and the number of rows from 51 to 60 (assuming that 10-point Arial is the Normal font). You adjust margins using the Page Setup dialog box. (See Chapter 16, "Printing a Workbook," for instructions on setting page margins.)

SUPER NOTE

Some laser printers don't enable you to set your margins smaller than 0.25 inches because of physical limitations.

Changing the Paper Size and Orientation

If you're having trouble fitting all your rows on a page, try printing on longer paper. Changing the paper size from 8 1/2 by 11 inches to 8 1/2 by 14 inches increases the number of rows per page from 51 to 68 (based on 10-point Arial). Use the Page Setup dialog box to select a paper size.

If you're having trouble getting all your columns to fit on a page, change the *paper orientation* from portrait to landscape in the Page Setup dialog box. When you switch to landscape orientation, Excel prints the worksheet sideways and increases the number of columns per page from 9 to 13. Just remember that this orientation reduces the number of rows printed per page.

Adjusting Rows and Columns

Make sure your rows are no taller (and your columns no wider) than they need to be. Select the entire print area and select both the F**o**rmat | **R**ow | **A**utoFit and F**o**rmat | **C**olumn | **A**utoFit Selection commands. Also, hiding any unnecessary rows and columns enables you to fit more important information on each page. (See Chapter 10, "Working with Columns and Rows," for more information.)

SUPER NOTE

You also can use row adjustments to reduce the number of lines printed per page. For example, if you want to produce a double-spaced report, select every row in the print area and select the Format | Row | Height command to double the height of each row.

Scaling Your Worksheet

If you have a PostScript printer or any other printer that accepts scalable fonts, you can scale your worksheets to fit on one page. When you specify a percentage reduction, Excel shrinks the printed worksheet proportionally and maintains all your layout and formatting options. (You also can enlarge your worksheets.) Procedure 17.3 outlines the steps to follow.

PROCEDURE 17.3. SCALING A WORKSHEET.

1. Select the File | Page Setup command and then select the Page tab from the Page Setup dialog box.
2. In the Scaling section, select the Adjust to option and then use the spinner beside it to enter a percentage. To reduce the printout, enter a value between 10 and 100. To enlarge the printout, enter a value between 100 and 400.
3. Click on OK or press Enter.

If you have to use a lot of trial and error to get the proper reduction setting, you can save some time by having Excel do it for you. All you do is specify the number of pages you want for the document, and Excel handles the reduction automatically. If necessary, you can enter both a length and width for the printout. Procedure 17.4 gives you the details.

PROCEDURE 17.4. SCALING A WORKSHEET AUTOMATICALLY.

1. Select File | Page Setup and then select the Page tab in the Page Setup dialog box.
2. In the Scaling section, select the Fit to option and use its spinners to enter the number of pages wide and tall you want the printout to be.
3. Click on OK or press Enter.

SUPER TIP

Even if your printer doesn't support scalable fonts, you can scale your worksheets to fit a page. Select the entire print area, hold down the Shift key while you select **Edit | Copy** Picture, and select the options you want from the Copy Picture dialog box. Click on OK to return to the worksheet. Finally, paste the picture and scale it to the size you want. See Chapter 28, "Working with Graphic Objects," for more information about working with pictures.

Adding a Header or Footer

You can add headers or footers that display information at the top (for a header) or bottom (for a footer) of every printed page. This is useful for keeping track of such items as page numbers and the current date and time. The next two sections show you how to work with Excel's predefined and custom headers and footers.

Adding a Predefined Header or Footer

Excel has a number of predefined headers and footers that can display page numbers, workbook and worksheet names, file revision dates, authors, and more. Follow the steps in Procedure 17.5 to add one of these headers or footers.

PROCEDURE 17.5. ADDING A PREDEFINED HEADER OR FOOTER TO A WORKSHEET.

1. Select **File | Page Setup** and select the Header/Footer tab in the Page Setup dialog box (see Figure 17.3).

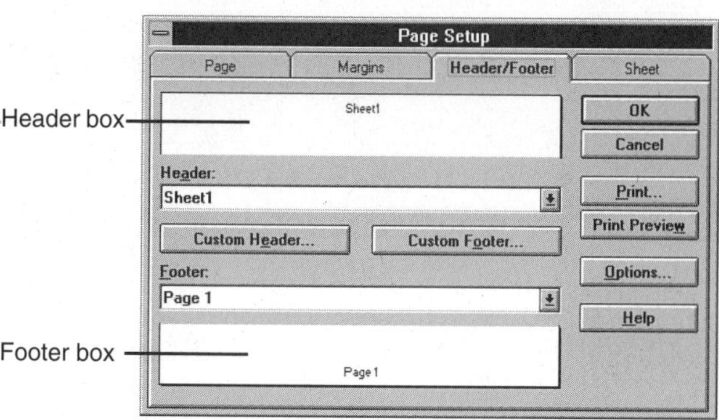

FIGURE 17.3.
The Header/Footer tab in the Page Setup dialog box.

2. Use the Header drop-down list to select a predefined header. Your selection appears in the header box above the list.
3. Use the Footer drop-down list to select a predefined footer. Your choice appears in the footer box below the list.
4. Click on OK or press Enter.

Creating a Custom Header or Footer

If none of the predefined headers or footers fits the bill, you can create your own custom version. You can enter seven different items in a customized header or footer: text (such as a workbook title or other explanatory comments), the current page number and total page count, the date and time, and the workbook and worksheet tab names. You can specify a font for any of these items, and you can place the items on the left or right side of the page (or in the center). Procedure 17.6 shows you the steps to follow.

PROCEDURE 17.6. CREATING A CUSTOM HEADER OR FOOTER.

1. Select File | Page Setup and then select the Header/Footer tab in the Page Setup dialog box.
2. To create a custom header, select the Custom Header button to display the Header dialog box (see Figure 17.4). To create a custom footer, select the Custom Footer button to display the Footer dialog box.

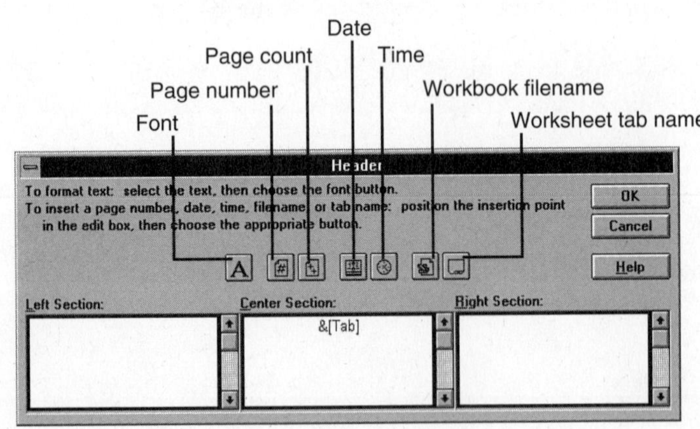

FIGURE 17.4.
Use the Header dialog box to create a custom header. The Footer dialog box works like the Header dialog box.

3. Select either the Left Section, Center Section, or Right Section edit box.

4. Enter text or select one of the buttons to insert any of the following codes: &[Page] (page number), &[Pages] (page count), &[Date] (date), &[Time] (time), &[File] (workbook filename), or &[Tab] (worksheet tab name).
5. (Optional) Select any text you want to format and then click on the Font button. In the font dialog box that appears, enter the font options you want to use. Click on OK or press Enter to return to the Header or Footer dialog box.
6. Repeat steps 3-5 to enter any other text or codes.
7. Click on OK or press Enter. Excel returns you to the Page Setup dialog box and displays the header or footer in the appropriate box.
8. Click on OK or press Enter. Excel adds the header or footer to the workbook.

Printing Patterns and Colors

Printing patterns and colors on a black-and-white printer can be tricky because different printers can reproduce these elements in different ways. To illustrate, this section compares the printed output of patterns and colors for a LaserJet and a PostScript printer.

As you learned in Chapter 11, "Using Color in Worksheets," you can produce shades of a foreground color by combining Excel's dot patterns with different background colors. Although this is a handy way to add attractive colors to your worksheet onscreen, your printer makes a big difference in how these colors are reproduced. Figure 17.5 shows a gray scale created by mixing dot patterns and colors. Figure 17.6 shows the same worksheet printed by a PostScript printer. As you can see, the dot pattern reproduction is inconsistent, and several of the shades are almost indistinguishable. The LaserJet, on the other hand, reproduces the gray scale perfectly, as shown in Figure 17.7. If you use dot patterns regularly in your worksheets, try to avoid using a PostScript printer.

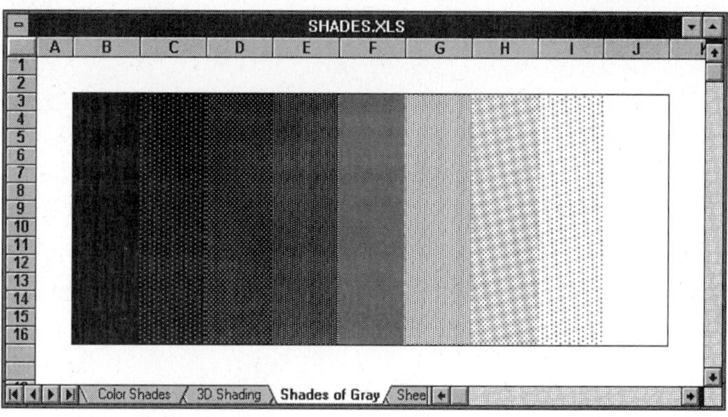

FIGURE 17.5.
A gray scale produced by combining dot patterns and colors.

FIGURE 17.6.
The gray scale printed on a PostScript printer.

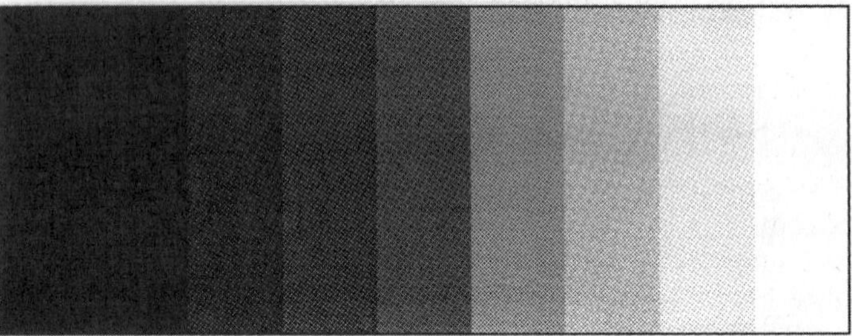

FIGURE 17.7.
The gray scale printed on a LaserJet printer.

Excel normally prints all text in black, no matter what color the text is on-screen. However, if you have a PostScript printer, you can get text colors to print in shades of gray by setting up your printer as a color printer. Procedure 17.7 lists the steps you need to follow.

PROCEDURE 17.7. SETTING UP A POSTSCRIPT PRINTER TO PRINT COLORED TEXT.

1. Using the Windows Control Panel, add a printer driver for a color PostScript printer (the NEC Colormate PS or the QMS ColorScript 100 will do the job). If you're not sure how to add a printer driver, see your Windows manual.
2. In Excel, select the **File** | **Print** command to display the Print dialog box.
3. Click on the P**r**inter button. Excel displays the Printer Setup dialog box.
4. Select the color PostScript printer from the **P**rinter list and then click on OK or press Enter to return to the Print dialog box. The printer name appears at the top of the dialog box.
5. If you want to print now, click on OK or press Enter. Otherwise, click on Cancel to return to the workbook.

Figure 17.8 shows a sample printout using this technique.

FIGURE 17.8.
Text colors printed as shades of gray.

This is blue text

This is red text

This is magenta text

This is green text

This is yellow text

Printing to a Text File

You can print your worksheets to a text file by using the Windows FILE: port. This is handy if you want to print a worksheet on an off-site printer, such as a color printer or a PostScript printer. You just select the appropriate printer driver and print the worksheet to a file (as outlined in Procedure 17.8). When you get to the printer site, use DOS to copy the file to the printer. The output will be exactly the same as if it were printed directly from Excel.

SUPER NOTE

Use Procedure 17.8 to copy worksheets to a file for printing later on a typesetting machine. Find out whether your typesetter uses a Linotronic or Compugraphic model. Select the appropriate printer driver and then print the worksheet to a disk.

Follow the steps in Procedure 17.8 to print a worksheet to a text file.

PROCEDURE 17.8. PRINTING A WORKSHEET TO A TEXT FILE.

1. Switch to the Windows Program Manager, activate the Control Panel, and select **S**ettings | **P**rinters. The Printers dialog box appears.
2. Highlight the appropriate printer in the Installed **P**rinters list box.
3. Click on the **C**onnect button. The Connect dialog box appears.
4. Select the FILE: port from the **P**orts list box.
5. Exit Control Panel and return to Excel.
6. Select the **F**ile | **P**rint command to display the Print dialog box.
7. Click on the P**r**inter button. Excel displays the Printer Setup dialog box.
8. Select the printer you've just configured to the FILE: port and then click on OK or press Enter to return to the Print dialog box.

9. Click on OK or press Enter. Excel displays the Print to File dialog box, shown in Figure 17.9.

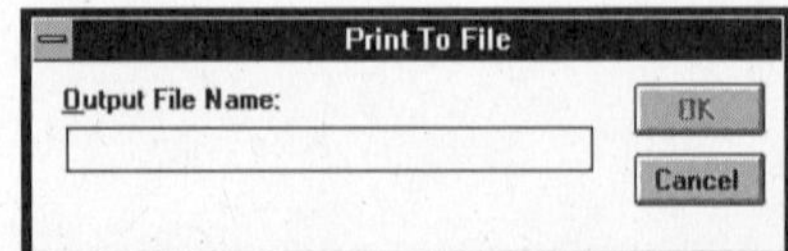

FIGURE 17.9.
Use the Print to File dialog box to enter a filename for the printout.

Enter the name you want the file to have. Be sure to include the appropriate drive and directory.

Click on OK or press Enter. Excel copies the worksheet to the file.

Chapter

18

Working with Reports

In Chapter 13, "Changing the Workbook View," you learned how to create different *views* of your worksheets. A view, you'll recall, contains specific settings for the display options, window position and size, row height and column width, and so on. These different views are real time-savers when you're manipulating a worksheet on-screen. Excel also includes a feature called the *Report Manager* that enables you to put together a sequence of views and print them in a *report*. For maximum flexibility, you can specify different print settings with each view, and use these settings when printing your reports.

This chapter introduces you to Excel reports and shows you how to create, edit, and print your own reports.

Creating Reports

If you're using views to create your report, you first need to define the print settings for each view. You can define page setup options, headers, footers, and even different printers (on different printer ports). Here are some guidelines to follow when defining your view print settings:

- Use the header or footer to display a title for each view.
- If a view is designed to show only a section of a worksheet (such as a list of account codes), be sure to set up a Print_Area range (see Chapter 16, "Printing a Workbook") to restrict the printout to the view's data.
- Set up your Print_Title range (see Chapter 16) and page breaks (see Chapter 17, "Advanced Print Operations") as needed with each view.

When you create a report, you enter a report name and then define the various *sections* of the report. (A section is a specific worksheet view, scenario, or a combination of the two.) Procedure 18.1 outlines the steps to follow.

PROCEDURE 18.1. CREATING A REPORT.

1. Select the **F**ile | Print Rep**o**rt command. Excel displays the Print Report dialog box.
2. Click on the **A**dd button. Excel displays the Add Report dialog box, shown in Figure 18.1.
3. Enter a name for the report in the **R**eport Name edit box.
4. Use the **S**heet drop-down list to select a worksheet to include in the report.
5. If you have a view to include in the report, select it from the **V**iew drop-down list.
6. If you have a scenario to include, select it from the S**c**enario drop-down list box.
7. Click on the **A**dd button. Excel displays the selected worksheet, view, and scenario in the S**e**ction in this Report list.
8. Repeat steps 4-7 to include other sections in the report.
9. Activate the Use Continuous Page **N**umbers check box to print the report with consecutive page numbers.

10. Click on OK or press Enter. Excel returns you to the Print Report dialog box.
11. Click on Close to return to the workbook.

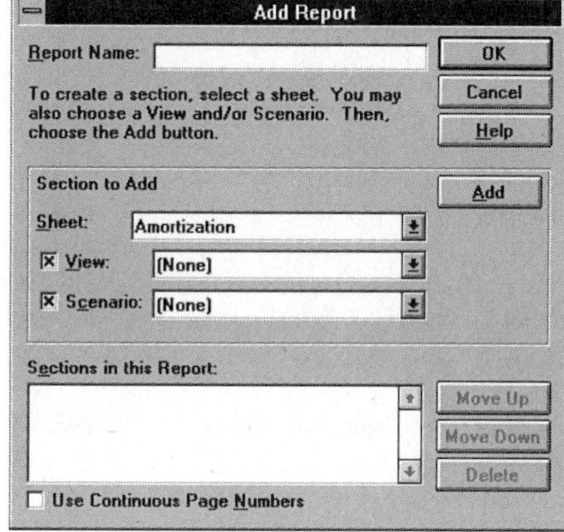

FIGURE 18.1.
The Add Report dialog box.

SUPER TIP

You can document your complex workbooks by printing hard copies of the results, formulas, variables used, and range names. Set up a view for each component and then create a report called "Documentation."

Editing Reports

Your reports will print in the order in which you selected the sections. If you want to change that order—or make any other modifications—you can edit your reports. Follow the steps in Procedure 18.2.

PROCEDURE 18.2. EDITING A REPORT.

1. Select the **F**ile | Print Re**p**ort command to display the Print Report dialog box.
2. In the **R**eports list box, highlight the report you want to edit.
3. Click on the **E**dit button. Excel displays the Edit Report dialog box.
4. To add a section (or to use a different combination of worksheets, views, and scenarios), choose the worksheet, view, and scenario from the Section to Add group, then click on the **A**dd button.
5. To change the section order, highlight the appropriate section in the S**e**ctions in this Report list and use the Move **U**p and Move **D**own buttons to place the section where you want it.

6. To delete a section, highlight the section in the Sections in this Report list and click on the Delete button.
7. Click on OK or press Enter. Excel returns you to the Print Report dialog box.
8. Click on the Close button to return to the workbook.

Printing Reports

When you've defined the report to your satisfaction, you can print it by following Procedure 18.3.

PROCEDURE 18.3. PRINTING A REPORT.

1. Select the **File** | Print Report command to display the Print Report dialog box.
2. In the **Reports** list box, highlight the report you want to print.
3. Click on the **Print** button. Excel displays the Print dialog box.
4. Select the print options you want.
5. Click on OK or press Enter. Excel prints the report.

Deleting Reports

Procedure 18.4 shows you how to delete a report you no longer need.

PROCEDURE 18.4. DELETING A REPORT.

1. Select the **File** | Print Report command to display the Print Report dialog box.
2. In the **Reports** list box, highlight the report you want to delete.
3. Click on the Delete button. Excel asks you to confirm the deletion (see Figure 18.2).

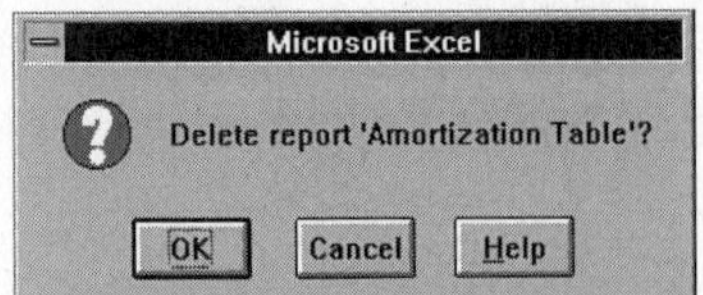

FIGURE 18.2.
Excel asks you to confirm a report deletion.

4. Click on **Yes** to proceed with the deletion. Excel removes the report from the **Reports** list.
5. Repeat steps 2-4 for other reports you want to delete.
6. Click on **Close**. Excel returns you to the workbook.

Workshop III

Graphics

Chapter

19

Creating Charts

One of the best ways to analyze your worksheet data—or get your point across to other people—is to display your data visually in a chart. Excel gives you tremendous flexibility when you're creating charts; it enables you to place charts in separate documents or directly on the worksheet itself. Not only that, but you have dozens of different chart formats to choose from—and you can further customize these charts to suit your needs.

This chapter shows you the basics of creating and saving your Excel charts. You'll learn how to create embedded charts and chart documents, as well as how to use Excel's new ChartWizard tool, which breaks chart creation into a series of easy steps.

Chart Basics

Worksheet charts have their own terminology that you need to become familiar with. Figure 19.1 points out the various parts of a typical chart. Each part is explained in Table 19.1.

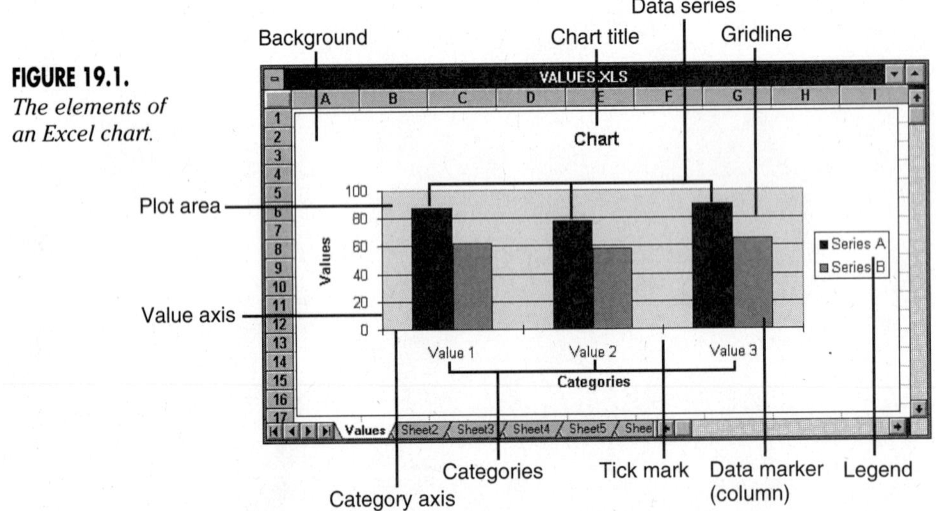

FIGURE 19.1.
The elements of an Excel chart.

Table 19.1. The elements of an Excel chart.

Element	*Description*
Background	The area on which the chart is drawn. You can change the color and border of this area.
Category	A grouping of data values on the category axis. Figure 19.1 has three categories: Value 1, Value 2, and Value 3.
Category axis	The axis (usually the X axis) that contains the category groupings.

Element	Description
Data marker	A symbol that represents a specific data value. The symbol used depends on the chart type. In a column chart such as the one shown in Figure 19.1, each column is a marker.
Data series	A collection of related data values. Normally, the marker for each value in a series has the same pattern. Figure 19.1 has two series: Series A and Series B. These are identified in the legend.
Data value	A single piece of data. Also called a *data point.*
Gridlines	Optional horizontal and/or vertical extensions of the axis tick marks. These make data values easier to read.
Legend	A guide that shows the colors, patterns, and symbols used by the markers for each data series.
Plot area	The area bounded by the category and value axes. It contains the data points and gridlines.
Tick mark	A small line that intersects the category axis or the value axis. It marks divisions in the chart's categories or scales.
Title	The title of the chart.
Value axis	The axis (usually the Y axis) that contains the data values.

How Excel Converts Worksheet Data into a Chart

Creating an Excel chart usually is straightforward and often can be done in only a few keystrokes or mouse clicks. However, a bit of background on how Excel converts your worksheet data into a chart will help you avoid some charting pitfalls.

When Excel creates a chart, it examines both the shape and the contents of the range you've selected. From this data, the program makes various assumptions to determine what should be on the category axis, what should be on the value axis, how to label the categories, and which labels should show within the legend.

The first assumption Excel makes is that *there are more categories than data series.* This makes sense, because most graphs plot a small number of series over many different intervals. For example, a chart showing monthly sales and profit over a year has two data series (the sales and profit numbers) but 12 categories (the monthly intervals). Consequently, Excel assumes that the category axis (the X axis) of your chart runs along the longest side of the selected worksheet range.

The chart shown in Figure 19.2 is a plot of the range A1:D3 in the Column Categories worksheet. Since, in this case, the range has more columns than rows, Excel uses each column as a category. Conversely, Figure 19.3 shows the plot of the range A1:C4, which has more rows than columns. In this case, Excel uses each row as a category.

SUPER NOTE

If a range has the same number of rows and columns, Excel uses the columns as categories.

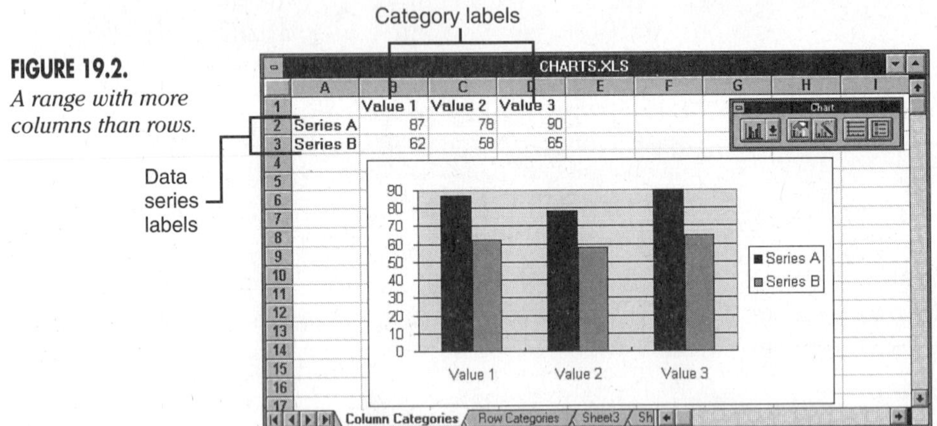

FIGURE 19.2.
A range with more columns than rows.

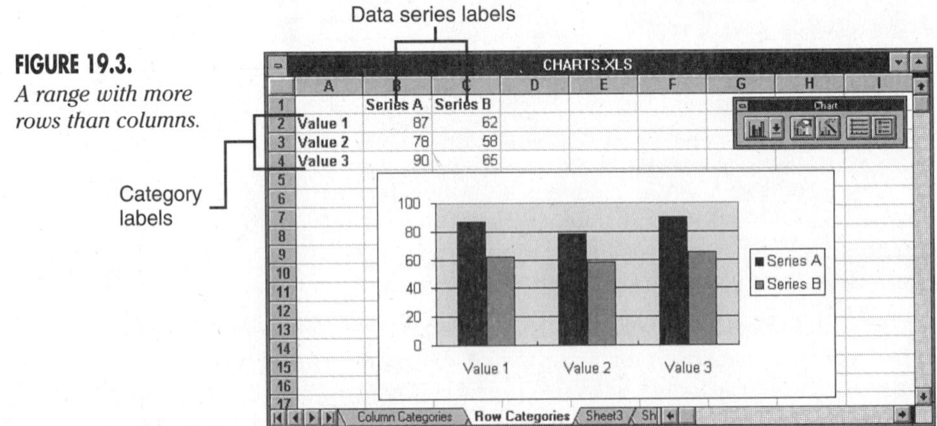

FIGURE 19.3.
A range with more rows than columns.

The second assumption Excel makes involves the location of labels for categories and data series:

- For a range with *more columns than rows* (such as in Figure 19.2), Excel uses the contents of the top row (row 1 in Figure 19.2) as the category labels and the leftmost column (column A in Figure 19.2) as the data series labels.
- For a range with *more rows than columns* (such as in Figure 19.3), Excel uses the contents of the leftmost column (column A in Figure 19.3) as the category labels and the top row (row 1 in Figure 19.3) as the data series labels.

SUPER NOTE

If a range has the same number of rows and columns, Excel uses the top row for the category labels and the leftmost column for the data series labels.

Creating a Chart

When plotting your worksheet data, you have two basic options: you can create an *embedded chart,* which sits on top of your worksheet and can be moved, sized, and formatted, or you can create a separate *chart sheet* by using the automatic or cut-and-paste methods. Whether you choose to embed your charts or store them in separate documents, the charts are linked with the worksheet data. Any changes you make to the data are automatically updated in the chart. The next few sections discuss each of these techniques.

Creating an Embedded Chart

When creating an embedded chart, you can use any of the following methods:

- Use the Default Chart tool to create a default chart.
- Use ChartWizard to set chart options such as the chart type and axis titles.
- Copy a chart from a separate chart sheet.

SUPER NOTE

Because you can print embedded charts along with your worksheet data, embedded charts are useful in presentations in which you need to show plotted data and worksheet information simultaneously.

Creating a Default Embedded Chart

Excel's default chart is a basic column chart. (See Chapter 20, "Working with Chart Types," to learn how to customize the default chart.) Follow the steps in Procedure 19.1 to create an embedded chart using the default format.

PROCEDURE 19.1. CREATING A DEFAULT EMBEDDED CHART.

1. Select the range you want to plot, including the row and column labels if there are any. Make sure that there are no blank rows between the column labels and the data.
2. Click on the Default Chart tool on the Chart toolbar. The mouse pointer changes to a crosshair with a chart icon.

The Default Chart tool from the Chart toolbar.

3. Position the mouse pointer at the top-left corner of the area where you want to put the chart.
4. Drag the mouse pointer to the bottom-right corner of that area. Excel displays a box as you drag. When you release the mouse button, Excel draws the chart.

SUPER TIP

To create a square chart area, hold down the Shift key while dragging the mouse pointer. To align the chart with the worksheet gridlines, hold down the Alt key while dragging.

SUPER NOTE

If, when you release the mouse button, you see a ChartWizard dialog box, Excel doesn't have enough information to automatically create the chart. Follow the steps in Procedure 19.2 to create the chart.

Creating an Embedded Chart with ChartWizard

If the default chart isn't what you want, Excel's ChartWizard tool takes you through the steps necessary for setting up an embedded chart and setting various customization options. Procedure 19.2 shows you how these procedures work.

PROCEDURE 19.2. CREATING AN EMBEDDED CHART WITH CHARTWIZARD.

1. (Optional) Select the cell range you want to plot. (You'll get a chance to select a range later in the process.)
2. Either click on the ChartWizard tool in the Standard toolbar (or the Chart toolbar) or select the **I**nsert | C**h**art | **O**n This Sheet command. The mouse pointer changes to a crosshair with a chart icon.

The ChartWizard tool from the Standard toolbar. (It's also on the Chart toolbar.)

3. Position the mouse pointer at the top-left corner of the area where you want to put the chart, then drag the pointer to the bottom-right corner of the area. Excel displays a box as you drag. When you release the mouse button, Excel displays the ChartWizard - Step 1 of 5 dialog box.
4. If you didn't do so earlier, select the cell range you want to chart, then click on the Next > button. The ChartWizard - Step 2 of 5 dialog box appears (see Figure 19.4).

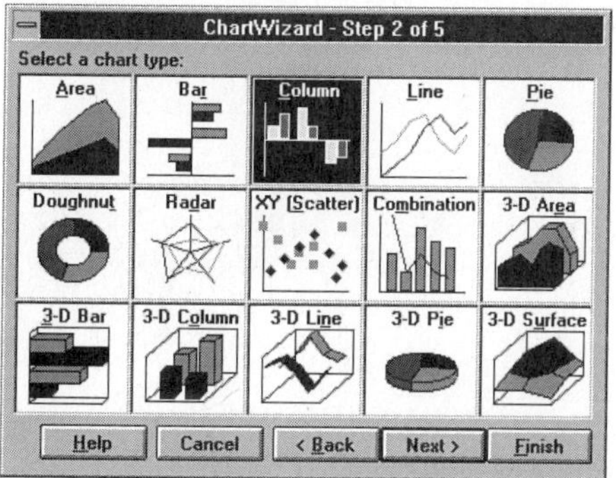

FIGURE 19.4.
The ChartWizard - Step 2 of 5 dialog box.

5. Select a chart type, then click on the Next > button. (See Chapter 20, "Working with Chart Types," and Chapter 25, "Combining Multiple Chart Types in a Single Chart," for an explanation of the various chart types.) Excel displays the ChartWizard - Step 3 of 5 dialog box, shown in Figure 19.5.

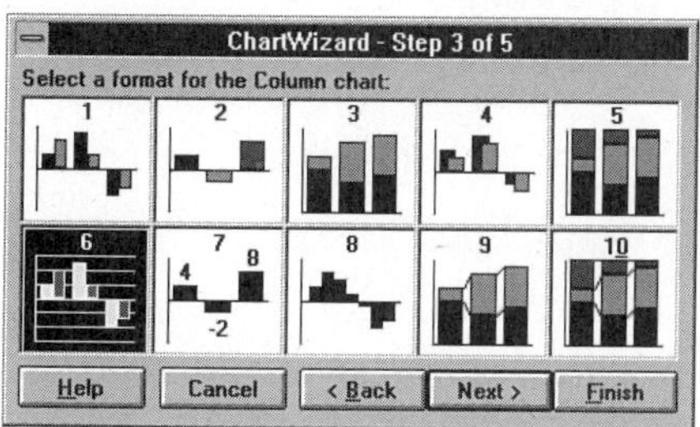

FIGURE 19.5.
The ChartWizard - Step 3 of 5 dialog box.

6. Select a chart format for the chart type you selected, then click on Next >. The ChartWizard - Step 4 of 5 dialog box appears (see Figure 19.6).

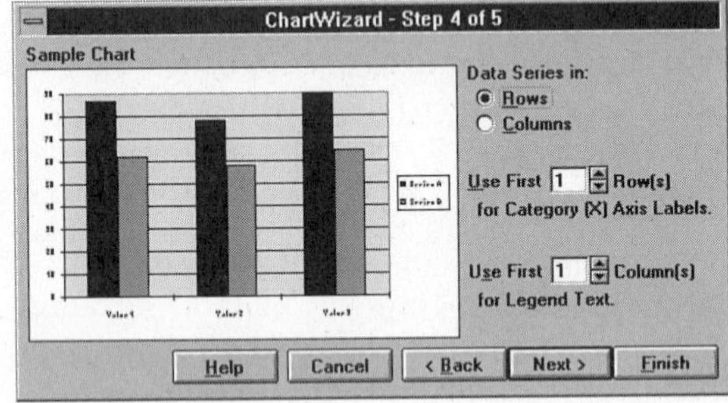

FIGURE 19.6.
The ChartWizard - Step 4 of 5 dialog box.

7. Select the options that define the layout of the data series and categories in your selected range. When you're done, click on Next >. Excel displays the ChartWizard - Step 5 of 5 dialog box, shown in Figure 19.7.

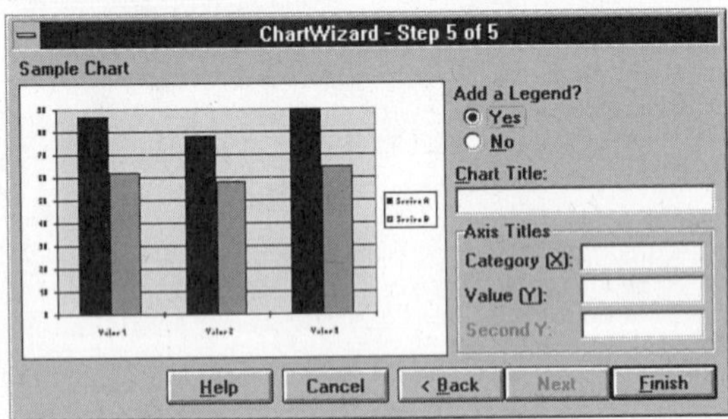

FIGURE 19.7.
The Chart Wizard - Step 5 of 5 dialog box.

8. Select a legend option and add any titles you need. When you're done, click on Finish. Excel draws the chart on the worksheet.

Embedding a Chart by Copying from a Chart Sheet

If you have a chart in a separate chart sheet (as explained in the next section), you can embed a copy in the current worksheet. This is a handy way to create an embedded chart if you don't have a mouse, because the normal Default Chart and ChartWizard methods require a mouse. Procedure 19.3 lists the steps to follow.

PROCEDURE 19.3. EMBEDDING A CHART FROM A CHART SHEET.

1. Activate the sheet that contains the chart you want to embed.
2. If you have a mouse, select the chart by clicking on the chart background. If you don't have a mouse, or if you prefer to use the keyboard, select the chart

by first pressing the Esc key to clear any current selections and then pressing the up arrow key. Excel puts black selection boxes around the chart and displays `Chart` in the formula bar's Name box, as shown in Figure 19.8.

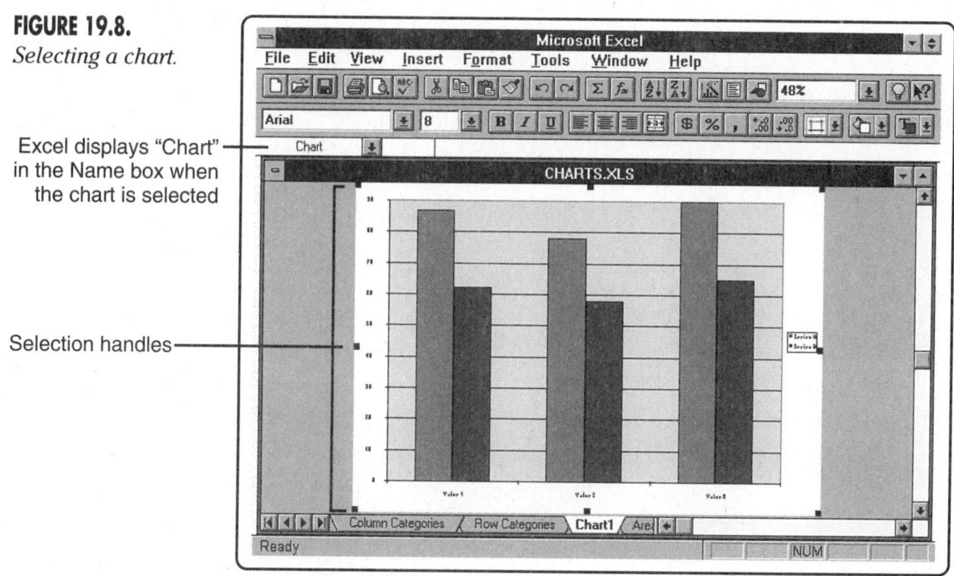

FIGURE 19.8.
Selecting a chart.

3. Select the **Edit** | **Copy** command.
4. Activate the worksheet in which you want to embed the chart.
5. Select the **Edit** | **Paste** command. Excel embeds the chart into the worksheet.

SUPER NOTE

You'll probably need to size the chart. See Chapter 21, "Enhancing Charts," for details.

Creating a Chart in a Separate Sheet

If you don't want a chart taking up space in a worksheet, or if you want to print a chart on its own, you can create a separate chart sheet. Procedure 19.4 outlines the steps.

PROCEDURE 19.4. CREATING A CHART IN A SEPARATE SHEET.

1. (Optional) Select the cell range you want to plot. (You'll get a chance to select a range later in the process.)

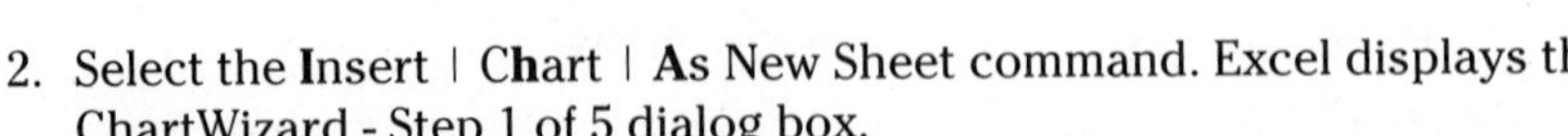

2. Select the **I**nsert | C**h**art | **A**s New Sheet command. Excel displays the ChartWizard - Step 1 of 5 dialog box.
3. Follow steps 4-8 in Procedure 19.2 to use ChartWizard. When you finish, Excel inserts a new chart sheet and displays your chart.

SUPER TIP

To create a new chart sheet quickly, select the cell range and press F11 (if you have an extended keyboard) or Alt+F1.

SUPER TIP

To get a better view of the chart in a separate chart sheet, select the **V**iew | Sized with **W**indow command. This command expands the chart to fill the entire window. It also means that the chart changes size when you change the size of the window.

Chapter

20

Working with Chart Types

For your various charting needs, Excel has no less than 14 unique *chart types*. Each chart type contains a number of predefined formats. All told, more than 100 different charts are available.

This chapter presents examples of eight of Excel's 2-D chart types: Area, Bar, Column, Line, Pie, Radar, XY, and Doughnut. (For information on Combination charts, see Chapter 25, "Combining Multiple Chart Types in a Single Chart." For information on 3-D charts, see Chapter 24, "Working with 3-D charts.") You'll learn how to select a different chart type by using either the Chart toolbar or the chart window's Format menu, and you'll learn how to change the default chart.

Activating a Chart

Before you can work with chart types, you need to activate a chart. How you do this depends on the kind of chart you're dealing with:

- For an embedded chart, double-click inside the chart box. The box border changes to a thicker, broken line.
- For a chart sheet, select the sheet tab.

Selecting a Chart Type

Depending on the chart, you can use one of three methods to select a different chart type:

- Use the Chart Type dialog box.
- Use the Chart Type tool's palette of types.
- Use the chart AutoFormat feature.

Selecting a Chart Type from the Chart Type Dialog Box

Follow the steps in Procedure 20.1 to use the Chart Type dialog box to select a chart type.

PROCEDURE 20.1. SELECTING A CHART TYPE FROM THE CHART TYPE DIALOG BOX.

1. Activate the chart you want to change.
2. Select the Format | Chart Type command. Excel displays the Chart Type dialog box, shown in Figure 20.1.

SUPER TIP

You also can display the Chart Type dialog box by right-clicking on the chart background and selecting the Chart Type command from the shortcut menu.

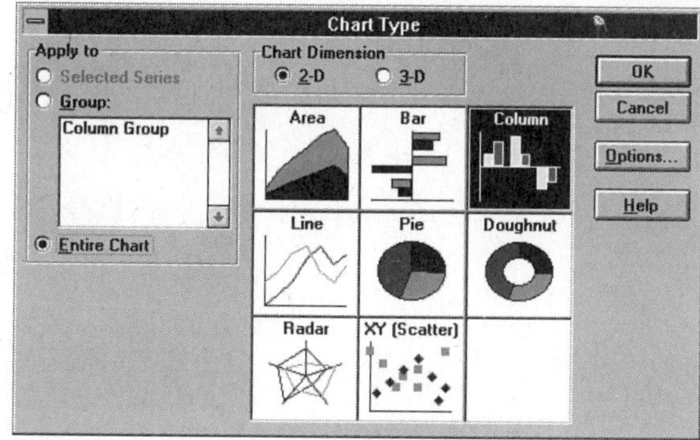

FIGURE 20.1.
The Chart Type dialog box.

3. In the Apply to group, select **E**ntire Chart. (To learn about the other options in this group, see Chapter 25.
4. In the Chart Dimension group, select either **2**-D or **3**-D. (This chapter covers just 2-D charts; refer to Chapter 24 to learn about Excel's 3-D chart types.)
5. Select a chart type.
6. To select a chart subtype (a variation on the main chart type), select the **O**ptions button, select the Subtype tab from the dialog box that appears, and select one of the **S**ubtype boxes.
7. Click on OK or press Enter.

Using the Chart Type Tool to Select a Chart Type

Procedure 20.2 shows you how to select a chart type using the Chart Type tool.

PROCEDURE 20.2. SELECTING A CHART TYPE USING THE CHART TYPE TOOL.

1. Activate the chart you want to change.
2. Display the Chart toolbar.
3. Drop down the Chart Type tool and select one of the chart types from the palette that appears. Using the selected chart type, Excel redraws the chart.

The Chart Type tool from the Chart toolbar.

> **SUPER TIP**
>
> If you want to experiment with a number of different chart types, you can "tear off" the Chart Type tool's palette. Drop the palette down, place the mouse pointer inside the palette, and drag the mouse until the palette separates. When you release the button, the Chart toolbar appears.

Selecting an AutoFormat Chart Type

To make your chart formatting chores easier, Excel comes with a number of built-in *AutoFormats*—predefined chart formats that you can apply easily. Procedure 20.3 shows you how to use the chart AutoFormat feature.

PROCEDURE 20.3. SELECTING AN AUTOFORMAT CHART TYPE.

1. Activate the chart you want to change.
2. Select the Format | AutoFormat command. Excel displays the AutoFormat dialog box, shown in Figure 20.2.

> **SUPER TIP**
>
> You also can display the AutoFormat dialog box by right-clicking on the chart background and selecting the shortcut menu's AutoFormat command.

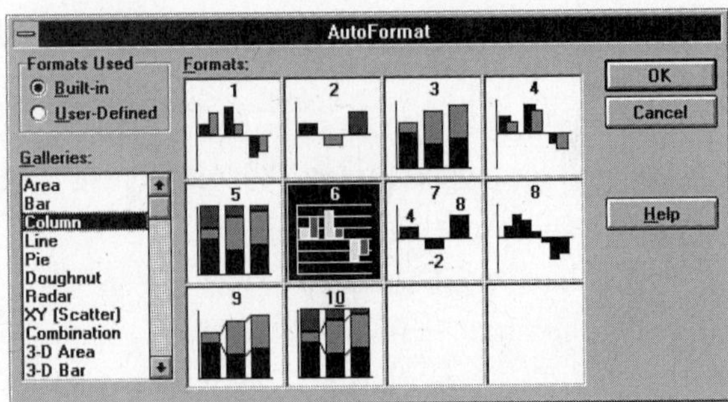

FIGURE 20.2.
The chart AutoFormat dialog box.

3. Select a chart type from the **G**alleries list.
4. Select a chart format from among the **F**ormats boxes.
5. Click on OK or press Enter.

SUPER NOTE

You can create your own chart AutoFormats. See Chapter 21, "Enhancing Charts," for details.

Working with 2-D Area Charts

Area charts show the relative contributions over time that each data series makes to the whole picture. The smaller the area a data series takes up, the smaller its contribution to the whole. For example, Figure 20.3 shows an area chart comparing yearly principal and interest over the 25-year term of a mortgage. The straight line across the top of the chart at about $19,000 indicates the total yearly mortgage payment. (The line is straight because the payments are constant over the term.) The two areas below this line show the relative contributions of principal and interest paid each year. As you can see, the area representing yearly principal increases over time, which means that the amount of principal in each payment will increase as the term of the loan progresses. You can use area charts to show the relative contributions over time of things such as individual expense categories, sales regions, and production costs.

To select an area chart, display the AutoFormat dialog box, choose the Area item from the **G**alleries list, and select an area chart from the **F**ormats section.

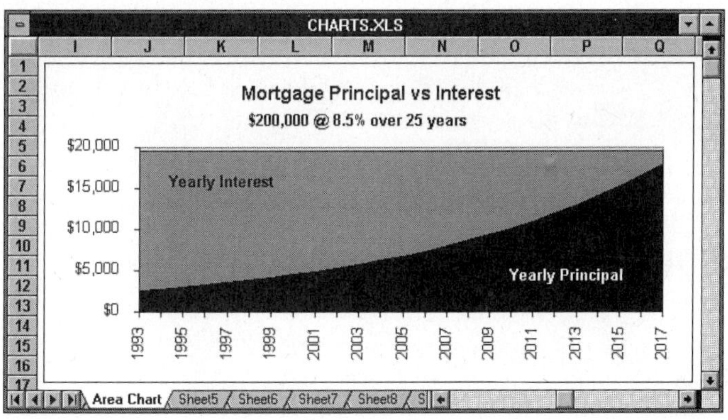

FIGURE 20.3.
An area chart that compares mortgage principal and interest.

Working with 2-D Bar Charts

Bar charts compare distinct items or show single items at distinct intervals. A bar chart is laid out with categories along the vertical axis and values along the horizontal axis. This format lends itself to competitive comparisons, because categories appear to be "ahead" or "behind." For example, Figure 20.4 shows a comparison of parking tickets written in a single month by four officers. You can easily see that the officer on top is the "winner," because the top bar extends farther to the right than anyone else's. You can use bar charts to show the results of sales contests, elections, sporting events, or any competitive activity.

To select a bar chart, display the AutoFormat dialog box, choose the Bar item from the **G**alleries list, and select a bar chart from the **F**ormats section.

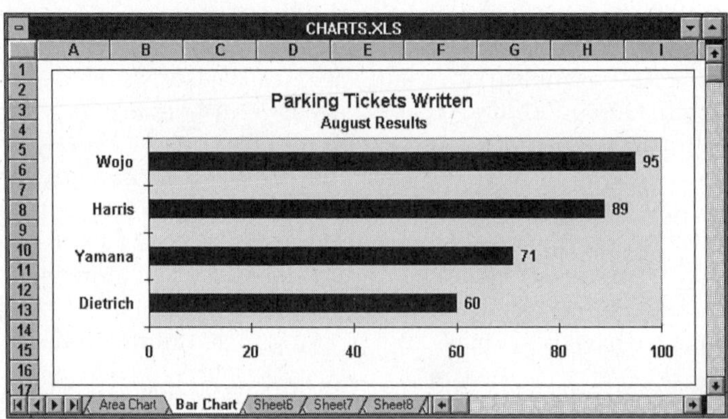

FIGURE 20.4.
Bar charts are useful for competitive comparisons.

SUPER TIP

Arrange bar charts with the longest bar on top and the others in descending order beneath it. This ensures that the chart looks "full," and it also emphasizes the competitive nature of this chart type.

Working with 2-D Column Charts

Like bar charts, *column charts* compare distinct items or show single items at distinct intervals. However, a column chart is laid out with categories along the *horizontal* axis and values along the *vertical* axis (as are most Excel charts). This format is best suited for comparing items over time. For example, Figure 20.5 uses a column chart to show another view of the mortgage principal and interest comparison. In this case, it's easier to see the individual amounts for principal and interest and how they change over time.

SUPER TIP

Try to keep the number of series in a column chart to a minimum. Having too many series causes the columns to become too narrow, making the chart confusing and difficult to read.

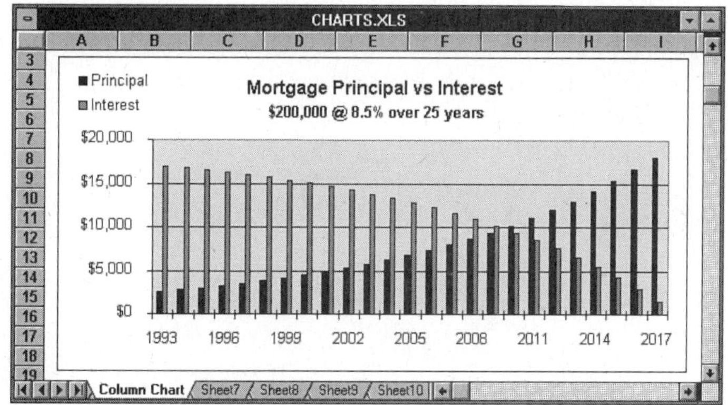

FIGURE 20.5.
A column chart that shows the comparison of mortgage principal and interest.

To select a column chart, display the AutoFormat dialog box, choose the Column item from the **G**alleries list, and select a column chart from the **F**ormats section.

Excel offers a number of different column chart formats, including *stacked* columns. A *stacked column chart* is similar to an area chart; series values are stacked on top of each other to show the relative contributions of each series. While an area chart is useful for showing the flow of the relative contributions over time, a stacked column chart is better for showing the contributions at discrete intervals. Figure 20.6 shows the mortgage principal and interest comparison as a stacked column chart.

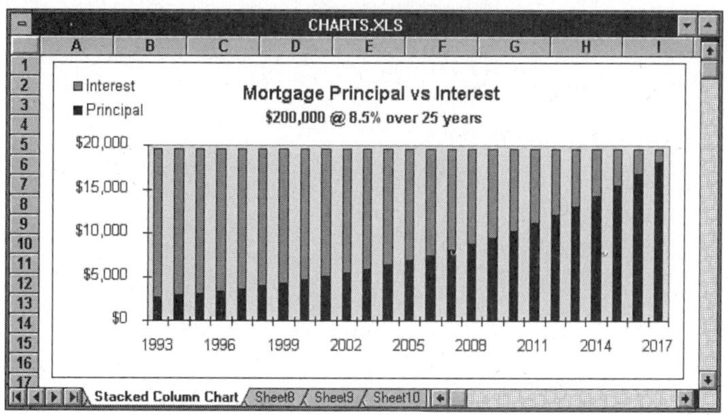

FIGURE 20.6.
The mortgage principal and interest comparison as a stacked column chart.

Working with 2-D Line Charts

Line charts show how a data series changes over time. The category (X) axis usually represents a progression of even increments (such as days or months), and the series points are plotted on the value (Y) axis. Figure 20.7 shows a simple line chart that displays a month of daily closing figures for a company's stock price. Use line charts when you're more concerned with the *trend* of a data series than with the actual quantities. For items such as interest rates, inflation, and profits, often it's just as important to know the *direction* of the data as it is to know the specific numbers.

To select a line chart, display the AutoFormat dialog box, choose the Line item from the **G**alleries list, and select a line chart from the **F**ormats section.

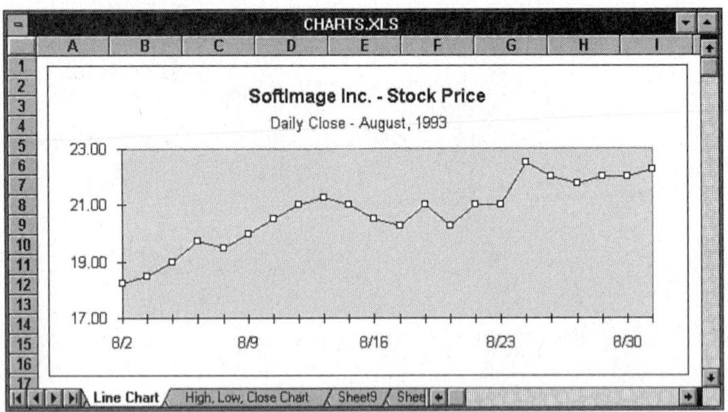

FIGURE 20.7. *A line chart showing daily closes for a company's stock price.*

Excel offers several line chart formats, including a *High, Low, Close chart,* which is useful for plotting stock market prices. Make sure your data is in High, Low, Close order, then select the format shown in Figure 20.8 from the collection of line chart formats in the AutoFormat dialog box.

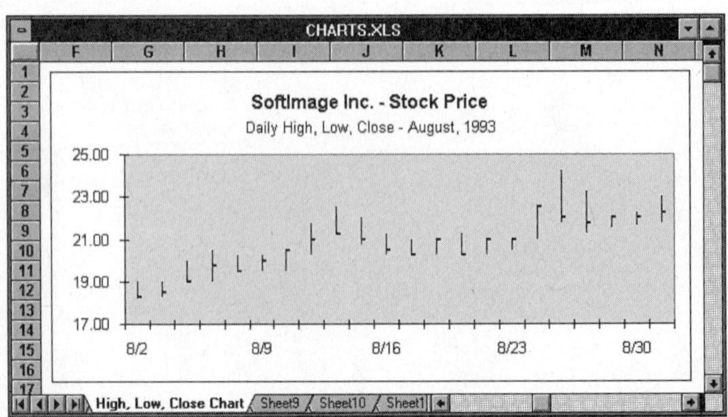

FIGURE 20.8. *A company's stock price plotted as a High, Low, Close chart.*

Working with 2-D Pie Charts

A *pie chart* shows the proportion of the whole that is contributed by each value in a single data series. The whole is represented as a circle (the "pie"), and each value is displayed as a proportional "slice" of the circle. Figure 20.9 shows a pie chart that plots the relative proportions of the Earth's most common elements. You can use pie charts to represent sales figures proportionally by region or by product, or to show population data such as age ranges or voting patterns.

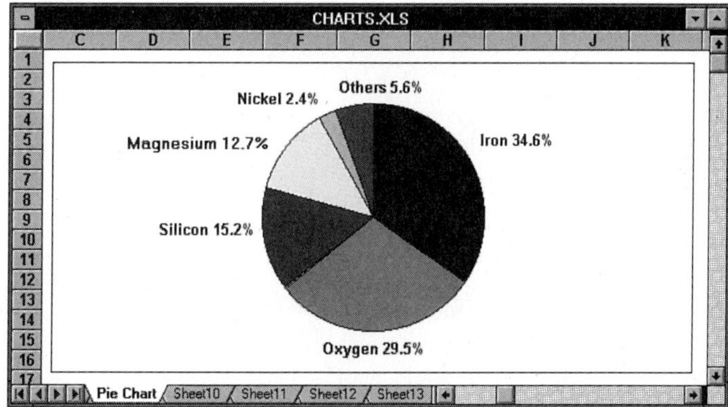

FIGURE 20.9.
Pie chart showing the proportions of terrestrial elements.

To select a pie chart, display the AutoFormat dialog box, choose the Pie item from the **G**alleries list, and select a pie chart from the **F**ormats section.

SUPER TIP

For best effect, try to keep the number of pie slices to a minimum. Using too many slices makes each one hard to read and lessens the impact of this type of chart.

Working with Radar Charts

Radar charts make comparisons within a data series and between data series relative to a center point. Each category is shown with a value axis extending from the center point. To understand this concept, think of a radar screen in an airport control tower. The tower itself is the central point, and the radar radiates a beam (a value axis). When the radar makes contact with a plane, a blip appears on the screen. In a radar chart, this is a data point that is shown with a data marker.

One common use for a radar chart is to make comparisons between products. For example, suppose you want to buy a new notebook computer. You decide to base your decision on six categories: price, weight, battery life, screen quality, keyboard quality, and service. To get a consistent scale, you rank each machine from 1 to 10 for each category. When you graph this data on a radar chart, the computer that covers the most area is the better computer. Figure 20.10 shows an example of this kind of analysis. In this case, Notebook "A" is a slightly better choice.

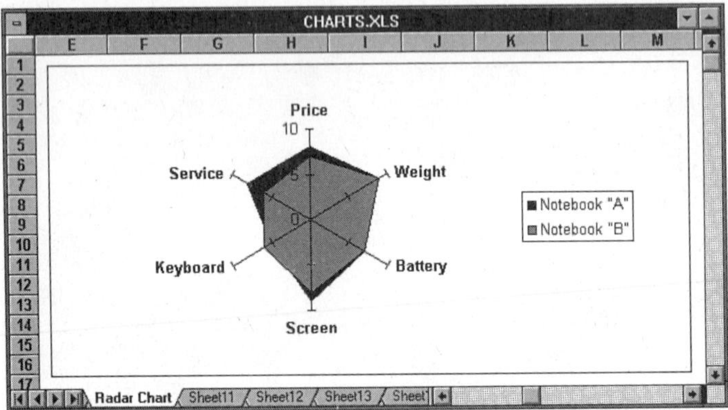

FIGURE 20.10. *Using a radar chart to compare products.*

To select a radar chart, display the AutoFormat dialog box, choose the Radar item from the **G**alleries list, and select a radar chart from the **F**ormats section.

Working with XY (Scatter) Charts

An *XY chart* (also called a *scatter chart*) shows the relationship between numeric values in two different data series. It also can plot a series of data pairs in XY coordinates. An XY chart is a variation of the line chart in which the category axis is replaced by a second value axis. Figure 20.11 shows a plot of the equation Y = SIN(X). You can use XY charts for plotting items such as survey data, mathematical functions, and experimental results.

To select an XY chart, display the AutoFormat dialog box, choose the XY (Scatter) item from the **G**alleries list, and select an XY chart from the **F**ormats section.

SUPER NOTE

In Figure 20.11, the X axis values are called the *independent variables* because you can control the series values. The result—SIN(X)—is called the *dependent variable* because you can't control these values. Excel always plots the independent variable on the X axis and the dependent variable on the Y axis.

FIGURE 20.11.
An XY chart of the `SIN()` *function.*

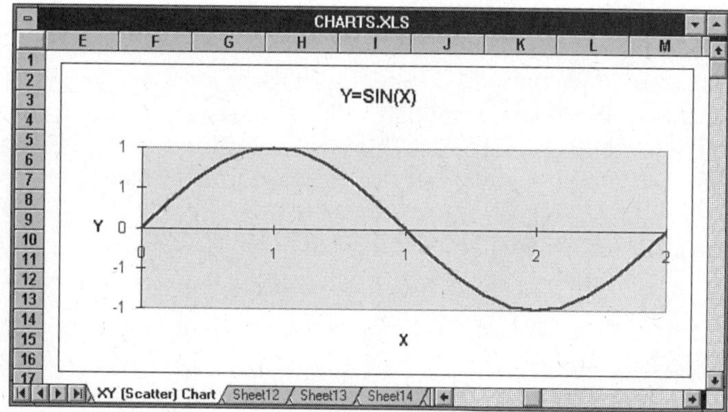

Working with Doughnut Charts

A *doughnut chart*, like a pie chart, shows the proportion of the whole that is contributed by each value in a data series. The advantage of a doughnut chart, however, is that you can plot multiple data series. (A pie chart can handle only a single series.)

Figure 20.12 shows a doughnut chart that plots the percentage of total revenues contributed by each of three products. Notice how the chart plots two data series—one for 1992 and another for 1993.

FIGURE 20.12.
A doughnut chart that shows yearly revenue by product.

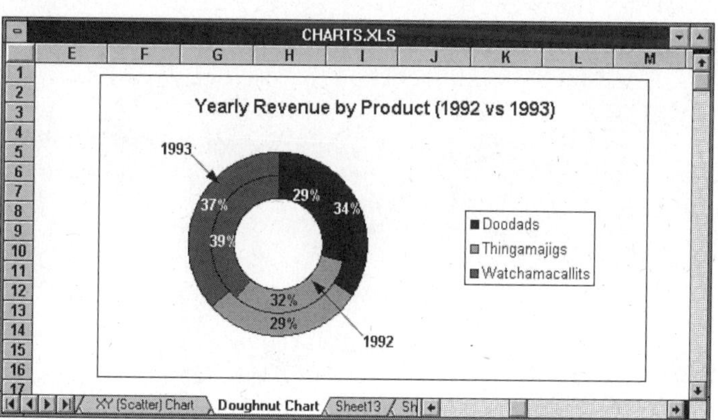

To select a doughnut chart, display the AutoFormat dialog box, choose the Doughnut item from the **G**alleries list, and select a doughnut chart from the **F**ormats section.

Setting the Default Chart Type

Many people use the same type of chart regularly. For example, stockbrokers use High, Low, Close line charts, scientists use XY charts, and so on. If you prefer a specific chart type, you can tell Excel to use this type or format as the *default* for any new charts you create with the Default Chart tool. Procedure 20.4 lists the steps to follow.

PROCEDURE 20.4. SETTING THE DEFAULT CHART TYPE.

1. Create a chart (or activate an existing chart) with the type you prefer.
2. Select the **T**ools | **O**ptions command, then select the Chart tab in the Options dialog box.
3. Click on the **U**se the Current Chart button. Excel displays the Add Custom AutoFormat dialog box, shown in Figure 20.13.

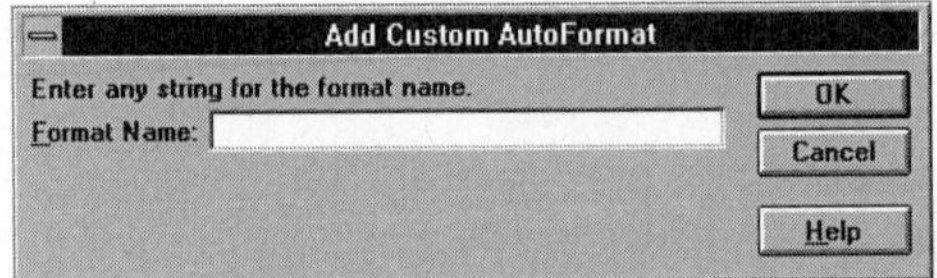

FIGURE 20.13.
Use this dialog box to enter a name for your new default format.

4. Use the **F**ormat Name edit box to enter a name for the new default format.
5. Click on OK or press Enter. Excel returns to the Options dialog box and adds the new name to the **D**efault Chart Format list.

SUPER NOTE

The new default format appears in the AutoFormat dialog box when you select the **U**ser-Defined option. By selecting this default format, you can apply it to any active chart.

Chapter 21

Enhancing Charts

After you've created a chart and selected the appropriate chart type, you can enhance the chart's appearance by formatting any of the various chart elements. This chapter shows you how to format chart axes, data markers, and gridlines, as well as how to move and size an embedded chart.

Selecting Chart Elements

An Excel chart is composed of elements such as axes, data markers, gridlines, and text, each with its own formatting options. Before you can format an element, however, you need to select it. Table 21.1 lists the mouse techniques for selecting various chart items. (Note that the chart must be activated before you try these techniques. See Chapter 20, "Working with Chart Types," to learn how to activate a chart.)

Table 21.1. Mouse techniques for selecting chart elements.

Action	*Result*
Click on the chart background	The entire chart is selected
Click on an empty part of the plot area	The plot area is selected
Click on an axis or an axis label	The axis is selected
Click on a gridline	The gridline is selected
Click on any marker in the series	The data series is selected
Click on a data marker while pressing the Ctrl key	The data marker is selected
Click on an object	The chart object is selected

If you don't have a mouse, or if you prefer to use the keyboard, you can navigate the chart elements using the arrow keys. To make navigating the chart easier, Excel groups related chart elements. For example, each data series is a group of individual data markers. The following is a list of the groups in a chart in their normal selection order:

Chart
Plot area
3-D floor
3-D walls
3-D corners
Legend
Axes
Titles
Gridlines
Data series
Other chart elements (such as hi-lo lines, trendlines, and error bars)
Other graphic objects (such as text and arrows)

SUPER NOTE

Excel provides no way to activate an embedded chart using the keyboard. To navigate an embedded chart using the keyboard, you must first activate the chart using the mouse.

You use the arrow keys to move between or within categories, as outlined in Table 21.2.

Table 21.2. Keyboard techniques for selecting chart elements.

Key to Press	*Result*
Up arrow	Selects the first element in the next chart group.
Down arrow	Selects the last element in the previous group.
Right arrow	Selects the next element in the current group. If the last element in the current group is selected, pressing the right arrow key selects the first element in the next group.
Left arrow	Selects the previous element in the current group. If the first element in the current group is selected, pressing the left arrow key selects the last element in the previous group.

When you select a chart element, Excel displays the name of the element in the Name box of the formula bar, and it attaches *selection handles* to the element. Figure 21.1 shows a chart with the plot area selected.

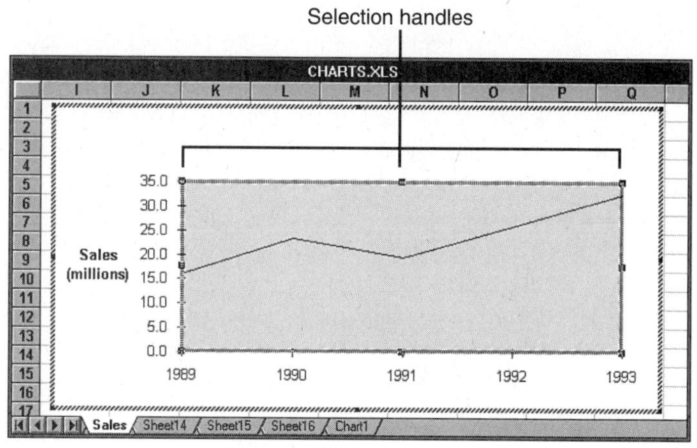

FIGURE 21.1.
Excel surrounds selected chart elements with selection handles.

Formatting Chart Axes

Excel gives you a number of options for controlling the appearance of your chart axes. You can hide axes; set the typeface, size, and style of axis labels; format the axis lines and tick marks; and adjust the axis scale. You'll find most of the axis formatting options in the Format Axis dialog box, shown in Figure 21.2. Procedure 21.1 shows you how to display this dialog box.

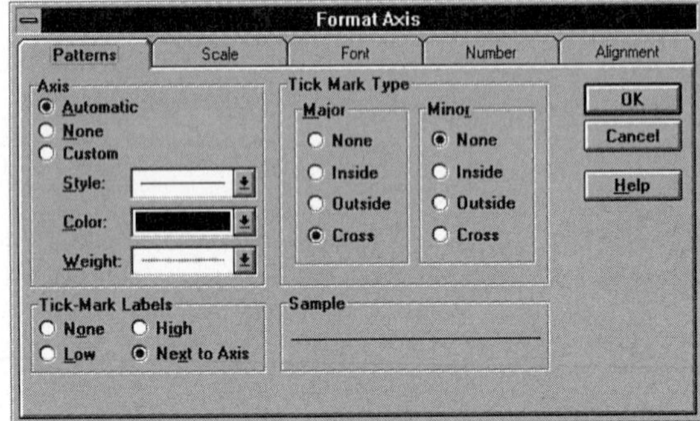

FIGURE 21.2.
The Format Axis dialog box.

PROCEDURE 21.1. DISPLAYING THE FORMAT AXIS DIALOG BOX.

1. Select the axis you want to format.
2. Select the Format | Selected Axis command. Excel displays the Format Axis dialog box.

> **SUPER TIP**
>
> To access the Format Axis dialog box quickly, you can either double-click on an axis or select the axis and press Ctrl+1.

Formatting Axis Patterns

The Patterns tab in the Format Axis dialog box enables you to set various options for the axis line and tick marks. Here's a summary of the control groups in the Patterns tab:

Axis	These options format the axis line. Select **N**one to remove the line and select Custom to adjust the **S**tyle, **C**olor, and **W**eight. The Sample box shows you how the line will look.
Tick Mark Type	These options control the position of the **M**ajor and Mino**r** tick marks.
Tick-Mark Labels	These options control the position of the tick mark labels.

Formatting an Axis Scale

You can format the scale of your chart axes to set things such as the range of numbers on an axis and where the category and value axes intersect.

To format the scale, select the Scale tab in the Format Axis dialog box. If you're formatting the value (Y) axis, you'll see the layout shown in Figure 21.3. These options format a number of scale characteristics, such as the range of values (Minimum and Maximum), the tick mark units (Major Unit and Minor Unit), and where the category (X) axis crosses the value axis (Category (X) Axis Crosses at Maximum Value).

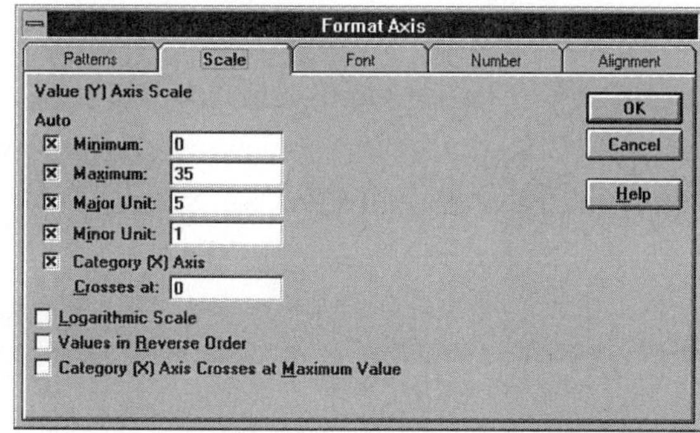

FIGURE 21.3.
The Scale tab for the value (Y) axis.

Formatting the value axis scale properly can make a big difference in the impact of your charts. For example, Figure 21.4 shows a chart with a value axis scale ranging from 0 to 50. Figure 21.5 shows the same chart with the value axis scale between 18 and 23. As you can see, the trend of the data is much clearer and more dramatic in Figure 21.5.

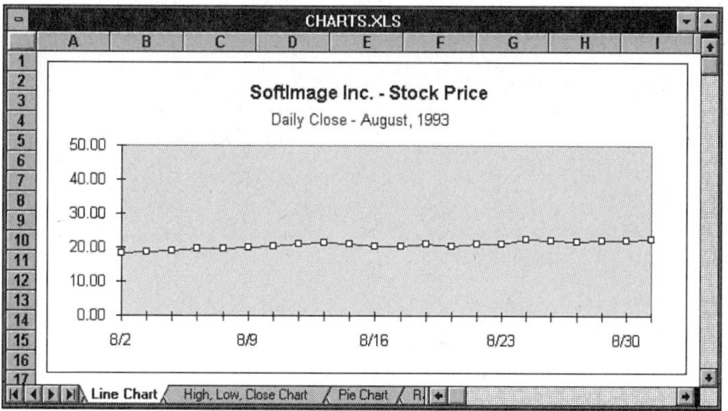

FIGURE 21.4.
A stock chart showing an apparently flat trend.

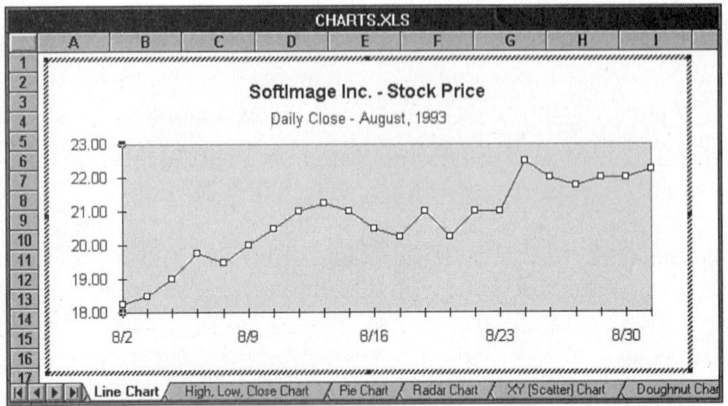

FIGURE 21.5.
The same stock chart with an adjusted scale shows an obvious up trend.

For the category (X) axis, the Scale tab appears as shown in Figure 21.6. These options mostly control where the value (Y) axis crosses the category (X) axis, and the frequency of categories.

Format Axis
Patterns | Scale | Font | Number | Alignment
Category (X) Axis Scale
Value (Y) Axis Crosses at Category Number: 1
Number of Categories between Tick-Mark Labels: 5
Number of Categories between Tick Marks: 1
Value (Y) Axis Crosses between Categories
Categories in Reverse Order
Value (Y) Axis Crosses at Maximum Category
OK
Cancel
Help

FIGURE 21.6.
The Scale tab for the category (X) axis.

Formatting Axis Labels

You can change the font, numeric format, and alignment of axis labels. To change the label font, select the Font tab in the Format Axis dialog box, then select the font options you want.

To change the numeric format of axis labels (where appropriate), you have two choices:

- Format the worksheet data series that generated the labels. Excel uses this formatting automatically.
- Select the Number tab in the Format Axis dialog box, then select a numeric format from the options provided.

To format the alignment of the axis labels, select the Alignment tab in the Format Axis dialog box, then select the option you want from the Orientation group.

SUPER TIP

You also can use the tools on the Formatting toolbar (such as Bold and Currency Style) to format the labels of a selected axis.

Hiding and Displaying Axes

If you like, you can hide a chart axis. This is useful when you add custom category or value labels to your chart. (This topic is covered in Chapter 27, "Editing Graphic Objects.") For example, Figure 21.7 shows a line chart in which custom category labels have been added to the plot area, making the category axis unnecessary.

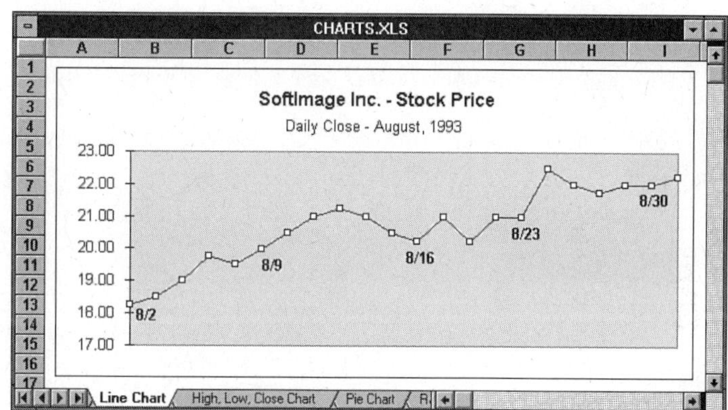

FIGURE 21.7.
Adding custom category labels often makes the category axis unnecessary.

Follow Procedure 21.2 to hide an axis.

PROCEDURE 21.2. HIDING A CHART AXIS.

1. Select the Insert | Axes command. The Axes dialog box appears.

SUPER TIP

To open the Axes dialog box quickly, right-click on an axis, then choose Insert Axes from the shortcut menu.

2. Deactivate the check box for the axis you want to hide.
3. Click on OK or press Enter. Excel hides both the axis and the axis labels from the chart.

Formatting Chart Data Markers

A *data marker* is a symbol Excel uses to plot each number. Examples of data markers are small circles or squares for line charts, rectangles for column and bar charts, and pie slices for pie charts. Depending on the type of marker, you can format the color, pattern, marker style, or border.

To begin, select a data marker. Next, select the F**o**rmat | S**e**lected Series command to display the Format Data Series dialog box. Finally, select the Patterns tab to display the formatting options for the series markers.

> **SUPER TIP**
>
> You also can display the Format Data Series dialog box by either double-clicking on an axis or by selecting the axis and pressing Ctrl+1.

Figure 21.8 shows the Patterns tab for an area, bar, column, pie, or doughnut chart marker. Use the Border group to either turn off the border or to define the **S**tyle, **C**olor, and **W**eight of the marker border. Use the Area section to assign marker colors and patterns.

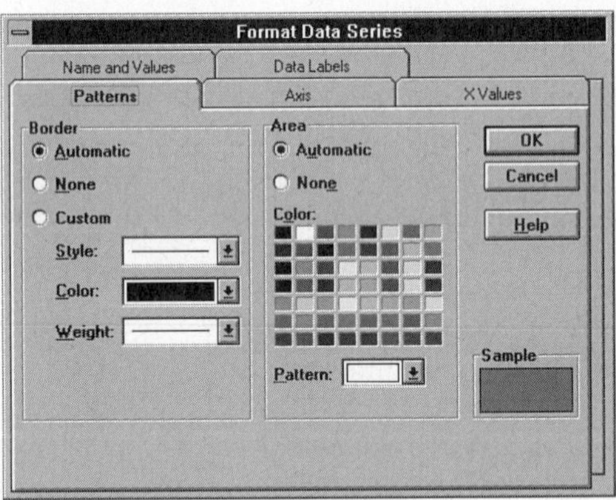

FIGURE 21.8.
The Patterns tab for area, bar, column, pie, and doughnut charts.

You get a different set of options when you format line, XY, or radar chart markers, as shown in Figure 21.9. Use the Line section to format the **S**tyle, **C**olor, and **W**eight of the data series line. The S**m**oothed Line option (available only for line and XY charts) smooths out some of the rough edges of a line. Use the Marker section to format the marker Sty**l**e as well as the **F**oreground and **B**ackground colors.

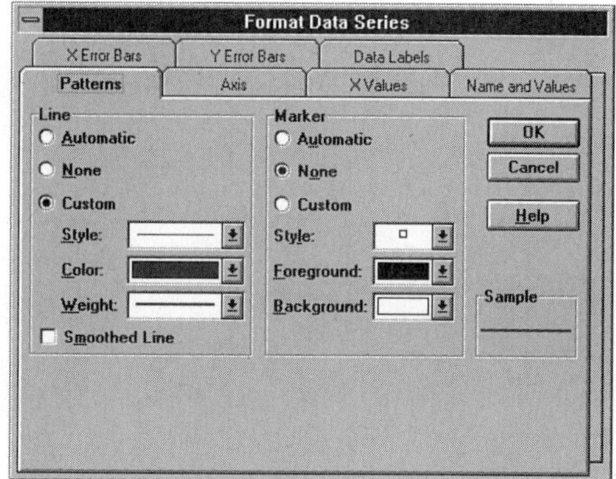

FIGURE 21.9.
The Patterns dialog box for line, XY, and radar charts.

Displaying and Formatting Chart Gridlines

Adding horizontal or vertical gridlines can make your charts easier to read. For each axis, you can display a major gridline, a minor gridline, or both. The positioning of these gridlines is determined by the numbers you enter for the axis scales. For a value axis, major gridlines are governed by the Major Unit, and minor gridlines are governed by the Minor Unit. (The Major and Minor Units are properties of the value axis scale. To learn how to adjust these values, see the section in this chapter titled "Formatting an Axis Scale.") For a category axis, major gridlines are governed by the number of categories between tick labels, and the minor gridlines are governed by the number of categories between tick marks.

Displaying Gridlines

Procedure 21.3 shows you how to display gridlines.

PROCEDURE 21.3. DISPLAYING CHART GRIDLINES.

1. Select the **Insert** | **Gridlines** command. Excel displays the Gridlines dialog box, shown in Figure 21.10.

SUPER TIP

To access the Gridlines dialog box quickly, right-click on the plot area and select Insert Gridlines from the shortcut menu.

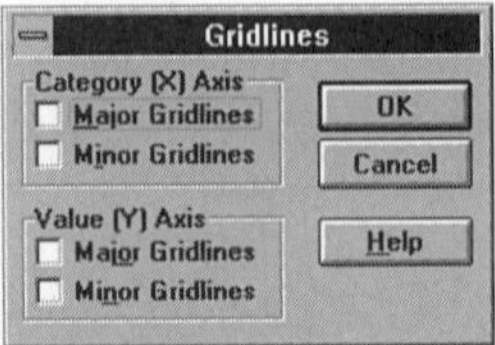

FIGURE 21.10.
The Gridlines dialog box.

2. Select the gridlines you want to display.
3. Click on OK or press Enter.

Click on this tool in the Chart toolbar to display value axis gridlines on your chart.

Formatting Gridlines

You can format the style, color, and weight of your gridlines by following the steps in Procedure 21.4.

PROCEDURE 21.4. FORMATTING CHART GRIDLINES.

1. Select a gridline.
2. Select the Format | Selected Gridlines command to display the Format Gridline dialog box.

SUPER TIP

You also can display the Format Gridline dialog box by double-clicking on a gridline or by selecting a gridline and pressing Ctrl+1.

3. Use the Patterns tab to select the gridline options you want.
4. Click on OK or press Enter.

Formatting the Plot Area and Background

You can format borders, patterns, and colors for both the chart plot area and the background. To format either of these areas, follow Procedure 21.5.

PROCEDURE 21.5. FORMATTING THE CHART PLOT AREA OR BACKGROUND.

1. Select the plot area or chart background.
2. Select either the Format | Selected Plot Area command or Format | Selected Chart Area to display the appropriate Format dialog box.

SUPER TIP

To quickly display the appropriate Format dialog box, you also can double-click on the plot area or background, or you can select either one and press Ctrl+1.

3. In the Patterns tab, select the options you want in the Border and Area groups.
4. If you're in the Format Chart Area dialog box, you also can select the Font tab to format the chart font.
5. Click on OK or press Enter.

Working with User-Defined Chart AutoFormats

Excel has so many chart formatting options that you can spend more time making your charts look good than you spend making them in the first place. To save time down the road, you can store your favorite chart formats as *user-defined AutoFormats*. This enables you to quickly apply these formats using the AutoFormat dialog box (as described in Chapter 20, "Working with Chart Types").

Adding a User-Defined AutoFormat

Procedure 21.6 shows you the steps to follow to add a user-defined AutoFormat.

PROCEDURE 21.6. ADDING A USER-DEFINED CHART AUTOFORMAT.

1. Apply the formatting options you want to save as an AutoFormat (or activate a chart that already uses the formatting).
2. Select the Format | AutoFormat command to display the AutoFormat dialog box.
3. Activate the User-Defined option.
4. Click on the Customize button. Excel displays the User-Defined AutoFormats dialog box.
5. Click on the Add button. The Add Custom AutoFormat dialog box appears, shown in Figure 21.11.
6. Use Format Name to name your AutoFormat and Description to enter a brief description (the maximum is 32 characters). When you're done, click on OK or press Enter.
7. Click on Close to return to the chart.

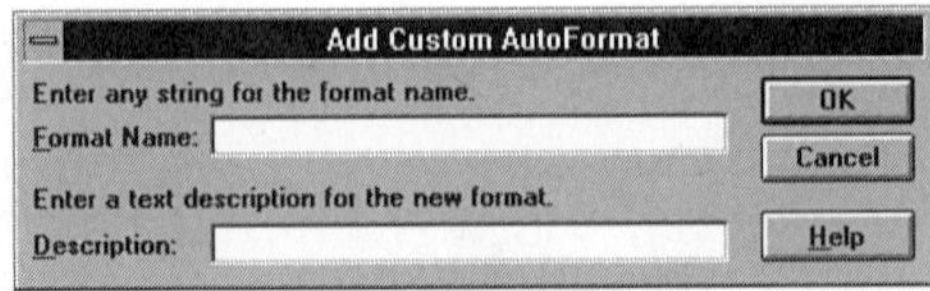

FIGURE 21.11.
Use the Add Custom AutoFormat dialog box to name and describe your AutoFormat.

Deleting a User-Defined AutoFormat

If you have some user-defined AutoFormats you no longer need, you should delete them. Procedure 21.7 shows you the necessary steps.

PROCEDURE 21.7. DELETING A USER-DEFINED CHART AUTOFORMAT.

1. Select the Format | AutoFormat command to display the AutoFormat dialog box.
2. Activate the User-Defined option.
3. Select the Customize button to display the User-Defined AutoFormats dialog box.
4. Use the Formats list to select the AutoFormat you want to delete.
5. Click on the Delete button. Excel asks you to confirm the deletion.
6. Click on OK or press Enter. Excel deletes the format.
7. Repeat steps 4-6 to delete other formats.
8. Click on Close to return to the chart.

Sizing an Embedded Chart

You can size charts embedded in a worksheet to suit your needs. As with other Excel objects, when you select an embedded chart, a number of *selection handles* appear around the chart. You size the chart by dragging these handles with the mouse pointer. Procedure 21.8 outlines the steps to follow.

PROCEDURE 21.8. SIZING AN EMBEDDED CHART.

1. Select the chart you want to size. Excel displays selection handles around the chart, as shown in Figure 21.12.
2. Position the mouse pointer over the appropriate handle to adjust the chart. The pointer changes to a two-headed arrow (see Figure 21.12).
3. Drag the handle to the position you want.
4. Release the mouse button. Excel changes the chart size.
5. Repeat steps 2-4 to adjust other sides of the chart.
6. Press the Esc key or click outside the chart.

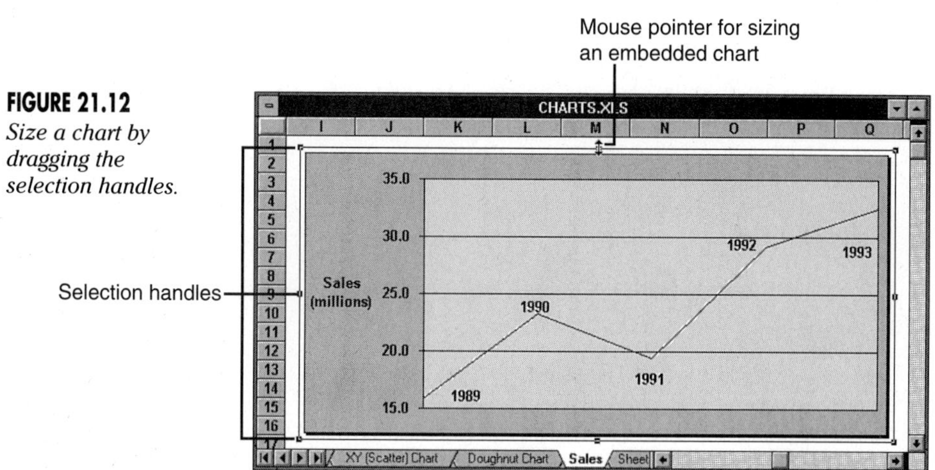

FIGURE 21.12
Size a chart by dragging the selection handles.

Moving an Embedded Chart

As your worksheets grow, you might find that embedded charts are getting in the way. You can move these charts by following the steps in Procedure 21.9.

PROCEDURE 21.9. MOVING AN EMBEDDED CHART.

1. Select the chart you want to move.
2. Position the mouse pointer inside the chart box.
3. Drag the mouse pointer to position the chart where you want it. Excel displays the new chart position with a dashed outline.
4. Release the mouse button. Excel moves the chart.

Chapter 22

Adding Objects to a Chart

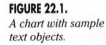

Using charts in a presentation is a great way to make a point or display important information. But even an attractively formatted chart can be difficult to interpret without some guidelines. This chapter shows you how to add text, legends, arrows, and other graphic objects to your charts to make them easier to understand.

Adding and Formatting Chart Text

One of the best ways to make your charts more readable is to attach some descriptive text to various chart elements. Excel works with three types of text: titles, data labels, and text boxes. I covered text boxes in Chapter 15, "Adding Comments with Text Boxes and Notes," so the next few sections show you how to use titles and data labels.

Adding Chart Titles

Excel enables you to add titles to the overall chart and to the chart axes, as shown in Figure 22.1. You have the following options:

Chart Title	Adds a title centered above the chart
Value (Y) Axis	Adds a title beside the value axis
Value (Z) Axis	Adds a title beside the value axis of a 3-D chart
Category (X) Axis	Adds a title below the category axis
Series (Y) Axis	Adds a title beside the series axis of a 3-D chart
Second Value (Y) Axis	Adds a title to a second value axis (see Chapter 25, "Combining Multiple Chart Types in a Single Chart")
Second Category (X) Axis	Adds a title to a second category axis (see Chapter 25)

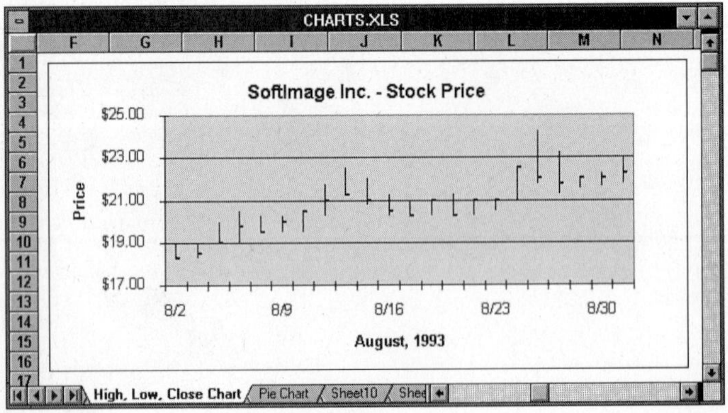

FIGURE 22.1.
A chart with sample text objects.

Follow the steps in Procedure 22.1 to add attached text to your chart. (If you're adding a label to a data point, select the appropriate data marker before beginning these steps.)

PROCEDURE 22.1. ADDING ATTACHED TEXT TO A CHART.

1. Select the **I**nsert | **T**itles command. Excel displays the Titles dialog box. Figure 22.2 shows the Titles dialog box for a 2-D chart.

FIGURE 22.2.
The Titles dialog box.

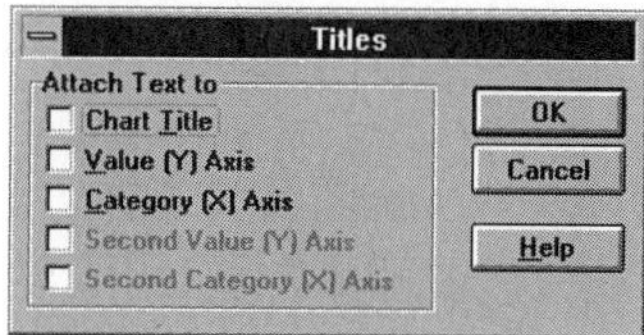

2. Select the titles you want to add to the chart.
3. Click on OK or press Enter. For each option you selected, Excel adds a temporary title to the chart.
4. Select a title box. Selection handles appear around the box.
5. Type the title you want to use and press Enter.
6. Repeat steps 4 and 5 for the other titles you added.

SUPER TIP

To start a new line when entering attached text, press Alt+Enter. To enter a tab, press Ctrl+Tab.

Adding Data Marker Labels

You can add text to individual data markers by following the steps in Procedure 22.2.

PROCEDURE 22.2. ADDING DATA MARKER LABELS.

1. Select the **I**nsert | **D**ata Labels command. Excel displays the Data Labels dialog box. The available options depend on the type of chart. Figure 22.3 shows the options for a pie chart series.
2. Select the label options you want to use.
3. Click on OK or press Enter.

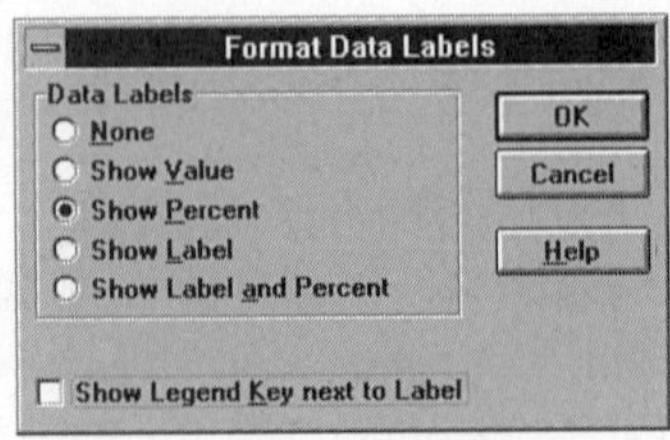

FIGURE 22.3.
The Data Labels dialog box for a pie chart data series.

Moving and Sizing Text

You can move and size chart text to suit your needs. To move text, make sure the box is selected, then drag the box to the new location. To size text, select the box and drag the appropriate selection handles to the dimensions you want.

Formatting Chart Text

You can format chart text to highlight the text or to make your chart conform to your presentation style. Procedure 22.3 shows you how it's done.

PROCEDURE 22.3. FORMATTING CHART TEXT.

1. Select the text box you want to format.
2. Select the F**o**rmat | S**e**lected [*ChartText*] command. *ChartText* is the type of text you selected (chart title, data label, and so on).
3. Select the Patterns tab to format the box Border and the Area colors and patterns.
4. Select the Font tab to format the text box's font.
5. Select the Alignment tab to format the Text Alignment and Orie**n**tation.
6. Click on OK or press Enter.

Using Worksheet Text in a Chart

You can add text to a chart by linking a text object to a cell in a worksheet. For example, you can link the title you use in a chart to the title of the underlying worksheet. That way, if you change the worksheet title, Excel updates the chart automatically. Procedure 22.4 shows you how to link chart text to a worksheet.

PROCEDURE 22.4. LINKING CHART TEXT TO A WORKSHEET CELL.

1. Select the chart text object that you want to link.
2. Type = (an equals sign) to let Excel know that you want to enter a formula.
3. Activate the worksheet and select the cell containing the text you want.

4. Select the Enter box or press Enter to confirm the formula. Excel adds the cell text to the chart edit box. The newly selected text replaces the text that had been in the chart edit box.

The reference that Excel uses for chart text has the form *worksheet!address*. *worksheet* is the worksheet tab name and *address* is the absolute cell address of the worksheet cell. For example, Figure 22.4 shows a chart title linked to a worksheet cell. The formula reference is 'High, Low, Close Chart'!$F$1.

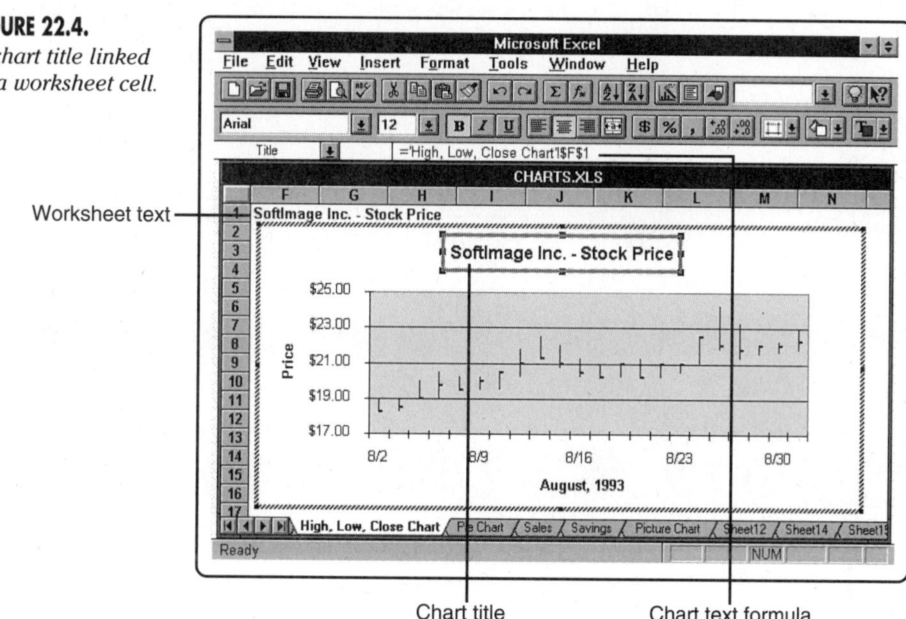

FIGURE 22.4.
A chart title linked to a worksheet cell.

Adding and Formatting a Chart Legend

If your chart includes multiple data series, you should add a legend to explain the series markers. This makes your chart more readable and makes it easier for others to distinguish each series.

To add a legend to a chart, simply select the **I**nsert | **L**egend command. Excel creates the legend automatically from the worksheet data. To delete a legend, select it and press the Delete key.

Click on this tool in the Chart toolbar to add a legend to a chart. Click on the tool again to delete the legend.

You can format your legends with the same options you used to format chart text. Select the legend, then select the F**o**rmat | S**e**lected Legend command to display the Format Legend dialog box. You can then use the Patterns and Font tabs to format the legend. You also can use the options in the Placement tab to change the position of the legend. (Alternatively, you can drag the legend to a different location.) Figure 22.5 shows a chart with a formatted legend.

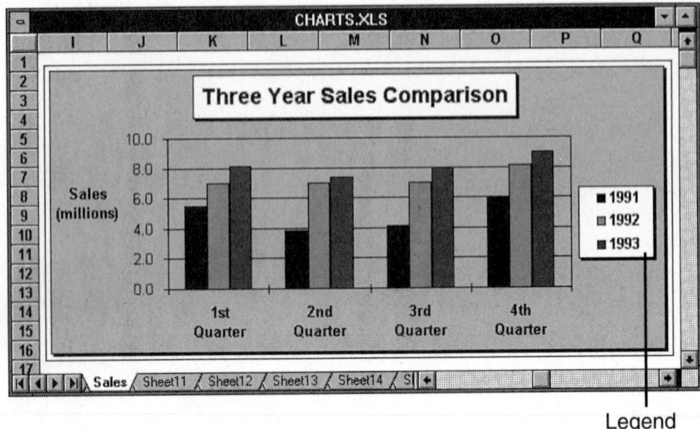

FIGURE 22.5.
A chart with a formatted legend.

Adding and Formatting Chart Arrows

Even though you'll often use chart text for general remarks, it's common to use text to point out a significant result or a specific piece of data that needs explanation. When you do this, you attach an arrow to the text that points at the appropriate data (see Figure 22.6).

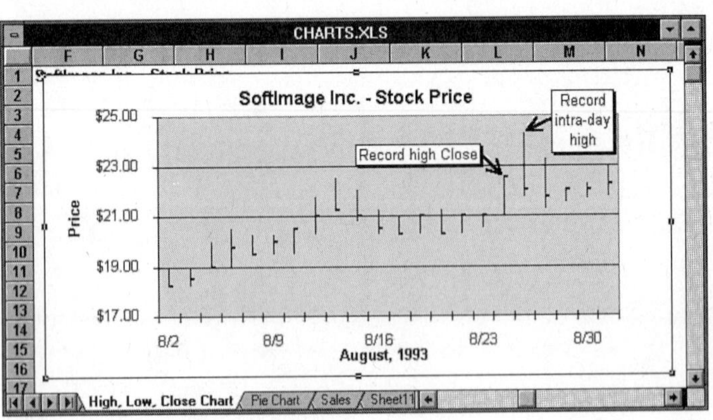

FIGURE 22.6.
Use arrows to point out significant results.

Follow the steps in Procedure 22.5 to add an arrow to a chart.

PROCEDURE 22.5. ADDING AN ARROW TO A CHART.

1. Display the Drawing toolbar and click on the Arrow tool.

Click on the Drawing Tool in the Standard toolbar to display the Drawing toolbar.

The Arrow tool from the Drawing toolbar.

2. Position the mouse pointer where you want the arrow to start.
3. Drag the pointer until the arrow has the length and direction you want, then release the button.

To move an arrow, position the mouse pointer on the shaft of the arrow and drag the arrow to the new position.

You can format an arrow by selecting it, executing the Format | Selected Object command, then using the Patterns tab in the Format Object dialog box.

Creating Picture Charts

For a different twist to your column, line, or radar charts, you can replace the regular data markers with graphic images imported from programs such as Windows Paintbrush or CorelDRAW!. Procedure 22.6 outlines the steps to follow.

PROCEDURE 22.6. CREATING A PICTURE CHART.

1. Copy the image you want from your graphics program to the Windows Clipboard.
2. In Excel, select the data series or data marker in which you want to use the picture.
3. Select the Edit | Paste command. Excel pastes the picture into the chart.

When you first paste the picture into the chart, Excel stretches the image according the number the marker represents. If you prefer, you can have Excel use stacks of the image to represent the number. Figure 22.7 shows an example of a stacked picture chart.

To change to a stacked picture, select the data series and then select the Format | Selected Series command to display the Format Data Series dialog box. Select the Patterns tab, then activate the Stack option to stack the images. To adjust the scale that Excel uses, select Stack and Scale and enter a number in the Units/Picture edit box.

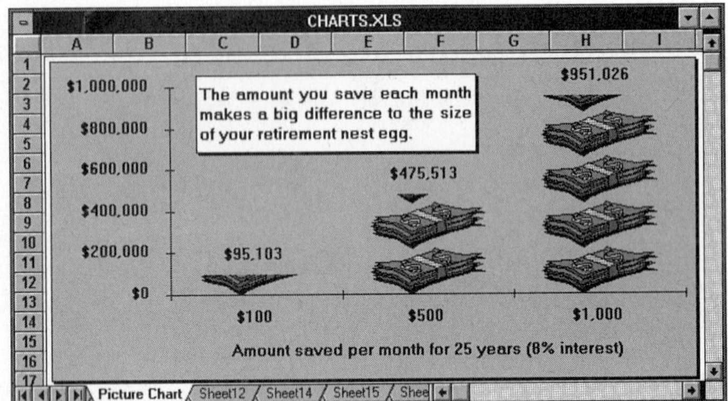

FIGURE 22.7.
A stacked picture chart.

Chapter

23

Data Series Editing

A chart is only as useful as the worksheet information on which it's based. If the chart data is out of date or erroneous, the chart itself will be of little use and might even be misleading. Excel makes it easy to update your charts whenever you add or edit worksheet data.

This chapter shows you the ins and outs of the series formulas used by Excel charts. It also shows you how to use these formulas to edit your chart data series and even add new data series.

Changing Data Series Values

The easiest way to update a chart is simply to edit the individual data series numbers in the associated worksheet. Because Excel maintains a link between the worksheet and the chart, the chart is adjusted automatically. This provides you with an extra "what-if" analysis tool. By arranging your worksheet and chart so that you can see both windows, you can plug numbers into the worksheet and watch the results on the chart.

> **SUPER NOTE**
>
> See Chapter 35, "Basic Analytic Methods," for more information on using Excel for what-if analysis.

For example, Figure 23.1 shows a worksheet that computes the future value of regular deposits to a retirement account. The accompanying chart shows the cumulative savings over time. (The numbers shown in the chart for 15, 20, and 25 years are linked to the appropriate cells. See Chapter 22, "Adding Objects to a Chart," for information on linking chart text and worksheet cells.) By plugging in different numbers for the interest rate, annual deposit, or deposit type, you can watch the effect on the total savings. Figure 23.2 shows the result when you change the annual deposit from $5,000 to $10,000.

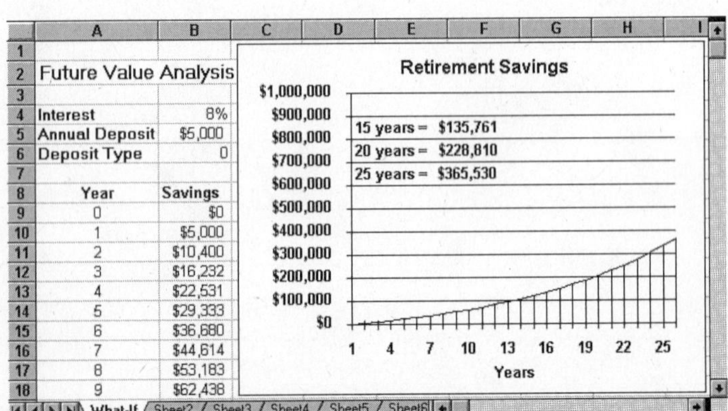

FIGURE 23.1.
Chart values are linked to the corresponding cells on the worksheet.

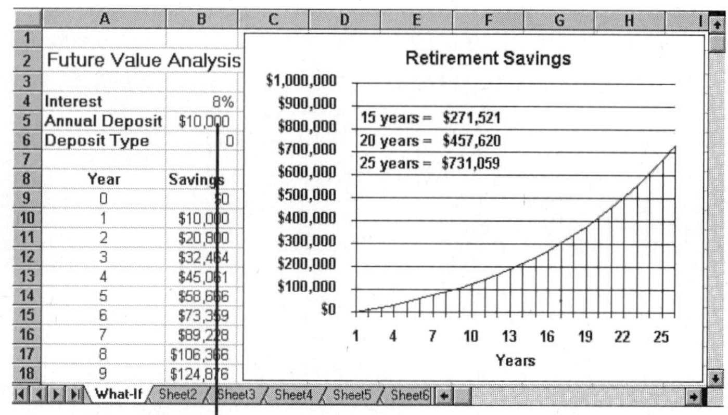

FIGURE 23.2.
When you change a variable in the worksheet, Excel updates the chart automatically.

Editing numbers in a worksheet and watching a linked chart update automatically is relatively straightforward. However, because the link extends both ways, it's possible to turn this process around. When you make changes to a chart data point, Excel updates the worksheet automatically. You can do this with 2-D bar, column, line, and XY charts by using the mouse to drag a data marker to a new position. If the data marker represents a worksheet value, Excel adjusts the contents of the corresponding cell. If the data marker represents a formula, Excel uses the Goal Seek tool to work backward and derive the appropriate formula input values.

SUPER NOTE

For an in-depth treatment of Goal Seek, see Chapter 37, "Working with Goal Seek."

An example helps explain this process. Suppose your goal is to retire in 25 years with $1,000,000 in savings. Assuming a constant interest rate, how much do you need to set aside annually to reach your goal? The idea is to adjust the chart data marker at 25 years so that it is $1,000,000. Procedure 23.1 lists the steps to follow to do this.

PROCEDURE 23.1. MOVING DATA MARKERS TO CHANGE WORKSHEET VALUES.

1. Activate the chart and select the specific data marker you want to adjust by first selecting the series and then selecting the marker. Excel adds selection handles to the marker. For example, select the data marker on the category axis that corresponds to 25 years.
2. Drag the black selection handle to the desired value. As you drag the handle, the current value appears in the formula bar's Name box. See the line chart in Figure 23.3.

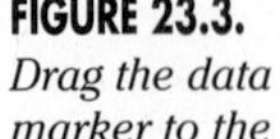

FIGURE 23.3.
Drag the data marker to the desired value.

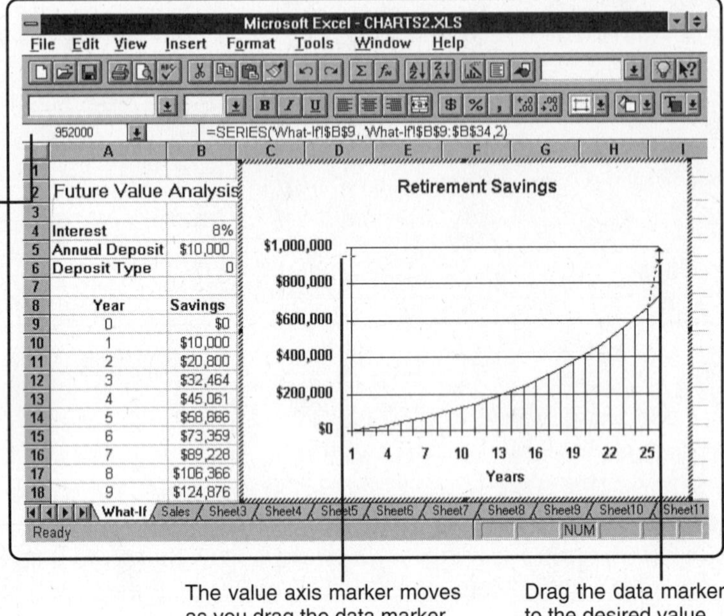

3. Release the mouse button. If the marker references a number in a cell, Excel changes the number and redraws the chart. If the marker references a formula, as in the example, Excel displays the Goal Seek dialog box, shown in Figure 23.4. The **S**et cell box shows the cell referenced by the data marker, the To **v**alue box shows the new number you selected, and the By **c**hanging cell box is the variable for the formula.

FIGURE 23.4.
If the data marker is derived from a formula, Excel runs Goal Seek.

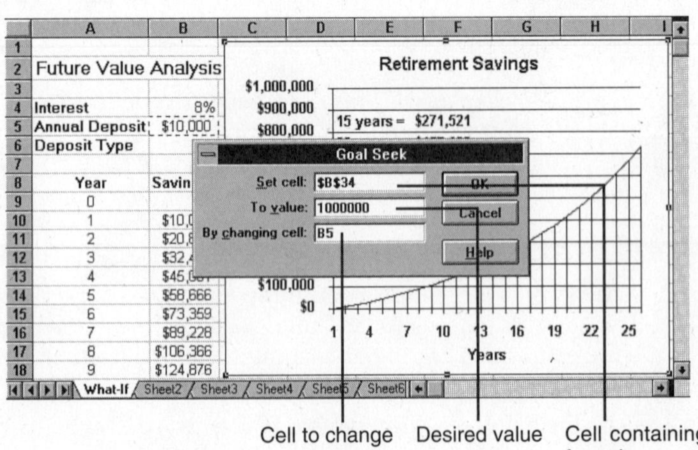

4. Enter the appropriate numbers. For the example, you would enter B5 in the By changing cell box to calculate the required annual deposit.
5. Click on OK or press Enter. Excel displays the Goal Seek Status dialog box as it solves for the new number.
6. When the iteration is complete, click on OK or press Enter.

SUPER NOTE

Use this technique to make visual adjustments to profit targets. You also can use Goal Seek to recalculate profit variables such as sales and expense budgets.

Working with Series Formulas

To understand how Excel links a worksheet and a chart, and to use the more complex series editing techniques presented in the rest of this chapter, you need to understand the *series formula*.

Whenever you create a chart, Excel sets up a series formula to define each chart data series. This formula has four parts:

Series name is the name of the series that appears in chart legends. It may be a reference to a worksheet label or a text string (in quotation marks). The general format is either `WorksheetName!CellReference` (`Sales!$A$3`, for example) or `"series name"` (`"1993 Sales"`, for example).

X axis labels appear as text on the category (X) axis (or as the X axis numbers in an XY chart). An X axis label may be a range or a range name. The general format is `WorksheetName!RangeReference` (`Sales!$B$1:$E$1`, for example).

Y axis values are plotted on the value (Y) axis. A Y axis value may be a range or a range name. The general format is `WorksheetName!RangeReference` (`Sales!$B$3:$E$3`, for example).

Plot order is an integer that represents the order in which each series is plotted on the chart.

As shown in Figure 23.5, the series formula appears in the formula bar whenever you select a chart data series.

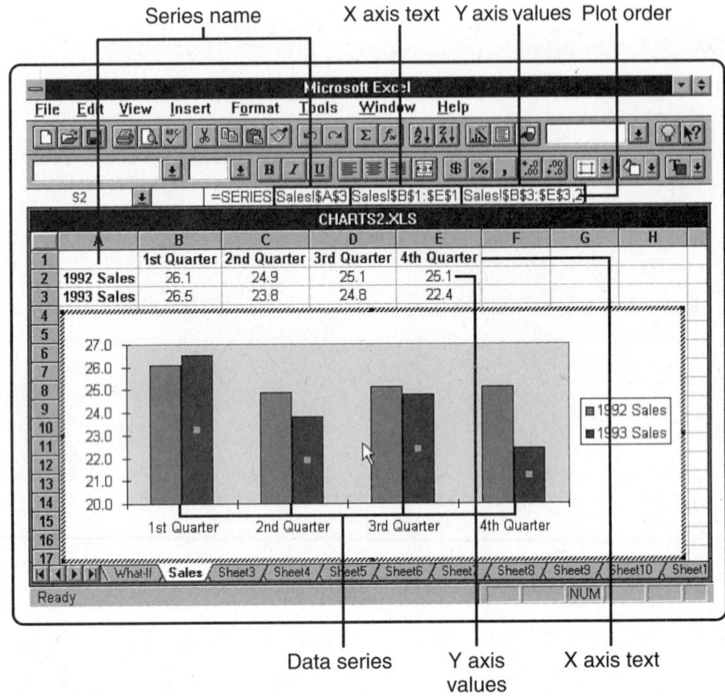

FIGURE 23.5.
When you select a data series, the series formula appears in the formula bar.

Editing a Data Series

When you make changes to an existing worksheet data series, Excel updates your charts automatically by referring to the series formula. However, if you make changes to an area of the worksheet not referenced by the series formula, Excel doesn't adjust the chart. If you extend or reduce a series on a worksheet, you have to tell Excel to extend or reduce the range in the series formula. For example, suppose a new column showing yearly totals is added to the Sales worksheet (see Figure 23.6). The formula for each series needs to be updated to include the new column.

Editing a Series Formula

Follow the steps in Procedure 23.2 to edit a series formula.

SUPER TIP

Besides following the steps outlined in Procedure 23.2, you also can edit the series formula in the formula bar. Just select the series you want to edit, activate the formula bar, and adjust the appropriate worksheet references.

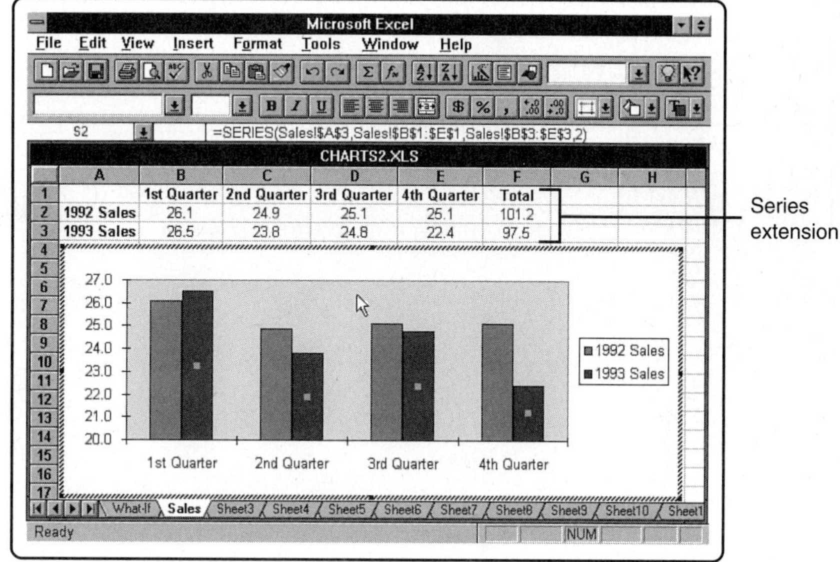

FIGURE 23.6.
When you extend a worksheet series, Excel doesn't extend the series on the chart.

PROCEDURE 23.2. EDITING A DATA SERIES.

1. Activate the chart you want to edit.
2. Select the **I**nsert | **N**ew Data command. Excel displays the New Data dialog box, shown in Figure 23.7.

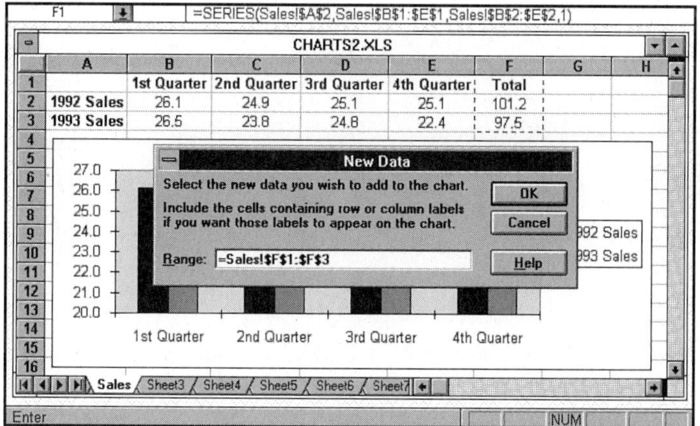

FIGURE 23.7.
Enter a reference for the new data in the New Data dialog box.

3. In the **R**ange edit box, enter a reference for the new data. You can either type the reference or select the range directly in the worksheet.
4. Click on OK or press Enter. Excel adds the data to the chart.

Figure 23.8 shows the Sales chart with the series extended.

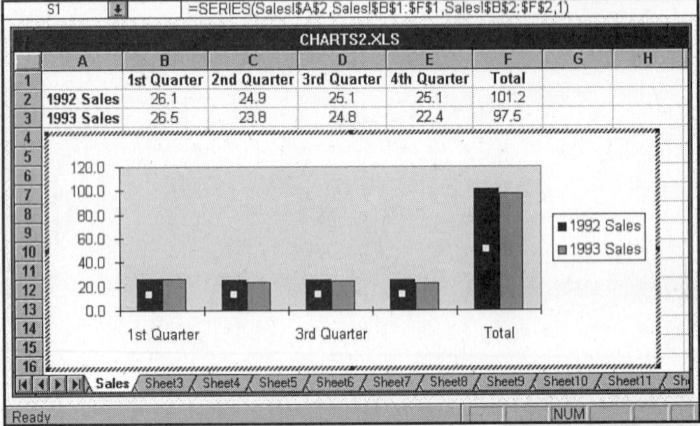

FIGURE 23.8.
The Sales chart with the extended series.

SUPER TIP

If you're extending a data series, Excel also supplies a simple drag-and-drop method for editing the series. Just select the new data, drag the range over to the chart, and release the mouse button. Excel updates the appropriate data series automatically.

Editing a Data Series with ChartWizard

If you extend or reduce a worksheet series, you can use ChartWizard to update the chart series formulas. (See Chapter 19, "Creating Charts," for details on using ChartWizard.) Procedure 23.3 outlines the steps to follow.

PROCEDURE 23.3. EDITING A DATA SERIES USING CHARTWIZARD.

1. Activate the chart you want to edit.
2. Select the ChartWizard tool from either the Chart toolbar or the Standard toolbar. Excel displays the ChartWizard - Step 1 of 2 dialog box. A moving line appears in the worksheet around the current chart range.

The ChartWizard tool.

3. In the **R**ange box, enter a new range or select the new range on the worksheet.
4. Click on Next >. Excel displays the ChartWizard - Step 2 of 2 dialog box.
5. Select any other adjustment options as needed.
6. Click on OK or press Enter.

Editing a Data Series by Copying

Another technique for editing a data series involves copying the new data points and then pasting the numbers onto the chart. Follow the steps in Procedure 23.4.

PROCEDURE 23.4. COPYING NEW DATA ONTO A CHART.

1. Activate the worksheet that contains the new data.
2. Select the range you want to copy and then select the **E**dit | **C**opy command. In this example, you would select the range F1:F3.
3. Activate the chart.
4. Select the **E**dit | Paste **S**pecial command. Excel displays the Paste Special dialog box, shown in Figure 23.9.

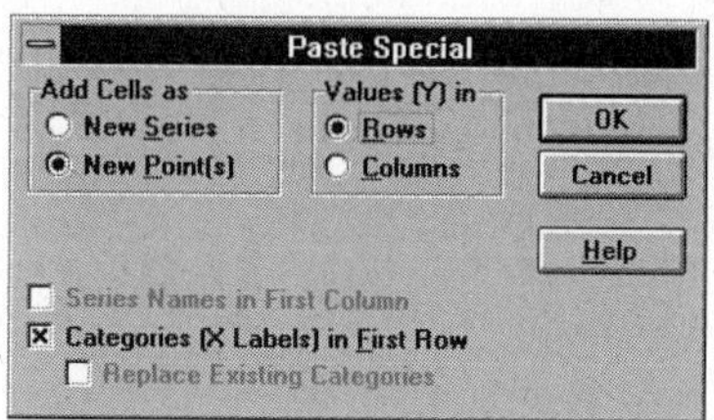

FIGURE 23.9.
The Paste Special dialog box, which appears when you paste new data onto a chart.

5. Select the appropriate options. In particular, be sure to activate the New **P**oint(s) option.
6. Click on OK or press Enter. Excel pastes the new data onto the chart.

Adding a Data Series

Besides editing existing data series, you'll often add new series to your worksheets. For example, Figure 23.10 shows the Sales worksheet with a new series added for 1994 sales. To add this series to the chart, you need to define a new series formula.

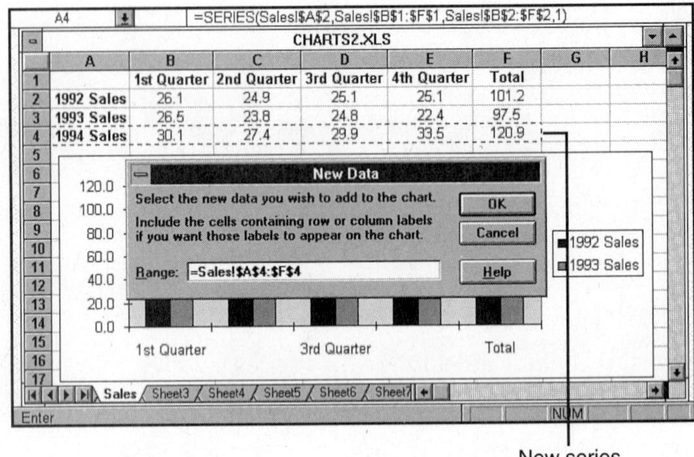

FIGURE 23.10.
To add a new data series to a chart, define a new data series formula.

To add a new series, you can follow the steps outlined in either Procedure 23.2, 23.3, (be sure to select the entire series when you enter the **R**ange reference; see Figure 23.9), or 23.4 (be sure to activate the New **S**eries option in the Paste Special dialog box).

SUPER TIP

Excel also enables you to use drag-and-drop to add a data series. Select the range that includes the data for the new series, drag the range to the chart, and release the mouse button. Excel adds the new series automatically.

Merging Charts

Another way of adding data series to a chart is to merge two similar charts. Follow the steps in Procedure 23.5 to merge charts.

SUPER NOTE

You can use this technique to combine charts from other departments for budget or sales presentations. For best results, the data in each chart should have the same layout.

PROCEDURE 23.5. MERGING TWO CHARTS.

1. Activate the chart that contains the data series you want to add.
2. Select the **E**dit | **C**opy command.
3. Activate the chart that will receive the copy.
4. Select the **E**dit | **P**aste command. Excel adds the new series to the chart.

SUPER CAUTION

When you paste the new series, Excel copies both the data series and their formats to the chart. To keep the formatting of the active chart, select the **E**dit | Paste **S**pecial command instead. In the Paste Special dialog box, activate the Fo**r**mulas option and then click on OK or press Enter.

Deleting Data Series

To delete a data series from a chart, select the series and then select the **E**dit | Cle**a**r | **S**eries command.

SUPER TIP

To delete a chart data series quickly, select it and press the Delete key.

SUPER CAUTION

After you delete a series, you can't retrieve it. As a precaution, save the chart before you perform any deletions. This way, if you accidentally delete a series, you can close the chart without saving changes and reopen it with the deleted series restored.

Chapter

24

Working with 3-D Charts

Besides the various 2-D chart types you learned about in Chapter 20, "Working with Chart Types," Excel also offers a number of 3-D charts. Because they're striking, 3-D charts are suitable for presentations, flyers, and newsletters. (If you need a chart to help with data analysis, or if you just need a quick chart to help visualize your data, you're probably better off sticking with the simpler 2-D charts.) Excel has six different 3-D chart types: area, bar, column, line, pie, and surface. You can select, format, and edit your 3-D charts using the same techniques you use with 2-D charts. This chapter introduces you to each 3-D chart type and shows you how to manipulate the depth and perspective for each chart.

Working with 3-D Area Charts

Like their 2-D counterparts, 3-D area charts show the relative contributions of each data series over time. You can use 3-D charts in presentations to show the relative contributions of items such as individual expense categories, sales regions, and production costs. Figure 24.1 shows the 3-D version of the Mortgage Principal vs. Interest chart.

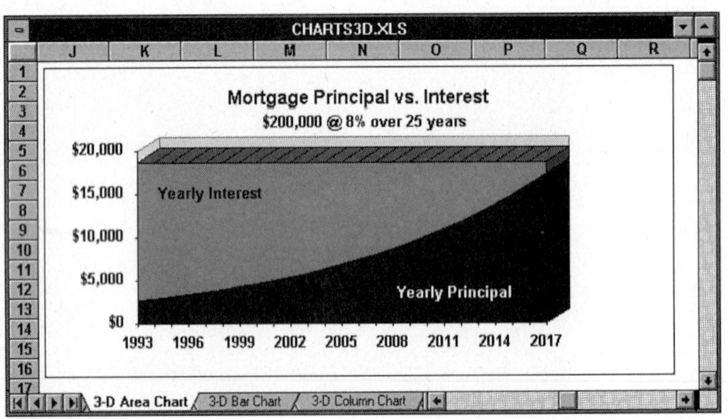

FIGURE 24.1.
3-D area chart comparing mortgage principal and interest.

Excel offers seven different 3-D area chart AutoFormats, three of which enable you to show separate area plots for each data series (something a 2-D area chart can't do). In this variation, the emphasis isn't on the relative contribution of each series to the whole; rather, it's on the relative differences among the series. Figure 24.2 shows an example.

To select a 3-D area chart, select **Format | Autoformat** to display the Autoformat dialog box, choose the 3-D Area item from the **Galleries** list, and select a 3-D area chart from the **Formats** section.

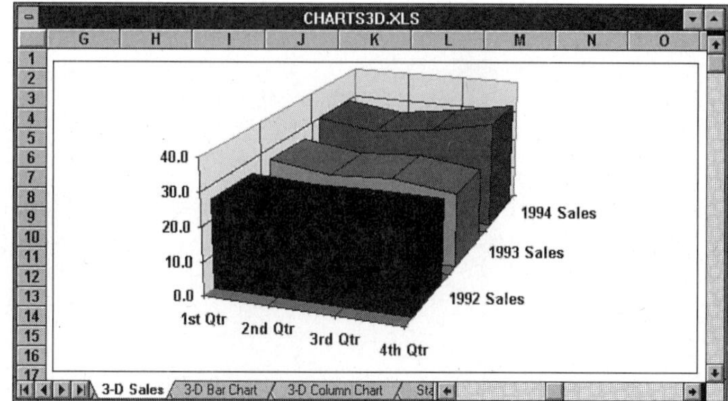

FIGURE 24.2.
A 3-D area chart showing separate series areas.

Working with 3-D Bar Charts

Like 2-D bar charts, 3-D bar charts are useful for portraying competitive comparisons. You can use 3-D bar charts to present the results of sales contests, elections, or sporting events. For example, Figure 24.3 shows a comparison of a company's sales increases by region. In this format, it's clear that the West region is the "winner" because its bar extends farthest to the right.

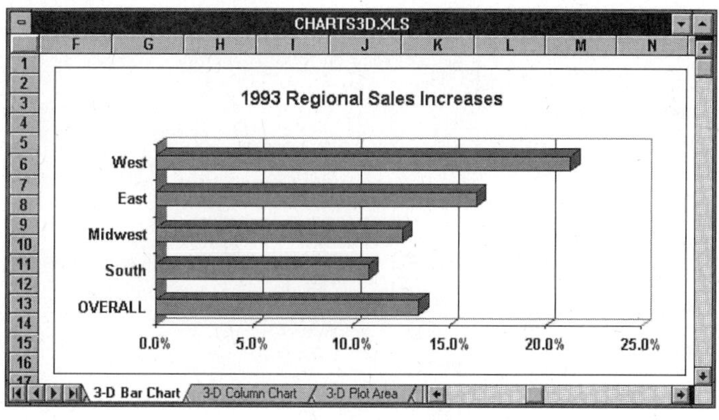

FIGURE 24.3.
Use 3-D bar charts for competitive comparisons.

To select a 3-D bar chart, select F**o**rmat | **A**utoformat to display the Autoformat dialog box, choose the 3-D Bar item from the **G**alleries list, and select a 3-D bar chart from the **F**ormats section.

Working with 3-D Column Charts

You use 3-D column charts to compare multiple, distinct data items or to show individual data items over distinct intervals. Figure 24.4 shows a basic 3-D column chart that compares quarterly sales data over three years.

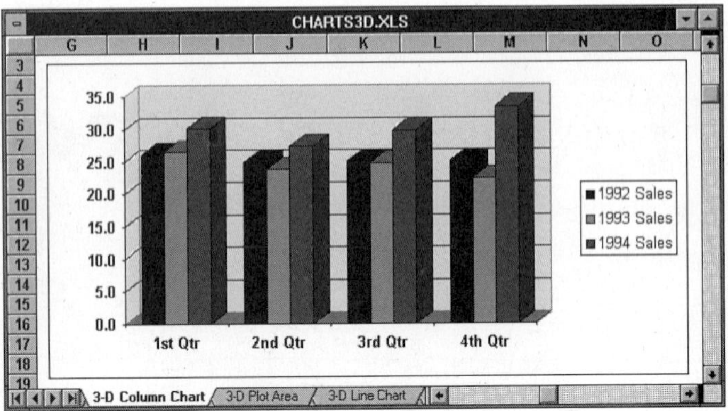

FIGURE 24.4.
3-D column charts compare multiple data series.

Excel has eight different 3-D column AutoFormats, including three that use a three-dimensional plot area. These charts have three axes: the category axis remains the X axis, a new *series axis* becomes the Y axis, and the value axis becomes the Z axis. The advantage of this design is that it enables you to compare data both within a data series and among data series in the same chart. For example, Figure 24.5 updates the sales chart to the three-axis format. To see the quarterly progression for each year (that is, each data series), read the data markers left to right *across* the graph. To compare series, read the data markers from front to back *into* the graph.

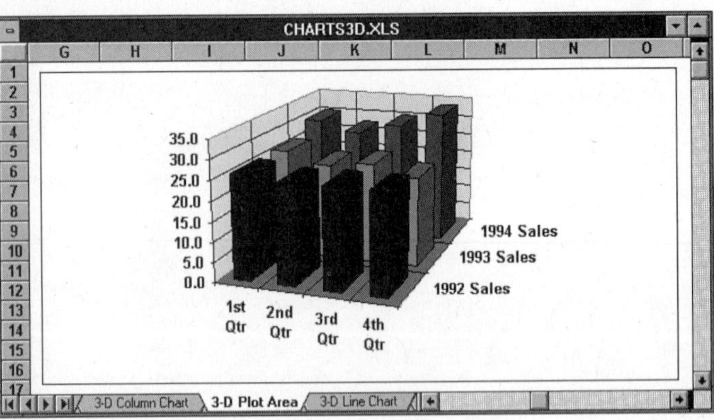

FIGURE 24.5.
An Excel column chart with a three-dimensional plot area.

To select a 3-D column chart, select **Format | Autoformat** to display the Autoformat dialog box, choose the 3-D Column item from the **Galleries** list, and select a 3-D column chart from the **Formats** section.

Working with 3-D Line Charts

3-D line charts, also called *ribbon* charts, show how data series change over time using a three-dimensional plot area that incorporates the category (X) axis, the series (Y) axis, and the value (Z) axis. The individual lines are plotted as ribbons, which makes it easier to see each line and to distinguish each series when they intersect. Use 3-D line charts to see the trends underlying stock, bond, and futures prices. Also, economic indicators such as interest rates, the money supply, and inflation are best seen with this type of chart. Figure 24.6 shows a 3-D plot of a company's stock price and its 10-day moving average.

FIGURE 24.6.
3-D line charts plot series as ribbons.

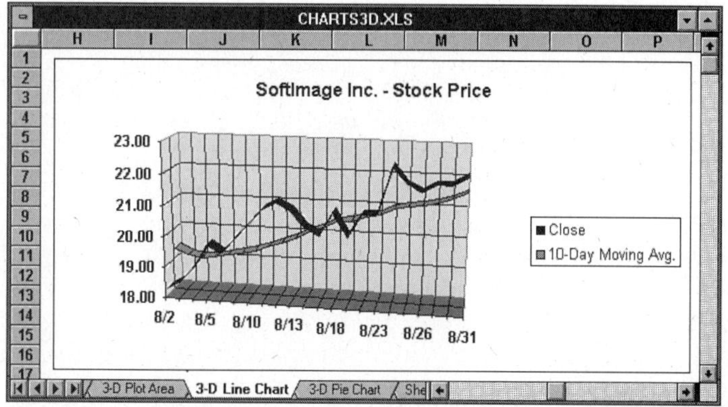

To select a 3-D line chart, select F**o**rmat | **A**utoformat to display the Autoformat dialog box, choose the 3-D Line item from the **G**alleries list, and select a 3-D line chart from the **F**ormats section.

Working with 3-D Pie Charts

Like 2-D pie charts, 3-D pie charts show the proportion of the whole that is contributed by each number in a single data series. A shallow cylinder (the "pie") represents the whole, and each "slice" represents an individual series value. Figure 24.7 shows a pie chart of the Earth's elements. As shown in the figure, you can highlight any of the pie slices by pulling them out from the pie. You move a slice by using the mouse pointer to drag the slice to the desired position. In Figure 24.7, the Iron slice has been moved out from the pie.

To select a 3-D pie chart, select F**o**rmat | **A**utoformat to display the Autoformat dialog box, choose the 3-D Pie item from the **G**alleries list, and select a 3-D pie chart from the **F**ormats section.

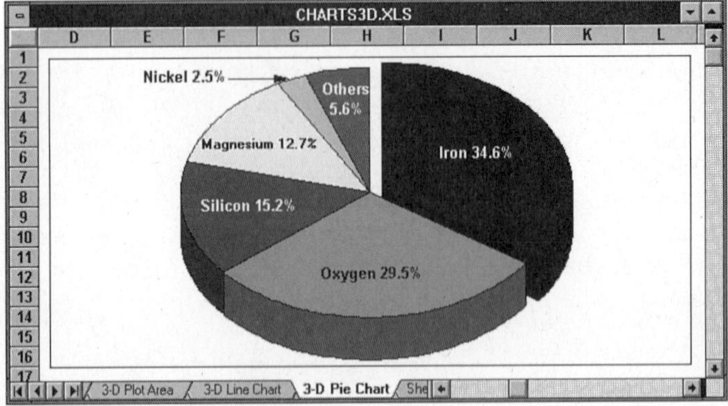

FIGURE 24.7.
A 3-D pie chart of the Earth's elements.

Working with 3-D Surface Charts

You use the 3-D surface chart to analyze two sets of data and determine the optimum combination of the two. For example, consider a simplified company where profit is a function of sales expenses and shipping costs. With too few salespeople or sales materials, revenues would drop and so would profits. Conversely, spending *too much* on sales support also would reduce profit. Using a similar analysis, you can determine that spending too little or too much on shipping costs also will lead to lower profits. These relationships are summarized in the surface chart shown in Figure 24.8.

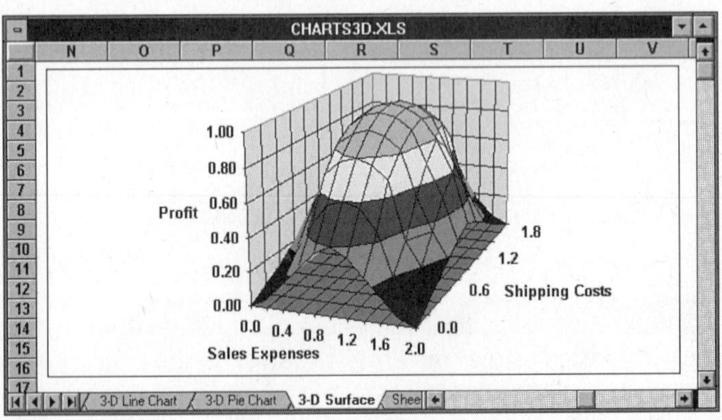

FIGURE 24.8.
A surface chart showing the relationship among sales, shipping costs, and profit.

To select a 3-D surface chart, select Format | Autoformat to display the Autoformat dialog box, choose the 3-D Surface item from the Galleries list, and select a 3-D surface chart from the Formats section.

A surface chart is like a topographical map. The chart colors don't represent individual data series; instead, they represent points from both series that are at the same value (that is, the same height on the Z axis). In Figure 24.8, each color represents a correlation between sales expenses and shipping costs that produces a certain level of profit. The area defined by the highest color, and therefore the highest profit, is the optimum combination of sales and shipping costs.

Excel has four different 3-D surface AutoFormats: a 3-D surface chart, a 3-D wireframe chart, a 2-D contour chart, and a 2-D wireframe contour chart.

SUPER NOTE

A contour chart shows you what the 3-D surface looks like from directly overhead. Use contour charts to help analyze the specific series combinations that produce an optimum result.

Changing the 3-D View

When you use 3-D charts, sometimes certain data points in the back of a chart get obscured behind taller data markers in the chart's foreground. This can mar the look of an otherwise attractive chart. Fortunately, Excel enables you to change a number of aspects of the 3-D view to try to get a better perspective on your data.

Excel's Format 3-D View dialog box, shown in Figure 24.9, handles these adjustments. (To display this dialog box, follow the steps in Procedure 24.1.)

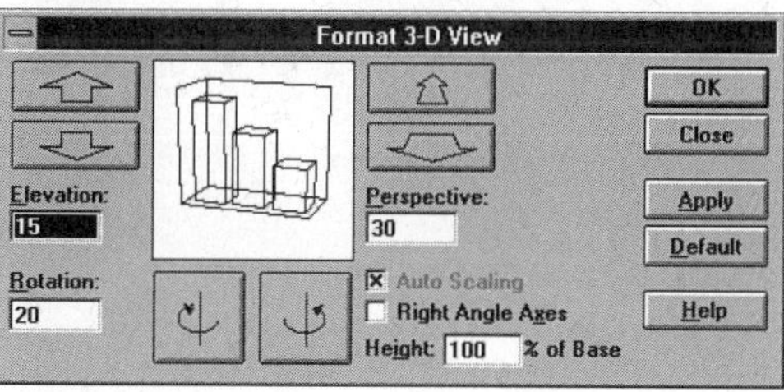

FIGURE 24.9.
The Format 3-D View dialog box.

Within this dialog box you can set six options: **E**levation, **R**otation, **P**erspective, Auto **S**caling, Right Angle A**x**es, and He**i**ght.

Elevation, which is measured in degrees, controls the height from which you look at the chart. For most 3-D charts, you can enter an elevation value between –90 and 90. A 0-degree elevation puts you on the floor of the plot area, 90 degrees means that you're looking at the chart from directly overhead, and –90 degrees means that you're looking at the chart from directly underneath. Figure 24.10 shows a 3-D column chart from an elevation of 80 degrees. For 3-D bar charts, the allowable range of elevation is between 0 and 44 degrees. For pie charts, the range is from 10 to 80 degrees.

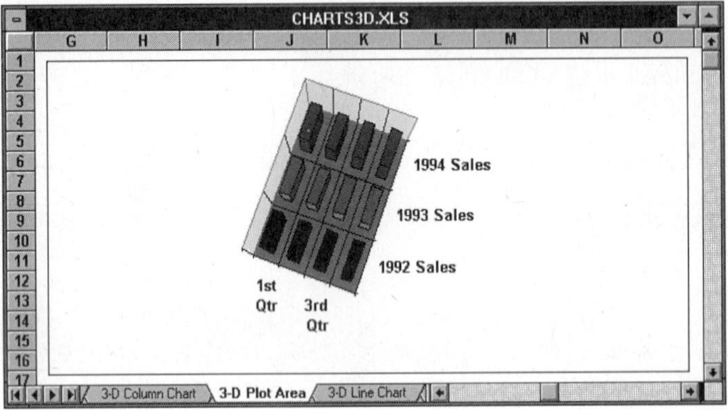

FIGURE 24.10.
A 3-D column chart from an elevation of 80 degrees.

Rotation, also measured in degrees, controls the rotation of the chart around the vertical (Z) axis. For most 3-D charts, you can enter a value between 0 and 360 degrees. A 0-degree rotation puts you directly in front of the chart, 90 degrees brings you to the side of the chart, and 180 degrees shows you the back of the chart with the series in reverse order. For 3-D bar charts, the acceptable range of rotation is between 0 and 44 degrees. For pie charts, the rotation represents the angle of the first slice where 0 degrees puts the left edge of the slice at 12 o'clock, 90 degrees puts it at 3 o'clock, and so on. Figure 24.11 shows the pie chart of the Earth's elements (first shown in Figure 24.7) rotated to 300 degrees.

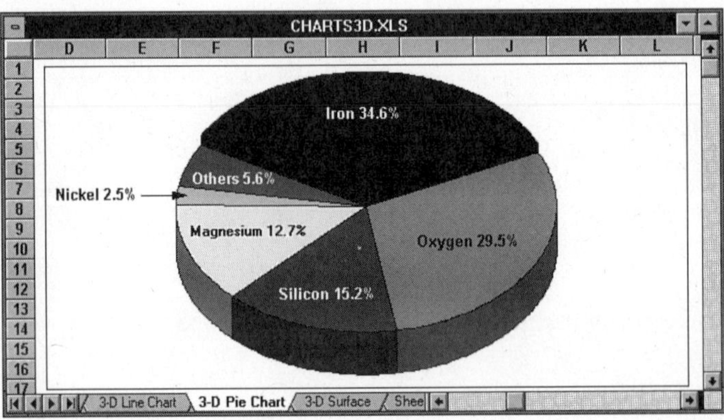

FIGURE 24.11.
Changing the rotation in a pie chart changes the angle of the first slice.

Perspective controls the sense of distance (or *perspective*) that a chart conveys. More perspective means that data markers at the back of the chart are shown relatively smaller than those at the front. (You can enter a value as high as 100 degrees.) Pie charts and 3-D bar charts don't have a perspective setting. Figure 24.12 shows a column chart with a high perspective value. This option is available only if the Right Angle Axes check box is deactivated.

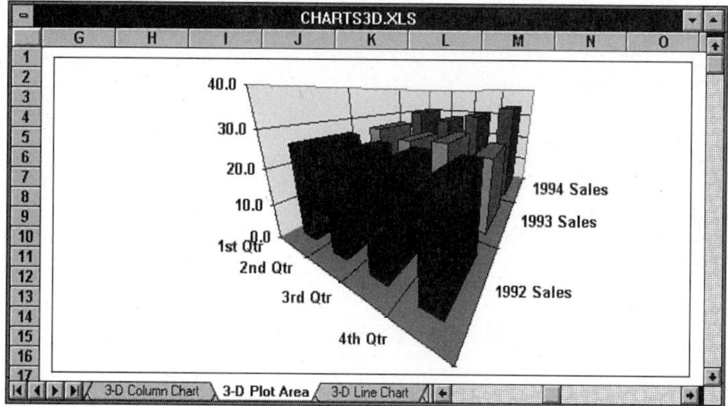

FIGURE 24.12.
Use a high perspective value to add a sense of distance to a chart.

The Auto Scaling option tells Excel to scale the chart automatically so that it always fills the entire chart window. This option is available only when the Right Angle Axes check box is selected.

The Right Angle Axes option controls the orientation of the chart axes. When you select this option, Excel draws the axes at right angles to each other and disables the Perspective option.

SUPER TIP

If your chart lines appear overly jagged, activate the Right Angle Axes option. The chart lines that define the walls and markers will run horizontally and vertically and should appear straight.

The Height option controls the height of the vertical (Z) axis. The height is measured as a percentage of the category (X) axis. This option is unavailable when you select Auto Scaling.

Follow the steps in Procedure 24.1 to adjust the 3-D view of a chart.

PROCEDURE 24.1. ADJUSTING THE 3-D VIEW.

1. Select the Format | 3-D View command. Excel displays the Format 3-D View dialog box.
2. Select the 3-D view options you want. The sample chart in the dialog box shows the effect of each change.
3. To see how your changes will look on the actual chart, click on the Apply button. Excel changes the chart view but leaves the dialog box open.
4. To change the view permanently, click on OK or press Enter.

SUPER TIP

To return a chart to its default view, click on the Default button.

Plotting a Multicategory 3-D Chart

The three-dimensional equivalent of the 2-D XY chart is called the *multicategory* chart. You'll recall that an XY chart (a variation of the line chart) plots the relationship between two sets of numbers—an independent variable and a dependent variable. Similarly, the multicategory 3-D chart (a variation of the 3-D column chart) plots the relationship among *two* independent variables (that is, two categories) and a dependent variable. Excel plots the categories on the X and Y axes and plots the values on the Z axis.

As an illustration, consider the earlier example of the company profit that is a function of both sales expenses and shipping costs. In that example, both types of costs are independent variables and the profit is the dependent variable. Figure 24.13 shows how you would set up a multicategory 3-D chart to analyze the relationship among these variables.

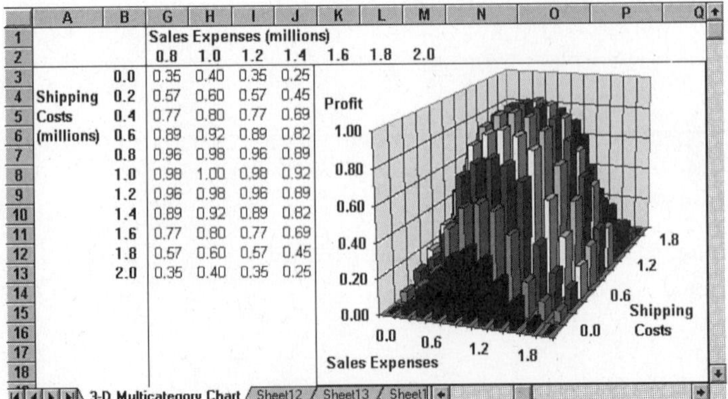

		Sales Expenses (millions)			
		0.8	1.0	1.2	1.4
	0.0	0.35	0.40	0.35	0.25
Shipping	0.2	0.57	0.60	0.57	0.45
Costs	0.4	0.77	0.80	0.77	0.69
(millions)	0.6	0.89	0.92	0.89	0.82
	0.8	0.96	0.98	0.96	0.89
	1.0	0.98	1.00	0.98	0.92
	1.2	0.96	0.98	0.96	0.89
	1.4	0.89	0.92	0.89	0.82
	1.6	0.77	0.80	0.77	0.69
	1.8	0.57	0.60	0.57	0.45
	2.0	0.35	0.40	0.35	0.25

FIGURE 24.13.
A multicategory 3-D chart.

Chapter

25

Combining Multiple Chart Types in a Single Chart

All the charts you've seen so far (except XY charts) have used a single value axis and a single chart type. With Excel, you can *overlay* one chart on another to produce combination charts that display two different chart types simultaneously. The two types can even use different units and different value axes.

This chapter shows you how to use Excel's preformatted combination charts and how to add and format your own overlay charts.

Working with Excel's AutoFormat Combination Charts

The easiest way to create a combination chart is to select one of Excel's six *combination* AutoFormats. Select the **F**ormat | **A**utoFormat command and, in the AutoFormat dialog box, select Combination from the **G**alleries list. You see the formats shown in Figure 25.1.

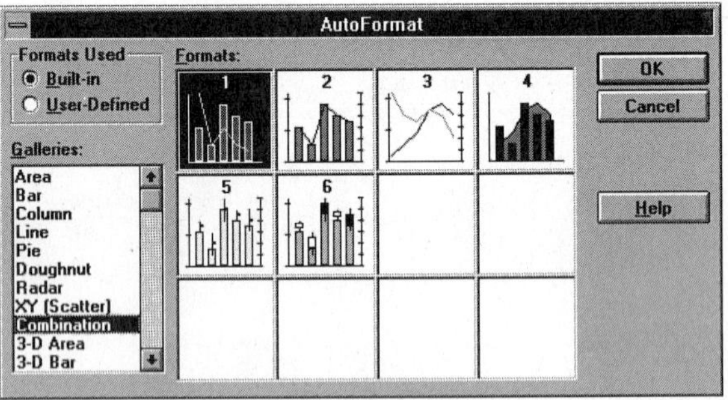

FIGURE 25.1.
Excel's combination chart formats.

SUPER CAUTION

Converting an existing chart to a combination type overwrites any formatting you've applied. To maintain your formatting, add your own overlay. See the section in this chapter titled "Converting a Series to a Different Chart Type" for instructions.

Excel creates combination charts by overlaying one chart type on another. Table 25.1 outlines the chart types used in each of the combination chart formats.

Table 25.1. Excel's combination chart AutoFormats.

Combination	*Description*
1	A column chart overlaid by a line chart.
2	A column chart overlaid by a line chart that uses a separate value (Y) axis. The overlay axis appears on the right side of the plot area.
3	A line chart overlaid by a second line chart that uses a separate value (Y) axis. The overlay axis appears on the right side of the plot area.
4	An area chart overlaid by a column chart.
5	A column chart overlaid by a high, low, close line chart that uses a separate value (Y) axis. The overlay axis appears on the right side of the plot area.
6	A column chart overlaid by an open, high, low, close chart that uses a separate value (Y) axis. The overlay axis appears on the right side of the plot area.

Combination charts are useful for showing how distinct series are related. For example, Figure 25.2 shows a stock price high, low, close line chart overlaid on a column chart showing daily volume. The line chart value axis (showing units in dollars) is on the right and the column chart value axis (showing units in shares) is on the left.

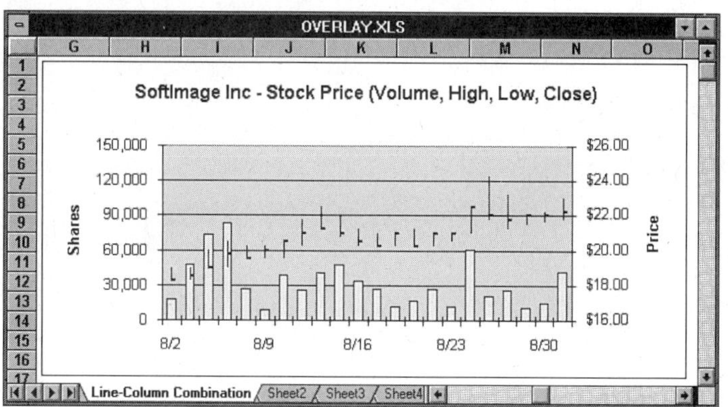

FIGURE 25.2.
A chart combining a high, low, close line chart type with a column chart type.

SUPER TIP

Scale the axes on your combination charts to prevent the series from interfering with each other. See Chapter 21, "Enhancing Charts," for information on formatting your chart axes.

Converting a Series to a Different Chart Type

If you want to create a combination chart not found among Excel's AutoFormat types, or if you have chart formatting you want to preserve, you can easily apply an overlay effect to an existing chart.

For example, Figure 25.3 shows a chart with three series: sales figures for 1992, sales figures for 1993, and a series that plots the growth from 1992 to 1993. Looking at the chart, it's clear that the growth series would make more sense as a line chart. Excel enables you to convert individual data series into chart types. To do so, follow the steps in Procedure 25.1.

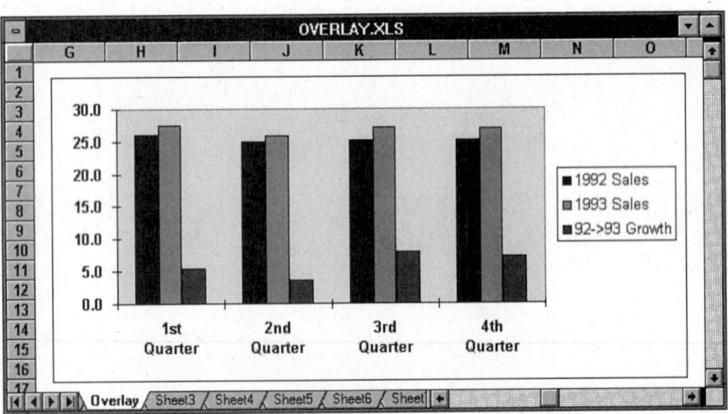

FIGURE 25.3.
The growth series would be better as a line chart.

PROCEDURE 25.1. CONVERTING A SERIES TO A DIFFERENT CHART TYPE.

1. Activate the chart you want to work with.
2. Select the series you want to convert.
3. Select the Format | Chart Type command to display the Chart Type dialog box.
4. In the Apply to group, activate the Selected Series option. (This option should already be selected.)
5. Select the chart type you want to use for the series.

6. Click on OK or press Enter. Excel converts the series to the chart type you selected. Figure 25.4 shows the previous chart with the Growth series converted to a line chart.

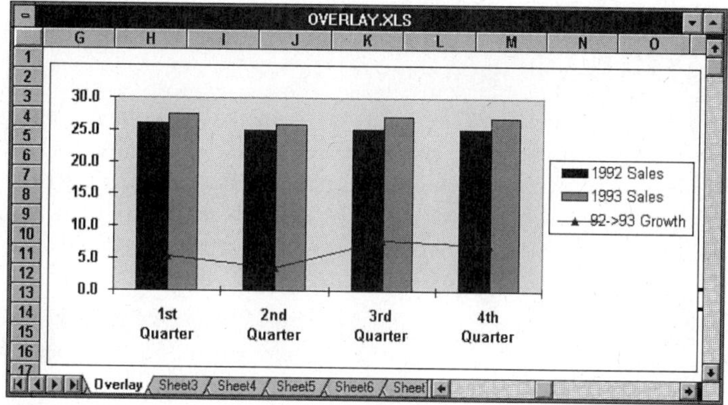

FIGURE 25.4.
The revised chart with the Growth series converted to a line chart.

Working with Chart Type Groups

Excel divides a chart's data series into different *chart type groups*. Because most charts use only one chart type, usually there is only one chart group. However, when you convert one or more series to a different type, Excel creates a new chart type group for those series. For example, the combination chart shown in Figure 25.4 has two chart groups: column and line.

You can work with series individually or as a group. The next few sections show you how to work with groups.

Changing the Chart Type of a Chart Group

If you want to convert the series in an existing chart group to a different chart type, follow the steps in Procedure 25.2.

PROCEDURE 25.2. CHANGING THE CHART TYPE OF A CHART GROUP.

1. Activate the chart you want to work with.
2. Select the F**o**rmat | Chart **T**ype command to display the Chart Type dialog box.
3. In the Apply to group, activate the **G**roup option.
4. Select the group you want to work with from the **G**roup list.
5. Select the chart type you want to use for the group.
6. Click on OK or press Enter. Excel converts the group to the chart type you selected.

Formatting Chart Groups

Excel gives you a number of formatting options for chart groups. These options enable you to control the appearance of certain aspects of the group's chart type. For example, with a line chart you can add drop lines, and with a column chart you can adjust the gap between categories. You also can change the series order within the group and even display a second value axis.

To get started, activate the chart you want to work with and then pull down the **For**mat menu. At the bottom of the menu is a list of groups in the chart. When you select one of these groups, Excel displays the Format [*Group*] Group dialog box, where *Group* is the group you chose. Figure 25.5 shows the Format Line Group dialog box. The next few sections take you through some of the options available in these dialog boxes.

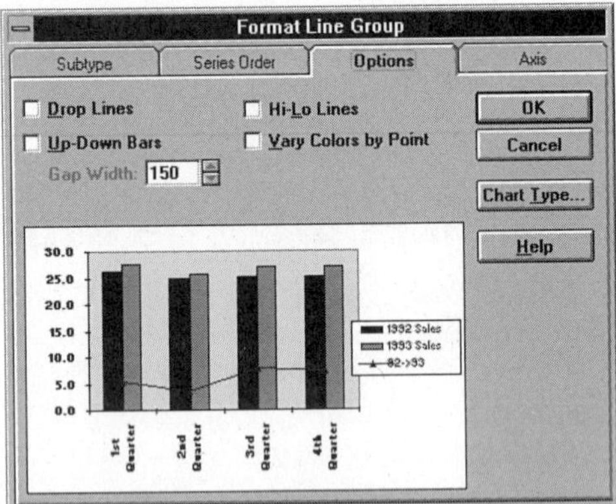

FIGURE 25.5.
The Format Line Group dialog box.

Setting Group Options

The Options tab of the Format Group dialog boxes contains various layout options specific to each chart type. In the Format Line Group dialog box, for example, you can add **D**rop Lines (see Figure 23.1 for an example), **U**p-Down Bars, and Hi-**L**o Lines (see Figure 25.2). (Up-down bars are used mostly in stock charts. If the close is less than the open, the stock is "down" and a black bar joins the two values. If the stock is up, a white bar joins them.)

Changing the Series Order of a Group

To change the order of the series in a group, select the Series Order tab in the appropriate Format Group dialog box. Figure 25.6 shows the Series Order tab for the Format Column Group dialog box. To change the order, select a series from the **S**eries Order list and then click on either the Move **U**p or Move **D**own button.

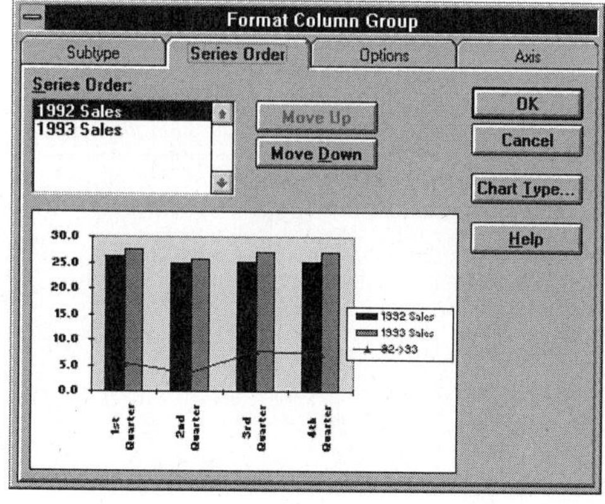

FIGURE 25.6.
Use the Series Order tab to change the order of a chart group's series.

Adding a Second Value Axis

If your chart groups use different units or have data series with different value ranges, you can add a second value axis for one of the groups. For example, consider the combination chart shown in Figure 25.7. This chart attempts to compare yearly sales with gross margin. However, the numbers in each series use completely different ranges. The sales numbers range from 95.9 to 119.5, and the gross margin figures range from 0.275 to 0.311. Because Excel has to allow for the larger range, the gross-margin line is almost invisible. The solution is to add a second value axis for the line group. Figure 25.8 shows the result.

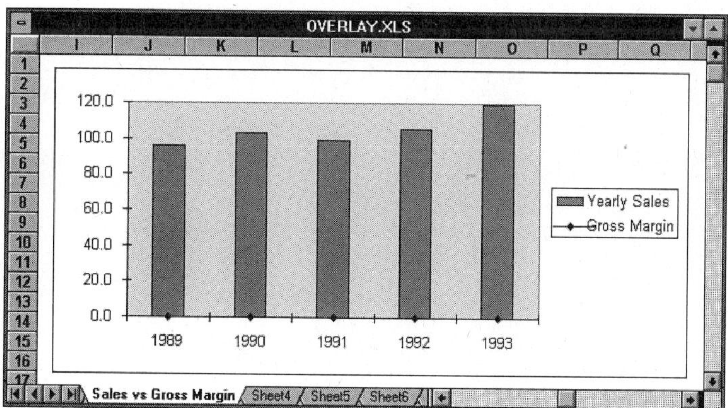

FIGURE 25.7.
Series with different ranges can produce ineffective charts.

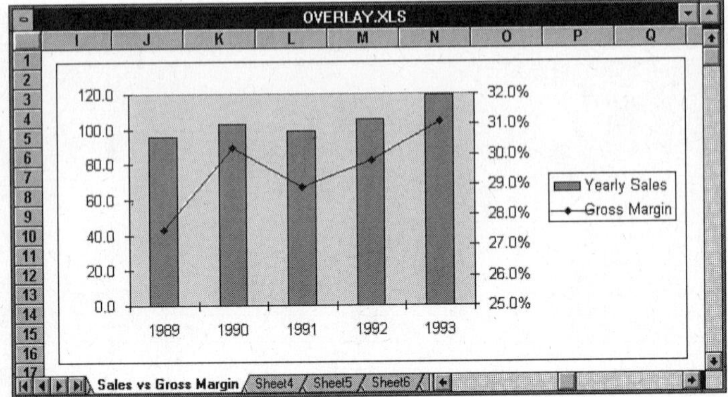

FIGURE 25.8. *Overlaying one series and adjusting the axes ranges leads to a better comparison.*

Follow the steps in Procedure 25.3 to add a second value axis for a chart group.

PROCEDURE 25.3. ADDING A DIFFERENT AXIS FOR A CHART GROUP.

1. Pull down the Format menu and select the group you want to work with from the list at the bottom of the menu.
2. Select the Axis tab from the dialog box that appears.
3. Activate the Secondary Axis option.
4. Click on OK or press Enter. Excel adds a new axis to the chart.
5. Scale each axis as needed.

Chapter

26

Adding Graphic Objects to a Worksheet

Excel gives you a powerful set of drawing tools to create and enhance graphic objects on your worksheets. You can add lines, circles, or polygons. You can import graphics from external sources, and you can even export pictures of your worksheets to use in other programs.

This chapter shows you the basics of adding graphic objects to a worksheet either by drawing them yourself using the Drawing toolbar or by importing graphics from outside Excel.

Using the Drawing Toolbar

The Drawing toolbar contains 11 tools you can use to create your own graphic objects. With these tools, you can add lines, rectangles, ovals, arcs, and polygons to your worksheets. Table 26.1 summarizes the 11 drawing tools.

Click on this tool in the Standard toolbar to display the Drawing toolbar.

Table 26.1. Excel's drawing tools.

Tool	*Name*	*Description*
	Line	Draws a straight line
	Arrow	Draws an arrow
	Freehand	Draws a freehand line
	Rectangle	Draws a rectangle or square
	Ellipse	Draws an ellipse or circle
	Arc	Draws an arc or circle segment
	Freeform Polygon	Draws a polygon from a combination of freehand and straight lines
	Filled Rectangle	Draws a rectangle or square filled with a background pattern and color

Tool	Name	Description
	Filled Ellipse	Draws an ellipse or circle filled with a background pattern and color
	Filled Arc	Draws an arc or circle segment filled with a background pattern and color
	Filled Freeform Polygon	Draws a freeform polygon filled with a background pattern and color

The Drawing toolbar makes creating your own graphic objects easy. In most cases, you just click on the tool and then drag on the worksheet to create the object. Figure 26.1 shows several examples of objects you can create with the drawing tools.

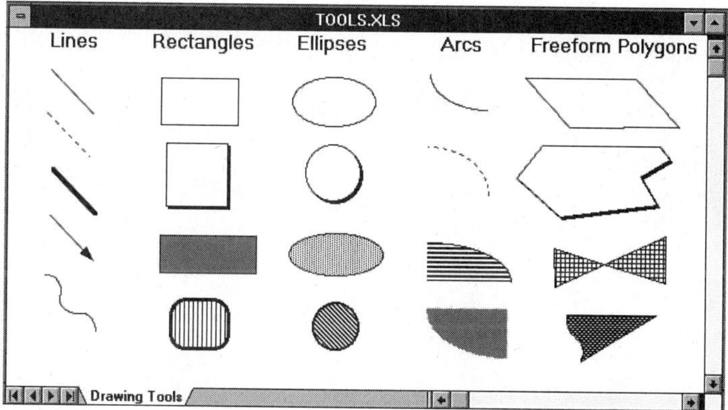

FIGURE 26.1.
Excel's drawing tools enable you to create many graphic objects.

Drawing Lines

You can create three kinds of lines with Excel's drawing tools: straight lines, arrows, and freehand lines. Use lines to point out important worksheet information or to design a more complex graphic, such as a company logo. Follow the steps in Procedure 26.1 to create a line.

PROCEDURE 26.1. DRAWING A LINE.

1. Click on a line-drawing tool. To draw multiple lines, double-click on the tool. The mouse pointer changes to a crosshair.
2. Position the crosshair where you want to begin the line.

3. Press and hold down the left mouse button.
4. Drag the mouse pointer to where you want the line to end. If you're drawing a freehand line, drag the mouse pointer in the shape of the line you want.
5. Release the mouse button. Excel places black selection handles on each end of the line. If you're drawing an arrow, Excel adds an arrowhead.
6. If you're drawing multiple lines, repeat steps 2-5.
7. To finish drawing multiple lines, click on an empty part of the worksheet or press the Esc key.

SUPER TIP

To restrict straight lines and arrows to horizontal, vertical, and 45-degree angles, hold down the Shift key while you draw. To create lines along the worksheet gridlines or diagonally between cell corners, hold down the Alt key while you draw.

Figure 26.2 demonstrates some ways to use lines in a worksheet.

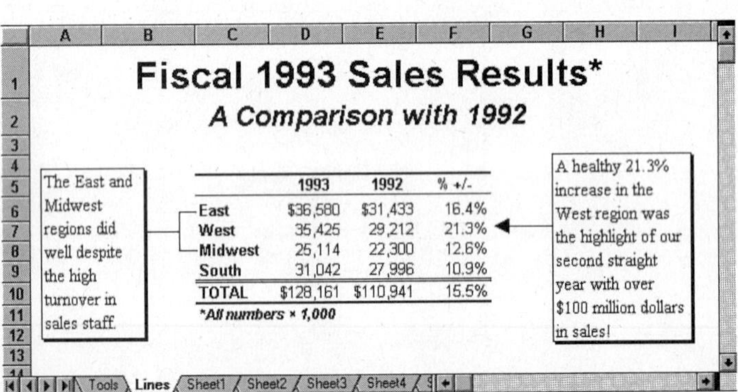

FIGURE 26.2. *Examples of line objects in a worksheet.*

Drawing Shapes

You can create three kinds of predefined shapes with Excel's drawing tools: rectangles, ellipses, and arcs (a fourth shape—the polygon—is discussed in the next section). You'll use shapes often as part of complex graphics, such as a company logo. Follow the steps in Procedure 26.2 to create a shape.

PROCEDURE 26.2. DRAWING A SHAPE.

1. Click on a shape-drawing tool. To draw multiple shapes, double-click on the tool. The mouse pointer changes to a crosshair.

2. Position the crosshair where you want to begin drawing the shape.
3. Press and hold down the left mouse button.
4. Drag the mouse pointer until the shape has the size and form you want.
5. Release the mouse button. Excel places black selection handles around the shape.
6. If you're drawing multiple shapes, repeat steps 2-5.
7. To finish drawing multiple shapes, click on an empty part of the worksheet or press the Esc key.

SUPER TIP

To make your rectangles square or your ellipses circular, hold down the Shift key while drawing. To align your shapes with the worksheet gridlines, hold down the Alt key while drawing.

You can use shapes to create your own custom worksheet formatting. For example, instead of using Excel's cell borders, create your own with the Rectangle tool, shown in Figure 26.3. This figure shows some examples of shapes used in a worksheet. The arrowhead on the end of the arc was accomplished by attaching an arrow with a very short shaft.

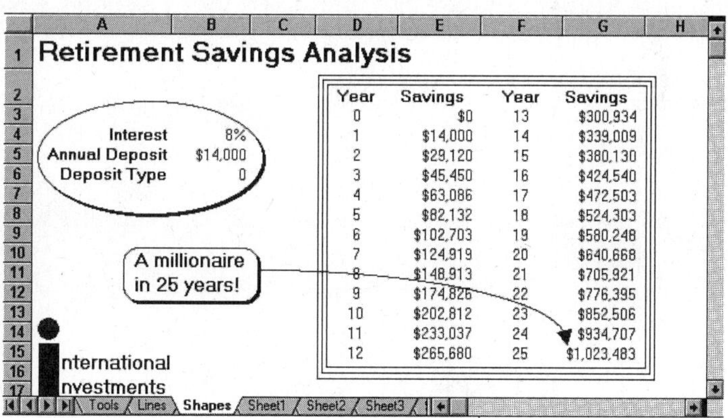

FIGURE 26.3.
Some sample shapes on a worksheet.

Drawing Polygons

The Freeform Polygon tool enables you to combine freehand lines with straight lines to create a polygon of any shape or size. Procedure 26.3 outlines the steps to follow to use this tool.

PROCEDURE 26.3. DRAWING A POLYGON.

1. Click on the Freeform Polygon tool. To draw multiple polygons, double-click on the tool. The mouse pointer changes to a crosshair.
2. Position the crosshair where you want to begin the polygon.
3. To draw freehand, press and hold down the left mouse button. To draw a straight line, click the left mouse button.
4. Move the mouse pointer to draw the object you want.
5. To finish freehand drawing, release the mouse button. To finish drawing a straight line, click the left mouse button.
6. Repeat steps 3-5 to add other freehand or straight lines.
7. Double-click to finish drawing the polygon.
8. If you're drawing multiple polygons, repeat steps 2-7.
9. To finish drawing multiple polygons, click on the Freeform Polygon tool or press the Esc key.

Polygons are useful for creating complex shapes. In Figure 26.4, a polygon has been added around the sales figures and shaded to create a 3-D effect.

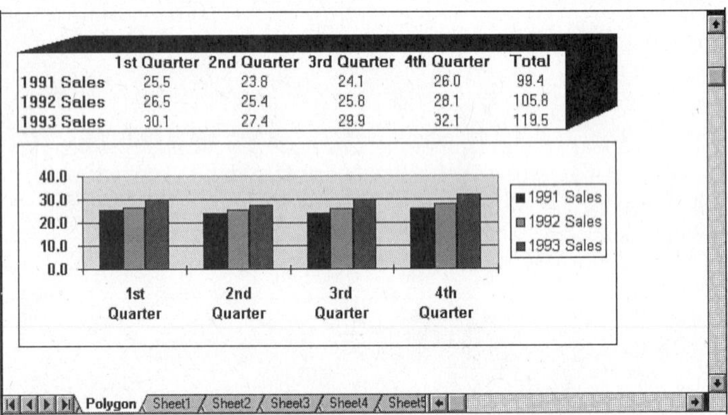

	1st Quarter	2nd Quarter	3rd Quarter	4th Quarter	Total
1991 Sales	25.5	23.8	24.1	26.0	99.4
1992 Sales	26.5	25.4	25.8	28.1	105.8
1993 Sales	30.1	27.4	29.9	32.1	119.5

FIGURE 26.4.
Use polygons for complex shapes.

Importing Graphics from Other Applications

Although the drawing tools that come with Excel are handy for creating simple graphics effects, a more ambitious image requires a dedicated graphics program, such as Windows Paintbrush or CorelDRAW!. With these programs you can create professional-quality graphics and then import them into your Excel worksheet. If an application supports Dynamic Data Exchange (DDE) or Object Linking and Embedding (OLE), you can maintain a link between the object and the original program. Follow the steps in Procedure 26.4 to import a graphic image from another application.

PROCEDURE 26.4. IMPORTING A GRAPHIC OBJECT.

1. Activate the graphics application.
2. Select the graphic image you want to import.
3. Copy the image to the Windows Clipboard. (In most Windows applications, select the **E**dit | **C**opy command.)
4. Activate Excel and select the worksheet you want to receive the graphic.
5. Select the **E**dit | **P**aste command to copy the image to the worksheet.

SUPER TIP

If the graphics application supports OLE, use the **E**dit | Paste **L**ink command to establish a link between the two applications, or select the **E**dit | Insert **O**bject command to embed an object from the application. If the application enables you to import the graphic as different data types, select the **E**dit | Paste **S**pecial command.

SUPER TIP

For more information on importing data into Excel, see Chapter 64, "Exchanging Data with Other Applications."

Use the images you import from dedicated graphics applications to enhance the appearance of your worksheets. Figure 26.5 shows a worksheet with an imported money-related graphic.

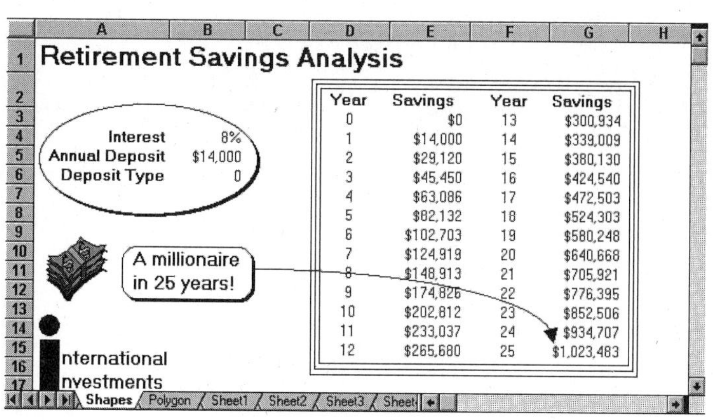

FIGURE 26.5.
Importing graphics from other programs can improve the appearance of your worksheets.

SUPER TIP

If you have access to a digital scanner, scan in your company logo and import the file to use for presentations and reports. If your computer has a fax/modem, you also can capture your logo by faxing it to the computer and then using your fax software to save the image as a graphics file. You then can use a dedicated graphics program such as Windows Paintbrush to clean up the image before you import it into Excel.

If you don't have the time or the skill to create your own images, consider using a *clip art* library. Clip art is professional-quality artwork that is commercially available in libraries of several hundred or more images. Some graphics programs, such as CorelDRAW! and Microsoft PowerPoint, include clip art collections. If you find you use certain images repeatedly, create a worksheet to hold copies of these images. This will save you from having to search through massive clip art libraries every time you need an image. Figure 26.6 shows a worksheet containing several images imported from the PowerPoint clip art library.

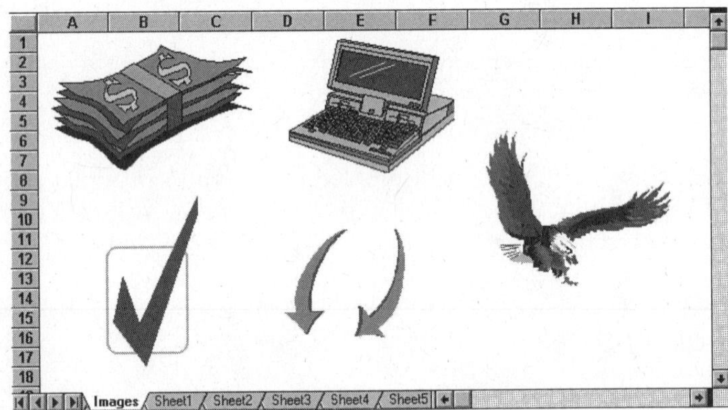

FIGURE 26.6.
Copy often-used images to a separate file for easy access.

Chapter 27

Editing Graphic Objects

After you've added a graphic object to a worksheet, you can edit the object by changing the line or border style, the fill pattern, or the size. You also can easily move, copy, and delete graphic objects. This chapter shows you how to perform these basic graphic-editing tasks.

Selecting Graphic Objects

Before you can edit a graphic object, you need to select it. Procedure 27.1 lists the steps to follow to select a graphic object.

PROCEDURE 27.1. SELECTING A GRAPHIC OBJECT.

1. Position the mouse pointer over the border of the graphic. The pointer changes to an arrow.
2. Click the mouse button. Excel displays selection handles around the object and shows the object identifier in the formula bar Name box (for example, Line 1 or Oval 5).
3. To select other objects, hold down the Shift key and repeat steps 1 and 2.

Every graphic object has an invisible rectangular *frame*. For a line or a rectangle, the frame is the same as the object itself. For all other objects, the frame is a rectangle that completely encloses the shape or image. When you select an object, Excel displays black *selection handles* around the frame. Figure 27.1 shows several selected objects.

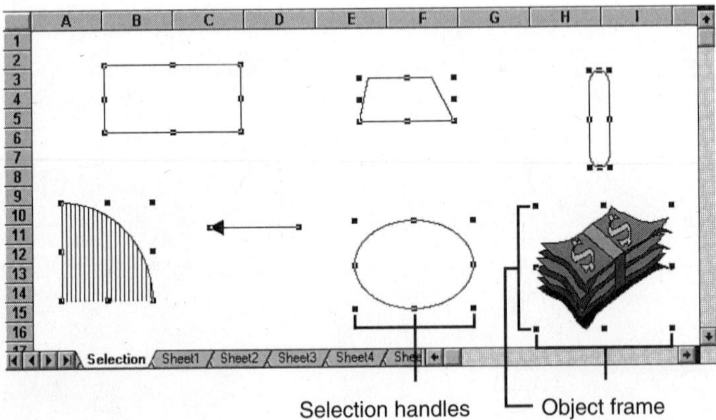

FIGURE 27.1. *Selected objects have handles around the object's frame.*

Formatting Lines

Figure 27.2 shows the Format Object dialog box for a line. Using the options in this dialog box, you can control the **S**tyle, **C**olor, and **W**eight of the line, and in the Arrowhead section, you can format the Sty**l**e, Wi**d**th, and Le**n**gth of an arrow's head. You also can add an arrowhead to a plain line or remove an arrowhead from an arrow. Figure 27.3 shows some formatted lines and arrows.

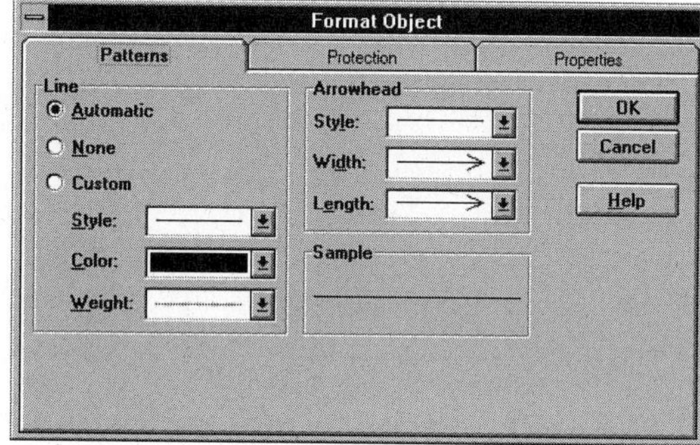

FIGURE 27.2.
The Format Object dialog box for a drawn line.

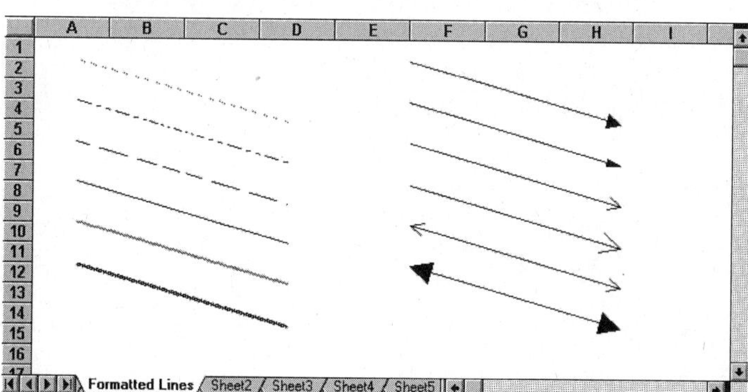

FIGURE 27.3.
Some formatted lines and arrows.

SUPER NOTE

To format a line drawn using the Freehand tool, see the next section.

Follow the steps in Procedure 27.2 to format a line.

PROCEDURE 27.2. FORMATTING A LINE.

1. Select the line you want to format.
2. Select the Format | Object command to display the Format Object dialog box.

SUPER TIP

You also can display the Format Object dialog box by double-clicking on the line, by selecting the line and pressing Ctrl+1, or by selecting Format Object from the line's shortcut menu.

3. Choose the line options you want.
4. Click on OK or press Enter.

Use this tool in the Drawing toolbar to select a line style and color.

Formatting Borders and Fill Patterns

For all other types of Excel graphic objects—including freehand lines—you can format the border and fill pattern using the Patterns tab in the Format Object dialog box, shown in Figure 27.4. In this dialog box, you can set the fill **P**attern, the foreground and background colors, and the **S**tyle, **C**olor, and **W**eight of the border. You also have the option of adding a Sha**d**ow to a rectangle, oval, polygon, or freehand line. The **R**ound Corners option is available only for rectangles. Figure 27.5 shows some sample objects with various border styles and fill patterns.

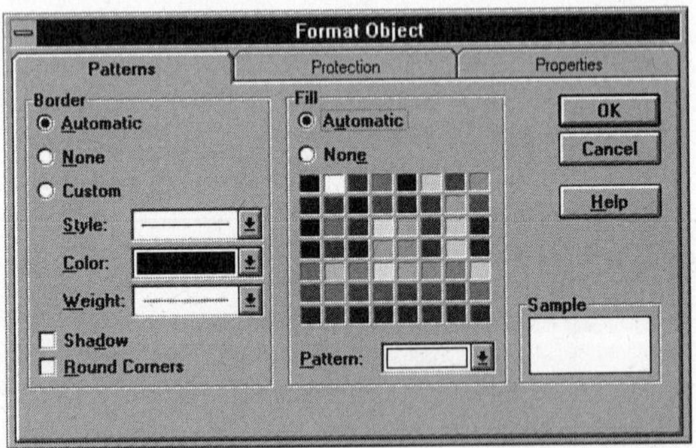

FIGURE 27.4.
The Patterns tab dialog box for formatting object borders and fills.

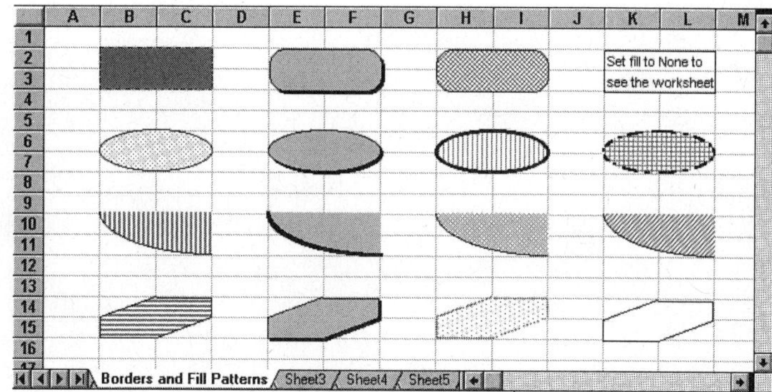

FIGURE 27.5.
Some sample objects with formatted borders and fill patterns.

Click on this tool in the Drawing toolbar to select a line style and color.

Click on this tool in the Drawing toolbar to add a shadow to a rectangle, oval, polygon, or freehand line.

Follow the steps in Procedure 27.3 to format borders and fill patterns.

PROCEDURE 27.3. FORMATTING BORDERS AND FILL PATTERNS.

1. Select the object you want to format.
2. Select the F**o**rmat | Ob**j**ect command to display the Format Object dialog box.

> **SUPER TIP**
>
> You also can display the Format Object dialog box by double-clicking on the object, by selecting the object and pressing Ctrl+1, or by selecting Format Object from the object's shortcut menu.

3. Use the Border group to select the border options you want. To remove the border, select **N**one. To create your own border, select Custom and choose the options you want from the **S**tyle, **C**olor, and **W**eight drop-down lists.
4. Use the Fill group to select the pattern options for the graphic. To set the background color, select one of the displayed color squares. To select the pattern and foreground color, open the **P**attern list and choose the pattern and color you want.
5. Click on OK or press Enter.

Sizing Graphic Objects

You can resize any graphic object to change its shape or dimensions. Procedure 27.4 outlines the steps to follow.

PROCEDURE 27.4. SIZING GRAPHIC OBJECTS.

1. Select the object you want to size. Excel displays black selection handles around the object's frame.
2. Position the mouse pointer over the handle you want to move. The pointer changes to a two-headed arrow (see Figure 27.6). To change the size horizontally or vertically, use the appropriate handle on the middle of a side. To change the size in both directions at once, use the appropriate corner handle.

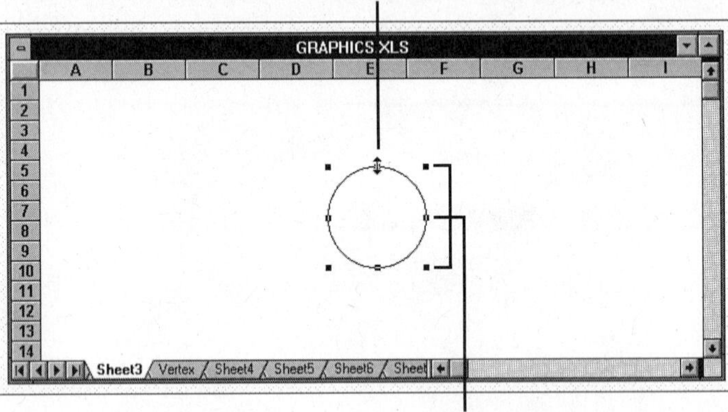

FIGURE 27.6. *Drag a selection handle to size a graphic object.*

3. Drag the handle to the position you want. The pointer changes to a crosshair.
4. Release the mouse button. Excel redraws the object and adjusts the frame size.

SUPER TIP

To keep the same proportions when sizing an object, hold down the Shift key and drag a corner handle. To size an object using the worksheet gridlines, hold down the Alt key while dragging.

SUPER NOTE

When you scale an image such as a clip art graphic, the scaling percentages for the height and width appear in the status bar at the bottom of the screen. The original graphic is 100% x 100%.

Editing Polygons

To change the size of a polygon, you can either use the procedure outlined in the preceding section or edit the polygon using the Reshape tool. When you click on the Reshape tool, Excel displays *selection squares* at each vertex of the selected polygon. (Several vertices appear along each freehand line, and one vertex appears at the beginning and end of every straight line.) You can then move, add, or delete vertices to get the shape you want. Procedure 27.5 takes you through the appropriate steps.

PROCEDURE 27.5. EDITING A POLYGON.

1. Select the polygon you want to edit.
2. Click on the Reshape tool. Excel displays selection squares at each vertex of the polygon.

The Drawing toolbar's Reshape tool.

3. To move a vertex, position the mouse pointer over the vertex. The pointer changes to a crosshair, as shown in Figure 27.7. Drag the vertex to the position you want and release the mouse button. Excel redraws the polygon with the new vertex position.

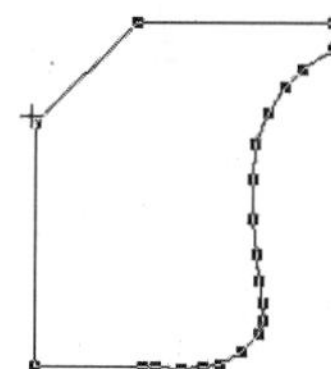

FIGURE 27.7.
The mouse pointer for moving a vertex.

4. To add a vertex, hold down the Ctrl key and position the mouse pointer over the appropriate polygon line. The pointer changes to a crosshair with a square in the middle, as shown in Figure 27.8. Drag the line to the new vertex point and release the mouse button and the Ctrl key. Excel adds the vertex and redraws the polygon.

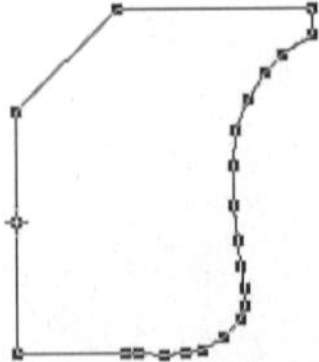

FIGURE 27.8.
The mouse pointer for adding a vertex.

5. To delete a vertex, hold down the Ctrl key and position the mouse pointer over the vertex. The pointer changes to an X, as shown in Figure 27.9. Click once. Excel deletes the vertex and redraws the polygon.

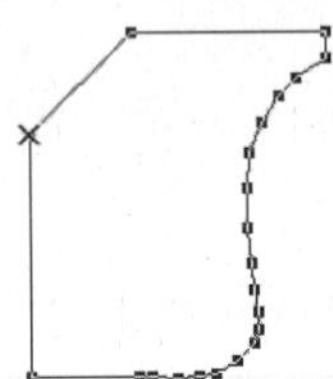

FIGURE 27.9.
The mouse pointer for deleting a vertex.

6. When you've finished editing the polygon, click on the Reshape tool.

Moving Graphic Objects

You can move any graphic object to a different part of the worksheet by following the steps in Procedure 27.6.

PROCEDURE 27.6. MOVING A GRAPHIC OBJECT.

1. Select the object you want to move. Excel displays black selection handles around the object's frame.
2. Position the mouse pointer on any edge of the object. The pointer changes to an arrow.
3. Drag the object to the position you want.
4. Release the mouse button. Excel redraws the object in the new position.

SUPER TIP

To move an object using the worksheet gridlines, hold down the Alt key while dragging. To move an object only horizontally or vertically, hold down the Shift key while dragging.

You also can move graphic objects using the cut-and-paste method. Procedure 27.7 shows you how it's done.

PROCEDURE 27.7. MOVING AN OBJECT BY CUTTING AND PASTING.

1. Select the object you want to move. Excel displays black selection handles around the object's frame.
2. Select the **Edit** | **Cut** command. Excel cuts the objects from the worksheet.
3. Move the cell selector to the new position.
4. Select **Edit** | **Paste**. Excel redraws the object in the new position.

SUPER TIP

Each graphic object's shortcut menu includes Cut and Paste commands.

Copying Graphic Objects

If you want multiple copies of the same object, you don't have to draw each one. Instead, follow the steps in Procedure 27.8 to make as many copies of the object as you need.

PROCEDURE 27.8. COPYING A GRAPHIC OBJECT.

1. Select the object you want to copy. Excel displays black selection handles around the object's frame.
2. Press the Ctrl key and position the mouse pointer on any edge of the object. The pointer changes to an arrow with a plus sign.
3. Drag the pointer to the position you want.
4. Release the mouse button. Excel copies the object to the new position.

You also can use the **Edit** | **Copy** command to copy graphic objects. Procedure 27.9 outlines the steps to follow.

PROCEDURE 27.9. COPYING A GRAPHIC OBJECT USING THE COPY COMMAND.

1. Select the object you want to copy. Excel displays black selection handles around the object's frame.
2. Select the **Edit** | **Copy** command.
3. Position the cell selector at the approximate position you want the copy to appear.
4. Select the **Edit** | **Paste** command. Excel pastes a copy of the object at the selected cell.

SUPER TIP

You also can select the Copy command from the object's shortcut menu.

Deleting Graphic Objects

To delete a graphic object, follow the steps in Procedure 27.10.

PROCEDURE 27.10. DELETING A GRAPHIC OBJECT.

1. Select the object you want to delete. Excel displays black selection handles around the object's frame.
2. Select the **E**dit | Cle**a**r | **A**ll command. Excel deletes the object.

SUPER TIP

To delete an object quickly, select it and press the Delete key. Alternatively, you can select Clear from the shortcut menu.

Chapter

28

Working with Graphic Objects

Now that you know how to create and edit graphic objects, this chapter illustrates several techniques that make working with graphics faster and more efficient. You'll learn about working with multiple objects, hiding objects, and taking pictures with Excel's Copy Picture command.

Selecting Multiple Graphic Objects

If you use graphics often, you could easily end up with a dozen or more objects in a worksheet. If you then want to rearrange or reformat a worksheet, it becomes time-consuming to move or format each object individually. To get around this, Excel enables you to select all the objects you want and work with them simultaneously.

Excel offers a couple methods for selecting multiple objects. If you need just a few objects, or if the objects you need are scattered widely throughout the worksheet, hold down the Shift key and select each object individually. If the objects you want are grouped, you can use Excel's Selection tool to select them all together. Procedure 28.1 takes you through the necessary steps.

PROCEDURE 28.1. SELECTING MULTIPLE OBJECTS WITH THE SELECTION TOOL.

1. Click on the Selection tool. The mouse pointer changes to a crosshair.

   The Selection tool from the Standard toolbar.

2. Position the pointer at the top-left corner of the area you want to select.
3. Press and hold down the left mouse button.
4. Drag the pointer to the bottom-right corner of the area you want to select. As you drag the pointer, Excel indicates the selected area with a dashed border, as shown in Figure 28.1.

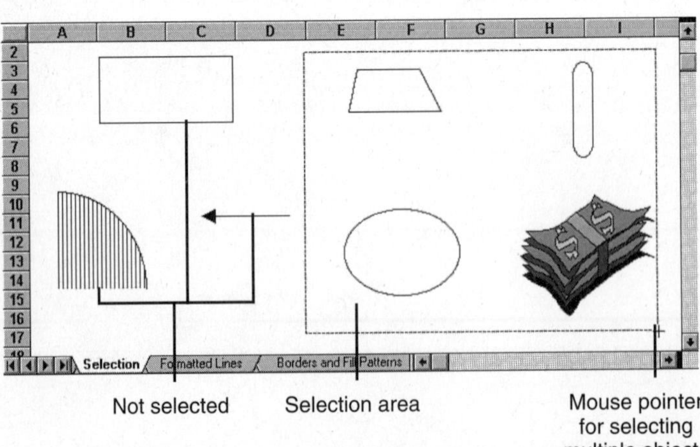

FIGURE 28.1. *Make sure the selection area completely encloses each object you want to select.*

5. Release the mouse button. Excel places selection handles around each object in the selection area.
6. To end the selection, click on the Selection tool or press the Esc key.

SUPER NOTE

The selection area must completely enclose an object to include it in the selection.

SUPER TIP

If you miss any objects, make sure the Selection key is still active. Then, while holding down the Shift key, repeat steps 2-5 for the other objects you want to include.

After you've made a multiple selection, you can format, size, move, copy, or delete all the objects at once. Note, however, that you'll need to format lines and shapes separately because they use different formatting options. To exclude an object from the selection, hold down the Shift key and click on the object's border. To exclude a number of objects from the selection, hold down Shift and use the Selection tool to reselect the objects.

SUPER TIP

To select all the graphic objects in a worksheet, select the **E**dit | **G**o To command and then click on the **S**pecial button in the Go To dialog box. In the Go To Special dialog box that appears, activate the O**b**jects option and click on OK or press Enter. To deselect all objects, click on any empty part of the worksheet or press the Esc key.

Grouping Graphic Objects

Excel enables you to create object *groups*. A group is a collection of objects that you can format, size, and move—similar to the way you format, size, and move a single object. To select an entire group, select just one object from the group. Procedure 28.2 lists the steps to follow.

PROCEDURE 28.2. GROUPING GRAPHIC OBJECTS.

1. Select the objects you want to group.
2. Select the Format | Placement | Group command. Excel creates an invisible, rectangular frame around the objects.

You also can use the Group Objects tool on the Drawing toolbar to group selected objects.

> **SUPER NOTE**
>
> If you've combined a number of graphic objects into a design or logo, group the elements so that you can move or size them together.

Excel treats a group as a single graphic object with its own frame. In Figure 28.2, for example, an oval, a rectangle, and an edit box have been grouped. Any sizing, moving, or copying operations act on each member of the group.

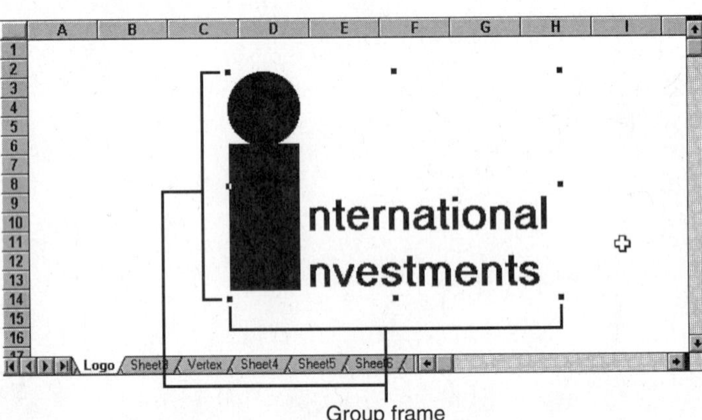

FIGURE 28.2. *Excel treats a group of graphics as a single object.*

To ungroup objects, follow the steps in Procedure 28.3.

PROCEDURE 28.3. UNGROUPING GRAPHIC OBJECTS.

1. Select a group.
2. Select the Format | Placement | Ungroup command. Excel removes the group but leaves the individual objects selected.

You can use the Ungroup Objects tool on the Drawing toolbar to ungroup graphic objects.

Hiding Graphic Objects

One problem with graphic objects is that they take longer to display than regular worksheet elements. The more detailed the graphic or the more graphics on-screen, the longer Excel takes to redraw the screen. Even with today's powerful 486 machines, redrawing can cause scrolling through a worksheet to be cumbersome and time-consuming.

To get around this problem, you can temporarily "hide" all the worksheet objects so that Excel doesn't redraw the objects every time you scroll past them. Follow the steps in Procedure 28.4 to hide graphic objects.

PROCEDURE 28.4. HIDING GRAPHIC OBJECTS.

1. Select the **T**ools | **O**ptions command and select the View tab in the Options dialog box.
2. Select the option you want from the Objects section. You have the following choices:

Show **A**ll	Displays all graphic objects normally.
Show **P**laceholders	Displays a gray rectangle in place of all embedded charts and pictures (see Figure 28.3). Lines, shapes, and polygons are still shown.
Hi**d**e All	Suppresses the display of all graphic objects.

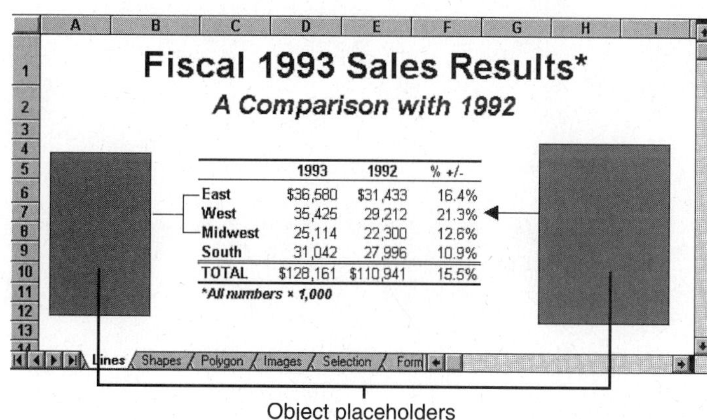

FIGURE 28.3.
For faster screen redraws, you can hide objects with placeholders.

3. Click on OK or press Enter.

SUPER TIP

Press Ctrl+6 to cycle through the Show **A**ll, Show **P**laceholders, and Hi**d**e All options without displaying the dialog box.

Controlling Object Placement

Most of your graphic objects are probably positioned relative to their specific worksheet cells. For example, you might have an edit box with an arrow to explain the contents of a cell or you might have a rectangle around a worksheet table. In either case, when you move or size the worksheet cells, you'll want the graphic to move or size along with the cells. You can control relative positioning with the options found in the Properties tab of the Format Object dialog box:

Move and **S**ize with Cells	Attaches the object to the cells underneath the object. When you move or size the cells, the object is moved or sized accordingly. This is the default option for drawn objects.
Move but Don't Size with Cells	Attaches the object only to the cell underneath its top-left corner. When you move this cell, the object moves with it but doesn't change size. This is the default option for embedded charts and pictures.
Don't Move or Size with Cells	The object isn't attached to the cell underneath it.

SUPER NOTE

Use the **M**ove but Don't Size with Cells option for logos and designs that you want to remain the same size.

SUPER NOTE

The Properties tab has a fourth option: **P**rint Object. Deactivate this option when you don't want the selected object to print with the worksheet.

Follow the steps in Procedure 28.5 to attach an object to its underlying cells.

PROCEDURE 28.5. SETTING AN OBJECT'S PLACEMENT.

1. Select the object.
2. Select the Format | Object command to display the Format Object dialog box.
3. Select the Properties tab.
4. Select the placement option you want.
5. Click on OK or press Enter.

> **SUPER TIP**
>
> A quick way to display the Format Object dialog box is to either select Format Object from the object's shortcut menu or select the object and press Ctrl+1.

To illustrate object placement, Figure 28.4 shows three copies of a graphic image. Each copy has a different placement option. Figure 28.5 shows the same graphics after one row has been inserted and another has had its height increased.

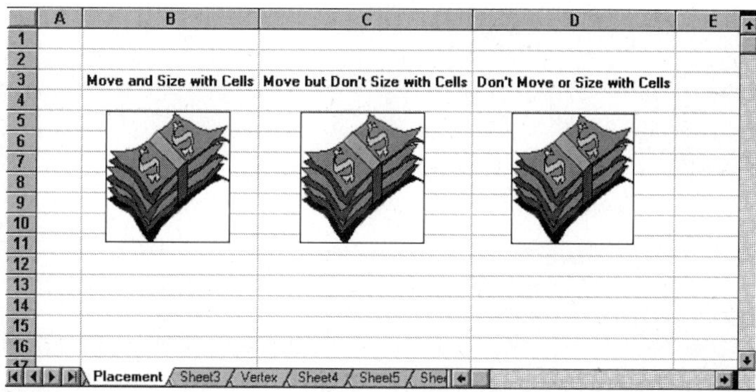

FIGURE 28.4.
Three objects with different placement options.

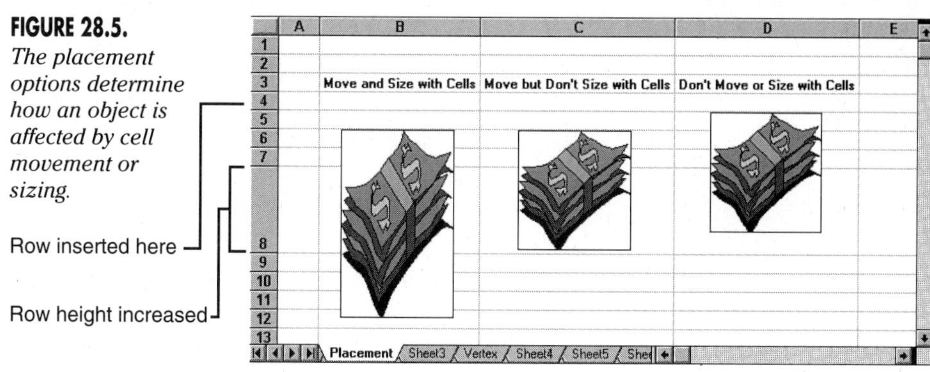

FIGURE 28.5.
The placement options determine how an object is affected by cell movement or sizing.

Ordering Overlapped Graphic Objects

When you have two graphic objects that overlap, the most recently created object covers part of the other object. The newer object is "in front" of the older one. You can change the order of the overlapped objects by selecting an object and then selecting either Format | Placement | Bring to Front or Format | Placement | Send to Back.

Figure 28.6 shows a filled rectangle in front of an edit box. When you select the rectangle and then select Format | Placement | Send to Back, the rectangle becomes an attractive shadow effect, as shown in Figure 28.7.

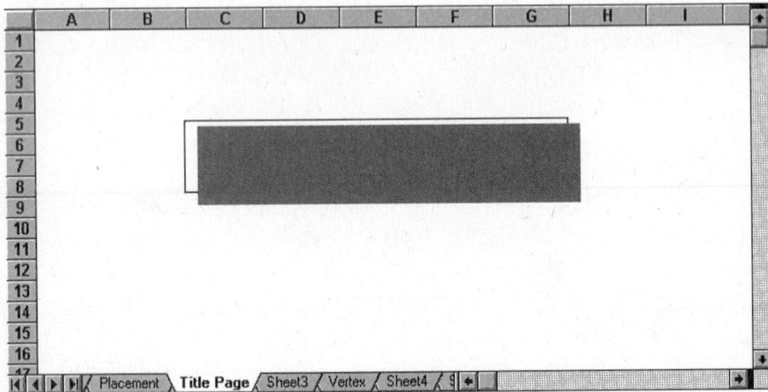

FIGURE 28.6.
The filled rectangle covers the edit box underneath.

FIGURE 28.7.
Selecting Send to Back enables you to use the rectangle to create a shadow effect.

Click on the Bring to Front tool in the Drawing toolbar to bring an object to the front.

Click on the Send to Back tool in the Drawing toolbar to send an object to the back.

Working with Pictures

Excel enables you to take *pictures* of your worksheet cells, graphic objects, and charts. Similar to the way a photograph captures an image of a particular scene, an Excel picture captures an image of the selected range or object. You can treat the picture as you would any other graphic object: you can place it anywhere in the current sheet or even in another workbook, size it, copy it, and even format it to suit your needs. If you take a picture of a range of cells, you also have the option of linking the picture to the original cells. This way, if any of the range values change, Excel automatically updates the picture.

SUPER NOTE

Use an unlinked picture of a chart (instead of an embedded chart) in your worksheets when you want the displayed chart to remain static as the numbers in the worksheet change.

When you copy a picture, you set the copy options using the Copy Picture dialog box, shown in Figure 28.8. To set the appearance of the picture, you have two options:

As Shown on **S**creen	Copies the picture as it appears on-screen, including the row and column headings for cell ranges.
As Shown when **P**rinted	Copies the picture as it appears when printed but doesn't copy row and column headings for cell ranges.

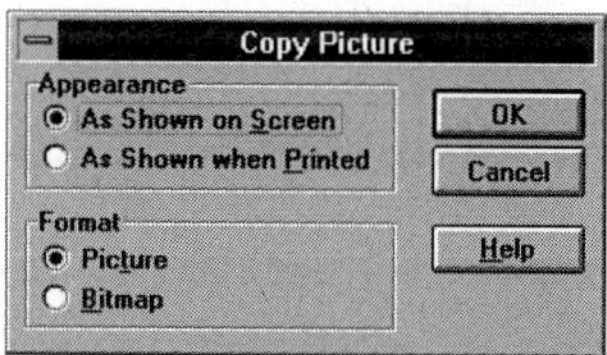

FIGURE 28.8.
The Copy Picture dialog box.

The option you choose depends on what you're copying and what kind of printer you have. The As Shown when **P**rinted option has the advantage of not copying row and column headers. However, if you select this option and are using a black-and-white printer, Excel converts all colors in the selection to black and white. In general, the best choice is As Shown on **S**creen. If you use this option and you don't want the row and column headers copied, select the **T**ools | **O**ptions command, select the View tab, and then deactivate the Row and Column H**e**aders check box before copying the range.

Sometimes, the Copy Picture dialog box gives you the choice of either a Picture or a Bitmap format. The Picture format, which is the default, copies a drawing of the image that scales proportionately when you size the picture. The Bitmap format gives you a picture made of different colored pixels.

Copying an Unlinked Picture

If you want to copy a picture of a cell range, graphic object, or chart, but you don't want Excel to update the picture every time the data changes, you need to copy an unlinked picture. Procedure 28.6 outlines the steps to follow.

PROCEDURE 28.6. COPYING AN UNLINKED PICTURE.

1. Select the range, object, or chart you want to copy.
2. Hold down Shift and select the **Edit** | **C**opy Picture command. Excel displays the Copy Picture dialog box.
3. Select the copy options you want.
4. Click on OK or press Enter.
5. Activate the worksheet that you want to receive the picture.
6. Select the cell at the upper-left corner of the area in which you want to copy the picture.
7. Hold down the Shift key and select the **Edit** | **P**aste Picture command. Excel pastes the picture onto the worksheet.

SUPER NOTE

Use Excel pictures when you need to view or print a range or chart on the same worksheet. Pictures are useful for performing worksheet analysis or data entry without having to set up separate windows or panes.

Copying a Linked Picture

If you want to copy a picture of a cell range, graphic object, or chart, and you want Excel to update the picture every time the data changes, you need to copy a linked picture. Follow the steps in Procedure 28.7.

PROCEDURE 28.7. COPYING A LINKED PICTURE OF A CELL RANGE.

1. Select the range you want to copy.
2. Select the **Edit** | **C**opy command to copy the range to the Clipboard.

3. Activate the worksheet you want to receive the picture.
4. Select the cell at the upper-left corner of the area in which you want to copy the picture.
5. Hold down the Shift key and select the **Edit** | Paste Picture Li**n**k command. Excel pastes the picture onto the worksheet and displays the linked range in the formula bar.

Excel updates linked pictures of ranges automatically, based on whether you change the numbers or the formatting of the original cells. For example, if you change the font or alignment in the original range, the picture, font, and alignment also change.

SUPER TIP

A quick way to make changes to a linked cell picture is by double-clicking on the picture. Excel activates the worksheet and automatically selects the range for you. When you change the cells, Excel updates the picture.

SUPER NOTE

Use Excel pictures to copy worksheet cells, objects, or charts to another Windows application. Copy the picture, activate the application, and choose its **Edit** | **P**aste command.

Chapter

29

Creating Slide Shows

Excel offers some powerful tools for creating slide show presentations. A template and add-in macro make creating slide shows fast and easy, and you can even include video and audio transition effects between slides. This chapter shows you how to create, edit, and run Excel slide shows.

Working with the Slide Template

You use a special template included with Excel to create your slide shows. To open the template, follow the steps in Procedure 29.1.

PROCEDURE 29.1. OPENING THE SLIDE TEMPLATE.

1. Select the **F**ile | **N**ew command. Excel displays the New dialog box.
2. In the **N**ew list box, highlight Slides.

> **SUPER NOTE**
>
> If you don't see a Slides item in the **N**ew list, the Slides template was not installed when you set up Excel. You need to rerun the setup program and install the Slide Show add-in.

3. Click on OK or press Enter. Excel opens the slide show template, shown in Figure 29.1.

FIGURE 29.1. *The slide show template.*

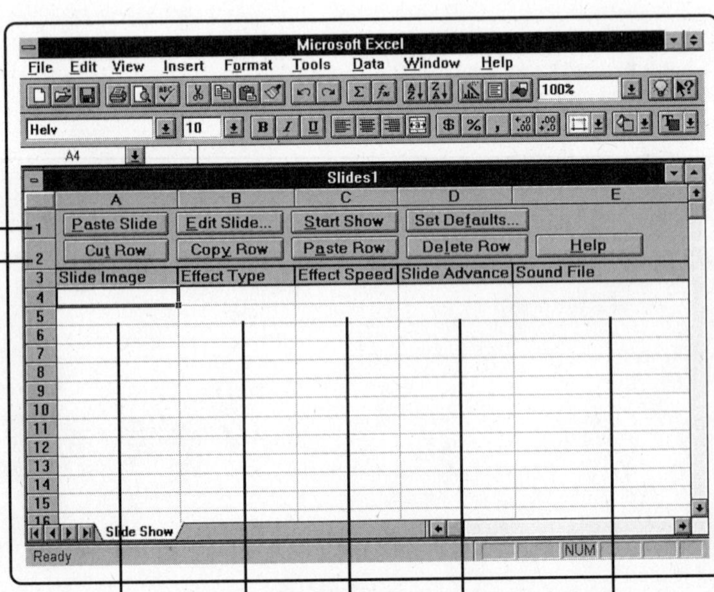

The first two rows of the template contain a number of macro buttons that you use to manipulate your slides. With these buttons, you can add or delete slides, edit the slide settings, and change the slide order. Excel stores the information for each slide in columns A through E, beginning in row 4. This information includes a reduced image of the slide and the settings for the transition effects.

Creating a Slide

To create a slide, you copy the desired cell range or chart into the Windows Clipboard. Excel uses the Clipboard contents to create a new slide in the slide template. Excel then displays the Edit Slide dialog box, shown in Figure 29.2. This dialog box contains three sections:

Transition Gallery: This section sets the video transition effects. The Effect list contains more than 40 different video transitions, and the Speed scroll bar controls the transition speed. Use the Test button to see an example of the transition effect.

Advance: Slide advance can be either Manual or Timed. If you choose Timed, you must enter the number of seconds between slides.

Sound: This section sets the audio transition effects. Click on Choose to open a sound file. The Test Sound button plays a sample of the sound. The Clear button closes the sound file.

SUPER NOTE

To use audio transition effects, you must have an appropriate sound board and at least Windows Multimedia Extensions version 1.0 or Windows 3.1.

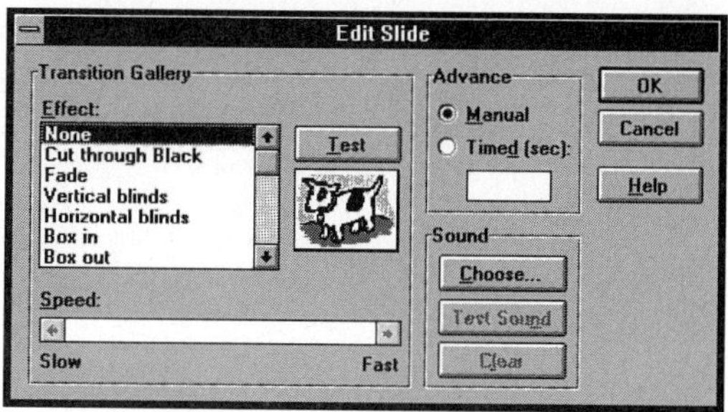

FIGURE 29.2.
The Edit Slide dialog box.

Follow Procedure 29.2 to create a slide from a worksheet range.

PROCEDURE 29.2. CREATING A SLIDE FROM A WORKSHEET RANGE.

1. Activate the worksheet containing the cell range you want to include in the slide.
2. Highlight the cell range.
3. Select the **E**dit | **C**opy command. Excel copies the range to the Clipboard.
4. Activate the slide template.
5. Click on the **P**aste Slide button on the slide template. (When you move the mouse pointer over the slide template buttons, the pointer changes to a hand with a pointing finger.) Excel pastes a reduced image of the range in the Slide Image column and displays the Edit Slide dialog box.
6. Select the options you want.
7. Click on OK or press Enter. Excel enters the slide settings on the template.

SUPER NOTE

The slide images are linked to the original worksheet. Excel automatically updates the slide whenever you make changes to the range.

SUPER NOTE

Make sure your slides are simple and readable with plenty of open space. Your audience should not have to guess what the point of the slide is. Try to use a consistent design scheme in all your slides. A company logo or other graphic in a corner and consistent colors will give your presentation continuity.

Figure 29.3 shows a slide template with three worksheet slides.

FIGURE 29.3.
An Excel slide show.

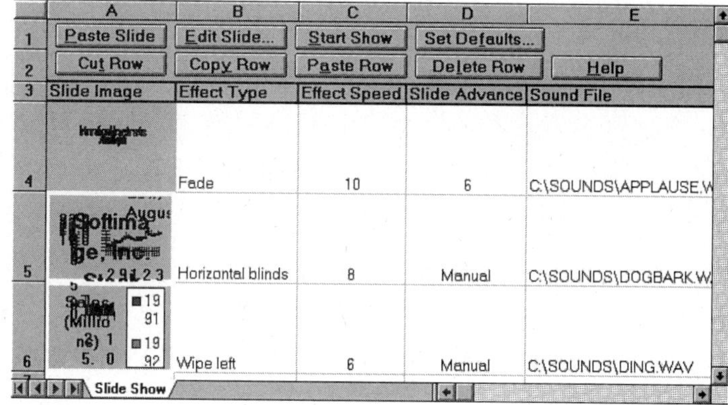

Follow the steps in Procedure 29.3 to create a slide from a chart.

PROCEDURE 29.3. CREATING A SLIDE FROM A CHART.

1. Activate the chart you want to include in the slide.
2. Select the **E**dit | **C**opy command. Excel copies the range to the Clipboard.
3. Activate the slide template.
4. Click on the **P**aste Slide button. Excel pastes a reduced image of the chart in the Slide Image column and displays the Edit Slide dialog box.
5. Select the options you want.
6. Click on OK or press Enter. Excel enters the slide settings on the template.

SUPER TIP

You can use graphics from other applications in your Excel slide shows. Simply copy the image to the Clipboard and select **P**aste Slide in the slide template.

Editing Slide Transition Effects

You can edit the transition effects of any slide or group of slides that appears on the slide show template. Procedure 29.4 provides the details.

PROCEDURE 29.4. EDITING SLIDE TRANSITION EFFECTS.

1. Select at least one cell from the row containing the slide information you want to edit (don't select the slide itself). To edit more than one slide, select a cell from each row.
2. Click on the Edit Slide button. Excel displays the Edit Slide dialog box.
3. Select the options you want.
4. Click on OK or press Enter. Excel updates the slide information.

If you find that you use the same transition settings for most of your slides, you can set up a default setting by following the steps in Procedure 29.5.

PROCEDURE 29.5. SETTING DEFAULT TRANSITION EFFECTS.

1. Click on the Set Defaults button. Excel displays the Set Defaults dialog box.
2. Select the transition effects you want to use as defaults.
3. Click on OK or press Enter.

SUPER NOTE

The new default transition effects don't change the settings for any existing slides. To change the transition options for existing slides, use Edit Slide instead.

Moving a Slide

Changing the order of a slide is as easy as cutting and pasting a row in the slide template. Procedure 29.6 shows you what to do.

PROCEDURE 29.6. MOVING A SLIDE.

1. Select at least one cell in the row containing the slide you want to move (don't select the slide itself).
2. Click on the Cut Row button. Excel cuts the slide from the template.
3. Select a cell in the row above which you want to insert the slide. To move the slide to the end, select a cell in any empty row.
4. Click on the Paste Row button. Excel inserts the slide above the selected row.

Copying a Slide

If you want to use the same slide at another point in your presentation, you don't have to create the slide again. Instead, follow the steps in Procedure 29.7 to copy the existing slide.

PROCEDURE 29.7. COPYING A SLIDE.

1. Select at least one cell in the row containing the slide you want to copy (don't select the slide itself).
2. Click on the Copy Row button.
3. Select a cell in the row above which you want to insert the copy. To copy the slide to the end, select a cell in any empty row.
4. Click on the Paste Row button. Excel inserts the copy above the selected row.

Deleting a Slide

If you no longer need a slide, you can delete it from the template by following Procedure 29.8.

PROCEDURE 29.8. DELETING A SLIDE.

1. Select at least one cell in the row containing the slide you want to delete (don't select the slide itself).
2. Click on the Delete Row button. Excel deletes the row.

Running a Slide Show

When you want to run a slide show, click on the **S**tart Show button. Excel displays the Start Show dialog box, shown in Figure 29.4. This dialog box enables you to set two options:

Repeat show until Esc is pressed	Select this option to run the slide show in a continuous loop.
Initial Slide	Use the scroll bar to specify the first slide in the show.

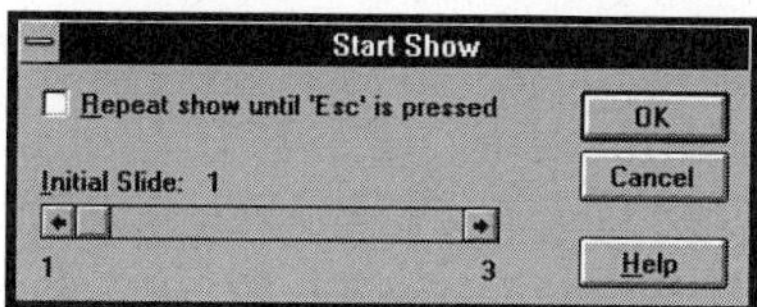

FIGURE 29.4.
The Start Show dialog box.

After you choose your options, click on OK or press Enter. Excel displays the first slide, sized to fit the screen.

If you set your slides to advance at timed intervals, Excel automatically performs the transition from one slide to the next. If you're using the manual advance, Excel pauses on each slide until you're ready. To advance to the next slide, click the left mouse button.

Interrupting a Slide Show

You can interrupt a slide show at any time by pressing the Esc key. When you do, Excel displays the Slide Show Options dialog box, shown in Figure 29.5. This dialog box provides you with the following options:

Slide **N**umber	If you want to switch to a different slide, use the scroll bar to select the slide number.
Goto	Click on this button to resume the slide show at the Slide **N**umber.
Stop	Click on this button to end the slide show.
Continue	Click on this button to resume the slide show from the same slide where it was interrupted.

FIGURE 29.5.
The Slide Show Options dialog box.

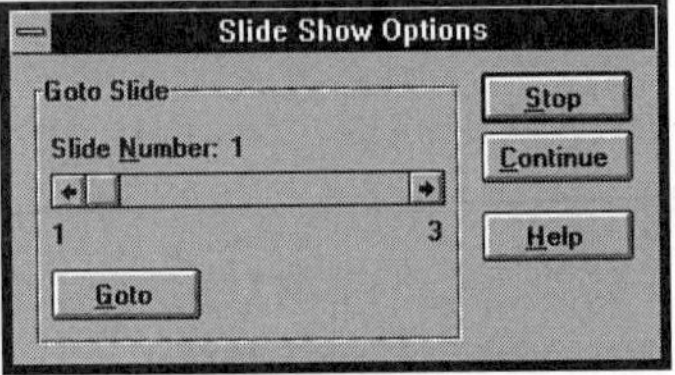

Running a Slide Show on a Different Computer

If you want to run your slide show on another computer equipped with Excel, you need to make sure the slide template is linked to the Slide Show Add-in file (called SLIDES.XLA) on the other computer. Procedure 29.9 takes you through the steps you need to follow.

PROCEDURE 29.9. RUNNING A SLIDE SHOW ON A DIFFERENT COMPUTER.

1. Activate Excel on the other computer.
2. Open the slide show template file as outlined in the section in this chapter titled "Working with the Slide Template."
3. Select the **T**ools | **P**rotection | Un**p**rotect Sheet command. This enables you to change the file's links.
4. Select the **E**dit | Lin**k**s command. Excel displays the Links dialog box.
5. Highlight SLIDES.XLA in the list box.
6. Click on the **C**hange Source button. Excel displays the Change Links dialog box.
7. Highlight SLIDES.XLA (this file should be in the \LIBRARY\SLIDES subdirectory).

8. Click on OK or press Enter. Excel updates the links and returns you to the Links dialog box.
9. Click on Close.
10. Run the slide show.

Workshop

IV

Databases and Lists

Chapter

30

Creating a List or Database

This chapter introduces you to Excel lists. You'll learn what lists are, how you can use them, and how to create them in your Excel worksheets.

What Is a List?

A *list* is a collection of related information with an organizational structure that makes it easy to find or extract data from its contents. Examples of lists are a phone book organized by name and a library card catalog organized by book title.

SUPER UPGRADE NOTE

If you've used previous versions of Excel (or if you're converting to Excel 5.0 from another spreadsheet), a list is equivalent to what used to be called a *database*. Excel 5.0 uses the term *list* so that you can differentiate between data on a worksheet and external data from a database management program (such as dBASE, Access, or SQL Server).

In Excel, the term *list* refers to a worksheet range that has the following properties:

Field: A single type of information, such as a name, address, or phone number. In Excel lists, each column (or any cell in a column) is a field.

Field value: A single item in a field. In an Excel list, the field values are the individual cells.

Field name: A unique name that you assign to every list field (worksheet column). These names are always found in the first row of the list.

Record: A collection of associated field values. In Excel lists, each row is a record.

List range: The worksheet range that includes all the records, fields, and field names of a list.

For example, suppose you want to set up an accounts receivable list. A simple system would include information such as the account name, account number, invoice number, invoice amount, due date, date paid, and a calculation of the number of days overdue. Figure 30.1 shows how this would be implemented as an Excel list.

SUPER NOTE

You can use lists for just about anything you need to keep track of: inventory, accounts payable, books, CDs, and even household possessions.

FIGURE 30.1.
An accounts receivable list.

AR_DATA.XLS

	A	B	C	D	E	F	G
1	Account Name	Account Number	Invoice Number	Invoice Amount	Due Date	Date Paid	Days Overdue
2	Emily's Sports Palace	08-2255	117316	$1,584.20	8-Dec-93		26
3	Refco Office Solutions	14-5741	117317	$ 303.65	9-Dec-93	9-Dec-93	-
4	Chimera Illusions	02-0200	117318	$3,005.14	10-Dec-93	15-Dec-93	-
5	Door Stoppers Ltd.	01-0045	117319	$ 78.85	12-Dec-93		22
6	Meaghan Manufacturing	12-3456	117320	$4,347.21	15-Dec-93	10-Dec-93	-
7	Brimson Furniture	10-0009	117321	$2,144.55	15-Dec-93		19
8	Katy's Paper Products	12-1212	117322	$ 234.69	16-Dec-93		18
9	Stephen Inc.	16-9734	117323	$ 157.25	18-Dec-93	17-Dec-92	-
10	Voyatzis Designs	14-1882	117324	$1,985.25	22-Dec-93		12
11	Lone Wolf Software	07-4441	117325	$2,567.12	25-Dec-93	20-Dec-93	-
12	O'Donoghue Inc.	09-2111	117326	$1,234.56	30-Dec-93		4
13	Renaud & Son	07-0025	117327	$ 565.77	4-Jan-94		-
14	Simpson's Ltd.	16-6658	117328	$ 898.54	3-Jan-94		-
15	Door Stoppers Ltd.	01-0045	117329	$1,584.20	7-Jan-94		-

Accounts Receivable Data / Customer Data

Field name — Record — Field value

Planning a List

You need to plan your list before you create it. What kind of information do you want to include? How much detail do you need for each record? What field names do you want to use? By asking yourself these questions in advance, you can save yourself the trouble of redesigning your list later.

The most important step in creating a list is determining the information you want it to contain. Although a list can be as large as the entire worksheet, in practice you should minimize the size of the range. This saves memory and makes managing the data easier. Therefore, you should strive to set up all your lists with only essential information.

For example, if you're building an accounts receivable list, you should include only data that relates to the receivables. In such a list, you need two kinds of information: invoice data and customer data. The invoice data would include the invoice number, the amount, the due date, and the date paid. You also would include a calculated field that determines the number of days overdue. For the customer, you would need at least a name and an account number. You don't need to include an address or phone number, because this information isn't essential to the receivables data.

This last point brings up the idea of *data redundancy*. In many cases, you'll be setting up a list as part of a larger application. For example, you might have lists not only for accounts receivable, but also for accounts payable, customer information, part numbers, and so on. You don't need to include information such as addresses and phone numbers in the receivables list, because you should have that data in a more general customer information list. To include this data in both places is redundant.

SUPER TIP

Different but related lists need to have a *key field* that is common to each. For example, the accounts receivable and customer information lists both could contain an account number field. This enables you to cross-reference entries in both lists.

As soon as you know what kind of information to include in your list, you need to determine the level of detail for each field. For example, if you're including address information, do you want separate fields for the street address, city, state, and zip code? For a phone number, do you need a separate field for the area code? In most cases, the best approach is to split the data into the smallest elements that make sense. This will give you maximum flexibility when you sort and extract information.

SUPER TIP

If you need to use a longer field name, turn on the Word Wrap alignment option to keep the field width small. See Chapter 9, "Formatting Other Cell Attributes."

The next stage in planning your list is to assign names to each field. Here are some guidelines to follow:

- Always use the top row of the list for the column labels.
- Although you can assign names as long as 255 characters, you should try to use shorter names to prevent your fields from becoming too wide.
- Field names must be unique, and they must be text or text formulas. If you need to use numbers, format them as text.
- You should format the column labels to help differentiate them from the list data. You can use bold text, a different font color, and a border along the bottom of each cell.

The final step in setting up your list is to plan its position in the worksheet. Here are some points to keep in mind:

- Some Excel commands can automatically identify the size and shape of a list. To avoid confusing such commands, try to use only one list per worksheet. If you have multiple, related lists, include them in other tabs in the same workbook.
- If you have any other nonlist data in a worksheet, leave at least one blank row or column between the data and the list. This will help Excel identify the list automatically.

- Excel has a command that enables you to filter your list data to show only records that match certain criteria. (See Chapter 31, "Managing List Records," for details.) This command works by hiding rows of data. Therefore, if you have nonlist data you need to access, it's important not to place it to the left or right of a list.

Entering List Data

As soon as you've set up your field names, you can start entering your list records. The following sections show you how to enter data directly on the worksheet or by using a data form.

Entering Data Directly on a Worksheet

The most straightforward way to enter information into a list is simply to directly type data in the worksheet cells. If you've formatted any of the fields (numeric formats, alignment, and so on), be sure to copy the formats to the new records.

SUPER TIP

Excel 5.0's new Format Painter tool makes copying cell formatting easy. See Chapter 12, "Working with Cell Formats," for details.

Entering and deleting records and fields within a list is analogous to inserting and deleting rows and columns in a regular worksheet model. Table 30.1 summarizes these list commands.

Table 30.1. Basic list commands.

List Action	*Excel Command*
Add a record	Select a row, then select **I**nsert | **R**ows
Add a field	Select a column, then select **I**nsert | **C**olumns
Delete a record	Select the entire row, then select **E**dit | **D**elete
Delete a field	Select the entire column, then select **E**dit | **D**elete

If you don't want to add or delete an entire row or column (for example, if other worksheet data is in the way), you can insert or delete data within the list range. If you're inserting or deleting a row, select a list record (make sure you include each field in the record). If you're inserting or deleting a column, select a list field (make sure you include each record in the field).

Entering list information can be a tedious chore. Excel offers a number of shortcut keys to speed up the process. These are summarized in Table 30.2.

Table 30.2. Excel data entry shortcut keys.

Key	*Action*
Tab	Confirms the entry and moves to the field on the right
Shift+Tab	Confirms the entry and moves to the field on the left
Enter	Confirms the entry and moves to the next record
Shift+Enter	Confirms the entry and moves to the previous record
Ctrl+"	Copies the number from the same field in the previous record
Ctrl+'	Copies the formula from the same field in the previous record
Ctrl+;	Enters the current date
Ctrl+:	Enters the current time

SUPER TIP

If pressing Enter or Shift+Enter doesn't move you to another record, select the **T**ools | **O**ptions command. Then select the Edit tab in the Options dialog box and activate the **M**ove Selection after Enter check box.

Entering Data Using a Data Form

Excel lists are powerful information-management tools, but creating and maintaining them can be tedious and time-consuming. To save you time and make data entry easier, Excel offers the *data form* dialog box. You can use this form to add, edit, delete, and find list records quickly.

What Is a Data Form?

A *data form* is a dialog box that simplifies list management in the following ways:

- The dialog box shows only one record at a time, which makes data entry and editing easier.

- You can view many more fields in a form than you can see on-screen. In fact, depending on the size of your screen, you can view as many as 18 fields in a single form.
- When you add or delete records using the data form, Excel automatically adjusts the list range.
- You get an extra level of safety when you add or delete records. Excel prevents you from overwriting existing worksheet data when you add records, and it seeks confirmation for record deletions.
- Novice users or data-entry clerks are insulated from the normal list commands. Simple command buttons enable users to add, delete, and find data.

You can view the form by following the steps in Procedure 30.1.

PROCEDURE 30.1. DISPLAYING A DATA FORM.

1. Select any cell from within the list. (You also can select one of the field name cells or a cell in a row or column immediately adjacent to the list.)
2. Select the **D**ata | F**o**rm command. Excel displays the data form.

Figure 30.2 shows the data form for the Accounts Receivable list. When constructing the data form, Excel begins with the field names and adds an edit box for each editable field. Excel includes fields that are the result of a formula or function (for example, the Days Overdue field in Figure 30.2) for display purposes only; you can't edit these fields. The scrollbar enables you to move quickly through the list. The record number indicator in the top-right corner of the dialog box keeps track of the current list row. The dialog box also includes several command buttons for adding, deleting, and finding records.

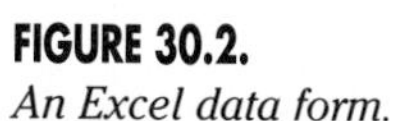

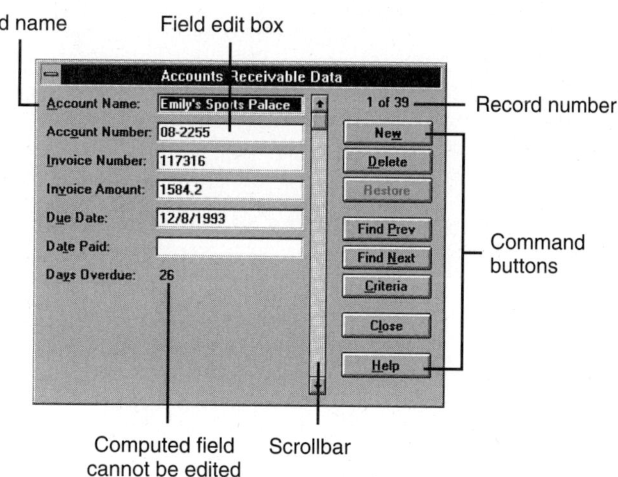

FIGURE 30.2.
An Excel data form.

SUPER NOTE

The record number indicator is unaffected by the list sort order. The first record below the field names is always record 1.

Editing Records

You can use the data form to edit any fields in your list records, with the exception of computed or protected fields. Procedure 30.2 lists the steps to follow.

PROCEDURE 30.2. EDITING A LIST WITH THE DATA FORM.

1. Display the data form.
2. Select the record you want to edit.
3. Edit the fields you want to change.
4. Repeat steps 2 and 3 for other records you want to edit.
5. Click on Close to finish editing the list.

SUPER CAUTION

When you make changes to a record, Excel saves the changes permanently when you scroll to another record. Before leaving a record, check each field to make sure it contains the data you want. To restore a record to its original data, click on the data form's **R**estore button before you move to another record.

If you prefer to use the keyboard to navigate the data form, you can use Excel's shortcuts to speed up the process. These are summarized in Table 30.3.

Table 30.3. Data form keyboard techniques.

Key	*Action*
Alt+underlined letter in a field name	Selects the field if it's editable
Alt+underlined letter in command button	Selects the command button

Key	Action
Tab	Moves to the next editable field
Shift+Tab	Moves to the previous editable field
Enter	Moves to the next record
Shift+Enter	Moves to the previous record
Down arrow	Moves to the same field in the next record
Up arrow	Moves to the same field in the previous record
Page Down	Moves to the same field 10 records down
Page Up	Moves to the same field 10 records back
Ctrl+Page Down	Displays a blank record
Ctrl+Page Up	Moves to the first record

Adding Records

Adding records with the data form is fast and easy. Procedure 30.3 outlines the steps to follow.

PROCEDURE 30.3. ADDING RECORDS WITH THE DATA FORM.

1. Display the data form.
2. Click on the New button or press Ctrl+Page Down. Excel creates a blank record and displays New Record as the record number indicator.
3. Fill in the fields for the new record.
4. Repeat steps 2 and 3 for other records you want to add.
5. Click on Close to finish adding new records.

When you add records with the data form, Excel adds them to the bottom of the list without inserting a new row. If there is no room to extend the list range, Excel displays the warning message shown in Figure 30.3. To add new records, you must either move or delete the other data.

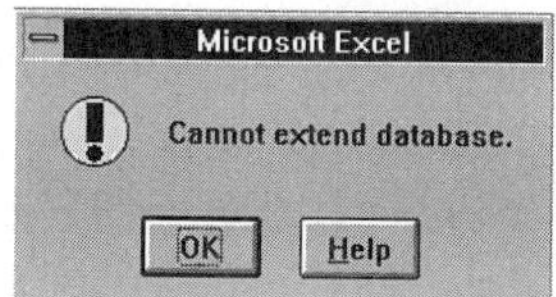

FIGURE 30.3.
Excel warns you when the list range runs out of room.

Deleting Records

Follow the steps in Procedure 30.4 to delete records using the data form.

PROCEDURE 30.4. DELETING RECORDS WITH THE DATA FORM.

1. Display the data form.
2. Select the record you want to delete.
3. Click on the **D**elete button. Excel warns you that the record will be deleted permanently.
4. Click on OK or press Enter to confirm the deletion. Click on Cancel to end the deletion. Excel returns you to the data form.
5. Repeat steps 2-4 to delete other records.
6. Click on C**l**ose to return to the worksheet.

SUPER NOTE

When you delete a record from the data form, Excel clears the data and shifts the records to fill in the gap.

Finding Records

Although the data form enables you to scroll through a list, you might find that, for larger lists, you need to use the form's search capabilities to quickly find what you want. You can find specific records in the list by first specifying the *criteria* that the search must match. Excel then compares each record with the criteria and displays the first record that matches. For example, you might want to find all invoices that are over $1,000.00 or those that are at least one day past due.

SUPER NOTE

You can perform only simple searches with the data form. For more complex search criteria, see Chapter 31, "Managing List Records."

You construct the search criteria using text, numbers, and comparison operators such as equal to (=) and greater than (>). For example, to find all the invoices that are over $1,000.00, you would type `>1000` in the Invoice Amount field. To find an account named Read Inc., you would type `read inc.` in the Account Name field. Procedure 30.5 takes you through the necessary steps.

PROCEDURE 30.5. FINDING RECORDS WITH THE DATA FORM.

1. Display the data form.
2. Click on the **C**riteria button. Excel displays a blank record and replaces the record number indicator with Criteria, as shown in Figure 30.4.

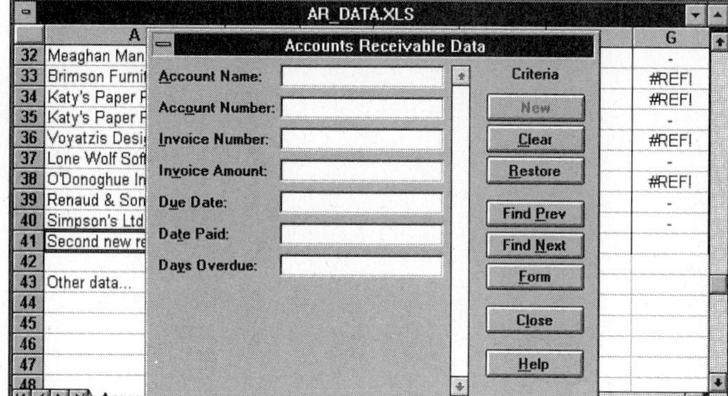

FIGURE 30.4.
The Criteria data form.

3. Select the field you want to use for the search.
4. Enter the criterion.
5. Repeat steps 3 and 4 if you want to use multiple criteria.
6. Use the Find **N**ext and Find **P**rev buttons to move up or down to the next record that matches the criteria.

To hone your searches, you can use multiple criteria. For example, Figure 30.5 shows a form with three criteria entered. In this case, Excel will search for all invoices for companies with the word *office* in their names, that are over $1,000.00, and that are past due. Note that all three criteria must be satisfied before Excel finds a match.

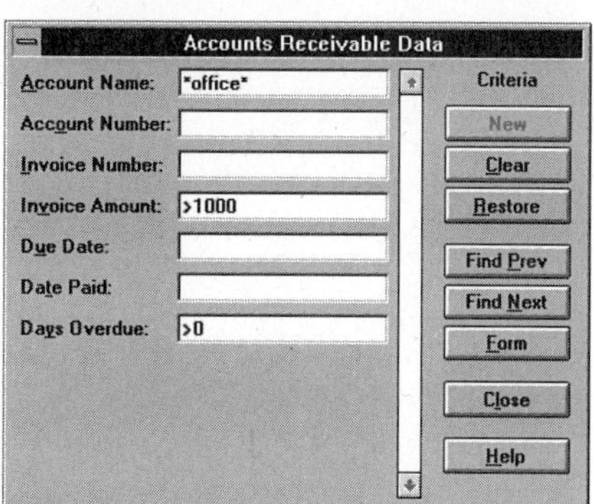

FIGURE 30.5.
You can enter multiple criteria to hone your searches.

Another feature demonstrated in Figure 30.5 is the use of *wildcard characters*. Use the asterisk (*) to substitute for any number of characters. In Figure 30.5, `*office*` finds Refco Office Solutions or Wilson Office Supplies. You also can use the question mark (?) to substitute for a single character. For example, enter `Re?d` to find Read, Reid, or Reed.

SUPER TIP

To search for an actual question mark (?) or asterisk (*), precede it with a tilde (~). For example, to find PAID?, enter `PAID~?`.

Chapter 31

Managing List Records

In the last chapter, you learned a few simple techniques for managing data either directly on the worksheet or with a data form. These techniques are fine for small lists, but they can be cumbersome and time-consuming with lists that contain dozens or even hundreds of records. This chapter shows you more sophisticated techniques for sorting and filtering records in large databases.

Sorting a List

One of the advantages of a list is that you can rearrange the records so they're sorted alphabetically or numerically. This enables you to view the data in order by customer name, account number, part number, or any other field. You can even sort on multiple fields, which would enable you, for example, to sort a client list by state and then by name within each state.

The sorting procedure is determined by the options in the Sort dialog box, shown in Figure 31.1.

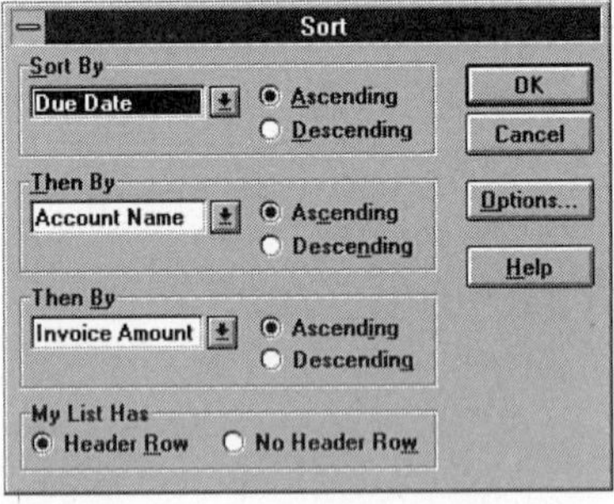

FIGURE 31.1.
The Sort dialog box.

Sort By — This drop-down list box contains the list field names. Select a field from this list to determine the overall order for the sort. In Figure 31.1, the Due Date field is selected; therefore, the entire database will be sorted by Due Date.

Then By — This drop-down list also contains the list field names. Select a field from this list to sort records that have the same data in the field specified in Sort By. In Figure 31.1, for example, all the records that have the same Due Date will be sorted by Account Name.

Then By — Select a field name from this list to sort the records that have the same data in the fields specified by both Sort By and Then By. Figure 31.1 shows that records that have the same Due Date and the same Account Name are sorted by the Invoice Amount field.

SUPER NOTE

Although Excel enables you to sort on as many as three fields, it isn't necessary to enter a field in all three lists. For most sorts, you'll need to choose a field in only the **S**ort By list.

My List Has — Excel usually can differentiate between field names (the header row) and data. If Excel finds what it thinks is a header row, it doesn't include it in the sort (and it activates the Header **R**ow option). If you want the top row included in the sort, select the No Header Ro**w** option.

SUPER NOTE

Excel identifies the header row of a list by looking for differences in data type (most field names are text entries), capitalization, and formatting. If your list doesn't have a header row, you still can sort by using column headings (Column A, Column B, and so on).

SUPER CAUTION

Be careful when you sort list records that contain formulas. If the formulas use relative addressing, the new sort order might change the references and produce erroneous results.

For each sort field, you can specify whether the field is sorted in ascending or descending order. Table 31.1 summarizes Excel's ascending sort priorities.

Table 31.1. Excel's ascending sort order.

Type (in Order of Priority)	*Order*
Numbers	Largest negative to largest positive
Text	Space ! " # $ % & ' ( ) * + , - . / 0 through 9 (when formatted as text) : ; < = > ? @ A through Z (Excel ignores case) [\ ] ^ _ ' { | } ~

continues

Table 31.1. continued

Type (in Order of Priority)	*Order*
Logical	FALSE before TRUE
Error	All error values are equal
Blank	Always sorted last (ascending or descending)

Procedure 31.1 shows you how to sort a list.

PROCEDURE 31.1. SORTING A LIST.

1. Select a cell inside the list.
2. Select the **D**ata | **S**ort command. Excel displays the Sort dialog box.
3. Enter the sort options you want.
4. Click on OK or press Enter. Excel sorts the range.

Sort Options

If you click on the **O**ptions button in the Sort dialog box, Excel displays the Sort Options dialog box (see Figure 31.2), which gives you the following choices:

First Key Sort Order — Sets a custom sort order for the field you chose in the **S**ort By list. For example, to sort by the days of the week, select the Sun, Mon, Tue,... option.

> **SUPER TIP**
>
> You can create your own custom sort orders. See Chapter 66, "Customizing Excel's Options and Workspace," for details.

Case Sensitive — Select this option to have Excel differentiate between uppercase and lowercase during sorting. For example, Excel would sort dBASE before DBASE.

Orientation	Excel normally sorts list rows (the Sort **T**op to Bottom option). To sort list columns, select Sort **L**eft to Right.

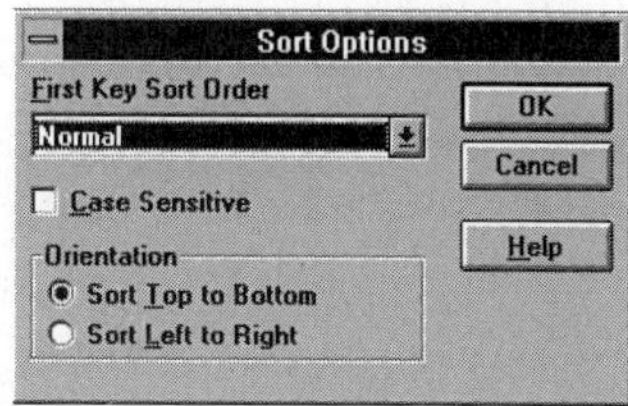

FIGURE 31.2.
The Sort Options dialog box.

Using the Standard Toolbar's Sorting Tools

Excel's Standard toolbar includes two tools that enable you to quickly sort a list on a single field. Just select a cell in the field and click on either the Sort Ascending tool (for an ascending sort) or the Sort Descending tool (for a descending sort). Excel sorts the entire list (except the field names) on the field you selected.

The Sort Ascending tool in the Standard toolbar.

The Sort Descending tool in the Standard toolbar.

> **SUPER NOTE**
>
> Both the Sort Ascending and Sort Descending tools use the currently selected options in the Sort Options dialog box.

Sorting on More Than Three Keys

You're not restricted to sorting on just three fields in an Excel list. By performing consecutive sorts, you can sort on any number of fields. For example, suppose you have a customer list that you want to sort by the following fields (in order of importance): Region, State, City, Zip Code, and Name. To use five fields, you need to perform two consecutive sorts. The first sort uses the three least important fields: City, Zip Code, and Name. Of these three, City is the most important, so it is sorted by the **S**ort By field, Zip Code is sorted by the **T**hen By field, and Name is sorted by the Then **B**y field. When this sort is complete, you need to run another using the remaining keys, Region and State. Select Region from the **S**ort By list and State from the **T**hen By list.

By running multiple sorts and always using the least important fields first, you can sort on as many fields as you like.

Using a List in Natural Order

It's convenient to see the order that records were entered into a list, or the *natural order* of the data. Normally, you can restore a list to its natural order by selecting the **E**dit | **U**ndo Sort command immediately after a sort.

Unfortunately, after several sort operations, it's no longer possible to restore the natural order. The solution is to create a new field, called Record, in which you assign consecutive numbers as you enter the data. The first record is 1, the second is 2, and so on. To restore the list to its natural order, you sort on the Record field. Figure 31.3 shows the Accounts Receivable list with a record field.

FIGURE 31.3.
The Record field tracks the order in which records are added to a list.

AR_DATA.XLS

	A	B	C	D	E	F	G	H
1	Record	Account Name	Account Number	Invoice Number	Invoice Amount	Due Date	Date Paid	Days Overdu
2	1	Emily's Sports Palace	08-2255	117316	$1,584.20	8-Dec-93		26
3	2	Refco Office Solutions	14-5741	117317	$ 303.65	9-Dec-93	9-Dec-93	-
4	3	Chimera Illusions	02-0200	117318	$3,005.14	10-Dec-93	15-Dec-93	-
5	4	Door Stoppers Ltd.	01-0045	117319	$ 78.85	12-Dec-93		22
6	5	Meaghan Manufacturing	12-3456	117320	$4,347.21	15-Dec-93	10-Dec-93	-
7	6	Brimson Furniture	10-0009	117321	$2,144.55	15-Dec-93		19
8	7	Katy's Paper Products	12-1212	117322	$ 234.69	16-Dec-93		18
9	8	Stephen Inc.	16-9734	117323	$ 157.25	18-Dec-93	17-Dec-92	-
10	9	Voyatzis Designs	14-1882	117324	$1,985.25	22-Dec-93		12
11	10	Lone Wolf Software	07-4441	117325	$2,567.12	25-Dec-93	20-Dec-93	-
12	11	O'Donoghue Inc.	09-2111	117326	$1,234.56	30-Dec-93		4
13	12	Renaud & Son	07-0025	117327	$ 565.77	4-Jan-94		-
14	13	Simpson's Ltd.	16-6658	117328	$ 898.54	3-Jan-94		-
15	14	Door Stoppers Ltd.	01-0045	117329	$1,584.20	7-Jan-94		-

Accounts Receivable Data / Customer Data / Sheet3

SUPER TIP

Use the Fill handle or the **E**dit | F**i**ll | **S**eries command to quickly enter a sequence of numbers (such as the record numbers for a list). See Chapter 4, "Working with Ranges," for more information.

Filtering List Data

One of the biggest problems with large lists is that it's often hard to find and extract the data you need. Sorting can help, but in the end you're still working with the entire list. What you need is a way to define the data you want to work with and then have Excel display only those records on-screen. This is called *filtering* your data; fortunately, Excel offers several techniques that get the job done.

Using AutoFilter to Filter a List

Excel 5.0's new AutoFilter feature makes filtering out subsets of your data as easy as selecting an option from a drop-down list. In fact, that is literally what happens. If you select the **D**ata | **F**ilter | Auto**F**ilter command, Excel adds drop-down arrows to the cells containing the list's column labels. Clicking on one of these arrows displays a list of all the unique entries in the column. Figure 31.4 shows the drop-down list for the Account Name field in an Accounts Receivable database.

AR_DATA.XLS

	A	B	C	D	E	F	G
1	Account Name	Account Numb	Invoice Numb	Invoice Amoun	Due Da	Date Paid	Days Overd
2	O'Donoghue Inc.	08-2255	117316	$1,584.20	8-Dec-93		26
3	Refco Office Solution Renaud & Son	14-5741	117317	$ 303.65	9-Dec-93		25
4	Simpson's Ltd.	02-0200	117318	$3,005.14	10-Dec-93	15-Dec-93	
5	Stephen Inc.	01-0045	117319	$ 78.85	12-Dec-93		22
6	Voyatzis Designs (Blanks)	12-3456	117320	$4,347.21	15-Dec-93	10-Dec-93	
7	(NonBlanks)	10-0009	117321	$2,144.55	15-Dec-93		19
8	Katy's Paper Products	12-1212	117322	$ 234.69	16-Dec-93		18
9	Stephen Inc.	16-9734	117323	$ 157.25	18-Dec-93	17-Dec-92	
10	Voyatzis Designs	14-1882	117324	$1,985.25	22-Dec-93		12
11	Lone Wolf Software	07-4441	117325	$2,567.12	25-Dec-93	20-Dec-93	
12	O'Donoghue Inc.	09-2111	117326	$1,234.56	30-Dec-93		4
13	Refco Office Solutions	14-5741	117327	$ 456.78	30-Dec-93		4
14	Renaud & Son	07-0025	117328	$ 565.77	4-Jan-94		
15	Simpson's Ltd.	16-6658	117329	$ 898.54	3-Jan-94		

Accounts Receivable Data / Customer Data / S

FIGURE 31.4.
For each list field, AutoFilter adds drop-down lists that contain only the unique entries in the column.

If you select an item from one these lists, Excel does the following:

- It displays only those records that include the item in that field. For example, Figure 31.5 shows the resulting records when the item Refco Office Solutions is selected from the list attached to the Account Name column. The other records are hidden and can be retrieved whenever you need them.
- It changes the color of the column's drop-down arrow. This enables you to know which column you used to filter the list.
- It displays the row headings of the filtered records in a different color.
- It displays a message in the status bar telling you how many records it found that matched the selected item.

FIGURE 31.5.
Selecting an item from a drop-down list displays only records that include the item in the field.

AR_DATA.XLS

	A	B	C	D	E	F	G
1	Account Name	Account Numb	Invoice Numb	Invoice Amoun	Due Da	Date Paid	Days Overdu
3	Refco Office Solutions	14-5741	117317	$ 303.65	9-Dec-93		25
13	Refco Office Solutions	14-5741	117327	$ 456.78	30-Dec-93		4
26	Refco Office Solutions	14-5741	117340	$1,234.56	29-Jan-94		
42	Refco Office Solutions	14-5741	117381	$ 854.50	17-Mar-94		
59	Refco Office Solutions	14-5741	117400	$3,210.98	31-Mar-94		
70	Refco Office Solutions	14-5741	117411	$1,642.75	15-Apr-94		
97	Refco Office Solutions	14-5741	117444	$ 422.76	6-May-94		
98							
99							
100							
101							
102							
103							
104							

Accounts Receivable Data / Customer Data / S

Filter Mode NUM

To continue filtering the data, you can select an item from one of the other lists. For example, you can select the nonblank cells in the Days Overdue column to see only those Refco Office Solutions invoices that are overdue. (To select nonblank fields, see the next section.)

AutoFilter Criteria Options

The items you see in each drop-down list are called the *filter criteria*. Besides selecting specific criteria (such as an account name), you also have the following choices in each drop-down list:

All: Removes the filter criterion for the column. If you have selected multiple criteria, you can remove all the filter criteria and display the entire list by selecting the **D**ata | **F**ilter | **S**how All command.

Custom: Enables you to enter more sophisticated criteria. For more information, see the next section.

Blanks: Displays records that have no data in the field. In the Accounts Receivable list, for example, you could use this criterion to find all the unpaid invoices (that is, those with a blank Date Paid field).

NonBlanks: Displays records that have data in the field. Selecting this criterion in the Days Overdue field of the Accounts Receivable list, for example, finds invoices that are overdue.

SUPER NOTE

To display the entire list and remove the column drop-down arrows, select the **D**ata | **F**ilter | Auto**F**ilter command again.

Setting Up Custom AutoFilter Criteria

In its basic form, AutoFilter enables you to select only a single item from each column drop-down list. AutoFilter's *custom filter criteria,* however, give you a way to select multiple items. In the Accounts Receivable list, for example, you could use custom criteria to display all the invoices with

- an Account Number that begins with 07
- a Due Date in January
- an amount between $1,000 and $5,000
- an Account Name of either Refco Office Solutions or Brimson Furniture

When you select the Custom item from a column drop-down list, you'll see the Custom AutoFormat dialog box, shown in Figure 31.6. The group box shows the name of the field you're using, and it contains four drop-down lists and a couple of option buttons. You use the two drop-down lists across the top to set up the first part of your criterion. The list on the left contains a list of Excel's *comparison operators,* shown in Table 31.2. The combination edit box drop-down list on the right enables you to select a unique item from the field or enter your own value.

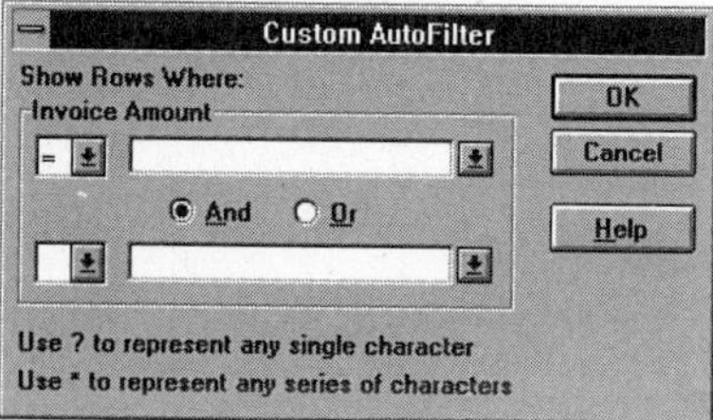

FIGURE 31.6.
Use the Custom AutoFormat dialog box to enter your custom criteria.

Table 31.2. Excel's comparison operators.

Operator	*Description*
=	Equal to
>	Greater than
<	Less than
>=	Greater than or equal to
<=	Less than or equal to
<>	Not equal to

For example, if you want to display invoices with an amount greater than or equal to $1,000, select the >= operator and enter `1000` in the edit box.

For text fields, you also can use *wildcard characters* to substitute for one or more characters. Use the question mark (?) wildcard to substitute for a single character. For example, if you enter `re?d`, Excel finds Read, Reid, and Reed. To substitute for groups of characters, use the asterisk (*). For example, if you enter `*carolina`, Excel finds all the entries that end with "carolina."

SUPER NOTE

If you enter a plain text criterion without any wildcards, Excel searches for items that begin with the text. Therefore, if you enter `R`, Excel matches all the entries that begin with R.

SUPER TIP

To include a wildcard as part of the criteria, precede the character with a tilde (~). For example, to find PAID?, enter `PAID~?`.

You can create *compound criteria* by clicking on the **And** or **Or** button and then entering another criterion in the bottom two drop-down lists. Use **And** when you want to display records that meet both criteria. Use **Or** when you want to display records that meet at least one of the two criteria.

For example, to display invoices with an amount greater than or equal to $1,000 and less than or equal to $5,000, you would fill in the dialog box as shown in Figure 31.7.

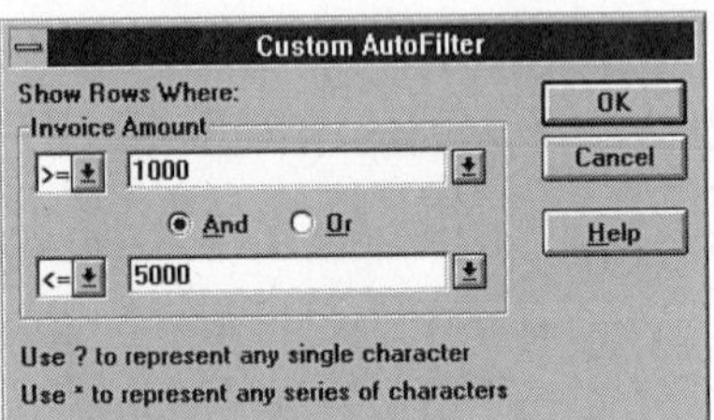

FIGURE 31.7.
A compound criterion that displays the records with invoice amounts between $1,000 and $5,000.

Procedure 31.2 takes you through the official steps to set up a custom AutoFilter criterion.

PROCEDURE 31.2. SETTING UP A CUSTOM AUTOFILTER CRITERION.

1. Select Custom from the drop-down list attached to the column you want to work with. Excel displays the Custom AutoFilter dialog box.

2. Select a comparison operator and enter a value for the first part of the criterion. If you don't want to create a compund criterion, skip to step 5.
3. Click on either the **A**nd or **O**r button, as appropriate.
4. Select a comparison operator and enter a value for the second part of the criterion.
5. Click on OK or press Enter. Excel filters the list.

Using Complex Criteria to Filter a List

The AutoFilter should take care of most of your filtering needs, but it's not designed for heavy-duty work. For example, AutoFilter doesn't handle the following Accounts Receivable criteria:

- Invoice Amounts greater than $100, less than $1,000, or greater than $10,000
- Account Numbers that begin with 01, 05, or 12
- Days Overdue greater than the value in cell J1

To work with these more sophisticated requests, you need to use *complex criteria.*

Setting Up a Criteria Range

Before you can work with complex criteria, you have to set up a *criteria range*. A criteria range has some or all of the list field names in the top row, with at least one blank row directly underneath. You enter your criteria in the blank row below the appropriate field name, and Excel searches the list for records with field values that satisfy the criteria. This setup gives you two major advantages over AutoFilter:

- By using either multiple rows or multiple columns for a single field, you can create compound criteria with as many terms as you like.
- Because you're entering your criteria in cells, you can use formulas to create *computed criteria.*

You can place the criteria range anywhere on the worksheet outside the list range. The most common position, however, is a couple of rows above the list range. Figure 31.8 shows the Accounts Receivable list with a criteria range. As you can see, the criteria are simply entered in the cell below the field name. In this case, the displayed criteria will find all Refco Office Solutions invoices that are overdue (that is, invoices that have a value greater than zero in the Days Overdue field).

FIGURE 31.8.
Set up a separate criteria range to enter complex criteria.

AR_DATA.XLS

	A	B	C	D	E	F	G
1	Account Name	Days Overdue					
2	Refco Office Solutions	>0					
3							
4							
5	Account Name	Account Number	Invoice Number	Invoice Amount	Due Date	Date Paid	Days Overdue
6	Emily's Sports Palace	08-2255	117316	$1,584.20	8-Dec-93		26
7	Refco Office Solutions	14-5741	117317	$ 303.65	9-Dec-93		25
8	Chimera Illusions	02-0200	117318	$3,005.14	10-Dec-93	15-Dec-93	
9	Door Stoppers Ltd.	01-0045	117319	$ 78.85	12-Dec-93		22
10	Meaghan Manufacturing	12-3456	117320	$4,347.21	15-Dec-93	10-Dec-93	
11	Brimson Furniture	10-0009	117321	$2,144.55	15-Dec-93		19
12	Katy's Paper Products	12-1212	117322	$ 234.69	16-Dec-93		18
13	Stephen Inc.	16-9734	117323	$ 157.25	18-Dec-93	17-Dec-92	
14	Voyatzis Designs	14-1882	117324	$1,985.25	22-Dec-93		12

Accounts Receivable Data / Customer Data

Filtering a List with a Criteria Range

Once you have your criteria range set up, you can use it to filter the list. Procedure 31.3 takes you through the basic steps.

PROCEDURE 31.3. FILTERING A LIST WITH A CRITERIA RANGE.

1. Copy the list field names you want to use for the criteria and paste them in the first row of the criteria range.
2. Below each field name in the criteria range, enter the criteria you want to use.
3. Select a cell in the list and then select the **Data | Filter | Advanced Filter** command. Excel displays the Advanced Filter dialog box.
4. The **List Range** edit box should contain the list range (if you selected a cell in the list beforehand). If not, activate the edit box and select the list (including the field names).
5. In the **Criteria Range** edit box, select the criteria range (again, including the field names you copied).
6. Click on OK or press Enter. Excel filters the list to show only those records that match your criteria.

SUPER TIP

When you define specific names for list and criteria, Excel always selects the correct list and criteria ranges in the Advanced Filter dialog box. Use Database for the list range and Criteria for the criteria range. (In both cases, be sure to include the column labels in the named range.)

Entering Compound Criteria

To enter compound criteria in a criteria range, use the following guidelines:

- To find records that match all the criteria, enter the criteria on a single row.
- To find records that match one or more of the criteria, enter the criteria in separate rows.

Finding records that match all the criteria is equivalent to clicking on the **And** button in the Custom AutoFormat dialog box. The sample criteria shown in Figure 31.8 matches records with the account name Refco Office Solutions and a positive number in the Days Overdue field. To narrow the displayed records, you can enter as many fields as you like.

You also can use the same field name more than once. For example, suppose you wanted to find all invoices with account names that begin with R and contain the strings "offic" and "sol." To do this, you would include the Account Name column label three times in the criteria range and enter the appropriate criteria below each label. Figure 31.9 shows the criteria range and the resulting filter.

FIGURE 31.9.
You can construct compound criteria on the same field by using multiple instances of the field name in the criteria range.

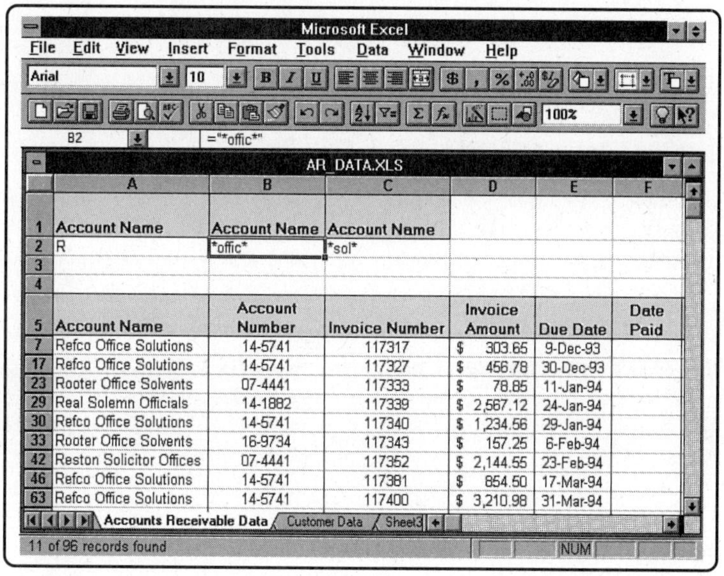

Microsoft Excel — AR_DATA.XLS

B2 ="*offic*"

	A	B	C	D	E	F
1	Account Name	Account Name	Account Name			
2	R	*offic*	*sol*			
3						
4						
5	Account Name	Account Number	Invoice Number	Invoice Amount	Due Date	Date Paid
7	Refco Office Solutions	14-5741	117317	$ 303.65	9-Dec-93	
17	Refco Office Solutions	14-5741	117327	$ 456.78	30-Dec-93	
23	Rooter Office Solvents	07-4441	117333	$ 78.85	11-Jan-94	
29	Real Solemn Officials	14-1882	117339	$ 2,567.12	24-Jan-94	
30	Refco Office Solutions	14-5741	117340	$ 1,234.56	29-Jan-94	
33	Rooter Office Solvents	16-9734	117343	$ 157.25	6-Feb-94	
42	Reston Solicitor Offices	07-4441	117352	$ 2,144.55	23-Feb-94	
46	Refco Office Solutions	14-5741	117381	$ 854.50	17-Mar-94	
63	Refco Office Solutions	14-5741	117400	$ 3,210.98	31-Mar-94	

Accounts Receivable Data / Customer Data / Sheet3

11 of 96 records found NUM

Finding records that match at least one out of several criteria is equivalent to clicking on the **Or** button in the Custom AutoFilter dialog box. In this case, you need to enter each criterion on a separate row. For example, to display all invoices with amounts greater than or equal to $10,000 or that are more than 15 days overdue, you would set up your criteria as shown in Figure 31.10.

FIGURE 31.10.
To display records that match one or more of the criteria, enter the criteria in separate rows.

AR_DATA.XLS

	A	B	C	D	E	F	G
1	Invoice Amount	Days Overdue					
2	>=10000						
3		>15					
4							
5	Account Name	Account Number	Invoice Number	Invoice Amount	Due Date	Date Paid	Days Overdue
6	Emily's Sports Palace	08-2255	117316	$ 1,584.20	8-Dec-93		26
7	Refco Office Solutions	14-5741	117317	$ 303.65	9-Dec-93		25
9	Door Stoppers Ltd.	01-0045	117319	$ 78.85	12-Dec-93		22
11	Brimson Furniture	10-0009	117321	$ 2,144.55	15-Dec-93		19
12	Katy's Paper Products	12-1212	117322	$ 234.69	16-Dec-93		18
28	Meaghan Manufacturing	12-3456	117338	$ 11,585.23	21-Jan-94		
36	Katy's Paper Products	12-1212	117346	$ 12,474.25	10-Feb-94		
102							
103							

Accounts Receivable Data / Customer Data / Sheet

7 of 96 records found NUM

SUPER CAUTION

Don't include any blank rows in your criteria range, because this throws off Excel when it tries to match the criteria.

Entering Computed Criteria

The fields in your criteria range aren't restricted to the list fields. You can create *computed criteria* that use a calculation to match records in the list. The calculation can refer to one or more list fields, or even to cells outside the list, and must return either `TRUE` or `FALSE`. Excel selects records that return `TRUE`.

To use computed criteria, add a column to the criteria range and enter the formula in the new field. Make sure that the name you give the criteria field is different from any field name in the list. When referencing the list cells in the formula, use the first row of the list. For example, to select all records in which the Date Paid is equal to the Due Date in the accounts receivable list, you would enter the following formula:

```
=F6=E6
```

Note the use of relative addressing. If you want to reference cells outside the list, use absolute addressing. See Chapter 5, "Building Formulas," to learn more about relative and absolute addressing.

SUPER TIP

Your computed criteria formulas will be easier to read if you use list field names instead of cell references. If a field name contains blanks, substitute an underscore character. For example, for the Due Date field, type `due_date`.

SUPER TIP

Use Excel's `AND`, `OR`, and `NOT` functions to create compound computed criteria. For example, to select all records in which the Days Overdue value is less than 90 and greater than 31, type `=AND(G6<90, G6>31)`.

Figure 31.11 shows a more complex example. The goal is to select all records whose invoices were paid after the due date. The new criteria—named Early—contains the following formula:

```
=IF(ISBLANK(F6),FALSE(),F6>E6)
```

FIGURE 31.11.
Use a separate criteria range column for calculated criteria.

Microsoft Excel — AR_DATA.XLS

A2 =IF(ISBLANK(F6),FALSE(),F6>E6)

	A	B	C	D	E	F	G
1	Early						
2	FALSE						
3							
4							
5	Account Name	Account Number	Invoice Number	Invoice Amount	Due Date	Date Paid	Days Overdue
6	Emily's Sports Palace	08-2255	117316	$ 1,584.20	8-Dec-93		26
7	Refco Office Solutions	14-5741	117317	$ 303.65	9-Dec-93		25
8	Chimera Illusions	02-0200	117318	$ 3,005.14	10-Dec-93	15-Dec-93	
9	Door Stoppers Ltd.	01-0045	117319	$ 78.85	12-Dec-93		22
10	Meaghan Manufacturing	12-3456	117320	$ 4,347.21	15-Dec-93	10-Dec-93	
11	Brimson Furniture	10-0009	117321	$ 2,144.55	15-Dec-93		19
12	Katy's Paper Products	12-1212	117322	$ 234.69	16-Dec-93		18
13	Stephen Inc.	16-9734	117323	$ 157.25	18-Dec-93	17-Dec-92	
14	Voyatzis Designs	14-1882	117324	$ 1,985.25	22-Dec-93		12

Accounts Receivable Data / Customer Data / Sheet1

Ready NUM

If the Date Paid field (column F) is blank, the invoice hasn't been paid and the formula returns `FALSE`. Otherwise, the logical expression `F6>E6` is evaluated. If the Date Paid (column F) is greater than Due Date field (column E), the expression returns `TRUE`, and Excel selects the record. In Figure 31.11, the Early field displays `FALSE`, because the formula evaluates to `FALSE` for the first row in the list.

Copying Filtered Data to a Different Range

If you want to work with the filtered data separately, you can copy it (or *extract* it) to a new location. Follow the steps in Procedure 31.4.

PROCEDURE 31.4. FILTERING A LIST TO A DIFFERENT LOCATION.

1. Set up the criteria you want to use to filter the list.
2. If you want to copy only certain columns from the list, copy the appropriate field names to the range you'll be using for the copy.
3. Select the **D**ata | **F**ilter | **A**dvanced Filter command to display the Advanced Filter dialog box.
4. In the Action group, select the C**o**py to Another Location option.
5. Enter your list and criteria ranges, if necessary.
6. In the Copy **t**o edit box, enter a reference for the copy location using the following guidelines (note that in each case you must select the cell or range in the same worksheet that contains the list):
   - To copy the entire filtered list, enter a single cell.
   - To copy only a specific number of rows, enter a range that contains the number of rows you want. If you have more data than will fit in the range, Excel asks whether you want to paste the remaining data.
   - To copy only certain columns, select the column labels you copied in step 2.

SUPER CAUTION

If you select a single cell to paste the entire filtered list, make sure you won't be overwriting any data. Otherwise, Excel will copy over the data without warning.

7. Click on OK or press Enter. Excel filters the list and copies the selected records to the location you specified.

Figure 31.12 shows the results of an extract in the Accounts Receivable list. I've hidden rows 9 through 100 to show all three ranges on-screen.

FIGURE 31.12.
The results of an extract in the Accounts Receivable list.

AR_DATA.XLS

	A	B	C	D	E	F	G
1	Days Overdue						
2	>0						
3							
4	Account Name	Account Number	Invoice Number	Invoice Amount	Due Date	Date Paid	Days Overdue
5	Emily's Sports Palace	08-2255	117316	$ 1,584.20	8-Dec-93		26
6	Refco Office Solutions	14-5741	117317	$ 303.65	9-Dec-93		25
7	Chimera Illusions	02-0200	117318	$ 3,005.14	10-Dec-93	15-Dec-93	
8	Door Stoppers Ltd.	01-0045	117319	$ 78.85	12-Dec-93		22
101							
102	Account Name	Invoice Number	Invoice Amount	Days Overdue			
103	Emily's Sports Palace	117316	$ 1,584.20	26			
104	Refco Office Solutions	117317	$ 303.65	25			
105	Door Stoppers Ltd.	117319	$ 78.85	22			
106	Brimson Furniture	117321	$ 2,144.55	19			

Accounts Receivable Data / Customer Data / Sheet

Chapter 32

Summarizing List Data

Because a list is just a worksheet range, you can analyze list data using many of the same methods you use for regular worksheet cells. Typically, this involves using formulas and functions to answer questions and produce results. To make your analysis chores easier, Excel enables you to create *automatic subtotals* that can give you instant subtotals, averages, and more. Excel goes one step further by also offering many list-specific functions. These functions work with entire lists or subsets defined by a criteria range. This chapter shows you how to use all these tools to analyze and summarize your data.

Creating Automatic Subtotals

Automatic subtotals enable you to summarize your sorted list data quickly. For example, if you have a list of invoices sorted by account name, you can use automatic subtotals to give you the following information for each account:

- The total number of invoices
- The sum of the invoice amounts
- The average invoice amount
- The maximum number of days an invoice is overdue

You can do all this and more without entering a single formula; Excel does the calculations and enters the results automatically. You also can just as easily create grand totals that apply to the entire list.

> **SUPER NOTE**
>
> As you can see, the term *automatic subtotal* is somewhat of a misnomer because you can summarize more than just totals. For this topic, at least, think of a subtotal as any summary calculation.

Setting Up a List for Automatic Subtotals

Excel calculates automatic subtotals based on data groupings in a selected field. For example, if you ask for subtotals based on account name, Excel runs down the account name column and creates a new subtotal *each time the name changes.* To get useful summaries, then, you need to sort a list on the field containing the data groupings you're interested in. Figure 32.1 shows the Accounts Receivable database sorted by account name. Subtotaling the Account Name field gives you summaries for Brimson Furniture, Chimera Illusions, Door Stoppers Ltd., and so on.

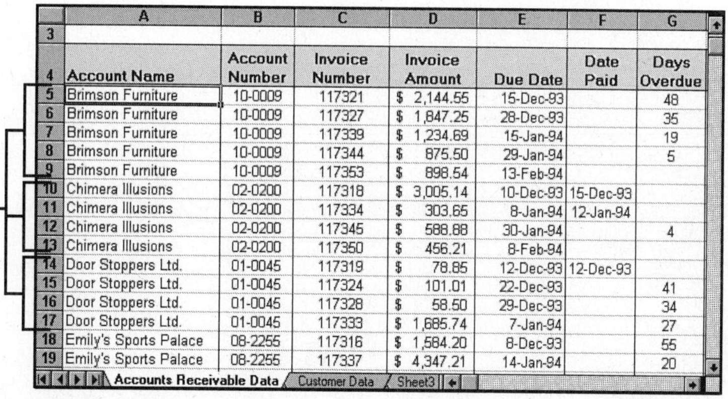

FIGURE 32.1.
A sorted list ready for displaying subtotals.

Data sorted into groups

	A	B	C	D	E	F	G
3							
4	Account Name	Account Number	Invoice Number	Invoice Amount	Due Date	Date Paid	Days Overdue
5	Brimson Furniture	10-0009	117321	$ 2,144.55	15-Dec-93		48
6	Brimson Furniture	10-0009	117327	$ 1,847.25	28-Dec-93		35
7	Brimson Furniture	10-0009	117339	$ 1,234.69	15-Jan-94		19
8	Brimson Furniture	10-0009	117344	$ 875.50	29-Jan-94		5
9	Brimson Furniture	10-0009	117353	$ 898.54	13-Feb-94		
10	Chimera Illusions	02-0200	117318	$ 3,005.14	10-Dec-93	15-Dec-93	
11	Chimera Illusions	02-0200	117334	$ 303.65	8-Jan-94	12-Jan-94	
12	Chimera Illusions	02-0200	117345	$ 588.88	30-Jan-94		4
13	Chimera Illusions	02-0200	117350	$ 456.21	8-Feb-94		
14	Door Stoppers Ltd.	01-0045	117319	$ 78.85	12-Dec-93	12-Dec-93	
15	Door Stoppers Ltd.	01-0045	117324	$ 101.01	22-Dec-93		41
16	Door Stoppers Ltd.	01-0045	117328	$ 58.50	29-Dec-93		34
17	Door Stoppers Ltd.	01-0045	117333	$ 1,685.74	7-Jan-94		27
18	Emily's Sports Palace	08-2255	117316	$ 1,584.20	8-Dec-93		55
19	Emily's Sports Palace	08-2255	117337	$ 4,347.21	14-Jan-94		20

Accounts Receivable Data / Customer Data / Sheet3

SUPER **NOTE**

If you want to display subtotals for a filtered list, make sure you filter the list before sorting it. See Chapter 31, "Managing List Records," for details on sorting and filtering.

Displaying Subtotals

When you subtotal your data, you use the Subtotal dialog box, shown in Figure 32.2. Before going through the steps necessary to display subtotals, let's look at the controls in this dialog box:

At Each Change in — This box contains the field names for your list. Select the field you want to use to group the subtotals.

Use Function — Select the function you want to use in the calculations. Excel gives you 11 choices, including Sum, Count, Average, Max, and Min.

A**d**d Subtotal to — This is a list of check boxes for each field. Activate the appropriate check boxes for the fields you want to subtotal.

Replace Current Subtotals	Activate this check box to display new subtotal rows. To add to the existing rows, deactivate this option.
Page Break Between Groups	If you intend to print the summary, activate this check box to insert a page break between each grouping.
Summary Below Data	Activate this check box if you want the subtotal rows to appear above the groupings.

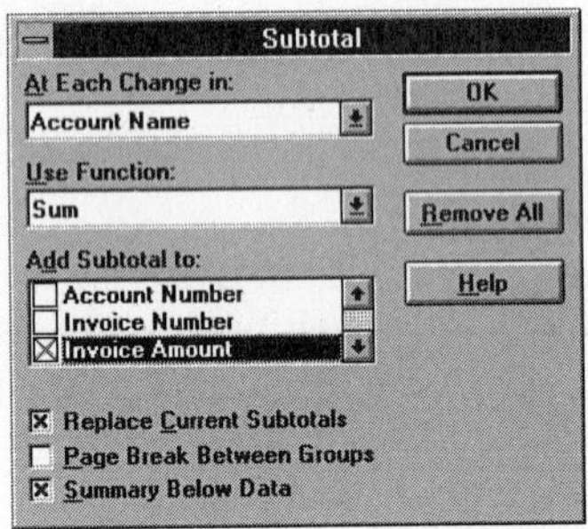

FIGURE 32.2.
You use the Subtotal dialog box to create subtotals for your list.

To subtotal a list, follow the steps in Procedure 32.1.

PROCEDURE 32.1. DISPLAYING LIST SUBTOTALS.

1. If you haven't already done so, sort your list according to the groupings you want to use for the subtotals.
2. Select the **D**ata | Su**b**totals command to display the Subtotal dialog box.
3. Enter the options you want to use for the subtotals, as described earlier.
4. Click on OK or press Enter. Excel calculates the subtotals and enters them into the list.

Figure 32.3 shows the Accounts Receivable list with the Invoice Amount field subtotaled.

Adding More Subtotals

You can add any number of subtotals to the current summary. Procedure 32.2 shows you what to do.

FIGURE 32.3.
A list showing Invoice Amount subtotals for each Account Name.

	A	B	C	D	E	F	G
4	Account Name	Account Number	Invoice Number	Invoice Amount	Due Date	Date Paid	Days Overdue
5	Brimson Furniture	10-0009	117321	$ 2,144.55	15-Dec-93		48
6	Brimson Furniture	10-0009	117327	$ 1,847.25	28-Dec-93		35
7	Brimson Furniture	10-0009	117339	$ 1,234.69	15-Jan-94		19
8	Brimson Furniture	10-0009	117344	$ 875.50	29-Jan-94		5
9	Brimson Furniture	10-0009	117353	$ 898.54	13-Feb-94		
10	**Brimson Furniture Total**			$ 7,000.53			
11	Chimera Illusions	02-0200	117318	$ 3,005.14	10-Dec-93	15-Dec-93	
12	Chimera Illusions	02-0200	117334	$ 303.65	8-Jan-94	12-Jan-94	
13	Chimera Illusions	02-0200	117345	$ 588.88	30-Jan-94		4
14	Chimera Illusions	02-0200	117350	$ 456.21	8-Feb-94		
15	**Chimera Illusions Total**			$ 4,353.88			
16	Door Stoppers Ltd.	01-0045	117319	$ 78.85	12-Dec-93	12-Dec-93	
17	Door Stoppers Ltd.	01-0045	117324	$ 101.01	22-Dec-93		41
18	Door Stoppers Ltd.	01-0045	117328	$ 58.50	29-Dec-93		34
19	Door Stoppers Ltd.	01-0045	117333	$ 1,685.74	7-Jan-94		27
20	**Door Stoppers Ltd. Total**			$ 1,924.10			

Accounts Receivable Data / Customer Data / Sheet3

Group subtotals

PROCEDURE 32.2. ADDING ANOTHER SUBTOTAL TO A SUMMARY.

1. Select the **D**ata | Su**b**totals command to display the Subtotal dialog box.
2. Enter the options you want to use for the new subtotal.
3. Deactivate the Replace **C**urrent Subtotals check box.
4. Click on OK or press Enter. Excel calculates the new subtotals and adds them to the list.

For example, Figure 32.4 shows the Accounts Receivable list with two new subtotals that count the invoices and display the maximum number of days overdue.

Count of Invoice Number field

Maximum of Days Overdue field

FIGURE 32.4.
You can use multiple subtotals in a list.

	A	B	C	D	E	F	G
4	Account Name	Account Number	Invoice Number	Invoice Amount	Due Date	Date Paid	Days Overdue
5	Brimson Furniture	10-0009	117321	$ 2,144.55	15-Dec-93		48
6	Brimson Furniture	10-0009	117327	$ 1,847.25	28-Dec-93		35
7	Brimson Furniture	10-0009	117339	$ 1,234.69	15-Jan-94		19
8	Brimson Furniture	10-0009	117344	$ 875.50	29-Jan-94		5
9	Brimson Furniture	10-0009	117353	$ 898.54	13-Feb-94		
10	**Brimson Furniture Total**			$ 7,000.53			
11	**Brimson Furniture Count**		5				
12	**Brimson Furniture Max**						48
13	Chimera Illusions	02-0200	117318	$ 3,005.14	10-Dec-93	15-Dec-93	
14	Chimera Illusions	02-0200	117334	$ 303.65	8-Jan-94	12-Jan-94	
15	Chimera Illusions	02-0200	117345	$ 588.88	30-Jan-94		4
16	Chimera Illusions	02-0200	117350	$ 456.21	8-Feb-94		
17	**Chimera Illusions Total**			$ 4,353.88			
18	**Chimera Illusions Count**		4				
19	**Chimera Illusions Max**						4
20	Door Stoppers Ltd.	01-0045	117319	$ 78.85	12-Dec-93	12-Dec-93	

Accounts Receivable Data / Customer Data / Sheet3

Nesting Subtotals

If the existing subtotal groups don't show enough detail, you can insert a subtotal within a subtotal group (this is called *nesting* subtotals). Follow the steps in Procedure 32.3.

PROCEDURE 32.3. NESTING A SUBTOTAL INSIDE AN EXISTING SUBTOTAL GROUP.

1. Select the **D**ata | Su**b**totals command to display the Subtotal dialog box.
2. Select the field you want to use for the new subtotal grouping from the **A**t Each Change in list.
3. Enter any other options you want to use for the new subtotal.
4. Deactivate the Replace **C**urrent Subtotals check box.
5. Click on OK or press Enter. Excel calculates the new subtotals and adds them to the list.

Figure 32.5 shows the original Accounts Receivable subtotals (the ones shown in Figure 32.3) with nested subtotals for each month.

FIGURE 32.5.
You also can nest subtotals inside existing subtotal groups.

	A	B	C	D	E	F	G
4	Account Name	Account Number	Invoice Number	Invoice Amount	Due Date	Date Paid	Days Overdu
5	Brimson Furniture	10-0009	117321	$2,144.55	Dec-93		48
6	Brimson Furniture	10-0009	117327	$1,847.25	Dec-93		35
7				$3,991.80	**Dec-93 Total**		
8	Brimson Furniture	10-0009	117339	$1,234.69	Jan-94		19
9	Brimson Furniture	10-0009	117344	$ 875.50	Jan-94		5
10				$2,110.19	**Jan-94 Total**		
11	Brimson Furniture	10-0009	117353	$ 898.54	Feb-94		
12				$ 898.54	**Feb-94 Total**		
13	**Brimson Furniture Total**			$7,000.53			
14	Chimera Illusions	02-0200	117318	$3,005.14	Dec-93	15-Dec-93	
15				$3,005.14	**Dec-93 Total**		
16	Chimera Illusions	02-0200	117334	$ 303.65	Jan-94	12-Jan-94	
17	Chimera Illusions	02-0200	117345	$ 588.88	Jan-94		4
18				$ 892.53	**Jan-94 Total**		
19	Chimera Illusions	02-0200	117350	$ 456.21	Feb-94		
20				$ 456.21	**Feb-94 Total**		

Accounts Receivable Data / Customer Data / Sheet3

Nested subtotals

SUPER TIP

Because Excel uses the format of the data to decide on the subtotal groupings, you also can control the subtotals by formatting the data appropriately. In Figure 32.5, I formatted the Due Date field as *mmm-yy*. This changes, for example, 15-Dec-93 to simply Dec-93 and enables Excel to group the invoices by month.

Working with a Subtotal's Outline Symbols

When Excel creates a subtotal, it displays various *outline symbols* to the left of the worksheet. You can use these symbols to hide or show detail data in the subtotals. Although you can find a complete discussion of outlining in Chapter 62, "Working with Templates and Outlines," this section gives you some basics to enable you to manipulate subtotals.

Outlines work by dividing your data into different *levels* that show different amounts of detail. The subtotaled data in Figure 32.6 has three levels:

> **Level 1:** The list grand total, which appears at the bottom of the list. It can't be seen in Figure 32.6.
> **Level 2:** The list subtotals.
> **Level 3:** The entire list.

Level symbols

Collapsed subtotals

Expand symbol

Collapse symbol

Level bars

	A	B	C	D	E	F	G
4	Account Name	Account Number	Invoice Number	Invoice Amount	Due Date	Date Paid	Days Overdue
5	Brimson Furniture	10-0009	117321	$ 2,144.55	15-Dec-93		48
6	Brimson Furniture	10-0009	117327	$ 1,847.25	28-Dec-93		35
7	Brimson Furniture	10-0009	117339	$ 1,234.69	15-Jan-94		19
8	Brimson Furniture	10-0009	117344	$ 875.50	29-Jan-94		5
9	Brimson Furniture	10-0009	117353	$ 898.54	13-Feb-94		
10	**Brimson Furniture Total**			$ 7,000.53			
15	**Chimera Illusions Total**			$ 4,353.88			
20	**Door Stoppers Ltd. Total**			$ 1,924.10			
21	Emily's Sports Palace	08-2255	117316	$ 1,584.20	8-Dec-93		55
22	Emily's Sports Palace	08-2255	117337	$ 4,347.21	14-Jan-94		20
23	Emily's Sports Palace	08-2255	117349	$ 1,689.50	7-Feb-94		
24	**Emily's Sports Palace Total**			$ 7,620.91			
25	Katy's Paper Products	12-1212	117322	$ 234.69	16-Dec-93		47
26	Katy's Paper Products	12-1212	117340	$ 1,157.58	17-Jan-94		17
27	Katy's Paper Products	12-1212	117351	$ 12,474.25	10-Feb-94		
28	Katy's Paper Products	12-1212	117354	$ 1,234.56	14-Feb-94		

Accounts Receivable Data / Customer Data / Sheet3

FIGURE 32.6.
You can use the outline symbols to the left of the worksheet to hide or show subtotal detail.

Here is a summary of the available outline tools:

> **Level bars:** These bars indicate the data included in the current level. Click on a bar to hide the rows marked by a bar.
> **Collapse symbol:** Click on this symbol to hide (or *collapse*) the rows marked by the attached level bar.
> **Expand symbol:** When you collapse a level, the collapse symbol changes to an expand symbol (+). Click on an expand symbol to display the hidden rows.
> **Level symbols:** These symbols tell you which level each level bar is on. Click on a level symbol to display all the detail data for that level.

In Figure 32.6, the detail data for Chimera Illusions and Door Stoppers Ltd. is collapsed, and the detail data for Brimson Furniture, Emily's Sports Palace, and Katy's Paper Products is expanded.

Removing Subtotals

To remove the subtotals from a list, follow the steps in Procedure 32.4.

PROCEDURE 32.4. REMOVING SUBTOTALS FROM A LIST.

1. Select the **D**ata | Su**b**totals command to display the Subtotal dialog box.
2. Click on the **R**emove All button. Excel removes the subtotals and returns you to the list.

Excel's List Functions

To get more control over your list analysis, you can use Excel's *list functions.* These functions are the same as those used in subtotals, but they have the following advantages:

- You can enter the functions into any cell in the worksheet.
- You can specify the range the function uses to perform its calculations.
- You can enter criteria or reference a criteria range to perform calculations on subsets of the list. (I cover criteria ranges in Chapter 31, "Managing List Records.")

About List Functions

If you want to calculate the sum of a list field, you can enter `SUM(`***`range`***`)`, and Excel produces the result. If you want to sum only a subset of the field, you must specify as arguments the particular cells to use. For lists containing hundreds of records, however, this process is impractical.

The solution is to use the list equivalent of the `SUM()` function: `DSUM()`. The `DSUM()` function takes three arguments: a list range, a field name, and a criteria range. `DSUM()` looks at the specified field in the list and sums only records that match the criteria in the criteria range.

The list functions come in two varieties: those that don't require a criteria range and those that do.

List Functions That Don't Require a Criteria Range

Excel has two list functions that enable you to specify the criteria as an argument instead of a range: `COUNTIF()` and `SUMIF()`.

Using *COUNTIF()*

The `COUNTIF()` function counts the number of cells in a range that meet a single criterion:

`COUNTIF(`*`range`*`,`*`criteria`*`)`

`range`	The range of cells to use for the count.
`criteria`	The criterion, entered as text, that determines which cells to count. Excel applies the criterion to *`range`*.

For example, Figure 32.7 shows a `COUNTIF()` function that calculates the total number of invoices that are more than 30 days overdue.

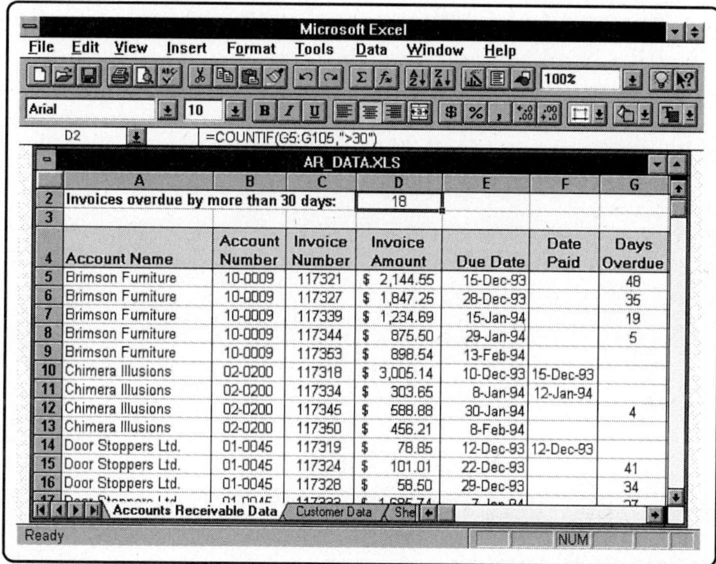

FIGURE 32.7.
Use `COUNTIF()` *to count the cells that meet a criterion.*

Using *SUMIF()*

The `SUMIF()` function is similar to `COUNTIF()`, except that it sums the range cells that meet its criterion:

`SUMIF(`***`range`***`,`***`criteria`***`,`*`sum_range`*`)`

`range`	The range of cells to use for the criterion.
`criteria`	The criterion, entered as text, that determines which cells to sum. Excel applies the criterion to ***`range`***.

sum_range	The range from which the sum values are taken. Excel sums only those cells in *sum_range* that correspond to the cells in ***range*** and meet the criterion. If you omit *sum_range*, Excel uses ***range*** for the sum.

Figure 32.8 shows a Parts database. The `SUMIF()` function in cell F12 sums the Total Cost (F3:F10) for the parts in Division 3 (A3:A10).

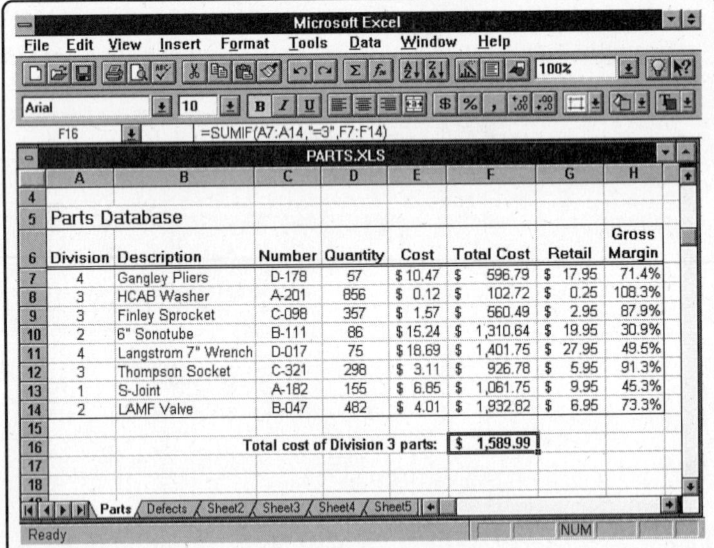

FIGURE 32.8.
Use SUMIF() to sum cells that meet a criterion.

List Functions That Require a Criteria Range

The remaining list functions require a criteria range. These functions take a little longer to set up, but the advantage is that you can enter compound and computed criteria.

All of these functions have the following structure:

```
Dfunction(database,field,criteria)
```

Dfunction	The function name, such as `DSUM()` or `DAVERAGE()`.
database	Specifies the range of cells that make up the list you want to work with. You can use either the range name, if one is defined, or the range address.

field	The name of the field on which you want to perform the operation. You can use either the field name or the *field number* as the argument (where the leftmost field is field number 1, the next field is field number 2, and so on). If you use the field name, enclose it in double quotation marks (for example, "total cost").
criteria	Specifies the range of cells that hold the criteria you want to work with. You can use either the range name, if one is defined, or the range address.

SUPER TIP

To perform an operation on every record in the list, leave all the ***criteria*** fields blank. This causes Excel to select every record in the list.

Table 32.1 summarizes the list functions.

Table 32.1. The list functions.

Function	*Description*
DAVERAGE()	Returns the average of the matching records in a specified field
DCOUNT()	Returns the count of the matching records
DCOUNTA()	Returns the count of the nonblank matching records
DGET()	Returns the value of a specified field for a single matching record
DMAX()	Returns the maximum value of a specified field for the matching records
DMIN()	Returns the minimum value of a specified field for the matching records
DPRODUCT()	Returns the product of the values of a specified field for the matching records
DSTDEV()	Returns the estimated standard deviation of the values in a specified field if the matching records are a sample of the population

continues

Table 32.1. continued

Function	*Description*
DSTDEVP()	Returns the standard deviation of the values of a specified field if the matching records are the entire population
DSUM()	Returns the sum of the values of a specified field for the matching records
DVAR()	Returns the estimated variance of the values of a specified field if the matching records are a sample of the population
DVARP()	Returns the variance of the values of a specified field if the matching records are the entire population

You enter list functions the same way you do any other Excel function. You type an equals sign (=) and then enter the function—either by itself or combined with other Excel operators in a formula. The following are all valid list functions:

```
=DSUM(A6:H14, "total cost", A1:H3)
=DSUM(List, "total cost", Criteria)
=DSUM(AR_List, 3, Criteria)
=DSUM(1993_Sales, "Sales", A1:H13)
```

The next two sections provide examples of the DAVERAGE() and DGET() list functions.

Using *DAVERAGE()*

The DAVERAGE() function calculates the average *field* value in the *database* records that match the *criteria*. In the Parts database, for example, suppose you wanted to calculate the average gross margin for all parts assigned to Division 2. You would set up a criteria range for the Division field and enter 2, as shown in Figure 32.9. You would then enter the following DAVERAGE() function (see cell H3):

```
=DAVERAGE(A6:H14, "gross margin", A2:A3)
```

TIP

As with all Excel formulas, your list functions will be much easier to read if you name your ranges.

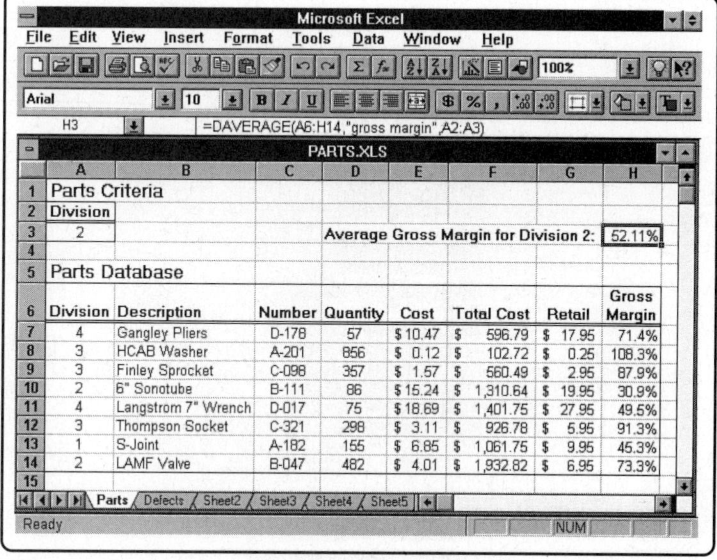

FIGURE 32.9.
Use DAVERAGE() to calculate the field average in the matching records.

Using *DGET()*

The `DGET()` function extracts the value of a single *`field`* from the record that matches the *`criteria`*. If there are no matching records, `DGET()` returns `#VALUE!`. If there is more than one matching record, `DGET()` returns `#NUM!`.

`DGET()` typically is used to query the list for a specific piece of information. For example, in the Parts list, you might want to know the cost of the Finley Sprocket. To extract this information, you would first set up a criteria range with the Description field and enter `Finley Sprocket`. You would then extract the information with the following formula (assuming that the list and criteria ranges are named Database and Criteria, respectively):

```
=DGET(Database, "Cost", Criteria)
```

A more interesting application of this function would be to extract the name of a part that satisfies a certain condition. For example, you might want to know the name of the part that has the highest gross margin. Creating this application requires two steps:

1. Set up the criteria to match the highest value in the Gross Margin field.
2. Add a `DGET()` function to extract the Description of the matching record.

Figure 32.10 shows how this is done. For the criteria, a new field called Highest Margin is created. As the text box shows, this field uses the following computed criteria:

```
=H7=MAX($H$7:$H$14)
```

FIGURE 32.10.
A DGET( ) function that extracts the name of the part with the highest margin.

Microsoft Excel — PARTS.XLS
G3: =DGET(Database,"Description",Criteria)

	A	B	C	D	E	F	G	H
1	Parts Criteria							
2	Highest Margin	=H7=MAX($H$7:$H$14)						
3	FALSE			Part with Highest Gross Margin:			HCAB Washer	
4								
5	Parts Database							
6	Division	Description	Number	Quantity	Cost	Total Cost	Retail	Gross Margin
7	4	Gangley Pliers	D-178	57	$10.47	$ 596.79	$ 17.95	71.4%
8	3	HCAB Washer	A-201	856	$ 0.12	$ 102.72	$ 0.25	108.3%
9	3	Finley Sprocket	C-098	357	$ 1.57	$ 560.49	$ 2.95	87.9%
10	2	6" Sonotube	B-111	86	$15.24	$1,310.64	$ 19.95	30.9%
11	4	Langstrom 7" Wrench	D-017	75	$18.69	$1,401.75	$ 27.95	49.5%
12	3	Thompson Socket	C-321	298	$ 3.11	$ 926.78	$ 5.95	91.3%
13	1	S-Joint	A-182	155	$ 6.85	$1,061.75	$ 9.95	45.3%
14	2	LAMF Valve	B-047	482	$ 4.01	$1,932.82	$ 6.95	73.3%

The range $H$7:$H$14 is the Gross Margin field. (Note the use of absolute references. See Chapter 5, "Building Formulas," for more information.) Excel matches only the record that has the highest Gross Margin. The `DGET()` function in cell G3 is straightforward:

```
=DGET(Database, "Description", Criteria)
```

This formula returns the Description of the part that has the highest Gross Margin.

Statistical List Functions

Many list functions are most often used to analyze statistical populations. Figure 32.11 shows a list of defects found among 12 work groups in a manufacturing process. In this example, the list (B3:D15) is named Defects, and two criteria ranges are used—one for each of the group leaders, Johnson (G3:G4 is Criteria1) and Perkins (H3:H4 is Criteria2).

The table shows several calculations. First, `DMAX()` and `DMIN()` are calculated for each criteria. The *range* (a statistic that represents the difference between the largest and smallest numbers in the sample; it's a crude measure of the sample's variance) is then calculated using the following formula (Johnson's groups):

```
=DMAX(Defects, "defects", Criteria1) - DMIN(Defects, "defects", Criteria1)
```

Instead of using `DMAX()` and `DMIN()` explicitly, you can, of course, simply refer to the cells containing the `DMAX()` and `DMIN()` results.

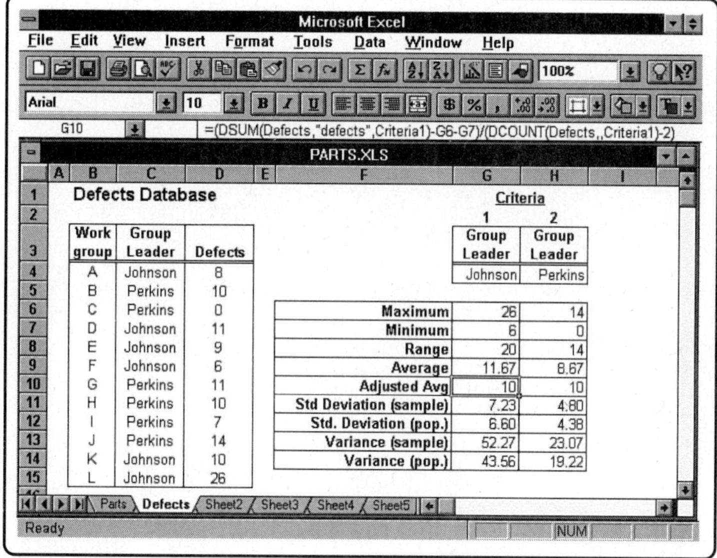

FIGURE 32.11.
Using functions to analyze a database of defects in a manufacturing process.

The next line uses `DAVERAGE()` to find the average number of defects for each group leader. Notice that the average for Johnson's groups (11.67) is significantly higher than that for Perkins' groups (8.67). However, Johnson's average is skewed higher by one anomalously large number (26), and Perkins' average is skewed lower by one anomalously small number (0).

To allow for this, the Adjusted Avg line uses `DSUM()`, `DCOUNT()`, and the `DMAX()` and `DMIN()` results to compute a new average without the largest and smallest number for each sample. As you can see, without the anomalies, the two leaders have the same average.

SUPER NOTE

As shown in cell G10 of Figure 32.11, if you don't include a *`field`* argument in the `DCOUNT()` function, it returns the total number of records in the list.

The rest of the calculations use the `DSTDEV()`, `DSTDEVP()`, `DVAR()`, and `DVARP()` functions.

Chapter 33

Using Microsoft Query

So far in this Workshop, you've used lists defined as ranges in Excel worksheets. You also can use Excel to access external database files from programs such as dBASE, Access, FoxPro, ORACLE, SQL Server, and more. Excel 5.0 comes with a separate program called Microsoft Query that enables you to work with these external files. This chapter shows you the basics of Microsoft Query and explains how to use external databases within Excel.

About Microsoft Query

Microsoft Query is a small but powerful database application designed to provide you with easy access to various database formats. You can use Microsoft Query as a stand-alone program or as an add-in to Excel. When used as a stand-alone program, you can display and manipulate database files in the Microsoft Query window. When used as an add-in, Microsoft Query provides links to an external database through *DDE* (*Dynamic Data Exchange*).

SUPER NOTE

Dynamic Data Exchange is a communications protocol that allows some Windows applications to send data back and forth and even execute each other's commands. You normally use DDE when you copy and paste data between applications.

A *query* is a request to a database for specific information. It combines criteria and extract conditions with functions to retrieve the data you want to see. Microsoft Query enables you to construct queries easily by using pull-down menu commands and drag-and-drop techniques.

You also can use Microsoft Query to edit and maintain your database files. You can add and delete records, modify field contents, join databases, and even create new database files. The beauty of Microsoft Query is that you can do all this with many different database formats and maintain a consistent interface.

The data you can work with in Microsoft Query depends on the *open database connectivity* (*ODBC*) *drivers* you installed with Excel. These drivers serve as intermediaries between Query and the external database. They take care of the messy problems of dealing with different database file structures and communicating between incompatible systems. Excel provides you with ODBC drivers for the following sources:

- Access (versions 1.0 and 1.1)
- Btrieve (version 5.1)
- dBASE (versions III and IV)
- Excel (.XLS files—versions 3.0, 4.0, and 5.0)

- FoxPro (versions 2.0 and 2.5)
- ODBC ODS Gateway
- ORACLE server (version 6.0)
- Paradox (versions 3.0 and 3.5)
- SQL Server (versions 1.1, 4.2, NT, Synbase 4.x)
- Text

If you installed Microsoft Query when you installed Excel, you can run it as a stand-alone program by double-clicking on the Microsoft Query icon in your Excel program group. See your Microsoft Query manual for complete instructions on using Microsoft Query as a stand-alone application. The rest of this chapter deals with using Microsoft Query as an Excel add-in.

Opening Microsoft Query Within Excel

You use Microsoft Query within Excel by opening the XLQUERY.XLA add-in file. This file normally is found in the \LIBRARY\MSQUERY subdirectory of your main Excel directory.

> **SUPER NOTE**
>
> If you can't find XLQUERY.XLA, you need to install it. Run the Excel setup program, select **A**dd/Remove, and, in the **O**ptions list, activate the Data Access check box.

When you open XLQUERY.XLA, Excel loads Query into memory and modifies the **D**ata menu by adding the Get E**x**ternal Data command that displays the Microsoft Query window so you can work with an external database.

Starting Microsoft Query

To retrieve data from an external database file, you need to switch to Microsoft Query and specify the information you need. To display the Microsoft Query window, follow the steps in Procedure 33.1.

PROCEDURE 33.1. STARTING MICROSOFT QUERY.

1. Select the **D**ata | Get E**x**ternal Data command. Query loads and then displays the Select Data Source dialog box, shown in Figure 33.1. If you're starting Query for the first time, this dialog box will be blank. Skip to the next section for instructions.

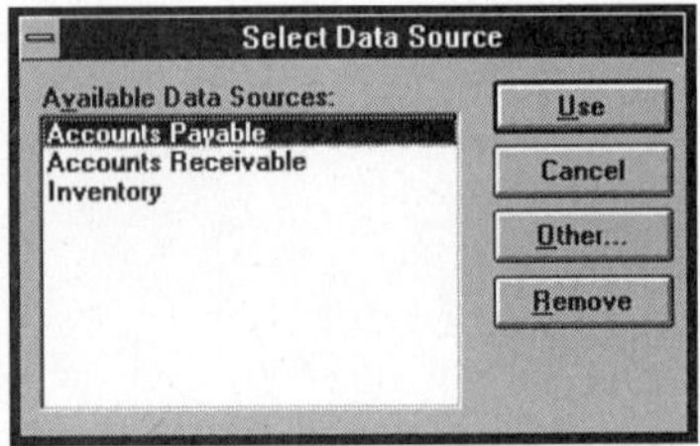

FIGURE 33.1.
Use the Select Data Source to choose the data source you want to work with.

2. Highlight a data source in the **A**vailable Data Sources list.
3. Select **U**se to open the source. Query displays the Add Tables dialog box.
4. For each database file you want to work with, highlight it in the Table **N**ame list and click on the **A**dd button. When you're done, click on **C**lose.

SUPER NOTE

In Microsoft Query, a *table* is synonymous with a database file.

Microsoft Query creates a new query file in a window divided into two areas (see Figure 33.2):

Database tables: The top pane displays one or more boxes that represent the tables you added to the query from the Add Tables dialog box. Each box displays a list of the database field names.

Data pane: The bottom pane displays the database records (also called the *result set*). This area is empty initially, so you have to add fields from the databases included in the query. Skip to the section titled "Adding Fields to the Data Pane" for details.

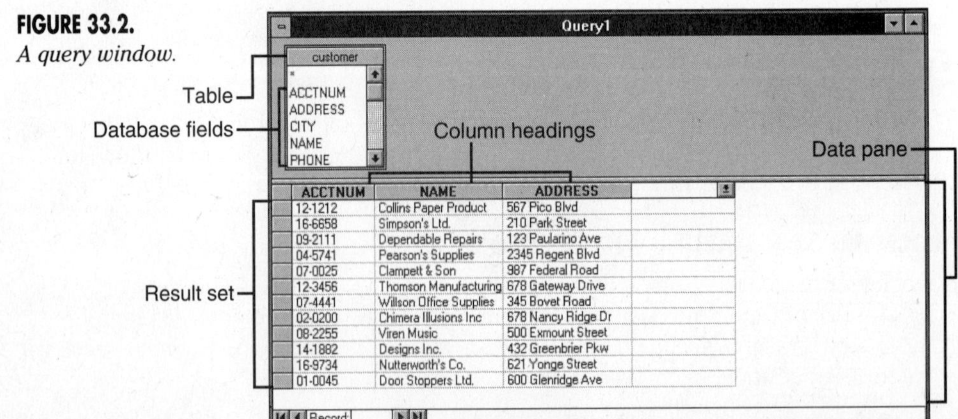

FIGURE 33.2.
A query window.

Defining a Data Source

A *data source* defines the data you want to work with. This includes the ODBC driver and the location of the files. (For example, a directory of FoxPro files is a data source.) Before you can work with Microsoft Query, you need to define at least one data source. Procedure 33.2 outlines the steps you need to follow.

PROCEDURE 33.2. DEFINING A DATA SOURCE IN MICROSOFT QUERY.

1. In the Select Data Source dialog box, click on the **O**ther button. Query displays the OBDC Data Sources dialog box.
2. Select **N**ew. The Add Data Source dialog box appears, shown in Figure 33.3.

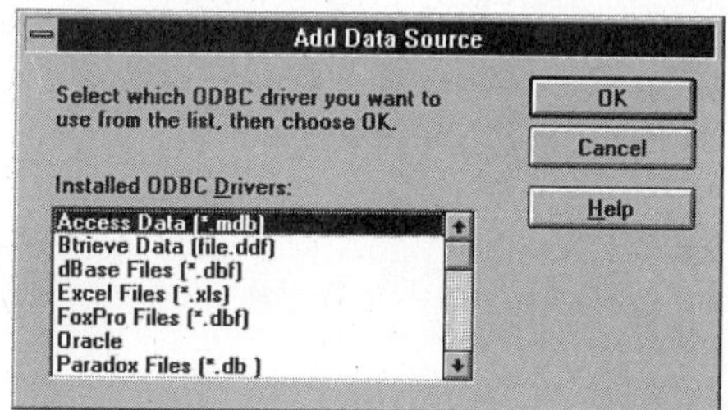

FIGURE 33.3. *Use the Add Data Source dialog box to select a driver for the database you want to work with.*

3. Highlight the driver for the database you want to work with and then click on OK or press Enter. Query displays a Setup dialog box for the driver. Figure 33.4 shows the Setup dialog box for a dBASE source.

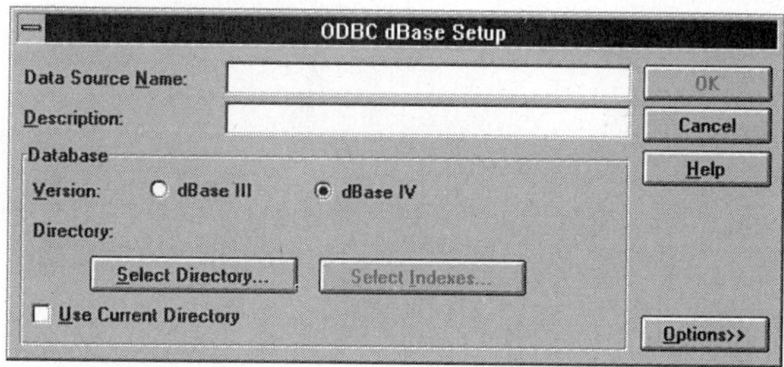

FIGURE 33.4. *The Setup dialog box for an ODBC dBASE source.*

4. In the Data Source **N**ame edit box, enter an identifier for the source. This is the name that will appear in the Select Data Source dialog box when you start Query.
5. Use the **D**escription edit box to enter a description for the source.
6. Fill in the other dialog box options, as appropriate.
7. Click on OK or press Enter to return to the ODBC Data Sources dialog box.
8. Repeat steps 2-7 to set up other data sources.

9. Click on OK or press Enter to return to the Select Data Source dialog box.
10. Highlight the source you want to work with and then select **U**se. The Add Tables dialog box appears.
11. For each database file you want to work with, highlight it in the Table **N**ame list and click on the **A**dd button. When you're done, click on **C**lose. Query displays a new query file.

Working with Database Fields

To get the information you want from an external database, you need to add one or more database fields to the query window's data pane. Once you've added fields, you can move them around, edit them, change their headings, and more. The next few sections take you through the basics of working with database fields.

Adding Fields to the Data Pane

To see any data in the data pane, you have to add one or more fields from the database field lists in the upper pane of the query window. Follow the steps in Procedure 33.3 to add a field to the data pane.

PROCEDURE 33.3. ADDING FIELDS TO THE MICROSOFT QUERY DATA PANE.

1. Select the **R**ecords | Add **C**olumn command. Query displays the Add Column dialog box, shown in Figure 33.5.

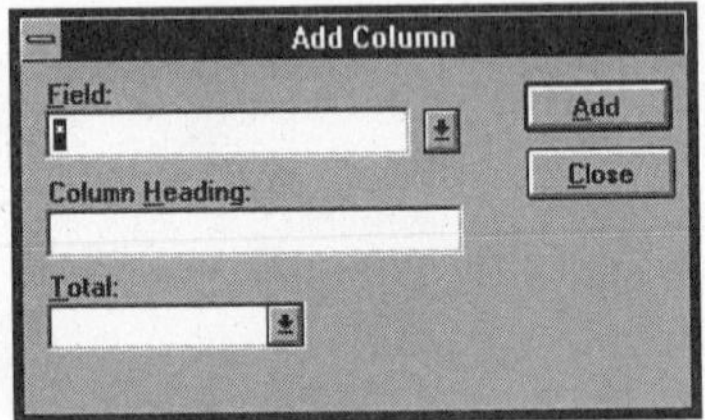

FIGURE 33.5.
Use the Add Column dialog box to add a field to the data pane.

2. In the **F**ield list, select the database field you want to add. To add all the fields, select the asterisk (*).

SUPER NOTE

If you have more than one database in the query, the field names use the format `database.field`. `database` is the name of the database file, and `field` is the name of the field.

3. Query uses the field name as the column heading. To specify a different heading, enter it in the Column **H**eading edit box.
4. To display summary data (that is, the field's sum, average, count, minimum, or maximum) instead of the field values, select the appropriate option from the **T**otal drop-down list.
5. Click on the **A**dd button. Query adds the field to the data pane.
6. Repeat steps 2-5 to add more fields.

You also can use any of the following techniques to add a field:

- Double-click on a field name to add it to the end of the data pane. To add all the fields, double-click on the asterisk (*) at the top of the list.
- Drag a field name from the field list into the data pane. Drop the name on an existing field to position the new field to its left.

Increasing the Size of the Data Pane

To see more records on-screen, you can increase the size of the data pane. You can use either of the following methods:

- Move the mouse pointer onto the bar that separates the data pane from the table area. The pointer will change to a two-sided arrow. Drag the bar towards the top of the screen.
- Select the **V**iew | **T**ables command. This removes the tables from the screen and gives the entire window to the data pane. To redisplay the table, select the **V**iew | **T**ables command again.

You also can click on the Show/Hide Tables tool in the Query toolbar to toggle the table display.

Editing Column Attributes

Once you've added some columns, you can navigate between them by using the left- and right-arrow keys or by clicking on a field. If you need to make changes to a column (such as changing the displayed field or editing the column heading), follow the steps in Procedure 33.4.

PROCEDURE 33.4. EDITING COLUMN ATTRIBUTES IN MICROSOFT QUERY.

1. Select the column you want to edit.
2. Select the **R**ecords | **E**dit Column command. The Edit Column dialog box appears.

SUPER TIP

You also can display the Edit Column dialog box by double-clicking on the column heading.

3. Make your changes and then click on OK or press Enter to return to the query.

Editing Field Data

The fields you add to the data pane are normally read-only. If you want to make changes to the data before retrieving it into Excel, select the **R**ecords | **A**llow Editing command. This removes the read-only status so you can make changes. You edit a field in a specific record the same as you do a worksheet cell—by pressing F2 or by double-clicking on the field.

Sorting the Data

Microsoft Query displays the records in the database's natural order (that is, the order the records were entered into the database). To change the sort order, follow the steps in Procedure 33.5.

PROCEDURE 33.5. SORTING DATA IN MICROSOFT QUERY.

1. Select the **R**ecords | **S**ort command. Query displays the Sort dialog box, shown in Figure 33.6.

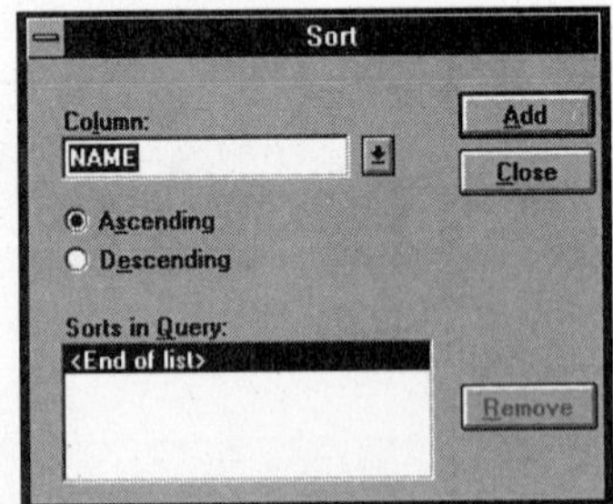

FIGURE 33.6.
Use the Sort dialog box to sort the query.

2. In the Co**l**umn list, select a field to use for the sort.
3. Select either A**s**cending or D**e**scending.
4. Click on the **A**dd button. Query adds the sort to the Sorts in **Q**uery list and sorts the data.

5. Repeat steps 2-4 to refine the sort order with other fields. If you want to remove a sort from the query, highlight it in the Sorts in **Q**uery list and click on the **R**emove button.
6. Click on **C**lose to return to the query.

Click on this tool to perform an ascending sort on the current field.

Click on this tool to perform a descending sort on the current field.

Deleting a Column

To remove a column from the data pane, follow the steps in Procedure 33.6.

PROCEDURE 33.6. REMOVING A COLUMN IN MICROSOFT QUERY.

1. Select the column you want to remove.
2. Select the **R**ecords | **R**emove Column command. Query removes the column.

Filtering Records with Criteria

Chapter 31, "Managing List Records," showed you how to filter records in an Excel list by setting up criteria. You also can filter the records in an external database, and the process is similar to the one you learned for lists. This section leads you through the basics of filtering records with criteria.

Creating Simple Criteria

Excel's AutoFilter enables you to set up simple criteria such as showing only records in which the State field is `CA` or in which the Account Number field is `12-3456` (see Chapter 31). Query enables you to create similar filters, and the process is almost as easy, as you'll see in Procedure 33.7.

PROCEDURE 33.7. CREATING SIMPLE FILTER CRITERIA IN MICROSOFT QUERY.

1. Move to the column that contains the field you want to use to filter the records.
2. Select the value in the field you want to use as a criterion.
3. Click on the Criteria Equals tool in the Query toolbar. Query filters the data based on the field value.

The Criteria Equals tool.

4. Repeat steps 1-3 to filter the records even further.

Working with the Criteria Pane

As you learned in Chapter 31, you can set up a criteria range in a worksheet to use when filtering your records. The equivalent in Microsoft Query is the *criteria pane*. You can add field names to this pane and then set up criteria that range from simple field values to complex expressions for compound and computed criteria.

Displaying the Criteria Pane

To display the criteria pane, use either of the following methods:

- Select the **View** | **Criteria** command.
- Click on the Show/Hide Criteria tool in the Query toolbar.

The Show/Hide Criteria tool.

Figure 33.7 shows a query window with the criteria pane added.

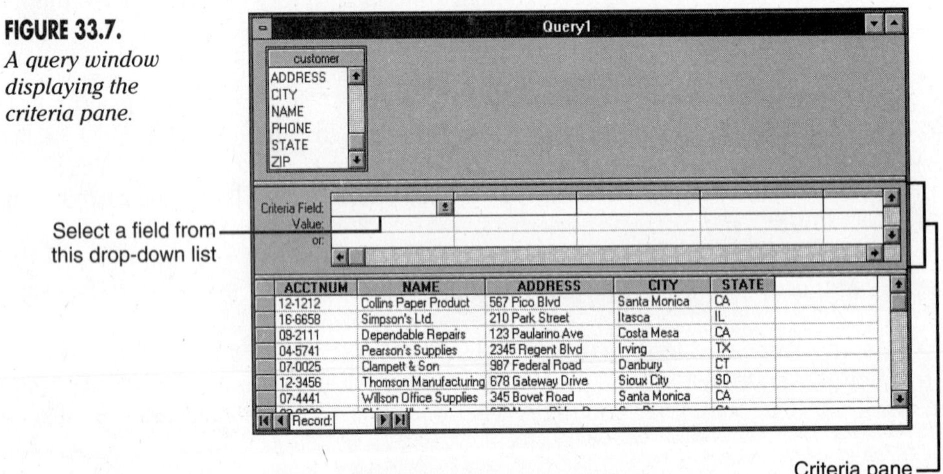

FIGURE 33.7.
A query window displaying the criteria pane.

Entering Simple Criteria in the Criteria Pane

If you now enter simple criteria as described in Procedure 33.7, you'll see that Query automatically adds the field names and values to the criteria pane. You also can enter simple criteria directly in the criteria pane (this is handy, for instance, if you don't have a mouse and can't use the Criteria Equals tool). Procedure 33.8 shows you the necessary steps.

PROCEDURE 33.8. ENTERING SIMPLE CRITERIA IN QUERY'S CRITERIA PANE.

1. Move to the criteria pane by clicking on it or by pressing F6 until you see a drop-down arrow appear in the top row of one of the pane's columns.
2. Select a field to use for the criterion by using one of the following methods:
   - Click on the top row of the column to get the drop-down arrow. Click on the arrow and then select a field name from the list.
   - Press Alt+down arrow, then select the field from the list that appears.
3. Select the cell below the field name and enter the field value you want to use for the criterion. Enclose text in single quotation marks (for example, `'CA'`) and dates in number signs (for example, `#1994-01-15#`). For more information, see the next section, "Entering Criteria Expressions in Microsoft Query."
4. Move the cursor to a different cell or select a different pane to put the criterion into effect.

Entering Criteria Expressions in Microsoft Query

Entering criteria expressions in Microsoft Query is similar to entering them in Excel (see Chapter 31 for details). However, you should be aware of the following differences:

- Use single quotation marks (for example, `'CA'`) around text instead of double quotation marks. In most cases, Query adds the single quotation marks for you.
- Enclose dates in number signs (for example, `#1994-01-15#`). Again, Query usually recognizes a date and adds the number signs for you.
- To use wildcard characters, you must include the keyword `Like` and then use an underscore to substitute for a single character or a percent sign to substitute for a group of characters. For example, to find all records in which the NAME field includes the word Office, you would type `Like '%Office%'` in the criteria pane's NAME field.
- Text criteria are case-sensitive in Microsoft Query. Therefore, you have to use the same uppercase and lowercase formats found in the database. For example, suppose you are setting criteria for a database with a STATE field that contains only two-letter state abbreviations in uppercase. If you enter, for example, `'ca'` (for California) as part of your criteria, Microsoft Query won't match any records because all the California records have `CA` in the STATE field.

Creating Complex Criteria

As you learned in Chapter 31, *complex criteria* come in two flavors: *compound criteria* that combine two or more criteria expressions and *computed criteria* that use formulas to filter data. You can enter your complex criteria either directly into the criteria pane or by using the Add Criteria dialog box.

Entering Complex Criteria in the Criteria Pane

You enter compound criteria in the criteria pane the same way you do in a criteria range on an Excel worksheet:

- Use the criteria pane column headers to select either multiple fields or multiple instances of a single field.
- If you enter criteria expressions in the same row, Query selects the records that match *all* the criteria.
- If you enter criteria expressions on different rows, Query selects the records that match *at least one* of the rows.

For example, Figure 33.8 shows a result set from the compound criteria shown in the criteria pane. This query selects records in which the STATE field is `CA` *and* the CITY field is `Santa Monica` (the first Value row in the criteria pane), *or* the STATE field is `NY` (the second row).

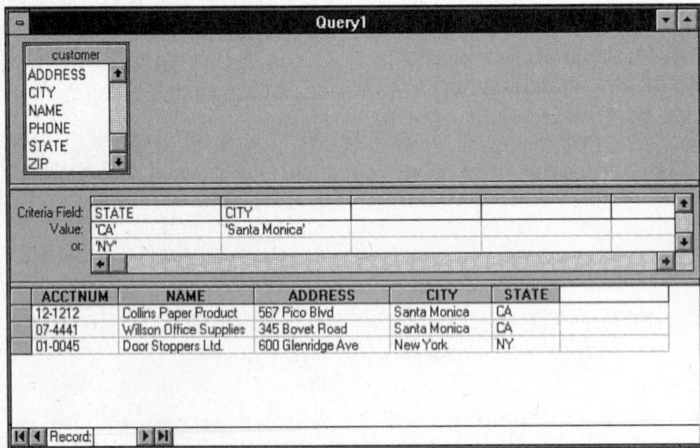

FIGURE 33.8.
The result set from a compound criterion.

Entering computed criteria is a little different than what you're familiar with in Excel:

- Use field names instead of cell references. For example, given an invoice database with DUE_DATE and DATE_PAID fields, you would use `DUE_DATE - DATE_PAID` to calculate the difference between the two fields.
- Query doesn't let you create new fields for computed criteria. Instead, you enter the expression you want to calculate in one of the column headings of the criteria pane.

For example, Figure 33.9 shows a query on a database named INVOICES. In this case, the goal is to display those invoices that were paid before the dates they were due. The formula to use for this calculation is the following:

```
DUE_DATE - DATE_PAID > 0
```

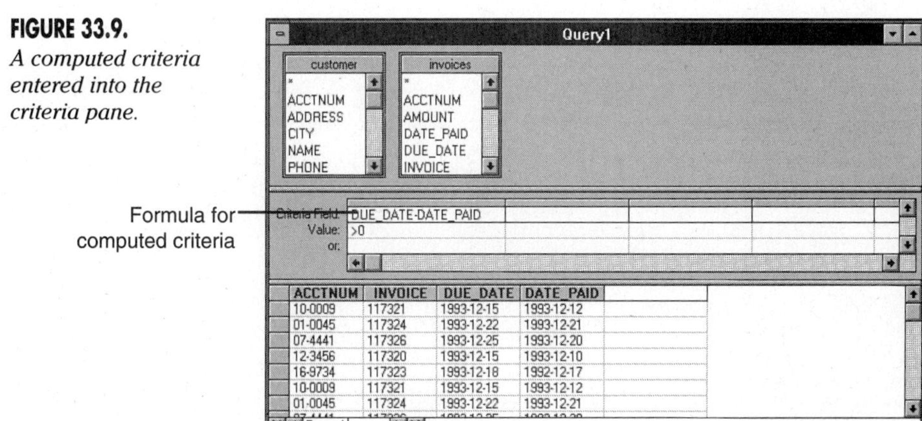

FIGURE 33.9.
A computed criteria entered into the criteria pane.

As you can see in Figure 33.9, you enter the left side of the calculation in the column heading and you enter the operator and value in the cell below it.

Entering Complex Criteria in the Add Criteria Dialog Box

You also can enter complex criteria using the Add Criteria dialog box shown in Figure 33.10. This dialog box contains the following features:

And/**Or** Use these options to create compound criteria. (When you add your first criterion, these options are disabled.) Select **And** when you want the records to match all the criteria; select **Or** when you want the records to match at least one of the criteria.

Total A list of summary functions (Sum, Avg, Count, Min, and Max).

Field A list of the database fields.

Operator A list of operators. Instead of logical operators (=, >, <=, and so on), Query uses English-language equivalents of the SQL (Structured Query Language) operators (equals, is greater than, is less than or equal to, and so on). SQL has many operators you might not be familiar with. Some, such as "begins with" and "ends with," are straightforward. Others are more obscure. Following is a list of a few of the other SQL operators you'll find in the **Operator** list:

Operator	*Description*
`is one of`	Selects records in which the selected field matches one of the elements in a list. You enter the list in the **Value** edit box and separate each element with a comma.

Operator	*Description*
`is between`	Selects records in which the selected field falls in between two values you enter into the **V**alue box (again, separated by commas).
`contains`	Selects records in which the text you enter into **V**alue is contained in the selected field.
`is Null`	Selects records in which the selected field value is empty.

Value The field value to use in the criterion. You can enter your own values or use the Va**l**ues button to select from a list of the unique values in the field.

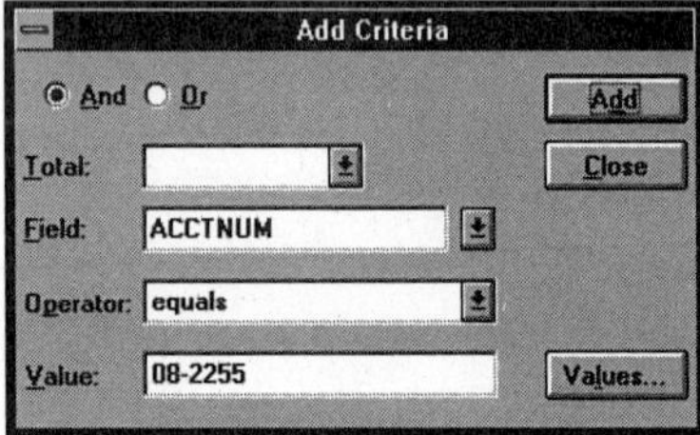

FIGURE 33.10.
You also can use the Add Criteria dialog box to add complex criteria to the query.

Follow the steps in Procedure 33.9 to add criteria using the Add Criteria dialog box.

PROCEDURE 33.9. ADDING CRITERIA USING THE ADD CRITERIA DIALOG BOX.

1. Select the **C**riteria | **A**dd Criteria command to display the Add Criteria dialog box.
2. Select the options you want to use in the criterion.
3. Click on the A**d**d button. Query adds the criterion and updates the result set.
4. If you want to add another criterion, select **A**nd or **O**r, as appropriate.
5. Repeat steps 2-4 to define more criteria.
6. When you're done, click on **C**lose to return to the query.

Removing Criteria

To remove a criterion from the query, use the steps outlined in Procedure 33.10.

PROCEDURE 33.10. REMOVING A CRITERION FROM THE QUERY.

1. Display the criteria pane (if it's not already displayed).
2. Select the entire column of the criterion you want to delete. You can use either of the following methods:

- Place the mouse pointer on the bar just above the Criteria Field row (the pointer will change to a downward pointing arrow) and click.
- Select the column and press Ctrl+Spacebar.

3. Press the Delete key. Query removes the column.

> **SUPER TIP**
>
> To delete all the criteria, select the **C**riteria | **R**emove All Criteria command.

Controlling Query Calculation

When you add fields or criteria, Microsoft Query normally calculates the query results automatically. If you're working with large tables or complicated criteria, it might take some time for Query to display the result set. To prevent Microsoft Query from updating the results every time you make a change, you can turn off the Automatic Query feature by using either of the following methods:

- Pull down the **R**ecords menu and select Automatic **Q**uery to remove the check mark from the command.
- Click on the Auto Query tool in the Query toolbar to return the tool to its normal (that is, nonpressed) state.

The Auto Query tool.

With Automatic Query turned off, you have to tell Query when you want to update the result set. Again, you have two methods:

- Select the **R**ecords | Query **N**ow command.
- Click on the Query Now tool in the Query toolbar.

The Query Now tool.

Joining Multiple Databases

Microsoft Query has a powerful feature that enables you to join two or more databases. In order for you to take advantage of this feature, your databases must have at least one field in common. The fields don't need to have the same name, but the data within each field must be of a common type. For example, if one database has an ACCTNUM field and another has a CUST_ID field, you can join the two databases as long as these fields have similar contents (account numbers, in this case).

Microsoft Query joins databases by using the common field to cross-reference information from one database to the other. As an example, I'll use two dBASE files—CUSTOMER.DBF and INVOICES.DBF—that contain the fields shown in Figure 33.11. As you can see, the databases have a single field in common: ACCTNUM. The goal is to join the two databases so that for each invoice you also see the account name and address.

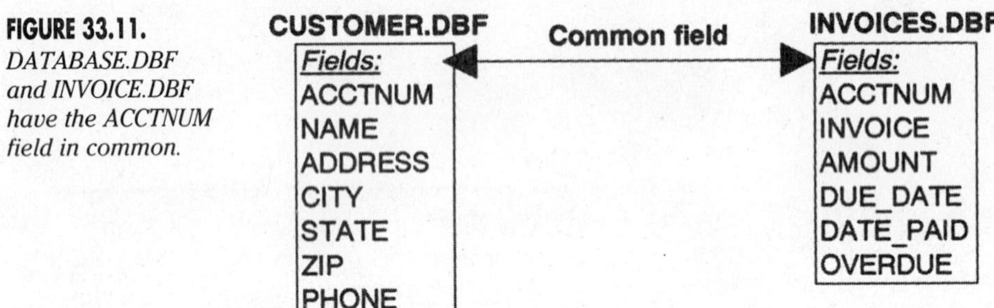

FIGURE 33.11.
DATABASE.DBF and INVOICE.DBF have the ACCTNUM field in common.

Adding Tables to the Query

Before you can join databases, you need to include them in the query. You can add the tables you need when you first start the query, or you can add new tables to an existing query by following the steps in Procedure 33.11.

PROCEDURE 33.11. ADDING TABLES TO A QUERY.

1. Select the Ta**b**le | **A**dd Tables command. Query displays the Add Tables dialog box.

You also can click on the Add Table(s) tool to display the Add Tables dialog box.

2. Highlight the table you want to add.
3. Click on the **A**dd button. Query adds the table to the query.
4. Repeat steps 2 and 3 to add more tables.
5. Click on the **C**lose button to return to the query.

Joining Tables

To join two tables, you use the Joins dialog box, shown in Figure 33.12. It includes the following features:

Left	A list of fields in the first database.
Right	A list of fields in the second database.

Operator	The operator to use for the join. Normally you use the equals sign (=), but you also can choose from a list of logical operators.
Join Includes	This group gives a selection of options for the join. (The available options depend on the operator you select.) In the example, you want to display all the invoices and match them with the corresponding records in CUSTOMER.DBF, so option 2 is the correct choice.
Joins in Query	Lists the current joins in the query (written in SQL). You can remove a join by highlighting it in this list and clicking on the Remove button.

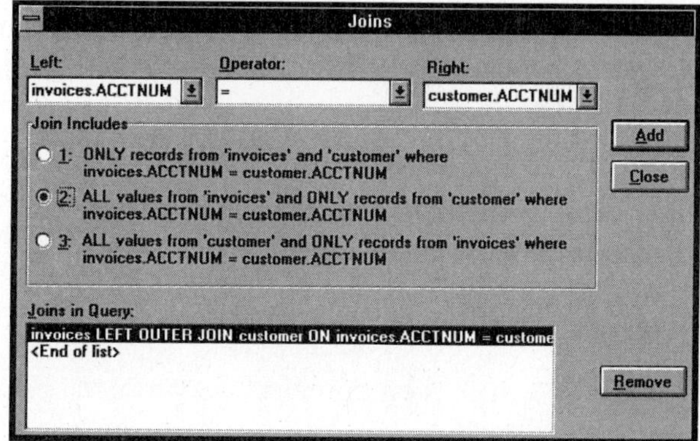

FIGURE 33.12.
Use the Joins dialog box to join two tables.

Follow the steps in Procedure 33.12 to add a join to the query.

PROCEDURE 33.12. ADDING A JOIN TO THE QUERY.

1. Add the tables you want to join.
2. Select the Table | Joins command to display the Joins dialog box.
3. Select the join options you want to use.
4. Click on the Add button. Query adds the join to the query.
5. Repeat steps 3 and 4 to add other joins.
6. Click on the Close button to return to the query. Query adds an arrow connecting the common fields in the table boxes.

As soon as you have your joins set up, you can add the appropriate fields to the query (if you haven't already done so). Figure 33.13 shows the result set after joining CUSTOMER.DBF and INVOICES.DBF.

FIGURE 33.13.
The result set of two joined databases.

Query1

customer: * ACCTNUM ADDRESS CITY NAME PHONE

invoices: * ACCTNUM AMOUNT DATE_PAID DUE_DATE INVOICE

NAME	ACCTNUM	ADDRESS	INVOICE	AMOUNT	DUE_DATE	DATE_PAID
Brimson Furniture	10-0009	621 Yonge Street	117321	2144.55	1993-12-15	1993-12-12
Brimson Furniture	10-0009	621 Yonge Street	117327	1847.25	1993-12-28	1994-01-06
Brimson Furniture	10-0009	621 Yonge Street	117339	1234.69	1994-01-15	
Brimson Furniture	10-0009	621 Yonge Street	117344	875.5	1994-01-29	
Brimson Furniture	10-0009	621 Yonge Street	117353	898.54	1994-02-13	
Chimera Illusions Inc	02-0200	678 Nancy Ridge Dr	117318	3005.14	1993-12-10	1993-12-15
Chimera Illusions Inc	02-0200	678 Nancy Ridge Dr	117334	303.65	1994-01-08	1994-01-12
Chimera Illusions Inc	02-0200	678 Nancy Ridge Dr	117345	588.88	1994-01-30	
Chimera Illusions Inc	02-0200	678 Nancy Ridge Dr	117350	456.21	1994-02-08	
Door Stoppers Ltd.	01-0045	600 Glenridge Ave	117319	78.85	1993-12-12	1993-12-12
Door Stoppers Ltd.	01-0045	600 Glenridge Ave	117324	101.01	1993-12-22	1993-12-21

Record: 1

Saving the Query

If you think you'll be using the query again in the future, you can save it by following the steps in Procedure 33.13.

PROCEDURE 33.13. SAVING A QUERY.

1. Select the **File** | **S**ave Query command. If you're saving the query for the first time, the Save As dialog box appears.

You also can click on the Save Query tool to save a query.

2. Enter a name and location for the query. You don't need to specify an extension, because Query automatically adds its default .QRY extension.
3. Click on OK or press Enter.

Starting a New Query

If you want to start with a fresh query file, follow the steps listed in Procedure 33.14.

PROCEDURE 33.14. STARTING A NEW QUERY.

1. Select the **File** | **N**ew Query command. Query displays the Select Data Source dialog box.

You also can click on the New Query tool to start a new query.

2. Highlight a data source in the **A**vailable Data Sources list.
3. Select **U**se to open the source. Query displays the Add Tables dialog box.
4. For each database file you want to work with, highlight the file in the Table **N**ame list and click on the **A**dd button.

5. Click on Close to display the new query.

Returning the Query Results to Excel

When you have the result set you want, you can import the data into Excel by following Procedure 33.15.

PROCEDURE 33.15. RETURNING THE QUERY RESULTS TO EXCEL.

1. Select the File | Return Data to Microsoft Excel command. Query switches to Excel and displays the Get External Data dialog box.

You also can click on the Return Data to Excel tool to return the query results.

2. Activate the appropriate check boxes in the Options group.
3. Use the Destination box to select the top-left corner of the range you want to use for the data.

> **SUPER TIP**
>
> If you think you'll need to update your data or edit the query later, make sure the Keep Query Definition check box is activated.

4. Click on OK or press Enter. Excel pastes the result set into the worksheet.

Working with the Result Set

Once you've retrieved the result set, you can work with the data as you would any Excel list. You also can refresh the data and edit the query, as explained in the next two sections.

Refreshing the Result Set

If the data in the external database changes, you can update the result set in your worksheet to reflect those changes. Procedure 33.16 shows you how.

> **SUPER NOTE**
>
> Excel refreshes the query results automatically only if you saved the query definition when you retrieved the result set.

PROCEDURE 33.16. REFRESHING A QUERY RESULT SET.

1. Select a cell in the result set.
2. Select the **D**ata | **R**efresh Data command. Excel runs the query again and then retrieves the new results.

SUPER CAUTION

When Excel retrieves the updated result set, it overwrites your existing data. Any sorting or rearranging of the data you may have done will be lost.

Editing the Query

To make changes to the query, follow the steps in Procedure 33.17.

PROCEDURE 33.17. EDITING A QUERY.

1. Select a cell in the result set.
2. Select the **D**ata | Get E**x**ternal Data command. The Get External Data dialog box appears.
3. Click on the **E**dit Query button. Excel switches to Microsoft Query and loads the query file.

SUPER NOTE

Excel loads the query file automatically only if you saved the query definition when you originally retrieved the result set.

4. Make your changes to the query.
5. Select the **F**ile | **R**eturn Data to Microsoft Excel command. Query switches to Excel and displays the Get External Data dialog box.
6. Click on OK or press Enter. Excel pastes the result set into the worksheet.

Chapter

34

Working with Pivot Tables

Lists and external databases can contain hundreds or even thousands of records. Analyzing that much data can be a nightmare without the right kinds of tools. Excel 5.0 offers a new data analysis tool called a *pivot table* that enables you to summarize hundreds of records into a concise tabular format. You can then manipulate the layout of the table to see different views of your data. This chapter introduces you to pivot tables and shows you a variety of ways to use them with your own data.

What Are Pivot Tables?

To understand pivot tables, you need to see where they fit in with Excel's other database analysis features. Database analysis has several levels of complexity. The simplest level involves the basic lookup and retrieval of information. For example, if you have a database that lists the company sales reps and their territory sales, you could use a data form to search for a specific rep and to look up the sales in his or her territory.

The next level of complexity involves more sophisticated lookup and retrieval systems in which the criteria and extract techniques discussed in Chapter 31, "Managing List Records," are used. You can then apply subtotals and the list functions described in Chapter 32, "Summarizing List Data," to find answers to your questions. For example, suppose each sales territory is part of a larger region, and you want to know the total sales in the eastern region. You could either subtotal by region or set up your criteria to match all territories in the eastern region and use the `DSUM()` function to get the total. To get more specific information, such as total eastern region sales in the second quarter, you just add the appropriate conditions to your criteria.

The next level of database analysis applies a single question to multiple variables. For example, if the company in the previous example has four regions, you might want to see separate totals for each region broken down by quarter. One solution would be to set up four different criteria and four different `DSUM()` functions. But what if there were a dozen regions? Or a hundred? Ideally, you need some way of summarizing the database information into a "sales table" that has a row for each region and a column for each quarter. This is exactly what pivot tables do. With Excel's PivotTable Wizard, you can create your own tables with just a few mouse clicks.

How Pivot Tables Work

In the simplest case, pivot tables work by summarizing the data in one field (called a *data field*) and breaking it down according to the data in another field. The unique values in the second field (called the *row field*) become the row headings. For example, Figure 34.1 shows a database of sales-by-sales representatives. With a pivot table, you can summarize the numbers in the Sales field (the data field) and break them down by Region (the row field). Figure 34.2 shows the resulting pivot table. Notice how Excel uses the four unique items in the Region field (East, West, Midwest, and South) as row headings.

FIGURE 34.1.
A database of sales by sales representatives.

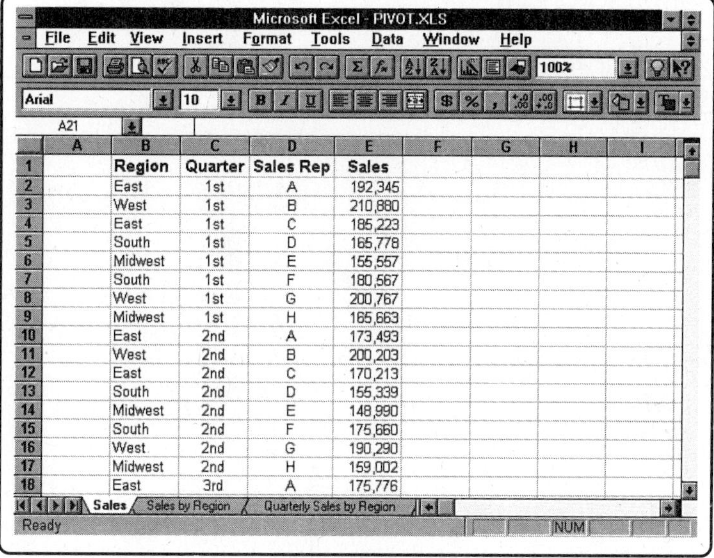

	Region	Quarter	Sales Rep	Sales
2	East	1st	A	192,345
3	West	1st	B	210,880
4	East	1st	C	185,223
5	South	1st	D	165,778
6	Midwest	1st	E	155,557
7	South	1st	F	180,567
8	West	1st	G	200,767
9	Midwest	1st	H	165,663
10	East	2nd	A	173,493
11	West	2nd	B	200,203
12	East	2nd	C	170,213
13	South	2nd	D	155,339
14	Midwest	2nd	E	148,990
15	South	2nd	F	175,660
16	West	2nd	G	190,290
17	Midwest	2nd	H	159,002
18	East	3rd	A	175,776

FIGURE 34.2.
A pivot table showing total sales by region.

Sum of Sales	
Region	Total
East	1,463,655
Midwest	1,340,875
South	1,409,544
West	1,477,884
Grand Total	5,691,958

You can further break down your data by specifying a third field (called the *column field*) to use for column headings. Figure 34.3 shows the resulting pivot table with the four unique items in the Quarter field (1st, 2nd, 3rd, and 4th) used to create the columns.

FIGURE 34.3.
A pivot table showing sales by region for each quarter.

Sum of Sales	Quarter				
Region	1st	2nd	3rd	4th	Grand Total
East	377,568	343,706	368,121	374,260	1,463,655
Midwest	321,220	307,992	365,790	345,873	1,340,875
South	346,345	330,999	376,658	355,542	1,409,544
West	411,647	390,493	361,091	314,653	1,477,884
Grand Total	1,456,780	1,373,190	1,471,660	1,390,328	5,691,958

The big news with pivot tables is the "pivoting" feature. If you want to see different views of your data, you can drag, for example, the column field over to the row field area, as shown in Figure 34.4. The result, as you can see, is that the table now shows each region as the main row category—with the quarters as regional subcategories.

FIGURE 34.4.
You can drag row or column fields to "pivot" the data and get a different view.

Sum of Sales		
Region	Quarter	Total
East	1st	377,568
	2nd	343,706
	3rd	368,121
	4th	374,260
East Total		1,463,655
Midwest	1st	321,220
	2nd	307,992
	3rd	365,790
	4th	345,873
Midwest Total		1,340,875
South	1st	346,345
	2nd	330,999
	3rd	376,658
	4th	355,542
South Total		1,409,544
West	1st	411,647
	2nd	390,493
	3rd	361,091
	4th	314,653
West Total		1,477,884
Grand Total		5,691,958

Some Pivot Table Terms

Pivot tables have their own terminology. Following is a quick glossary of some terms you need to become familiar with:

Source list: The original data. You can use one or more Excel lists, an external database, an existing pivot table, or a crosstab table from Excel 4.

Field: A category of data, such as Region, Quarter, or Sales. Because most pivot tables are derived from lists or databases, a pivot table field is directly analogous to a list or database field.

Item: An element in a field.

Row field: A field with a limited set of text values to use as row headings in the pivot table. In the previous example, *Region* is the row field.

Column field: A field with a limited set of text values to use as column headings for the pivot table. In the second pivot table shown in Figure 34.3, the Quarter field is the column field.

Page field: A field with a limited set of text values that you use to filter the pivot table view. For example, you could use the Sales Rep field to create separate *pages* for each rep. Selecting a different sales rep filters the table to show data only for that person.

Pivot table items: The items from the source list used as row, column, and page labels.

Data field: A field that contains the data you want to summarize in the table.

Data area: The interior section of the table in which the data summaries appear. In Figure 34.3, for example, the data area is the range C8:G12.

Layout: The overall arrangement of fields and items in the pivot table.

Building Pivot Tables

Excel provides the PivotTable Wizard to make it easy to create and modify your pivot tables. The PivotTable Wizard uses a four-step approach that enables you to build a pivot table from scratch. Following is a summary of the four steps:

1. Specify the type of source list to use for the pivot table.
2. Identify the location of the data.
3. Define the row, column, page, and data fields for the table.
4. Select a location, name, and other options for the table. Then create the table.

Throughout the rest of this chapter, I'll use the list shown in Figure 34.5 as an example. This is a list of orders placed in response to a three-month marketing campaign. Each record shows the date of the order, the product ordered (there are four types: Printer stand, Glare filter, Mouse pad, and Copy holder), the quantity and net dollars ordered, the promotional offer selected by the customer (1 Free with 10 or Extra Discount), and the advertisement to which the customer is responding (Direct mail, Magazine, or Newspaper).

FIGURE 34.5.
The Orders database that will be used as an example throughout this chapter.

SUMMER SALES PROMOTION - ORDERS

	A	B	C	D	E	F	G
2		Date	Product	Quantity	Net $	Promotion	Advertisement
3		6/1/93	Printer stand	11	119.70	1 Free with 10	Direct mail
4		6/1/93	Glare filter	6	77.82	Extra Discount	Magazine
5		6/1/93	Mouse pad	15	100.95	Extra Discount	Newspaper
6		6/1/93	Glare filter	11	149.71	1 Free with 10	Magazine
7		6/2/93	Mouse pad	22	155.40	1 Free with 10	Magazine
8		6/2/93	Mouse pad	3	20.19	Extra Discount	Newspaper
9		6/2/93	Copy holder	5	33.65	Extra Discount	Direct mail
10		6/2/93	Printer stand	22	239.36	1 Free with 10	Newspaper
11		6/2/93	Glare filter	10	129.70	Extra Discount	Magazine
12		6/3/93	Mouse pad	22	155.40	1 Free with 10	Magazine
13		6/3/93	Printer stand	8	82.96	Extra Discount	Direct mail
14		6/3/93	Printer stand	22	239.40	1 Free with 10	Direct mail
15		6/3/93	Copy holder	55	388.50	1 Free with 10	Magazine
16		6/3/93	Mouse pad	25	168.25	Extra Discount	Newspaper
17		6/3/93	Glare filter	22	299.42	1 Free with 10	Magazine
18		6/4/93	Printer stand	11	119.70	1 Free with 10	Magazine

Orders / Sheet5 / Sheet6 / Sheet7 / Sheet8 / She

Figure 34.6 shows a simple pivot table for the Orders database. In this example, the quantity shipped is summarized by product and advertisement. The row headings were taken from the Product field, and the column headings were taken from the Advertisement field. The Promotion field is used as the page field to filter the data.

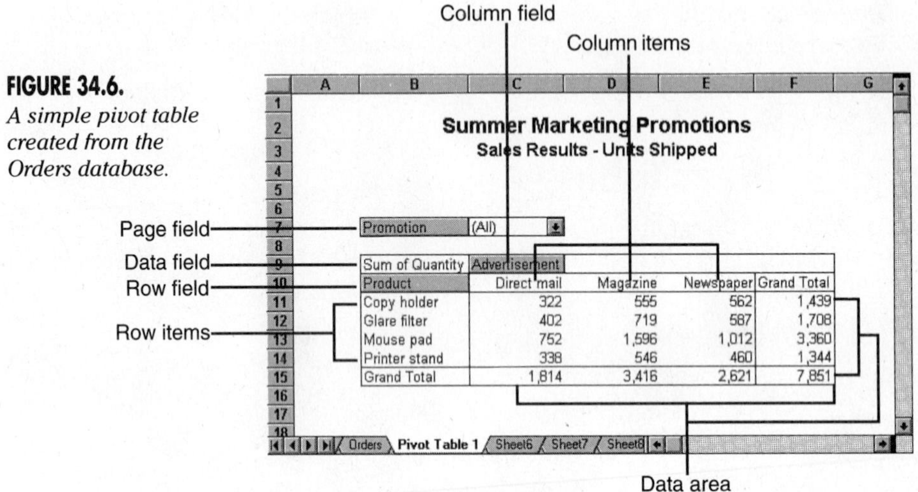

FIGURE 34.6.
A simple pivot table created from the Orders database.

Navigating the PivotTable Wizard

The PivotTable Wizard dialog boxes, like other Excel Wizard tools, contain a number of buttons that enable you to quickly navigate the PivotTable Wizard. These buttons are summarized in Table 34.1.

Table 34.1. PivotTable Wizard navigation buttons.

Button	*Description*
Help	Displays a Help window for the current step
Cancel	Closes the PivotTable Wizard without creating the table
< Back	Goes back to the previous step
Next >	Goes to the next step
Finish	Creates the pivot table

Creating a Pivot Table

The steps you use to create a pivot table vary depending on the source data you're using. There are four types you can use:

Microsoft Excel List or Database: A multicolumn list on a worksheet. The list must have labeled columns.

External Data Source: A separate database file in dBASE, FoxPro, ORACLE, or some other format. You retrieve the data from Microsoft Query.

Multiple Consolidation Ranges: A collection of lists with row and column labels in one or more worksheets. Each range must have a similar layout and identical row and column labels.

Another Pivot Table: Another pivot table in the same workbook.

The next few sections show you how to create a pivot table for each type of source.

Creating a Pivot Table from an Excel List

Follow the steps in Procedure 34.1 to create a pivot table from an Excel list. (Make sure the list's columns are labeled before beginning.)

PROCEDURE 34.1. CREATING A PIVOT TABLE FROM A LIST.

1. Select a cell inside the list you want to use. Doing so will save you a step later on.
2. Select the **D**ata | **P**ivotTable command. Excel displays the PivotTable Wizard - Step 1 of 4 dialog box, shown in Figure 34.7.

You also can start the PivotTable Wizard by clicking on this tool in the Query and Pivot toolbar.

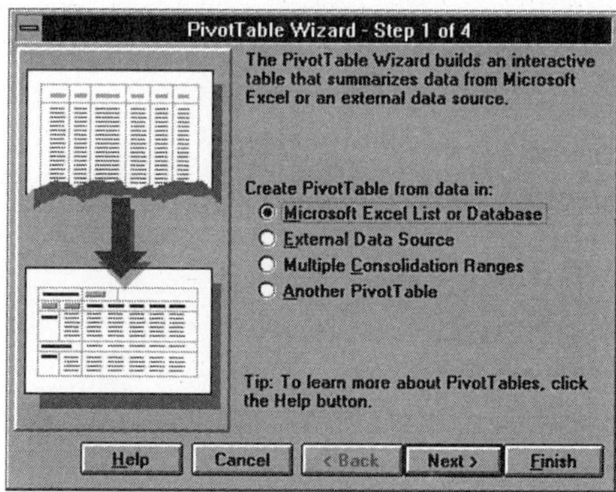

FIGURE 34.7. *The PivotTable Wizard - Step 1 of 4 dialog box that appears when you start the PivotTable Wizard.*

3. Make sure the **M**icrosoft List or Database option is activated and then click on Next >. The PivotTable Wizard - Step 2 of 4 dialog box appears, shown in Figure 34.8.

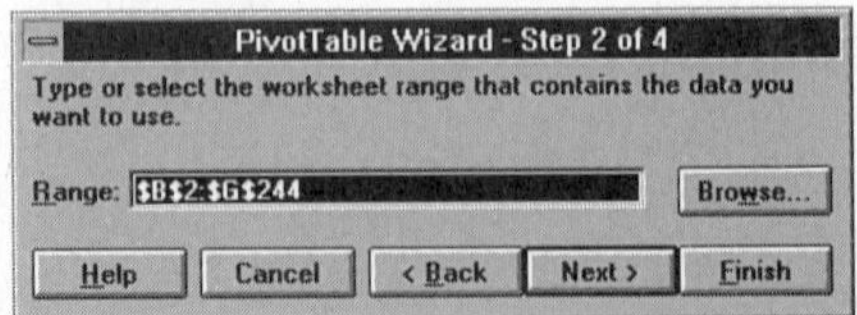

FIGURE 34.8.
The PivotTable Wizard - Step 2 of 4 dialog box for an Excel list.

4. If you selected a cell in the list, the correct range coordinates should already be displayed in the **R**ange edit box. If not, enter the range by either typing the address or selecting the range directly on the worksheet. Use Browse to enter a range from an unopened workbook. Click on Next > to display the PivotTable Wizard - Step 3 of 4 dialog box.
5. Specify the layout of the pivot table by dragging the field labels on the right to the appropriate areas. Figure 34.9 shows the layout used to create the pivot table in Figure 34.6. When you're done, click on Next > to display the PivotTable Wizard - Step 4 of 4 dialog box, shown in Figure 34.10.

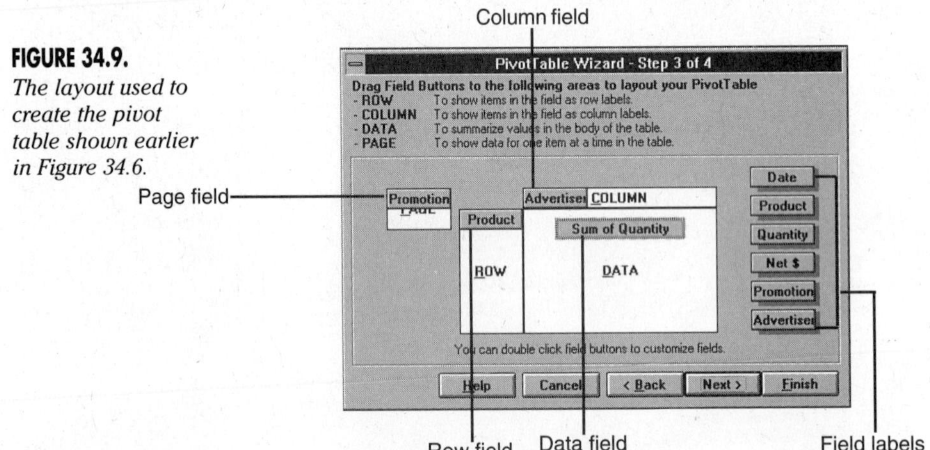

FIGURE 34.9.
The layout used to create the pivot table shown earlier in Figure 34.6.

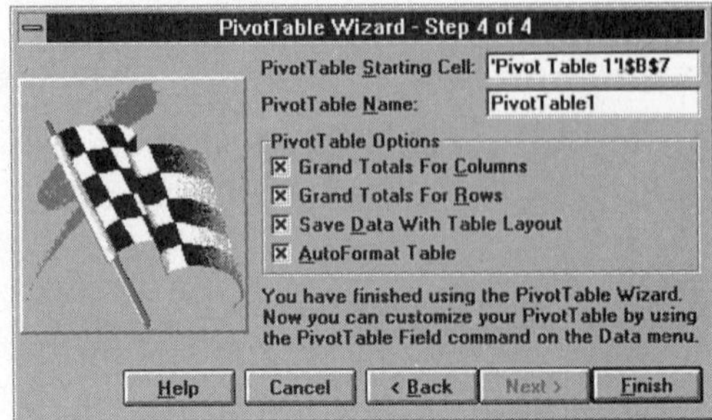

FIGURE 34.10.
Use the PivotTable Wizard - Step 4 of 4 dialog box to specify the table location and display options.

SUPER TIP

You can customize each field by double-clicking on the label. (You also can customize the fields after you've created the pivot table.) See the section titled "Customizing Pivot Table Fields" later in this chapter.

6. Use the PivotTable **S**tarting Cell box to select the upper-left corner of the range you want to use for the table. You can type a reference or select it directly on the worksheet (or even on another sheet).
7. Enter a name for the table in the PivotTable **N**ame box.
8. Use the check boxes in the PivotTable Options group to refine the table's display.

SUPER NOTE

To make pivot table updating faster, Excel normally stores a hidden copy of the source data with the table layout. If the source list contains a large amount of data, you may not want Excel to store a copy. In this case, deactivate the Save **D**ata With Table Layout check box. Now, when you make changes to the pivot table layout, Excel will use the source data directly to update the table.

9. Click on the **F**inish button. Excel creates the pivot table in the location you specified.

Creating a Pivot Table from an External Database

If the source data exists in an external database (for example, dBASE, FoxPro, or SQL Server), you can create a pivot table from the data by following Procedure 34.2.

PROCEDURE 34.2. CREATING A PIVOT TABLE FROM AN EXTERNAL DATABASE.

1. Select the **D**ata | **P**ivotTable command to display the PivotTable Wizard - Step 1 of 4 dialog box.

You also can start the PivotTable Wizard by clicking on this tool in the Query and Pivot toolbar.

2. Activate the **E**xternal Data Source option and then click on Next >. Excel displays the PivotTable Wizard - Step 2 of 4 dialog box.
3. Click on the **G**et Data button. Excel loads Microsoft Query.

4. Use Query to display the result set you want to use for the pivot table and then return the data to Excel. (To learn how to use Microsoft Query, refer to Chapter 33, "Using Microsoft Query.") The PivotTable Wizard stores the result set, but doesn't display it in the worksheet. Click on Next > to continue.
5. Follow steps 5-9 of Procedure 34.1 to create the pivot table.

SUPER TIP

If you think you'll be creating similar pivot tables with the same external data, you won't have to run the query again if you activate the Save **D**ata With Table Layout check box. This tells Excel to store a hidden copy of the data with the table layout, so you can use this hidden data to build other pivot tables. (See the section in this chapter titled "Creating a Pivot Table Using the Data From an Existing Table.")

Creating a Pivot Table from Multiple Ranges

Your source data may exist in multiple ranges or even on multiple worksheets. For example, you may have separate budget worksheets for different divisions or product lines. If the ranges have row and column labels (and they use identical labels), you can consolidate the data into a pivot table by following Procedure 34.3.

PROCEDURE 34.3. CREATING A PIVOT TABLE FROM MULTIPLE RANGES.

1. Select the **D**ata | **P**ivotTable command to display the PivotTable Wizard - Step 1 of 4 dialog box.

You also can start the PivotTable Wizard by clicking on this tool in the Query and Pivot toolbar.

2. Activate the Multiple **C**onsolidation Ranges option and then click on Next > to display the PivotTable Wizard - Step 2a of 4 dialog box.
3. To have PivotTable Wizard create a page field for each range, activate the **C**reate a single page for me option. To create your own page fields, choose the **I** will create the page option. Click on Next > to display the PivotTable Wizard - Step 2b of 4 dialog box.
4. For each range you want to include in the pivot table, enter a reference in the **R**ange box (or select it on the sheet), and then click on the **A**dd button. Use Bro**w**se to enter a range from an unopened workbook. Click on Next > when you're done.
5. Follow steps 5-9 of Procedure 34.1 to create the pivot table.

SUPER NOTE

PivotTable Wizard gives your pivot table generic names such as Row and Column. To change these names, see the section titled "Customizing Pivot Table Fields" later in this chapter.

Creating a Pivot Table Using the Data from an Existing Table

You can use the data stored with an existing pivot table layout to create a new pivot table. This is handy if the original data is not accessible for some reason, or if the data was created with a query and you don't want to run the query again. Procedure 34.4 shows you the necessary steps.

PROCEDURE 34.4. CREATING A PIVOT TABLE FROM AN EXISTING PIVOT TABLE.

1. Select the **D**ata | **P**ivotTable command to display the PivotTable Wizard - Step 1 of 4 dialog box.

You also can start the PivotTable Wizard by clicking on this tool in the Query and Pivot toolbar.

2. Activate the **A**nother PivotTable option and then click on Next > to display the PivotTable Wizard - Step 2 of 4 dialog box.
3. Highlight the pivot table that contains the data you want to use and then click on Next >.
4. Follow steps 5-9 of Procedure 34.1 to create the pivot table.

Refreshing a Pivot Table

If the source data changes, you'll need to update the pivot table to reflect the latest data. You can do this by following the steps in Procedure 34.5.

PROCEDURE 34.5. REFRESHING A PIVOT TABLE.

1. Activate the worksheet containing the pivot table.
2. Select a cell inside the pivot table.
3. Select the **D**ata | **R**efresh Data command. Excel updates the table values.

Click on the Refresh Data tool in the Query and Pivot toolbar to refresh your pivot table data.

SUPER TIP

You also can refresh pivot table data by right-clicking on pivot table cell and selecting Refresh Data from the shortcut menu.

Customizing a Pivot Table

As you've seen, even a simple pivot table is a powerful tool for summarizing and consolidating large amounts of data. However, Excel doesn't stop there. Once you've created a pivot table, you have a myriad of options available for rearranging the layout, adding and removing fields, and even redefining the entire table. The next few sections look at many of these customization options.

Adding Fields to a Pivot Table

To further refine your pivot tables, you can add new row, column, page, or data fields. The effect on the table depends on what type of field you add:

- Adding a row or column field creates subcategories for each row or column. For example, Figure 34.11 shows a new pivot table for the Orders list. In this case, the Promotion field has been added as a subcategory of the row fields. As you can see, each Product is broken down by Promotion and given its own subtotal.

FIGURE 34.11.
A pivot table with two row fields.

	A	B	C	D	E	F	G
1							
2		Sum of Quantity		Advertisement			
3		Product	Promotion	Direct mail	Magazine	Newspaper	Grand Total
4		Copy holder	1 Free with 10	154	341	297	792
5			Extra Discount	168	214	265	647
6		Copy holder Total		322	555	562	1,439
7		Glare filter	1 Free with 10	220	352	242	814
8			Extra Discount	182	367	345	894
9		Glare filter Total		402	719	587	1,708
10		Mouse pad	1 Free with 10	385	836	484	1,705
11			Extra Discount	367	760	528	1,655
12		Mouse pad Total		752	1,596	1,012	3,360
13		Printer stand	1 Free with 10	176	264	198	638
14			Extra Discount	162	282	262	706
15		Printer stand Total		338	546	460	1,344
16		Grand Total		1,814	3,416	2,621	7,851
17							
18							

Pivot Table 2 / Sheet8 / Sheet9 / Sheet10 / Shee

- Inserting another page field adds a new filter to the list. The pivot table reflects only data that meets the criteria specified by both items in the page field lists. (See the section later in this chapter titled "Working with Page Fields.")
- Adding a second data field changes the data area so that summary data is shown for both fields. In Figure 34.12, for example, a second data field has been added to show the data for the Net $ field in the Orders list.

FIGURE 34.12.
A pivot table with two data fields.

		Advertisement			
Product	Data	Direct mail	Magazine	Newspaper	Grand Total
Copy holder	Sum of Quantity	322	555	562	1,439
	Sum of Net $	$2,327	$4,051	$4,091	$10,469
Glare filter	Sum of Quantity	402	719	587	1,708
	Sum of Net $	$5,654	$9,985	$8,097	$23,736
Mouse pad	Sum of Quantity	752	1,596	1,012	3,360
	Sum of Net $	$5,461	$11,579	$7,314	$24,355
Printer stand	Sum of Quantity	338	546	460	1,344
	Sum of Net $	$3,751	$6,072	$5,063	$14,886
Total Sum of Quantity		1,814	3,416	2,621	7,851
Total Sum of Net $		$17,193	$31,687	$24,566	$73,446

Pivot Table 3 / Sheet9 / Sheet10 / Sheet11 / She

Procedure 34.6 shows you the steps to follow to add a field to a pivot table.

PROCEDURE 34.6. ADDING A FIELD TO A PIVOT TABLE.

1. Select a cell inside the pivot table you want to work with.
2. Select the **D**ata | **P**ivotTable command. Excel displays the PivotTable Wizard - Step 3 of 4 dialog box.

SUPER TIP

You also can display the PivotTable Wizard - Step 3 of 4 dialog box by right-clicking a pivot table cell and selecting PivotTable from the shortcut menu.

3. Select the field label you want to add and drag it to the appropriate pivot table area.
4. Click on the **F**inish button. Excel adds the new field and redisplays the pivot table.

SUPER TIP

You can quickly add fields by first right-clicking the area in which you want to add the field. In the shortcut menu, select the Add *type* Field command, in which *type* is either Row, Column, Page, or Data, depending on the area you selected. In the menu of field names that appears, select the field you want to add.

Deleting Fields from a Pivot Table

To remove a field from the pivot table, follow the steps in Procedure 34.7.

PROCEDURE 34.7. DELETING A FIELD FROM A PIVOT TABLE.

1. Select a cell inside the pivot table you want to work with.
2. Select the **D**ata | **P**ivotTable command to display the PivotTable Wizard - Step 3 of 4 dialog box.

SUPER TIP

You also can display the PivotTable Wizard - Step 3 of 4 dialog box by right-clicking on a pivot table cell and selecting PivotTable from the shortcut menu.

3. Select the field label you want to remove and drag it off the table area.
4. Click on the **F**inish button. Excel removes the new field and redisplays the pivot table.

Customizing Row, Column, and Page Fields

You can customize the table's row, column, and page fields to change things such as the field name and the field items to hide or display. These chores are handled by the PivotTable Field dialog box, shown in Figure 34.13. Following is a summary of the options:

N**a**me	The name of the field.
Orientation	Determines whether the field appears in the **R**ow, **C**olumn, or **P**age area.
Subtotals	If you have multiple fields in the row or column area, this group determines what kind of subtotals are displayed.

Hide **I**tems	Shows the items for the selected field. Selecting an item in the list hides it from the pivot table.
Delete	This button gives you an alternative method for deleting a field.

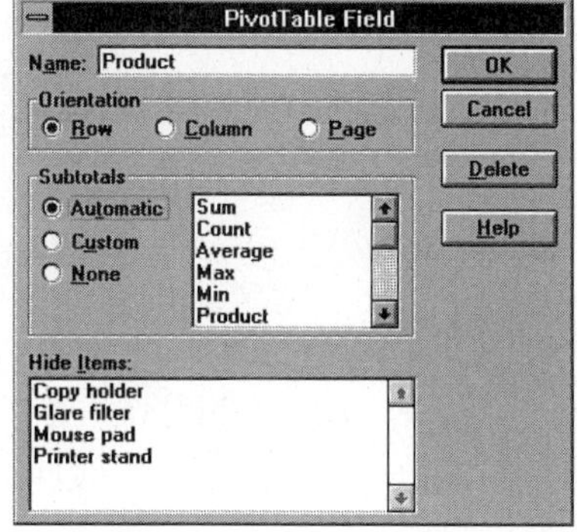

FIGURE 34.13.
Use the PivotTable Field dialog box to customize the pivot table's row, column, and page fields.

Procedure 34.8 shows you how to customize a row, column, or page pivot table field.

PROCEDURE 34.8. CUSTOMIZING A PIVOT TABLE FIELD.

1. Select a cell in the pivot table field you want to customize.
2. Select the **D**ata | PivotTable F**i**eld command to display the PivotTable Field dialog box.

> **SUPER TIP**
>
> You also can display the PivotTable Field dialog box by right-clicking on a cell in the pivot table field and selecting PivotTable Field from the shortcut menu.

Select a cell in the pivot table field and click on the PivotTable Field tool to display the PivotTable Field dialog box.

3. Enter the options you want for the field.
4. Click on OK or press Enter. Excel modifies the field and redisplays the pivot table.

Customizing a Data Field

Excel normally displays the sum of the data field values. You can use a different summary function and set other data field customization options with the version of the

PivotTable Field dialog box, shown in Figure 34.14. This dialog has the following options:

Name	The name of the field.
Summarize by	A list of the available summary functions, including Sum, Count, Average, Max, and Min.
Delete	The button that deletes the data field.
Number	The button that displays the Format Cells dialog box so you can specify a numeric format for the data field cells.
Options	The button that expands the dialog box to display the Show D**a**ta as group. You can use the controls in this group to determine the calculation type for the data field. For example, Figure 34.15 shows the Orders list pivot table using the % of total calculation.

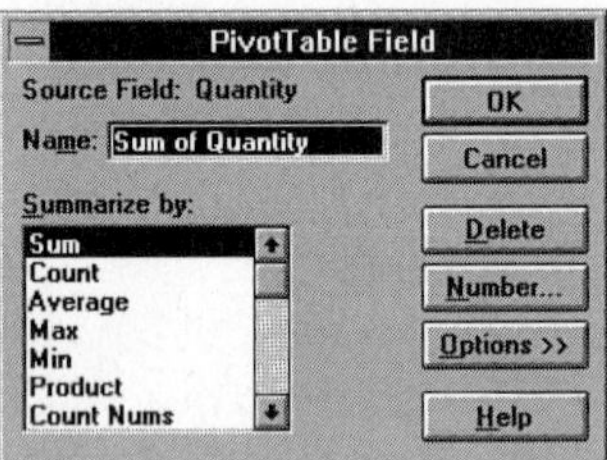

FIGURE 34.14.
Use this PivotTable Field dialog box to customize the pivot table's data fields.

Sum of Quantity		Advertisement			
Product	Promotion	Direct mail	Magazine	Newspaper	Grand Total
Copy holder	1 Free with 10	1.96%	4.34%	3.78%	10.09%
	Extra Discount	2.14%	2.73%	3.38%	8.24%
Copy holder Total		4.10%	7.07%	7.16%	18.33%
Glare filter	1 Free with 10	2.80%	4.48%	3.08%	10.37%
	Extra Discount	2.32%	4.67%	4.39%	11.39%
Glare filter Total		5.12%	9.16%	7.48%	21.76%
Mouse pad	1 Free with 10	4.90%	10.65%	6.16%	21.72%
	Extra Discount	4.67%	9.68%	6.73%	21.08%
Mouse pad Total		9.58%	20.33%	12.89%	42.80%
Printer stand	1 Free with 10	2.24%	3.36%	2.52%	8.13%
	Extra Discount	2.06%	3.59%	3.34%	8.99%
Printer stand Total		4.31%	6.95%	5.86%	17.12%
Grand Total		23.11%	43.51%	33.38%	100.00%

Pivot Table 1 / Pivot Table 2 / Pivot Table 3 / Sh

FIGURE 34.15.
A pivot table generated using the% of total calculation.

Procedure 34.9 shows you how to customize a data field.

PROCEDURE 34.9. CUSTOMIZING A PIVOT TABLE DATA FIELD.

1. Select a cell in the data field.

2. Select the **Data** | PivotTable F**i**eld command to display the PivotTable Field dialog box.

SUPER TIP

You also can display the PivotTable Fields dialog box by right-clicking on a cell in the data field and selecting PivotTable Field from the shortcut menu.

Select a cell in the data field and click on the PivotTable Field tool to display the PivotTable Field dialog box.

3. Enter the options you want for the field.
4. Click on OK or press Enter. Excel modifies the field and redisplays the pivot table.

Changing the Pivot Table View

In their most basic form, pivot tables consolidate large amounts of complex data into a comprehensive, readable summary. But the real beauty of pivot tables is how they enable you to view your data from different angles. Simply by selecting a page from a drop-down list, or by dragging fields to different table locations, you can see the numbers in an entirely different way. The next two sections show you how to use page fields and data pivoting to change the table view.

Working with Page Fields

Page fields filter your data the same way criteria do. (Criteria and filtering are covered in Chapter 31, "Managing List Records.") When you include a page field in your pivot table, Excel creates a drop-down list that contains the unique items from the field. You use these items to filter the list and display a different "page" of the table.

Displaying a Different Page

To display a different pivot table page, drop down the page field list and select one of the items. Excel filters the data to include only those records that match the page field item and then updates the table. When you want to remove the filter, select All from the list.

In the Orders list pivot table, for example, the page field is based on the Promotion column, which has two unique values: 1 Free with 10 and Extra Discount. To show only the totals for orders generated by the Extra Discount promotion, you would select Extra Discount from the page field drop-down list.

Displaying All Pages

If you want to include the various pivot table pages in a report, you can tell Excel to create new worksheets for each page view. There are two methods you can use:

- Select the Show Pages tool from the Query and Pivot toolbar.

The Show Pages tool from the Query and Pivot toolbar.

- Right-click on the page field and select Show Pages from the shortcut menu.

Pivoting the Table

Pivot tables "pivot" because the data area acts as a kind of fulcrum around which you can move row, column, and page fields. As you saw earlier, you can use the PivotTable Field dialog box to change the orientation of a field, but Excel gives you a much easier method. Specifically, you can pivot a table just by dragging the field labels to different locations. Here's a summary:

- To change the orientation of a row, column, or page field, drag the field label to the appropriate area. For example, to display a row field as a column field, drag the field label into the column area.
- To change the field order within an area, drag the field label to a new location within the area. For example, the pivot table in Figure 34.12 has two row fields: Promotion is a subcategory of the Product field. To reverse this, you would drag the Promotion label to the left of the Product label.
- To remove a field from the pivot table, drag the field label off the table.

Workshop

V

Data Analysis

Chapter 35

Basic Analytic Methods

This Workshop begins with a look at a few simple analytic techniques that have a wide variety of uses. You'll learn how to use Excel's numerous methods for what-if analysis, how to use iteration to solve problems, and how to use trend analysis.

Using What-If Analysis

What-if analysis is perhaps the most basic method for interrogating your spreadsheet data. In fact, it's probably safe to say that most spreadsheet work involves what-if analysis of one form or another.

With what-if analysis, you first calculate a formula D, based on the input from variables A, B, and C. You then say, "What if I change variable A? Or B or C? What happens to the result?"

For example, Figure 35.1 shows a worksheet that calculates the future value of an investment based on five variables: the interest rate, period, annual deposit, initial deposit, and the deposit type. Cell C10 shows the result of the `FV()` function. Now the questions begin. What if the interest rate were 7 percent? What if you deposited $8,000 per year? Or $12,000? What if you reduced the initial deposit? Answering these questions is a simple matter of changing the appropriate variables and watching the effect on the result.

C10 =FV(C3,C4,C5,C6,C7)*-1

ANALYSIS.XLS

	A	B	C	D
1		The Future Value of an Investment		
2				
3		Interest Rate	5%	
4		Period	10	
5		Annual Deposit	$10,000	
6		Initial Deposit	$25,000	
7		Deposit Type	1	
8				
9			Future Value	
10			$172,790	

Future Value / Sheet2 / Sheet3 / Sheet4 / Sheet
Ready NUM

FIGURE 35.1.
The simplest what-if analysis involves changing worksheet variables and watching the result.

Setting Up a One-Input Data Table

The problem with modifying formula variables is that you see only a single result at one time. If you're interested in studying the effect a range of values has on the formula, you need to set up a *data table*. In the investment analysis worksheet, for example, suppose you would like to see the future value of the investment with the annual deposit varying between $7,000 and $13,000. You could just enter these values in a row or column and then create the appropriate formulas. However, setting up a data table is much easier, as Procedure 35.1 shows.

PROCEDURE 35.1. SETTING UP A ONE-INPUT DATA TABLE.

1. Enter the values you want to input into the formula. You have two choices for the placement of these values:
   - If you want to enter the values in a row, start the row one cell up and one cell to the right of the formula.
   - If you want to enter the values in a column, start the column one cell down and one cell to the left of the cell containing the formula (see Figure 35.2).

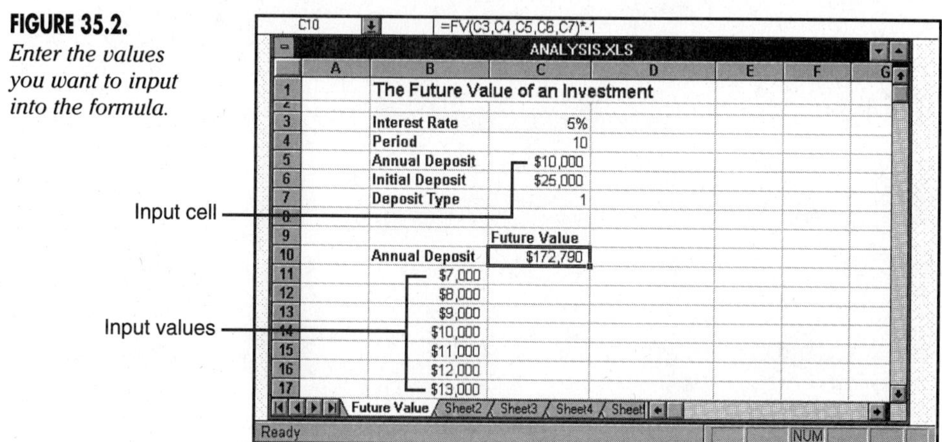

FIGURE 35.2.
Enter the values you want to input into the formula.

2. Select the range that includes the input values and the formula. (In Figure 35.2, this would be B10:C17.)
3. Select the **D**ata | **T**able command. Excel displays the Table dialog box.
4. If you entered the input values in a row, select the **R**ow Input Cell box and enter the cell address of the input cell. If the input values are in a column, enter the input cell's address in the **C**olumn Input Cell edit box instead. In the investment analysis example, you enter C5 in the **C**olumn Input Cell, as shown in Figure 35.3.
5. Click on OK or press Enter. Excel takes each of the input values and places them in the input cell; Excel then displays the results in the data table, as shown in Figure 35.4.

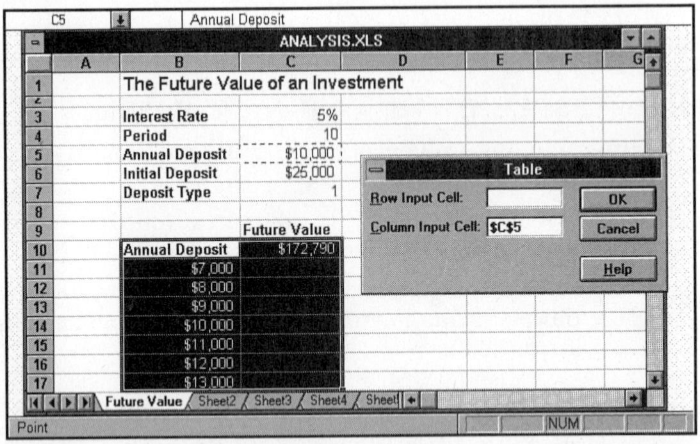

FIGURE 35.3.
In the Table dialog box, enter the input cell you want Excel to use for the input values.

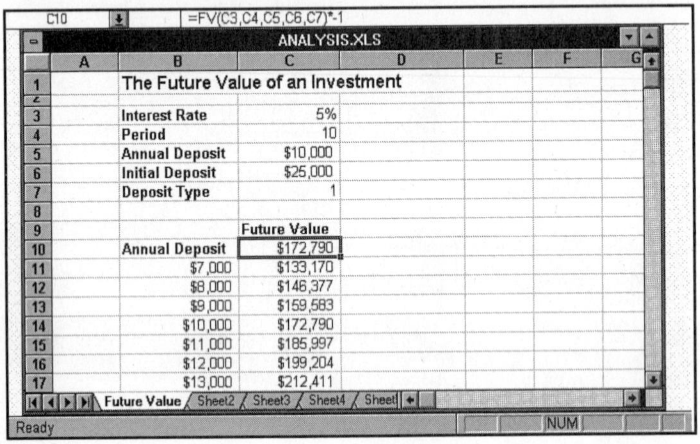

FIGURE 35.4.
Excel substitutes each input value into the input cell and displays the result in the data table.

Adding More Formulas to the Input Table

You're not restricted to just a single formula in your data tables. If you want to see the effect of the various input values on different formulas, you can easily add them to the data table. For example, in our future value worksheet, it would be interesting to factor inflation into the calculations so that the user could see how the investment appears in today's dollars. Figure 35.5 shows the revised worksheet with a new `Inflation Rate` variable and a formula that converts the calculated future value into today's dollars (cell D10).

FIGURE 35.5.
To add a formula to a data table, enter the new formula next to the existing one.

D10 =C10/(1+C8)^C4

ANALYSIS.XLS

	A	B	C	D	E	F	G
1		The Future Value of an Investment					
2							
3		Interest Rate	5%				
4		Period	10				
5		Annual Deposit	$10,000				
6		Initial Deposit	$25,000				
7		Deposit Type	1				
8		Inflation	3%				
9			Future Value	Today's Dollars			
10		Annual Deposit	$172,790	$128,572			
11		$7,000					
12		$8,000					
13		$9,000					
14		$10,000					
15		$11,000					
16		$12,000					
17		$13,000					

Future Value / Sheet2 / Sheet3 / Sheet4 / Sheet
Ready NUM

SUPER NOTE

The formula for converting a future value into today's dollars is as follows:

```
Future Value / (1 + Inflation Rate) ^ Period
```

Here, `Period` is the number of years from now that the future value exists.

To create the new data table, follow the steps in Procedure 35.1. However, the range you select in step 2 includes the input values and both formulas (that is, the range B10:D17 in Figure 35.5). Figure 35.6 shows the results.

FIGURE 35.6.
The results of the data table with multiple formulas.

D10 =C10/(1+C8)^C4

ANALYSIS.XLS

	A	B	C	D	E	F	G
1		The Future Value of an Investment					
2							
3		Interest Rate	5%				
4		Period	10				
5		Annual Deposit	$10,000				
6		Initial Deposit	$25,000				
7		Deposit Type	1				
8		Inflation	3%				
9			Future Value	Today's Dollars			
10		Annual Deposit	$172,790	$128,572			
11		$7,000	$133,170	$99,091			
12		$8,000	$146,377	$108,918			
13		$9,000	$159,583	$118,745			
14		$10,000	$172,790	$128,572			
15		$11,000	$185,997	$138,399			
16		$12,000	$199,204	$148,226			
17		$13,000	$212,411	$158,053			

Future Value / Sheet2 / Sheet3 / Sheet4 / Sheet
Ready NUM

SUPER NOTE

As soon as you have a data table set up, you can do regular what-if analysis by adjusting the other worksheet variables. Each time you make a change, Excel recalculates every formula in the table.

Setting Up a Two-Input Table

You also can set up data tables that take two input variables. This would enable you, for example, to see the effect on an investment's future value when you enter different values for the annual deposit and the interest rate. Procedure 35.2 shows how to set up a two-input data table.

PROCEDURE 35.2. SETTING UP A TWO-INPUT DATA TABLE.

1. Enter one set of values in a column below the formula and the second set of values in the row beside the formula, as shown in Figure 35.7.

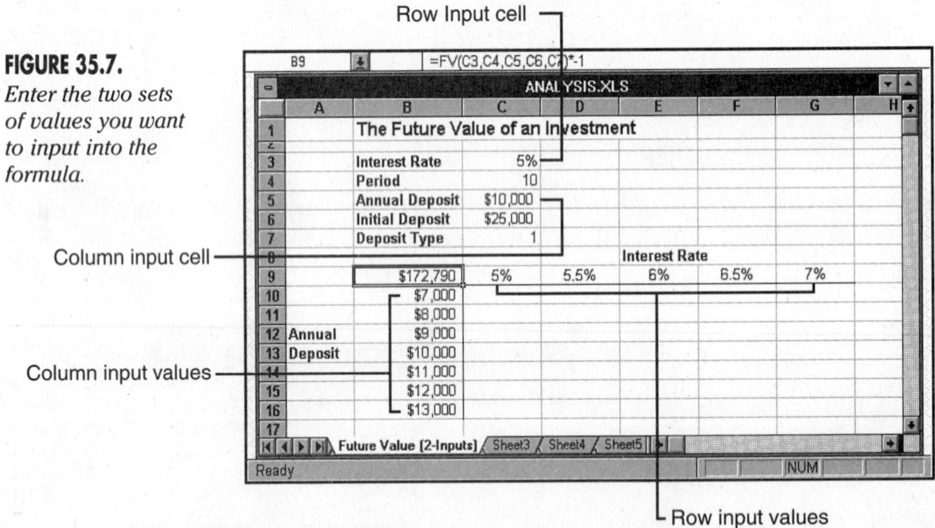

FIGURE 35.7. *Enter the two sets of values you want to input into the formula.*

2. Select the range that includes input values and the formula (B9:G16 in Figure 35.7).
3. Select the **Data** | **Table** command to display the Table dialog box.
4. In the **R**ow Input Cell edit box, enter the cell address of the input cell that corresponds to the row values you entered (C3 in Figure 35.7). In the **C**olumn

Input Cell edit box, enter the cell address of the input cell you want to use for the column values (C5 in Figure 35.7).

5. Click on OK or press Enter. Excel runs through the various input combinations and then displays the results in the data table, as shown in Figure 35.8.

FIGURE 35.8.
Excel substitutes each input value into the input cell and displays the result in the data table.

B9 =FV(C3,C4,C5,C6,C7)*-1

ANALYSIS.XLS

	A	B	C	D	E	F	G
1		The Future Value of an Investment					
2							
3		Interest Rate	5%				
4		Period	10				
5		Annual Deposit	$10,000				
6		Initial Deposit	$25,000				
7		Deposit Type	1				
8					Interest Rate		
9		$172,790	5%	5.5%	6%	6.5%	7%
10		$7,000	$133,170	$137,788	$142,573	$147,529	$152,664
11		$8,000	$146,377	$151,372	$156,544	$161,901	$167,448
12	Annual	$9,000	$159,583	$164,955	$170,516	$176,272	$182,231
13	Deposit	$10,000	$172,790	$178,539	$184,488	$190,644	$197,015
14		$11,000	$185,997	$192,122	$198,459	$205,016	$211,798
15		$12,000	$199,204	$205,706	$212,431	$219,387	$226,582
16		$13,000	$212,411	$219,289	$226,403	$233,759	$241,366
17							

Future Value (2-Inputs) / Sheet3 / Sheet4 / Sheet5

Ready NUM

SUPER TIP

As I mentioned earlier, if you make changes to any of the variables in a table formula, Excel recalculates the entire table. This isn't a problem in small tables, but large ones can take forever to calculate. If you prefer to control the table recalculation, select the **T**ools | **O**ptions command, select the Calculation tab, then activate the Automatic Except Tables check box. To recalculate a table, press F9 (or Shift+F9 for the current worksheet only).

Editing a Data Table

When you select the **D**ata | **T**able command, Excel enters an *array formula* in the interior of the data table. This formula is a `TABLE()` function with the following form:

`{=TABLE(`*`row_input_ref`*`,`*`column_input_ref`*`)}`

Here, *`row_input_ref`* and *`column_input_ref`* are the cell references you entered in the Table dialog box. The braces ({ }) tell you that this is an array. Therefore, you can't change or delete individual elements of the table. (To learn more about arrays, see Chapter 60, "Advanced Range Topics.") If you want to delete or move the data table, you have to select the entire table.

SUPER NOTE

Excel has other features that perform even more sophisticated what-if analysis. These features—Goal Seek, Solver, and Scenario Manager—are covered in the next three chapters.

Trend Analysis with Best-Fit Lines

Whether you're looking at stock prices, putting together a business plan, or setting up a budget, you'll need to analyze the overall trend of your data to get the big picture and to make short-term predictions.

Excel offers a number of tools for trend analysis, and this section explains a few of them. Specifically, you'll look at two methods that calculate the trend based on the *line of best-fit*. This is a straight line through the data points in which the differences between the points above and below the line cancel each other out (more or less). For example, in Figure 35.9, I've charted the worksheet sales figures and then inserted a trendline. This line clearly shows the trend of the data and, by visually extending the line, you can project the sales into the future.

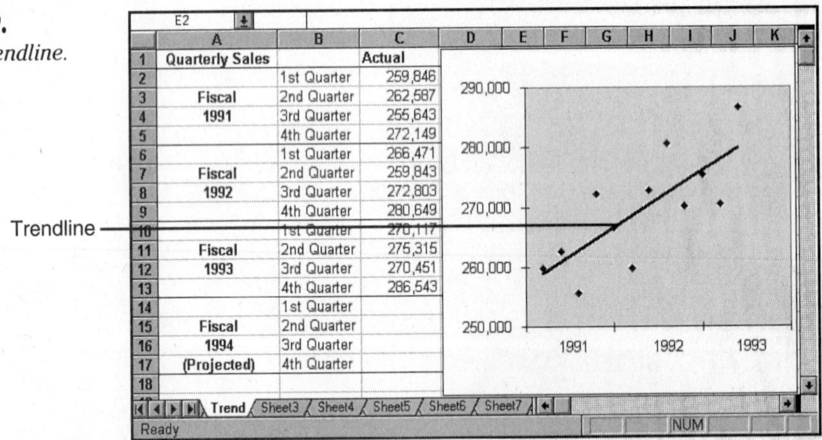

	A	B	C
1	Quarterly Sales		Actual
2		1st Quarter	259,846
3	Fiscal	2nd Quarter	262,587
4	1991	3rd Quarter	255,643
5		4th Quarter	272,149
6		1st Quarter	266,471
7	Fiscal	2nd Quarter	259,843
8	1992	3rd Quarter	272,803
9		4th Quarter	280,649
10		1st Quarter	270,117
11	Fiscal	2nd Quarter	275,315
12	1993	3rd Quarter	270,451
13		4th Quarter	286,543
14		1st Quarter	
15	Fiscal	2nd Quarter	
16	1994	3rd Quarter	
17	(Projected)	4th Quarter	
18			

FIGURE 35.9.
A best-fit trendline.

SUPER NOTE

To add a trendline to a chart, select the data series and then select the **Insert | Trendline** command. From the Trendline dialog box that appears, select the Type tab and choose one of the Trend types.

How accurate is such a prediction? A linear projection based on historical data assumes that the factors influencing the data over the historical period will remain constant. If this is a reasonable assumption in your case, the projection will be a reasonable one. Of course, the longer you extend the line, the more likely it is that some of the factors will change or that new ones will arise. As a result, best-fit extensions should be used only for short-term projections.

> **SUPER NOTE**
>
> Excel provides the `TREND()` function for more sophisticated trend analysis. To learn how to use this function, see Chapter 70, "Building a Sales Forecasting Model."

Extending a Series with the Fill Handle

The fill handle introduced in Excel 4 is probably the easiest method to project a best-fit line into the future. All you do is highlight the historical data and then drag the fill handle to extend the selection. Excel calculates the best-fit line from the existing data and then projects this line into the new data.

Figure 35.10 shows an example. Here, I've used the fill handle to project the quarterly sales figures over the next fiscal year. The accompanying chart clearly shows the extended best-fit line.

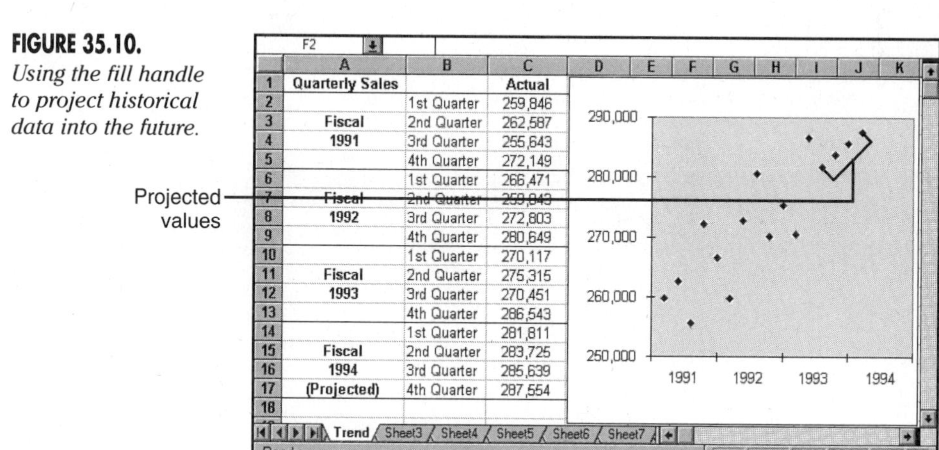

	A	B	C
1	Quarterly Sales		Actual
2		1st Quarter	259,846
3	Fiscal	2nd Quarter	262,587
4	1991	3rd Quarter	255,643
5		4th Quarter	272,149
6		1st Quarter	266,471
7	Fiscal	2nd Quarter	259,843
8	1992	3rd Quarter	272,803
9		4th Quarter	280,649
10		1st Quarter	270,117
11	Fiscal	2nd Quarter	275,315
12	1993	3rd Quarter	270,451
13		4th Quarter	286,543
14		1st Quarter	281,811
15	Fiscal	2nd Quarter	283,725
16	1994	3rd Quarter	285,639
17	(Projected)	4th Quarter	287,554
18			

FIGURE 35.10. *Using the fill handle to project historical data into the future.*

Using the Series Command

You also can use the Series command to project a best-fit line. Procedure 35.3 shows you how it's done.

PROCEDURE 35.3. PRODUCING A BEST-FIT PROJECTION WITH THE SERIES COMMAND.

1. Select the range that includes both the historical data and the cells that will contain the projections (make sure the projection cells are blank).
2. Select the **Edit** | **Fill** | **Series** command. Excel displays the Series dialog box.
3. Select the AutoFill check box.
4. Click on OK or press Enter. Excel fills in the blank cells with the best-fit projection.

You also can use the **Data** | **Series** command to produce the full best-fit line so that you can see the trend. Follow the steps in Procedure 35.4.

PROCEDURE 35.4. DISPLAYING THE BEST-FIT LINE WITH THE SERIES COMMAND.

1. Copy the historical data onto an adjacent row or column.
2. Select the range that includes both the copied historical data and the cells that will contain the projections (again, make sure the projection cells are blank).
3. Select the **Edit** | **Fill** | **Series** command. Excel displays the Series dialog box.
4. Activate the **Trend** check box and make sure the **Linear** check box is also activated.
5. Click on OK or press Enter. Excel replaces the copied historical data with the best-fit numbers and projects the trend onto the blank cells.

Figure 35.11 shows a chart with the best-fit line on top of the historical data.

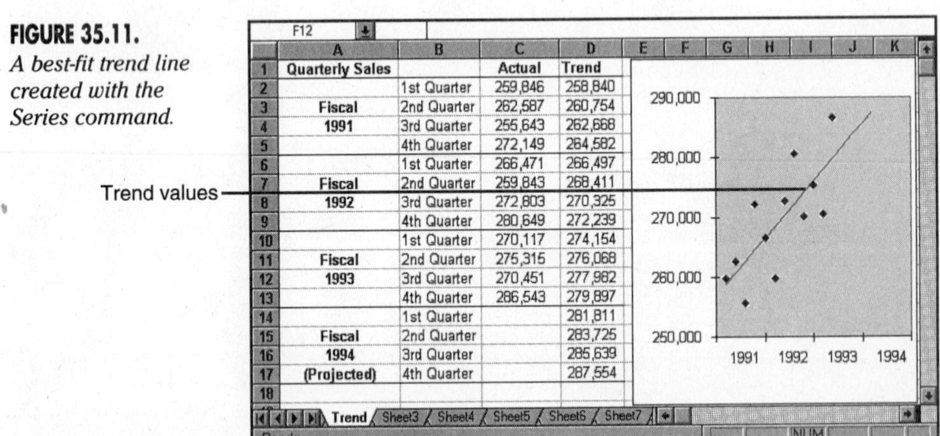

Quarterly Sales		Actual	Trend
	1st Quarter	259,846	258,840
Fiscal	2nd Quarter	262,587	260,754
1991	3rd Quarter	255,643	262,668
	4th Quarter	272,149	264,582
	1st Quarter	266,471	266,497
Fiscal	2nd Quarter	259,843	268,411
1992	3rd Quarter	272,803	270,325
	4th Quarter	280,649	272,239
	1st Quarter	270,117	274,154
Fiscal	2nd Quarter	275,315	276,068
1993	3rd Quarter	270,451	277,982
	4th Quarter	286,543	279,897
	1st Quarter		281,811
Fiscal	2nd Quarter		283,725
1994	3rd Quarter		285,639
(Projected)	4th Quarter		287,554

FIGURE 35.11.
A best-fit trend line created with the Series command.

Using Iteration

A common business problem involves calculating a profit-sharing plan contribution as a percentage of a company's net profits. This isn't a simple multiplication problem, because the net profit is determined, in part, by the profit-sharing figure. For example, suppose a company has a gross margin of $1,000,000 and expenses of $900,000, which leaves a gross profit of $100,000. The company also sets aside 10 percent of net profits for profit sharing. The net profit is calculated with the following formula:

```
Net Profit = Gross Profit - Profit Sharing Contribution
```

This is called a *circular reference formula* because there are terms on the left and right side of the equals sign (=) that depend on each other.

One way to solve such a formula is to guess at an answer and see how close you come. For example, because profit sharing should be 10 percent of net profits, a good first guess might be 10 percent of *gross* profits, or $10,000. If you plug this into the formula, you end up with a net profit of $90,000. This isn't right, however, because 10 percent of $90,000 is $9,000. Therefore, the profit-sharing guess is off by $1,000.

So you can try again. This time, use $9,000 as the profit-sharing number. Plugging this new value into the formula gives a net profit of $91,000. This would translate into a profit-sharing contribution of $9,100—which is off by only $100.

If you continue this process, your profit-sharing guesses will get closer to the calculated value (this is called *convergence*). When the guesses are close enough (for example, within a dollar), you can stop and pat yourself on the back for finding the solution. This process is called *iteration.*

Of course, you didn't spend your (or your company's) hard-earned money on a computer to do this sort of thing by hand. Excel makes iterative calculations a breeze, as you'll see in Procedure 35.5.

PROCEDURE 35.5. USING ITERATION TO SOLVE CIRCULAR REFERENCE FORMULAS.

1. Set up your worksheet and enter your circular reference formula. Figure 35.12 shows a worksheet for the example I used earlier.

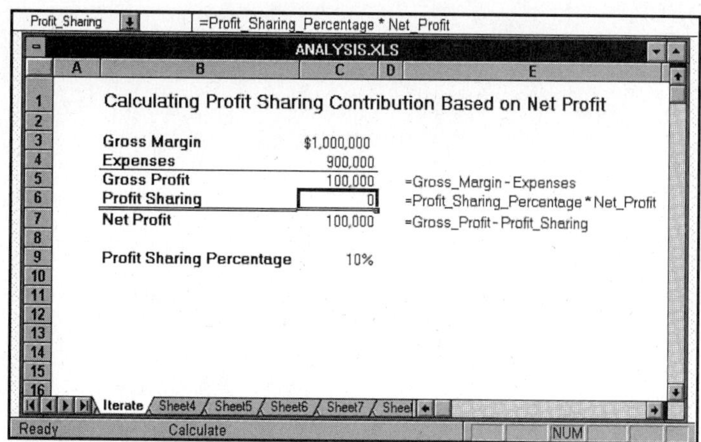

FIGURE 35.12.
A worksheet with a circular reference formula.

2. Select the Tools | Options command and then select the Calculation tab in the Options dialog box.
3. Activate the Iteration check box.
4. Use the Maximum Iterations edit box to specify the number of iterations you need. In most cases, the default figure of 100 is more than enough.
5. Use the Maximum Change edit box to tell Excel how accurate you want your results calculated. The smaller the number, the longer the iteration takes and the more accurate the calculation will be.
6. Click on OK or press Enter. Excel begins the iteration and stops when it has found a solution (see Figure 35.13).

FIGURE 35.13.
The solution to the iterative profit-sharing problem.

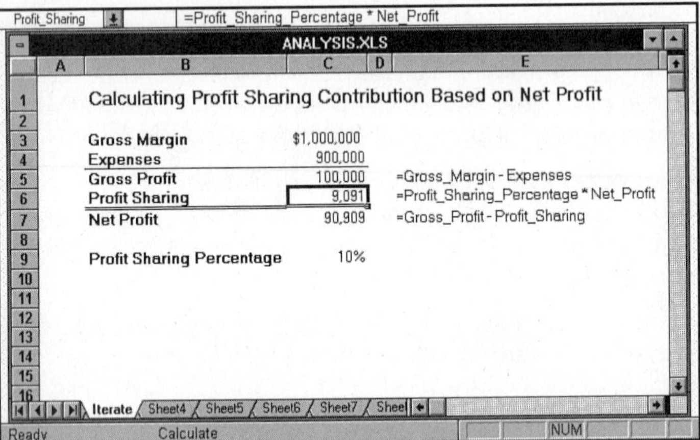

SUPER TIP

If you want to watch the progress of the iteration, turn on the Manual check box in the Calculation tab and enter 1 in the Maximum Iterations edit box. When you return to your worksheet, each time you press F9, Excel performs a single pass of the iteration.

SUPER NOTE

Excel's Solver utility is a powerful iterative method. See Chapter 38, "Working with Solver," for details.

Chapter

36

Working with the Analysis Toolpack

Excel's Analysis Toolpack is a large collection of powerful statistical functions and commands. Most of these tools use advanced statistical techniques and were designed with only a limited number of technical users in mind. However, in this chapter, I'll discuss a few tools that do have general applications.

Loading the Analysis Toolpack

To use the tools and functions in the Analysis Toolpack, you need to load the add-in macro that makes them available to Excel. Procedure 36.1 takes you through the steps.

PROCEDURE 36.1. LOADING THE ANALYSIS TOOLPACK.

1. Select the Tools | Add-Ins command. Excel displays the Add-ins dialog box.
2. Activate the Analysis check box in the Add-ins Available list.

> **SUPER NOTE**
>
> If you don't see an Analysis check box in the Add-ins Available list, you didn't install the Analysis Toolpack when you installed Excel. You need to run the Excel setup program and use it to install the Analysis Toolpack.

3. Click on OK or press Enter.

New Analysis Toolpack Functions

The Analysis Toolpack adds over 90 new functions to Excel's already impressive function list. The next few sections take a look at some of the most useful of these new functions.

New Date Functions

The Analysis Toolpack features a number of new date functions; I'll look at four of them here: EDATE(), WORKDAY(), NETWORKDAYS(), and YEARFRAC().

The EDATE() function calculates a date that is a given number of months before or after a specified date. This is useful for calculating maturity dates or due dates that fall on the same day of the month as the date of issue. EDATE() has the following syntax:

EDATE(***start_date***,***months***)

start_date	The date from which you want to start the calculation.
months	The number of months from ***start_date***.

Use a positive number to get a date after ***start_date*** and a negative number to get a date before ***start_date***.

`WORKDAY()` returns a date that is a specified number of working days before or after a given date. Working days exclude weekends; you also can provide the function a list of holidays to exclude. Use the following syntax to do so:

`WORKDAY(`***start_date***`,`***days***`,`*holidays*`)`

start_date	The date from which to begin the calculation.
days	The number of working days before or after ***start_date***. Use a positive number to get a later date, and a negative number to get an earlier date.
holidays	An array or a reference to a range of dates to exclude as work days (such as federal or state holidays).

The `NETWORKDAYS()` function is similar to `WORKDAY()`. However, `NETWORKDAYS()` returns the number of whole working days between two dates. Again, weekends are excluded, and you can specify holidays as well. `NETWORKDAYS()` has the following syntax:

`NETWORKDAYS(`***start_date***`,`***end_date***`,`*holidays*`)`

start_date	The beginning date.
end_date	The ending date.
holidays	An array or a reference to a range of dates to exclude as work days.

`YEARFRAC()` calculates the fraction of a year represented by the number of days between two dates. This is ideal for calculating items such as benefits and vacation days owed to new employees. Following is the syntax for `YEARFRAC()`:

`YEARFRAC(`***start_date***`,`***end_date***`,`*basis*`)`

start_date	The beginning date.
end_date	The ending date.
basis	The day count basis you want Excel to use. You have four options:

basis	*Day Count Basis*
0 (or omitted)	30 days per month and 360 days per year
1	Actual number of days per month and per year
2	Actual number of days per month and 360 days per year
3	Actual number of days per month and 365 days per year

For example, if cell A1 contains 1/1/93 and cell A2 contains 6/30/93, the formula `=YEARFRAC(A1,A2,0)` returns 0.5. However, `YEARFRAC(A1,A2,1)` returns 0.49589 because there are actually 181 days between January 1st and June 30th, which is slightly less than half a year.

New Math Functions

The Analysis Toolpack adds a fistful of new math functions, but I'll talk about three here: `CONVERT()`, `COMBIN()`, and `MROUND()`.

The `CONVERT()` function converts a number between different measurement systems. For example, you can use `CONVERT()` to change inches to centimeters, or liters to gallons. Following is the structure of the `CONVERT()` function:

CONVERT(***number***,***from_unit***,***to_unit***)

number	The number you want to convert.
from_unit	The unit of measurement currently used by ***number***.
to_unit	The unit you want to convert ***number*** to.

Both ***from_unit*** and ***to_unit*** accept abbreviations such a "g" for gram and "mi" for mile. See the Excel Function Reference for the complete list of abbreviations.

`COMBIN()` computes the number of possible combinations of groups of a certain size when selected from a population of a certain size. Following is its syntax:

COMBIN(***number***,***number_chosen***)

number	The population size.
number_chosen	The number chosen from the population to form each group.

For example, to find out the number of five-card hands that are possible with a 52-card deck, you would enter `=COMBIN(52,5)` to get the answer 2,589,960.

The `MROUND()` function goes `ROUND()` one better by enabling you to round a value to the nearest multiple of any number. This is handy for setting prices to the nearest 25 cents or for ordering items that come in packs (of 12 for example). Following is `MROUND()`'s syntax:

MROUND(***number***,***multiple***)

number	The value you want to round.
multiple	The multiple to which you want ***number*** rounded.

Here are some examples:

```
=MROUND(14.68,0.25) returns 14.75

=MROUND(500,12) returns 504

=MROUND(-272,-5) returns -270
```

Analysis Toolpack Statistical Tools

The Analysis Toolpack comes with 19 new statistical tools that handle everything from correlation to regression. The next few sections look at five of these tools: correlation, descriptive statistics, histograms, random numbers, and rank and percentile.

Determining the Correlation Between Data

Correlation is a measure of the relationship between two or more sets of data. For example, you might have monthly figures for advertising expenses and sales, and you might wonder if they're related. That is, do higher advertising expenses lead to more sales?

To determine this, you need to calculate the *correlation coefficient.* The coefficient is a number between –1 and 1 that has the following properties:

Correlation Coefficient	*Interpretation*
1	The two sets of data are perfectly and positively correlated. For example, a 10 percent increase in advertising produces a 10 percent increase in sales.
Between 0 and 1	The two sets of data are positively correlated (an increase in advertising leads to an increase in sales). The higher the number the higher the correlation between the data.
0	There is no correlation between the data.
Between 0 and –1	The two sets of data are negatively correlated (an increase in advertising leads to a *decrease* in sales). The lower the number, the more negatively correlated the data.
–1	The data sets have a perfect negative correlation. For example, a 10 percent increase in advertising leads to a 10 percent decrease in sales (and, presumably, a new advertising department).

To calculate the correlation between data sets, follow the steps in Procedure 36.2.

PROCEDURE 36.2. CALCULATING THE CORRELATION BETWEEN SETS OF DATA.

1. Select the **T**ools | **D**ata Analysis command. Excel displays the Data Analysis dialog box.
2. Highlight the Correlation option and then click on OK. The Correlation dialog box appears.

3. In the Input group, select the data range, including the row or column headings.
4. If you included labels in your range, make sure **Labels in First Row** is checked. (If your data is arranged in rows, this check box will say **Labels in First Column**.)
5. Excel displays the correlation coefficients in a table, so use the **Output Range** box to enter a reference to the upper-left corner of the table. (If you're comparing two sets of data, the output range is three columns wide by three rows high.) You also can select a different sheet or workbook.
6. Click on OK or press Enter. Excel calculates the correlation and displays the table.

Figure 36.1 shows a worksheet that compares advertising expenses with sales. For a control, I've also included a column of random numbers. The Correlation table lists the various correlation coefficients. In this case, the high correlation between advertising and sales (0.74) means that these two factors are strongly (and positively) correlated. As you can see, there is almost no correlation among the advertising, sales data, and the random numbers (as you might expect).

FIGURE 36.1.
The correlation between advertising expenses, sales, and a set of randomly generated numbers.

		Advertising	Sales	Tea in China
Fiscal 1991	1st Quarter	512,450	8,123,965	125,781
	2nd Quarter	447,840	7,750,500	499,772
	3rd Quarter	500,125	7,860,405	735,374
	4th Quarter	515,600	8,005,800	620,991
Fiscal 1992	1st Quarter	482,754	8,136,444	894,312
	2nd Quarter	485,750	7,950,426	101,451
	3rd Quarter	460,890	7,875,500	225,891
	4th Quarter	490,400	7,952,600	823,969
Fiscal 1993	1st Quarter	510,230	8,100,145	869,564
	2nd Quarter	515,471	8,034,125	495,102
	3rd Quarter	525,850	8,350,450	119,939
	4th Quarter	520,365	8,100,520	875,057

Correlation	*Advertising*	*Sales*	*Tea in China*
Advertising	1.00		
Sales	0.74	1.00	
Tea in China	0.07	-0.09	1.00

SUPER NOTE

The 1s in the Correlation table signify that any set of data is always perfectly correlated to itself.

SUPER NOTE

Use the CORREL() function to calculate a correlation without going through the Data Analysis dialog box.

Generating Descriptive Statistics

Excel has separate statistical functions for calculating things such as the mean, standard deviation, and maximum and minimum values of a sample. If you need this sort of basic analysis, entering all those functions can be a pain. Instead, use the Analysis Toolpack's Descriptive Statistics tool. This tool automatically calculates 16 of the most common statistical functions and lays them all out in a table. Follow the steps in Procedure 36.3.

SUPER NOTE

Keep in mind that the Descriptive Statistics tool outputs only numbers, not formulas. Therefore, if your data changes, you'll have to select the tool again.

PROCEDURE 36.3. USING THE ANALYSIS TOOLPACK'S DESCRIPTIVE STATISTICS TOOL.

1. Select the range that includes the data you want to analyze (including the row and column headings, if any).
2. Select the **T**ools | **D**ata Analysis command and in the Data Analysis dialog box, highlight the Descriptive Statistics option. Then click on OK. Excel displays the Descriptive Statistics dialog box.
3. Use the Output options group to select a location for the output. For each set of data included in the input range, Excel creates a table that is two columns wide and up to 18 rows high.
4. Select the statistics you want to include in the output:

   Summary Statistics: Select this option to include statistics such as the mean, median, mode, standard deviation, and more.

   Kth L**a**rgest: Select this option to add a row to the output that specifies the *k*th largest value in the sample. The default value for *k* is 1 (that is, the largest value), but if you want to see any other number, enter a value for *k* in the edit box.

Kth Smallest: Select this option to include the sample's *k*th smallest value in the output. Again, if you want *k* to be something other than 1 (that is, the smallest value), enter a number in the edit box.

Confidence Level for Mean: Select this option if your data set is a sample of a larger population and you want Excel to calculate the confidence interval for the population mean. A confidence level of 95 percent means that you can be 95 percent confident that the population mean will fall within the confidence interval. For example, if the sample mean is 10 and Excel calculates a confidence interval of 1.5, you can be 95 percent sure that the population mean will fall between 8.5 and 11.5.

5. Click on OK. Excel calculates the various statistics and displays the output table, shown in Figure 36.2.

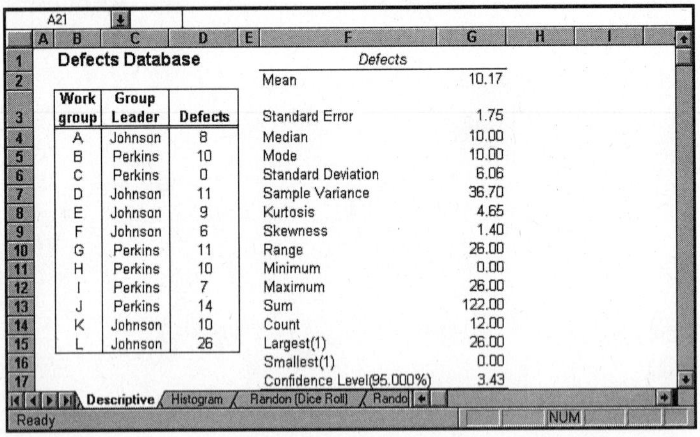

Defects Database

Work group	Group Leader	Defects
A	Johnson	8
B	Perkins	10
C	Perkins	0
D	Johnson	11
E	Johnson	9
F	Johnson	6
G	Perkins	11
H	Perkins	10
I	Perkins	7
J	Perkins	14
K	Johnson	10
L	Johnson	26

Defects	
Mean	10.17
Standard Error	1.75
Median	10.00
Mode	10.00
Standard Deviation	6.06
Sample Variance	36.70
Kurtosis	4.65
Skewness	1.40
Range	26.00
Minimum	0.00
Maximum	26.00
Sum	122.00
Count	12.00
Largest(1)	26.00
Smallest(1)	0.00
Confidence Level(95.000%)	3.43

FIGURE 36.2. *Use the Analysis Toolpack's Descriptive Statistics tool to generate the most common statistical measures for a sample.*

Working with Histograms

The Analysis Toolpack's Histogram tool calculates the frequency distribution of a range of data. It also calculates cumulative frequencies for your data and produces a bar chart that shows the distribution graphically.

Before you use the Histogram tool, you need to decide which groupings (or *bins*) you want Excel to use for the output. These bins are numeric ranges, and the Histogram tool works by counting the number of observations that fall into each bin. You enter the bins as a range of numbers, where each number defines a boundary of the bin. For example, Figure 36.3 shows a worksheet with two ranges. One is a list of student grades. The second range is the bin range. For each number in the bin range, Histogram counts the number of observations that are greater than or equal to the bin value, and less than (but *not* equal to) the next higher bin value. Therefore, in Figure 36.3, the six bin values correspond to the following ranges:

```
0 <= Grade < 50
50 <= Grade < 60
60 <= Grade < 70
70 <= Grade < 80
80 <= Grade < 90
90 <= Grade < 100
```

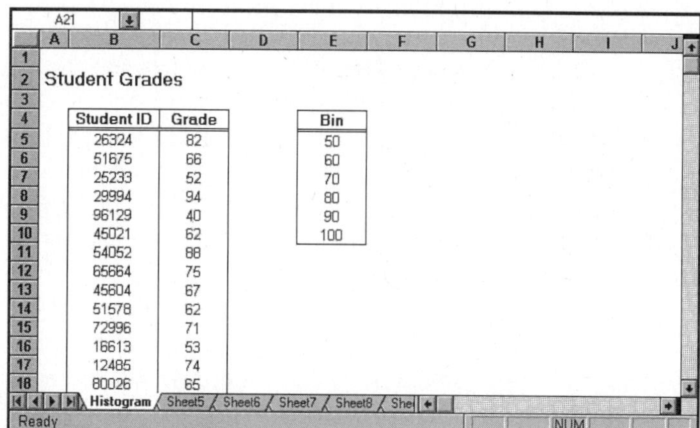

Student Grades

Student ID	Grade
26324	82
51675	66
25233	52
29994	94
96129	40
45021	62
54052	88
65664	75
45604	67
51578	62
72996	71
16613	53
12485	74
80026	65

Bin
50
60
70
80
90
100

FIGURE 36.3.
A worksheet set up to use the Histogram tool. Notice how you have to enter the bin range in ascending order.

SUPER CAUTION

Make sure you enter your bin values in ascending order.

SUPER NOTE

How many bins should you use? The answer usually depends on the data. If you want to calculate the frequency distribution for a set of student grades, for example, you would probably set up six bin values (0, 50, 60, 70, 80, and 90). For less obvious distributions, you can use the following rule:

If *n* is the number of cells in the input range, enclose *n* between two successive powers of 2 and take the higher exponent to be the number of bins.

For example, if *n* is 100, you would use 7 bins, because 100 lies between 2^6 (64) and 2^7 (128). You also can use the following formula to calculate the number of bins:

```
=CEILING(LOG(COUNT(input_range),2),1)
```

Follow the steps in Procedure 36.4 to use the Histogram tool.

PROCEDURE 36.4. USING THE ANALYSIS TOOLPACK'S HISTOGRAM TOOL.

1. Select the Tools | Data Analysis command. Excel displays the Data Analysis dialog box.
2. Select the Histogram option and then click on OK. Excel displays the Histogram dialog box.
3. Use the Input Range and Bin Range boxes to enter the ranges holding your data and bin values, respectively.
4. Use the Output options group to select a location for the output. The output range will be one row taller than the bin range, and it could be up to six columns wide (depending on which of the following options you choose).
5. Select the other options you want to use for the frequency distribution:

   Pareto: If you activate this check box, Excel displays a second output range with the bins sorted in order of descending frequency. (This is called a *Pareto distribution*.)

   Cumulative Percentage: If you activate this option, Excel adds a new column to the output that tracks the cumulative percentage for each bin.

   Chart Output: If you select this option, Excel automatically generates a chart for the frequency distribution.
6. Click on OK or press Enter. Excel displays the histogram data, as shown in Figure 36.4.

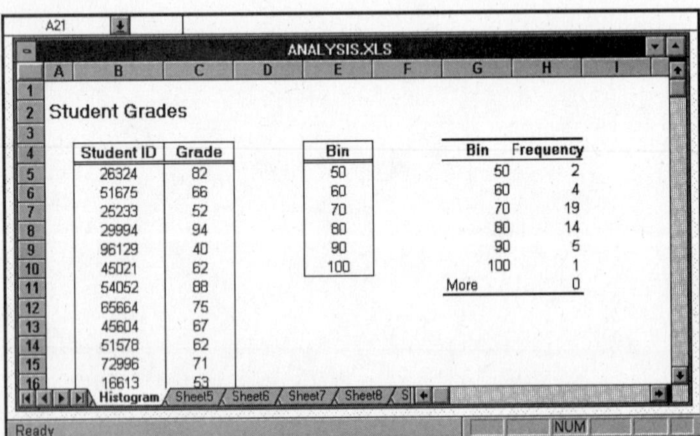

FIGURE 36.4.
The output of the Histogram tool.

SUPER NOTE

The problem with the Histogram tool's output is that there are no formulas linking the output to your data. If the data changes, you have to run the Histogram tool again. For simple frequency distributions, use the `FREQUENCY()` function to set up a link between your data and the distribution output.

Generating Random Numbers

If you're using a worksheet to set up a simulation, you'll need realistic data on which to do your testing. You could make up the numbers, but it's possible to unconsciously skew the data. A better approach is to use the Analysis Toolpack's Random Number Generation tool to generate the data for you.

Unlike the `RAND()` function that only generates real numbers between 0 and 1, the Random Number Generation tool can produce numbers in any range and can generate different distributions, depending on the application. Table 36.1 summarizes the seven available distribution types.

Table 36.1. The distributions available with the Random Number Generation tool.

Distribution	*Description*
Uniform	Generates numbers with equal probability from the range of values you provide. Using the range 0 to 1 produces the same distribution as the `RAND()` function.
Normal	Produces numbers in a bell curve (that is, normal) distribution based on the mean and standard deviation you enter. This is good for generating samples of test scores and population heights.
Bernoulli	Generates a random series of 1s and 0s based on the probability of success on a single trial. A common example of a Bernoulli distribution is a coin toss (in which the probability of success is 50 percent; in this case, as in all Bernoulli distributions, you would have to assign either heads or tails to be 1 or 0).

continues

Table 36.1. continued

Distribution	*Description*
Binomial	Generates random numbers characterized by the probability of success over a number of trials. For example, you could use this type of distribution to model the number of responses received for a direct mail campaign. The probability of success would be the average (or projected) response rate, and the number of trials would be the number of mailings in the campaign.
Poisson	Generates random numbers based on the probability of a designated number of events occurring in a time frame. The distribution is governed by a value Lambda that represents the mean number of events known to occur over the time frame.
Patterned	Generates random numbers according to a pattern that is characterized by a lower and upper bound, a step value, and a repetition rate for each number and the entire sequence.
Discrete	Generates random numbers from a series of values and probabilities for these values (in which the sum of the probabilities equals 1). You could use this distribution to simulate the rolling of dice (where the values would be 1 through 6, each with a probability of 1/6; see the following example).

Follow the steps outlined in Procedure 36.5 to use the Random Number Generation tool.

NOTE

If you'll be using a Discrete distribution, be sure to enter the appropriate values and probabilities before starting the Random Number Generation tool.

PROCEDURE 36.5. GENERATING RANDOM NUMBERS.

1. Select the Tools | Data Analysis command. Excel displays the Data Analysis dialog box.
2. Select the Random Number Generation option and then click on OK. The Random Number Generation dialog box appears.

3. If you want to generate more than one set of random numbers, enter the number of sets (or variables) you need in the Number of **V**ariables box. Excel enters each set in a separate column. If you leave this box blank, Excel uses the number of columns in the **O**utput Range.
4. Use the Number of Random Num**b**ers edit box to enter how many random numbers you need. Excel enters each number in a separate row. If you leave this box blank, Excel fills the **O**utput Range.
5. Use the **D**istribution drop-down list to select the distribution you want to use.
6. In the Parameters group, enter the appropriate parameters for the distribution you selected.
7. The **R**andom Seed number is the value Excel uses to generate the random numbers. If you leave this box blank, Excel generates a different set each time. If you enter a value (which must be an integer between 1 and 32,767), you can reuse the value later to reproduce the same set of numbers.
8. Use the Output options group to select a location for the output.
9. Click on OK or press Enter. Excel calculates the random numbers and displays them in the worksheet.

SUPER NOTE

You also can use the `RANDOM()` function to generate random numbers. The function parameters are the same as those you enter into the Random Number Generation dialog box.

As an example, Figure 36.5 shows a worksheet set up to simulate rolling two dice. The Probabilities box shows the values (the numbers one through six) and their probabilities (=1/6 for each). A Discrete distribution is used to generate the two numbers in cells H2 and H3. The Discrete distribution's Value and Probability **I**nput Range parameter is the range $D$2:$E$7. Figure 36.6 shows the formulas used to display Die #1. (The formulas for Die #2 are similar, except that $H$2 is replaced with $H$3.)

SUPER NOTE

The die markers in Figure 36.5 were generated using a 24-point Wingdings font.

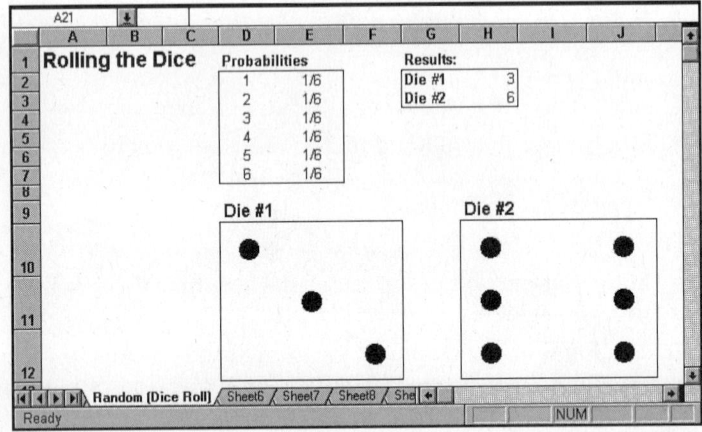

FIGURE 36.5.
A worksheet that simulates the rolling a pair of dice.

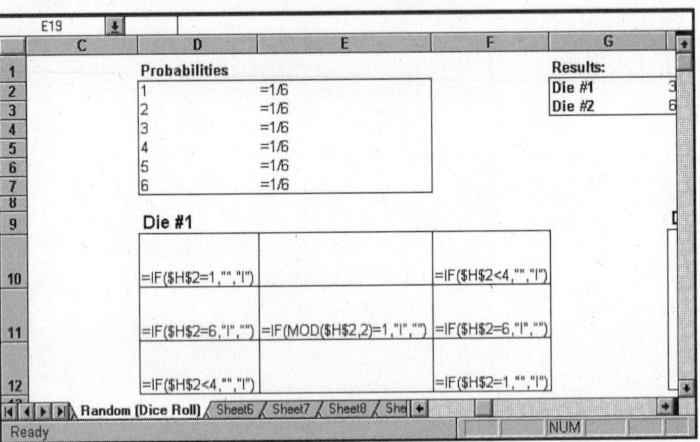

FIGURE 36.6.
The formulas used to display Die #1.

Working with Rank and Percentile

If you need to rank data, use the Analysis Toolpack's Rank and Percentile tool. This command not only ranks your data from first to last, but it also calculates the percentile—the percentage of items in the sample that are at the same or a lower level than a given value. Follow the steps in Procedure 36.6 to use the Rank and Percentile tool.

PROCEDURE 36.6. USING THE RANK AND PERCENTILE TOOL.

1. Select the **T**ools | **D**ata Analysis command. Excel displays the Data Analysis dialog box.
2. Select the Rank and Percentile option and then click on OK. Excel displays the Rank and Percentile dialog box.

3. Use the **I**nput Range edit box to enter a reference for the data you want to rank.
4. Select the appropriate Grouped By option (**C**olumns or **R**ows).
5. If you included row or column labels in your selection, activate the **L**abels in First Row check box. (If your data is in rows, the check box will read **L**abels in First Column.)
6. Use the Output options group to select a location for the output. For each sample, Excel displays a table that is four columns wide and the same height as the number of values in the sample.
7. Click on OK or press Enter. Excel calculates the results and displays them in a table similar to the one shown in Figure 36.7.

FIGURE 36.7.
Sample output from the Rank and Percentile tool.

ANALYSIS.XLS

Defects Database

Workgroup	Group Leader	Defects
1	Johnson	28
2	Perkins	30
3	Perkins	18
4	Johnson	21
5	Johnson	29
6	Johnson	26
7	Perkins	31
8	Perkins	30
9	Perkins	27
10	Perkins	34
11	Johnson	30
12	Johnson	46

Point	Defects	Rank	Percent
12	46	1	100.00%
10	34	2	90.90%
7	31	3	81.80%
2	30	4	54.50%
8	30	4	54.50%
11	30	4	54.50%
5	29	7	45.40%
1	28	8	36.30%
9	27	9	27.20%
6	26	10	18.10%
4	21	11	9.00%
3	18	12	.00%

Rank & Percentile / Goal Seek / Margin / Break Even

Ready NUM

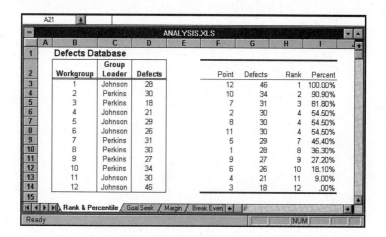

SUPER NOTE

Use the `RANK()` and `PERCENTRANK()` functions to calculate rank and percentile without using the Analysis Toolpack.

Chapter

37

Working with Goal Seek

As you learned in Chapter 35, "Basic Analytic Methods," a what-if analysis enables you to see how changing one or more variables in a formula affects the formula results. Sometimes you already know what result you want. For example, you might know that you want to have $100,000 in a college fund 18 years from now, or that you need to achieve a 30 percent gross margin in your next budget. If you need to manipulate only a single variable to achieve these results, you can use Excel's Goal Seek feature. You tell Goal Seek the final value you need and which variable to change, and it finds a solution for you (if one exists). This chapter shows you how to use Goal Seek.

SUPER NOTE

For more complicated scenarios with multiple variables and constraints, you'll need to use Excel's Solver feature. See Chapter 38, "Working with Solver," for details.

How Does Goal Seek Work?

When you set up a worksheet to use Goal Seek, you usually have a formula in one cell and the formula's variable—with an initial value—in another. (Your formula can have multiple variables, but Goal Seek enables you to manipulate only one variable at a time.) Goal Seek operates by using an *iterative method* to find a solution. That is, Goal Seek first tries the variable's initial value to see if that produces the result you want. If not, Goal Seek tries different values until (hopefully) it converges on a solution. This essentially is the same method as the iterative technique you learned in Chapter 35—when you looked at solving circular reference formulas. The difference is that Goal Seek already knows the final result.

Running Goal Seek

Suppose you want to set up a college fund for your newborn child. Your goal is to have $100,000 in the fund 18 years from now. Assuming five percent interest, how much will you need to deposit into the fund every year? Procedure 37.1 shows how to use Goal Seek to calculate the answer.

PROCEDURE 37.1. USING EXCEL'S GOAL SEEK FEATURE.

1. Set up your worksheet to use Goal Seek. Figure 37.1 shows the COLLEGE.XLS worksheet, which I've set up as follows:
   - Cell C8 contains the `FV()` function that calculates the future value of the college fund. This value should be $50,000.
   - Cell C6 contains the annual deposit into the fund. This is the value Goal Seek will adjust to find a solution.
   - The other cells (C4 and C5) are used in the `FV()` function; however, assume that they are constants.

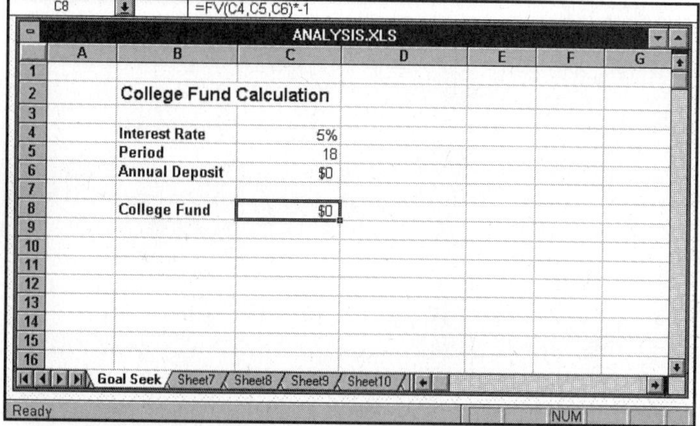

FIGURE 37.1.
A worksheet set up to use Goal Seek.

2. Select the **T**ools | **G**oal Seek command. Excel displays the Goal Seek dialog box.
3. In the **S**et cell edit box, enter a reference to the cell that contains your goal. For the example, you would enter C8.
4. In the To **v**alue box, enter the final value you want for the goal cell. The example's value is 50000.
5. Use the By **c**hanging cell box to enter a reference to the variable cell. In the example, enter C6. Figure 37.2 shows the completed dialog box.

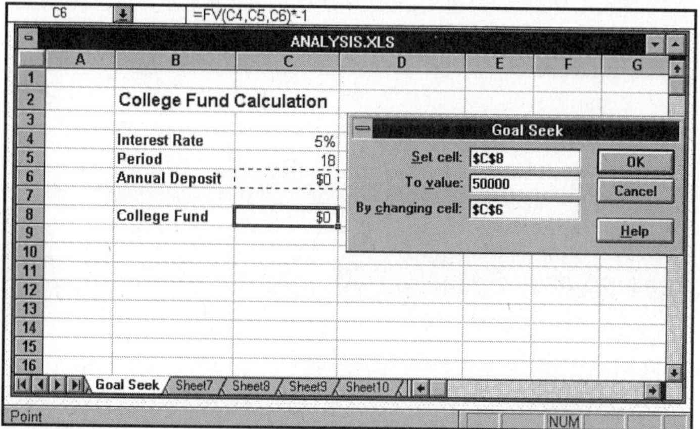

FIGURE 37.2.
A worksheet set up to use Goal Seek.

6. Click on OK or press Enter. Excel begins the iteration and displays the Goal Seek Status dialog box. When finished, Goal Seek displays the Goal Seek Status dialog box to tell you whether or not it found a solution (see Figure 37.3).

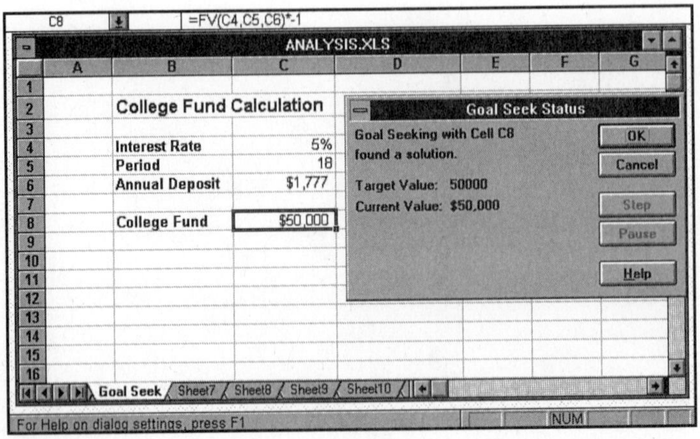

FIGURE 37.3.
The Goal Seek Status dialog box shows you the solution (if one was found).

SUPER NOTE

Most of the time, Goal Seek finds a solution relatively quickly. For longer operations, you can use the **P**ause button in the Goal Seek Status dialog box to stop Goal Seek. To walk through the process one iteration at a time, click on the **S**tep button. To resume Goal Seek, click on **C**ontinue.

7. If Goal Seek found a solution, you can accept the solution by clicking on OK. To ignore the solution, click on Cancel.

Goal Seek Examples

Goal Seek is a simple tool, but it can handle many different types of problems. This section looks at a few more examples of Goal Seek.

Optimizing Product Margin

Many businesses use product margin as a measure of health. If the margin is strong, it usually means that expenses are under control and that the market is satisfied with your price points. Product margin depends on many factors, of course, but you can use Goal Seek to find the optimum margin based on a single variable.

For example, suppose you want to introduce a new product line, and you would like the product to return a margin of 30 percent during the first year. You're making the following assumptions:

- The sales during the year will be 100,000 units.
- The average discount to your customers will be 40 percent.
- The total fixed costs will be $750,000.
- The cost per unit will be $12.63.

Given all this, you want to know what price point will produce the 30 percent margin.

Figure 37.4 shows a worksheet set up to handle this. An initial value of $1.00 is entered into the Price cell, and Goal Seek is set up as follows:

- The **S**et cell reference is C14, the Margin calculation.
- A value of .3 (the Margin goal) is entered in the To **v**alue box.
- A reference to the Price cell (C4) is entered into the By **c**hanging cell box.

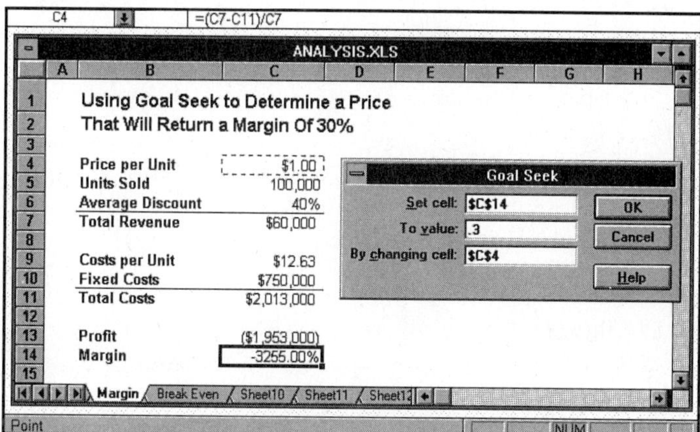

FIGURE 37.4.
A worksheet set up to calculate a price point that will optimize gross margin.

When you run Goal Seek, it produces a solution of $47.87 for the price, as shown in Figure 37.5. This solution can be rounded up to $47.95.

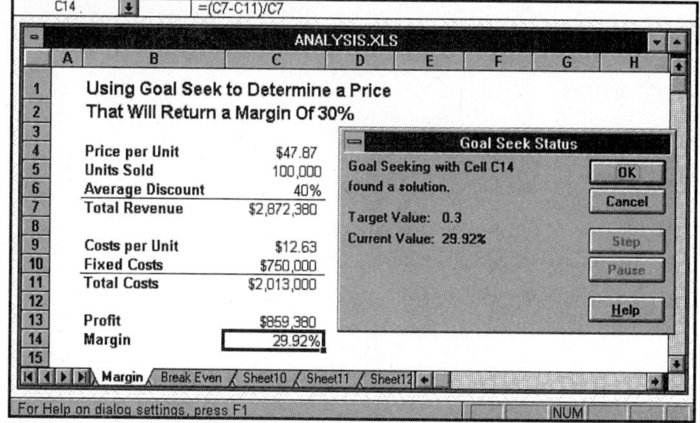

FIGURE 37.5.
Goal Seek has found a solution for the price variable.

SUPER NOTE

The solution in Figure 37.5 is an approximate figure (the margin value is 29.92 percent). To get an exact solution, you need to change the threshold Excel uses to determine if it has converged on a solution. The default value is 0.001, which is not small enough for Excel to arrive at the proper solution. In this example, a value of 0.0001 would do the job. (Select the **T**ools | **O**ptions command. In the Calculation tab, enter this number in the Maximum **C**hange edit box.)

Performing a Break Even Analysis

In a *break even analysis,* you determine the number of units you have to sell of a product so that your total profits are 0 (that is, the product revenue equals the product costs). Setting up a profit equation with a goal of 0 and varying the units sold is perfect for Goal Seek.

To try this, use the example from the previous section. In this case, assume a unit price of $47.95 (the solution found to optimize product margin). Figure 37.6 shows the Goal Seek dialog box filled out as follows:

- The **S**et cell reference is C13, the Profit calculation.
- A value of 0 (the Profit goal) is entered in the To **v**alue box.
- A reference to the Units Sold cell (C5) is entered into the By **c**hanging cell box.

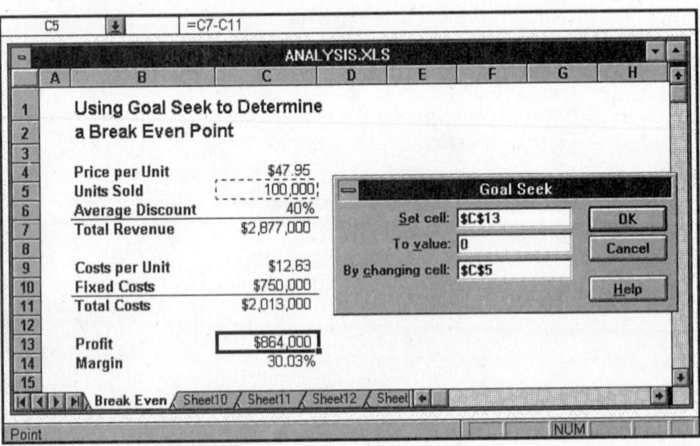

FIGURE 37.6.
A worksheet set up to calculate a price point that optimizes gross margin.

Figure 37.7 shows the solution: 46,468 units must be sold to break even.

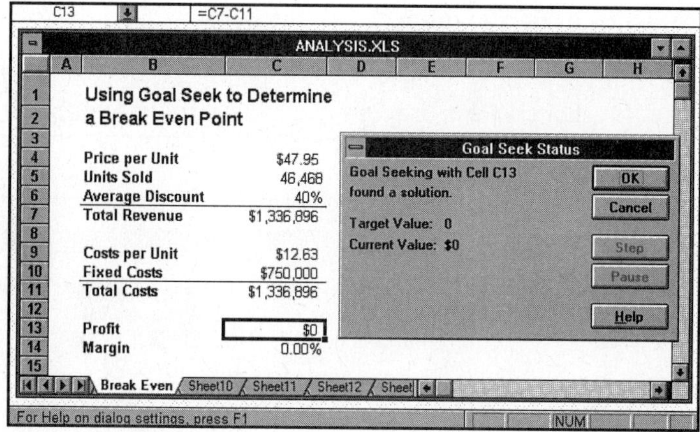

FIGURE 37.7.
The break even solution.

Solving Algebraic Equations

Goal Seek also is useful for solving complex algebraic equations of one variable. For example, suppose you need to find the value of *x* in order to solve the following rather nasty equation:

$$\frac{(3x - 8)^2(x - 1)}{4x^2 - 5} = 1$$

This equation, although too complex for the quadratic formula, can be easily rendered in Excel. The left side of the equation can be represented with the following formula:

```
=(((3*A2 - 8)^2)*(A2-1))/(4*A2^2-5)
```

Cell A2 represents the variable *x*. You can solve this equation in Goal Seek by setting the goal for this equation to 1 (the right side of the equation) and by varying cell A2. Figure 37.8 shows a worksheet and the completed Goal Seek dialog box.

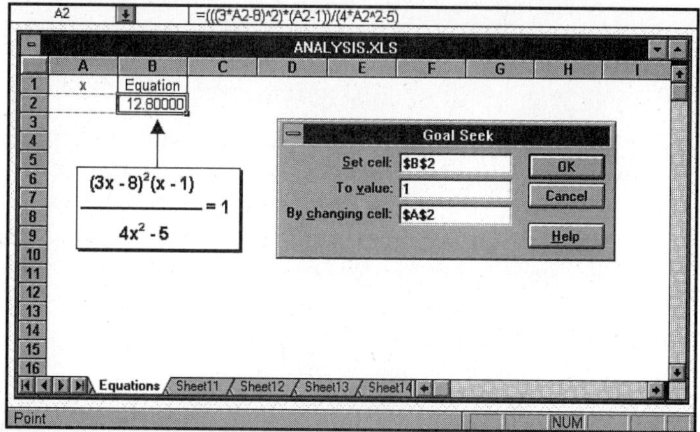

FIGURE 37.8.
Solving an algebraic equation with Goal Seek.

Figure 37.9 shows the result. The value in cell A2 is the solution *x* that satisfies the equation. Notice that the equation result (cell A1) is not quite 1. As I mentioned earlier in this chapter, if you need higher accuracy, you need to change Excel's convergence threshold. In this example, select the **T**ools | **O**ptions command, and in the Calculation tab, type `0.000001` in the Maximum **C**hange edit box.

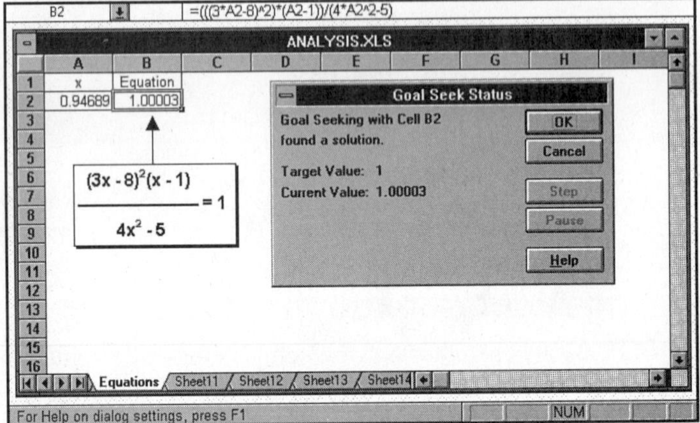

FIGURE 37.9.
Cell A2 holds the solution for the equation in cell A1.

Goal Seeking with Charts

If you have your data graphed in a 2-D bar, column, line, or XY chart, you can run Goal Seek by using the mouse to drag a data marker to a new position. If the data marker represents a formula, Excel uses Goal Seek to work backward and derive the appropriate formula input values.

The following example helps explain this process. Suppose you want to invest some money every year, so that in 10 years, you'll have $150,000. Assuming a constant interest rate, how much do you need to set aside annually to reach your goal? The solution is to adjust the chart data marker at 10 years so that it has the value $150,000. Procedure 37.2 shows you the steps to follow.

PROCEDURE 37.2. USING GOAL SEEK WITH A CHART.

1. Activate the chart and select the specific data marker you want to adjust. Excel adds selection handles to the marker. For the example, select the data marker corresponding to 10 years on the category axis.
2. Drag the black selection handle to the desired value. As you drag the handle, the current value appears in the formula bar's Name box, shown in Figure 37.10.

FIGURE 37.10.
Drag the data marker to the desired value.

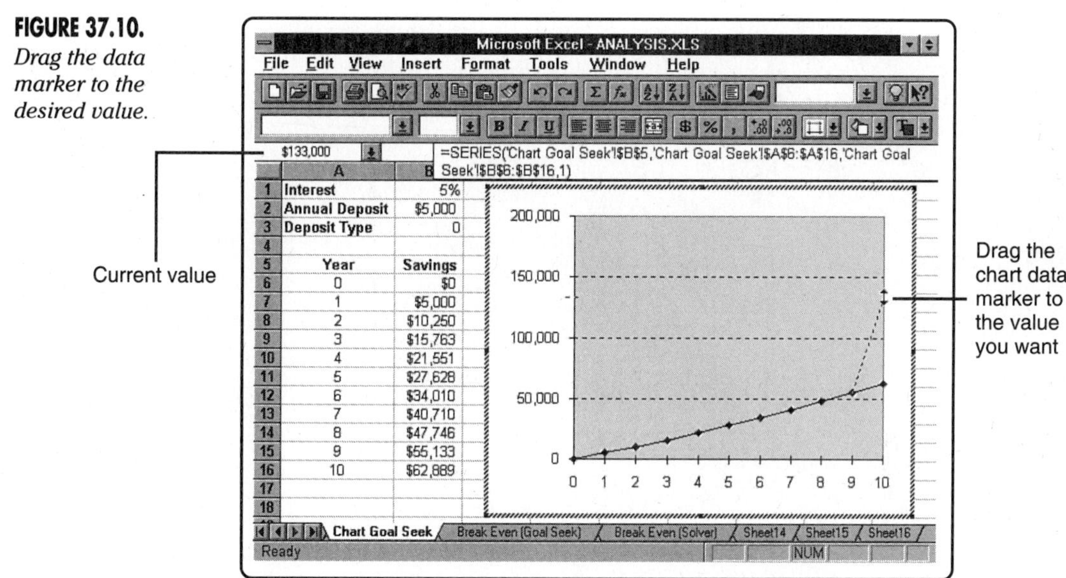

3. Release the mouse button. If the marker references a number in a cell, Excel changes the number and redraws the chart. If the marker references a formula, as in the example, Excel displays the Goal Seek dialog box shown in Figure 37.11. The **S**et cell box shows the cell referenced by the data marker, the To **v**alue box shows the new number you selected, and the By **c**hanging cell box shows the variable for the formula.

FIGURE 37.11.
If the data marker is derived from a formula, Excel runs Goal Seek.

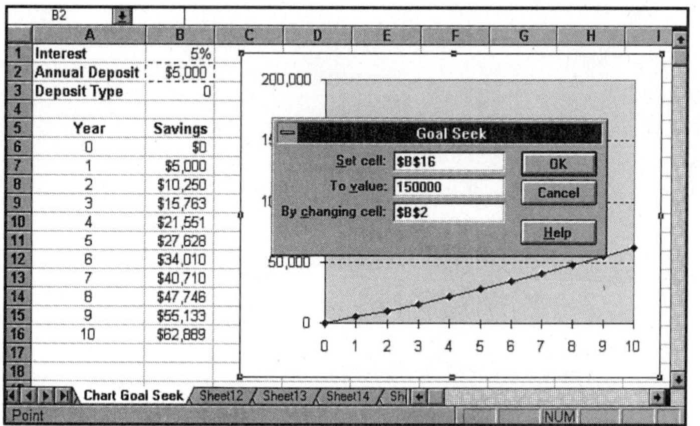

4. Enter the appropriate numbers. For the example, you would enter B2 in the By changing cell box to calculate the required annual deposit.
5. Click on OK or press Enter. The Goal Seek Status dialog box appears while Excel solves for the new number.
6. When the iteration is complete, click on OK.

Chapter 38

Working with Solver

In Chapter 37, "Working with Goal Seek," you learned how to use Goal Seek to find solutions to formulas by changing a single variable. Unfortunately, most problems in business and science aren't so easy. You'll usually face formulas with at least two and sometimes even dozens of variables. Often a problem will have more than one solution, and your challenge will be to find the *optimal* solution (that is, the one that maximizes profit, minimizes costs, and so forth). For these bigger challenges, you need a more muscular tool. Excel has just the answer: Solver. Solver is a sophisticated optimization program that enables you to find the solutions to complex problems that would otherwise require high-level mathematical analysis. This chapter introduces you to Solver (a complete discussion would require a book in itself) and takes you through a few examples.

Some Background on Solver

Problems such as "What product mix will maximize profit?" or "What transportation routes will minimize shipping costs while meeting demand?" traditionally have been solved by numerical methods such as *linear programming* and *nonlinear programming*. An entire mathematical field—*operations research*—has been developed to handle such problems, which are found in all kinds of disciplines. The drawback to linear and nonlinear programming is that solving even the simplest problem by hand is a complicated, arcane, and time-consuming business. In other words, it's a perfect job to slough off on a computer.

This is where Solver comes in. Solver incorporates many of these algorithms from operations research, but it keeps the sordid details in the background. All you do is fill out a dialog box or two, and Solver does the rest (the hard part).

The Advantages of Solver

Solver, like Goal Seek, uses an iterative method to perform its magic. This means that Solver tries a solution, analyzes the results, tries another solution, and so on. However, this cyclic iteration isn't just guesswork on Solver's part. The program looks at how the results change with each new iteration and, through some sophisticated mathematical trickery, it can tell (usually) what direction it should head for the solution.

However, the fact that Goal Seek and Solver are both iterative doesn't make them equal. In fact, Solver brings a number of advantages to the table:

- Solver enables you to specify multiple adjustable cells. You can use up to 200 adjustable cells in all.
- Solver enables you to set up *constraints* on the adjustable cells. For example, you could tell Solver to find a solution that not only maximizes profit, but that also satisfies certain conditions, such as achieving a gross margin between 20 percent and 30 percent or keeping expenses under $100,000. These conditions are said to be *constraints* on the solution.

- Solver seeks not only a desired result (the "goal" in Goal Seek), but also the optimum one. This means you can find a solution that is the maximum or minimum possible.
- For complex problems, Solver can generate multiple solutions. You then can save these different solutions under different scenarios. (See Chapter 39, "Working with Scenarios," to learn how to use Excel's scenarios.)

When Do You Use Solver?

Solver is a powerful tool that isn't needed by most Excel users. It would be overkill, for example, to use Solver to compute net profit given fixed revenue and cost figures. Many problems, however, require nothing less than the Solver approach. These problems cover many different fields and situations, but they all have the following characteristics in common:

- They have a single *target cell* that contains a formula you want to maximize, minimize, or set to a specific value. This formula could be a calculation, such as total transportation expenses or net profit.
- The target cell formula contains references to one or more *changing cells* (also called *unknowns* or *decision variables*). Solver adjusts these cells to find the optimal solution for the target cell formula. These changing cells might include items such as units sold, shipping costs, or advertising expenses.
- Optionally, there are one or more *constraint cells* that must satisfy certain criteria. For example, you might require that advertising be less than 10 percent of total expenses, or that the discount to customers be a number between 40 percent and 60 percent.

What types of problems exhibit these kinds of characteristics? A surprisingly broad range, as the following list shows:

The transportation problem: This problem involves minimizing shipping costs from multiple manufacturing plants to multiple warehouses while meeting demand.

The allocation problem: This problem requires minimizing employee costs while maintaining appropriate staffing requirements.

The product mix problem: This problem requires generating the maximum profit with a mix of products, while still meeting customer requirements. You solve this problem when you sell multiple products with different cost structures, profit margins, and demand curves.

The blending problem: This problem involves manipulating the materials used for one or more products to minimize production costs, meet consumer demand, and maintain a minimum level of quality.

Linear algebra: This involves solving sets of linear equations.

Using Solver

So that you can see how Solver works, I'll show you an example. In Chapter 37, "Working with Goal Seek," you used Goal Seek to compute the break even point for a new product (that is, the number of units that need to be sold to produce a profit of 0). I'll extend this analysis by computing the break even for two products: a Finley sprocket and a Langstrom wrench. The goal is to compute the number of units to sell for both products so that the total profit is 0.

The most obvious way to proceed is to use Goal Seek to determine the break even points for each product separately. Figure 38.1 shows the results.

B8 =B7*B4

SOLVER.XLS

	A	B	C
1			
2		Finley Sprocket	Langstrom Wrench
3	Price	$24.95	$19.95
4	Units	8032	7177
5	Revenue	$200,402	$143,182
6			
7	Unit Cost	$12.50	$9.50
8	Variable Costs	$100,402	$68,182
9	Fixed Costs	$100,000	$75,000
10	Total Costs	$200,402	$143,182
11			
12	Product Profit	$0	$0
13			
14	Total Profit	$0	
15			

Break Even (Goal Seek) / Break Even (Solver) / Tr

FIGURE 38.1.
The break even points for two products (using separate Goal Seek calculations on the Product Profit cells).

Using this works, but the problem is that the two products don't exist in a vacuum. For example, there will be cost savings associated with each product because of joint advertising campaigns, combined shipments to customers (larger shipments usually mean better rates), and so on. To allow for this, you need to reduce the cost for each product by a factor related to the number of units sold by the other product. In practice, this would be difficult to estimate, but to keep things simple, I'll use the following assumption: the costs for each product are reduced by one dollar for every unit sold of the other product. For instance, if the Finley sprocket sells 10,000 units, the costs for the Langstrom wrench are reduced by $10,000. I'll make this adjustment in the Variable Costs formula. Therefore, the formula that calculates Variable Costs for the Langstrom wrench becomes the following:

```
=C4*C7 - B4
```

By making this change, you move out of Goal Seek's territory. The Variable Costs formulas now have two variables: the units sold for the Finley sprocket and the units sold for the Langstrom wrench. I've changed the problem from one of two single-variable formulas, which are easily handled by Goal Seek, to a single formula with two variables—which is the terrain of Solver.

To see how Solver handles such a problem, follow the steps outlined in Procedure 38.1.

PROCEDURE 38.1. USING SOLVER.

1. Select the **T**ools | Sol**v**er command. Excel displays the Solver Parameters dialog box.
2. In the S**e**t Target Cell edit box, enter a reference to the target cell—that is, the cell with the formula you want to optimize. In the example, you would enter `B14`.
3. In the Equal to section, click on the appropriate option button. Click on **M**ax to maximize the target cell, Mi**n** to minimize it, or **V**alue of to solve for a particular value (in which case you also need to enter the value in the edit box provided). In the example, you would click on **V**alue of and enter `0` in the edit box.
4. Use the **B**y Changing Cells box to enter the cells you want Solver to change while it looks for a solution. In the example, select cells B4 and C4 (see Figure 38.2).

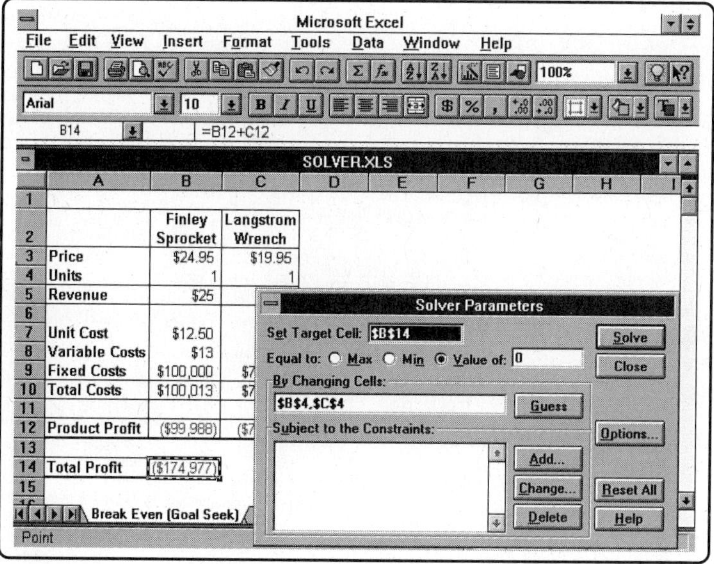

FIGURE 38.2.
The Solver Parameters dialog box.

SUPER TIP

The **G**uess button enters all the non-formula cells referenced by the target cell formula into the **B**y Changing Cells box.

> **SUPER NOTE**
>
> You can enter a maximum of 200 changing cells.

5. Click on OK or press Enter. (I discuss constraints and other Solver options in the next few sections.) Solver works on the problem and then displays the Solver Results dialog box, which tells you whether or not it found a solution. (See the section later in this chapter titled "Making Sense of Solver's Messages.")
6. If Solver found a solution that you want to use, select the **K**eep Solver Solution option and then click on OK. If you don't want to accept the new numbers, select Restore **O**riginal Values and click on OK, or just click on Cancel. (To learn how to save a solution as a scenario, see the section later in this chapter titled "Saving a Solution as a Scenario.")

Figure 38.3 shows the results for the example. As you can see, Solver has produced a Total Profit of 0 by running one product (the Langstrom wrench) at a slight loss and the other at a slight profit. While this is certainly a solution, it's not really the one you want. Ideally, for a true break even analysis, both products should end up with a Product Profit of 0. The problem is that you haven't told Solver that. In other words, you haven't set up any *constraints*.

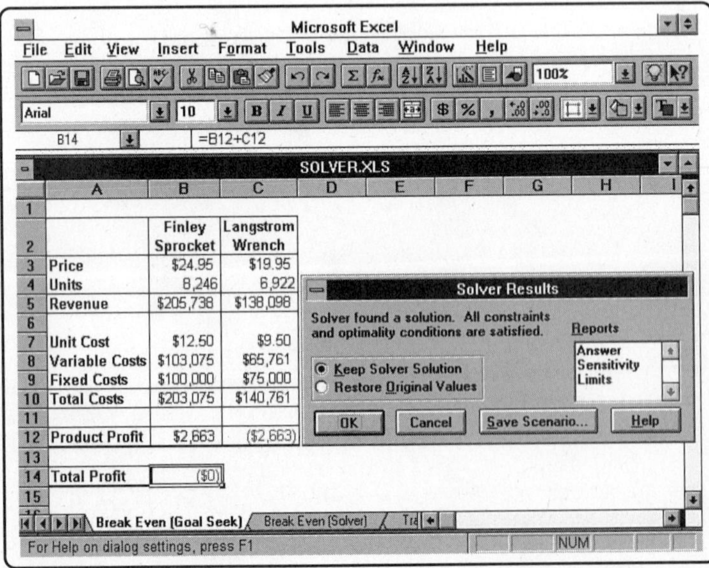

FIGURE 38.3.
When Solver finishes its calculations, it displays a completion message and enters the solution (if it found one) into the worksheet cells.

Adding Constraints

The real world puts restrictions and conditions on formulas. A factory might have a maximum capacity of 10,000 units a day; the number of employees in a company might have to be a number greater than or equal to zero (negative employees would really reduce staff costs, but nobody has been able to figure out how to do it yet); your advertising costs might be restricted to 10 percent of total expenses. All these are examples of what Solver calls *constraints*. Adding constraints tells Solver to find a solution so that these conditions are not violated.

To find the best solution for the break even analysis, you need to tell Solver to optimize both Product Profit formulas to 0. The steps in Procedure 38.2 show you how to do this.

> **SUPER NOTE**
>
> If Solver's completion message is still on-screen from the last section, click on Cancel to return to the worksheet without saving the solution.

PROCEDURE 38.2. ADDING CONSTRAINTS TO SOLVER.

1. Select the **T**ools | Sol**v**er command to display the Solver Parameters dialog box. Solver reinstates the options you entered the last time you used Solver.
2. To add a constraint, click on the **A**dd button. Excel displays the Add Constraint dialog box.
3. In the Cell **R**eference box, enter the cell you want to constrain. For the example, you would enter cell B12 (the Product Profit formula for the Finley sprocket).
4. The drop-down list in the middle of the dialog box contains several logical operators for the constraint. The available operators are less than or equal to (<=), equal to (=), greater than or equal to (>=), or integer (int). (Use the integer operator when you need a constraint, such as *total employees*, to be an integer instead of a real number.) Select the appropriate operator for your constraint. For the example, select the equal to operator (=).
5. In the **C**onstraint box, enter the value by which you want to restrict the cell. The sample value is 0 (see Figure 38.4).

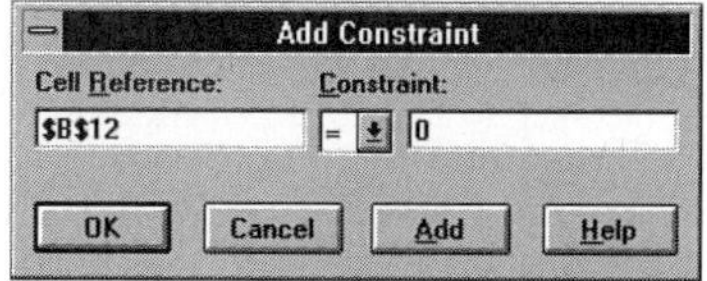

FIGURE 38.4.
The Add Constraint dialog box.

6. If you want to enter more constraints, click on the **A**dd button and repeat steps 3-5. For the example, you also need to constrain cell C12 (the Product Profit formula for the Langstrom wrench) so that it, too, equals 0. When you're done, click on OK to return to the Solver Parameters dialog box. Excel displays your constraints in the S**u**bject to the Constraints list box.

> **SUPER NOTE**
>
> You can add a maximum of 100 constraints.

7. Click on OK or press Enter. Solver again tries to find a solution, but this time it uses your constraints as guidelines.

> **SUPER TIP**
>
> If you need to make a change to a constraint, highlight the constraint in the S**u**bject to the Constraints list box, click on the **C**hange button, and then make your adjustments in the Change Constraint dialog box that appears. If you want to delete a constraint you no longer need, highlight it, and click on the **D**elete button.

Figure 38.5 shows the results of the break even analysis after adding the constraints. As you can see, Solver was able to find a solution in which both Product Margins are 0.

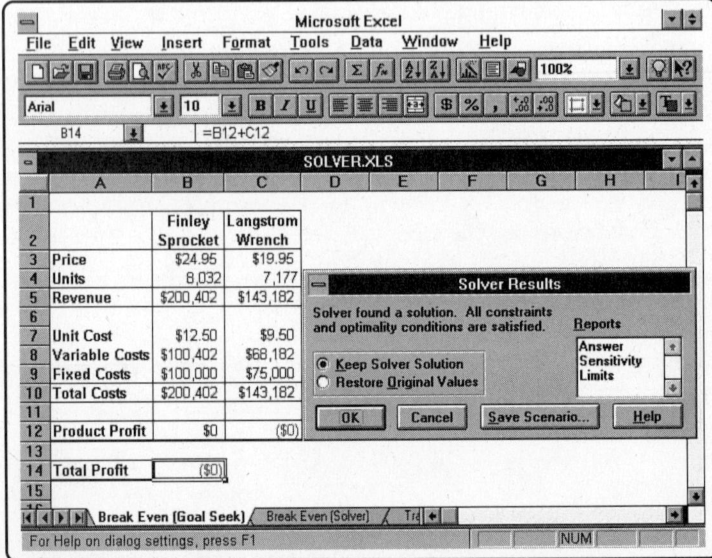

FIGURE 38.5.
The solution to the break even analysis after adding the constraints.

Saving a Solution as a Scenario

If Solver finds a solution, you can save the changing cells as a scenario that you can display at any time. (See Chapter 39, "Working with Scenarios," to learn how to work with Excel's scenarios.) Follow the steps in Procedure 38.3 to save a solution as a scenario.

PROCEDURE 38.3. SAVING A SOLVER SOLUTION AS A SCENARIO.

1. Select the Tools | Solver command to display the Solver Parameters dialog box.
2. Enter the appropriate target cell, changing cells, and constraints, if necessary.
3. Click on OK or press Enter to begin solving.
4. If Solver finds a solution, click on the Save Scenario button in the Solver Results dialog box. Excel displays the Save Scenario dialog box.
5. Use the Scenario Name edit box to enter a name for the scenario.
6. Click on OK or press Enter. Excel returns you to the Solver Results dialog box.
7. Keep or discard the solution, as appropriate.

Setting Other Solver Options

Most Solver problems should respond to the basic target cell/changing cell/constraint cell model you've looked at so far. However, if you're having trouble getting a solution for a particular model, Solver has a number of options that might help. In the Solver Parameters dialog box, click on the Options button to display the Solver Options dialog box, shown in Figure 38.6.

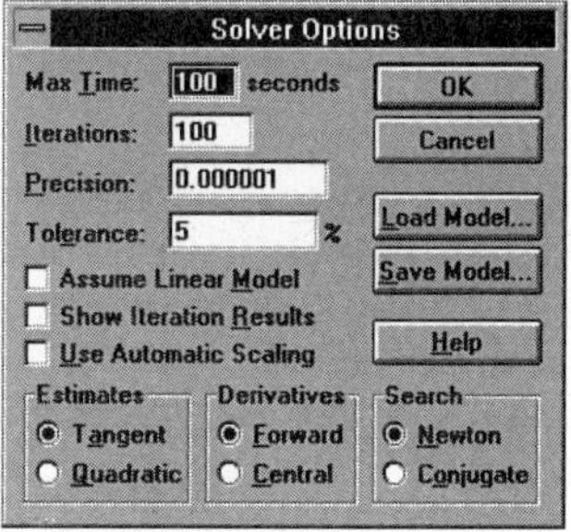

FIGURE 38.6.
The Solver Options dialog box controls how Solver solves a problem.

Controlling Solver

The following options control how solver works:

Max Time — The amount of time Solver takes is a function of the size and complexity of the model, the number of changing cells and constraint cells, and the other Solver options you've chosen. If you find that Solver runs out of time before finding a solution, increase the number in this edit box.

SUPER CAUTION

Integer programming (where you have integer constraints) can take a long time because of the complexity involved in finding solutions that satisfy exact integer constraints. If you find your models taking an abnormally long time to solve, increase the value in the Tolerance box to get an approximate solution (see "Tolerance" in the following list).

Iterations	This box controls the number of iterations Solver tries before giving up on a problem. Increasing this number gives Solver more of a chance to solve the problem, but it will take correspondingly longer.
Precision	This number determines how close a constraint cell must be to the constraint value you entered before Solver declares the constraint satisfied. The higher the precision (that is, the lower the number), the more accurate the solution (and the longer it takes Solver to find it).
Tolerance	If you have integer constraints, this box determines what percentage of the integer Solver has to be within before declaring the constraint satisfied. For example, if the integer tolerance is set to 0.05 percent, Solver will declare a cell with the value 99.95, to be close enough to 100 to declare it an integer.
Assume Linear Model	In the simplest possible terms, a *linear model* is one in which the variables are not raised to any powers and none of the so-called *transcendent* functions—such as `SIN()` and `COS()`—are used. These models can be charted as straight lines. Therefore, they're called linear models. If your formulas are linear, make sure this check box is activated, because this will greatly speed up the solution process.
Show Iteration Results	Select this option to have Solver pause and show you its trial solutions. To resume, select Continue from the Show Trial Solution dialog box.
Use Automatic Scaling	Select this check box if your model has changing cells that are significantly different in magnitude. For

example, you might have a changing cell that controls customer discount (a number between 0 and 1) and sales (a number that might be in the millions).

Selecting the Method Used by Solver

The options in the Estimates, Derivatives, and Search groups at the bottom of the dialog box control the method used by Solver. The default options perform the job in the vast majority of cases. However, following is a quick rundown of the options:

Estimates	These two options determine how Solver obtains its initial estimates of the model variables. The Tangent option is the default, and you need to select Quadratic only if your model is highly nonlinear.
Derivatives	Some models require Solver to calculate partial derivatives. These two options specify the method Solver uses to do this. Forward differencing is the default method. The Central differencing method takes longer than forward differencing, but you might want to try it when Solver reports that it can't improve a solution. (See the section later in this chapter titled "Making Sense of Solver's Messages.")
Search	When finding a solution, Solver starts with the initial values in the model and then must decide which direction to take to adjust the variables. These options determine the method Solver uses to make this decision. The default Newton option tells Solver to use a quasi-Newton search method. This method uses more memory, but it's faster than the Conjugate method, which uses a conjugate gradient search method. Usually you'll need to select Conjugate only for large models in which memory is at a premium.

Working with Solver Models

Excel attaches your most recent Solver parameters to the worksheet when you save it. If you would like to save different sets of parameters, you can do so by following the steps in Procedure 38.4.

PROCEDURE 38.4. SAVING A SOLVER MODEL.

1. Select the Tools | Solver command to display the Solver Parameters dialog box.
2. Enter the parameters you want to save.
3. Click on the Options button to display the Solver Options dialog box.
4. Enter the options you want to save.

5. Click on the **S**ave Model button. Solver prompts you to enter a range in which to store the model.
6. Select an empty range large enough to hold the data. You'll need one cell for the target cell reference, one for the changing cells, one for each constraint, and one to hold the array of Solver options.
7. Click on OK or press Enter. Solver gathers the data and enters it into your selected range.

To use your saved settings, click on the **L**oad Model button from the Solver Options dialog box, enter the range containing the settings in the Load Model dialog box, and then click on OK.

Making Sense of Solver's Messages

When Solver finishes its calculations, it displays the Solver dialog box and a message that tells you what happened. Some of these messages are straightforward, but others are more than a little cryptic. This section looks at the most common messages and gives their translations.

If Solver found a solution successfully, you'll see one of the following messages:

`Solver found a solution. All constraints and optimality conditions are satisfied.` This is the message you hope to see. It means that the value you wanted for the target cell has been found, and Solver was able to find the solution while meeting your constraints within the precision and integer tolerance levels you set.

`Solver has converged to the current solution. All constraints are satisfied.` Solver normally assumes it has a solution if the value of the target cell formula remains virtually unchanged during a few iterations. This is called converging to a solution. Such is the case with this message, but it doesn't necessarily mean that Solver has found a solution. It may be that the iterative process is just taking a long time or that the initial values in the changing cells were set too far from the solution. You should try rerunning Solver with different values. You also can try using a higher precision setting (that is, entering a smaller number in the **P**recision box).

If Solver didn't find a solution, you'll see one of the following messages telling you why:

`Solver cannot improve the current solution. All constraints are satisfied.` This message tells you that Solver has found a solution, but it may not be the optimal one. Try setting the precision to a smaller number, or try using the central differencing method for partial derivatives.

`The Set Cell values do not converge.` This means that the value of the target cell formula has no finite limit. For example, if you're trying to maximize profit based on product price and unit costs, Solver won't find a solution; the reason is that continually higher prices and lower costs lead to higher profit. You need to add (or change) constraints in your model, such as setting a maximum price or minimum cost level (for example, the amount of fixed costs).

`Solver could not find a feasible solution.` Solver couldn't find a solution that satisfied all your constraints. Check your constraints to make sure they are realistic and consistent.

`Stop chosen when the maximum x limit was reached.` This message appears when Solver bumps up against either the maximum time limit or the maximum iteration limit. If it appears that Solver is heading toward a solution, click on the **K**eep Solver Solution button and try again.

`The conditions for Assume Linear Model are not satisfied.` Solver based its iterative process on a linear model, but when the results are put into the worksheet, they don't conform to the linear model. You need to clear the Assume Linear **M**odel check box and try again.

Displaying Solver's Reports

When Solver finds a solution, the Solver dialog box gives you the option of generating three reports: the Answer report, the Sensitivity report, and the Limits report. Select the reports you want to see from the **R**eports list box and then click on OK. Excel displays each report on its own sheet.

SUPER TIP

If you've named the cells in your model, Solver uses these names to make its reports easier to read. If you haven't already done so, you should define names for the target cell, changing cells, and constraint cells before creating a report.

The Answer Report

The Answer report, shown in Figure 38.7, displays information about the model's target cell, changing cells, and constraints. For the target cell and changing cells, Solver shows original and final values. For the constraints, the report shows the final value and two values called the *binding* and the *slack*. The binding can take one of three values:

Binding — Signifies that the final value in the constraint cell equals the constraint value (or the constraint boundary, if the constraint is an inequality).

Not Binding	This value tells you that the constraint cell value satisfied the constraint, but it doesn't equal the constraint boundary.
Not Satisfied	Signifies that the constraint was not satisfied.

The slack is the difference between the final constraint cell value and the value of the original constraint (or its boundary).

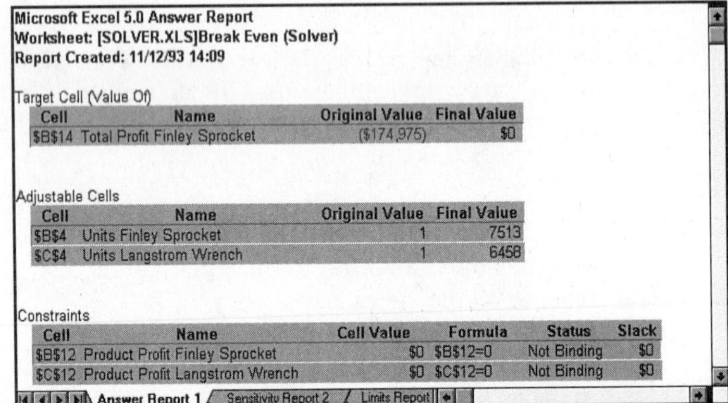

Microsoft Excel 5.0 Answer Report
Worksheet: [SOLVER.XLS]Break Even (Solver)
Report Created: 11/12/93 14:09

Target Cell (Value Of)

Cell	Name	Original Value	Final Value
$B$14	Total Profit Finley Sprocket	($174,975)	$0

Adjustable Cells

Cell	Name	Original Value	Final Value
$B$4	Units Finley Sprocket	1	7513
$C$4	Units Langstrom Wrench	1	6458

Constraints

Cell	Name	Cell Value	Formula	Status	Slack
$B$12	Product Profit Finley Sprocket	$0	$B$12=0	Not Binding	$0
$C$12	Product Profit Langstrom Wrench	$0	$C$12=0	Not Binding	$0

Answer Report 1 / Sensitivity Report 2 / Limits Report

FIGURE 38.7.
Solver's Answer report.

The Sensitivity Report

The Sensitivity report attempts to show how sensitive a solution is to changes in the model's formulas. Figure 38.8 shows the Sensitivity report for a linear problem. (The nonlinear report is slightly different.)

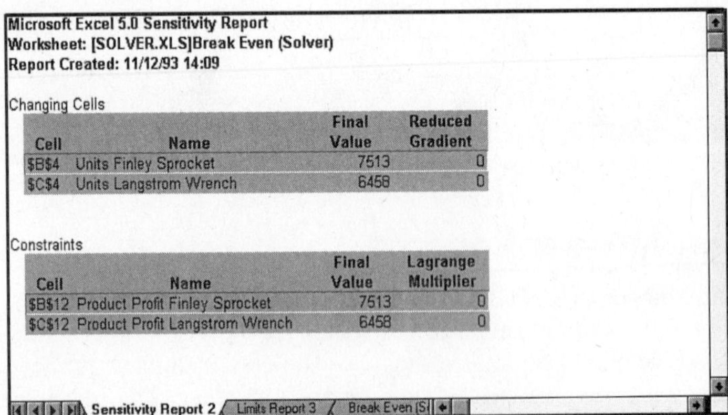

Microsoft Excel 5.0 Sensitivity Report
Worksheet: [SOLVER.XLS]Break Even (Solver)
Report Created: 11/12/93 14:09

Changing Cells

Cell	Name	Final Value	Reduced Gradient
$B$4	Units Finley Sprocket	7513	0
$C$4	Units Langstrom Wrench	6458	0

Constraints

Cell	Name	Final Value	Lagrange Multiplier
$B$12	Product Profit Finley Sprocket	7513	0
$C$12	Product Profit Langstrom Wrench	6458	0

Sensitivity Report 2 / Limits Report 3 / Break Even (S

FIGURE 38.8.
Solver's Sensitivity report.

The Limits Report

The Limits report, shown in Figure 38.9, displays the target cell and its value, as well as the changing cells and their values, upper and lower limits, and target results.

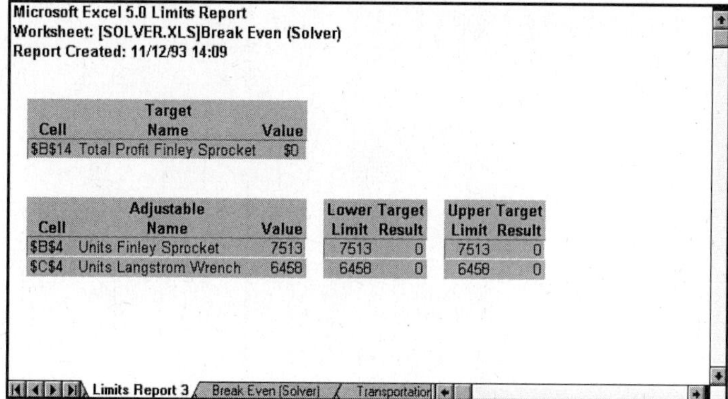

Microsoft Excel 5.0 Limits Report
Worksheet: [SOLVER.XLS]Break Even (Solver)
Report Created: 11/12/93 14:09

Cell	Target Name	Value
$B$14	Total Profit Finley Sprocket	$0

Cell	Adjustable Name	Value	Lower Limit	Target Result	Upper Limit	Target Result
$B$4	Units Finley Sprocket	7513	7513	0	7513	0
$C$4	Units Langstrom Wrench	6458	6458	0	6458	0

Limits Report 3 / Break Even (Solver) / Transportation

FIGURE 38.9.
Solver's Limits report.

A Solver Example

The best way to learn how to use a complex tool such as Solver is to get your hands dirty with some examples. Thoughtfully, Excel comes with several sample worksheets that use simplified models to demonstrate the various problems Solver can handle. I look at one of these worksheets in detail in this section.

The Transportation Problem

The *transportation problem* is the classic model for solving linear programming problems. The basic goal is to minimize the costs of shipping goods from several production plants to various warehouses scattered around the country. Your constraints are as follows:

1. The amount shipped from each plant can't exceed the plant's supply of goods.
2. The amount shipped to each warehouse must meet the warehouse's demand for goods.
3. The amount shipped from each plant must be greater than or equal to 0.

Figure 38.10 shows the model for solving the transportation problem.

SUPER TIP

The worksheet in Figure 38.10 is a slightly modified version of the file SOLVSAMP.XLS in the \EXAMPLES\SOLVER subdirectory of your main Excel directory.

FIGURE 38.10.
A worksheet for solving the transportation problem.

File Edit View Insert Format Tools Data Window Help

B20 =SUM(B18:F18)

Number to ship from plant X to warehouse Y (at intersection).

Plants:	San Fran	Denver	Chicago	Dallas	N.Y.	TOTALS	Supply
	Warehouses						
S. Carolina	1	1	1	1	1	5	310
Tennessee	1	1	1	1	1	5	260
Arizona	1	1	1	1	1	5	280
TOTALS	3	3	3	3	3		
Warehouse Demands	180	80	200	160	220		

Plants:	San Fran	Denver	Chicago	Dallas	N.Y.
	Warehouses				
S. Carolina	10	8	6	5	4
Tennessee	6	5	4	3	6
Arizona	3	4	5	5	9
TOTALS	19	17	15	13	19

Shipping Total: 83

Shipping costs from plant X to warehouse Y (at intersection).

Break Even (Solver) | Transportation Problem

The top table (A6:F10) lists the three plants (A7:A9) and the five warehouses (B6:F6). This table will hold the number of units shipped from each plant to each warehouse. In the Solver model, these will be the changing cells. The total shipped from each plant (G7:G9) must be less than or equal to the available supply for each plant (H7:H9) to satisfy constraint #1. The total shipped to each warehouse (B10:F10) must match the warehouse demands (B11:F11) to satisfy constraint #2.

SUPER NOTE

When you need to use a range of values in a constraint, you don't need to set up a separate constraint for each cell. Instead, you can compare entire ranges. For example, the constraint that the total shipped from each plant be less than or equal to the plant supply can be entered as follows:

```
G7:G9<=H7:H9
```

The bottom table (A14:F18) holds the corresponding shipping costs from each plant to each warehouse. The total shipping cost (cell B20) is the target cell you want to minimize.

Chapter

39

Working with Scenarios

What-if analysis by definition is not an exact science. All what-if models make guesses and assumptions based on history, expected events, or whatever voodoo comes to mind. A particular set of guesses and assumptions that you plug into a model is called a *scenario.* Because most what-if worksheets can take a wide range of input values, you usually end up with a large number of scenarios to examine. Instead of making you tediously insert all these values into the appropriate cells, Excel has a Scenarios feature that manages the process for you. This chapter completes the Data Analysis Workshop by examining this useful tool.

How Scenarios Work

As you've seen in this Workshop, Excel has powerful features that enable you to build sophisticated models that can answer even the most complex questions. The problem, though, isn't answering questions but *asking* them. For example, Figure 39.1 shows a worksheet model that analyzes a mortgage. You use this model to decide how much of a down payment to make, how long the term should be, and whether to include a principal paydown every month. The Results section compares the monthly payment and total paid for the regular mortgage and for the mortgage with a paydown. It also shows the savings and reduced term that result from the paydown.

Payment | =PMT(Interest/12,Term*12,House_Price-Down_Payment)

	A	B	C	D	E	F	G	H
1	**Mortgage Analysis**							
2								
3	**Fixed Cells:**							
4	House Price	$100,000						
5	Interest	8.0%						
6								
7	**Changing Cells:**							
8	Down Payment	$15,000						
9	Term	25						
10	Paydown	($50)						
11								
12	**Results:**	**Regular Mortgage**	**With Paydown**					
13	Monthly Payment	($656.04)	($706.04)					
14	Total Paid	($196,813.14)	($172,404.90)					
15	Total Savings	-	($24,408.23)					
16	Revised Term	-	20.3					
17								

Mortgage Scenarios / Sheet3 / Sheet4 / Sheet5 / Sh

Ready NUM

FIGURE 39.1.
A mortgage analysis worksheet.

Here are some possible questions to ask this model:

- How much will I save over the term of the mortgage if I use a shorter term, a larger down payment, and include a monthly paydown?
- How much more will I end up paying if I extend the term, reduce the down payment, and forego the paydown?

These are examples of *scenarios* that you would plug into the appropriate cells in the model. Excel's Scenarios feature helps by enabling you to define a scenario separately from the worksheet. You can save specific values for any or all of the model's input cells, give the scenario a name, and then recall the name (and all the input values it contains) from a list.

Setting Up Your Worksheet for Scenarios

Before creating a scenario, you need to decide which cells in your model will be the input cells. These will be the worksheet variables—the cells that, when you change them, change the results of the model. (Not surprisingly, Excel calls these the *changing cells.*) You can have as many as 32 changing cells in a scenario. For best results, follow these guidelines when setting up your worksheet for scenarios:

- The changing cells should be constants. Formulas can be affected by other cells, and that can throw off the entire scenario.
- To make it easier to set up each scenario and to make your worksheet easier to understand, group the changing cells and label them.
- For even greater clarity, name each changing cell.

Using the Scenario Manager

To work with scenarios, you use Excel's Scenario Manager tool. This feature enables you to add, edit, display, and delete scenarios as well as create summary scenario reports.

Adding a Scenario

Once your worksheet is set up the way you want, you can add a scenario to the sheet by following the steps in Procedure 39.1.

PROCEDURE 39.1. ADDING SCENARIOS WITH SCENARIO MANAGER.

1. Select the Tools | Scenarios command. Excel displays the Scenario Manager dialog box, shown in Figure 39.2.
2. Click on the Add button. The Add Scenario dialog box appears.
3. In the Scenario Name box, enter a name for the scenario.
4. In the Changing Cells box, enter references to your worksheet's changing cells. You can type in the references (be sure to separate noncontiguous cells with commas) or select the cells directly on the worksheet (see Figure 39.3).
5. In the Comment box, enter a description for the scenario. This will appear in the Comment section of the Scenario Manager dialog box.
6. Click on OK or press Enter. Excel displays the Scenario Values dialog box, shown in Figure 39.4.

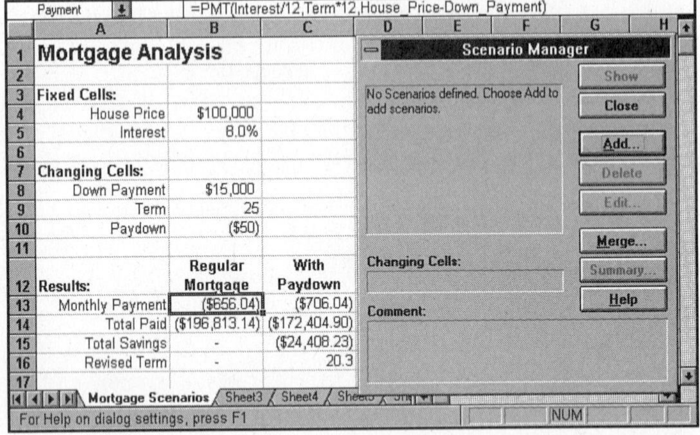

FIGURE 39.2.
Excel's Scenario Manager.

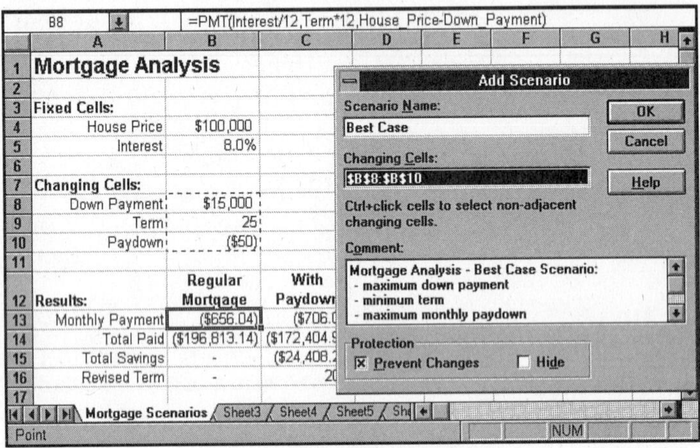

FIGURE 39.3.
Use the Add Scenario dialog box to add scenarios to a workbook.

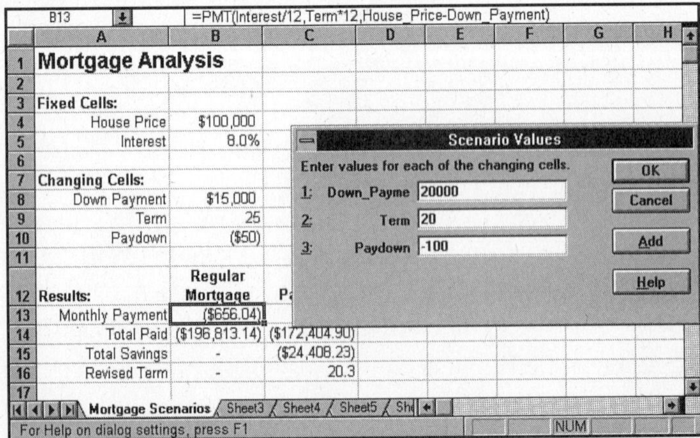

FIGURE 39.4.
Use the Scenario Values dialog box to enter the values you want to use for the scenario's changing cells.

7. Use the edit boxes to enter values for the changing cells.

> **SUPER NOTE**
>
> To learn about protecting and hiding scenarios, see Chapter 63, "Other Advanced Workbook Topics."

8. To add more scenarios, click on the **A**dd button to return to the Add Scenario dialog box and repeat steps 3-7. Otherwise, click on OK or press Enter to return to the Scenario Manager dialog box.
9. Click on the Close button to return to the worksheet.

Displaying a Scenario

After you define a scenario, you can enter its values into the changing cells simply by selecting the scenario from the Scenario Manager dialog box. Procedure 39.2 gives you the details.

PROCEDURE 39.2. DISPLAYING SCENARIOS WITH SCENARIO MANAGER.

1. Select the **T**ools | Scenarios command to display the Scenario Manager.
2. In the **S**cenarios list, highlight the scenario you want to display.
3. Click on the **S**how button. Excel enters the scenario values into the changing cells, as shown in Figure 39.5.
4. Repeat steps 2 and 3 to display other scenarios.
5. Click on the Close button to return to the worksheet.

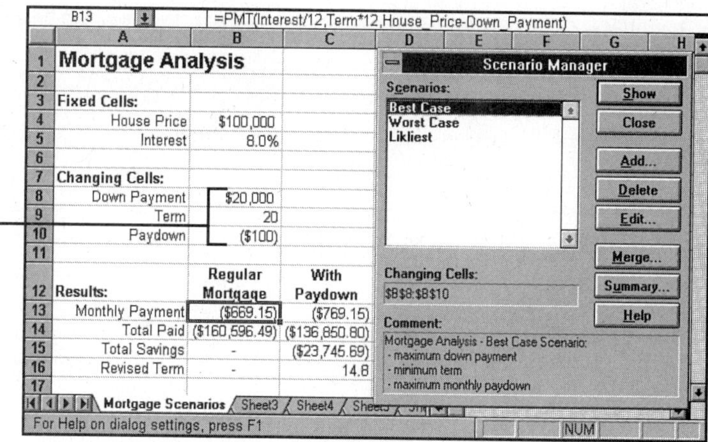

FIGURE 39.5. *When you select a scenario in Scenario Manager, Excel enters its values into the changing cells.*

Editing a Scenario

If you need to make changes to a scenario—whether it's changing the scenario's name, selecting different changing cells, or entering new values—follow the steps in Procedure 39.3.

PROCEDURE 39.3. EDITING SCENARIOS WITH SCENARIO MANAGER.

1. Select the **T**ools | Sc**e**narios command to display the Scenario Manager.
2. Use the S**c**enarios list to highlight the scenario you want to edit.
3. Click on the **E**dit button. Excel displays the Edit Scenario dialog box.
4. Make your changes, if necessary, and click on OK or press Enter. The Scenario Values dialog box appears.
5. Enter the new values, if necessary, and then click on OK or press Enter to return to the Scenario Manager dialog box.
6. Repeat steps 2-5 to edit other scenarios.
7. Click on the Close button to return to the worksheet.

Merging Scenarios

The scenarios you create are stored with each worksheet in a workbook. If you have similar models in different sheets (for example, budget models for different divisions), you can create separate scenarios for each sheet and then merge them later on. Procedure 39.4 outlines the steps to follow.

PROCEDURE 39.4. MERGING SCENARIOS.

1. Activate the worksheet you want to contain the merged scenarios.
2. Select the **T**ools | Sc**e**narios command to display the Scenario Manager.
3. Click on the **M**erge button. Excel displays the Merge Scenarios dialog box.
4. In the **B**ook list, select the workbook that contains the scenario sheet.
5. In the **S**heet list, select the worksheet that contains the scenario.
6. Click on OK or press Enter. Excel returns you to the Scenario Manager.
7. Repeat steps 3-6 to merge other scenarios.
8. Click on Close to return to the worksheet.

Generating a Summary Report

You can create a summary report that shows the changing cells in each of your scenarios along with selected result cells. This is a handy way to compare different scenarios. You can try it by following Procedure 39.5.

SUPER NOTE

When Excel sets up the scenario summary, it uses either the cell addresses or defined names of the changing cells and results cells. Your reports will be more readable if you name in advance the cells you'll be using.

PROCEDURE 39.5. GENERATING A SCENARIO SUMMARY REPORT.

1. Select the **T**ools | Scenarios command to display the Scenario Manager.
2. Click on the S**u**mmary button. Excel displays the Scenario Summary dialog box, shown in Figure 39.6.

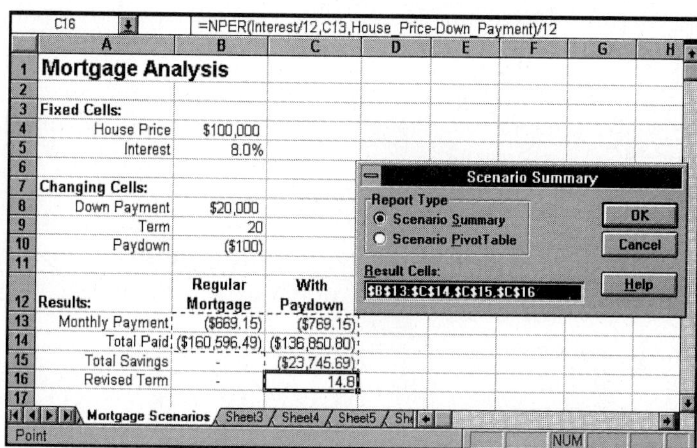

FIGURE 39.6.
Use the Scenario Summary dialog box to select the report type and result cells.

3. In the Report Type group, select either Scenario **S**ummary or Scenario **P**ivotTable.
4. In the **R**esult Cells box, enter references to the result cells you want to appear in the report (see Figure 39.6). You can select the cells directly on the sheet or type in the references. (Separate noncontiguous cells with commas.)
5. Click on OK or press Enter. Excel displays the report.

Figure 39.7 shows the Scenario Summary for the Mortgage Analysis worksheet.

FIGURE 39.7.
The Scenario Summary report for the Mortgage Analysis worksheet.

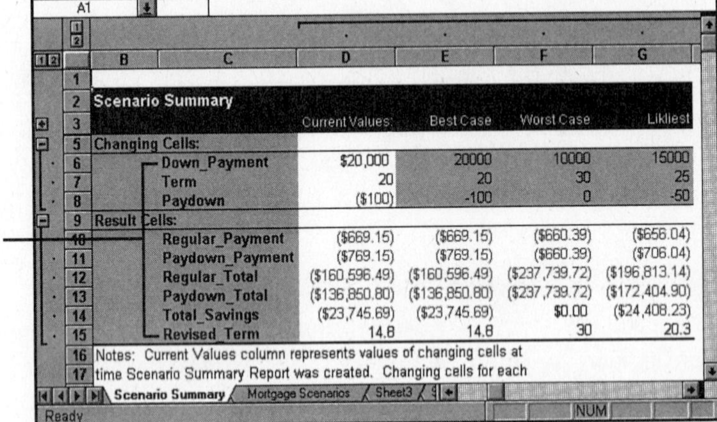

Deleting a Scenario

If you have scenarios you no longer need, you can delete them by following the steps in Procedure 39.6.

PROCEDURE 39.6. DELETING SCENARIOS.

1. Select the **T**ools | Scenarios command to display the Scenario Manager.
2. In the Scenarios list, highlight the scenario you want to delete.

SUPER CAUTION

Excel doesn't warn you when it's about to delete a scenario, so be sure the scenario you highlighted is one you can live without.

3. Click on the **D**elete button. Excel deletes the scenario.
4. Repeat steps 2 and 3 to delete other scenarios.
5. Click on Close to return to the worksheet.

Using the Scenarios Box

The Scenarios box on the WorkGroup toolbar, shown in Figure 39.8, offers an easy way to add, display, and edit scenarios. The next three sections fill you in on the details.

FIGURE 39.8.
The Scenarios box on the WorkGroup toolbar.

Adding a Scenario

To add a scenario with the Scenario box, follow the steps in Procedure 39.7.

PROCEDURE 39.7. ADDING A SCENARIO WITH THE SCENARIOS BOX.

1. Enter the values into the changing cells that you want to use for the scenario.
2. Select the changing cells.
3. In the Scenarios box, enter a name for the scenario, and then press Enter.

Displaying a Scenario

Displaying a scenario with the Scenarios box is simplicity itself: just pull down the list and select the scenario you want to display. One caveat, though: if you select the same scenario twice in succession, Excel asks whether you want to redefine the scenario. Click on **N**o to keep the current scenario definition. (If you *do* want to make changes to a scenario, see the next section.)

Editing a Scenario

To revise the values in the changing cells of a scenario, work through the steps in Procedure 39.8.

PROCEDURE 39.8. EDITING A SCENARIO WITH THE SCENARIOS BOX.

1. Use the Scenarios box to display the scenario you want to edit.
2. Make your changes to the changing cells.
3. Select the scenario again. Excel asks whether you want to redefine the scenario.
4. Click on **Y**es. Excel changes the scenario.

Workshop

VI

Excel 4.0 Macro Language

Chapter

40

Macro Basics

Excel is one of the most powerful spreadsheet programs around. You probably could spend years learning its various features without even touching a macro. However, if you want to get the most out of Excel (or if you want to make your life just plain easier), some familiarity with macros is a must. This chapter introduces you to Excel macros and gets you started with a few examples of command macros.

SUPER NOTE

Excel 5.0 includes Visual Basic for Applications, Microsoft's new common macro language. Microsoft has stated that it will be putting all its macro development efforts behind Visual Basic from now on. Although the Excel macro language has a few new features in Excel 5.0, it will receive few (if any) improvements in future versions. Keep this in mind when deciding which language to use for your macros.

What Is a Macro?

A macro is a small program that contains a list of instructions that you want Excel to execute. Similar to batch files, macros combine several operations into a single procedure that you can invoke quickly. This list of instructions is composed mostly of *macro functions* that work similar to regular worksheet functions. Some of these functions perform specific macro-related tasks, but most just correspond to Excel's menu commands and dialog box options. For example, the `FILE.CLOSE` macro function works much like the **File** | **Close** command.

The Three Types of Macros

Macros come in three flavors: *command macros, function macros,* and *subroutine macros*. Following is a summary of their differences:

- Command macros are the most common type of macro; they usually contain functions that are the equivalent of menu options and other Excel commands. The distinguishing feature of a command macro is that, similar to regular Excel commands, they have an effect on their surroundings (the worksheet, workspace, and so on). Whether you're formatting a range, printing a worksheet, or creating custom menus, command macros *change* things. I'll show you how to create command macros later in this chapter.
- Function macros work similar to Excel's built-in functions. Their distinguishing characteristics are that they accept arguments, manipulate those arguments, and return a result. A properly designed function macro has no effect on the current environment. See Chapter 41, "Creating Function Macros," for more information.

- Subroutine macros are a combination of command and function macros. They can take arguments and return values similar to a function macro, but they also can affect their surroundings similar to a command macro. Subroutines are invoked from within other macros and their usual purpose is to streamline macro code. If you have a task that you need to run several times in a macro, you'll typically split off the task into a subroutine instead of cluttering up your macro. See Chapter 42, "Macro Programming Concepts," for the lowdown on subroutine macros.

Working with Macro Sheets

You'll be entering your macros on special sheets called *macro sheets*. Your entries will be formulas that contain macro functions. However, to make macros easier to read, a macro sheet doesn't show the results of each formula; it shows the actual formulas.

As soon as you open a workbook containing a macro sheet, the sheet's macros become available to all other open documents. However, if you have any macros you think you'll be using regularly, you should consider storing them in a special file called the Personal Macro Workbook (PERSONAL.XLS). Excel keeps this workbook in the XLSTART directory and opens the workbook automatically at startup. This ensures that your regular macros are always available to your worksheets.

Recording a Command Macro

To create a command macro, Excel gives you two choices. Using the Macro Recorder to record the appropriate menu choices and dialog box selections, you can automatically create the macro on a macro sheet. Or you can use a macro sheet to build a macro from scratch. The next few sections show you how to record a command macro.

How to Record a Command Macro

The easiest way to create a command macro is to use the Macro Recorder. With this option, you just run through the task you want to automate (including selecting ranges, menu commands, and dialog box options), and Excel translates everything into the appropriate macro functions. These are copied to a macro sheet in which you can replay the entire procedure any time you like.

When you record a macro, you name it, and then you can set up other options. For example, you might set up a shortcut key to run the macro, or specify the workbook in which you want the macro stored. You'll be using the Record New Macro dialog box, shown in Figure 40.1. Following is a review of the options:

Macro Name — The name of the macro. Excel displays a proposed name for the macro (such as *Macro1*), but you can change the name to anything you like. Of course, you must follow Excel's usual

	naming conventions. The macro name can't be longer than 255 characters, the first letter must be a letter or an underscore (_), and spaces aren't allowed.
Description	An optional description of what the macro does.
Assign To	To make the macro easy to run, you can create a new command on the Tools menu or create a shortcut key combination. To add the command to the menu, activate the Menu Item on Tools Menu check box and enter the command name in the edit box. Include an ampersand (&) before the letter you want to use. This ampersand serves as the command's accelerator key. For a shortcut key, activate the Shortcut Key check box and then either accept Excel's suggestion or enter your own key in the Ctrl+ text box.
Store in	The location to store the macro.
Language	The macro language to use for the macro. Select the MS Excel 4.0 Macro option.

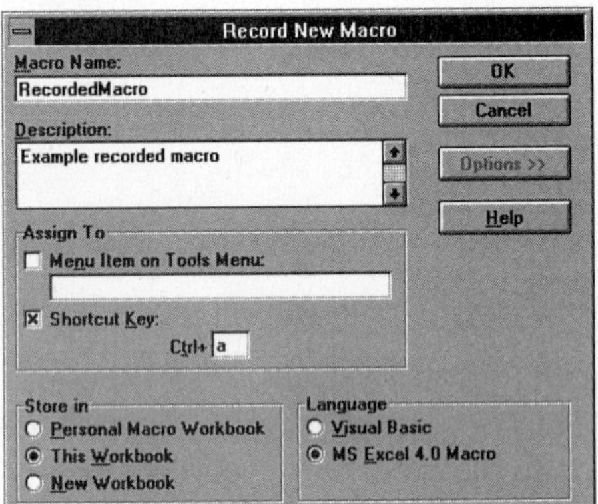

FIGURE 40.1.
The expanded Record New Macro dialog box.

Procedure 40.1 takes you through the steps required to record a command macro.

PROCEDURE 40.1. RECORDING A COMMAND MACRO.

1. Select the Tools | Record Macro | Record New Macro command. Excel displays an abbreviated version of the Record New Macro dialog box.

Click on this tool in the Visual Basic toolbar to display the Record New Macro dialog box.

2. Enter a name and description, if required.
3. Click on the Options button to expand the dialog box to the size shown in Figure 40.1.

4. Enter the options you want to use with the macro. In particular, be sure to select the MS Excel 4.0 Macro option.
5. Click on OK or press Enter. Excel returns you to the worksheet and displays Recording in the status line.
6. Perform the tasks you want to include in the macro.
7. When you've finished, select the **T**ools | **R**ecord Macro | **S**top Recording command.

Click on this tool to stop recording a macro.

To see your creation, either activate the last sheet in the workbook (if you used the current workbook to store the macro), or open the appropriate workbook. (If you used the Personal Macro Workbook, you need to unhide the workbook by selecting the **W**indow | Un**h**ide command and unhiding PERSONAL.XLS.) As you can see in Figure 40.2, Excel translates your actions into macro functions and writes them in a column. A typical macro has the following features:

Macro name:	The first cell holds the macro name you entered in the Record New Macro dialog box.
Shortcut key:	If you assigned a shortcut key to the macro, that key appears in parentheses beside the macro name. (It's understood that a shortcut key shown as (a) means Ctrl+a.)
Macro functions:	The main body of the macro consists of a series of formulas. These are Excel's interpretations of the actions you performed during the recording. Excel replays each task by "calculating" each of these formulas when you run the macro.
`RETURN()` function:	When you stop recording, Excel adds the `RETURN()` function to designate the end of the macro.

Here are some notes to keep in mind when recording command macros:

- You can control where a macro appears in a sheet by selecting a cell and then selecting the **T**ools | **R**ecord Macro | **M**ark Position for Recording command. When you're ready to record, select the **T**ools | **R**ecord Macro | **R**ecord at Mark command.
- The shortcut keys Excel suggests are ones that don't conflict with Excel's built-in shortcuts (such as Ctrl+B for Bold or Ctrl+C for Copy). There are twelve letters not assigned to Excel commands that you can use with your macros: a, e, g, h, j, k, l, m, q, t, w, and y.
- You can have an extra 26 shortcut keys by using capital letters. For example, Excel differentiates between Ctrl+a and Ctrl+A (or, more explicitly, Ctrl+Shift+a).

- By default, Excel uses absolute references during recording. If you prefer to use relative references, select the **T**ools | **R**ecord Macro | **U**se Relative References command. To change back, select the command again.
- If you perform the wrong action while recording, just continue with the correct sequence. I'll show you later in this chapter how to take out your mistakes. Don't try to fix the problem by selecting the Undo command, because doing so will only add an `UNDO()` function to the macro.
- You can pause recording by selecting the **T**ools | **R**ecord Macro | **S**top Recording command. To resume, use the **T**ools | **R**ecord Macro | **R**ecord at Mark command.

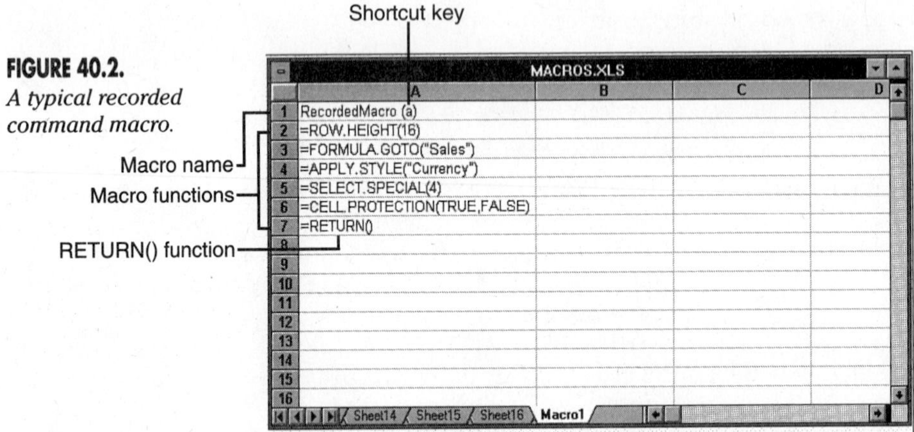

FIGURE 40.2.
A typical recorded command macro.

Procedural Macros Versus Keystroke Macros

If you're familiar with Lotus 1-2-3 or Quattro Pro macros, Excel's macros probably will look a little strange. In Lotus 1-2-3, for example, a macro command to format a number as currency with 0 decimal places appears as follows:

```
/RFC0~
```

This macro command is just a list of the appropriate keystrokes you would use to enter this command (with ~ as the Enter key). Not surprisingly, these kinds of macros are called *keystroke* macros.

Excel, on the other hand, uses *procedural* macros. A procedural macro doesn't care about the individual keystrokes you use to perform an action. Instead, the macro records the final result of each separate procedure. There are several examples of this in the macro shown in Figure 40.2. For example, consider the following formula (cell A2):

```
=ROW.HEIGHT(16)
```

I generated this formula by selecting the Format | Row | Height command, entering 16 in the Row Height text box, and then clicking on OK. Excel ignored the individual keystrokes and mouse clicks I used and, instead, just noted what was important: the end result.

Procedural macros operate by compressing an entire procedure (such as selecting a menu command and entering options in a dialog box) into a single macro function. To interpret many of these macro functions properly, you need to know how Excel translates dialog box options into function arguments. Here's a rundown:

- Excel arranges the function arguments in the same order they appear in the dialog box. (That is, the order you select options when you tab through them.)
- Numbers or text you type in a text box are shown as numeric or text arguments. For example, entering `16` in the Row Height dialog box produced the `ROW.HEIGHT(16)` macro function. Similarly, selecting Edit | Go To and entering the name `Sales` in the Reference text box records the function `FORMULA.GOTO("Sales")`.
- A list box selection is shown as a text argument. For example, selecting Format | Style and choosing Currency from the Style Name list produces the function `APPLY.STYLE("Currency")`.
- Option buttons are represented as numeric arguments. The number corresponds to the button's order in its group. For example, if you select the Special button in the Go To dialog box, and then choose the Blanks option in the Go To Special dialog box (the fourth button), Excel enters the function `SELECT.SPECIAL(4)`.
- Check box arguments are shown as `TRUE` (if activated) or `FALSE` (if deactivated). For example, if you select Format | Cells and activate the Locked check box (but not the Hidden check box) in the Protection tab, you end up with the function `CELL.PROTECTION(TRUE,FALSE)`.

Keep these guidelines in mind, and you'll find that procedural macros are much easier to understand and debug than their cryptic keystroke cousins.

Editing a Recorded Command Macro

Although procedural macros are almost always cleaner than their keystroke counterparts, you'll have plenty of recorded macros that don't turn out quite right the first time. Whether it's giving a command you shouldn't have or missing a command altogether, often you'll have to patch things up after the fact.

If your macro contains functions that you want to remove, just delete the offending cells from the macro sheet. (To keep things tidy, it's best to delete the cells instead of just clearing them.)

If you left out a step or two, follow the instructions in Procedure 40.2 to insert new recorded actions into an existing macro.

SUPER NOTE

If you just want to add new actions to the end of your macro, you can skip steps 1-3 of Procedure 40.2.

PROCEDURE 40.2. RECORDING CHANGES TO AN EXISTING MACRO.

1. Activate the macro sheet that contains the macro you want to change.

SUPER NOTE

If you need to make changes to a macro stored in PERSONAL.XLS, you must first unhide the sheet by selecting the **W**indow | **U**nhide command.

2. Decide where in the macro you want the new recording to begin and, at that position, insert enough blank cells to hold all of your actions. To be safe, you probably should insert a few more cells than you need (see Figure 40.3).

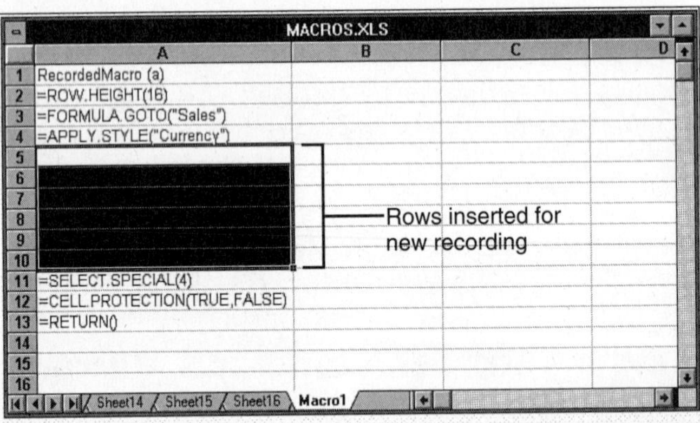

FIGURE 40.3. *Insert more than enough cells to handle your new recorded actions.*

3. Select the topmost blank cell and choose **T**ools | **R**ecord Macro | **M**ark Position for Recording. This tells Excel where you want the new actions recorded.
4. Activate the worksheet or chart you want to use for the recording.
5. Select the **T**ools | **R**ecord Macro | Record at Mark command to resume the recording.

6. Perform the actions you want to add to the macro.
7. When you're done, select **T**ools | **R**ecord Macro | **S**top Recorder.
8. Activate the macro sheet and clean up things by deleting any remaining blank cells or, if necessary, the extra `RETURN()` function that Excel added (see Figure 40.4).

FIGURE 40.4.
When you finish inserting your recording, you'll need to clean up the macro.

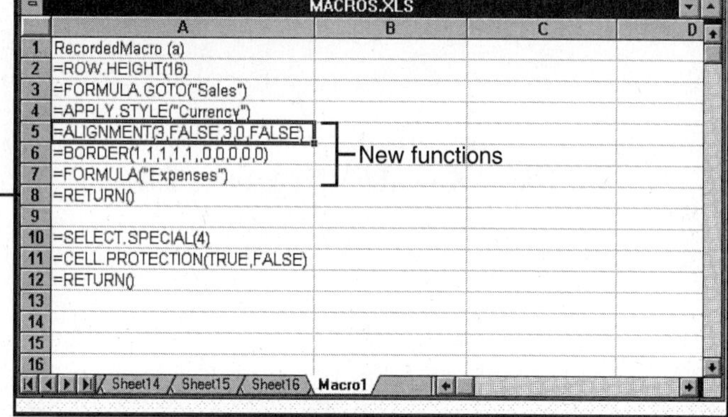

Writing Your Own Command Macro

Although the Macro Recorder makes it easy to create your own homegrown macros, there are plenty of macro features that you can't access with mouse or keyboard actions or by selecting menu options. For example, Excel has a couple dozen information macro functions that return data about cells, worksheets, the workspace, and more. (I discuss many of these functions in later chapters of this Workshop.) Also, the control functions enable you to add true programming constructs, such as looping, branching, and decision making.

To access these macro elements, you need to write your own macros from scratch. This is easier than it sounds, because all you'll really be doing is entering a series of formulas in a macro sheet and then defining a name for the macro. It's not all that different from what you've been doing with regular worksheets. The next few sections take you through the various steps.

Inserting a New Macro Sheet

If you want to enter your macro on an existing macro sheet, just select the sheet's tab. (If you want to use PERSONAL.XLS, you need to unhide it first.)

If you want to start a new macro sheet, follow the steps in Procedure 40.3.

PROCEDURE 40.3. INSERTING A NEW EXCEL 4.0 MACRO SHEET.

1. Activate the sheet before which you want to insert the macro sheet.
2. Select the **I**nsert | **M**acro | MS **E**xcel 4.0 Macro command. Excel inserts the new sheet.

> **SUPER TIP**
>
> You can create a new macro sheet by pressing Ctrl+F11 or Ctrl+Alt+F1.

How to Write a Command Macro

With a macro sheet active, follow the steps in Procedure 40.4 to write your own command macro.

PROCEDURE 40.4. WRITING A COMMAND MACRO.

1. Select the first cell you want to use for the macro.
2. Enter a name for the macro. (Make sure you use a legal Excel name.)
3. Enter your macro formulas and functions in the column immediately below the macro name. Remember that every macro entry is a formula, so you have to begin each cell with an equals sign (=).

> **SUPER NOTE**
>
> For complex command functions, it's probably faster to use the Macro Recorder than trying to remember the syntax of something such as `FORMAT.FONT()`, which has nine arguments.

4. When you're finished, type `=RETURN()` to mark the end of the macro.

> **SUPER NOTE**
>
> Properly written macros also include documentation that explains each macro step. See Chapter 42, "Macro Programming Concepts," for more information on macro documentation.

Pasting Macro Functions

Some macro functions have very long argument lists. (The `WORKSPACE()` function, for example, has no less than 16 arguments.) Rather than looking up the proper order for these arguments, you can simply paste the function into the cell. Procedure 40.5 lists the required steps.

PROCEDURE 40.5. PASTING A MACRO FUNCTION INTO A CELL.

1. In the cell, enter an equals sign (=) and then select the **I**nsert | **F**unction command (or press Shift+F3). The Function Wizard - Step 1 of 2 dialog box appears.
2. Use the Function **C**ategory list to select a category. You'll find that most macro functions are in the Commands, Customizing, and Macro control categories.
3. Select the function you want from the Function **N**ame list.
4. Click on the Next > button. If the function has multiple syntaxes, the Function Wizard - Step 1a of 2 dialog box appears. In this case, select the syntax you want and then select the Next > button. Excel displays the Function Wizard - Step 2 of 2 dialog box.

SUPER NOTE

Why would a function have more than one syntax? Well, some functions can do double (or even triple) duty. For example, you can apply the `FORMAT.FONT()` function to worksheet cells, graphic objects, or chart items. Each of these applications requires a different argument list.

5. Enter the arguments you want to use with the function.
6. Click on **F**inish to paste the function.

SUPER TIP

If you know the name of the function you want, you can paste its arguments by entering the function name followed by the left parenthesis and then pressing Ctrl+A.

Naming a Command Macro

When you've finished writing your macro, you need to name it (and, optionally, assign a shortcut key). Procedure 40.6 shows you how you name a macro.

PROCEDURE 40.6. NAMING A COMMAND MACRO.

1. Activate the macro sheet containing the macro you want to name.
2. Select the cell containing the name of the macro.
3. Select the **I**nsert | **N**ame | **D**efine command. The Define Name dialog box appears, shown in Figure 40.5.

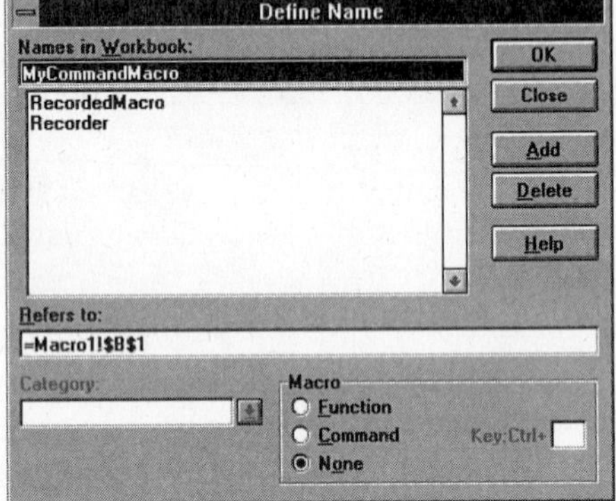

FIGURE 40.5.
Use this version of the Define Name dialog box to name your macros.

4. If necessary, change the macro name shown in the Names in **W**orkbook edit box.
5. Make sure the reference in the **R**efers to box is the correct address for the macro name.
6. In the Macro box, select the **C**ommand option.
7. If you want the macro to appear in the Function Wizard's list of functions, select Ca**t**egory and choose the User Defined option. You normally use this option only for function and subroutine macros.
8. If you would like to use a shortcut key with the macro, enter a letter in the **K**ey:Ctrl+ text box.
9. Click on OK or press Enter.

Running a Command Macro

Excel offers several methods for running your command macros. The next few sections discuss a few of these methods.

SUPER NOTE

For information about more ways to run macros, see Chapter 49, "Macro Tips and Techniques."

Using the Macro Dialog Box

Excel takes all the command macros it finds in the macro sheets of any open workbook and in the PERSONAL.XLS file and stores their names in a list in the Macro dialog box. To run any of these macros, you can select the name from the list, as described in Procedure 40.7.

PROCEDURE 40.7. RUNNING A MACRO FROM THE MACRO DIALOG BOX.

1. Open the workbook with the macro sheet that contains the macro you want to run. (You can skip this step if the macro exists in the Personal Macro Workbook.) Note that the macro sheet just has to be open in memory; it doesn't have to be the active sheet.
2. If the macro will be affecting a worksheet, activate the sheet and position the active cell where you need it.
3. Select the **T**ools | **M**acro command. The Macro dialog box appears, shown in Figure 40.6.

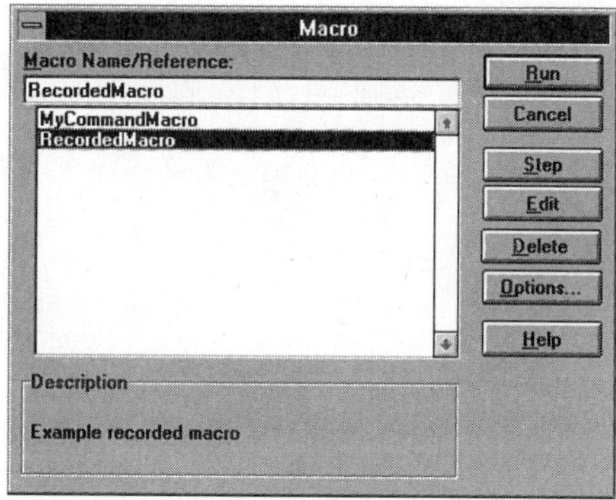

FIGURE 40.6.
Use the Macro dialog box to run your macros.

4. Select the name of the macro you want to run from the **M**acro Name/Reference list.
5. Click on **R**un or press Enter. Excel runs the macro.

SUPER TIP

If the active sheet is a macro sheet, you also can run a macro from a shortcut menu. Right-click on the name of the macro and select the Run command. Excel displays the Macro dialog box and enters the cell address in the **M**acro Name/Reference box. Click on **R**un to start the macro.

SUPER NOTE

If you want to stop a macro before it's finished, press the Esc key. In the Macro Error dialog box that appears, select Halt to shut down the macro or Continue to resume.

Using Macro Shortcut Keys

Running a macro with a shortcut key is easy. Hold down the Ctrl key and press the letter you assigned to the macro. If the macro doesn't run, check for these possibilities:

- Is the workbook that contains the macro open?
- Did you assign a shortcut key to the macro?
- Is there another macro with the same shortcut key? If two or more macros have the same shortcut key, Excel runs the first macro in the list.
- Did you assign a capital letter shortcut key? As mentioned earlier, Excel differentiates between Ctrl+A and Ctrl+Shift+A.

SUPER TIP

You can assign a shortcut key to an existing macro by highlighting the macro in the Macro dialog box and selecting the Options button. In the Macro Options dialog box that appears, activate the Shortcut Key check box and enter the letter in the Ctrl+ edit box.

Using the Visual Basic Toolbar

The Visual Basic toolbar includes a Run Macro tool. Procedure 40.8 explains how to use it.

PROCEDURE 40.8. RUNNING A MACRO USING THE VISUAL BASIC TOOLBAR.

1. Activate the macro sheet containing the macro you want to run.
2. Select the cell containing the name of the macro.
3. Click on the Run Macro tool.

The Run Macro tool.

SUPER TIP

If you don't want the macro to start at the beginning, select whatever cell you want to use as a starting point and then click on the Run Macro tool.

Chapter

41

Creating Function Macros

Excel comes with hundreds of built-in functions that make up one of the largest function libraries of any spreadsheet. However, even with this vast collection, you'll still find plenty of applications these functions don't cover. For example, you might need to calculate the area of a circle of a specified radius, or the gravitational force between two objects. You could easily calculate these things on a worksheet, of course, but if you need them frequently, it makes sense to create your own functions that you can use anytime. This chapter shows you how to create your own function macros.

Understanding Function Macros

As I mentioned in the last chapter, the defining characteristic of function macros is that they return a result. They can perform any number of calculations on numbers, text, logical values, and so on, but they're not allowed to affect their surroundings. They can't move the active cell or format a range or change the workspace settings. In fact, anything you can access using the menus is off-limits in a function macro.

What *can* you put in a function macro? Well, all of Excel's built-in worksheet functions are fair game, and you can use any macro function that isn't the equivalent of a menu command or a desktop action. You can, of course, combine these functions and other items to create formulas using Excel's basic operators.

The simplest function macro is one that does nothing but return a value. Figure 41.1 shows a function macro called Return57 that consists of a single formula: `=RETURN(57)`. This is the same `RETURN()` function you used to terminate your command macros in the last chapter. `RETURN()` performs the same task in a function macro, but it also serves to send the function result back to the worksheet that called it. And, as you can see in the accompanying worksheet, you use a function macro just like you use a regular function (except, of course, that you have to precede the macro name with the name of the macro sheet's workbook so that Excel knows where to find it).

Most function macros (like most of the built-in functions) actually accept *arguments*. This enables you to send data to the macro, which then manipulates it and sends back the result. For example, Excel has a `SQRT()` function for calculating square roots, but it doesn't have a cube root function. Figure 41.2 shows a CubeRoot function macro that fits the bill.

The macro's first line is an `ARGUMENT()` function that tells Excel to expect an argument with this function. This line also gives the argument a name (`Num`). As you can see in the accompanying worksheet, the macro is called and a value is sent (the contents of cell A1, in this case). The macro's second line—`=Num^(1/3)`—takes the `Num` argument and calculates its cube root. Finally, the `RETURN()` function sends back the result (from cell A6 in the macro sheet).

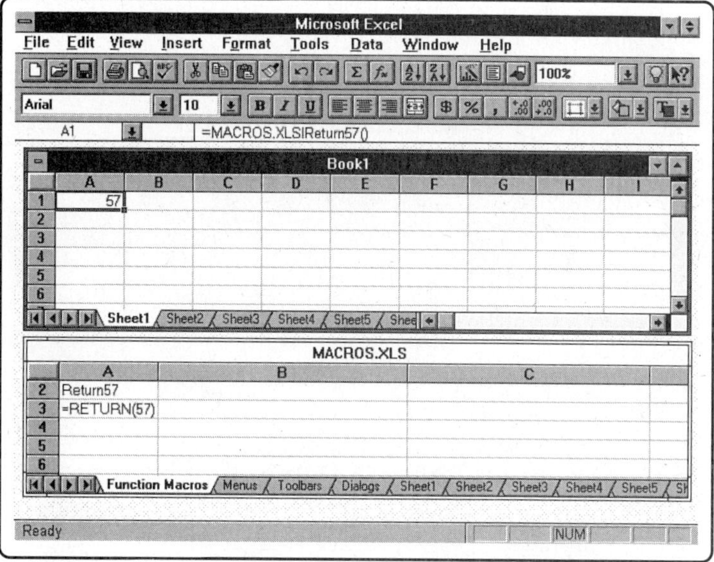

FIGURE 41.1.
A simple function macro that only returns a value.

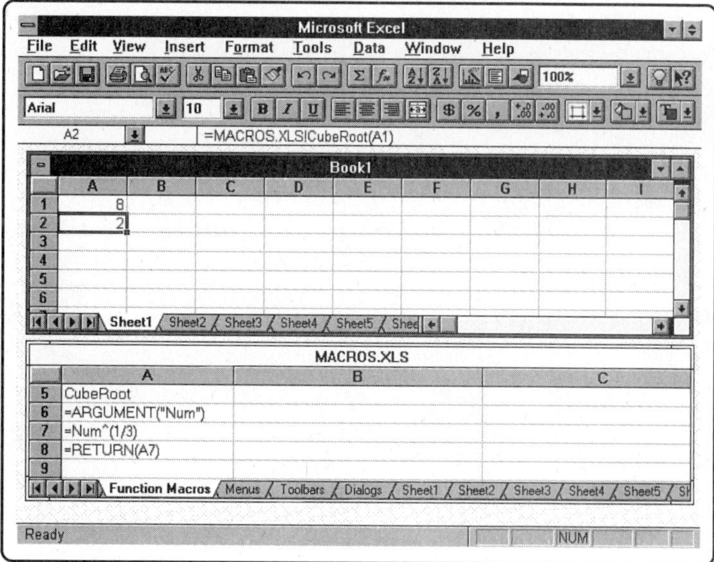

FIGURE 41.2.
A function macro that calculates cube roots.

All your function macros will have this basic structure. Therefore, you need to keep three things in mind when you design these kinds of macros:

- What arguments will the macro take?
- What formulas will you use within the macro?
- What value or values will be returned?

SUPER NOTE

You can use arrays to return multiple values from a function macro. See Chapter 60, "Advanced Range Topics," to learn about array formulas.

Writing a Function Macro

As I've said, function macros can't contain menu commands or mouse and keyboard actions. This means, of course, that there is no way to record a function macro. You have to type them out by hand. The process is very similar to creating a command macro from scratch. Follow the steps in Procedure 41.1 to write a function macro.

PROCEDURE 41.1. WRITING A FUNCTION MACRO.

1. In the macro sheet you want to use, select the first cell for the macro and enter a name.
2. Enter your macro formulas and functions in the column immediately below the macro name. When entering your `ARGUMENT()` functions, make sure you place them in the same order that the arguments will appear when the function is called. (See the section in this chapter titled "Common Function Macro Functions" to learn more about `ARGUMENT()` and other functions commonly used in function macros.)

SUPER NOTE

As with command macros, you can paste functions and arguments into the formula bar. See Chapter 40, "Macro Basics," for details.

3. Finish the macro by including a `RETURN()` function that returns a value to the worksheet.
4. Select the cell containing the name of the macro.
5. Select the **I**nsert | **N**ame | **D**efine command to display the Define Name dialog box.

6. In the Macro group, select the Function option.
7. If you want the macro to appear in the FunctionWizard dialog box, select Category and choose the User Defined option.
8. Click on OK or press Enter.

Using a Function Macro

You can use function macros only within worksheet or macro sheet formulas. First you need to make sure that the sheet containing the macro is open (unless the macro is stored in PERSONAL.XLS). Then you have two choices:

- In the formula bar, type the name of the macro's workbook, an exclamation point (!), the macro name, and any arguments enclosed in parentheses.

> **SUPER TIP**
>
> If you're entering the formula in a worksheet in the same workbook as the macro, you don't need to include the workbook name and exclamation point.

- Select the Insert | Function command, highlight User Defined in the Function Category list, and select the macro from the Function Name list. (You can do this only if you chose to save the macro in the User Defined category when you defined the macro name.)

Common Function Macro Functions

Despite the function restrictions you face when you're creating function macros, there are still hundreds of functions to choose from. However, four functions are used often in function macros: `RESULT()`, `ARGUMENT()`, `CALLER()`, and `VOLATILE()`. Let's take a closer look at each of these important functions.

The *RESULT()* Function

You use the `RESULT()` function to specify the data type of the value returned by a function macro. Make sure that you use `RESULT()` before any other formulas in the macro (including `ARGUMENT()` functions) and that it has the following syntax:

RESULT(***type_num***)

type_num indicates the data type of the result according to the values displayed in the following table:

type_num	*Data Type*
1	Numeric
2	Text
4	Logical
8	Reference
16	Error
64	Array

In most cases, RESULT() is an optional function. Therefore, you don't have to use it in macros where the data type of the result is obvious, such as in the CubeRoot macro discussed earlier. If you don't include RESULT(), Excel assumes that the data type value is 7. Why 7? That's the sum of the values for the numeric, text, and logical data types. This means that you can return a value that is any of those three types. To specify any other combination of data types, just add the appropriate values together.

SUPER NOTE

RESULT() is not optional when a macro returns values that are either references or arrays.

You'll use RESULT() most often in complex macros where there is a chance that you could accidentally return an incorrect value. RESULT() can save you lots of debugging time. For example, it can prevent you from returning text when the calling program is expecting a logical value.

SUPER CAUTION

You might still get unexpected results even if you use the RESULT() function. If the returned value is a different type than that specified in the RESULT() function, Excel tries to convert the result to the required data type. This is another example of Excel's *data coercion:* you might end up with numbers converted to text, or something similar. If Excel can't make the conversion, the macro returns the #VALUE! error.

The *ARGUMENT()* Function

You've seen how the ARGUMENT() function adds flexibility to a function macro by enabling the user to input data to the function. The ARGUMENT() function actually serves three important purposes:

- It defines the names of the arguments.
- It determines the order of the arguments between the function's parentheses.
- Optionally, it specifies the data type of each argument.

Unless you're using `RESULT()`, the `ARGUMENT()` functions must appear at the beginning of the macro. You have a choice of two syntaxes, depending on how you want to store the arguments.

To store the arguments as names, use the following:

`ARGUMENT(`***`name_text`***`,`*`type_num`*`)`

name_text	The name you want to define for the argument.
type_num	The data type value.

As soon as you've defined a name for the argument, any formula in the macro sheet may use the name in its calculations.

If you prefer to store the arguments in cells, use this form:

`ARGUMENT(`*`name_text`*`,`*`type_num`*`,`***`reference`***`)`

name_text	The name you want to define for the argument.
type_num	The data type value.
reference	A cell address that Excel uses to store the data.

To refer to the argument in other formulas, you can use *name_text* or ***reference***. Most macro programmers avoid using ***reference*** because the arguments take up unnecessary space on the macro sheet. The exception is if your function will be returning an array. In this case, you'll usually want to enter the array values into a range on the macro sheet and then return that range.

When designing your `ARGUMENT()` functions, keep the following points in mind:

- Function macros can have a maximum of 29 arguments.
- If your function has any optional arguments, put them at the end of the argument list to make things easier for the user.
- Use an `IF()` function to test for incorrect values entered by the user. For example, if one of your arguments requires a positive number, you should check for negative numbers and report an error if anything is amiss. Chapter 42, "Macro Programming Concepts," tells you how to use `IF()` in a macro. See Chapter 43, "Using Macros to Get and Display Information," to learn how to display error messages.

The *CALLER()* Function

The `CALLER()` function returns information about which cell, range, menu command, tool, or object called the currently running macro. `CALLER()` is invaluable for macros that need to behave differently depending on where they were called.

For example, you might have several worksheets that call the same macro. If these sheets have slightly different structures, your macro might have to allow for this in some way. The simple macro shown in Figure 41.3 passes `CALLER()` to the `GET.CELL()` function to determine the name of the calling worksheet. A more advanced macro would test for possible filenames and react accordingly.

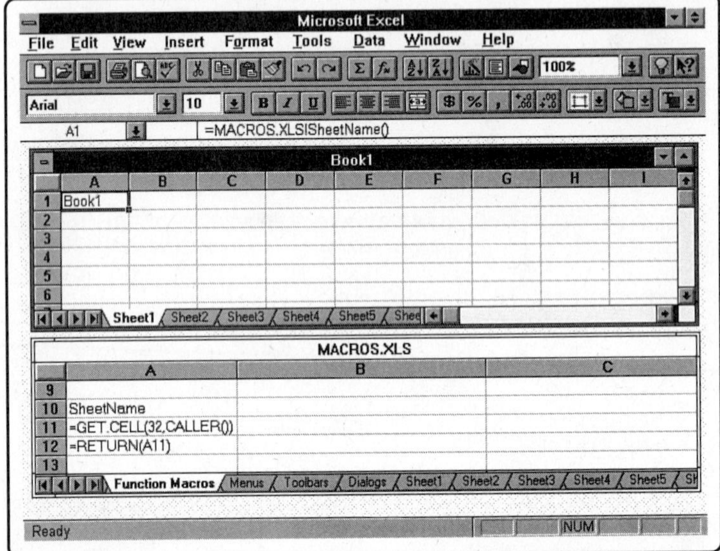

FIGURE 41.3.
A macro that uses CALLER() to determine the name of the worksheet that called the macro.

Here are some points you should keep in mind when using `CALLER()`:

- If you want to determine the cell or range from which a macro was called, you can't use `CALLER()` by itself. Instead, use `GET.CELL()` or `REFTEXT()` to convert the reference to text.
- If the macro was chosen from a menu command, `CALLER()` returns a horizontal array of three elements that includes the command's position number, the menu number, and the menu bar number.
- If the macro was invoked by selecting an object such as a macro button (see Chapter 49, "Macro Tips and Techniques"), `CALLER()` returns a text string that identifies the object.
- If the macro was started from a toolbar, `CALLER()` returns a horizontal array that includes the tool's position and the toolbar name.

The *VOLATILE()* Function

As you may know, Excel normally recalculates your worksheet formulas only when you change any data that affects the formula either directly or indirectly. Unfortunately, this *doesn't* apply to function macros. This means that you might end up with out-of-date results in some of your worksheet formulas that use function macros for their calculations.

To overcome this problem, include the `VOLATILE()` function in all your function macros. This function tells Excel to always recalculate the macro whenever it recalculates a worksheet. Enter `VOLATILE()` before all other macro formulas except `RESULT()` and `ARGUMENT()`.

Chapter 42

Macro Programming Concepts

The macros you've seen so far have been simple, linear beasts designed to carry out only a few tasks or calculations. To build truly powerful (and truly useful) macros, you need to learn about the Excel's programming features. This is, after all, a programming language (albeit a simple one). As such, it enables you to make decisions, branch to other parts of a macro, set up loops, and create subroutines. This chapter shows you all these features and more.

Documenting Your Macros

Before diving in to the programming features of Excel's macro language, I want to make a quick point about documentation. As your macros grow more complex, they also grow harder to decipher, either by someone else looking at the macro for the first time, or by yourself looking at your code a few months down the road. Excel's often cryptic function arguments (all those numbers and TRUE/FALSE values) can make some macros downright impenetrable.

To avoid this fate, you should enter a short comment into the cell next to each of your macro formulas. This note can be a brief explanation of what the formula is doing or a clarification of the function arguments used. Figure 42.1 shows a macro formatted for documentation. Here are some of the features of this format:

- The right column holds the formula documentation.
- The left column lists any cell names used in the macro. (To learn about using names in macros, see Chapter 44, "Macro Worksheet Skills.")
- You can include text entries among the macro formulas to add comments that separate each of the macro's tasks. (Excel ignores text cells when processing the macro.) To make the comments easier to spot, use a bold italic font.
- Borders separate the various parts and make the macro easier to read.

MACROS.XLS

	A	B	C
1	Names	Commands	Documentation
2			
3		RecordedMacro (a)	
4		=ROW.HEIGHT(16)	Change row height to 16
5		=FORMULA.GOTO("Sales")	Select the "Sales" range
6		=APPLY.STYLE("Currency")	Apply the "Currency" style
7		***This comment is ignored***	
8		=SELECT.SPECIAL(4)	Select the blank cells
9		=CELL.PROTECTION(TRUE,FALSE)	Turn on cell protection
10		=RETURN()	Stop the macro
11			
12			
13			
14			
15			
16			

Command Macros / Function Macros / Sheet1 / Sh

FIGURE 42.1.
Document your macros to make them easier to understand.

Macros That Make Decisions

A smart macro performs tests on its environment and then, based on the results of each test, decides what to do next. For example, suppose you've written a function macro that uses one of its arguments as a divisor in a formula. You should test the argument before using it in the formula to make sure it isn't `0` (to avoid producing a `#DIV/0!` error). If it is, you could display a message to alert the user to the illegal argument.

Using *IF()* to Make True/False Decisions

Simple true/false decisions are handled by the `IF()` function that you learned about in Chapter 6, "Working with Functions." Recall that the `IF()` function has the following syntax:

`IF(`***`logical_test`***`,`*`true_expr`*`,`*`false_expr`*`)`

`logical_test`	A logical expression that evaluates to either TRUE or FALSE.
`true_expr`	The value returned by the `IF()` function if ***`logical_test`*** evaluates to TRUE.
`false_expr`	The value returned if the ***`logical_test`*** is FALSE.

Figure 42.2 shows a simple function macro that tests an argument and returns a different string based on the results of that test.

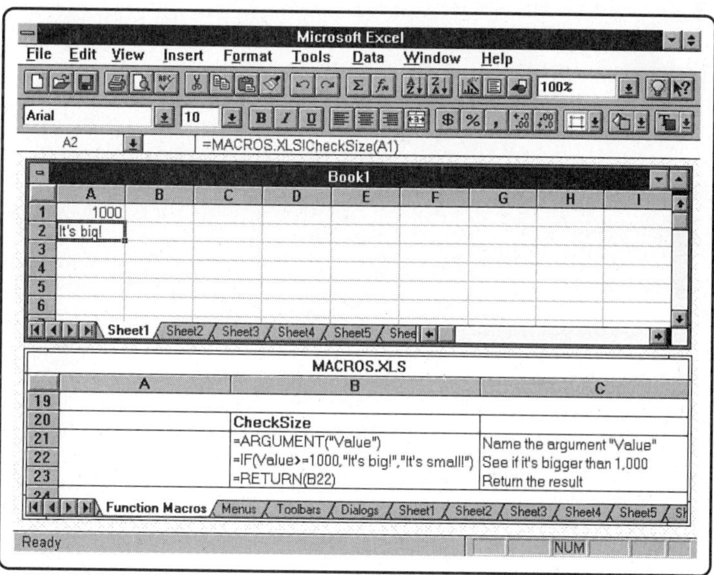

FIGURE 42.2.
A simple function macro that returns a different value based on a logical test.

Although most `IF()` functions return constants, you can use formulas and even other functions for the *`true_expr`* and *`false_expr`*. For example, the `CubeRoot` function from the last chapter should check to see if the argument is negative:

```
=IF(Num < 0, "Num < 0!", Num^(1/3))
```

If the `Num` argument is negative, the function returns `Num < 0!`; otherwise, the cube root expression is evaluated. In fact, you could make this expression truly efficient by including the `RETURN()` function right in the `IF()`:

```
=IF(Num < 0, RETURN("Num < 0!"), RETURN(Num^(1/3)))
```

Using a Block *IF* to Run Multiple Expressions

Using the `IF()` function to calculate a formula or run another function adds a powerful new weapon to your macro arsenal. However, this technique suffers from an important drawback: whatever the result of the logical test, you only can execute a single expression. This is fine in many cases, but there will be times when you'll need to run one group of expressions if the test is `TRUE` and a different group if the test if `FALSE`. To handle such a situation, you need to use a *block `IF`*.

A block `IF` is actually a combination of three functions: `IF()`, `ELSE()`, and `END.IF()`. The block is set up in the following manner:

=IF(***logical_test***)

(Expressions to run if ***logical_test*** is TRUE go here.)

=ELSE()

(Expressions to run if ***logical_test*** is FALSE go here.)

=END.IF()

SUPER NOTE

In contrast to a block `IF`, the `IF()` function by itself is called an *in-line `IF`*, because everything happens in a single line.

The block begins with the usual `IF()` function, without the *`true_expr`* and *`false_expr`* arguments. If the `logical_test` returns `TRUE`, all the statements between the `IF()` and `ELSE()` functions are executed (you can insert any number of formulas). However, if ***`logical_test`*** returns `FALSE`, all the statements between the `ELSE()` and `END.IF()` functions are executed.

For example, suppose you want to calculate the future value of a series of regular deposits, but you want to differentiate between monthly deposits and quarterly deposits. Figure 42.3 shows a function macro called FutureValue that does the job.

FIGURE 42.3.
A function macro that uses a block `IF` *to differentiate between monthly and quarterly deposits.*

MACROS.XLS

	A	B	C
1	Names	Commands	Documentation
25			
26		FutureValue	
27		=ARGUMENT("Rate")	The annual interest rate
28		=ARGUMENT("Nper")	The number of years in the term
29		=ARGUMENT("Pmt")	The annual deposit available
30		=ARGUMENT("Frequency")	The frequency of deposits
31		=IF(Frequency="Monthly")	If the frequency is monthly,
32		= RETURN(FV(Rate/12,Nper*12,Pmt/12))	Use monthly values for FV()
33		=ELSE()	Otherwise,
34		= RETURN(FV(Rate/4,Nper*4,Pmt/4))	Use quarterly values
35		=END.IF()	
36			
37			
38			

Function Macros / Sheet1 / Sheet2 / Sheet3 / Sheet4

The first three arguments (`Rate`, `Nper`, and `Pmt`) are the annual interest rate, the number of years in the term of the investment, and the total deposit available annually. The fourth argument—`Frequency`—is either "Monthly" or "Quarterly." The goal is to adjust the first three arguments based on the `Frequency`. For example, if `Frequency` is "Monthly," you need to divide the interest rate by 12, multiply the term by 12, and divide the annual deposit by 12. The `IF()` function (cell B31) runs a test on the `Frequency` argument:

```
=IF(Frequency = "Monthly")
```

If this argument is true, the function adjusts `Rate`, `Nper`, and `Pmt` accordingly and returns the future value. Otherwise, a quarterly calculation is assumed and different adjustments are made to the arguments.

Following are some notes on the block `IF`:

- The `ELSE()` function is optional. If you can ignore a `FALSE` result in the `IF()` function (which is often the case), you can leave out the `ELSE()` and its associated statements. Therefore, the structure of the block `IF` becomes the following:

  =IF(***logical_test***)

  (Expressions to run if ***logical_test*** is `TRUE` go here.)

  =END.IF()

- Block `IF`s are much easier to read if you indent the expressions between `IF()`, `ELSE()`, and `END.IF()`, as I've done in Figure 42.3. This enables you to easily identify which group of statements will be run if there is a `TRUE` result and which group will be run if the result is `FALSE`. Just add three or four spaces after the equals sign (=).

Using a Block *IF* to Make Multiple Decisions

Another problem with the in-line `IF()` is that normally you can make only one decision. The function calculates a single logical result and performs one of two actions. However, there are plenty of situations that require multiple decisions before you can decide which action to take.

One solution is to use the `AND()` and `OR()` functions to evaluate a series of logical tests. For example, the FutureValue macro probably should test the `Frequency` argument to make sure it's either "Monthly" or "Quarterly." The following `IF()` function uses `OR()` to accomplish this:

```
IF(OR(Frequency = "Monthly", Frequency = "Quarterly"))
```

If `Frequency` doesn't equal either of the values, the `OR()` function returns `FALSE`, and the macro can return a message to the user.

This approach works, but you're really just performing multiple logical tests; in the end, you only make a single decision. A second solution would be to *nest* *`IF()`* functions. Nesting involves running an `IF()` and using another `IF()` as part of either the `true_expr` or `false_expr`. Excel enables you to nest up to seven `IF()` functions. Following is an example that checks the number of days an invoice is past due:

```
IF(PastDue>30, IF(PastDue>90, "Really late!", "Late"), "OK")
```

If the invoice is less than or equal to 30 days past due, the function returns `OK`. For invoices more than 30 days past due, a second `IF()` checks to see if the invoice is more than 90 days past due. If it is, the function returns `Really late!`. Otherwise, the function returns `Late`.

At the cost of added complexity, nested `IF()` functions accomplish the goal of multiple decision making. The further you nest `IF()` functions, the harder they get to read and understand. The best solution is to return to the block `IF` and add a new function: `ELSE.IF()`. This function combines `ELSE()` and `IF()` to make it easy to make multiple decisions. The syntax of `ELSE.IF()` is as follows:

```
ELSE.IF(logical_test)
```

Here is the basic structure of a block `IF` that includes this function:

`=IF(`***`logical_test1`***`)`

(Expressions to run if ***`logical_test1`*** is true)

`=ELSE.IF(`***`logical_test2`***`)`

(Expressions to run if ***`logical_test2`*** is true)

`=ELSE()`

(Expressions to run if all tests are false)

`=END.IF()`

As you can see, you keep adding `ELSE.IF()` functions for each new decision you want to make. For example, suppose you want to write a function that converts a raw score into a letter grade according to the following table:

Raw Score	*Letter Grade*
Less than 50	F
Between 50 and 59	D
Between 60 and 69	C
Between 70 and 79	B
80 and over	A

Figure 42.4 shows the LetterGrade macro, which uses a block `IF` with several `ELSE.IF()` functions to make the conversion.

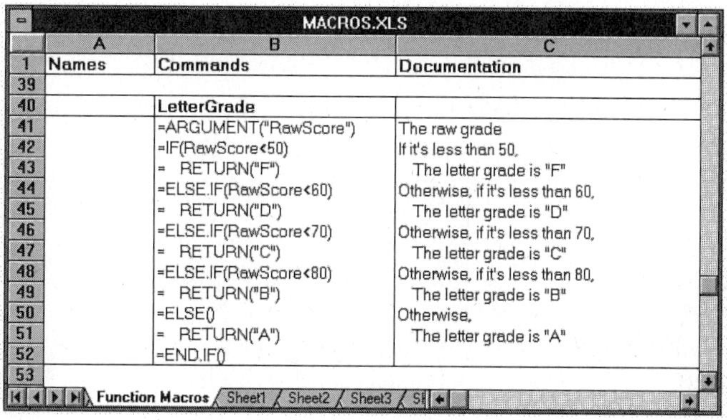

FIGURE 42.4.
A macro that makes multiple decisions using a block `IF` *with a number of* `ELSE.IF()` *functions.*

MACROS.XLS

	A	B	C
1	Names	Commands	Documentation
39			
40		LetterGrade	
41		=ARGUMENT("RawScore")	The raw grade
42		=IF(RawScore<50)	If it's less than 50,
43		= RETURN("F")	The letter grade is "F"
44		=ELSE.IF(RawScore<60)	Otherwise, if it's less than 60,
45		= RETURN("D")	The letter grade is "D"
46		=ELSE.IF(RawScore<70)	Otherwise, if it's less than 70,
47		= RETURN("C")	The letter grade is "C"
48		=ELSE.IF(RawScore<80)	Otherwise, if it's less than 80,
49		= RETURN("B")	The letter grade is "B"
50		=ELSE()	Otherwise,
51		= RETURN("A")	The letter grade is "A"
52		=END.IF()	
53			

Function Macros / Sheet1 / Sheet2 / Sheet3 / Sł

Macros That Loop

If your macro needs to repeat a section of code, you can set up a loop that tells Excel how many times to run through the code. The next few sections look at Excel's three different loop types.

Using *FOR()* Loops

The most common type of loop is the `FOR()` loop (also called the `FOR-NEXT` loop). Use this loop when you know exactly how many times you want to repeat a group of formulas. The structure of a `FOR()` loop is similar to the following:

=FOR(***counter_text***,***start_num***,***end_num***,*step_num*)

(Statements to be repeated go here.)

=NEXT()

counter_text	A text string that defines the name of the loop counter. The loop counter is a number that counts how many times the macro has gone through the loop.
start_num	A value that tells the macro what value the loop counter starts with. (This usually is 1, but you can enter any value.)
end_num	A value that tells the macro the last number the loop counter can have before exiting the loop.
step_num	A value that defines an increment for the loop counter. (If you leave this out, the default value is 1.)

When Excel encounters the `FOR()` function, it follows this five-step process:

1. It sets ***counter_text*** equal to ***start_num***.
2. It tests ***counter_text*** to see whether it's greater than ***end_num***. If so, Excel exits the loop (that is, it processes the first statement after the `NEXT()` function). Otherwise, it continues.
3. It processes each statement between the `FOR()` and `NEXT()` functions.
4. It adds ***step_num*** to ***counter_text***. (It adds 1 to ***counter_text*** if ***step_num*** is not specified.)
5. It repeats steps 2-4 until it's done.

Figure 42.5 shows a simple command macro (LoopTest) that uses a `FOR()` loop. Each time the macro goes through the loop, it invokes the `MESSAGE()` function to display the value of `Counter` (the loop counter) in the status bar. (To learn more about the `MESSAGE()` function, see Chapter 43, "Using Macros to Get and Display Information.") When you run the LoopTest macro, `Counter` gets incremented by one each time it goes through the loop. Also, the new value gets displayed in the status bar.

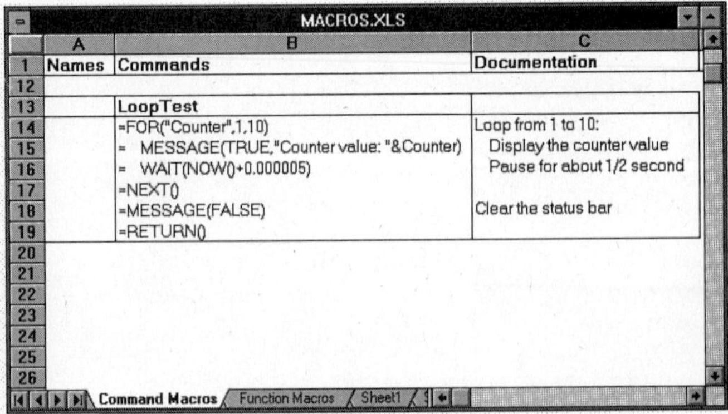

FIGURE 42.5.
A simple FOR() loop.

SUPER NOTE

The LoopTest macro also uses the WAIT(***serial_text***) function to slow things down a bit. The ***serial_text*** argument is the time serial number (enclosed in quotes) that you want Excel to wait until before resuming processing. LoopTest uses the argument NOW() + 0.000005 to pause the macro for about half a second.

Following are some notes on FOR() loops:

- The loop counter doesn't always have to be incremented. By using a negative value for step_num, you can start at a higher number and work down to a lower value.
- As with block IFs, indent the statements inside a FOR() loop for increased readability.
- To keep the number of names defined on a macro sheet to a minimum, always try to use the same name for all your FOR() loop counters. The letters i through n are traditionally used for counters in programming. For greater clarity, names such as Counter are best. The only time you need to be careful is when a FOR() loop statement calls another macro that has its own FOR() loop. If the two loops use the same name for the counter, the results probably won't be what you intended.
- If you need to break out of a FOR() loop before the defined number of repetitions are completed, use the BREAK() function, described in the section titled "Using BREAK() to Exit a Loop."

Using *FOR.CELL()* Loops

A useful variation of the FOR() loop is the FOR.CELL() loop that operates on each cell in a range. You don't need a loop counter, because Excel loops through the individual cells in the range and performs whatever operations are inside the loop on each cell. Following is the structure of the basic FOR.CELL() loop:

=FOR.CELL(***cell_name***,*range_ref*,*skip_blanks*)

(Statements to be performed on each cell go here.)

=NEXT()

cell_name	A defined name that Excel uses to represent the reference for each cell in the range.
range_ref	A reference to the range of cells through which FOR.CELL() will loop. If you leave this out, Excel will use the current selection.

skip_blanks	A logical value that determines whether or not `FOR.CELL()` skips blanks. Set *skip_blanks* to `TRUE` (or omit it) to make `FOR.CELL()` skip blanks. To include blanks, use `FALSE`.

For example, you can create a command macro that converts a range of text into proper case (that is, with the first letter of each word capitalized). This is a useful function if you import mainframe data into your worksheets, because mainframe records usually are displayed entirely in uppercase. This macro uses the following three steps:

1. Loop through the selected cells with `FOR.CELL()`.
2. Convert each cell's text to proper case. Use the `PROPER()` function to handle this:

   `PROPER(`***`text`***`)`

   text is the text to convert to proper case.
3. Enter the converted text into the selected cell. This is the job of the `FORMULA()` function:

   `FORMULA(`***`formula`***`,`*`reference`*`)`

   formula is the value or formula you want to enter. *reference* specifies where you want the formula entered. (If you omit *reference*, Excel enters *formula* in the active cell.)

Figure 42.6 shows the resulting macro, ConvertToProper.

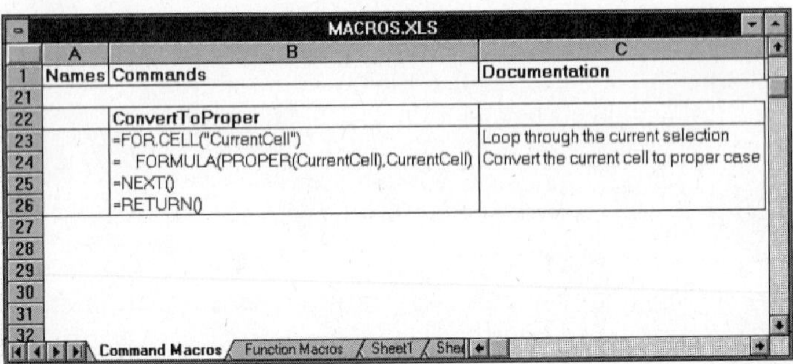

FIGURE 42.6.
This command macro uses FOR.CELL() to loop through a selection and convert each cell to proper text.

Using *WHILE()* Loops

What do you do if you need to loop, but you don't know in advance how many times to repeat the loop? This could happen, for example, if you want to loop only until a certain condition is met (such as encountering a blank cell). The solution is to use the third type of loop: the `WHILE()` (or `WHILE-NEXT`) loop.

Following is the basic structure of a `WHILE()` loop:

```
=WHILE(logical_test)
```

(Statements to be repeated go here.)

```
=NEXT()
```

As long as ***logical_test*** returns `TRUE`, Excel repeats the loop. As soon as ***logical_test*** changes to `FALSE`, the loop ends.

Figure 42.7 shows a macro called BoldText that runs down a worksheet column and, whenever a cell contains text, adds bold formatting to the cell. The idea is to loop until the macro encounters a blank cell. This is controlled by the following `WHILE()` function:

```
=WHILE(NOT(ISBLANK(ACTIVE.CELL())))
```

The `ACTIVE.CELL()` function returns the reference for the active cell. The `ISBLANK()` function checks the active cell to see whether it's blank. Entering `ISBLANK(ACTIVE.CELL())` inside the `NOT()` function tells the macro to continue looping while the active cell is not blank. Then, an `IF()` function uses `ISTEXT()` to check whether the active cell contains a text value. If the cell does contain text, the `FORMAT.FONT(,,TRUE)` formula adds bold formatting. The `SELECT("R[1]C")` function moves down one row, and the whole thing repeats. (For details on the `SELECT()` function, see Chapter 44, "Macro Worksheet Skills.")

MACROS.XLS

	A	B	C
1	Names	Commands	Documentation
28			
29		BoldText	
30		=WHILE(NOT(ISBLANK(ACTIVE.CELL())))	Loop while the active cell is not blank
31		= IF(ISTEXT(ACTIVE.CELL()))	If the active cell is text
32		= FORMAT.FONT(,,TRUE)	Set the bold attribute
33		= END.IF()	
34		= SELECT("R[1]C")	Move down one row
35		=NEXT()	
36		=RETURN()	
37			
38			
39			

Command Macros / Function Macros / Sheet1 / She

FIGURE 42.7.
A macro that uses a `WHILE()` loop to process cells until it encounters a blank cell.

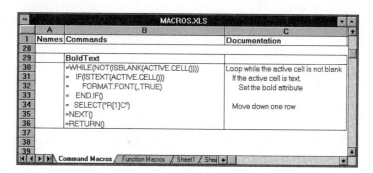

Using *BREAK()* to Exit a Loop

Most loops run their natural course, and then the macro moves on. However, there might be times that you want to prematurely exit a loop—times, for example, that you find a certain type of cell, an error, or when the user has entered an unexpected value. To exit the loop, include a `BREAK()` function. (Usually, you also need an `IF()` function to test for the exit condition.)

Figure 42.8 shows a revised version of the previous macro (BoldText2) that exits the `WHILE()` loop when it encounters a cell that doesn't contain text.

FIGURE 42.8.
In the BoldText2 macro, the `BREAK()` function terminates the `WHILE()` loop if the active cell contains text.

MACROS.XLS

	A	B	C
1	Names	Commands	Documentation
37			
38		BoldText2	
39		=WHILE(NOT(ISBLANK(ACTIVE.CELL())))	Loop while the active cell is not blank
40		= IF(ISTEXT(ACTIVE.CELL()))	If the active cell is text,
41		= FORMAT.FONT(,,TRUE)	Set the bold attribute
42		= ELSE()	Otherwise,
43		= BREAK()	Exit the WHILE() loop
44		= END.IF()	
45		= SELECT("R[1]C")	Move down one row
46		=NEXT()	
47		=RETURN()	
48			

Command Macros / Function Macros / Sheet1 / She

Using Subroutine Macros

As you work with macros, you'll find that certain tasks keep cropping up regularly. For example, if you import a lot of mainframe data into your worksheets, you may be constantly using the code from the ConvertToProper macro, discussed earlier. However, adding code from frequently used macros to your new macros creates large programs. You should be using *subroutine macros* to streamline your work.

A subroutine is a separate macro that gets invoked from within the main macro. Control is passed over to the subroutine, and the subroutine's macro formulas are then executed. When Excel processes the subroutine's `RETURN()` function, control is passed back to the main macro, and this macro resumes executing. There are many advantages to using subroutines in this way:

- Your main macro remains uncluttered and easy to read. As long as you give the subroutine a descriptive name, the reader will know what is happening in the macro.
- A well-written subroutine will be set up to accomplish only a single, specific task. Keeping subroutines simple and focused makes figuring out what they do and debugging them easier.
- Once you have a subroutine working perfectly, you can confidently use it in your other macros. You don't have to reinvent the wheel each time.

You create subroutine macros just like you create any other macro. After you define a macro's name, you can invoke the subroutine from the main program the same way you would a regular Excel function. For example, to run the ConvertToProper macro as a subroutine, you would just include the following formula in a macro:

```
=ConvertToProper()
```

If the macro exists in a different workbook, precede the name with the name of the workbook and an exclamation point:

```
=MACROS.XLS!ConvertToProper()
```

Of course, if the subroutine takes arguments, you need to include them as well.

Chapter

43

Using Macros to Get and Display Information

Most macros have an essentially antisocial nature. They do their jobs quietly in the background without much fuss or fanfare. Other macros, however, are more gregarious; they tell you things, ask you questions, and even listen to your answers. This chapter presents the macro functions that enable you to display information and get input from the user.

Displaying Information to the User

One of the cardinal rules in successful macro design (indeed, in all of programming) is to keep the user involved. If an operation is going to take a long time, let the user know and keep him or her informed of its progress. If they make an error (for example, by entering the wrong argument in a function macro), they need to be gently admonished so they'll be less likely to do it again.

Excel has four functions that display information in one form or another: `BEEP()`, `SOUND.PLAY()`, `MESSAGE()`, and `ALERT()`.

> **SUPER NOTE**
>
> You can display information also by setting up your own custom dialog boxes. See Chapter 47, "Creating Custom Dialog Boxes," for details.

Beeping the Speaker

Excel's most basic form of communication is the simple, attention-getting beep. It's Excel's way of saying "Ahem!" or "Excuse me!," and it's handled, appropriately enough, by the `BEEP()` function.

`BEEP(`*`tone_num`*`)`

`tone_num` is a number between 1 and 4 that specifies the sound you want to hear. (To hear different sounds, you need to have a sound driver installed on your system.) Without *`tone_num`*, `BEEP()` simply reproduces the usual sound that you hear on your system when, for example, you try to close a file without saving it.

If you have a sound board, you can use `BEEP()` to produce up to five different sounds, depending on what you use for *`tone_num`*. Table 43.1 lists the various values you can use with the `BEEP()` function and the corresponding system sounds they produce.

Table 43.1. System sounds generated by the BEEP() function.

tone_num	*System Sound*
None	Default beep
1	Critical stop
2	Question
3	Exclamation
4	Asterisk

SUPER CAUTION

Avoid overusing the BEEP() function. The idea is to get the user's attention, and constant beeping will only defeat that purpose. Besides, most users quickly become annoyed at any program that barks at them incessantly. Signaling errors and the ends of long operations are good uses for the BEEP() function.

Using Other Sounds

The BEEP() function is useful, but it's primitive, to say the least. If you have the necessary hardware, you can get your macros to play much more sophisticated sounds and even your own recorded voice.

Adding a Sound to a Cell Note

It all begins with the SOUND.NOTE() function, which has two syntaxes. The first form enables you to import a sound from a sound file into a cell note:

```
SOUND.NOTE(cell_ref,file_text)
```

`cell_ref`	A reference to the cell that will receive the sound. If you omit *cell_ref*, Excel enters the note into the active cell.
`file_text`	The name of the file containing the sound. If you don't include this argument, Excel uses the active worksheet.

For example, the following function imports a sound file called DOGBARK.WAV into the active cell:

```
=SOUND.NOTE(,"C:\SOUNDS\DOGBARK.WAV")
```

The second form of the `SOUND.NOTE()` function enables you to record or erase sounds in a cell note:

```
SOUND.NOTE(cell_ref,erase_sound)
```

cell_ref A reference to the cell where the sound will be recorded or erased. Excel uses the active cell if you omit *cell_ref*.

erase_sound A logical value that determines whether you're recording or erasing a sound note. Set it to `TRUE` if you want to erase the sound note; set it to `FALSE` (or omit it) to record a sound note.

SUPER NOTE

To record sound notes, you must have the appropriate hardware installed and you must have Windows 3.1 (or Windows 3.0 with at least version 1.0 of the Multimedia Extensions).

If you use the `SOUND.NOTE()` function to record a sound, you'll see the Record dialog box, shown in Figure 43.1, when you run the macro. Just choose **R**ecord, record your note, choose **S**top when you're done, and then click on OK.

FIGURE 43.1. *If you have the necessary hardware, you can use the Record dialog box to record messages in a sound note.*

Playing a Sound

Once you have inserted a sound note, you can use the `SOUND.PLAY()` function to play it (assuming, as usual, that the user's computer has the appropriate hardware):

```
SOUND.PLAY(cell_ref,file_text)
```

cell_ref A reference to the cell that contains the sound. Excel uses the active cell if you omit *cell_ref*.

file_text The name of a file containing the sound you want to play. If you include *cell_ref*, Excel ignores *file_text*.

For example, the following function plays a message recorded in a cell named ErrorMessage in the active worksheet:

```
=SOUND.PLAY(!ErrorMessage)
```

SUPER NOTE

Prefacing a cell reference or range name with an exclamation mark tells Excel that the reference applies to the active worksheet. See Chapter 44, "Macro Worksheet Skills," for more information.

Instead of adding sounds to cell notes, you can play them right from a file. The following function plays the TADA.WAV file:

```
=SOUND.PLAY(,"C:\WINDOWS\TADA.WAV")
```

Adding Sound Checks to Your Macros

As you've seen, using sounds in your macros requires special hardware and software. A well-written macro should verify that a computer is capable of playing or recording sounds before trying to use them. You do this by using the `GET.WORKSPACE()` function, which has the following syntax:

GET.WORKSPACE(**type_num**)

type_num tells Excel what type of workspace information you need. Your Excel manual lists the dozens of available values, but Table 43.2 shows the two that serve our purpose here.

Table 43.2. Values for `type_num` that return system sound information.

type_num	*Returns*
42	`TRUE` if the system is capable of playing sounds and `FALSE` otherwise
43	`TRUE` if the system is capable of recording sounds and `FALSE` otherwise

When adding sounds to a cell note, you should always check that no sound note already exists. If one does exist and you try to add another, your macro will crash. Figure 43.2 shows a macro that uses the `GET.CELL(47)` function to first check for the existence of a sound note in the active cell. If one exists, the macro uses `SOUND.NOTE()` to erase it before proceeding.

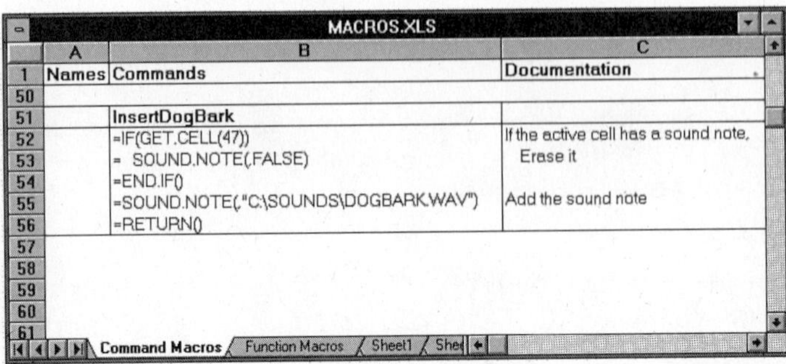

MACROS.XLS
Names
Commands
Documentation
InsertDogBark
=IF(GET.CELL(47))
= SOUND.NOTE(,FALSE)
=END.IF()
=SOUND.NOTE(,"C:\SOUNDS\DOGBARK.WAV")
=RETURN()
If the active cell has a sound note,
Erase it
Add the sound note
Command Macros
Function Macros
Sheet1

FIGURE 43.2.
This macro checks for a sound note before adding one.

Displaying a Message in the Status Bar

The `MESSAGE()` function displays text messages on the left side of the status bar at the bottom of the screen. This provides you with an easy way to keep the user informed about what the macro is doing or how much there is left to process.

Here's the syntax for this function:

`MESSAGE(`***`logical`***`,`*`message_text`*`)`

`logical`	A logical value that controls the message displayed in the status bar. Use `TRUE` to display the message given by *`message_text`*. To remove a message and return control of the status bar back to Excel, set ***`logical`*** to `FALSE`.
`message_text`	The message you want to display.

As an example of the `MESSAGE()` function, Figure 43.3 shows a revised version of the ConvertToProper macro (called ConvertToProper2). The idea here is to display a message of the form "Converting cell *x* of *y*" where *x* is the number of cells converted so far and *y* is the total number of cells to be converted.

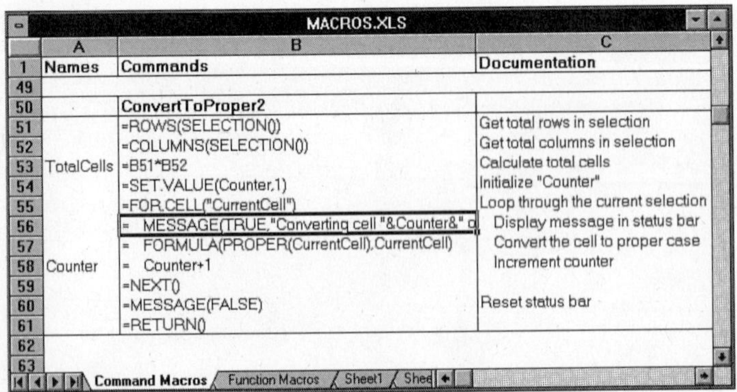

MACROS.XLS
Names
Commands
Documentation
ConvertToProper2
=ROWS(SELECTION())
=COLUMNS(SELECTION())
TotalCells
=B51*B52
=SET.VALUE(Counter,1)
=FOR.CELL("CurrentCell")
= MESSAGE(TRUE,"Converting cell "&Counter&" o
= FORMULA(PROPER(CurrentCell),CurrentCell)
Counter
= Counter+1
=NEXT()
=MESSAGE(FALSE)
=RETURN()
Get total rows in selection
Get total columns in selection
Calculate total cells
Initialize "Counter"
Loop through the current selection
Display message in status bar
Convert the cell to proper case
Increment counter
Reset status bar
Command Macros
Function Macros
Sheet1

FIGURE 43.3.
A macro that uses MESSAGE() to inform the user of the progress of the operation.

The first two lines use the `ROWS()` and `COLUMNS()` functions to return the total number of rows and columns in the current selection. The third line (cell B53) just multiplies these numbers to get the total number of cells in the selection (cell B53 is named TotalCells). The final bit of preparation requires the `SET.VALUE()` function (which I discuss in detail in Chapter 44, "Macro Worksheet Skills") to initialize a counter variable (named `Counter`).

In the `FOR.CELL()` loop, the `MESSAGE()` function displays the progress of the operation. (Note the use of the concatenation operator (`&`) to combine text and values.) Then, before looping, the `Counter` variable gets incremented.

SUPER NOTE

The ConvertToProper2 macro uses range names in the macro itself (`TotalCells` and `Counter`). I describe this handy technique in more depth in Chapter 44.

SUPER NOTE

You can use the `MESSAGE()` function when debugging your macros. See Chapter 48, "Debugging Macros," for more information.

Displaying an Alert Dialog Box

The problem with the `MESSAGE()` display is that it's often a bit too subtle. Unless users know to look down at the status bar, they might miss your messages altogether. For those times when users must see a message, you can use the `ALERT()` function to display an Alert dialog box.

Here is the syntax for the `ALERT()` function:

```
ALERT(message_text,type_num,help_ref)
```

message_text	The message you want to display in the dialog box.
type_num	Specifies which of the three dialog box types you want to use (see Table 43.3).
help_ref	A reference to a custom help topic. If you include *help_ref*, a **H**elp button appears in the dialog box.

SUPER NOTE

See Chapter 49, "Macro Tips and Techniques," to learn how to set up your own custom help topics.

Table 43.3 explains each type of Alert dialog box and shows an example for each.

Table 43.3. Excel's Alert dialog box types.

`type_num`	*Description*	*Example*
1	Displays a question mark icon and OK and Cancel buttons. Use this Alert when you want the user to make a choice about whether or not to proceed with an action.	Microsoft Excel A type 1 Alert box. OK Cancel
2	Displays an information icon and an OK button. Use this Alert to display important information to the user.	Microsoft Excel A type 2 Alert box. OK
3	Displays an exclamation icon and an OK button. Use this Alert to display errors or warnings.	Microsoft Excel A type 3 Alert box. OK

SUPER TIP

For long alert messages, Excel automatically wraps the text inside the dialog box. If you want to create your own line breaks, use the carriage-return character (ASCII 13) between each line:

```
=ALERT("First line."&CHAR(13)&"Second line.",1)
```

Type 2 and 3 Alert dialog boxes are straightforward. They simply display information to the user, who must then click on OK before the macro will resume.

Type 1 Alert dialog boxes are a little different. In this case, users have a choice between OK and Cancel, which gives them some control over the progress of the macro.

If they click on OK, the `ALERT()` function returns `TRUE`; if they click on Cancel, `ALERT()` returns `FALSE`. This means that you can use an `IF()` function to test the user's choice and branch accordingly. The following macro fragment asks users whether they would like to see a preview before printing a document:

```
Preview=ALERT("Preview print job?",1)
=IF(Preview)
=     PRINT.PREVIEW()
=END.IF()
```

Getting Input from the User

As you've seen, a type 1 Alert dialog box enables your macros to interact with the user and get some feedback. Unfortunately, this method limits you to simple yes/no answers. For more varied user input, you need to use more sophisticated techniques.

Prompting the User for Input

The most common way to get input from the user is through the `INPUT()` function. This function displays a dialog box with a message that prompts the user to enter data, and it provides an edit box for the data itself. The syntax for this function is

`INPUT(`**`message_text`**`,`*`type_num`*`,`*`title_text`*`,`*`default`*`,`*`x_pos`*`,`*`y_pos`*`,`*`help_ref`*`)`

message_text The prompt text that appears in the dialog box.

type_num A number that specifies the type of data to be entered. You can use any of the following values (if omitted, `INPUT()` assumes a value of 2):

type_num	*Data Type*
0	Formula
1	Number
2	Text
4	Logical
8	Reference
16	Error
64	Array

title_text The title of the dialog box. If you omit this argument, Excel uses the title "Input."

default Specifies the default value shown in the edit box.

x_pos,y_pos Specifies the horizontal and vertical positions of the upper left corner of the dialog box. The values are measured in *points;* there are 72 points in an inch. If you omit these values, Excel centers the dialog box.

help_ref A reference to a custom help topic. See Chapter 49, "Macro Tips and Techniques," for details.

In addition, the dialog box has OK and Cancel buttons. If users click on OK, `INPUT()` returns the value entered into the edit box; if they click on Cancel, `INPUT()` returns the logical value `FALSE`.

As an example of the `INPUT()` function, Figure 43.4 shows a macro that starts a command macro.

FIGURE 43.4.
A macro to start a command macro.

MACROS.XLS

	A	B	C
1	Names	Commands	Documentation
75			
76		StartCommandMacro	
77	MacroName	=INPUT("Enter the macro name:",2,"Macro Starter")	Get the name of the macro
78		=IF(NOT(MacroName),HALT())	If Cancel selected, quit
79		=FORMULA(MacroName)	Enter the name in the active cell
80		=DEFINE.NAME(MacroName,,2)	Define the macro name
81		=RETURN()	
82			
83			
84			
85			
86			

Command Macros / Function Macros / Sheet1 / Shee

The `INPUT()` function prompts for the name of the macro, which is stored in `MacroName`. Figure 43.5 shows the dialog box displayed by the `INPUT()` function. If users click on Cancel, `INPUT()` returns `FALSE`, the `IF()` test in cell B78 fails, and the macro runs a `HALT()` function to stop the macro. Otherwise, the macro enters the name in the appropriate cell (using the `FORMULA()` function) and then defines the name (using the `DEFINE.NAME()` function; see the Excel Function Reference for details).

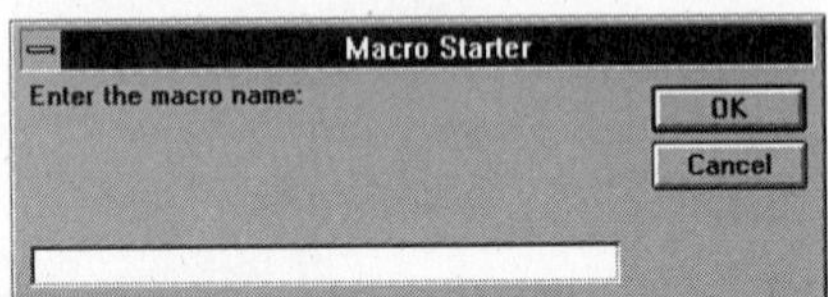

FIGURE 43.5.
The dialog box displayed by the `INPUT()` function.

SUPER NOTE

`HALT()` stops all running macros. This prevents the current macro from returning to the macro that called it. This precaution probably is not necessary in this case, but it's a good idea to get in the habit of running `HALT()` whenever the user clicks on Cancel.

SUPER TIP

You can easily modify this macro to create another that starts a function macro. Just change the `2` in the `DEFINE.NAME()` function to a `1`.

SUPER NOTE

You can create your own dialog boxes for more sophisticated data entry needs. See Chapter 47, "Creating Custom Dialog Boxes," to learn how it's done.

Accessing Excel's Standard Dialog Boxes

Many macro functions are known as *dialog box equivalents* because they enable you to select the same options that are available in Excel's standard dialog boxes. This works fine if your macro knows which options to select, but this isn't always the case.

For example, if your macro prints a document (using the `PRINT()` function), you might need to know how many copies the user wants or how many pages to print. You could use `INPUT()` functions to get this data, but it's usually easier just to display the Print dialog box. All you have to do is add a question mark after the function name. For the Print dialog box, you would use the following formula:

```
=PRINT?()
```

If you know *some* of the data beforehand, you can still fill in the appropriate function arguments. This data then appears in the dialog box as the defaults. For example, when you display the Open dialog box, Excel enters `*.XL?` as the default file specification. If you want to open non-Excel files, you have to change the file specification or select a different item from the List Files of **T**ype box. To avoid this, you can specify a different file type when you invoke the Open dialog box. For example, to display files with a .TXT extension, you would use the following formula:

```
=OPEN?("*.TXT")
```

Chapter

44

Macro Worksheet Skills

Most command macros eventually do *something* to a worksheet. It might be selecting a cell or a range, entering a formula, or even copying and moving data. Knowing how a macro interacts with a worksheet is crucial if you ever hope to write useful routines. This chapter looks closely at that interaction. First, I show you how macros use references, and then I show you basic tasks such as selecting ranges, cutting and copying data, and getting cell information.

Working with References

Mastering cell and range references is perhaps the most fundamental of all spreadsheet skills because most worksheet chores involve cells, ranges, and range names. However, this skill takes on added importance when you work with macros. On a worksheet, for example, you can select cells and ranges easily with the mouse or keyboard, or you can paste range names into formulas. In a macro, though, you are, in a sense, flying blind. Because most macros operate on some *other* sheet (that is, a sheet other than the one on which the macro resides), you usually end up having to describe—or even calculate—the range you want to work with.

This, unfortunately, tends to add a layer of complexity to macro references, which can sometimes leave even experienced macro jockeys shaking their heads. The good news is that you really only have to learn a few fundamental concepts (and use them often) to get comfortable. The next few sections tell you everything you need to know.

Understanding A1 Versus R1C1 References

Perhaps the biggest source of confusion in macro references is Excel's use of the so-called *R1C1* reference style. The normal A1 style that you're used to numbers a worksheet's rows from 1 to 16384 and assigns the letters A through IV to the worksheet's 256 columns. In R1C1 style, though, Excel numbers both the rows and the columns. In general, the notation R*x*C*y* refers to the cell at row *x* and column *y*. Here are some examples:

A1 Style	*R1C1 Style*
$A$1	R1C1
$D$8	R8C4
$B$4:$E$10	R4C2:R10C5
$B:$B	C2 (that is, column B)
$3:$3	R3 (that is, row 3)

As you can see, these are all absolute references. To use relative references in R1C1 notation, enclose the numbers in square brackets. For example, R[2]C[2] refers to the cell two rows down and two columns to the right of the active cell. Similarly, R[-1]C[-3] refers to the cell one row above the active cell and three columns to the left. Here are a few more examples of relative references:

Relative Reference	*Description*
R[1]C[-1]	One row down and one column left
R[-5]C[3]	Five rows up and three columns right
R[2]C	Two rows down, same column
RC[-1]	Same row, one column left
R	The current row
C	The current column

Should You Use A1 or R1C1 Notation?

The reference style you use in your macros depends on the context. If a formula or function requires a *true* reference (that is, a cell or range address), then you can use either A1 or R1C1 notation. Note, though, that using R1C1 for true references requires changing Excel's workspace options. (See the next section).

Some functions, however, require arguments to be *text* references (that is, a reference in the form of a text string). In this case, you have to use R1C1 notation and enclose the reference in quotation marks (for example, `"R[1]C[2]"`.)

You're left, then, with two choices:

- If you want to maintain a consistent notation throughout your macros, use the R1C1 style for true references.
- If the users of your macros might not be familiar with R1C1 notation, then you should stick to A1 style for true references (especially if the user will be selecting ranges).

Switching Excel to R1C1 Notation

If you decide to use R1C1 notation, you need to change your workspace setup to switch true references from the default A1 style to the R1C1 style. Follow the steps in Procedure 44.1.

PROCEDURE 44.1. SWITCHING TO R1C1 NOTATION.

1. Select the **T**ools | **O**ptions command and select the General tab in the Options dialog box.
2. Activate the R1**C**1 check box.
3. Click on OK or press Enter. Excel returns you to the worksheet and converts all the A1 notation in your formulas to the R1C1 style.

Referencing Worksheets

One of the crucial questions to keep asking yourself when building your command macros is, "What sheet do I want this formula to affect?" When answering this question, you have three choices:

- The macro sheet. This is called a *local reference.*
- The active sheet. This is an *active reference.*
- A specific sheet. This is an *external reference.*

The next three sections present each type of reference in more detail.

Using Local References

Local references are straightforward. Because they refer to the sheet on which the macro formula resides, you simply use the appropriate cell or range address in either A1 or R1C1 style. For example, Figure 44.1 shows the ConvertToProper2 macro. To calculate the `TotalCells` variable, cell B53 multiplies the values for the rows (cell B51) and columns (cell B52) in the selection:

```
=B51*B52
```

MACROS.XLS

	A	B	C
1	Names	Commands	Documentation
49			
50		ConvertToProper2	
51		=ROWS(SELECTION())	Get total rows in selection
52		=COLUMNS(SELECTION())	Get total columns in selection
53	TotalCells	=B51*B52	Calculate total cells
54		=SET.VALUE(Counter,1)	Initialize "Counter"
55		=FOR.CELL("CurrentCell")	Loop through the current selection
56		= MESSAGE(TRUE,"Converting cell "&Counter&" o	Display message in status bar
57		= FORMULA(PROPER(CurrentCell),CurrentCell)	Convert the cell to proper case
58	Counter	= Counter+1	Increment counter
59		=NEXT()	
60		=MESSAGE(FALSE)	Reset status bar
61		=RETURN()	
62			

Command Macros / Function Macros / Sheet1 / She

FIGURE 44.1.
For local references, just use the cell or range address.

SUPER CAUTION

You should always use relative references in macros. This way, if you alter the macro by adding or deleting lines, your existing formulas will adjust accordingly.

Using Active References

Two methods are available for referencing a cell or range on the active worksheet. The method you use depends on whether you need a true reference or a text reference.

For a true reference, simply enter an exclamation point followed by an absolute address in either A1 or R1C1 style. (Remember, though, that to use R1C1 notation for true references you need to set up your workspace to handle them, as described in the section earlier in this chapter titled "Switching Excel to R1C1 Notation.") For example, the following function enters the label Expenses into cell C3 of the active worksheet:

```
=FORMULA("Expenses",!$C$3)
```

Notice that I said you must use an *absolute* address when entering a true reference. The problem with relative addresses is that, contrary to what you might expect, Excel doesn't assume the reference is relative to the active cell. Instead, it assumes the reference is relative *to the cell that contains the formula on the macro sheet.* This can lead to two types of problems. For example, suppose you're using A1 notation and you enter the following formula in cell B10 of the macro sheet:

```
=FORMULA("Expenses",!C3)
```

This will work, but if you subsequently delete a line from the macro, the formula changes to the following:

```
=FORMULA("Expenses",!C2)
```

The second type of problem occurs when you're using R1C1 notation. Suppose you enter the following formula in cell R10C2:

```
=FORMULA("Expenses",!R[-1]C)
```

Theoretically, you're trying to enter the label `Expenses` in the cell above the active cell. However, Excel interprets the relative address `R[-1]C` to mean R9C2 (the cell above the one containing the formula), so it enters the label in cell R9C2 of the active worksheet (no matter which cell is active).

If you need to enter a text reference to a cell on the active worksheet, just enter the reference in R1C1 style enclosed in quotation marks. (You don't have to change the workspace options for text references.) The following formula enters the Expenses label in row 3, column 3:

```
=FORMULA("Expenses","R3C3")
```

Unlike true references, you *can* use relative addresses with text references. For example, the following formula adds the Expenses label to the cell one row above the active cell:

```
=FORMULA("Expenses","R[-1]C")
```

SUPER NOTE

Why is there a difference between how Excel sees a true relative reference and a text relative reference? The reason has to do with when Excel calculates the reference. A true relative reference is calculated as soon as you enter the formula (so it's interpreted relative to the formula's cell). A text relative reference, on the other hand, is calculated only when you run the macro (so it's interpreted relative to the active cell).

One of the handiest functions in the Excel 4.0 macro language is the `ACTIVE.CELL()` function. This function simply returns a reference to the active cell (including the sheet name and workbook filename, if necessary). For example, to find out the row number of the active cell, you would use the following formula:

```
=ROW(ACTIVE.CELL())
```

Using External References

To reference a cell or range on a sheet other than the active sheet, enter the name of the sheet, an exclamation point, and the absolute address in either A1 or R1C1 style. If the sheet name uses two or more words, enclose the name in single quotation marks. For example, the following formula enters an Expenses label in cell C3 on a sheet named August Expenses:

```
=FORMULA("Expenses",'August Expenses'!$C$3)
```

If the sheet resides in a different workbook, precede the sheet name with the workbook filename (including the extension and the drive and directory, if necessary) in square brackets:

```
=FORMULA("Expenses",'[BUDGET.XLS]August Expenses'!$C$3)
```

For a text reference, enter the sheet name, an exclamation point, and the absolute cell address in R1C1 style, and surround everything with quotation marks:

```
=FORMULA("Expenses","'August Expenses'!R3C3")
```

As with referencing the active worksheet, relative references to an external worksheet are dangerous. If you use a true relative reference, the reference is calculated relative to the formula's cell on the macro sheet. For example, if you enter the following formula in cell R10C2 on the macro sheet, it will always enter the label in cell R9C2 of August Expenses:

```
=FORMULA("Expenses",'August Expenses'!R[-1]C)
```

If you use a text relative reference, Excel calculates the reference relative to the *active cell* (which could be on any sheet). For example, if the active cell is R5C5, the following formula enters Expenses in cell R6C6 of August Expenses (this assumes that August Expenses is not the active worksheet):

```
=FORMULA("Expenses","'August Expenses'!R[1]C[1]")
```

Calculating References with *OFFSET()*

In the preceding section, you saw that the only way to reference a relative address on the active worksheet was to use a text reference (and you also saw that you can never safely use relative addresses for external references). There are several disadvantages to this approach:

- Excel doesn't check the syntax of references enclosed in quotation marks.
- It's difficult to create relative text references from existing macro variables. (However, it's not impossible: you could just use the concatenation operator (&) to construct the appropriate string. The problem is that these statements are unintuitive and tough to decipher.)
- Only five functions accept text references—`ABSREF()`, `FORMULA()`, `INDIRECT()`, `SELECT()`, and `TEXTREF()`—and, of these, only `ABSREF()`, `FORMULA()`, and `SELECT()` accept relative text references.

The way to overcome these problems, and add tremendous flexibility to your macros in the process, is to *calculate* references using the `OFFSET()` function. With this method, you begin with a reference and then specify a certain number of rows and columns to indicate where the new reference should start.

Here is the syntax for this function:

`OFFSET(`***`reference`***`,`***`rows`***`,`***`cols`***`,`*`height`*`,`*`width`*`)`

`reference`	The original reference upon which the returned reference is based.
`rows`	The number of rows (up or down) from the top-left cell of ***`reference`*** to where the returned reference will start.
`cols`	The number of columns (left or right) from the top-left cell of ***`reference`*** to where the returned reference will start.
`height`	The number of rows in the returned reference.
`width`	The number of columns in the returned reference.

For example, the following `OFFSET()` function returns a reference to the cell that is one row above and two columns to the right of the active cell:

```
OFFSET(ACTIVE.CELL(),-1,2)
```

Figure 44.2 shows a simple macro that concatenates (combines) two text strings. This is handy, for instance, if you have a list with separate first-name and last-name fields and you want to combine them. As you can see in Sheet1, the active cell is C2, and the first-name and last-name fields are in columns A and B, respectively.

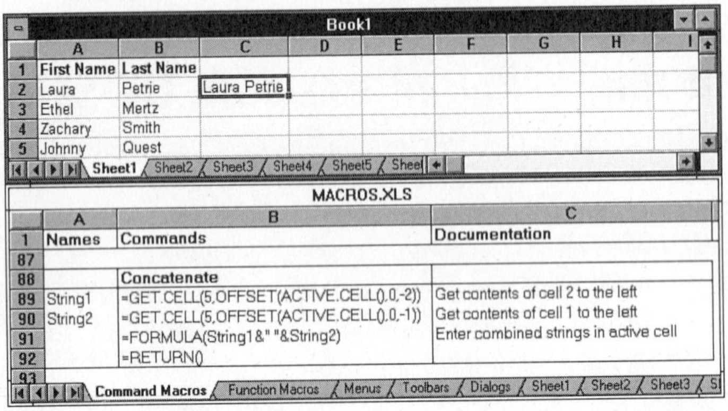

FIGURE 44.2.
A macro that concatenates two text strings.

The first `GET.CELL()` function (its name is *String1*) returns the contents of the cell two columns to the left of the active cell by using the following `OFFSET()` function:

```
OFFSET(ACTIVE.CELL(),0,-2)
```

Similarly, the second `GET.CELL()` function (*String2*) returns the contents of the cell one column to the left of the active cell. Finally, the `FORMULA()` function concatenates `String1` and `String2` (with a space in between) and enters the new string in the active cell.

Converting Between Text and True References

Your macros will often have to convert between text and true references. For example, suppose the active cell contains the string *Sales* and you want to store the active cell's address in cell C2. You know the `ACTIVE.CELL()` function returns a reference to the active cell, so your first guess might be to use the following formula in a macro:

```
=FORMULA(ACTIVE.CELL(),!$C$2)
```

When you run the macro, you get *Sales* in cell C2 instead of the reference you wanted. This happens because of an assumption that Excel makes. For functions that return references, Excel usually assumes you want to work with the contents of the referenced cell, instead of the reference itself. (The exception to this is when you use the function as an argument in another function that accepts a reference argument.) In this case, Excel stores the contents of the active cell (the string *Sales*) in cell C2.

To get around this, you have to convert the reference to text with the `REFTEXT()` function:

`REFTEXT(`***reference***`,`*a1*`)`

reference	The reference you want to convert.
a1	A logical value that determines whether `REFTEXT()` returns the text in A1 style (`TRUE`) or R1C1 style (`FALSE` or omitted).

To fix the previous problem, you would convert `ACTIVE.CELL()` to text:

```
=FORMULA(REFTEXT(ACTIVE.CELL(),TRUE),!$C$2)
```

One of the most common uses for `REFTEXT()` is to capture a reference entered with the `INPUT()` function. Again, without converting, `INPUT()` would store the contents of the reference. To capture the reference itself, you need to use `REFTEXT()`, as in the following example:

```
=REFTEXT(INPUT("Enter a reference",8))
```

To convert text references into true references, use the `TEXTREF()` function:

`TEXTREF(`***text***`,`*a1*`)`

text	The text reference you want to convert.
a1	A logical value that determines whether `TEXTREF()` returns the text in A1 style (`TRUE`) or R1C1 style (`FALSE` or omitted).

For example, the following macro fragment gets a range from the user and then selects the range (assuming that the first formula resides in cell B10):

```
=REFTEXT(INPUT("Enter a range",8))
=SELECT(TEXTREF(B10))
```

NOTE

I discuss the `SELECT()` function in the section later in this chapter titled "Using the `SELECT()` Function."

Working with Names in Macros

Using range names in your macros is generally straightforward. You can refer to names on the active worksheet (by preceding the name with an exclamation point (`!`); for example, `!Database`) or on an external worksheet (by preceding the name with the workbook filename, the sheet name, and an exclamation point; for example, `'[DATA.XLS]Customer Data'!Database`).

You also have access to six functions that are the macro equivalents of Excel's range commands: `DEFINE.NAME()`, `CREATE.NAMES()`, `LIST.NAMES()`, `DELETE.NAME()`, `GET.NAME()`, and `GET.DEF()`. I won't discuss these functions in detail here. (See Chapter 43, "Using Macros to Get and Display Information," for an example of the `DEFINE.NAME()` function. To learn more about the rest of the functions, see your Excel Function Reference.) There are, however, two other functions that you need to look at more closely: `SET.NAME()` and `SET.VALUE()`.

Defining Macro Sheet Names with *SET.NAME()*

Use the `SET.NAME()` function to define a name for a value on a macro sheet. Here is its syntax:

```
SET.NAME(name_text,value)
```

name_text	The name you want to define.
value	The value you want to store in ***name_text***. If you omit *value*, Excel deletes ***name_text***.

Figure 44.3 shows a revised version of the Concatenate macro (called Concatenate2) that uses `SET.NAME()`. In this macro, the `OFFSET()` functions in cells B101 and B102 need to access the active cell. Rather than running the `ACTIVE.CELL()` function each time, the macro uses the following formula to assign the name `Active` to the result of the `ACTIVE.CELL()` function:

```
=SET.NAME("Active",ACTIVE.CELL())
```

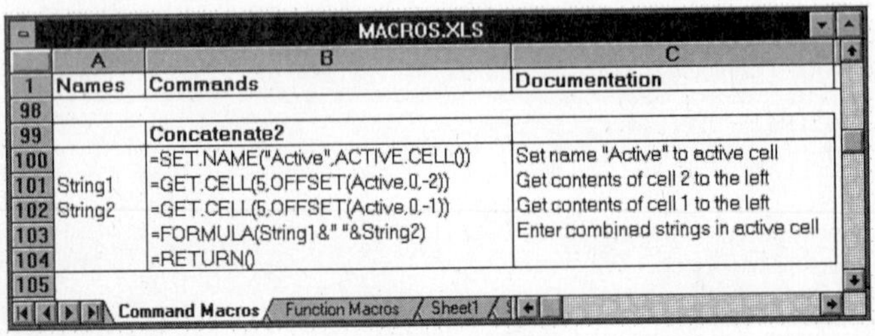

FIGURE 44.3.
Use SET.NAME() to assign a name to a frequently used value.

MACROS.XLS

	A	B	C
1	Names	Commands	Documentation
98			
99		Concatenate2	
100		=SET.NAME("Active",ACTIVE.CELL())	Set name "Active" to active cell
101	String1	=GET.CELL(5,OFFSET(Active,0,-2))	Get contents of cell 2 to the left
102	String2	=GET.CELL(5,OFFSET(Active,0,-1))	Get contents of cell 1 to the left
103		=FORMULA(String1&" "&String2)	Enter combined strings in active cell
104		=RETURN()	
105			

Command Macros / Function Macros / Sheet1

This means that any subsequent function that needs to refer to the active cell just uses the name Active. You gain two advantages with this method:

- Substituting shorter names for long-winded functions makes the macro less cluttered and easier to read.
- Because the macro has to run the function only once, it executes faster.

SUPER TIP

In addition to using the `SET.NAME()` function, you also can assign names to values using the following syntax:

name_text=*value*

This saves you from having to enter the name in a separate cell, and it often makes the macro code easier to read. For example, to assign the value 1 to the name Counter, just type `Counter = 1` in a cell. To increment Counter, you would type the formula `Counter = Counter + 1` in another cell.

SUPER NOTE

To avoid wasting memory, it's good practice to delete any range names in the macro sheet that are not used by any other macro. Use the `DELETE.NAME(`***name_text***`)` function, where ***name_text*** is the name you want to delete.

Storing Macro Sheet Values with *SET.VALUE()*

Instead of storing a value in a name, you may need to store it in a cell or range on the macro sheet. You can do this with the `SET.VALUE()` function:

`SET.VALUE(`***reference***`,`*value*`)`

reference	The cell (or range) on the macro sheet where you want to store the value.
value	The value you want to store.

Note that if ***reference*** contains a formula, the formula does *not* change; only the value of the cell changes. To see how this works, take a look at the macro in Figure 44.4.

The purpose of this macro is to enter numeric data in a column until the user clicks on Cancel in the `INPUT()` dialog box. The first `SET.VALUE()` function sets the value of the cell named *Done* (cell B114) to `FALSE`:

```
=SET.VALUE(Done,FALSE)
```

Although this cell contains the formula `=TRUE()`, setting `Done` to `FALSE` has no affect on the formula. (Remember: Excel doesn't evaluate macro formulas until it comes across them when you run the macro. This means that you're free to assign any value you

like to any cell.) The second `SET.VALUE()` function simply initializes a counter (the cell named *EntryRow*) that tracks which row the data goes in:

```
=SET.VALUE(EntryRow,0)
```

MACROS.XLS

	A	B	C
1	Names	Commands	Documentation
107			
108		DataEntry	
109		=SET.VALUE(Done,FALSE)	Initialize Done to FALSE
110		=SET.VALUE(EntryRow,0)	Initialize EntryRow to 0
111		=WHILE(NOT(Done))	Loop while Done is FALSE
112	InputValue	= INPUT("Enter a value",,"Data Entry")	Get the next value
113		= IF(InputValue=FALSE)	If the user selected Cancel,
114	Done	= TRUE()	Set Done to TRUE to exit loop
115		= ELSE()	Otherwise,
116		= FORMULA(InputValue,OFFSET(ACTIVE.CELL(	Enter the value
117	EntryRow	= EntryRow+1	Increment EntryRow
118		= END.IF()	
119		=NEXT()	
120		=RETURN()	
121			

Command Macros / Function Macros / Sheet1 / Shee

FIGURE 44.4.
`SET.VALUE()` initializes `Done` and `EntryRow` but doesn't alter their formulas.

Next, a `WHILE()` function loops as long as `Done` is `FALSE` (because you don't know in advance how much data the user will enter). As long as the user clicks on OK, the macro enters the data (the new cell is offset from the active cell by *EntryRow* rows) and increments the *EntryRow* counter. When the user clicks on Cancel, however, the `INPUT()` function returns `FALSE`, and *Done* is set to `TRUE`. This exits the loop on the next pass and you are, literally, done.

Selecting a Cell or Range

Selecting a cell or range is one of the most common worksheet tasks, so you need to be comfortable with the corresponding macro methods. The next two sections take you through the basics.

Using the *SELECT()* Function

The `SELECT()` function will handle most of your range selection needs. Here is its syntax:

```
SELECT(selection,active_cell)
```

`selection` — The cell or range you want to select on the active worksheet. If you use A1 notation, it must be an absolute reference as in `SELECT(!$B$3)`, for example. You can also use the R1C1 style as in, for example, `SELECT("R3C2")`. If you omit *`selection`*, the current selection is used.

active_cell	The cell in *selection* that you want to make the active cell. If you omit this argument, Excel makes the upper-left cell of *selection* the active cell. Again, you can use A1 (absolute) or R1C1 notation.

It's important to remember that SELECT() applies only to the active worksheet. If you try to use it with an external reference, Excel generates an error. If you need to select a range on an external worksheet, use the FORMULA.GOTO() function. (See the section later in this chapter titled "Selecting a Range with FORMULA.GOTO().")

SUPER NOTE

If you need to, you can make a worksheet active before using SELECT() by running the WORKBOOK.SELECT(*sheet_name*) function, where *sheet_name* is the name of a sheet in the active workbook (enclosed in quotation marks). To activate a different workbook, use the ACTIVATE(*window_text*) function, where *window_text* is the name of the open workbook you want to activate. (Technically, it's the name that appears in the window title bar.) You also can use ACTIVATE.PREV() to activate the previous workbook window and ACTIVATE.NEXT() to activate the next workbook window.

The most basic use of the SELECT() function is to simulate the keys you normally use to navigate through a worksheet. Table 44.1 lists some SELECT() functions and their key equivalents.

Table 44.1. Some SELECT() functions and their key equivalents.

SELECT() Function	*Key Equivalent*
SELECT("RC[1]")	Right arrow or Tab
SELECT("RC[-1]")	Left arrow or Shift+Tab
SELECT("R[1]C")	Down arrow
SELECT("R[-1]C")	Up arrow

If you want to select a range of cells, just enter the range coordinates in SELECT(). For example, the following formula selects the range A1:E10 in the active worksheet:

```
=SELECT(!$A$1:$E$10)
```

SUPER TIP

Use the `SELECTION()` function if you need the reference of the current selection.

SUPER CAUTION

`SELECT()` is fairly slow, so don't use it if you don't have to. For many functions that take reference arguments, you often can use an `OFFSET()` function to specify the reference instead of selecting it in advance. For example, consider the following formula:

```
=FORMULA("Sales",OFFSET(ACTIVE.CELL(),1,1)
```

This executes slightly faster than these two formulas:

```
=SELECT("R[1]C[1]")
=FORMULA("Sales")
```

Selecting a Range with *FORMULA.GOTO()*

`SELECT()` only selects ranges in the active worksheet. If you need to select an external reference, use `FORMULA.GOTO()` instead:

`FORMULA.GOTO(`*`reference`*`,`*`corner`*`)`

reference	An active or external reference for the cell or range you want to select.
corner	A logical value that determines the position of the upper-left cell of the selection. If *corner* is `TRUE`, Excel places the upper-left cell of *reference* in the upper-left corner of the window. If *corner* is `FALSE` (or if you omit it), Excel positions *reference* normally.

`FORMULA.GOTO()` is the command equivalent of the **E**dit | **G**o To command, and it works just like the `SELECT()` function.

SUPER TIP

After you select a range with `FORMULA.GOTO()`, run the function again without the *reference* argument to return to your previous position.

Cutting and Copying Data with Macros

If you need to cut and copy data within your macros, you can do it easily with the `CUT()` and `COPY()` functions. These functions have identical syntaxes:

`CUT(`*`from_reference`*`,`*`to_reference`*`)`

`COPY(`*`from_reference`*`,`*`to_reference`*`)`

from_reference	The reference of the source cell or range you want to cut or copy. If you omit *from_reference*, Excel uses the current selection.
to_reference	The reference of the destination cell or range. If you omit *to_reference*, Excel cuts or copies *from_reference* to the Clipboard. You can enter these references in either A1 or R1C1 style for either the active worksheet or an external document.

SUPER NOTE

By specifying the *from_reference* argument in `CUT()` or `COPY()`, you don't need to use `SELECT()` to select a cell or range beforehand.

Although Excel has a `PASTE()` function, you don't need to use it as long as you specify a *to_reference* argument in your `CUT()` and `COPY()` functions. However, there also is a `PASTE.SPECIAL()` function that is the equivalent of the selecting the **S**pecial button in the Go To dialog box:

`PASTE.SPECIAL(`***`paste_num`***`,`***`operation_num`***`,`***`skip_blanks`***`,`***`transpose`***`)`

paste_num A number that specifies what you want to paste:

paste_num	*Description*
1	All
2	Formulas
3	Values
4	Formats
5	Notes

operation_num A number that specifies what type of operation to perform:

operation_num	*Operation*
1	None
2	Add

	operation_num	*Operation*
	3	Subtract
	4	Multiply
	5	Divide
skip_blanks	Set this logical value to TRUE if you want to skip blank cells when pasting. Set it to FALSE to paste normally.	
transpose	Set this logical value to TRUE if you want Excel to transpose rows and columns when pasting. Set it to FALSE to paste the data without transposing.	

SUPER NOTE

Before you use PASTE.SPECIAL(), make sure you use SELECT() to select the area where you want the data pasted. Also, be sure not to specify a destination range in your CUT() or COPY() function.

Chapter

45

Creating Custom Menus

Macros are only as useful as they are convenient. There just isn't much point in creating a macro that saves you a few keystrokes if you have to spend time opening the appropriate sheet and then searching for the routine you need. The Personal Macro Workbook helps, but overloading it can make navigating the Macro dialog box a nightmare. Shortcut keys are true time-savers, but Excel has only so many (and our brains can memorize only so many Ctrl+*key* combinations).

One elegant solution is to turn command macros into menu commands. You can add them to existing menus, or you can create new menus and even entire menu bars. Not only is this convenient for you, but it also is just about essential if you're creating an application that other people will use. This chapter shows you how to create custom menus.

SUPER NOTE

Excel 5.0 features a new Menu Editor that makes it easy to customize menus. See Chapter 65, "Customizing Excel's Menus and Toolbars," for details.

About Excel's Menus

Excel has four different menu bars, and the one you see depends on what you're doing with the program. Excel uses a *bar_num* variable to identify each of the menu bars. These are listed in Table 45.1.

Table 45.1. Some of Excel's built-in menu bars.

Menu Bar	*bar_num*
Excel 4.0 worksheet	1
Excel 4.0 chart	2
No Documents Open	3
Info window	4
Excel 5.0 worksheet	10
Excel 5.0 chart	11
Visual Basic module	12

Each menu bar option is identified by a *menu* variable that can be either the name of the option or a number that represents its position in the menu bar. For example, in the Worksheet menu bar, the **F**ile menu is 1, the **E**dit menu is 2, and so on.

Shortcut menu options also are classified by *bar_num* and *menu* parameters. Table 45.2 lists these variables and their corresponding shortcut menus.

Table 45.2. Using the bar_num and menu variables to identify Excel's shortcut menus.

bar_num	*menu*	*Shortcut Menu*
7	1	Toolbars
7	2	Toolbar tools
7	3	Workbook paging icons
7	4	Worksheet cells
7	5	Column selections
7	6	Row selections
7	7	Workbook items
7	8	Macro sheet cells
7	9	Workbook title bar
7	10	Excel desktop
8	1	Drawn or imported objects
8	2	Macro Buttons
8	3	Text boxes
9	1	Chart series
9	2	Chart text
9	3	Chart plot area, walls
9	4	Entire charts
9	5	Chart axes
9	6	Chart gridlines
9	7	Chart floor, arrows
9	8	Chart legends
9	9	Visual Basic module
9	10	Watch Pane
9	11	Immediate Pane
9	12	Code Window

SUPER NOTE

Excel also defines *bar_num* values 5 and 6. These refer to the short menus used in Excel versions prior to 4.0.

When working with these menus, you have three customization options:

- Customize an existing menu by adding your own commands or by renaming, disabling, or deleting existing commands.
- Customize an existing menu bar by adding your own menus or by renaming, disabling, or deleting existing menus.
- Create your own menu bar that includes existing Excel menus or your own custom menus.

Customizing an Existing Menu

One of Excel's most powerful features is its easily customizable menus. Using only a few simple functions, you can add your own commands; disable, rename, and delete existing commands; and even toggle a command check mark on and off.

Adding a Command to a Menu

If you have command macros that you use regularly or if you're creating a custom application and want to give users easy access to your macros, add them to one of Excel's menus. This not only saves you from using the Macro dialog box or shortcut key combinations, but it also adds a classy touch to your work.

Before adding a command, you have to set up a table in your macro sheet to define various aspects of the command. As you can see in Figure 45.1, this *command table* has five columns:

MACROS.XLS

	B	C	D	E	F
1	Command Name	Macro Name	Key	Status Bar	Help Topic
2					
3	&Concatenate Text	MACROS.XLS!Concatenate		Concatenate two left columns	HELP.TXT!12
4	&Proper Case	MACROS.XLS!ConvertToProper		Convert cell to proper case	HELP.TXT!47
5	-				
6	&Start Command Macro	PERSONAL.XLS!StartCommandMacro		Start a command macro	HELP.TXT!33
7	&Data Entry	MACROS.XLS!DataEntry		Enter numbers in a column	HELP.TXT!57
8					
9					
10					
11					
12					
13					
14					
15					

Menus / Sheet1 / Sheet2 / Sheet3 / Sheet4 / Sheet5

FIGURE 45.1.
The command table describes the commands you want to add to your menus.

Command Name	This is the name of the command as it will appear in the menu. If you want to include an accelerator key in the command, precede the appropriate letter with an ampersand (&). If you want the entry to be a separator line (such as the line between **C**lose and **S**ave on the **F**ile menu), just enter a hyphen (-).
Macro Name	This is the name of the macro you want to run when the user selects the command. Include the workbook name so that Excel can find the macro easily.
Key	Leave this column blank (it's only used to define shortcut keys in Excel for the Macintosh).
Status Bar	This is the text you want Excel to display in the status bar when the user highlights the command. Although this is optional, it's usually best to include a brief description of what the command does.
Help Topic	This column specifies a custom help topic for the command. See Chapter 49, "Macro Tips and Techniques," to learn how to create custom help topics.

When you have your command table set up, use the `ADD.COMMAND()` function to add the commands to a menu:

`ADD.COMMAND(`***`bar_num`***`,`***`menu`***`,`***`command_ref`***`,`*`position`*`)`

bar_num	The number of the menu bar you want to add the command to.
menu	The menu you want to use for the command.
command_ref	A reference to the cells in the command table that describe the command you want to add. You must include at least the first two columns (the Command Name and Macro Name) of the table.
position	Specifies where you want the command to appear in the menu. You can enter either the position number (commands are numbered from the top of the menu starting with 1) or the name of an existing command. The new command is inserted above the existing command. If you omit *position*, Excel places the command at the bottom of the menu.

SUPER TIP

For clarity, you should define a range name for each command definition. This enables you to use the range name for the ***command_ref*** argument, which will make your `ADD.COMMAND()` functions more readable.

Figure 45.2 shows a macro (AddR1C1Command) that adds a separator line (`Separator` from the command table) and a new command (`ToggleCmd`) to Excel's Tools menu. This new command—**R**1C1 Notation—calls the ToggleR1C1 macro which toggles the workspace between A1 and R1C1 notation.

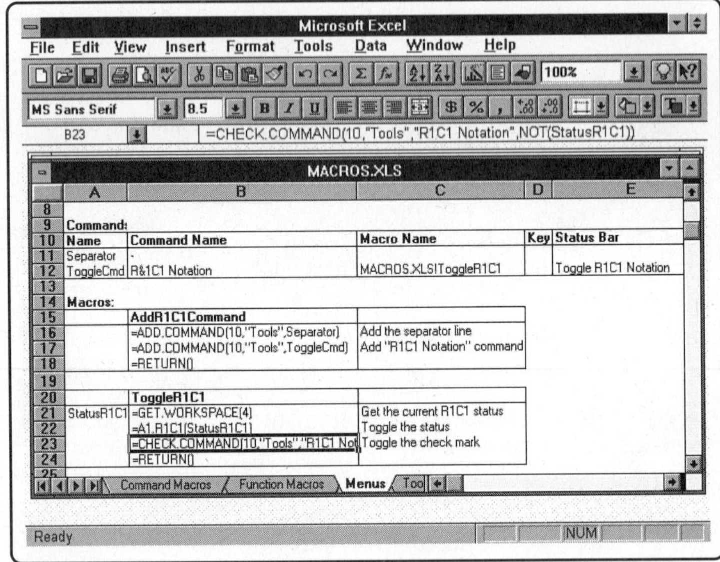

FIGURE 45.2.
A macro to add commands to a menu.

Adding a Check Mark to a Command

Some menu commands toggle settings on and off. When a setting is on, Excel indicates this by placing a check mark beside the command. You can do the same thing for your custom commands by using the `CHECK.COMMAND()` function:

```
CHECK.COMMAND(bar_num,menu,command,check)
```

- ***bar_num*** The menu bar number.
- ***menu*** The menu containing the command.
- ***command*** Identifies the command using either its name, a reference to the command table range that defines it, or its position number (the top command is 1).
- ***check*** A logical value that toggles the check mark. Use `TRUE` to add the check mark and `FALSE` to remove it.

In the ToggleR1C1 macro (see Figure 45.2), the following command toggles a check mark beside the **T**ool menu's new **R**1C1 Notation command:

```
CHECK.COMMAND(10,"Tools","R1C1 Notation",NOT(StatusR1C1))
```

The name `StatusR1C1` comes from the first line of the macro—`=GET.WORKSPACE(4)`—that determines the status of R1C1 notation (`TRUE`, if on).

Disabling and Enabling a Command

Excel dims menu commands to show you when a command has been disabled. You use the `ENABLE.COMMAND()` function to disable (and enable) your custom commands:

`ENABLE.COMMAND(`***`bar_num,menu,command,enable`***`)`

bar_num	The menu bar number.
menu	The menu containing the command.
command	Identifies the command using either its name, a reference to the command table range that defines it, or its position number (the top command is 1).
enable	Controls the dimming. Set ***enable*** to `FALSE` to disable a command, and set it to `TRUE` to enable it again.

For example, to disable the **R**1C1 Notation command, you would use the following formula:

```
=ENABLE.COMMAND(10,"Tools","R1C1 Notation",FALSE)
```

Renaming a Command

To change the name of a command, use the `RENAME.COMMAND()` function:

`RENAME.COMMAND(`***`bar_num,menu,command,name_text`***`)`

bar_num	The menu bar number.
menu	The menu containing the command.
command	Identifies the command using either its name, a reference to the command table range that defines it, or its position number (the top command is 1).
name_text	Specifies the new name. You can just enter a text string, but it's best to add the new name to the command table and then use ***name_text*** to reference the table range that defines the name.

The most common use for renaming commands is to indicate a different workspace state. For instance, instead of naming the command "R1C1 Notation" as in the earlier example, you could have used "Switch to R1C1 Notation." Then, after the user has run this command to change to the R1C1 style, you could rename the command to "Switch to A1 Notation."

Deleting a Command

If you no longer need a command or if you want to remove a command that might be dangerous for novice users, use the DELETE.COMMAND() function:

DELETE.COMMAND(***bar_num***,***menu***,***command***)

bar_num	The menu bar number.
menu	The menu containing the command.
command	Identifies the command using either its name, a reference to the command table range that defines it, or its position number (the top command is 1).

> SUPER NOTE
>
> Because separator bars don't have names, to delete them you must specify the menu position of the separator bar when you use the DELETE.COMMAND() function.

> SUPER TIP
>
> As you know, the **F**ile menu shows a list of the most recently opened files, and the **W**indow menu shows a list of the open windows. To delete these lists, use File List or Window List, respectively, for the ***command*** argument.

Getting Command Information

To get either the name of a command (given its position) or the position of a command (given its name), use the GET.MENU() function:

GET.MENU(***bar_num***,***menu***,***command***)

bar_num	The number of the menu bar that contains the menu.
menu	The menu that contains the command.
command	The command you want information on. If you enter the name of the command, the function returns the command's position in the menu (the top command is 1). If you enter the command's position, the function returns its name.

For example, the following formula returns the position of the **O**ptions command from the Worksheet menu bar's **T**ools menu:

```
=GET.MENU(10,"Tools","Options")
```

Customizing an Existing Menu Bar

You can customize any of Excel's menu bars the same way you can customize an individual menu. You can add new menus, and you can disable, rename, and delete menus.

Adding a Menu to a Menu Bar

If you have a number of macros that you would like to add to Excel's menu structure, you might not want to clutter the existing menus with all kinds of new commands. The alternative is to create an entirely new menu and add it to a menu bar.

As was the case with adding commands, you must first set up a table—called a *menu table*—to define your new creation before you add a menu. A menu table uses the same five-column structure that you use for your command tables (see Figure 45.3). The first cell of the first column holds the menu name, and subsequent rows define the individual commands for the menu.

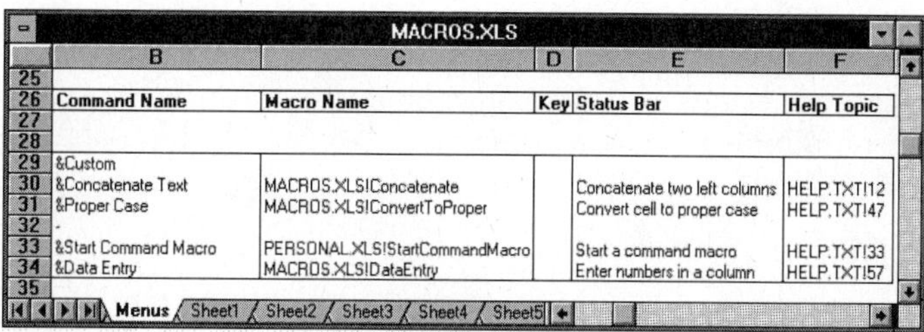

MACROS.XLS

	B	C	D	E	F
25					
26	Command Name	Macro Name	Key	Status Bar	Help Topic
27					
28					
29	&Custom				
30	&Concatenate Text	MACROS.XLS!Concatenate		Concatenate two left columns	HELP.TXT!12
31	&Proper Case	MACROS.XLS!ConvertToProper		Convert cell to proper case	HELP.TXT!47
32	-				
33	&Start Command Macro	PERSONAL.XLS!StartCommandMacro		Start a command macro	HELP.TXT!33
34	&Data Entry	MACROS.XLS!DataEntry		Enter numbers in a column	HELP.TXT!57
35					

FIGURE 45.3.
Set up a menu table to define a new menu.

After you've set up your menu table, you use the `ADD.MENU()` function to add the menu to an existing menu bar:

ADD.MENU(***bar_num***,***menu_ref***,*position*)

bar_num	The number of the menu bar you want to customize.
menu_ref	A reference to the menu table.
position	Specifies where you want Excel to insert the menu. You can enter a menu name or position number (the leftmost menu is 1), and Excel will insert the new menu to its left. If you omit *position*, the menu is added to the right end of the menu bar (but to the left of the **H**elp menu).

Figure 45.4 shows the menu table and a macro named AddCustomMenu, which adds the new menu by invoking the following formula:

```
=ADD.MENU(10,CustomMenu)
```

Here, `CustomMenu` is the range name of the menu table (B29:F34).

FIGURE 45.4.
A macro that adds the new menu.

MACROS.XLS

	A	B	C	D	E
25					
26	Name	Command Name	Macro Name	Key	Status Bar
27					
28	Menu:				
29	CustomMenu	&Custom			
30		&Concatenate Text	MACROS.XLS!Concatenate		Concatenate two left columns
31		&Proper Case	MACROS.XLS!ConvertToProper		Convert cell to proper case
32		-			
33		&Start Command Macro	PERSONAL.XLS!StartCommandMacro		Start a command macro
34		&Data Entry	MACROS.XLS!DataEntry		Enter numbers in a column
35					
36	Macro:				
37		AddCustomMenu			
38		=ADD.MENU(10,CustomMenu)	Add the Custom menu		
39		=RETURN()			
40					

Menus / Sheet1 / Sheet2 / Sheet3 / Sheet4 / Sheet5

Disabling and Enabling a Menu

As I stated in the section titled "Disabling and Enabling a Command," you can disable or enable a menu command using the following function:

ENABLE.COMMAND(***bar_num***,***menu***,***command***,***enable***)

You use the same command to disable and enable a menu, except that you must specify a zero (0) for the ***command*** argument.

Renaming a Menu

To rename a menu, use the RENAME.COMMAND() function:

RENAME.COMMAND(***bar_num***,***menu***,***command***,***name_text***)

Again, be sure to specify a zero (0) for the ***command*** argument.

Deleting a Menu from a Menu Bar

When you're done with a menu, you can delete it with the DELETE.MENU() function:

DELETE.MENU(***bar_num***,***menu***)

bar_num The number of the menu bar that contains the menu.

menu Specifies which menu you want to delete. You can use either the name of the menu or its position number (the leftmost menu is 1).

For example, to delete the Custom menu added earlier, you would use the following formula:

```
=DELETE.MENU(10,"Custom")
```

Getting Menu Information

If you need to know either the name of a menu (given its position) or the position of a menu (given its name), use the following syntax for the GET.MENU() function:

```
GET.MENU(bar_num,menu)
```

bar_num	The number of the menu bar that contains the menu.
menu	Specifies the menu you want the information about. If you enter the name of the menu, the function returns its position in the menu bar (the leftmost menu is 1). If you enter the menu's position, the function returns its name.

For example, the following formula returns the position of the Worksheet menu bar's Tools menu:

```
=GET.MENU(10,"Tools")
```

Creating a Custom Menu Bar

If you're building a custom application in Excel, you'll often want to shield novice users from parts of Excel that they might not be familiar with. One of the best ways to do that is to create a custom menu bar that includes only the commands you want the user to see.

Setting up your own menu bar is just an extension of the techniques you learned for custom menus and commands. There are three steps to follow:

1. Run the ADD.BAR() function to create a new, empty menu bar.
2. Use the ADD.MENU() function to add menus to the new menu bar.
3. Display the menu bar by running the SHOW.BAR() function.

Adding a Menu Bar

To add a menu bar, just run the ADD.BAR() function. This function creates a new, empty menu bar and returns the new bar's number. You can then use this number to add your own menus to the menu bar with the ADD.MENU() function.

SUPER NOTE

You can define a maximum of 15 custom menu bars.

Displaying a Menu Bar

After you've created your new menu bar and attached some menus to it, you display it by running the `SHOW.BAR()` function:

`SHOW.BAR(`*`bar_num`*`)`

`bar_num` The number of the menu bar you want to display.

Figure 45.5 shows a macro called NewMenuBar, which creates a new menu bar with two menus: the File menu shown and the Custom menu defined earlier.

FIGURE 45.5.
A macro that creates and displays a new menu bar.

MACROS.XLS

	A	B	C	D	E
41					
42	Name	Command Name	Macro Name	Key	Status Bar
43					
44	Menu:				
45	FileMenu	&File			
46		&Save	MACROS.XLS!FileSave		Saves the current workbook
47		&Print	MACROS.XLS!FilePrint		Prints the current sheet
48		-			
49		E&xit	MACROS.XLS!FileExit		Quits the application
50					
51		NewMenuBar			
52	BarNumber	=ADD.BAR()	Create a new, empty menu bar		
53		=ADD.MENU(BarNumber,FileMenu)	Add the File menu		
54		=ADD.MENU(BarNumber,CustomMenu)	Add the Tools menu		
55		=SHOW.BAR(BarNumber)	Show the new menu bar		
56		=RETURN()			
57					

Menus / Sheet1 / Sheet2 / Sheet3 / Sheet4 / Sheet5

SUPER TIP

If you omit the *`bar_num`* argument from `SHOW.BAR()`, Excel displays the appropriate built-in menu bar. For example, if the active sheet is a worksheet, Excel displays the Worksheet menu bar.

Deleting a Menu Bar

To delete a menu bar you no longer need, you have to do two things:

1. If necessary, run the `SHOW.BAR()` function to display a different menu bar.
2. Run the `DELETE.BAR(`***`bar_num`***`)` function, where ***`bar_num`*** is the number of the menu bar you want to delete.

Getting the Menu Bar Number

If you need to know the number of the active menu bar, use the `GET.BAR()` function with no arguments.

For example, the following macro fragment saves the number of the current menu bar, displays a custom menu bar, and then restores the original:

```
=SET.NAME("OriginalBar",GET.BAR())
=SHOW.BAR(CustomBar)
```

(Macro commands that work with `CustomBar`)

```
=SHOW.BAR(OriginalBar)
```

Chapter

46

Creating Custom Toolbars

Excel's built-in toolbars give you easy access to many of the program's most-used features. You can add the same "point-and-click" functionality to your macros by adding new tools and assigning procedures to them. The user clicks on a tool, and the procedure runs. You can design your own tool icons and create entire toolbars for your macros. This chapter shows you how to do these things and more.

> **SUPER NOTE**
>
> See Chapter 65, "Customizing Excel's Menus and Toolbars," to learn how to create custom toolbars without programming.

About Excel's Toolbars

Excel has 13 different toolbars, and it identifies each one with a number called the `bar_id` variable. These are shown in Table 46.1.

Table 46.1. Excel's toolbar names and numbers.

Name	*Number*
Standard	1
Formatting	2
Query and Pivot	3
Chart	4
Drawing	5
TipWizard	6
Forms	7
Stop Recording	8
Visual Basic	9
Auditing	10
WorkGroup	11
Microsoft	12
Full Screen	13

For custom toolbars, `bar_id` is the name of the toolbar.

In addition, each tool is identified by a tool ID number. Excel's Visual Basic User's Guide lists all the built-in tools and their corresponding ID numbers.

Creating a Custom Tool

You can customize individual tools by assigning macros to them, adding new tools to a toolbar, and disabling or deleting tools.

Assigning a Macro to a Tool

The easiest way to customize a tool is to assign one of your macros to it using the `ASSIGN.TO.TOOL()` function:

`ASSIGN.TO.TOOL(`***`bar_id`***`,`***`position`***`,`*`macro_ref`*`)`

`bar_id` The number of the toolbar that contains the tool (or, for a custom toolbar, ***`bar_id`*** is the name of the toolbar).

`position` The location of the tool on the toolbar, in which the leftmost tool (if the toolbar is horizontal) or topmost tool (if the toolbar is vertical) is `1`.

`macro_ref` A reference to the macro you want to assign to the tool. If you omit *`macro_ref`*, the tool no longer runs the previously assigned macro and, if it's a built-in tool, it reverts to its default action.

For example, if you have a macro called FileOpen that replaces the **File** | **O**pen command (for example, by running the `OPEN()` function with your own defaults), you could use the following formula to assign it to the Open File tool:

```
=ASSIGN.TO.TOOL(1,2,FileOpen)
```

Adding a Tool to a Toolbar

The layout of Excel's predefined toolbars is not set in stone. You're free to add as many tools as you like, whether they're Excel's standard tools or your own command macros.

Before adding a tool, you have to set up a table in your macro sheet to define the tool. As you can see in Figure 46.1, this *tool table* has eight columns.

MACROS.XLS

	A	B	C	D	E	F	G	H
3								
4								
5	**Tools:**							
6	**Tool ID**	**Macro Name**	**Down**	**Enabled**	**Face**	**Help Text**	**Balloon**	**Help Topic**
7	2							
8	0							
9	201	MACROS.XLS!ConvertToProper	FALSE	TRUE		Convert to proper case		
10	202	PERSONAL.XLS!StartCommandMacro	FALSE	TRUE	Picture 2	Start command macro		
11	203	MACROS.XLS!ToggleR1C1	FALSE	TRUE	Picture 3	Toggle R1C1 notation		
12								
13								
14								

Toolbars / Sheet1 / Sheet2 / Sheet3 / Sheet4 / Shee

FIGURE 46.1. *The tool table describes the tools to add to your toolbars.*

Tool ID	The tool number. You can use the tool ID for one of Excel's built-in tools, or you can assign your own number (starting at 200). If you want to place a gap between tools, enter a 0 for the tool number.
Macro Name	The name of the macro to run when the user selects the tool. If Tool ID is a built-in tool, and you leave Macro Name blank, Excel runs the command associated with the built-in tool.
Down	A logical value that determines whether the tool appears pressed (`TRUE`) or normal (`FALSE`).
Enabled	A logical value that specifies whether the tool is initially enabled (`TRUE`) or disabled (`FALSE`).
Face	A reference to the picture object you want to appear on the face of the tool. If Tool ID is a built-in tool, leave the Face column blank to use the default face. For custom picture objects, use the name of the object (for example, "Picture 1"). For clarity, insert the picture object in the tool table right below the reference. (See the section in this chapter titled "Using a Custom Tool Face.")

SUPER TIP

Excel also has a number of custom tool faces you can use. These are associated with tool ID numbers 201 through 231.

Help Text	Text that appears in the status bar and Customize Toolbar dialog box.
Balloon	A column that is only used by Excel for the Macintosh.
Help Topic	The column that specifies a custom help topic for the command. To learn how to create custom help topics, see Chapter 49, "Macro Tips and Techniques."

In the tool table in Figure 46.1, the first line (Tool ID = 2) refers to the Save tool, and the second line (Tool ID = 0) defines a space. The other lines define custom tools.

As soon as you have your tool table set up, use the `ADD.TOOL()` function to add a tool to a toolbar:

`ADD.TOOL(`***`bar_id,position,tool_ref`***`)`

bar_id	The number or name of the toolbar.
position	The location that you want Excel to insert the tool on the toolbar. The leftmost tool (if the toolbar is horizontal) or topmost tool (if the toolbar is vertical) is 1.
tool_ref	The tool ID of a built-in tool, or a reference to the cells in the tool table that describe the tool you want to add.

For example, the AddTools macro, shown in Figure 46.2, adds a tool for the ConvertToProper macro (Tool ID 201 in Figure 46.1) to the WorkGroup toolbar (***bar_id*** 11). It then adds a space to the toolbar. (Even though the space appears before the new tool, you have to add it second because Excel doesn't let you add a space to the end of a toolbar.) The WorkGroup toolbar shows the new tool.

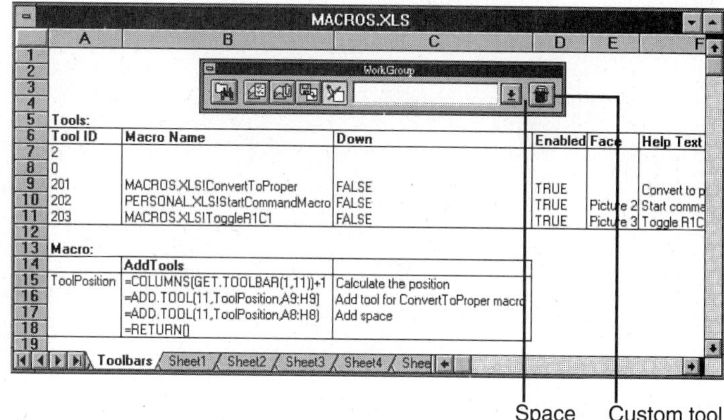

FIGURE 46.2.
A macro to add a tool and a space to the WorkGroup toolbar.

In most cases, you'll want to add your tools to the end of a toolbar. Rather than counting the number of existing tools, you can use the following formula to calculate the total number of tools:

```
=COLUMNS(GET.TOOLBAR(1,bar_id))
```

Here, `GET.TOOLBAR(1,`*`bar_id`*`)` returns an array consisting of all the tool IDs for the *`bar_id`* toolbar. The `COLUMNS()` function returns the number of elements in the array (that is, the number of tools, including spaces, in the toolbar). Therefore, to place a tool at the end of the toolbar, you need to add 1 to this result and use this as your *`position`* argument in the `ADD.TOOL()` function (shown in the AddTools macro in Figure 46.2).

SUPER NOTE

For more information on the `GET.TOOLBAR()` function, see the section in this chapter titled "Getting Toolbar Information."

Using a Custom Tool Face

You'll normally want to use a custom tool face for any tools assigned to macros (unless the macro closely emulates the default action of a built-in tool). You have three options for creating a custom tool face:

- Use one of Excel's custom tool faces.
- Use Excel 5.0's new Button Editor feature.
- Create your own tool face in a graphics program such as Paintbrush.

To use one of Excel's custom tool faces, you can use the appropriate tool ID (201 to 231). You also can copy the face you want to the macro sheet and reference the object in the Face column of the definition table. Follow the steps in Procedure 46.1 to insert one of Excel's custom tool faces in the Face column of your tool table.

PROCEDURE 46.1. USING EXCEL'S CUSTOM TOOL FACES.

1. Select the **V**iew | **T**oolbars command. The Toolbars dialog box appears.
2. Click on the **C**ustomize button. Excel displays the Customize dialog box.

> **SUPER TIP**
>
> You also can display the Customize dialog box by right-clicking on a toolbar and selecting Customize from the shortcut menu.

3. In the **C**ategories list, select Custom. The Buttons area displays Excel's custom tool faces, as shown in Figure 46.3.

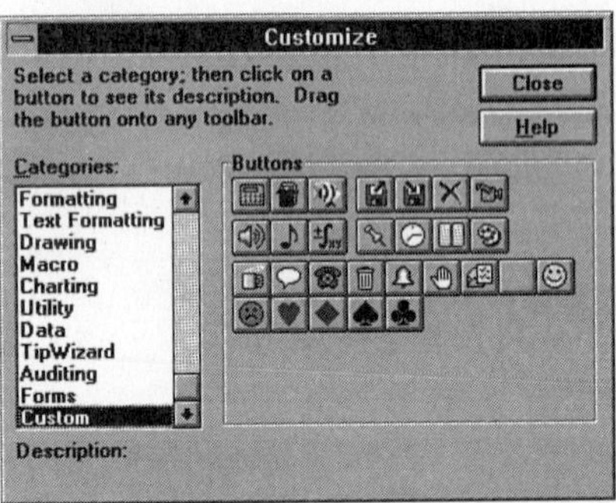

FIGURE 46.3.
Excel's custom tool faces.

4. Click on the tool face you want to use and then select the **E**dit | **C**opy Button Image command.
5. Click on Close to return to the macro sheet.
6. In the tool table, select the cell in the Face column where you want the tool face pasted; then select the **E**dit | **P**aste command. Excel pastes the face.
7. In the Face column, enter the name of the object. Excel assigns the names Picture 1, Picture 2, and so on. To find out the name of the tool face object, select it. Excel displays the name in the formula bar's Name box.

The easiest way to create your own tool face is to use the Button Editor. I'll save the Button Editor for Chapter 65, "Customizing Excel's Menus and Toolbars." You also can use a graphics program such as Paintbrush. For the best results, create a bitmap image on a gray background that is 16 pixels wide by 15 pixels high. (Excel scales down larger images, but you usually lose too much detail to make the image useful.) When you're finished, copy the image, switch to Excel, and paste the tool face into the appropriate cell in the tool table.

If you don't want to start a face from scratch, you can copy one of Excel's tool faces and modify it in your graphics program. Follow the steps in Procedure 46.2.

PROCEDURE 46.2. CREATING A CUSTOM TOOL FACE FROM A BUILT-IN FACE.

1. Select the **V**iew | **T**oolbars command. The Toolbars dialog box appears.
2. Click on the **C**ustomize button. Excel displays the Customize dialog box.

> **SUPER TIP**
>
> You also can display the Customize dialog box by right-clicking on the toolbar and selecting Customize from the shortcut menu.

3. In the **C**ategories list, select Custom and then click on the face you want to use.

> **SUPER TIP**
>
> If you want to start with a blank tool face, select the Custom category and click on the blank face.

4. Select the **E**dit | **C**opy Button Image command and then click on Close to return to the worksheet.
5. Start the graphics program and paste the tool face. Figure 46.4 shows the blank tool pasted into Paintbrush. (Select the **V**iew | Zoom **I**n command to get the view shown in Figure 46.4.)
6. Make your changes to the tool face, copy the image, and return to Excel.
7. In the tool table, select the cell in the Face column where you want the tool face pasted and then select the **E**dit | **P**aste command. Excel pastes the face.
8. In the Face column, enter the name of the object. Again, Excel assigns the names Picture 1, Picture 2, and so on.

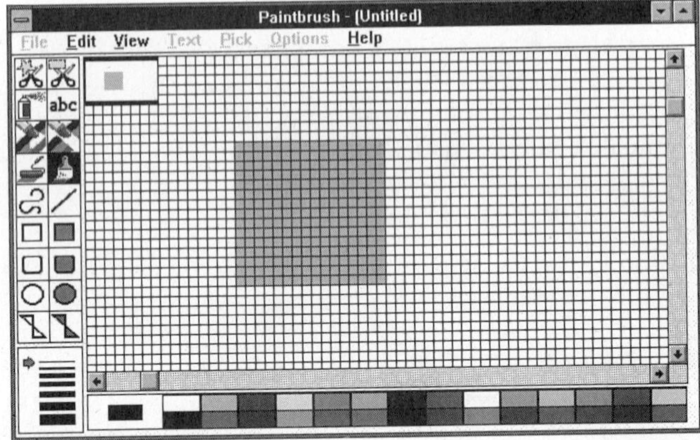

FIGURE 46.4.
Excel's blank tool face pasted into Paintbrush.

Making a Tool Appear Pressed

Some tools toggle workspace or worksheet settings on and off. Excel indicates that a setting is on by leaving the tool in the "pressed" position. You can do the same thing for your custom tools by using the `PRESS.TOOL()` function:

`PRESS.TOOL(`***`bar_id`***`,`***`position`***`,`*`down`*`)`

bar_id	The number or name of the toolbar.
position	The location of the tool on the toolbar, where the leftmost tool (if the toolbar is horizontal) or topmost tool (if the toolbar is vertical) is 1.
down	A logical value that toggles the tool. Use `TRUE` to display the tool pressed and `FALSE` to display it normally.

Disabling and Enabling a Tool

If you need to control a user's access to a tool, use the `ENABLE.TOOL()` function:

`ENABLE.TOOL(`***`bar_id`***`,`***`position`***`,`*`enable`*`)`

bar_id	The number or name of the toolbar.
position	The location of the tool on the toolbar, where the leftmost tool (if the toolbar is horizontal) or topmost tool (if the toolbar is vertical) is 1.
enable	Controls access to the tool. Set *enable* to `FALSE` to disable the tool and to `TRUE` to enable it again.

For example, to disable the New Workbook tool in the Standard toolbar, you would use the following formula:

```
=ENABLE.TOOL(1,1,FALSE)
```

Deleting a Tool

If you no longer need a tool, or if you want to remove a tool that might be dangerous in the hands of novice users, you can delete any tool by using the `DELETE.TOOL()` function:

```
DELETE.TOOL(bar_id,position)
```

bar_id	The number or name of the toolbar.
position	The location of the tool on the toolbar, where the leftmost tool (if the toolbar is horizontal) or topmost tool (if the toolbar is vertical) is 1.

Resetting a Toolbar

If you've been working with a built-in toolbar and would like to reset it to its default set of tools, use the `RESET.TOOLBAR()` function:

```
RESET.TOOLBAR(bar_id)
```

bar_id is the number of the built-in toolbar.

Getting Tool Information

If you need information such as a tool's ID number or which macro is assigned to the tool, use the `GET.TOOL()` function:

```
GET.TOOL(type_num,bar_id,position)
```

type_num A number that specifies the type of information the function returns:

type_num	*Returns*
1	The ID number of the tool. Toolbar spaces return `0`.
2	A reference to the macro assigned to the tool. Built-in tools return `0`.
3	`FALSE` if the button is pressed, `TRUE` otherwise.
4	`TRUE` if the tool is enabled, `FALSE` otherwise.
5	`TRUE` if the face is a bitmap image, `FALSE` if it's a default tool face.
6	The *`help_text`* reference associated with a custom tool. Built-in tools return `#NA`.
7	Used with Excel for the Macintosh only.

bar_id The number or name of the toolbar.

position The location of the tool on the toolbar, where the leftmost tool (if the toolbar is horizontal) or topmost tool (if the toolbar is vertical) is 1.

For example, the following formula returns a logical value that indicates whether or not the second tool in a toolbar called MyToolbar is pressed:

```
=GET.TOOL(3,"MyToolbar",2)
```

Creating a Custom Toolbar

Many macro programmers prefer to leave Excel's built-in toolbars intact and create their own custom toolbars. This is handy for adding large numbers of macros and also for designing a custom application. The next few sections show you how to create and work with custom toolbars.

Adding a Toolbar

If you have a number of macros that you would like to access from a toolbar, you might not want to clutter the built-in toolbars with all kinds of new tools. The alternative is to create an entirely new toolbar.

As with adding individual tools, before you add a toolbar you must first set up a *toolbar table* to define it. A toolbar table uses the same eight-column structure that you use for tool tables.

Once you've set up your toolbar table, you use the ADD.TOOLBAR() function to create the new toolbar:

ADD.TOOLBAR(***bar_name***,*tool_ref*)

bar_name	A text string that identifies the new toolbar.
tool_ref	A reference to the toolbar table that defines the new toolbar. For clarity, you should define a name for the toolbar table.

For example, suppose you've set up the name CustomToolbar for a toolbar table. To create a toolbar named Custom from this table, you would need to include the following formula in a macro:

```
=ADD.TOOLBAR("Custom",CustomToolbar)
```

Displaying a Toolbar

Once you've created your custom toolbar, you can display it for the user by running the SHOW.TOOLBAR() function:

SHOW.TOOLBAR(***bar_id***,***visible***,*dock*,*x_pos*,*y_pos*,*width*)

bar_id	The number or name of the toolbar.
visible	A logical value that displays (TRUE) or hides (FALSE) the toolbar.
dock	A number that specifies the location of the toolbar:

	dock	*Toolbar Position*
	1	Top of the workspace
	2	Left edge of the workspace
	3	Right edge of the workspace
	4	Bottom of the workspace
	5	Floating
x_pos	The horizontal position of the toolbar measured in points (there are 72 points in an inch).	
y_pos	The vertical position of the toolbar (also measured in points).	
width	The width of the toolbar (in points).	

For example, to display the "Custom Toolbar" discussed in the preceding section, you would include the following formula in your macro:

```
=SHOW.TOOLBAR("Custom",TRUE)
```

Figure 46.5 shows a toolbar definition table. Two macros—AddToolbar and Show-Toolbar—define, create, and display a custom toolbar and the toolbar itself.

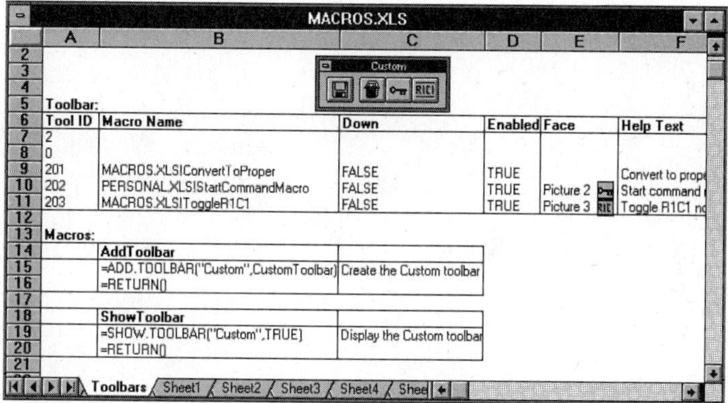

FIGURE 46.5.
A toolbar definition table, macros to create and display it, and the custom toolbar itself.

Deleting a Toolbar

Use the `DELETE.TOOLBAR()` function to delete any custom toolbars you no longer need. (You can't delete built-in toolbars.)

`DELETE.TOOLBAR(`***`bar_name`***`)`

`bar_name` is the name of the custom toolbar you want to delete.

For example, to delete the toolbar named "Custom," you would use the following formula:

```
=DELETE.TOOLBAR("Custom")
```

Getting Toolbar Information

If you need information such as the ID numbers of a toolbar's tools, or you need to know whether a toolbar is visible, use the GET.TOOLBAR() function:

GET.TOOLBAR(***type_num***,*bar_id*)

type_num A number that specifies the type of information the function returns:

type_num	*Returns*
1	A horizontal array of all tool IDs in order of position. Toolbar spaces are returned as 0.
2	The horizontal position of the toolbar (in points)
3	The vertical position of the toolbar (points)
4	The width of the toolbar (points)
5	The height of the toolbar (points)
6	The toolbar location: 1 = Top dock 2 = Left dock 3 = Right dock 4 = Bottom dock 5 = Floating
7	TRUE, if the toolbar is visible—otherwise, FALSE.
8	A horizontal array of the tool IDs for all toolbars.
9	A horizontal array of tool IDs for all visible toolbars.

bar_id The number or the name of the toolbar.

For an example that uses the GET.TOOLBAR() function, see the section earlier in this chapter titled "Adding a Tool to the Toolbar."

Chapter

47

Creating Custom Dialog Boxes

In Chapter 43, "Using Macros to Get and Display Information," you learned how to use the `INPUT()` function to display a simple dialog box. This works fine if you need a single item of information, but what if you need four or five? Or what happens when you want the user to choose from a list of items? In some cases, you can use Excel's standard dialog boxes. However, these dialog boxes might not have the exact controls you need, and your macros can't access the user's selections from these dialog boxes.

The solution is to build your own dialog boxes. You can add as many controls as you need (including list boxes, option buttons, and check boxes), and your macros have complete access to all the dialog box results. This chapter shows you how to create dialog boxes and integrate them into your applications.

Using the Dialog Editor

Compared to menus and toolbars, dialog boxes are relatively complicated affairs. However, you can reduce this complexity by taking advantage of Excel's Dialog Editor. This program enables you to build a dialog box by drawing each control on-screen. You add some basic definitions to each control, copy everything to a macro sheet, and you're ready to go.

> **SUPER NOTE**
>
> Microsoft decided not to include the Dialog Editor in Excel 5.0 (presumably to encourage people to use Visual Basic for Applications). If you upgraded to version 5.0 from a previous version of Excel, you'll still have the Dialog Editor. If you're new to Excel 5.0, you can create dialog boxes by hand. Skim through the Dialog Editor material to familiarize yourself with the controls, then move to the section later in this chapter titled "Understanding the Dialog Box Definition Table."

Starting the Dialog Editor

The Dialog Editor is a separate program that comes with Excel. Follow Procedure 47.1 to start the Dialog Editor.

PROCEDURE 47.1. STARTING THE DIALOG EDITOR.

1. Switch to Program Manager or File Manager.
2. Select the **F**ile | **R**un command. The Run dialog box appears.
3. In the **C**ommand Line box, type `c:\excel\excelde.exe`.
4. Click on OK or press Enter. The Dialog Editor program loads, and you see the screen shown in Figure 47.1.

FIGURE 47.1.
The Dialog Editor screen.

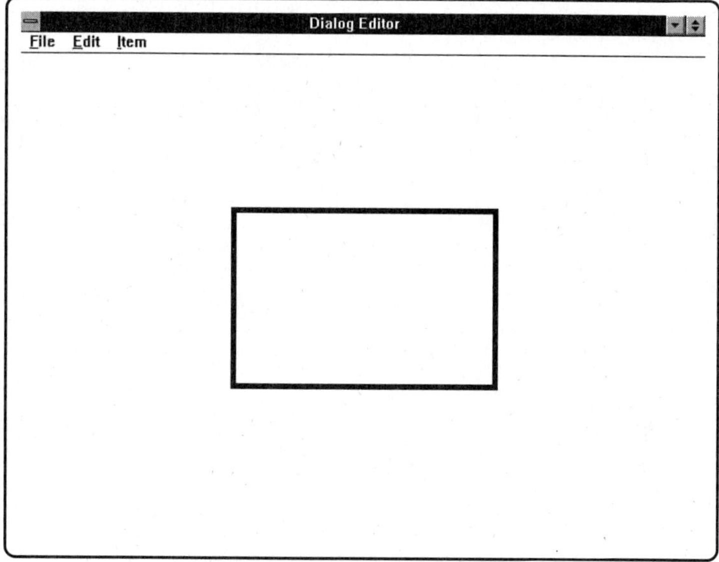

The Dialog Editor screen is simple enough. The box you see in the middle of your screen is the outline of an empty dialog box. The controls you add will appear inside this box, and you can move or resize them. You also can resize the dialog box itself. (See the section later in this chapter titled "Editing a Dialog Box Item.")

Building a dialog box involves adding various items and making adjustments. This is a four-step process:

1. Add an item to the dialog box.
2. Edit the item's information (such as its initial value, whether or not it's dimmed, and so forth).
3. Move or size the item, as needed.
4. If necessary, add any explanatory text for the item.

Adding Items to the Dialog Box

The dialog editor enables you to add six different items to your dialog boxes: buttons, edit boxes, group boxes, list boxes, text, and icons. Several of these items represent a number of different controls. For example, a button can be, among other things, a command button, an option button, or a check box.

As soon as you've added an item, you need to give some information about the item. With the item selected, choose the **Edit | Info** command. An Info dialog box similar to the one shown in Figure 47.2 appears.

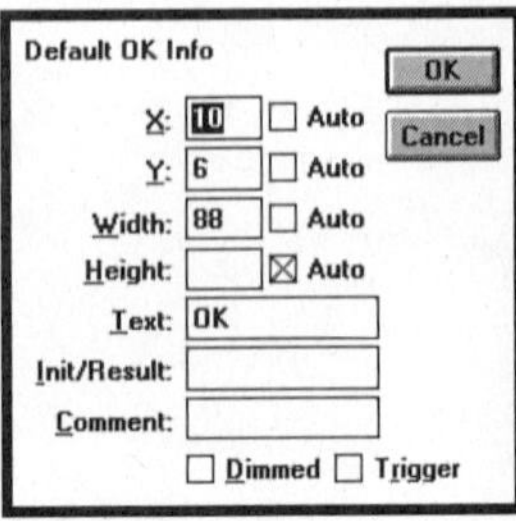

FIGURE 47.2. *You use these Info dialog boxes to define an item's information.*

The Info dialog box contains the following fields:

X	The number of pixels from the left edge of the dialog box to the left edge of the item.
Y	The number of pixels from the top edge of the dialog box to the top edge of the item.
Width	The width of the item (in pixels).
Height	The height of the item (in pixels).
Auto	Activate these check boxes to tell Dialog Editor to automatically position and size the item.

SUPER NOTE

Normally you adjust the position and size of an item using the mouse or the arrow keys. (See the section later in this chapter titled "Editing a Dialog Box Item.") Use the X, Y, **W**idth, and **H**eight boxes to make fine-tuned adjustments.

Text	The text associated with some items (such as the text on the face of a command button). Include an ampersand (&) before a letter to make the letter the item's accelerator key.

SUPER TIP

To give your dialog box a title, select the **E**dit | **I**nfo command before adding any items. Then enter the title in the **T**ext box. If you already added items, double-click on an empty area of the dialog box.

Init/Result	The initial value of the item when you display the custom dialog box, and the final value of the item when you close the dialog box.

Comment	Descriptive comments about the item. This field has no effect on the dialog box definition.
Dimmed	Determines whether an item is available to the user. If you activate this check box, the item will appear in lighter text (that is, *dimmed*) and the user won't be able to select it.
Trigger	Determines whether an item is a *trigger*. When the user selects an item defined as a trigger, Excel returns control to the macro that called the dialog box. However, the dialog box stays on-screen. This enables the macro to change the dialog box definition, or to display a second dialog box or alert message. See the section later in this chapter titled "Using Triggers to Create Dynamic Dialog Boxes."

SUPER CAUTION

The order you add items in the Dialog Editor is the order the user will navigate them in the dialog box (although you can make adjustments when you paste the dialog box definition in the macro sheet, as you'll see later). For this reason, you should plan your dialog box ahead of time and add items in the order you want them navigated.

Adding a Button

The steps displayed in Procedure 47.2 show you how to add a button to the dialog box.

PROCEDURE 47.2. ADDING A BUTTON TO A DIALOG BOX.

1. Select the **I**tem | **B**utton command. The Dialog Editor displays a dialog box of button types, shown in Figure 47.3.

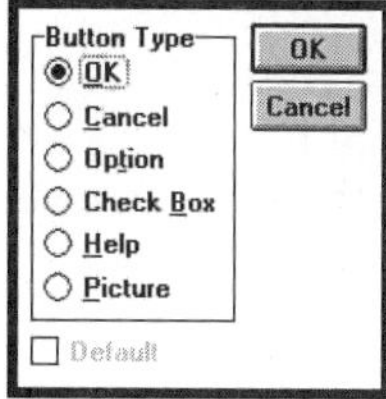

FIGURE 47.3.
The Dialog Editor's button options.

2. Select the button type you want to add. (See the description of each type in the following table.)

3. To define the OK or Cancel buttons as the default—that is, as the button that will execute when the user presses Enter—activate the **D**efault check box.
4. Click on OK or press Enter. Dialog Editor adds the button to the dialog box.
5. Select the **E**dit | **I**nfo command (or double-click on the item) and enter the appropriate information for the item.

You can choose from six different button types. The following list gives a summary of the button types:

Button	*Description*	*Info Dialog Box*
OK	A command button that closes the custom dialog box and enters the results of the other items in their respective Init/Result fields.	The Text field appears on the button face. The Dialog Editor uses OK by default, but you can enter whatever you like.
Cancel	A command button that closes the dialog box but doesn't return the results of the other items.	The Text field appears on the button face. The default is Cancel, but you can enter whatever you like.
Option	Option buttons normally appear in groups of two or more. (See the next section.) You need to define a group box before adding any option buttons.	The Text field holds the name of the button.
Check Box	Control that enables the user to turn an option on or off. Init/Result field returns `TRUE` if selected, `FALSE` if deselected, and `#N/A` if grayed (partially selected).	The Text field holds the name of the check box. The Init/Result field holds the initial value of the check box: `TRUE` if the check box is selected, `FALSE` if it is deselected, and `#N/A` if the check box is grayed.
Help	A command button that displays a custom help topic. You have to add	

Button	Description	Info Dialog Box
	by hand the name of the help topic to the dialog box definition table. (See the section titled "Understanding the Dialog Box Definition Table.")	
Picture	A picture button that works much like an OK command button.	Enter a reference to the picture in the Text field (for example, Picture 1).

SUPER TIP

After you've added an item to your custom dialog box, you usually can press Enter to immediately add another instance of the same item. However, if you've just entered an OK button, pressing Enter will produce a Cancel button.

Adding a Group Box

To make dialog boxes more readable, you should place related controls close together and surround them with a group box. (The Button Type group from the dialog box shown in Figure 47.3 is a good example.) You can add a group box for any collection of controls, but you must add a group box for option buttons (so that the user can select one button from the group). Always create an option group before adding your option buttons.

To add a group box, select the **I**tem | **G**roup Box command. To change the name of the group, select **E**dit | **I**nfo and enter a different name in the **T**ext field.

For an option group, use the **I**nit/Result field to specify which option is selected when the user displays the dialog box (that is, 1 for the first option button, 2 for the second, and so on). When the user exits the dialog box, the option group's Init/Result field contains the number of the selected option.

SUPER TIP

If you press Enter after adding a group box, Excel automatically adds an option button inside the box.

What happens if you want to include an existing item in a group? If you try moving the item into the group, it disappears behind the group box. To add the item to the group, you need to follow the steps in Procedure 47.3.

PROCEDURE 47.3. ADDING AN EXISTING ITEM TO A GROUP BOX.

1. Click on an item or press the Tab key until it is selected.
2. Select the **E**dit | Cu**t** command.
3. Click on the group or press the Tab key until it is selected.
4. Select the **E**dit | **P**aste command.
5. Move the item into the group.

Adding Text

Text items are static text strings that you can use to label edit boxes and list boxes, or to provide instructions for the user. Select the **I**tem | **T**ext command to add the text item. Then select **E**dit | **I**nfo and enter the text in the **T**ext field.

TIP

If you want an edit box or list box label to have an accelerator key, add the text item for the label immediately before adding the edit box or list box. In the text item's Info dialog box, enter the label in the **T**ext box and precede the designated letter with an ampersand (&).

Adding an Edit Box

Edit boxes enable the user type in data. Five different edit boxes are available:

Edit Box	*Accepts*	*Returns*
Text	Anything	Text
Integer	Integer values between –32765 and 32767	Integer values between –32765 and 32767
Number	Any number	Numeric
Formula	Anything	Text in R1C1 notation
Reference	References	Text in R1C1 notation

If you want the edit box to display an initial value, enter the value in the Init/Result field. When the user exits the dialog box, Init/Result contains the contents of the edit box.

> **SUPER NOTE**
>
> To name an edit box, don't use the Text field. Instead, you need to add a Text item to the dialog box. (See the section earlier in this chapter titled "Adding Text.")

Follow the steps in Procedure 47.4 to add an edit box to your custom dialog box.

PROCEDURE 47.4. ADDING AN EDIT BOX TO A DIALOG BOX.

1. Select the **I**tem | **E**dit Box command. The Dialog Editor displays a dialog box of edit box types, shown in Figure 47.4.

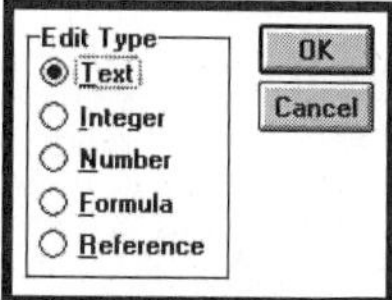

FIGURE 47.4.
The Dialog Editor's edit box options.

2. Select the edit box type you want.
3. Click on OK or press Enter. Dialog Editor adds the edit box.
4. Select **E**dit | **I**nfo (or double-click on the item) and enter the appropriate information for the item.

Adding a List Box

List boxes display lists of items that the user can choose. You can select one of the following list box types (see Figure 47.5):

> *Standard List Box:* A simple list of items. You'll enter the list in a range on a worksheet (in a database, for example) or on the macro sheet. In the Info dialog box, you need to enter a reference to the list in the **T**ext field. Init/Result returns the number of the item selected (the first item in the list is 1).
>
> *Linked List Box:* Links a standard list box to an edit box. An item selected from the list appears in the edit box, and the user can edit the selection. As with the standard list box, you need to set up a list and add a reference to the range in the **T**ext field of the Info dialog box. The returned value in Init/Result depends on whether the user edited the item:

If the user didn't edit the item, Init/Result for the list box returns the number of the selected item.

If the user did edit the item, the list box returns #N/A, and the edit box returns the edited text in its Init/Result field.

Linked File/Directory List Box: If you need a dialog box similar to Excel's Open dialog box, use this item to display a file list linked to an edit box, and use a drive and directory list box. If you select the **T**racking Text option, you also get a *directory* text item that displays the initial directory. In the Info dialog box, enter an initial file spec in the **I**nit/Result field for the edit box. If you don't enter a file specification, Excel uses *.*. The selected file is returned in the Init/Result field of the edit box.

SUPER TIP

You can link the drive and directory list box to a text item that displays the current directory. Just add a text item immediately after adding the Linked file/directory list box.

Drop-Down List Box: Shows a single item, but displays a list of items when the user selects it. In the Info dialog box, enter a reference to the list in the **T**ext field. Init/Result returns the number of the selection.

Combination Drop-Down List Box: Combines a drop-down list with an edit box. The user can drop down the list to select an item or edit the selection in the edit box. Enter a reference to the list in the Info dialog box **T**ext field. The returned value depends on whether the user edited the item:

If the user didn't edit the item, the Init/Result field for the list box returns the number of the selected item.

If the user did edit the item, the list box returns #N/A, and the edit box returns the edited text in its Init/Result field.

SUPER NOTE

To name a list box, use a Text item.

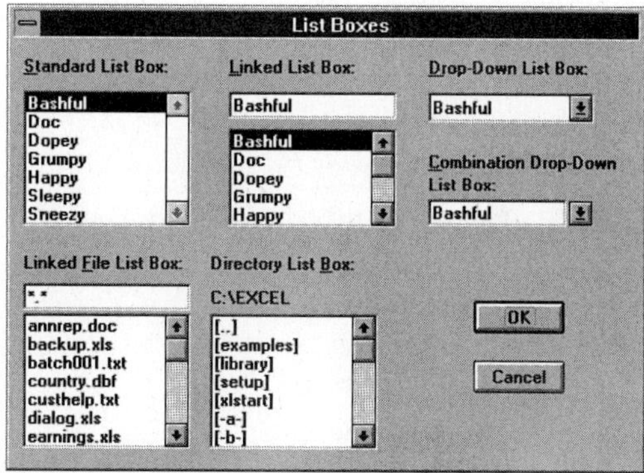

FIGURE 47.5.
Examples of Excel's list box types.

Procedure 47.5 shows you how to add a list box to your custom dialog box.

PROCEDURE 47.5. ADDING A LIST BOX TO A DIALOG BOX.

1. Select the **Item** | **List Box** command. The Dialog Editor displays a dialog box of list box types, shown in Figure 47.6.

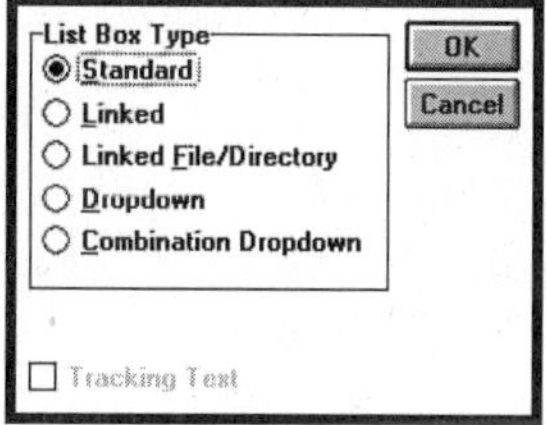

FIGURE 47.6.
The Dialog Editor's list box options.

2. Select the list box type you want.
3. Click on OK or press Enter. Dialog Editor adds the list box.
4. Select **Edit** | **Info** (or double-click on the item) and enter the appropriate information for the list box.

Adding an Icon

For emphasis or to jazz things up a little, you can add an icon or picture to your custom dialog boxes. The Dialog Editor icons are the same three that are available with the ALERT() function. Follow the steps in Procedure 47.6 to add an icon or picture to a dialog box.

PROCEDURE 47.6. ADDING AN ICON TO A DIALOG BOX.

1. Select the **I**tem | **I**con command. Dialog Editor displays a dialog box showing the available icons.
2. Select the icon you want or select **P**icture.
3. Click on OK or press Enter. Dialog Editor adds the icon to the dialog box.
4. Select **E**dit | **I**nfo (or double-click on the item) and enter the appropriate information for the icon. If you selected the **P**icture option, enter a reference for the picture object (for example, "Picture 1") in the Text field.

Editing a Dialog Box Item

Dialog Editor places newly added items below the previous item, so you'll need to move and size some of the items to get your dialog box set up the way you want. Table 47.1 lists some mouse and keyboard techniques for editing items.

Table 47.1. Editing techniques for dialog box items.

Result	*Action*
Select an item	Click on the item or use the Tab key
Select multiple items	Hold down the Shift key and click on the items
Select a group box	Select the group and then select **E**dit	Select **G**roup
Select all items	Select the Select **A**ll Items command
Move an item	Drag the item. Alternatively, select the item and use the arrow keys
Size an item	Drag the item's edges. Alternatively, select the item, hold down the Shift key, and use the arrow keys
Delete an item	Select the item and choose **E**dit	Cl**e**ar (or press the Delete key)

TIP

If you can't move or size an item, display its Info dialog box (by double-clicking on it or by selecting **E**dit | **I**nfo) and deselect the appropriate Auto check boxes.

SUPER TIP

To make items easier to line up, change the grid size. Select the **E**dit | **G**rid Si**z**e command and enter larger numbers for the **H**orizontal (x) and **V**ertical (y) grids. (Values of 5 or 10 pixels work well.)

Copying the Dialog Box to Excel

Once you've set up a custom dialog box, you can't use it in your macros until you copy it to a macro sheet. Procedure 47.7 outlines the steps to follow.

PROCEDURE 47.7. COPYING A CUSTOM DIALOG BOX TO EXCEL.

1. Select the **E**dit | **S**elect Dialog command.
2. Select **E**dit | **C**opy to copy the dialog box to the Clipboard.
3. Switch to Excel and activate the macro sheet you want to use to store the dialog box.
4. Select a cell in an empty area of the macro sheet.
5. Select **E**dit | **P**aste. Excel pastes a dialog box definition table to the macro sheet.
6. Select the **I**nsert | **N**ame | **D**efine command. Excel displays the Define Name dialog box.
7. In the Names in **W**orkbook edit box, enter a name for the table.
8. Click on OK or press Enter.

Understanding the Dialog Box Definition Table

The numbers and text that Excel pastes into the dialog box definition table can seem meaningless at first. To knock some sense into them, format the definition table as shown in Figure 47.7. The custom dialog box defined by this table is shown in Figure 47.8.

Excel designates each type of dialog box item with a unique *item number* (see Table 47.2). The first column of the dialog box table (*Item*) lists the item number for each element in your custom dialog box. The rest of the columns are the corresponding fields from the Info dialog box. The individual rows in the table define a single item in your custom dialog box. (The first row always defines the dialog box as a whole; that's why the item number is blank.) In Figure 47.7, for example, the last two rows define the OK and Cancel buttons (item numbers 1 and 2, respectively). Blank values in the X, Y, Width, and Height columns signify that Excel automatically calculates these properties.

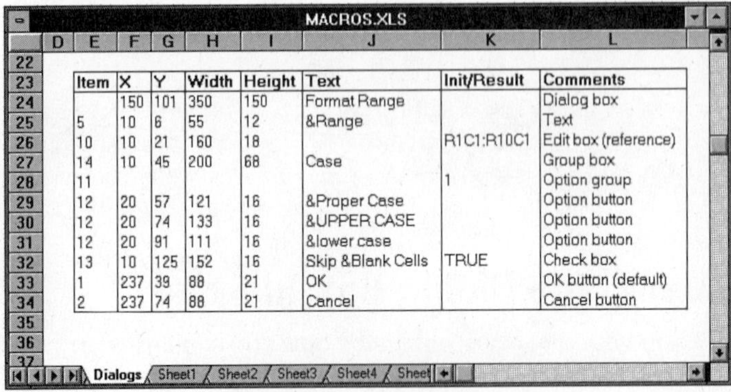

Item	X	Y	Width	Height	Text	Init/Result	Comments
	150	101	350	150	Format Range		Dialog box
5	10	6	55	12	&Range		Text
10	10	21	160	18		R1C1:R10C1	Edit box (reference)
14	10	45	200	68	Case		Group box
11						1	Option group
12	20	57	121	16	&Proper Case		Option button
12	20	74	133	16	&UPPER CASE		Option button
12	20	91	111	16	&lower case		Option button
13	10	125	152	16	Skip &Blank Cells	TRUE	Check box
1	237	39	88	21	OK		OK button (default)
2	237	74	88	21	Cancel		Cancel button

FIGURE 47.7.
A formatted dialog box definition table.

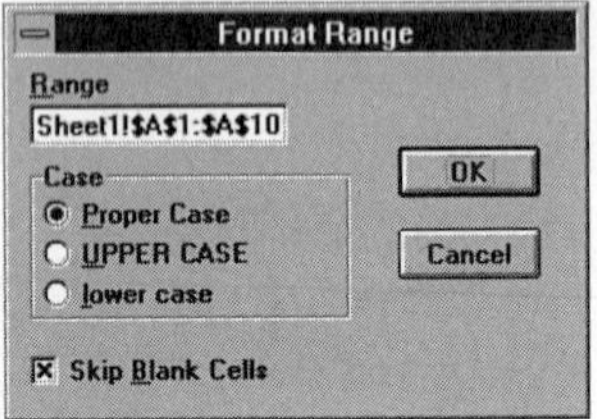

FIGURE 47.8.
The custom dialog box defined by the dialog box table shown in Figure 47.7.

Table 47.2. Item numbers for the various dialog box items.

Number	*Item*
1	OK button (default)
2	Cancel button (nondefault)
3	OK button (nondefault)
4	Cancel button (default)
5	Text
6	Text edit box
7	Integer edit box
8	Number edit box
9	Formula edit box
10	Reference edit box
11	Option group
12	Option button
13	Check box
14	Group box
15	Standard list box

Number	*Item*
16	Linked list box
17	Icon
18	Linked file list box
19	Linked drive.directory list box
20	Directory text
21	Drop-down list box
22	Combination drop-down list box
23	Picture button
24	Help button

SUPER NOTE

If you included a Help button in your dialog box, you need to add a help topic reference in the upper-left corner of the dialog box table (for example, cell E24 in Figure 47.7). For information on creating custom help topics, see Chapter 49, "Macro Tips and Techniques."

Editing the Dialog Box Table

If you need to make changes to your dialog box, you can edit the dialog box table or load the definition back into the Dialog Editor and make your changes there.

If you would prefer to edit the table, select each cell you want to change and enter the new values. You can delete rows to remove items from the dialog box, and you can add new items by inserting a row and filling in the appropriate fields. You can even build an entire dialog box table from scratch and bypass the Dialog Editor altogether (which is a must if you're new to Excel 5.0 and don't have the Dialog Editor program).

SUPER TIP

Add 200 to an item number to define it as dimmed. Add 100 to an item number to define it as a trigger. See the section later in this chapter titled "Using Triggers to Create Dynamic Dialog Boxes."

SUPER CAUTION

Don't leave any blank rows in the table or Excel will generate an error when you try to display the dialog box.

If you want to load the dialog box back into the Dialog Editor, follow the steps in Procedure 47.8.

PROCEDURE 47.8. LOADING A DIALOG BOX INTO THE DIALOG EDITOR.

1. Select the dialog box table (don't include any column headings or other cells you added yourself).
2. Select the **E**dit | **C**opy command.
3. Start (or switch to) the Dialog Editor.
4. Select the **E**dit | **P**aste command.

Using Dialog Boxes in Macros

To display your custom macro in a dialog box, use the `DIALOG.BOX()` function:

`DIALOG.BOX(`***`dialog_ref`***`)`

`dialog_ref` is a reference to the dialog box definition table.

If a user clicks on the OK button, `DIALOG.BOX()` returns the position number of the button (the second row of the dialog box table is position 1, the third row is 2, and so on). The function also enters the return values for the dialog box fields in their respective cells in the Init/Result column. If the user clicks on the Cancel button, `DIALOG.BOX()` returns `FALSE`.

Figure 47.9 shows a macro named DisplayDialog that displays the dialog box from the definition shown in Figure 47.7. The next two sections explain this macro in detail.

Setting Dialog Box Initial Values

Some dialog box items (such as OK and Cancel buttons, text, and group boxes) don't need initial values. Others (such as edit boxes, check boxes, and lists) accept initial values that appear in the dialog box when the user displays it. For the latter, you have two choices when setting initial values:

- If you want the dialog box to use the same defaults every time the user displays it, use `SET.VALUE()` before every `DIALOG.BOX()` function to enter values in the appropriate Init/Result cells.

- If you want the dialog box to use its previous results as the new initial values, enter initial values into the table's Init/Result cells before the first `DIALOG.BOX()` call. Subsequent calls will automatically use the values returned to Init/Result.

FIGURE 47.9.
A macro to initialize, display, and process a custom dialog box.

	A	B	C
23		**DisplayDialog**	
24		=ECHO(FALSE)	Turn off screen echoing
25		=SET.VALUE(RefResult,REFTEXT(SELECTION()))	Initialize edit box
26		=SET.VALUE(OptionResult,1)	Initialize option group
27		=SET.VALUE(CheckResult,TRUE)	Initialize check box
28	DialogResult	=DIALOG.BOX(FormatDialog)	Display dialog box
29		=IF(DialogResult=FALSE,RETURN())	If Cancelled, stop
30		=SELECT(TEXTREF(RefResult))	Select entered range
31		=FOR.CELL("CurrentCell",,GET.CELL(5,CheckResult))	Loop through current selection
32		= IF(OptionResult=1)	If Proper case,
33		= FORMULA(PROPER(CurrentCell),CurrentCell)	Use PROPER()
34		= ELSE.IF(OptionResult=2)	If Upper case
35		= FORMULA(UPPER(CurrentCell),CurrentCell)	Use UPPER()
36		= ELSE()	Otherwise,
37		= FORMULA(LOWER(CurrentCell),CurrentCell)	Use LOWER()
38		= END.IF()	
39		=NEXT()	
40		=RETURN()	

Dialogs / Sheet1 / Sheet2 / Sheet3 / Sheet4 / Sheet5

In the DisplayDialog macro, the first three lines set values for the reference edit box, the option group, and the check box. (For clarity, I've named the Init/Result cells for these items RefResult, OptionResult, and CheckResult, respectively.)

Processing Dialog Box Results

Once you've initialized your items, you call the `DIALOG.BOX()` function to display the dialog box to the user. When the user exits, use an `IF()` function to test the return value of `DIALOG.BOX()`. A `FALSE` result means the user selected a Cancel button; a non-zero (`TRUE`) result means the user clicked on the OK button.

When `IF()` detects a `TRUE` result, your macro needs to process the dialog box results returned in the Init/Result fields. In the DisplayDialog macro, for example, a `SELECT()` function first selects the range the user entered. Then, the `FOR.CELL()` function loops through the range and formats each cell according to the options the user selected.

Using Triggers to Create Dynamic Dialog Boxes

A *dynamic dialog box* is a dialog box that changes its state whenever the user selects a certain item. An example is the Series dialog box that appears when you select the **E**dit | F**i**ll | **S**eries command. When you first display this dialog box, Excel dims the option buttons in the Date Unit group. If you select the **D**ate type, however, Excel activates the Date Unit options. An item such as the **D**ate option button that changes a dynamic dialog box is called a *trigger*.

You create a trigger in the Dialog Editor by selecting the Trigger option in the item's Info dialog box or by adding 100 to the item number in the dialog box table. For example, to make a nondefault OK button a trigger, change its item number to 103.

SUPER NOTE

To define an item as dimmed, add 200 to its regular item number. For example, to dim an option button, change its item number to 212.

To process a trigger, you set up a loop (usually a `WHILE()` function) in your macro. When the user selects the trigger, Excel returns control to the macro but leaves the dialog box on-screen. You can then make your changes (for example, by altering the dialog box definition or displaying an `ALERT()` box) and loop back and redisplay the dialog box.

As an example, I'll show you how to create a dynamic dialog box similar to the one shown in Figure 47.10. When the user clicks on the **M**ore>> button, the dialog box expands to show more options (see Figure 47.11).

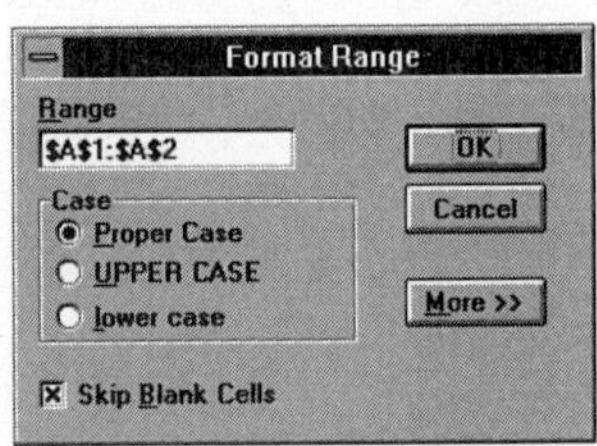

FIGURE 47.10. *A dynamic dialog box that expands when the user clicks on the More>> button.*

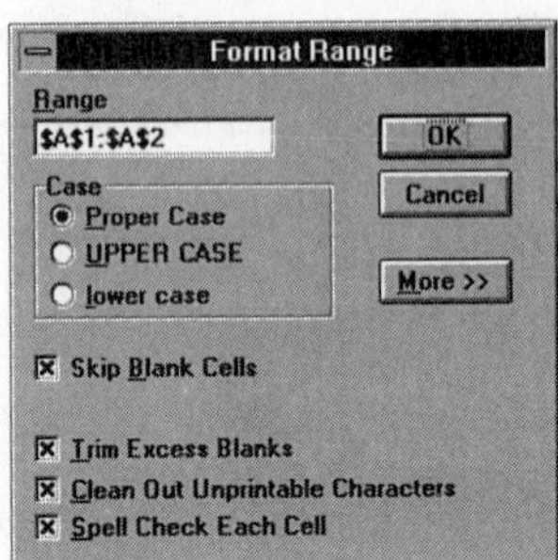

FIGURE 47.11. *The expanded dynamic dialog box.*

The idea is to create a dialog box that looks similar to the expanded dialog box, shown in Figure 47.11. Then, in the definition table, you define two range names: one for the regular dialog box and one for the expanded one. Figure 47.12 shows the definition table. The range E43:L54 is named RegDialog, and it includes all the items in the regular dialog box. Notice, in particular, that it includes the **M**ore>> button, which is the trigger. The range E43:L57 is named ExpDialog, and it includes all the items in the expanded dialog box.

FIGURE 47.12.
The definition table for the dynamic dialog box.

	E	F	G	H	I	J	K	L
41								
42	Item	X	Y	Width	Height	Text	Init/Result	Comments
43		150	101	350	150	Format Range		Dialog box
44	5	10	6	55	12	&Range		Text
45	10	10	21	160	18		R1C1:R2C1	Edit box (referen
46	14	10	45	200	68	Case		Group box
47	11						1	Option group
48	12	20	57	121	16	&Proper Case		Option button
49	12	20	74	133	16	&UPPER CASE		Option button
50	12	20	91	111	16	&lower case		Option button
51	13	10	125	152	16	Skip &Blank Cells	TRUE	Check box
52	1	237	20	88	21	OK		OK button (defaul
53	2	237	45	88	21	Cancel		Cancel button
54	103	237	84	88	21	&More >>		OK button
55	13	10	161	176	16	&Trim Excess Blanks	TRUE	Check box
56	13	10	178	283	16	&Clean Out Unprintable Characters	TRUE	Check box
57	13	10	195	197	16	&Spell Check Each Cell	TRUE	Check box
58								

Dialogs / Sheet1 / Sheet2 / Sheet3 / Sheet4 / Sheet5

Finally, Figure 47.13 shows the DisplayDynamicDialog macro, which displays the dynamic dialog box. (To keep things simple, I've left out the commands that initialize the items and process the results.) The first line uses `SET.NAME()` to define a variable—*`DialogName`*—that holds the range name of the dialog box (either RegDialog or ExpDialog, as explained previously). The second line defines the height of the dialog box to be 150 pixels (the name DialogHeight refers the cell in the dialog box table that defines the dialog box height).

FIGURE 47.13.
A macro to display a dynamic dialog box.

	A	B	C
42			
43		DisplayDynamicDialog	
44		=SET.NAME("DialogName",RegDialog)	Initialize dialog range name
45		=SET.VALUE(DialogHeight,150)	Initialize dialog box height
46		***Other initializations go here***	
47		=WHILE(TRUE)	Loop,
48	DynamicResult	= DIALOG.BOX(DialogName)	Display dialog box
49		= IF(DynamicResult=FALSE)	If Cancelled,
50		= RETURN()	Stop the macro
51		= ELSE.IF(DynamicResult=11)	If the More button selected,
52		= SET.NAME("DialogName",ExpDialog)	Change the dialog range
53		= SET.VALUE(DialogHeight,220)	Change the dialog height
54		= ELSE()	Otherwise,
55		= BREAK()	Exit the loop
56		= END.IF()	
57		=NEXT()	
58		***Formatting commands go here***	
59		=RETURN()	

Dialogs / Sheet1 / Sheet2 / Sheet3 / Sheet4 / Sheet5

The macro then loops (using the `WHILE()` function) and displays the regular dialog box (shown in Figure 47.10). The `IF()` function (cell B28) tests for a result of 11 from the `DIALOG.BOX()` function. This corresponds to the **M**ore>> button (the trigger). If this returns `TRUE`, the macro changes the *`DialogName`* variable to *`ExpDialog`* and redefines the dialog box height to 220 pixels. The macro then loops back and redisplays the dialog box with the new settings (see Figure 47.11). If the user clicks on OK or Cancel, the macro processes the result accordingly.

Chapter

48

Debugging Macros

It usually isn't very difficult to get short command and function macros up and running, but as your macros grow larger and more complex, errors inevitably will creep in. Many will be simple syntax problems you can fix easily, but others will be more subtle and harder to find. For the latter—whether they have to do with incorrect values being returned or problems in the overall logic of a macro—you'll need to be able to look "inside" your macros to determine what's wrong. This chapter covers several debugging techniques that should help you recover from most macro errors.

Monitoring Macro Values

If a macro isn't doing what it's supposed to, it could be that some formulas are returning values you didn't expect. For example, in an IF-END.IF block, if the statements between the `IF()` and `ELSE()` functions never seem to execute, it's probably because the `IF()` function is always returning `FALSE`. To check this, you need to look either at the result of the `IF()` function or at the individual values that make up its logical test.

Monitoring macro sheet values is the most basic (and one of the most useful) debugging techniques. The next three sections show you several methods for keeping an eye on macro results and values.

Viewing Macro Sheet Results

The simplest way to monitor a macro is to view the results of each formula after the macro has finished. To do this, follow the steps in Procedure 48.1.

PROCEDURE 48.1. VIEWING VALUES IN A MACRO SHEET.

1. If necessary, activate the macro sheet that contains the macro.
2. Select the **T**ools | **O**ptions command to display the Options dialog box.
3. In the View tab, deactivate the Fo**r**mulas check box.
4. Click on OK or press Enter.

SUPER TIP

You can toggle between Formulas view and Values view by pressing Ctrl+' (back quote).

With the Values view on, Excel replaces each macro formula with the result the macro returned the last time you ran it. The values you see depend on the contents of the formula. Most macro functions return `TRUE` if they ran successfully and return `FALSE` or an error value, otherwise. `INPUT()` functions return either the entered data or `FALSE` if the user clicked on Cancel. Calculations return the result of the calculation.

You also can use this method to view macro results while the macro is running. Just open a second window on the macro sheet (by selecting the **W**indow | **N**ew Window command) and change one of the windows to Values view. By arranging your windows strategically, you can see the result of each formula as the macro runs.

Storing Macro Sheet Values

If you have a large macro that either doesn't fit inside a window or has only a few values you want to monitor, a Values view of the macro sheet isn't practical. Instead, you can set up a table in an empty part of the macro sheet and include `SET.VALUE()` functions in your macro to store the results you want.

For example, in the DataEntry macro in Figure 48.1, I added `SET.VALUE()` functions to monitor three variables: `InputValue`, `Done`, and `EntryRow`. These values are stored in the range F109:F111. To monitor them, I arranged the windows as shown in Figure 48.2.

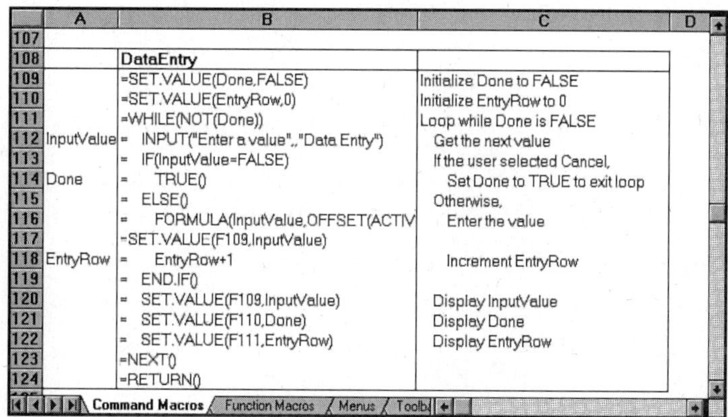

A
B
C
D
DataEntry
=SET.VALUE(Done,FALSE)
Initialize Done to FALSE
=SET.VALUE(EntryRow,0)
Initialize EntryRow to 0
=WHILE(NOT(Done))
Loop while Done is FALSE
InputValue
= INPUT("Enter a value",,"Data Entry")
Get the next value
= IF(InputValue=FALSE)
If the user selected Cancel,
Done
= TRUE()
Set Done to TRUE to exit loop
= ELSE()
Otherwise,
= FORMULA(InputValue,OFFSET(ACTIV
Enter the value
=SET.VALUE(F109,InputValue)
EntryRow
= EntryRow+1
Increment EntryRow
= END.IF()
= SET.VALUE(F109,InputValue)
Display InputValue
= SET.VALUE(F110,Done)
Display Done
= SET.VALUE(F111,EntryRow)
Display EntryRow
=NEXT()
=RETURN()
Command Macros
Function Macros
Menus

FIGURE 48.1.
Use SET.VALUE() functions to store macro values in a separate macro sheet table.

SUPER NOTE

For best results, enter your `SET.VALUE()` functions immediately after any formula that changes a value you are tracking (where possible).

Another use for `SET.VALUE()` is to store function results that are embedded inside a formula. For example, in the DataEntry macro, consider the following formula (this is the complete formula in cell B116):

```
=FORMULA(InputValue,OFFSET(ACTIVE.CELL(),EntryRow,0))
```

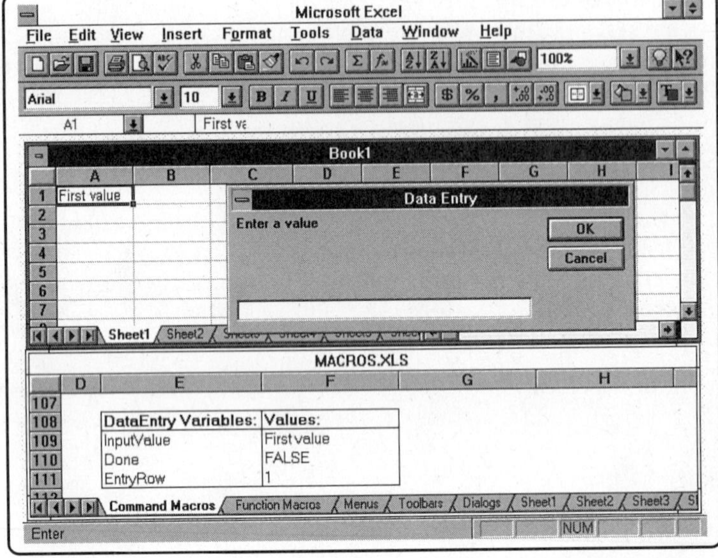

FIGURE 48.2.
Arrange your windows so you can monitor your SET.VALUE() functions.

The Values view can tell you the result of the `FORMULA()` function and the values for `InputValue` and `EntryRow`. However, it won't show the results of the embedded functions `OFFSET()` and `ACTIVE.CELL()`. To track these values, include them in `SET.VALUE()` functions before the formula.

> **SUPER CAUTION**
>
> Be sure to remove these `SET.VALUE()` functions once your macro is working properly. Leaving them in only slows down the macro.

Displaying Macro Sheet Values in the Status Bar

Watching values on a macro sheet doesn't work if you need to keep the worksheet maximized or if you have several worksheets open at once. Instead, you can use the `MESSAGE()` function to display individual values in the status bar. (See Chapter 43, "Using Macros to Get and Display Information," for a full discussion of the `MESSAGE()` function.)

For example, the following formula displays the values for the DataEntry macro's `Done` and `EntryRow` variables (along with some explanatory text) in the status line:

```
=MESSAGE(TRUE,"Done = "&Done&"; EntryRow = "&EntryRow)
```

Controlling the Operation of a Macro

Monitoring values in the DataEntry macro is easy because the macro regularly stops to get user input. While Excel waits for you to enter some data, you can peruse leisurely the macro's values and look for anomalies. However, for a macro that never pauses for input, either from a dialog box or an `ALERT()` or `INPUT()` function, you need some special techniques that control the operation of the macro.

Pausing Macro Operation

The easiest way to pause a macro is, naturally, to use the `PAUSE()` function. When Excel encounters a `PAUSE()` function, it suspends the macro and returns you to the active sheet. This enables you either to make changes to the sheet or to switch to the macro sheet to view the current values.

To resume a paused macro, you have two choices:

- Click on the Resume tool in the Visual Basic toolbar.

Click on this tool to resume a paused macro.

- Run a macro containing the `RESUME()` function:

  `RESUME(type_num)`

  `type_num` A number that specifies how Excel resumes:

  1 If the macro was paused by a `PAUSE()` function, the macro continues where it left off. If it was paused in Single Step mode (see the next section), the macro returns to the Single Step dialog box.

  2 The macro halts.

  3 The macro continues where it left off.

  4 Puts the macro in Single Step mode.

Include `PAUSE()` functions in your macros wherever you want to stop and take stock of the situation. Alternatively, you can test variables and pause when they meet certain conditions. For example, the following formula pauses the DataEntry macro when the `EntryRow` variable equals 10:

```
=IF(EntryRow=10,PAUSE())
```

Stepping Through a Macro

The methods you've seen so far have dealt mostly with macro values in one form or another, but many macro problems are the result of *logic errors,* especially in larger programs. A logic error is when your macro zigs instead of zags. It could be a loop that gets missed, a `GOTO()` that goes to the wrong place, or a call to another macro at the wrong time.

To solve these kinds of problems, you need a more powerful tool: Excel's Single Step mode. Single Step mode enables you to work through a macro one line at a time so that you can see the logical progression of the code. You can monitor macro values, too, so you get the best of both worlds.

There are five ways to get into Single Step mode:

- In the Macro dialog box, select a macro and then click on the **S**tep button.
- Include a `STEP()` function in the macro at the point where you want to start stepping through the code.
- After an error, click on the **S**tep button in the Macro Error dialog box.
- While a macro is running, press the Esc key.
- In a macro sheet, select the cell containing the macro name and then click on the Step tool in the Visual Basic toolbar.

Click on this tool in the Visual Basic toolbar to step through a selected macro.

After Excel enters Single Step mode, you see the Single Step dialog box, shown in Figure 48.3. The first line (Cell) shows the macro cell that Excel is about to execute. The second line (Formula) shows the formula contained in the cell.

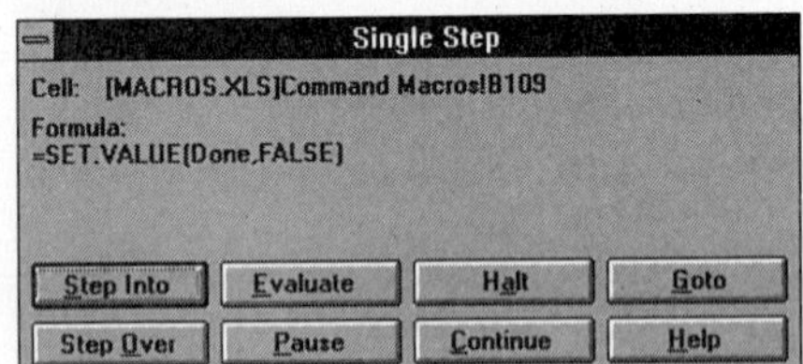

FIGURE 48.3.
Use the Single Step dialog box to step through a macro one line at a time.

The buttons at the bottom of the Single Step dialog box control the stepping procedure. Table 48.1 summarizes these buttons.

Table 48.1. The Single Step dialog box buttons.

Button	*Description*
Step Into	Executes the displayed formula. If the formula is a call to a subroutine, Excel also steps through the subroutine formulas. In this case, the next formula displayed will be the first formula in the subroutine. When you've stepped through the entire subroutine, Excel returns you to the original macro.
Step **O**ver	Executes the displayed formula. If the formula calls a subroutine, Excel executes the entire subroutine without stepping into it.

Button	Description
Evaluate	Calculates the formula one operator or function at a time. See the next section for details.
Pause	Suspends operation of the macro. This works just like the PAUSE() function described earlier.
Halt	Stops the macro and returns to the active sheet.
Continue	Exits Single Step mode and resumes running the macro.
Goto	Stops the macro and selects the cell shown in the Single Step dialog box.

Evaluating Macro Formulas in Single Step Mode

One of the most useful features of Single Step mode is the Evaluate button. As I mentioned earlier, one of the obstacles you face when debugging your macros is unraveling functions embedded either in formulas or in other functions. The Evaluate feature solves this problem elegantly by enabling you to calculate a formula one function at a time.

As an example, let's return to the formula in the DataEntry macro that enters the data in the active worksheet:

```
=FORMULA(InputValue,OFFSET(ACTIVE.CELL(),EntryRow,0))
```

The purpose of this formula is to enter `InputValue` in the worksheet cell that is offset from the active cell by `EntryRow` rows. Figures 48.4 through 48.7 display the formula in the Single Step dialog box after four successive clicks of the Evaluate button.

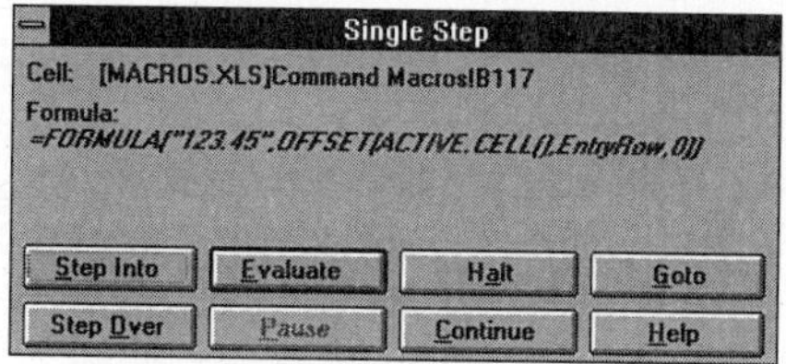

FIGURE 48.4. *The formula after you click on the Evaluate button the first time.*

FIGURE 48.5. *The formula after you click on the Evaluate button the second time.*

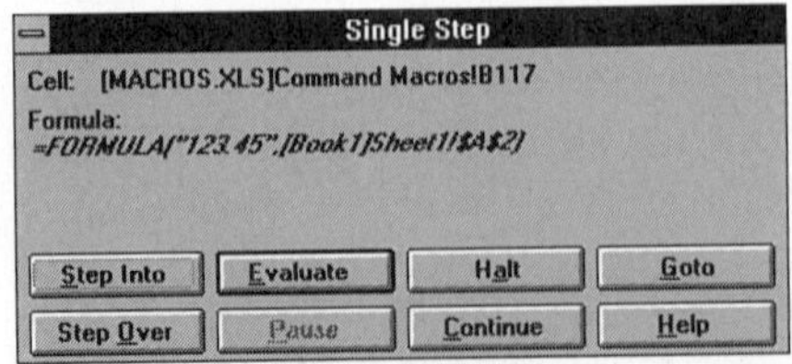

FIGURE 48.6.
The formula after you click on the Evaluate button the third time.

FIGURE 48.7.
The formula after you click on the Evaluate button the fourth time.

With this formula displayed in the Single Step dialog box, clicking once on the **Evaluate** button replaces the `InputValue` variable with the value entered by the user (as you can see in Figure 48.4, the value in this case is `123.45`). A second click on **Evaluate** replaces the arguments of the `OFFSET()` function with their existing values. That is, Excel replaces `ACTIVE.CELL()` with `[Book1]Sheet1!$A$1` and `EntryRow` with `1` (see Figure 48.5). Figure 48.6 shows that when you evaluate the formula for a third time, Excel calculates the result of the `OFFSET()` function (`[Book1]Sheet1!$A$2`). Finally, a fourth click on **Evaluate** returns the result of the `FORMULA()` function—`TRUE` (see Figure 48.7).

Debugging Tips

Debugging your macros can be a frustrating job at the best of times. To help, here are several tips to keep in mind when tracking down macro problems.

Break Down Complex Macros

Don't try to solve all your problems at once. If you have a large macro that isn't working right, test it in small chunks to try to narrow down the problem. To test a piece of a macro, add a `RETURN()` function after the last line of the code you want to run, move to the first line, and then run the macro from there.

Enter Formulas in Lowercase

When you press Enter to accept a macro formula (or if you click on the Enter button in the formula bar), Excel converts the case of the formula text as follows:

- The names of built-in functions are converted to uppercase.
- Range names are converted to the case you used when you originally defined the name.

One easy way to detect macro problems is to enter your formulas entirely in lowercase. If you see that Excel hasn't converted a function name or a range name to the correct case, you know that Excel didn't recognize the name—either because you misspelled the name or because the range name hasn't been defined.

If a Macro Name Doesn't Appear in the Macro Dialog Box

If you don't see the macro's name in the Macro dialog box, check these things out:

- Is the workbook that contains the macro sheet open? The Macro dialog lists macros only from open workbooks.
- Did you define the macro's name? Run the **I**nsert | **N**ame | **D**efine command, and look for the name. If it's not there, define it.
- When you defined the name, did you remember to select the **C**ommand option?

If a Macro Refuses to Run

If your macro refuses to run at all, check the following:

- Make sure the appropriate workbook is open.
- If you're trying to run the macro from a shortcut key, make sure you've defined one. In the Macro dialog box, highlight the file and then click on the **O**ptions button to see if a shortcut has been defined.
- Check to see whether another macro has the same shortcut key. If one does, and it appears earlier in the Macro dialog box list, your macro won't run. You need to change the shortcut key for one of the macros.
- Make sure the macro name refers to the proper cell in the macro sheet.

Deactivate Problem Formulas

If a particular formula is giving you problems, you can temporarily deactivate it by removing the equals sign (=). This at least enables you to check the rest of the macro.

This trick also works if you've entered several `SET.VALUE()` or `STEP()` functions to aid your debugging. If you want to leave them in just in case you need them later, but you want to deactivate them for now, follow these steps:

1. Select the cells containing the macro.
2. Select the **E**dit | R**e**place command.
3. Enter `=step` in the Fi**n**d What box and `step` in the Re**p**lace with box.
4. Click on Replace **A**ll.

5. Repeat steps 2-4, but this time enter `=set.value` in the Find What box and `set.value` in the Replace with box.

Break Up Long Formulas

One of the most complicated aspects of macro debugging is making sense out of long formulas. The `STEP()` function's Evaluate feature can help, but it's usually best to keep your formulas as short as you can. Once you get things working properly, you can often recombine formulas for more efficient code.

For example, consider the following formula (from the DataEntry macro I showed you earlier):

```
=FORMULA(InputValue,OFFSET(ACTIVE.CELL(),EntryRow,0))
```

That's a real mouthful, but I originally wrote it as two formulas:

```
=OFFSET(ACTIVE.CELL(),EntryRow,0)
=FORMULA(InputValue,NextCell)
```

Here, `NextCell` was the name I assigned to the result of the `OFFSET()` function. This was more comprehensible and more easily debugged. When I was sure things worked right, I combined them into the larger formula.

Use Range Names Whenever Possible

Macros are much easier to read and debug if you use range names in place of cell references. Not only is a name such as *Expenses!Summary* more comprehensible than, for example, *Expenses!$A$1:$F$10,* but it's safer, too. If you add rows or columns to the *Summary* range, the name changes as well. With cell addresses, you would have to adjust the references yourself.

Name Constant Values

If your macro uses constant values in several different formulas, you can give yourself one less debugging chore by assigning a name to the value and then using that name in all the formulas. This ensures that you don't enter the wrong value in a formula, and you get the added benefit of making your macro easier to understand.

Chapter

49

Macro Tips and Techniques

This chapter concludes the Macro Workshop with a look at a few tips and techniques that will help you get the most out of Excel's macros. I show you how to assign your macros to worksheet buttons and other objects, how to create your own add-in macros, how to set up a custom Help system, and more.

Creating a Macro Button

As you learned in Chapters 45 and 46, you can assign your macros to either menu commands or custom tools. These approaches have advantages and disadvantages:

- Toolbar tools give the user push-button access to a macro, but it's often hard to tell what a tool does by looking at the picture on the tool face.
- Menu commands describe the actions they perform, but the user must navigate the menu system to execute them.

You can get the best of both worlds by assigning your macros to *macro buttons.* A macro button is an object you draw right on the worksheet. As you can see in Figure 49.1, they look just like dialog box command buttons. The user simply clicks on a button, and the macro assigned to it executes.

	A	B	C	D	E	F	G
1	Monthly Sales - Historical Trend						
2							
3	Correlation to Actual Sales:						
4		Normal Trend –>	0.42				
5		Reseasoned Trend –>	0.96				
6							
7			Actual	Normal Trend	Deseasoned Actual	Deseasoned Trend	Reseasoned Trend
8		January	90.0	109.2	108.7	112.0	92.7
9		February	90.0	109.4	107.0	112.2	94.4
10		March	110.0	109.7	118.0	112.4	104.8
11		April	105.0	109.9	114.9	112.6	102.9
12		May	100.0	110.2	110.9	112.8	101.7
13	Year 1	June	100.0	110.4	109.0	113.0	103.7
14		July	105.0	110.7	108.9	113.2	109.2
15		August	105.0	110.9	103.6	113.4	114.9

FIGURE 49.1.
You draw macro buttons right on the worksheet to give the user quick access to commonly used features.

Follow the steps in Procedure 49.1 to create a macro button.

PROCEDURE 49.1. CREATING A MACRO BUTTON.

1. Open the workbook that contains the macro, and activate the worksheet where you want to draw the button.
2. Display the Drawing toolbar, and click on the Create Button tool. The mouse pointer changes to a crosshair.

The Create Button tool from the Drawing toolbar.

3. Move the mouse pointer to where you want one corner of the button to appear.
4. Drag the mouse pointer until the button is the size and shape you want. To make the button a square, hold down the Shift key while you drag the mouse pointer. To align the button with the worksheet gridlines, hold down the Alt key while you drag the mouse pointer. When you release the mouse button, Excel displays the Assign Macro dialog box, shown in Figure 49.2.

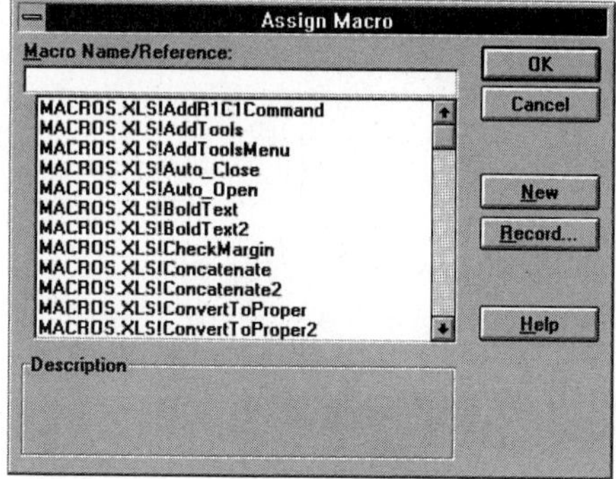

FIGURE 49.2.
Use the Assign Macro dialog box to assign a procedure to the macro button.

5. Use the **M**acro Name/Reference list to select the macro you want to assign to the button.

   or

   To record the macro, click on the **R**ecord button, and record the macro as you normally would.
6. If you selected a macro from the list, click on OK or press Enter.

To run the macro, simply position the mouse pointer over the button (it will change to a hand) and click.

SUPER TIP

You can assign macros to any worksheet graphic object (pictures, charts, drawings, and so on). Just click on the object, run the Tools | Assign Macro command, and select the macro from the Assign Macro dialog box.

Changing the Button Text

After you create a macro button, you need to edit the button text so it describes the action performed by the procedure. Procedure 49.2 shows you how to do this.

PROCEDURE 49.2. CHANGING MACRO BUTTON TEXT.

1. Hold down the Ctrl key and double-click on the button. An insertion point cursor appears inside the button text.
2. Delete the existing text, and type in the text you want.
3. Exit the button by clicking on the worksheet.

> **SUPER NOTE**
>
> If you need to move, size, or format a button, refer to Chapter 27, "Editing Graphic Objects," for instructions. When you select a button to edit, however, you need to hold down the Ctrl key to prevent Excel from running the procedure.

Controlling Other Applications

Excel offers a number of functions for starting and working with other applications inside your macros. The next few sections present some of these functions.

Starting Another Application

You can start another application by using the `EXEC()` function:

`EXEC(`***`program_text`***`,`*`window_num`*`)`

`program_text` — The name of the file that starts the application (or the name of a data file associated with the executable file). Include the drive and directory to make sure Excel can find the file.

`window_num` — A number that specifies the appearance of the application window:

window_num	*Window Appearance*
1	Normal size
2 (or omitted)	Minimized
3	Maximized

If successful, `EXEC()` returns a number (called the *Task ID* number). If unsuccessful, `EXEC()` returns `#VALUE!`.

For example, the following formula starts the Windows Cardfile application:

```
=EXEC("C:\WINDOWS\CARDFILE.EXE",1)
```

As soon as another application is open, use the APP.ACTIVATE() function to switch between it and Excel:

```
APP.ACTIVATE(title_text,wait)
```

title_text	The name of the application as it appears in the title bar. If you omit *title_text*, APP.ACTIVATE() switches to Excel.
wait	A logical value that determines when Excel switches to the application. If *wait* is TRUE, APP.ACTIVATE() waits until you activate Excel before switching. If it's FALSE, APP.ACTIVATE() switches to the application immediately.

SUPER CAUTION

Note that, for some applications, the title bar may include both the name of the application and the name of the active document.

Using DDE to Work with Another Application

Dynamic Data Exchange (or *DDE*) is a communications protocol that enables some Windows applications to send data back and forth and even execute each other's commands. You normally use DDE when you copy and paste data between applications. However, you can control the DDE protocol also at the macro level. Although I won't go into this subject in any depth, the basics you learn here will be enough to add some powerful functionality to your Excel applications.

DDE: The Basic Steps

Using DDE is a three-step process:

1. **Establish a link between Excel and the other application.** This link—called a *channel*—is the path along which the two applications communicate.
2. **Work with the other application.** This usually means either sending data back and forth or operating the other application by invoking its internal commands or by sending keystrokes.
3. **Close the link.** When you finish working with the application, your macro needs to close the channel.

The next three sections look at each step more closely.

Establishing a Link Between Excel and Another Application

To establish a channel between Excel and another DDE application, use the `INITIATE()` function:

`INITIATE(`***app_text***`,`***topic_text***`)`

app_text	This is the DDE name of the application with which you want to open a link. The DDE name depends on the application. For example, the DDE name for Excel is "Excel," and for Word for Windows it's "Winword." For other applications, check their documentation or contact their technical support department.
topic_text	This is, if you will, the "topic of conversation" that the two applications will be using. For most applications, you use either "System" (the application as a whole) or the name of a document in the application (that is, the name as it appears in the title bar).

If the `INITIATE()` function was successful, Excel returns a number identifying the channel. If it was unsuccessful, Excel returns #N/A.

For example, to open a channel between Excel and a document named SUMMARY.DOC in Word for Windows, you would use the following formula:

```
=INITIATE("Winword","SUMMARY.DOC")
```

SUPER NOTE

If the topic document isn't already open, be sure to include its full path name in the `INITIATE()` function.

If the application isn't open when you run the `INITIATE()` function, Excel displays the dialog box shown in Figure 49.3. Just click on **Y**es to start the application. Better yet, you can avoid this message altogether by including an `=ERROR(FALSE)` command just before running `INITIATE()`.

SUPER CAUTION

If the application isn't in the current directory or the search path, the `INITIATE()` function won't be able to find it. One solution is to first use the `DIRECTORY()` function to change to the application's directory (`DIRECTORY("C:\WINWORD")`, for example). Another solution is to use an `EXEC()` function to start the application before invoking `INITIATE()`.

FIGURE 49.3.
When you use INITIATE(), Excel asks whether you want to start the application if it isn't already running.

Controlling the Other Application

Once you have an open channel, you can use the `EXECUTE()` and `SEND.KEYS()` functions to control the other application. `EXECUTE()` has the following syntax:

`EXECUTE(`***`channel_num,execute_text`***`)`

channel_num	The channel returned by the `INITIATE()` function.
execute_text	A text string representing the commands to run in the application. The format depends on the application. For some applications (such as Excel and Word for Windows), you can use their macro commands. Other applications use special DDE commands (refer to your manual or contact technical support).

`EXECUTE()` returns `#VALUE!` if ***channel_num*** is invalid, `#N/A` if the application is busy, `#DIV/0!` if the application doesn't respond after a specific amount of time, and `#REF!` if the application refused the `EXECUTE()` request.

The tricky part of the `EXECUTE()` command is the ***execute_text*** argument, because its form depends entirely on the application. For Excel and Word for Windows, you can use their macro commands as long as you enclose them in square brackets ([ ]). For some other applications, you also can use their macro commands, but they don't support the square brackets standard. Still other programs have no macro language, but they do have special DDE commands you can use. Finally, there are applications with no special commands you can use, but it's still possible to control them by sending keystroke sequences with the `EXECUTE()` function.

SUPER NOTE

To send keystrokes with `EXECUTE()`, use the key formats I discuss later for the `SEND.KEYS()` function. Note, however, that you can't use `EXECUTE()` to send keys to a dialog box. For that you need to use the `SEND.KEYS()` function.

Figure 49.4 shows a macro called WordDDETest, which uses `EXECUTE()` to manipulate Word for Windows. The channel is opened first (and the returned value is stored in `Channel` so the other DDE functions can reference it). Then three `EXECUTE()` functions each run a command from Word for Windows' macro language. These lines move to the start of SUMMARY.DOC, select the first five lines, and copy them to the Clipboard. Then the channel is closed, and an Excel `PASTE()` function pastes the data into the active cell.

FIGURE 49.4.
A macro that uses `EXECUTE()` functions to manipulate Word for Windows using a DDE channel.

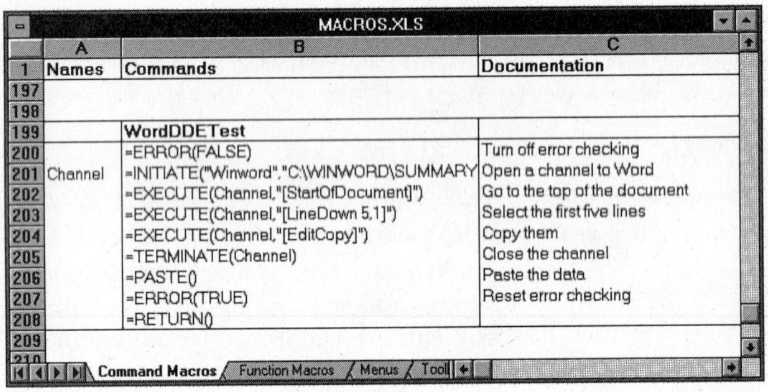

MACROS.XLS

	A	B	C
1	Names	Commands	Documentation
197			
198			
199		WordDDETest	
200		=ERROR(FALSE)	Turn off error checking
201	Channel	=INITIATE("Winword","C:\WINWORD\SUMMARY	Open a channel to Word
202		=EXECUTE(Channel,"[StartOfDocument]")	Go to the top of the document
203		=EXECUTE(Channel,"[LineDown 5,1]")	Select the first five lines
204		=EXECUTE(Channel,"[EditCopy]")	Copy them
205		=TERMINATE(Channel)	Close the channel
206		=PASTE()	Paste the data
207		=ERROR(TRUE)	Reset error checking
208		=RETURN()	
209			

Command Macros / Function Macros / Menus / Tool

For applications with no specific macro language or DDE commands, you can use the `SEND.KEYS()` function to send keystrokes to the program:

```
SEND.KEYS(key_text,wait)
```

key_text This is the key or key combination that will run the procedure. For letters, numbers, or punctuation marks, simply enclose the character in quotes (for example, `"a"`). For other keys, use the following:

Key Name	***key_text***
Backspace	`"{BACKSPACE}"` or `"{BS}"`
Break	`"{BREAK}"`
Caps Lock	`"{CAPSLOCK}"`
Delete	`"{DELETE}"` or `"{DEL}"`
Down arrow	`"{DOWN}"`
End	`"{END}"`
Enter (keypad)	`"{ENTER}"`
Enter	`"~"` (tilde)
Esc	`"{ESCAPE}"` or `"{ESC}"`
Home	`"{HOME}"`
Insert	`"{INSERT}"`
Left arrow	`"{LEFT}"`
Num Lock	`"{NUMLOCK}"`
Page Down	`"{PGDN}"`

	Page Up	`"{PGUP}"`
	Right arrow	`"{RIGHT}"`
	Scroll Lock	`"{SCROLLLOCK}"`
	Tab	`"{TAB}"`
	Up arrow	`"{UP}"`
	F1 through F12	`"{F1}"` through `"{F12}"`

You also can combine these keys with the Shift, Ctrl, and Alt keys. You just precede the above codes with one or more of the following:

Key Name	***key_text***
Alt	`%` (percent)
Ctrl	`^` (caret)
Shift	`+` (plus)

wait — A logical value that determines whether Excel waits for the keys to be processed before continuing the macro. If *wait* is TRUE, Excel waits for the application to finish processing the keys. It doesn't wait if *wait* is FALSE.

For example, if you've initiated a channel between Excel and Word for Windows, the following SEND.KEYS() functions select Word's Forma**t** | **C**haracter command, select the **B**old option, and click on OK:

```
=SEND.KEYS("%tc")
=SEND.KEYS("%b~")
```

You don't need to initiate a DDE link to use SEND.KEYS(). All you need to do is activate a program with EXEC() or APP.ACTIVATE(), and then you can send keystrokes to your heart's content. Figure 49.5, for example, shows the PhoneCustomer macro, which does the following:

- Copies a phone number from the active cell and starts Cardfile.
- Uses SEND.KEYS() to add a new card (F7), paste the phone number (Ctrl+V and Enter), and then start Cardfile's AutoDial feature (F5 and Enter).
- Delays for five seconds to give the phone time to dial.
- Uses SEND.KEYS() to exit Cardfile (Enter, Alt+F4, then N to answer "no" when Cardfile asks whether you want to save changes).

Terminating the Link

When you finish communicating with the other application, use the TERMINATE() function to close the channel between them:

TERMINATE(***channel_num***)

channel_num is the channel number returned by the INITIATE() function.

FIGURE 49.5.
A procedure that uses SEND.KEYS() to control the Cardfile.

MACROS.XLS

	A	B	C
1	Names	Commands	Documentation
209			
210		PhoneCustomer	
211		=COPY()	Copy phone number in active cell
212		=EXEC("C:\WINDOWS\CARDFILE.EXE",1)	Start CardFile
213		=SEND.KEYS("{F7}",TRUE)	Display a new card
214		=SEND.KEYS("^v~",TRUE)	Paste the phone number
215		=SEND.KEYS("{F5}~",TRUE)	Start AutoDial
216		=WAIT(NOW()+"00:00:5")	Wait five seconds fro the phone to dial
217		=SEND.KEYS("~%{F4}n",TRUE)	Exit CardFile
218		=CANCEL.COPY()	Cancel the Copy command
219		=ERROR(TRUE)	Turn error checking back on
220		=RETURN()	
221			

Command Macros / Function Macros / Menus / Tool

Creating an Add-In Macro

If you've used any of Excel's add-in applications, you know they're handy because they add extra functions and commands and make them look as though they were built right into the program. For your own applications, you can convert your workbooks to add-ins and gain the following advantages:

- Your function macros appear in the FunctionWizard dialog box.
- Your command macros do *not* appear in the Macro dialog box.
- You can refer to the macros on the add-in without using an external reference. For example, if the MACROS.XLS workbook is not an add-in, you would refer to a macro named `DisplayDialog` in the `Macros` sheet as follows:

  ```
  =[MACROS.XLM]Macros!DisplayDialog()
  ```

  If the workbook is an add-in, you would need to refer only to the macro name:

  ```
  =DisplayDialog()
  ```

- Add-ins execute faster than normal files.
- The code is converted into a compressed format that no one else can read or modify.

Follow the steps in Procedure 49.3 to save a workbook as an add-in.

PROCEDURE 49.3. SAVING A WORKBOOK AS AN ADD-IN.

1. Activate a macro sheet in the workbook that you want to save as an add-in.
2. Select the Tools | Make Add-In command to display the Make Add-In dialog box.
3. Enter a new name, drive, and directory (if required) for the file.

SUPER CAUTION

Because you can't edit an add-in, make sure you save the workbook under a new name. Using the default .XLA extension should do the job.

4. Make sure Microsoft Excel Add-In is selected in the Save File as Type drop-down list.
5. Click on OK or press Enter.

Creating a Custom Help Topic

As you've seen in earlier chapters, you can add a help system to your Excel applications. This system can display help information for custom menu commands, `ALERT()` boxes, dialog boxes, and custom tools. Setting up your help system requires three steps:

1. Create a text file containing Help topics.
2. Convert the text file to the Windows' Help file format.
3. Add Help references to the macro functions and definition tables that need them.

Creating a Help Text File

Your Help system begins with one or more text files that contain several *Help topics*. A Help topic is a section of text that appears in the Help window. This text usually offers an explanation of what the user is doing and instructions on how to proceed. Because these are simple text files, you can use any text editor to create them. (Windows Notepad does the job nicely.) If you use a word processor, be sure to save the file as pure text.

The first line of a Help topic (the *header line*) always begins with an asterisk, followed by a topic number, followed by an optional comment. The topic number can be any positive integer, and it serves as the identifier for the topic. The rest of the Help topic consists of the actual Help information.

For example, suppose Help topic 12 covers a custom dialog box called Format Range. The topic might look something like the one shown in Figure 49.6.

To include other Help topics in the same file, just keep adding header lines and Help text. The topic numbers don't have to be in a particular order, but each topic in a given Help file must have a unique number.

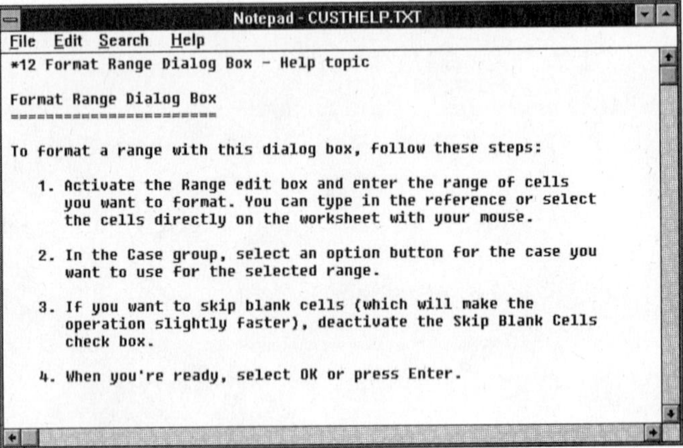
```
*12 Format Range Dialog Box - Help topic

Format Range Dialog Box
=======================

To format a range with this dialog box, follow these steps:

    1. Activate the Range edit box and enter the range of cells
       you want to format. You can type in the reference or select
       the cells directly on the worksheet with your mouse.

    2. In the Case group, select an option button for the case you
       want to use for the selected range.

    3. If you want to skip blank cells (which will make the
       operation slightly faster), deactivate the Skip Blank Cells
       check box.

    4. When you're ready, select OK or press Enter.
```

FIGURE 49.6.
The text file for a custom Help topic.

Converting the Text File to a Help File

Before you can use the Help topics in your application, you have to convert the text file into Windows' Help file format. The disk that comes with this book includes the Microsoft Excel Custom Help File Conversion Utility that will do this for you. The converter—HELPCONV.EXE—is a DOS program that uses the following syntax:

HELPCONV *filename* [/T "*title_text*"]

filename	The name of the text file containing the Help topics.
/T "*title_text*"	(Optional) This parameter specifies the text that will appear in the Help window title bar. If you omit this parameter, the default string *Excel Macro* is used.

To run the converter, start a DOS session and switch to the directory where you installed this book's files. For convenience, you should store the Help file in the same directory as your application. (This saves you from having to specify the file's drive and directory when you reference the file in your macros). Be sure to specify the complete path of the text file when you run HELPCONV.EXE.

For example, to convert a text file named `CUSTHELP.TXT` and add the string `Custom Application - Help` to the Help window title bar, you would run the following command:

```
HELPCONV C:\EXCEL\CUSTHELP.TXT /T "Custom Application - Help"
```

The conversion utility saves a backup copy of the text file (with the extension .BAK) and then creates the Help file (it has the same name as the original).

Referencing a Help Topic

To add Help to your application, you need to add Help references with the following syntax:

```
filename!topic_number
```

filename is the name of the Help file, and *topic_number* is the appropriate topic number from the file.

You can add Help references in any of the following ways:

- For an Alert box, enter a *help_ref* argument in the `ALERT()` function.
- For a custom command or menu, enter the reference in the fifth column of the definition table.
- For a custom tool, enter the reference in the eighth column of the definition table.
- For a custom dialog box, add a Help button, and include the reference in the first cell of the Item column.
- Run the `HELP(`*help_ref*`)` function, where *help_ref* is the help reference.

For example, to add a Help reference for the Format Range dialog box, you would add the following to the upper-left corner of the dialog box definition table:

```
CUSTHELP.TXT!12
```

When the user clicks on the Help button, he or she sees the Help window, shown in Figure 49.7.

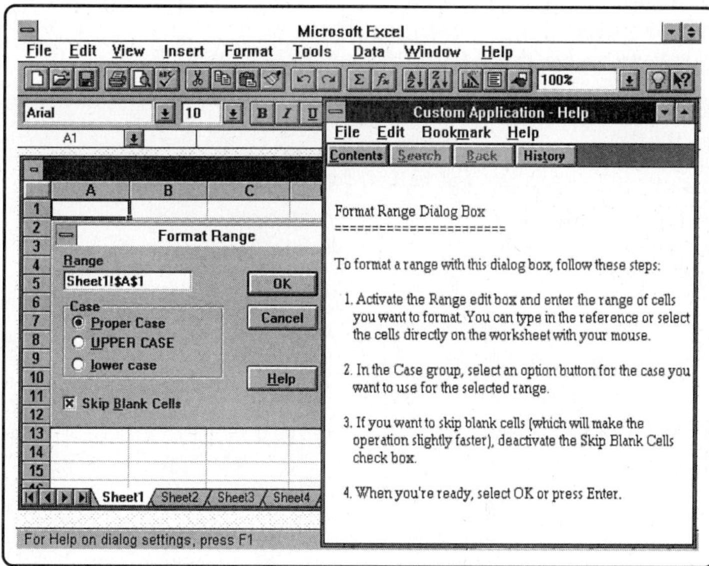

FIGURE 49.7.
A custom Help topic.

Tips for Faster Macros

Short macros usually are over in the blink of an eye. However, as your macros get longer, the time they take to complete their tasks becomes noticeable. For these more complex routines, you need to start thinking not only about *what* the macro does, but *how* it does it. The more efficient you make your code, the zippier the macro executes. This section gives several tips for writing efficient code that runs quickly.

Use *ECHO()* to Turn Off Screen Updates

One of the biggest drags on macro performance is the constant screen updating that occurs. If your macro uses large numbers of functions such as `SELECT()`, `FORMULA()`, `CUT()`, and `COPY()`, then the macro will spend most of its time updating the screen to show the results of these functions. This not only slows everything down, it looks unprofessional. It's much nicer if the macro performs all its chores "behind the scenes" and then presents the user with the finished product at the end of the macro. You can do this with the `ECHO()` function:

```
ECHO(logical)
```

`logical` is a logical value that turns screen updating on or off. Use`FALSE` to turn off screen updates and `TRUE` to turn them back on again.

Hide Your Windows

If your macro does a lot of switching between windows, you can speed things up by hiding the windows with the `HIDE()` function. `HIDE()` is the equivalent of the **W**indow | **H**ide command. You can still work with hidden windows normally, and then, when your macro is done, you can use the `UNHIDE()` function to display the results to the user:

```
UNHIDE(window_text)
```

`window_text` is the name of the window you want to unhide.

SUPER CAUTION

As soon as you hide an active window, Excel deactivates it. If your macros reference the active sheet, you need to activate the window (with the `ACTIVATE()` function) immediately after hiding it.

Don't Select Worksheets or Ranges If You Don't Have To

Three of Excel's slowest macro functions are `ACTIVATE()`, `WORKBOOK.SELECT()`, and `SELECT()`, so you should use them sparingly. In many cases you can substitute these functions with an active reference to a range on the active sheet or an external reference to another worksheet.

For example, suppose you wanted to enter the text string `Expenses` in cell A1 of a sheet named `August Expenses` in the `BUDGET.XLS` workbook. The slow way would be to use the following four formulas:

```
=ACTIVATE("BUDGET.XLS")
=WORKBOOK.SELECT("August Expenses")
=SELECT("R1C1")
=FORMULA("Expenses")
```

The fast way is to combine everything into a single formula:

```
=FORMULA("Expenses",'[BUDGET.XLS]August Expenses'!$A$1)
```

Don't Recalculate Until You Have To

As you know, manual calculation mode prevents Excel from recalculating a worksheet until you say so. This saves you time in sheets with complicated models where you don't necessarily want to see a recalculation every time you change a variable.

You can get the same benefits in your macros by using the `CALCULATION()` command. Here's the short version of this command's syntax (see your Excel Function Reference for all 11 arguments):

`CALCULATION(`***`mode_num`***`)`

mode_num A number that defines the calculation mode:

mode_num	Calculation mode
1	Automatic
2	Automatic except tables
3	Manual

The following formula places Excel in manual calculation mode:

```
=CALCULATION(3)
```

When you need to update your formula results, use the `CALCULATE.DOCUMENT()` function to recalculate the active worksheet only, and use `CALCULATE.NOW()` to recalculate all the open worksheets.

Optimize Your Loops

One of the cornerstones of efficient programming (whether you're dealing with macros or high-level languages such as C) is loop optimization. Because a macro might run the code inside a loop hundreds or even thousands of times, a minor improvement in loop efficiency can result in drastically reduced execution times.

When you analyze your loops, make sure you're particularly ruthless about applying the previous tips. One `SELECT()` command is slow; a thousand will drive you crazy.

Also, weed out from your loops any functions that return the same value each time. For example, consider the following macro fragment:

```
=FOR("n",1,1000)
=     FORMULA(GET.CELL(5,ACTIVE.CELL()),OFFSET(ACTIVE.CELL(),n,0))
=NEXT()
```

The purpose of this somewhat useless code is to loop 1,000 times and each time get the contents of the active cell and enter them in the cell offset from the active cell by *n* rows. However, the results of the `GET.CELL()` function and both the `ACTIVE.CELL()` functions never change. These function calls take time, though, and this slows the loop drastically. A better approach would be the following:

```
=SET.NAME("ActiveCell",ACTIVE.CELL())
=SET.NAME("CellContents",GET.CELL(5,ActiveCell))
=FOR("n",1,1000)
=     FORMULA(CellContents,OFFSET(ActiveCell,n,0))
=NEXT()
```

By moving the unchanging `ACTIVE.CELL()` and `GET.CELL()` calculations outside the loop and naming their results, this code not only reduces the number of function calls by some 3,000, but it also has the added benefit of being easier to read.

Workshop

VII

Visual Basic for Applications

Chapter

50

Getting Started with Visual Basic

Excel 5.0 includes Microsoft's long-awaited common macro language: Visual Basic for Applications (which I'll refer to simply as "Visual Basic" from now on). This chapter introduces you to this powerful new tool and shows you how to use Visual Basic to record simple macros that help automate routine tasks. To get the most out of Visual Basic, however, you need to do some programming. This chapter gets you started with simple command macros and user-defined functions.

What Is a Macro?

A *macro*

is a small program that contains a list of instructions that you want Excel to perform. Like batch files, macros combine several operations into a single procedure that you can invoke quickly. This list of instructions is composed mostly of *macro statements* that are closely related to Excel commands. Some of these statements perform specific macro-related tasks, but most just correspond to Excel's menu commands and dialog box options. For example, the `ActiveWindow.Close` function works just like the **File | Close** command.

How Does Visual Basic Fit In?

Visual Basic for Applications is a programming environment designed specifically for application macros. Excel is the first program to include Visual Basic, but soon other Microsoft applications (such as Word for Windows and PowerPoint) will feature Visual Basic as well. It's also possible that Microsoft will license the technology to other vendors so they can incorporate Visual Basic in their applications. At the very least, you're likely to see other macro programming languages that are "Visual Basic-compatible."

This all means that Visual Basic likely will become the de facto standard for macro programming. The advantage of this is obvious: a standard language means that, no matter which program you use, you have to learn only one set of statements and techniques. And it also means that applications will get along better than they ever have, because Visual Basic "knows" the functions and commands used by every program. Eventually, you'll be able to use Visual Basic to design your own applications that consist of bits and pieces from other programs.

The power of Visual Basic is clear, but perhaps its biggest advantage is that it's just plain easier to use than most programming languages (including the Excel 4.0 macro language). If you don't want to do any programming, Visual Basic enables you to record macros and attach them to buttons either on the worksheet or on a toolbar. You also can create dialog boxes by simply drawing the appropriate controls onto a worksheet or onto a separate dialog sheet. Other visual tools enable you to customize menus and toolbars as well, so you have everything you need to create simple applications without writing a line of code.

Of course, if you want to get the most out of Visual Basic, you'll need to augment your interface with programming code. Unlike the Excel 4.0 macro language, Visual Basic is a full-blown programming environment that includes most high-level programming constructs as well as every Excel function. Add the powerful debugging tool and a Help system compiler to the mix, and you have everything you need to create professional-level applications.

The Three Types of Macros

Visual Basic macros come in three flavors: *command macros, user-defined functions,* and *subroutine macros.* Here's a summary of the differences:

- Command macros (which also are known as `Sub` procedures for reasons that will become clear later in this chapter) are the most common type of macro, and they usually contain statements that are the equivalent of menu options and other Excel commands. The distinguishing feature of a command macro is that, like regular Excel commands, they have an effect on their surroundings (the worksheet, workspace, and so on). Whether it's formatting a range, printing a worksheet, or creating custom menus, command macros *change* things. I show you how to create command macros in the section in this chapter titled "Writing Your Own Command Macro."
- User-defined functions (also called `Function` procedures) work just like Excel's built-in functions. Their distinguishing characteristic is that they accept arguments, manipulate those arguments, and then return a result. A properly designed function macro has no effect on the current environment. I show you how to create these functions in the section in this chapter titled "Creating User-Defined Functions with Visual Basic."
- Subroutine macros are a combination of command and function macros. They can take arguments and return values like a function macro, but they also can affect their surroundings like a command macro. You invoke subroutines from within other macros, and their usual purpose is to streamline macro code. If you have a task that you need to run several times in a macro, you'll typically split off the task into a subroutine instead of cluttering up your macro.

Recording a Visual Basic Macro

By far the easiest way to create a command macro is to use the Macro Recorder. With this method, you just run through the task you want to automate (including selecting ranges, menu commands, and dialog box options), and Excel translates everything into the appropriate Visual Basic statements. These are copied to a separate sheet called a *module* where you can then replay the entire procedure any time you like. Procedure 50.1 takes you through the steps required to record a command macro.

PROCEDURE 50.1. RECORDING A VISUAL BASIC COMMAND MACRO.

1. Select the Tools | Record Macro | Record New Macro command. Excel displays the Record Macro dialog box.

Click on this tool in the Visual Basic toolbar to display the Record New Macro dialog box.

2. Excel proposes a name for the macro (such as Macro1), but you can change the name to anything you like. (You must follow Excel's usual naming conventions: no more than 255 characters, the first character must be a letter or an underscore (_), and no spaces or periods are allowed.)
3. Enter a description of the macro in the Description edit box.
4. Click on OK or press Enter. Excel returns you to the worksheet and displays Recording in the status bar.
5. Perform the tasks you want to include in the macro.
6. When you finish, select the Tools | Record Macro | Stop Recording command.

Click on this tool in either the Visual Basic toolbar or the Stop Recording Macro toolbar to stop macro recording.

Viewing the Resulting Module

Excel stores your recorded macros in a special sheet called a *module*. By default, Excel uses a sheet named Module1 for recorded macros, and it places this sheet at the end of the current workbook. To see your macro, move to the last sheet in the workbook and select the tab labeled Module1.

If you've renamed the module or you're not sure where the macro is stored, follow the steps in Procedure 50.2 to display the module.

PROCEDURE 50.2. VIEWING A VISUAL BASIC MODULE.

1. Select the Tools | Macro command. Excel displays the Macro dialog box.
2. In the Macro Name/Reference list, highlight the macro you want to display.
3. Click on the Edit button. Excel opens the module and displays the macro.

As you can see in Figure 50.1, Excel translates your actions into Visual Basic code and combines everything into a single macro.

A typical macro has the following features:

> **Comments:** The first few lines display the name of the macro and the description you entered in the Record New Macro dialog box. Each line begins with a quotation mark (') to tell Excel that the line is only a comment and that it shouldn't be processed.

Sub/End Sub: These keywords mark the beginning and end of a macro. The `Sub` keyword is the reason why command macros also are called `Sub` procedures.

Macro Name: After the `Sub` keyword, Excel enters the name of the macro followed by a left and right parenthesis (the parentheses are used for *arguments,* as you'll see later).

Macro code: The main body of the macro consists of a series of statements. These are Excel's interpretations of the actions you performed during the recording. In the example, three actions were performed: cell A1 was selected; the string *Expenses* was typed into the cell and the Enter button on the formula bar was clicked; and the cell was formatted as boldface.

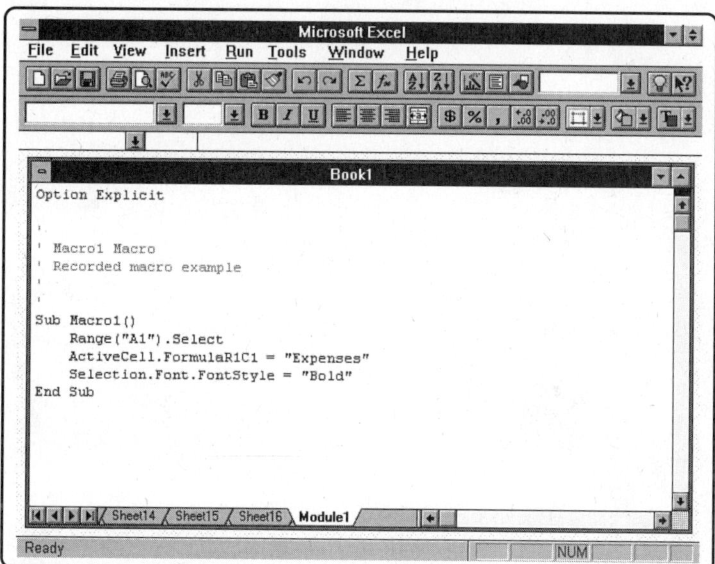
Microsoft Excel
File Edit View Insert Run Tools Window Help
Book1
Option Explicit
' Macro1 Macro
' Recorded macro example
Sub Macro1()
Range("A1").Select
ActiveCell.FormulaR1C1 = "Expenses"
Selection.Font.FontStyle = "Bold"
End Sub
Sheet14 Sheet15 Sheet16 Module1
Ready
NUM

FIGURE 50.1.
A sample recorded macro.

SUPER NOTE

If your recorded macro doesn't have the preceding features, you might have recorded an Excel 4.0 macro instead. To make sure you record in Visual Basic, click on the **O**ptions button in the Record New Macro dialog box and select the **V**isual Basic option from the expanded dialog box.

Setting Recording Options

Excel provides you with several options for recording macros. To check them out, display the Record New Macro dialog box, then click on the **O**ptions button. The dialog box expands to the one shown in Figure 50.2.

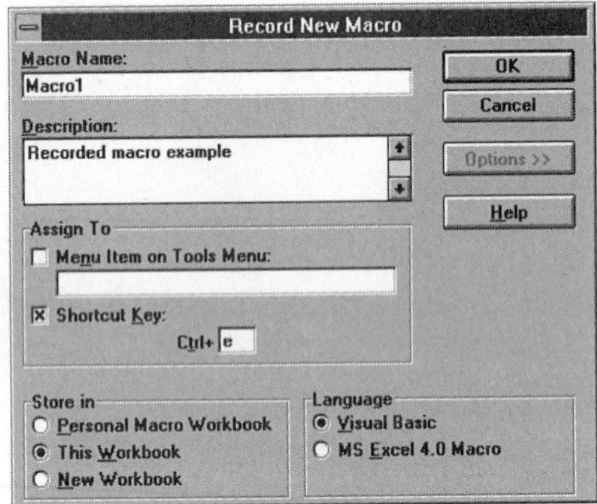

FIGURE 50.2.
Use the Record New Macro dialog box to name your macro and assign a shortcut key and storage location.

SUPER NOTE

By default, Excel uses absolute references during recording. If you prefer to use relative references, select the **T**ools | **R**ecord Macro | **U**se Relative References command before you start recording.

SUPER NOTE

If you want to adjust the options for a macro you've already recorded, select the **T**ools | **M**acro command, highlight the macro you want to work with from the list that appears, and then click on the **O**ptions button.

Here's a rundown of the available options:

- If you think you will use the macro often, you can add a command that automatically runs the macro to the **T**ools menu. Activate the Me**n**u Item on Tools Menu check box, and then enter the command name you want to use in the edit box. To make one of the letters an accelerator key, place an ampersand (&) before the letter (for example, `E&xpenses Macro`).
- To assign a shortcut key to the macro, activate the Shortcut **K**ey check box and use the C**t**rl+ edit box to enter the letter you want to use with Ctrl for the

key combination. For example, if you enter a, you can run the macro by pressing Ctrl+a. Note that Excel shortcut keys are case-sensitive. That is, if you enter A in the Ctrl+ edit box, you would have to press Ctrl+Shift+A to run the macro.

SUPER CAUTION

The shortcut keys Excel suggests are ones that don't conflict with Excel's built-in shortcuts (such as Ctrl+B for Bold or Ctrl+C for Copy). There are 12 letters not assigned to Excel commands that you can use with your macros: *a, e, g, h, j, k, l, m, q, t, w,* and *y*. You can get an extra 26 shortcut keys by using uppercase letters. For example, Excel differentiates between Ctrl+a and Ctrl+A (or, more explicitly, Ctrl+Shift+a). You also can use the `OnKey` method to trigger a macro when the user presses a specific key combination. See Chapter 57, "Visual Basic Procedures That Respond to Events," for details.

- As you've seen, Excel normally stores your recorded macros in a separate sheet at the end of the current workbook. These macros are available only when the workbook is open; if you close it, you can't use the macros. Although this is often desirable behavior, you'll no doubt have some macros you want available all the time. To ensure this, you can store the macros in the Personal Macro Workbook. This is a hidden workbook (its filename is PERSONAL.XLS) that is opened automatically when you start Excel. To store a macro in the Personal Macro Workbook, select the **P**ersonal Macro Workbook option.

SUPER NOTE

If you used the Global macro sheet (GLOBAL.XLM) in Excel 4.0, you still can use it in version 5.0. Note, however, that all global macros in version 5.0, regardless of the language you use, are stored in the Personal Macro Workbook.

- If you want to store your macro in a new workbook, select the **N**ew Workbook option.

Editing a Recorded Macro

As you're learning Visual Basic, you'll often end up with recorded macros that don't turn out quite right the first time. Whether the macro runs a command it shouldn't or is missing a command altogether, you'll often have to patch things up after the fact.

A Visual Basic module is more like a word-processing document than a worksheet, so you make changes the same way you would in a word processor or text editor. If your macro contains statements that you want to remove, just delete the offending lines from the module.

If you left out a step or two, follow the instructions in Procedure 50.3 to insert new recorded actions into an existing macro.

PROCEDURE 50.3. RECORDING CHANGES TO AN EXISTING VISUAL BASIC MACRO.

1. Activate the module that contains the macro you want to change.

> **SUPER NOTE**
>
> If you need to make changes to a macro stored in the Personal Macro Workbook (PERSONAL.XLS), you must first unhide it by selecting the **W**indow | **U**nhide command.

2. Position the insertion point where you want the new statements recorded.
3. Select the **T**ools | **R**ecord Macro | **M**ark Position for Recording command. This tells Excel where you want the new actions recorded.
4. Activate the worksheet or chart you want to use for the recording.
5. Select **T**ools | **R**ecord Macro | **R**ecord at Mark to resume the recording.
6. Perform the actions you want added to the macro.
7. When you finish, select **T**ools | **R**ecord Macro | **S**top Recording.

Writing Your Own Command Macro

Although the Macro Recorder makes it easy to create your own homegrown macros, there are plenty of macro features that you can't access with mouse or keyboard actions or by selecting menu options. For example, Visual Basic has a couple of dozen information macro functions that return data about cells, worksheets, workspaces, and more. Also, the control functions enable you to add true programming constructs such as looping, branching, and decision-making.

To access these macro elements, you need to write your own Visual Basic routines from scratch. This is easier than it sounds, because all you really need to do is enter a series of statements in a module. The next two sections take you through the various steps.

SUPER NOTE

Although the next two sections tell you how to create Visual Basic macros, I realize there's an inherent paradox here: how can you write your own macros when you haven't learned anything about them yet? Making you familiar with Visual Basic's statements and functions is the job of the other nine chapters in this Workshop. The remaining sections in this chapter at least get you started, and then you can use subsequent chapters to build your knowledge slowly.

Creating a New Module

If you want to enter your macro in an existing module, just display the sheet as described in the section in this chapter titled "Viewing the Resulting Module." If you want to start a new module sheet, follow the steps in Procedure 50.4.

PROCEDURE 50.4. CREATING A NEW VISUAL BASIC MODULE.

1. Open the workbook you want to use for the macros.
2. Select the sheet before which you want to insert the module.
3. Select the **I**nsert | **M**acro | **M**odule command. Excel adds a new module to the workbook.

Click on this tool in the Visual Basic toolbar to create a new module.

Writing a Command Macro

With a module open and active, follow the steps in Procedure 50.5 to write your own command macro.

PROCEDURE 50.5. WRITING A VISUAL BASIC COMMAND MACRO.

1. Place the insertion point where you want to start the macro.
2. If you want to begin your macro with a few comments that describe what the macro does, type a single quotation mark (') at the beginning of each comment line.
3. To start the macro, type `Sub`, followed by a space and the name of the macro. When you press Enter at the end of this line, Excel automatically adds a pair of parentheses at the end of the macro name.
4. Enter the Visual Basic statements you want to include in the macro. For clarity, indent each line by pressing the Tab key at the beginning of the line.
5. When you're finished, type `End Sub` to mark the end of the macro.

Running a Visual Basic Macro

Excel offers several methods for running your Visual Basic macros. Here's a quick rundown:

- From any sheet in a workbook, select the **T**ools | **M**acro command to display the Macro dialog box. Highlight the macro you want to run in the **M**acro Name/Reference list, and then click on the **R**un button.

You also can click on the Run Macro tool in the Visual Basic toolbar to display the Macro dialog box.

- In a module, place the insertion point anywhere inside the macro, and then either select the **R**un | S**t**art command, press the F5 key, or click on the Run Macro tool in the Visual Basic toolbar.

SUPER CAUTION

Before you run a macro directly from a module, make sure the macro doesn't include statements that make changes to a worksheet. For example, if the macro enters data and formats cells, you need to have a worksheet active before you run the macro, or Visual Basic will display an error message.

- If you assigned a shortcut key to the macro, press the key combination.
- If you added a new command to the **T**ools menu for the macro, select the command.

SUPER NOTE

See Chapter 57, "Visual Basic Procedures That Respond to Events," for more ways to run macros.

Creating User-Defined Functions with Visual Basic

Excel comes with hundreds of built-in functions—one of the largest function libraries of any spreadsheet. However, even with this vast collection, you'll still find plenty of applications they don't cover. For example, you might need to calculate the area of a circle of a given radius, or the gravitational force between two objects. You could, of course, easily calculate these things on a worksheet, but if you need them frequently, it makes sense to define your own functions that you can use anytime. The next four sections show you how it's done.

Understanding User-Defined Functions

As I mentioned earlier in this chapter, the defining characteristic of user-defined functions is that they return a result. They can perform any number of calculations on numbers, text, logical values, or whatever, but they're not allowed to affect their surroundings. They can't move the active cell, format a range, or change the workspace settings. In fact, anything you can access using the menus is off-limits in a user-defined function.

So, what *can* you put in a user-defined function? All of Excel's built-in worksheet functions are fair game, and you can use any Visual Basic function that isn't the equivalent of a menu command or desktop action.

All user-defined functions have the same basic structure, as illustrated in Figure 50.3. This is a procedure named `HypotenuseLength` that calculates the length of a right triangle's hypotenuse given the other two sides.

FIGURE 50.3.
A user-defined function that calculates the length of a right triangle's hypotenuse.

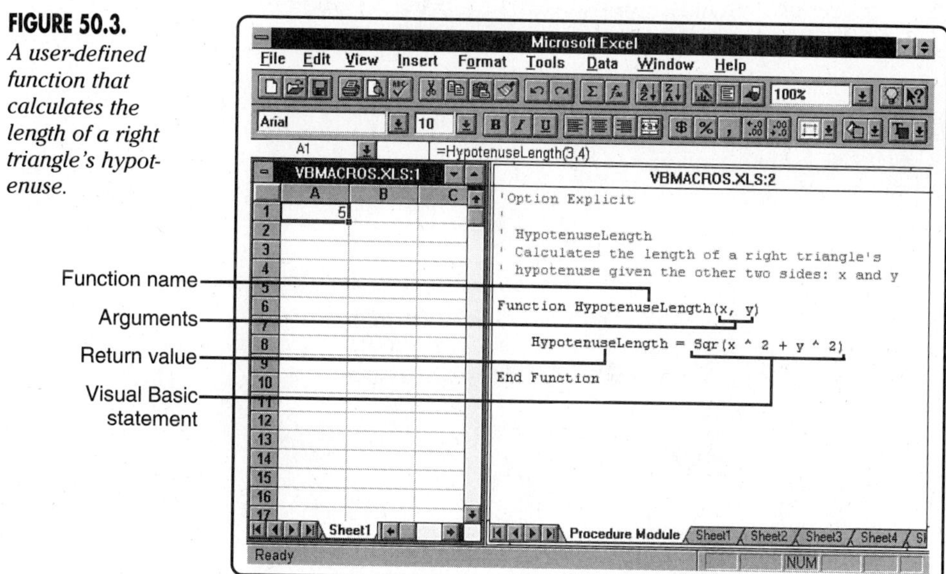

Here's a summary of the various parts of a user-defined function:

The `Function` statement: This keyword identifies the procedure as a user-defined function. The `Function` keyword is the reason that user-defined functions also are called `Function` procedures.

The function name: This is a unique name for the function. Names must begin with an alphabetic character; they can't include a space or a period; and they can't be any longer than 255 characters.

The function arguments: Just as many of Excel's built-in worksheet functions accept arguments, so do user-defined functions. Arguments are typically one or more values that the function uses to make its calculations. You always enter arguments between parentheses after the function name, and you separate multiple arguments with commas.

The Visual Basic statements: This is the code that actually performs the calculations. Each expression is a combination of values, operators, variables, and Visual Basic or Excel functions that produce a result.

The return value: User-defined functions usually return a value. To do this, include a statement where you set the name of the function equal to an expression. For example, in the `HypotenuseLength` function, the following statement defines the return value:

```
HypotenuseLength = Sqr(x ^ 2 + y ^ 2)
```

The `End Function` keywords: These keywords indicate the end of the procedure.

All your user-defined functions will have this basic structure, so you need to keep three things in mind when designing these kinds of macros:

- What arguments will the macro take?
- What formulas will you use within the macro?
- What value or values will be returned?

Writing User-Defined Functions

User-defined functions can't contain menu commands or mouse and keyboard actions. This means, of course, there is no way to record user-defined functions. You have to write them out by hand, and the process is very similar to creating a command macro from scratch. Follow the steps in Procedure 50.6 to write a user-defined function.

> **SUPER NOTE**
>
> As with command macros, I don't expect you to sit down and start cranking out user-defined functions right away. The knowledge of what statements to include in a user-defined function will come only after you've read more chapters in this Workshop.

PROCEDURE 50.6. WRITING A USER-DEFINED FUNCTION IN VISUAL BASIC.

1. Activate the module you want to use for the function.
2. Place the insertion point where you want to start the macro.

3. If you like, enter one or more comments that describe what the macro does. Be sure to type a single quotation mark (') at the beginning of each comment line.
4. Start the macro by typing `Function` followed by a space and then the name of the macro. If your function uses arguments, enclose them in parentheses after the function name (be sure to separate each argument with a comma).
5. Enter the Visual Basic statements that you want to include in the function. As with `Sub` procedures, you should indent each line for clarity by pressing the Tab key at the beginning of the line.
6. When you finish, type `End Function` to mark the end of the procedure.

SUPER TIP

When you press Enter to start a new line, Visual Basic automatically formats the previous line and checks for syntax errors. One of the formatting chores Visual Basic performs is to convert keywords to their proper case. For example, if you type `end function`, Visual Basic converts this to `End Function`. By always entering keywords in lowercase letters, you'll be able to catch typing errors by looking for those keywords that Visual Basic doesn't recognize (that is, the ones not converted).

Employing User-Defined Functions

You can employ user-defined functions only within worksheet formulas or in other macro statements. After you make sure that the sheet containing the module is open (unless, of course, the macro is stored in the Personal Macro Workbook), you have two choices:

- In the cell, enter the function the same way you would any of Excel's built-in functions. That is, enter the name of the function and then the necessary arguments enclosed in parentheses. In Figure 50.3, the window on the right shows the `HypotenuseLength` function in action. Cell A1 contains the following formula:

  ```
  =HypotenuseLength(3,4)
  ```

- Select the **I**nsert | **F**unction command, highlight User Defined in the Function **C**ategory list, and then select the macro from the Function **N**ame list. Click on Next and enter the arguments. When you're done, click on **F**inish.

Assigning User-Defined Functions to Function Categories

By default, Excel places user-defined functions in the User Defined category. If you would like to see your function in one of Excel's other function categories (for example, the `HypotenuseLength` function would fit nicely in the Math & Trig category), follow the steps in Procedure 50.7.

PROCEDURE 50.7. ASSIGNING A CATEGORY TO A USER-DEFINED FUNCTION.

1. Activate the module that contains the user-defined function.
2. Select the **V**iew | **O**bject Browser command. Excel displays the Object Browser dialog box.

Click on this tool in the Visual basic toolbar to display the Object Browser.

> **SUPER TIP**
>
> Press the F2 key to display the Object Browser quickly.

3. If necessary, use the **L**ibraries/Workbooks drop-down list to select the appropriate workbook, and the O**b**jects/Modules list to select the appropriate module.
4. In the **M**ethods/Properties list, highlight the user-defined function you want to work with.
5. Click on the **O**ptions button. Excel displays the Macro Options dialog box.
6. Use the Function **C**ategory drop-down list to select a category for the user-defined function.
7. Click on OK to return to the Object Browser, and then click on **S**how.

Chapter 51

Introduction to Visual Basic Programming

Although it's possible to create useful Visual Basic applications without programming, most macro developers occasionally have to write at least a little bit of code. And it goes without saying that if you hope to build anything even remotely complex or powerful, a knowledge of Visual Basic programming is a must. This chapter gets you started with some programming fundamentals. If you combine these with the control structures I talk about in Chapter 52, "Controlling Visual Basic Code," you'll have a solid base from which to explore further programming topics.

Visual Basic Procedures

The basic unit of Visual Basic programming is the *procedure,* which is a block of code in a module that you refer to as a unit. In Chapter 50, "Getting Started with Visual Basic," you learned about the two most common types of procedures: command macros (also known as `Sub` procedures) and user-defined functions (or `Function` procedures).

SUPER NOTE

In this chapter and in the rest of this Workshop, the terms *macro* and *procedure* are equivalent. I use *procedure* almost exclusively because that's the preferred term in Visual Basic parlance.

The Structure of a Procedure

To recap what you learned in the preceding chapter, a `Sub` procedure is allowed to modify its environment, but it can't return a value. Here is the basic structure of a `Sub` procedure:

```
Sub ProcedureName (argument1, argument2, ...)
    [Visual Basic statements]
    End Sub
```

For example, here's a `Sub` procedure that enters some values for a loan in various ranges and then adds a formula to calculate the loan payment:

```
Sub EnterLoanData()
    Range("InterestRate").Value = .08
    Range("Term").Value = 10
    Range("Principal").Value = 10000
    Range("Payment").Formula = "=PMT(InterestRate/12, Term*12,
                                Principal)"
End Sub
```

A `Function` procedure, on the other hand, can't modify its environment, but it does return a value. Here is its structure:

```
Function ProcedureName (argument1, argument2, ...)
     [Visual Basic statements]
     ProcedureName = returnValue
End Function
```

For example, here's a `Function` macro that sums two ranges, stores the results in variables named `totalSales` and `totalExpenses` (see the section in this chapter titled "Working with Variables"), and then uses these values and the `fixedCosts` argument to calculate the net margin:

```
Function NetMargin(fixedCosts)
     totalSales = Application.Sum(Range("Sales"))
     totalExpenses = Application.Sum(Range("Expenses"))
     NetMargin = (totalSales-totalExpenses-fixedCosts)/totalSales
End Function
```

Calling a Procedure

Once you've written a procedure, you can use it either in a worksheet formula or in another procedure. This is known as *calling* the procedure.

Calling a Unique Procedure Name in the Same Workbook

If a procedure has a unique name in a workbook, you call it by entering the procedure name, and then including any necessary arguments. For example, as you learned in the previous chapter, you called the `HypotenuseLength` procedure from a worksheet cell by entering a formula such as the following:

```
=HypotenuseLength(3,4)
```

If you like, you also can call a procedure from another procedure. For example, the following Visual Basic statement sets a variable named `TotalPerimeter` equal to the total perimeter of a right triangle that has two sides of length `X` and `Y`:

```
TotalPerimeter = X + Y + HypotenuseLength(X,Y)
```

Calling a Nonunique Procedure Name in the Same Workbook

Every procedure in a module must have a unique name, but you can have multiple modules in a workbook. Although you should try to give all your procedures unique names, that may not always be convenient. If you have a workbook with two or more procedures that have the same name, you can differentiate between them by calling each procedure with the following general format:

```
ModuleName.ProcedureName
```

For example, to call a procedure named `NetMargin` in a module named Financial, you would use the following form:

```
Financial.NetMargin
```

If the module name contains more than one word, enclose the name in square brackets, like this:

```
[Financial Functions].NetMargin
```

SUPER TIP

Some procedures are used only inside their own modules and shouldn't be called from another module or from a worksheet. To make sure of this, you can declare the procedure to be *private*. This means that no other module or worksheet can access the procedure. To declare a procedure as private, include the keyword `Private` before either `Sub` or `Function`. For example, the following statement declares the `SupportCode` procedure as private:

```
Private Sub SupportCode()
```

Calling a Procedure in Another Workbook

If you have a Visual Basic statement that needs to call a procedure in another workbook, you first need to set up a *reference* to the workbook. Doing this gives you access to all the workbook's procedures. Procedure 51.1 shows you what to do.

PROCEDURE 51.1. SETTING UP A REFERENCE BETWEEN VISUAL BASIC AND ANOTHER WORKBOOK.

1. Activate the module containing the procedure that must access the other workbook.
2. Select the Tools | References command. The References dialog box appears, shown in Figure 51.1.

FIGURE 51.1.
Use the References dialog box to set up a reference between Visual Basic and a workbook.

3. If the workbook is open, it will appear in the Available References list. Highlight the workbook and activate the check box. If the workbook isn't open, click on the Browse button and choose the workbook you want from the Browse dialog box that appears. Click on OK to return to the References dialog box.
4. Click on OK to return to the module.

Once you have the reference established, you call the procedure the same way you call the procedures in the current workbook. If the two workbooks have procedures with the same names, you need to add the workbook name and module name to the call:

```
[WorkbookName].ModuleName.ProcedureName
```

For example, the following statement calls the `NetMargin` procedure in the Financial module of the `BUDGET.XLS` workbook:

```
[BUDGET.XLS].Financial.NetMargin
```

Again, if the module name uses multiple words, enclose it in square brackets.

SUPER TIP

In the same way that you can make an individual procedure private, you also can make an entire module private. This prevents any other module or workbook from accessing the module's procedures. To declare a module as private, include the following statement near the top of the module (that is, before you define any procedures):

```
Option Private Module
```

Using Objects

Many of your Visual Basic procedures will perform calculations using simple combinations of numbers, operators, and Excel's built-in functions. You'll probably find, however, that the majority of your code manipulates the Excel environment in some way, whether it's entering data in a range, formatting a chart, or setting Excel workspace options. Each of these items—the range, the chart, the Excel workspace—is called an *object* in Visual Basic. Objects are perhaps the most crucial concept in Visual Basic programming, and I explain them in detail in this section.

What Is an Object?

The dictionary definition of an object is "anything perceptible by one or more of the senses, especially something that can be seen and felt." Now, of course, you can't feel anything in Excel, but you can see all kinds of things. To Visual Basic, an object is anything in Excel that you can see *and* manipulate in some way. For example, a range is something you can see, and you can manipulate it by entering data, changing colors, setting fonts, and so on. A range, therefore, is an object.

What isn't an object? Excel 5.0 is so customizable that most things you can see qualify as objects, but not everything does. For example, the Maximize and Minimize buttons in workbook windows are not objects. Yes, you can operate them, but you can't change them. Instead, the window itself is the object, and you manipulate it so that it is maximized or minimized.

You can manipulate objects in Visual Basic in one of two ways:

- You can make changes to the object's *properties*.
- You can make the object perform a task by activating a *method* associated with the object.

I discuss properties and methods later in this chapter.

Common Excel Objects

Excel has dozens of objects that range from chart axes to menus to workbooks. There are, however, a few that you'll use over and over, so it's a good idea to get familiar with them right off the bat:

Application	This object refers to Excel as a whole (although it can also refer to a custom application built with Excel). The Application object contains global settings such as the calculation mode, the standard font, and the name that appears in the Excel title bar. It also contains Excel's built-in worksheet functions.
Workbook	This object controls whether or not a workbook is read-only, which sheet in a workbook is the active sheet, the file format of a workbook, and more. `ActiveWorkbook` is a Workbook object that refers to the currently active workbook.
Worksheet	You can use this object for such things as copying and deleting a worksheet, hiding or displaying a sheet, and recalculating a sheet's formulas. `ActiveSheet` is a Worksheet object that refers to the currently active sheet.
Window	Use this object to maximize or minimize a window, split a window, or freeze a window's panes. `ActiveWindow` is a Window object that refers to the currently active window.
Range	With this object, you can set a range's font, return the contents of a cell, cut or copy a range, and more. `ActiveCell` is a Range object that refers to the active cell.

SUPER NOTE

There is no such thing as a "cell" object. Individual cells are special cases of Range objects.

Working with Object Properties

Every Excel object has a defining set of characteristics. These characteristics are called the object's *properties,* and they control the appearance and position of the object. For example, each Window object has a `WindowState` property you can use to display a window as maximized, minimized, or normal. Similarly, a Range object has a `Font` property that defines the range font, a `Formula` property for the range data, a `Name` property to hold the range name, and many more.

When you refer to a property, you use the following syntax:

```
Object.Property
```

For example, the following expression refers to the `WindowState` property of the `ActiveWindow` object:

```
ActiveWindow.WindowState
```

One of the most confusing aspects of objects and properties is that some properties do double-duty as objects. Figure 51.2 illustrates this. The Application object has an `ActiveWindow` property that tells you the name of the active window. However, as I mentioned earlier, `ActiveWindow` is also a Window object. Similarly, the Window object has an `ActiveCell` property, but `ActiveCell` is also a Range object. Finally, a Range object has a `Font` property, but a font is also an object with its own properties (`Italic`, `Name`, `Size`, and so on).

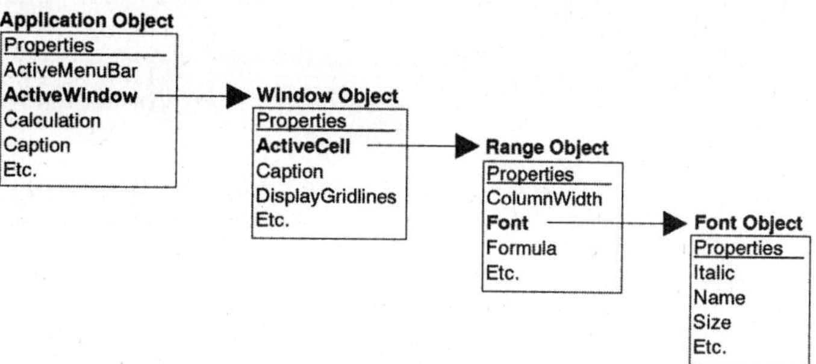

FIGURE 51.2.
Some Excel properties also can be objects.

In effect, you have a hierarchy of objects beginning with the Application object at the highest level and working down through lower-level objects such as Window, Range, and Font. To refer to these lower-level objects, you'll sometimes need to use a syntax similar to the following example:

```
Application.ActiveWindow.ActiveCell.Font.Italic
```

However, an object such as `ActiveCell` implicitly refers to the `ActiveWindow` and `Application` objects, so you can save yourself some typing by using the following reference instead:

```
ActiveCell.Font.Italic
```

Common Object Properties

Each Excel object has a number of properties. Table 51.1 is a list of frequently used properties associated with the common objects described earlier.

Table 51.1. Frequently used properties of some common Excel objects.

Property	*Description*
	Application
`ActiveWindow`	The active window
`ActiveWorkbook`	The active workbook
`Calculation`	The calculation mode
`Caption`	The name that appears in the title bar of the main Excel window
`ScreenUpdating`	Turns screen updating on or off
`StandardFont`	The standard font name for new worksheets
	Workbook
`ActiveSheet`	The active sheet
`FullName`	The full name of the workbook, including the path
`Name`	The name of the workbook
`Path`	The full path of the workbook, excluding the name of the workbook
`Saved`	Returns `False` if changes have been made to the workbook
	Worksheet
`Name`	The name of the worksheet
`ProtectContents`	Protects the worksheet cell contents
`Visible`	Hides or unhides the worksheet

Property	Description
	Window
`ActiveCell`	The active cell
`Caption`	The name that appears in the window's title bar
`DisplayGridlines`	Turns the grid lines on or off
`DisplayHeadings`	Turns the row and column headings on or off
`Visible`	Hides or unhides the window
`WindowState`	Sets the window view to maximized, minimized, or normal
	Range
`Column`	The first column of the range
`Font`	The font of the range
`Formula`	The range formula
`Name`	The range name
`Row`	The first row of the range
`Style`	The range style
`Value`	The value of a cell
`Worksheet`	The worksheet that contains the range

SUPER NOTE

To learn how to refer to individual workbooks, worksheets, and windows, see the section in this chapter titled "Working with Object Collections."

Setting the Value of a Property

To set a property to a certain value, you use the following syntax:

`Object.Property=value`

Here, *`value`* is the value you want to use. *`value`* can be either a constant or a formula that returns a constant, and it can be any one of the following types:

- A numeric value. For example, the following statement sets the size of the font in the active cell to `14`:

  ```
  ActiveCell.Font.Size = 14
  ```

- A string value. You denote a string by surrounding it with double quotation marks. The following example sets the font name in the active cell to Times New Roman:

  ```
  ActiveCell.Font.Name = "Times New Roman"
  ```

- A logical value (that is, `True` or `False`). The following statement turns on the `Italic` property in the active cell:

  ```
  ActiveCell.Font.Italic = True
  ```

Returning the Value of a Property

Sometimes you need to know the current setting of a property before changing the property or performing some other action. You can find out the current value of a property by using the following syntax:

```
variable=Object.Property
```

Here, *`variable`* is a variable or another property. (I explain Visual Basic variables in the section in this chapter titled "Working with Variables.") For example, the following statement stores the contents of the active cell in a variable named `cellContents`:

```
cellContents = ActiveCell.Value
```

Working with Object Methods

An object's properties describe what the object is, whereas its *methods* describe what the object *does*. For example, a Worksheet object can recalculate its formulas using the `Calculate` method. Similarly, a Range object can sort its cells by using the `Sort` method.

How you refer to a method depends on whether or not the method uses any arguments. If it doesn't, the syntax is similar to that of properties:

```
Object.Method
```

For example, the following statement saves the active workbook:

```
ActiveWorkbook.Save
```

If the method requires arguments, you use the following syntax:

```
Object.Method (argument1, argument2, ...)
```

SUPER NOTE

Technically, the parentheses around the argument list are necessary only if you'll be storing the result of the method in a variable or object property.

For example, the Range object has an `Offset` method that returns a range offset from the specified range. Here's the syntax:

```
Object.Offset(rowOffset, columnOffset)
```

Object	The range object.
rowOffset	The number of rows to offset.
columnOffset	The number of columns to offset.

For example, the following expression returns a cell offset 5 rows and 3 columns from the active cell:

```
ActiveCell.Offset(5, 3)
```

To make your methods clearer to read, you can use Visual Basic's predefined *named arguments*. For example, the syntax of the `Offset` method has two named arguments: *rowOffset* and *columnOffset*. Here's how you would use them in the previous example:

```
ActiveCell.Offset(rowOffset:=5, columnOffset:=3)
```

Notice how the named arguments are assigned values by using the := operator.

SUPER TIP

Another advantage to using named arguments is that you can enter the arguments in any order you like, and you can ignore any arguments you don't need (except necessary arguments, of course).

SUPER NOTE

In this example, the `Offset` method returns a Range object. It is quite common for methods to return objects, and it's perfectly acceptable to change the properties or use a method of the returned object.

Common Object Methods

Each Excel object has several methods you can use. Table 51.2 summarizes a few of the most frequently used methods associated with the common objects discussed earlier.

Table 51.2. Frequently used methods for common Excel objects.

Method	*Description*
	Application
`FindFile`	Displays the Find File dialog box
`Quit`	Exits Excel
`Undo`	Cancels the last action
	Workbook
`Activate`	Activates a workbook
`Close`	Closes a workbook
`Protect`	Protects a workbook
`Save`	Saves a workbook
`Save As`	Saves a workbook under a different name
`Unprotect`	Unprotects a workbook
	Worksheet
`Activate`	Activates a worksheet
`Calculate`	Recalculates a worksheet
`Copy`	Copies a worksheet
`Delete`	Deletes a worksheet
`Move`	Moves a worksheet
`Protect`	Protects a worksheet
`Unprotect`	Unprotects a worksheet
	Window
`Activate`	Activates a window
`Close`	Closes a window
	Range
`Clear`	Clears everything from the range
`ClearContents`	Clears the contents of each cell in the range
`ClearFormats`	Clears the formatting of every cell in the range
`Copy`	Copies the range
`Cut`	Cuts the range
`Offset`	Returns a range that is offset from the specified range
`Paste`	Pastes the Clipboard contents into the range
`Select`	Selects a range
`Sort`	Sorts the range

Working with Object Collections

A *collection* is a set of similar objects. For example, the `Workbooks` collection is the set of all the open Workbook objects. Similarly, the `Worksheets` collection is the set of all Worksheet objects in a workbook. Collections are objects, so they have their own properties and methods, and you can use the properties and methods to manipulate one or more objects in the collection.

The members of a collection are called the *elements* of the collection. You can refer to individual elements using either the object's name or by using an *index*. For example, the following statement closes a workbook named `BUDGET.XLS`:

```
Workbooks("BUDGET.XLS").Close
```

On the other hand, the following statement uses an index to make a copy of the first picture object in the active worksheet:

```
ActiveSheet.Pictures(1).Copy
```

If you don't specify an element, Visual Basic assumes you want to work with the entire collection.

> **SUPER NOTE**
>
> It's important here to reiterate that you can't refer to many Excel objects by themselves. Instead, you must refer to the object as an element in a collection. For example, when referring to the BUDGET.XLS workbook, you can't just use `BUDGET.XLS`. You have to use `Workbooks("BUDGET.XLS")` so that Visual basic knows you're talking about a currently open workbook.

Common Object Collections

Here's a list of collections that you are likely to use most frequently:

Sheets	Contains all the sheets in a workbook. This includes not only worksheets, but also modules, charts, and dialog sheets as well. The available methods include `Add` (to create a new sheet), `Copy`, `Delete`, `Move`, and `Select`.
Workbooks	Contains all the open workbooks. Use this collection's `Open` method to open a workbook. The `Add` method creates a new workbook.
Worksheets	Contains all the worksheets in a workbook. The `Visible` property enables you to hide or unhide the collection. The methods are the same as for `Sheets`.

Windows	Contains all the open windows. The `Arrange` method enables you to arrange the collection on-screen (for example, tile or cascade).

Using the Object Browser

The Object Browser is a handy tool that shows you the objects available for your procedures as well as the properties and methods of each object. You also can use it to move quickly between procedures and to paste code templates into a module. To display the Object Browser, select the View | **O**bject Browser command. You'll see the Object Browser dialog box, shown in Figure 51.3.

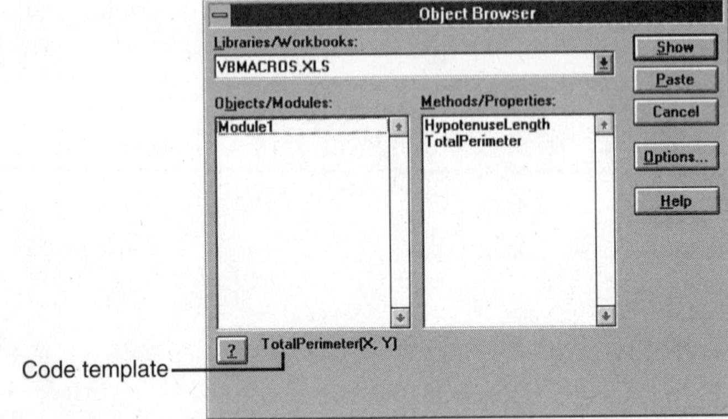

FIGURE 51.3.
Visual Basic's Object Browser.

SUPER TIP

You also can press F2 to display the Object Browser.

Click on this tool in the Visual Basic toolbar to display the Object Browser.

Here's a rundown of the Object Browser window's features:

- Libraries/Workbooks: This drop-down list contains all the libraries and workbooks referenced by any module in the current workbook. A *library* is a file that contains information about the objects in an application. You'll always see at least two libraries in this list: the Excel library lists the Excel objects you can use in your code, and the VBA (Visual Basic for Applications) library lists the functions and language constructs specific to Visual Basic.

- **Objects/Modules**: When you highlight a library in **Libraries/Workbooks**, the **Objects/Modules** list shows the available objects in the library. When you highlight a workbook, **Objects/Modules** shows the modules in the workbook.
- **Methods/Properties**: When you highlight an object in the **Objects/Modules** list, **Methods/Properties** shows the methods and properties available for that object. When you highlight a module, **Methods/Properties** shows the procedures contained in the module. To move to one of these procedures, highlight it, and then click on the **Show** button.
- Code template: This section displays code templates you can paste into your modules. These templates list the method, property, or function name followed by the appropriate named arguments, if there are any (see Figure 51.4). You can paste this template into a procedure and then edit the template. Follow the steps in Procedure 51.2 to paste code templates.

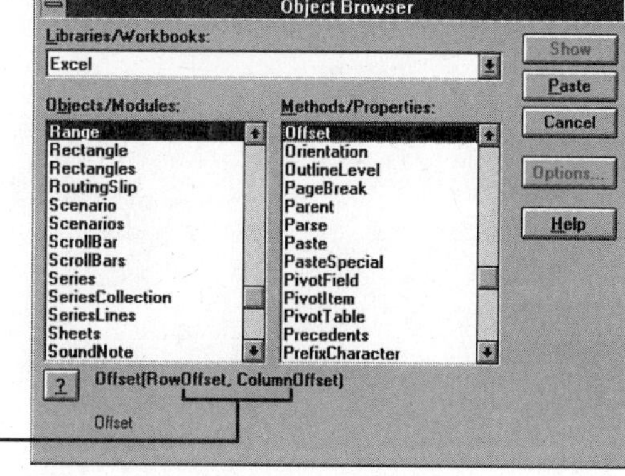

FIGURE 51.4.
The Object Browser displays code templates that you can paste into your procedures.

PROCEDURE 51.2. PASTING OBJECT BROWSER CODE TEMPLATES.

1. In a Visual Basic module, place the insertion point where you want the code template to appear.
2. Select the **View | Object** Browser command to display the Object Browser.
3. Select a library from the **Libraries/Workbooks** list, and then select an object from the **Objects/Modules** list.
4. Use the **Methods/Properties** list to highlight the method or property you want to use.
5. Click on the **Paste** button. Visual Basic returns you to the module and pastes the code template into the procedure.

Working with Multiple Properties or Methods

Because most Excel objects have many different properties and methods, you'll often need to perform multiple actions on a single object. This is accomplished easily with multiple statements that set the appropriate properties or run the necessary methods. However, this can be a pain if you have a long object name. For example, take a look at the `FormatRange` procedure in Figure 51.5. This procedure formats a range in the `Sales` worksheet with six statements. The `Range` object name—`Worksheets("Sales").Range("A1:C5")`—is quite long and is repeated in all six statements.

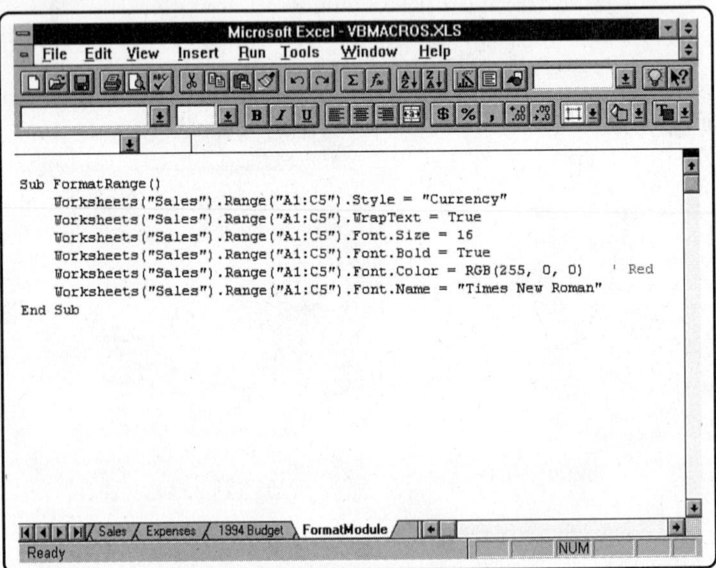
Microsoft Excel - VBMACROS.XLS
File Edit View Insert Run Tools Window Help
Sub FormatRange()
Worksheets("Sales").Range("A1:C5").Style = "Currency"
Worksheets("Sales").Range("A1:C5").WrapText = True
Worksheets("Sales").Range("A1:C5").Font.Size = 16
Worksheets("Sales").Range("A1:C5").Font.Bold = True
Worksheets("Sales").Range("A1:C5").Font.Color = RGB(255, 0, 0) ' Red
Worksheets("Sales").Range("A1:C5").Font.Name = "Times New Roman"
End Sub
Sales
Expenses
1994 Budget
FormatModule
Ready
NUM

FIGURE 51.5.
A long object name makes it cumbersome to perform multiple actions on the object.

To shorten this procedure, Visual Basic provides the `With` statement. Here's the syntax:

```
With object
    [statements]
End With
```

object	The name of the object.
statements	The statements you want to execute on *object*.

Figure 51.6 shows the `FormatRange2` procedure that uses the `With` statement to make the previous macro more efficient.

FIGURE 51.6.
Use the `With` statement to save typing and make your procedures more efficient.

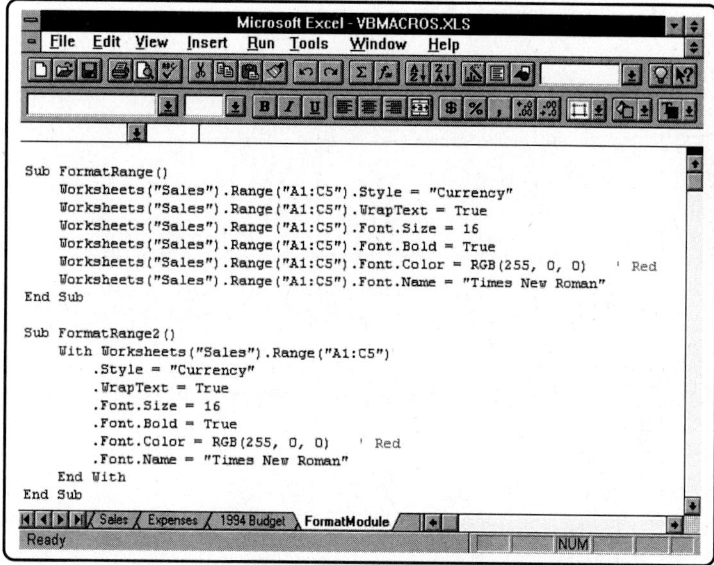

SUPER NOTE

You can make the `FormatRange2` procedure even more efficient when you realize that the `Font` object also is repeated several times. In this case, you can *nest* another `With` statement inside the original one. The new `With` statement would look like this:

```
With .Font
     .Size = 16
     .Bold = True
     .Color = RGB(255, 0, 0)
     .Name = "Times New Roman"
End With
```

Working with Variables

Your Visual Basic procedures often will need to store temporary values for use in later statements and calculations. For example, you might want to store values for total sales and total expenses to use later in a gross margin calculation. In Visual Basic, as in most programming languages, you store temporary values in *variables*. This section explains this important topic and shows you how to use variables in your Visual Basic procedures.

Declaring Variables

Declaring a variable tells Visual Basic the name of the variable you're going to use. You declare variables by including `Dim` statements (`Dim` is short for *dimension*) at the beginning of each `Sub` or `Function` procedure. A `Dim` statement has the following syntax:

```
Dim variableName
```

`variableName` is the name of the variable. The name must begin with an alphabetic character, it can't be longer than 255 characters, it can't be a Visual basic keyword, and it can't contain a space or any of the following characters:

```
. ! # $ % & @
```

For example, the following statement declares a variable named `totalSales`:

```
Dim totalSales
```

SUPER NOTE

To avoid confusing variables with the names of objects, properties, or methods, many macro programmers begin their variable names with a lowercase letter. This is the style I use in this book.

Most programmers set up a declaration section at the beginning of each procedure and use it to hold all their `Dim` statements. Then, once the variables have been declared, you can use them throughout the procedure. Figure 51.7 shows a `Function` procedure that declares two variables—`totalSales` and `totalExpenses`—and then uses Excel's `Sum` function to store a range sum in each variable. Finally, the `GrossMargin` calculation uses each variable to return the function result.

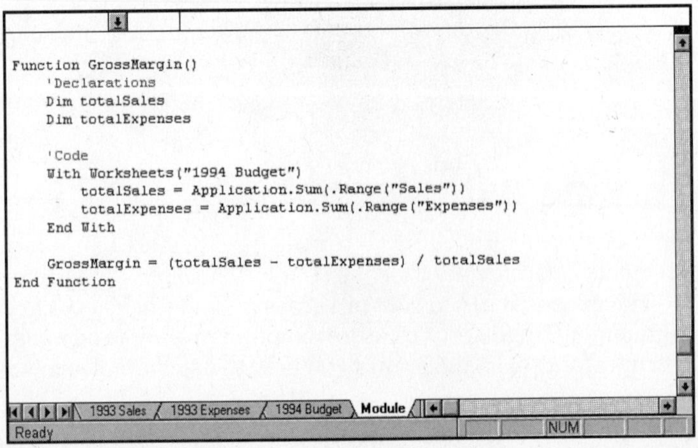

FIGURE 51.7.
A function that uses variables to store the intermediate values of a calculation.

```
Function GrossMargin()
    'Declarations
    Dim totalSales
    Dim totalExpenses

    'Code
    With Worksheets("1994 Budget")
        totalSales = Application.Sum(.Range("Sales"))
        totalExpenses = Application.Sum(.Range("Expenses"))
    End With

    GrossMargin = (totalSales - totalExpenses) / totalSales
End Function
```

1993 Sales | 1993 Expenses | 1994 Budget | Module
Ready NUM

In the `GrossMargin` function, notice that you store a value in a variable with a simple assignment statement of the following form:

```
variableName = value
```

SUPER TIP

To conserve space, you can declare multiple variables on a single line. In the `GrossMargin` function, for example, you could declare `totalSales` and `totalExpenses` using the following statement:

```
Dim totalSales, totalExpenses
```

SUPER NOTE

If you want to use a variable in all the procedures in a module, place the declaration at the top of the module before your first procedure. This is called a *global* declaration.

Avoiding Variable Errors

One of the most common errors in Visual Basic procedures is to declare a variable and then later misspell the name. For example, suppose I had entered the following statement in the `GrossMargin` procedure from the preceding section:

```
totlExpenses = Application.Sum(.Range("Expenses"))
```

Visual Basic supports *implicit declarations,* which means that if it sees a name it doesn't recognize, it assumes that the name belongs to a new variable. In this case, Visual Basic would assume that `totlExpenses` is a new variable, proceed normally, and calculate the wrong answer for the function.

To avoid this problem, you can tell Visual Basic to generate an error whenever it comes across a name that hasn't been declared explicitly with a `Dim` statement. There are two ways to do this:

- For an individual module, enter the following statement before the first procedure:

  ```
  Option Explicit
  ```

- To do it for all your modules, select the **T**ools | **O**ptions command, select the Module General tab, and activate the **R**equire Variable Declaration check box.

SUPER NOTE

Activating the **R**equire Variable Declaration check box forces Visual Basic to add the `Option Explicit` statement at the beginning of each new module. However, it *doesn't* add this statement to any existing modules; you need to do that by hand.

Variable Data Types

The *data type* of a variable determines the kind of data the variable can hold. Table 51.3 lists all the Visual Basic data types.

Table 51.3. The Visual Basic data types.

Data Type	*Description*
`Array`	A set of variables where each element in the set is referenced by an index number. Storage size: Depends on the size of the array.
`Boolean`	Takes one of two logical values: `TRUE` or `FALSE`. Storage size: 2 bytes.
`Currency`	Used for monetary or fixed-decimal calculations where accuracy is important. The value range is from –922,337,203,685,477.5808 to 922,337,203,685,477.5807. Storage size: 8 bytes. Type-declaration character: `@`
`Date`	Used for holding date data. The range is from January 1, 0100, to December 31, 9999. Storage size: 8 bytes.
`Double`	Double-precision floating point. Negative numbers range from –1.79769313486232E308 to –4.94065645841247E–324. Positive numbers range from 4.94065645841247E–324 to 1.79769313486232E308. Storage size: 8 bytes. Type-declaration character: `#`
`Integer`	Small integer values only. The range is from –32,768 to 32,767. Storage size: 2 bytes. Type-declaration character: `%`

Data Type	Description
`Long`	Large integer values. The range is from –2,147,483,648 to 2,147,483,647. Storage size: 4 bytes. Type-declaration character: `&`
`Object`	Refers to objects only. Storage size: 4 bytes.
`Single`	Single-precision floating point. Negative numbers range from –3.402823E38 to –1.401298E–45. Positive numbers range from 1.401298E–45 to 3.402823E38. Storage size: 4 bytes. Type-declaration character: `!`
`String`	Holds string values. The strings can be up to 64K. Storage size: 1 byte per character. Type-declaration character: `$`
`Variant`	Can take any kind of data.

You specify a data type by including the `As` keyword in a `Dim` statement. Here is the general syntax:

```
Dim variableName As DataType
```

`variableName`	The name of the variable.
`DataType`	One of the data types from Table 51.3.

For example, the following statement declares a variable named `textString` to be of type `String`:

```
Dim textString As String
```

Here are a few notes to keep in mind when using data types:

- If you don't include a data type when declaring a variable, Visual Basic assigns the `Variant` data type. This enables you to store any kind of data in the variable.
- If you declare a variable to be one data type and then try to store a value of a different data type in the variable, Visual Basic displays an error. To help avoid this, many programmers like to use the *type-declaration characters* (see Table 51.3). By appending one of these characters to the end of a variable name, you automatically declare the variable to be of the type represented by the character. For example, `$` is the type-declaration character for a string, so

the variable `textString$` is automatically a `String` data type variable. Having the `$` (or whatever) at the end of the variable name also reminds you of the data type, so you'll be less likely to store the wrong type of data.

- To specify the data type of a procedure argument, use the `As` keyword in the argument list. For example, the following `Function` statement declares variables `x` and `y` to be `Single`:

  ```
  Function HypotenuseLength(x As Single, y As Single)
  ```

- To specify the data type of the return value in a `Function` procedure, use the `As` keyword at the end of the `Function` statement:

  ```
  Function HypotenuseLength(x, y) As Single
  ```

Assigning an Object to a Variable

To assign an object to a variable, use the `Set` statement. `Set` has the following syntax:

```
Set variableName = ObjectName
```

variableName	The name of the variable.
ObjectName	The object you want to assign to the variable.

For example, the following statements declare a variable named `budgetSheet` to be an `Object` and then assign it to the `1994 Budget` worksheet in the `BUDGET.XLS` workbook:

```
Dim budgetSheet As Object
Set budgetSheet = Workbooks("BUDGET.XLS").Worksheets("1994 Budget")
```

Working with Constants

Constants are values that don't change. They can be numbers, strings, or other values, but, unlike variables, they keep their value throughout your code. Visual Basic recognizes two types of constants: built-in and user-defined.

Using Built-In Constants

Many properties and methods have their own predefined constants. For Excel objects, these constants begin with the letters `xl`. For Visual Basic objects, the constants begin with `vb`.

For example, the Window object's `WindowState` property recognizes three built-in constants: `xlNormal` (to set a window in its normal state), `xlMaximized` (to maximize a window), and `xlMinimized` (to minimize a window). To maximize the active window, for example, you would use the following statement:

```
ActiveWindow.WindowState = xlMaximized
```

Creating User-Defined Constants

To create your own constants, use the `Const` statement:

```
Const CONSTANTNAME = expression
```

CONSTANTNAME	The name of the constant. Most programmers use all-uppercase names for constants.
expression	The value (or a formula that returns a value) that you want to use for the constant.

For example, the following statement creates a constant named `DISCOUNT` and assigns it the value `0.4`:

```
Const DISCOUNT = 0.4
```

Chapter

52

Controlling Visual Basic Code

One of the advantages of writing your own Visual Basic procedures instead of simply recording them is that you end up with much more control over what your code does and how it performs its tasks. In particular, you can create procedures that make decisions based on certain conditions and that can perform *loops*—the running of several statements repeatedly. The statements that handle this kind of processing—*control structures*—are the subject of this chapter.

Code That Makes Decisions

A smart procedure performs tests on its environment and then decides what to do next based on the results of each test. For example, suppose you've written a `Function` procedure that uses one of its arguments as a divisor in a formula. You should test the argument before using it in the formula to make sure that it isn't 0 (to avoid producing a `Division by zero` error). If it is, you could then display a message to the user that alerts him or her to the illegal argument.

Using *If..Then* to Make True/False Decisions

Simple true/false decisions are handled by the `If..Then` statement. You can use either the single-line syntax or the *block* syntax:

```
If condition Then statement
```

or

```
If condition Then
     [statements]
End If
```

`condition`	You can use either a logical expression that returns `True` or `False`, or you can use any expression that returns a numeric value. In the latter case, a return value of zero is functionally equivalent to `False`, and any nonzero value is equivalent to `True`.
`statement(s)`	The Visual Basic statement or statements to run if *`condition`* returns `True`. If *`condition`* returns `False`, Visual Basic skips over the *`statements`*.

Whether you use the single-line or block syntax depends on the statements you want to run if the *`condition`* returns a `True` result. If you have only one statement, you can use either syntax. If you have multiple statements, you must use the block syntax.

Figure 52.1 shows a revised version of the `GrossMargin` procedure that uses `If...Then` to check the `totalSales` variable. The procedure calculates the gross margin only if `totalSales` is not zero.

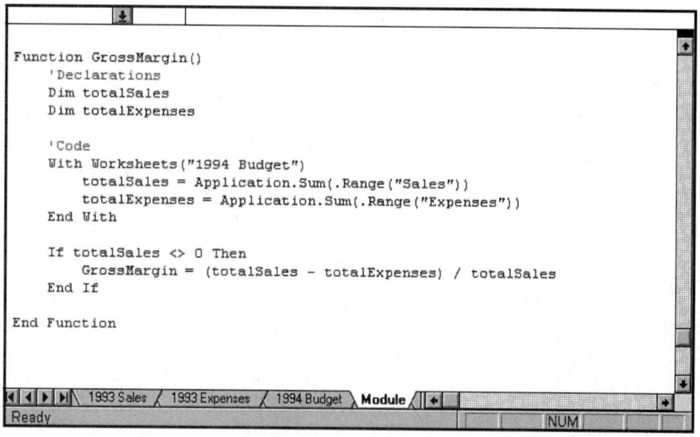

FIGURE 52.1.
Using `If...Then` to make sure that the `totalSales` variable isn't zero before dividing.

```
Function GrossMargin()
    'Declarations
    Dim totalSales
    Dim totalExpenses

    'Code
    With Worksheets("1994 Budget")
        totalSales = Application.Sum(.Range("Sales"))
        totalExpenses = Application.Sum(.Range("Expenses"))
    End With

    If totalSales <> 0 Then
        GrossMargin = (totalSales - totalExpenses) / totalSales
    End If

End Function
```

SUPER TIP

You can make the `If...Then` statement in Figure 52.1 slightly more efficient by taking advantage of the fact that in the condition, zero is equivalent to `False`, and any other number is equivalent to `True`. This means you don't have to explicitly test the `totalSales` variable to see whether it is zero. Instead, you can use the following statements:

```
If totalSales Then
    GrossMargin = (totalSales-totalExpenses)/totalSales
End If
```

To demonstrate the `GrossMargin` procedure in action, Figure 52.2 shows a worksheet with a Sales range (B2:B4) and an Expenses range (B7:B13). Cell B15 calls the `GrossMargin` procedure to calculate the gross margin.

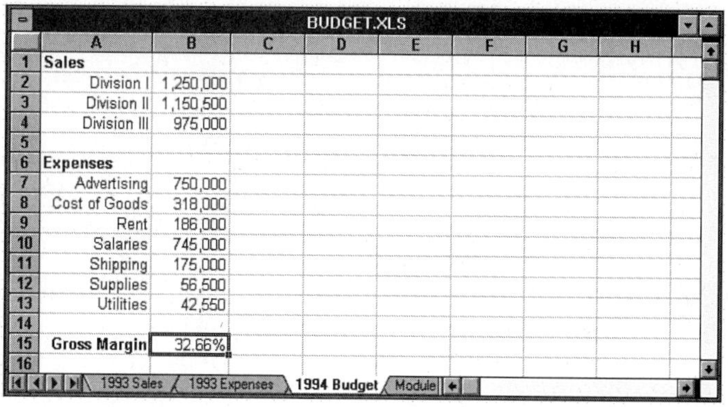

FIGURE 52.2.
A worksheet that uses the `GrossMargin` procedure.

BUDGET.XLS

	A	B	C	D	E	F	G	H
1	**Sales**							
2	Division I	1,250,000						
3	Division II	1,150,500						
4	Division III	975,000						
5								
6	**Expenses**							
7	Advertising	750,000						
8	Cost of Goods	318,000						
9	Rent	186,000						
10	Salaries	745,000						
11	Shipping	175,000						
12	Supplies	56,500						
13	Utilities	42,550						
14								
15	**Gross Margin**	32.66%						
16								

1993 Sales / 1993 Expenses / **1994 Budget** / Module

Using *If...Then...Else* to Handle a *False* Result

Using the `If...Then` statement to make decisions adds a powerful new weapon to your Visual Basic arsenal. However, this technique suffers from an important drawback: a `False` result only avoids one or more statements; it doesn't execute any of its own. This is fine in many cases, but there will be times when you need to run one group of statements if the condition returns `True` and a different group if the result is `False`. To handle this, you need to use an `If...Then...Else` statement:

```
If condition Then
    [TrueStatements]
Else
    [FalseStatements]
End If
```

condition	The test that returns `True` or `False`.
TrueStatements	The statements to run if *condition* returns `True`.
FalseStatements	The statements to run if *condition* returns `False`.

If the *condition* returns `True`, Visual Basic runs the group of statements between the `If...Then` and the `Else`. If it returns `False`, Visual Basic runs the group of statements between the `Else` and the `End If`.

Let's look at an example. Suppose you want to calculate the future value of a series of regular deposits, but you want to differentiate between monthly deposits and quarterly deposits. Figure 52.3 shows a `Function` procedure called `FutureValue` that does the job.

FIGURE 52.3.
A function procedure that uses `If...Then...Else` to differentiate between monthly and quarterly deposits.

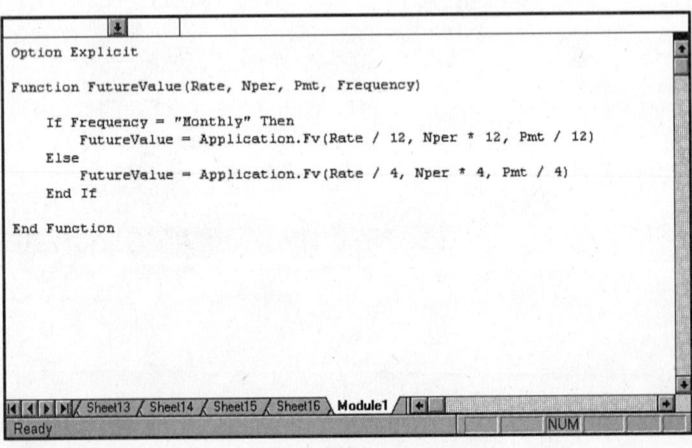
Option Explicit
Function FutureValue(Rate, Nper, Pmt, Frequency)
If Frequency = "Monthly" Then
FutureValue = Application.Fv(Rate / 12, Nper * 12, Pmt / 12)
Else
FutureValue = Application.Fv(Rate / 4, Nper * 4, Pmt / 4)
End If
End Function
Sheet13
Sheet14
Sheet15
Sheet16
Module1
Ready
NUM

The first three arguments—`Rate`, `Nper`, and `Pmt`—are the annual interest rate, the number of years in the term of the investment, and the total deposit available annually. The fourth argument—`Frequency`—is either `"Monthly"` or `"Quarterly"`. The idea is to adjust the first three arguments based on the `Frequency`. For example, if `Frequency` is

"Monthly", you need to divide the interest rate by 12, multiply the term by 12, and divide the annual deposit by 12. The If...Then...Else statement runs a test on the Frequency argument:

```
If Frequency = "Monthly" Then
```

If this is True, the function adjusts Rate, Nper, and Pmt accordingly and returns the future value. Otherwise, a quarterly calculation is assumed, and different adjustments are made to the arguments.

SUPER TIP

If..Then...Else statements are much easier to read when you indent the expressions between If...Then, Else, and End If, as I've done in Figure 52.2. This enables you to easily identify which group of statements will be run if there is a True result and which group will be run if the result is False. Pressing the Tab key once does the job.

Using *Select Case* to Make Multiple Decisions

The problem with If...Then...Else is that normally you can make only a single decision. The statement calculates a single logical result and performs one of two actions. But there are plenty of situations that require multiple decisions before you can decide which action to take.

One solution is to use the And and Or operators to evaluate a series of logical tests. For example, the FutureValue procedure probably should test the Frequency argument to make sure it's either "Monthly" or "Quarterly" and not something else. The following If...Then statement uses the Or operator to accomplish this:

```
If Frequency = "Monthly" Or Frequency = "Quarterly" Then
```

If Frequency doesn't equal either of these values, the entire condition returns False and the procedure can return a message to the user.

This approach works, but you're really only performing multiple logical tests; in the end, you're still making a single decision. A better approach is to use Visual Basic's Select Case statement:

```
Select Case TestExpression
     Case FirstExpressionList
          [FirstStatements]
     Case SecondExpressionList
          [SecondStatements]...
     Case Else
          [ElseStatements]
End Select
```

TestExpression	This expression is evaluated at the beginning of the structure. It must return a value (logical, numeric, string, and so on).
ExpressionList	A list of one or more expressions in which each expression is separated by a comma. Visual Basic examines each element in the list to see whether one matches the `TestExpression`. These expressions can take any one of the following forms: *Expression* *Expression* To *Expression* Is *LogicalOperator Expression* The `To` keyword defines a range of values (for example, `1 To 10`). The `Is` keyword defines an open-ended range of values (for example, `Is >= 100`).
Statements	These are the statements Visual Basic runs if any part of the associated *ExpressionList* matches the *TestExpression*. Visual Basic runs the optional *ElseStatements* if no *ExpressionList* matches the *TestExpression*.

For example, suppose you want to write a procedure that converts a raw score into a letter grade according to the following table:

Raw Score	*Letter Grade*
80 and over	A
Between 70 and 79	B
Between 60 and 69	C
Between 50 and 59	D
Less than 50	F

Figure 52.4 shows the `LetterGrade` procedure, which uses a `Select Case` statement to make the conversion.

SUPER NOTE

If more than one *ExpressionList* contains an element that matches the *TestExpression*, Visual Basic runs only the statements associated with the *ExpressionList* that appears first in the `Select Case` structure.

FIGURE 52.4.
A procedure that makes multiple decisions using a `Select Case` *statement.*

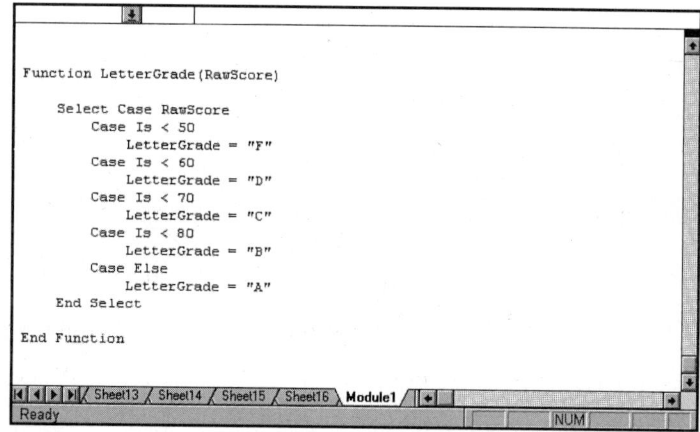

```
Function LetterGrade(RawScore)

    Select Case RawScore
        Case Is < 50
            LetterGrade = "F"
        Case Is < 60
            LetterGrade = "D"
        Case Is < 70
            LetterGrade = "C"
        Case Is < 80
            LetterGrade = "B"
        Case Else
            LetterGrade = "A"
    End Select

End Function
```


Code That Loops

If your procedure needs to repeat a section of code, you can set up a loop that tells Visual Basic how many times to run through the code. The next few sections look at Visual Basic's three different loop types.

Using *Do...Loops*

What do you do when you need to loop but you don't know in advance how many times to repeat the loop? This could happen if, for example, you wanted to loop only until a certain condition was met, such as encountering a blank cell. The solution is to use a `Do...Loop`.

The `Do...Loop` has four different syntaxes:

`Do While` *`condition`* *`[statements]`* `Loop`	Checks *`condition`* before entering the loop. Executes the *`statements`* only while *`condition`* is `True`.
`Do` *`[statements]`* `Loop while` *`condition`*	Checks *`condition`* after running through the loop once. Executes the *`statements`* only while *`condition`* is `True`. Use this form when you want the loop to be processed at least once.
`Do Until` *`condition`* *`[statements]`*	Checks *`condition`* before entering the loop. Executes the *`statements`* only while `Loop` *`condition`* is `False`.
`Do` *`[statements]`* `Loop Until` *`condition`*	Checks *`condition`* after running through the loop once. Executes the *`statements`* only while *`condition`* is `False`. Again, use this form when you want the loop to be processed at least once.

Figure 52.5 shows a procedure called `BigNumbers` that runs down a worksheet column and, whenever a cell contains a number greater than or equal to 1,000, changes the font color to magenta. The idea is to loop until the procedure encounters a blank cell. This is controlled by the following `Do While` statement:

```
Do While currCell.Value <> ""
```

Next, the first `If...Then` uses the `IsNumeric` function to check cells containing numbers, and the second `If...Then` checks the size of the numbers. If both conditions are `True`, the font color is set to magenta—`RGB(255,0,255)`.

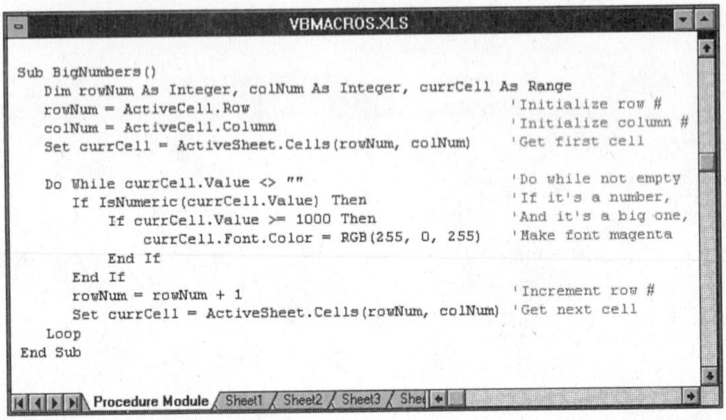

FIGURE 52.5.
A procedure that uses a `Do...Loop` to process cells until it encounters a blank cell.

VBMACROS.XLS

```
Sub BigNumbers()
    Dim rowNum As Integer, colNum As Integer, currCell As Range
    rowNum = ActiveCell.Row                                     'Initialize row #
    colNum = ActiveCell.Column                                  'Initialize column #
    Set currCell = ActiveSheet.Cells(rowNum, colNum)            'Get first cell

    Do While currCell.Value <> ""                               'Do while not empty
        If IsNumeric(currCell.Value) Then                       'If it's a number,
            If currCell.Value >= 1000 Then                      'And it's a big one,
                currCell.Font.Color = RGB(255, 0, 255)          'Make font magenta
            End If
        End If
        rowNum = rowNum + 1                                     'Increment row #
        Set currCell = ActiveSheet.Cells(rowNum, colNum)        'Get next cell
    Loop
End Sub
```

Procedure Module / Sheet1 / Sheet2 / Sheet3 / She

Using *For...Next* Loops

The most common type of loop is the `For...Next` loop. Use this loop when you know exactly how many times you want to repeat a group of statements. The structure of a `For...Next` loop looks like this:

```
For counter = start To end [Step increment]
     [statements]
Next [counter]
```

`counter` A numeric variable used as a *loop counter*. The loop counter is a number that counts how many times the procedure has gone through the loop.

`start` The initial value of *`counter`*. This is usually 1, but you can enter any value.

`end` The final value of *`counter`*.

`increment` This optional value defines an increment for the loop counter. If you leave this out, the default value is 1. Use a negative value to decrement *`counter`*.

`statements` The statements to execute each time through the loop.

The basic idea is simple. When Excel encounters the `For...Next` statement, it follows this five-step process:

1. Set *`counter`* equal to *`start`*.
2. Test *`counter`*. If it's greater than *`end`*, exit the loop (that is, process the first statement after the `Next` statement). Otherwise, continue. If *`increment`* is negative, Visual Basic checks to see whether *`counter`* is less than *`end`*.
3. Execute each statement between the `For` and `Next` statements.
4. Add *`increment`* to *`counter`*. Add 1 to *`counter`* if *`increment`* is not specified.
5. Repeat steps 2-4 until done.

Figure 52.6 shows a simple `Sub` procedure—`LoopTest`—that uses a `For...Next` statement. Each time through the loop, the procedure uses the `StatusBar` property to display the value of `Counter` (the loop counter) in the status bar. (See Chapter 54, "Using Visual Basic to Get and Display Information," to learn more about the `StatusBar` property.) When you run this procedure, `Counter` gets incremented by one each time through the loop, and the new value gets displayed in the status line.

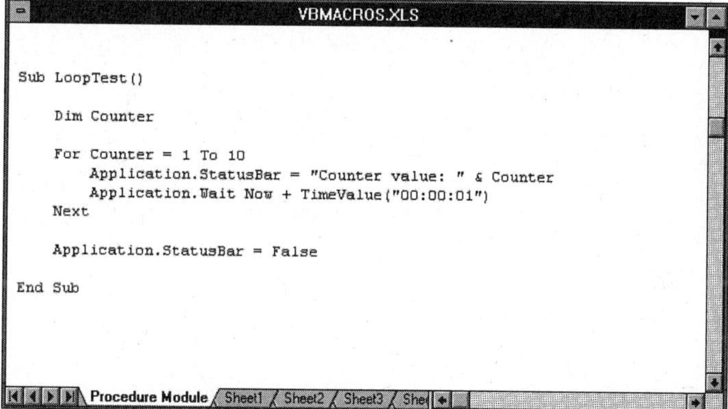
VBMACROS.XLS
Sub LoopTest()
Dim Counter
For Counter = 1 To 10
Application.StatusBar = "Counter value: " & Counter
Application.Wait Now + TimeValue("00:00:01")
Next
Application.StatusBar = False
End Sub
Procedure Module
Sheet1
Sheet2
Sheet3

FIGURE 52.6.
A simple `For...Next` loop.

SUPER NOTE

The `LoopTest` procedure also uses the `Wait` method to slow things down a bit. The argument `Now + TimeValue("00:00:01")` pauses the procedure for a second before continuing.

Following are some notes on `For...Next` loops.

- If you use a positive number for *`increment`* (or if you omit *`increment`*), *`end`* must be greater than or equal to *`start`*. If you use a negative number for *`increment`*, *`end`* must be less than or equal to *`start`*.

- If *start* equals *end*, the loop will execute once.
- As with `If...Then...Else` structures, indent the statements inside a `For...Next` loop for increased readability.
- To keep the number of variables defined in a procedure to a minimum, always try to use the same name for all your `For...Next` loop counters. The letters *i* through *n* traditionally are used for counters in programming. For greater clarity, names such as `Counter` are best.
- If you need to break out of a `For...Next` loop before the defined number of repetitions is completed, use the `Exit For` statement, described in the section titled "Using `Exit For` or `Exit Do` to Exit a Loop."

Using *For Each...Next* Loops

A useful variation of the `For...Next` loop is the `For Each...Next` loop, which operates on a collection of objects. You don't need a loop counter, because Visual Basic just loops through the individual elements in the collection and performs on each element whatever operations are inside the loop. Here's the structure of the basic `For Each...Next` loop:

```
For Each element In group
    [statements]
Next [element]
```

element	A variable used to hold the name of each element in the collection.
group	The name of the collection.
statements	The statements to be executed for each element in the collection.

As an example, let's create a command procedure that converts a range of text into proper case (that is, the first letter of each word is capitalized). This function can come in handy if you import mainframe data into your worksheets, because mainframe reports usually appear entirely in uppercase. This process involves three steps:

1. Loop through the selected range with `For Each...Next`.
2. Convert each cell's text to proper case. Use Excel's `PROPER()` function to handle this:

   `PROPER(`***`text`***`)`

   `text` is the text to convert to proper case.
3. Enter the converted text into the selected cell. This is the job of the `Range` object's `Formula` method:

   `Object``.Formula = `*`Expression`*

Object	The Range object in which you want to enter *Expression*.
Expression	The data you want to enter into *Object*.

Figure 52.7 shows the resulting procedure, `ConvertToProper`.

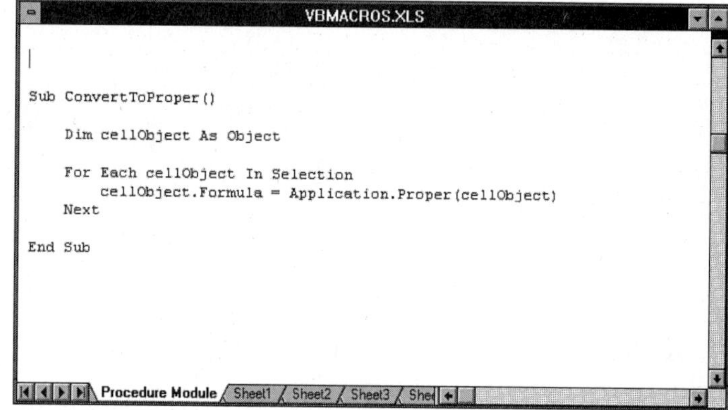


```
Sub ConvertToProper()

    Dim cellObject As Object

    For Each cellObject In Selection
        cellObject.Formula = Application.Proper(cellObject)
    Next

End Sub
```

FIGURE 52.7.
This Sub procedure uses `For Each...Next` to loop through a selection and convert each cell to proper text.

Using *Exit For* or *Exit Do* to Exit a Loop

Most loops run their natural course and then the procedure moves on. There might be times, however, when you want to exit a loop prematurely. For example, you might come across a certain type of cell or an error, or the user might enter an unexpected value. To exit a `For...Next` loop or a `For Each...Next` loop, use the `Exit For` statement. To exit a `Do...Loop`, use the `Exit Do` statement.

Figure 52.8 shows a revised version of the `BigNumbers` procedure, which exits the `Do...Loop` if it comes across a cell that isn't a number.

FIGURE 52.8.
In this version of the `BigNumbers` procedure, the `Do...Loop` is terminated with the `Exit Do` statement if the current cell isn't a number.

VBMACROS.XLS

```
Sub BigNumbers()
    Dim rowNum As Integer, colNum As Integer, currCell As Range
    rowNum = ActiveCell.Row                                  'Initialize row #
    colNum = ActiveCell.Column                               'Initialize column #
    Set currCell = ActiveSheet.Cells(rowNum, colNum)         'Get first cell

    Do While currCell.Value <> ""                            'Do while not empty
        If IsNumeric(currCell.Value) Then                    'If it's a number,
            If currCell.Value >= 1000 Then                   'And it's a big one,
                currCell.Font.Color = RGB(255, 0, 255)       'Make font magenta
            End If
        Else                                                 'If it's not,
            Exit Do                                          'Exit the loop
        End If
        rowNum = rowNum + 1                                  'Increment row #
        Set currCell = ActiveSheet.Cells(rowNum, colNum)     'Get next cell
    Loop
End Sub
```

Procedure Module / Sheet1 / Sheet2 / Sheet3

SUPER NOTE

If you want to exit a procedure before reaching `End Sub` or `End Function`, use `Exit Sub` or `Exit Function`.

Chapter

53

Visual Basic Worksheet Skills

Most Visual Basic procedures eventually do *something* to a worksheet. They might select a cell or range, enter a formula, or even copy and move data. Therefore, knowing how Visual Basic interacts with a worksheet is crucial if you ever hope to write useful routines. This chapter looks closely at that interaction. I'll show you a number of ways to reference Range objects, and then you'll learn about selecting ranges, entering data, copying ranges, and more.

You'll learn how macros use references, and then I'll show you basic tasks such as selecting ranges, cutting and copying data, and getting cell information.

Working with Range Objects

Mastering cell and range references is perhaps the most fundamental skill to learn when working with spreadsheets. After all, most worksheet chores involve cells, ranges, and range names. However, this skill takes on added importance when dealing with Visual Basic procedures. When you're working on a worksheet, you can easily select cells and ranges with the mouse or the keyboard, or you can paste range names into formulas. In a procedure, though, you always have to describe—or even calculate—the range with which you want to work.

What you describe is the most common of all Visual Basic objects: the Range object. A Range object can be a single cell, a row or column, a selection of cells, or a 3D range. The following sections look at various methods and properties that return Range objects.

Using the *Range* Method

The `Range` method is the most straightforward way to identify a cell or range. It has two syntaxes. The first requires only a single argument:

```
object.Range(name)
```

object	The Worksheet object to which the `Range` method applies. If you omit *object*, Visual Basic assumes the method applies to the `ActiveSheet` object.
name	A range reference or name entered as text.

For example, the following statement enters a data series in the range B2:E10 of the active worksheet:

```
Range("B2:B13").DataSeries Type:=xlDate, Date:=xlMonth
```

The `Range` method also works with named ranges. For example, the following statement clears the contents of a range named *Criteria* in the Data worksheet:

```
Worksheets("Data").Range("Criteria").ClearContents
```

The second syntax for the `Range` method requires two arguments:

```
object.Range(cell1,cell2)
```

object	The Worksheet object to which the `Range` method applies. If you omit *object*, Visual Basic assumes that the method applies to the `ActiveSheet` object.
cell1*,*cell2	The cells that define the upper-left corner (***cell1***) and lower-right corner (***cell2***) of the range. Each can be a cell address as text, a Range object consisting of a single cell, or an entire column or row.

The advantage of this syntax is that it separates the range corners into separate arguments. This enables you to modify each corner under procedural control. For example, you could set up variables named *upperLeft* and *lowerRight*, then return Range objects of different sizes:

```
Range(upperLeft,lowerRight)
```

Working with Cells

The `Cells` method returns a single cell as a Range object. Here's the syntax:

```
object.Cells(rowIndex,columnIndex)
```

object	A Worksheet or Range object. If you omit *object*, the method applies to the `ActiveSheet` object.
rowIndex	The row number of the cell. If `object` is a worksheet, a ***rowIndex*** of `1` refers to row 1 on the sheet. If `object` is a range, ***rowIndex*** `1` refers to the first row of the range.
columnIndex	The column of the cell. You can enter a letter as text or a number. If *object* is a worksheet, a ***columnIndex*** of `"A"` or `1` refers to column A on the sheet. If `object` is a range, ***columnIndex*** `"A"` or `1` refers to the first column of the range.

For example, the following procedure fragment loops five times and enters the values `Field1` through `Field5` in cells A1 through E1:

```
For colNumber = 1 To 5
    Cells(1, colNumber).Value = "Field" & colNumber
```

SUPER TIP

You also can refer to a cell by enclosing an A1-style reference in square brackets ([]). For example, the following statement justifies the text in the cell C4:

```
[C4].Justify
```

SUPER NOTE

The `Cells` method has a second syntax that doesn't require arguments: *`object`*`.Cells`. When *`object`* is a worksheet, this method returns a collection of all the cells in the sheet.

Working with Rows and Columns

If you need to work with entire rows or columns, Visual Basic has several methods and properties you can use. In each case, the object returned is a Range.

Returning a Row

The most common way to refer to a row in Visual Basic is to use the `Rows` method. This method uses the following syntax:

`object``.Rows(`*`index`*`)`

`object`	The Worksheet or Range object to which the method applies. If you omit *`object`*, Visual Basic uses the `ActiveSheet` object.
`index`	The row number. If *`object`* is a worksheet, an *`index`* of `1` refers to row 1 on the sheet. If *`object`* is a range, *`index`* `1` refers to the first row of the range. If you omit *`index`*, the method returns a collection of all the rows in *`object`*.

For example, Figure 53.1 shows a procedure named `InsertRangeRow`. This procedure inserts a new row before the last row of whatever range is passed as an argument (`rangeObject`). This would be a useful subroutine in programs that need to maintain ranges (such as a database).

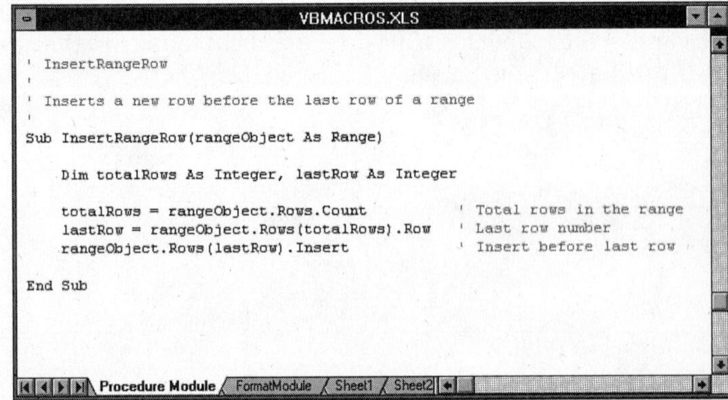

VBMACROS.XLS
' InsertRangeRow
'
' Inserts a new row before the last row of a range
'
Sub InsertRangeRow(rangeObject As Range)
Dim totalRows As Integer, lastRow As Integer
totalRows = rangeObject.Rows.Count ' Total rows in the range
lastRow = rangeObject.Rows(totalRows).Row ' Last row number
rangeObject.Rows(lastRow).Insert ' Insert before last row
End Sub
Procedure Module
FormatModule
Sheet1
Sheet2

FIGURE 53.1.
A procedure that uses the Rows method to insert a row.

After declaring the variables, the first statement uses the `Rows` method without *`index`* to return a collection of all the rows in `rangeObject` and uses the `Count` property to get the total number of `rangeObject` rows:

```
totalRows = rangeObject.Rows.Count
```

`Count` is a handy property that returns the number of elements in any collection:

```
object.Count
```

`object` is the collection object.

The second statement uses the `totalRows` variable as an argument in the `Rows` method to return the last row of `rangeObject`, and then the `Row` property returns the row number:

```
lastRow = rangeObject.Rows(totalRows).Row
```

The `Row` property returns the number of the first row in a Range object:

```
object.Row
```

`object` is the Range object.

Finally, the last statement uses the `Insert` method to insert a row before `lastRow`. (`Insert` has three different syntaxes. See the Help system for details.)

NOTE

You also can use the `EntireRow` property to return a row. The syntax *`object`*`.EntireRow` returns the entire row or rows that contain the Range object. This is most often used to mimic the Shift+Spacebar shortcut key that selects the entire row of the active cell. To do this, you use the following statement:

```
ActiveCell.EntireRow.Select
```

Returning a Column

To return a column, use the `Columns` method. The syntax for this method is almost identical to the `Rows` method:

```
object.Columns(index)
```

`object`	The Worksheet or Range object to which the method applies. If you omit *`object`*, Visual Basic uses the `ActiveSheet` object.

index — The column number. If *object* is a worksheet, an *index* of "A" or 1 refers to column A on the sheet. If *object* is a range, *index* "A" or 1 refers to the first column of the range. If you omit *index*, the method returns a collection of all the columns in *object*.

For example, the following statement sets the width of column B on the active worksheet to 20:

```
Columns("B").ColumnWidth = 20
```

To return the number of the first column in a Range object, use the `Column` property:

```
object.Column
```

object is the Range object.

SUPER NOTE

The syntax *object*.`EntireColumn` returns the entire column or columns that contain the Range object.

Using the Offset Method

When defining your Range objects, you often won't know the specific range address to use. For example, you may need to refer to the cell that is two rows down and one column to the right of the active cell. You could find out the address of the active cell and then calculate the address of the other cell, but Visual Basic gives you an easier (and more flexible) way: the `Offset` method. `Offset` returns a Range object that is offset from a specified range by a certain number of rows and columns. Here is its syntax:

```
object.Offset(rowOffset,ColumnOffset)
```

object — The original Range object.

rowOffset — The number of rows to offset *object*. You can use a positive number (to move down), a negative number (to move up), or 0 (to use the same rows). If you omit *rowOffset*, Visual Basic uses 0.

columnOffset — The number of columns to offset *object*. Again, you can use a positive number (to move right), a negative number (to move left), or 0 (to use the same columns). If you omit *columnOffset*, Visual Basic uses 0.

For example, the following statement formats the range B2:D6 as bold:

```
Range("A1:C5").Offset(1,1).Font.Bold = True
```

Figure 53.2 shows a procedure called `ConcatenateStrings` that concatenates two text strings. This is handy, for instance, if you have a list with separate first and last name fields and you want to combine them.

FIGURE 53.2.
A procedure that uses the Offset method to concatenate two text strings.

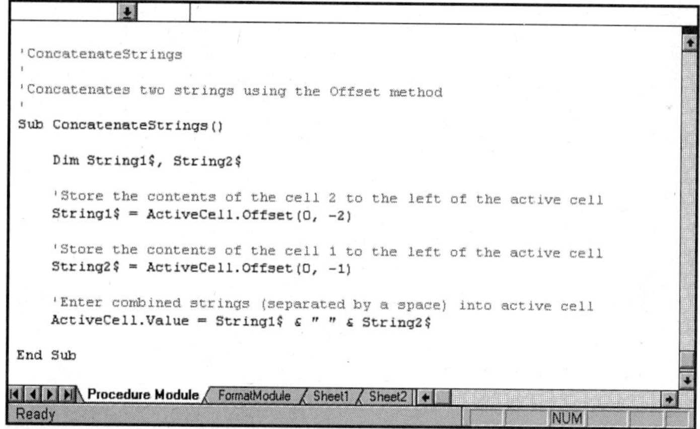

```
'ConcatenateStrings
'
'Concatenates two strings using the Offset method
'
Sub ConcatenateStrings()

    Dim String1$, String2$

    'Store the contents of the cell 2 to the left of the active cell
    String1$ = ActiveCell.Offset(0, -2)

    'Store the contents of the cell 1 to the left of the active cell
    String2$ = ActiveCell.Offset(0, -1)

    'Enter combined strings (separated by a space) into active cell
    ActiveCell.Value = String1$ & " " & String2$

End Sub
```


The procedure begins by declaring `String1$` and `String2$`. (The `$` type declaration characters automatically declare these variables as string types; see Chapter 51, "Introduction to Visual Basic Programming," for details.) The next statement stores in `String1$` the contents of the cell two columns to the left of the active cell by using the `Offset` method as follows:

```
String1$ = ActiveCell.Offset(0, -2)
```

Similarly, the next statement stores in `String2$` the contents of the cell one column to the left of the active cell. Finally, the last statement combines `String1$` and `String2$` (with a space in between) and enters the new string in the active cell.

Assigning Range Objects to Variables

The `ConcatenateStrings` procedure mentioned in the preceding section illustrates another important concept for working with Range objects in Visual Basic: variables can refer to either the contents of a cell, or to the cell itself (that is, as a Range object). For example, suppose that A1 is the active cell and that it contains the string `"Expenses"`. Consider the following statement:

```
cellVar = ActiveCell
```

Setting a variable equal to a cell reference stores the contents of the cell in the variable. In this case, `cellVar` equals "Expenses."

Now consider the following statement:

```
Set cellVar = ActiveCell
```

The `Set` statement (as explained in Chapter 51), assigns an object to a variable. Therefore, the preceding code line assigns the Range object A1 to `cellVar`.

This is an excellent example of why it's always good programming practice to specify a data type when declaring your variables. The `cellVar` variable can be either a Range object or some other data type (depending on the contents of cell A1). If you want to use `cellVar` as a Range object, but you forget to include the `Set` statement, your procedure won't run properly, or it will return unexpected results.

However, if you declare the variable to be a `Range` data type, Visual Basic will warn you if you forget to include `Set`. Figure 53.3 shows a procedure in which a variable named `cellVar` is declared as a `Range` data type. The assignment statement doesn't include `Set`, so Visual basic displays an error message when you try to run the program.

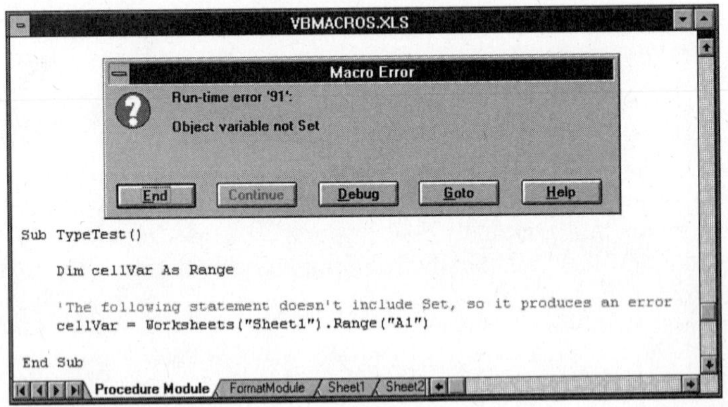
VBMACROS.XLS
Macro Error
Run-time error '91':
Object variable not Set
End
Continue
Debug
Goto
Help
Sub TypeTest()
Dim cellVar As Range
'The following statement doesn't include Set, so it produces an error
cellVar = Worksheets("Sheet1").Range("A1")
End Sub
Procedure Module
FormatModule
Sheet1
Sheet2

FIGURE 53.3.
When you include a data type in a variable declaration, Visual Basic will warn you if you try to use the variable as a different data type.

Defining a Range Name

Range names in Visual Basic are Name objects. To define them, you use the `Add` method for the `Names` collection (which is usually the collection of defined names in a workbook). Here is an abbreviated syntax for the `Names` collection's `Add` method (this method has nine arguments; see the Visual Basic Reference in the Help system):

```
object.Add(text,refersTo)
```

object	The Names object.
text	The text you want to use as the range name.
refersTo	The item to which you want the name. You can enter a constant, a formula as text (such as `"=Sales-Expenses"`), or a worksheet reference (such as `"Sales!A1:C6"`).

For example, the following statement adds the range name `SalesRange` to the Names collection of the active workbook:

```
ActiveWorkbook.Names.Add _
     Text:="SalesRange", _
     RefersTo:="Sales!A1C6"
```

SUPER NOTE

The Add method example uses an underscore (_), which is Visual Basic's *line continuation character.* This character tells Visual Basic to treat the next line as part of the current line. Always include a space before the underscore.

Selecting a Cell or Range

If you've used the Excel 4.0 macro language, you know that most of its range operations require you to first select the range and then do something to it. For example, changing the font to Times New Roman in the range B1 to B10 of the active sheet requires two commands:

```
=SELECT(!$B$1:$B$10)
=FORMAT.FONT("Times New Roman")
```

Visual Basic, however, enables you to access objects directly without having to select them first. This means that your Visual Basic procedures rarely have to select a range. The preceding example can be performed with a single (and faster) Visual Basic statement:

```
Range("B1:B10").Font.Name = "Times New Roman"
```

However, there are times when you do need to select a range. For example, to create a chart with Visual Basic, you first select a range and then run the `Charts.Add` method. To select a range, use the `Select` method:

```
object.Select
```

object is the Range object you want to select.

For example, the following statement selects the range A1:E10 in the Sales worksheet:

```
Worksheets("Sales").Range("A1:E10").Select
```

SUPER TIP

To return the currently selected range, use the `Selection` property.

Working with Range Data

If you need to get the contents of a cell, or if you need to enter data into a range, Visual Basic offers two Range object properties: `Value` and `Formula`.

To get the contents of a cell, use its `Value` property when you're concerned only with the result of the formula that is in the cell. For example, if cell A1 contains the formula `=2*2`, `Range("A1").Value` returns `4`. The `Formula` property, on the other hand, returns the following:

- If the cell contains a constant, it returns the constant.
- If the cell contains a formula, it returns the formula as a text string.

In the example, `Range("A1").Formula` returns `=2*2`.

To enter data in a cell or range, you can use `Value` or `Formula` interchangeably. For example, the following two statements do the same thing:

```
Worksheets("Data").Range("A1:F6").Value = "=PI()*Radius^2"

Worksheets("Data").Range("A1:F6").Formula = "=PI()*Radius^2"
```

Methods for Cutting, Copying, and Clearing Data

If your procedures need to do some basic worksheet editing chores, Visual Basic's `Cut`, `Copy`, and `Clear` methods do the job.

The `Cut` method uses the following syntax:

```
object.Cut(destination)
```

`object`	The Range object to cut.
`destination`	The cell or range where you want the cut range to be pasted.

For example, the following statement cuts the range A1:B3 and moves it to the range B4:C6:

```
Range("A1:B3").Cut Destination:=Range("B4")
```

Copying a range is similar to cutting a range. Here is the syntax for the `Copy` method:

```
object.Copy(destination)
```

`object`	The range to copy.
`destination`	The cell or range where you want the copied range to be pasted.

To remove data from a range, you could either use the `Cut` method without the *`destination`* argument, or you could use the `Clear` method:

```
object.Clear
```

`object` is the range to clear.

`Clear` removes everything from the range (contents, formats, and notes). To remove only selected elements from a range, use the `ClearContents`, `ClearFormats`, or `ClearNotes` methods, instead.

Working with Worksheet Objects

Worksheet objects contain a number of properties and methods you can exploit in your code. These include options for activating and hiding worksheets, adding new worksheets to a workbook, and moving, copying, and deleting worksheets. The next few sections discuss each worksheet operation.

Activating a Worksheet

To make a worksheet active (so that it becomes the `ActiveSheet` property of the workbook), use the `Activate` method:

```
object.Activate
```

`object` is the worksheet you want to activate.

For example, the following statement activates the Sales worksheet in the FINANCE.XLS workbook:

```
Workbooks("FINANCE.XLS").Worksheets("Sales").Activate
```

Hiding a Worksheet

Worksheet objects have a `Visible` property that controls whether or not the user can see the sheet. Setting this property to `False` is equivalent to running the F**o**rmat | S**h**eet | **H**ide command. Here is the syntax:

```
object.Visible
```

`object` is the worksheet you want to hide.

For example, to hide a worksheet named Expenses, you would use the following statement:

```
Worksheets("Expenses").Visible = False
```

To unhide the sheet, set its `Visible` property to `True`.

Creating a New Worksheet

The `Worksheets` collection, which consists of all the worksheets in the current workbook, has an `Add` method you can use to insert new sheets into the workbook. Following is the syntax for this method:

```
object.Add(before,after,count,type)
```

object	The `Worksheets` collection.
before	The sheet before which the new sheet is added. If you omit both *before* and *after*, the new worksheet is added before the active sheet.
after	The sheet after which the new sheet is added. You can't specify both the *before* and *after* arguments.
count	The number of new worksheets to add. Visual Basic adds one worksheet if you omit *count*.
type	The type of worksheet. You have three choices: `xlWorksheet` (the default), `xlExcel4MacroSheet`, or `xlExcel4IntlMacroSheet`.

In the following statement, a new worksheet is added to the active workbook before the Sales sheet:

```
Worksheets.Add Before:=Worksheets("Sales")
```

Renaming a Worksheet

Use the Worksheet object's `Name` property to rename a worksheet:

```
object.Name
```

object is the worksheet you want to rename.

For example, the following statement renames the Sheet1 worksheet to 1994 Budget:

```
Worksheets("Sheet1").Name = "1994 Budget"
```

Copying and Moving a Worksheet

You can use the `Copy` and `Move` methods to rearrange the sheets in a workbook. Both methods have identical syntaxes:

```
object.Copy(before,after)
```

```
object.Move(before,after)
```

object	The worksheet you want to copy or move.
before	The sheet before which the sheet will be copied or moved. If you omit both *before* and *after*, Visual Basic creates a new workbook for the copied or moved sheet.
after	The sheet after which the new sheet is added. You can't specify both the *before* and *after* arguments.

In the following statement, the Budget 1993 worksheet is moved before the Budget 1994 worksheet:

```
Worksheets("Budget 1993").Move Before:=Worksheets("1994 Budget")
```

Deleting a Worksheet

To delete worksheets you no longer need, use the `Delete` method:

```
object.Delete
```

object is the worksheet you want to delete.

For example, the following statement deletes the active worksheet:

```
ActiveSheet.Delete
```

Chapter

54

Using Visual Basic to Get and Display Information

A well-designed application is one that keeps the user involved. It should display messages at appropriate times and ask the user for input. When interacting with the application, the user feels that he or she is a part of the process and has enough control over what the program does—which means that the user won't lose interest in the program.

Displaying Information to the User

Displaying information is one of the best (and easiest) ways to keep your users involved. If an operation is going to take a long time, keep the user informed of the operation's time and progress. If a user makes an error (for example, enters the wrong argument in a user-defined function), the user should be gently admonished so that he or she will be less likely to repeat the error.

Visual Basic gives you four main ways to display information: the `Beep` statement, the `SoundNote` property, the `StatusBar` property, and the `MsgBox` function.

Beeping the Speaker

Visual Basic's most rudimentary form of communication is the simple, attention-getting beep. It's Excel's way of saying "Ahem!" or "Excuse me!," and it's handled, appropriately enough, by the `Beep` statement.

For example, the following procedure recalculates all the open workbooks and then sounds two beeps to mark the end of the process:

```
Sub RecalcAll()
    Application.Calculate
    For i = 1 To 2
        Beep
    Next i
End Sub
```

SUPER CAUTION

Avoid overusing the `Beep` statement. You need to get the user's attention, but constant beeping only defeats that purpose; most users get annoyed at any program that barks at them incessantly. Good uses for the `Beep` statement are signaling errors and signaling the end of long operations.

Using Other Sounds

The `Beep` statement is useful, but it's primitive. If you have the necessary hardware, you can get your procedures to play much more sophisticated sounds, including your own recorded voice!

Chapter 15, "Adding Comments with Text Boxes and Notes," showed you how to add a sound note to a cell. You also can work with sound notes in Visual Basic. A `SoundNote` is a Range object property that is also an object in its own right. SoundNote objects have methods that enable you to import sound files, record sounds, and play a cell's sound note.

SUPER NOTE

To record and play sound notes, you must have the appropriate hardware installed and Windows 3.1 (or Windows 3.0 with at least version 1.0 of the Multimedia Extensions).

Importing a Sound File

The SoundNote object includes an `Import` method that imports a sound file directly into a sound note. Following is the proper syntax:

```
object.Import(file,resource)
```

`object`	The SoundNote object.
`file`	The full pathname of the sound file.
`resource`	An argument used only in Excel for the Macintosh.

For example, the following statement imports a sound file called DOGBARK.WAV into the active cell:

```
ActiveCell.SoundNote.Import "C:\SOUNDS\DOGBARK.WAV"
```

Recording a Sound Note

If you prefer to record your own sounds, the SoundNote object also includes a `Record` method:

```
object.Record
```

`object` is the SoundNote object.

If you use the Record method to record a sound, you'll see the Record dialog box when you run the procedure. Choose **R**ecord, record your note, choose **S**top when you're done, and then click on OK. The following statement records a sound note in the active cell:

```
ActiveCell.SoundNote.Record
```

Playing a Sound

After you've inserted a sound note, you can use the Play method to play it (assuming that the user's computer has the appropriate hardware):

```
object.Play
```

object is the SoundNote object.

For example, the following statement plays a message recorded in a cell named ErrorMessage in the active worksheet:

```
Range("ErrorMessage").SoundNote.Play
```

Adding Sound Checks to Your Procedures

As you've seen, using sounds in your procedures requires special hardware and software. A well-written procedure should check that a computer is capable of playing or recording sounds before trying to use them. You do this by testing the Application object's CanPlaySounds or CanRecordSounds properties. If these properties return True, you can play and record sounds, respectively.

In the following example, the code first checks the CanPlaySounds property before playing a sound:

```
If Application.CanPlaySounds Then
     Range("ErrorMessage").SoundNote.Play
End If
```

Displaying a Message in the Status Bar

You can use the Application object's StatusBar property to display text messages in the status bar at the bottom of the screen. This provides you with an easy way to keep the user informed about what a procedure is doing or how much is left to process.

Figure 54.1, an example of the StatusBar property, shows a revised version of the ConvertToProper procedure. The goal is to display a message of the form Converting cell x of y, in which x is the number of cells converted so far and y is the total number of cells to be converted.

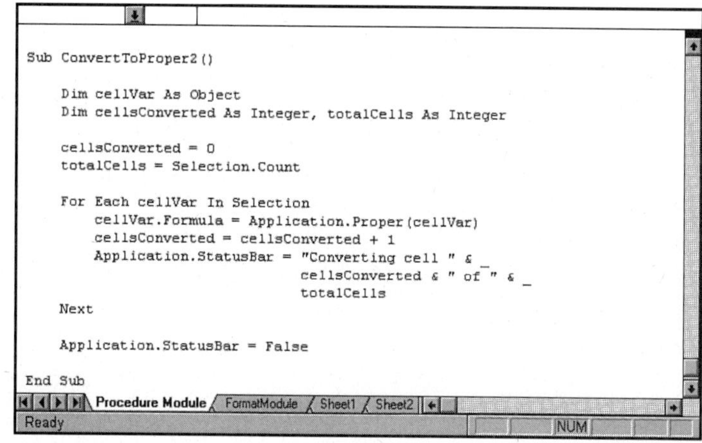

```
Sub ConvertToProper2()

    Dim cellVar As Object
    Dim cellsConverted As Integer, totalCells As Integer

    cellsConverted = 0
    totalCells = Selection.Count

    For Each cellVar In Selection
        cellVar.Formula = Application.Proper(cellVar)
        cellsConverted = cellsConverted + 1
        Application.StatusBar = "Converting cell " & _
                                cellsConverted & " of " & _
                                totalCells
    Next

    Application.StatusBar = False

End Sub
```


FIGURE 54.1.
A procedure that uses the `StatusBar` property to inform the user of the progress of the operation.

The `cellsConverted` variable tracks the number of cells converted, and the `totalsCells` variable stores the total number of cells in the selection (given by `Selection.Count`).

The `For Each...Next` loop does three things:

- Converts one cell at a time to proper case.
- Increments the `cellsConverted` variable.
- Sets the `StatusBar` property to display the progress of the operation (note the use of the concatenation operator (&) to combine text and variable values).

When the loop is done, the procedure sets the `StatusBar` property to `False` to clear the status bar.

Displaying a Message Using *MsgBox*

The problem with using the `StatusBar` property to display messages is that it's often a bit too subtle. Unless the user knows to look in the status bar, he or she might miss your messages altogether. When the user really needs to see a message, you can use the `MsgBox` function:

```
MsgBox(prompt,buttons,title,helpFile,context)
```

prompt	The message you want to display in the dialog box.
buttons	A number or constant that specifies, among other things, the command buttons that appear in the dialog. (See the next section.) The default value is `0`.
title	The text that appears in the dialog box title bar. If you omit *title*, Visual Basic uses "Microsoft Excel."

`helpFile` The text that specifies the Help file that contains the custom help topic. If you enter *`helpFile`*, you also have to include *`context`*. If you include *`helpFile`*, a **H**elp button appears in the dialog box.

`context` A number that identifies the help topic in *`helpFile`*.

> **SUPER NOTE**
>
> To learn how to set up your own custom help topics, see Chapter 59, "Visual Basic Tips and Techniques."

For example, the following statement displays the message dialog box shown in Figure 54.2:

```
MsgBox "You must enter a number between 1 and 100",,"Warning"
```

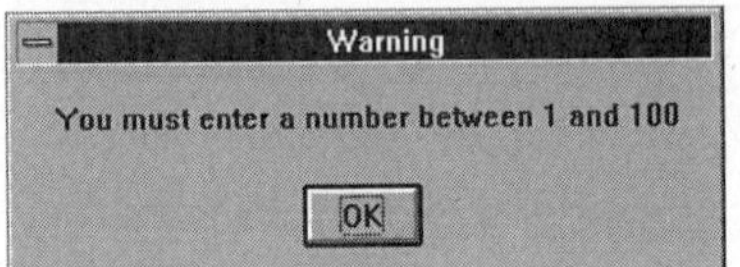

FIGURE 54.2.
A simple message dialog box produced by the `MsgBox` *function.*

> **SUPER NOTE**
>
> The `MsgBox` function, like all Visual Basic functions, needs parentheses around its arguments only when you use the function's return value. See the section later in this chapter titled "Getting Return Values from the Message Dialog Box."

> **SUPER TIP**
>
> For long prompts, Visual Basic wraps the text inside the dialog box. If you would like to create your own line breaks, use the `Chr` function and the carriage-return character (ASCII 13) between each line:
>
> ```
> MsgBox "First line" & Chr(13) & "Second line"
> ```

Setting the Style of the Message

The default message dialog box displays only an OK button. You can include other buttons and icons in the dialog box by using different values for the *buttons* parameter. Table 54.1 lists the available options.

Table 54.1. The MsgBox buttons parameter options.

Constant	*Value*	*Description*
		Buttons
`vbOKOnly`	0	Displays only an OK button (the default)
`vbOKCancel`	1	Displays the OK and Cancel buttons
`vbAbortRetryIgnore`	2	Displays the **A**bort, **R**etry, and **I**gnore buttons
`vbYesNoCancel`	3	Displays the **Y**es, **N**o, and Cancel buttons
`vbYesNo`	4	Displays the **Y**es and **N**o buttons
`vbRetryCancel`	5	Displays the **R**etry and Cancel buttons
		Icons
`vbCritical`	16	Displays the Critical Message icon
`vbQuestion`	32	Displays the Warning Query icon
`vbExclamation`	48	Displays the Warning Message icon
`vbInformation`	64	Displays the Information Message icon
		Defaults
`vbDefaultButton1`	0	The first button is the default
`vbDefaultButton2`	256	The second button is the default
`vbDefaultButton3`	512	The third button is the default
		Modality
`vbApplicationModal`	0	The user must respond to the message box before continuing work in the current application
`vbSystemModal`	4096	All applications are suspended until the user responds to the message box

You derive the *buttons* argument in one of two ways:

- By adding up the values for each option
- By using the Visual Basic constants separated by plus signs (+)

For example, Figure 54.3 shows a procedure named `ButtonTest` and its dialog box. Here, three variables—*msgPrompt*, *msgButtons*, and *msgTitle*—store the values for the `MsgBox` function's ***prompt***, *buttons*, and *title* arguments. In particular, the following statement derives the *buttons* argument:

```
msgButtons = vbYesNoCancel + vbQuestion + vbDefaultButton2
```

You also could derive the *buttons* argument by adding up the values that these constants represent (3, 32, and 256, respectively), although the procedure becomes less readable.

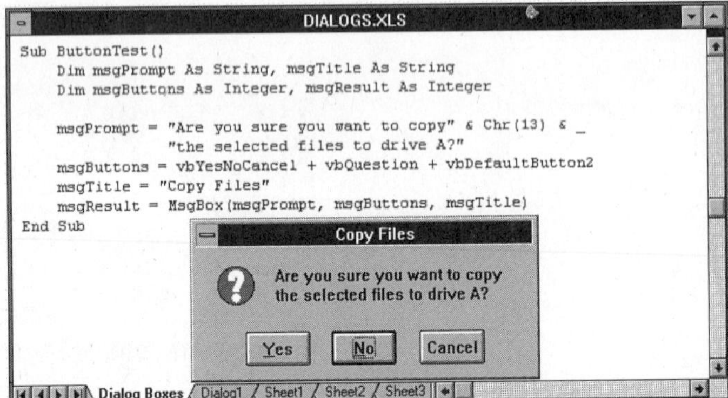

FIGURE 54.3.
A procedure that creates a message dialog box.

Getting Return Values from the Message Dialog Box

A message dialog box that displays only an OK button is straightforward. The user either clicks on OK or presses Enter to remove the dialog from the screen. The multi-button styles are a little different, however; the user has a choice of buttons to select. Your procedure should have a way to find out what the user chose.

You do this by storing the `MsgBox` function's return value in a variable. Table 54.2 lists the seven possibilities.

Table 54.2. The `MsgBox` function's return values.

Constant	*Value*	*Button Selected*
`vbOK`	1	OK
`vbCancel`	2	Cancel
`vbAbort`	3	Abort
`vbRetry`	4	Retry
`vbIgnore`	5	Ignore

Constant	Value	Button Selected
vbYes	6	Yes
vbNo	7	No

To process the return value, you can use an `If...Then...Else` or `Select Case` structure to test for the appropriate values. For example, the `ButtonTest` procedure shown earlier used a variable named *`msgResult`* to store the return value of the `MsgBox` function. Figure 54.4 shows a revised version of `ButtonTest` that uses a `Select Case` statement to test for the three possible return values. (Note that the `vbYes` case runs a procedure named `CopyFiles`. The `ButtonTest` procedure assumes that the `CopyFiles` procedure already exists elsewhere in the module.)

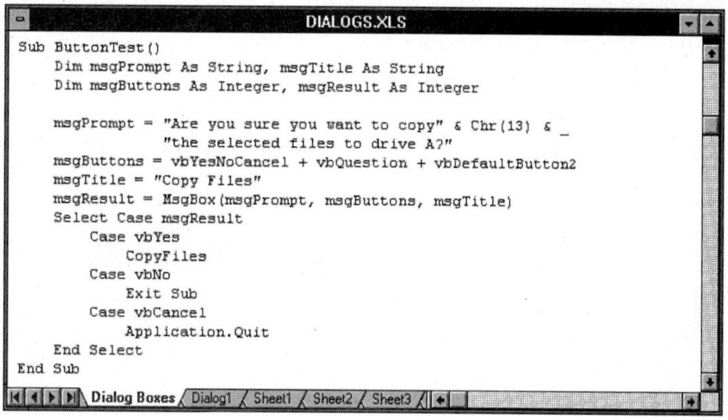

FIGURE 54.4.
This example uses `Select Case` to test the return values of the `MsgBox` function.

DIALOGS.XLS

```
Sub ButtonTest()
    Dim msgPrompt As String, msgTitle As String
    Dim msgButtons As Integer, msgResult As Integer

    msgPrompt = "Are you sure you want to copy" & Chr(13) & _
                "the selected files to drive A?"
    msgButtons = vbYesNoCancel + vbQuestion + vbDefaultButton2
    msgTitle = "Copy Files"
    msgResult = MsgBox(msgPrompt, msgButtons, msgTitle)
    Select Case msgResult
        Case vbYes
            CopyFiles
        Case vbNo
            Exit Sub
        Case vbCancel
            Application.Quit
    End Select
End Sub
```

Dialog Boxes / Dialog1 / Sheet1 / Sheet2 / Sheet3

Getting Input from the User

As you've seen, the `MsgBox` function enables your procedures to interact with the user and get some feedback. Unfortunately, this method limits you to simple command button responses. For more varied user input, you need to use more sophisticated techniques.

Prompting the User for Input

The `InputBox` method displays a dialog box with a message that prompts the user to enter data, and it provides an edit box for the data itself. The syntax for this method appears as the following:

`object``.InputBox(`***`prompt`***`,`*`title`*`,`*`default`*`,`*`xpos`*`,`*`ypos`*`,`*`helpFile`*`,`*`context`*`)`

`object`	An `Application` object.

prompt	The message you want to display in the dialog box.
title	Text that appears in the dialog box title bar. The default value is the null string (nothing).
default	The default value displayed in the edit box. If you omit *default*, the edit box is displayed empty.
xpos	The horizontal position of the dialog box from the left edge of the screen. The value is measured in points (there are 72 points in an inch). If you omit *xpos*, the dialog box is centered horizontally.
ypos	The vertical position, in points, from the top of the screen. If you omit *ypos*, the dialog is centered vertically in the current window.
helpFile	Text specifying the Help file that contains the custom help topic. If you enter *helpFile*, you also have to include *context*. If you include *helpFile*, a **H**elp button appears in the dialog box.
context	A number that identifies the help topic in *helpFile*.

For example, Figure 54.5 shows a dialog box generated by the following statement:

```
Application.InputBox _
    prompt:="Enter a number between 1 and 100:", _
    title:="Enter Data", _
```

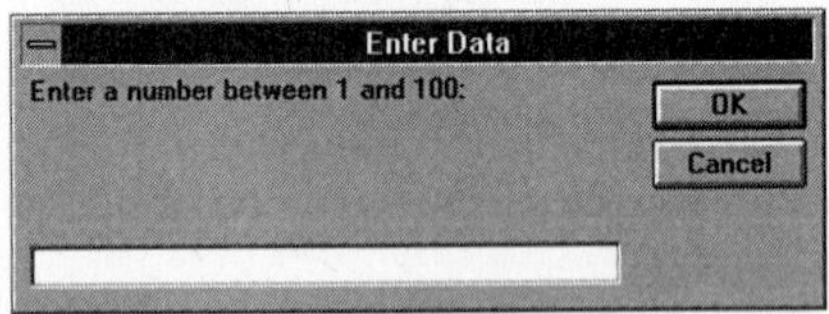

FIGURE 54.5.
A dialog box generated by the InputBox method.

The InputBox method returns one of the following values:

- The value entered into the edit box, if the user clicks on OK.
- An empty string, if the user clicks on Cancel.

You can store the result by assigning a variable to the InputBox statement. You can then use this variable to test the result (with If...Then...Else or Select Case), or you can use the variable in other statements and calculations.

Accessing Excel's Built-In Dialog Boxes

Many Visual Basic methods are known as *dialog box equivalents* because they enable you to select the same options that are available in Excel's built-in dialog boxes. Using dialog box equivalents works fine if your procedure knows which options to select, but there are times when you might want the user to specify some of the dialog box options.

For example, if your procedure will print a document (using the `PrintOut` method), you might need to know how many copies the user wants or how many pages to print. You could use the `InputBox` method to get this data, but it's usually easier just to display the Print dialog box.

The built-in dialog boxes are Dialog objects, and `Dialogs` is the collection of all the dialog boxes. To reference a particular dialog box, use one of the predefined Excel constants. Table 54.3 lists a few of the more common ones.

Table 54.3. Some of Excel's built-in dialog box constants.

Constant	*Dialog Box*
`xlDialogOpen`	Open
`xlDialogSaveAs`	Save As
`xlDialogPrint`	Print
`xlDialogFindFile`	Find File
`xlDialogDefineName`	Define Name
`xlDialogSort`	Sort

To display any of these dialog boxes, use the `Dialog` object's `Show` method. For example, the following statement displays the Print dialog box:

```
Application.Dialogs(xlDialogPrint).Show
```

If the user clicks on Cancel to exit the dialog box, the `Show` method returns `False`. This means you can use `Show` inside an `If` statement to determine what the user did:

```
If Not Application.Dialogs(xlDialogPrint).Show Then
    MsgBox "File was not printed"
End If
```

Chapter

55

Creating Custom Dialog Boxes in Visual Basic

The `InputBox` method you learned about in Chapter 54, "Using Visual Basic to Get and Display Information," works fine if you need just a single item of information, but what if you need four or five? Or what if you want the user to choose from a list of items? In some cases, you can use Excel's built-in dialog boxes, but these might not have the exact controls you need, or they might have controls you don't want the user to have access to.

The solution is to build your own dialog boxes. You can add as many controls as you need (including list boxes, option buttons, and check boxes), and your procedures have complete access to all the results. Best of all, Visual Basic makes constructing even the most sophisticated dialog boxes as easy as dragging the mouse pointer. This chapter shows you how to create dialog boxes and integrate them into your applications.

Inserting a New Dialog Sheet

You create a custom dialog box in a separate *dialog sheet.* A dialog sheet is a special sheet that has a *dialog frame*—an empty dialog box—and a grid you add controls to. The first thing you need to do is to insert a dialog sheet into the workbook, as described in Procedure 55.1.

PROCEDURE 55.1. INSERTING A DIALOG SHEET.

1. Select the workbook you want to use to store the dialog box.
2. Excel inserts the dialog sheet before the active sheet, so you need to activate the sheet you want the dialog sheet to appear before. For example, to have the dialog sheet appear before Sheet1, activate Sheet1.
3. Select the **I**nsert | **M**acro | **D**ialog command. Excel inserts a new sheet and displays the Forms toolbar, as shown in Figure 55.1.
4. To change the name of the displayed dialog frame, double-click on its title bar and then enter the name you want to use.

Adding Controls to a Dialog Sheet

The new dialog sheet displays a default dialog box frame with the OK and Cancel buttons already added. The idea is that you use this frame to "draw" the controls you need. Later, you can either link the controls directly to worksheet cells or you can create procedures to handle the selections.

The Forms toolbar contains tools for all the controls you can add to a dialog box. Procedure 55.2 lists the basic steps to follow to add any control to the dialog box.

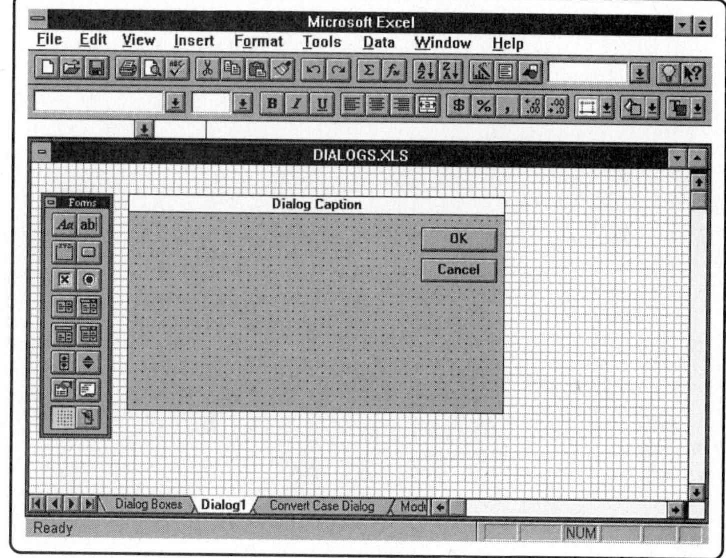

FIGURE 55.1.
A new dialog sheet is added to a workbook.

PROCEDURE 55.2. ADDING A CONTROL TO A DIALOG BOX.

1. Click on the tool you want to use.
2. Move the mouse pointer into the dialog box and position it where you want the top-left corner of the control to appear.
3. Drag the mouse pointer. Visual Basic displays a gray border indicating the outline of the control.
4. Release the mouse button. Visual Basic creates the control and gives it a default name (such as Check Box *n*; *n* signifies that this is the *n*th control you've created on this dialog box).

As soon as you've added a control, you can move it around, size it, or delete it. Table 55.1 summarizes the techniques for these actions.

Table 55.1. Mouse techniques for working with controls.

Action	*Result*
Click on the control	Selects the control
Hold down the Shift key and click on each control	Selects multiple controls
Drag the control	Moves the control

continues

Table 55.1. continued

Action	*Result*
Select the control and then drag any of the selection handles that appear	Sizes a control
Select the control and press the Delete key	Deletes a control

SUPER NOTE

To size the dialog box itself, click on the title bar and then use the selection handles that appear.

Setting the Tab Order

As you know, you can navigate a dialog box by pressing the Tab key. The order in which the controls are selected is called the *tab order* (or the *z-order*). Visual Basic sets the tab order according to the order you create the controls on the dialog sheet. In most cases, this order isn't what you want to end up with; Visual Basic enables you to control the tab order yourself. Procedure 55.3 shows you how.

PROCEDURE 55.3. SETTING THE TAB ORDER OF A CUSTOM DIALOG BOX.

1. Select the Tools | Tab Order command. Excel displays the Tab Order dialog box, shown in Figure 55.2.

SUPER TIP

You also can display the Tab Order dialog box by right-clicking on an empty part of the dialog box and selecting Tab Order from the shortcut menu.

2. In the Tab Order list, highlight the control you want to move.
3. Use the Move control to move the item up (by clicking the up arrow) or down (by clicking the down arrow).
4. Repeat steps 2 and 3 for other controls you want to move.
5. Click on OK or press Enter.

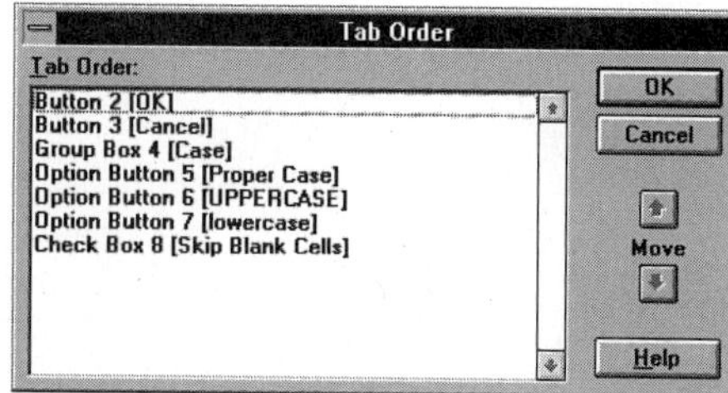

FIGURE 55.2.
The Tab Order dialog box.

Setting Control Properties

Dialog box controls are objects with their own set of properties and methods. A check box, for example, is a CheckBox object, and it has properties that control the name of the check box, whether or not it is initially checked, its accelerator key, and more. There are also collections of control objects. `CheckBoxes`, for example, is a collection of all the check boxes on a dialog sheet.

SUPER NOTE

You can reference each control in a collection in one of two ways:

- You can use a number that corresponds to the control's position in the tab order among similar controls. For example, CheckBoxes(2) refers to the second check box in the tab order, not the second control in the tab order.
- You can use the unique name Excel defines for each control. These names take the form control_type n, where control_type is the type of control (Check Box or Button, for example) and n means that the control was the *n*th control added to the dialog box. For example, if a check box was the third item added to a dialog box, you could reference the check box as CheckBoxes("Check Box 3"). The name of a control appears in the formula bar's Name box whenever you select a control.

You can manipulate control properties at runtime, before you display the dialog box, while displaying it, or after. However, you can set some control properties at design time (that is, in the dialog sheet) by following the steps in Procedure 55.4.

PROCEDURE 55.4. SETTING CONTROL PROPERTIES IN THE DIALOG SHEET.

1. Select the control you want to work with.
2. Select the Format | Object command. Excel displays the Format Object dialog box.

SUPER TIP

You also can display the Format Object dialog box by either selecting the control and pressing Ctrl+1 or by right-clicking on the control and selecting Format Object from the shortcut menu.

Click on this tool in the Forms toolbar to display the selected object's Format Object dialog box.

3. Select the Control tab.
4. Enter your options.
5. Click on OK or press Enter.

Figure 55.3 shows the Control tab for a check box. Each type of control has its own unique options, but there are two you'll see for most objects:

Accelerator Key	Defines which letter in the control's name (or *caption,* as it's called in Visual Basic) will be the accelerator key. This letter appears underlined in the caption, and the user can select the control by holding down the Alt key and pressing the letter.
Cell Link	A worksheet cell that holds the value of the control when the user exits the dialog box. If a check box is activated, for example, its linked cell will contain the value `TRUE`.

FIGURE 55.3.
The Control tab for a check box.

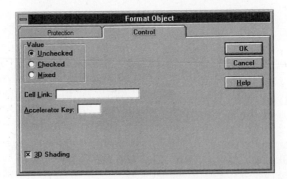

SUPER CAUTION

A cell linked to a control changes value if the control changes, even when the user clicks on Cancel to exit the dialog box. It's usually better (and safer) to assign the value of a control to a variable and then, if appropriate, place the value in the cell under program control.

Types of Controls

Visual Basic offers a dozen different controls for your custom dialog boxes. The next few sections look at each type of control.

Command Buttons

Most dialog boxes include command buttons to enable the user to carry out a command at the click of the mouse. The default dialog sheet, in fact, starts with the two most common command buttons: OK and Cancel. A command button is a Button object, and `Buttons` is the collection of all the buttons on a dialog sheet.

To create other buttons, use the Create Button tool in the Forms toolbar. Once you've added a button, you can change its name by double-clicking on the button and entering the text.

The Create Button tool.

The Format Object dialog box for command buttons includes the following options:

Default	The button appears surrounded by a thin black border, and it is selected automatically when the user presses Enter. The default OK button has this option activated.
Cancel	The button is selected if the user presses the Esc key. The default Cancel button has this option activated.
Di**s**miss	The dialog box exits if the user selects the button. The default OK button has this option activated.
Help	The button is selected if the user presses F1. Use this option if you plan to include context-sensitive Help in your application. (See Chapter 59, "Visual Basic Tips and Techniques.")

Labels

The Label tool adds text labels to the dialog box. A label is a Label object, and `Labels` is the collection of all the labels on a dialog sheet.

To create labels, use the Label tool in the Forms toolbar. Once you've added a label, you can change its caption by double-clicking on the label and entering the text.

The Label tool.

Although labels are mostly used to display text, you also can use them to name controls that don't have their own captions: edit boxes, list boxes, scrollbars, and spinners. You can even add accelerator keys to the text so the user has a shortcut to access these controls. Procedure 55.5 shows you the steps to follow.

PROCEDURE 55.5. ASSIGNING A LABEL AND ACCELERATOR KEY TO A CONTROL.

1. Before creating the control you want to name, add a label and change the text to the name of the control.
2. In the label's Format Object dialog box, select the Control tab, enter a letter in the **A**ccelerator Key box, and then click on OK or press Enter.
3. Add the control and position it just below the label.

SUPER TIP

To assign a label and accelerator key to an existing control, add the label and then adjust the tab order so the label comes immediately before the control.

Edit Boxes

Edit boxes are versatile controls that enable the user to enter text, numbers, cell references, and formulas. An edit box is an EditBox object, and `EditBoxes` is the collection of all edit boxes on a dialog sheet.

To create an edit box, use the Edit tool in the Forms toolbar.

The Edit tool.

The Format Object dialog box for an edit box includes the following options:

Edit Validation	These option buttons determine the type of data the user enters into the edit box.
Multiline Edit	Enables the user to enter multiple lines of text. The text wraps automatically.
Vertical Scrollbar	Adds a scrollbar to the side of the edit box to enable the user to navigate the text.

Group Boxes

You use group boxes to create a group of two or more option buttons. The user can then select only one option from the group. A group box is a GroupBox object, and `GroupBoxes` is the collection of all group boxes on a dialog sheet.

Use the Group Box tool to create a group box. You can change its caption by double-clicking on the default caption and then entering your text.

SUPER NOTE

To group two or more option buttons together, create the group box and then create the option buttons inside it.

The Group Box tool.

Option Buttons

Option buttons are controls that usually appear in groups of two or more, and the user can only select one of the options. An option button is an OptionButton object, and `OptionButtons` is the collection of all option buttons on a dialog sheet.

To create an option button, use the Option Button tool. As usual, you can change the caption by double-clicking on the option button.

The Option Button tool.

The Format Object dialog box for an option button enables you to determine which of the buttons is initially selected. Display the Format Object dialog box for that button and activate the **Checked** option.

SUPER NOTE

If you don't surround the option buttons with a group box, Visual Basic treats all the option buttons in a dialog box as one group.

Check Boxes

Check boxes enable you to include options that the user can toggle on or off. A check box is a CheckBox object, and `CheckBoxes` is the collection of all the check boxes on a dialog sheet.

To create a check box, use the Check Box tool in the Forms toolbar and then double-click on the caption to change it.

The Check Box tool.

As with option buttons, you also can control whether or not a check box is initially activated (checked). In the Control tab of a check box's Format Object dialog box, select either **C**hecked or **U**nchecked.

List Boxes

Visual Basic offers two different list boxes you can use to present the user with a list of choices:

List Box: A simple list of items. The user selects an item from the list. Use the List Box tool to create a list box.

The List Box tool.

Combination List-Edit Box: A control that combines an edit box with a list box. The user either selects an item from the list or enters an item in the edit box. Use the Combination List-Edit tool to create this control.

The Combination List-Edit tool.

Both these controls are ListBox objects, and `ListBoxes` is the collection of all list boxes on a dialog sheet.

You generate the items that appear in the list by entering them in a worksheet range and then specifying the range in the **I**nput Range edit box in the list's Format Object dialog box.

Drop-Down Lists

Visual Basic gives you a choice of two different drop-down lists:

Drop-Down List: A non-editable list of items. Use the Drop-Down tool to create a drop-down list.

The Drop-Down tool.

Combination Drop-Down Edit List: A control that combines an edit box with a drop-down list. The user either selects an item from the list or enters an item in the edit box. Use the Combination Drop-Down Edit tool to create this control.

The Combination Drop-Down Edit tool.

Both these controls are DropDown objects, and `DropDowns` is the collection of all list boxes on a dialog sheet.

As with list boxes, use a worksheet range to define the list of items and then use **I**nput Range in the list's Format Object dialog box to reference the range.

Scroll Bars

Scroll bars are normally used to navigate windows, but by themselves you can use them to enter values between a predefined maximum and minimum. A scroll bar is a ScrollBar object, and `ScrollBars` is the collection of all scroll bars on a dialog sheet.

Use the Scroll Bar tool to create either a vertical or horizontal scroll bar.

The Scroll Bar tool.

The Format Object dialog box for a scroll bar includes the following options:

Current Value	The initial value of the scroll bar
Minimum Value	The minimum value of the scroll bar
Ma**x**imum Value	The maximum value of the scroll bar
Incremental Change	The amount the scroll bar changes when the user clicks on a scroll arrow
Page Change	The amount the scroll bar changes when the user clicks between the scroll box and a scroll arrow

Spinners

A spinner is similar to a scroll bar because the user can click the spinner arrows to increment or decrement a value. A spinner is a Spinner object, and `Spinners` is the collection of all the spinners on a dialog sheet.

To create a spinner, use the Spinner tool in the Forms toolbar.

The Spinner tool.

The options in a spinner's Format Object dialog box are the same as those for a scroll bar (except you can't enter a **P**age Change value).

Using a Custom Dialog Box in a Procedure

After you've created your dialog box, the next step is to incorporate your handiwork into some Visual Basic code. This involves two separate techniques:

- Displaying the dialog box
- Processing the dialog box results

Displaying the Dialog Box

The DialogSheet object has a `Show` method you use to display the dialog box to the user. For example, consider the dialog sheet shown in Figure 55.4. To display this dialog box, you use the following statement:

```
DialogSheets(1).Show
```

Alternatively, you could use the sheet name to reference the appropriate sheet in the `DialogSheets` collection:

```
DialogSheets("Convert Case Dialog").Show
```

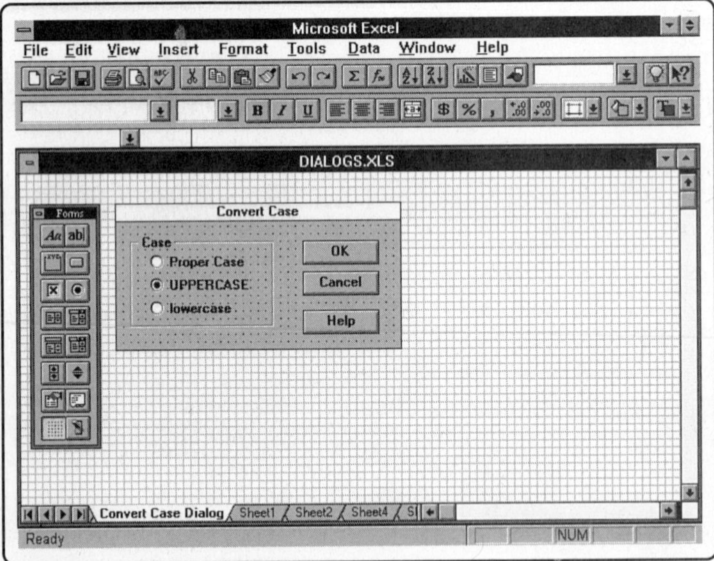

FIGURE 55.4.
A custom dialog box.

SUPER TIP

Before you get to the code stage, you might want to first try out your dialog box in the dialog sheet to make sure it looks okay. To do this, either select the **T**ools | Run **D**ialog command or click on the Run Dialog tool in the Forms toolbar.

The Run Dialog tool.

Processing the Dialog Box Results

When the user clicks on OK or Cancel (or any other button in which the **D**ismiss option was activated), you usually need to examine the dialog box results and process them.

In most cases, the first thing to find out is whether the user clicked on OK or Cancel because, presumably, this determines whether or not you ignore the other dialog box selections. If you click on OK in a dialog box, the `Show` method returns the value `True`; if you click on Cancel, `Show` returns `False`. A simple `If...Then...Else` usually does the job:

```
If DialogSheets(1).Show Then
     (process the other results)
Else
     Exit Sub (or whatever)
End If
```

If you do need to process the results of the other dialog box controls, you can use the control object to get the current value of the control. Table 55.2 lists some control objects, the property that returns the control's current state, and a description of what kind of data gets returned.

Table 55.2. Return value properties for some dialog box controls.

Object	*Property*	*What It Returns*
`CheckBox`	`Value`	One of `xlOn`, `xlOff`, or `xlMixed`
`DropDown`	`Value`	The position of the selected item in the list (where 1 is the first item)
`Edit Box`	`Caption`	The value entered in the box

continues

Table 55.2. continued

Object	*Property*	*What It Returns*
`ListBox`	`Value`	The position of the selected item in the list (where 1 is the first item)
`OptionButton`	`Value`	Either `xlOn` or `xlOff`
`ScrollBar`	`Value`	A number between the scrollbar's minimum and maximum values
`Spinner`	`Value`	A number between the spinner's minimum and maximum values

For example, Figure 55.5 shows a procedure that displays the Convert Case dialog box and then, if OK was selected, examines the state of each option button to see if it was selected (and now set to xlOn).

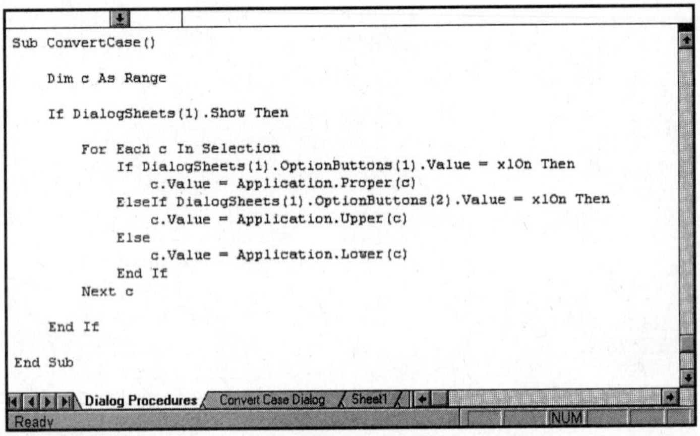

```
Sub ConvertCase()

    Dim c As Range

    If DialogSheets(1).Show Then

        For Each c In Selection
            If DialogSheets(1).OptionButtons(1).Value = xlOn Then
                c.Value = Application.Proper(c)
            ElseIf DialogSheets(1).OptionButtons(2).Value = xlOn Then
                c.Value = Application.Upper(c)
            Else
                c.Value = Application.Lower(c)
            End If
        Next c

    End If

End Sub
```

Dialog Procedures / Convert Case Dialog / Sheet1
Ready NUM

FIGURE 55.5.
A procedure to show and process the Convert Case custom dialog box.

Creating Event Handler Code

Visual Basic is an *event-driven* language, which means that your code can respond to specific events such as a user clicking on a command button or selecting an item from a list. The procedure can then take appropriate action, whether it's validating the user's input or asking for confirmation of the requested action.

The procedures that perform these tasks are called *event handlers*; you create them by following the steps in Procedure 55.6.

PROCEDURE 55.6. CREATING AN EVENT HANDLER FOR A DIALOG BOX CONTROL.

1. Select the control for which you want to create an event handler.
2. Click on the Edit Code tool in the Forms toolbar. Excel displays a Visual Basic module and enters the appropriate `Sub` and `End Sub` statements.

The Edit Code tool.

3. Enter the rest of the procedure code between the `Sub` and `End Sub` statements.

SUPER TIP

If you want to assign an existing procedure to a control event, select the control and then select the **T**ools | Assig**n** Macro command. In the Assign Macro dialog box, select the procedure you want to use.

For example, the following event handler gets processed whenever the user selects the `Option Button 5` control:

```
Sub OptionButton5_Click()
     DialogSheets(1).ListBoxes(1).Enabled = True
     DialogSheets(1).Focus = DialogSheets(1).ListBoxes(1)
End Sub
```

A list box is enabled, and the dialog box focus is switched to the list box.

Chapter

56

Creating Custom Menus and Toolbars in Visual Basic

Visual Basic procedures are only as useful as they are convenient. There isn't much point in creating a procedure that saves you a few keystrokes if you have to expend a lot of energy hunting down the routine you need. The Personal Macro Library helps, but overloading it can make navigating the Macro dialog box a nightmare. Shortcut keys are true time-savers, but Excel has only so many (and our brains can memorize only so many Ctrl+*key* combinations).

One elegant solution to the problem of running procedures conveniently is to turn command macros into menu commands. You can add commands to existing menus, or you can create new menus and even entire menu bars. This is not only convenient for you, but essential if you're creating an application that other people will use. Another solution is to create your own toolbars to give your applications pushbutton access. This chapter takes you through the basics of creating both custom menus and custom toolbars with Visual Basic.

SUPER NOTE

Excel 5.0 offers several tools that make it easy to customize menus and toolbars. See Chapter 65, "Customizing Excel's Menus and Toolbars," for details.

Using Visual Basic to Modify Menus

You can use Visual Basic properties and methods to make modifications to Excel's menus within procedures. This includes adding menus and entire menu bars, renaming commands, and disabling or enabling commands. This section takes you on a brief tour of some of these techniques.

Working with Menu Bars

When working with menu bars, you can either use a custom menu bar that you created, or you can use one of the built-in menu bars listed in Table 56.1.

Table 56.1. Excel's built-in menu bars.

Menu Bar	*Description*
Worksheet	Appears when a worksheet is active
Chart	Appears when a chart is active
No Documents Open	Appears when no workbooks are open

Menu Bar	*Description*
Module	Appears when a Visual Basic module is active
Shortcut Menus 1	Appears when the user right-clicks on a toolbar, tool, cell, row or column header, workbook tab, window title bar, or desktop
Shortcut Menus 2	Appears when the user right-clicks on a drawn object, macro button, or text box
Shortcut Menus 3	Appears when the user right-clicks on the following chart elements: data series, text, arrow, plot area, gridline, floor, legend, or the entire chart

SUPER NOTE

Excel stores your customized menus in the current workbook. If you close the workbook, Excel reverts to the default menus. If you want your custom menus to appear all the time, unhide the Personal Macro Workbook (PERSONAL.XLS) and use it to customize your menus.

Menu bars are MenuBar objects, and `MenuBars` is the collection of all menu bars. You can refer to a menu bar in one of three ways:

- Use `ActiveMenuBar` to refer to the currently displayed menu bar.
- Use the name of a custom menu bar.
- Use the Excel constants listed in Table 56.2.

Table 56.2. Excel menu bar constants.

Constant	*Menu Bar*
`xlWorksheet`	Worksheet
`xlChart`	Chart
`xlNoDocuments`	No Documents Open
`xlModule`	Visual Basic Module

For example, `MenuBars("CustomBar")` refers to a custom menu bar named *`CustomBar`*, and `MenuBars(xlWorksheet)` refers to the Worksheet menu bar.

Following are a few common methods used with menu bars:

Method	*Description*	*Example*
`Add`	Creates a new menu bar	`MenuBars.Add "CustomBar"`
`Activate`	Displays a menu bar	`MenuBars("CustomBar").Activate`
`Delete`	Deletes a custom menu bar	`MenuBars("CustomBar").Delete`
`Reset`	Restores a built-in menu bar	`MenuBars(xlWorksheet).Reset`

Working with Menus

Menus are Menu objects, and `Menus` is the collection of all menus on a menu bar. You can refer to a menu in one of two ways:

- Use the name of the menu.
- Use the position of the menu on the menu bar, where the leftmost menu is 1.

For example, `MenuBars(xlWorksheet).Menus("File")` and `MenuBars(xlWorksheet).Menus(1)` both refer to the Worksheet menu bar's **F**ile menu.

Adding a Menu

To add a menu to a menu bar, use the `Add` method for the `Menus` collection:

`object``.Add(`***`caption`***`,`*`before`*`,`*`restore`*`)`

`object`	The `Menus` object.
`caption`	The menu name. Include an ampersand before a letter to make the letter the menu's accelerator key.
`before`	The menu to the left of which you want the new menu added. You can use either the menu's name or its position in the menu bar. If you omit *`before`*, the menu is added to the left of the **H**elp menu.
`restore`	If *`restore`* is `True`, Excel restores the previously deleted built-in menu named ***`caption`***. If *`restore`* is `False` or omitted, Excel adds the menu.

For example, the following statement adds a **P**rocedures menu to the end of the Worksheet menu bar:

```
MenuBars(xlWorksheet).Menus.Add caption:="&Procedures"
```

Deleting a Menu

To delete a built-in or custom menu, use the `Delete` method:

```
object.Delete
```

`object` is the Menu object you want to delete.

The following statement deletes the **P**rocedures menu from the active menu bar:

```
ActiveMenuBar.Menus("Procedures").Delete
```

Working with Menu Commands

Menu commands are MenuItem objects, and `MenuItems` is the collection of all commands on a menu. As with menus, you can refer to a menu command in one of two ways:

- Use the name of the command.
- Use the position of the command on the menu, where the top command is 1.

Adding a Command

To add a command to a menu, use the `Add` method for the `MenuItems` collection:

```
object.Add(caption,onAction,shortcutKey,before,restore)
```

`object`	The `MenuItems` object.
`caption`	The command name. Include an ampersand before a letter to make the letter the command's accelerator key. To create a separator bar, use a hyphen (-).
`onAction`	The procedure to run when the user selects the command.
`shortcutKey`	Used only on Macintosh systems.
`before`	The command above which you want the new command added. You can use either the command's name or its position in the menu. If you omit *`before`*, the command is added to the bottom of the menu.
`restore`	If *`restore`* is `True`, Excel restores the previously deleted built-in command named *`caption`*. If *`restore`* is `False` or omitted, Excel adds the command.

For example, the following statement adds a command named **H**ide Gridlines to the **T**ools menu:

```
MenuBars(xlWorksheet).Menus("Tools").MenuItems.Add _
    caption:="&Hide Gridlines", _
    onAction:="PERSONAL.XLS!HideGridlines"
```

Adding a Check Mark to a Command

Some menu commands toggle settings on and off. When a setting is on, Excel indicates it by placing a check mark beside the command. You can do the same thing for your custom commands by setting the `Checked` property to `True` for a MenuItem object. (To remove the check mark, set `Checked` to `False`.)

For example, the following statements add a check mark beside the **H**ide Gridlines command (I'm using the *`menuVar`* variable to save space; it isn't necessary for setting the property):

```
Set menuVar = MenuBars(xlWorksheet).Menus("Tools")
menuVar.MenuItems("Hide Gridlines").Checked = True
```

Disabling and Enabling a Command

Excel dims menu commands to show you when a command has been disabled. The `Enabled MenuItem` property enables you to disable (when it's set to `False`) and enable (when it's set to `True`) commands in your procedures.

To disable the **H**ide Gridlines command, for example, you use the following code:

```
Set menuVar = MenuBars(xlWorksheet).Menus("Tools")
menuVar.MenuItems("Hide Gridlines").Enabled = False
```

Renaming a Command

To change the name of a command, you can alter its `Caption` property. The most common use for renaming commands is to reflect a different workspace state. For example, instead of placing a check mark beside the **H**ide Gridlines command, you could rename it to S**h**ow Gridlines as follows:

```
Set menuVar = MenuBars(xlWorksheet).Menus("Tools")
menuVar.MenuItems("Hide Gridlines").Caption = "S&how Gridlines"
```

TIP

To avoid confusing your users, try to keep the same accelerator key when you rename a command.

Deleting a Command

When you no longer need a command, or when you want to remove a command that might be dangerous for novice users, use the `Delete` method:

```
object.Delete
```

object is the MenuItem object you want to delete.

The following statement deletes the **H**ide Gridlines command:

```
Set menuVar = MenuBars(xlWorksheet).Menus("Tools")
menuVar.MenuItems("Hide Gridlines").Delete
```

Using Visual Basic to Customize Excel's Toolbars

Excel's built-in toolbars give you easy access to many of the program's most-used features. You can add the same point-and-shoot functionality to your Visual Basic procedures by adding new tools and assigning procedures to them. Then when a user clicks on the tool, the procedure runs. You can even design your own tool icons and create entire toolbars for your macros. This section shows you how to do these things and more.

Working with Toolbars

Toolbars are Toolbar objects, and `Toolbars` is the collection of all the toolbars in the workspace. You can refer to a toolbar in one of two ways:

- Use the name of the toolbar.
- Use the toolbar number shown in Table 56.3.

Table 56.3. Excel's toolbar names and numbers.

Name	*Number*
Standard	1
Formatting	2
Query and Pivot	3
Chart	4
Drawing	5
TipWizard	6
Forms	7
Stop Recording	8
Visual Basic	9
Auditing	10
Workgroup	11
Microsoft	12
Full Screen	13

Displaying a Toolbar

To display a toolbar, set the Toolbar object's `Visible` property to `True`. For example, the following statement displays the Drawing toolbar:

```
Toolbars("Drawing").Visible = True
```

When you want to hide the toolbar again, set the `Visible` property to `False`.

Changing the Position of a Toolbar

Toolbars can either be *docked* at the top or bottom of the screen, or on the left or right side. They also can be *floating* in the desktop area. You can use the `Position` property to control these attributes. Table 56.4 lists the constants to use with the `Position` property.

Table 56.4. Excel constants to use with the `Position` property.

Constant	*Where It Positions the Toolbar*
`xlTop`	In the top docking area
`xlBottom`	In the bottom docking area
`xlLeft`	In the left docking area
`xlRight`	In the right docking area
`xlFloating`	Floating

You also can use the `Width` and `Height` properties to change the dimensions of a floating toolbar. You specify a value in *points;* one point equals 1/72 of an inch.

In the following statement, the Drawing toolbar is displayed in the floating position with a width of 100 points:

```
With Toolbars("Drawing")
     .Position = xlFloating
     .Width = 100
End With
```

Adding a Toolbar

Many macro programmers prefer to leave Excel's built-in toolbars intact and create their own custom toolbars. This is handy for giving easy access to large numbers of procedures; it also can add a nice touch to an application.

You add a toolbar with the `Add` method of the `Toolbars` collection:

```
object.Add(name)
```

object	The `Toolbars` object.
name	The *name* you want to use for the toolbar. If you omit name, Visual Basic assigns a default name of "Toolbar *n*." *n* signifies the *n*th unnamed toolbar.

For example, the following statement creates a new toolbar named Custom Tools:

```
Toolbar.Add Name:="Custom Tools"
```

Deleting a Toolbar

To delete a toolbar you no longer use, use the `Delete` method:

```
object.Delete
```

object is the Toolbar object you want to delete.

The following statement deletes the Custom Tools toolbar:

```
Toolbars("Custom Tools").Delete
```

Restoring a Built-In Toolbar

If you've made changes to one of Excel's built-in toolbars, you can revert the toolbar to its default state by using the `Reset` method:

```
object.Reset
```

object is the built-in Toolbar object you want to reset.

For example, following is a code fragment that loops through the `Toolbars` collection and resets the toolbar if it's built-in, or deletes it if it isn't:

```
For Each toolbarVar In Toolbars
     If toolbarVar.BuiltIn Then
          toolbarVar.Reset
     Else
          toolbarVar.Delete
     End If
Next toolbarVar
```

SUPER NOTE

The `BuiltIn` property returns `True` if the toolbar is built-in and `False` otherwise.

Attaching a Toolbar to a Workbook

To distribute a custom toolbar along with your Visual Basic application, you need to attach the toolbar to the application's workbook. Procedure 56.1 shows you how.

PROCEDURE 56.1. ATTACHING A TOOLBAR TO A WORKBOOK.

1. Open the workbook you want to use and activate a Visual Basic module.
2. Select the Tools | Attach Toolbars command. Excel displays the Attach Toolbars dialog box, shown in Figure 56.1.

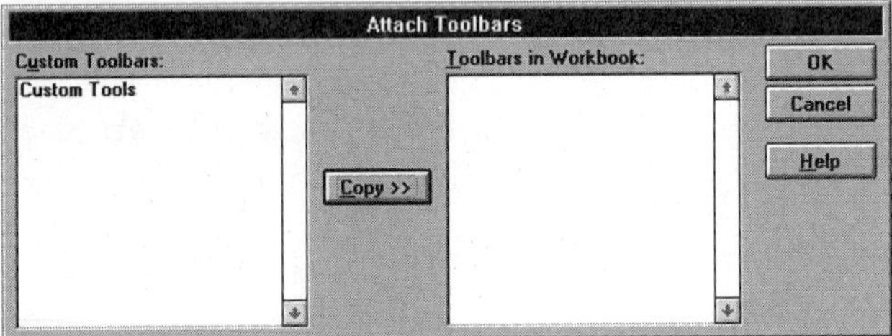

FIGURE 56.1.
Use the Attach Toolbars dialog box to attach a toolbar to a workbook.

3. In the Custom Toolbars list, highlight the toolbar you want to attach.
4. Click on the Copy>> button. Excel adds the name to the Toolbars in Workbook list.
5. Repeat steps 3 and 4 to attach any other toolbars to the workbook.

SUPER TIP

If you accidentally copy a toolbar, you can remove it by highlighting it in the Toolbars in Workbook list and clicking on the Delete button.

6. Click on OK or press Enter.

After you've attached a toolbar, it automatically gets copied into the Excel workspace whenever the user opens the workbook.

Working with Toolbar Buttons

You can customize toolbar buttons by assigning procedures to them, adding new buttons, disabling and enabling buttons, and deleting buttons you don't need. A button is a ToolbarButton object, and `ToolbarButtons` is a collection of the buttons on a toolbar.

To reference a toolbar button, you can use one of the following three methods (depending on the context):

- The button name
- The button ID number
- The button's position on the toolbar

SUPER NOTE

See your Visual Basic User's Guide for a complete list of button names and ID numbers.

Adding a Button to a Toolbar

To add a button to any toolbar, use the `Add` method of the `ToolbarButtons` collection:

object.Add(*button*,*before*,*onAction*,*pushed*,*enabled*)

object	The `ToolbarButtons` object.
button	The button ID number or its name. If you want to enter a space, set *button* to 0.
before	The position of the button before which you want to position the new button. If you omit *before,* the button appears at the end of the toolbar. If the toolbar is empty, set *before* to 1.
onAction	The procedure to run when the user clicks on the button.
pushed	If `True`, the button appears pressed. If `False` or omitted, the button appears normal.
enabled	If `True` or omitted, the button is enabled. If `False`, the button is disabled.

For example, the following statement adds a happy face button (ID 211) to the beginning of a custom toolbar named Custom Tools:

```
Toolbars("Custom Tools").Toolbars.Add _
     button:=211, _
     before:= 1, _
     onAction:="PERSONAL.XLS!HideGridlines"
```

SUPER NOTE

You can create your own toolbar button faces with the Button Image Editor. See Chapter 65, "Customizing Excel's Menus and Toolbars," for more information.

Making a Button Appear Pressed

The `Add` method enables you to initialize a button to appear either pressed or normal, but you also can control this attribute during runtime. To make a button appear pressed, set the button's `Pushed` property to `True`. To revert the button to its normal appearance, set `Pushed` to `False`.

For example, the following statements toggle the `Pushed` property of the first button on the Custom Tools toolbar between `True` and `False`:

```
With Toolbars("Custom Tools").ToolbarButtons(1)
     .Pushed = Not .Pushed
End With
```

Disabling and Enabling a Button

You also can control the enabling and disabling of buttons at runtime. To disable a button, set the `Enabled` property to `False`. When a button is disabled, the computer will beep if the user tries to select it. To enable the button, set the `Enabled` property to `True`.

Deleting a Button

To delete a toolbar button, use the `Delete` method:

```
object.Delete
```

object is the ToolbarButton object you want to delete.

The following statement deletes the first tool in the Custom Tools toolbar:

```
Toolbars("Custom Tools").ToolbarButtons(1).Delete
```

Chapter

57

Visual Basic Procedures That Respond to Events

You have learned how to start your procedures from the Macro dialog box, with a shortcut key, or with a customized menu command or tool. In each case, you had to do something to get the procedure up and running. However, Excel also enables you to create procedures that automatically run, for example, when a workbook is opened. This chapter shows you how to create such procedures.

Running a Procedure When You Open a Workbook

Excel can automatically run a procedure when you open a workbook. This is useful for setting up the workbook environment (the calculation mode, view settings, custom menus and toolbars) or displaying a dialog box of options.

You set up this automatic routine by creating a `Sub` procedure named `Auto_Open` in any Visual Basic module in the workbook. When Excel is opening a workbook and sees an `Auto_Open` procedure, it automatically runs the code. Figure 57.1 shows an `Auto_Open` procedure that uses `MsgBox` (see Chapter 54, "Using Visual Basic to Get and Display Information") to ask whether a custom menu should be loaded. If the user clicks on **Yes**, the `LoadProceduresMenu` code (partially shown in Figure 57.1) is run. `Auto_Open` then displays a custom toolbar.

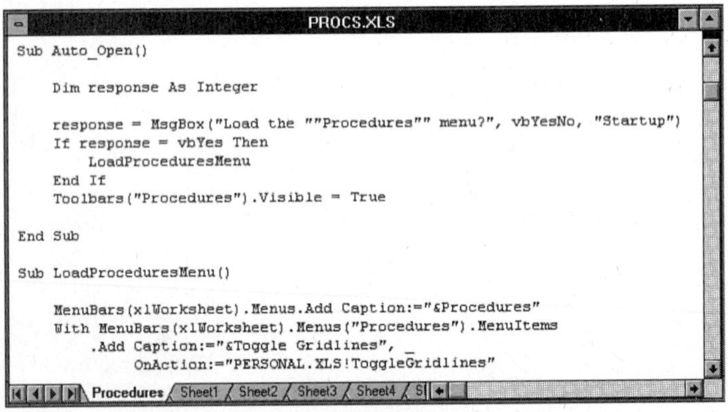

FIGURE 57.1.
The `Auto_Open` procedure automatically runs when this workbook is opened.

PROCS.XLS

```
Sub Auto_Open()

    Dim response As Integer

    response = MsgBox("Load the ""Procedures"" menu?", vbYesNo, "Startup")
    If response = vbYes Then
        LoadProceduresMenu
    End If
    Toolbars("Procedures").Visible = True

End Sub

Sub LoadProceduresMenu()

    MenuBars(xlWorksheet).Menus.Add Caption:="&Procedures"
    With MenuBars(xlWorksheet).Menus("Procedures").MenuItems
        .Add Caption:="&Toggle Gridlines", _
            OnAction:="PERSONAL.XLS!ToggleGridlines"
```

Procedures / Sheet1 / Sheet2 / Sheet3 / Sheet4 / S

SUPER TIP

To prevent an `Auto_Open` procedure from running, hold down the Shift key while opening the workbook.

SUPER CAUTION

You can't have more than one Auto_Open procedure in a workbook. If you do, Excel won't run any of them.

Running a Procedure When You Close a Workbook

Because most Auto_Open procedures change the Excel environment in some way, you usually need to reset everything when you close the worksheet. To reset the environment automatically, include a procedure named Auto_Close in the workbook. Here is an Auto_Close procedure that resets the Worksheet menu bar and then hides the custom Procedures toolbar:

```
Sub Auto_Close()
     MenuBars(xlWorksheet).Reset
     Toolbars("Procedures").Visible = False
End Sub
```

SUPER NOTE

Excel doesn't run an Auto_Close procedure when you close a workbook from another procedure using the Close method.

SUPER CAUTION

As with Auto_Open, you can't have more than one Auto_Close procedure in a workbook.

Working with Event Handler Procedures

Some Visual Basic objects include properties and methods that enable you to run a procedure when a specific event occurs. You can set up these *event handler* procedures (also called OnEvent procedures) to automatically execute when the user activates a worksheet, at a certain time of day, or when a specified key combination is pressed. The next few sections take you through each of Visual Basic's event handlers.

Running a Procedure When You Activate a Sheet

Many of your applications use multiple workbooks or multiple sheets in a single workbook. For example, you might have a customer database, an invoice entry sheet, and an accounts receivable aging report all in different sheets in a single workbook. As the user activates each sheet, you may need to perform various actions such as modifying an application menu, displaying a toolbar, or asking the user whether he or she wants to save changes.

You can do this by using the `OnSheetActivate` property to specify an event handler to run when the user activates a sheet. The six objects listed in Table 57.1 use the `OnSheetActivate` property.

Table 57.1. Excel objects that use the `OnSheetActivate` property.

Object	*Description*
`Application`	Runs event handler when any sheet in any workbook is activated
`Chart`	Runs event handler when a specified chart sheet is activated
`DialogSheet`	Runs event handler when a specified dialog sheet is activated
`Module`	Runs event handler when a specified Visual Basic module is activated
`Workbook`	Runs event handler when any sheet in the specified workbook is activated
`Worksheet`	Runs event handler when a specified worksheet is activated

For example, Figure 57.2 shows an `Auto_Open` procedure that sets up an event handler for a worksheet named Data Entry. When the user selects the Data Entry tab, the `DataEntryHandler` procedure automatically runs. In this case, the event handler sets the calculation mode to manual and then displays a dialog box.

SUPER NOTE

Excel doesn't run an `OnSheetActivate` handler when you open the workbook.

FIGURE 57.2.
An event handler for a worksheet.

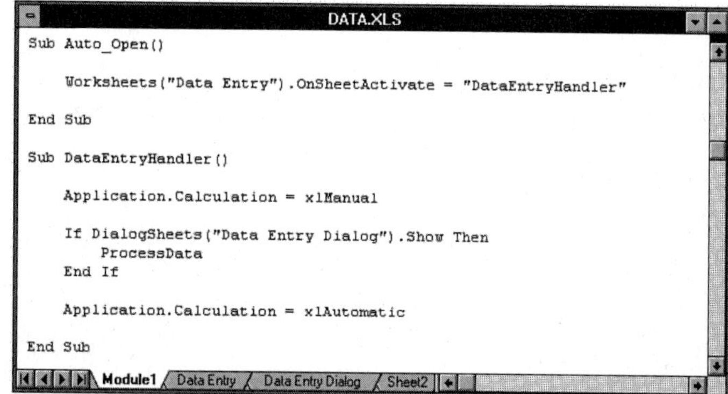

SUPER CAUTION

When specifying an `OnSheetActivate` handler for the `Application` object, be sure to include the name of the workbook and module where the event handler resides. Otherwise, Excel might not be able to find the procedure, and you'll get an error.

Running a Procedure When You Deactivate a Sheet

The `OnSheetDeactivate` property enables you to set up an event handler that automatically runs when the user deactivates a sheet. The objects that use `OnSheetActivate` use `OnSheetDeactivate` in the same way (see Table 57.1).

For example, the following statement sets up an event handler that runs when the user deactivates the DATA.XLS workbook:

```
Workbooks("DATA.XLS").OnSheetDeactivate = "ResetAll"
```

SUPER CAUTION

Avoid using the `ActiveWorkbook` or `ActiveSheet` objects with the `OnSheetDeactivate` property. Excel switches to the new workbook or sheet before running the event handler, so the code that references the active workbook or sheet might not run properly.

Running a Procedure When You Activate a Window

The `OnWindow` property is similar to `OnSheetActivate`. However, `OnWindow` specifies an event handler that runs whenever the user activates a window (and not just a sheet). Recall that you can have multiple windows opened for the same worksheet.

You can use the `OnWindow` property with the `Window` object (in which case the event handler runs when the user switches to a specified window) or the `Application` object (the event handler runs when the user switches to any window).

In Figure 57.3, for example, the `SetWindowHandler` procedure defines an `OnWindow` handler for the DATA.XLS:2 window. The event handler, `DataWindowHandler`, sets several `Window` object properties.

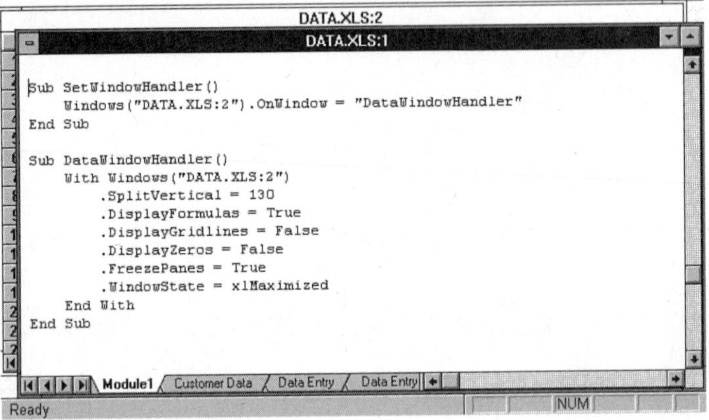

FIGURE 57.3.
Setting up an `OnWindow` event handler.

To cancel an event handler associated with a window, assign the `OnWindow` property to the null string (`""`), such as

```
Windows("DATA.XLS:2").OnWindow = ""
```

> **SUPER NOTE**
>
> `OnSheetActivate` or `OnSheetDeactivate` event handlers execute after the `OnWindow` procedure.

Running a Procedure When You Press a Key

Excel enables you to assign a Ctrl+*key* shortcut to a procedure, but there are two major drawbacks to this method:

- Excel uses some Ctrl+*key* combinations internally; therefore, your choices are limited.
- It doesn't help if you would like your procedures to respond to "meaningful" keys such as Delete and Esc.

To remedy these problems, use the `OnKey` method to run a procedure when the user presses a specific key or key combination:

```
object.OnKey(key,procedure)
```

key The key or key combination that runs the procedure. For letters, numbers, or punctuation marks, enclose the character in quotes (for example, `"a"`). For other keys, use the following strings:

Key	*What to Use*
Backspace	`"{BACKSPACE}"` or `"{BS}"`
Break	`"{BREAK}"`
Caps Lock	`"{CAPSLOCK}"`
Delete	`"{DELETE}"` or `"{DEL}"`
Down arrow	`"{DOWN}"`
End	`"{END}"`
Enter (keypad)	`"{ENTER}"`
Enter	`"~"` (tilde)
Esc	`"{ESCAPE}"` or `"{ESC}"`
Home	`"{HOME}"`
Insert	`"{INSERT}"`
Left arrow	`"{LEFT}"`
Num Lock	`"{NUMLOCK}"`
Page Down	`"{PGDN}"`
Page Up	`"{PGUP}"`
Right arrow	`"{RIGHT}"`
Scroll Lock	`"{SCROLLLOCK}"`
Tab	`"{TAB}"`
Up arrow	`"{UP}"`
F1 through F12	`"{F1}"` through `"{F12}"`

You also can combine these keys with the Shift, Ctrl, and Alt keys. You just precede the preceding codes with one or more of the following:

Key	*What to Use*
Alt	% (percent)
Ctrl	^ (caret)
Shift	+ (plus)

procedure The name (entered as text) of the procedure to run when the user presses a key. If you enter the null string ("") for *procedure*, a key is disabled. If you omit *procedure*, Excel resets the key to its normal state.

For example, pressing Delete normally wipes out only a cell's contents. If you would like a quick way of deleting everything in a cell (contents, formats, notes, and so on), you could set up (for example) Ctrl+Delete to do the job. Figure 57.4 shows three procedures in the Personal Macro Workbook:

SetKey: This procedure sets up the Ctrl+Delete key combination to run the `DeleteAll` event handler. Notice how the *procedure* argument includes the name of the workbook so this key combination will operate in any workbook.
DeleteAll: This procedure runs the `Clear` method on the current selection.
ResetKey: Use this procedure to reset Ctrl+Delete to its default behavior.

FIGURE 57.4.
Use the OnKey method to run a procedure when the user presses a key combination.

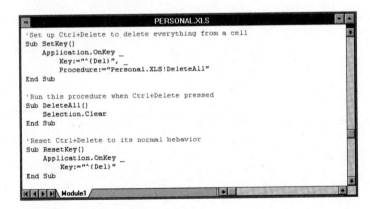

```
'Set up Ctrl+Delete to delete everything from a cell
Sub SetKey()
    Application.OnKey _
        Key:="^{Del}", _
        Procedure:="Personal.XLS!DeleteAll"
End Sub

'Run this procedure when Ctrl+Delete pressed
Sub DeleteAll()
    Selection.Clear
End Sub

'Reset Ctrl+Delete to its normal behavior
Sub ResetKey()
    Application.OnKey _
        Key:="^{Del}"
End Sub
```

Procedures That Respond to the Mouse

In Excel, double-clicking on an object with the mouse produces different results depending on the object involved. For example, double-clicking on a cell activates in-cell editing, and double-clicking on a graphics object displays the Format Object dialog box for that object. Either of these behaviors could be dangerous because they enable the user to edit cells or objects. To intercept double-clicks, you can set the `OnDoubleClick` property to run a procedure whenever the user double-clicks.

You can set the `OnDoubleClick` property for the `Application` object (to trap double-clicks in any sheet), or for `Chart`, `DialogSheet`, `Module`, and `Worksheet` objects (to trap double-clicks in specific sheets).

If you just want to disable double-clicks, assign `OnDoubleClick` to a null string (`""`). More usefully, you could assign a different behavior to a double-click. For example, Figure 57.5 shows three procedures that take advantage of the `OnDoubleClick` property:

`SetDoubleClick`: This procedure sets the `Application` object's `OnDoubleClick` property to run the `DisplayTime` procedure whenever the user double-clicks.

`DisplayTime`: This procedure uses the `MsgBox` method to display the time. The `Now` function returns the current date and time, and the `Format` function converts the date to text in the specified date format.

`ResetDoubleClick`: This procedure resets double-clicking to its default behavior.

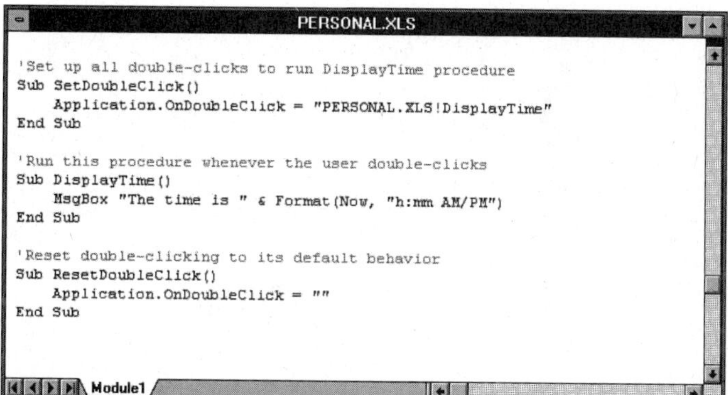

```
'Set up all double-clicks to run DisplayTime procedure
Sub SetDoubleClick()
    Application.OnDoubleClick = "PERSONAL.XLS!DisplayTime"
End Sub

'Run this procedure whenever the user double-clicks
Sub DisplayTime()
    MsgBox "The time is " & Format(Now, "h:mm AM/PM")
End Sub

'Reset double-clicking to its default behavior
Sub ResetDoubleClick()
    Application.OnDoubleClick = ""
End Sub
```

FIGURE 57.5.
Procedures that display the time when the user double-clicks.

Running a Procedure at a Specific Time

If you need to run a procedure at a specific time, use the `OnTime` method:

object.OnTime(***earliestTime***,***procedure***,*latestTime*,*schedule*)

object	The Application object.
earliestTime	The time (and date, if necessary) you want the procedure to run. Enter a date/time serial number.
procedure	The name (entered as text) of the procedure to run when the ***earliestTime*** arrives.

latestTime	If Excel isn't ready to run the procedure at ***earliestTime*** (that is, if it's not in Ready, Cut, Copy, or Find mode), it will keep trying until *latestTime* arrives. If you omit *latestTime*, Excel waits until it is ready. Enter a date/time serial number.
schedule	A logical value that determines whether the procedure runs at ***earliestTime*** or not. If *schedule* is True or omitted, the procedure runs. Use False to cancel a previous OnTime setting.

The easiest way to enter the time serial numbers for ***earliestTime*** and *latestTime* is to use the TimeValue function:

TimeValue(***time***)

time is a string representing the time you want to use (such as "5:00PM" or "17:00"). For example, the following formula runs a procedure called Backup at 5:00 PM:

```
Application.OnTime _
     earliestTime:=TimeValue("5:00PM"), _
     procedure:="Backup"
```

SUPER TIP

If you want the OnTime handler to run after a specified time interval (for example, an hour from now), use Now + TimeValue(***time***) for ***earliestTime***; ***time*** is the interval you want to use. For example, the following statement schedules a procedure to run in 30 minutes:

```
Application.OnTime _
    earliestTime:=Now + TimeValue("00:30"), _
    procedure:="Backup"
```

Procedures That Respond to Data Entry

To run a procedure when the user enters data in a worksheet, set the OnEntry property of the Application or a Worksheet object.

Figure 57.6 shows a procedure called SetDataEntry that sets the Statistics worksheet's OnEntry property to run a procedure called VerifyNumbers whenever a user enters data. If the data entered is not a number, the procedure displays a message box to warn the user.

To cancel a data entry event handler, assign the OnEntry property to the null string (""):

```
Workbooks("STAT.XLS").Worksheets("Statistics").OnEntry = ""
```

FIGURE 57.6.
Procedure to verify data entered in a worksheet.

```
'Set up OnEntry to run VerifyNumbers procedure after data entry
Sub SetDataEntry()
    Workbooks("STATS.XLS").Worksheets("Statistics").OnEntry = _
        "PERSONAL.XLS!VerifyNumbers"
End Sub

'Run this procedure whenever the user enters data
Sub VerifyNumbers()
    Dim cellValue

    cellValue = ActiveCell
    If Not IsNumeric(cellValue) Then
        MsgBox "You must enter a number"
    End If

End Sub
```

Running a Procedure After Recalculation

On a complex worksheet, changing one variable can affect dozens of formulas. If you can't keep an eye on all these formulas (to check, for example, that a boundary condition is still being met), you can have Excel do it for you. Just set the `OnCalculate` property of the `Application` or a `Worksheet` object.

For example, the `SetCalculate` procedure in Figure 57.7 sets the Budget worksheet's `OnCalculate` property to run the `CheckMargin` procedure whenever the worksheet recalculates. `CheckMargin` watches a value named `GrossMargin` in Budget. If, after a recalculation, this value dips below 20 percent, the procedure displays a warning message.

FIGURE 57.7.
The `SetCalculate` *procedure runs* `CheckMargin` *whenever the Budget worksheet recalculates.*

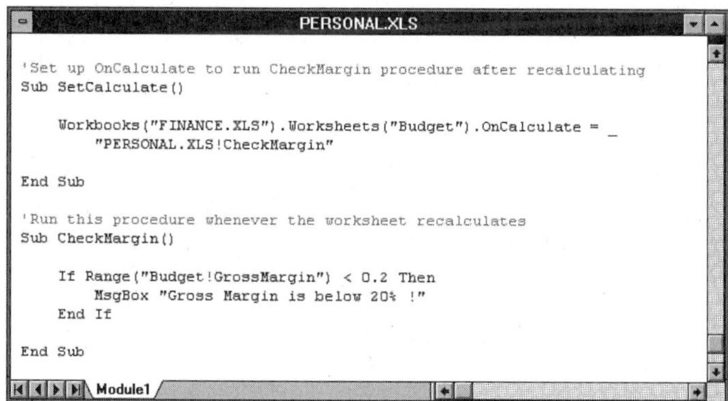

```
'Set up OnCalculate to run CheckMargin procedure after recalculating
Sub SetCalculate()

    Workbooks("FINANCE.XLS").Worksheets("Budget").OnCalculate = _
        "PERSONAL.XLS!CheckMargin"

End Sub

'Run this procedure whenever the worksheet recalculates
Sub CheckMargin()

    If Range("Budget!GrossMargin") < 0.2 Then
        MsgBox "Gross Margin is below 20% !"
    End If

End Sub
```

To cancel an `OnCalculate` event handler, assign the property to the null string (`""`).

Running a Procedure When an Error Occurs

Properly designed procedures don't leave the user out in the cold if an error occurs. Instead, they designate an *error handling routine* to process errors and (usually) report back to the user.

To trap errors, use the `On Error GoTo line` statement; *line* is a label that indicates the start of your error handling code. (A *label* is a text string—without spaces or periods—followed by a colon.)

Figure 57.8 shows an example. The `BackUpToFloppy` procedure is designed to get a drive letter from the user and then save the active workbook to the drive. If a problem occurs (such as having no disk in the drive), the routine displays an error message and gives the user the option of trying again or quitting.

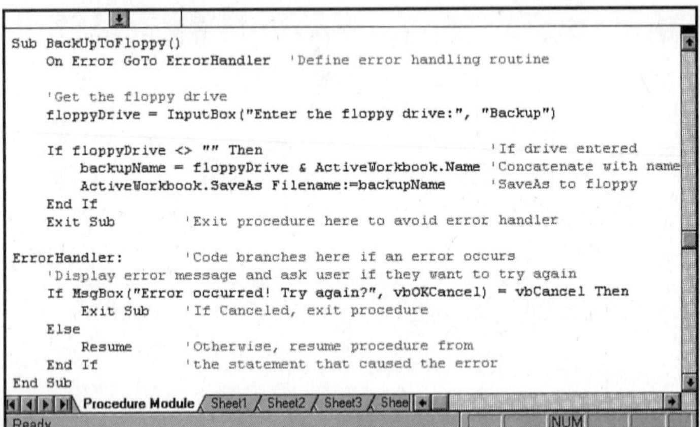

Sub BackUpToFloppy()
On Error GoTo ErrorHandler 'Define error handling routine
'Get the floppy drive
floppyDrive = InputBox("Enter the floppy drive:", "Backup")
If floppyDrive <> "" Then 'If drive entered
backupName = floppyDrive & ActiveWorkbook.Name 'Concatenate with name
ActiveWorkbook.SaveAs Filename:=backupName 'SaveAs to floppy
End If
Exit Sub 'Exit procedure here to avoid error handler
ErrorHandler: 'Code branches here if an error occurs
'Display error message and ask user if they want to try again
If MsgBox("Error occurred! Try again?", vbOKCancel) = vbCancel Then
Exit Sub 'If Canceled, exit procedure
Else
Resume 'Otherwise, resume procedure from
End If 'the statement that caused the error
End Sub
Procedure Module
Sheet1
Sheet2
Sheet3
Ready
NUM

FIGURE 57.8.
A procedure with an error-handling routine.

The error routine is set up with the following statement:

```
On Error GoTo ErrorHandler
```

The `ErrorHandler` argument refers to the *ErrorHandler:* label. If an error occurs, the procedure jumps to this label and runs the code between the label and the `End Sub` statement. In this case, a message is displayed, and the user can click on Cancel (in which case the procedure exits) or OK. In the latter case, a `Resume` statement tells Visual Basic to rerun the statement that caused the error.

SUPER NOTE

For more sophisticated error handling, use the `Err` function to return the error number. You then can use `Select Case` to test for different errors and process the result accordingly. For a list of error codes, see the Visual Basic Help system and look for the trappable errors topic.

Chapter

58

Debugging Visual Basic Procedures

It's usually easy to get short `Sub` and `Function` procedures up and running. However, as your code grows larger and more complex, errors inevitably will creep in. Many will be simple syntax problems you can fix easily, but others will be more subtle and harder to find. For the latter—whether the errors are incorrect values being returned or problems in the overall logic of a procedure—you'll need to be able to look "inside" your code to scope out what's wrong. The good news is that Visual Basic provides you with several sophisticated debugging tools that can remove some of the burden of program problem solving. This chapter looks at these tools and shows you how to use them to help recover from most programming errors.

SUPER NOTE

A *bug* is a logical or syntactical error in a computer program. The term descends from the earliest days of room-size computers, when problems occasionally were traced to insects getting stuck between vacuum tubes!

A Basic Strategy for Debugging

Debugging, like most computer skills, involves no great secrets. In fact, all debugging is usually a matter of taking a good, hard, dispassionate look at your code. Although there are no set-in-stone techniques for solving programming problems, you can formulate a basic strategy that will get you started.

When a problem occurs, the first thing you need to determine is what kind of error you're dealing with. There are four basic types:

Syntax errors: These errors arise from misspelled or missing keywords and incorrect punctuation. Visual Basic catches most (but not all) of these errors when you enter your statements.

Compile errors: When you try to run a procedure, Visual Basic takes a quick look at the code to make sure things look right. If it sees a problem (such as an `If...Then` statement without a corresponding `End If`), it highlights the statement where the problem occurred and displays an error message.

Runtime errors: These errors occur during the execution of a procedure. They generally mean that Visual Basic has stumbled on a statement that it can't figure out. It might be a formula attempting to divide by zero or using a property or method with the wrong object.

Logic errors: If your code zigs instead of zags, the cause is usually a flaw in the logic of your procedure. It might be a loop that never ends or a `Select Case` that doesn't select.

After you've determined what species of error has occurred, you need to decide how to deal with it. Syntax errors are flagged right away by Visual Basic, which means that you just have to read the error message and then clean up the offending statement.

Unfortunately, not all of Visual Basic's error messages are helpful. For example, one common syntax error is to forget to include a closing quotation mark in a string. When this happens, Visual Basic reports the following unhelpful message:

```
Expected: To or list separator or )
```

Fixing compile errors also usually is straightforward. Read the error message and see where Visual Basic has highlighted the code. Doing so almost always gives you enough information to fix the problem.

Runtime errors produce a dialog box such as the one shown in Figure 58.1. These error messages usually are a little more vague than the ones you see for syntax and compile errors. It often helps to see the statement where the offense occurred. You can do this by clicking on the **G**oto button. This activates the module and places the insertion point on the appropriate line. If you still can't see the problem, you need to rerun the procedure and pause at or near the point in which the error occurs. This enables you to examine the state of the program when it tries to execute the statement. These techniques are explained later in this chapter.

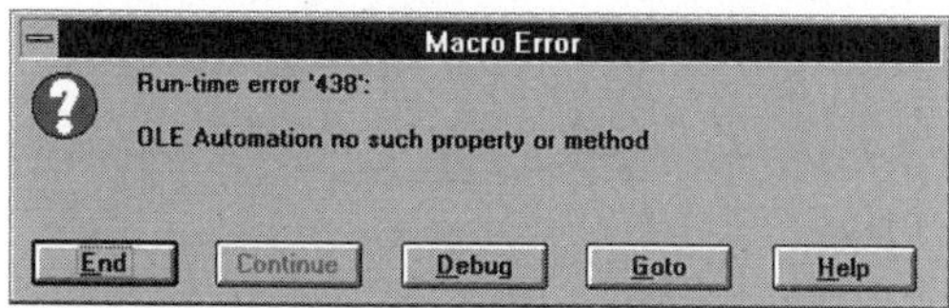

FIGURE 58.1.
A typical runtime error message.

Logic errors are the toughest to pin down because you don't get any error messages to give you clues about what went wrong and where. To help, Visual Basic enables you to trace through a procedure one statement at a time. This enables you to watch the flow of the procedure and to see if the code does what you want it to do. You also can keep an eye on the values of individual variables and properties to make sure they're behaving as expected.

Pausing a Procedure

Pausing a procedure in midstream enables you to see certain elements, such as the current values of variables and properties. It also enables you to execute program code one statement at a time so you can monitor the flow of a procedure.

When you pause a procedure, Visual Basic enters *break mode* and displays the Debug window, shown in Figure 58.2. The Debug window is divided into two parts:

> **The Watch Pane:** This area enables you to monitor the values of procedure variables, properties, or expressions. See the section later in this chapter titled "Monitoring Procedure Values."

The Code Pane: This area shows a section of the currently running procedure. The current statement (that is, the one that Visual Basic will execute next) is surrounded by a box. See the section later in this chapter titled "Stepping into a Procedure."

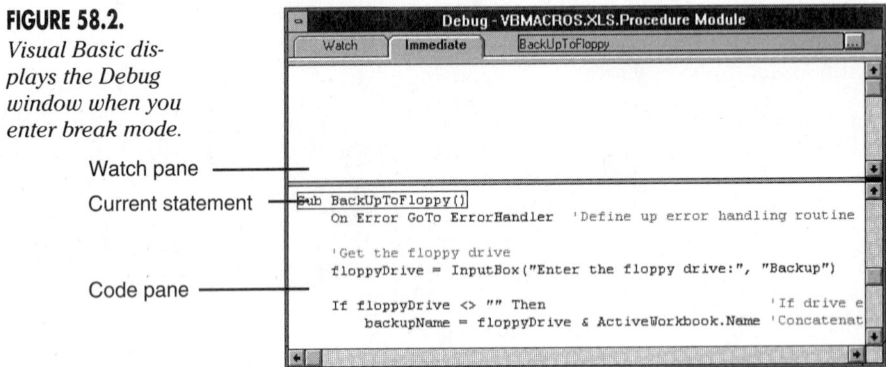
Debug - VBMACROS.XLS.Procedure Module
Watch
Immediate
BackUpToFloppy
Watch pane
Current statement
Code pane
Sub BackUpToFloppy()
On Error GoTo ErrorHandler 'Define up error handling routine
'Get the floppy drive
floppyDrive = InputBox("Enter the floppy drive:", "Backup")
If floppyDrive <> "" Then 'If drive e
backupName = floppyDrive & ActiveWorkbook.Name 'Concatenat

FIGURE 58.2.
Visual Basic displays the Debug window when you enter break mode.

Entering Break Mode

Visual Basic gives you no less than five ways to enter break mode:

- From a runtime error dialog box
- At the beginning of a procedure
- By pressing Esc or Ctrl+Break
- By setting *breakpoints*
- By using a `Stop` statement

Entering Break Mode from an Error Dialog Box

As I mentioned earlier, when a runtime error occurs, you should first try clicking on the **G**oto button in the dialog box. This takes you to the statement causing the problem and, in many cases, enables you to fix the error right away.

For more obscure problems, you'll need to enter break mode and take a look around. You can do this by clicking on the **D**ebug button from the error message dialog box.

Entering Break Mode at the Beginning of a Procedure

If you're not sure where to look for the cause of an error, you can start the procedure in break mode. Place the insertion point inside the procedure and select the **R**un | Step **I**nto command. Visual Basic displays the Debug window and highlights the `Sub` statement.

Click on the Step Into tool in the Visual Basic toolbar to start a procedure in break mode.

TIP

You also can press F8 to start a procedure in break mode.

Entering Break Mode by Pressing the Esc Key

If your procedure isn't producing an error, but appears to be behaving strangely, you can enter break mode by pressing Esc (or Ctrl+Break). Visual Basic pauses on whatever statement it was about to execute.

Click on the Step Macro tool in the Visual Basic toolbar to place a running procedure in break mode.

Setting a Breakpoint

If you know approximately where an error or logic flaw is occurring, you can enter break mode at a specific statement in the procedure by setting up a *breakpoint*. Procedure 58.1 shows you what to do.

PROCEDURE 58.1. SETTING A BREAKPOINT IN VISUAL BASIC.

1. Activate the module containing the procedure you want to run.
2. Place the insertion point on the statement where you want to enter break mode. Visual Basic will run every line of code up to, but not including, this statement.
3. Select the **R**un | Toggle **B**reakpoint command. Visual Basic highlights the entire line, as shown in Figure 58.3.

Breakpoint

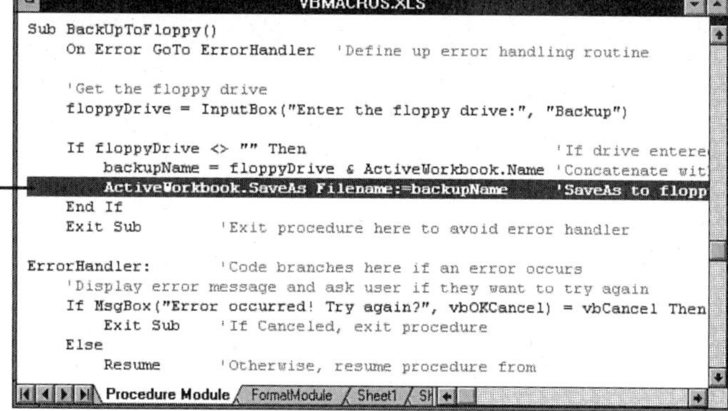
VBMACROS.XLS
Sub BackUpToFloppy()
On Error GoTo ErrorHandler 'Define up error handling routine
'Get the floppy drive
floppyDrive = InputBox("Enter the floppy drive:", "Backup")
If floppyDrive <> "" Then 'If drive entere
backupName = floppyDrive & ActiveWorkbook.Name 'Concatenate wit
ActiveWorkbook.SaveAs Filename:=backupName 'SaveAs to flopp
End If
Exit Sub 'Exit procedure here to avoid error handler
ErrorHandler: 'Code branches here if an error occurs
'Display error message and ask user if they want to try again
If MsgBox("Error occurred! Try again?", vbOKCancel) = vbCancel Then
Exit Sub 'If Canceled, exit procedure
Else
Resume 'Otherwise, resume procedure from
Procedure Module
FormatModule
Sheet1

FIGURE 58.3.
When you set a breakpoint, Visual Basic highlights the entire line.

4. Repeat steps 2 and 3 to set other breakpoints.

Click on the Toggle Breakpoint tool in the Visual Basic toolbar to add (or remove) a breakpoint.

> **SUPER TIP**
>
> You also can set a breakpoint by pressing F9.

> **SUPER NOTE**
>
> To remove a breakpoint, place the insertion point on the same line and select the **R**un | Toggle **B**reakpoint command. To remove all the breakpoints, select the **R**un | **C**lear All Breakpoints command.

Entering Break Mode Using a *Stop* Statement

When developing your applications, you'll often test the robustness of a procedure by sending it various test values or by trying it out under different conditions. In many cases, you'll want to enter break mode to make sure things look okay. You could set breakpoints at specific statements, but you lose them if you close the file. For something a little more permanent, you can include a `Stop` statement in a procedure. Visual Basic automatically enters break mode whenever it encounters a `Stop` statement.

Figure 58.4 shows the `BackUpToFloppy` procedure with a `Stop` statement inserted just before the statement that runs the `SaveAs` method.

FIGURE 58.4.
You can insert `Stop` *statements to enter break mode at specific procedure locations.*

Stop statement

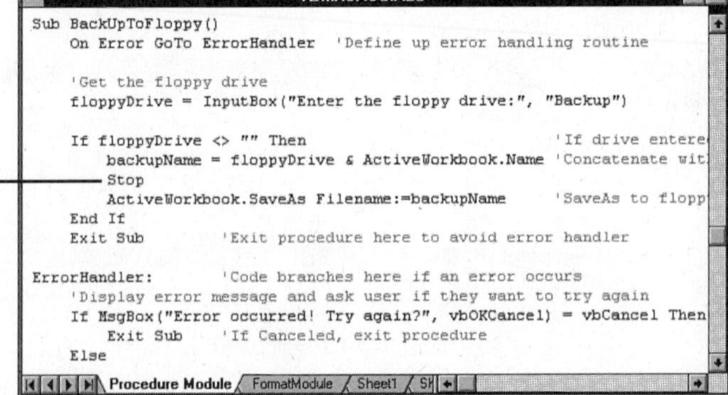
VBMACROS.XLS
Sub BackUpToFloppy()
On Error GoTo ErrorHandler 'Define up error handling routine
'Get the floppy drive
floppyDrive = InputBox("Enter the floppy drive:", "Backup")
If floppyDrive <> "" Then 'If drive entere
backupName = floppyDrive & ActiveWorkbook.Name 'Concatenate wit
Stop
ActiveWorkbook.SaveAs Filename:=backupName 'SaveAs to flopp
End If
Exit Sub 'Exit procedure here to avoid error handler
ErrorHandler: 'Code branches here if an error occurs
'Display error message and ask user if they want to try again
If MsgBox("Error occurred! Try again?", vbOKCancel) = vbCancel Then
Exit Sub 'If Canceled, exit procedure
Else
Procedure Module
FormatModule
Sheet1

Exiting Break Mode

To exit break mode, you can use either of the following methods:

- Resume normal program execution by selecting the **R**un | Con**t**inue command or by pressing F5.

You also can click on the Resume Macro tool in the Visual Basic toolbar to resume the procedure.

- End the procedure by selecting the **R**un | **E**nd command.

Stepping Through a Procedure

One of the most common (and most useful) debugging techniques is to step through the code one statement at a time. This enables you to get a feel for the program flow to make sure that things such as loops and procedure calls are executing properly. You can either step *into* procedures or step *over* them.

Stepping into a Procedure

Stepping into a procedure means you execute one line at a time. Procedure 58.2 shows you how to step into a procedure.

PROCEDURE 58.2. STEPPING INTO A VISUAL BASIC PROCEDURE.

1. Enter break mode as described earlier in this chapter. The Debug window appears, and Visual Basic places a box around the current statement.
2. Select the **R**un | Step **I**nto command. Visual Basic executes the current statement and displays the box around the next statement.

Click on the Step Into tool in the Visual Basic toolbar to step into a procedure.

TIP

You also can step into a procedure by pressing F8.

3. Repeat step 2 until the procedure ends or until you're ready to resume normal execution.

Stepping over a Procedure

Some statements call other procedures. If you're not interested in stepping through a called procedure, you can *step over* it. This means that Visual Basic executes the procedure normally and then resumes break mode at the next statement after the procedure call. Procedure 58.3 shows you how to step over a procedure.

PROCEDURE 58.3. STEPPING OVER A VISUAL BASIC PROCEDURE.

1. Enter break mode as described earlier in this chapter. The Debug window appears, and Visual Basic displays a box around the current statement.
2. Step into the procedure until you come to a procedure call you want to step over.
3. Select the **R**un | Step **O**ver command. Visual Basic executes the procedure and then places the box around the next statement.

Click on the Step Over tool in the Visual Basic toolbar to step over a procedure.

> **SUPER TIP**
>
> You also can step over a procedure by pressing Shift+F8.

4. Repeat steps 2 and 3 until the procedure ends or until you're ready to resume normal execution.

> **SUPER TIP**
>
> I'm always accidentally stepping into procedures I'd rather step over. If the procedure is short, I just step through it until I'm back in the original procedure. If it's long, however, I don't want to waste time going through every line. Instead, I set a breakpoint at the `End Sub` (or `End Function`) statement and then resume normal execution. The procedure reenters break mode at the end of the procedure, and I continue stepping from there.

Monitoring Procedure Values

Many runtime and logic errors are the result of (or, in some cases, can result in) variables or properties assuming unexpected values. If your procedure uses or changes these elements in several places, you'll need to enter break mode and monitor the values of these elements to see where things go awry. Visual Basic enables you to set up *watch expressions* to do just that. These watch expressions appear in the Watch pane of the Debug window.

Adding a Watch Expression

To add a watch expression, you use the Add Watch dialog box, shown in Figure 58.5. This dialog box contains the following elements:

Expression	The watch expression. You can enter a variable name, property, user-defined function name, or any other valid Visual Basic expression.
Context	Specifies the context of the variable (that is, where the variable is used).
Watch Type	Specifies how Visual Basic watches the expression. The Watch Expression option displays the expression in the Watch pane when you enter break mode. Break When Value is True tells Visual Basic to automatically enter break mode when the expression value becomes `True` (or nonzero). Break When Value Changes automatically enters break mode whenever the value of the expression changes.

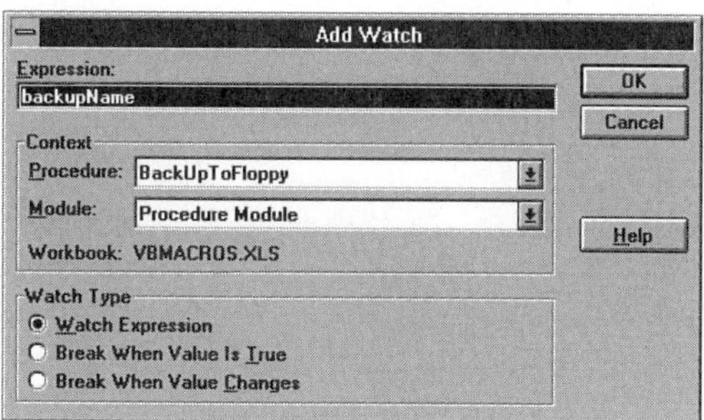

FIGURE 58.5.
Use the Add Watch dialog box to add watch expressions.

Follow the steps in Procedure 58.4 to add a watch expression.

PROCEDURE 58.4. ADDING A WATCH EXPRESSION TO THE DEBUG WINDOW.

1. Select the Tools | Add Watch command to display the Add Watch dialog box.
2. Enter the expression you want to watch in the Expression edit box.

> **SUPER TIP**
>
> Excel automatically enters the expression for you if you place the insertion point inside the expression before displaying the Add Watch dialog box.

3. Select the Context and Watch Type options, as appropriate.
4. Click on OK or press Enter.

Once you've added a watch expression, you monitor it by entering break mode and selecting the Watch tab in the Debug window. Figure 58.6 shows an example.

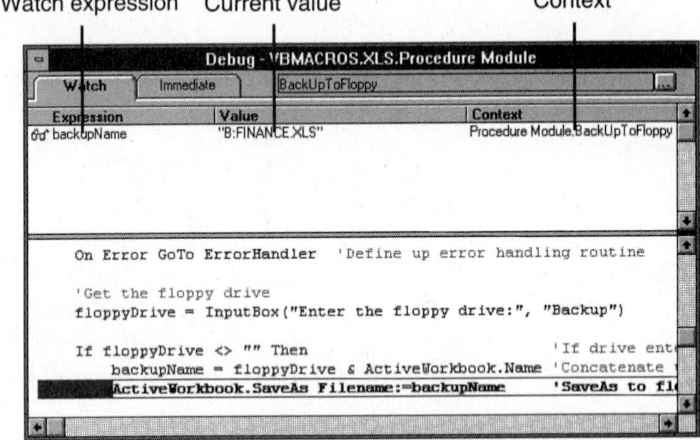
Watch expression
Current value
Context
Debug - VBMACROS.XLS.Procedure Module
Watch
Immediate
BackUpToFloppy
Expression
Value
Context
backupName
"B:FINANCE.XLS"
Procedure Module.BackUpToFloppy
On Error GoTo ErrorHandler 'Define up error handling routine
'Get the floppy drive
floppyDrive = InputBox("Enter the floppy drive:", "Backup")
If floppyDrive <> "" Then
backupName = floppyDrive & ActiveWorkbook.Name
ActiveWorkbook.SaveAs Filename:=backupName

FIGURE 58.6.
The Debug window with a watch expression.

> **SUPER TIP**
>
> The Tools | Add Watch command is available when the Debug window is active. Therefore, you can add watch expressions while in break mode.

Editing a Watch Expression

You can make changes to a watch expression while in break mode. Procedure 58.5 takes you through the steps.

PROCEDURE 58.5. EDITING A WATCH EXPRESSION.

1. Select the Watch pane by clicking on it or by pressing Ctrl+F6.
2. Highlight the watch expression you want to edit.
3. Select the Tools | Edit Watch command. Visual Basic displays the Edit Watch dialog box.

> **SUPER TIP**
>
> You also can display the Edit Watch dialog box by double-clicking on the watch expression.

4. Make your changes to the watch expression.
5. Click on OK or press Enter to return to the Debug window.

Deleting a Watch Expression

To delete a watch expression you no longer need to monitor, follow the steps in Procedure 58.6.

PROCEDURE 58.6. DELETING A WATCH EXPRESSION.

1. Select the Watch pane by clicking on it or by pressing Ctrl+F6.
2. Highlight the watch expression you want to delete.
3. Select the **T**ools | **E**dit Watch command. Visual Basic displays the Edit Watch dialog box.
4. Click on the **D**elete button. Visual Basic deletes the expression and returns you to the Debug window.

SUPER TIP

You can quickly delete a watch expression by highlighting it in the Watch pane and pressing Delete.

Displaying an Instant Watch

Many variables and properties are set once, and they don't change for the rest of the procedure. To avoid cluttering the Watch pane with these expressions, you can use an Instant Watch to quickly check the expressions' values. Procedure 58.7 shows you how it's done.

PROCEDURE 58.7. DISPLAYING AN INSTANT WATCH FROM THE DEBUG WINDOW.

1. In the Debug window's Code pane, place the insertion point inside the expression you want to display.
2. Select the **T**ools | Instant **W**atch command. Visual Basic displays the Instant Watch dialog box, shown in Figure 58.7.

Click on this tool in the Visual Basic toolbar to display the Instant Watch dialog box.

SUPER TIP

You also can display the Instant Watch dialog box by pressing Shift+F9.

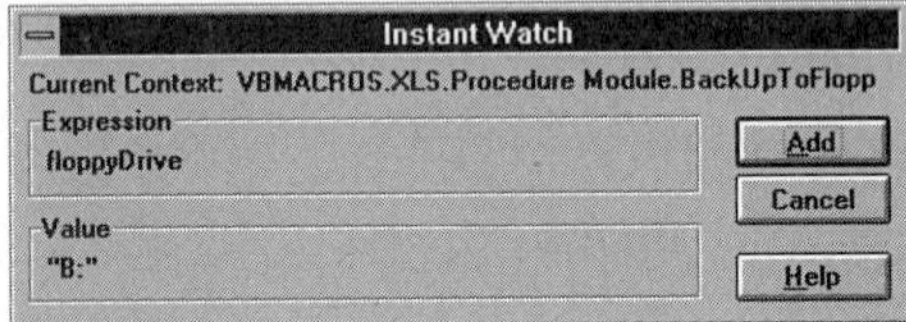

FIGURE 58.7. *Use the Instant Watch dialog box to quickly display the value of an expression.*

3. If you would like to add an expression to the Watch pane, click on the **Add** button. To return to the Debug window without adding the expression, click on Cancel.

Using the Immediate Pane

The Watch pane tells you the current value of an expression, but you'll often need more information than this. You also might want to plug in different values for an expression while in break mode. You can perform these tasks with the Debug window's Immediate pane.

Printing Data in the Immediate Pane

Using the special `Debug` object, you can use its `Print` method to print text and expression values in the Immediate pane. There are two ways to do this:

- Run the `Print` method from the procedure
- Enter the `Print` method directly into the Immediate pane

The `Print` method uses the following syntax:

```
object.Print outputList
```

`object` is the Debug object, and *`outputList`* is an expression or list of expressions to print in the Immediate pane. Separate multiple expressions with semicolons. If you omit *`outputList`*, a blank line is printed.

Running the *Print* Method from a Procedure

If you know that a variable or expression changes at a certain place in your code, enter a `Debug.Print` statement at that spot. When you enter break mode, the `Print` expressions appear in the Immediate pane. For example, Figure 58.8 shows a procedure in break mode. The information displayed in the Immediate pane was generated by the following statement:

```
Debug.Print "The backup filename is "; backupName
```

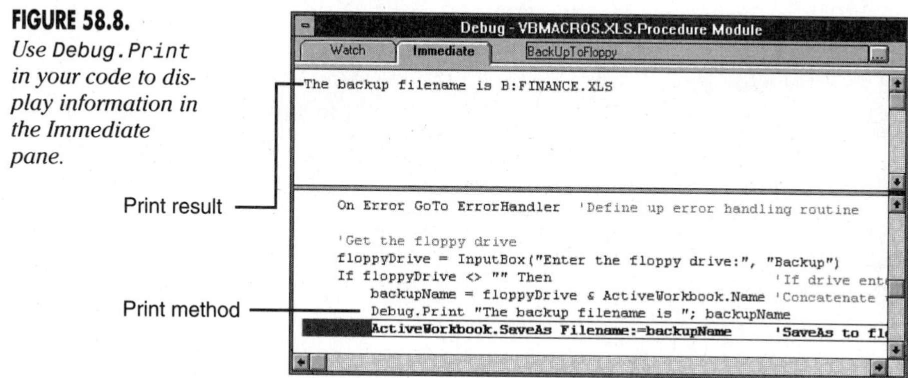
Debug - VBMACROS.XLS.Procedure Module
Watch
Immediate
BackUpToFloppy
The backup filename is B:FINANCE.XLS
Print result
On Error GoTo ErrorHandler 'Define up error handling routine
'Get the floppy drive
floppyDrive = InputBox("Enter the floppy drive:", "Backup")
If floppyDrive <> "" Then 'If drive ent
backupName = floppyDrive & ActiveWorkbook.Name 'Concatenate
Print method
Debug.Print "The backup filename is "; backupName
ActiveWorkbook.SaveAs Filename:=backupName 'SaveAs to fl

FIGURE 58.8. *Use `Debug.Print` in your code to display information in the Immediate pane.*

Running the *Print* Method in the Immediate Pane

You also can use the `Print` method directly in the Immediate pane to display information; because you're already in the Debug window, you don't need to specify the `Debug` object.

Figure 58.9 shows a couple of examples. In the first line, I typed `Print floppyDrive` and pressed Enter. Visual Basic responded with B:. In the second example, I typed `? backupName` (? is the short form for the `Print` method), and Visual Basic responded with B:FINANCE.XLS.

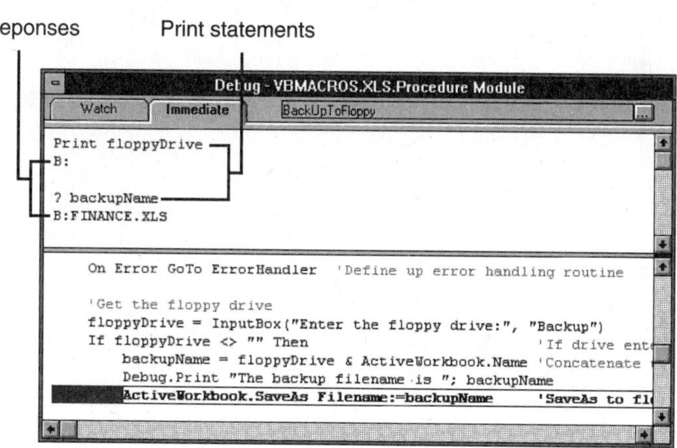
Reponses
Print statements
Debug - VBMACROS.XLS.Procedure Module
Watch
Immediate
BackUpToFloppy
Print floppyDrive
B:
? backupName
B:FINANCE.XLS
On Error GoTo ErrorHandler 'Define up error handling routine
'Get the floppy drive
floppyDrive = InputBox("Enter the floppy drive:", "Backup")
If floppyDrive <> "" Then 'If drive ent
backupName = floppyDrive & ActiveWorkbook.Name 'Concatenate
Debug.Print "The backup filename is "; backupName
ActiveWorkbook.SaveAs Filename:=backupName 'SaveAs to fl

FIGURE 58.9. *You can enter `Print` statements directly in the Immediate pane. Note the use of the question mark (?) as a short form for the `Print` method.*

Executing Statements in the Immediate Pane

Perhaps the most effective use of the Immediate pane, however, is to execute statements. There are many uses for this feature:

- To try some experimental statements to see their effect on the procedure.
- To change the value of a variable or property. For example, if you see that a variable with a value of zero is about to be used as a divisor, you could change the variable to a nonzero value to avoid crashing the procedure.
- To run other procedures or user-defined functions to see if they operate properly under the current conditions.

You enter statements in the Immediate pane just as you do in the module itself. For example, entering the following statement in the Immediate pane changes the value of the `backupName` variable:

```
backupName = "A:FINANCE.XLS"
```

Debugging Tips

Debugging your procedures can be a frustrating job—even during the best of times. Following are a few tips to keep in mind when tracking down programming problems.

Indent Your Code for Readability

Visual Basic code is immeasurably more readable when you indent your control structures; readable code is that much easier to trace and decipher, so your debugging efforts have one less hurdle to negotiate. Indenting code is a simple matter of pressing Tab an appropriate number of times at the beginning of a statement.

It helps if Visual Basic's automatic indentation feature is enabled. To check this, select the **T**ools | **O**ptions command, select the Module General tab, and activate the **A**uto Indent check box.

SUPER NOTE

By default, Visual Basic moves the insertion point four spaces to the right when you press the Tab key. You can change the default by entering a new value in the **T**ab Width spinner in the Module General tab of the Options dialog box.

Turn on Syntax Checking

Visual Basic's automatic syntax checking is a real time-saver. To make sure this option is turned on, activate the **D**isplay Syntax Errors check box in the Module General tab of the Options dialog box.

Require Variable Declarations

To avoid errors caused by using variables improperly, you should always declare your procedure variables. To make Visual Basic display an error if you don't declare a variable, add the following statement to the top of the module:

```
Option Explicit
```

> **SUPER TIP**
>
> To have Visual Basic include the `Option Explicit` statement in every new module, activate the **R**equire Variable Declarations check box in the Module General tab of the Options dialog box.

Break Down Complex Procedures

Don't try to solve all your problems at once. If you have a large procedure that isn't working right, test it in small chunks to try and narrow down the problem. To test a piece of a procedure, add an `Exit Sub` statement after the last line of the code you want to test.

Enter Visual Basic Keywords in Lowercase

If you always enter keywords in lowercase letters, you can easily detect a problem when you see that Visual Basic doesn't change the word to its normal case when you enter the line.

When a Procedure Refuses to Run

If your procedure refuses to run, check the following:

- Make sure the workbook containing the module is open.
- If you're trying to run the procedure by pressing a shortcut key, make sure the shortcut key has been defined.
- Check to see whether another procedure has the same shortcut key. If one does, and it appears earlier in the Macro dialog box list, your procedure won't run. You'll need to change the shortcut key for one of the procedures.

- Make sure that another open module doesn't have a procedure with the same name.

Comment Out Problem Statements

If a particular statement is giving you problems, you can temporarily deactivate it by placing an apostrophe at the beginning of the line. This tells Visual Basic to treat the line as a comment.

Break Up Long Statements

One of the most complicated aspects of procedure debugging is making sense out of long statements (especially formulas). The Immediate pane can help (you can use it to print parts of the statement), but it's usually best to keep your statements as short as you can. Once you get things working properly, you often can recombine statements for more efficient code.

Use Range Names Whenever Possible

Procedures are much easier to read and debug if you use range names in place of cell references. Not only is a name such as Expenses!Summary more comprehensible than Expenses!A1:F10, it's safer too. If you add rows or columns to the Summary range, the name changes as well. With cell addresses, you have to adjust the references yourself.

Take Advantage of User-Defined Constants

If your procedure uses constant values in several different statements, you can give yourself one less debugging chore by creating a user-defined constant for the value. (See Chapter 51, "Introduction to Visual Basic Programming.") This gives you three important advantages:

- It ensures that you don't enter the wrong value in a statement.
- It's easier to change the value because you only have to change the constant declaration.
- Your procedures will be easier to understand.

Chapter

59

Visual Basic Tips and Techniques

This chapter concludes the Visual Basic for Applications Workshop. You'll read about a few tips and techniques that will help you get the most out of your Visual Basic procedures. I'll show you how to assign your procedures to worksheet buttons and other objects, how to create your own add-in procedures, how to set up a custom Help system, and more.

Assigning a Procedure to a Macro Button

As you learned in Chapter 56, "Creating Custom Menus and Toolbars in Visual Basic," you can assign your procedures to menu commands or custom tools. These approaches have advantages and disadvantages:

- Toolbar tools give the user push-button access to a procedure, but it's often hard to tell what a tool does just by looking at the picture on the tool face.
- Menu commands describe the action they perform, but the user must navigate the menu system to execute them.

You can get the best of both worlds by assigning your procedures to *macro buttons*. A macro button is an object you draw on the worksheet. As you can see from Figure 59.1, macro buttons appear similar to dialog box command buttons. When the user clicks on a button, the procedure assigned to it executes.

FIGURE 59.1.
You draw macro buttons on the worksheet to give the user quick access to commonly used features.

Monthly Sales - Historical Trend

Correlation to Actual Sales:
Normal Trend -> 0.42
Reseasoned Trend -> 0.96

Recalculate Sheet | Print Sheet | Display Chart

		Actual	Normal Trend	Deseasoned Actual	Deseasoned Trend	Reseasoned Trend
	January	90.0	109.2	108.7	112.0	92.7
	February	90.0	109.4	107.0	112.2	94.4
	March	110.0	109.7	118.0	112.4	104.8
	April	105.0	109.9	114.9	112.6	102.9
	May	100.0	110.2	110.9	112.8	101.7
Year 1	June	100.0	110.4	109.0	113.0	103.7
	July	105.0	110.7	108.9	113.2	109.2
	August	105.0	110.9	103.6	113.4	114.9

Monthly Data | Monthly Trend | Monthly Forecast

Ready Calculate NUM

Follow the steps in Procedure 59.1 to assign a procedure to a macro button.

PROCEDURE 59.1. ASSIGNING A PROCEDURE TO A MACRO BUTTON.

1. Open the workbook that contains the procedure and activate the worksheet on which you want to draw the button.
2. Display the Drawing toolbar and click on the Create Button tool. The mouse pointer changes to a crosshair.

The Create Button tool from the Drawing toolbar.

3. Move the mouse pointer to where you want one corner of the button to appear.
4. Drag the mouse pointer until the button is the size and shape you want. Hold down the Shift key while dragging to make the button a square. Hold down the Alt key to align the button with the worksheet gridlines. When you release the mouse button, Visual Basic displays the Assign Macro dialog box, shown in Figure 59.2.

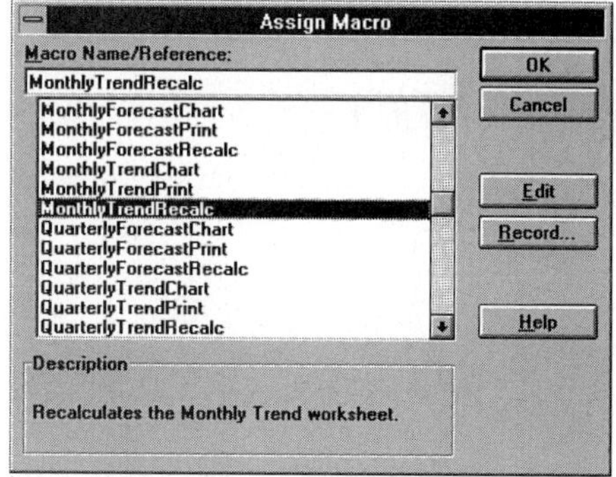

FIGURE 59.2.
Use the Assign Macro dialog box to assign a procedure to the macro button.

5. Select the procedure from the **M**acro Name/Reference list.

   or

   To record the procedure, click on the **R**ecord button and record the procedure as you normally would.
6. If you selected a procedure from the list, click on OK or press Enter.

To run the procedure, position the mouse pointer over the button (it will change to a hand) and click.

SUPER TIP

You can assign procedures to worksheet graphic objects (such as pictures, charts, and drawings). Just select the object, run the **T**ools | Assig**n** Macro command, and then select the procedure from the Assign Macro dialog box.

Changing the Button Text

Once you've created a macro button, you'll need to edit the button text so that it describes the action performed by the procedure. Procedure 59.2 shows you how to do this.

PROCEDURE 59.2. CHANGING MACRO BUTTON TEXT.

1. Hold down the Ctrl key and double-click on the button. An insertion point cursor appears inside the button text.
2. Delete the existing text and type in the text you want.
3. Exit the button by clicking on the worksheet.

> **SUPER NOTE**
>
> If you need to move, size, or format a button, refer to Chapter 27, "Editing Graphic Objects," for instructions. When clicking on a button, however, you need to hold down the Ctrl key to prevent Visual Basic from running the procedure.

Controlling Other Applications

Visual Basic offers a number of functions and methods for starting and working with other applications inside your procedures. The next few sections take a look at some of these techniques.

Starting Another Application

You can start another application by using the `Shell` function:

`Shell(`***`pathname`***`,`*`windowStyle`*`)`

`pathname`	The name of the file that starts the application (or the name of a data file associated with the executable file). Include the drive and directory to make sure that Visual Basic can find the file.
`windowStyle`	A number that specifies how the application window will appear:

`window Style`	*Window Appearance*
1, 5, 9	Normal size with focus
2 (or omitted)	Minimized with focus
3	Maximized with focus
4, 8	Normal without focus
6, 7	Minimized without focus

If successful, `Shell` returns a number (called the *task ID* number). If unsuccessful, `Shell` generates an error.

For example, the following statement starts the Windows Cardfile in a normal-sized window without focus:

```
taskID = Shell("C:\WINDOWS\CARDFILE.EXE",4)
```

When another application is open, use the `AppActivate` statement to switch between it and Excel:

```
AppActivate(title,wait)
```

title	The name of the application as it appears in the title bar, or its `task ID` number.
wait	A logical value that determines when Excel switches to the application. If *wait* is `True`, `AppActivate` waits until you activate Excel before switching. If *wait* is `False` or omitted, `AppActivate` immediately switches to the application.

SUPER CAUTION

For some applications, the title bar might include both the name of the application and the name of the active document. If ***title*** doesn't match any application's title bar exactly, Visual Basic tries to find a title bar that begins with ***title***.

In the following statements, Cardfile is started and then activated using the `task ID` number:

```
taskID = Shell("C:\WINDOWS\CARDFILE.EXE",4)
AppActivate taskID
```

Using DDE to Work with Another Application

Dynamic Data Exchange (*DDE*) is a communications protocol that enables some Windows applications to send data back and forth and even execute each other's commands. You normally use DDE when you copy and paste data between applications. However, you also can control the DDE protocol at the procedure level. Although I don't go into this subject in depth, I'll cover the basics, which are enough to add some powerful functionality to your Visual Basic applications.

DDE's Basic Steps

Using DDE is a three-step process:

1. **Establish a link between Visual Basic and the other application.** This link—called a *channel*—is the path along which the two applications communicate.
2. **Work with the other application.** Send data back and forth between the two applications or operate the other application by invoking its internal commands and by sending keystrokes.
3. **Close the link.** When you've finished working with the application, your procedure needs to close the channel.

The next few sections look at each step more closely.

Establishing a Link Between Visual Basic and Another Application

To establish a channel between Visual Basic and another DDE application, use the `DDEInitiate` method:

```
object.DDEInitiate(app,topic)
```

object	The Application object.
app	The DDE name of the application with which you want to open a link. The DDE name depends on the application. For example, the DDE name for Excel is `Excel`, and for Word for Windows it's `Winword`. For other applications, check your documentation or contact the application's technical support department.
topic	This is the "topic of conversation" that the two applications will be using. For most applications, you use either `System` (the application as a whole) or the name of a document in the application (that is, the name as it appears in the title bar).

If `DDEInitiate` is successful, it returns a number identifying the channel.

For example, to open a channel between Visual Basic and a document named SUMMARY.DOC in Word for Windows, you would use the following statement:

```
Channel = DDEInitiate("Winword","SUMMARY.DOC")
```

SUPER NOTE

If the topic document isn't already open, be sure to include its full pathname in the `DDEInitiate` method.

If the application isn't open when you run `DDEInitiate`, Visual Basic displays the dialog box shown in Figure 59.3. Click on **Yes** to start the application. Better yet, you can avoid seeing this dialog box altogether by setting the `DisplayAlerts` property to `False`:

```
Application.DisplayAlerts = False
```

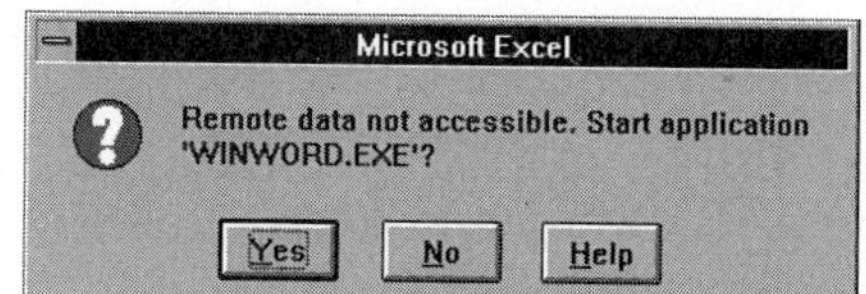

FIGURE 59.3.
When you use `DDEInitiate`, *Visual Basic asks whether you want to start the application (if it's not already running).*

SUPER **CAUTION**

If the application isn't in the current directory or the search path, the `DDEInitiate` method won't be able to find it. You can use the `ChDir` statement to change to the application's directory:

```
ChDir "C:\WINWORD"
```

You also can use the `Shell` function to start the application before invoking `DDEInitiate`.

Controlling the Other Application

Once you have an open channel, you can use the `DDEExecute` and `SendKeys` methods to control the other application. `DDEExecute` has the following syntax:

```
object.DDEExecute(channel,string)
```

channel	The channel returned by the `DDEInitiate` method.
string	A text string representing the commands to run in the application. The format depends on the application. Some applications (such as Word for Windows) enable you to use their macro commands. Other applications use special DDE commands. Check your documentation or contact technical support.

The tricky part of the `DDEExecute` method is the ***string*** argument; its form entirely depends on the application. Excel and Word for Windows enable you to use their macro commands, provided that you enclose the commands in square brackets ([ ]). Other applications also enable you to use their macro commands, but they don't support the square-brackets standard. Other programs have no macro language, but they do

have special DDE commands. Finally, there are applications without special commands to use, but which enable you to control the application by sending keystroke sequences with the `DDEExecute` method.

> **SUPER NOTE**
>
> To send keystrokes with `DDEExecute`, use the same key formats I showed you for the `OnKey` method in Chapter 57, "Visual Basic Procedures That Respond to Events." For example, the `DDEExecute(Channel,"^v")` statement sends the key combination Ctrl+V to the application linked to Visual Basic by `Channel`. Note, however, that you can't use `DDEExecute` to send keys to a dialog box. For that you need to use the `SendKeys` method, which I discuss later in this section.

Figure 59.4 shows a procedure called `WordDDETest` that uses `DDEExecute` to manipulate Word for Windows. The channel is opened first and the returned value is stored in `wordChannel` so that the other DDE statements can reference it. Then three `DDEExecute` statements each run a command from Word for Windows' macro language. These lines move to the start of SUMMARY.DOC, select the first five lines, and then copy them to the Clipboard. Then the channel is closed, and the `Paste` method pastes the data at the active cell.

FIGURE 59.4.
A procedure that uses `DDEExecute` *statements to manipulate Word for Windows through a DDE channel.*

VBMACROS.XLS

```
Sub WordDDETest()
    Dim wordChannel
    Application.DisplayAlerts = False   'Turn off alert messages

    'Open a channel to Word
    wordChannel = DDEInitiate( _
        App:="Winword", _
        Topic:="C:\WINWORD\SUMMARY.DOC")

    'Run word commands
    DDEExecute wordChannel, "[StartOfDocument]"
    DDEExecute wordChannel, "[LineDown 5,1]"
    DDEExecute wordChannel, "[EditCopy]"
    DDETerminate wordChannel

    ActiveCell.Paste                      'Paste data copied from Word
    Application.DisplayAlerts = True      'Turn on alert messages
End Sub
```

Procedure Module / FormatModule / Sheet1 / Sh

For applications with no specific procedure language or DDE commands, you can use the `SendKeys` method to send keystrokes to the program:

`SendKeys(`***keys***`,`*wait*`)`

keys	The key or key combination you want to send to the application. Use the same format for the keys that I described for the `OnKey` method in Chapter 57.

wait — A logical value that determines whether Visual Basic waits for the keys to be processed before continuing a procedure. If *wait* is True, Visual Basic waits for the application to finish processing the keys. If *wait* is False or omitted, Visual Basic doesn't wait.

For example, if you've initiated a channel between Visual Basic and Word for Windows, the following statements use SendKeys to select Word's Forma**t** | **C**haracter command, select the **B**old option, and then click on OK:

```
=SendKeys("%tc")
=SendKeys("%b~")
```

You don't need to initiate a DDE link to use SendKeys. All you have to do is activate a program with Shell or AppActivate, and then you can send keystrokes to your heart's content. Figure 59.5, for example, shows the PhoneCustomer procedure, which does the following:

- Copies a phone number from the active cell and starts Cardfile.
- Uses SendKeys to add a new card (F7), pastes the phone number (Ctrl+V and Enter), and then starts Cardfile's AutoDial feature (F5 and Enter).
- Delays for five seconds to give the phone time to dial.
- Uses SendKeys to exit CardFile (Enter, Alt+F4, and N to click on **N**o when Cardfile asks whether you want to save changes).

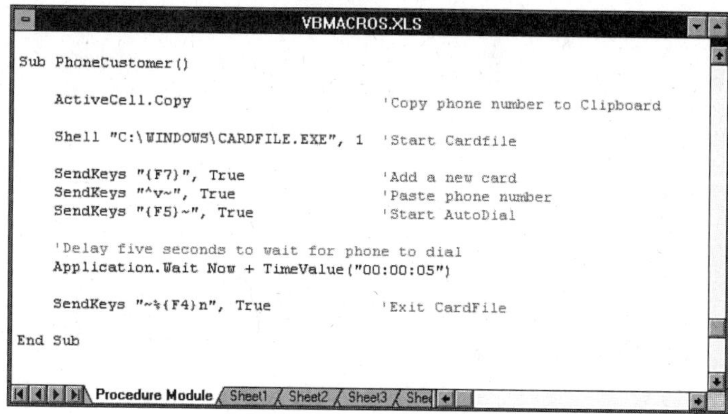

```
Sub PhoneCustomer()

    ActiveCell.Copy                             'Copy phone number to Clipboard

    Shell "C:\WINDOWS\CARDFILE.EXE", 1          'Start Cardfile

    SendKeys "{F7}", True                       'Add a new card
    SendKeys "^v~", True                        'Paste phone number
    SendKeys "{F5}~", True                      'Start AutoDial

    'Delay five seconds to wait for phone to dial
    Application.Wait Now + TimeValue("00:00:05")

    SendKeys "~%{F4}n", True                    'Exit CardFile

End Sub
```


FIGURE 59.5.
A procedure that uses SendKeys to control the Cardfile application.

Terminating the Link

When you've finished communicating with the other application, use the DDETerminate method to close the channel:

```
DDETerminate(channel)
```

channel is the channel number returned by the DDEInitiate method.

Creating an Add-In Application

If you've used any of Excel's add-in applications, you know they're convenient because they add extra functions and commands that appear as though they were built right into the program. For your own applications, you can convert your workbooks to add-ins and gain the following advantages:

- Your `Function` procedures appear in the Function Wizard dialog box.
- Your `Sub` procedures do not appear in the Macro dialog box.
- Add-ins execute faster than normal files.
- The code is converted into a compressed format that no one else can read or modify.

Follow the steps in Procedure 59.3 to save a workbook as an add-in.

PROCEDURE 59.3. SAVING A VISUAL BASIC WORKBOOK AS AN ADD-IN.

1. Activate a module in the workbook you want to save as an add-in.
2. Select the **T**ools | Ma**k**e Add-In command to display the Make Add-In dialog box.
3. Enter a new name, drive, and directory (if required) for the file.

> **SUPER CAUTION**
>
> Because you can't edit an add-in, make sure you save the workbook under a new name. Using the default .XLA extension should do the job.

4. Make sure Microsoft Excel Add-In is selected in the Save File as **T**ype drop-down list.
5. Click on OK or press Enter.

Creating a Custom Help Topic

As you've seen in earlier chapters, you can add a help system to your Visual Basic applications. This system can display help information for custom menu commands, `MsgBox` boxes, dialog boxes, and custom tools. Setting up your help system requires three steps:

1. Create a text file containing Help topics.
2. Convert the text file to the Windows Help file format.
3. Add Help references to the procedure statements and definition tables that need them.

Creating a Help Text File

Your Help system begins with one or more text files that contain several *Help topics*. A Help topic is a section of text that appears in the Help window. This text usually offers explanations of what the user is doing and instructions on how to proceed. Because these are simple text files, you can use any text editor to create them. (Windows' Notepad does the job nicely.) If you use a word processor, be sure to save the file as a text file.

The first line of a Help topic (the *header line*) always begins with an asterisk, followed by a topic number, and an optional comment. The topic number can be any positive integer, and it serves as the identifier for the topic. The rest of the Help topic consists of the actual Help information.

For example, suppose Help topic 12 covers an `InputBox` that prompts the user to enter a drive letter for a floppy drive. Figure 59.6 shows a text file named CUSTHELP.TXT that displays the topic.

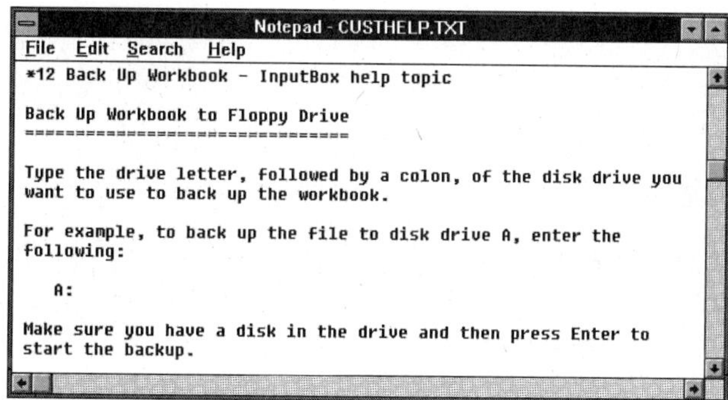

Notepad - CUSTHELP.TXT
File Edit Search Help
*12 Back Up Workbook - InputBox help topic
Back Up Workbook to Floppy Drive
==============================
Type the drive letter, followed by a colon, of the disk drive you want to use to back up the workbook.
For example, to back up the file to disk drive A, enter the following:
A:
Make sure you have a disk in the drive and then press Enter to start the backup.

FIGURE 59.6.
A text file displaying a custom help topic.

To include other Help topics in the same file, keep adding header lines and Help text. The topic numbers don't have to be in any order, but all the topics in a given Help file must have a unique number.

Converting a Text File to a Help File

Before you can use the Help topics in your application, you have to convert the text file into Windows' Help file format. The Super Disk includes the Microsoft Excel Custom Help File Conversion Utility, which will do this for you. The converter—HELPCONV.EXE—is a DOS program that uses the following syntax:

```
HELPCONV filename [/T "title_text"]
```

filename	The name of the text file containing the Help topics.
/T "*title_text*"	(Optional) This parameter specifies the text that will appear in the Help window title bar. If you omit this parameter, the default string `"Excel Macro"` is used.

To run the converter, start a DOS session and switch to the directory where you installed this book's files. For convenience, you should store the Help file in the same directory as your application (this saves you from having to specify the file's drive and directory when referencing the file in your procedures). Be sure to specify the complete path of the text file when you run HELPCONV.EXE.

For example, to convert a text file named C:\EXCEL\CUSTHELP.TXT and add the string `"My Application Help"` to the Help window title bar, you would run the following command:

```
HELPCONV C:\EXCEL\CUSTHELP.TXT /T "My Application Help"
```

The conversion utility saves a backup copy of the text file (with the extension .BAK) and then creates the Help file (with the same name as the original file).

Referencing a Help Topic

To add Help to your application, you need to use one of the following methods:

- Include a **H**elp button in a `MsgBox` or `InputBox` dialog box.
- Run the Application object's `Help` method.
- Include a **H**elp button in a custom dialog box.

Adding Help to *MsgBox* and *InputBox* Dialog Boxes

To include a **H**elp button in a `MsgBox` or `InputBox` dialog box, enter both the `helpFile` and `context` arguments in the `MsgBox` or `InputBox` function.

For example, to add Help to the `InputBox` dialog box mentioned earlier, you would use a statement such as this:

```
floppyDrive = InputBox( _
     prompt:="Enter the floppy drive:", _
     title:="Backup", _
     helpFile:="C:\EXCEL\CUSTHELP.TXT",
     context:=12)
```

Figure 59.7 shows the dialog box and the Help window that appears when the user selects **H**elp.

FIGURE 59.7.
A custom Help topic for an `InputBox` *dialog box.*

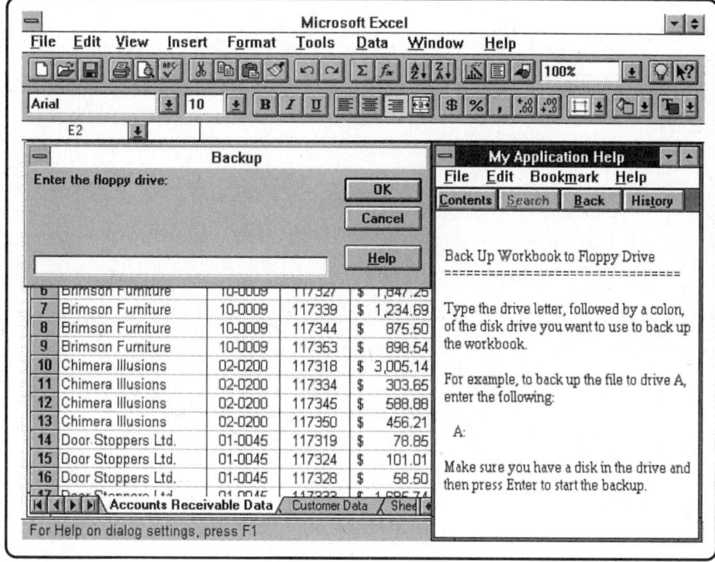

Using the *Help* Method

You can display a topic in the Help window anytime by using the `Help` method:

`object.Help(helpFile,helpContextID)`

`object`	The Application object.
`helpFile`	A string specifying the Help file to use. If you omit *`helpFile`*, the Excel Help file is used.
`helpContextID`	The Help topic in *`helpFile`*. If you omit *`helpContextID`*, the contents topic is displayed.

For example, the following statement displays Help topic 57 in C:\EXCEL\CUSTHELP.TXT:

```
Application.Help "C:\EXCEL\CUSTHELP.TXT", 57
```

Adding Help to a Custom Dialog Box

To add Help to a custom dialog box, follow the steps in Procedure 59.4.

PROCEDURE 59.4. ADDING HELP TO A CUSTOM DIALOG BOX.

1. Create a command button and change its caption to Help.
2. Click on the Help button, then run the Format | Object command.

3. In the Format object dialog box, activate the Help check box, enter `H` in the Accelerator Key box (optional), and click on OK or press Enter.
4. Click on the Edit Code button in the Visual Basic toolbar. Visual Basic displays a procedure stub for the button.

The Edit Code button from the Visual Basic toolbar.

5. Add the appropriate `Help` method to the procedure, as described in the preceding section.

For example, if your Help button was the third button added to the dialog box, your procedure would look something like this:

```
Sub Button3_Click()
    Application.Help "C:\EXCEL\CUSTHELP.TXT", 16
End Sub
```

Tips for Faster Procedures

Short procedures usually are over in the blink of an eye. As your procedures get longer, however, the time they take to complete their tasks becomes more noticeable. For these more complex routines, you need to start thinking not only about *what* the procedure does, but *how* it does it. The more efficient you can make your code, the zippier the procedure will execute. This section gives a few tips for writing efficient code that runs quickly.

Turn Off Screen Updating

One of the biggest drags on procedure performance is the constant screen updating that occurs. If your procedure uses many statements that format ranges, enter formulas, or cut and copy cells, the procedure will spend most of its time updating the screen to show the results of these operations. This not only slows everything down, it looks unprofessional. It's much nicer when the procedure performs all its chores "behind the scenes" and then presents the user with the finished product at the end of the procedure.

You can do this with the `Application` object's `ScreenUpdating` property. Set `ScreenUpdating` to `False` to turn off screen updates and set it back to `True` to resume updating.

Hide Your Worksheets

If your procedure does a lot of switching between worksheets, you can speed things by hiding the worksheets while you work with them. To do this, set the worksheet's

`Visible` property to `False`. You can work with hidden worksheets, and when your procedure is done, you can set `Visible` to `True` to display the results to the user.

SUPER CAUTION

As soon as you've hidden an active worksheet, Visual Basic deactivates it. Therefore, if your procedures reference the active sheet, you need to activate the window (using the `Activate` method) right after hiding it.

Don't Select Worksheets or Ranges If You Don't Have To

Two of Visual Basic's slowest methods are `Activate` and `Select`, so they should be used sparingly. In the majority of cases, you can indirectly work with ranges and worksheets by referencing them as arguments in the `Range` method (or any other Visual Basic statement that returns a `Range` object) and the `Worksheets` collection.

Don't Recalculate Until You Have To

As you know, manual calculation mode prevents Excel from recalculating a worksheet until you say so. This saves you time when using sheets with complicated models—models in which you don't necessarily want to see a recalculation every time you change a variable.

You can get the same benefits in your procedures by using the `Application` object's `Calculation` property. Use the constants in Table 59.1 to set the calculation mode you want.

Table 59.1. Excel calculation mode constants.

Constant	*Calculation Mode*
`xlAutomatic`	Automatic
`xlManual`	Manual
`xlSemiautomatic`	Automatic except tables

The following statement places Excel in manual calculation mode:

```
Application.Calculation = xlManual
```

When you need to update your formula results, use the `Calculate` method. This method applies to either the `Application` object (in which case it recalculates all open workbooks) or the Worksheet object (in which case it recalculates a specific sheet).

Optimize Your Loops

One of the cornerstones of efficient programming is loop optimization. Because a procedure might run the code inside a loop hundreds or even thousands of times, a minor improvement in loop efficiency can result in considerably reduced execution times.

When analyzing your loops, make sure you're particularly ruthless about applying the previous tips. One `Select` method is slow; a thousand will drive you crazy.

Also, weed out from your loops any statements that return the same value each time. For example, consider the following procedure fragment:

```
For n = 1 To 1000
     Application.StatusBar = "Path: " & CurDir()
Next n
```

The idea of this somewhat useless code is to loop 1,000 times, each time displaying the current directory in the status bar. The result of the `CurDir` function never changes, but this function call takes time, slowing the loop considerably. A better approach would be the following:

```
currDirectory = CurDir()
For n = 1 To 1000
     Application.StatusBar = "Path: " & currDirectory
Next n
```

Transferring the unchanging `CurDir` calculation outside the loop, and assigning it to a variable, means that the procedure has to call the function only once.

Workshop

VIII

Advanced Topics

Chapter

60

Advanced Range Topics

Way back in Chapter 3, "Getting Started with Ranges," and Chapter 4, "Working with Ranges," you learned how to select and work with ranges and range names. Because ranges are such an important feature of the Excel landscape and they make worksheets (especially large ones) so much easier to manage, it's worthwhile to take a closer look at what ranges can do. This chapter presents some advanced techniques for working with ranges.

Advanced Range Selection Techniques

Because selecting a range is one of the most common worksheet tasks, Excel gives you a fistful of ways to do it. You saw many of them in Chapter 3, but now I'll show you a few advanced techniques that can make your selection chores faster and easier.

Using Go To to Select a Range

For very large ranges, Excel's **E**dit | **G**o To command comes in handy. You normally use **G**o To to jump quickly to a specific cell address or range name. Procedure 60.1 shows you how to exploit the power of Go To to select a range.

PROCEDURE 60.1. SELECTING A RANGE WITH THE GO TO COMMAND.

1. Select any cell in the range.
2. Select the **E**dit | **G**o To command, or press the F5 key. The Go To dialog box appears.
3. Use the **R**eference text box to enter the cell address of the lower-right corner of the range.

> **SUPER TIP**
>
> If the range is named, select the name from the **G**o to list box.

4. Hold down the Shift key and click on OK or press Enter. Excel selects the range.

> **SUPER TIP**
>
> You also can select a range using **G**o To by entering the range coordinates in the **R**eference text box.

SUPER TIP

Another way to select very large ranges is to use the **V**iew | **Z**oom command to reduce the size of the worksheet and then select the range using the reduced view.

Using the Go To Special Dialog Box

You normally select cells according to their position within a worksheet, but Excel includes a powerful feature that enables you to select cells according to their contents or other special properties. If you select the **E**dit | **G**o To command and then click on the **S**pecial button in the Go To dialog box, the Go To Special dialog box appears (see Figure 60.1).

FIGURE 60.1.
The Go To Special dialog box.

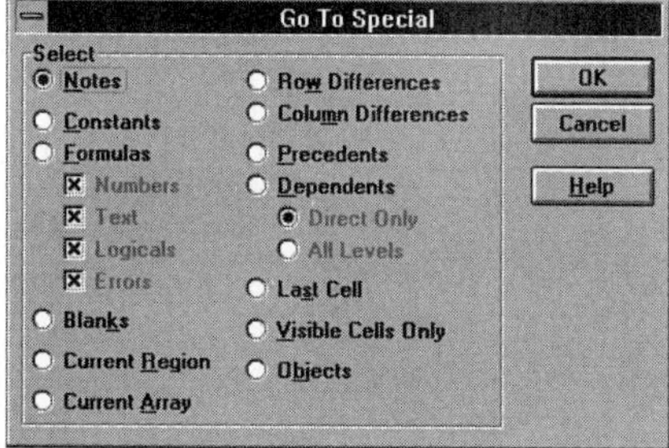

Selecting Cells by Type

The Go To Special dialog box contains four options to select cells according to the type of contents they contain. Table 60.1 presents these options.

Table 60.1. Options for selecting a cell by type.

Option	*Description*
Notes	Selects all cells that contain a note
Constants	Selects all cells that contain constants of the types specified in one or more of the check boxes listed under the **F**ormulas option
Formulas	Selects all cells containing formulas that produce results of the types specified in one or more of the following four check boxes: N**u**mbers — Selects all cells that contain numbers

continues

Table 60.1. continued

Option	Description	
	Text	Selects all cells that contain text
	Logicals	Selects all cells that contain logical values
	Errors	Selects all cells that contain errors
Blanks	Selects all cells that are blank	

SUPER TIP

Press Ctrl+? to select all cells containing notes.

Selecting Adjacent Cells

If you need to select cells adjacent to the active cell, the Select Special dialog box gives you two options. Choose the Current **R**egion option to select a rectangular range that includes all the nonblank cells that touch the active cell.

If the active cell is part of an array, choose the Current **A**rray option to select all the cells in the array.

SUPER NOTE

To learn more about arrays, see the section in this chapter titled "Working with Arrays."

SUPER TIP

Press Ctrl+* to select the current region quickly. For the current array, press Ctrl+/.

Selecting Cells by Differences

Excel also enables you to select cells by comparing rows or columns of data and selecting only cells that are different. Procedure 60.2 shows you how it's done.

PROCEDURE 60.2. SELECTING CELLS BY DIFFERENCES.

1. Select the rows or columns you want to compare. (Make sure the active cell is in the row or column with the comparison values you want to use.)
2. In the Go To Special dialog box, select one of the following options:

Row Differences	This option uses the data in the active cell's column as the comparison values. Excel compares each of these cells with the corresponding cells in each row and selects those that are different.
Column Differences	This option uses the data in the active cell's row as comparison values. Excel selects those cells in the corresponding columns that are different.

3. Click on OK or press Enter.

SUPER TIP

Excel provides shortcut keys for these options. Press Ctrl+\ to select row differences and Ctrl+| to select column differences.

For example, Figure 60.2 shows a selected range of numbers. Suppose you wanted to compare the numbers in columns B and C with those in column A and select the ones that are different. Because you are comparing rows of data, you would select the Row Differences option from the Select Special dialog box. Figure 60.3 shows the results.

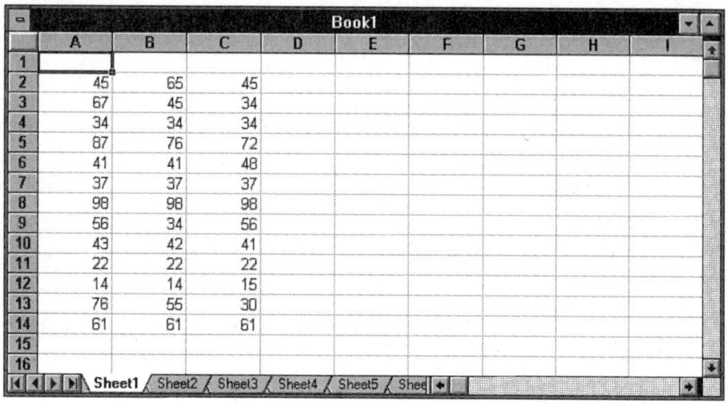

Book1

	A	B	C	D	E	F	G	H	I
1									
2	45	65	45						
3	67	45	34						
4	34	34	34						
5	87	76	72						
6	41	41	48						
7	37	37	37						
8	98	98	98						
9	56	34	56						
10	43	42	41						
11	22	22	22						
12	14	14	15						
13	76	55	30						
14	61	61	61						
15									
16									

Sheet1 Sheet2 Sheet3 Sheet4 Sheet5 Shee

FIGURE 60.2.
The Go To Special feature can compare rows (or columns) of data and select only the different cells.

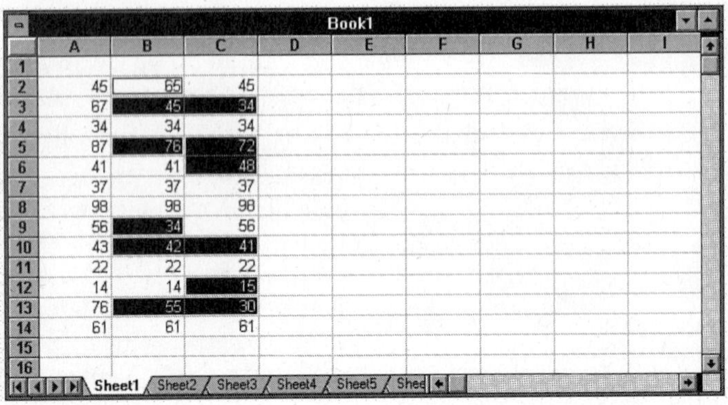

Book1

	A	B	C	D	E	F	G	H	I
1									
2	45	65	45						
3	67	45	34						
4	34	34	34						
5	87	76	72						
6	41	41	48						
7	37	37	37						
8	98	98	98						
9	56	34	56						
10	43	42	41						
11	22	22	22						
12	14	14	15						
13	76	55	30						
14	61	61	61						
15									
16									

Sheet1 / Sheet2 / Sheet3 / Sheet4 / Sheet5 / Shee

FIGURE 60.3. *The results of the Go To Special operation.*

Selecting Cells by Reference

If a cell contains a formula, Excel defines the cell's *precedents* as those cells that the formula refers to. For example, if cell A4 contains the formula =SUM(A1:A3), then cells A1, A2, and A3 are the precedents of A4. A *direct* precedent is a cell referred to explicitly in the formula. In the previous example, A1, A2, and A3 are direct precedents of A4. An *indirect* precedent is a cell referred to by a precedent. For example, if cell A1 contained the formula =B3*2, cell B3 would be an indirect precedent of cell A4.

Excel also defines a cell's *dependents* as those cells with a formula that refers to the cell. In the previous example, cell A4 would be a dependent of cell A1. Like precedents, dependents can be direct or indirect.

The Go To Special dialog box enables you to select precedents and dependents as described in Procedure 60.3.

PROCEDURE 60.3. SELECTING CELLS BY REFERENCE.

1. Select the range you want to work with.
2. Display the Go To Special dialog box.
3. Select either the **P**recedents or **D**ependents option.
4. Select the D**i**rect Only option to select only direct precedents or dependents. If you need to select both the direct and indirect precedents or dependents, select the All **L**evels option.
5. Click on OK or press Enter.

Table 60.2 lists the shortcut keys you can use to select precedents and dependents.

Table 60.2. Shortcut keys for selecting precedents and dependents.

Shortcut Key	*Description*
Ctrl+[	Selects direct precedents
Ctrl+]	Selects direct dependents
Ctrl+{	Selects all levels of precedents
Ctrl+}	Selects all levels of dependents

Other Go To Special Options

The Go To Special dialog box also includes a few more options:

Option	*Description*
Last Cell	Selects the last cell in the worksheet (that is, the lower-right corner) that contains data or formatting
Visible Cells Only	Selects only cells that are unhidden
Objects	Selects all the worksheet's graphic objects

TIP

To select the last cell quickly, press Ctrl+End. For the visible cells, press Alt+;.

Advanced Range Copying

The **E**dit | **C**opy command normally copies the entire contents of each cell in a range: the value or formula, the formatting, and any attached cell notes. If you like, you can tell Excel to copy only some of these attributes, you can transpose rows and columns, or you can combine the source and destination ranges arithmetically. All this is possible with Excel's **E**dit | Paste **S**pecial command. These techniques are outlined in the next three sections.

Copying Selected Cell Attributes

When rearranging a worksheet, you can save time by combining cell attributes. For example, if you need to copy several formulas to a range but you don't want to disturb the existing formatting, you can tell Excel to copy only the formulas.

If you want to copy only selected cell attributes, follow the steps in Procedure 60.4.

PROCEDURE 60.4. COPYING SELECTED CELL ATTRIBUTES.

1. Select the range you want to copy and then select the **E**dit | **C**opy command.
2. Select the destination range.
3. Select the **E**dit | Paste **S**pecial command. Excel displays the Paste Special dialog box, shown in Figure 60.4.

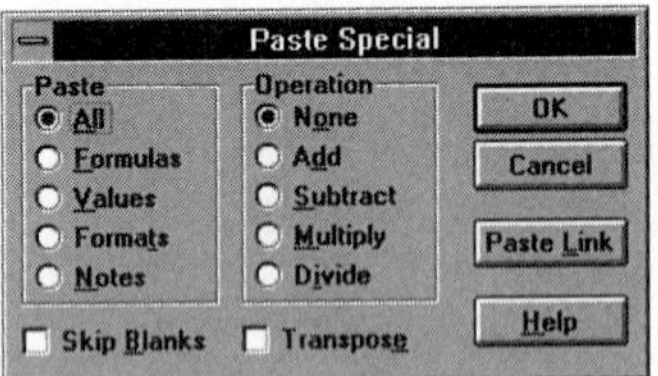

FIGURE 60.4.
Use the Paste Special dialog box to select the cell attributes you want to copy.

4. In the Paste group, select the attribute that you want to paste into the destination range.

All	Pastes all the cell attributes
Formulas	Pastes only the cell formulas
Values	Converts the cell formulas to values and pastes only the values
Forma**t**s	Pastes only the cell formatting
Notes	Pastes only the cell notes

5. If you don't want Excel to paste any blank cells included in the selection, activate the Skip **B**lanks check box.
6. Click on OK or press Enter to paste the range.

Combining the Source and Destination Arithmetically

Excel enables you to combine two ranges arithmetically. For example, suppose you have a range of constants that you want to double. Instead of creating formulas that multiply each cell by two, you can create a range of the same size that consists of nothing but twos (the fill handle makes this easy). You then combine this new range with the old one and tell Excel to multiply them. Procedure 60.5 shows you what to do.

PROCEDURE 60.5. COMBINING SOURCE AND DESTINATION RANGES ARITHMETICALLY.

1. Select the source you want to copy and select the **E**dit | **C**opy command.
2. Select the destination range. (Make sure it's the same shape as the source range.)
3. Select the **E**dit | Paste **S**pecial command to display the Paste Special dialog box.

4. Use the following options in the Operation group to select the arithmetic operator you want to use:

None	Performs no operation
Add	Adds the destination cells to the source cells
Subtract	Subtracts the destination cells from the source cells
Multiply	Multiplies the destination cells by the source cells
Divide	Divides the destination cells by the source cells

5. If you don't want Excel to include any blank cells in the operation, activate the Skip Blanks check box.
6. Click on OK or press Enter. Excel pastes the results of the operation into the destination range.

Transposing Rows and Columns

If you have row data that you would prefer to see in columns (or vice versa), the **Edit** | Paste **S**pecial command can do the job. Follow the steps in Procedure 60.6.

PROCEDURE 60.6. TRANSPOSING ROWS AND COLUMNS.

1. Select the source you want to copy and then select the **Edit** | **C**opy command.
2. Select the upper-left corner of the destination range.
3. Select the **Edit** | Paste **S**pecial command to display the Paste Special dialog box.
4. Activate the Transpos**e** check box.
5. Click on OK or press Enter. Excel transposes the source range, as shown in Figure 60.5.

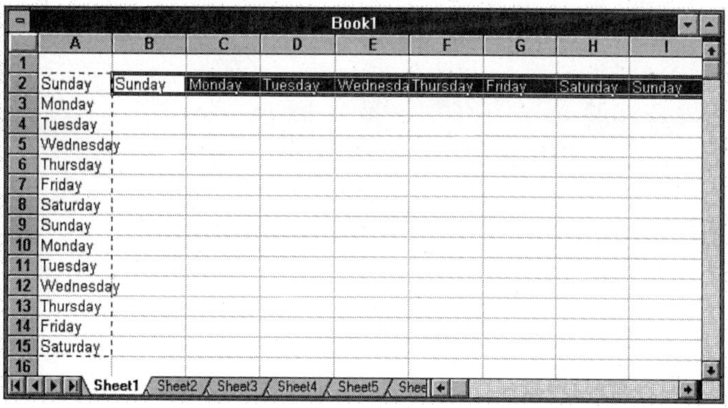

FIGURE 60.5.
You can use the Edit | Paste Special command to transpose rows and columns.

Using Excel's Reference Operators

You learned about Excel's various operators (such as +, *, and &) in Chapter 5, "Building Formulas." Excel also has three *reference operators* that you can use when working with cell references. The next three sections discuss each of these operators.

Using the Range Operator

The *range* operator is just the familiar colon (:) that you've been using all along. You simply insert a colon between two references, and Excel creates a range (for example, A1:C5). Until now, you've probably been creating your ranges by using the reference on the left side of the colon to define the upper-left corner of the range and the reference on the right side of the colon to define the lower-left corner. There are other ways to create ranges with the range operator, however. Table 60.3 points out a few of them.

Table 60.3. Sample ranges created with the range operator.

Range	*Description*
A:A	Column A (the entire column)
A:C	Columns A through C
1:1	Row 1
1:5	Rows 1 through 5

You also can use a range name on either side of the colon. In this case, the named range becomes a *corner* for the larger range. For example, Figure 60.6 shows a worksheet with the named range Rent that refers to C7:E7. Table 60.4 shows some sample ranges you can create with Rent as one corner.

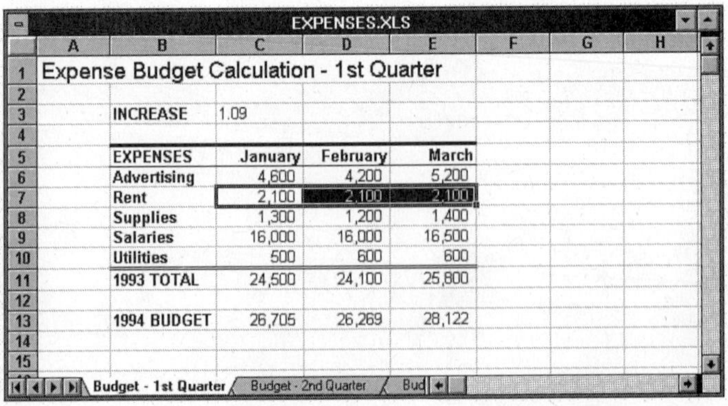

EXPENSES.XLS

	A	B	C	D	E	F	G	H
1	Expense Budget Calculation - 1st Quarter							
2								
3		INCREASE	1.09					
4								
5		EXPENSES	January	February	March			
6		Advertising	4,600	4,200	5,200			
7		Rent	2,100	2,100	2,100			
8		Supplies	1,300	1,200	1,400			
9		Salaries	16,000	16,000	16,500			
10		Utilities	500	600	600			
11		1993 TOTAL	24,500	24,100	25,800			
12								
13		1994 BUDGET	26,705	26,269	28,122			
14								
15								

Budget - 1st Quarter / Budget - 2nd Quarter / Bud

FIGURE 60.6.
The named range Rent used in Table 60.4.

Table 60.4. Sample ranges created with a range name.

Range	*What It Refers To*
Rent:A1	A1:E7
Rent:G2	C2:G7
Rent:E10	C7:E10
Rent:A13	A7:E13

Using the Intersection Operator

If you have ranges that overlap, you can use the *intersection* operator (a space) to refer to the overlapping cells. For example, Figure 60.7 shows two ranges: C5:E10 and D9:G12. To refer to the overlapping cells (C9:E10), you would use the following notation: C5:E10 D9:G12.

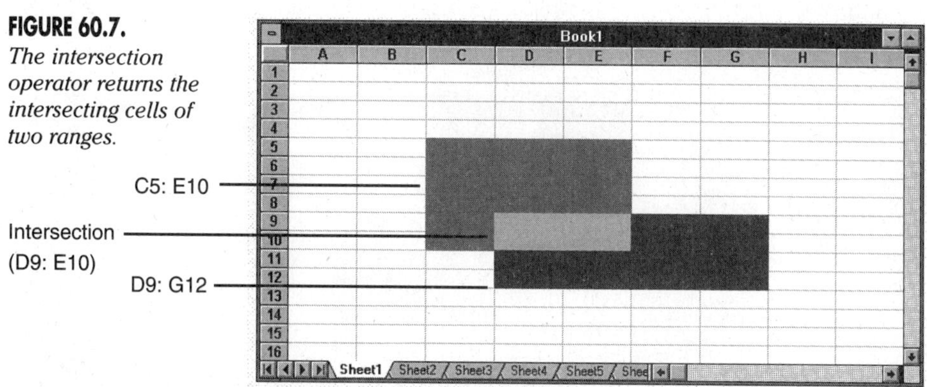

FIGURE 60.7.
The intersection operator returns the intersecting cells of two ranges.

If you've named the ranges on your worksheet, the intersection operator can make things much easier to read because you can refer to individual cells by using the names of the cell's row and column. For example, in Figure 60.8, the range C6:C13 is named January and the range C7:E7 is named Rent. This means that you can refer to cell C7 as January Rent (see cell G3).

SUPER CAUTION

If you try to define an intersection name and Excel displays `#NULL!` in the cell, it means that the two ranges don't have any overlapping cells.

EXPENSES.XLS

	A	B	C	D	E	F	G
1	Expense Budget Calculation - 1st Quarter						
2							
3		INCREASE	1.09			Rent for January:	2,100
4							
5		EXPENSES	January	February	March		
6		Advertising	4,600	4,200	5,200		
7		Rent	2,100	2,100	2,100		
8		Supplies	1,300	1,200	1,400		
9		Salaries	16,000	16,000	16,500		
10		Utilities	500	600	600		
11		1993 TOTAL	24,500	24,100	25,800		
12							
13		1994 BUDGET	26,705	26,269	28,122		
14							
15							

Budget - 1st Quarter / Budget - 2nd Quarter / Bud

January range

Rent range

FIGURE 60.8.
After you name ranges, you can combine row and column headings to create intersecting names for individual cells.

Using the Union Operator

To create a reference that combines two or more ranges, use the *union* operator (,). For example, Figure 60.9 shows the range C5:E10,D9:G12, the union of C5:E10 and D9:G12.

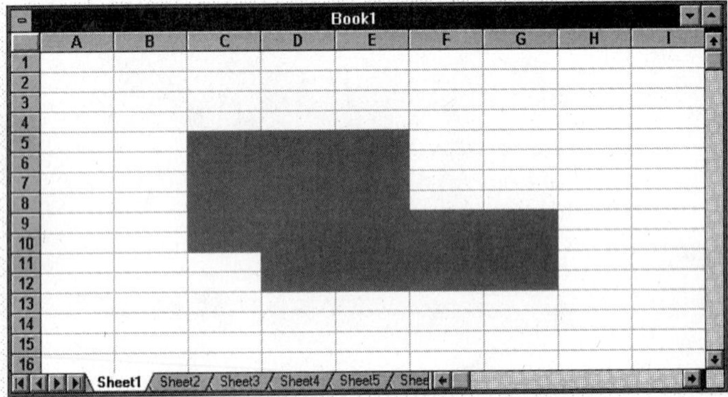

FIGURE 60.9.
Use the union operator to create a single reference that combines two or more ranges.

Working with Arrays

An *array* is a group of cells or values that Excel treats as a unit. You create arrays either by running a function that returns an array result (such as `DOCUMENTS()`; see the section in this chapter titled "Functions That Use or Return Arrays"), or by entering an *array formula*, which is a single formula that either uses an array as an argument or enters results in multiple cells.

Using Array Formulas

Here is a simple example that illustrates how array formulas work. In the EXPENSES.XLS workbook shown in Figure 60.10, the 1994 BUDGET totals are calculated using a separate formula for each month as follows:

January 1994 BUDGET	=C11*INCREASE
February 1994 BUDGET	=D11*INCREASE
March 1994 BUGET	=E11*INCREASE

You can replace all three formulas with a single array formula by following the steps in Procedure 60.7.

FIGURE 60.10.
This worksheet uses three separate formulas to calculate the 1994 BUDGET figures.

EXPENSES.XLS

	A	B	C	D	E	F	G	H
1	Expense Budget Calculation - 1st Quarter							
2								
3		INCREASE	1.09					
4								
5		EXPENSES	January	February	March			
6		Advertising	4,600	4,200	5,200			
7		Rent	2,100	2,100	2,100			
8		Supplies	1,300	1,200	1,400			
9		Salaries	16,000	16,000	16,500			
10		Utilities	500	600	600			
11		1993 TOTAL	24,500	24,100	25,800			
12								
13		1994 BUDGET	26,705	26,269	28,122			
14								
15								

Budget - 1st Quarter / Budget - 2nd Quarter / Bud

PROCEDURE 60.7. ENTERING AN ARRAY FORMULA.

1. Select the range that you want to use for the array formula. In the 1994 BUDGET example, you would select C11:E11.
2. Type in the formula and, in the places where you would normally enter a cell reference, enter a range reference that includes the cells you want to use. *Don't,* I repeat, *don't* press Enter when you're done. In the example, you would enter `=C11:E11*INCREASE`.
3. To enter the formula as an array, press Ctrl+Shift+Enter.

The 1994 BUDGET cells now all contain the same formula:

```
{=C11:E11*INCREASE}
```

The braces ({}) are just Excel's designation for an array.

SUPER NOTE

Because Excel treats arrays as a unit, you can't move or delete part of an array. If you need to work with an array, you have to select the whole thing. If you want to reduce the size of an array, select it, activate the formula bar, and then press Ctrl+Enter to change the entry to a normal formula. You can then select the smaller range and reenter the array formula.

SUPER TIP

To select an array quickly, activate one of its cells and press Ctrl+/.

Understanding Array Formulas

To understand how Excel processes an array, you need to keep in mind that Excel always sets up a correspondence between the array cells and the cells of whatever range you entered into the array formula. In the 1994 BUDGET example, the array consists of cells C13, D13, and E13, and the range used in the formula consists of cells C11, D11, and E11. Excel sets up a correspondence between array cell C13 and input cell C11, D13 and D11, and E13 and E11. To calculate the value of cell C13 (the January 1994 BUDGET), for example, Excel just grabs the input value from cell C11 and substitutes that in the formula. Figure 60.11 shows a diagram of this process.

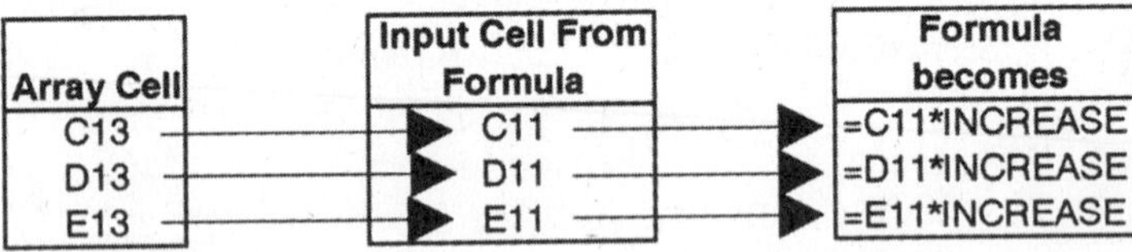

FIGURE 60.11. *When processing an array formula, Excel sets up a correspondence between the array cells and the range used in the formula.*

Array formulas can be confusing, but if you keep these correspondences in mind, you should have no trouble figuring out what's going on.

Array Formulas That Operate on Multiple Ranges

In the previous example, the array formula operated on a single range, but array formulas also can operate on multiple ranges. For example, consider the Invoice Template worksheet shown in Figure 60.12. The totals in the Extension column (cells F12 through F16) are generated by a series of formulas that multiply the item's price by the quantity ordered. For example, the formula in cell F12 is the following:

```
=B12*E12
```

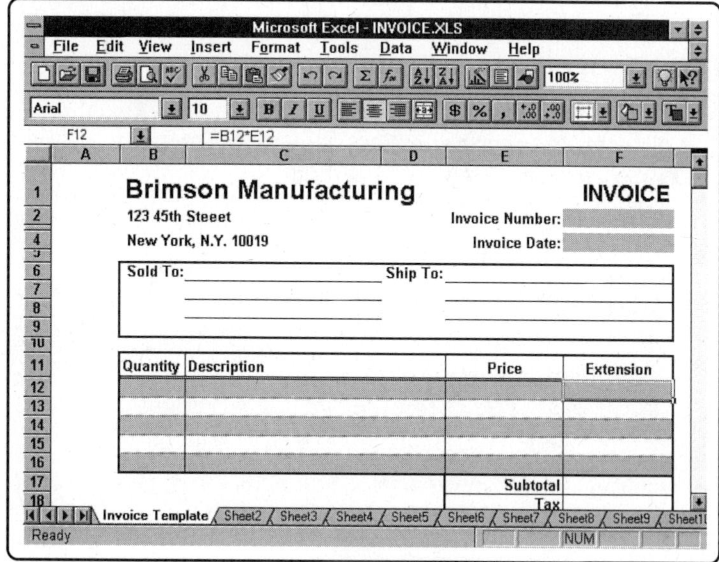

FIGURE 60.12.
This worksheet uses several formulas to calculate the extended totals for each line.

You can replace all these formulas by entering the following as an array formula into the range F12:F16:

```
=B12:B16*E12:E16
```

Again, you've created the array formula by replacing each individual cell reference with the corresponding ranges (and by pressing Ctrl+Shift+Enter).

> **SUPER NOTE**
>
> You don't have to enter array formulas in multiple cells. For example, if you didn't need the Extended totals in the Invoice Template worksheet, you could still calculate the Subtotal by entering the following as an array formula in cell F17:
>
> ```
> =SUM(B12:B16*E12:E16)
> ```

Using Array Constants

In the array formulas you've seen so far, the array arguments have been cell ranges. You also can use constant values as array arguments. This enables you to input values into a formula without having them clutter your worksheet.

To enter an array constant in a formula, just enter the values right in the formula and observe the following guidelines:

- Enclose the values in braces ({}).
- If you want Excel to treat the values as a row, separate each value with a semicolon.
- If you want Excel to treat the values as a column, separate each value with a comma.

For example, the following array constant is the equivalent of entering the individual values in a column on your worksheet:

```
{1;2;3;4}
```

Similarly, the following array constant is equivalent to entering the values in a worksheet range of three columns and two rows:

```
{1,2,3;4,5,6}
```

As a practical example, Figure 60.13 shows two different array formulas. The one on the left (used in the range E4:E7) calculates various loan payments given the different interest rates in the range C5:C8. The array formula on the right (used in the range F4:F7) does the same thing, but the interest rate values are entered as an array constant directly in the formula.

FIGURE 60.13.
Using array constants in your array formulas means you don't have to clutter your worksheet with the input values.

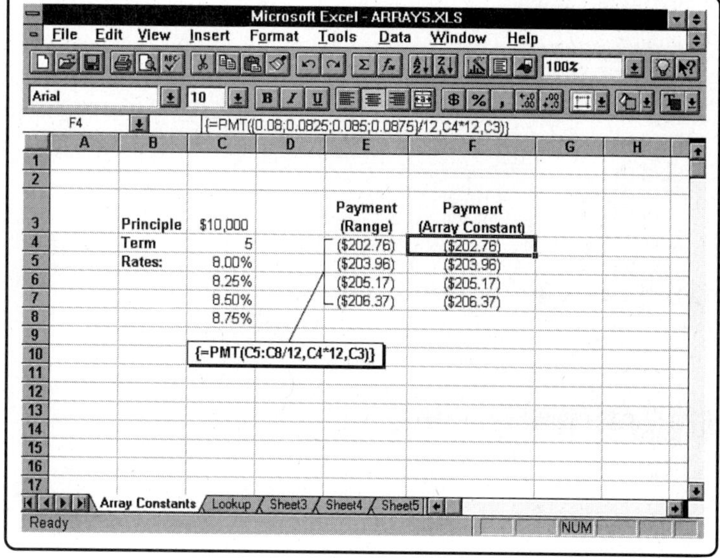

Functions That Use or Return Arrays

Many of Excel's worksheet and macro functions either require an array argument or return an array result (or both). Table 60.5 lists several of these functions and explains how each one uses arrays.

Table 60.5. Some Excel functions that use arrays.

Function Uses	*Array Argument?*	*Returns Array Result?*
`APPLY.NAMES()`	Yes	No
`COLUMN()`	No	Yes, if the argument is a range
`COLUMNS()`	Yes	No
`CONSOLIDATE()`	Yes	No
`DOCUMENTS()`	No	Yes, if multiple documents are open
`FILES()`	No	Yes
`GET.DOCUMENT()`	No	Yes, depending on the arguments
`GET.WINDOW()`	No	Yes, depending on the arguments
`GROWTH()`	Yes	Yes
`HLOOKUP()`	Yes	No

continues

Table 60.5. continued

Function Uses	*Array Argument?*	*Returns Array Result?*
`INDEX()`	Yes	Yes
`LINEST()`	No	Yes
`LOGEST()`	No	Yes
`LOOKUP()`	Yes	No
`MATCH()`	Yes	No
`MDETERM()`	Yes	No
`MINVERSE()`	No	Yes
`MMULT()`	No	Yes
`NAMES()`	No	Yes
`ROW()`	No	Yes, if the argument is a range
`ROWS()`	Yes	No
`SUMPRODUCT()`	Yes	No
`TRANSPOSE()`	Yes	Yes
`TREND()`	Yes	Yes
`VLOOKUP()`	Yes	No
`WINDOWS()`	No	Yes
`WORKGROUP()`	Yes	No

When you use functions that return arrays, be sure to select a range large enough to hold the resulting array and then enter the function as an array formula.

Chapter 61

Advanced Formulas and Functions

Formulas and functions are what spreadsheets are all about. Once you enter your data, you need to do something to it—such as adding up a few numbers, taking an average, or performing a regression analysis. This chapter looks at some techniques that will take your formulas and functions to new heights. You'll learn about using range names in formulas, using Excel's extensive lookup functions, and more.

Working with Range Names in Formulas

You probably use range names often in formulas. Something such as =Sales-Expenses is easier to understand than =F12-F5. The next few sections show you a few techniques that make using range names in formulas easy.

Pasting a Name into a Formula

When entering a range name in a formula, you could type the name in the formula bar. But what if you can't remember the name? Or what if the name is a long one? For such situations, Excel has a feature that enables you to select the name you want from a list and paste it right into the formula. Procedure 61.1 gives you the details.

PROCEDURE 61.1. PASTING A RANGE NAME INTO A FORMULA.

1. In the formula bar, place the insertion point where you want the name to appear.
2. Select the **I**nsert | **N**ame | **P**aste command. Excel displays the Paste Name dialog box, shown in Figure 61.1.

> **SUPER TIP**
> A quick way to display the Paste Name dialog box is to press F3.

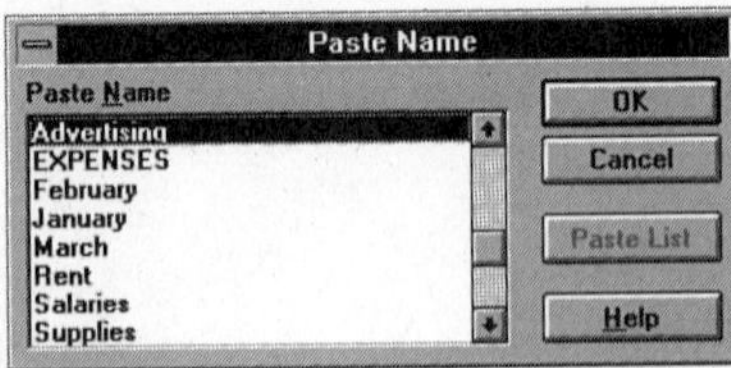

FIGURE 61.1.
Use the Paste Name dialog box to paste a range name into a formula.

3. Highlight the range name you want to use from the Paste **N**ame list.
4. Click on OK or press Enter.

SUPER TIP

A quick way to paste names is to use the Name box in the formula bar. When you're ready to paste a name, drop down the Name list and select the name you want.

Applying Names to Formulas

If you've been using ranges in your formulas, and you name those ranges later, Excel doesn't automatically apply the new names to the formulas. Instead, you have to apply new names to your existing formulas. To do so, follow the steps in Procedure 61.2.

PROCEDURE 61.2. APPLYING NAMES TO FORMULAS.

1. Select the range in which you want to apply the names, or select a single cell if you want to apply the names to the entire worksheet.
2. Select the **I**nsert | **N**ame | **A**pply command. Excel displays the Apply Names dialog box, shown in Figure 61.2.

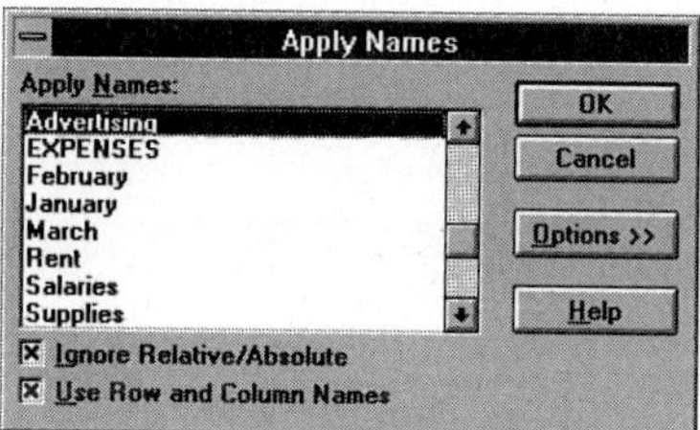

FIGURE 61.2.
Use the Apply Names dialog box to select the names you want to apply to your formula ranges.

3. Select the names you want applied from the Apply **N**ames list.
4. Use the **I**gnore Relative/Absolute check box to ignore relative and absolute references when applying names. (See the next section for more information.)
5. The **U**se Row and Column Names check box tells Excel whether or not to use the worksheet's row and column names when applying names. If you activate this check box, you also can click on the **O**ptions button to see more choices. (See the section in this chapter titled "Using Row and Column Names When Applying Names" for details.)
6. Click on OK or press Enter to apply the names.

Ignoring Relative and Absolute References When Applying Names

If you activate the **I**gnore Relative/Absolute option in the Apply Names dialog box, Excel will ignore relative and absolute reference formats when applying names to a formula. If you deactivate this option, Excel will only replace relative references with names that refer to relative references, and it will only replace absolute references with names that refer to absolute references.

For example, suppose you have a formula such as =SUM(A1:A10) and a range named Sales that refers to $A$1:$A$10. With the **I**gnore Relative/Absolute option turned off, Excel will not apply the name Sales to the range in the formula; Sales refers to an absolute range, and the formula contains a relative range. In most cases, you should leave the Ignore Relative/Absolute option activated.

Using Row and Column Names When Applying Names

For extra clarity in your formulas, select the **U**se Row and Column Names check box in the Apply Names dialog box. This tells Excel to rename all cell references that can be described as the intersection of a named row and a named column. In Figure 61.3, for example, the range C6:C13 is named January, and the range C7:E7 is named Rent. This means that cell C7—the intersection of these two ranges—can be referenced as January Rent.

FIGURE 61.3.
The intersection of the January and Rent ranges (cell C7) can be referenced as January Rent.

C11 =C6+C7+C8+C9+C10

EXPENSES.XLS

	A	B	C	D	E	F	G	H
1	Expense Budget Calculation - 1st Quarter							
2								
3		INCREASE	1.09					
4								
5		EXPENSES	January	February	March			
6		Advertising	4,600	4,200	5,200			
7		Rent	2,100	2,100	2,100			
8		Supplies	1,300	1,200	1,400			
9		Salaries	16,000	16,000	16,500			
10		Utilities	500	600	600			
11		1993 TOTAL	24,500	24,100	25,800			
12								
13		1994 BUDGET	26,705	26,269	28,122			
14								
15								

Budget - 1st Quarter / Budget - 2nd Quarter / Bud

Ready NUM

SUPER NOTE

The space character is Excel's intersection operator. For more information, see Chapter 60, "Advanced Range Topics."

The January 1993 TOTAL (cell C11) currently contains the formula =C6+C7+C8+C9+C10. Applying range names to this worksheet and selecting the **U**se Row and Column Names option changes this formula to the one shown in Figure 61.4.

FIGURE 61.4.
The January 1994 TOTAL formula after applying names.

C11 =Advertising+Rent+Supplies+Salaries+Utilities

EXPENSES.XLS

	A	B	C	D	E	F	G	H
1	Expense Budget Calculation - 1st Quarter							
2								
3		INCREASE	1.09					
4								
5		EXPENSES	January	February	March			
6		Advertising	4,600	4,200	5,200			
7		Rent	2,100	2,100	2,100			
8		Supplies	1,300	1,200	1,400			
9		Salaries	16,000	16,000	16,500			
10		Utilities	500	600	600			
11		1993 TOTAL	24,500	24,100	25,800			
12								
13		1994 BUDGET	26,705	26,269	28,122			
14								
15								

Budget - 1st Quarter / Budget - 2nd Quarter / Bud

Ready NUM

The formula in cell C11 is more comprehensible, but if you look at cells D11 and E11, you'll see that they have what appears to be the same formula. The reason is that when Excel is applying names, it omits the column name if the formula is in the same column. In cell C11, for example, Excel omits January in each term because C11 is in the January column.

Omitting column headings isn't a problem in a small model, but it can be confusing in a large worksheet where you may not be able to see the column names. Therefore, if you are applying names to a large worksheet, you'll probably prefer to include the column headings when applying names.

If you click on the Options button in the Apply Names dialog box, the expanded dialog box (shown in Figure 61.5) includes extra options that enable you to include column (and row) headings. When you work with the Expense Budget sheet, for example, you can include column names by deactivating the Omit **C**olumn Name if Same Column check box. You can include rows by deactivating the Omit **R**ow Name if Same Row check box. The expanded dialog box also enables you to choose the order of names in the reference (Ro**w** Column or Co**l**umn Row).

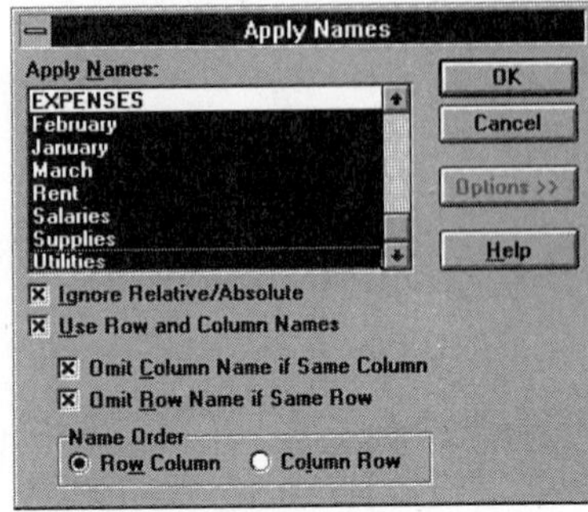

FIGURE 61.5.
The expanded Apply Names dialog box.

Naming Formulas

In Chapter 3, "Getting Started with Ranges," I showed you how to set up names for often-used constants. You can apply a similar naming concept for frequently used formulas and, as with the constants, the formula doesn't have to physically appear in a cell. This not only saves memory, but it often makes your worksheets easier to read. Follow the steps in Procedure 61.3 to name a formula.

PROCEDURE 61.3. NAMING A FORMULA.

1. Select the **I**nsert | **N**ame | **D**efine command. Excel displays the Define Name dialog box.
2. Enter the name you want to use for the formula in the Names in **W**orkbook edit box.
3. In the **R**efers to box, enter the formula exactly as you would in the formula bar.

> **SUPER TIP**
>
> Press F2 to put Excel into Edit mode before you move around inside the **R**efers to box with the arrow keys. If you don't press F2 first, Excel assumes you're trying to select a cell on the worksheet.

4. Click on OK or press Enter.

Now you can enter the formula name in your worksheet cells (instead of the formula itself). For example, the formula for the volume of a sphere is the following (r is the radius of the sphere):

$4\pi r^3/3$

Figure 61.6 shows the Define Name dialog box with this formula named as SphereVolume (assuming that the worksheet has the sphere's radius defined as the name Radius).

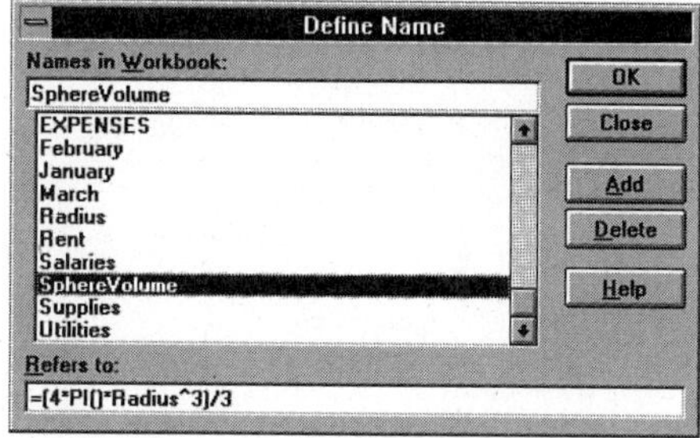

FIGURE 61.6.
A formula named SphereVolume that calculates the volume of a sphere.

SUPER NOTE

To see some good examples of named formulas, refer to Chapter 74, "The Game of Life, Excel Style."

Looking Up a Value in a List

Many spreadsheet applications require you to look up a value in a list. For example, you might have a table of customer discounts in which the percentage discount is based on the number of units ordered. For each customer order, you need to look up the appropriate discount, based on the total units in the order. Similarly, a teacher might convert a raw test score into a letter grade by referring to a table of conversions.

Using an Array Formula

The array formulas you learned about in Chapter 60, "Advanced Range Topics," offer some tricks for looking up values. For example, suppose you want to know if a certain value exists in an array. You could use the following general formula, entered as an array:

```
=OR(value=array)
```

value is the value you want to search for, and *array* is the range of cells in which to search. For example, Figure 61.7 shows a list of customers with overdue accounts. You enter the account number of the customer in cell B1, and cell B2 tells you whether or not the number appears in the list.

FIGURE 61.7.

An array formula that tells you if a value appears in a list.

B2 {=OR(B1=B6:B39)}

ARRAYS.XLS

	A	B	C	D	E	F	G
1	**Account Number:**	09-2111					
2	**In the List?**	TRUE					
3							
4							
5	**Account Name**	**Account Number**	**Invoice Number**	**Invoice Amount**	**Due Date**	**Date Paid**	**Days Overdue**
6	Emily's Sports Palace	08-2255	117316	$1,584.20	8-Dec-93		55
7	Refco Office Solutions	14-5741	117317	$ 303.65	9-Dec-93		54
8	Brimson Furniture	10-0009	117321	$2,144.55	15-Dec-93		48
9	Katy's Paper Products	12-1212	117322	$ 234.69	16-Dec-93		47
10	Door Stoppers Ltd.	01-0045	117324	$ 101.01	22-Dec-93		41
11	Voyatzis Designs	14-1882	117325	$1,985.25	22-Dec-93		41
12	Brimson Furniture	10-0009	117327	$1,847.25	28-Dec-93		35
13	Door Stoppers Ltd.	01-0045	117328	$ 58.50	29-Dec-93		34
14	O'Donoghue Inc.	09-2111	117329	$1,234.56	30-Dec-93		33
15	Refco Office Solutions	14-5741	117330	$ 456.78	30-Dec-93		33
16	Renaud & Son	07-0025	117331	$ 565.77	4-Jan-94		30

Lookup / Sheet3 / Sheet4 / Sheet5 / Sheet6 / Sheet

Ready NUM

Following is the array formula in cell B2:

```
{=OR(B1=B6:B39)}
```

The `OR()` function returns `TRUE` if any one of its arguments is true. The array formula checks each value in the range B6:B39 to see if it equals the value in B1. If any one of those comparisons is `TRUE`, `OR()` returns `TRUE`. Therefore, you'll know the value is in the list.

SUPER NOTE

Recall from Chapter 60 that you don't include braces ({ }) when you enter an array formula. Just type the formula without the braces, then press Ctrl+Shift+Enter.

SUPER TIP

As a similar example, the following is an array formula that returns `TRUE` if a particular account number is not in the list:

```
{=AND(B1<>B6:B39)}
```

I'll leave figuring out how this formula works as an exercise for you.

Now you know how to find out whether or not a value appears in a list, but what if you need to know how many times the value appears? The following array formula does the job:

```
=SUM(IF(value=array,1,0))
```

Again, *value* is the value you want to look up, and *array* is the range for searching. In this formula, the `IF()` function compares *value* with every cell in array. The values that match return 1, and the `SUM()` function adds up all the 1s. The final total is the number of occurrences of *value*. Figure 61.8 shows this formula in action using the list of overdue invoices.

FIGURE 61.8.
An array formula that counts the number of times a value appears in a list.

B3 {=SUM(IF(B1=B6:B39,1,0))}

ARRAYS.XLS

	A	B	C	D	E	F	G	H
1	Account Number:	09-2111						
2	In the List?	TRUE						
3	How Many Times?	2						
4								
5	Account Name	Account Number	Invoice Number	Invoice Amount	Due Date	Date Paid	Days Overdue	
6	Emily's Sports Palace	08-2255	117316	$1,584.20	8-Dec-93		55	
7	Refco Office Solutions	14-5741	117317	$ 303.65	9-Dec-93		54	
8	Brimson Furniture	10-0009	117321	$2,144.55	15-Dec-93		48	
9	Katy's Paper Products	12-1212	117322	$ 234.69	16-Dec-93		47	
10	Door Stoppers Ltd.	01-0045	117324	$ 101.01	22-Dec-93		41	
11	Voyatzis Designs	14-1882	117325	$1,985.25	22-Dec-93		41	
12	Brimson Furniture	10-0009	117327	$1,847.25	28-Dec-93		35	
13	Door Stoppers Ltd.	01-0045	117328	$ 58.50	29-Dec-93		34	
14	O'Donoghue Inc.	09-2111	117329	$1,234.56	30-Dec-93		33	
15	Refco Office Solutions	14-5741	117330	$ 456.78	30-Dec-93		33	
16	Renaud & Son	07-0025	117331	$ 565.77	4-Jan-94		30	

Lookup / Sheet3 / Sheet4 / Sheet5 / Sheet6 / Sheet

Ready NUM

Selecting a Value from a List

Excel's `CHOOSE()` function enables you to select a value from a list. Following is this function's syntax:

```
CHOOSE(index_num,value1,value2,...)
```

index_num	Determines which of the values in the list is returned. If ***index_num*** is 1, ***value1*** is returned. If ***index_num*** is 2, ***value2*** is returned (and so on). ***index_num*** must be a number (or a formula or function that returns a number) between 1 and 29.
value1,value2...	Signifies the list of up to 29 values from which `CHOOSE()` selects the return value. The values can be numbers, text strings, references, names, formulas, or functions.

For example, the following formula returns the text string `"Place"`:

```
=CHOOSE(2,"Win, "Place", "Show")
```

One common use for CHOOSE() is to calculate weighted questionnaire responses. For example, suppose you just completed a survey in which the respondents had to enter a value between 1 and 5 for each question. Some questions and answers were more important than others, so each question was assigned a set of weights. You use these weighted responses for your data. How do you assign the weights? The easiest way is to set up a CHOOSE() function for each question. For instance, suppose question 1 used the following weights for answers 1 through 5: 1.5, 2.3, 1.0, 1.8, and 0.5. If so, the following formula could be used to derive the weighted response:

```
=CHOOSE(Question1, 1.5, 2.3, 1.0, 1.8, 0.5)
```

(Assume that the answer for question 1 is in a cell named Question1.)

Looking Up Values in Tables

In many worksheet formulas, the value of one argument often depends on the value of another. For example, in a formula that calculates an invoice total, the customer's discount might depend on the number of units purchased. The usual way to handle this kind of problem is to look up the appropriate value in a table. Excel has two functions that will do just that: VLOOKUP() and HLOOKUP().

The VLOOKUP() function works by looking in the first column of a table for the value you specify. (Remember that the V in VLOOKUP() is short for "vertical.") More specifically, the VLOOKUP() function looks for the largest value that is less than or equal to the one you specify. It then looks across the appropriate number of columns (which you specify) and returns whatever value it finds there.

Following is the syntax for VLOOKUP():

VLOOKUP(***lookup_value***,***table_array***,***col_index_num***)

lookup_value	The value you want to find in the first column of ***table_array***. You can enter a number, a string, or a reference. Excel looks for the largest value that is less than or equal to ***lookup_value***.
table_array	The table to use for the lookup. You can use a range reference or a name.
col_index_num	If VLOOKUP() finds a match, ***col_index_num*** is the column number in the table that contains the data you want returned (when the first column is column 1).

SUPER CAUTION

To get reliable results from VLOOKUP(), the values in the first column of the table must be in alphabetical order.

Figure 61.9 shows a worksheet that uses `VLOOKUP()` to determine the discount a customer gets on an order, based on the number of units purchased. For example, cell D4 uses the following formula:

```
=VLOOKUP(A4, $H$5:$I$11,2)
```

Cell A4 contains the number of units purchased (20), and the range $H$5:$I$11 is the discount schedule table. `VLOOKUP()` searches down the first column (H5:H11) for the largest value that is less than or equal to 20. The first such cell is H6 (because the value in H7—24—is larger than 20); therefore, `VLOOKUP()` moves to the second column of the table (cell I6) and grabs the value there (40%).

FIGURE 61.9.
A worksheet that uses VLOOKUP() to look up a customer's discount in a discount schedule.

D4 =VLOOKUP(A4,$H$5:$I$11,2)

LOOKUP.XLS

Units Ordered	Part	List Price	Discount	Net Price	Extension		Discount Schedule	
							Units	Discount
20	D-178	$17.95	40%	$10.77	$215.40		0	20%
10	B-047	$6.95	40%	$4.17	$41.70		4	40%
1000	C-098	$2.95	50%	$1.48	$1,475.00		24	42%
50	B-111	$19.95	44%	$11.17	$558.60		49	44%
2	D-017	$27.95	20%	$22.36	$44.72		99	46%
25	D-178	$17.95	42%	$10.41	$260.28		249	48%
100	A-182	$9.95	46%	$5.37	$537.30		499	50%
250	B-047	$6.95	48%	$3.61	$903.50			

Discount Schedule / Sheet2 / Sheet3 / Sheet4 / Sh

Ready NUM

The `HLOOKUP()` function is similar, except that it works by looking in the first row of a table for the largest value that is less than or equal to the one you specify. (The H in `HLOOKUP()` stands for "horizontal.") If successful, it then looks down the specified number of rows and returns the value it finds there. Following is the syntax for `HLOOKUP()`:

`HLOOKUP(`***`lookup_value,table_array,row_index_num`***`)`

`lookup_value`	The value to find in the first row of **`table_array`**. You can enter a number, a string, or a reference. Excel looks for the largest value that is less than or equal to ***`lookup_value`***.
`table_array`	The table you want to use for the lookup. You can use a range reference or a name.
`row_index_num`	If `HLOOKUP()` finds a match, this is the row number in the table that contains the data you want returned (where the first row is row 1).

SUPER CAUTION

As with VLOOKUP(), HLOOKUP() only works reliably when the values in the first row of the table are in alphabetical order.

Finding Exact Matches

VLOOKUP() and HLOOKUP() have two major drawbacks as lookup tools:

- They look only for the largest entries that are less than or equal to the value you enter as an argument. In most lookups, you'll probably want to find an exact match.
- The column or row that these functions use for searching must be in alphabetical or numerical order. You can sort the table, but this isn't always convenient.

To get around these limitations, you need to use two more functions: MATCH() and INDEX().

The MATCH() function looks through a row or column of cells for a value. If MATCH() finds an exact match, it returns the relative position of the match in the row or column. Following is the syntax:

MATCH(***lookup_value***,***lookup_array***,***match_type***)

lookup_value The value you want to find. You can use a number, string, reference, or logical value.

lookup_array The row or column of cells you want to use for the lookup.

match_type Specifies how you want Excel to match ***lookup_value*** with the entries in ***lookup_array***. You have three choices:

0	Finds the first value that exactly matches ***lookup_value***. ***lookup_array*** can be in any order.
1	Finds the largest value that is less than or equal to ***lookup_value***. ***lookup_array*** must be in ascending order. This is the default value.
–1	Finds the smallest value that is greater than or equal to ***lookup_value***. ***lookup_array*** must be in descending order.

SUPER TIP

Another advantage you get with MATCH() is that you can use the usual wildcard characters within ***lookup_value*** (provided that ***match_type*** is 0

> and **`lookup_value`** is text). You can use the question mark (?) for single characters and the asterisk (*) for multiple characters.

Normally you don't use the `MATCH()` function by itself; rather, you combine it with the `INDEX()` function. `INDEX()` returns the value of a cell at the intersection of a row and column inside a reference. Following is the syntax for `INDEX()`:

```
INDEX(reference,row_num,column_num,area_num)
```

`reference`	A reference to one or more cell ranges.
`row_num`	The number of the row in reference from which to return a value. You can omit ***`row_num`*** if ***`reference`*** is a single row.
`column_num`	The number of the column in reference from which to return a value. You can omit ***`column_num`*** if ***`reference`*** is a single column.
`area_num`	If you entered more than one range for ***`reference`***, ***`area_num`*** is the range you want to use. The first range you entered is 1, the second is 2, and so on.

You use `MATCH()` to get ***`row_num`*** or ***`column_num`*** (depending on how your table is laid out) and then use `INDEX()` to return the value you need. For example, Figure 61.10 shows a simple data entry screen that automatically adds a customer name after the user enters the account number. The function that accomplishes this is in cell B4:

```
=INDEX(D3:E18,MATCH(B2,D3:D18,0),2)
```

B4 =INDEX(D3:E18,MATCH(B2,D3:D18,0),2)

LOOKUP.XLS

	A	B	C	D	E
1					
2	Enter Account Number:	10-0009		Account Number	Account Name
3				10-0009	Brimson Furniture
4	Account Name is:	Brimson Furniture		02-0200	Chimera Illusions
5				01-0045	Door Stoppers Ltd.
6				08-2255	Emily's Sports Palace
7				12-1212	Katy's Paper Products
8				16-1616	Lone Wolf Software
9				12-3456	Meaghan Manufacturing
10				09-2111	O'Donoghue Inc.
11				14-1882	Real Solemn Officials
12				14-5741	Refco Office Solutions
13				07-0025	Renaud & Son
14				11-1111	Reston Solicitor Offices
15				07-4441	Rooter Office Solvents
16				16-6658	Simpson's Ltd.

Account Name / Sheet3 / Sheet4 / Sheet5 / Sheet6

Ready NUM

FIGURE 61.10.
A simple data entry worksheet that uses `INDEX()` and `MATCH()` to look up a customer's name based on the entered account number.

SUPER TIP

To access values in a two-dimensional table, use `MATCH()` functions for both the ***row_num*** and ***column_num*** arguments in `INDEX()`.

Working with Links in Formulas

If you have data in one workbook that you want to use in another, you can set up a link between them. This enables your formulas to use references to cells or ranges in the other workbook. When the other data changes, Excel automatically updates the link.

For example, Figure 61.11 shows two linked workbooks. The Budget Summary sheet in SUMMARY.XLS includes data from the 1994 Budget worksheet in BUDGET.XLS. The formula shown for cell B2 in SUMMARY.XLS contains an external reference to cell R7 in the 1994 Budget worksheet of BUDGET.XLS. If the value in R7 changes, Excel immediately updates SUMMARY.XLS.

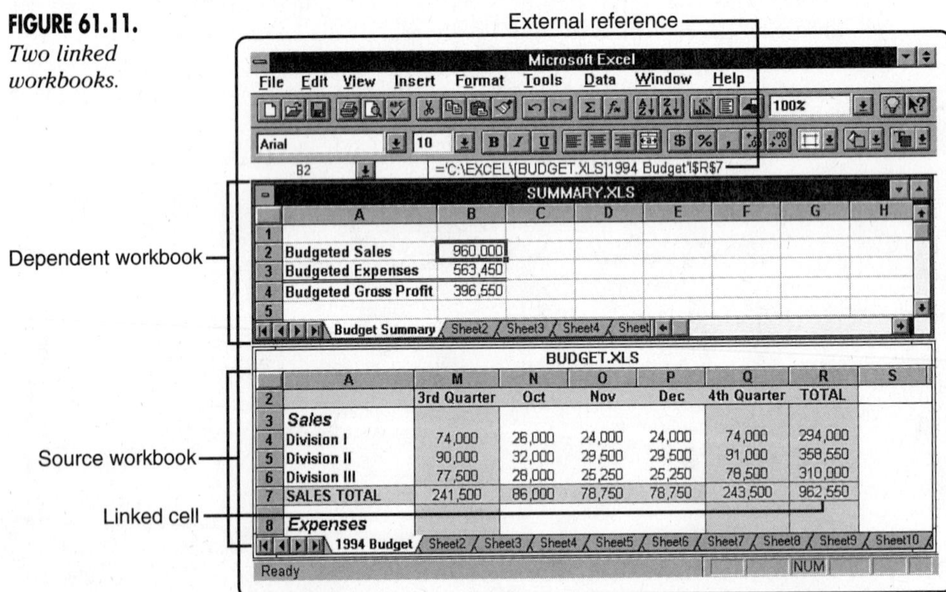

FIGURE 61.11. *Two linked workbooks.*

SUPER NOTE

The workbook that contains the external reference is called the dependent workbook (or the client workbook). The workbook that contains the original data is called the source workbook (or the server workbook).

Understanding External References

There is no big mystery behind Excel links. You set up links by including an external reference to a cell or range in another workbook (or in another worksheet from the same workbook). The only thing you need to be comfortable with is the structure of an external reference. Following is the general syntax:

```
'path[workbookname]sheetname'!reference
```

path	The drive and directory in which the workbook is located. You need to include the path only when the workbook is closed.
workbookname	The name of the workbook, including an extension. Always enclose the workbook name in square brackets ([ ]). You can omit *workbookname* if you're referencing a cell or range in another sheet from the same workbook.
sheetname	The name of the worksheet's tab. You can omit *sheetname* if reference is a defined name in the same workbook. For example, in SUMMARY.XLS, you could use the external reference `SUMMARY.XLS!BudgetedSales` to refer to a cell named BudgetedSales that exists elsewhere in the SUMMARY.XLS workbook.
reference	A cell or range reference, or a defined name.

For example, if you were to close the BUDGET.XLS workbook, Excel would automatically change the external reference shown in Figure 61.11 to the following:

```
='C:\EXCEL\[BUDGET.XLS]1994 Budget'!$R$7
```

SUPER NOTE

You need the single quotation marks around the path, workbook name, and sheet name only if the workbook is closed or if the sheet name contains spaces. If in doubt, include the single quotation marks anyway; Excel will ignore them if they're not required.

Updating Links

The purpose of a link is to avoid duplicating formulas and data in multiple worksheets. If one workbook contains the information you need, you can use a link to reference the data without re-creating it in another workbook.

The data in the dependent workbook should always reflect what actually is in the source workbook. You maintain this by updating the link as follows:

- If both the source and dependent workbooks are open, Excel automatically updates the link whenever the data in the source file changes.
- If the source workbook is open when you open the dependent workbook, Excel automatically updates the links again.
- If the source workbook is closed when you open the dependent workbook, Excel displays a dialog box asking if you want to update the links. Click on **Y**es to update or **N**o to cancel.
- If you didn't update a link when you opened the dependent document, you can update it any time by selecting the **E**dit | Lin**k**s command. In the Links dialog box that appears, highlight the link and then click on the **U**pdate Now button.

Editing Links

If the name of the source document changes, you'll need to edit the link to keep the data up to date. You can edit the external reference directly, or you can change the source by following the steps in Procedure 61.4.

PROCEDURE 61.4. EDITING A LINK.

1. With the dependent workbook active, select the **E**dit | Lin**k**s command. Excel displays the Links dialog box, shown in Figure 61.12.

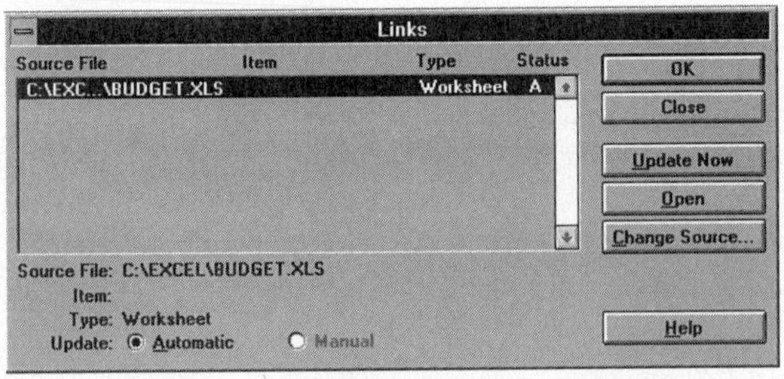

FIGURE 61.12.
Use the Links dialog box to change the source workbook for a link.

2. Highlight the link you want to change.
3. Click on the Change Source button. Excel displays the Change Links dialog box.
4. Select the new source document and then click on OK or press Enter to return to the Links dialog box.
5. Click on Close to return to the workbook.

Sample Formulas

This section runs through a few sample formulas that take advantage of some of the techniques looked at in this chapter. Studying these formulas will give you an idea of the kinds of things you can do with your newly found knowledge.

Calculating the Day of the Week

Excel's `WEEKDAY()` function returns a number that corresponds to the day of the week: Sunday is 1, Monday is 2, and so on. Here's the syntax of `WEEKDAY()`:

```
WEEKDAY(date)
```

date is the date you want to use. It can be a serial number, a text string in one of Excel's date formats, or a function that returns a date, such as `NOW()`.

However, what if you want to know the actual day (not the number) of the week? If you need to display only the day of the week, you format the cell as dddd. If you need to use the day of the week in a formula, you need a way of converting the `WEEKDAY()` result into the appropriate string. Fortunately, the `CHOOSE()` function makes this easy. For example, suppose cell B5 contains a date. You can find the day of the week it represents with the following formula:

```
=CHOOSE(WEEKDAY(B5),"Sun","Mon","Tue","Wed","Thu","Fri","Sat")
```

I've used abbreviations for each day to save space, but you can use whatever you like.

Generating a Series of Letters

Excel's Fill handle and Data | Series command are great for generating a series of numbers or dates, but they don't do the job when you need a series of letters (such as a, b, c, and so on). However, you can use the `CHAR()` function in an array formula for generating a series.

The `CHAR()` function's purpose is to convert a character's ANSI code number into the character itself. Here's the syntax:

```
CHAR(number)
```

number is the code number from the Windows ANSI character set. For example, CHAR(162) returns the cents symbol (¢), and CHAR(188) returns the one-quarter symbol (¼). We're concerned with the characters a through z, which correspond to ANSI codes 97 to 122, and A through Z (65 to 90). To generate a series of these letters, follow the steps in Procedure 61.5.

PROCEDURE 61.5. GENERATING A SERIES OF LETTERS.

1. Select the range you want to use for the series.
2. Activate in-cell editing by pressing F2.
3. Type in the following formula:

   `=CHAR(97+ROW(range)-ROW(first_cell))`

   where *range* is the range you selected in step 1, and *first_cell* is a reference to the first cell in *range*. For example, if the selected range is B10:B20, you would type the following:

   `=CHAR(97+ROW(B10:B20)-ROW(B10))`

> **SUPER NOTE**
>
> I'm assuming that you've selected a column for your series. If you selected a row, replace the `ROW()` functions in the formula with `COLUMN()`.

4. Press Ctrl+Shift+Enter to enter the formula as an array.

Because you entered this as an array formula, the `ROW(range)-ROW(first_cell)` calculation generates a series of numbers (0, 1, 2, and so on) which represent the offset of each cell in the range from the first cell. These offsets are added to 97 to produce the appropriate ANSI codes for the lowercase letters. If you want uppercase letters, replace the 97 with 65.

> **SUPER TIP**
>
> If you want to generate your letters starting in row 1, you can use the following version of the formula:
>
> `{=CHAR(96+ROW(range))}`

Calculating Cumulative Totals

Many worksheets need to calculate cumulative totals. Most budget worksheets, for example, show cumulative totals for sales and expenses over the course of the fiscal year. Similarly, loan amortizations often show the cumulative interest and principal paid over the life of the loan.

Calculating these straightforward cumulative totals is easy. See the worksheet shown in Figure 61.13. Column F is supposed to track the cumulative interest on the loan, and cell F6 contains the following `SUM()` formula:

```
=SUM($D$6:D6)
```

This formula sums cell D6, which is no great feat. However, when you fill the range F6:F53 with this formula, the left part of the `SUM()` range ($D$6) remains anchored; the right side (D6) is relative, therefore it changes. So, for example, the corresponding formula in cell F10 would be the following:

```
=SUM($D$6:D10)
```

F6 =SUM($D$6:D6)

LOAN.XLS

	A	B	C	D	E	F	G	H
1			Loan Amortization Schedule					
2	Rate	8%						
3	Months	48						
4	Amount	$10,000						
5	Period	Month	Payment	Interest	Principle	Total Interest	Prinicipal % Paid	
6	1	Jun-93	($244.13)	($66.67)	($177.46)	($66.67)	1.77%	
7	2	Jul-93	($244.13)	($65.48)	($178.65)	($132.15)	3.56%	
8	3	Aug-93	($244.13)	($64.29)	($179.84)	($196.44)	5.36%	
9	4	Sep-93	($244.13)	($63.09)	($181.04)	($259.54)	7.17%	
10	5	Oct-93	($244.13)	($61.89)	($182.24)	($321.42)	8.99%	
11	6	Nov-93	($244.13)	($60.67)	($183.46)	($382.10)	10.83%	
12	7	Dec-93	($244.13)	($59.45)	($184.68)	($441.54)	12.67%	
13	8	Jan-94	($244.13)	($58.22)	($185.91)	($499.76)	14.53%	
14	9	Feb-94	($244.13)	($56.98)	($187.15)	($556.74)	16.40%	

Amortization / Sheet2 / Sheet3 / Sheet4 / Sheet5

Ready NUM

FIGURE 61.13.
A worksheet that calculates cumulative totals.

Summing Only the Positive or Negative Values in a Range

If you have a range of numbers that contains both positive and negative values, what do you do if you need a total of only the negative values? Or only the positive ones? You could enter the individual cells into a `SUM()` function. However, an easier way uses a simple array formula.

To sum the negative values in a range called *range*, you would use the following formula:

```
{=SUM((range<0)*range)}
```

The *range*<0 test returns 1 for those range values that are less than 0; otherwise, it returns 0. Therefore, only negative values get included in the SUM().

Similarly, you would use the following array formula to sum only the positive values in *range*:

```
{=SUM((range>0)*range)}
```

Determining Whether or Not a Year is a Leap Year

If you need to determine whether or not a given year is a leap year, you use the MOD() function. MOD() calculates the remainder (or modulus) after dividing one number into another. Following is the syntax for this very useful function:

MOD(***number***,***divisor***)

number	The dividend (that is, the number to be divided).
divisor	The number by which you want to divide ***number***.

For example, MOD(24,10) equals 4 (that is, 24 divided by 10 is 2 with remainder 4).

Leap years (with some exceptions) are years divisible by 4. So a year would be a leap year if the following formula returned 0:

```
=MOD(year,4)
```

This formula works for the years 1901 to 2099, which should take care of most people's needs. The formula doesn't work for 1900 and 2100, because those years, despite being divisible by four, aren't leap years. The general rule is that a year is a leap year if it's divisible by 4 and it's not divisible by 100, *unless* it's also divisible by 400. Therefore, because 1900 and 2100 are divisible by 100 and not by 400, they aren't leap years. The year 2000, however, is a leap year. If you want a formula that takes the full rule into account, use the following:

```
=(MOD(year,4)=0)-(MOD(year,100)=0)+(MOD(year,400)=0)
```

The three parts of the formula that compare a MOD() function to 0 will return 1 or 0. Therefore, the result of this formula will always be 0 for leap years and nonzero for all other years.

Chapter

62

Working with Templates and Outlines

Although many of Excel's advanced features are designed with specific groups of users in mind (scientists, engineers, and so on), others are intended to make everyone's life easier. These tools reward a bit of effort in the short term with improved productivity in the long term. Such is the case with the two features that are the subjects of this chapter: templates and outlines. Although they're not directly related, both features have two things in common: they can make your day-to-day work more efficient, and they can help you get more out of your Excel investment.

Working with Templates

A *template* is a document that contains a basic layout (sheets, labels, formulas, formatting, styles, names, and so on) that you can use as a skeleton for similar documents. This ensures that worksheets, charts, or macro sheets that you use frequently all have a consistent look and feel. For example, if you need to consolidate budget numbers from various departments, your task will be much easier if all the worksheets have the same layout. To that end, you can issue each department a budget template containing the worksheet layout you want everyone to use.

Creating a Template

Creating a template is similar to creating any other workbook. Procedure 62.1 outlines the required steps.

PROCEDURE 62.1. CREATING A TEMPLATE.

1. Set up the workbook with the settings you want to preserve in the template. You can either use an existing document or create a new one from scratch.
2. Select the **F**ile | Save **A**s command to display the Save As dialog box.
3. Enter a name for the template in the File **N**ame edit box (you don't need to add an extension; see step 5).
4. Use the Directories and Drives lists to select the location for the template.

> **SUPER TIP**
>
> If you save the template in your Excel startup directory (usually the \XLSTART subdirectory), you can open it quickly by selecting the **F**ile | **N**ew command (see the next section).

5. In the Save File as **T**ype drop-down list, select the Template option. Excel adds a .XLT extension to the filename.
6. Click on OK or press Enter.

Creating a New Document Based on a Template

As soon as you've created a template, you can use either of the following methods to create a new document based on the template:

- If you saved the template in your Excel startup directory, select the **F**ile | **N**ew command to display the New dialog box, shown in Figure 62.1. Highlight the template in the **N**ew list and click on OK or press Enter.

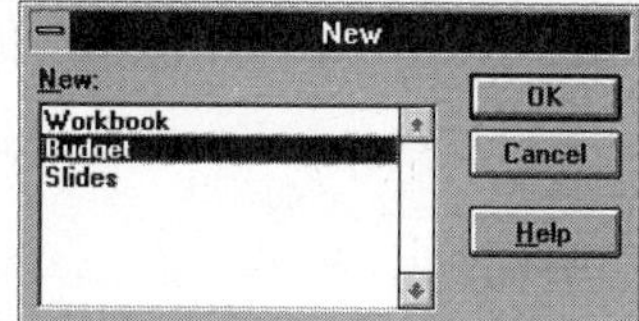

FIGURE 62.1.
When you save a template in the startup directory, its name appears in the New dialog box.

- Select the **F**ile | **O**pen command, highlight the template file in the Open dialog box, and then click on OK or press Enter.

In both cases, Excel opens a copy of the file and gives the window the same name as the template and adds a number. The number indicates how many times you've used this template to create a new document in the current Excel session. For example, if the template is called BUDGET.XLT, the first new document you create will be called Budget1, the second will be Budget2, and so on.

Customizing the Startup Workbook

By default, Excel opens a workbook called Book1 when you start the program. This default workbook is referred to as the *startup workbook.* If you find yourself constantly changing the default formatting, display options, or other settings, you can create a customized version of the startup workbook. Follow the steps in Procedure 62.2.

PROCEDURE 62.2. CUSTOMIZING EXCEL'S STARTUP WORKBOOK.

1. Open a new workbook (or an existing one) and specify the settings you want to use for your startup document.
2. Follow the steps in Procedure 62.1 to save the sheet as a template with the name BOOK.XLT. You must save the template to your startup directory (usually \XLSTART).
3. Click on OK or press Enter.

Whenever you start Excel, the program now automatically opens a copy of BOOK.XLT with your customized settings.

SUPER TIP

If you often begin your Excel sessions by creating a new document based on a template, you can get Excel to do it for you automatically. You need to do the following two things:

1. Change the name of the template so that it begins with START (for example, STARTEMP.XLT).
2. Save the template in your main Excel directory.

Now, every time you start Excel, it will create a new document based on your template. You're not restricted to a single START template. You can create as many templates as you like, and Excel will open a new document based on each template whenever you start the program (subject to your computer's memory limitations, of course). Note, however, that Excel will no longer open a new workbook based on the BOOK template.

Making Changes to a Template

When you want to make changes to a template, hold down the Shift key as you open the template. (Otherwise, Excel just opens a copy of it.) As soon as the template is open, you can make changes as you would to any other workbook. When you finish, save the file. (You don't need to specify the Template type this time, because Excel automatically saves the file as a template.)

Using Outlines

Outlines? In a spreadsheet? Yes, those same creatures that caused you so much grief in high school English class also are available in Excel. In a worksheet outline, though, you can *collapse* sections of the sheet to display only summary cells (such as quarterly or regional totals, for example), or you can *expand* hidden sections to show the underlying detail.

The worksheet in Figure 62.2 displays monthly budget figures for various sales and expense items. The columns include quarterly subtotals and, although you can't see it in Figure 62.2, a grand total. The rows include subtotals for sales, expenses, and gross profit.

FIGURE 62.2.
A budget worksheet showing detail and summary data.

A21

	A	B	C	D	E	F	G	H
1								
2		Jan	Feb	Mar	1st Quarter	Apr	May	Jun
3	*Sales*							
4	Division I	23,500	23,000	24,000	70,500	25,100	25,000	25,400
5	Division II	28,750	27,800	29,500	86,050	31,000	30,500	30,000
6	Division III	24,400	24,000	25,250	73,650	26,600	27,000	26,750
7	SALES TOTAL	76,650	74,800	78,750	230,200	82,700	82,500	82,150
8	*Expenses*							
9	Cost of Goods	6,132	5,984	6,300	18,416	6,616	6,600	6,572
10	Advertising	4,600	4,200	5,200	14,000	5,000	5,500	5,250
11	Rent	2,100	2,100	2,100	6,300	2,100	2,100	2,100
12	Supplies	1,300	1,200	1,400	3,900	1,300	1,250	1,400
13	Salaries	16,000	16,000	16,500	48,500	16,500	16,500	17,000
14	Shipping	14,250	13,750	14,500	42,500	15,000	14,500	14,750
15	Utilities	500	600	600	1,700	550	600	650
16	EXPENSES TOTAL	44,882	43,834	46,600	135,316	47,066	47,050	47,722
17	GROSS PROFIT	31,768	30,966	32,150	94,884	35,634	35,450	34,428

Budget / Sheet2 / Sheet3 / Sheet4 / Sheet5 / Sheet6

Ready NUM

Suppose you don't want to see so much detail. For example, you might need to see only the quarterly totals for each row, or you might want to hide the salary figures for a presentation you're making. An outline is the easiest way to do this. Figure 62.3 shows the same worksheet with an outline added (I explain shortly what the various symbols mean). Using this outline, you can hide whatever details you don't need to see. Figure 62.4 shows the worksheet with data hidden for the individual months and salaries. You can go even further. The view in Figure 62.5 shows only the sales and expenses subtotals and the grand totals.

FIGURE 62.3.
The budget worksheet with outlining added.

A1

	A	B	C	D	E	F	G	H
1								
2		Jan	Feb	Mar	1st Quarter	Apr	May	Ju
3	*Sales*							
4	Division I	23,500	23,000	24,000	70,500	25,100	25,000	25,4
5	Division II	28,750	27,800	29,500	86,050	31,000	30,500	30,0
6	Division III	24,400	24,000	25,250	73,650	26,600	27,000	26,7
7	SALES TOTAL	76,650	74,800	78,750	230,200	82,700	82,500	82,1
8	*Expenses*							
9	Cost of Goods	6,132	5,984	6,300	18,416	6,616	6,600	6,57
10	Advertising	4,600	4,200	5,200	14,000	5,000	5,500	5,2
11	Rent	2,100	2,100	2,100	6,300	2,100	2,100	2,10
12	Supplies	1,300	1,200	1,400	3,900	1,300	1,250	1,40
13	Salaries	16,000	16,000	16,500	48,500	16,500	16,500	17,0
14	Shipping	14,250	13,750	14,500	42,500	15,000	14,500	14,7
15	Utilities	500	600	600	1,700	550	600	65

Budget / Sheet2 / Sheet3 / Sheet4 / Sheet5 / Sheet6

Ready NUM

FIGURE 62.4.
Outlining enables you to hide detail data you don't need to see.

	A	E	I	M	Q	R
1						
2		1st Quarter	2nd Quarter	3rd Quarter	4th Quarter	TOTAL
3	Sales					
4	Division I	70,500	75,500	74,000	74,000	294,000
5	Division II	86,050	91,500	90,000	91,000	358,550
6	Division III	73,650	80,350	77,500	78,500	310,000
7	SALES TOTAL	230,200	247,350	241,500	243,500	962,550
8	Expenses					
9	Cost of Goods	18,416	19,788	19,320	19,480	77,004
10	Advertising	14,000	15,750	15,900	14,900	60,550
11	Rent	6,300	6,300	6,300	6,300	25,200
12	Supplies	3,900	3,950	4,100	4,000	15,950
14	Shipping	42,500	44,250	44,000	45,500	176,250
15	Utilities	1,700	1,800	1,850	1,850	7,200
16	EXPENSES TOTAL	135,316	141,838	142,470	144,030	563,654

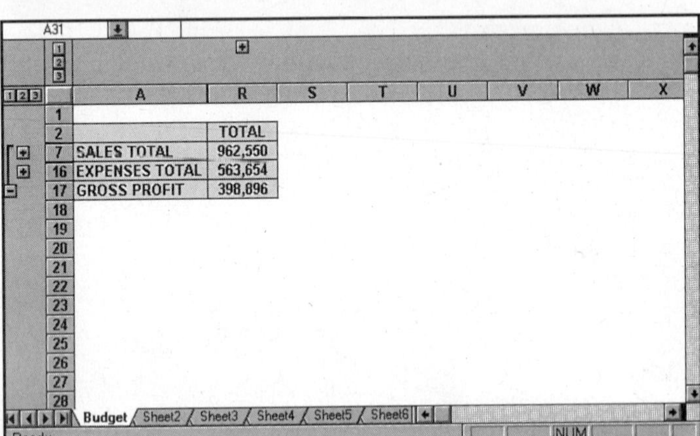

FIGURE 62.5.
Outlines usually have several levels that enable you to hide even subtotals.

One of the big advantages of outlines is that, as soon as you've hidden some data, you can work with the visible cells as though they were a single range. This means that you can format those cells quickly, print them, create charts, and so on.

Creating an Outline Automatically

The easiest way to create an outline is to have Excel do it for you. (You can create an outline manually too, as you'll see later.) Before you create an outline, you need to make sure your worksheet is a candidate for outlining. There are two main criteria:

- The worksheet must contain formulas that reference cells or ranges directly adjacent to the formula cell. Worksheets with `SUM()` functions that subtotal cells above or to the left (such as the budget worksheet presented earlier) are particularly good candidates for outlining.

- There must be a consistent pattern to the direction of the formula references. For example, you can outline a worksheet containing formulas that always reference cells above or to the left. However, you can't outline a worksheet with, for example, `SUM()` functions that reference ranges above *and* below a formula cell.

After you determine that your worksheet is outline material, follow the steps in Procedure 62.3.

PROCEDURE 62.3. OUTLINING A WORKSHEET AUTOMATICALLY.

1. Select the range of cells you want to outline. If you want to outline the entire worksheet, select only a single cell.
2. Select the **D**ata | **G**roup and Outline | **A**uto Outline command. Excel creates the outline and displays the outline tools (see Figure 62.6).

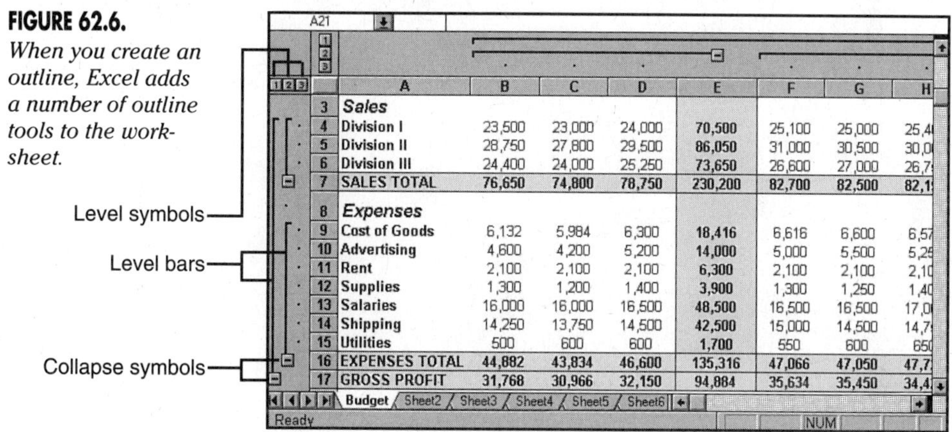

	A	B	C	D	E	F	G	H
3	*Sales*							
4	Division I	23,500	23,000	24,000	70,500	25,100	25,000	25,4
5	Division II	28,750	27,800	29,500	86,050	31,000	30,500	30,0
6	Division III	24,400	24,000	25,250	73,650	26,600	27,000	26,7
7	SALES TOTAL	76,650	74,800	78,750	230,200	82,700	82,500	82,1
8	*Expenses*							
9	Cost of Goods	6,132	5,984	6,300	18,416	6,616	6,600	6,57
10	Advertising	4,600	4,200	5,200	14,000	5,000	5,500	5,25
11	Rent	2,100	2,100	2,100	6,300	2,100	2,100	2,10
12	Supplies	1,300	1,200	1,400	3,900	1,300	1,250	1,40
13	Salaries	16,000	16,000	16,500	48,500	16,500	16,500	17,0
14	Shipping	14,250	13,750	14,500	42,500	15,000	14,500	14,7
15	Utilities	500	600	600	1,700	550	600	650
16	EXPENSES TOTAL	44,882	43,834	46,600	135,316	47,066	47,050	47,7
17	GROSS PROFIT	31,768	30,966	32,150	94,884	35,634	35,450	34,4

FIGURE 62.6.
When you create an outline, Excel adds a number of outline tools to the worksheet.

Understanding the Outline Tools

When Excel creates an outline, it divides your worksheet into a hierarchy of *levels*. These levels range from the worksheet detail (the lowest level) to the grand totals (the highest level). Excel outlines can handle up to eight levels of data.

In the Budget worksheet, for example, Excel created three levels for both the column and the row data:

- In the columns, the monthly figures are the details, so they're the lowest level (level 3). The quarterly totals are the first summary data, so they're the next level (level 2). Finally, the grand totals are the highest level (level 1).
- In the rows, the individual sales and expense items are the details (level 3). The sales and expenses subtotals are the next level (level 2). The Gross Profit row is the highest level (level 1).

SUPER NOTE

Somewhat confusingly, Excel has set things up so that lower outline levels have higher level numbers. The way I remember it is that the higher the number, the more detail the level contains.

To help you work with your outlines, Excel adds the following tools to your worksheet:

Level bars: These bars indicate the data included in the current level. Click on a bar to hide the rows or columns marked by a bar.

Collapse symbol: Click on this symbol to hide (or *collapse*) the rows or columns marked by the attached level bar.

Expand symbol: When you collapse a level, the collapse symbol changes to an expand symbol (+). Click on this symbol to display (or *expand*) the hidden rows or columns.

Level symbols: These symbols tell you which level each level bar is on. Click on a level symbol to display all the detail data for that level.

SUPER TIP

To toggle the outline symbols on and off, press Ctrl+8.

Creating an Outline Manually

If you would like more control over the outlining process, you easily can do it yourself. The idea is that you selectively *group* or *ungroup* rows or columns. When you group a range, you assign it to a lower outline level (that is, you give it a higher level number). When you ungroup a range, you assign it to a higher outline level.

Grouping Rows and Columns

Procedure 62.4 shows you how to group rows and columns.

PROCEDURE 62.4. GROUPING ROWS AND COLUMNS.

1. If your detail data is in rows, select the rows you want to group. To save a step later on, select the entire row (see Figure 62.7). If your detail data is in columns, select the columns you want to group.

SUPER TIP

To select an entire row, click on the row heading or press Shift+Spacebar. To select an entire column, click on the column heading or press Ctrl+Spacebar.

A4 | Division I

	A	B	C	D	E	F	G	H
1								
2		Jan	Feb	Mar	1st Quarter	Apr	May	Jun
3	*Sales*							
4	Division I	23,500	23,000	24,000	70,500	25,100	25,000	25,400
5	Division II	28,750	27,800	29,500	86,050	31,000	30,500	30,000
6	Division III	24,400	24,000	25,250	73,650	26,600	27,000	26,750
7	SALES TOTAL	76,650	74,800	78,750	230,200	82,700	82,500	82,150
8	*Expenses*							
9	Cost of Goods	6,132	5,984	6,300	18,416	6,616	6,600	6,572
10	Advertising	4,600	4,200	5,200	14,000	5,000	5,500	5,250
11	Rent	2,100	2,100	2,100	6,300	2,100	2,100	2,100
12	Supplies	1,300	1,200	1,400	3,900	1,300	1,250	1,400
13	Salaries	16,000	16,000	16,500	48,500	16,500	16,500	17,000
14	Shipping	14,250	13,750	14,500	42,500	15,000	14,500	14,750
15	Utilities	500	600	600	1,700	550	600	650
16	EXPENSES TOTAL	44,882	43,834	46,600	135,316	47,066	47,050	47,722
17	GROSS PROFIT	31,768	30,966	32,150	94,884	35,634	35,450	34,428

Budget / Sheet2 / Sheet3 / Sheet4 / Sheet5 / Sheet6

Ready NUM

FIGURE 62.7.
The Sales detail rows selected for grouping.

2. Select the Data | Group and Outline | Group command. If you selected entire rows or columns, Excel groups the selection and adds the outline symbols to the sheet (see Figure 62.8); skip to step 4. If you selected something other than entire rows or columns, Excel displays the Group dialog box; proceed to step 3.

SUPER TIP

You also can group selected rows or columns by pressing Alt+Shift+right arrow.

Click on this tool in the Query and Pivot toolbar to group a selection.

FIGURE 62.8.
When you group a selection, Excel adds the appropriate outline symbols to the worksheet.

A4 | Division I

	A	B	C	D	E	F	G	H
1								
2		Jan	Feb	Mar	1st Quarter	Apr	May	Jun
3	*Sales*							
4	Division I	23,500	23,000	24,000	70,500	25,100	25,000	25,400
5	Division II	28,750	27,800	29,500	86,050	31,000	30,500	30,000
6	Division III	24,400	24,000	25,250	73,650	26,600	27,000	26,750
7	SALES TOTAL	76,650	74,800	78,750	230,200	82,700	82,500	82,150
8	*Expenses*							
9	Cost of Goods	6,132	5,984	6,300	18,416	6,616	6,600	6,572
10	Advertising	4,600	4,200	5,200	14,000	5,000	5,500	5,250
11	Rent	2,100	2,100	2,100	6,300	2,100	2,100	2,100
12	Supplies	1,300	1,200	1,400	3,900	1,300	1,250	1,400
13	Salaries	16,000	16,000	16,500	48,500	16,500	16,500	17,000
14	Shipping	14,250	13,750	14,500	42,500	15,000	14,500	14,750
15	Utilities	500	600	600	1,700	550	600	650
16	EXPENSES TOTAL	44,882	43,834	46,600	135,316	47,066	47,050	47,722
17	GROSS PROFIT	31,768	30,966	32,150	94,884	35,634	35,450	34,428

Budget / Sheet2 / Sheet3 / Sheet4 / Sheet5 / Sheet6

Ready NUM

3. In the Group dialog box, select either **R**ows or **C**olumns, then click on OK or press Enter to create the group.
4. Repeat steps 1-3 either to group other rows or columns or to move existing groups to a lower outline level.

Ungrouping Rows and Columns

Procedure 62.5 shows you how to ungroup rows and columns.

PROCEDURE 62.5. UNGROUPING ROWS AND COLUMNS.

1. If you're working with rows, select the rows you want to ungroup. Again, you can save a step if you select the entire row. If you're working with columns, select the columns you want to ungroup.
2. Select the **D**ata | **G**roup and Outline | **U**ngroup command. If you selected entire rows or columns, Excel ungroups the selection and removes the outline symbols; skip to step 4. If you selected something other than entire rows or columns, Excel displays the Ungroup dialog box; proceed to step 3.

SUPER TIP

You also can ungroup selected rows or columns by pressing Alt+Shift+left arrow.

Click on this tool in the Query and Pivot toolbar to ungroup a selection.

3. In the Ungroup dialog box, select either **R**ows or **C**olumns, then click on OK or press Enter to ungroup the selection.
4. Repeat steps 1-3 either to ungroup other rows or columns or to move existing groups to a higher outline level.

Hiding and Showing Detail Data

The whole purpose of an outline is to enable you to move easily between views of greater or lesser detail. The next two sections tell you how to hide and show detail data in an outline.

Hiding Detail Data

To hide details in an outline, you have three methods to choose from:

- Click on the collapse symbol at the bottom (for rows) or right (for columns) of the level bar that encompasses the detail data.
- Select a cell in a row or column marked with a collapse symbol, and then select the **D**ata | **G**roup and Outline | **H**ide Detail command.
- Select a cell in a row or column marked with a collapse symbol and click on the Hide Detail tool in the Query and Pivot toolbar.

The Hide Detail tool.

Showing Detail Data

To show collapsed detail, you have four methods to choose from:

- Click on the appropriate expand symbol.
- To see the detail for an entire level, click on the level marker.
- Select a cell in a row or column marked with an expand symbol, and then select the **D**ata | **G**roup and Outline | **S**how Detail command.
- Select a cell in a row or column marked with an expand symbol, and then click on the Show Detail tool in the Query and Pivot toolbar.

The Show Detail tool.

Selecting Outline Data

When you collapse an outline level, the data is only temporarily hidden from view. If you select the outline, your selection includes the collapsed cells. If you want to copy, print, or chart only the visible cells, you need to follow the steps in Procedure 62.6.

PROCEDURE 62.6. SELECTING ONLY EXPANDED OUTLINE DATA.

1. Hide the outline data you don't need.
2. Select the outline cells you want to work with.
3. Select the **E**dit | **G**o To command to display the Go To dialog box.
4. Click on the **S**pecial button. Excel displays the Go To Special dialog box.
5. Click on the **V**isible Cells Only option button.
6. Click on OK or press Enter. Excel modifies your selection to include only those cells in the selection that are part of the expanded outline.

TIP

You also can select visible cells by pressing Alt+; (semicolon).

Removing an Outline

You can remove selected rows or columns from an outline, or you can remove the entire outline. Follow the steps in Procedure 62.7.

PROCEDURE 62.7. REMOVING SOME OR ALL OF AN OUTLINE FROM A WORKSHEET.

1. If you want to remove only part of an outline, select the appropriate rows or columns. If you want to remove the entire outline, select a single cell.
2. Select the **D**ata | **G**roup and Outline | **C**lear Outline command. Excel adjusts or removes the outline.

Chapter

63

Other Advanced Workbook Topics

So far in this Workshop, you've read about such advanced workbook features as arrays, templates, and outlines. This chapter covers four other important topics: protecting your worksheet data, troubleshooting formulas, auditing worksheets, and adding dialog box controls to worksheets.

Protecting Workbook Data

When you've labored long and hard to get your worksheet formulas or formatting just right, the last thing you need is to have a cell or range accidentally deleted or copied over. You can prevent this by using Excel's workbook protection features that enable you to prevent changes to anything from a single cell to an entire workbook.

Protecting Individual Cells, Objects, and Scenarios

Protecting cells, objects, and scenarios in Excel is a two-step process:

1. Set up the item's protection formatting. You have three options:
   - Cells, objects, and scenarios can be either *locked* or *unlocked*. As soon as protection is turned on (see step 2), a locked item can't be changed, deleted, moved, or copied over.
   - Cell formulas and scenarios can be either *hidden* or *visible*. With protection on, a hidden formula doesn't appear in the formula bar when the cell is selected; a hidden scenario doesn't appear in the Scenario Manager dialog box.
   - Text boxes, macro buttons, and some worksheet dialog box controls (see the section later in this chapter titled "Using Dialog Box Controls on a Worksheet") also can have *locked text,* which prevents the text they contain from being altered.
2. Turn on the worksheet protection.

These steps are outlined in more detail in the following sections.

Setting Up Protection Formatting for Cells

By default, all worksheet cells are formatted as locked and visible. This means that you have three options when setting up your protection formatting:

- If you want to protect every cell, leave the formatting as it is and turn on the worksheet protection.
- If you want certain cells unlocked (for data entry, for example), select the appropriate cells and unlock them before turning on worksheet protection. Similarly, if you want certain cells hidden, select the cells and hide them.

- If you want only selected cells locked, select all the cells and unlock them. Then select the cells you want protected and lock them. To keep only selected formulas visible, hide every formula and then make the appropriate range visible.

Follow the steps in Procedure 63.1 to set up protection formatting for worksheet cells.

PROCEDURE 63.1. SETTING UP PROTECTION FORMATTING FOR WORKSHEET CELLS.

1. Select the cells for which you want to adjust the protection formatting.
2. Select the Format | Cells command and, in the Format Cells dialog box, activate the Protection tab. Excel displays protection options for the range (see Figure 63.1).

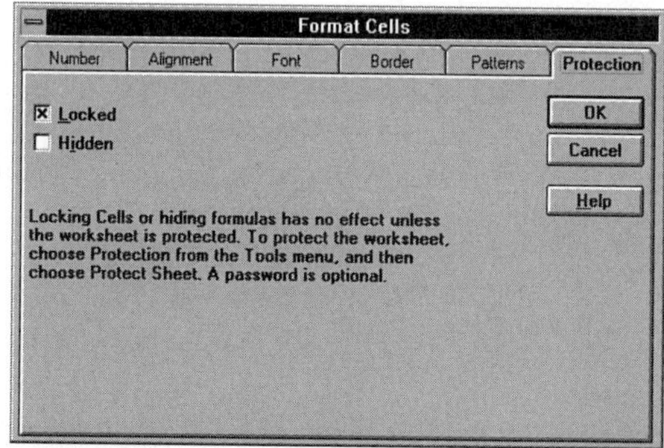

FIGURE 63.1.
Use the Protection tab in the Format Cells dialog box to set up the protection formatting for individual worksheet cells.

3. To lock the cells' contents, activate the **L**ocked check box. To unlock cells, deactivate this check box.
4. To hide the cells' formulas, activate the H**i**dden check box. To make the cells' formulas visible, deactivate the check box.

SUPER TIP

Hiding a formula prevents only the formula from being displayed in the formula bar; the results appear inside the cell itself. If you also want to hide the cell's contents, create an empty custom numeric format (;;;) and assign this format to the cell. For details on creating a custom numeric format, see Chapter 7, "Formatting Numbers, Dates, and Times."

5. Click on OK or press Enter.

Setting Up Protection Formatting for Objects

Excel locks all worksheet objects by default (and it locks the text in text boxes, macro buttons, and some worksheet dialog box controls; see the section in this chapter titled "Using Dialog Box Controls on a Worksheet"). As with cells, you have three options for protecting objects:

- If you want to protect every object, leave the formatting as it is and turn on the worksheet protection.
- If you want certain objects unlocked, select the appropriate objects and unlock them before turning on worksheet protection.
- If you want only selected objects locked, select all the objects and unlock them. Then select the objects you want protected and lock them.

SUPER TIP

To select all the objects in a sheet, choose the **E**dit | **G**o To command, click on the **S**pecial button in the Go To dialog box, and then activate the O**b**jects option.

Follow the steps in Procedure 63.2 to set up protection formatting for worksheet objects.

PROCEDURE 63.2. SETTING UP PROTECTION FORMATTING FOR WORKSHEET OBJECTS.

1. Select the objects for which you want to adjust the protection formatting.
2. Select the F**o**rmat | Object command and, in the Format Object dialog box, activate the Protection tab. Excel displays protection options for objects.
3. To lock the objects, activate the **L**ocked check box. To unlock them, deactivate this check box.
4. For text boxes or macro buttons, activate the Lock **T**ext check to protect the text. Deactivate this check box to unlock the text.
5. Click on OK or press Enter.

Setting Up Protection Formatting for Scenarios

Similar to cells, scenarios are normally locked and visible. However, you can't work with scenarios in groups, so you have to set up their protection formatting individually. Procedure 63.3 shows you the steps.

PROCEDURE 63.3. SETTING UP PROTECTION FORMATTING FOR SCENARIOS.

1. Select the Tools | Scenarios command. The Scenario Manager dialog box appears.
2. Highlight the scenario in the Scenarios list and then click on the Edit button. Excel displays the Edit Scenario dialog box, shown in Figure 63.2.

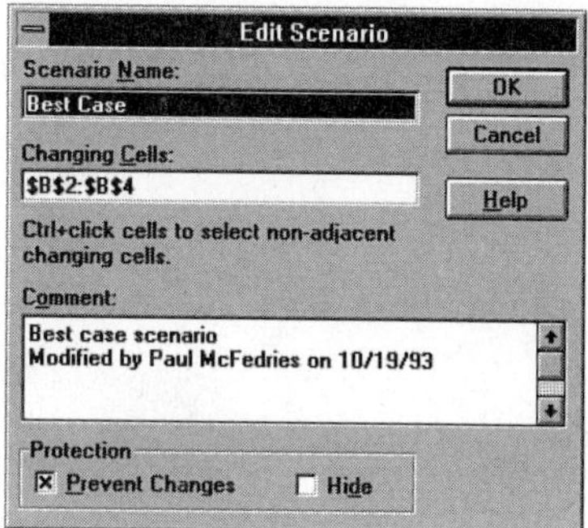

FIGURE 63.2.
Use the Edit Scenario dialog box to set up protection formatting for a scenario.

3. To lock the scenario, activate the Prevent Changes check box. To unlock it, deactivate this check box.
4. To hide the scenario, activate the Hide check box, or deactivate it to unhide the scenario.
5. Click on OK or press Enter. Excel displays the Scenario Values dialog box.
6. Enter new values, if necessary, and then click on OK or press Enter.
7. Repeat steps 2-6 to set the protection formatting for other scenarios.
8. When you're done, click on Close to return to the worksheet.

Protecting a Worksheet

At this point, you've formatted the cells, objects, or scenarios for protection. To activate the protection, follow the steps in Procedure 63.4.

PROCEDURE 63.4. PROTECTING A WORKSHEET.

1. Select the Tools | Protection | Protect Sheet command. Excel displays the Protect Sheet dialog box, shown in Figure 63.3.

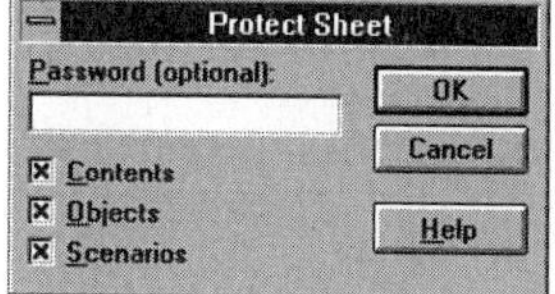

FIGURE 63.3.
Use the Protect Sheet dialog box to activate your protection formatting.

2. For added security, you can enter a password in the **P**assword edit box. This means that no one can turn off the worksheet's protection without first entering the password. If you decide to enter a password, keep the following guidelines in mind:
   - When you enter a password, Excel masks it with asterisks. If you're not sure whether you entered the word correctly, don't worry. Excel will ask you to confirm it.
   - Passwords can be up to 255 characters long, and you can use any combination of letters, numbers, spaces, and other symbols.
   - Keep passwords short and meaningful so they're easier to remember.

> **SUPER CAUTION**
>
> If you forget your password, there is no way to retrieve it, and you will never be able to access your worksheet. As an added precaution, you might want to write down your password and store it in a safe place.

   - Excel differentiates between uppercase and lowercase letters, so remember the capitalization you use.
3. Select what you want to protect: **C**ontents, **O**bjects, or **S**cenarios.
4. Click on OK or press Enter.
5. If you entered a password, Excel asks you to confirm it. Reenter the password and then click on OK or press Enter.

> **SUPER TIP**
>
> To navigate only the unlocked cells in a protected document, use the Tab key (or Shift+Tab to move backwards). Tab avoids the locked cells altogether (which you can still move to by using the arrow keys or the mouse) and always jumps to the next unlocked cell. If you happen to be on the last unlocked cell, Tab wraps around to the first unlocked cell.

To turn off the protection, select the **T**ools | **P**rotection | Un**p**rotect Sheet command. If you entered a password, Excel displays the Unprotect Sheet dialog box. Type the password in the **P**assword edit box and then click on OK or press Enter.

Protecting Windows and Workbook Structures

You also can protect your windows and workbook structures. When you protect a window, Excel does the following:

- The window's maximize and minimize buttons, Control-menu box, and borders are hidden. This means the window can't be moved, sized, or closed.
- When the window is active, the following commands are disabled on the **W**indow menu: **N**ew Window, **S**plit, and **F**reeze Panes. The **A**rrange command remains active, but it has no effect on the protected window. The **H**ide and **U**nhide commands remain active.

When you protect a workbook's structure, Excel does the following:

- The **E**dit menu's De**l**ete Sheet and **M**ove or Copy Sheet commands are disabled.
- The **I**nsert menu's **W**orksheet, C**h**art, and **M**acro commands have no effect on the workbook.
- The Scenario Manager can't create a summary report.

Follow the steps in Procedure 63.5 to protect windows and workbook structures.

PROCEDURE 63.5. PROTECTING A WINDOW OR WORKBOOK STRUCTURE.

1. Activate the window or workbook you want to protect.
2. Select the **T**ools | **P**rotection | Protect **W**orkbook command. Excel displays the Protect Workbook dialog box, shown in Figure 63.4.

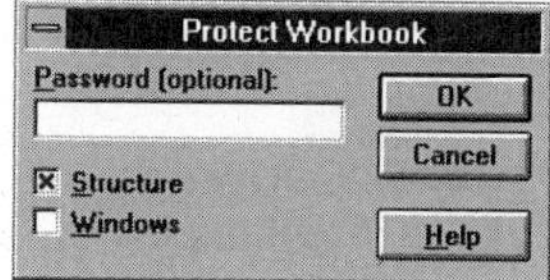

FIGURE 63.4.
The Protect Workbook dialog box.

3. Enter a password in the **P**assword edit box, if required. Follow the same guidelines outlined in Procedure 63.4.
4. Select what you want to protect: **S**tructure or **W**indows.
5. Click on OK or press Enter.
6. If you entered a password, Excel asks you to confirm it. Reenter the password and click on OK or press Enter.

Protecting a File

For workbooks with confidential data, merely protecting cells or sheets may not be enough. For a higher level of security, Excel gives you three options (listed in order of increasing security):

- You can have Excel recommend that a workbook be opened as *read-only*. A read-only document can be changed, but you can't save your changes. Or, more accurately, you can save changes, but only to a file with a different name. The original file always remains intact. Note that Excel only recommends that the file be opened as read-only. You also can open the file with full read/write privileges.

- You can assign a password for saving changes. Users who know this password (the *write reservation password*) are assigned write privileges and can save changes to the workbook. All others can open the file as read-only.
- You can assign a password for opening a document. This is useful for workbooks with confidential information, such as payroll data. Only users who know the password can open the file.

To set these security options, follow the steps in Procedure 63.6.

PROCEDURE 63.6. PROTECTING A FILE.

1. Activate the workbook and select the **F**ile | Save **A**s command (or press F12).
2. In the Save As dialog box, click on the **O**ptions button. Excel displays the Save Options dialog box, shown in Figure 63.5.

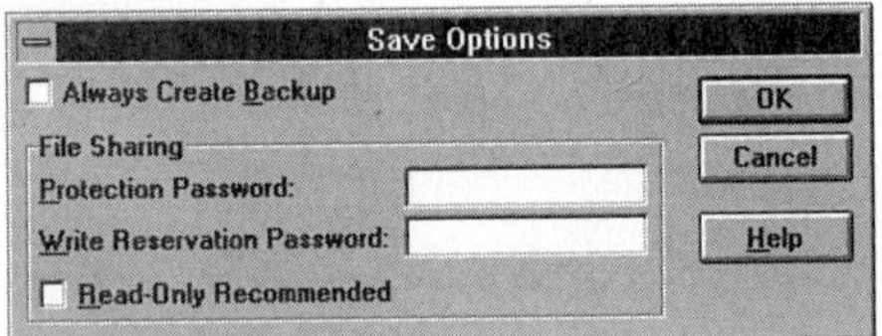

FIGURE 63.5.
Use the Save Options dialog box to set up various levels of security for a worksheet file.

3. If you want Excel to recommend the file be opened as read-only, activate the **R**ead-Only Recommended check box.
4. To restrict the write privileges when opening the worksheet, enter a password in the **W**rite Reservation Password edit box.
5. To prevent unauthorized users from opening the file, enter a password in the **P**rotection Password edit box.

SUPER NOTE

When entering passwords, follow the same guidelines I outlined earlier for worksheet protection (see Procedure 63.4).

6. Click on OK or press Enter.
7. If you entered passwords, Excel asks you to confirm them. Reenter the passwords and click on OK or press Enter. Excel returns you to the Save As dialog box.

8. Click on OK or press Enter. Excel asks whether you want to replace the existing file.
9. Click on OK or press Enter.

Troubleshooting Formulas

Despite your best efforts, errors might appear in your formulas. These errors can be mathematical (for example, dividing by zero) or simply that Excel can't interpret the formula. In the latter case, problems can be caught while you're entering the formula. For example, if you try to enter a formula that has unbalanced parentheses, Excel won't accept the entry; it displays an error message instead.

SUPER TIP

If you try to enter an incorrect formula, Excel won't enable you to do anything else until you either fix the problem or cancel the operation (which means you lose your work). If the formula is a complex one, you may not be able to see the problem right away. Rather than deleting all your work, place an apostrophe (') at the beginning of the formula to convert it to text. This way, you can save your work while you try to figure out the problem.

Excel's Error Values

For other kinds of errors, Excel displays one of the following error values in the cell:

`#DIV/0!` This error almost always means that the cell's formula is trying to divide by 0. The cause is usually a reference to a cell that is either blank or contains the value `0`. Check the cell's precedents to look for possible culprits. You'll also see `#DIV/0!` if you enter an inappropriate argument in some functions. `MOD()`, for example, returns `#DIV/0!` if the second argument is `0`.

SUPER NOTE

To check items such as cell precedents and dependents, see the section later in this chapter titled "Auditing a Worksheet."

`#N/A`	This value is short for "not available," and it means that the formula couldn't return a legitimate result. You usually see `#N/A` when you use an inappropriate argument in a function. `HLOOKUP()` and `VLOOKUP()`, for example, return `#N/A` if the lookup value is smaller than the first value in the lookup range.
`#NAME?`	You'll see the `#NAME?` error when Excel doesn't recognize a name you used in a formula. Make sure you've defined the name and that you've spelled it correctly. You'll also see `#NAME?` if you enter a string without surrounding it with quotation marks, or if you enter a range and accidentally omit the colon.
`#NULL!`	Excel displays this error when you use the intersection operator (see Chapter 60, "Advanced Range Topics") on two ranges that have no cells in common.
`#NUM!`	This error means there is a problem with a number in your formula. For example, you'll see `#NUM!` if you enter a negative number as the argument for the `SQRT()` or `LOG()` functions.
`#REF!`	The `#REF!` error means that your formula contains an invalid reference. You usually see this error when you delete a cell to which the formula refers. You need to add the cell back in or adjust the formula reference.
`#VALUE!`	When Excel generates a `#VALUE!` error, you've used an inappropriate argument in a function. For example, you might have entered a string instead of a number or reference.

Troubleshooting Techniques

Tracking down formula errors is one of the necessary evils you'll face when building your worksheets. To make this chore a little easier, this section presents the following simple techniques you can use to sniff out problems:

- To help you avoid mismatched parentheses, Excel provides two visual clues in the formula bar. The first clue occurs when you type a right parenthesis. Excel highlights both the right parenthesis and its corresponding left parenthesis. If you type what you think is the last right parenthesis and Excel doesn't highlight the first left parenthesis, your parentheses are unbalanced. The second clue occurs when you use the left and right arrow keys to navigate a formula. When you cross over a parenthesis, Excel highlights the other parenthesis in the pair.
- When entering function names and defined names, use all lowercase letters. If Excel recognizes a name, it will convert the function to all uppercase and the defined name to its original case. If no conversion occurs, you either misspelled the name, you haven't defined it yet, or you're using a function from an add-in macro that isn't loaded.

SUPER TIP

You also can use the **I**nsert | **F**unction (shortcut key Shift+F3) or **I**nsert | **N**ame | **P**aste (shortcut F3) commands to enter functions and names safely.

- You can calculate complex formulas one term at a time. In the formula bar, highlight the term you want to calculate and then press F9. Excel converts the highlighted section into its value. Make sure you press the Esc key when you're done to avoid entering the formula with just the calculated values.

Auditing a Worksheet

Some formula errors are the result of referencing other cells that contain errors or inappropriate values. To find out, you can use Excel 5.0's new auditing features to trace cell precedents, dependents, and errors.

How Auditing Works

If a formula refers to a number of cells, and some of those cells also refer to other cells, tracking down the source of a problem can become a nightmare. To help out, Excel's auditing features can create *tracers*—arrows that literally point out the cells involved in a formula. You can use tracers to find three kinds of cells:

Precedents	Cells that are directly or indirectly referenced in a formula. For example, suppose cell B4 contains the formula =B2; B2 is a direct precedent of B4. Now suppose that cell B2 contains the formula =A2/2; A2 is a direct precedent of B2, but it's also an *indirect* precedent of cell B4.
Dependents	Cells that are directly or indirectly referenced by a formula. In the previous example, cell B2 is a direct dependent of A2, and B4 is an indirect dependent of A2.
Errors	Cells that contain an error value and are directly or indirectly referenced in a formula (and therefore cause the same error to appear in the formula).

Figure 63.6 shows a worksheet with three examples of tracer arrows:

- Cell B4 contains the formula =B2, and B2 contains =A2/2. The arrows (they're blue on-screen) point out the precedents (direct and indirect) of B4.
- Cell D4 contains the formula =D2, and D2 contains =D1/0. The latter produces the `#DIV/0!` error. Therefore, the same error appears in cell D4. The arrow (it's red on-screen) is pointing out the source of the error.

- Cell G4 contains the formula =Sheet2!A1. Excel displays the dashed arrow with the worksheet icon whenever the precedent or dependent exists on a different worksheet.

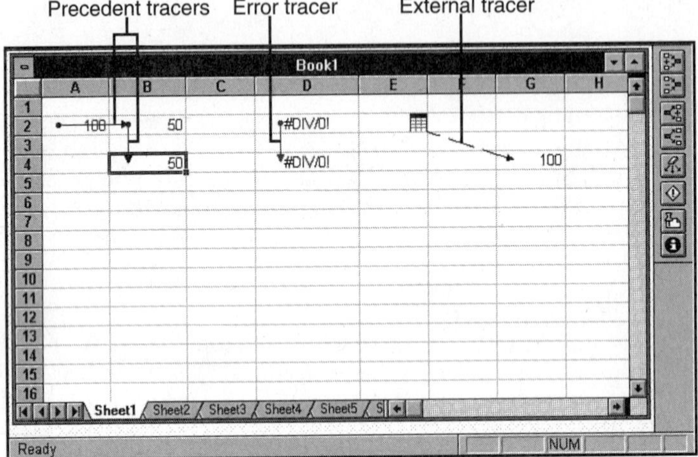

FIGURE 63.6.
The three types of tracer arrows.

Tracing Cell Precedents

To trace cell precedents, follow the steps in Procedure 63.7.

PROCEDURE 63.7. TRACING CELL PRECEDENTS.

1. Select the cell containing the formula whose precedents you want to trace.
2. Select the **T**ools | Au**d**iting | **T**race Precedents command. Excel adds a tracer arrow to each direct precedent.

You also can click on this tool in the Auditing toolbar to trace precedents.

3. Keep repeating step 2 to see more levels of precedents.

SUPER TIP

You also can trace precedents by double-clicking on the cell, provided you turn off in-cell editing. You do this by selecting the **T**ools | **O**ptions command and then deactivating the **E**dit Directly in Cell check box in the Edit tab. Now when you double-click on a cell, Excel selects the cell's precedents.

Tracing Cell Dependents

To trace cell dependents, follow the steps in Procedure 63.8.

PROCEDURE 63.8. TRACING CELL DEPENDENTS.

1. Select the cell whose dependents you want to trace.
2. Select the Tools | Auditing | Trace Dependents command. Excel adds a tracer arrow to each direct dependent.

You also can click on this tool in the Auditing toolbar to trace dependents.

3. Keep repeating step 2 to see more levels of dependents.

Tracing Cell Errors

To trace cell errors, follow the steps in Procedure 63.9.

PROCEDURE 63.9. TRACING CELL ERRORS.

1. Select the cell containing the error you want to trace.
2. Select the Tools | Auditing | Trace Error command. Excel adds a tracer arrow to each cell that produced the error.

You also can click on this tool in the Auditing toolbar to trace errors.

Removing Tracer Arrows

To remove the tracer arrows, you have three choices:

- Select the Tools | Auditing | Remove All Arrows command to remove all the tracer arrows.
- Click on the Remove All Arrows tool in the Auditing toolbar to remove all tracer arrows.

Click on the Remove All Arrows tool in the Auditing toolbar to remove all tracer arrows.

- Use the following buttons on the Auditing toolbar to remove precedent and dependent arrows one level at a time.

Click on the Remove Precedent Arrows tool in the Auditing toolbar to remove precedent arrows one level at a time.

Click on the Remove Dependent Arrows tool in the Auditing toolbar to remove dependent arrows one level at a time.

Using Dialog Box Controls on a Worksheet

One of the slick new features of Excel 5.0 is that it enables you to place dialog box controls such as spinners, check boxes, and list boxes directly on a worksheet. You can then link the values returned by these controls to a cell to create an elegant method for entering data.

Using the Forms Toolbar

You add the dialog box controls by selecting tools from the Forms toolbar, shown in Figure 63.7. Following is a summary of the tools you can use to place controls on a worksheet.

SUPER NOTE

The following descriptions are purposely brief. For a more complete discussion of each control, see Chapter 55, "Creating Custom Dialog Boxes in Visual Basic."

Group box	Creates a box to hold option buttons.
Check box	Creates a check box. If activated, a check box returns the value TRUE in its linked cell. If it is deactivated, it returns FALSE.
Option button	Creates an option button. In each group of option buttons, the user can select only one option. The returned value is a number indicating which option button was activated. The value 1 represents the first button added to the group, 2 signifies the second button, and so on.
List box	Creates a list box from which the user can select an item. The list is given by a worksheet range, and the value returned to the linked cell is the number of the item chosen.
Drop-down	Creates a drop-down list box. This box is similar to a list box; however, the control shows only one item at a time—until it is dropped down.
Scrollbar	Creates a scrollbar control. Unlike window scrollbars, a scrollbar control can be used to select a number from a range of values. Clicking on the arrows or dragging the scrollbox changes the value of the control. This value is what is returned to the linked cell.

Spinner	Creates a spinner. Similar to a scrollbar, you can use spinners to select a number between a maximum and minimum value by clicking on the arrows. The number is returned to the linked cell.

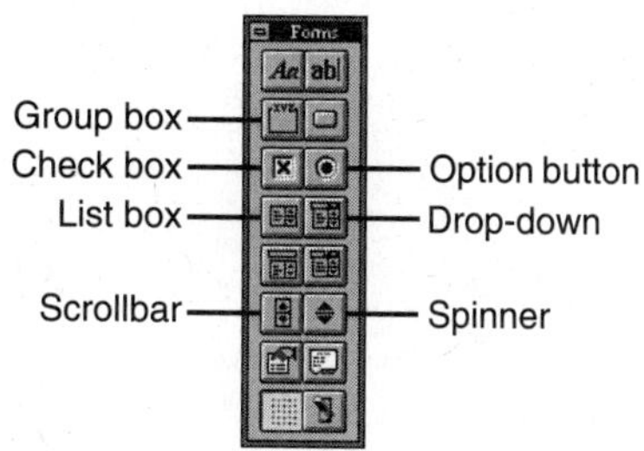

FIGURE 63.7.
Use the Forms toolbar to draw dialog box controls on a worksheet.

SUPER NOTE

You can add a command button to a worksheet, but you have to assign a macro to it. See Chapter 59, "Visual Basic Tips and Techniques" and Chapter 49, "Macro Tips and Techniques," to learn how to create macro buttons.

Adding a Control to a Worksheet

You add controls to a worksheet using the same steps you use to create any graphic object. Procedure 63.10 takes you through the steps.

PROCEDURE 63.10. ADDING A DIALOG BOX CONTROL TO A WORKSHEET.

1. Click on the control you want to create. The mouse pointer changes to a crosshair.
2. Move the pointer onto the worksheet and drag the mouse pointer to create the object.
3. Excel assigns a default caption to group boxes, check boxes, and option buttons. To edit this caption, double-click on it and enter the text you want.

Once you've added a control, you can move it and size it as needed. See Chapter 27, "Editing Graphic Objects," for instructions.

SUPER CAUTION

The controls you add are "live" in the sense that when you click on them, you're working the control (activating it and changing its value). To select a control for sizing or moving, you need to hold down the Ctrl key before clicking on it.

Linking a Control to a Cell Value

To use the dialog box controls for inputting data, you need to associate each control with a worksheet cell. Procedure 63.11 shows you how it's done.

PROCEDURE 63.11. LINKING A DIALOG BOX CONTROL TO A WORKSHEET CELL.

1. Select the control with which you want to work.
2. Select the Format | Object command to display the Format Object dialog box.

SUPER TIP

A quick way to display the Format Object dialog box is by either selecting the control and pressing Ctrl+1 or right-clicking on the control and selecting Format Object from the shortcut menu.

You also can click on this tool in the Forms toolbar to display the Format Object dialog box.

3. Activate the Control tab and then use the Cell Link box to enter the cell's reference. You can either type in the reference or select it directly on the worksheet.
4. Click on OK or press Enter to return to the worksheet.

SUPER TIP

Another way to link a control to a cell is to select the control and enter a formula in the formula bar of the form `=cell`. `cell` is an absolute reference to the cell you want to use. For example, to link a control to cell A1, you would enter the following formula:

```
=$A$1
```

SUPER NOTE

When working with option buttons, you only have to enter the linked cell for one of the buttons in a group. Excel automatically adds the reference to the rest.

Figure 63.8 shows a worksheet with several controls and their corresponding linked cells. (To make things a little clearer, I added the numbers you see beside the scroll-bar and spinner; they don't come with the control.)

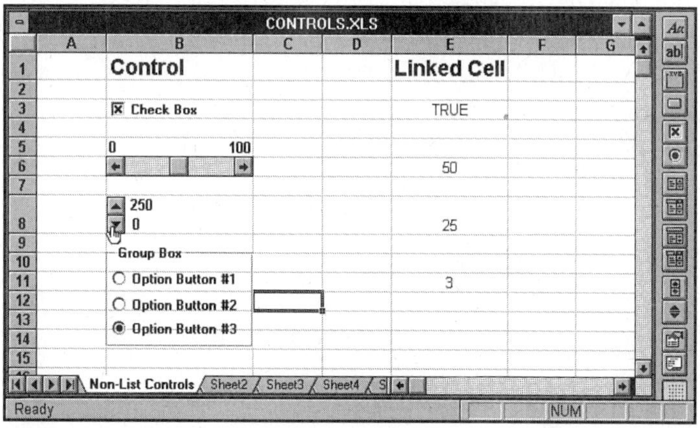

FIGURE 63.8.
A worksheet with several controls and their corresponding linked cells.

Working with List Boxes

List boxes and drop-down lists are different from other controls because you also have to specify a range that contains the items to appear in the list. Follow the steps in Procedure 63.12.

PROCEDURE 63.12. DEFINING A RANGE OF ITEMS FOR A LIST BOX CONTROL.

1. Enter the list items in a range.
2. Select the list control with which you want to work.
3. Select the Format | Object command to display the Format Object dialog box.

SUPER TIP

A quick way to display the Format Object dialog box is by either selecting the list and pressing Ctrl+1 or right-clicking on the list and selecting Format Object from the shortcut menu.

You also can click on this tool in the Forms toolbar to display the Format Object dialog box.

4. Activate the Control tab and then use the **I**nput Range box to enter a reference to the range of items. You can either type in the reference or select it directly on the worksheet.
5. Click on OK or press Enter to return to the worksheet.

Figure 63.9 shows a worksheet with a list box and a drop-down list. The list used by both controls is range A2:A8. Notice that the linked cells display the number of the list selection, not the selection itself. To get the selected list item, you could use an `INDEX()` function with the following syntax:

`INDEX(`*`list_range`*`,`*`list_selection`*`)`

`list_range`	The range used in the list box or drop-down list.
`list_selection`	The number of the item selected in the list.

FIGURE 63.9.
A worksheet with a list box and drop-down list control.

For example, to find out the item selected from the list box in Figure 63.9, you would use the following formula:

```
=INDEX(A2:A8,F3)
```

Chapter

64

Exchanging Data with Other Applications

Excel doesn't exist in a vacuum. You often have to import data to Excel from other applications (such as a database file or a text file from a mainframe), and just as often you have to export Excel data to other programs (such as a word processor or presentation graphics package). Although these tasks usually are straightforward, you can still run into some problems. Therefore, Excel provides a number of features that can help you avoid these problems. This chapter looks at the various ways you can exchange data between Excel and other applications.

Moving Workbooks Between Excel and Lotus 1-2-3

If it's not overly dramatic to discuss software in terms of geopolitical forces, then I can summarize the current struggle for domination in the spreadsheet market as the struggle between two countries: Excel (in Windows) and Lotus 1-2-3 (in DOS). Both countries seek to expand their borders and increase their populations by offering new perks and features in their software and by encouraging immigration with attractive incentives and entitlement programs.

Even though their governments may have declared a spreadsheet war, the citizens of both countries still need to work together and cross each other's borders with a minimum of culture shock. In this section, I show you how to make Excel and 1-2-3 work together. I also show you how to transfer files back and forth so that you preserve not only worksheet accuracy but also your careful formatting.

SUPER NOTE

If you're switching from 1-2-3 to Excel, Appendix A, "Notes for Lotus 1-2-3 Users Switching to Excel," gives you some helpful hints on making the transition.

Many offices today use a mixture of Excel and 1-2-3. For example, the Accounting department may use 1-2-3 exclusively, whereas the Sales and Marketing departments may have switched to Excel when they converted their machines to Windows. Both types of users often need to exchange information, so it's important that the transition be as smooth as possible. Because Excel recognized this fact long ago, they've made it easy to import 1-2-3 files into Excel and to export Excel files to 1-2-3 format. You have to watch out for some pitfalls, however. I discuss these later.

Importing a 1-2-3 File into Excel

Excel can import 1-2-3 files that are in the following formats:

Lotus Release	*Format*
1A	WKS
2.*x*	WK1
2.3, 2.4 (formatting)	FMT
3.*x*	WK3
3.1, 3.1+ (formatting)	FM3
1-2-3/W	WK3, FM3

To import a 1-2-3 file, follow the steps in Procedure 64.1.

PROCEDURE 64.1. IMPORTING A 1-2-3 FILE INTO EXCEL.

1. Select the **F**ile | **O**pen command.
2. Use the Dri**v**es and **D**irectories lists to select the drive and directory containing the 1-2-3 file you want to import.
3. To see only 1-2-3 files in the File **N**ame list, select Lotus 1-2-3 Files (*.WK*) from the List Files of **T**ype drop-down list.
4. Select the file in the File **N**ame list.
5. Click on OK or press Enter.

How Excel Imports 1-2-3 Files

Excel usually imports 1-2-3 files without fuss, but you should be aware of the following characteristics of the importing process:

- 3-D worksheets (WK3 format) are imported as multiple-tab workbooks. The 3-D formulas are preserved, and each 3-D level is given its own workbook tab.
- If Excel can't interpret a formula, it uses the calculated value of the formula.
- If the worksheet's FMT or FM3 formatting file has the same name as the worksheet and is in the same directory, Excel reads the formatting and tries to duplicate it.
- If the worksheet has no formatting file, Excel uses Courier 10 as the Normal style font.
- Unprotected cells appear in a blue font.
- Formula comments (that is, any text that follows a semicolon in a formula) get imported into a cell note.

Figure 64.1 shows a typical 1-2-3 worksheet (without an associated FMT file) imported into Excel.

FIGURE 64.1.
A 1-2-3 worksheet imported into Excel.

LOANCOST.WK1

	A	B	C	D	E	F	G
1							
2					Loan Cost Analysis		
3							
4							
5		Loan Amount			100,000.00		
6		Beginning Interest Rate			9.25%		
7		Points/costs paid for loan			2.00		
8		Number of payments/year			12.00		
9		Payout length of loan in yrs			30.00	Yrs	
10		Prepare Amort Table for			4.00	Yrs	
11							
12		Base Payment Amount			822.68		
13		Computed Effective Rate of Interest				9.70%	
14							
15			Int.			----Cumulative----	
16		Beg Bal	Rate	Interest	Princ.	Princ.	Interest
17							
18	1	102,000.00	9.25%	786.25	36.43	36.43	786.25

Sheet1
Ready Calculate NUM

Excel Changes Its Settings When You Import a 1-2-3 File

When you import a 1-2-3 file, Excel changes some option settings to make using a 1-2-3 worksheet easier for you. The settings it changes are in the Transition tab of the Options dialog box, shown in Figure 64.2. You can display this dialog box by selecting the **T**ools | **O**ptions command.

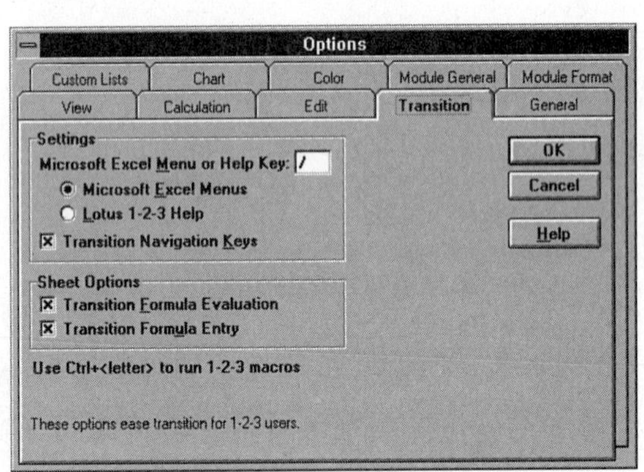

FIGURE 64.2.
The Transition tab in the Options dialog box controls settings that make Excel operate more like 1-2-3.

Transition Navigation **K**eys: Excel activates this check box, which changes the functions of the following keys:

Key	*New Function*
Home	Moves to cell A1
Tab	Moves right one page
Shift+Tab	Moves left one page
Ctrl+Right arrow	Moves right one screen
Ctrl+Left arrow	Moves left one screen

"	Right-aligns the cell text
^	Centers the cell text
\	Fills the cell with the characters that follow the backslash (\)

Transition Formula Evaluation: Excel also activates this check box. This option causes Excel to handle formula evaluation in the following ways:

- If the lookup value in the `HLOOKUP()` and `VLOOKUP()` functions is text, Excel does three things differently: (1) it looks for exact matches instead of the largest value that is less than or equal to the lookup value; (2) the row or column you're using for the search can be in any order; and (3) if the third argument (the one that tells Excel how many rows or columns into the table to look for the desired value) is `1`, Excel returns the offset of the matched lookup value, not the value itself. For example, if you're using `VLOOKUP()` and the lookup value is in the fourth row of the lookup column, Excel returns 4 if `VLOOKUP()`'s third argument is `1`.
- Conditional tests return 1 instead of `TRUE` and 0 instead of `FALSE`.
- When one of its arguments is negative, the `MOD()` function returns different values depending on the setting of this check box. For example, the formula =MOD(-24,10) returns 6 when Transition Formula Evaluation is off and –4 if it's on.
- Text strings are assigned the value 0.
- You can't concatenate numeric values. If you try to, Excel returns a `#VALUE!` error.
- You can't use string functions on numeric values. If you try to, Excel returns a `#VALUE!` error.

Transition Formula Entry: Excel activates this check box if there are any macro names on the worksheet. This option causes Excel to handle formula entry in the following ways:

- If you enter a reference that corresponds to a named range you've defined, Excel automatically converts the reference to the appropriate name after you confirm the entry. Note that this works only for contiguous ranges. Because Excel enables you to define noncontiguous ranges, this feature might not always work.
- If a formula contains a range name, activating the formula bar changes the name to its underlying reference.
- If you delete a range name, formulas containing the name automatically convert to their underlying reference.
- If you add a dollar sign ($) before a range name, Excel makes the name absolute.

SUPER CAUTION

As soon as you've opened a 1-2-3 worksheet, don't change the settings of these three check boxes. Changing them while you are working on the sheet can throw off the worksheet calculations.

You should be aware that Excel also turns off its automatic number formatting feature when you're working with a 1-2-3 worksheet. In an Excel worksheet, if you enter `3-mar-94`, Excel knows you've entered a date and formats the cell automatically with the dd-mmm-yy format. In a Lotus 1-2-3 worksheet, however, entering `3-mar-94` produces a `#NAME?` error.

Saving a 1-2-3 Worksheet as an Excel File

If you apply Excel-specific formatting or features to a 1-2-3 worksheet, you lose these changes when you save the sheet in a 1-2-3 format. If you want to keep these nontranslatable changes, you need to save the file in Excel's format. (You can just rename the file with an .XLS extension.) Procedure 64.2 takes you through the steps.

PROCEDURE 64.2. SAVING A 1-2-3 WORKSHEET AS AN EXCEL FILE.

1. Select the **F**ile | Save **A**s command. Excel displays the Save As dialog box.
2. In the Save File as **T**ype drop-down list, select Microsoft Excel Workbook.
3. If necessary, use the Dri**v**es and **D**irectories lists to select a location for the file.
4. Use the File **N**ame box to enter a name for the worksheet (Excel adds its default .XLS extension automatically).
5. Click on OK or press Enter. Excel converts the file into an Excel worksheet.

Exporting an Excel File in 1-2-3 Format

If you need to export an Excel file in 1-2-3 format, follow the steps in Procedure 64.3.

PROCEDURE 64.3. EXPORTING AN EXCEL WORKSHEET IN 1-2-3 FORMAT.

1. Select the **F**ile | Save **A**s command to display the Save As dialog box.
2. In the Save File as **T**ype drop-down list, select one of the Lotus 1-2-3 file formats. If you want to create a Lotus formatting file as well, make sure you select either the WK3,FM3 (1-2-3) or the WK1,FMT (1-2-3) option.
3. If necessary, use the Dri**v**es and **D**irectories lists to select a location for the file.

4. Use the File Name box to enter a name for the worksheet (Excel automatically adds the required extension).
5. Click on OK or press Enter. Excel converts the file into a Lotus worksheet.

Some Notes About Exporting Excel Files to 1-2-3

Exporting Excel files, like importing 1-2-3 files, is generally straightforward. However, you should keep the following points in mind when exporting your Excel workbooks:

- If you select a 1-2-3 format other than WK3, Excel exports only the active sheet.
- If Excel can't convert a formula into something 1-2-3 understands, it exports the value of the formula instead.
- References to noncontiguous ranges are not exported (because they are not supported by 1-2-3). Intersection and union operators (see Chapter 60, "Advanced Range Topics") also are not exported.
- The WKS format can handle only 2,048 rows, and the WK1 and WK3 formats can handle only 8,192 rows. References above these limits are wrapped around to the top of the worksheet. For example, converting a sheet with a reference to A8193 into the WK1 format changes the reference to A1. Because this probably is undesirable, you should adjust the layout of the worksheet before exporting it.
- All Excel error values are exported as 1-2-3's `@ERR` function, except `#N/A`, which is exported as the `@NA` function.
- Named constants and formulas are not exported. Excel converts the name to the constant or formula instead.
- Arrays are not exported. Excel uses the values in the array instead.

Exchanging Data with Windows Applications

To use text and graphics from another Windows application in Excel (or to use Excel data in another Windows application), you can use any of the following methods:

Cut and paste using the Clipboard: With this method, you cut or copy data from one Windows application and paste it into the other.
Linking: With this method, you use a special paste command that sets up a link between the original data and the new copy. When you change the original data, the linked copy is updated automatically.
Embedding: With this method, you create a special copy of a file or object from another application and paste the copy into Excel. This copy contains not only the data but also all the underlying information associated with the originating application (file structure, formatting codes, and so on).

These methods are described in the next three sections.

SUPER NOTE

Linking and embedding are possible only with applications that support the object linking and embedding (OLE) standard.

Using the Clipboard

The *Clipboard* is a temporary storage location in memory for cut or copied data. It can store text, numbers, graphics, or anything you can cut or copy in a Windows application. You then can switch to a completely different program and paste the Clipboard data. If you don't want to embed or link the data, follow the steps in Procedure 64.4 to exchange data using the Clipboard.

PROCEDURE 64.4. EXCHANGING DATA USING THE CLIPBOARD.

1. Activate the application containing the original data (this is called the *server* application).
2. Select the data, and then select either the **Edit** | **Cut** or **Edit** | **Copy** command. The data is transferred to the Clipboard. Figure 64.3 shows a table in Word for Windows that has been selected and copied.

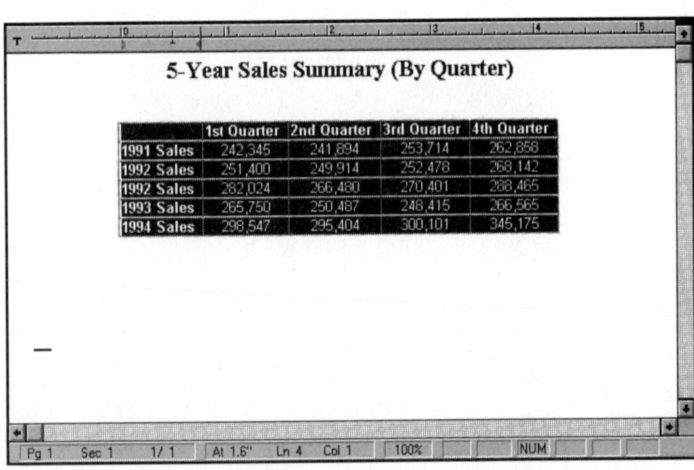

5-Year Sales Summary (By Quarter)

	1st Quarter	2nd Quarter	3rd Quarter	4th Quarter
1991 Sales	242,345	241,894	253,714	262,858
1992 Sales	251,400	249,914	252,478	268,142
1992 Sales	282,024	266,480	270,401	288,465
1993 Sales	265,750	250,487	248,415	266,565
1994 Sales	298,547	295,404	300,101	345,175

FIGURE 64.3.
A Word for Windows table that has been selected and copied.

SUPER TIP

If you want to copy an Excel range to another application as a picture, select the range, hold down the Shift key, and select the **Edit** | **Copy Picture** command.

3. Switch to the application that you want to receive the data (the *client* application).
4. Move to where you want the data to appear and select the **E**dit | **P**aste command. The data is pasted from the Clipboard. Figure 64.4 shows the Word for Windows table pasted into an Excel worksheet.

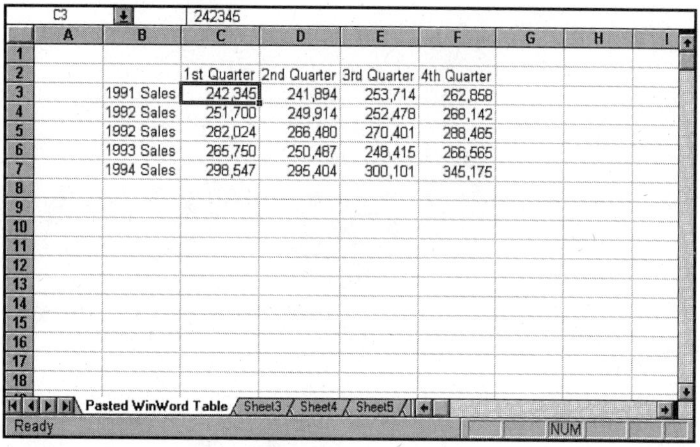
C3
242345
1st Quarter 2nd Quarter 3rd Quarter 4th Quarter
1991 Sales 242,345 241,894 253,714 262,858
1992 Sales 251,700 249,914 252,478 268,142
1992 Sales 282,024 266,480 270,401 288,465
1993 Sales 265,750 250,487 248,415 266,565
1994 Sales 298,547 295,404 300,101 345,175
Pasted WinWord Table
Sheet3
Sheet4
Sheet5
Ready
NUM

FIGURE 64.4.
The Word for Windows table pasted to an Excel worksheet.

If you're pasting text into Excel, follow these guidelines when you select a location for the text:

- If you want to place the text in a text box, double-click on the text box to get the insertion point, and then position the insertion point where you want the text to appear.
- If you want to position the text within a single cell (provided that there are less than 255 characters in the selection), activate either in-cell editing or the formula bar, and then position the insertion point.
- If you've selected any object before pasting (such as a graphics image or text box), Excel embeds the text as a Picture object. (See the section in this chapter titled "Embedding Objects in a Worksheet.")

Linking Data

If you use the normal paste command to paste data from a server file into a client application, you must manually change the copied data in the client file whenever the data in the server file is changed. By including a special *link* reference when you perform the paste, however, you can eliminate this extra work, because the link changes the copied data automatically. This link tells the client application where the document came from so that the link can check the server file for changes. If the server file has been altered, the link automatically updates the client application's copy. Procedure 64.5 shows you how to copy and link data in Excel.

PROCEDURE 64.5. LINKING COPIED DATA IN EXCEL.

1. Activate the application containing the original data (the *server*).
2. Select the data, then select **E**dit | **C**opy to copy the data to the Clipboard.
3. Switch to Excel (the *client*) and activate the cell or object that you want to receive the data.
4. Select the **E**dit | Paste **S**pecial command. Excel displays the Paste Special dialog box, shown in Figure 64.5.

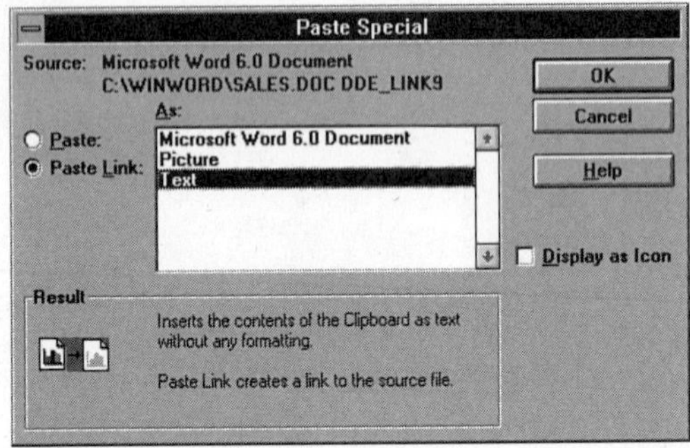

FIGURE 64.5.
Use the Paste Special dialog box to select the type of object to paste and to set up the link.

5. In the **As** list, select the format you want to use for the copied data. The options you see depend on the type of data. If you're copying text, you need to select the Text option.
6. Select the Paste **L**ink option.
7. Click on OK or press Enter. Excel pastes the data and sets up the link.

Figure 64.6 shows the same Word for Windows table, but this time it was pasted with a link. The array formula displayed in the formula bar is called a *remote reference formula.* It tells Excel where the server document is located so that it can update the link when necessary.

SUPER NOTE

The steps to link data copied from Excel to another application are similar to those in Procedure 64.5. Some applications have a Paste Link command on their Edit menu that enables you to paste and link at the same time.

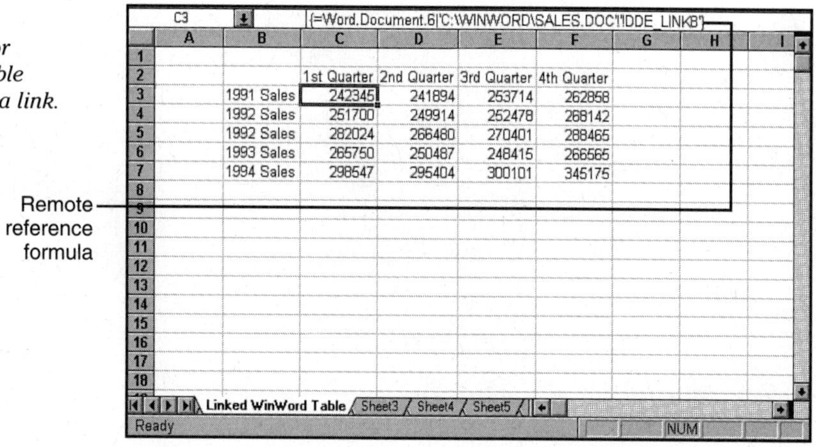

FIGURE 64.6.
The Word for Windows table pasted with a link.

C3 {=Word.Document.6|'C:\WINWORD\SALES.DOC'!'DDE_LINK8'}

	1st Quarter	2nd Quarter	3rd Quarter	4th Quarter
1991 Sales	242345	241894	253714	262858
1992 Sales	251700	249914	252478	268142
1992 Sales	282024	266480	270401	288465
1993 Sales	265750	250487	248415	266565
1994 Sales	298547	295404	300101	345175

Remote reference formula

Linked WinWord Table / Sheet3 / Sheet4 / Sheet5
Ready NUM

Updating Links

After you've pasted and linked some data, Excel maintains the links as follows:

- If both the server application and the Excel workbook (the client) are open, Excel updates the link automatically whenever the data in the server file changes.
- When you open a client workbook that contains automatic links (see the next section), Excel displays a dialog box asking whether you want to update the links. Click on **Y**es to update or **N**o to cancel.
- If you didn't update a link when you opened the client workbook, you can update it at any time by selecting the **E**dit | Lin**k**s command. Then, in the Links dialog box that appears, highlight the link and select the **U**pdate Now button.

Controlling a Link

The problem with linked objects is that they tend to slow you down. Even the smallest change in the server data can cause a delay in the client while the two programs exchange pleasantries. Therefore, many people prefer to control the link themselves by switching from an *automatic* link (where the data gets updated automatically) to a *manual* link (where the data gets updated only when you say so). Procedure 64.6 shows you how to convert to a manual link.

PROCEDURE 64.6. CONVERTING A LINK TO A MANUAL LINK.

1. Activate the workbook containing the link.
2. Select the **E**dit | Lin**k**s command. Excel displays the Links dialog box, shown in Figure 64.7.

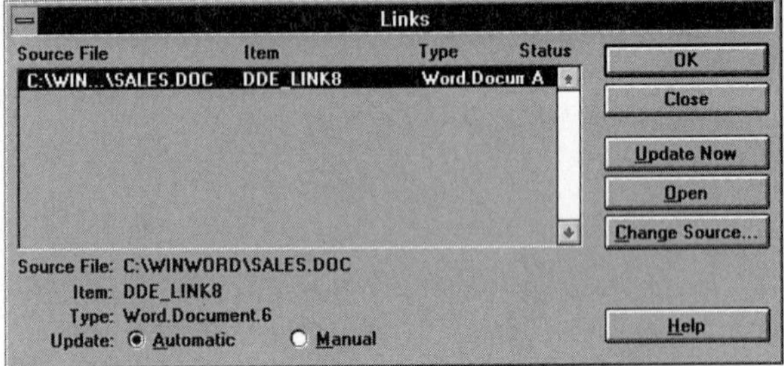

FIGURE 64.7.
Use the Links dialog box to change a link from automatic to manual.

3. Highlight the link you want to change.
4. Select the **M**anual option.
5. Click on OK or press Enter.

With a manual link established, you can update the link by displaying the Links dialog box, highlighting the link, and selecting the **U**pdate Now button.

SUPER TIP

If a workbook contains many links, you might not want to convert them all to manual. Instead, select the **T**ools | **O**ptions command and, in the Calculation tab, deactivate the **U**pdate Remote References check box. This prevents Excel from updating any link, even if you select the Update Now button in the Links dialog box.

Editing a Link

If the name of the server document changes, you need to edit the link to keep the data up-to-date. You can edit the external reference directly, or you can change the source by following the steps in Procedure 64.7.

PROCEDURE 64.7. EDITING A LINK.

1. With the client workbook active, select the **E**dit | Lin**k**s command to display the Links dialog box.
2. Highlight the link you want to change.
3. Select the **C**hange Source button. Excel displays the Change Links dialog box.

SUPER NOTE

The term *source document* is just another name for a server document.

4. Select the new server document, then click on OK or press Enter to return to the Links dialog box.
5. Click on Close to return to the workbook.

Embedding Objects in a Worksheet

When you paste a linked object in a worksheet, Excel doesn't paste the data. Instead, it sets up a remote reference formula that *points to* the data. If Excel can't find the server file—for example, if the file has been moved, renamed, or deleted—the link breaks and Excel displays a `#NAME?` error in any cell that used the remote reference.

Embedding differs from linking in that embedded data becomes part of the worksheet. There is no link to the original server document, so it doesn't matter what happens to the original document. In fact, there is no need for a server file at all because the embedded object maintains its native format. Also, you can easily start the server application simply by double-clicking on one of its objects in the client worksheet. The downside to this convenience is that storing all the information about an embedded object increases the size of the workbook accordingly.

SUPER NOTE

In applications that support the OLE standard, an *object* is, in simplest terms, any data you can place on the Clipboard. It could be a section of text, a graphic image, a chart, or anything else you can select and copy.

There are three ways to embed an object in a worksheet:

- Copy the object from the server application and paste it in the worksheet as an embedded object.
- Insert a new embedded object from within Excel.
- Insert an existing file as an embedded object from within Excel.

Embedding an Object by Pasting

If the object you want to embed already exists, you can place it on the Clipboard and then embed it in the worksheet using the Paste Special command. Procedure 64.8 shows you the steps to follow.

PROCEDURE 64.8. EMBEDDING AN OBJECT BY PASTING.

1. Activate the server application, and open or create the document that contains the object.
2. Select the object you want to embed.

3. Select the **E**dit | **C**opy command to place the data on the Clipboard.
4. Activate Excel and open or create the worksheet that you want to receive the data.
5. Select the cell where you want to paste the data.
6. Select the **E**dit | Paste **S**pecial command to display the Paste Special dialog box.
7. In the **A**s list, select the option that will paste the data as an embedded object. You generally look for one of two clues, depending on the server application:
   - The data type contains the word *Object.*
   - The data type contains the name of the server application.
8. If you want to see the data in the worksheet, skip to step 10. Otherwise, you can display the object as an icon by activating the **D**isplay as Icon check box. The default icon and the Change **I**con button appear (see Figure 64.8).

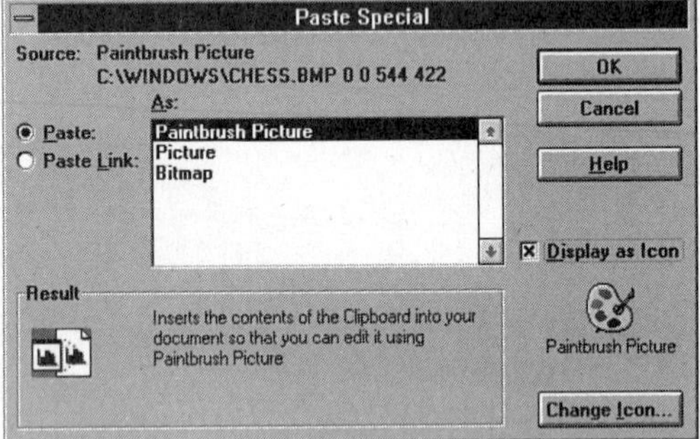

FIGURE 64.8.
You can display an embedded object as an icon.

SUPER NOTE

Why would you want to display the object as an icon? The most common reason is that you don't need to see the data all the time. For example, the object might contain explanatory text for a worksheet model. If users of the model need to read the text, they can double-click on the icon.

9. To choose a different icon, select Change **I**con, and then select the image from the Change Icon dialog box. To use a different icon file, select the **B**rowse button, and then select the file from the Browse dialog box. (The MORICONS.DLL file in your Windows directory contains dozens of icons.) Click on OK or press Enter until you return to the Paste Special dialog box.
10. Click on OK or press Enter. Excel embeds the object in the worksheet.

Figure 64.9 shows a worksheet with a Paintbrush object embedded normally and as an icon.

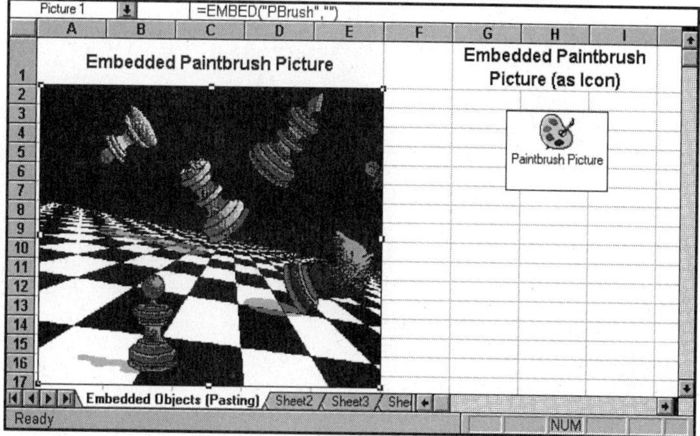

FIGURE 64.9.
A Paintbrush object embedded normally and as an icon.

Embedding a New Object by Inserting

If the object you want to embed doesn't exist, you can use Excel to create a new object in the server application and embed it without creating a separate server document. This is, in fact, the only way to embed an object from one of the mini-applications that ship with Excel and other products. Programs such as Microsoft WordArt and Microsoft Draw are not stand-alone applications, so you can't create separate files. You can use their objects only by inserting them in the client application. Follow the steps in Procedure 64.9 to insert a new server object in an Excel worksheet.

PROCEDURE 64.9. INSERTING A NEW EMBEDDED OBJECT IN A WORKSHEET.

1. Select the cell where you want the object embedded. (This cell represents the upper-left corner of the object.)
2. Select the **I**nsert | **O**bject command and, in the Object dialog box that appears, select the Create New tab, shown in Figure 64.10.
3. In the **O**bject Type list, select the type of object you want to create.

> **SUPER NOTE**
>
> You can display the new object as an icon by activating the Displ**a**y as Icon check box.

4. Click on OK or press Enter. Excel starts the server application.

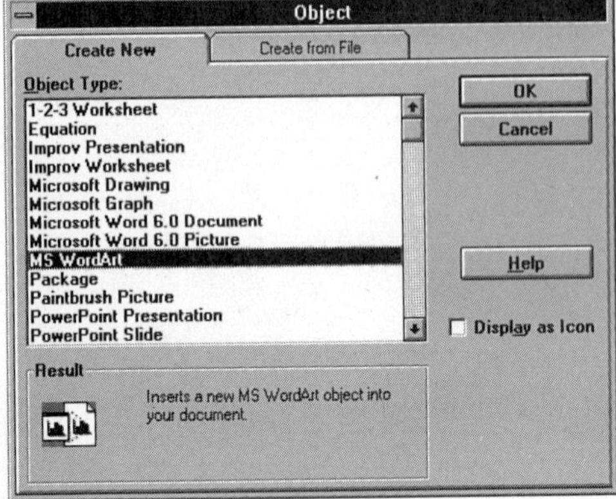

FIGURE 64.10.
Use the Create New tab to create a new object for embedding.

5. Create the object you want to embed.
6. Exit the server application. In most cases, you'll select the **File** | **Exit & Return to *Worksheet*** command, where *Worksheet* is the name of the active Excel worksheet. (In other cases—such as WordArt—click on OK to exit.) The server application asks whether you want to update the embedded object.

SUPER TIP

In most server applications, you can embed the object without leaving the application by selecting the **File** | **Update** command.

7. Click on **Yes**. Excel embeds the object.

Figure 64.11 shows a Microsoft WordArt object embedded in a worksheet.

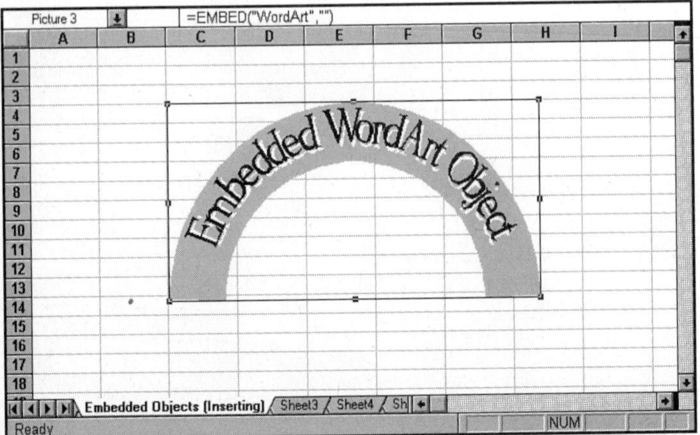

FIGURE 64.11.
A new WordArt object embedded in a worksheet.

Embedding a File by Inserting

You can insert an entire existing file (as opposed to an object within a file) as an embedded object. This is useful if you want to make changes to the file from within Excel without disturbing the original. Follow the steps in Procedure 64.10.

PROCEDURE 64.10. INSERTING A FILE AS AN EMBEDDED OBJECT.

1. Select the cell where you want to embed the object. (This cell represents the upper-left corner of the object.)
2. Select the **I**nsert | **O**bject command and, in the Object dialog box that appears, select the Create from File tab.
3. Use the Dri**v**es, **D**irectories, and File **N**ame lists to select the file you want to insert.
4. Click on OK or press Enter. Excel embeds the file.

Editing an Embedded Object

If you need to make changes to an embedded object, you can start the server application and automatically load the object by using either of the following methods:

- Double-click on the object.
- Select the object, and then select the **E**dit | *ObjectType* **O**bject | **E**dit command, where *ObjectType* is the type of object you selected (for example, MS WordArt or Document).

Working with OLE 2 Applications

The latest version of object linking and embedding—version 2—includes many new features that make embedded objects even easier to create and maintain. Here's a summary of just a few of these features:

Drag and drop objects between applications: You can copy information between two open OLE 2 applications simply by dragging selected data from one and dropping it in the other. If you want to copy the data, you need to hold down the Ctrl key while dragging.

In-place inserting: If you select an OLE 2 object from the Create New tab in the Object dialog box, Excel activates *in-place* inserting. This means that instead of displaying the server application in a separate window, certain features of the Excel window are temporarily hidden so that the server's features can be displayed:

- Excel's title bar changes to the name of the server application.
- The Excel menu bar (with the exception of the **F**ile and **W**indow menus) is replaced by the server's menu bar.

- The Excel toolbars are replaced by the server's toolbars.
- Any other features you need for creating the server object (such as the Ruler in Word for Windows 6) also are added to the window.

To exit in-place editing and embed the object, click outside the object frame. Figure 64.12 shows what happens to the Excel window when you insert a Word for Windows 6 document object.

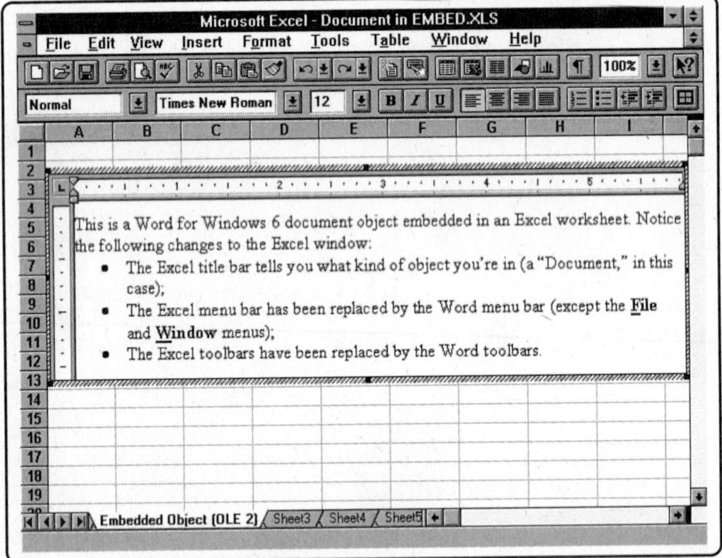

FIGURE 64.12.
The Excel window displays many features of the Word for Windows 6 window when you insert a Word 6 document object.

In-place editing: When you edit an OLE 2 object, the object remains where it is, and the Excel window changes as it does with in-place inserting. Make your changes and then click outside the object to complete the edit.

Exchanging Data with DOS Applications

Many Excel users have a foot in both the Windows and DOS camps. They use some Windows applications (such as Excel), but they also use some DOS programs (such as dBASE or WordPerfect). If you're one of those people, this section shows you how to exchange data between Excel and a DOS application.

Opening DOS Files in Excel

Excel can open and work with files from the following DOS applications: Lotus 1-2-3 (as described in the section in this chapter titled "Moving Workbooks Between Excel and Lotus 1-2-3"), Quattro Pro, Microsoft Works, dBASE (or any database management program—such as FoxPro—that produces dBASE-compatible files), and Microsoft Multiplan. (Excel also can import text files created by DOS applications. See the section in this chapter titled "Importing Text Files.")

To open a file for one of these programs, follow the steps in Procedure 64.11.

PROCEDURE 64.11. OPENING A DOS FILE IN EXCEL.

1. Select the **F**ile | **O**pen command.
2. Use the Dri**v**es and **D**irectories lists to select the drive and directory containing the file you want to open.
3. Use the List Files of **T**ype drop-down list to select the type of file you want to open.
4. Select the file in the File **N**ame list.
5. Click on OK or press Enter.

SUPER NOTE

If Excel doesn't recognize the structure of the file you're opening, the Text Import Wizard dialog box might appear. See the section in this chapter titled "Importing Text Files" to learn how to use the Text Import Wizard.

Copying Text from a DOS Application

If you want to copy some text from a DOS application, the method you use depends on whether you're using a 286 computer or a computer with a 386 or higher processor.

Copying DOS Text in 386 Enhanced Mode

The best way to copy text from a DOS application is to place the program in a window and highlight the text you want. However, you can place DOS programs in windows only if you have at least a 386 computer and Windows is operating in 386 Enhanced mode. Procedure 64.12 takes you through the required steps.

PROCEDURE 64.12. COPYING DOS TEXT IN 386 ENHANCED MODE.

1. Switch to the DOS application and place it in a window (if it's not already in a window) by pressing Alt+Enter.

SUPER NOTE

If the DOS application has a graphics mode, copying a section of the screen will copy a graphic image of the text, not the text itself. If you want text only, make sure the program is running in character mode before continuing.

2. When the text you want to copy is on-screen, pull down the window's Control menu (by clicking on the Control-menu box or by pressing Alt+Spacebar).
3. Select the Control menu's **E**dit | Mar**k** command. A blinking cursor appears just below the Control menu box.
4. Highlight the information you want to copy.
5. Press Enter to copy the selection.
6. Switch to Excel and select the cell or object that you want to receive the text.
7. Select the **E**dit | **P**aste command. Excel pastes the text.

SUPER NOTE

If you want to copy a graphic image from a DOS application, activate the program and press the Print Screen key. Because this method makes a copy of the *entire* window, you first have to edit the image in a dedicated graphics program such as Paintbrush.

Copying DOS Text with a 286 Computer

If you have a 286 computer, you can still copy text from a DOS application by following the steps in Procedure 64.13.

PROCEDURE 64.13. COPYING DOS TEXT WITH A 286 COMPUTER.

1. Switch to the DOS application, and display the text you want to copy.
2. Press the Print Screen key (on some older machines, you may have to press Alt+Print Screen).

SUPER NOTE

If the DOS application has a graphics mode, copying the screen will copy a graphic image of the screen. If you want text only, be sure the program is running in character mode before continuing.

3. Switch back to Excel.
4. Select the **Edit | Paste** command. Excel pastes a text version of the entire screen.
5. Delete any text you don't need (such as menu names and status line information).

Pasting Excel Data to a DOS Application

As with copying, the method you use to paste data to a DOS application depends on your computer, as the next two sections illustrate.

Pasting to a DOS Application in 386 Enhanced Mode

Follow the steps in Procedure 64.14 to paste Excel data to a DOS application while Windows is in 386 Enhanced mode.

PROCEDURE 64.14. PASTING DATA TO A DOS PROGRAM IN 386 ENHANCED MODE.

1. Select the data you want to copy, and then run the **Edit | Copy** command. This places the data into the Clipboard.
2. Switch to the DOS application and place it in a window.
3. Position the cursor where you want the data to appear.
4. Pull down the window's Control menu and select the **Edit | Paste** command. The Clipboard copies the data to the application and places a Tab between each cell's data.

Pasting to a DOS Application with a 286 Computer

Follow the steps in Procedure 64.15 to paste Excel data to a DOS application if you have a 286 computer.

PROCEDURE 64.15. PASTING DATA TO A DOS APPLICATION WITH A 286 COMPUTER.

1. Select the data you want to copy, and then run the **Edit | Copy** command to place the data on the Clipboard.
2. Switch to the DOS application, and press Alt+Esc to reduce the program to an icon.
3. Click on the icon to display its Control menu. Alternatively, you can display the icon's Control menu by pressing Alt+Esc until the icon is highlighted and then pressing Alt+Spacebar.
4. Select the **Paste** command. Windows redisplays the program and pastes the text.

Importing Text Files

When you import text data, Excel usually breaks up the file according to the position of the carriage return and line feed characters. This means that each line in the text file gets inserted into a cell. In most cases, this will not be the behavior you want. For example, if you've downloaded some stock data, you'll need the date, volume, and pricing values in separate columns.

Instead of dividing each line by hand, Excel 5.0 includes a new TextWizard tool that can parse text files in the usual step-by-step fashion of the Wizards. How you use the TextWizard depends on the format of the text. There are two possibilities:

Delimited: Each field is separated by characters such as commas, spaces, or tabs.
Fixed Width: The fields are aligned in columns.

If you're not sure which type of file you're dealing with, just start the TextWizard as described in either of the following two procedures. In most cases, the TextWizard will be able to determine the data type for you.

To import a text file (or to convert worksheet text into columns), follow the steps in Procedure 64.16.

PROCEDURE 64.16. IMPORTING A TEXT FILE.

1. To open the text file, select the **F**ile | **O**pen command, and then select the file from the Open dialog box. (To help out, select the Text Files option from the List Files of **T**ype list.) Excel displays the Text Import Wizard - Step 1 of 3 dialog box, shown in Figure 64.13.

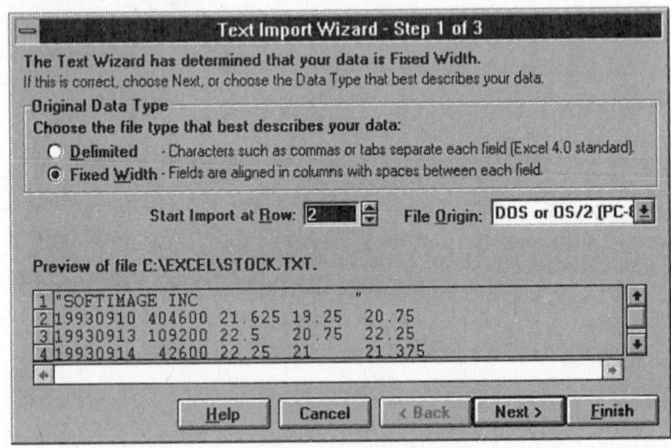

FIGURE 64.13.
The Text Import Wizard - Step 1 of 3 dialog box.

Or, if you want to convert worksheet text, select the text and run the **D**ata | Text to Columns command. Excel displays the Convert Text to Columns Wizard - Step 1 of 3 dialog box.

2. In the Original Data Type group, select the data type, if necessary.
3. If you're importing a text file, enter a number in the Start Import at **R**ow spinner, and then select the file's native environment from the File **O**rigin drop-down list.
4. Click on the Next > button to move to the Wizard's Step 2 dialog box, shown in Figure 64.14.

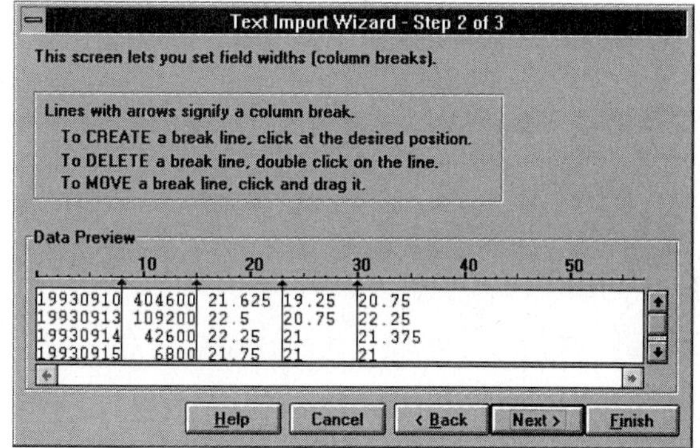

FIGURE 64.14.
The Text Import Wizard - Step 2 of 3 dialog box for fixed-width data.

5. If you're using a delimited file, select the appropriate delimiting character from the Delimiters check boxes. If the data includes text in quotation marks, select the appropriate quotation mark character from the Text **Q**ualifier list.

   If you're using a fixed-width file, you can set up the column breaks by using the following techniques:

   - To create a column break, click inside the Data Preview area at the spot where you want the break to occur.
   - To move a column break, drag it to the new location.
   - To delete a column break, double-click on it.

6. Click on the Next> button to move to the Wizard's Step 3 dialog box.
7. Select each column, and then choose one of the options from the Column Data Format group. (You select a column by clicking on the column header.)
8. Click on **F**inish.

Chapter

65

Customizing Excel's Menus and Toolbars

The Microsoft programmers have designed Excel so that the commands and features most commonly used by the majority of people are within easy reach. This means that the setup of the menu system and toolbars reflects what the average user might want. However, no one qualifies as an average user. We all work with Excel in our own unique ways; what one person uses every day, another needs only once a year; one user's obscure technical feature is another's bread and butter.

To address these differences, Excel provides what may be the most customizable interface on the market today. The Menu Editor enables you to create custom menus either by deleting some of Excel's built-in commands or by adding new commands and attaching macros to them. The toolbars, too, are easily configured simply by dragging buttons on or off a toolbar. You can even create your own button faces with the Button Editor. This chapter gives you the details.

Customizing Excel's Menus

Excel 5.0 comes with a powerful new tool called the Menu Editor. This feature enables you to modify Excel's menus or create your own from scratch. Here's a list of some of the things you can do with the Menu Editor:

- Add commands to or delete commands from an existing menu or shortcut menu.
- Create your own custom menus and attach them to any menu bar.
- Delete menus from any menu bar.
- Create your own menu bars.

The next few sections show you how to do all this and more.

Starting the Menu Editor

To start the Menu Editor, follow the steps in Procedure 65.1.

PROCEDURE 65.1. STARTING THE MENU EDITOR.

1. Either activate an existing Visual Basic module or create a new one by selecting the **I**nsert | **M**acro | **M**odule command.
2. Select the **T**ools | Menu E**d**itor command. Excel displays the Menu Editor dialog box, shown in Figure 65.1.

You also can click on this tool in the Visual Basic toolbar to start the Menu Editor.

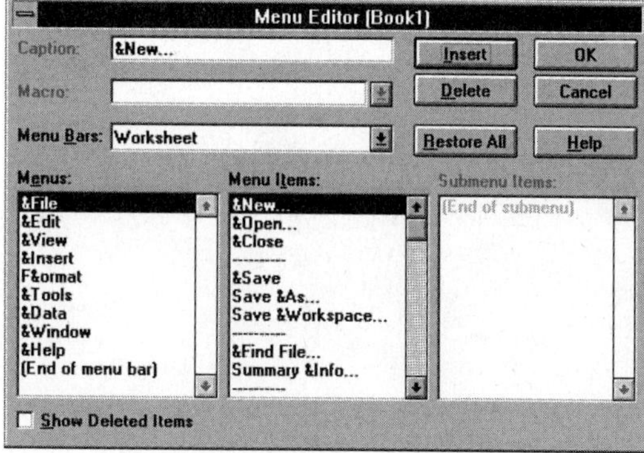

FIGURE 65.1.
Use the Menu Editor to customize Excel's menus.

The Menu Editor screen contains the following features:

Caption	An edit box containing the name of the item currently highlighted in the Menu Items list.
Macro	Use this edit box to enter the name of the macro you want to attach to a custom menu item.
Menu Bars	The name of the current menu bar.
Menus	A list of the menus in the current menu bar.
Menu Items	A list of the menu items in the highlighted menu.
Submenu Items	A list of items on the submenu attached to the highlighted menu item.

When working with menu bars, you can use either a custom menu bar you created or one of the built-in menu bars listed in Table 65.1.

Table 65.1. Excel's built-in menu bars.

Menu Bar	*Description*
Worksheet	Appears when a worksheet is active
Chart	Appears when a chart is active
No Documents Open	Appears when there are no open workbooks
Visual Basic Module	Appears when a Visual Basic module is active
Shortcut Menus 1	Appears when you right-click a toolbar, tool, cell, row or column header, workbook tab, window title bar, or desktop
Shortcut Menus 2	Appears when you right-click a drawn object, macro button, or text box
Shortcut Menus 3	Appears when you right-click the following chart elements: data series, text, arrow, plot area, gridline, floor, legend, or the entire chart

SUPER NOTE

Excel stores your customized menus in the current workbook. If you close the workbook, Excel reverts to the default menus. If you want your custom menus to appear all the time, you can use either the Personal Macro Workbook (unhide the file PERSONAL.XLS) or a template that you store in the startup directory (see the section in Chapter 62 titled "Working with Templates").

Customizing an Existing Menu

You can customize an existing Excel menu either by adding new commands to run your macros or by deleting some of Excel's built-in commands.

Adding a Command to a Menu

To add a command to an existing menu, follow the steps in Procedure 65.2.

PROCEDURE 65.2. ADDING A COMMAND WITH THE MENU EDITOR.

1. Start the Menu Editor as described in Procedure 65.1.
2. Use the Menu **B**ars list to select the menu bar or shortcut menu group you want to work with.
3. Use the M**e**nus list to select the menu you want to add the command to.
4. Use the Menu **I**tems list to select where on the menu you want the command added:
   - To add the command to the end of the menu, select the [End of menu] item.
   - Otherwise, select the command above which you want the new command to appear.
5. Click on the **I**nsert button. Excel adds a blank command and activates the **C**aption edit box.
6. Use the **C**aption box to enter a name for the command. Type an ampersand (&) before the letter you want to use as an accelerator key for the command. To add a separator bar, type a hyphen (-).
7. To attach a macro to the command, move to the **M**acro drop-down list and either type in the name or select it from the list. If the macro resides in another workbook, be sure to include the name of the workbook (for example, `PERSONAL.XLS!ToggleGridlines`).
8. Click on OK or press Enter. Excel adds the command.

SUPER NOTE

If you add the command to any menu bar other than the Visual Basic Module menu bar, you have to activate the appropriate sheet to see your changes. For example, if you add a command to the Worksheet menu bar, activate a worksheet.

Adding Submenu Commands

As soon as you've added a command, you can attach a submenu by following the steps in Procedure 65.3.

PROCEDURE 65.3. ADDING SUBMENU COMMANDS WITH THE MENU EDITOR.

1. Start the Menu Editor as described in Procedure 65.1.
2. Use the Menu **B**ars list to select the menu bar or shortcut menu group you want to work with.
3. Use the M**e**nus list to select the menu that contains the submenu command.
4. Use the Menu **I**tems list to select the submenu command.
5. Use the S**u**bmenu Items list to select where on the submenu you want the command added:
   - To add the command to the end of the submenu, select the [End of submenu] item.
   - Otherwise, select the command above which you want the new command to appear.
6. Click on the **I**nsert button. Excel adds a blank command and activates the **C**aption edit box.
7. Use the **C**aption box to enter a name for the command. Type an ampersand (&) before the letter you want to use as an accelerator key for the command. To add a separator bar, type a hyphen (-).
8. To attach a macro to the command, move to the **M**acro drop-down list and either type in the name or select it from the list. If the macro resides in another workbook, be sure to include the name of the workbook (for example, `PERSONAL.XLS!ToggleGridlines`).
9. Repeat steps 5-8 to add other commands to the submenu.
10. Click on OK or press Enter. Excel creates the submenu.

Deleting a Command from a Menu

Procedure 65.4 shows you the steps to follow to delete a command from an existing menu.

PROCEDURE 65.4. DELETING A COMMAND WITH THE MENU EDITOR.

1. Start the Menu Editor as described in Procedure 65.1.
2. Select the menu bar or shortcut menu group you want to work with from the Menu **B**ars list.
3. Select the menu that contains the command you want to delete.
4. Highlight the command in the Menu **It**ems list.
5. Click on the **D**elete button. Excel deletes the command.
6. Click on OK or press Enter to return to the module.

> SUPER CAUTION
>
> Excel doesn't ask for confirmation before deleting a command. If you accidentally delete a custom command, click on Cancel. If you accidentally delete a built-in command, see the section later in this chapter titled "Undeleting a Built-In Menu or Command."

Customizing an Existing Menu Bar

The Menu Editor enables you to customize any of Excel's menu bars the same way you customize an individual menu. You can add new menus and delete existing menus.

Adding a Menu to a Menu Bar

If you have some macros you would like to add to Excel's menu structure, you might not want to clutter the existing menus with all kinds of new commands. The alternative is to create an entirely new menu and add it to a menu bar. Procedure 65.5 shows you the steps to follow.

PROCEDURE 65.5. CREATING A MENU WITH THE MENU EDITOR.

1. Start the Menu Editor as described in Procedure 65.1.
2. Select the menu bar or shortcut menu group you want to work with from the Menu **B**ars list.
3. Use the Me**n**us list to select where on the menu bar you want the menu added:

- To add the menu to the end of the menu bar, select the [End of menu bar] item.
- Otherwise, select the menu to the left of which you want the new command to appear.

4. Click on the **I**nsert button. Excel adds a blank menu and activates the **C**aption edit box.
5. Use the **C**aption box to enter a name for the menu. As with commands, type an ampersand (&) before the letter you want to use as an accelerator key for the menu.
6. Follow Procedure 65.2 to add commands to the new menu.
7. Click on OK or press Enter. Excel adds the menu.

Deleting a Menu from a Menu Bar

Procedure 65.6 shows you the steps to follow to delete a menu from an existing menu bar.

PROCEDURE 65.6. DELETING A MENU WITH THE MENU EDITOR.

1. Start the Menu Editor as described in Procedure 65.1.
2. Use the Menu **B**ars list to select the menu bar or shortcut menu group you want to work with.
3. Use the M**e**nus list to select the menu you want to delete.
4. Click on the **D**elete button. Excel deletes the command.
5. Click on OK or press Enter to return to the module.

SUPER CAUTION

Excel doesn't ask for confirmation before deleting a menu. If you accidentally delete a custom menu, click on Cancel. If you accidentally delete a built-in menu, see the section later in this chapter titled "Undeleting a Built-In Menu or Command."

Working with Custom Menu Bars

The Menu Editor also enables you to create your own custom menu bars from scratch and to delete any custom menu bars you no longer need (although you can't delete any of the built-in menu bars).

Creating a Custom Menu Bar

If you're building a custom application in Excel, you'll often need to satisfy two goals:

- Give your users easy access to commands that directly affect the application.
- Hide any other Excel commands that are not related to the application.

One of the best ways to accomplish this is to create a custom menu bar that includes only the commands you want the user to see. Follow the steps in Procedure 65.7 to create a custom menu bar.

PROCEDURE 65.7. CREATING A CUSTOM MENU BAR WITH THE MENU EDITOR.

1. Start the Menu Editor as described in Procedure 65.1.
2. In the Menu **B**ars list, select one of the menu bars or shortcut menu groups (it doesn't matter which one) to clear any selections you might have in the other lists.
3. Click on the **I**nsert button. Excel creates a blank menu bar and activates the **C**aption edit box.
4. Enter a name for the new menu bar.
5. Follow the steps in Procedures 65.5 and 65.2 to add new menus and commands, respectively, to the menu bar.
6. Click on OK or press Enter.

Deleting a Custom Menu Bar

If you no longer need a custom menu bar, follow the steps in Procedure 65.8 to delete it.

PROCEDURE 65.8. DELETING A CUSTOM MENU BAR WITH THE MENU EDITOR.

1. Start the Menu Editor as described in Procedure 65.1.
2. In the Menu **B**ars list, select the custom menu bar you want to delete.
3. Click on the **D**elete button. Excel deletes the menu bar.
4. Click on OK or press Enter.

Undeleting a Built-In Menu or Command

If you delete any of Excel's built-in menus or commands, you can restore them by following the steps in Procedure 65.9.

PROCEDURE 65.9. UNDELETING A BUILT-IN MENU OR COMMAND.

1. Start the Menu Editor as described in Procedure 65.1.

2. Activate the **S**how Deleted Items check box. The deleted menus or commands appear in grayed text.
3. Highlight the menu or command you want to restore.
4. Click on the Un**d**elete button. Excel restores the command.
5. Click on OK or press Enter to return to the module.

Customizing Excel's Toolbars

Excel 5.0's new tabbed dialog boxes and revamped menu structure make it much easier to find the commands and features you want. However, you still can't beat the toolbars for making short work of common tasks. The problem is that Excel has 13 displayable toolbars in all, and there is a finite amount of screen real estate to work with (especially if you use Excel in VGA mode). The solution is to customize the toolbars so that they display buttons for only the features you use the most.

Setting Toolbar Options

Before you learn how to customize toolbars, there are a few toolbar options you should know about. Procedure 65.10 tells you about them.

PROCEDURE 65.10. SETTING TOOLBAR OPTIONS.

1. Select the **V**iew | **T**oolbars command. Excel displays the Toolbars dialog box, shown in Figure 65.2.

TIP

You also can display the Toolbars dialog box by right-clicking on a toolbar and selecting the Toolbars command from the shortcut menu.

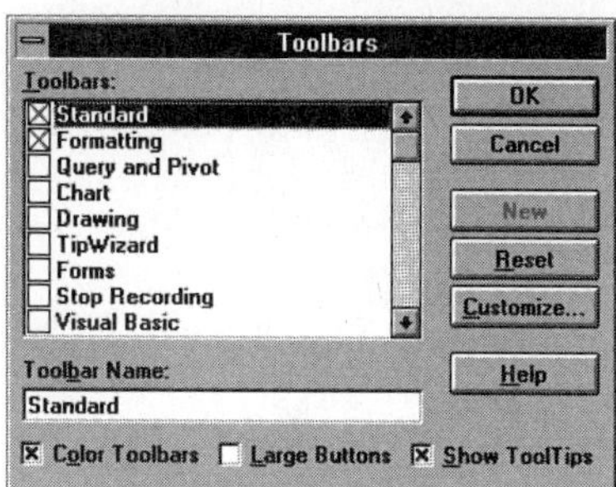

FIGURE 65.2.
Use the Toolbars dialog box to set toolbar options.

2. Excel usually displays color in some of the toolbar buttons. If you don't have a color screen, you might be able to see these buttons better if you deactivate the Color Toolbars check box.
3. The toolbar buttons can be quite small in higher video resolutions. You can increase the size of the buttons by activating the Large Buttons check box.
4. The ToolTips that appear when the mouse pointer lingers for a second or two over a button are convenient when you're first learning the lay of the toolbar land. After a while, however, you might find them distracting. You can turn them off by deactivating the Show ToolTips check box.
5. Click on OK or press Enter to put these options into effect.

Customizing an Existing Toolbar

With the Toolbars dialog box displayed, use the following techniques to modify any displayed toolbar:

- To move a button to a different location, drag it within the toolbar. If you drag the button only slightly, you'll create a space between buttons.
- To change the size of a toolbar drop-down list, click on it and drag either the left or right edge.
- To delete a button, drag it off the toolbar.

Adding a Button to a Toolbar

Excel actually has more toolbar buttons than the ones you see on its default toolbars. In fact, most Excel features have their own button, and it's possible to add any of these buttons to a toolbar. For example, if you regularly use Excel's worksheet protection, you can add the Lock Cell button that toggles protection on and off. This is more convenient than constantly selecting the **T**ools | **P**rotection | **P**rotect Sheet command.

You add buttons to a toolbar by using the Customize dialog box, shown in Figure 65.3. This dialog box is divided into three sections:

Categories	Excel divides all its toolbar buttons into the 14 categories contained in this list. The Custom category contains buttons you can use for your macros.
Buttons	These are the available buttons in the selected category.
Description	If you click on a button, Excel displays a description of the button's function at the bottom of the dialog box.

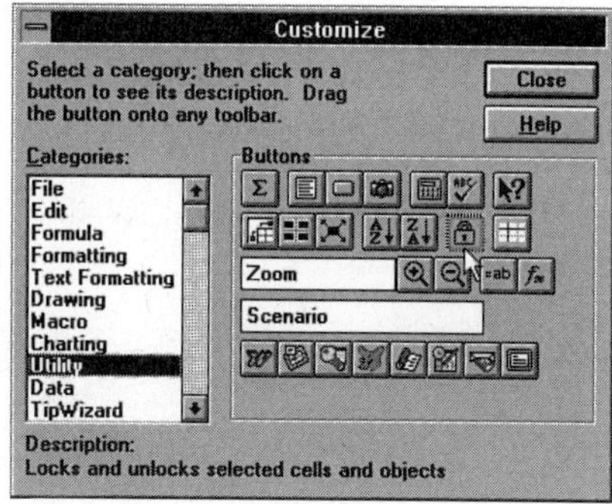

FIGURE 65.3.
Use the Customize dialog box to add buttons to a toolbar.

To add buttons to a toolbar, follow the steps in Procedure 65.11.

PROCEDURE 65.11. ADDING BUTTONS TO A TOOLBAR.

1. Display the toolbar you want to add buttons to.
2. Select the **V**iew | **T**oolbars command to display the Toolbars dialog box.
3. Click on the **C**ustomize button to display the Customize dialog box.

> **SUPER TIP**
>
> A quick way to display the Customize dialog box is to right-click on a toolbar and select the Customize command from the shortcut menu.

4. Use the **C**ategories list to select a button category.
5. Drag the button you want to add from the Buttons section to the toolbar location. Excel inserts the button between the existing buttons.
6. Repeat steps 4 and 5 to add other buttons.
7. When you're done, click on the Close button.

Assigning a Macro to a Button

If you have a macro you would like to assign to a button, you can assign it either to one of Excel's built-in buttons or to one of the custom buttons.

If you have a macro that mimics or improves upon an existing Excel feature, you can assign the macro to the feature's toolbar button. Follow the steps in Procedure 65.12.

PROCEDURE 65.12. ASSIGNING A MACRO TO A BUILT-IN BUTTON.

1. Display the toolbar that contains the button you want to work with.
2. Select the **V**iew | **T**oolbars command to display the Toolbars dialog box.

3. Click on the button.
4. Select the **T**ools | Assig**n** Macro command. Excel displays the Assign Macro dialog box, shown in Figure 65.4.

> **SUPER TIP**
>
> You can display the Assign Macro dialog box also by right-clicking on the button and selecting the Assign Macro command from the shortcut menu.

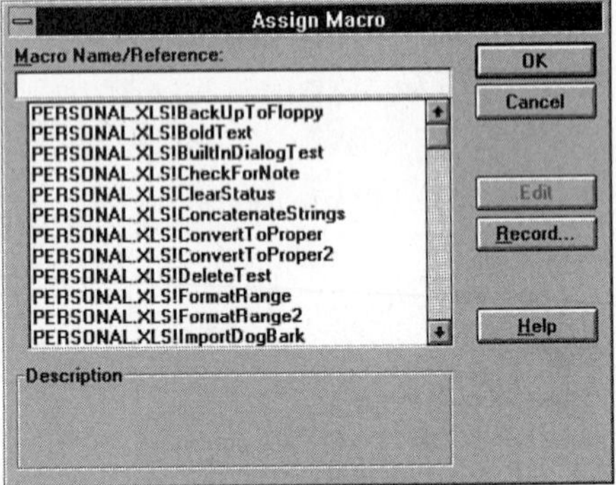

FIGURE 65.4.
Use the Assign Macro dialog box to assign a macro to a toolbar button.

5. Select the macro from the **M**acro Name/Reference list.
   or
   To record the macro, click on the **R**ecord button and record the macro as you normally would. When you finish recording the macro, Excel assigns the macro to the button you selected and then returns you to the worksheet.
6. If you selected a macro from the list, click on OK or press Enter to return to the Customize dialog box, and then click on Close to return to the workbook.

Instead of altering the behavior of Excel's built-in buttons, you can use one of the buttons in the Custom category. Procedure 65.13 shows you how to assign a macro to one of these buttons.

PROCEDURE 65.13. ASSIGNING A MACRO TO A CUSTOM BUTTON.

1. Display the toolbar you want to use for the custom button.
2. Select the **V**iew | **T**oolbars command to display the Toolbars dialog box.
3. Click on the **C**ustomize button and then select Custom from the **C**ategories list.

4. Drag the custom button you want to use to the toolbar. When you release the button, Excel displays the Assign Macro dialog box.
5. Select the macro from the **M**acro Name/Reference list.
   or
   To record the macro, click on the **R**ecord button and record the macro as you normally would. When you finish recording the macro, Excel assigns the macro to the button you selected and then returns you to the worksheet.
6. If you selected a macro from the list, click on OK or press Enter to return to the Customize dialog box, and then click on Close to return to the workbook.

Resetting a Toolbar

If you've customized one of Excel's built-in toolbars, you reset it to its default configuration by following the steps in Procedure 65.14.

PROCEDURE 65.14. RESETTING A BUILT-IN TOOLBAR.

1. Select the **V**iew | **T**oolbars command to display the Toolbars dialog box.
2. In the **T**oolbars list, highlight the toolbar you want to reset.
3. Click on the **R**eset button.
4. Click on OK or press Enter.

Creating a New Toolbar

Rather than messing around with Excel's own toolbars, you might prefer to create a toolbar from scratch and add built-in and custom buttons to it. Procedure 65.15 shows you the steps to follow.

PROCEDURE 65.15. CREATING A NEW TOOLBAR.

1. Select the **V**iew | **T**oolbars command to display the Toolbars dialog box.
2. In the Toolbar **N**ame edit box, enter the name you want to use for the toolbar.
3. Click on the **N**ew button. Excel displays a new, empty toolbar and displays the Customize dialog box (see Figure 65.5).
4. Add the buttons you want for the new toolbar as described earlier in the section titled "Adding a Button to a Toolbar."
5. When you're done, click on Close to return to the workbook.

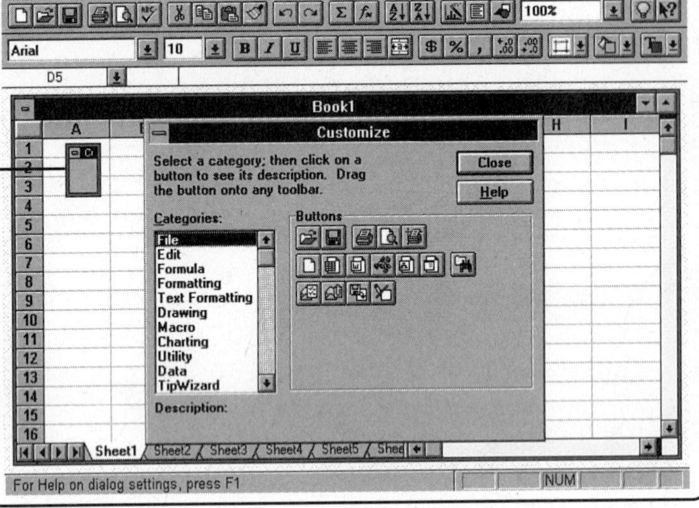

FIGURE 65.5.
When you create a new toolbar, Excel displays it and opens the Customize dialog box.

Using the Button Editor

Excel 5.0's new Button Editor enables you to modify an existing button face or create your own. Procedure 65.16 shows you how it's done.

PROCEDURE 65.16. USING THE BUTTON EDITOR.

1. Display the toolbar containing the button you want to edit.
2. Select the **View** | **Toolbars** command to display the Toolbars dialog box.
3. Right-click on the button you want to edit, and select Edit Button Image from the shortcut menu. Excel displays the Button Editor dialog box, shown in Figure 65.6.

SUPER TIP

If you want to start a button from scratch, click on the **C**lear button.

4. Select a color by clicking on one of the boxes in the Colors group.
5. Add the color to the image by clicking on one or more boxes in the Picture area. To clear a box, click on it again. The Preview area shows you what the button will look like at regular size.

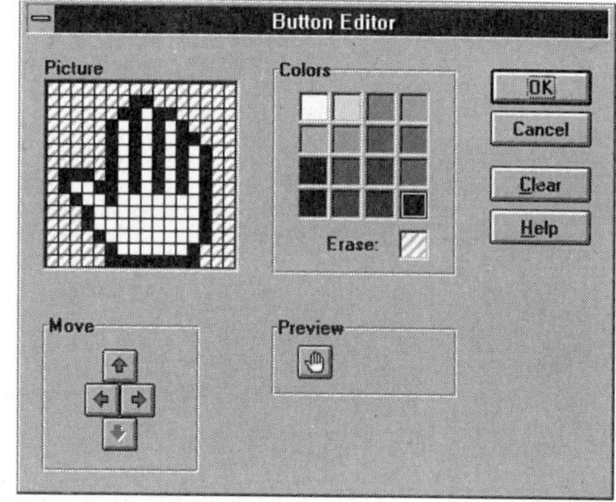

FIGURE 65.6.
The Button Editor enables you to design your own toolbar buttons.

6. Repeat steps 4 and 5 to draw the complete image.
7. Click on OK or press Enter.

Attaching a Toolbar to a Workbook

If you need a custom toolbar only for a specific workbook, you can attach the toolbar to the workbook by following Procedure 65.17.

PROCEDURE 65.17. ATTACHING A TOOLBAR TO A WORKBOOK.

1. Open the workbook you want to use and activate a Visual Basic module.
2. Select the Tools | Attach Toolbars command. Excel displays the Attach Toolbars dialog box, shown in Figure 65.7.
3. In the Custom Toolbars list, highlight the toolbar you want to attach.
4. Click on the Copy>> button. Excel adds the name to the Toolbars in Workbook list.

SUPER TIP

If you accidentally copy a toolbar, you can remove it by highlighting it in the Toolbars in Workbook list and then clicking on the Delete button.

5. Click on OK or press Enter.

As soon as you've attached a toolbar, it is automatically copied into the Excel workspace whenever you open the workbook.

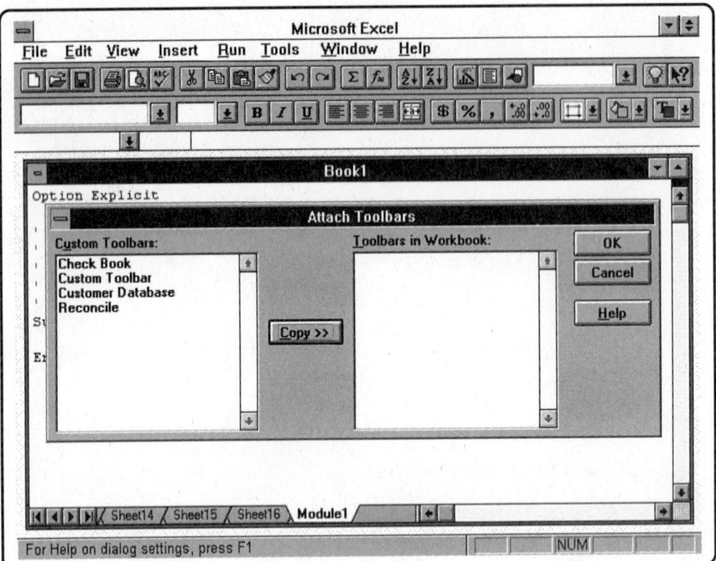

FIGURE 65.7.
Use the Attach Toolbars dialog box to attach a toolbar to a workbook.

Chapter

66

Customizing Excel's Options and Workspace

Chapter 65, "Customizing Excel's Menus and Toolbars," showed you how to modify Excel's menus and toolbars, but Excel's customization options don't stop there. Excel has dozens of settings you can use to control everything from automatic recalculation to displaying zero values. You also can create *workspace files* that "remember" which workbooks you had open and where they were positioned on-screen. This chapter takes you through all of Excel's options and shows you how to save and use workspace files.

Customizing Excel's Options

I've already introduced you to the Options dialog box and showed you how to modify some of Excel's default settings. This section takes a comprehensive look at every option available in this dialog box.

Displaying the Options Dialog Box

To get started, you need to display the Options dialog box by selecting the **T**ools | **O**ptions command. In this dialog box, shown in Figure 66.1, you use the 10 tabs to modify Excel's settings and default values.

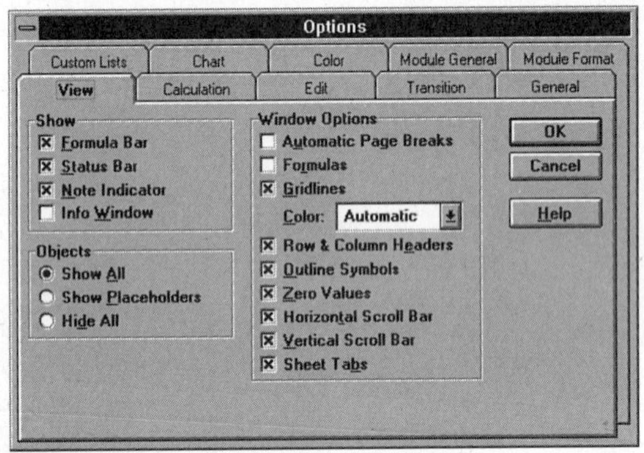

FIGURE 66.1.
You use the Options dialog box to change Excel's default settings.

Although it may not be necessary at this point, here is a summary of the navigation techniques for a multi-level tabbed dialog box:

- Using the mouse, click on a tab to select it.
- Using the keyboard, press Ctrl+Tab to move right and Ctrl+Shift+Tab to move left.
- If the tab name is selected, you can press Ctrl+right arrow to move right, Ctrl+left arrow to move left, Ctrl+up arrow to move up, and Ctrl+down arrow to move down.

When you finish choosing your options, click on OK or press Enter to return to the worksheet.

Changing the View

The View tab options control several display settings for the Excel screen, workbooks, objects, and windows.

The Show group has four check boxes:

Formula Bar: Deactivate this check box to hide the formula bar. If you use in-cell editing, turning off the formula bar gives you more room on-screen. The downside is that you lose access to the Name box and the FunctionWizard button. You also can hide the formula bar by selecting the **View | Formula Bar** command.

Status Bar: Deactivate this check box to hide the status bar. This option also gives you some extra screen real estate. You also can hide the status bar by selecting the **View | Status Bar** command.

SUPER TIP

If you want to maximize the work area, the easiest way to do it is to select the **View | Full Screen** command. This removes everything from the screen except the menu bar, row and column headers, scroll bars, and sheet tabs (as you'll soon see, you can use the View tab to turn these off as well). To return to the normal view, either click on the Full Screen button or select **View | Full Screen** again.

Note Indicator: Deactivate this check box to remove the small red squares that Excel places in the upper-right corner of cells that have notes attached to them.

Info Window: Activate this check box to display the Info window, which gives you information about various cell properties. Figure 66.2 shows the Info window containing data for cell R17 in the 1994 Budget worksheet. Use the Info menu (which appears when you activate the Info window) to select which properties you want displayed.

The Objects group sets the display options for worksheet objects. If you have a worksheet with a lot of graphics, these options can make it easier to scroll through the sheet. Select Show Placeholders to show a gray box where the graphics would normally be. Select Hide All to hide the graphics entirely. When you want to display objects normally, select the Show All option.

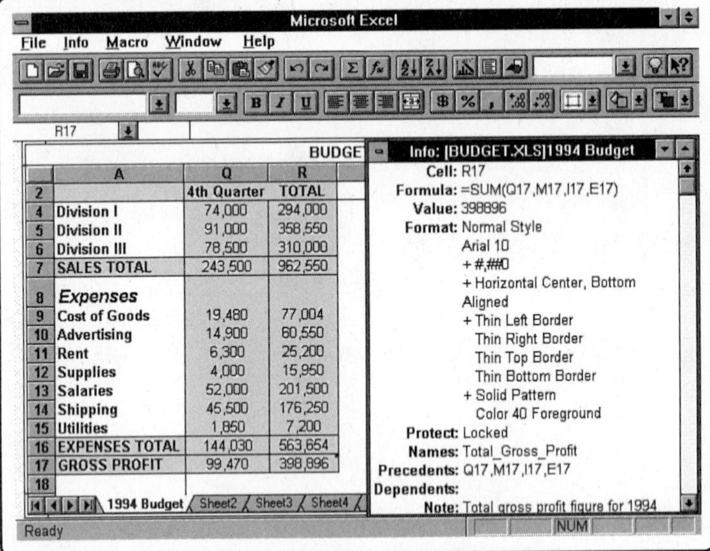

FIGURE 66.2.
The Info window can show you many properties of the active cell.

SUPER TIP

You also can cycle through these options without displaying the Options dialog box. Just press Ctrl+6 repeatedly.

The nine check boxes in the Window Options group control the display of each Excel window:

Automatic Page Breaks: Activate this check box to display the dashed lines that mark the borders of each printed page.

Formulas: Activate this check box to display cell formulas instead of values.

SUPER TIP

You also can switch between formulas and values by pressing Ctrl+` (backquote).

Gridlines: Use this check box to toggle gridlines on and off. When gridlines are on, you can use the Color drop-down list to select a color for the gridlines.

Click on this button in the Forms toolbar to toggle gridlines on and off.

Row and Column Headers: Use this check box to toggle row and column headers on and off.

Outline Symbols: If the current worksheet is outlined, use this check box to toggle the outline symbols on and off.

SUPER TIP

You also can press Ctrl+8 to toggle outline symbols on and off.

Zero Values: Deactivate this check box to hide cells containing zero.

Horizontal Scroll Bar: Use this check box to toggle the horizontal scroll bar on and off.

Vertical Scroll Bar: Use this check box to toggle the vertical scroll bar on and off.

Sheet Tabs: Use this check box to toggle the sheet tabs on and off.

Changing the Calculation Options

The Calculations tab options contain several settings used to control worksheet calculations (see Figure 66.3).

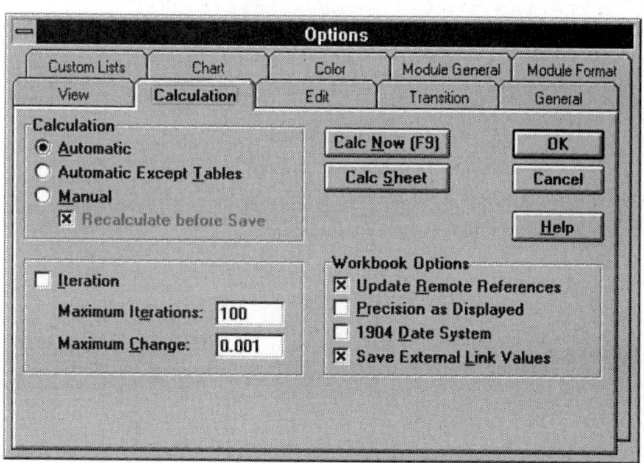

FIGURE 66.3.
Use the Calculation tab to set several calculation settings.

You use the Calculation group options to set the calculation mode, which determines when Excel recalculates a worksheet. See Chapter 5, "Building Formulas," to learn about Excel calculation modes.

Activating the Iteration check box sets up the worksheet for iterative calculations. For an example, see the material on circular reference formulas in Chapter 35, "Basic Analytic Methods." You also can use the Maximum Iterations and Maximum Change edit boxes with Goal Seek (see Chapter 37, "Working with Goal Seek").

The Workbook Options group contains the following options:

Update **R**emote References: This check box controls whether or not Excel recalculates formulas that contain references to other applications. If you find that remote references are increasing the time Excel takes to recalculate formulas, deactivate this option.

Precision as Displayed: When this check box is deactivated (the default), Excel stores values with full (15-digit) precision. When you activate this check box, Excel uses the displayed value in each cell to determine the precision it uses. For example, if a cell contains 123.456, Excel uses three-digit precision for this cell.

1904 **D**ate System: Activate this check box to calculate dates using January 2, 1904, as the starting point (instead of January 1, 1900). Because Excel for the Macintosh uses this date system, this option enables you to work with the same worksheet in both the PC and Mac environments.

Save External **L**ink Values: If this check box is activated (the default) and a workbook contains links to another workbook, Excel saves copies of the linked values from the client workbook in the server workbook. If a large amount of data is involved, this may bloat the dependent workbook beyond a reasonable size. If this happens, deactivate this check box to prevent Excel from storing the source values.

Changing Editing Options

The options in the Edit tab control cell and range editing settings (see Figure 66.4):

Edit Directly in Cell: Toggles in-cell editing on and off. If you turn in-cell editing off, Excel's double-click behavior changes: if the cell contains a note, the Cell Note dialog box appears; if the cell contains a formula, the formula's precedents are selected.

Allow Cell **D**rag and Drop: Toggles Excel's drag-and-drop feature. When this check box is activated, you can move or copy a range by dragging it with the mouse pointer.

Alert before Overwriting Cells: When you use drag-and-drop to move or copy a range, Excel warns you if non-blank cells in the destination range will be overwritten. Deactivate this check box to disable this warning.

Move Selection after Enter: If you activate this check box, Excel moves down one row when you press Enter to confirm a cell entry (or it moves up one row when you press Shift+Enter). If you deactivate this check box, Excel stays on the same cell when you press Enter (or Shift+Enter).

Fi**x**ed Decimal: Activate this check box to cause Excel to automatically insert a decimal place into numbers you enter. Use the **P**laces spinner to specify the location of the decimal. For example, if **P**laces is 2, Excel converts a number entered as 12345 to 123.45.

Cut, Copy, and Sort **O**bjects with Cells: Activate this check box to keep graphic objects together with their underlying cells when you cut or copy the cells or when you sort or filter a list.

Ask to **U**pdate Automatic Links: When you open a workbook that contains automatic links to a server document in another application (see Chapter 64, "Exchanging Data with Other Applications"), Excel displays a dialog box asking whether you want to update the links. Deactivate this check box to prevent this dialog box from appearing.

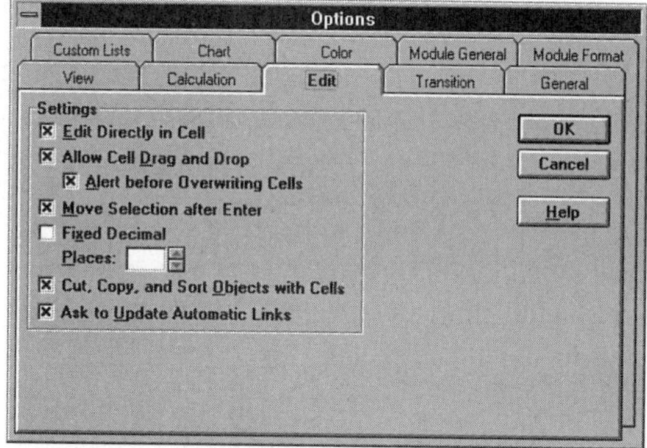

FIGURE 66.4.
The Edit tab options control Excel's editing settings.

Changing the Lotus 1-2-3 Transition Options

The options in the Transition tab control settings that make it easier to make the switch from Lotus 1-2-3 to Excel. See Chapter 64 and Appendix A, "Notes for Lotus 1-2-3 Users Switching to Excel," for details.

Changing the General Workspace Options

The controls on the General tab affect miscellaneous workspace options (see Figure 66.5):

Reference Style: Select A**1** to use A1-style references or R1**C**1 to use R1C1-style references. (See Chapter 44, "Macro Worksheet Skills," for an explanation of these two styles.)

Menus: Activate the **R**ecently Used File List check box to display at the bottom of the **F**ile menu a list of the last four files you used. If you prefer the Excel 4.0 menu structure, activate the Microsoft E**x**cel 4.0 Menus check box.

Ignore Other Applications: Activate this check box to cause Excel to ignore Dynamic Data Exchange (DDE) requests from other applications.

Reset Tip**W**izard: The TipWizard—new to Excel 5.0—is a toolbar that displays tips related to actions you have recently performed in Excel. Activate this check box to clear the list of tips.

Click on this tool in the Standard toolbar to display the TipWizard.

Prompt for Summary Info: Activate this check box to have Excel display the Summary Info dialog box whenever you save a new workbook.
Sheets in New Workbook: This option specifies the default number of sheets in new workbooks. You can enter a number between 1 and 255.
St**a**ndard Font: This drop-down list contains the typefaces available on your system. The typeface you select becomes the one Excel uses for all new worksheets and workbooks. You also can set the default type size by selecting a number in the Si**z**e list.
Default File Location: This option determines the initial directory that appears when you first display the Open or Save As dialog boxes. To make it easy to find your Excel documents, save them all in a single subdirectory and enter the full path in this edit box.
Alternate Startup File **L**ocation: Excel uses the XLSTART subdirectory as its default startup directory. Any files placed in this directory are opened automatically when you start Excel, and any templates in this directory appear in the New dialog box. Use this edit box to specify a startup directory in addition to XLSTART.
User **N**ame: In this edit box, enter the user name you want to be displayed in the document summary, scenarios, views, and file sharing.

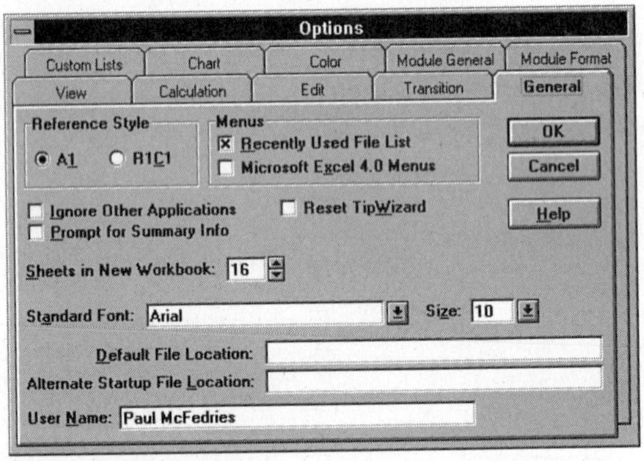

FIGURE 66.5.
The General tab controls various workspace options.

Creating a Custom AutoFill List

As you learned in Chapter 4, "Working with Ranges," you can use the AutoFill tool to enter a series of values simply by dragging the mouse pointer. Excel recognizes certain values (for example, January, Sunday, 1st Quarter) as part of a larger list and creates the series accordingly. You can use the Custom Lists tab (see Figure 66.6) to create your own lists for AutoFill. Procedure 66.1 takes you through the steps.

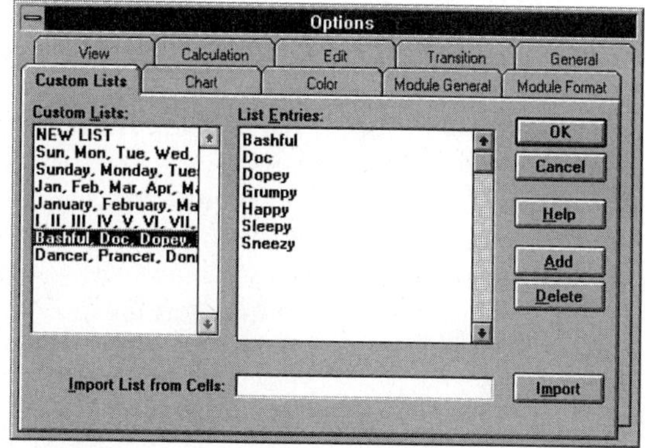

FIGURE 66.6.
Use the Custom Lists tab to create your own custom lists.

PROCEDURE 66.1. CREATING CUSTOM AUTOFILL LISTS.

1. In the Custom **L**ists box, select NEW LIST. An insertion point appears in the List **E**ntries box.
2. Type the list item into the List **E**ntries box and press Enter. Repeat this step for each item.
3. Click on **A**dd to add the list to the Custom **L**ists box.

SUPER TIP

If you already have the list in a worksheet range, activate the **I**mport List from Cells edit box and enter a reference to the range (you can type the reference or select the cells directly on the worksheet). Click on the **Im**port button to add the list to the Custom **L**ists box.

SUPER NOTE

If you need to delete a custom list, highlight it in the Custom **L**ists box, and then click on the **D**elete button.

Changing the Chart Options

The Chart tab shown in Figure 66.7 controls several default chart settings:

Empty Cells Plotted as: This group specifies how Excel should handle blank cells in a data series. Select **N**ot Plotted to ignore blanks, **Z**ero to plot blanks as zeros, and **I**nterpolated to have Excel draw a straight line between the points on either side of the blank cell.

Plot Visible Cells Only: Excel normally ignores cells you've hidden yourself or that have been hidden by an outline or filter. Deactivate this check box to include hidden cells in the chart data series.

Chart Sizes with Window Frame: If your chart is displayed in a separate chart sheet, activate this check box to cause Excel to change the size of the chart whenever you change the size of the window. You also can size a chart with its window frame by selecting the View | Sized with Window command. (This command is available only when you activate a chart sheet.)

Default Chart Format: This group determines the chart type for new charts that are created using the Default Chart button. See Chapter 20, "Working with Chart Types," for instructions.

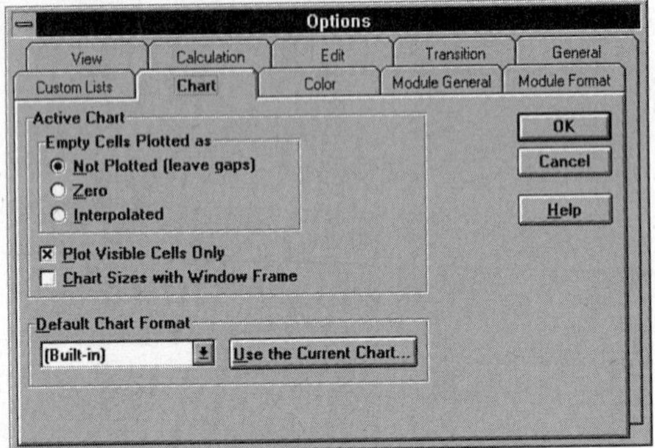

FIGURE 66.7.
The Chart tab controls various default chart settings.

Working with Custom Color Palettes

You can use the Color tab to customize Excel's default 56-color palette. For the full details, see Chapter 11, "Using Color in Worksheets."

Changing the General Module Options

If you use Visual Basic for Applications, the options in the Module General tab (see Figure 66.8) control several module sheet settings:

Auto Indent: If this check box is activated, Visual Basic indents the next line to the same point as the line you just entered. If it is deactivated, Visual Basic moves the insertion point to the beginning of each new line.

Tab Width: Use this option to set the number of spaces Visual Basic moves whenever you press the Tab key in a module.

Display Syntax Errors: Activate this check box to force Visual Basic to check the syntax of each line when you enter it. If a mistake is detected, a dialog box pops up to warn you.

Break on All Errors: Activate this check box to force Excel to halt execution if any procedure in the current module contains an error.

Require Variable Declarations: When this check box is activated, it adds the following statement to each new module:

```
Option Explicit
```

This tells Visual Basic to generate an error if you try to use an undeclared variable.

International: This group controls the international settings used in the module. Select Current Settings to use the settings defined in the Windows Control Panel. Select Default Settings and choose an item from the Language/Country list to specify settings for Visual Basic modules only.

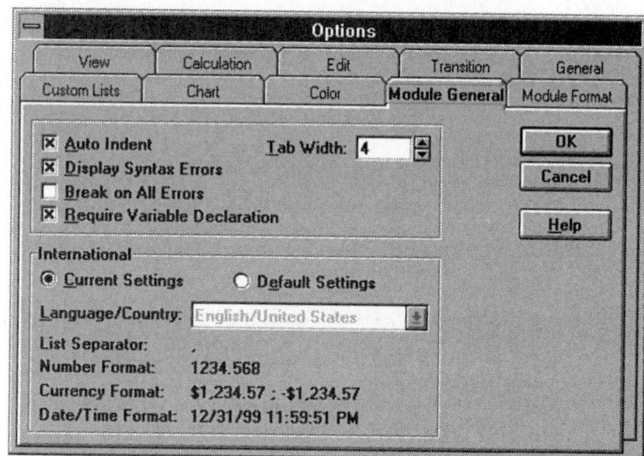

FIGURE 66.8.
The Module General tab controls the default settings for Visual Basic modules.

Changing the Module Format Options

Visual Basic displays text such as keywords, comments, and syntax errors in a different color. The Module Format tab (see Figure 66.9) enables you to customize these colors as well as the font used in a module. Procedure 66.2 shows you how to use this tab to format the appearance of module code.

PROCEDURE 66.2. FORMATTING VISUAL BASIC MODULE TEXT.

1. Use the Font list to select a typeface for the code.
2. Use the Size list to select a type size.
3. Use the Code Colors list to select the type of code you want to work with.
4. Use the Foreground and Background lists to select the colors to use for the code type you selected in step 3.
5. Repeat steps 3 and 4 to set the colors for other code types.

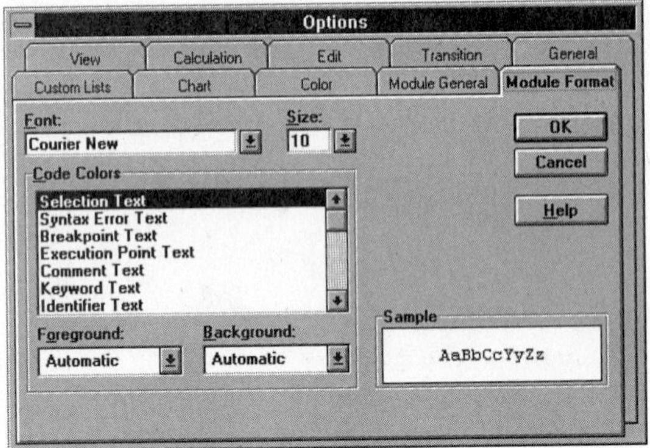

FIGURE 66.9.
Use the Module Format options to format the text in your Visual Basic modules.

Using Workspace Files

Although Excel 5.0's new worksheet tabs mean that you will probably have fewer files open at once, there will still be plenty of times when you need multiple workbooks open. If you regularly use the same workbooks, you can create a *workspace file* that contains not only the workbooks, but also their current position. When you open the workspace file, Excel opens the specified workbooks and positions them accordingly. Follow the steps in Procedure 66.3 to save a workspace file.

PROCEDURE 66.3. SAVING A WORKSPACE FILE.

1. Open the workbooks you want to use and position them where you want them to appear.
2. Select the **F**ile | Save **W**orkspace command. Excel displays the Save Workspace dialog box.
3. Use the Dri**v**es and **D**irectories lists to select a location for the file.

> **SUPER TIP**
>
> If you want the file opened automatically when you start Excel, save it in the XLSTART directory (or in your alternative startup directory, if you have one; see the section in this chapter titled "Changing the General Workspace Options").

4. Enter a name for the file in the File **N**ame box. (You don't need to include an extension; Excel adds the default .XLW extension automatically.)
5. Click on OK or press Enter.

After you save a workspace file, you can open it at any time just like a regular Excel file.

SUPER CAUTION

If you make changes to the workspace (such as closing a file or changing the position of a window), you need to follow Procedure 66.3 again to save the new settings.

IX

Projects

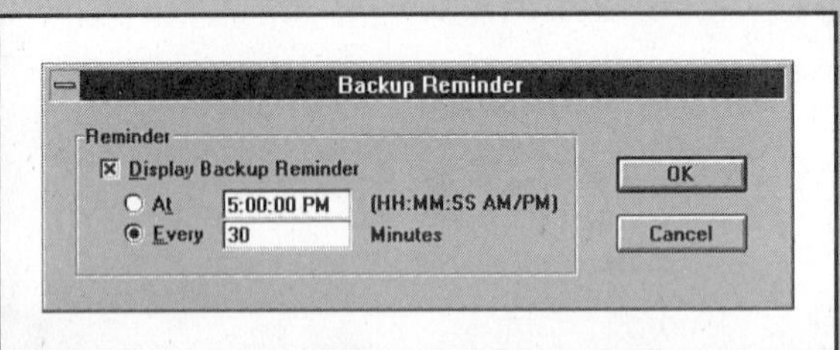

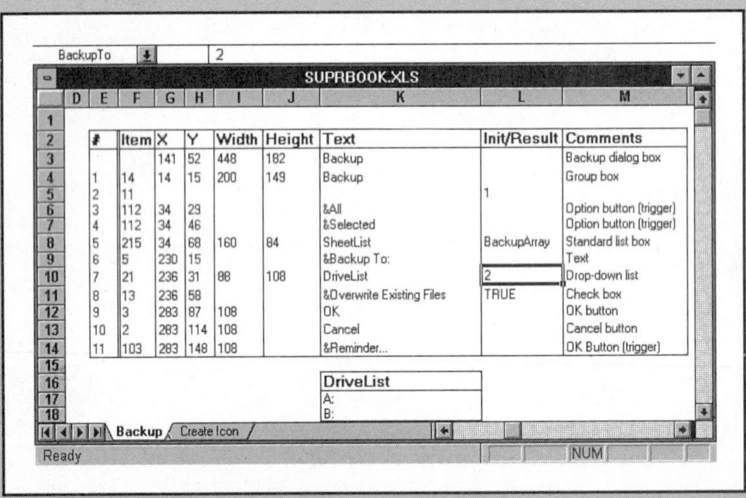

#	Item	X	Y	Width	Height	Text	Init/Result	Comments
		141	52	448	182	Backup		Backup dialog box
1	14	14	15	200	149	Backup		Group box
2	11						1	
3	112	34	29			&All		Option button (trigger)
4	112	34	46			&Selected		Option button (trigger)
5	215	34	68	160	84	SheetList	BackupArray	Standard list box
6	5	230	15			&Backup To:		Text
7	21	236	31	88	108	DriveList	2	Drop-down list
8	13	236	58			&Overwrite Existing Files	TRUE	Check box
9	3	283	87	108		OK		OK button
10	2	283	114	108		Cancel		Cancel button
11	103	283	148	108		&Reminder...		OK Button (trigger)

DriveList
A:
B:

Chapter

67

Backing Up Worksheets from Within Excel

Your Excel data is precious and, in most cases, irreplaceable. I hope you already have a backup strategy in which you make a full backup about once a month and an incremental backup every couple of days. However, even such an ambitious strategy has its drawbacks. If you backed up yesterday, and your hard disk crashes today, you might lose a full day's work—and that's a best-case scenario.

My credo is that you can never back up too often. Of course, you don't want to be cranking up your backup software every 15 minutes, but if you set things up right, you don't have to. In this project I take you through the Backup macro sheet included on the Super Disk. This application enables you to make quick backups of your open workbooks to a floppy disk. You never have to leave the friendly confines of Excel, and everything takes only a few seconds. You can even make Backup remind you to back up your data.

Excel 5.0 Features Used

Excel 4.0 Macro Language
Custom dialog boxes
Custom menu commands
Dynamic dialog boxes
Multiple-selection lists
Arrays
Automatic macros (Auto_Open, Auto_Close, ON.TIME)

Files Used

SUPRBOOK.XLS

Special Instructions

To have the Backup application available all the time, copy the SUPRBOOK.XLS file to your XLSTART directory.

About SUPRBOOK.XLS

The Backup application is part of the SUPRBOOK.XLS workbook. When you open SUPRBOOK.XLS, it adds a new SuperBook menu to the worksheet menu bar. This menu contains the following commands:

Back Up Open Workbooks: The command to run the backup application discussed in this project.
Create Workbook Icon: The command to run the Create Icon application presented in Chapter 68, "Using DDE to Create Icons for Excel Workbooks."

Close SUPRBOOK.XLS: Because SUPRBOOK.XLS is hidden, you can use this command to close SUPRBOOK.XLS and remove the SuperBook menu without having to unhide the file.

> SUPER NOTE
>
> Many of this book's projects add commands and submenus to the SuperBook menu. If any other applications are using this menu, the Close SUPRBOOK.XLS command removes only the three commands used by SUPRBOOK.XLS.

If you would like to see either the Backup or Create Icon applications, you need to unhide SUPRBOOK.XLS by selecting the **W**indow | **U**nhide command.

Using Backup

The Backup application uses the Backup dialog box, shown in Figure 67.1. The Backup dialog box gives you the following options:

Backup	This group gives you two options: **A**ll or **S**elected. Choose **A**ll to back up all the open workbooks to a floppy disk. Choose **S**elected to activate the list of open workbooks from which you can select the workbooks you want to back up. You can select multiple items from this list.
Backup To	Use this drop-down list to select the floppy drive you want to use for the backup.
Overwrite Existing Files	Activate this check box to enable Backup to overwrite files that already exist on the floppy disk.
Reminder	Click on this button to display the Backup Reminder dialog box (see Figure 67.2). You can use this dialog box to have Backup remind you to back up your files. To learn how to set a reminder, see the section in this chapter titled "Setting a Backup Reminder."

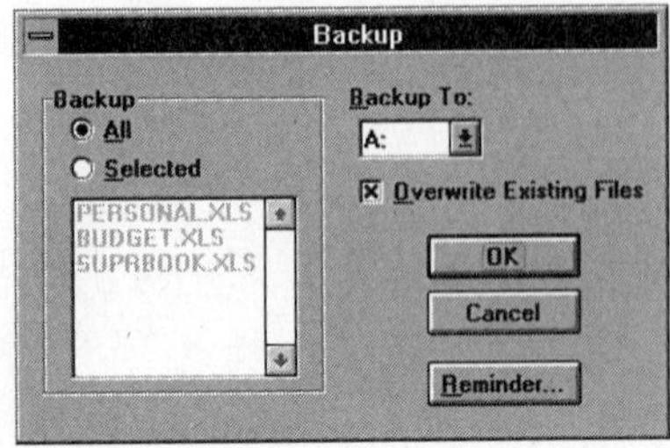

FIGURE 67.1.
The Backup dialog box.

Backing Up Open Workbooks

Follow the steps in Procedure 67.1 to perform a backup.

PROCEDURE 67.1. PERFORMING A BACKUP WITH THE BACKUP APPLICATION.

1. Open the SUPRBOOK.XLS workbook.
2. Select the **S**uperBook | **B**ack Up Open Workbooks command. The Backup dialog box appears.
3. In the Backup group, select either **A**ll or **S**elected. If you choose the **S**elected option, you also have to select one or more files from the attached list.
4. Use the **B**ackup To drop-down list to select the floppy drive to use for the backup.
5. If you want Excel to warn you if Backup is going to overwrite a file on the floppy disk, deactivate the Overwrite Existing Files check box.
6. Click on OK or press Enter. Backup begins backing up the file. If you selected a new, unsaved file, Backup displays the Save As dialog box to enable you to save the file.

Setting a Backup Reminder

The Backup application can remind you to back up your files. You set reminders using the Backup Reminder dialog box, shown in Figure 67.2. The dialog box gives you the following options:

Display Backup Reminder	Activate this check box if you want Backup to display a reminder about backing up your files.
A**t**	Select this option to display the reminder at a specific time (which you enter in the edit box in HH:MM:SS AM/PM format).

Every	Select this option to display the backup reminder at regular intervals. Enter the interval in minutes in the edit box.

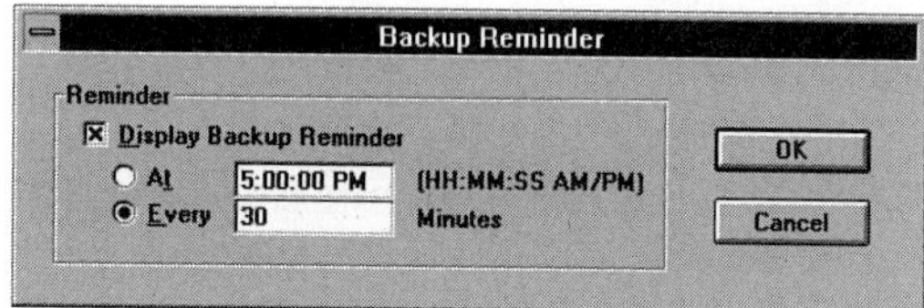

FIGURE 67.2.
The Backup Reminder dialog box.

If you would like the Backup application to display a reminder to back up your files, follow the steps in Procedure 67.2.

PROCEDURE 67.2. SETTING A BACKUP REMINDER.

1. Select the **S**uperBook | **B**ack Up Open Workbooks command to display the Backup dialog box.
2. Click on the **R**eminder button. Backup displays the Backup Reminder dialog box.
3. Make sure the **D**isplay Backup Reminder check box is activated.
4. Select when you want the reminder to be displayed. If you select the **A**t option, enter a time in the edit box provided. If you select **E**very, enter a number (representing the frequency, in minutes, at which you would like to see the reminder) in the edit box.
5. Click on OK or press Enter to return to the Backup dialog box.
6. Click on Cancel to return to the worksheet.

Understanding the Backup Macros

The backup macro sheet is a collection of nine macros that handle displaying the dialog boxes, setting the time for the next reminder, performing the backup, and more. Three of these macros control the backup process; they're the subject of the next few sections.

Displaying the Backup Dialog Box

The main macro, DisplayBackupDialog, initializes the Backup dialog box, sets up a loop to display the dialog box and process the triggers, and then calls other macros to back up the files and reset the reminder time.

The Backup Dialog Box Definition Table

The Backup dialog box was originally prototyped in Excel 4's Dialog Editor. The definition was then copied to the Backup macro sheet and tweaked into the final state shown in Figure 67.3.

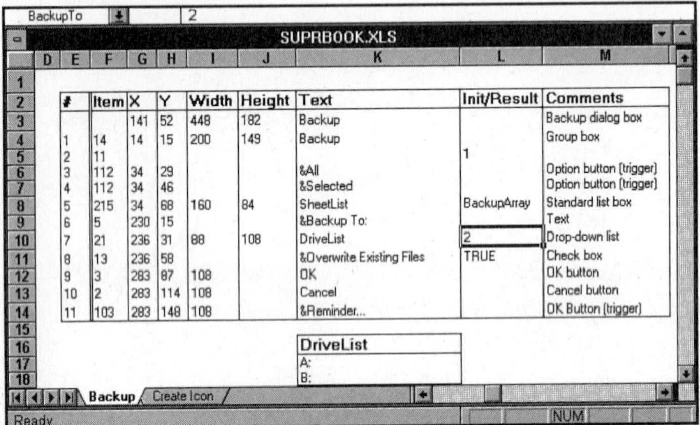

#	Item	X	Y	Width	Height	Text	Init/Result	Comments
		141	52	448	182	Backup		Backup dialog box
1	14	14	15	200	149	Backup		Group box
2	11						1	
3	112	34	29			&All		Option button (trigger)
4	112	34	46			&Selected		Option button (trigger)
5	215	34	68	160	84	SheetList	BackupArray	Standard list box
6	5	230	15			&Backup To:		Text
7	21	236	31	88	108	DriveList	2	Drop-down list
8	13	236	58			&Overwrite Existing Files	TRUE	Check box
9	3	283	87	108		OK		OK button
10	2	283	114	108		Cancel		Cancel button
11	103	283	148	108		&Reminder...		OK Button (trigger)

DriveList
A:
B:

FIGURE 67.3.
The Backup dialog box definition table.

This dialog box has the following named ranges:

Range	*Name*	*Purpose*
L5	BooksToBackup	Holds the option chosen from the Backup option group
L10	BackupTo	Holds the item selected from the **B**ackup To drop-down list
L11	OverwriteFiles	Holds the state of the **O**verwrite Existing Files check box
F8	WorkbookListBox	Holds the item number of the list box that contains the list of open workbooks
K17:K18	DriveList	Holds the list of floppy drives for the **B**ackup To list

Following are some notes about this dialog box:

- The option buttons **A**ll and **S**elected are triggers. If you select **A**ll, you don't need the list of open workbooks, so it gets disabled. Conversely, if you choose **S**elected, the list is enabled.

- The list of open workbooks is a multiple-selection list. To set this up, first you enter a name in the list's Init/Result cell. In this case, the name BackupArray was entered in cell L8. Later, you define this name in the dialog box initialization; this creates an array to hold the selected items from the list.
- The DriveList range contains items for floppy drives A: and B:. You can, of course, substitute appropriate drive letters for your system. In fact, you don't have to use floppy drives at all. You can expand the DriveList to include another directory on the same hard disk, a different hard disk, a network drive, and so forth. Just be sure to include both the drive and directory of the backup location. For example, to include the D:\BACKUP directory in the **B**ackup To list, you enter `D:\BACKUP` in the DriveList range.

Initializing the Backup Dialog Box

Figure 67.4 shows the code that initializes the Backup dialog box. The first `SET.NAME()` function creates an array named `WorkbookList` to hold the list of open workbooks generated by the `DOCUMENTS()` function. The second `SET.NAME()` function creates the name `BackupArray` to hold the selections from the list of open workbooks (when you choose the **S**elected option).

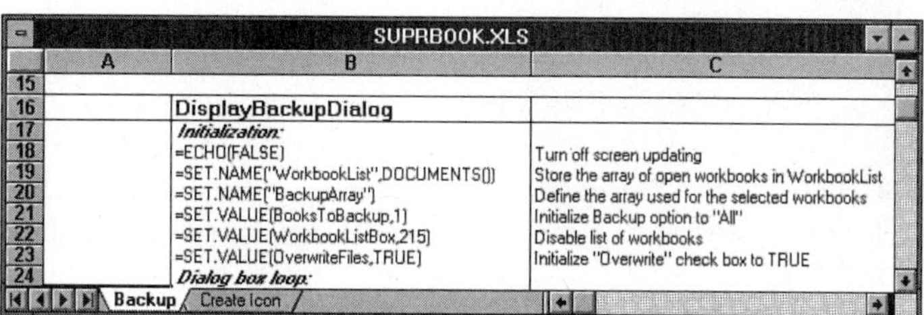

FIGURE 67.4.
The Backup dialog box initialization commands.

The next three `SET.VALUE()` functions initialize the Backup group to **A**ll, disable the list of open workbooks (by setting the item number of the list to 215), and set the **O**verwrite Existing Files check box to `TRUE`.

The Backup Dialog Box Loop

Figure 67.5 shows the `WHILE()` loop that displays and processes the Backup dialog box. Using `WHILE(TRUE)` forces the loop to continue indefinitely. Breaking out of the loop is handled within the loop itself.

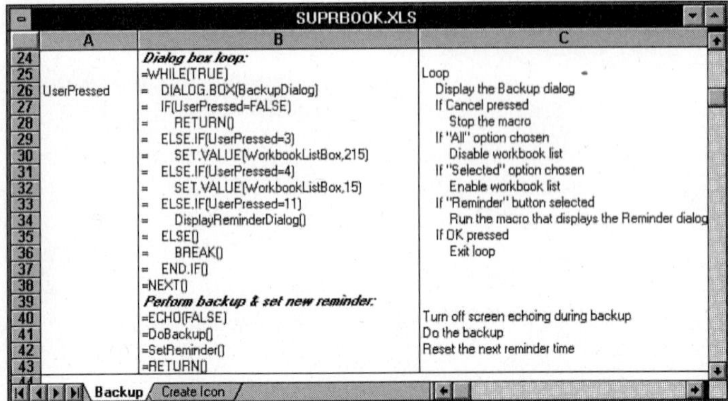

SUPRBOOK.XLS

	A	B	C
24		***Dialog box loop:***	
25		=WHILE(TRUE)	Loop
26	UserPressed	= DIALOG.BOX(BackupDialog)	Display the Backup dialog
27		= IF(UserPressed=FALSE)	If Cancel pressed
28		= RETURN()	Stop the macro
29		= ELSE.IF(UserPressed=3)	If "All" option chosen
30		= SET.VALUE(WorkbookListBox,215)	Disable workbook list
31		= ELSE.IF(UserPressed=4)	If "Selected" option chosen
32		= SET.VALUE(WorkbookListBox,15)	Enable workbook list
33		= ELSE.IF(UserPressed=11)	If "Reminder" button selected
34		= DisplayReminderDialog()	Run the macro that displays the Reminder dialog
35		= ELSE()	If OK pressed
36		= BREAK()	Exit loop
37		= END.IF()	
38		=NEXT()	
39		***Perform backup & set new reminder:***	
40		=ECHO(FALSE)	Turn off screen echoing during backup
41		=DoBackup()	Do the backup
42		=SetReminder()	Reset the next reminder time
43		=RETURN()	

Backup / Create Icon

FIGURE 67.5.
The Backup dialog box loop.

The dialog box result is stored in the `UserPressed` variable. The dialog box is "exited" if you select any of the following five controls: the Cancel button, the three triggers (the **A**ll or **S**elected options, or the **R**eminder button), or the OK button. The `IF-ELSE.IF` functions inside the loop check for each possibility:

- If you select Cancel, the macro is stopped.
- If you select **A**ll (the third line in the dialog box definition), the list of open workbooks is disabled.
- If you choose **S**elected (the fourth line in the table), the workbook list is enabled.
- If you select **R**eminder (line 11), the DisplayReminderDialog macro is run (see the section in this chapter titled "Understanding the Backup Reminder Macros").
- If you select OK, the loop ends with a `BREAK()` function.

Once out of the loop after selecting OK, the DoBackup macro is called to perform the backup and then SetReminder is run to reset the backup reminder.

Getting Ready to Back Up

The DoBackup macro shown in Figure 67.6 gets ready for the backup by processing the dialog box options and getting the names of the files to be backed up.

The first `IF()` test checks the state of the **O**verwrite Existing Files check box. If it's `TRUE` (that is, activated), you turn off error checking to prevent Excel from asking whether the user wants to overwrite files in the destination.

The next two lines (cells B49 and B50) set two variables: `CurrentWindow` holds the name of the active window. This enables the macro to return to that window when it's done. The second variable—`Drive`—uses the `INDEX()` function to return the drive letter selected from the **B**ackup To list.

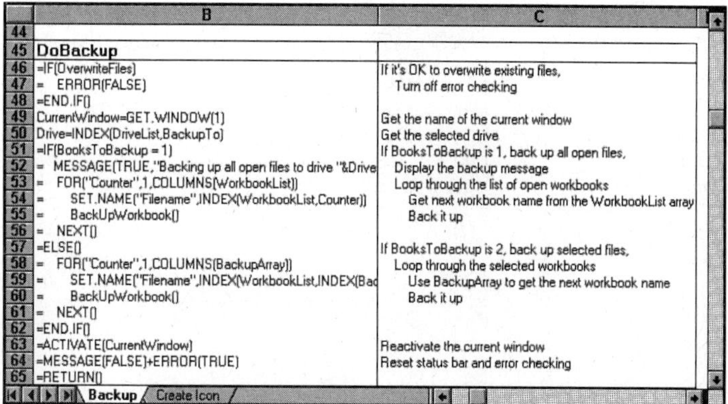

	B	C
44		
45	**DoBackup**	
46	=IF(OverwriteFiles)	If it's OK to overwrite existing files,
47	= ERROR(FALSE)	Turn off error checking
48	=END.IF()	
49	CurrentWindow=GET.WINDOW(1)	Get the name of the current window
50	Drive=INDEX(DriveList,BackupTo)	Get the selected drive
51	=IF(BooksToBackup = 1)	If BooksToBackup is 1, back up all open files,
52	= MESSAGE(TRUE,"Backing up all open files to drive "&Drive	Display the backup message
53	= FOR("Counter",1,COLUMNS(WorkbookList))	Loop through the list of open workbooks
54	= SET.NAME("Filename",INDEX(WorkbookList,Counter))	Get next workbook name from the WorkbookList array
55	= BackUpWorkbook()	Back it up
56	= NEXT()	
57	=ELSE()	If BooksToBackup is 2, back up selected files,
58	= FOR("Counter",1,COLUMNS(BackupArray))	Loop through the selected workbooks
59	= SET.NAME("Filename",INDEX(WorkbookList,INDEX(Bac	Use BackupArray to get the next workbook name
60	= BackUpWorkbook()	Back it up
61	= NEXT()	
62	=END.IF()	
63	=ACTIVATE(CurrentWindow)	Reactivate the current window
64	=MESSAGE(FALSE)+ERROR(TRUE)	Reset status bar and error checking
65	=RETURN()	

Backup / Create Icon

FIGURE 67.6.
The DoBackup macro.

SUPER NOTE

Using the `CurrentWindow` variable to restore the active window illustrates an important point in good macro programming: whenever possible, try to leave the user in the same place he or she started. If your macro changes windows, cells, or workspace options, reset everything to its original state before leaving the macro (if appropriate).

Next, another `IF()` function (cell B51) checks the `BooksToBackup` variable to see which option button was selected. If **A**ll (option 1) was selected, the macro uses a `FOR()` loop (B53:B56) to go through every item in the `WorkbookList` array (the array of all open workbooks). The `INDEX()` function (cell B54) extracts each filename and stores it in the `Filename` variable. Then the BackUpWorkbook macro is called to perform the actual backup (see the next section).

If the **S**elected option was chosen, a different `FOR()` loop (B58:B67) goes through the `BackupArray` list (the list of selected workbooks). Because `BackupArray` is an array of numbers (specifically, an array of the item numbers corresponding to the workbooks selected from the WorkbookList), you need two `INDEX()` functions to extract the name. The first—`BACKUP(BackupArray,Counter)`—extracts the item number of the workbook, and the second uses this number to get the workbook name. The name is then stored in the `Filename` variable and BackUpWorkbook is called.

When the `FOR()` loop is complete, the last two lines return to the active window and reset the status bar and error checking.

Performing the Backup

The first part of the BackUpWorkbook macro, shown in Figure 67.7, saves the workbook (or enables you to assign a name to an unsaved workbook).

FIGURE 67.7.
The first part of the BackUpWorkbook macro.

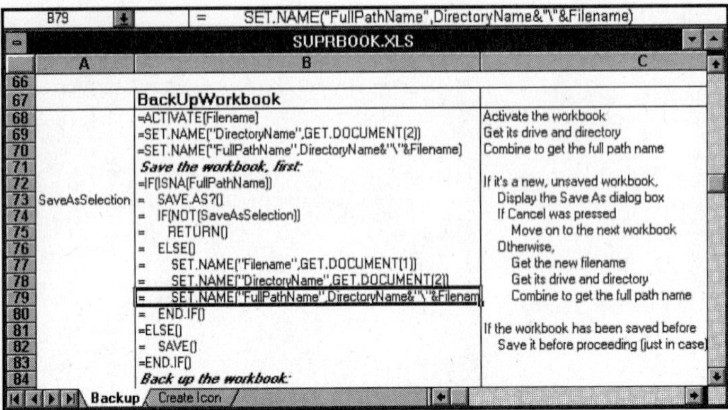

	A	B	C
66			
67		**BackUpWorkbook**	
68		=ACTIVATE(Filename)	Activate the workbook
69		=SET.NAME("DirectoryName",GET.DOCUMENT(2))	Get its drive and directory
70		=SET.NAME("FullPathName",DirectoryName&"\"&Filename)	Combine to get the full path name
71		***Save the workbook, first:***	
72		=IF(ISNA(FullPathName))	If it's a new, unsaved workbook,
73	SaveAsSelection	= SAVE.AS?()	Display the Save As dialog box
74		= IF(NOT(SaveAsSelection))	If Cancel was pressed
75		= RETURN()	Move on to the next workbook
76		= ELSE()	Otherwise,
77		= SET.NAME("Filename",GET.DOCUMENT(1))	Get the new filename
78		= SET.NAME("DirectoryName",GET.DOCUMENT(2))	Get its drive and directory
79		= SET.NAME("FullPathName",DirectoryName&"\"&Filenam	Combine to get the full path name
80		= END.IF()	
81		=ELSE()	If the workbook has been saved before
82		= SAVE()	Save it before proceeding (just in case)
83		=END.IF()	
84		***Back up the workbook:***	

After activating the workbook (cell B68), two new variables are created: `DirectoryName` uses `GET.DOCUMENT(2)` to return the workbook's drive and directory; `FullPathName` concatenates `DirectoryName` and `Filename` to get the full path for the file.

The `IF()` function in cell B72 checks out `FullPathName`. If it's an `#N/A!` error, the file is a new, unsaved workbook. (The `#N/A!` error is generated by the `GET.DOCUMENT(2)` function.) In this case, the macro displays the Save As dialog box to enable you to save the workbook. If you click on Cancel in the Save As dialog, the macro returns; otherwise, the `Filename`, `DirectoryName`, and `FullPathName` are reassigned. If `FullPathName` is not `#N/A!`, the macro saves the workbook.

The second part of the BackUpWorkbook macro is shown in Figure 67.8. Here, a `WHILE()` loop is set up to safeguard against an error during the backup process. The `WHILE()` loop is controlled by the `SavedOK` variable.

FIGURE 67.8.
The second part of the BackUpWorkbook macro.

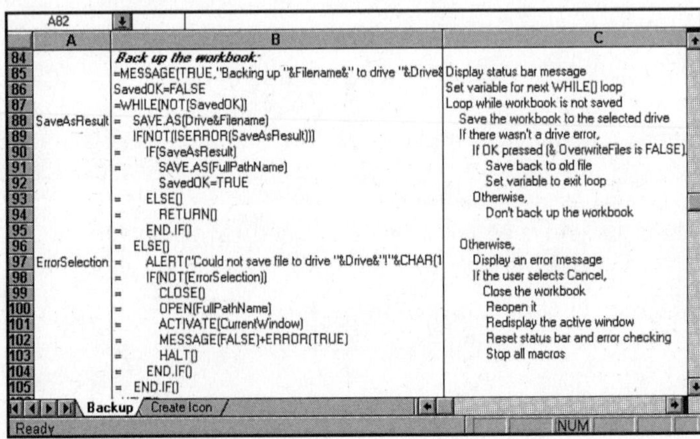

	A	B	C
84		***Back up the workbook:***	
85		=MESSAGE(TRUE,"Backing up "&Filename&" to drive "&Drive&	Display status bar message
86		SavedOK=FALSE	Set variable for next WHILE() loop
87		=WHILE(NOT(SavedOK))	Loop while workbook is not saved
88	SaveAsResult	= SAVE.AS(Drive&Filename)	Save the workbook to the selected drive
89		= IF(NOT(ISERROR(SaveAsResult)))	If there wasn't a drive error,
90		= IF(SaveAsResult)	If OK pressed (& OverwriteFiles is FALSE)
91		= SAVE.AS(FullPathName)	Save back to old file
92		SavedOK=TRUE	Set variable to exit loop
93		= ELSE()	Otherwise,
94		= RETURN()	Don't back up the workbook
95		= END.IF()	
96		= ELSE()	Otherwise,
97	ErrorSelection	= ALERT("Could not save file to drive "&Drive&"!"&CHAR(1	Display an error message
98		= IF(NOT(ErrorSelection))	If the user selects Cancel,
99		= CLOSE()	Close the workbook
100		= OPEN(FullPathName)	Reopen it
101		= ACTIVATE(CurrentWindow)	Redisplay the active window
102		= MESSAGE(FALSE)+ERROR(TRUE)	Reset status bar and error checking
103		= HALT()	Stop all macros
104		= END.IF()	
105		= END.IF()	

The actual backup is performed by the `SAVE.AS()` function (cell B88), and the result is stored in the `SaveAsResult` variable. When determining whether or not the backup was successful, the macro needs to allow for two possibilities:

- There was an error during the `SAVE.AS()` function. This could be caused, for example, by having no diskette in the drive or by not having enough room on the disk.
- If the **O**verwrite Existing Files check box is deactivated, you could click on Cancel when Excel asks whether you want to overwrite a file already on the floppy.

The first `IF()` function (cell B89) checks for an error. If none occurred, the second `IF()` function (cell B90) checks `SaveAsResult`. If it's `TRUE`, another `SAVE.AS()` function reinstates the original file. Then `SavedOK` is set to `TRUE` to exit the loop. If `SaveAsResult` is `FALSE`, the macro exits without backing up the file.

If there was an error, an `ALERT()` box is displayed. This box explains that an error occurred and asks whether you want to retry the backup. If you click on Cancel, the macro needs to reset Excel by closing the workbook and reopening it. (Problems would occur if the backup application didn't do this.) If you click on OK, the macro loops and tries the `SAVE.AS()` function again.

Understanding the Backup Reminder Macros

Four macros control the backup reminders you can set. The next few sections look at these macros and at the definition of the Backup Reminder dialog box.

Displaying the Backup Reminder Dialog Box

The DisplayReminderDialog macro displays the Backup Reminder dialog box and processes its various triggers.

The Backup Reminder Dialog Box Definition Table

The Backup Reminder dialog box definition table, shown in Figure 67.9, has the following named ranges:

Range	*Name*	*Purpose*
L23	DisplayReminder	Holds the state of the **D**isplay Backup Reminder check box
L24	ReminderOption	Holds the selection from the Reminder group

continues

Range	Name	Purpose
L27	ReminderTime	Holds the time of the reminder if the **At** option was selected
L28'	ReminderMinutes	Holds the number of minutes between reminders if the **Every** option was selected
F25	AtOption	Holds the item number of the **At** option button
F26	EveryOption	Holds the item number of the **Every** option button
F27	AtEditBox	Holds the item number of the edit box associated with the **At** option
F28	EveryEditBox	Holds the item number of the edit box associated with the **Every** option
F29	AtText	Holds the item number of the text label associated with the **At** option (that is, HH:MM:SS AM/PM)
F30	EveryText	Holds the item number of the text label associated with the **Every** option (that is, Minutes)

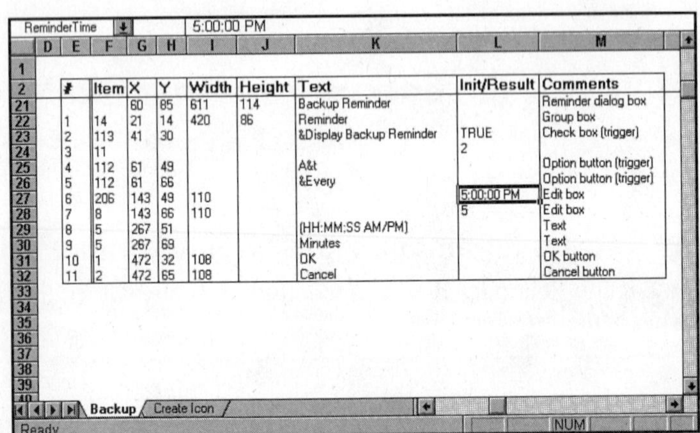

#	Item	X	Y	Width	Height	Text	Init/Result	Comments
		60	85	611	114	Backup Reminder		Reminder dialog box
1	14	21	14	420	86	Reminder		Group box
2	113	41	30			&Display Backup Reminder	TRUE	Check box (trigger)
3	11						2	
4	112	61	49			A&t		Option button (trigger)
5	112	61	66			&Every		Option button (trigger)
6	206	143	49	110			5:00:00 PM	Edit box
7	8	143	66	110			5	Edit box
8	5	267	51			(HH:MM:SS AM/PM)		Text
9	5	267	69			Minutes		Text
10	1	472	32	108		OK		OK button
11	2	472	65	108		Cancel		Cancel button

FIGURE 67.9.
The definition table for the Backup Reminder dialog box.

This dialog box uses three triggers to toggle the various controls:

- If you deactivate the **D**isplay Backup Reminder check box, the trigger disables the other options.
- If you select the **A**t option, the **E**very option and its associated controls are disabled.
- If you select the **E**very option, the **A**t option and its associated controls are disabled.

The Backup Reminder Dialog Box Loop

To process the triggers in the Backup Reminder dialog box, the DisplayReminderDialog macro sets up a `WHILE(TRUE)` loop, shown in Figure 67.10. The dialog box result is stored in the `UserSelected` variable, and then a series of `IF-ELSE.IF` tests check for specific results.

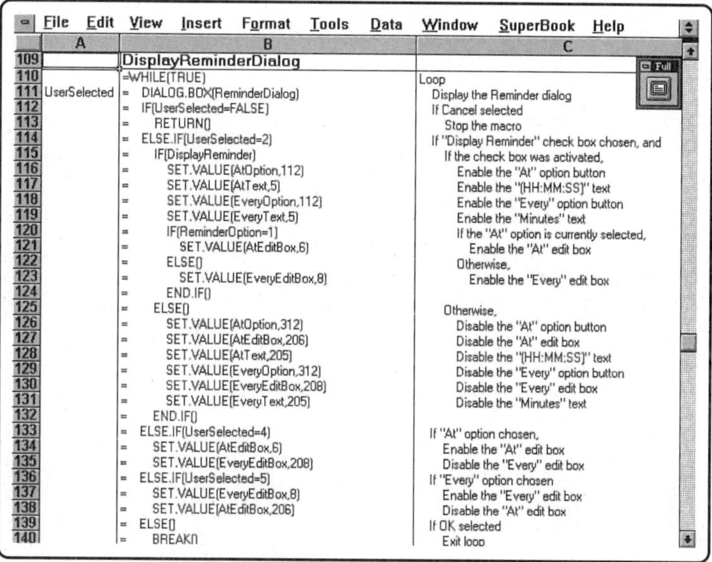

	A	B	C
109		DisplayReminderDialog	
110		=WHILE(TRUE)	Loop
111	UserSelected	= DIALOG.BOX(ReminderDialog)	Display the Reminder dialog
112		= IF(UserSelected=FALSE)	If Cancel selected
113		= RETURN()	Stop the macro
114		= ELSE.IF(UserSelected=2)	If "Display Reminder" check box chosen, and
115		= IF(DisplayReminder)	If the check box was activated,
116		= SET.VALUE(AtOption,112)	Enable the "At" option button
117		= SET.VALUE(AtText,5)	Enable the "(HH:MM:SS)" text
118		= SET.VALUE(EveryOption,112)	Enable the "Every" option button
119		= SET.VALUE(EveryText,5)	Enable the "Minutes" text
120		= IF(ReminderOption=1)	If the "At" option is currently selected,
121		= SET.VALUE(AtEditBox,6)	Enable the "At" edit box
122		= ELSE()	Otherwise,
123		= SET.VALUE(EveryEditBox,8)	Enable the "Every" edit box
124		= END.IF()	
125		= ELSE()	Otherwise,
126		= SET.VALUE(AtOption,312)	Disable the "At" option button
127		= SET.VALUE(AtEditBox,206)	Disable the "At" edit box
128		= SET.VALUE(AtText,205)	Disable the "(HH:MM:SS)" text
129		= SET.VALUE(EveryOption,312)	Disable the "Every" option button
130		= SET.VALUE(EveryEditBox,208)	Disable the "Every" edit box
131		= SET.VALUE(EveryText,205)	Disable the "Minutes" text
132		= END.IF()	
133		= ELSE.IF(UserSelected=4)	If "At" option chosen,
134		= SET.VALUE(AtEditBox,6)	Enable the "At" edit box
135		= SET.VALUE(EveryEditBox,208)	Disable the "Every" edit box
136		= ELSE.IF(UserSelected=5)	If "Every" option chosen
137		= SET.VALUE(EveryEditBox,8)	Enable the "Every" edit box
138		= SET.VALUE(AtEditBox,206)	Disable the "At" edit box
139		= ELSE()	If OK selected
140		= BREAK()	Exit loop

FIGURE 67.10.
The `WHILE()` loop for the Backup Reminder dialog box.

If you click on Cancel, the macro quits without doing anything. Otherwise, another `IF()` function (cell B115) checks the state of the **D**isplay Reminder check box. If this box was activated, the other options are enabled (B116:B123). Otherwise, they're disabled (B126:B131).

Subsequent `ELSE.IF()` tests (cells B133 and B136) check for option button selections. For example, if you select the **A**t option, its associated edit box is enabled, and the edit box for the **E**very option is disabled.

If OK was selected, a `BREAK()` function (cell B140) exits the loop.

Setting the Reminder Time

As soon as the DisplayReminderDialog macro exits the loop, it needs to either set the reminder time or clear the reminder time, depending on the state of the **D**isplay Reminder check box.

As Figure 67.11 shows, an `IF()` function (cell B143) tests the `DisplayReminder` variable. If it's `TRUE` (that is, the check box was activated), the SetReminder macro is called. Otherwise, ClearReminder is called to clear out any existing reminder (see the next section).

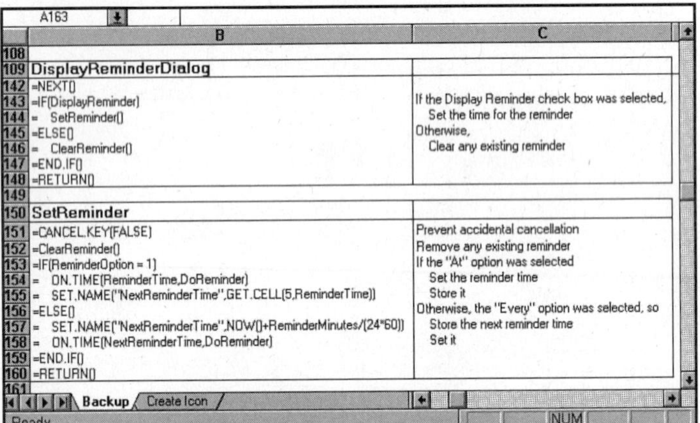

FIGURE 67.11.
The macro commands that set or delete the reminder.

The SetReminder macro (see Figure 67.11) sets up the reminder based on the selections in the Backup Reminder dialog box. The first line, `CANCEL.KEY(FALSE)`, disables the Esc key for the duration of the macro. This prevents an accidental cancellation before the macro has had time to do its work. The second line calls `ClearReminder` (see the next section) to remove any existing reminder before continuing.

The `IF()` test in cell B153 checks the `ReminderOption` variable. If it corresponds to the **A**t option, an `ON.TIME()` function sets up the DoReminder macro (see the next section) to run at the time given by `ReminderTime`. Also, the time is stored in a variable named `NextReminderTime`. You'll need this variable when clearing the `ON.TIME()` function.

If you selected the **E**very option, the time of the next reminder is calculated with the following formula (cell B157):

```
NOW() + ReminderMinutes/(24*60)
```

This is stored in the `NextReminderTime` variable; then the `ON.TIME()` function sets up the reminder.

Other Reminder Macros

The ClearReminder and DoReminder macros are shown in Figure 67.12. ClearReminder turns off the current reminder by setting the fourth argument of the `ON.TIME()` function to `FALSE` (cell B165). You have to turn off error checking in cell B163 because Excel will generate an error message if you try to reset an `ON.TIME()` function that has already expired.

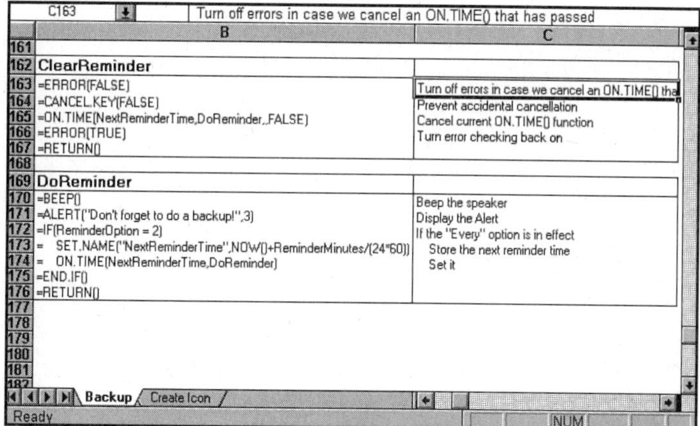

FIGURE 67.12.
The ClearReminder and DoReminder macros.

The DoReminder macro beeps the speaker and displays a simple `ALERT()` box for the reminder. If you selected **E**very (option 2), the macro then sets up the time for the next reminder (B173 and B174).

The Automatic Macros

The Backup sheet also includes the Auto_Open_Backup and Auto_Close_Backup macros, shown in Figure 67.13. Auto_Open_Backup calls `SetReminder` if the **D**isplay Reminder check box was activated in the last session. The Auto_Close_Backup macro calls ClearReminder to clear the `ON.TIME()` function, then it activates and saves SUPRBOOK.XLS to preserve any changed dialog box preferences.

FIGURE 67.13.
The Auto_Open_Backup and Auto_Close_Backup macros.

SUPRBOOK.XLS

	A	B	C
1	Macros		
2	Names	Commands	Comments
3			
4		Auto_Open_Backup	
5		=IF(DisplayReminder)	If the Display Reminder check box is activated
6		= SetReminder()	Set the time for the reminder
7		=END.IF()	
8		=RETURN()	
9			
10		Auto_Close_Backup	
11		=ClearReminder()	Clear any pending ON.TIME() functions
12		=ACTIVATE("SUPRBOOK.XLS")	Activate SUPRBOOK.XLS
13		=SAVE()	Save reminder preferences
14		=RETURN()	
15			

Backup / Create Icon / SuperBook Menu

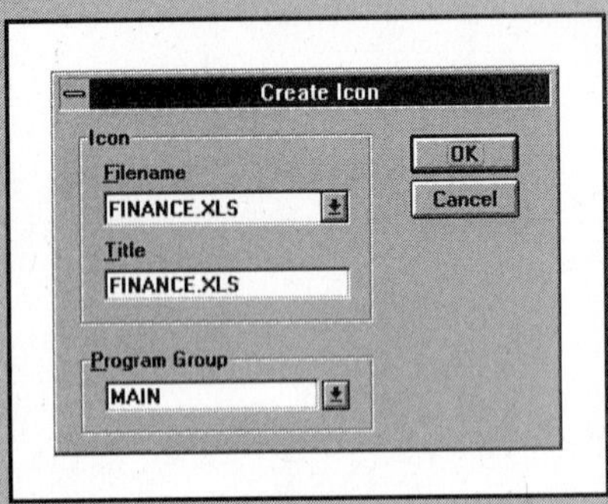

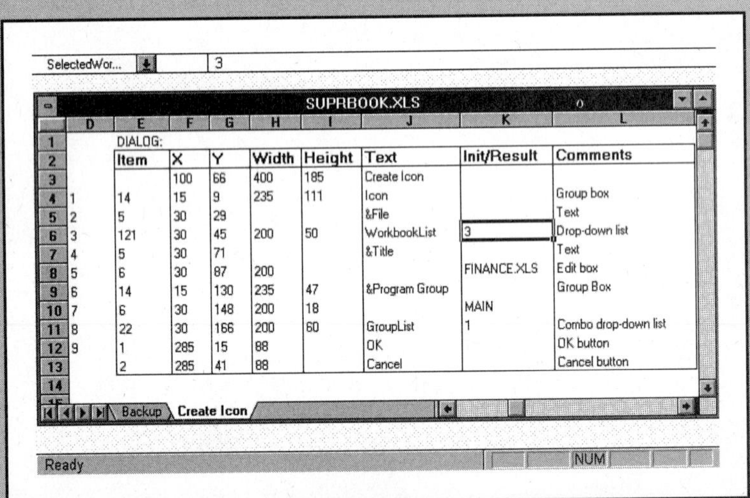

	D	E	F	G	H	I	J	K	L
1		DIALOG:							
2		Item	X	Y	Width	Height	Text	Init/Result	Comments
3			100	66	400	185	Create Icon		
4	1	14	15	9	235	111	Icon		Group box
5	2	5	30	29			&File		Text
6	3	121	30	45	200	50	WorkbookList	3	Drop-down list
7	4	5	30	71			&Title		Text
8	5	6	30	87	200			FINANCE.XLS	Edit box
9	6	14	15	130	235	47	&Program Group		Group Box
10	7	6	30	148	200	18		MAIN	
11	8	22	30	166	200	60	GroupList	1	Combo drop-down list
12	9	1	285	15	88		OK		OK button
13		2	285	41	88		Cancel		Cancel button
14									

Chapter 68

Using DDE to Create Icons for Excel Workbooks

Excel 5.0's new tabbed workbooks enable you to combine worksheets, charts, modules, and macro sheets in one package. Although there are many advantages to this approach, one of the biggest is that you'll have fewer files to manage. Instead of opening half a dozen files to work with, you'll need just one or two. Therefore, you'll probably find yourself using the same few workbooks every day. To make life easier, you can create icons in Program Manager for individual Excel workbooks. When you double-click on the icon, Excel starts and automatically loads the workbook.

This project takes you through a collection of Excel 4.0 macros that enable you to create a workbook icon in Program Manager without leaving Excel. You'll be able to create an icon for any open workbook, and you'll even be able to create new program groups.

Excel 5.0 Features Used

Excel 4.0 Macro Language
Dynamic Data Exchange
Low-level file functions
Custom dialog boxes
Dynamic dialog boxes
Arrays

Files Used

SUPRBOOK.XLS

Creating an Icon for an Open Workbook

The sheet that contains the macros for this project is called Create Icon, and it resides in the SUPRBOOK.XLS file that is included on the Super Disk. As soon as you load this file, a new **S**uperBook menu appears in the Worksheet menu bar. You can create a Program Manager icon for an open workbook by following the steps in Procedure 68.1.

PROCEDURE 68.1. CREATING AN ICON FOR AN OPEN WORKBOOK.

1. Select the **S**uperBook | **C**reate Workbook **I**con command. The Create Icon dialog box appears, shown in Figure 68.1.
2. In the **F**ile list, select the workbook for which you want to create an icon. The filename also appears in the **T**itle edit box.
3. In the **T**itle edit box, enter the text you want to appear beneath the icon. The default is the name of the file, but you can enter any description. Although you can use up to 255 characters, keep in mind that Windows limits icon titles to 40 characters.

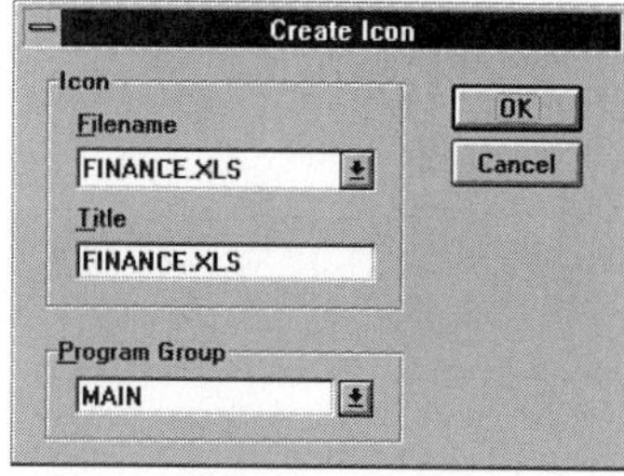

FIGURE 68.1.
The Create Icon dialog box.

4. In the **P**rogram Group list, select the program group in which you want the icon to appear. To create a new group, enter the group name in the edit box.
5. Click on OK or press Enter. An Alert box appears to inform you that the icon has been created, as shown in Figure 68.2.

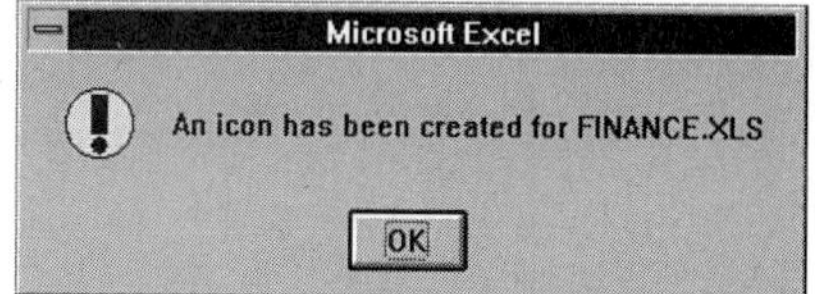

FIGURE 68.2.
This dialog box appears when the icon has been created.

Examining the Create Icon Macros

Now that you know how to use the Create Icon command, it's time to look under the hood and see how things work. Run the **W**indow | Un**h**ide command and unhide the SUPRBOOK.XLS workbook. With the workbook visible, select the Create Icon macro sheet.

Initializing the Environment

The macro that gets things started is called CreateIcon. Figure 68.3 shows the macro's opening lines, which serve to set up the environment. After turning off screen updating and error checking, the next three cells initialize two of the dialog box controls. Three variables are used here:

`WorkbookList`: This variable stores the result of the `DOCUMENTS()` function. `DOCUMENTS()` returns an array of all the open workbooks. Therefore, you'll use `WorkbookList` as the data for the **F**ile list box.

`SelectedWorkbook`: This variable holds the name of the workbook selected from the **F**ile list. The formula in cell B9 (seen in the full entry in the formula bar) initializes the variable to the name of the active workbook: `GET.DOCUMENT(1)` returns the file's name, and `MATCH()` finds its position in the `WorkbookList` array.

`IconTitle`: This variable is the title that appears under the icon. Cell B10 initializes it as the name of the active workbook.

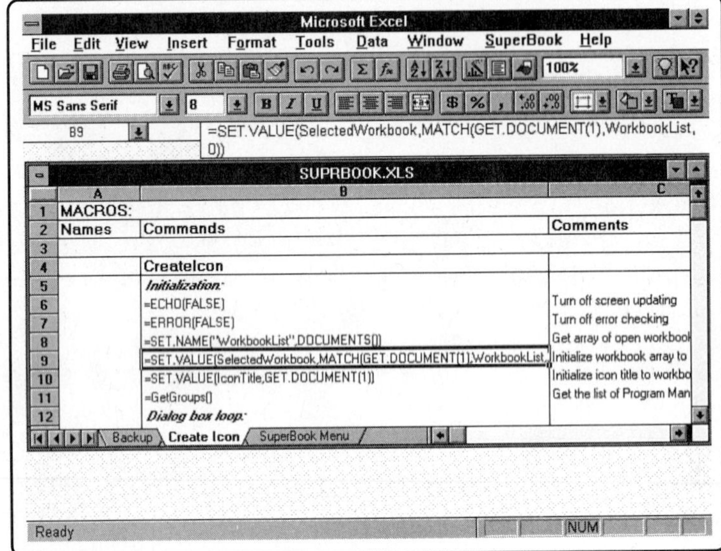

FIGURE 68.3.
The opening lines of the CreateIcon macro.

As the final initialization chore, cell B11 calls the `GetGroups` procedure (examined in the next section) to get the list of your program groups.

Creating the Program Group List

For Windows users who have customized Program Manager, there is no way to tell in advance what program groups exist on any system. Therefore, to get the list of program groups that appears in the **P**rogram Group list box, the `GetGroups` procedure has to take the direct route: it reads the program groups from the PROGMAN.INI file. PROGMAN.INI is the Program Manager initialization file that includes, among other things, several lines that define the program groups.

To do this, you need to use some of Excel's low-level file functions. These functions work with files directly from the disk, instead of loading them into memory. This enables you to read the file one character or (in this case) one line at a time. To find program groups, you read the PROGMAN.INI lines, look for those with "Group" in them, and then extract the group name from those lines.

Figure 68.4 shows the beginning of the `GetGroups` procedure. The third line (cell B41) uses `FOPEN()`, the first of the low-level file functions:

`FOPEN(`***`file_text`***`,`*`access_num`*`)`

`file_text`	The name of the file to open.
`access_num`	A number specifying how the file is to be opened, as follows:

`access_num`	*Opened As*
1	Read/write
2	Read-only
3	New read/write file

`FOPEN()` creates a link to the file on the disk and, if successful, returns a file handle that identifies the file for future operations. In `GetGroups`, this file handle is assigned to the `FileHandle` variable. The next five lines use an `IF()` test to make sure that PROGMAN.INI was opened properly.

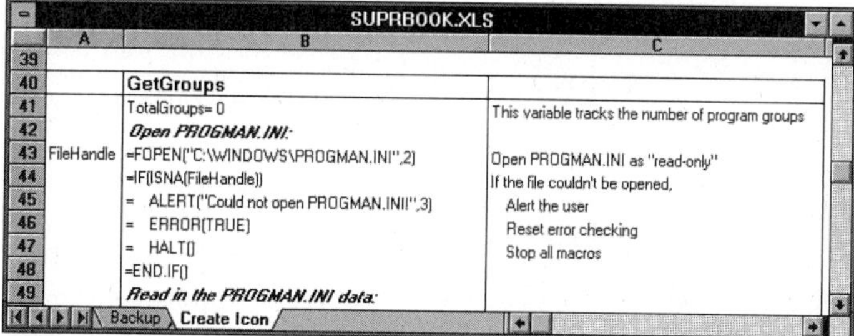

FIGURE 68.4.
The `GetGroups` procedure begins by establishing a low-level connection to PROGMAN.INI.

SUPER CAUTION

PROGMAN.INI is always found in the main Windows directory. If you installed Windows in a location other than C:\WINDOWS, you'll need to edit cell B43 and enter the correct drive and directory.

The second half of `GetGroups`, shown in Figure 68.5, reads in and processes data from PROGMAN.INI. You'll be using three more low-level file functions here (in each case, *`FileHandle`* is the number returned by the `FOPEN()` function):

`FSIZE(`*`FileHandle`*`)`: Returns the size, in bytes, of PROGMAN.INI.

`FREADLN(`*`FileHandle`*`)`: Reads in characters from PROGMAN.INI one line at a time. Each line is stored in the `LineRead` variable.

`FPOS(`*`FileHandle`*`)`: Returns your current position in PROGMAN.INI. `FPOS()` is updated each time `FREADLN()` is called.

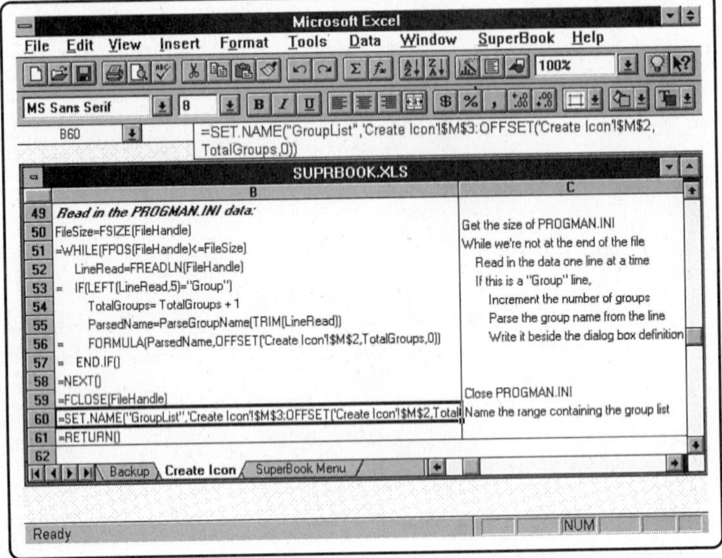

FIGURE 68.5.
The second part of `GetGroups` *reads and processes PROGMAN.INI.*

The `WHILE()` loop set up in cell B51 compares `FPOS()` with the file size. While `FPOS()` is less than `FileSize`, you continue reading lines from the file. What do you do with these lines you're reading? Because you know you want program groups, you take advantage of the fact that all the lines you need look something like this:

```
Group1=C:\WINDOWS\MAIN.GRP
```

Therefore, the formula in cell B53 checks the five leftmost characters in each line to see if they contain the word "Group." If they do, you have a program group line.

The next challenge is to extract the group name from the line. In the previous example, you would only want "MAIN" to appear in the list. Therefore, the formula in B55 sends `LineRead` to a function macro named `ParseGroupName` that does the job, as shown in Figure 68.6. I won't go into the details of this function, but its operation can be summarized as follows:

1. Look for the first backslash (\).
2. Discard all the characters up to and including the backslash.
3. Repeat steps 1 and 2 until there are no more backslashes.
4. Discard the extension (the last four characters, including the period).
5. Return the group name.

After you have extracted the group name, it is stored on the macro sheet, and the process repeats until PROGMAN.INI is exhausted. The `FCLOSE()` low-level file function closes the connection, and then the name `GroupList` is defined as the range containing the group names you extracted.

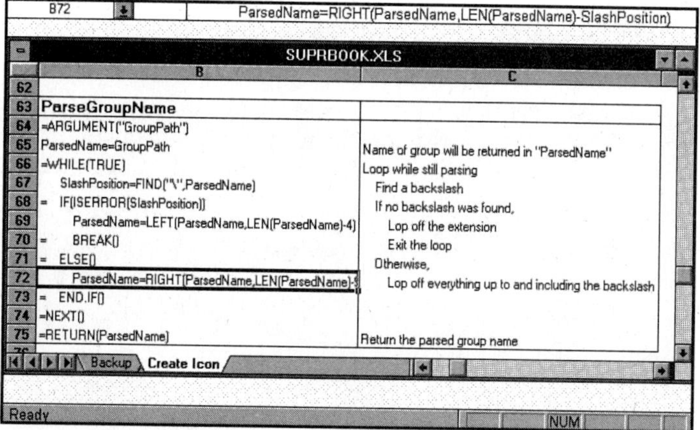

B72 | ParsedName=RIGHT(ParsedName,LEN(ParsedName)-SlashPosition)

SUPRBOOK.XLS

	B	C
62		
63	**ParseGroupName**	
64	=ARGUMENT("GroupPath")	
65	ParsedName=GroupPath	Name of group will be returned in "ParsedName"
66	=WHILE(TRUE)	Loop while still parsing
67	SlashPosition=FIND("\",ParsedName)	Find a backslash
68	= IF(ISERROR(SlashPosition))	If no backslash was found,
69	ParsedName=LEFT(ParsedName,LEN(ParsedName)-4)	Lop off the extension
70	= BREAK()	Exit the loop
71	= ELSE()	Otherwise,
72	ParsedName=RIGHT(ParsedName,LEN(ParsedName)-S	Lop off everything up to and including the backslash
73	= END.IF()	
74	=NEXT()	
75	=RETURN(ParsedName)	Return the parsed group name

Backup | Create Icon

Ready NUM

FIGURE 68.6.
A function macro to extract the group name from the PROGMAN.INI line.

The Create Icon Dialog Box

The application is now ready to display the Create Icon dialog box. Before you examine the code, the next section takes a look at the definition table for the dialog box.

The Dialog Box Definition Table

Figure 68.7 shows the definition table for the Create Icon dialog box. This table is fairly straightforward, but I would like to point out a few features.

SelectedWor... | 3

SUPRBOOK.XLS

	D	E	F	G	H	I	J	K	L
1		DIALOG:							
2		**Item**	**X**	**Y**	**Width**	**Height**	**Text**	**Init/Result**	**Comments**
3			100	66	400	185	Create Icon		
4	1	14	15	9	235	111	Icon		Group box
5	2	5	30	29			&File		Text
6	3	121	30	45	200	50	WorkbookList	3	Drop-down list
7	4	5	30	71			&Title		Text
8	5	6	30	87	200			FINANCE.XLS	Edit box
9	6	14	15	130	235	47	&Program Group		Group Box
10	7	6	30	148	200	18		MAIN	
11	8	22	30	166	200	60	GroupList	1	Combo drop-down list
12	9	1	285	15	88		OK		OK button
13		2	285	41	88		Cancel		Cancel button
14									

Backup | Create Icon

Ready NUM

FIGURE 68.7.
The definition table for the Create Icon dialog box.

- The **File** drop-down list is defined by the range E6:L6. Its item number (121) signifies that it's a trigger. Specifically, when you select a different filename, the **Title** edit box adjusts accordingly (see the next section). Recall that you're using the `WorkbookList` array for this list. Therefore, as expected, the name `WorkbookList` appears in its Text cell (J6). Also, its Init/Result cell (K6) is defined as the *SelectedWorkbook* name you saw earlier.
- The **Title** edit box is defined in E8:L8. Cell K8 is defined as the *IconTitle* name.
- The **Program Group** control is a combination drop-down edit list that is defined in two rows—E10:L11. Its elements are given by the GroupList created from PROGMAN.INI (cell J11), and its Init/Result is defined as the *SelectedGroup* name (cell K10).

Handling the Trigger

Because this dialog box has a trigger control (the **File** list), you need to set up a `WHILE()` loop, as shown in Figure 68.8. (To learn more about dialog box triggers, see Chapter 47, "Creating Custom Dialog Boxes.") This loop simply checks for various results (returned in the `DialogSelection` variable):

- If you click on Cancel, the routine jumps to a cell named `TheEnd` to end the procedure.
- If you select an item from the **File** drop-down list (the third control in the definition table), the filename is looked up in the `WorkbookList` and assigned to `IconTitle` (cell B18).
- If you click on OK, the loop exits.

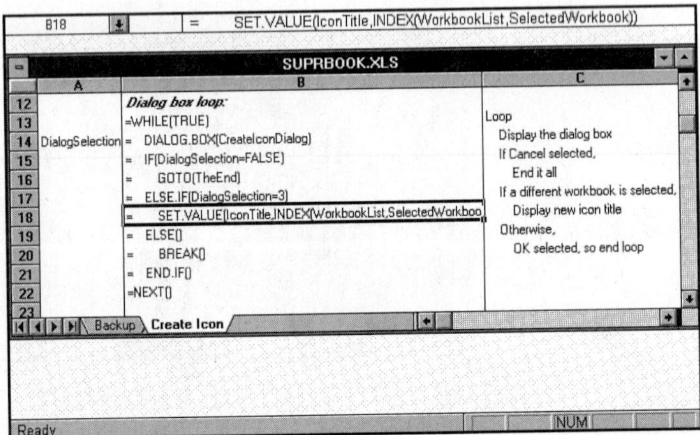

FIGURE 68.8. *The `WHILE()` loop that displays the Create Icon dialog box.*

Constructing the File's Full Pathname

As soon as you're out of the dialog box loop, all you have to do is construct the full pathname for the file before creating the icon.

Figure 68.9 shows the remainder of the code in the CreateIcon macro. The first two lines (cells B25 and B26) create two variables. `WorkbookName` uses the `INDEX()` function to return the name of the selected workbook from the `WorkbookList` array. `WorkbookPath` uses `GET.DOCUMENT()` to return the drive and directory for the workbook.

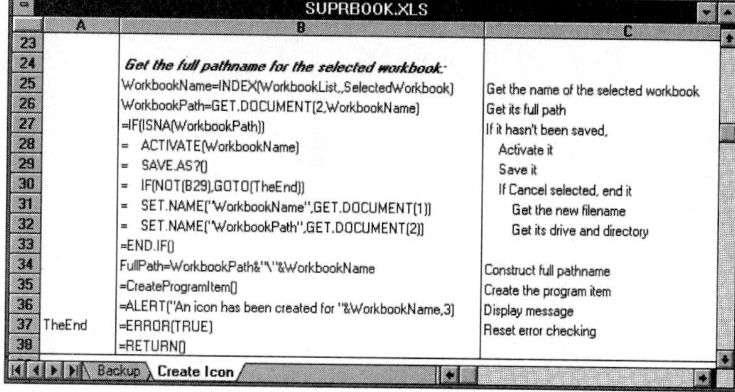

	A	B	C
23			
24		***Get the full pathname for the selected workbook:***	
25		WorkbookName=INDEX(WorkbookList,,SelectedWorkbook)	Get the name of the selected workbook
26		WorkbookPath=GET.DOCUMENT(2,WorkbookName)	Get its full path
27		=IF(ISNA(WorkbookPath))	If it hasn't been saved,
28		= ACTIVATE(WorkbookName)	Activate it
29		= SAVE.AS?()	Save it
30		= IF(NOT(B29),GOTO(TheEnd))	If Cancel selected, end it
31		= SET.NAME("WorkbookName",GET.DOCUMENT(1))	Get the new filename
32		= SET.NAME("WorkbookPath",GET.DOCUMENT(2))	Get its drive and directory
33		=END.IF()	
34		FullPath=WorkbookPath&"\"&WorkbookName	Construct full pathname
35		=CreateProgramItem()	Create the program item
36		=ALERT("An icon has been created for "&WorkbookName,3)	Display message
37	TheEnd	=ERROR(TRUE)	Reset error checking
38		=RETURN()	

FIGURE 68.9.
The code that constructs the workbook's full pathname.

The `IF()` test in cell B27 checks `WorkbookPath`. If `GET.DOCUMENT()` returned the `#N/A!` error, the workbook is a new, unsaved file. In this case, the macro activates the workbook and calls the `SAVE.AS()` function to give you a chance to save the file. If you do save it, two `SET.NAME()` functions (cells B31 and B32) get the new workbook name, drive, and directory.

The next step is to construct a full pathname. This happens in cell B32, in which the `FullPath` variable is assigned the concatenation of `WorkbookPath` and `WorkbookName`.

Finally, the CreateProgramItem macro is called to create the icon.

Creating the Icon

Figure 68.10 shows the final Create Icon macro: CreateProgramItem. The first line opens a channel to Program Manager using the Dynamic Data Exchange (DDE) function `INITIATE()`. (See Chapter 49, "Macro Tips and Techniques," for details on using DDE in macros.) The first `EXECUTE()` function (cell B79) sends the Program Manager function `CreateGroup` through the opened channel. This function either activates the program group you selected or, if you entered a new group name, it creates the group.

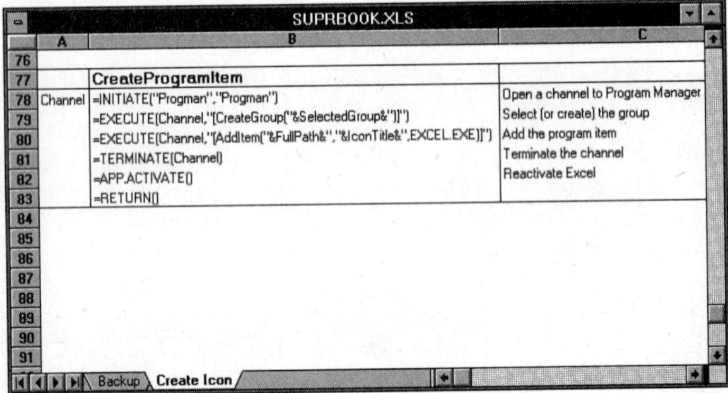

FIGURE 68.10.
The macro that creates the Program Manager icon.

The second `EXECUTE()` function sends the Program Manager function `AddItem`. This creates the program item using `FullPath` as the command line, Icon Title as the description, and the EXCEL.EXE icon.

The macro finishes by closing the channel and activating Excel.

Saving for Retirement

Personal Data		
Date of Birth	8/23/59	
Age Now	34	
Retirement Age/Date	55	8/23/14
Yrs/Mths to Retirement	21	249
Life Expectancy	80	
Yrs/Mths Retired	25	300

Statistical Data	
Inflation Rate	3.0%
Investment Rate	6.0%
Tax Rate	15.0%

Retirement Income	Today's $	Retirement
Desired Retirement Income	50,000	93,015
Pension Income	6,000	11,162
Social Security Income	10,000	18,603
Net Income Needed	34,000	63,250
Total Needed for Retirement	439,753	818,070

Savings Calculations		
Current Retirement Plans	25,000	84,989
Current Tax-Free Investments	100,000	339,956
Current Taxable Investments	15,000	42,633
Total Current Investments	125,000	416,585

Total Amount to Save	314,753	401,484
Amount to Save/Month (Non-Tax)	639	
Amount to Save/Month (Taxable)	713	

Chapter

69

Personal Financial Planning Examples

Spreadsheets were invented by a business school graduate student in the late 1970s to take the drudgery out of working with financial data. Ever since then, spreadsheets have been used mostly for financial applications—although, as you've seen, a powerful, modern program like Excel is capable of much more than dollar crunching.

This project returns to Excel's roots and looks at several personal finance applications. The sheets in this project include a net worth statement, a monthly budget, a retirement savings calculator, and three mortgage worksheets that cover analysis, amortization, and refinancing.

Excel 5.0 Features Used

Financial functions
Linking formulas
Outlining
Worksheet dialog box controls
Visual Basic for Applications

Files Used

FINANCES.XLS

Special Instructions

Open the FINANCES.XLS file from the directory where you installed the Super Disk files.

Creating a Net Worth Statement

Your *net worth* is the difference between your assets and your liabilities. In this sense, we define an *asset* as something you own and a *liability* as something you owe. A *net worth statement* is an itemized list of your assets and liabilities that shows totals for each, as well as the difference (your net worth).

Most financial institutions require a net worth statement as part of the application process for large loans and mortgages. Also, a net worth statement is a convenient measure of your financial stability and progress.

Examining the Net Worth Worksheet

The FINANCES.XLS workbook contains a Net Worth worksheet you can use to calculate your net worth. This worksheet is divided into two sections:

The ASSETS section, which begins in row 4 (see Figure 69.1), lists various asset items. These items are grouped into three categories:

Liquid Assets: These are assets that are readily convertible into cash. They include cash and cash equivalents, bank accounts, and short-term investments and deposits.

Investments: Use this section to record the current value of longer-term investments. These include items such as mutual funds, stocks, bonds, IRAs, and real estate purchased for investment purposes.

Personal Assets: This section records the current value of your possessions, including your home, vehicles, furnishings, and collectibles.

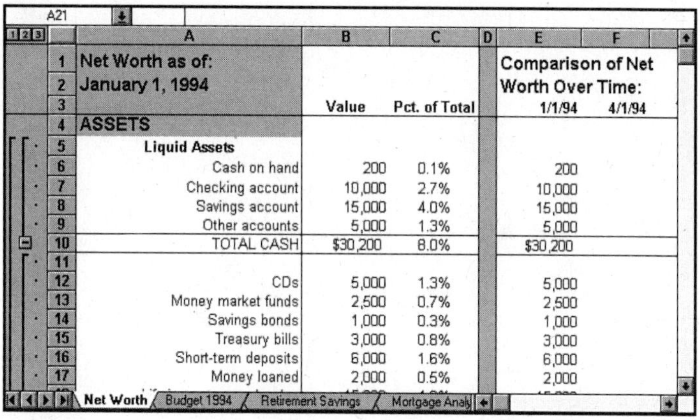

	A	B	C	E	F
1	Net Worth as of:			Comparison of Net	
2	January 1, 1994			Worth Over Time:	
3		Value	Pct. of Total	1/1/94	4/1/94
4	ASSETS				
5	Liquid Assets				
6	Cash on hand	200	0.1%	200	
7	Checking account	10,000	2.7%	10,000	
8	Savings account	15,000	4.0%	15,000	
9	Other accounts	5,000	1.3%	5,000	
10	TOTAL CASH	$30,200	8.0%	$30,200	
11					
12	CDs	5,000	1.3%	5,000	
13	Money market funds	2,500	0.7%	2,500	
14	Savings bonds	1,000	0.3%	1,000	
15	Treasury bills	3,000	0.8%	3,000	
16	Short-term deposits	6,000	1.6%	6,000	
17	Money loaned	2,000	0.5%	2,000	

Net Worth / Budget 1994 / Retirement Savings / Mortgage Analy

FIGURE 69.1. *The Net Worth worksheet showing part of the ASSETS section.*

The LIABILITIES section, which begins in row 46 (see Figure 69.2), lists your liability items. These items are grouped into two categories:

Short Term: Debts you expect to repay in the short term. They include rent, accrued taxes, credit cards, and monthly bills.

Long Term: Debts you pay off over time. They include your mortgage, car loans, and investment loans.

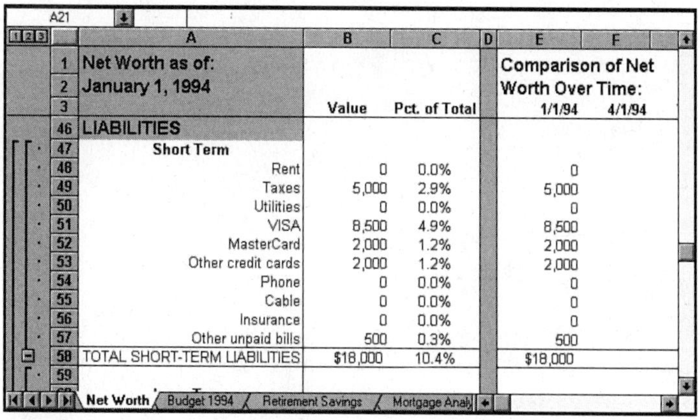

	A	B	C	E	F
1	Net Worth as of:			Comparison of Net	
2	January 1, 1994			Worth Over Time:	
3		Value	Pct. of Total	1/1/94	4/1/94
46	LIABILITIES				
47	Short Term				
48	Rent	0	0.0%	0	
49	Taxes	5,000	2.9%	5,000	
50	Utilities	0	0.0%	0	
51	VISA	8,500	4.9%	8,500	
52	MasterCard	2,000	1.2%	2,000	
53	Other credit cards	2,000	1.2%	2,000	
54	Phone	0	0.0%	0	
55	Cable	0	0.0%	0	
56	Insurance	0	0.0%	0	
57	Other unpaid bills	500	0.3%	500	
58	TOTAL SHORT-TERM LIABILITIES	$18,000	10.4%	$18,000	
59					

Net Worth / Budget 1994 / Retirement Savings / Mortgage Analy

FIGURE 69.2. *The LIABILITIES section of the Net Worth worksheet.*

The Net Worth worksheet provides two columns for each asset and liability item. Use the Value column (column B) to enter the present value of each item as of the current date (which you enter in cell A2). The Pct. of Total column calculates the percentage contribution for each item. Note that these percentages are relative to the asset and liability totals, not your net worth. For example, a figure of 4.0% for your savings account means that this item represents 4.0% of your total assets.

Calculating Your Net Worth

Calculating your net worth is a simple matter of filling in the Value fields for asset and liability items that apply to you. Enter a 0 for items with no value. Totals are calculated for each subcategory (for example, `TOTAL CASH` in cell B10), as well as for total assets (cell B44) and total liabilities (cell B68). Your net worth appears at the bottom of the sheet in cell B70.

SUPER NOTE

If you use the mortgage worksheets included in the FINANCES.XLS workbook, the Mortgage Refinance sheet includes a `CurrentBalance` cell (B12) that constantly tracks the current principal balance for your mortgage. The Net Worth worksheet's Mortgage liability item (cell B61) is linked to this cell.

SUPER NOTE

There probably will be items in the default Net Worth sheet that don't apply to you. For example, if you own your home, you don't need the Rent liability item. To make it easier to navigate the list, you can safely delete what you don't use. To avoid possible complications, you should delete the entire row. Similarly, if you need to add items to the list, just insert a new row in the appropriate area and copy one of the percentage formulas in column C. The total formulas in column B will adjust automatically.

Hiding and Showing Detail in the Net Worth Statement

The Net Worth sheet is outlined so that you can hide and show asset and liability items. Chapter 62, "Working with Templates and Outlines," explains outlines in depth, but I'll summarize the techniques you can use to hide and show the worksheet detail.

To hide items, do one of the following:

- Select one or more cells in a row that has a collapse outline symbol (the minus sign) and select the **D**ata | **G**roup and Outline | **H**ide Detail command.
- Click on a collapse symbol.

To show items, do one of the following:

- Select one or more cells in a row that has an expand outline symbol (the plus sign) and select the **D**ata | **G**roup and Outline | **S**how Detail command.
- Click on an expand symbol.

Figure 69.3 shows the worksheet with only the asset, liability, and net worth totals displayed.

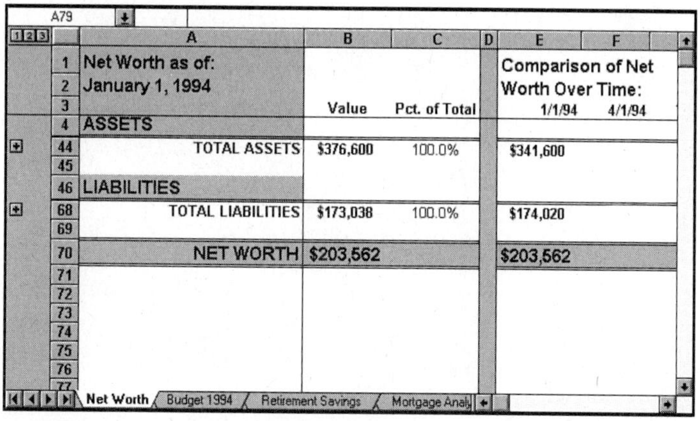

FIGURE 69.3.
The Net Worth worksheet with the detail collapsed.

	A	B	C	D	E	F
1	Net Worth as of:				Comparison of Net	
2	January 1, 1994				Worth Over Time:	
3		Value	Pct. of Total		1/1/94	4/1/94
4	ASSETS					
44	TOTAL ASSETS	$376,600	100.0%		$341,600	
45						
46	LIABILITIES					
68	TOTAL LIABILITIES	$173,038	100.0%		$174,020	
69						
70	NET WORTH	$203,562			$203,562	

Net Worth / Budget 1994 / Retirement Savings / Mortgage Analy

Comparing Net Worth Over Time

Besides using the Net Worth worksheet to get a snapshot of your current financial picture, you also can use it to track your financial progress over several periods. The Comparison of Net Worth Over Time section (beginning in column E) includes columns with dates separated at quarterly intervals. (You can change these dates to whatever interval you want.) When you've completed your net worth statement, copy the figures from the Value column into the appropriate Comparison column.

Setting Up a Personal Budget

Many people, when they think about budgets at all, think of them as monetary straightjackets. When they look at a budget, all they see are limits imposed on their spending. But just as a glass that's half empty also can be seen as half full, so too can budgets be seen in a more positive light. I prefer to think of budgets as *blueprints* to help you achieve your financial goals. Think of it this way: if you wanted to build a house, you wouldn't just start hammering boards together at random. You'd get some plans made up and use them to carefully construct your house. Your financial house is no different: you set a monetary goal and then create a budget to help yourself meet that goal.

The Budget worksheet included in FINANCES.XLS enables you to set up a personal budget by month. This sheet, shown in Figure 69.4, is divided into two sections:

Income: This section contains various income categories such as Advances, Bonuses, and Salary.
Expenses: This section includes expense categories for things such as Clothing, Entertainment, Rent, and Utilities.

FIGURE 69.4.
The Budget worksheet.

	A	B	C	D	E	F	G	H	I	J
1	Budget	Amount	Y/M	Jan	Feb	Mar	Apr	May	Jun	Jul
2	Income									
3	Advances	500	M	500	500	500	500	500	500	500
4	Bonuses	5,000	Y	417	417	417	417	417	417	417
5	Consulting	500	M	500	500	500	500	500	500	500
6	Dividends	50	M	50	50	50	50	50	50	50
7	Gifts	500	Y	42	42	42	42	42	42	42
8	Interest	25	M	25	25	25	25	25	25	25
9	Miscellaneous	1,000	Y	83	83	83	83	83	83	83
10	Other Investments	5,000	Y	417	417	417	417	417	417	417
11	Royalties	1,000	M	1,000	1,000	1,000	1,000	1,000	1,000	1,000
12	RRSP Inc	0	M	0	0	0	0	0	0	0
13	Salary #1	50,000	Y	4,167	4,167	4,167	4,167	4,167	4,167	4,167
14	Salary #2	35,000	Y	2,917	2,917	2,917	2,917	2,917	2,917	2,917
15	TOTAL INCOME			10,117	10,117	10,117	10,117	10,117	10,117	10,117

Each section has its own subtotal (row 15 for Income and row 75 for Expenses), and the DIFFERENCE row (row 77) calculates the difference between income and expenses. Ideally, the numbers that appear in this row should be positive, because this means that you're earning more than you're spending.

Each budget category has 16 columns:

Amount: The amount you want to budget for the category. You enter a monthly or a yearly amount, as appropriate.
Y/M: This column designates the Amount as either Monthly or Yearly. For example, if you're budgeting $500 per month for rent, you would enter `500` in the Rent category's Amount column and `M` in the Y/M column. The letter can be in either uppercase or lowercase.
Jan, Feb, and so on: The monthly breakdowns for each income and expense category. The number that appears here depends on three things:

- If you entered `M` in the Y/M column, the Amount figure appears in each month.

- If you entered Y in the Y/M column, each month displays the Amount figure divided by 12.
- If you prefer to use different figures in different months for some categories, delete the existing formulas and enter the appropriate amounts by hand.

TOTAL: The yearly total for each category.
Pct of TOTAL: The percentage contribution for each category. Note that the percentages are relative to the section containing the category. For example, if 10% appears for the Bonuses category, it means that bonuses represent 10% of all income.

SUPER NOTE

As with the Net Worth worksheet, you can safely delete any budget categories you don't need. Again, delete the entire row to be safe. You also can add your own categories by inserting a row and copying the formulas from one of the existing rows.

SUPER NOTE

The Budget worksheet also contains an outline. See the section titled "Hiding and Showing Detail in the Net Worth Statement" for a quick review of outline basics. For more detailed coverage, see Chapter 62, "Working with Templates and Outlines."

Filling Out the Budget

Follow the steps in Procedure 69.1 to use the Budget worksheet.

PROCEDURE 69.1. USING THE BUDGET WORKSHEET.

1. Select a category and enter a figure in the Amount row. If the income is earned monthly, or if the expense is paid monthly, enter the monthly figure. Otherwise, enter an amount for the entire year.

SUPER NOTE

This worksheet also has a link to the mortgage application in FINANCES.XLS. The Mortgage expense category (cell B57) is linked to a cell in the Payment column in the Mortgage Amortization worksheet.

2. In the Y/M column, enter `M` if the Amount is a monthly figure or `Y` if it's a yearly figure. The application fills in the month columns automatically.
3. When you've entered the budget values, examine the DIFFERENCE row. If it shows negative numbers, this means that your ways are exceeding your means and that you need to cut back somewhere. Try adjusting some of the Expense items to see whether you can get the DIFFERENCE to 0 or a positive number.

Saving for Retirement

When you've had enough of the rat race and decide it's time to retire to a life of leisure, you need to make sure you have enough money to live in the style to which you're accustomed.

No matter how far away your retirement is, it pays to start planning now. The Retirement Savings worksheet can help. This sheet looks at items such as the number of years you have until retirement, the number of years you'll be retired (approximately), the value of your current investments, and the income you think you'll need during your retirement. From this data, it calculates what you must save per month to reach your goal.

Figure 69.5 shows the Retirement Savings worksheet. The next few sections look at the four areas of this sheet: Personal Data, Statistical Data, Retirement Income, and Savings Calculations.

FIGURE 69.5.
The Retirement Savings worksheet.

A21

	A	B	C	D	E	F	G
1	**Saving for Retirement**						
2							
3	**Personal Data**				**Retirement Income**	**Today's $**	**Retirement**
4	Date of Birth	8/23/59			Desired Retirement Income	50,000	93,015
5	Age Now	34			Pension Income	6,000	11,162
6	Retirement Age/Date	55	8/23/14		Social Security Income	10,000	18,603
7	Yrs/Mths to Retirement	21	249		Net Income Needed	34,000	63,250
8	Life Expectancy	80			Total Needed for Retirement	439,753	818,070
9	Yrs/Mths Retired	25	300				
10					**Savings Calculations**		
11	**Statistical Data**				Current Retirement Plans	25,000	84,989
12	Inflation Rate	3.0%			Current Tax-Free Investments	100,000	339,956
13	Investment Rate	6.0%			Current Taxable Investments	15,000	42,633
14	Tax Rate	15.0%			Total Current Investments	125,000	416,585
15							
16					Total Amount to Save	314,753	401,484
17					Amount to Save/Month (Non-Tax)	639	
18					Amount to Save/Month (Taxable)	713	

Net Worth / Budget 1994 / **Retirement Savings** / Mortgage Analy

Entering Personal Data

The Personal Data area shows how many years and months you have until retirement and how many years and months you'll be retired. There are six fields:

Date of Birth: Use this cell to enter your date of birth. This cell is named `Birthday`.

Age Now: This cell calculates your current age using the `CalculateAge Function` procedure (see the section titled "Calculating Your Age"). This cell is named `AgeNow`.

Retirement Age/Date: Enter the age at which you think you'll be retiring in cell B6. This cell is named `RetirementAge`. Cell C6 automatically calculates the date of your retirement (assuming that you'll retire on your birthday) with the following formula:

```
=DATE(YEAR(Birthday)+RetirementAge,MONTH(Birthday),DAY(Birthday))
```

This formula creates a new date with the same day and month as `Birthday`, but `RetirementAge` years in the future. Cell C6 is named `RetirementDate`.

Yrs/Mths to Retirement: Cell B7 (named `YearsToRetire`) calculates the number of years between `RetirementAge` and `AgeNow`. Cell C7 (`MonthsToRetire`) uses a `Function` procedure named `MonthsBetween` to calculate the exact number of months until you retire. (See the section in this chapter titled "Calculating the Number of Months Between Two Dates.")

Life Expectancy: Enter an approximate age for your life expectancy in cell B8 (named `LifeExpectancy`).

Yrs/Mths Retired: Cell B9 (`YearsRetired`) calculates the number of years you'll be retired (`LifeExpectancy-RetirementAge`) and cell C9 (`MonthsRetired`) converts this number into months.

Calculating Your Age

The FINANCES.XLS workbook also includes a Procedures sheet that contains several supporting procedures for various applications. Figure 69.6 shows two of these procedures: `CalculateAge` and `MonthsBetween`.

`CalculateAge` is a `Function` procedure that calculates how old you are given your date of birth (the `birthDate` argument). In the Retirement Savings worksheet, this saves you from having to constantly update the Age Now cell.

The procedure begins by calculating the difference in the year components of `birthDate` and `Now`. (The `Now` function returns today's date.) This will be your true age only if your birthday has already passed this year, so the procedure has to check this. The first `If` statement tests the month components (as returned by the `Month` function). If the current month is less than the `birthDate` month, your birthday is yet to come, so the procedure subtracts 1 from `CalculateAge`. If the month components are the same, then the day components must be checked (as given by the `Day` function). If the current day is less than the `birthDate` day, 1 must be subtracted from `CalculateAge`.

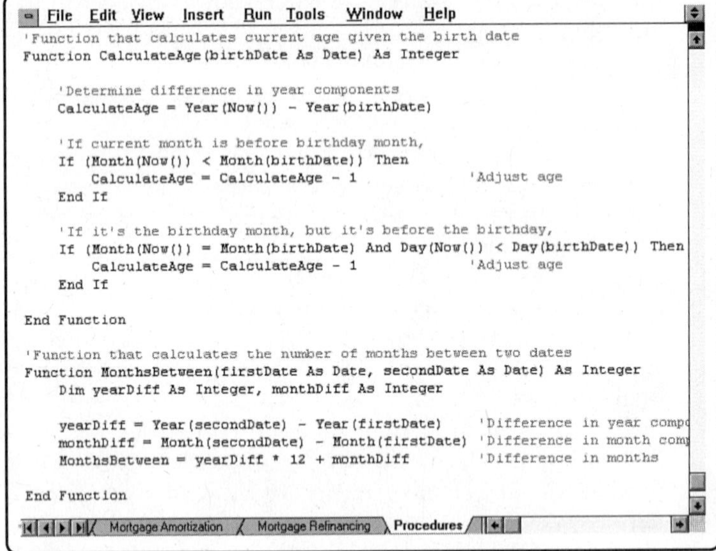

File Edit View Insert Run Tools Window Help
'Function that calculates current age given the birth date
Function CalculateAge(birthDate As Date) As Integer
'Determine difference in year components
CalculateAge = Year(Now()) - Year(birthDate)
'If current month is before birthday month,
If (Month(Now()) < Month(birthDate)) Then
CalculateAge = CalculateAge - 1
'Adjust age
End If
'If it's the birthday month, but it's before the birthday,
If (Month(Now()) = Month(birthDate) And Day(Now()) < Day(birthDate)) Then
CalculateAge = CalculateAge - 1
'Adjust age
End If
End Function
'Function that calculates the number of months between two dates
Function MonthsBetween(firstDate As Date, secondDate As Date) As Integer
Dim yearDiff As Integer, monthDiff As Integer
yearDiff = Year(secondDate) - Year(firstDate)
'Difference in year comp
monthDiff = Month(secondDate) - Month(firstDate)
'Difference in month com
MonthsBetween = yearDiff * 12 + monthDiff
'Difference in months
End Function
Mortgage Amortization
Mortgage Refinancing
Procedures

FIGURE 69.6.
The `CalculateAge` and `MonthsBetween` procedures.

SUPER NOTE

To learn more about `Function` procedures, see Chapter 50, "Getting Started with Visual Basic."

Calculating the Number of Months Between Two Dates

The `MonthsBetween` `Function` procedure calculates the number of months between two dates (the *`firstDate`* and *`secondDate`* arguments). The procedure first calculates *`yearDiff`*—the difference in the year components of the two dates. Then *`monthDiff`* is assigned the difference in the month components. The number of months between the two dates is calculated by the following formula:

```
MonthsBetween = yearDiff * 12 + monthDiff
```

Entering Statistical Data

Use the Statistical Data section to enter the following three pieces of information:

Inflation Rate: The average rate of inflation you expect between now and the day you retire. Cell B12 is named `InflationRate`.

Investment Rate: The expected average rate of return on the money you invest both before and during your retirement. Cell B13 is named `InvestmentRate`.

Tax Rate: Your expected average tax rate until you retire. Cell B14 is named `TaxRate`.

Calculating Retirement Income

Use the Retirement Income section to enter your expected (or needed) retirement income. The cells calculate the total amount you'll need based on the number of years you'll be retired. Each field has two columns: Today's $ expresses each amount in today's dollars (that is, before inflation) and Retirement expresses the numbers in future dollars at the time of your retirement, including inflation. (See the section titled "Allowing for Inflation.") This section has five fields:

Desired Retirement Income: The annual pre-tax amount you would like to receive throughout your retirement. Enter a value in cell F4 (`DesiredIncome`) in today's dollars.

Pension Income: The annual pre-tax amount you expect to receive from your pension plans. Again, enter a value in today's dollars in cell F5 (`PensionIncome`).

Social Security Income: The annual pre-tax amount you expect to receive from Social Security. Enter a value in today's dollars in cell F6 (`SocialSecurityIncome`).

Net Income Needed: The calculated annual amount you need over and above pension and Social Security income. (Cell F7 is named `NetIncomeNeeded`.)

Total Needed for Retirement: The calculated amount of money you'll need on the day you retire. In other words, you need to invest this amount at `InvestmentRate` percent for `MonthsRetired` months to earn `NetIncomeNeeded` annually. The following `PV()` function in cell F8 performs the calculation:

```
=PV(InvestmentRate/12,MonthsRetired,NetIncomeNeeded/12)*-1
```

Allowing for Inflation

To get an accurate picture of your financial needs 10, 20, or more years down the road, you have to take inflation into account. Because inflation erodes the purchasing power of savings, what you can buy for $100 today might cost $150 or even $200 in the future. This means a nest egg that appears comfortable now might not be all that attractive by the time you retire.

The cells in column G of the Retirement Savings worksheet factor inflation into the calculations. Using the `InflationRate` variable, you use the following formula to express an amount given by *`PresentValue`* in dollars *`N`* years from now:

```
=PresentValue*(1 + InflationRate)^N
```

For example, if inflation is 2.5%, having $420,000 30 years from now is equivalent to only $200,000 in today's dollars, as calculated by the following formula:

```
=200000*(1.025)^30
```

Determining How Much You Need to Save

As soon as you know the total amount you need to save, you need to determine how much to save per month. The *Savings Calculation* section accomplishes this. The first part calculates the total value of your current investments:

Current Retirement Plans: Use cell F11 (`PlansToday`) to enter the current amount you have in any IRA, Keogh, or 401(K) plans.

Current Tax-Free Investments: Use cell F12 (`TaxFreeToday`) to enter the current value of any tax-free investments such as your home or municipal bonds.

Current Taxable Investments: Use cell F13 (`TaxableToday`) to enter the current value of your taxable investments.

Total Current Investments: Cell F14 (`TotalAssetsToday`) calculates the total of all your investments. The taxable investments are assumed to be taxed at your marginal rate (*TaxRate*).

The Total Amount to Save field (cells F16—named `TotalToSave`—and G16) calculates the difference between what you need for your retirement and what you already have. This is the amount you must save between now and the time you retire.

Cell F17 shows the amount to save in tax-free investments per month. It uses the following formula:

```
=PMT(InvestmentRate/12,MonthsToRetire,0,TotalToSave)*-1
```

Cell F18 shows the amount to save in taxable investments per month. Here's the formula:

```
=PMT(InvestmentRate*(1-TaxRate)/12,MonthsToRetire,0,TotalToSave)*-1
```

The Mortgage Application

If you have a mortgage, or you're thinking of getting one, FINANCES.XLS includes three worksheets that help you get a handle on what might be the biggest financial transaction of your life:

Mortgage Analysis: This sheet performs the basic mortgage calculations and also shows the effect of making extra payments monthly.

Mortgage Amortization: This is an amortization table for the mortgage.

Mortgage Refinance: This sheet sets up a cost/benefit analysis for mortgage refinancing.

Analyzing Your Mortgage

The Mortgage Analysis sheet shown in Figure 69.7 enables you to set up basic mortgage data and calculate the results for both a regular mortgage and a mortgage in which you pay an extra amount each month.

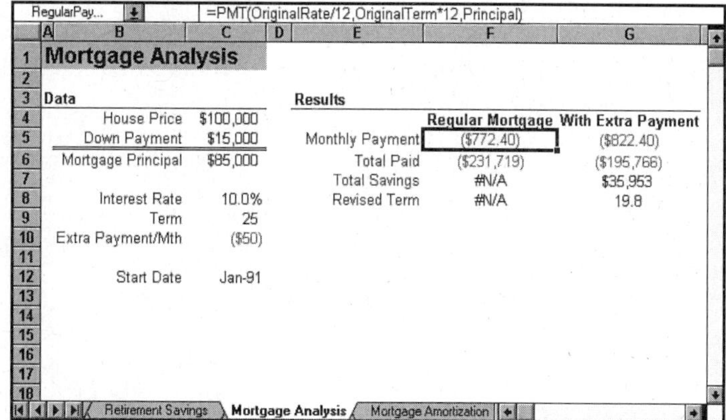

FIGURE 69.7.
The Mortgage Analysis worksheet.

The Data area contains the following fields:

House Price: The purchase price of the house.
Down Payment: The down payment on the house.
Mortgage Principal: The amount you need to finance. Cell C6 is named `Principal`.
Interest Rate: The annual interest rate for the mortgage. Cell C8 is named `Rate`.
Term: The term of the mortgage in years. Cell C9 is named `Term`.
Extra Payment/Mth: The amount you want to pay on top of your regular mortgage payment each month. Enter a *negative* number (money you pay is always a negative number in Excel) in cell C10 (named `ExtraPayment`).
Start Date: The date of the first payment. Cell C12 is named `StartDate`.

The Results area makes the following calculations for both the regular mortgage and the mortgage including the extra payment:

Monthly Payment: The amount you pay each month. Cell F5 (`RegularPayment`) uses the `PMT()` function. Cell G5 (`PaymentWithExtra`) adds `ExtraPayment` to `RegularPayment`.
Total Paid: The total principal and interest you'll pay over the course of the mortgage. Cell G6 uses the `RevisedTerm` variable calculated at the end of this section.
TotalSavings: The difference between the `Total Paid` for the regular mortgage and the mortgage with the extra payment.

Revised Term: Cell G8 (`RevisedTerm`) calculates how long it will take you to pay off the mortgage if you include an extra payment each month. This cell uses the following `NPER()` function:

```
=NPER(Rate/12,PaymentWithExtra,Principal)/12
```

The Mortgage Amortization Table

Figure 69.8 shows the amortization table for the mortgage. The table itself is straightforward, but the sheet contains a couple of unusual features: the check box and the macro button.

FIGURE 69.8.
The mortgage amortization table.

J1

Mortgage Amortization — Does Table Need Updating? No

☐ Include Extra Payment — Update Amortization Table

Period	Date	Current Balance	Payment	Interest	Principal	Cumulative Interest	Cumulative Principal
1	Jan-91	85,000	(772.40)	(708.33)	(64.06)	(708.33)	(64.06)
2	Feb-91	84,936	(772.40)	(707.80)	(64.60)	(1,416.13)	(128.66)
3	Mar-91	84,871	(772.40)	(707.26)	(65.13)	(2,123.39)	(193.79)
4	Apr-91	84,806	(772.40)	(706.72)	(65.68)	(2,830.11)	(259.47)
5	May-91	84,741	(772.40)	(706.17)	(66.22)	(3,536.28)	(325.69)
6	Jun-91	84,674	(772.40)	(705.62)	(66.78)	(4,241.90)	(392.47)
7	Jul-91	84,608	(772.40)	(705.06)	(67.33)	(4,946.97)	(459.80)
8	Aug-91	84,540	(772.40)	(704.50)	(67.89)	(5,651.47)	(527.70)
9	Sep-91	84,472	(772.40)	(703.94)	(68.46)	(6,355.40)	(596.16)
10	Oct-91	84,404	(772.40)	(703.37)	(69.03)	(7,058.77)	(665.19)
11	Nov-91	84,335	(772.40)	(702.79)	(69.61)	(7,761.56)	(734.79)
12	Dec-91	84,265	(772.40)	(702.21)	(70.19)	(8,463.77)	(804.98)
13	Jan-92	84,195	(772.40)	(701.63)	(70.77)	(9,165.39)	(875.75)

Mortgage Analysis | Mortgage Amortization | Mortgage Refinanci

The Worksheet Check Box

In particular, look at the check box in the upper-left corner. As you saw in the Mortgage Analysis worksheet, you can calculate two different monthly payments: the normal payment and one that includes an extra payment each month. Rather than create a separate amortization table for each result, you use the check box to toggle the amortization table between the two payments.

Activating the check box enters a `TRUE` value in cell A3 (named `IncludeExtraPmt`), and deactivating it enters `FALSE`. The first cell in the Payment column (cell D6, named `FirstPmt`) contains the following formula:

```
=IF(IncludeExtraPmt,PaymentWithExtra,RegularPayment)
```

If `IncludeExtraPmt` is `TRUE`, the `PaymentWithExtra` value appears in the Payment column; otherwise, the `RegularPmt` value appears. Similarly, the Interest and Principal columns use the `IncludeExtraPmt` variable to determine which term to use in the `IPMT()` and `PPMT()` functions, respectively:

```
IF(IncludeExtraPmt,RevisedTerm,Term)
```

SUPER NOTE

To learn more about using dialog box controls on worksheets, see Chapter 63, "Other Advanced Workbook Topics."

SUPER TIP

If you don't have a mouse, you can still toggle the table between payments by entering either TRUE or FALSE in cell A3. Note, however, that this cell has been formatted with a gray font, so the value won't appear in the cell. (You will be able to see it in the formula bar, however.)

The Worksheet Macro Button

The other unusual feature of the Mortgage Amortization worksheet is the Update Amortization Table macro button. This button recreates the entire table from scratch based on the values you entered in the Mortgage Analysis worksheet.

SUPER TIP

If you don't have a mouse, you can update the table by selecting the **T**ools | **M**acro command, highlighting FillAmortizationTable in the **M**acro Name/Reference list, and clicking on the **R**un button.

SUPER NOTE

See Chapter 59, "Visual Basic Tips and Techniques," for more information on macro buttons.

You know the table needs to be updated by looking at the Does Table Need Updating? field (cell H1, named UpdateNeeded). A *Yes* appears in this cell whenever you make changes to the Mortgage Analysis worksheet or when you toggle the Include Extra Payment check box. This is accomplished by running the following two Visual Basic statements:

```
Worksheets("Mortgage Analysis").OnEntry = "TableNeedsUpdate"

Worksheets("Mortgage Amortization").CheckBoxes("Check Box 1").OnAction = _
  "TableNeedsUpdate"
```

These commands are in the `Auto_Open` procedure in the Procedures module. They tell Excel to run the `TableNeedsUpdate` procedure every time you make changes to the Mortgage Analysis worksheet or when you toggle the Include Extra Payment check box. `TableNeedsUpdate` contains the following statement:

```
Range("UpdateNeeded").Formula = "Yes"
```

This statement simply enters a *Yes* in the `UpdateNeeded` cell.

The *FillAmortizationTable* Procedure

The Update Amortization Table button is assigned to the `FillAmortizationTable` procedure in the Procedures sheet. Figure 69.9 shows the first part of this procedure. After declaring a few variables, the first two lines save the current calculation mode and then turn on manual calculations to make the update perform faster.

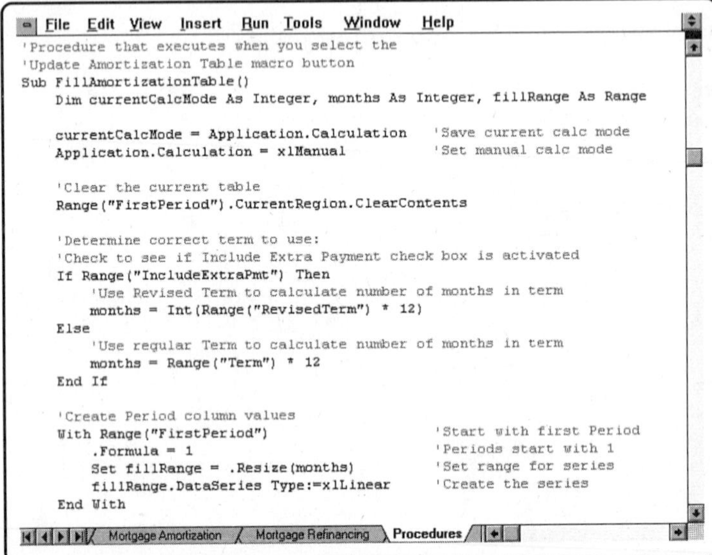

```
'Procedure that executes when you select the
'Update Amortization Table macro button
Sub FillAmortizationTable()
    Dim currentCalcMode As Integer, months As Integer, fillRange As Range

    currentCalcMode = Application.Calculation     'Save current calc mode
    Application.Calculation = xlManual            'Set manual calc mode

    'Clear the current table
    Range("FirstPeriod").CurrentRegion.ClearContents

    'Determine correct term to use:
    'Check to see if Include Extra Payment check box is activated
    If Range("IncludeExtraPmt") Then
        'Use Revised Term to calculate number of months in term
        months = Int(Range("RevisedTerm") * 12)
    Else
        'Use regular Term to calculate number of months in term
        months = Range("Term") * 12
    End If

    'Create Period column values
    With Range("FirstPeriod")                     'Start with first Period
        .Formula = 1                              'Periods start with 1
        Set fillRange = .Resize(months)           'Set range for series
        fillRange.DataSeries Type:=xlLinear       'Create the series
    End With
```


FIGURE 69.9.
The first part of the `FillAmortizationTable` *procedure.*

The next statement uses the `CurrentRegion` property to return the range of non-empty cells surrounding the cell named `FirstPeriod`. (`FirstPeriod` is cell A6 in the Mortgage Amortization worksheet.) This region includes all the cells in the amortization table below the column headings. Why doesn't `CurrentRegion` select the column headings as well? Because row 5 (which is hidden) is blank. Then the `ClearContents` method clears the contents of the range returned by `CurrentRegion`.

The next `If` statement determines how many months are in the term. It checks the value of the `IncludeExtraPmt` cell (cell A3 in the Mortgage Amortization worksheet): if it's `TRUE`, the procedure uses `RevisedTerm` from the Mortgage Analysis worksheet; otherwise, it just uses `Term`.

The rest of the procedure fills in the table. There are a couple dozen statements, so I won't examine them in detail. As you're looking through them, though, it will help you to know that all the range names beginning with `First` (for example, `FirstPeriod` and `FirstMonth`) refer to the first cell in each column of the amortization table. For example, `FirstMonth` refers to cell B6 in the Mortgage Amortization worksheet.

Refinancing Your Mortgage

If interest rates have gone down since you first took on your mortgage, you might be thinking about refinancing. You know your payments will be lower, but is the cost of refinancing worth it? The Mortgage Refinancing worksheet, shown in Figure 69.10, will help you answer that question. The next four sections cover the four areas of this sheet: Original Data, New Data, Refinancing Costs, and Analysis.

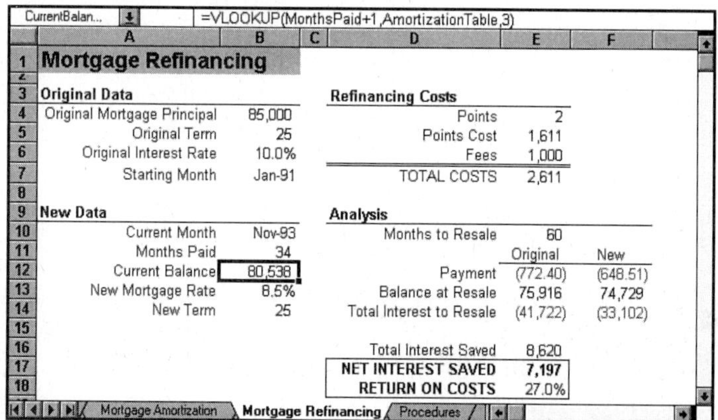

CurrentBalan... =VLOOKUP(MonthsPaid+1,AmortizationTable,3)

	A	B	C	D	E	F
1	**Mortgage Refinancing**					
2						
3	**Original Data**			**Refinancing Costs**		
4	Original Mortgage Principal	85,000		Points	2	
5	Original Term	25		Points Cost	1,611	
6	Original Interest Rate	10.0%		Fees	1,000	
7	Starting Month	Jan-91		TOTAL COSTS	2,611	
8						
9	**New Data**			**Analysis**		
10	Current Month	Nov-93		Months to Resale	60	
11	Months Paid	34			Original	New
12	Current Balance	80,538		Payment	(772.40)	(648.51)
13	New Mortgage Rate	8.5%		Balance at Resale	75,916	74,729
14	New Term	25		Total Interest to Resale	(41,722)	(33,102)
15						
16				Total Interest Saved	8,620	
17				**NET INTEREST SAVED**	**7,197**	
18				**RETURN ON COSTS**	27.0%	

Mortgage Amortization / **Mortgage Refinancing** / Procedures

FIGURE 69.10.
The Mortgage Refinancing worksheet.

The Original Data

The four fields in the Original Data section are linked to the corresponding cells in the Mortgage Analysis worksheet. To make some of the formulas you'll see later more comprehensible, I've named cell B5 `OriginalTerm` and cell B6 `OriginalRate`.

The New Data

The New Data section contains some current data as well as the inputs for the new mortgage:

Current Month: Today's date, as given by the `TODAY()` function.

Months Paid: The number of months between the Starting Month and the Current Month. This cell uses the `MonthsBetween Function` procedure discussed earlier. This cell is named `MonthsPaid`.

Current Balance: The current principal balance for the present mortgage. This cell (named `CurrentBalance`) uses `VLOOKUP()` to extract the balance from the amortization table.
New Mortgage Rate: The rate for the refinanced mortgage. Cell B13 is named `NewRate`.
New Term: The term you want to use for the new mortgage (`NewTerm`).

Calculating Refinancing Costs

The Refinancing Costs section calculates how much you'll have to pay for the privilege of refinancing:

Points: The number of points you have to pay.
Points Cost: The calculated cost of the points.
Fees: Enter your total fees for the title, application, lawyers, and whatever other expenses you incur.
TOTAL COSTS: The total costs for refinancing.

Analyzing the Refinancing

The Analysis section gets down to brass tacks to see whether refinancing is a good idea or not. The idea is that, between now and the time you sell your house, you want to accomplish two goals:

- Recoup your refinancing costs through lower interest payments.
- Generate a return on your refinancing costs greater than you would get with any other investment.

The first order of business is to enter a value in the `Months To Resale` cell (E10). The next three lines compare your existing mortgage with the refinanced one:

Payment: The monthly payment.

SUPER NOTE

This analysis assumes that you're not making any extra payments each month.

Balance at Resale: The principal owing on both mortgages at the time of resale. Both cell E13 and cell F13 use the `PV()` function to calculate this.
Total Interest to Resale: The amount of interest you'll pay between now and the resale date.

The difference between the two `Total Interest to Resale` figures is computed in the `Total Interest Saved` cell (E16). The important number, though, is the `NET INTEREST`

SAVED cell (E17). This is the Total Interest Saved result, minus the total refinancing costs, minus whatever extra principal you have to pay off at the time of resale.

A second, slightly different, analysis is the RETURN ON COSTS calculation (cell E18). If you think of the refinancing costs as an investment, then your return is the Total Interest Saved figure. The percentage in cell E18 is the rate of interest at which you'd have to invest the refinancing costs to end up with the Total Interest Saved number. In general, if this number is lower than what you can get in another investment, you're better off holding on to your existing mortgage and investing the refinancing costs.

Monthly Sales - Forecast		Normal Trend Forecast	Deseasoned Trend Forecast	Reseasoned Trend Forecast
	January, 1994	138.2	134.8	111.6
	February, 1994	138.4	135.0	113.6
	March, 1994	138.7	135.2	126.0
	April, 1994	138.9	135.4	123.7
	May, 1994	139.2	135.6	122.3
1994	June, 1994	139.4	135.8	124.6
	July, 1994	139.7	136.0	131.1
	August, 1994	139.9	136.2	138.0
	September, 1994	140.2	136.4	141.7
	October, 1994	140.4	136.6	154.2
	November, 1994	140.7	136.8	164.8
	December, 1994	140.9	136.9	180.1
	January, 1995	141.2	137.1	113.5
	February, 1995	141.4	137.3	115.6
	March, 1995	141.7	137.5	128.2
	April, 1995	141.9	137.7	125.8
	May, 1995	142.2	137.9	124.4
1995	June, 1995	142.4	138.1	126.8
	July, 1995	142.7	138.3	133.4
	August, 1995	142.9	138.5	140.4
	September, 1995	143.2	138.7	144.1
	October, 1995	143.4	138.9	156.8
	November, 1995	143.7	139.1	167.7
	December, 1995	143.9	139.3	183.1
	January, 1996	144.2	139.5	115.4
	February, 1996	144.4	139.7	117.5
	March, 1996	144.7	139.9	130.4
	April, 1996	144.9	140.1	128.0
	May, 1996	145.2	140.3	126.5
1995	June, 1996	145.4	140.5	128.9
	July, 1996	145.7	140.6	135.6
	August, 1996	145.9	140.8	142.8
	September, 1996	146.2	141.0	146.5
	October, 1996	146.4	141.2	159.4
	November, 1996	146.6	141.4	170.5
	December, 1996	146.9	141.6	186.2

Chapter

70

Building a Sales Forecasting Model

In these complex and uncertain times, forecasting business performance is increasingly important. Today, more than ever, managers at all levels need to make intelligent predictions of future sales and profit trends as part of their overall business strategy. By forecasting sales six months, a year, or even three years down the road, managers can anticipate related needs such as employee acquisitions, warehouse space, and raw material requirements. Similarly, a profit forecast enables the planning of the future expansion of a company.

Business forecasting has been around for many years, and a number of methods have been developed—some more successful than others. The most common forecasting method is the qualitative "seat-of-the-pants" approach in which a manager (or a group of managers) estimates future trends based on experience and knowledge of the market. This method, however, suffers from an inherent subjectivity and a short-term focus, because many managers tend to extrapolate from recent experience and ignore the long-term trend. Other methods (such as averaging past results) are more objective, but generally are useful for forecasting only a few months in advance.

This project uses a technique called *linear regression analysis*. Regression is a powerful statistical procedure that has become a popular business tool. In its general form, you use regression analysis to determine the relationship between a dependent variable (car sales, for example) and one or more independent variables (interest rates and disposable income, for example). The worksheets created for this project explore two relatively simple cases:

- Sales are a function of time. Essentially, this case determines the trend over time of past sales and extrapolates the trend in a straight line to determine future sales.
- Sales are a function of the season (in a business sense). Many businesses are seasonal; that is, their sales are traditionally higher or lower during certain periods of the fiscal year. Retailers, for example, usually have higher sales in the fall leading up to Christmas. If your business' sales are a function of the season, you need to remove these seasonal biases to calculate the true, underlying trend.

This project uses sales as an example; however, you can use this application to forecast expenses, profits, or any other quantity for which you have historical data.

Excel 5.0 Features Used

Trend analysis
Correlation
Arrays
Linking
Named formulas
Relative range names
Advanced worksheet functions such as `OFFSET()` and `INDEX()`

Files Used

FORECAST.XLS

Special Instructions

If you'll be using FORECAST.XLS to forecast different quantities, use the **File** | Save **As** command to save the file under a different name before filling in any data.

About FORECAST.XLS

The FORECAST.XLS workbook contains the following eight worksheets:

Monthly Data: Use this worksheet to enter up to ten years of monthly historical data. This worksheet also calculates the 12-month moving averages used by the Monthly Seasonal Index worksheet.
Monthly Seasonal Index: Calculates the seasonal adjustment factors (the seasonal indexes) for the monthly data.
Monthly Trend: Calculates the trend of the monthly historical data. Both a normal trend and a seasonally adjusted trend are computed.
Monthly Forecast: Derives a three-year monthly forecast based on both the normal trend and the seasonally adjusted trend.
Quarterly Data: Consolidates the monthly actuals into quarterly data and also calculates the four-quarter moving average (used by the Quarterly Seasonal Index worksheet).
Quarterly Seasonal Index: Calculates the seasonal indexes for the quarterly data.
Quarterly Trend: Calculates the trend of the quarterly historical data. Both a normal trend and a seasonally adjusted trend are computed.
Quarterly Forecast: Derives a three-year quarterly forecast based on both the normal trend and the seasonally adjusted trend.

SUPER TIP

FORECAST.XLS contains dozens of formulas. You'll probably want to switch to manual calculation mode when working with this file. (Recall that you activate manual calculation mode by selecting the **T**ools | **O**ptions command and then activating the **M**anual option in the Calculation tab. While you're at it, deactivate the Recalc**u**late Before Save check box as well.)

Entering Historical Data

The sales forecast workbook is driven entirely by the historical data you enter into the Monthly Data worksheet, shown in Figure 70.1. Use the Actual column to enter the data in the appropriate rows for each month.

SUPER NOTE

The worksheet shown in Figure 70.1 contains dummy data for illustration purposes. The Super Disk version has 1s in all the Actual cells.

FIGURE 70.1.
Use the monthly data worksheet to enter your historical data.

	A	B	C	D
1	Monthly Sales - Data		Actual	12-Month Moving Avg
2		January, 1984	90.0	-
3		February, 1984	95.0	-
4		March, 1984	110.0	-
5		April, 1984	105.0	-
6		May, 1984	100.0	-
7	1984	June, 1984	100.0	-
8		July, 1984	105.0	-
9		August, 1984	105.0	-
10		September, 1984	110.0	-
11		October, 1984	120.0	-
12		November, 1984	130.0	-
13		December, 1984	140.0	109.2
14		January, 1985	90.0	109.2
15		February, 1985	95.0	109.2
16		March, 1985	115.0	109.6
17		April, 1985	110.0	110.0

Keep the following points in mind when working with this table:

- All cells are locked except for those in the Actual column. If you need to work with any other part of the sheet, you'll have to unprotect it (by selecting the Tools | Protection | Unprotect Sheet command).
- The worksheet is set up to handle ten years of data—from 1984 to 1993. If you'll be starting with a different year, begin with row two and change the year in cell A7. The other years (cells A19, A31, and so on) are derived from formulas. Therefore, you have to make only one change.
- The years displayed in column A are linked to various other cells in the workbook (including the cells in column B), so their format shouldn't be changed.
- If you'll be entering less than ten years of data, you have to delete the moving average formulas that you don't need. If you don't, your seasonal index calculations will be wrong.

- If you add new historical data later, you can insert the corresponding moving average formulas by filling down from one of the existing formulas.

Calculating a Normal Trend

As I mentioned earlier, you can use FORECAST.XLS to calculate either a normal trend that treats all sales as a simple function of time or a deseasoned trend that takes seasonal factors into account. This section covers the normal trend.

All the trend calculations in FORECAST.XLS use a variation of Excel's `TREND()` function. `TREND()` calculates the best-fit line through your data; that is, the differences between the line and the actual data are minimized. The line takes the following general form:

```
y = mx + b
```

y is the dependent variable, *x* is the independent variable, and *m* and *b* represent the line's slope and y-intercept, respectively. The dependent variable is sales, and the independent variable is time.

Following is the syntax of the `TREND()` function:

TREND(***known_y's***,*known_x's*,*new_x's*,*const*)

known_y's	Make up the range representing the known dependent variables. You'll be using the actual monthly sales you entered in the Monthly Data worksheet.
known_x's	Make up the range or array representing the known independent variables. If you omit *known_x's*, Excel uses the array {1,2,3,...,*n*}, in which *n* is the number of cells in the ***known_y's*** range. You use this array when the independent variable is time. Therefore, the formulas will omit the *known_x's*.
new_x's	Make up a range or array representing the new independent variable values for which you want `TREND()` to calculate the corresponding dependent variable values. If you omit *new_x's*, Excel uses the same values as *known_x's*.
const	A logical value that determines whether or not the constant *b* is forced to equal 0. If *const* is `True` or omitted, *b* is calculated normally. If it's `False`, *b* is set to `0`.

For example, suppose you have a range named Actual that contains 12 months of sales data, and you're assuming sales is dependent on time. Then you would use the following formula to calculate a forecast value for the 13th month:

```
=TREND(Actual,,13)
```

Similarly, to calculate the trend of the existing data, you enter the following array formula in a range of 12 cells:

```
{=TREND(Actual)}
```

which is equivalent to the following:

```
{=TREND(Actual,,{1;2;3;4;5;6;7;8;9;10;11;12})}
```

Calculating the Monthly Trend

The latter example is the basis for the Normal Trend calculation in the Monthly Trend worksheet (see Figure 70.2). This worksheet displays (in column B) a linked copy of the sales you entered in Monthly Data. Because the data is linked, you easily can update the Monthly Trend values whenever you make changes to the Monthly Data worksheet.

FIGURE 70.2.
The Monthly Trend worksheet.

	A	B	C	D	E	F	G
1				Correlation to Actual Sales:			
2	Monthly Sales - Historical Trend			Normal Trend --> 0.42			
3				Reseasoned Trend --> 0.96			
4		Actual	Normal Trend	Deseasoned Actual	Deseasoned Trend	Reseasoned Trend	
5	January, 1984	85.0	108.1	108.8	111.4	92.2	
6	February, 1984	95.0	108.4	112.9	111.6	93.9	
7	March, 1984	110.0	108.7	118.0	111.8	104.2	
8	April, 1984	105.0	108.9	114.9	112.0	102.3	
9	May, 1984	100.0	109.2	110.9	112.2	101.2	
10	June, 1984	100.0	109.4	109.0	112.4	103.2	
11	July, 1984	105.0	109.7	108.9	112.6	108.6	
12	August, 1984	105.0	109.9	103.6	112.8	114.3	
13	September, 1984	110.0	110.2	105.9	113.0	117.4	
14	October, 1984	120.0	110.4	106.3	113.2	127.8	
15	November, 1984	130.0	110.7	107.9	113.4	136.7	
16	December, 1984	140.0	110.9	106.4	113.6	149.4	
17	January, 1985	90.0	111.2	108.8	113.8	94.2	

Monthly Trend / Monthly Forecast / Quarterly Data

Ready Calculate NUM

SUPER NOTE

You'll be using the values in the Monthly Data worksheet to calculate the trend, so technically you don't need the figures in column B. However, I included them to make it easier to compare the trend and the actuals. Including the Actual values is also handy if you want to create a chart that includes these values.

To avoid entering dozens of linking formulas, I used a named range and an array. I defined the name Actual for the range of historical sales figures in the Monthly Data worksheet. I then selected the corresponding range in Monthly Trend and entered the following as an array formula:

```
=Actual
```

Recall that you enter a formula as an array by pressing Ctrl+Shift+Enter; see Chapter 60, "Advanced Range Topics," for more information.

SUPER NOTE

If you don't have enough data to fill in the entire 10-year range, you first need to remove the existing array in Monthly Trend (because you can't change part of an existing array). To do this quickly, select a cell within the array, press Ctrl+/ to select the entire array, activate the formula bar, and then press Ctrl+Enter. Note that later you'll also have to use this method to remove the array in the Normal Trend column.

SUPER NOTE

If you make changes to the values in the Monthly Data worksheet, Excel won't update automatically the corresponding values in the Monthly Trend worksheet's Actual column (because you can't change part of an array). To update these values, select a cell within the array, press Ctrl+/ to select the entire array, activate the formula bar, and then press Ctrl+Shift+Enter to re-enter the array.

As soon as the data is in place, calculating the trend line for the historical sales requires three steps:

1. In the Normal Trend column, select the entire range that corresponds to the number of months of historical sales figures you've entered (C5:C124 if you filled in the entire 10-year range in the Monthly Data worksheet).
2. Type in the following formula, but don't press Enter:

   ```
   =TREND(Actual)
   ```

3. Press Ctrl+Shift+Enter to enter the formula as an array.

To get some idea whether the trend is close to your data, cell F2 calculates the *correlation* between the trend values and the actual sales figures. (See Chapter 36, "Working with the Analysis Toolpack," to learn more about correlation.) A positive number signifies that the trend line approximates the sales direction; the closer the number is to 1, the better the approximation.

Calculating the Forecast Trend

To get a sales forecast, extend the historical trend line into the future. This is the job of the Monthly Forecast worksheet, shown in Figure 70.3.

FIGURE 70.3.
The Monthly Forecast worksheet.

C2 =TREND(Actual,,ROWS(Actual)+ROW()-1)

	A	B	C	D	E	F
1	Monthly Sales - Forecast		Normal Trend Forecast	Deseasoned Trend Forecast	Reseasoned Trend Forecast	
2		January, 1994	138.3	134.8	111.6	
3		February, 1994	138.5	135.0	113.6	
4		March, 1994	138.8	135.2	126.0	
5		April, 1994	139.0	135.4	123.7	
6		May, 1994	139.3	135.6	122.3	
7	1994	June, 1994	139.5	135.8	124.6	
8		July, 1994	139.8	136.0	131.1	
9		August, 1994	140.0	136.2	138.0	
10		September, 1994	140.3	136.4	141.6	
11		October, 1994	140.5	136.6	154.2	
12		November, 1994	140.8	136.8	164.8	
13		December, 1994	141.0	136.9	180.1	
14		January, 1995	141.3	137.1	113.5	
15		February, 1995	141.5	137.3	115.6	
16		March, 1995	141.8	137.5	128.2	
17		April, 1995	142.0	137.7	125.8	

Monthly Forecast / Quarterly Data / Quarterly Seasonal
Ready Calculate NUM

Calculating a forecast trend is a little different than calculating a historical trend, because you have to specify the *new_x's* argument for the `TREND()` function. In this case, the *new_x's* are the sales periods in the forecast interval. For example, suppose you have a ten-year period of monthly data from January 1984 to December 1993. This involves 120 periods of data. Therefore, to calculate the trend for January 1994 (the 121st period), you use the following formula:

```
=TREND(Actual,,121)
```

You use 122 as the *new_x's* argument for February 1994, 123 for March 1994, and so on.

The Monthly Forecast worksheet uses the following formula to calculate these *new_x's* values:

```
ROWS(Actual)+ROW()-1
```

`ROWS(Actual)` returns the number of sales periods in the Actual range in the Monthly Data worksheet. `ROW()-1` is a trick that returns the number you need to add to get the forecast sales period. For example, the January 1994 forecast is in cell C2; therefore, `ROW()-1` returns 1.

Calculating the Seasonal Trend

Many businesses experience predictable fluctuations in sales throughout their fiscal year. Resort operators see most of their sales during the summer months; retailers look forward to the Christmas season for the revenue that will carry them the rest of the year. Figure 70.4 shows a sales chart for a company that experiences a large increase in sales during the fall.

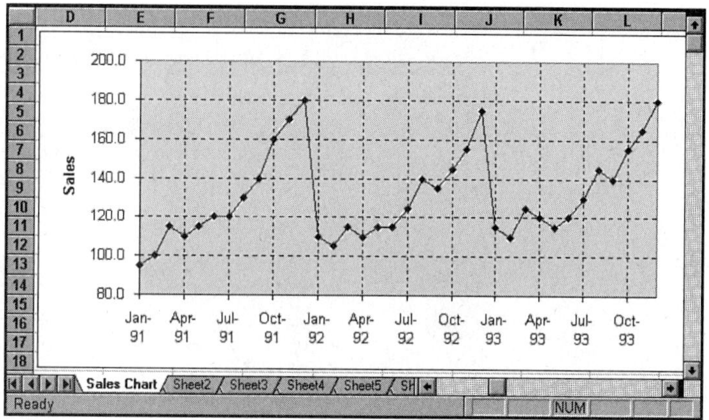

FIGURE 70.4. *A sales chart for a company showing seasonal variations.*

Because of the nonlinear nature of the sales in companies that see seasonal fluctuations, the normal trend calculation won't give an accurate forecast. You need to include seasonal variations in your analysis. This involves four steps:

1. For each month (or quarter), calculate a *seasonal index* that identifies seasonal influences.
2. Use these indexes to calculate seasonally adjusted (or *deseasoned*) values for each month.
3. Calculate the trend based on these deseasoned values.
4. Compute the true trend by adding the seasonal indexes to the calculated trend (from Step 3).

The next few sections show how FORECAST.XLS implements each step.

Computing the Monthly Seasonal Indexes

A *seasonal index* is a measure of how the average sales in a given month compare to a "normal" value. For example, if January has an index of 90, January's sales are (on average) only 90 percent of what they are in a normal month.

Therefore, you first must define what "normal" signifies. Because you're dealing with monthly data, you define normal as the 12-month moving average. (An *n*-month moving average is the average taken over the last *n* months.) The 12-Month Moving Avg column in the Monthly Data sheet uses a formula named `TwelveMonthMovingAvg` to handle this calculation. This is a relative range name, so its definition changes with each cell in the column. Figure 70.5 shows how the formula appears in the Define Name dialog box when cell D13 is selected. As you would expect, the formula calculates the average for the range C2:C13, or for the previous 12 months.

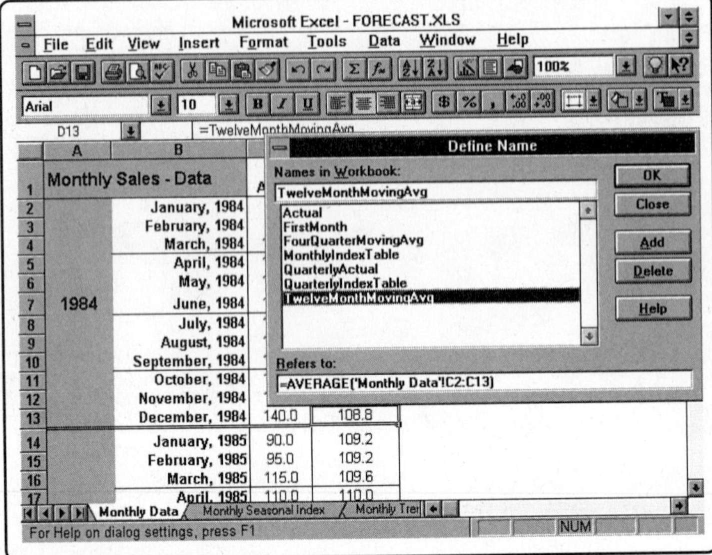

FIGURE 70.5.
The *TwelveMonthMovingAvg* *named formula.*

This moving average defines the "normal" value for any given month. The next step is to compare each month to the moving average. Do this by dividing each monthly sales figure by its corresponding moving average calculation and multiplying by 100—which equals the sales *ratio* for the month. For example, the sales in December 1984 (cell C13) were 140.0, and the moving average is 109.2 (D13). Dividing C13 by D13 and multiplying by 100 returns a ratio of about 128. You can loosely interpret this to mean that the sales in December were 28 percent higher than the sales in a normal month.

To get an accurate seasonal index for December (or any month) however, you must calculate ratios for every December that you have historical data. Take an average of all these ratios to reach a true seasonal index (except for a slight adjustment, as you'll see).

The purpose of the Monthly Seasonal Index worksheet, shown in Figure 70.6, is to derive a seasonal index for each month. The worksheet's table calculates the ratios for every month over the span of the historical data. The Avg Ratio column then calculates the average for each month. To get the final values for the seasonal indexes, however, you need to make a small adjustment. The indexes should add up to 1200 (100 per month, on average) in order to be true percentages. As you can see in cell B15, however, the sum is 1214.0. This means that you have to reduce each average by a factor of 1.0116 (1214/1200). The Seasonal Index column does that, thereby producing the true seasonal indexes for each month.

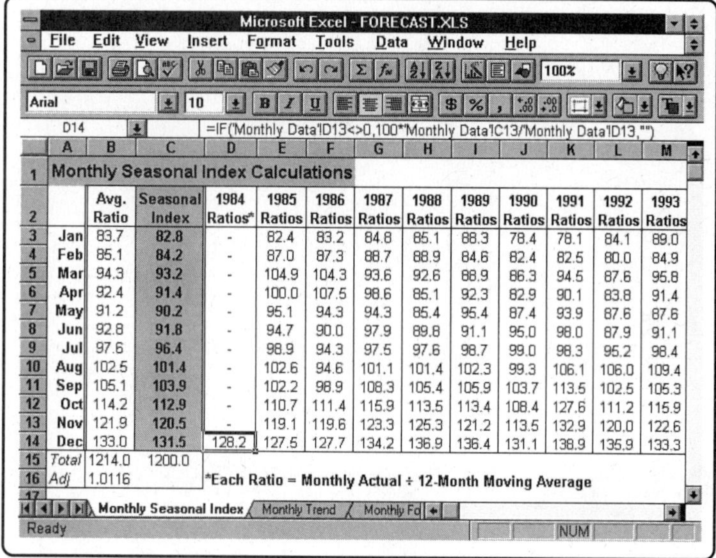

Microsoft Excel - FORECAST.XLS

D14 =IF('Monthly Data'!D13<>0,100*'Monthly Data'!C13/'Monthly Data'!D13,"")

Monthly Seasonal Index Calculations

	Avg. Ratio	Seasonal Index	1984 Ratios*	1985 Ratios	1986 Ratios	1987 Ratios	1988 Ratios	1989 Ratios	1990 Ratios	1991 Ratios	1992 Ratios	1993 Ratios
Jan	83.7	82.8	-	82.4	83.2	84.8	85.1	88.3	78.4	78.1	84.1	89.0
Feb	85.1	84.2	-	87.0	87.3	88.7	88.9	84.6	82.4	82.5	80.0	84.9
Mar	94.3	93.2	-	104.9	104.3	93.6	92.6	88.9	86.3	94.5	87.6	95.8
Apr	92.4	91.4	-	100.0	107.5	98.6	85.1	92.3	82.9	90.1	83.8	91.4
May	91.2	90.2	-	95.1	94.3	94.3	85.4	95.4	87.4	93.9	87.6	87.6
Jun	92.8	91.8	-	94.7	90.0	97.9	89.8	91.1	95.0	98.0	87.9	91.1
Jul	97.6	96.4	-	98.9	94.3	97.5	97.6	98.7	99.0	98.3	95.2	98.4
Aug	102.5	101.4	-	102.6	94.6	101.1	101.4	102.3	99.3	106.1	106.0	109.4
Sep	105.1	103.9	-	102.2	98.9	108.3	105.4	105.9	103.7	113.5	102.5	105.3
Oct	114.2	112.9	-	110.7	111.4	115.9	113.5	113.4	108.4	127.6	111.2	115.9
Nov	121.9	120.5	-	119.1	119.6	123.3	125.3	121.2	113.5	132.9	120.0	122.6
Dec	133.0	131.5	128.2	127.5	127.7	134.2	136.9	136.4	131.1	138.9	135.9	133.3
Total	1214.0	1200.0										
Adj	1.0116											

*Each Ratio = Monthly Actual ÷ 12-Month Moving Average

Monthly Seasonal Index / Monthly Trend / Monthly Fo

FIGURE 70.6. *The Monthly Seasonal Index worksheet.*

Calculating the Deseasoned Monthly Values

When you have the seasonal indexes, you need to put them to work to "level the playing field." Basically, you divide the actual sales figures for each month by the appropriate monthly index (and also multiply them by 100 to keep the units the same). This effectively removes the seasonal factors from the data (this is called *deseasoning* or *seasonally adjusting* the data).

The Deseasoned Actual column in the Monthly Trend worksheet performs these calculations (see Figure 70.7). Following is a typical formula (from cell D5):

```
=100*B5/INDEX(MonthlyIndexTable,MONTH(A5),3)
```

`B5` refers to the sales figure in the Actual column, and `MonthlyIndexTable` is the range A3:C14 in the Monthly Seasonal Index worksheet. The `INDEX()` function finds the appropriate seasonal index for the month (given by the `MONTH(A5)` function).

FIGURE 70.7.
Calculation from the Monthly Trend worksheet.

Microsoft Excel - FORECAST.XLS

D5 =100*B5/INDEX(MonthlyIndexTable,MONTH(A5),3)

	Actual	Normal Trend	Deseasoned Actual	Deseasoned Trend	Reseasoned Trend
January, 1984	90.0	108.3	108.7	111.4	92.2
February, 1984	95.0	108.6	112.9	111.6	93.9
March, 1984	110.0	108.8	118.0	111.8	104.2
April, 1984	105.0	109.1	114.9	112.0	102.3
May, 1984	100.0	109.3	110.9	112.2	101.2
June, 1984	100.0	109.6	109.0	112.4	103.2
July, 1984	105.0	109.8	108.9	112.6	108.6
August, 1984	105.0	110.1	103.6	112.8	114.3
September, 1984	110.0	110.3	105.9	113.0	117.4
October, 1984	120.0	110.6	106.3	113.2	127.8
November, 1984	130.0	110.8	107.9	113.4	136.7
December, 1984	140.0	111.1	106.5	113.6	149.3
January, 1985	90.0	111.3	108.7	113.8	94.2

Monthly Sales - Historical Trend

Correlation to Actual Sales:
Normal Trend --> 0.42
Reseasoned Trend --> 0.96

Monthly Trend / Monthly Forecast / Quarterly Data

Ready NUM

Calculating the Deseasoned Trend

The next step is to calculate the historical trend based on the new deseasoned values. The Deseasoned Trend column uses the following array formula to accomplish this:

```
{=TREND('Monthly Trend'!DeseasonedActual)}
```

The name `DeseasonedActual` refers to the values in the Deseasoned Actual column.

Calculating the Reseasoned Trend

By itself, the deseasoned trend doesn't amount to much. To get the true historical trend, you need to add the seasonal factor back in to the deseasoned trend (this is called *reseasoning* the data). The Reseasoned Trend column does the job with a formula similar to the one used in the Deseasoned Actual column:

```
=E5*INDEX(MonthlyIndexTable,MONTH(A5),3)/100
```

Calculating the Seasonal Forecast

To derive a forecast based on seasonal factors, combine the techniques you used to calculate a normal trend forecast and a reseasoned historical trend. In the Monthly Forecast worksheet (see Figure 70.3), the Deseasoned Trend Forecast column computes the forecast for the deseasoned trend:

```
=TREND('Monthly Trend'!DeseasonedTrend,,
       ROWS('Monthly Trend'!Deseasoned Trend)+ROW()-1)
```

The Reseasoned Trend Forecast column adds the seasonal factors back in to the deseasoned trend forecast:

```
=D2*Index(MonthlyIndexTable,MONTH(B2),3)/100
```

D2 is the value from the Deseasoned Trend Forecast column, and B2 is the forecast month.

Figure 70.8 shows a chart comparing the actual sales and the reseasoned trend for the last three years of the sample data. The chart also shows two years of the reseasoned forecast.

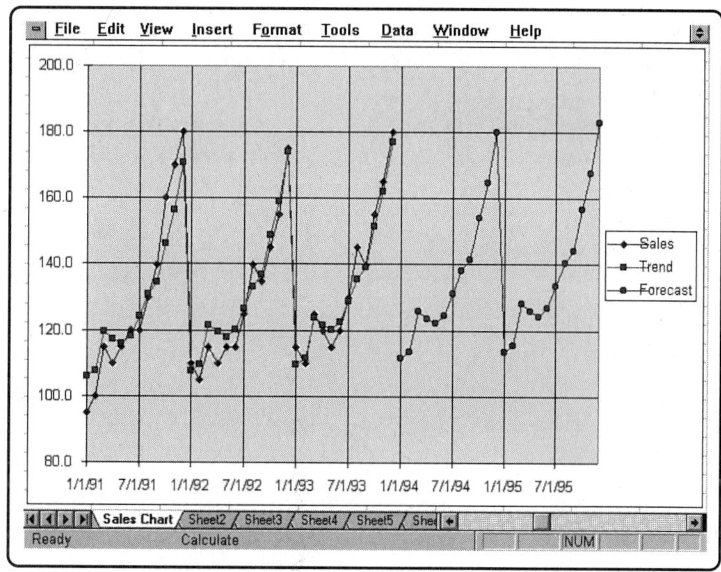

FIGURE 70.8.
A chart of the sample data, which compares actual sales, the reseasoned trend, and the reseasoned forecast.

Working with Quarterly Data

If you prefer to work with quarterly data, the Quarterly Data, Quarterly Seasonal Index, Quarterly Trend, and Quarterly Forecast worksheets perform the same functions as their monthly counterparts. You don't have to reenter your data, because the Quarterly Data worksheet consolidates the monthly numbers by quarter.

Trip Information

Destination	Florence, Italy	**Travel Agency**	Brimson's Travel
		Travel Agent	Lorraine Brimson
Flight Information (Departure)		**Flight Information (Return)**	
Date	Friday Apr 1, 1994	**Date**	Tuesday Apr 19, 1994
Airline	Alitalia	**Airline**	Alitalia
Flight #	740	**Flight #**	742
Departs	9:30 AM	**Departs**	4:25 PM
Arrives	10:45 PM	**Arrives**	5:40 PM
Hotel Information		**Miscellaneous**	
Name	Villa Villoresi		Heathrow
Address	2 Via Campi Localito Collonnata Sesto Fiorentino		
Phone #	55-448-9032		

Chapter 71

Trip Planner

Whether you're traveling for business or pleasure, across the country or across the ocean, for a few days or a few weeks, planning your trip carefully is the best way to avoid headaches and problems. By taking care of the details before you leave, you'll be free to get the most out of your trip.

To help you with these details, this project presents a trip planner workbook. No matter what kind of trip you take, you can use this workbook to

- record vital trip information
- calculate trip costs
- set up a preparation schedule
- run through a packing checklist

Excel 5.0 Features Used

Excel 4.0 Macro Language
Custom toolbar
Custom menu commands
Custom dialog box
Macro buttons
Automatic macros (Auto_Open, Auto_Close)

Files Used

TRIPPLAN.XLS

Special Instructions

If you'll be using TRIPPLAN.XLS for more than one trip, use the **F**ile | Save **A**s command to save the file under a different name before filling in the fields.

Opening the Workbook

The trip planner workbook is called TRIPPLAN.XLS. To follow along with the steps in this project, you need to open this workbook, as described in Procedure 71.1.

PROCEDURE 71.1. OPENING THE TRIP PLANNER WORKBOOK (TRIPPLAN.XLS).

1. Select the **F**ile | **O**pen command.
2. Select the drive and directory where you copied the Super Disk files.
3. Highlight the TRIPPLAN.XLS file.
4. Click on OK or press Enter. Excel opens TRIPPLAN.XLS.

About TRIPPLAN.XLS

TRIPPLAN.XLS consists of six worksheets:

Trip Info: Use this section to record basic information about your trip, such as the destination, departure and return dates, and flight data.
Emergency Info: Use this section to record important data such as your passport number, ticket information, and credit card numbers.
Cost Calculation: Use this section to calculate the costs of your trip. You can enter costs for the flight, hotel, car rental, and more.
Preparation Schedule: Use this section to set up a schedule for your trip preparation.
Packing Checklists: Use this section to run through various checklists of items to pack for your trip.
Macros: This macro sheet contains the supporting macros for the workbook.

Each of these sheets has been set up to be as general as possible. You may find that individual worksheets contain too much or too little information. In these cases, you easily can customize each worksheet to suit your needs.

Using Trip Planner

Trip Planner is simple to use: you'll spend most of your time moving between sheets and filling in cells. The next few sections talk about navigating Trip Planner, using each of the worksheets, and printing the information.

Navigating Trip Planner

Trip Planner gives you three ways to navigate the five main worksheets:

- You can select the worksheet tabs, as you would in any Excel workbook.
- You can use the commands on the **S**uperBook | **T**rip Planner submenu. This submenu is added automatically to the **S**uperBook menu when you open TRIPPLAN.XLS.
- You can use the Trip Planner toolbar.

Recording Basic Information About Your Trip

You use the Trip Info worksheet, shown in Figure 71.1, to enter some basic information about your trip. This information includes your destination, travel agent, flight data, and hotel particulars.

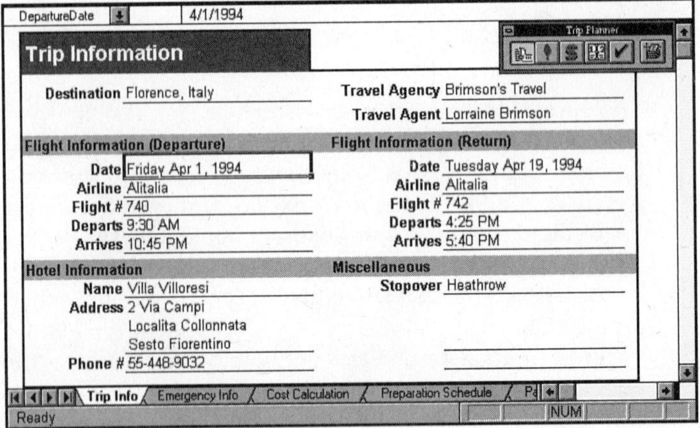

FIGURE 71.1.
The Trip Info worksheet.

If you're in a different sheet, you can display the Trip Info sheet either by selecting the **S**uperBook | **T**rip Planner | **T**rip Information command or by clicking on the Trip Info button in the Trip Planner toolbar.

The Trip Info button from the Trip Planner toolbar.

Three items worth noting about the Trip Info worksheet are

- The two date fields accept data entered in any Excel date format. The display format is *dddd mmm dd, yyyy*.
- The departure and arrival time cells accept any Excel time format. The display format is *hh:mm AM/PM*.
- Use the Miscellaneous section to enter any other information you need. This might include stopovers, flight meals, extra hotel information, and so on.

Recording Vital Information Useful in an Emergency

You use the Emergency Info worksheet, shown in Figure 71.2, to record vital data about your airline tickets, passport, home bank, traveler's checks, and credit cards. Most flight information is linked to the corresponding cells in the Trip Info worksheet, so you don't need to fill in these areas.

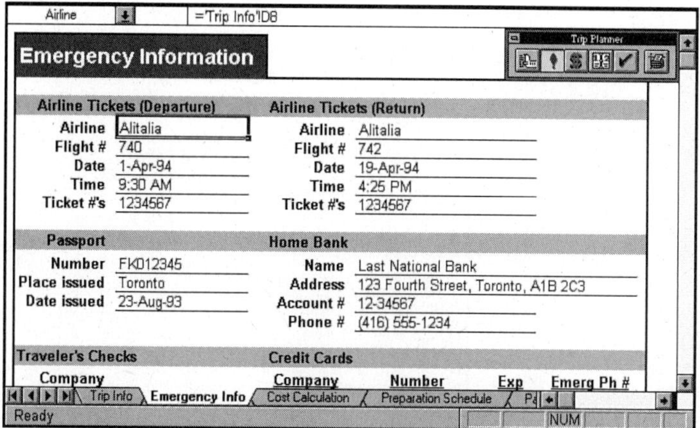

FIGURE 71.2.
The Emergency Info worksheet.

SUPER TIP

Print this information and take it with you when you travel. (See the section in this chapter titled "Printing the Trip Planner" for details.) When you arrive at your destination, store the printout in a safety deposit box or other secure place. If any of these items are lost or stolen, having a record of the appropriate information will make it easier to obtain replacements.

To display the Emergency Info worksheet, you either can select the **S**uperBook | **T**rip Planner | **E**mergency Information command or click on the Emergency Info button in the Trip Planner toolbar.

The Emergency Info button from the Trip Planner toolbar.

Calculating Trip Costs

The total cost of a trip is more than your airfare and a few nights at a hotel. You also need to factor in meals, entertainment, car rentals, and fees such as trip insurance. The Cost Calculation worksheet, shown in Figure 71.3, enables you to itemize these expenses and, where appropriate, to break them down by day to get the most accurate estimate of your total costs.

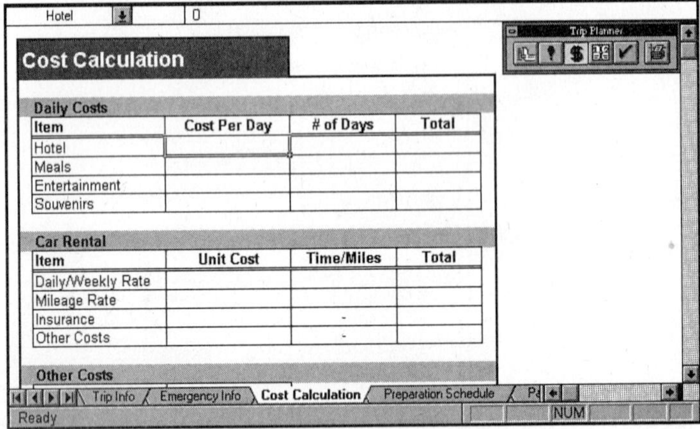

FIGURE 71.3.
The Cost Calculation worksheet.

Either select the **S**uperBook | **T**rip Planner | **C**ost Calculation command, or click on the Cost Calculation button in the Trip Planner toolbar to display the Cost Calculation worksheet.

The Cost Calculation button from the Trip Planner toolbar.

Use the Daily Costs section to calculate the total cost for your hotel, meals, entertainment, and souvenirs. Enter the approximate daily rate for each item in the Cost Per Day field, and enter the number of days you'll be using each item in the # of Days field. The Total is calculated automatically.

Entering car rental costs is similar. In the Car Rental section, enter the daily or weekly rate for the car, the mileage rate, the insurance fee (if applicable), and any other costs such as a drop-off fee.

Use the Other Costs section to enter expenses such as your flight, other transportation costs (parking, buses, taxis), fees (passport, visa, trip insurance), and any miscellaneous expenses you can think of. After you've entered all your trip costs, the overall total appears in the `Grand Total` cell (D25).

Tracking Trip Preparation

Successful trip planning involves more than simply attending to details. You must attend to the details at the *proper time*. For example, if the country you're traveling to requires a visa, it won't do you much good to apply the day before you leave. Instead, you need to get your application in at least three months before departing.

To help you avoid any last-minute rushing around, the trip planner includes a Preparation Schedule worksheet. This sheet is set up much like a time line. The first column lists a number of trip preparation tasks, and each task is scheduled for one of the times shown in the time-line column headings. These values represent the number of months, weeks, or days before your departure that you should consider performing the task. You add *shading* to the appropriate cell to indicate the status of a task:

> **SUPER NOTE**
>
> The dates listed in the Actual Date cells are derived from the `DepartureDate` cell (D7) in the Trip Info worksheet.

- Use light shading to schedule each task. The default worksheet uses a suggested schedule, but you're free to make whatever changes suit your needs.
- Use dark shading to indicate tasks that are partially completed.
- Use black shading to indicate tasks that are completed.

To display the Preparation Schedule worksheet, you can select the **S**uperBook | **T**rip Planner | **P**reparation Schedule command, or you can click on the Preparation Schedule button in the Trip Planner toolbar.

The Preparation Schedule button from the Trip Planner toolbar.

Figure 71.4 shows part of the Preparation Schedule worksheet with several cells demonstrating the task shading. The sheet also includes four macro buttons to make the shading easier:

Clear: Click on this button to clear the shading from a cell.
Schedule: Click on this button to mark a task as scheduled.
Partial: Click on this button to mark a task as partially completed.
Done: Click on this button to mark a task as completed.

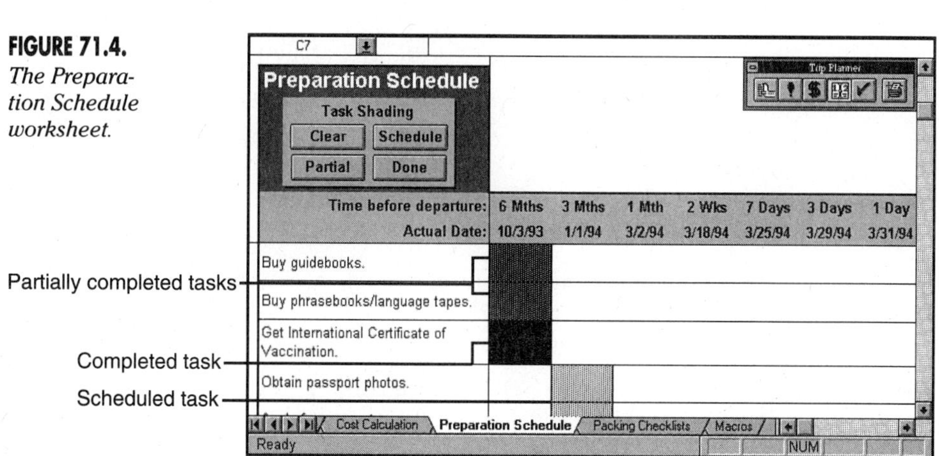

FIGURE 71.4.
The Preparation Schedule worksheet.

Using the Packing Checklists

Forgetting to pack something seems to be one of those inevitable travel problems. It's not surprising, however, when you consider that even a short trip might require you to pack a few dozen items. The Packing Checklists worksheet includes several checklists that will help make sure you have everything you need. There are five checklists: Clothes, Toiletries, First Aid, Laundry, and Miscellaneous.

You can display the Packing Checklists worksheet by selecting the **S**uperBook | **T**rip Planner | P**a**cking Checklists command or by clicking on the Packing Checklists button in the Trip Planner toolbar.

The Packing Checklists button from the Trip Planner toolbar.

Figure 71.5 shows the Packing Checklists worksheet. To enter a check mark in a cell, use either of the following methods:

- Activate the cell and click on the Toggle Checkmark macro button.
- Enter Alt+0252 in the cell. You must use the keyboard's numeric keypad to enter the numbers.

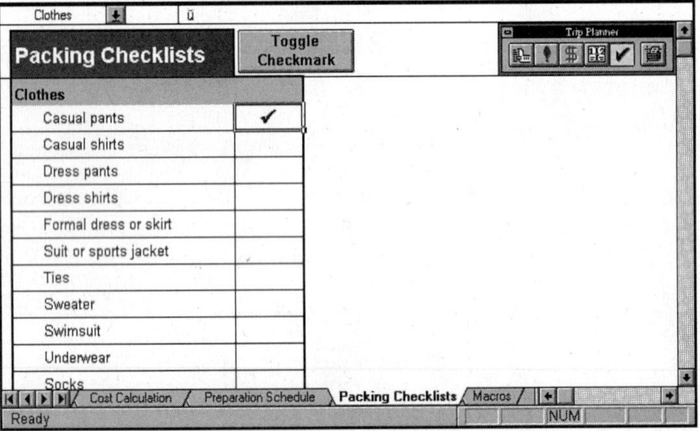

FIGURE 71.5.
The Packing Checklists worksheet.

Printing Trip Planner

You can print any or all of the Trip Planner worksheets. You'll need to do this, for example, if you want to take a copy of the Emergency Info data with you, or if you want to refer to a hard copy of the Packing Checklists while you pack.

To print the Trip Planner, follow the steps in Procedure 71.2.

PROCEDURE 71.2. PRINTING THE TRIP PLANNER WORKSHEETS.

1. Select the SuperBook | Trip Planner | Print Trip Planner command. The Print Trip Planner dialog box appears, shown in Figure 71.6.

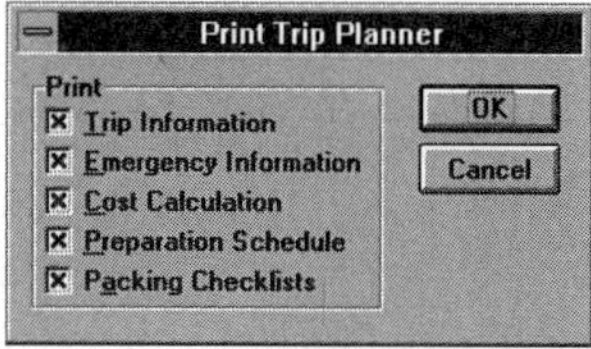

FIGURE 71.6.
Use the Print Trip Planner dialog box to select the worksheets you want to print.

You also can display the Print Trip Planner dialog box by clicking on the Print Trip Planner tool in the Trip Planner toolbar.

2. In the Print group, activate the check boxes for the worksheets you want to print.
3. Click on OK or press Enter. The Print dialog box appears.
4. Enter your print options.
5. Click on OK or press Enter. Excel prints the worksheets.

Understanding the Trip Planner Macros

The Macros sheet contains a number of macros that perform some of the behind-the-scenes work for the Trip Planner. The rest of this chapter looks at these macros in detail.

The Auto_Open Macro

The Auto_Open macro, shown in Figure 71.7, initializes the Trip Planner and sets up things such as the submenu and toolbar.

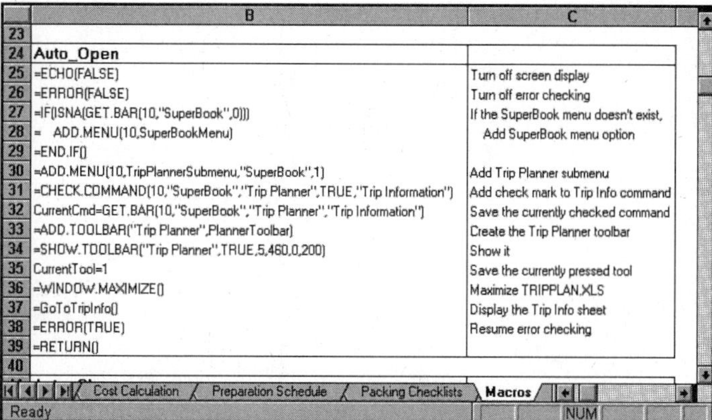

	B	C
23		
24	**Auto_Open**	
25	=ECHO(FALSE)	Turn off screen display
26	=ERROR(FALSE)	Turn off error checking
27	=IF(ISNA(GET.BAR(10,"SuperBook",0)))	If the SuperBook menu doesn't exist,
28	= ADD.MENU(10,SuperBookMenu)	Add SuperBook menu option
29	=END.IF()	
30	=ADD.MENU(10,TripPlannerSubmenu,"SuperBook",1)	Add Trip Planner submenu
31	=CHECK.COMMAND(10,"SuperBook","Trip Planner",TRUE,"Trip Information")	Add check mark to Trip Info command
32	CurrentCmd=GET.BAR(10,"SuperBook","Trip Planner","Trip Information")	Save the currently checked command
33	=ADD.TOOLBAR("Trip Planner",PlannerToolbar)	Create the Trip Planner toolbar
34	=SHOW.TOOLBAR("Trip Planner",TRUE,5,460,0,200)	Show it
35	CurrentTool=1	Save the currently pressed tool
36	=WINDOW.MAXIMIZE()	Maximize TRIPPLAN.XLS
37	=GoToTripInfo()	Display the Trip Info sheet
38	=ERROR(TRUE)	Resume error checking
39	=RETURN()	
40		

FIGURE 71.7.
The Trip Planner's Auto_Open macro.

After turning off screen updates and error checking, the macro checks to see whether the **S**uperBook menu already exists (as it might if you have one of the other projects already loaded). This is the job of the `IF()` function in cell B27. If the menu doesn't exist, the macro adds it. The `ADD.MENU()` command in cell B30 then adds the **T**rip Planner submenu. The menu definition table is shown in Figure 71.8.

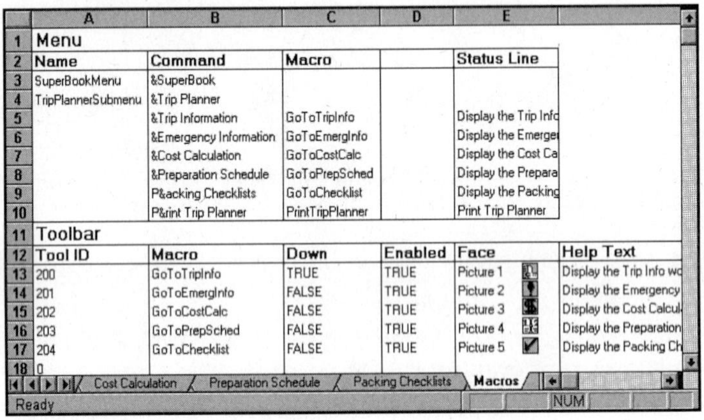

	A	B	C	D	E	
1	Menu					
2	Name	Command	Macro		Status Line	
3	SuperBookMenu	&SuperBook				
4	TripPlannerSubmenu	&Trip Planner				
5		&Trip Information	GoToTripInfo		Display the Trip Info	
6		&Emergency Information	GoToEmergInfo		Display the Emerge	
7		&Cost Calculation	GoToCostCalc		Display the Cost Ca	
8		&Preparation Schedule	GoToPrepSched		Display the Prepara	
9		P&acking Checklists	GoToChecklist		Display the Packing	
10		P&rint Trip Planner	PrintTripPlanner		Print Trip Planner	
11	Toolbar					
12	Tool ID	Macro	Down	Enabled	Face	Help Text
13	200	GoToTripInfo	TRUE	TRUE	Picture 1	Display the Trip Info wo
14	201	GoToEmergInfo	FALSE	TRUE	Picture 2	Display the Emergency
15	202	GoToCostCalc	FALSE	TRUE	Picture 3	Display the Cost Calcul
16	203	GoToPrepSched	FALSE	TRUE	Picture 4	Display the Preparation
17	204	GoToChecklist	FALSE	TRUE	Picture 5	Display the Packing Ch
18	0					

Cost Calculation / Preparation Schedule / Packing Checklists / Macros

Ready NUM

FIGURE 71.8.
The menu and toolbar definition tables for the Trip Planner.

As you move through the Trip Planner worksheets, the application does two things:

- It adds a check mark beside the appropriate **T**rip Planner submenu command.
- It presses the appropriate tool in the Trip Planner toolbar.

Because the Trip Planner always starts in the Trip Info sheet (as you'll see in a second), the `CHECK.COMMAND()` function in cell B31 places a check mark beside the `Trip Information` command. The `CurrentCmd` variable tracks which command is currently checked.

The next two commands create and display the Trip Planner toolbar, shown in Figure 71.8. The `CurrentTool` variable tracks which tool is currently pressed.

The last three commands maximize the window, call the GoToTripInfo macro (see the next section), and reset error checking.

Moving Between Worksheets

Each worksheet has its own macro that handles various chores when you move between worksheets. They're all basically the same, so I explain only one of them here.

Figure 71.9 shows the GoToTripInfo macro. The first three commands handle the checking (and unchecking) of the submenu commands. The first `CHECK.COMMAND()` function removes the check mark from the current command (as given by the `CurrentCmd` variable). Then, by using the `GET.BAR()` function, `CurrentCmd` is updated to, in this case, the `Trip Information` command (cell B54). The second `CHECK.COMMAND()` function places a check mark beside the **T**rip Information command.

FIGURE 71.9.
The GoToTripInfo macro.

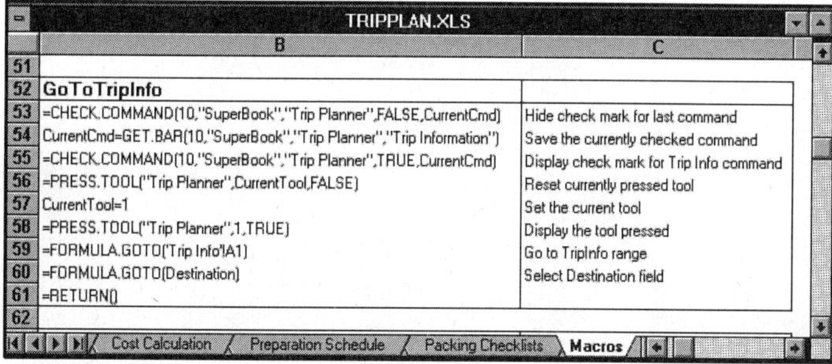

TRIPPLAN.XLS

	B	C
51		
52	GoToTripInfo	
53	=CHECK.COMMAND(10,"SuperBook","Trip Planner",FALSE,CurrentCmd)	Hide check mark for last command
54	CurrentCmd=GET.BAR(10,"SuperBook","Trip Planner","Trip Information")	Save the currently checked command
55	=CHECK.COMMAND(10,"SuperBook","Trip Planner",TRUE,CurrentCmd)	Display check mark for Trip Info command
56	=PRESS.TOOL("Trip Planner",CurrentTool,FALSE)	Reset currently pressed tool
57	CurrentTool=1	Set the current tool
58	=PRESS.TOOL("Trip Planner",1,TRUE)	Display the tool pressed
59	=FORMULA.GOTO("Trip Info!A1")	Go to TripInfo range
60	=FORMULA.GOTO(Destination)	Select Destination field
61	=RETURN()	
62		

Cost Calculation / Preparation Schedule / Packing Checklists / Macros

The next three formulas perform the same function for the Trip Planner toolbar. The first `PRESS.TOOL()` function (cell B56) resets the currently pressed tool (as given by the `CurrentTool`) variable. `CurrentTool` is then set to `1` (because the Trip Info tool is the first tool in the toolbar). A second `PRESS.TOOL()` function presses the Trip Info tool.

The macro finishes with two `FORMULA.GOTO()` functions. The first goes to cell A1 in the worksheet. This makes sure the top of the worksheet is always displayed initially. The second `FORMULA.GOTO()` selects the first field in the worksheet. In this case, it selects the `Destination` field of the Trip Info sheet.

The Printing Macro

Printing the Trip Planner is handled by the PrintTripPlanner macro, shown in Figure 71.10. After turning off screen echoing, the macro displays the dialog box defined by the table shown in Figure 71.11. The result is stored in the `PrintSelection` variable.

FIGURE 71.10.
The Trip Planner's printing macros.

C112 | If Trip Info check box selected, add Trip Info to print group

	A	B	C
106			
107		PrintTripPlanner	
108		=ECHO(FALSE)	Turn off screen echoing
109	PrintSelection	=DIALOG.BOX(PrintTripDialog)	Display dialog box
110		=IF(NOT(PrintSelection),RETURN())	If Cancel selected, return
111		FirstSheetSelected= TRUE	Initialize "first sheet" variable
112		=IF(PrintTripInfo,AddToPrintGroup("Trip Info"))	If Trip Info check box selected, add Trip Info
113		=IF(PrintEmergInfo,AddToPrintGroup("Emergency Info"))	If Emergency Info, add to print group
114		=IF(PrintCostCalc,AddToPrintGroup("Cost Calculation"))	If Cost Calculation, add to print group
115		=IF(PrintPrepSched,AddToPrintGroup("Preparation Schedule"))	If Prep Schedule, add to print group
116		=IF(PrintChecklists,AddToPrintGroup("Packing Checklists"))	If Checklists, add to print group
117		=PRINT?()	Display the Print dialog box
118		=ACTIVATE("Macros")	Activate "Macros" to ungroup sheets
119		=CHOOSE(CurrentTool,GoToTripInfo(),GoToEmergInfo(),GoToC	Return to the current sheet
120		=RETURN()	
121			
122		AddToPrintGroup	
123		=ARGUMENT("PrintSheet")	Sheet to add to print group
124		=IF(FirstSheetSelected,ACTIVATE(PrintSheet))	If adding first sheet to group, activate it
125		=WORKBOOK.SELECT(PrintSheet,,FALSE)	Add sheet to group
126		FirstSheetSelected= FALSE	Turn off "first sheet" variable
127		=RETURN()	

Cost Calculation / Preparation Schedule / Packing Checklists / Macros

Ready NUM

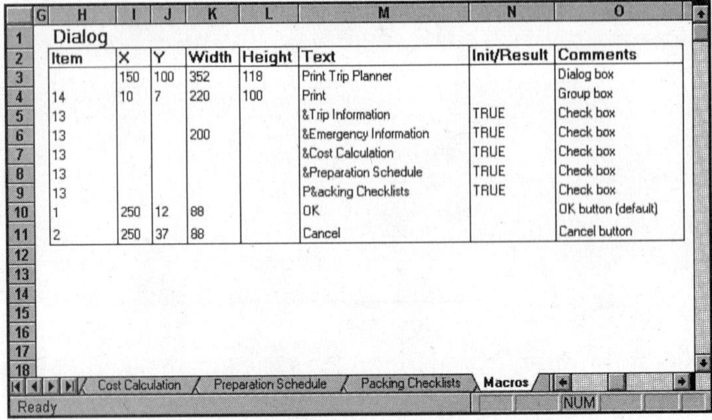

Dialog

Item	X	Y	Width	Height	Text	Init/Result	Comments
	150	100	352	118	Print Trip Planner		Dialog box
14	10	7	220	100	Print		Group box
13					&Trip Information	TRUE	Check box
13			200		&Emergency Information	TRUE	Check box
13					&Cost Calculation	TRUE	Check box
13					&Preparation Schedule	TRUE	Check box
13					P&acking Checklists	TRUE	Check box
1	250	12	88		OK		OK button (default)
2	250	37	88		Cancel		Cancel button

FIGURE 71.11.
The Print Trip Planner dialog box definition table.

If you click on Cancel, the macro quits (cell B110). Otherwise, a variable named `FirstSheetSelected` is set to `TRUE` (I explain this variable shortly). Next, a series of `IF()` functions tests the various checkbox results from the dialog box. In each case, if the check box is activated, the macro calls another macro, AddToPrintGroup (see Figure 71.10), and sends the name of the appropriate worksheet as an argument. AddToPrintGroup does three things:

1. It checks the `FirstSheetSelected` variable. If it's `TRUE`, it activates the sheet represented by the `PrintSheet` argument.
2. It uses the `WORKGROUP.SELECT()` function to add the sheet to the current selection.
3. It sets `FirstSheetSelected` to `FALSE` (because the first sheet—at least—has been selected).

To see why the `FirstSheetSelected` variable is necessary, you need to examine the syntax of the `WORKBOOK.SELECT` function:

`WORKBOOK.SELECT(`*`name_array`*`,`*`active_sheet`*`,`*`replace`*`)`

`name_array`	An array of sheet names to include in the group.
`active_sheet`	The selected sheet that should be the active sheet.
`replace`	A logical value that determines whether *`name_array`* is added to the current group. If *`replace`* is `TRUE`, *`name_array`* becomes the current group; if it's `FALSE`, *`name_array`* is added to the current group.

If you just ran the `WORKBOOK.SELECT()` command by itself, the sheet that was active when the Print Trip Planner command was chosen always would be included in the print group. The `FirstSheetSelected` variable enables you to avoid this. When this variable is TRUE, it means you haven't selected any sheets for the group, so you activate the first sheet to be added. After the first sheet is activated, the variable is set to FALSE so that Excel ignores it when you add subsequent sheets to the group.

After the print group has been selected, the built-in Print dialog box is displayed so that you can select any other print options.

Finally, the Macros sheet is activated to ungroup the sheets (cell B118). The CHOOSE() function then sends control back to whatever sheet was active.

The Auto_Close Macro

When you close TRIPPLAN.XLS, its Auto_Close macro (shown in Figure 71.12) runs so that the application can clean up after itself. The second formula (cell B43) deletes the Trip Planner submenu. The IF() function in cell B44 checks the SuperBook menu to see if it has any commands left. If it doesn't, it is deleted. The macro then deletes the toolbar (cell B47) and resets error checking (B48). The macro finishes by checking for changes using the GET.WORKBOOK(24) function. If this function returns TRUE, the workbook has unsaved changes, so an ALERT() box is displayed to ask whether you want to save these changes. If you click on OK, the SAVE() function saves the workbook.

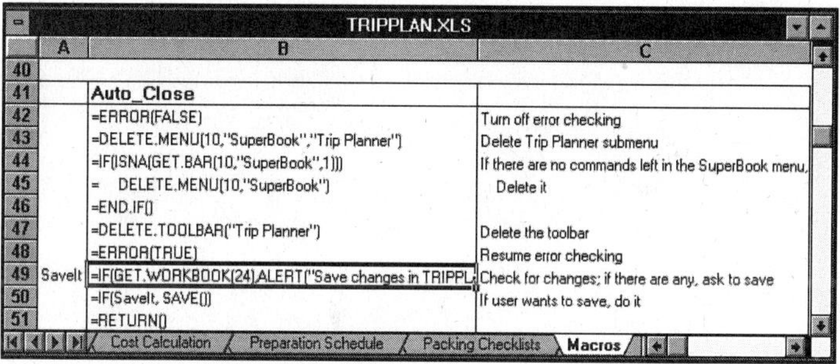

TRIPPLAN.XLS

	A	B	C
40			
41		Auto_Close	
42		=ERROR(FALSE)	Turn off error checking
43		=DELETE.MENU(10,"SuperBook","Trip Planner")	Delete Trip Planner submenu
44		=IF(ISNA(GET.BAR(10,"SuperBook",1)))	If there are no commands left in the SuperBook menu,
45		= DELETE.MENU(10,"SuperBook")	Delete it
46		=END.IF()	
47		=DELETE.TOOLBAR("Trip Planner")	Delete the toolbar
48		=ERROR(TRUE)	Resume error checking
49	SaveIt	=IF(GET.WORKBOOK(24),ALERT("Save changes in TRIPPL	Check for changes; if there are any, ask to save
50		=IF(SaveIt, SAVE())	If user wants to save, do it
51		=RETURN()	

Cost Calculation / Preparation Schedule / Packing Checklists / Macros

FIGURE 71.12.
The Auto_Close macro.

Rec	Date	Chk Num	Payee/Description	Category	Debit	Credit	✓	Balance
1	12/10/93		Initial deposit			5,000.00	✓	5,000.00
2	12/13/93	1	Bell	Phone - L. Dist	(87.25)		✓	4,912.75
3	12/15/93	2	Lawyer	L&P Fees	(750.00)		✓	4,162.75
4	12/17/93		Paycheck	Salary		1,237.45	✓	5,400.20
5	12/20/93		Presents	Christmas	(500.00)		✓	4,900.20
6	12/22/93	3	Eaton's	Clothing	(149.37)		✓	4,750.83
7	12/23/93		Food City	Groceries	(187.50)		✓	4,563.33
8	12/27/93		Last National Bank	Bank Charge	(12.50)		✓	4,550.83
9	12/27/93		Last National Bank	Interest		13.87	✓	4,564.70
10	12/31/93		Paycheck	Salary		1,237.45	✓	5,802.15
11	1/5/94	4	Hockey Tickets	Entertainment	(90.00)		✓	5,712.15
12	1/6/94		Texaco	Auto - Fuel	(25.00)		✓	5,687.15
13	1/8/94	5	Baby-sitter	Household	(20.00)		✓	5,667.15
14	1/10/94		Year-End Bonus	Bonus		2,500.00	✓	8,167.15
15	1/13/94	6	VISA	Christmas	(847.96)		✓	7,319.19
16	1/14/94		Paycheck	Salary		1,237.45	✓	8,556.64
17	1/15/94		Deposit	Consulting	(137.45)		✓	8,419.19
18	1/15/94		Withdrawal	Miscellaneous	(500.00)		✓	7,919.19
19	1/16/94	7	Mega-Hydro Inc.	Utilities	(57.00)		✓	7,862.19
20	1/17/94	8	Last National Bank	Auto - Loan	(257.64)		✓	7,604.55
21	1/20/94	9	Clascom Computers	Comp Software	(247.47)		✓	7,357.08
22	1/20/94		Withdrawal	Miscellaneous	(100.00)		✓	7,257.08
23	1/23/94	10	P. Bond Insurance	Insurance	(857.00)		✓	6,400.08
24	1/25/94	11	O'Donoghue Contractors	Home Repair	(475.00)		✓	5,925.08
25	1/28/94		Paycheck	Salary		1,237.45	✓	7,162.53

Chapter

72

Check Book Application

If you've ever wondered where all your money goes, this project's for you. This chapter looks at a checkbook application—Check Book—that enables you to record all the financial activity from a bank account into a worksheet. You can use Check Book to record checks, deposits, withdrawals, ATM (automated teller machine) transactions, bank charges, and more. You can categorize each transaction so that you can see how much you're spending on clothing, groceries, and entertainment. The application even keeps a running balance for the account so that you know how much money you have before you write that check.

Excel 5.0 Features Used

Visual Basic for Applications
Custom dialog boxes
Criteria and extract ranges
Named formulas
Linked cells

Files Used

CHECKBK.XLS

Special Instructions

Open the CHECKBK.XLS file from the directory in which you installed the Super Disk files. If you want to use CHECKBK.XLS for more than one bank account, use the **File** | Save **As** command to save the file under a different name before you start entering transactions.

Using Check Book

When you open CHECKBK.XLS, you'll see the Register worksheet, shown in Figure 72.1. This worksheet is similar to the paper check register you're familiar with, and it's where you enter the information for each transaction. You have the following fields:

Rec: The record number of the transaction. If you use the custom dialog boxes, this field is automatically incremented.
Date: The date of the transaction.
Chk Num: The check number (if the transaction is a check).
Payee/Description: If the transaction is a check, use this field to enter the name of the payee. For deposits or withdrawals, enter a short description.
Category: The application comes with more than 50 predefined income and expense categories that cover Advances and Advertising, Salary, Utilities, and

more. The dialog boxes list all the categories in drop-down list boxes, so you can easily select the category you want from the list.

Debit: Cash outflows are placed in this column. Although the numbers are formatted to appear in a red font with parentheses around them, they are *not* negative numbers.

Credit: Cash inflows are placed in this column.

The **"checkmark"** column is used to indicate transactions that have cleared the bank (that is, transactions that appear on your bank statement). Normally this is done by the Reconciliation feature, but you can enter a check mark by pressing Ctrl+Shift+K or Alt+0252. (You must use the keyboard's numeric keypad to enter the numbers.)

Balance: The running balance in the account. With the exception of cell I2, which contains the formula `=G2-F2`, the cells in this column contain the following formula:

```
=Balance
```

This is a named formula that computes the balance at the time of the highlighted transaction. This is a relative reference formula, so its definition changes with each cell. For example, here is the formula when cell I3 is selected:

```
=I2 + G3 - F3
```

This translates as follows: take the previous Balance amount, add the current Credit amount and subtract the current Debit amount.

	A	B	C	D	E	F	G	H	I
1	Rec	Date	Chk Num	Payee/Description	Category	Debit	Credit	✓	Balance
2	1	12/10/93		Initial deposit			5,000.00	✓	5,000.00
3	2	12/13/93	1	Bell	Phone - L. Dist	(87.25)		✓	4,912.75
4	3	12/15/93	2	Lawyer	L&P Fees	(750.00)		✓	4,162.75
5	4	12/17/93		Paycheck	Salary		1,237.45	✓	5,400.20
6	5	12/20/93		Presents	Christmas	(500.00)		✓	4,900.20
7	6	12/22/93	3	Eaton's	Clothing	(149.37)		✓	4,750.83
8	7	12/23/93		Food City	Groceries	(187.50)		✓	4,563.33
9	8	12/27/93		Last National Bank	Bank Charge	(12.50)		✓	4,550.83
10	9	12/27/93		Last National Bank	Interest		13.87	✓	4,564.70
11	10	12/31/93		Paycheck	Salary		1,237.45		5,802.15
12	11	1/5/94	4	Hockey Tickets	Entertainment	(90.00)			5,712.15
13	12	1/6/94		Texaco	Auto - Fuel	(25.00)			5,687.15
14	13	1/8/94	5	Baby-sitter	Household	(20.00)			5,667.15
15	14	1/10/94		Year-End Bonus	Bonus		2,500.00		8,167.15
16	15	1/13/94	6	VISA	Christmas	(847.96)			7,319.19
17	16	1/14/94		Paycheck	Salary		1,237.45		8,556.64

FIGURE 72.1.
The Check Book worksheet.

Entering Account Information

When you first open Check Book, you need to tell the application some basic information about the bank account, such as the name of the bank and the account number. This information, which appears in the transaction dialog boxes, can be handy if you're using the application for more than one account. You also can add or delete categories for the account.

Entering Basic Account Data

Procedure 72.1 shows you how to enter basic account data.

PROCEDURE 72.1. ENTERING ACCOUNT INFORMATION FOR THE CHECK BOOK APPLICATION.

1. Select the **S**uperBook | Check **B**ook | **A**ccount Information command. The Account Information dialog box appears, shown in Figure 72.2.

You also can click on this button in the Check Book toolbar to display the Account Information dialog box.

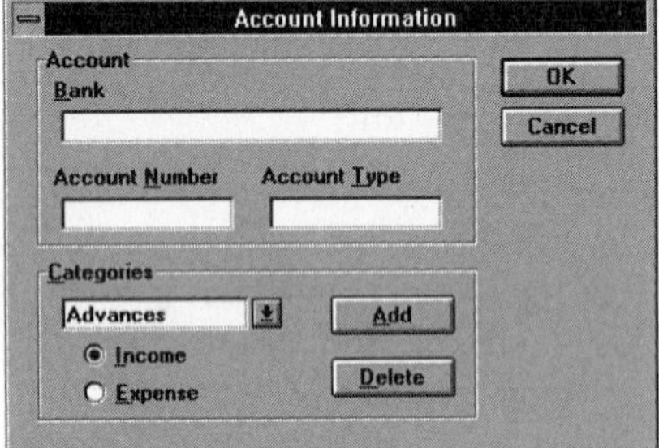

FIGURE 72.2. *The Account Information dialog box.*

2. In the **B**ank edit box, enter the name of the bank for this account.
3. In the Account **N**umber edit box, enter the account number.
4. In the Account **T**ype edit box, enter the type of account (for example, Checking or Savings).
5. Click on OK or press Enter.

Adding Check Book Categories

As I've mentioned, the Check Book application comes with dozens of predefined categories for your transactions. However, this list is by no means exhaustive, so there may be categories you would like to add. Procedure 72.2 tells you how to do it.

PROCEDURE 72.2. ADDING CHECK BOOK CATEGORIES.

1. Display the Account Information dialog box, as described in Procedure 72.1.
2. In the **C**ategories drop-down list, enter a name for the category. You can enter up to 255 characters, but only about 15 or so will appear in the Category column.
3. Select a type for the new category (**I**ncome or **E**xpense).
4. Click on the **A**dd button. Check Book adds the new category and displays a message.

5. Click on OK to return to the Account Information dialog box.
6. To add other categories, repeat steps 2-5.
7. Click on OK or press Enter.

Deleting Check Book Categories

To delete categories you'll never use, follow the steps in Procedure 72.3.

PROCEDURE 72.3. DELETING CHECK BOOK CATEGORIES.

1. Display the Account Information dialog box, as described in Procedure 72.1.
2. Select the type of category you want to delete (**I**ncome or **E**xpense).
3. Select the category in the **C**ategories drop-down list.
4. Click on the **D**elete button. Check Book asks whether you're sure you want to delete the category.
5. Select **Y**es to proceed with the deletion.
6. Repeat steps 2-5 to delete other categories.
7. Click on OK or press Enter.

Entering a Starting Balance

Before processing any transactions, you should enter a starting balance in the first row of the register. You can enter either the current balance in the account or the balance on your last bank statement. If you choose the latter, you'll also have to enter any subsequent transactions that transpired since the date of the last statement. Procedure 72.4 shows you the steps to follow.

PROCEDURE 72.4. ENTERING A STARTING BALANCE IN THE CHECK BOOK REGISTER.

1. In row 2, enter the appropriate date in the Date field. If you're using the balance from your last statement, enter the statement date.
2. If the account has a positive balance, enter the amount in the Credit field. Otherwise, enter it in the Debit field (remember to enter the debit balance as a positive number). The Balance field automatically lists the new balance.

Recording Checks

If you can write checks on your account, follow the steps in Procedure 72.5 to record checks in the Check Book register.

PROCEDURE 72.5. RECORDING CHECKS IN THE CHECK BOOK APPLICATION.

1. Select the **S**uperBook | Check **B**ook | Record **C**heck command. Check Book displays the Check dialog box, shown in Figure 72.3.

You also can click on this button in the Check Book toolbar to display the Check dialog box.

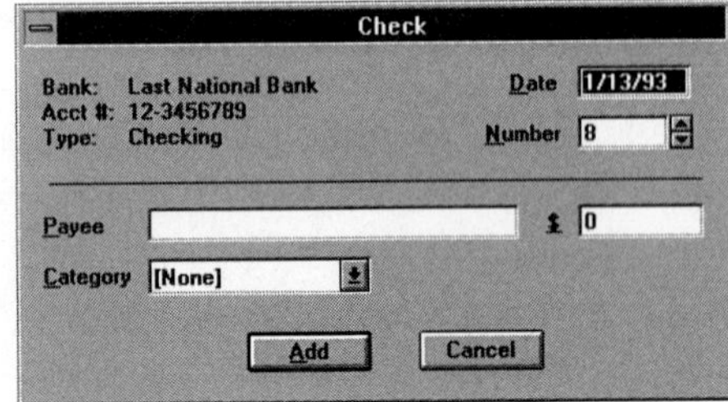

FIGURE 72.3.
The Check dialog box.

2. Enter the check date in the **D**ate edit box. You can use any Excel data format, but the Date field is formatted as *d/mm/yy*.
3. Enter the check number in the **N**umber spinner.
4. Use the **P**ayee edit box to enter the name of the person or company to whom the check is payable.
5. In the **$** edit box, enter the check amount.
6. Select a category from the **C**ategory drop-down list. If you don't want to use a category for this transaction, select [None].
7. Click on the **A**dd button. Check Book records the check and displays a fresh Check dialog box.
8. Repeat steps 2-7 to record other checks.
9. Click on Close to return to the register.

Recording Withdrawals

When you withdraw money from the account, follow Procedure 72.6 to record the withdrawal.

PROCEDURE 72.6. RECORDING WITHDRAWALS IN THE CHECK BOOK APPLICATION.

1. Select the **S**uperBook | Check **B**ook | Record **W**ithdrawal command. The Withdrawal Slip dialog box appears, shown in Figure 72.4.

You also can click on this button in the Check Book toolbar to display the Withdrawal Slip dialog box.

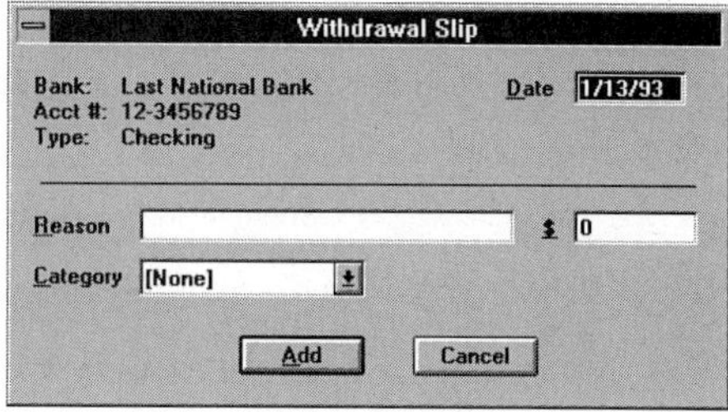

FIGURE 72.4.
The Withdrawal Slip dialog box.

2. Enter the withdrawal date in the **D**ate edit box.
3. Enter a reason for the withdrawal in the **R**eason edit box.
4. In the **$** edit box, enter the amount of the withdrawal.
5. Select a category from the **C**ategory drop-down list (or select [None] to enter no category).
6. Click on the **A**dd button. Check Book records the withdrawal and displays a fresh Withdrawal Slip dialog box.
7. Repeat steps 2-6 to record other withdrawals.
8. Click on Close to return to the register.

Recording Deposits

Procedure 72.7 shows you how to record deposits to your account.

PROCEDURE 72.7. RECORDING DEPOSITS IN THE CHECK BOOK APPLICATION.

1. Select the **S**uperBook | Check **B**ook | Record **D**eposit command. Check Book displays the Deposit Slip dialog box, shown in Figure 72.5.

You also can click on this button in the Check Book toolbar to display the Deposit Slip dialog box.

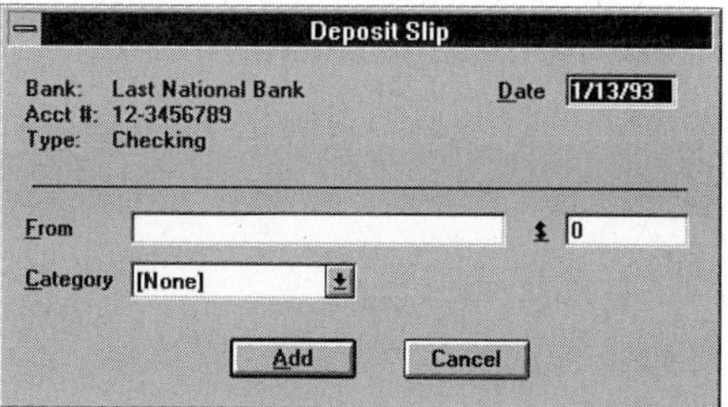

FIGURE 72.5.
The Deposit Slip dialog box.

2. Enter the date of the deposit in the **Date** edit box.
3. In the **From** edit box, enter the source of the deposit.
4. Enter the deposit amount in the **$** edit box.
5. Select a category from the **Category** drop-down list (or select [None] to enter no category).
6. Click on the **Add** button. Check Book records the deposit and displays a fresh Deposit Slip dialog box.
7. To record other deposits, repeat steps 2-6.
8. Click on Close to return to the register.

Balancing the Check Book

The Check Book application includes a Reconciliation feature that enables you to balance the account by reconciling the Check Book register with your bank statement. You supply the application with the date and balance of your last statement and the date and balance of your current statement. Check Book then extracts the transactions you entered between those dates (and any older, uncleared transactions) and you check them off (one by one) with your statement.

Figure 72.6 shows the screen you'll be using. The area on the left shows the statement data. The Difference field is the value to watch. The area on the right displays the uncleared transactions that occurred before or on the current statement date. You use the field with a check mark to check off these transactions with the corresponding items on the new statement. If all goes well, the two transaction lists will be identical and the Difference field will show a 0. You've balanced the account!

FirstCheckm...

	K	L
1	Reconciliation	
2		
3	Last Statement	
4	Date	12/28/93
5	Balance	5802.15
6		
7	Current Statement	
8	Date	1/28/94
9	Balance	7162.53
10		
11	Difference	1,360.38
12	Reconcile	
13		
14		
15	Ctrl+Shift+K - Toggle Checkmark	
16	Ctrl+Shift+R - Record Changes	
17	Ctrl+Shift+X - Cancel	

N Rec	O Date	P Chk Num	Q Payee/Description	R Debit	S Credit	T ✓
10	12/31/93		Paycheck		1,237.45	
11	1/5/94	4	Hockey Tickets	(90.00)		
12	1/6/94		Texaco	(25.00)		
13	1/8/94	5	Baby-sitter	(20.00)		
14	1/10/94		Year-End Bonus		2,500.00	
15	1/13/94	6	VISA	(847.96)		
16	1/14/94		Paycheck		1,237.45	
17	1/15/94		Deposit	(137.45)		
18	1/15/94		Withdrawal	(500.00)		
19	1/16/94	7	Mega-Hydro Inc.	(57.00)		
20	1/17/94	8	Last National Bank	(257.64)		
21	1/20/94	9	Clascom Computers	(247.47)		
22	1/20/94		Withdrawal	(100.00)		
23	1/23/94	10	P. Bond Insurance	(857.00)		
24	1/25/94	11	O'Donoghue Contractin	(475.00)		

Register / Account Info / Transaction Procedures
Ready NUM

FIGURE 72.6.
The Reconciliation screen.

If the Difference field is not 0, you need to look for the discrepancy. You might have missed a transaction or you may have entered the wrong amount. If you find the problem, cancel the reconciliation, fix (or add) the transaction, and try again.

Procedure 72.8 takes you through the required steps for completing the reconciliation.

PROCEDURE 72.8. BALANCING THE CHECK BOOK REGISTER.

1. With your statement in hand, enter any new bank charges or interest payments that appear in the statement.
2. Select the **S**uperBook | Check **B**ook | **R**econciliation command. The Reconciliation dialog box appears.

You also can click on this button in the Check Book toolbar to display the Reconciliation dialog box.

3. The Last Bank Statement group displays the information from the last reconciliation. (Or, if this is your first reconciliation, it shows the date and amount of your starting balance.) Edit this data if it is incorrect.
4. In the Current Bank Statement group, use the D**a**te edit box to enter the statement date and the Ba**l**ance edit box to enter the final balance on the statement.
5. Click on OK or press Enter. The Reconciliation screen appears (see Figure 72.6).
6. In the field with the check mark, enter check marks for each transaction that appears on the statement. To enter a check mark, press Ctrl+Shift+K or Alt+0252 (make sure you use the keyboard's numeric keypad to enter the numbers).

You also can click on this button in the Reconcile toolbar to add a check mark to the active cell.

7. If the reconciliation was successful (that is, the Difference field is 0), press Ctrl+Shift+R to record the changes in the register. If you need to cancel the reconciliation and return to the register to make adjustments, press Ctrl+Shift+X.

You also can click on the Record Reconciliation button in the Reconcile toolbar to record the changes to the register.

You also can click on this button in the Reconcile toolbar to cancel the reconciliation.

How the Check Book Application Works

Other than the Register worksheet, the Check Book application includes seven other sheets that perform behind-the-scenes duties:

> **Account Info:** This is the sheet where your account information, including the income and expense categories, is stored.
>
> **Transaction Procedures:** This module contains the Visual Basic procedures that support the three Check Book transactions: recording checks, withdrawals, and deposits.
>
> **Transaction Dialog:** This is a dialog sheet that contains the basic layout of the dialog boxes used for the transactions. Properties such as the dialog box title are modified within the procedures.
>
> **Info Procedures:** This module contains the Visual Basic procedures behind the Account Information command.
>
> **Info Dialog:** This dialog sheet defines the layout of the Account Information dialog box.
>
> **Reconciliation Procedures:** This module contains the Visual Basic procedures used by the Reconciliation feature.
>
> **Reconciliation Dialog:** This is the dialog sheet for the Reconciliation dialog box.

Understanding the Account Info Worksheet

Figure 72.7 shows the Account Info worksheet. Many of the procedures (which you'll be looking at later) refer to cells or ranges on this sheet, so it's important to understand how it's set up. The worksheet is divided into four areas: Account Data, Reconciliation Data, Income Categories, and Expense Categories.

FIGURE 72.7.
The Account Info worksheet.

SelectedInco... =IF(IncomeLink<>1,INDEX(Income,IncomeLink),"")

	A	B	C	D	E
1	Account Data		Reconciliation Data		
2	Bank	Last National Bank		Last	Current
3	Account Number	12-3456789	Date	12/28/93	1/28/94
4	Account Type	Checking	Balance	4,564.70	7,162.53
5	Records	25		✓	Date
6	Next Check Num	12	Criteria	<>ü	<=1/28/94
8	Income Categories	Drop-Down Value	Selected Income Category		
9	[None]	8	Salary		
10	Advances				
11	Consulting				
12	Interest Inc				
13	Miscellaneous				
14	Royalties				
15	RRSP Inc				
16	Salary				
18	Expense Categories	Drop-Down Value	Selected Expense Category		
19	[None]	24	Home Repair		

Register | Account Info | Transaction Procedures

Ready NUM

The Account Data Area

This area contains the account information and data that applies to the Register worksheet. Following is a summary of the cells, their names, and their descriptions:

Cell	*Name*	*Description*
B2	`Bank`	The name of the bank, as entered into the Account Information dialog box.
B3	`AccountNumber`	The account number from the Account Information dialog box.
B4	`AccountType`	The type of account from the Account Information dialog box.
B5	`Records`	The number of records (transactions) in the Register worksheet. The range of transactions is named Register, so the value in this cell is given by the formula `=ROWS(Register-1)`. (You have to subtract one, because the Register range includes the column headings.)
B6	`NextCheckNum`	The next likely check number you'll be using. This is given by the formula `=MAX(Register!C:C)+1`. (Column C is the Chk Num column in the Register worksheet.)

The Reconciliation Data Area

This area holds data used by the Reconciliation feature. It contains the following ranges and names:

Range	*Name*	*Description*
D3	`LastDate`	The date of the last bank statement.
D4	`LastBalance`	The balance on the last statement.
E3	`CurrentDate`	The date of the current statement.
E4	`CurrentBalance`	The balance on the current statement.
D5:E6	`Criteria`	The criteria range used to extract the transactions for the reconciliation. The checkmark field selects the uncleared transactions. (The checkmark character is the normal text representation of the ANSI 252 character used to create a check mark.) The Date field selects transactions that were entered on or before the `CurrentDate`.

The Income Categories Area

This area holds the list of income categories that appear in the Deposit Slip dialog box (or when you select the **I**ncome option in the Account Information dialog box). Following is a summary of the defined names in this area:

Range	*Name*	*Description*
A9:A16	`Income`	The range of income categories.
B9	`IncomeLink`	The linked cell associated with either the **C**ategory drop-down list in the Deposit Slip dialog box, or the **C**ategories drop-down in the Account Information dialog box when the **I**ncome option is selected. The value represents the item number of the list selection (where [None] is 1, Advances is 2, and so on).

C9	`SelectedIncome`	The category that corresponds to the value in the IncomeLink cell. This value is given by the following formula:
		`=IF(IncomeLink<>1,`
		`INDEX(Income,IncomeLink),"")`
		If `IncomeLink` is not `1`, use `INDEX()` to find the category; otherwise, [None] was selected, so display a blank.

The Expense Categories Area

This area holds the list of expense categories that appear in the Check and Withdrawal Slip dialog boxes (or when you select the **E**xpense option in the Account Information dialog box). Following is a summary of the defined names in this area:

Range	*Name*	*Description*
A19:A68	`Expense`	The range of expense categories.
B19	`ExpenseLink`	The linked cell associated with the **C**ategory drop-down list in the Check and Withdrawal Slip dialog boxes, or the **C**ategories drop-down in the Account Information dialog box when the **E**xpense option is selected. The value represents the item number of the list selection.

Range	Name	Description
C9	`SelectedExpense`	The category that corresponds to the value in the ExpenseLink cell. This value is given by the following formula: `=IF(ExpenseLink<>1,INDEX(Expense, ExpenseLink),"")` If `ExpenseLink` is not `1`, use `INDEX()` to find the category; otherwise, [None] was selected, so display a blank.

The Transaction Procedures

The Transaction module contains a number of procedures that set up the application, display the transaction dialog boxes, and process the results. The next few sections discuss the procedures related to the transaction dialog boxes.

Recording a Check

When you select the Record Check command, Check Book runs the `RecordCheck` procedure, shown in Figure 72.8. Because the different transactions all use the same basic dialog box layout, most of this procedure (and the similar procedures for recording withdrawals and deposits) is spent modifying the dialog box properties.

FIGURE 72.8.
The `RecordCheck` procedure.

```
Sub RecordCheck()
    Set transDialog = DialogSheets("Transaction Dialog")
    'Initialize dialog box controls for recording a check
    With transDialog
        .DialogFrame.Caption = "Check"
        .DialogFrame.OnAction = "TransactionDialogShow"
        .Labels("Label 6").Caption = "Payee"
        .Labels("Label 6").Accelerator = "P"
        .Labels("Label 15").Visible = True
        .EditBoxes("Edit Box 16").Visible = True
        .EditBoxes("Edit Box 16").Caption = Range("NextCheckNum")
        .EditBoxes("Edit Box 16").OnAction = "Transaction_EditBox16_Change"
        .Spinners("Spinner 24").Visible = True
        .Spinners("Spinner 24").Value = Range("NextCheckNum")
        .Spinners("Spinner 24").OnAction = "Transaction_Spinner24_Change"
        .DropDowns("Drop Down 14").ListFillRange = "Expenses"
        .DropDowns("Drop Down 14").LinkedCell = "ExpenseLink"
    End With
    'Display Check dialog box
    transDialog.Show
End Sub
```

Register / Account Info / Transaction Procedures

The first order of business, however, is to initialize a variable named `transDialog`. This variable is used by most of the procedures in this module, so it was declared with the following statement at the top of the module:

```
Public transDialog As DialogSheet
```

The `Public` keyword makes the variable available to every procedure in the module. In `RecordCheck`, the variable is assigned to the Transaction Dialog dialog sheet.

Then a `With` statement initializes the dialog box properties that apply to the Check dialog box. In particular, note the following:

- When you set the `OnAction` property of the `DialogFrame`, you're setting up an `OnShow` event handler for the dialog box. This is a procedure that runs automatically whenever you display a dialog box with the `Show` method. In this case, `RecordCheck` defines a procedure named `TransactionDialogShow` as the `OnShow` event handler. (See the section in this chapter titled "The `OnShow` Event Handler for the Transaction Dialog Boxes.")
- The Withdrawal Slip and Deposit Slip dialog boxes don't use the **N**umber control for entering a check number, so (as you'll see) they hide the label ("Label 15"), edit box ("Edit Box 16"), and spinner ("Spinner 24"). `RecordCheck` sets the `Visible` property for these controls to `TRUE` to make sure they're visible in the Check dialog box.
- The **N**umber edit box ("Edit Box 16") is initialized to the `NextCheckNum` range from the Account Info worksheet. Also, its `OnAction` property is set to the `Transaction_EditBox16_Change` procedure.
- The **N**umber spinner ("Spinner 24") is also initialized to the `NextCheckNum` range and its `OnAction` property is set to the `Transaction_Spinner24_Change` procedure. (See the section in this chapter titled "The Event Handlers for the Check Dialog Box.")
- For the drop-down list ("Drop Down 14"), you change the list of items by changing the `ListFillRange` property (if the list is in a worksheet range). `RecordCheck` sets this property to the `Expenses` range from the Account Info worksheet.
- The cell linked to the drop-down is governed by the `LinkedCell` property. `RecordCheck` sets this to the Account Info worksheet's `ExpenseLink` cell.

When the dialog box is ready, the `Show` method is run to display it. The next three sections discuss the event handlers associated with this dialog box.

The *OnShow* Event Handler for the Transaction Dialog Boxes

An `OnShow` event handler is useful for statements that initialize common properties in a dialog box. In the Check Book application, each type of transaction has its own specific dialog box properties, but there are many properties common to all three. These are set by the `TransactionDialogShow` procedure, shown in Figure 72.9.

FIGURE 72.9.
The `TransactionDialogShow` procedure.

```
'OnShow event handler for Transaction dialog boxes
Sub TransactionDialogShow()

    'Initialize dialog box controls
    With transDialog
        .Buttons("Button 2").OnAction = "Transaction_Button2_Click"
        .Buttons("Button 3").Caption = "Cancel"
        .Labels("Label 22").Caption = Range("Bank")
        .Labels("Label 23").Caption = Range("AccountNumber")
        .Labels("Label 26").Caption = Range("AccountType")
        .EditBoxes("Edit Box 7").Caption = ""
        .EditBoxes("Edit Box 9").Caption = Format(Now, "m/d/yy")
        .EditBoxes("Edit Box 12").Caption = 0
        .EditBoxes("Edit Box 12").OnAction = "Transaction_EditBox12_Change"
        .DropDowns("Drop Down 14").Value = 1
        .Focus = .EditBoxes("Edit Box 9").Name
    End With

End Sub
```

Transaction Procedures / Transaction Dialog / Info R

As you can, the entire procedure is spent initializing dialog box properties. Here are some highlights:

- The **A**dd button ("Button 2") has its `OnAction` property set to the procedure `Transaction_Button2_Click`. This procedure will then run whenever you click on the **A**dd button (see the section in this chapter titled "The Event Handler for Adding a Transaction").
- The account information from the Account Info worksheet (Bank, AccountNumber, and AccountType) is assigned to three label captions.
- The **D**ate field ("Edit Box 9") is initialized to today's date.
- The **$** field ("Edit Box 12") has its `OnAction` property set to the procedure `Transaction_EditBox12_Change`. This procedure checks to make sure you enter a number in the **$** field.
- The `Value` property of the drop-down list ("Drop Down 14") is set to 1 (that is, the first item in the list).
- The dialog box `Focus` property (the *focus* is the currently selected control) is set to the **D**ate field.

The Event Handlers for the Check Dialog Box

The Check dialog box has two event handlers that set up a link between the edit box and spinner associated with the **N**umber option. These are shown in Figure 72.10.

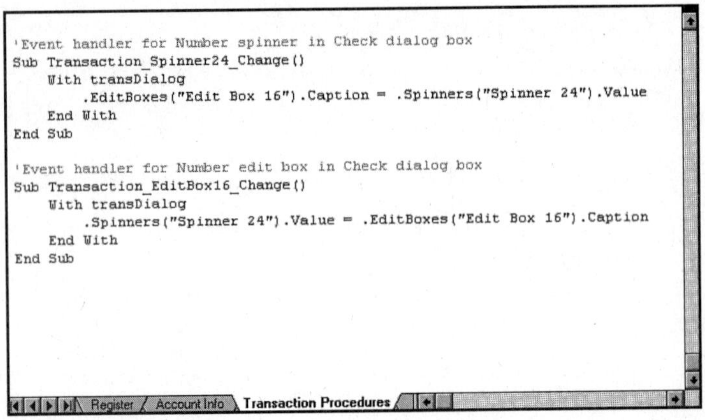

```
'Event handler for Number spinner in Check dialog box
Sub Transaction_Spinner24_Change()
    With transDialog
        .EditBoxes("Edit Box 16").Caption = .Spinners("Spinner 24").Value
    End With
End Sub

'Event handler for Number edit box in Check dialog box
Sub Transaction_EditBox16_Change()
    With transDialog
        .Spinners("Spinner 24").Value = .EditBoxes("Edit Box 16").Caption
    End With
End Sub
```

Register / Account Info / Transaction Procedures

FIGURE 72.10.
The event handlers for the Check dialog box.

When you change the value of one control, you want the other to change as well. For example, the `Transaction_Spinner24_Change` procedure is called whenever you click one of the spinner arrows. The procedure sets the edit box caption equal to the new value of the spinner.

Similarly, the `Transaction_EditBox16_Change` procedure is called whenever you change the value in the edit box. The procedure sets the `Value` property of the spinner equal to the new value in the edit box.

The Event Handler for Adding a Transaction

In each transaction dialog box, when you click on the **A**dd button, Check Book records the information in the Register and then displays a fresh dialog box for the next transaction. This process is controlled by `Transaction_Button2_Click`—the event handler for the **A**dd button. Figure 72.11 shows the first part of this procedure.

The first two statements declare and initialize a variable named `newTransRow`. This is the row number in which the new transaction will appear in the Register worksheet. `newTransRow` is the sum of the `Row` and `Rows.Count` properties of the `Register` range. The next statement changes the caption of the other command button to Close (it appears initially as Cancel). This is standard practice for this kind of dialog box. A Cancel button is supposed to exit a dialog box without doing anything. By clicking on **A**dd, you've done something (added a transaction), so you can no longer "cancel" the dialog box; you can only "close" it.

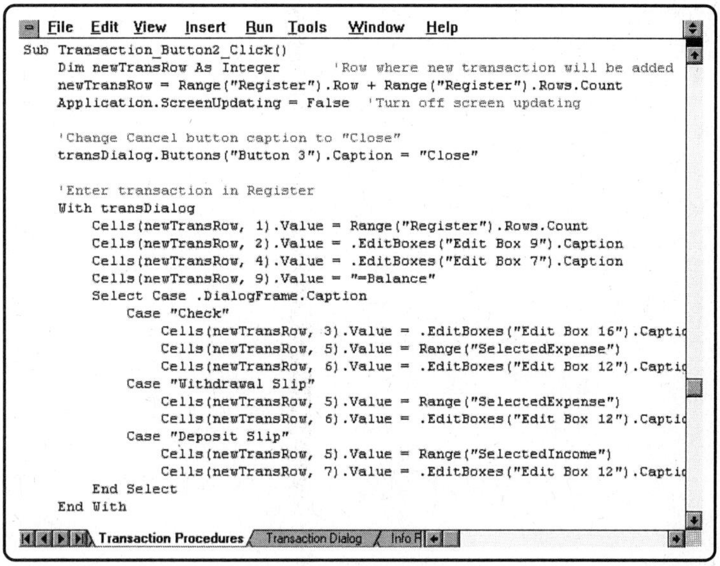

FIGURE 72.11.
The first part of the Add button event handler.

```
File  Edit  View  Insert  Run  Tools  Window  Help
Sub Transaction_Button2_Click()
    Dim newTransRow As Integer      'Row where new transaction will be added
    newTransRow = Range("Register").Row + Range("Register").Rows.Count
    Application.ScreenUpdating = False  'Turn off screen updating

    'Change Cancel button caption to "Close"
    transDialog.Buttons("Button 3").Caption = "Close"

    'Enter transaction in Register
    With transDialog
        Cells(newTransRow, 1).Value = Range("Register").Rows.Count
        Cells(newTransRow, 2).Value = .EditBoxes("Edit Box 9").Caption
        Cells(newTransRow, 4).Value = .EditBoxes("Edit Box 7").Caption
        Cells(newTransRow, 9).Value = "=Balance"
        Select Case .DialogFrame.Caption
            Case "Check"
                Cells(newTransRow, 3).Value = .EditBoxes("Edit Box 16").Captic
                Cells(newTransRow, 5).Value = Range("SelectedExpense")
                Cells(newTransRow, 6).Value = .EditBoxes("Edit Box 12").Captic
            Case "Withdrawal Slip"
                Cells(newTransRow, 5).Value = Range("SelectedExpense")
                Cells(newTransRow, 6).Value = .EditBoxes("Edit Box 12").Captic
            Case "Deposit Slip"
                Cells(newTransRow, 5).Value = Range("SelectedIncome")
                Cells(newTransRow, 7).Value = .EditBoxes("Edit Box 12").Captic
        End Select
    End With
Transaction Procedures / Transaction Dialog / Info R
```

The `With` statement takes care of adding the dialog box data into the worksheet cells. The various `Cells` methods return the cells in the new transaction row, and the `Value` properties of the returned cells are set to the appropriate dialog box properties. Also, the `=Balance` formula is entered into the Balance field (column 9). To handle the differences between checks, withdrawals, and deposits, a `Select Case` statement is used:

- For a check, a check number is entered, the Account Info worksheet's `SelectedExpense` range is used for the Category field, and the amount is entered in the Debit field (column 6).
- For a withdrawal, `SelectedExpense` is used for the Category, and the amount is entered in the Debit field.
- For a deposit, `SelectedIncome` is used for the Category, and the amount is entered into the Credit field (column 7).

Figure 72.12 shows the second half of the `Transaction_Button2_Click` event handler. The first statement redefines the `Register` range name by using the Name object's `Add` method. The new range is calculated by using the `Resize` method to increase the number of rows in the `Register` range. The number of rows is determined by the following formula:

```
Range("Records") + 2
```

The `Records` cell, you'll recall, contains the number of transactions in the Check Book register. This number is one less than the number of rows in `Register`, and because you're adding a row for the new transaction, you have to add `2` to the `Records` value.

FIGURE 72.12.
The second half of the Add button event handler.

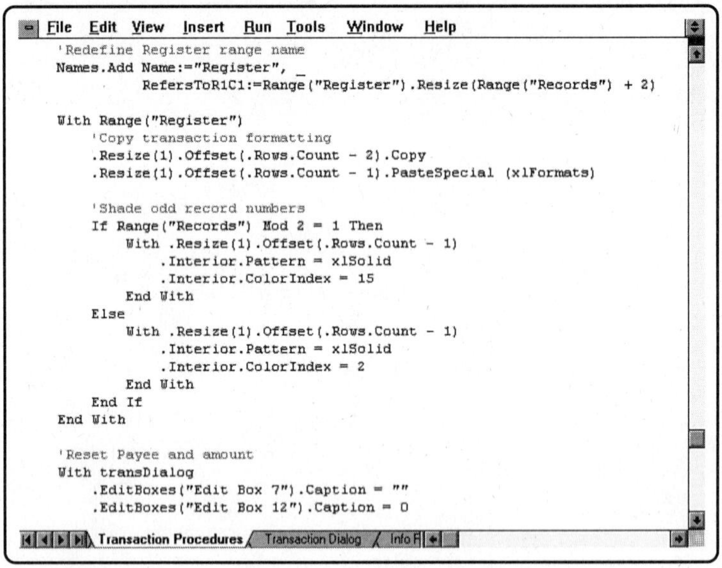

```
File  Edit  View  Insert  Run  Tools  Window  Help
'Redefine Register range name
Names.Add Name:="Register", _
        RefersToR1C1:=Range("Register").Resize(Range("Records") + 2)

With Range("Register")
    'Copy transaction formatting
    .Resize(1).Offset(.Rows.Count - 2).Copy
    .Resize(1).Offset(.Rows.Count - 1).PasteSpecial (xlFormats)

    'Shade odd record numbers
    If Range("Records") Mod 2 = 1 Then
        With .Resize(1).Offset(.Rows.Count - 1)
            .Interior.Pattern = xlSolid
            .Interior.ColorIndex = 15
        End With
    Else
        With .Resize(1).Offset(.Rows.Count - 1)
            .Interior.Pattern = xlSolid
            .Interior.ColorIndex = 2
        End With
    End If
End With

'Reset Payee and amount
With transDialog
    .EditBoxes("Edit Box 7").Caption = ""
    .EditBoxes("Edit Box 12").Caption = 0
Transaction Procedures / Transaction Dialog / Info F
```

In the first `With` statement, the first two lines copy the transaction above the new transaction and then paste the formatting onto the new transaction cells.

The Register worksheet uses shading on odd-numbered transactions to make them more readable. The next section adds this shading automatically. It first checks to see if the new record number is odd with the following statement:

```
If Range("Records") Mod 2 = 1
```

Visual Basic's `Mod` operator returns the remainder when you divide the number to the left of `Mod` by the number to the right of `Mod`. In this example, the procedure divides the value in the `Records` range by `2`. If the remainder equals 1, the number is odd, so you need to shade the transaction. A combination of the `Resize` and `Offset` methods returns the transaction. Then the `Interior` property is set to a solid pattern (the `xlSolid` constant), and the color is set to gray (15). If the record is not odd, the application colors the transaction cells white (`ColorIndex 2`) instead.

The final `With` statement resets the dialog box controls for the next transaction. The **P**ayee/**R**eason/From control ("Edit Box 7") is cleared, the **$** edit box ("Edit Box 12") is set to 0, and the **N**umber edit box and spinner are set to the new value in the NextCheckNum range. (This value is automatically updated when you add a transaction. See the section in this chapter titled "Understanding the Account Info Worksheet.")

Recording a Withdrawal

Recording a withdrawal is handled by the `RecordWithdrawal` procedure. This is almost identical to the `RecordCheck` procedure (discussed earlier). It initializes its specific dialog box properties and then shows the dialog box. Following is a summary of some of the changes it makes:

- The title of the dialog box (the `DialogFrame.Caption` property) is set to "Withdrawal Slip."
- The label that appears as **P**ayee in the Check dialog box is changed to **R**eason.
- The edit box and spinner associated with the **N**umber option are hidden.

Recording a Deposit

As you might expect, the procedure for recording a deposit—`RecordDeposit`—is similar to that for recording a check or a withdrawal. Following are a few of the dialog box properties that get changed in this procedure:

- The title of the dialog box is set to "Deposit Slip."
- The label that appears as **P**ayee in the Check dialog box and **R**eason in the Withdrawal Slip dialog box, is set to **F**rom.
- The edit box and spinner associated with the **N**umber option are hidden.
- The `ListFillRange` property of the drop-down list is set to the `Income` range on the Account Info worksheet. Also the `LinkedCell` property is set to the `IncomeLink` cell.

The Account Information Procedures

The Info Procedures module contains five procedures that display and process the Account Information dialog box. The next few sections look at each of these procedures.

Displaying the Dialog Box

The **A**ccount Information command is attached to the `DisplayInfoDialog` procedure, shown in Figure 72.13. The `InfoDialog` variable (which is declared as `Public` at the top of the module) is set to the Info Dialog dialog sheet. Then, a `With` statement initializes the dialog box control properties. Here are some things to note:

- The three edit boxes are assigned the account information data from the Account Info worksheet.
- The drop-down list is initialized to contain the items from the `Income` range.
- The **I**ncome option ("Option Button 11") is activated (that is, its `Value` property is set to `TRUE`), and its `OnAction` property is set to the `Income_Button_Click` event handler. Also, the **E**xpense option button's `OnAction` property is set to the `Expense_Button_Click` procedure. (Both procedures are discussed in the section in this chapter titled "The Event Handlers for the Option Buttons.")

- The `OnAction` properties for the **Add** and **Delete** buttons are set to `Add_Button_Click` and `Delete_Button_Click`, respectively. (See the sections in this chapter titled “Adding a Category” and “Deleting a Category.”)

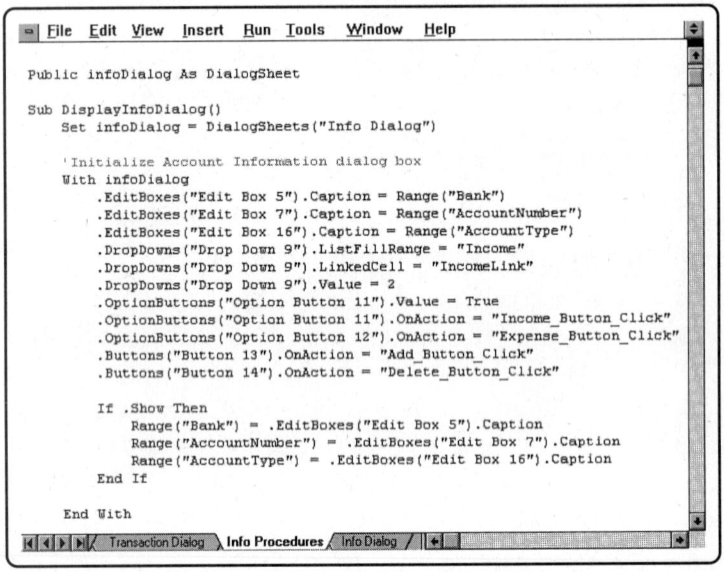

FIGURE 72.13.
The `DisplayInfoDialog` *procedure.*

```
Public infoDialog As DialogSheet

Sub DisplayInfoDialog()
    Set infoDialog = DialogSheets("Info Dialog")

    'Initialize Account Information dialog box
    With infoDialog
        .EditBoxes("Edit Box 5").Caption = Range("Bank")
        .EditBoxes("Edit Box 7").Caption = Range("AccountNumber")
        .EditBoxes("Edit Box 16").Caption = Range("AccountType")
        .DropDowns("Drop Down 9").ListFillRange = "Income"
        .DropDowns("Drop Down 9").LinkedCell = "IncomeLink"
        .DropDowns("Drop Down 9").Value = 2
        .OptionButtons("Option Button 11").Value = True
        .OptionButtons("Option Button 11").OnAction = "Income_Button_Click"
        .OptionButtons("Option Button 12").OnAction = "Expense_Button_Click"
        .Buttons("Button 13").OnAction = "Add_Button_Click"
        .Buttons("Button 14").OnAction = "Delete_Button_Click"

        If .Show Then
            Range("Bank") = .EditBoxes("Edit Box 5").Caption
            Range("AccountNumber") = .EditBoxes("Edit Box 7").Caption
            Range("AccountType") = .EditBoxes("Edit Box 16").Caption
        End If

    End With
```

The `Show` method displays the dialog box. If you click on OK, the three edit box captions are entered into the appropriate Account Info worksheet cells.

The Event Handlers for the Option Buttons

The `Income_Button_Click` and `Expense_Button_Click` event handlers are shown in Figure 72.14. The `Income_Button_Click` procedure runs whenever you activate the **Income** option button. This routine modifies the drop-down list’s `ListFillRange` property to point to the `Income` range on the Account Info worksheet and the `LinkedCell` property to point to the `IncomeLink` cell. The `Value` is set to `2` to bypass the [None] item.

The `Expense_Button_Click` procedure is similar to the `Income_Button_Click` procedure. When you activate the **Expenses** button, the `Expense_Button_Click` procedure is executed, and this procedure changes the `ListFillRange` to the `Expenses` range and the `LinkedCell` to `ExpensesLink`.

FIGURE 72.14.
The event handlers for the Income and Expense option buttons.

```
'Event handler for Income option button
Sub Income_Button_Click()

    With infoDialog.DropDowns("Drop Down 9")
        .ListFillRange = "Income"
        .LinkedCell = "IncomeLink"
        .Value = 2
    End With

End Sub

'Event handler for Expense option button
Sub Expense_Button_Click()

    With infoDialog.DropDowns("Drop Down 9")
        .ListFillRange = "Expenses"
        .LinkedCell = "ExpenseLink"
        .Value = 2
    End With

End Sub
```

Transaction Dialog | Info Procedures | Info Dialog

Adding a Category

When you click on the **Add** button to add a category, Check Book runs the `Add_Button_Click` procedure, shown in Figure 72.15. The procedure begins by declaring two variables: `newCategory` is the name of the new category, and `rowNum` is the row number in which the new category will be inserted.

FIGURE 72.15.
The `Add_Button_Click` event handler.

File Edit View Insert Run Tools Window Help

```
Sub Add_Button_Click()
    Dim newCategory, rowNum As Integer
    Application.ScreenUpdating = False

    With infoDialog
        newCategory = .DropDowns("Drop Down 9").Caption
        'Determine if category is Income or Expense
        If .OptionButtons("Option Button 11").Value = 1 Then
            rowNum = Range("Income").Row + 1
            With Worksheets("Account Info")
                .Cells(rowNum, 1).EntireRow.Insert
                .Cells(rowNum, 1).Value = newCategory
                .Range("Income").Sort Key1:=.Cells(rowNum, 1)
            End With
        Else
            rowNum = Range("Expenses").Row + 1
            With Worksheets("Account Info")
                .Cells(rowNum, 1).EntireRow.Insert
                .Cells(rowNum, 1).Value = newCategory
                .Range("Expenses").Sort Key1:=.Cells(rowNum, 1)
            End With
        End If
    End With

    MsgBox Prompt:="The " & newCategory & " category has been added.", _
          Buttons:=vbOKOnly + vbInformation, _
          Title:="Add Category"
End Sub
```

The With statement adds the new category. The newCategory variable is set to the drop-down list's Caption property. Then an If statement checks to see which type of category you're adding.

- In an income category (the **I**ncome button, "Option Button 11", has the Value 1), rowNum is assigned a row within the Income range. (The actual location within the Income range isn't important, because you'll be sorting the range later.) Then an entire row is inserted at Cells(rowNum,1), newCategory is placed in the cell, and the Income range is sorted to keep things in alphabetical order.
- In an expense category, the process is similar. The new row is set within the Expenses range, the new category is inserted, and Expenses is sorted.

The procedure ends by displaying a MsgBox function telling the user that the new category has been added.

Deleting a Category

The Delete_Button_Click procedure is shown in Figure 72.16. Check Book runs this procedure when you click on the **D**elete button to delete a category.

FIGURE 72.16.
The Delete_Button_Click procedure.

```
Sub Delete_Button_Click()
    Dim rowNum As Integer, categoryToDelete, categoryNumber As Integer
    Dim alertMsg As String, alertButtons As Integer, response As Integer

    'Determine if category is Income or Expense
    With infoDialog
        If .OptionButtons("Option Button 11").Value = 1 Then
            categoryToDelete = Range("SelectedIncome")
            rowNum = Range("Income").Row + .DropDowns("Drop Down 9").Value -
        Else
            categoryToDelete = Range("SelectedExpense")
            rowNum = Range("Expenses").Row + .DropDowns("Drop Down 9").Value
        End If
        categoryNumber = .DropDowns("Drop Down 9").Value
    End With

    'Check for [None] selected
    If categoryToDelete = "" Then
        alertMsg = "Can't delete the [None] category!"
        alertButtons = vbOKOnly + vbExclamation
    Else
        alertMsg = "Are you sure you want to delete the" & _
                   " " & categoryToDelete & " " & "category?"
        alertButtons = vbYesNo + vbQuestion
    End If

    'Ask for confirmation
    response = MsgBox(Prompt:=alertMsg, _
```

The With statement checks to see whether you're deleting an income or expense category:

- In an income category, a variable named categoryToDelete is set to the value in the SelectedIncome range. Then rowNum is set to the row number in the Income range of the category to be deleted.

- In an expense category, `categoryToDelete` is set to `SelectedExpense`, and `rowNum` is set to the appropriate row number within the `Expenses` range.

The procedure then checks to make sure you don't select the [None] item. The [None] item shouldn't be deleted, because you need it for entering transactions that don't have categories. If [None] is selected, the `alertMsg` and `alertButtons` variables are set up to display an appropriate message. Otherwise, these variables are set up to display a confirmation message.

In either case, a `MsgBox` function displays the constructed message, and the result is stored in the `response` variable. If you're deleting a legitimate category, the `response` variable is checked with an `If` statement (not shown in Figure 72.16). If `response` equals `vbYes`, the category's row is deleted with the following statement:

```
=Worksheets("Account Info").Cells(rowNum,1).EntireRow.Delete
```

The Reconciliation Procedures

The Reconciliation Procedures module contains several procedures that support the Check Book's Reconciliation feature. This section takes a look at these procedures.

Displaying the Reconciliation Dialog Box

The `DisplayReconciliationDialog` procedure, shown in Figure 72.17, displays and processes the Reconciliation dialog box. The `reconDialog` variable holds the Reconciliation Dialog sheet, and a `With` statement uses this variable to initialize, show, and process the dialog box. The initialization statements read the appropriate cells from the Account Info worksheet. The `If` statement runs the `Show` method and, if you click on OK, the procedure records the new data in Account Info. Then the `SetUpReconciliation` procedure is called to run the reconciliation.

FIGURE 72.17.
The `Display-Reconciliation-Dialog` *procedure.*

```
Public reconDialog As DialogSheet, totalTrans As Integer
Sub DisplayReconciliationDialog()

    Set reconDialog = DialogSheets("Reconciliation Dialog")

    'Initialize the dialog box controls and then show it
    With reconDialog
        .EditBoxes("Edit Box 6").Caption = Range("LastDate").Text
        .EditBoxes("Edit Box 8").Caption = Range("LastBalance")
        .EditBoxes("Edit Box 11").Caption = ""
        .EditBoxes("Edit Box 13").Caption = 0

        If .Show Then    'Record new data and set up reconciliation
            Range("LastDate").Value = .EditBoxes("Edit Box 6").Caption
            Range("LastBalance").Value = .EditBoxes("Edit Box 8").Caption
            Range("CurrentDate").Value = .EditBoxes("Edit Box 11").Caption
            Range("CurrentBalance").Value = .EditBoxes("Edit Box 13").Caption
            SetUpReconciliation
        End If
    End With
End Sub
```
Reconciliation Procedures / Reconciliation Dialog

Setting Up the Reconciliation Screen

As you'll soon see, Check Book creates the reconciliation transactions by extracting them from the Register—based on the values in the Account Info worksheet's `Criteria` range. However, Excel doesn't enable you to extract list records to a different worksheet, so the Reconciliation area must reside on the Register worksheet. I've placed the Reconciliation area to the right of the Register range, starting in column K. The problem with this arrangement is that rows may accidentally get deleted if you're performing maintenance within the register.

To guard against this possibility, the `SetUpReconciliation` procedure reconstructs the entire Reconciliation screen from scratch. Figure 72.18 shows the first part of this procedure. The first statement turns off screen updating. Then a `With` statement adds and formats the labels and data used in the Reconciliation screen. A cell named `Reconciliation` (cell K1 in the Register worksheet) is the starting point, and the rest of the statements use either `Resize` or `Offset` to enter and format the cell values.

FIGURE 72.18.
The first part of the `SetUpReconciliation` procedure.

```
Sub SetUpReconciliation()

    Application.ScreenUpdating = False  'Turn off screen updating

    'Add and format reconciliation labels and data
    With Range("Reconciliation")
        With .Resize(20, 2)
            .Clear
            .Interior.Pattern = xlSolid
            .Interior.ColorIndex = 15
            .BorderAround
        End With
        .Value = "Reconciliation"
        .Font.Bold = True
        .Font.Size = 12
        .Offset(2, 0).Value = "Last Statement"
        .Offset(2, 0).Font.Bold = True
        .Offset(3, 0).Value = "Date"
        .Offset(3, 0).HorizontalAlignment = xlRight
        .Offset(3, 1).Value = Range("LastDate")
        .Offset(3, 1).NumberFormat = "m/d/yy"
```

Reconciliation Procedures / Reconciliation Dialog

Most of the statements are straightforward, but there is one that may create a few furrows in your brow. Toward the end of the `With` statement, you'll see the following (take a deep breath):

```
With .Offset(10,1).FormulaArray = "=CurrentBalance-LastBalance-
SUM(IF(NOT(ISBLANK(Checkmarks)),Credits-Debits,0))"
```

This is the array formula that appears in the Difference cell in the Reconciliation screen (L11). `CurrentBalance` and `LastBalance` are the balances from the Account Info sheet. The `Checkmarks` name refers to the range of cells under the checkmark column in the extracted reconciliation transactions. Similarly, `Credits` refers to the range of cells under the Credit column, and `Debits` refers to the cells under the Debit column. The `IF()` part of the formula translates to the following:

For each reconciliation transaction, if the checkmark field is not blank (that is, it contains a check mark), return the difference between the Credit value and the Debit value; otherwise, return `0`.

The `SUM()` function adds up all these values.

The second part of `SetUpReconciliation` sets up the new reconciliation transactions, as shown in Figure 72.19. The `With` statement uses the cell `FirstCheckmark` as the starting point (cell T2). The old transactions are cleared by first offsetting the `CurrentRegion` (the transactions plus the column headings) by one row (to move it off the headings) and by using the `Clear` method.

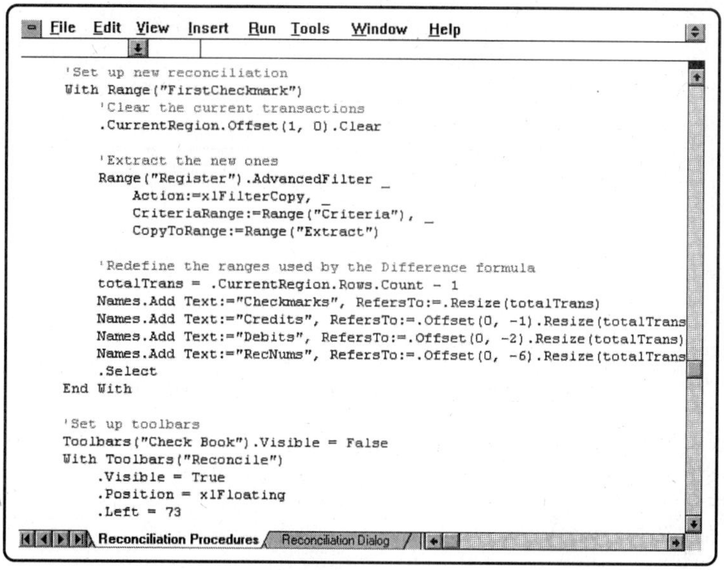

FIGURE 72.19.
The second part of the `SetUp-Reconciliation` procedure.

```
'Set up new reconciliation
With Range("FirstCheckmark")
    'Clear the current transactions
    .CurrentRegion.Offset(1, 0).Clear

    'Extract the new ones
    Range("Register").AdvancedFilter _
        Action:=xlFilterCopy, _
        CriteriaRange:=Range("Criteria"), _
        CopyToRange:=Range("Extract")

    'Redefine the ranges used by the Difference formula
    totalTrans = .CurrentRegion.Rows.Count - 1
    Names.Add Text:="Checkmarks", RefersTo:=.Resize(totalTrans)
    Names.Add Text:="Credits", RefersTo:=.Offset(0, -1).Resize(totalTrans
    Names.Add Text:="Debits", RefersTo:=.Offset(0, -2).Resize(totalTrans)
    Names.Add Text:="RecNums", RefersTo:=.Offset(0, -6).Resize(totalTrans
    .Select
End With

'Set up toolbars
Toolbars("Check Book").Visible = False
With Toolbars("Reconcile")
    .Visible = True
    .Position = xlFloating
    .Left = 73
```

The `AdvancedFilter` method is used to extract the transactions. Notice how the `xlFilterCopy` constant is used to tell Excel to extract the records to a different location. The new location is governed by the `CopyToRange` named variable, which in this case is the `Extract` range (this is the range of column headings in the Reconciliation screen; that is, N1:T1).

The next few statements redefine the Checkmarks, Credits, and Debits names used in the Difference formula, as well as the RecNums name you'll use later on. The size of each range is determined by the number of extracted transactions, and that value is stored in the `totalTrans` variable (which is declared as `Public` at the top of the module).

The rest of the procedure hides the Check Book toolbar, displays the Reconcile toolbar, and sets up the shortcut keys for recording or canceling the reconciliation (not shown in Figure 72.19).

Recording the Reconciliation

When you record the reconciliation, the `RecordReconciliation` procedure, shown in Figure 72.20, is executed. The job of the `For Each...Next` loop is to copy the contents of the Reconciliation screen's checkmark field into the corresponding field in the `Register` range. The `RecNums` name refers to the range of cells below the Rec column. Each loop through these cells (each cell is named `recCell`) does three things:

1. The contents of the checkmark field (offset from recCell by six columns) are stored in `checkCell`.
2. The `MATCH()` worksheet function looks for the record number (the Value of `recCell`) in column A (the Rec column of the Register). The result is the row number of the transaction, which is stored in `registerRow`.
3. `checkCell` is stored in the checkmark field of the Register range. (The `CheckField` name refers to the column heading of the field.)

FIGURE 72.20.
The final procedures for the Reconciliation feature.

File Edit View Insert Run Tools Window Help

```
Sub RecordReconciliation()
    Dim registerRow As Integer, recCell As Range, checkCell As Variant

    'Record check marks
    For Each recCell In Range("RecNums")
        checkCell = recCell.Offset(0, 6).Value
        registerRow = Application.Match(recCell.Value, [a1].EntireColumn, 0)
        Cells(registerRow, Range("CheckField").Column).Value = checkCell
    Next recCell

    'Record statement data
    Range("LastDate").Value = Range("CurrentDate")
    Range("CurrentDate") = ""
    Range("LastBalance").Value = Range("CurrentBalance")
    Range("CurrentBalance") = 0

    EndReconciliation         'End it all
End Sub

'Procedure that ends the reconciliation
Sub EndReconciliation()
    Toolbars("Reconcile").Visible = False         'Hide Reconcile toolbar
    Toolbars("Check Book").Visible = True         'Display Check Book toolbar
    Cells(Range("Register").Row + 1, 1).Select    'Select first cell
    Application.OnKey Key:="^+r"                  'Reset Ctrl+Shift+R
    Application.OnKey Key:="^+x"                  'Reset Ctrl+Shift+K
End Sub
```

Reconciliation Procedures / Reconciliation Dialog

The next four statements record the statement data in the Account Info worksheet: `CurrentDate` is moved to `LastDate` and cleared, and `CurrentBalance` is moved to `LastBalance` and set to `0`. The final statement calls the `EndReconciliation` procedure.

Ending the Reconciliation

The `EndReconciliation` procedure (see Figure 72.20) performs several tasks that reset the Register worksheet: the Check Book toolbar is displayed, the Reconcile toolbar is hidden, the first cell of the Register range is selected, and the Ctrl+Shift+R and Ctrl+Shift+K shortcut keys are reset.

Customer Database

Title	First Name	Last Name	Position	Company	Acct Num	Address1
Mr.	Louis	DePalma	Dispatcher	Sunshine Cab Company	123456	123 45th Street
Mr.	Rob	Petrie	Screenwriter	The Alan Brady Show	987654	987 Somwhere Drive
Mr.	Herb	Tarlek	Sales Mgr	WKRP	121212	456 Pitty-Pat Lane
Mr.	Bert	Campbell	Owner	Campbell Construction	654321	1234 Harris Avenue
Mr.	Ricky	Riccardo	Bandleader	DesiLu	456789	456 Lucy Street
Ms.	Mary	Richards	Producer	WJN News	876543	6543 Tinker Way
Mr.	Woody	Boyd	Bartender	Cheers	456654	432 Hayseed Road
Ms.	Edith	Bunker	Housewife		111111	63 Hauser St
Mr.	Homer	Simpson	Nuclear Oper	Springfield Nuclear Plant	246802	742 Evergreen Terrace

City	State	ZIP Code	Phone Num	Fax Num	Memo
New York	NY	10019	1-212-123-4567	1-212-987-6543	Birthday: Feb 29
New Rochelle	NY	98765-4321	1-203-987-6543	1-203-876-5432	Wife's name is Laura
Cincinnati	OH	45678	555-6988	1-513-555-3456	Likes plaid suits
Danbury	CT	12345-0001	1-203-444-5566	1-203-444-5567	Wife: Mary; Sons: Danny, Jody, Bob
New York	NY	65432-0002	1-987-654-3210	1-987-654-3211	Friend of Fred Mertz
Minneapolis	MI	11111-9999	1-345-678-9999	1-345-678-8888	Has spunk
Hanover	IN	46032	1-111-222-3333	1-111-222-4444	Wife: Kelly (K-E-L-L-Y)
New York	NY	10019	555-9876	555-8765	Husband: Archie; Daughter: Gloria
Springfield	CA	12345	555-1234	555-2345	Likes doughnuts; LOTS of doughnuts

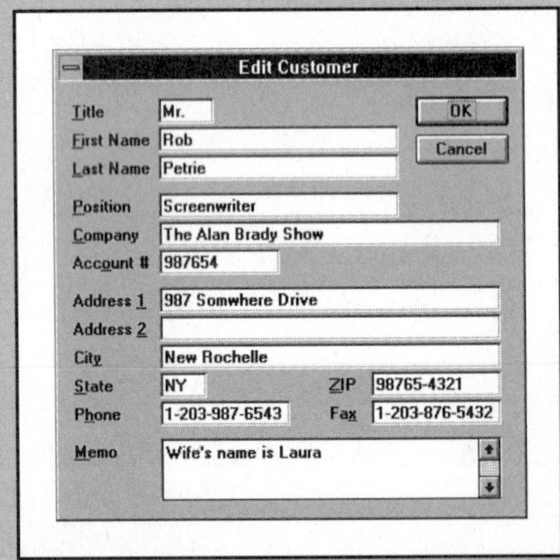

Chapter

73

Setting Up a Customer Database

In business, managing information is often as important as crunching numbers. Excel provides extensive list and database capabilities that enable you to enter, edit, sort, find, and filter the information you want. Each of these list features and some advanced topics, such as pivot tables and querying external databases, are explained thoroughly in the Databases and Lists Workshop (see Chapters 30-34).

This project provides you with a ready-to-use Excel database designed to hold customer information. With this database, you can enter your customer's name, company, position, account number, address, phone number, and fax number. Also provided is a memo field that can hold general comments. As soon as you've entered some data, you can use the application to edit, filter, and delete records; if you have a modem, you can even phone a customer from Excel.

Of course, you don't have to restrict yourself to entering only customer data. You can use this database for contacts, colleagues, friends, family, or even a mailing list. Be sure to save each type of database under a different name.

This project assumes you're familiar with Excel databases and with terminology such as *criteria* and *filter*. If you need to refresh your memory, read the relevant chapters in the Databases and Lists Workshop.

Excel 5.0 Features Used

Visual Basic for Applications
List criteria and filtering
Custom dialog boxes
Controlling a remote application

Files Used

CUSTOMER.XLS

Special Instructions

Open the CUSTOMER.XLS file from the directory in which you installed the Super Disk files. If you want to use CUSTOMER.XLS as the basis for different lists, use the **File | Save As** command to save the file under a different name before you start entering data.

About CUSTOMER.XLS

The customer database consists of the following 14 fields:

Field	*Description*
Title	The form of address you use with the customer (for example, Miss, Ms., or Mr.).
First Name	The customer's first name.
Last name	The customer's surname.
Position	The customer's job title.
Company	The name of the company the customer works for.
Acct Num	The account number of either the customer or the company the customer works for.
Address1	The first part of the customer's street address.
Address2	The second part of the address.
City	The customer's city.
State	The customer's state.
ZIP Code	The customer's zip code. This field has been formatted to accept both the normal five-digit zip codes and the newer nine-digit codes. Note that a dash is added automatically whenever you enter a nine-digit code. For example, if you enter `123456789`, the data appears as 12345-6789.
Phone Num	The customer's phone number. This field has been formatted to accept a number with or without the area code and to enter the dash automatically. For example, if you enter `1234567`, the number appears as 123-4567. If you enter `12345678901`, the number appears as 1-234-567-8901.
Fax Num	The customer's fax number. This field uses the same formatting as the Phone Num field.
Memo	Miscellaneous comments about the customer (for example, birthdays, children's names, favorite color). The field is formatted as word wrap, so you can enter as much information as you need.

When you open CUSTOMER.XLS, you'll see the screen shown in Figure 73.1. The workbook contains three sheets:

Customer Database	This is the worksheet on which you'll enter and work with your data. There are two sections: enter your data in Customer Database and your advanced filter criteria in Customer Criteria.
Module	A collection of Visual Basic macros.
Dialog	A custom dialog box you can use to add, edit, and delete customers.

FIGURE 73.1.
The Customer Database screen.

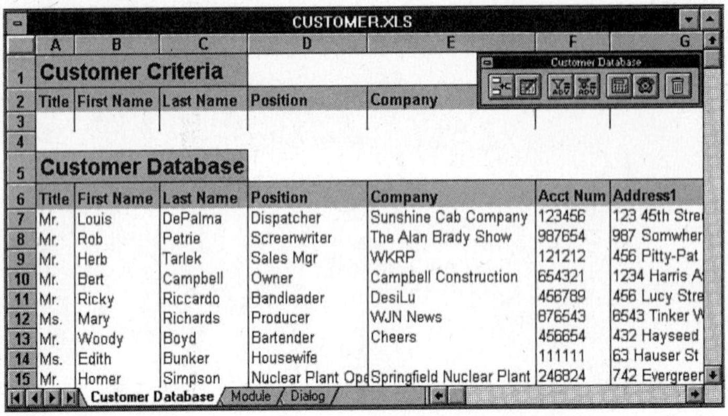

Title	First Name	Last Name	Position	Company	Acct Num	Address1
Mr.	Louis	DePalma	Dispatcher	Sunshine Cab Company	123456	123 45th Stre
Mr.	Rob	Petrie	Screenwriter	The Alan Brady Show	987654	987 Somwher
Mr.	Herb	Tarlek	Sales Mgr	WKRP	121212	456 Pitty-Pat
Mr.	Bert	Campbell	Owner	Campbell Construction	654321	1234 Harris A
Mr.	Ricky	Riccardo	Bandleader	DesiLu	456789	456 Lucy Stre
Ms.	Mary	Richards	Producer	WJN News	876543	6543 Tinker W
Mr.	Woody	Boyd	Bartender	Cheers	456654	432 Hayseed
Ms.	Edith	Bunker	Housewife		111111	63 Hauser St
Mr.	Homer	Simpson	Nuclear Plant Op	Springfield Nuclear Plant	246824	742 Evergreen

Entering Data

You can use either of the following methods to add data to the customer database:

- Enter the information directly in the worksheet cells.
- Use the Add Customers dialog box.

Entering Data Directly on the Worksheet

Follow the steps in Procedure 73.1 to add a customer record directly into the worksheet cells.

PROCEDURE 73.1. ENTERING CUSTOMER DATABASE RECORDS DIRECTLY.

1. Select the Title cell in the first empty row of the Customer Database section.
2. Enter the customer data in the appropriate fields.

> **SUPER TIP**
>
> Press the Tab key after each entry to move the active cell to the next field.

3. Repeat steps 1 and 2 to add other customers.
4. Select the entire database, including the column headings.

SUPER TIP

If the database is quite large, you can quickly select it by first choosing Database from the Name box. Doing so selects the old database range. Next, hold down the Shift key and click on the Memo cell of the last record you entered. Excel adjusts the selection to include all the records.

5. Select the **I**nsert | **N**ame | **D**efine command to display the Define Name dialog box.
6. In the Names in **W**orkbook box, type `Database`.
7. Click on OK or press Enter.

SUPER CAUTION

Many of the other features in this application use the Database range name, so it's important to keep this name up to date.

Entering Data Using the Custom Dialog Box

Although entering data directly on the worksheet is simple, it suffers from two major drawbacks:

- Not all the fields appear on-screen at once. This means you can never see the entire record you're adding and it can be a chore to navigate between fields at either end of the database.
- If you add new records at the end of the list, you have to redefine the Database range manually. (You don't have to do this if you insert rows within the existing Database range.)

To overcome these problems, CUSTOMER.XLS comes with the custom dialog box shown in Figure 73.2. Using this dialog box to enter your customers gives you the following advantages:

- There is an edit box for every field in the database, so you always see the entire record before you add it.
- Navigating the fields is easy. If you have a mouse, just click on the field you want to work with. From the keyboard, use each field's accelerator key (the underlined letter) to select the field.
- When you select **A**dd, the dialog box stays on-screen so you can add another customer.

- The Database range name is updated automatically.

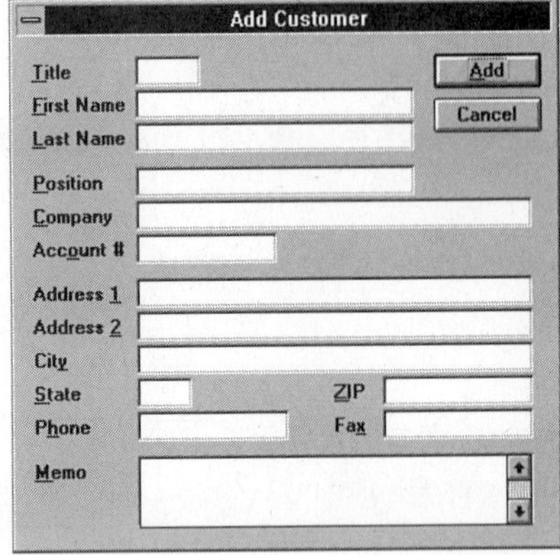

FIGURE 73.2.
The custom Add Customer dialog box.

Procedure 73.2 shows you how to add customers with the custom dialog box.

PROCEDURE 73.2. ENTERING CUSTOMER DATABASE RECORDS USING THE CUSTOM DIALOG BOX.

1. Select the **S**uperBook | Customer **D**atabase | **A**dd Customers command. The Add Customer dialog box appears.

   You also can click on this button in the Customer Database toolbar to display the Add Customer dialog box.

2. Fill in the fields for the customer.
3. Click on the **A**dd button. The customer is added to the database and a fresh Add Customer dialog box appears.
4. Repeat steps 2 and 3 to add more customers.
5. When you're done, click on Close to return to the worksheet.

Editing a Customer Record

If you need to make changes to a record, you can just edit the worksheet cells directly. However, if you prefer the convenience of a custom dialog box, follow the steps in Procedure 73.3 to edit a record.

PROCEDURE 73.3. EDITING A CUSTOMER RECORD USING A CUSTOM DIALOG BOX.

1. Select any cell within the record you want to edit.
2. Select the **S**uperBook | Customer **D**atabase | **E**dit Customer command. The Edit Customer dialog box appears, shown in Figure 73.3.

You also can click on this button in the Customer Database toolbar to display the Edit Customer dialog box.

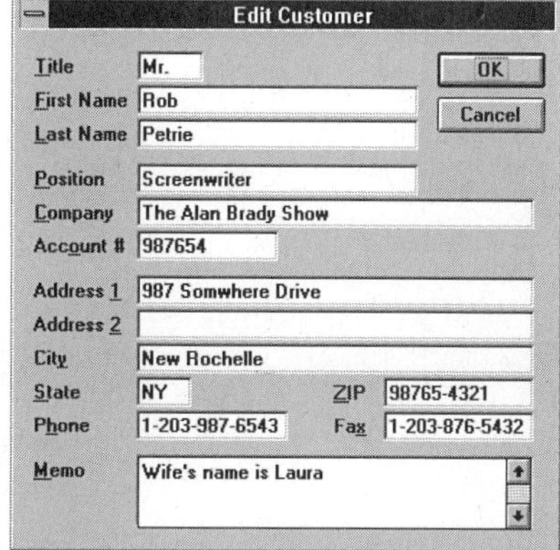

FIGURE 73.3.
The Edit Customer dialog box.

SUPER CAUTION

Be sure to select a cell within the database when you run the Edit Customer command. If you don't, the application displays a warning message. If you get this message and you've selected a record, you may have to redefine the Database range name to include the entire list. See Procedure 73.1, steps 4-7.

3. Make your changes to the record.
4. Click on OK or press Enter. The application writes the changes to the worksheet.

Filtering the Customer Database

Chapter 31, "Managing List Records," showed you how to filter a list to see only certain records. You can use the same techniques to filter the customer database. If you have simple criteria, the AutoFilter feature probably is your best bet.

For more complex filtering, use the Customer Criteria range to enter your compound or computed criteria. When you're ready to filter the list, you can do it in one step by clicking on the Advanced Filter button in the Customer Database toolbar. When you want to exit filter mode and return to the normal view, click on the Show All button.

The Advanced Filter button from the Customer Database toolbar.

The Show All button from the Customer Database toolbar.

If you don't have a mouse, you can use Excel's regular menu commands:

- Select the **D**ata | **F**ilter | **A**dvanced Filter command to run the advanced filter.
- Select the **D**ata | **F**ilter | **S**how All command to exit filter mode.

SUPER CAUTION

The Advanced Filter button uses a range named Criteria to filter the records. By default, this range consists of the Customer Criteria column headings and the first row beneath them (A2:N3). If you'll be using multiline criteria to display records that match one criterion or another, you'll need to redefine the Criteria range appropriately.

Getting a Count of the Database Records

As your database grows, you may need to know how many records it contains. You can find out by following the steps in Procedure 73.4.

PROCEDURE 73.4. GETTING A COUNT OF THE CUSTOMER DATABASE RECORDS.

1. Select the **S**uperBook | Customer **D**atabase | **C**ount Customers command. A dialog box appears with the current count, shown in Figure 73.4.

You also can click on this button in the Customer Database toolbar to get a count of the customers.

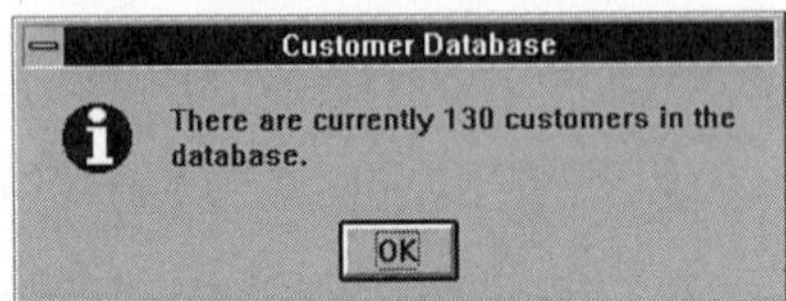

FIGURE 73.4.
You can get a quick count of the customer records.

2. Click on OK or press Enter to return to the worksheet.

Phoning a Customer Using a Modem

If you have a modem, you can use it to automatically dial a customer from the customer database. Procedure 73.5 shows you the steps to follow.

PROCEDURE 73.5. PHONING A CUSTOMER USING A MODEM.

1. Select any cell within the record of the customer you want to phone.
2. Select the **S**uperBook | Customer **D**atabase | **P**hone Customer command. The Phone Customer dialog box appears, shown in Figure 73.5.

You also can click on this button in the Customer Database toolbar to phone the current customer.

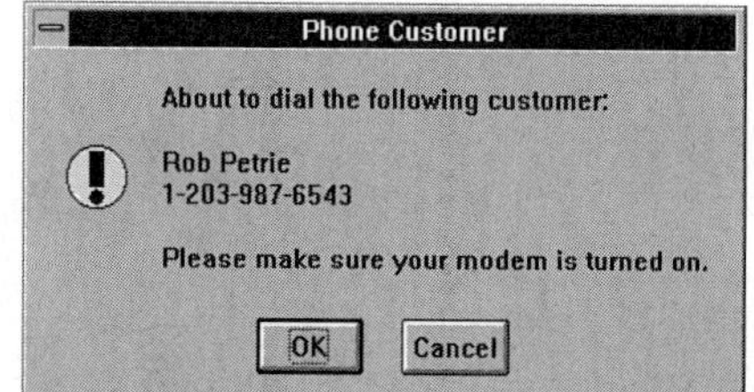

FIGURE 73.5.
The application displays the customer name and phone number before phoning the customer.

SUPER CAUTION

The customer database application displays a warning message if you select a record outside the Database range or if there is no phone number for the current customer.

3. If necessary, turn on your modem.
4. Click on OK or press Enter. The application starts the Windows Cardfile program and uses Cardfile's AutoDial feature to dial the phone. After a few seconds, you'll see the dialog box shown in Figure 73.6.

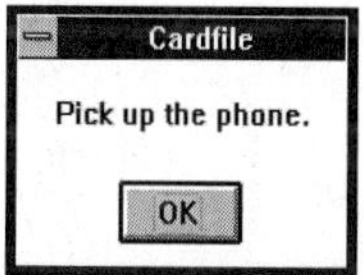

FIGURE 73.6.
You'll see this dialog box while your modem is dialing.

5. When you hear your modem dialing, pick up the receiver. Note, however, that you *don't* need to click on the OK button on the dialog box. After about seven seconds, the customer application does it for you automatically and then returns you to Excel.

Deleting a Customer Record

To save memory and make the database easier to manage, you should delete customer records you no longer need. Follow the steps in Procedure 73.6.

PROCEDURE 73.6. DELETING A CUSTOMER RECORD.

1. Select any cell within the record of the customer you want to delete.
2. Select the **S**uperBook | Customer **D**atabase | **D**elete Customer command. The Delete Customer dialog box appears, shown in Figure 73.7.

You also can click on this button in the Customer Database toolbar to delete the current customer.

FIGURE 73.7.
The Delete Customer dialog box.

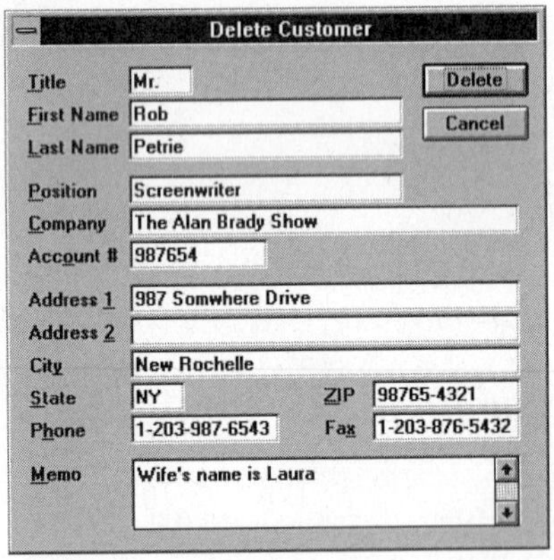

3. If you're sure you want to delete this customer, click on the Delete button. The application deletes the record and returns you to the worksheet.

Looking at the Customer Database Procedures

The Module sheet contains a number of Visual Basic procedures that supply the underlying functionality of the customer database application. The rest of this chapter takes a look at these procedures.

The Custom Dialog Box

Several of the procedures display the custom dialog box from the Dialog sheet in CUSTOMER.XLS (see Figure 73.8). This dialog box is a fairly simple affair with its two command buttons and 14 edit boxes (one for each field in the database). The dialog box shown in Figure 73.8 is used for adding customers, but as you'll soon see, it's quite simple to customize the dialog box for use with other procedures.

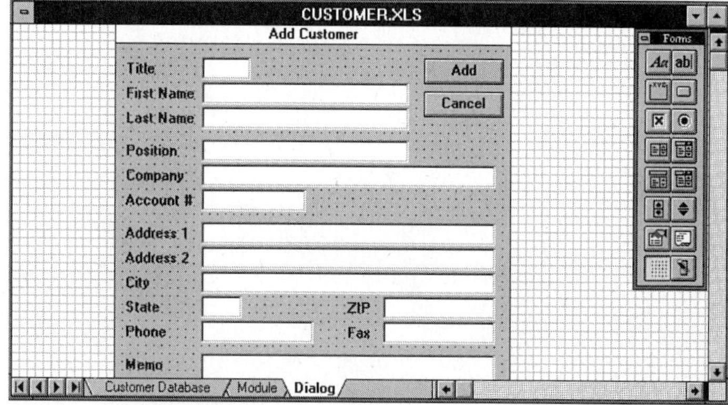

FIGURE 73.8.
The custom dialog box used in the customer database application.

SUPER NOTE

The dialog box on your screen likely will look different than the one shown in Figure 73.8. The dialog controls and data that are displayed depend on the last operation you performed in the application.

Adding Customers

The commands for adding a customer are in the `AddCustomer` procedure in the Module sheet, shown in Figure 73.9. The procedure first sets up the `dbDialog` variable to refer to `DialogSheets("Dialog")` and then uses a `With` statement to set up the dialog box.

FIGURE 73.9.
The `AddCustomer` procedure.

```
Sub AddCustomer()

    'Set up dialog box
    Set dbDialog = DialogSheets("Dialog")
    With dbDialog
        .DialogFrame.Caption = "Add Customer"    'Set dialog title
        .EditBoxes.Caption = ""                  'Clear edit boxes
        .EditBoxes.Enabled = True                'Enable edit boxes
        .Buttons(1).Caption = "Add"             'Make sure first button is Add
        .Buttons(2).Caption = "Cancel"          'Start second button as Cancel
    End With

    'Display dialog and loop until done
    Do While dbDialog.Show
        WriteNewData                             'Write the new record
        dbDialog.Buttons(2).Caption = "Close"   'Change button to Close
        dbDialog.EditBoxes.Caption = ""          'Clear edit boxes
    Loop

End Sub
```

SUPER NOTE

The dbDialog variable is declared at the top of the module with the following statement:

```
Public dbDialog As DialogSheet
```

The Public keyword tells Visual Basic to make this variable available to all procedures in the module.

- The dialog box title is changed to Add Customer.
- The edit boxes are cleared and enabled. (The DeleteCustomer procedure disables the edit boxes, so you have to enable them here just in case.)
- The caption for the first command button is set to Add.
- The caption for the second button is set to Cancel.

A Do...Loop is set up to display (dbDialog.Show) and process the dialog box. If you click on the second command button, the loop ends and the procedure is done. Otherwise, the loop statements get executed. The first statement calls a procedure named WriteNewData to create the new customer record, as shown in Figure 73.10. The next line changes the name of the second command button to Close. (Because you're adding a customer, it's too late to cancel the procedure. Therefore, it's normal programming practice to rename a Cancel button "Close" in this situation.) The last line clears the edit boxes for the next record.

FIGURE 73.10.
The WriteNewData procedure.

```
'The WriteNewData procedure records the new data from the
'Add Customer dialog box and redefines the Database range.
Sub WriteNewData()
    Dim i As Integer, dbTopRow As Integer, dbNewRow As Integer
    Dim dbRows As Integer, dbColumns As Integer

    'Get Database range data
    With Range("Database")
        dbRows = .Rows.Count
        dbColumns = .Columns.Count
        dbTopRow = .Row
        dbNewRow = dbTopRow + dbRows
    End With

    'Enter new data in fields
    For i = 1 To dbColumns
        Cells(dbNewRow, i).Value = dbDialog.EditBoxes(i).Caption
    Next i

    'Define new Database range name
    Range("Database").Select
    Selection.Resize(RowSize:=dbRows + 1, ColumnSize:=dbColumns).Select
    Names.Add Name:="Database", RefersToR1C1:=Selection

    Cells(dbNewRow, 1).Select    'Select first cell in new record
End Sub
```

Figure 73.10 shows the `WriteNewData` procedure, which is used to add the new data to the worksheet cells and redefine the Database range name. The `With` statement sets several variables that define the boundaries of the Database range. In particular, the `dbNewRow` variable points to the first row below the database.

Then a `For...Next` loop adds the new data. The `Cells` method is used to return the individual cells in the new row. In each case, the cell value is assigned the appropriate edit box caption.

SUPER TIP

In this `For...Next` loop, column *i* corresponds to edit box *i*. To get this correspondence, you need to add the edit boxes to the dialog frame in the same order they appear in the worksheet (working from left to right).

The next three statements redefine the Database name. The existing range is selected and the `Resize` method adds one row. With this new range selected, the `Names.Add` method redefines Database to refer to the selection.

The last line selects the first cell of the new record.

Editing a Customer Record

When you select the **E**dit Customer command, the application runs the `EditCustomer` procedure, shown in Figure 73.11. The first part of this procedure checks to make sure the active cell is within the Database range. The variable `currRow` holds the row number of the active cell. If this number is less than or equal to the first row of the database (as given by the `Row` property), or below the database (that is, greater than or equal to the sum of `Row` and `Rows.Count`), a `MsgBox` function displays a warning message.

The next section performs the dialog box setup. A `For...Next` loop reads the record into the edit boxes. Then a `With` statement sets the dialog title, enables the edit boxes, and sets the captions for the two command buttons.

Following is the rest of the code for the `EditCustomer` procedure:

```
If Not dbDialog.Show Then
     Exit Sub
End If

For i = 1 To lastCol
     Cells(currRow, i).Value = dbDialog.EditBoxes(i).Caption
Next i
```

FIGURE 73.11.
The `EditCustomer` *procedure.*

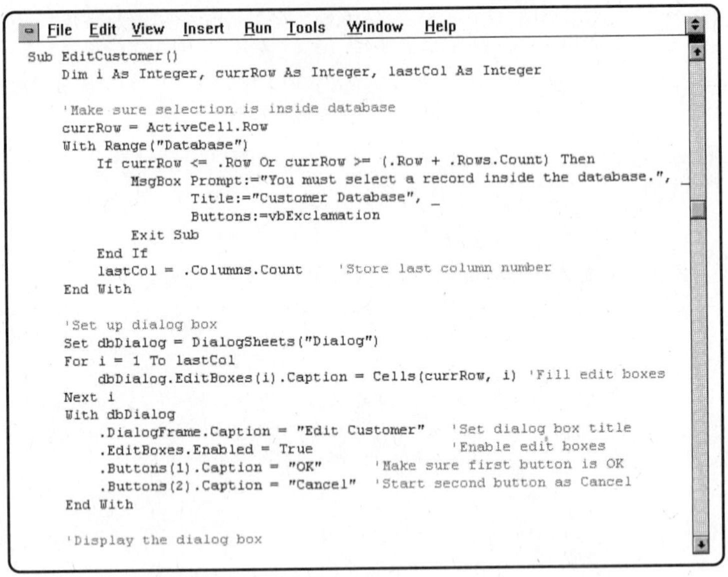

```
File  Edit  View  Insert  Run  Tools  Window  Help
Sub EditCustomer()
    Dim i As Integer, currRow As Integer, lastCol As Integer

    'Make sure selection is inside database
    currRow = ActiveCell.Row
    With Range("Database")
        If currRow <= .Row Or currRow >= (.Row + .Rows.Count) Then
            MsgBox Prompt:="You must select a record inside the database.", _
                   Title:="Customer Database", _
                   Buttons:=vbExclamation
            Exit Sub
        End If
        lastCol = .Columns.Count     'Store last column number
    End With

    'Set up dialog box
    Set dbDialog = DialogSheets("Dialog")
    For i = 1 To lastCol
        dbDialog.EditBoxes(i).Caption = Cells(currRow, i) 'Fill edit boxes
    Next i
    With dbDialog
        .DialogFrame.Caption = "Edit Customer"    'Set dialog box title
        .EditBoxes.Enabled = True                 'Enable edit boxes
        .Buttons(1).Caption = "OK"       'Make sure first button is OK
        .Buttons(2).Caption = "Cancel"   'Start second button as Cancel
    End With

    'Display the dialog box
```

This displays the dialog box and, if you click on Cancel, exits the procedure. Otherwise, the `For...Next` loop enters the new data into the record.

Filtering the List

The Advanced Filter and Show All buttons in the Customer Database toolbar are attached to the `FilterCustomers` and `ShowAllCustomers` procedures, shown in Figure 73.12.

FIGURE 73.12.
The `FilterCustomers` *and* `ShowAllCustomers` *procedures.*

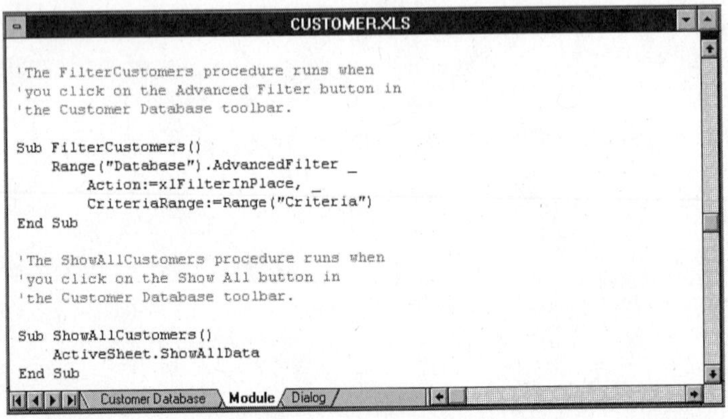

```
CUSTOMER.XLS
'The FilterCustomers procedure runs when
'you click on the Advanced Filter button in
'the Customer Database toolbar.

Sub FilterCustomers()
    Range("Database").AdvancedFilter _
        Action:=xlFilterInPlace, _
        CriteriaRange:=Range("Criteria")
End Sub

'The ShowAllCustomers procedure runs when
'you click on the Show All button in
'the Customer Database toolbar.

Sub ShowAllCustomers()
    ActiveSheet.ShowAllData
End Sub
Customer Database  Module  Dialog
```

`FilterCustomers` runs the `AdvancedFilter` method on the Database range object. The `Action` argument uses the `xlFilterInPlace` constant to filter the range in place, and the `CriteriaRange` argument uses the Criteria named range. (This is why, when you use multiple lines for your criteria, you have to redefine the Criteria name before running this procedure.)

The `ShowAllCustomers` procedure runs the `ShowAllData` method for the active sheet.

Counting the Customers

The Count Customers command and the Count Customers button are attached to the `CountCustomers` procedure, shown in Figure 73.13. The `totalRows` variable holds the count, which is given by the `Rows.Count` property, minus 1 (because you don't count the column headings). Then three variables `alertMsg`, `alertButtons`, and `alertTitle`, are assigned values. The `MsgBox` function then displays the count message.

FIGURE 73.13.
The `CountCustomers` procedure.

```
'The CountCustomers procedure runs when
'you select the Count Customers command
'or click on the Count Customers button.

Sub CountCustomers()
    Dim totalRows As Integer
    Dim alertMsg As String, alertButtons As Integer, alertTitle As String

    'Customer count is total rows in Database, minus 1
    totalRows = Range("Database").Rows.Count - 1

    alertMsg = "There are currently " & _
        totalRows & _
        " customers in the database."
    alertButtons = vbInformation
    alertTitle = "Customer Database"
    MsgBox alertMsg, alertButtons, alertTitle

End Sub
```

Customer Database | Module | Dialog

Phoning a Customer

Phoning a customer is handled by the `PhoneCustomer` procedure. The first part of the procedure sets up a few variables, including `currCell`, which holds the active cell, and `currRow`, which holds the row number of the active cell. The `PhoneCustomer` procedure also checks to make sure the active cell is within the database.

The next part of the procedure sets up and displays the dialog box that shows the customer to be phoned and reminds you to turn on your modem (see Figure 73.14). The `firstName` and `lastName` variables get the data from the First Name and Last Name fields for the current record. (The range name FirstNameField refers to the column heading of the First Name field.) Then the cell containing the phone number is selected, and the number is stored in the `phoneNumber` variable. (The PhoneNumberField name refers to the column heading of the Phone Num field.)

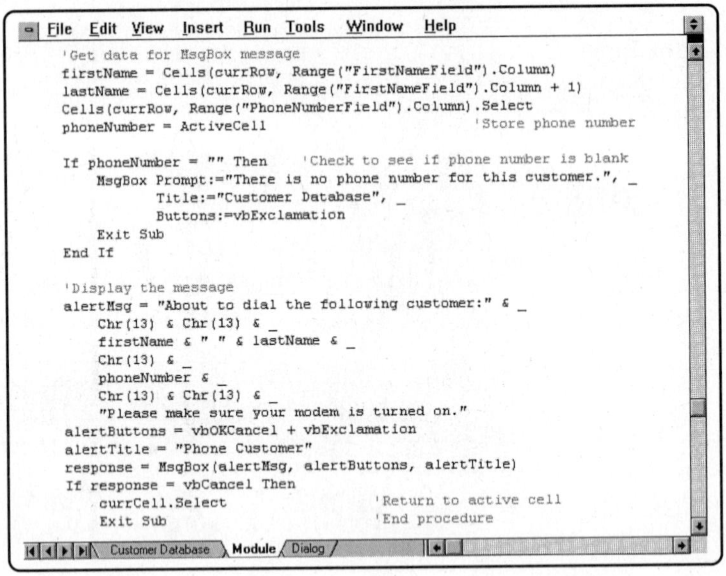

FIGURE 73.14.
A partial listing of the `PhoneCustomer` *procedure.*

```
File  Edit  View  Insert  Run  Tools  Window  Help
'Get data for MsgBox message
firstName = Cells(currRow, Range("FirstNameField").Column)
lastName = Cells(currRow, Range("FirstNameField").Column + 1)
Cells(currRow, Range("PhoneNumberField").Column).Select
phoneNumber = ActiveCell                                   'Store phone number

If phoneNumber = "" Then     'Check to see if phone number is blank
    MsgBox Prompt:="There is no phone number for this customer.", _
          Title:="Customer Database", _
          Buttons:=vbExclamation
    Exit Sub
End If

'Display the message
alertMsg = "About to dial the following customer:" & _
    Chr(13) & Chr(13) & _
    firstName & " " & lastName & _
    Chr(13) & _
    phoneNumber & _
    Chr(13) & Chr(13) & _
    "Please make sure your modem is turned on."
alertButtons = vbOKCancel + vbExclamation
alertTitle = "Phone Customer"
response = MsgBox(alertMsg, alertButtons, alertTitle)
If response = vbCancel Then
    currCell.Select                  'Return to active cell
    Exit Sub                         'End procedure
Customer Database  Module  Dialog
```

An `If` statement checks `phoneNumber`; if it's empty, a `MsgBox` function displays a warning and exits the procedure. Otherwise, a different `MsgBox` function displays the name and number to be phoned. (Note the use of `Chr(13)` functions to add new lines in the dialog box.)

The rest of the macro phones the customer. The technique takes advantage of the AutoDial feature of the Windows Cardfile applet. This feature uses a modem to dial automatically a phone number listed in a card. By sending keystrokes to the program, you can insert a new card, paste in the customer's phone number, and then start AutoDial.

Figure 73.15 shows the remainder of the `PhoneCustomer` procedure. The active cell (that is, the phone number) is copied to the Clipboard. Then a `Shell` statement starts Cardfile, and three `SendKeys` functions do the following:

- Add a new card (F7)
- Paste the phone number from the Clipboard (Ctrl+V and Enter)
- Start Cardfile's AutoDial feature (F5 and Enter)

At this point, you see the `Pick up the phone` message. The procedure delays seven seconds to give the phone time to dial; then another `SendKeys` function exits CardFile by sending three keystrokes: an Enter (to remove the dialog box), Alt+F4, and then N to answer no to CardFile's question about saving changes. Finally, the `CutCopyMode` property is set to `FALSE` to exit Copy mode, and the cell in which you started is reselected.

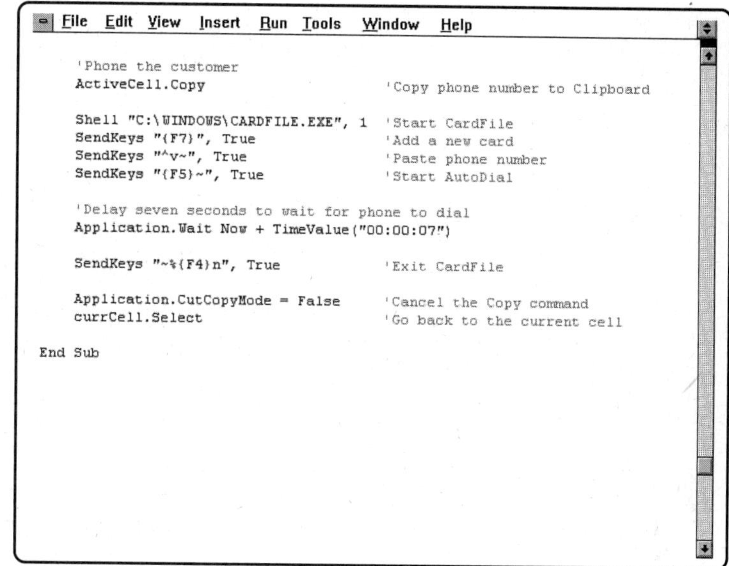

File Edit View Insert Run Tools Window Help
'Phone the customer
ActiveCell.Copy 'Copy phone number to Clipboard
Shell "C:\WINDOWS\CARDFILE.EXE", 1 'Start CardFile
SendKeys "{F7}", True 'Add a new card
SendKeys "^v~", True 'Paste phone number
SendKeys "{F5}~", True 'Start AutoDial
'Delay seven seconds to wait for phone to dial
Application.Wait Now + TimeValue("00:00:07")
SendKeys "~%{F4}n", True 'Exit CardFile
Application.CutCopyMode = False 'Cancel the Copy command
currCell.Select 'Go back to the current cell
End Sub

FIGURE 73.15.
The rest of the `PhoneCustomer` *procedure.*

Deleting a Customer

The `DeleteCustomer` procedure handles the customer deletions. This procedure is almost identical to the `EditCustomer` procedure discussed earlier. The major difference is that if you click on the Delete button, the procedure runs the following statement:

```
ActiveCell.EntireRow.Delete
```

The `EntireRow` property returns the entire row of, in this case, the selected customer. The `Delete` method deletes the row.

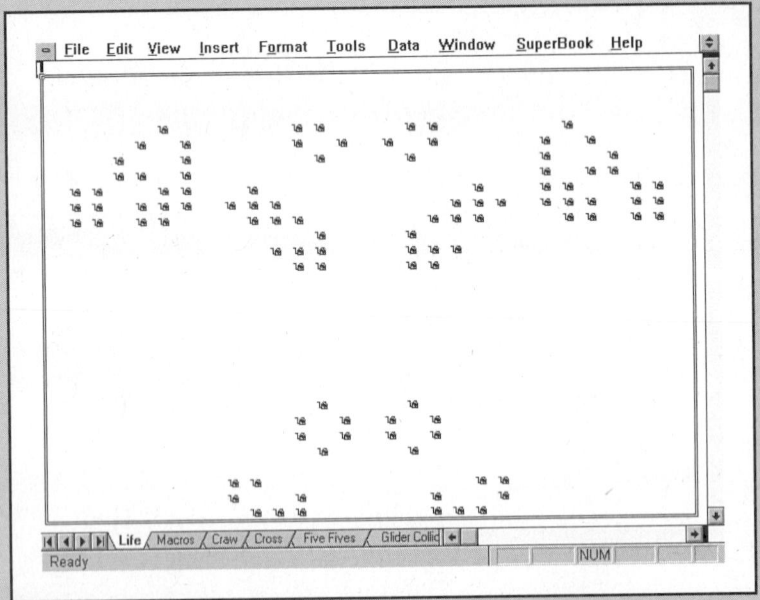
File Edit View Insert Format Tools Data Window SuperBook Help
Life Macros Craw Cross Five Fives Glider Collic
Ready
NUM

Chapter

74

The Game of Life, Excel Style

The final project is an application that is both fun and highly addictive. (Don't try this one if you have deadlines to meet!) It's an Excel version of the popular game called Life. This is a game in which living cells survive, die, or are reborn based on simple rules that take into account overcrowding and isolation. A habitat is set up where you can watch the population through successive generations. After a while, the birth and death of individual cells become secondary to the spellbinding patterns that always seem to emerge. You can use any of the 10 initial populations supplied with the game, or you can create your own populations.

Don't worry, this project isn't totally frivolous; there are also plenty of more serious things to learn. You will explore concepts such as named formulas and relative range names, and there are several macros for you to dissect.

Excel 5.0 Features Used

Excel 4.0 Macro Language
Custom dialog boxes
Custom menu commands
Named formulas
Relative range names
Circular references
Automatic macros (ON.KEY, ON.DOUBLECLICK)

Files Used

LIFE.XLS

What Is the Game of Life?

The Game of Life was invented by the Cambridge mathematician John Horton Conway in the 1960s. It involves a two-dimensional, grid-like world populated with *cells.* The fate of each cell depends entirely on how many *neighbors* it has; a neighbor is any other immediately adjacent living cell.

As you might expect, you use individual worksheet cells to represent the Life cells. A living cell will be represented by a *nonzero* worksheet cell, and a dead cell by a worksheet cell containing *zero.*

There are three simple rules that determine the destiny of each cell:

- A living cell survives into the next generation if it has either two or three neighbors.
- A living cell dies if it has four or more neighbors (overpopulation), or if it has either one or zero neighbors (isolation).
- A dead cell is reborn if it has exactly three neighbors.

In Life, you apply each of these rules to every cell in the population *simultaneously*. In other words, you don't start with one cell, determine whether it lives or dies, and then move on to the next. Instead, you take a snapshot of the population at a given moment and apply the rules to all the cells at once. This is called a *generation*. When the calculations are done, you remove the dead cells, add the reborn ones, and start again. Because each generation takes only a second or two (depending on the speed of your computer), it's easy to watch dozens of generations to see what fate befalls your population.

Playing the Game of Life

When you open the LIFE.XLS file, the worksheet and dialog box shown in Figure 74.1 appear. The bordered worksheet area is called the *Habitat*. It's the Life world where the cells live and die. You can use the Life dialog box to select an initial population, clear the Habitat, or create your own world.

FIGURE 74.1.
The Life worksheet and dialog box.

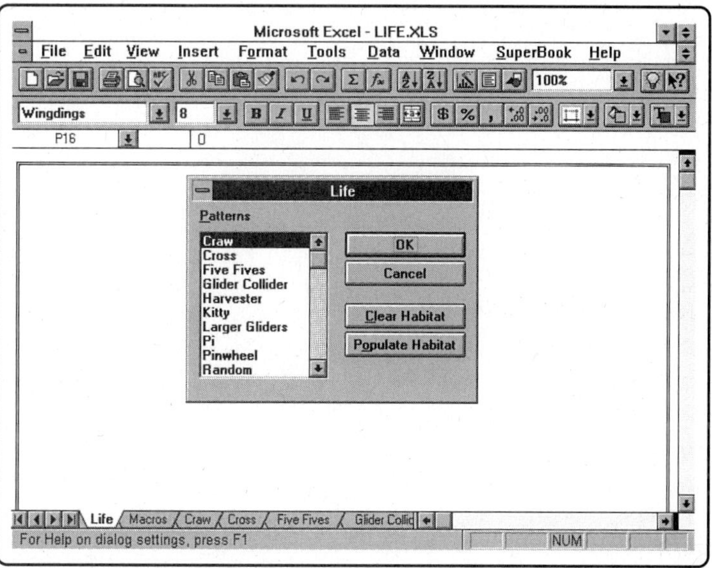

Before looking under the hood of the Life application, let's see how the game is played. The next two sections give you the basics.

Playing with the Predefined Population Patterns

Life comes with 10 predefined population patterns. These are initial populations that demonstrate how Life works. Procedure 74.1 shows you how to run Life using one of these patterns.

PROCEDURE 74.1. PLAYING LIFE WITH A PREDEFINED PATTERN.

1. Open the LIFE.XLS file. If it's already open but the Life dialog box isn't on your screen, select the **S**uperBook | **L**ife command.
2. Select an initial population pattern from the **P**atterns list. Figure 74.2 shows the initial population for the Kitty pattern.

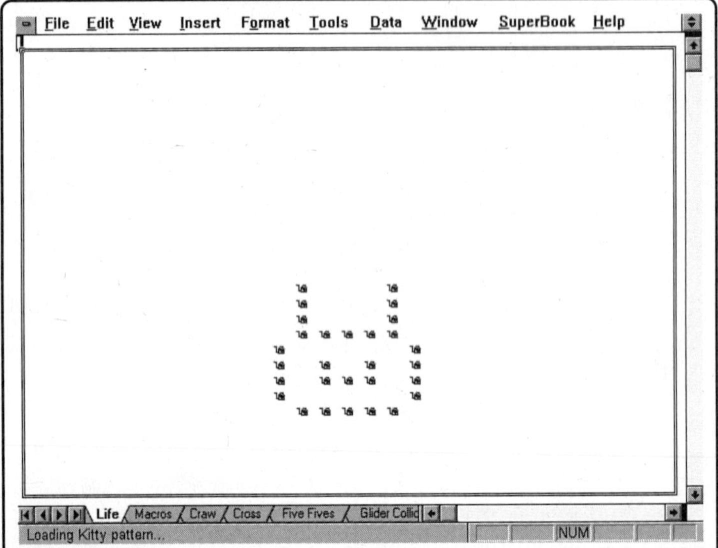

FIGURE 74.2.
The initial population for the Kitty pattern.

SUPER TIP

To start with something different every time, try the Random pattern.

3. Click on OK or press Enter. The initial population is seeded, and the generations begin. The status bar tells you how many generations have passed and what the current population is. Figure 74.3 shows the Kitty pattern after about 100 generations.
4. Press the Esc key to stop the game and return to the Life dialog box.

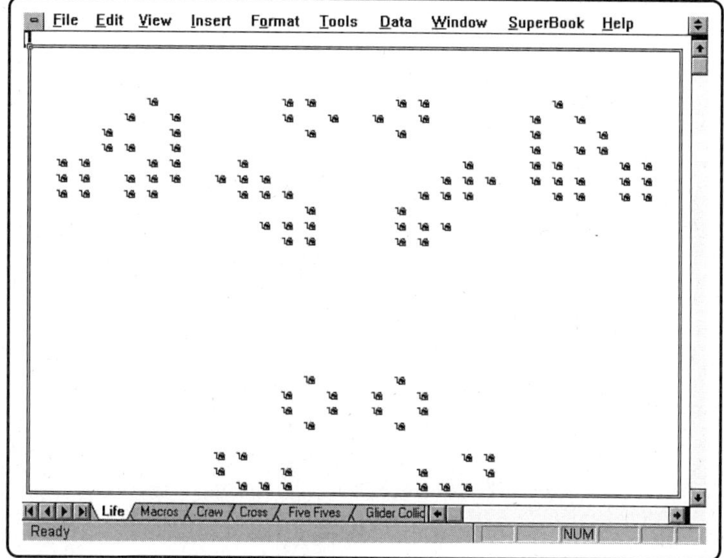

FIGURE 74.3.
The Kitty patterns after about 100 generations.

Creating Your Own Population

If you would like to enter your own population, follow the steps in Procedure 74.2.

PROCEDURE 74.2. CREATING YOUR OWN LIFE POPULATION.

1. Open the LIFE.XLS file (or select the **S**uperBook | **L**ife command to display the Life dialog box).
2. To start with a fresh habitat, click on the **C**lear Habitat button.
3. Click on the P**o**pulate Habitat button. Life removes the dialog box and activates the Habitat.
4. To create a living cell, select a worksheet cell and either press the Insert key or double-click on the cell. You can remove the cell by pressing Insert or double-clicking again.
5. After you enter all the living cells you want for your initial population, press Enter to start the game. (If you would prefer to return to the Life dialog box, press the Esc key instead.)
6. Press the Esc key to stop the game and return to the Life dialog box.

How Life Works

Breaking down the Life application into the following four areas makes it easier to understand: the Habitat, the Neighbor Table, the New Generation Table, and the Macros sheet.

The Habitat

As I mentioned earlier, the *Habitat* is the Life world where the cells live, die, and are reborn. There is nothing terribly fancy about this area: to designate a living cell, the program enters a `9` in one of the worksheet cells. Why a 9? The Habitat is formatted with the Wingdings font, and a 9 prints a small mouse, which was the most life-like symbol I could find. For dead cells, the programs enters a `0` (which display as blanks because I turned off the zeros for this worksheet).

The Neighbor Table

To find out what happens to each cell, you have to look at its neighbors. In this case, you have to examine the worksheet cells surrounding each cell in the Habitat. For example, consider cell C3. To find out whether it lives, dies, or is reborn in the next generation, you have to count the number of neighbors that exist in its eight surrounding cells: B2, C2, D2, B3, D3, B4, C4, and D4. This is the job of the *Neighbor Table.*

The Neighbor Table consists of the range B43:AD71, and each cell in this table corresponds to a cell in the Habitat. After each generation, the Neighbor Table tells you how many neighbors each cell in the Habitat has. You can then use this data to create the next generation.

Every cell in the Neighbor Table has what appears to be the same formula:

```
=Neighbors
```

`Neighbors` is the defined name for the formula that calculates how many neighbors each cell has. Figure 74.4 illustrates how this works. The selected cell is C44, which corresponds to C3 in the Habitat. As you can see in the Define Name dialog box, the Neighbors formula is as follows:

```
=SUM(Life!B2:D2,Life!B3,Life!D3,Life!B4:D4)
```

This formula adds the values of the cells surrounding C3. Because dead cells have the value 0 and live cell have the value 9, this will tell us how many living neighbors C3 has. (Technically, it gives the number of neighbors multiplied by 9; this is why the values you see in the Neighbor Table in Figure 74.4 are all multiples of 9.)

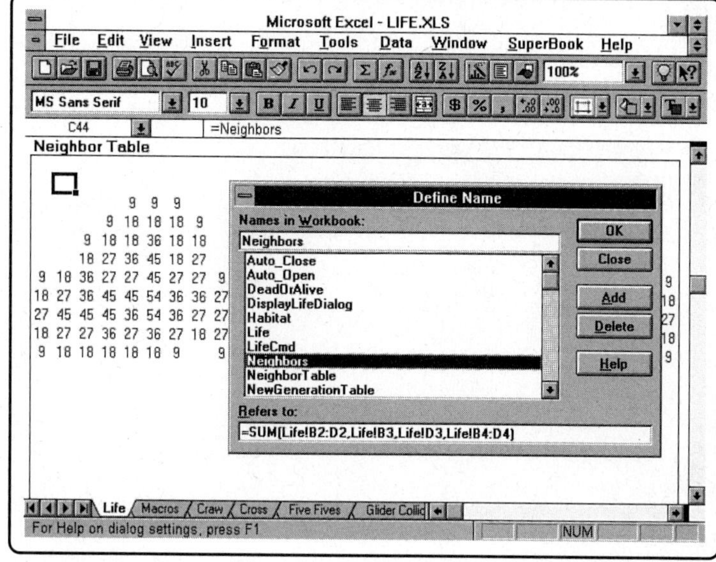

FIGURE 74.4.
The Neighbor Table and the Neighbors formula.

Note that `Neighbors` is a relative range name. The references in the formula are relative, so they change for each cell in the Neighbor Table. For example, the Neighbors formula for cell D44 (which counts the neighbors for cell D3 in the Habitat), is the following:

```
=SUM(Life!C2:E2,Life!C3,Life!E3,Life!C4:E4)
```

The other thing to note about the Neighbor Table is that the formulas overlap each other. This overlap creates circular references, so you have to control the calculations manually (as you'll see later).

The New Generation Table

Once you know how many neighbors each cell has, you need to apply the Life rules to determine the fate of the cell. This is accomplished by the *New Generation Table.* This table has the coordinates B74:AD102, and each cell corresponds to a cell in the Neighbor Table (and so, indirectly, to a cell in the Habitat).

Like the Neighbor Table, the New Generation Table also appears to have the same formula in every cell:

```
=DeadOrAlive
```

This is another named formula, but this one applies the Life rules to determine whether the corresponding Habitat cell is dead or alive in the next generation. In Figure 74.5, cell C75 is selected, which corresponds to C44 in the Neighbor Table and C3 in the Habitat.

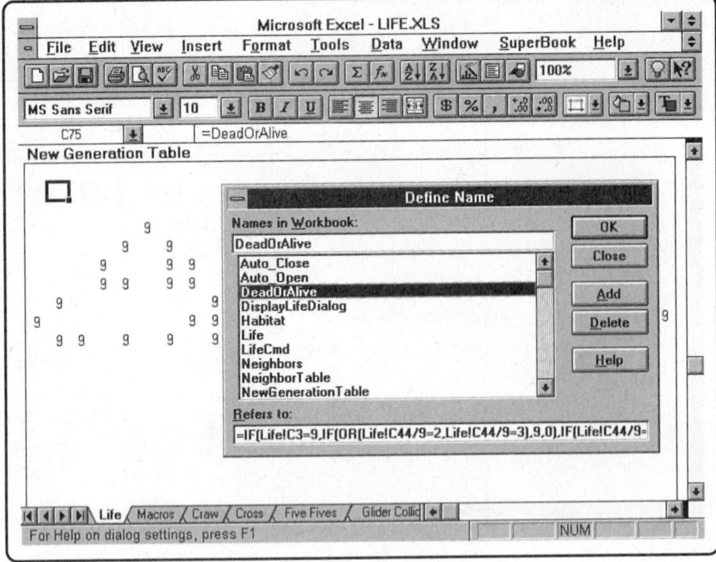

FIGURE 74.5. *The New Generation Table and the DeadOrAlive formula.*

As you can see, this formula is a real mouthful. Here's a revised version where I've taken out all the references to the Life worksheet:

```
=IF(C3=9,IF(OR(C44/9=2,C44/9=3),9,0),IF(C44/9=3,9,0))
```

The main `IF()` function tests whether or not the cell is currently alive (`C3=9`). If it is, then the following `IF()` function is executed:

```
IF(OR(C44/9=2,C44/9=3),9,0)
```

`C44` is the corresponding Neighbor Table cell that tells you how many neighbors the Habitat cell has. Recall that these are in multiples of 9, so you have to divide C44 by 9 to get the true number. This `IF()` function says that if the cell now has either two or three neighbors (that is, if it will survive into the next generation), enter a `9` in the New Generation Table cell; otherwise, enter a `0` (that is, it dies).

If the Habitat cell is currently dead, then the second part of the main `IF()` function executes instead:

```
IF(C44/9=3,9,0)
```

Again, you have to divide C44 by 9 to get the number of neighbors. If the result is 3 (that is, the dead cell has enough neighbors to be reborn), enter a `9` in the New Generation Table cell; otherwise, enter a `0` (the cell remains dead).

Note, too, that `DeadOrAlive` is a relative range name. This means the formula changes for each cell in the New Generation Table.

The final step is to create the new generation by copying the New Generation Table and pasting it on to the Habitat. Because the New Generation Table consists of 0s and 9s, these will appear as dead or alive cells, respectively, in the Habitat.

The Life Macros

The Macros sheet contains a number of macros that handle the nitty-gritty of the Life application. DisplayLifeDialog is the main macro. Its job is to display the Life dialog box and process the results. Figure 74.6 shows the dialog box definition table. This is a straightforward dialog box. It consists of four command buttons (two of which are triggers) and a list box. The list box uses the `PatternList` range for its items, where `PatternList` is the range N11:N21 (you can see part of it in Figure 74.6).

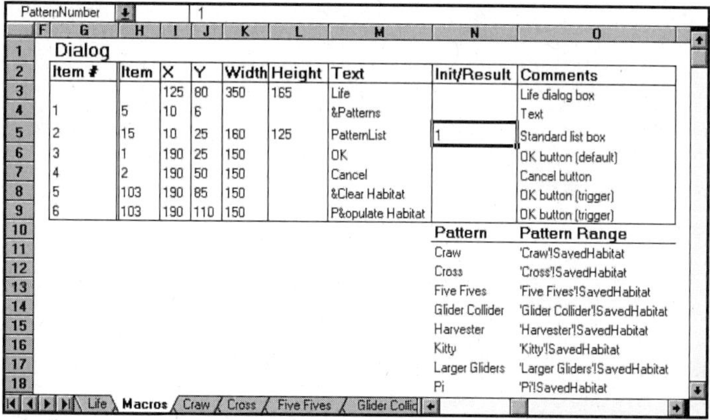

PatternNumber: 1

Dialog

Item #	Item	X	Y	Width	Height	Text	Init/Result	Comments
		125	80	350	165	Life		Life dialog box
1	5	10	6			&Patterns		Text
2	15	10	25	160	125	PatternList	1	Standard list box
3	1	190	25	150		OK		OK button (default)
4	2	190	50	150		Cancel		Cancel button
5	103	190	85	150		&Clear Habitat		OK button (trigger)
6	103	190	110	150		P&opulate Habitat		OK button (trigger)

Pattern	Pattern Range
Craw	'Craw'!SavedHabitat
Cross	'Cross'!SavedHabitat
Five Fives	'Five Fives'!SavedHabitat
Glider Collider	'Glider Collider'!SavedHabitat
Harvester	'Harvester'!SavedHabitat
Kitty	'Kitty'!SavedHabitat
Larger Gliders	'Larger Gliders'!SavedHabitat
Pi	'Pi'!SavedHabitat

FIGURE 74.6.
The definition table for the Life dialog box.

DisplayLifeDialog is a rather long macro, so I'll approach it according to the three main tasks you can execute with it:

- Run Life with a predefined population pattern.
- Clear the Habitat.
- Populate the Habitat manually.

The next four sections look at each of these features.

The Macros That Run Life with a Predefined Pattern

Figure 74.7 shows a partial listing of the DisplayLifeDialog macro. The macro begins with a `CANCEL.COPY()` function. This is needed in case the last game was interrupted during a `COPY()` operation. (See the section later in this chapter titled "The StartLife Macro.") A `FORMULA.GOTO()` function then selects a cell in the center of the Habitat, turns off screen echoing, and initializes the list box to the first item.

FIGURE 74.7.
A partial listing for the DisplayLifeDialog macro.

	A	B	C
28		**DisplayLifeDialog**	
29		=CANCEL.COPY()	Cancel copy, just in case
30		=FORMULA.GOTO(!$P$16)	Move active cell to center of Habitat
31		=ECHO(FALSE)	Turn off screen echoing
32		=SET.VALUE(PatternNumber,1)	Initialize Pattern list to first value
33		=WHILE(TRUE)	Loop
34	LifeSelection	= DIALOG.BOX(LifeDialog)	Display the Life dialog
35		= IF(LifeSelection=FALSE)	If Cancel was selected,
36		= MESSAGE(FALSE)	Reset status bar
37		= HALT()	Stop everything
38		= ELSE.IF(LifeSelection=5)	If "Clear Habitat" selected,
39		= FORMULA.FILL(0,!Habitat)	Fill Habitat with 0s
40		= ECHO(TRUE)	Turn on screen echoing
41		= CALCULATE.DOCUMENT()	Recalculate new population
42		= ECHO(FALSE)	Turn screen echoing back off
43		= ELSE.IF(LifeSelection=6)	If "Populate Habitat" selected,
44		= ON.DOUBLECLICK("[LIFE.XLS]Life",ToggleCell)	Set mouse double-click
45		= ON.KEY("{INSERT}",ToggleCell)	Set Insert key

Life | Macros | Craw | Cross | Five Fives | Glider Collid
Ready NUM

Because the dialog box includes triggers, a `WHILE(TRUE)` loop is set up. This loops indefinitely until you either click on OK, Cancel, or Populate Habitat. The dialog box is then displayed (cell B35), and the result is stored in the variable `LifeSelection`. If you click on Cancel, the macro resets the status bar (you'll be using it later) and halts all macros (cells B36 and B37).

Otherwise, a series of `ELSE.IF()` functions checks to see whether you pressed one of the other buttons. Because I'm only concerned with running Life patterns in this section, I'll skip to the OK button case, shown in Figure 74.8.

FIGURE 74.8.
The rest of the DisplayLifeDialog macro.

	A	B	C
52		= ELSE()	Otherwise, OK was selected,
53		= SetUpScreen()	Get the screen ready
54		= FORMULA.FILL(0,!Habitat)	Clear the Habitat
55		PatternName=INDEX(PatternList,PatternNumber)	Get the pattern name
56		= IF(PatternName="Random")	If "Random" was selected,
57		= RandomPopulation()	Add random cells
58		= ELSE()	Otherwise,
59		= ECHO(FALSE)	Turn off screen echoing
60		= MESSAGE(TRUE,"Loading "&PatternName&" pattern...	Display loading message
61		= COPY(TEXTREF(VLOOKUP(PatternName,PatternTable	Look up and copy the pattern
62		= FORMULA.GOTO(!Habitat)	Select Habitat
63		= PASTE()	Paste the pattern
64		= FORMULA.GOTO(!$A$1)	Move pointer out of the way
65		= ECHO(TRUE)	Display the pattern
66		= WAIT(NOW()+"00:00:01")	Hold for 1 second
67		= END.IF()	
68		= BREAK()	Exit loop
69		= END.IF()	
70		=NEXT()	
71		=StartLife()	Start Life generations
72		=RETURN()	
73			

Life | Macros | Craw | Cross | Five Fives | Glider Collid

First, the `SetUpScreen` macro is called (cell B53). This macro consists of the following three formulas (they're in cells B75:B77, if you want to take a look):

```
=FULL.SCREEN(TRUE)
=OPTIONS.VIEW(,TRUE)
=SHOW.TOOLBAR(13,FALSE)
```

These commands set up the Life screen by switching to Full Screen view, reinstating the status bar (which is normally not displayed in the Full Screen view), and hiding the Full Screen toolbar.

With the screen ready to go, the Habitat is then cleared by using the `FORMULA.FILL()` function to fill the range with 0s (cell B54). Cell B55 uses `INDEX()` to get the name of the pattern you selected. (The `PatternNumber` variable comes from the dialog box definition table. It's the name of the Init/Result cell for the list box; see cell N5 in Figure 74.6.) If you chose the `Random` pattern, the macro calls the RandomPopulation macro, shown in Figure 74.9.

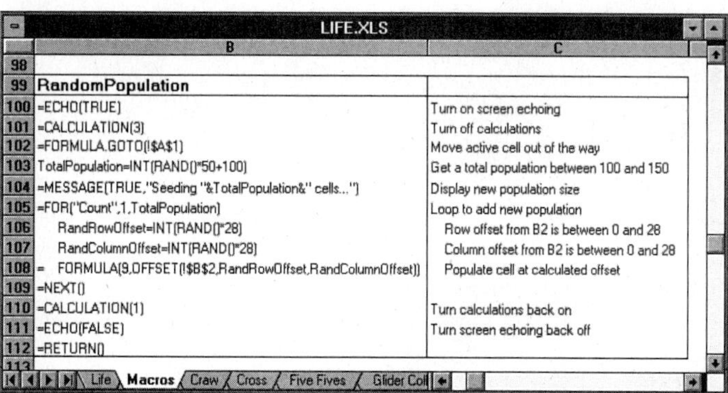

LIFE.XLS

	B	C
98		
99	**RandomPopulation**	
100	=ECHO(TRUE)	Turn on screen echoing
101	=CALCULATION(3)	Turn off calculations
102	=FORMULA.GOTO(!$A$1)	Move active cell out of the way
103	TotalPopulation=INT(RAND()*50+100)	Get a total population between 100 and 150
104	=MESSAGE(TRUE,"Seeding "&TotalPopulation&" cells...")	Display new population size
105	=FOR("Count",1,TotalPopulation)	Loop to add new population
106	RandRowOffset=INT(RAND()*28)	Row offset from B2 is between 0 and 28
107	RandColumnOffset=INT(RAND()*28)	Column offset from B2 is between 0 and 28
108	= FORMULA(9,OFFSET(!$B$2,RandRowOffset,RandColumnOffset))	Populate cell at calculated offset
109	=NEXT()	
110	=CALCULATION(1)	Turn calculations back on
111	=ECHO(FALSE)	Turn screen echoing back off
112	=RETURN()	

Life | Macros | Craw | Cross | Five Fives | Glider Col

FIGURE 74.9.
The RandomPopulation macro.

The RandomPopulation macro begins by turning screen echoing back on (so you can see the population being added), and then it sets the calculation mode to manual (this speeds up the whole process). The `FORMULA.GOTO()` function in cell B102 puts the active cell out of the way, and then you're ready to go.

The first order of business is to determine the size of the population. A number between 100 and 150 seems to work best, so the `TotalPopulation` variable is set to the following formula:

```
=INT(RAND()*50+100)
```

A `FOR()` function then loops `TotalPopulation` times and calculates an offset from cell A1 for each cell in the population. (The offsets are between 0 and 28 because the Habitat has 29 rows and 29 columns.) A `9` is entered into the offset cell to mark the cell as alive. When the loop completes, calculation is returned to automatic, screen echoing is turned back off, and the macro ends.

If you selected a pattern other than Random, the macro must load the appropriate pattern into the Habitat. It does this by copying the corresponding range from one of the pattern worksheets. The LIFE.XLS workbook comes with 10 pattern worksheets (Craw, Cross, Kitty, and so on). The `PatternTable` range (N11:O21; see Figure 74.6) lists the worksheet and range that corresponds to each pattern name. Cell B61 uses `VLOOKUP()` to find the range and then copies it. The Habitat is selected, and then the range is pasted (cells B62 and B63).

The next three commands move the active cell out of the way, turn on screen echoing, and then delay for a second so you can get a good look at the pattern before starting. When that's done, a `BREAK()` function (cell B68) exits the loop, and the StartLife macro is called.

The StartLife Macro

Figure 74.10 shows the StartLife macro. The `CANCEL.KEY()` macro tells Excel to run the `ResetLife` macro when you press the Esc key. The `ERROR()` function tells Excel to run `ResetLife` if an error occurs. `ResetLife` (see Figure 74.11) disables any automatic macros that might be running (see the discussion of the Populate button in the section titled "The Macros That Enable You to Populate the Habitat Manually"), returns the screen to its normal state, and displays the Life dialog box.

FIGURE 74.10.
The StartLife and DoNextGeneration macros.

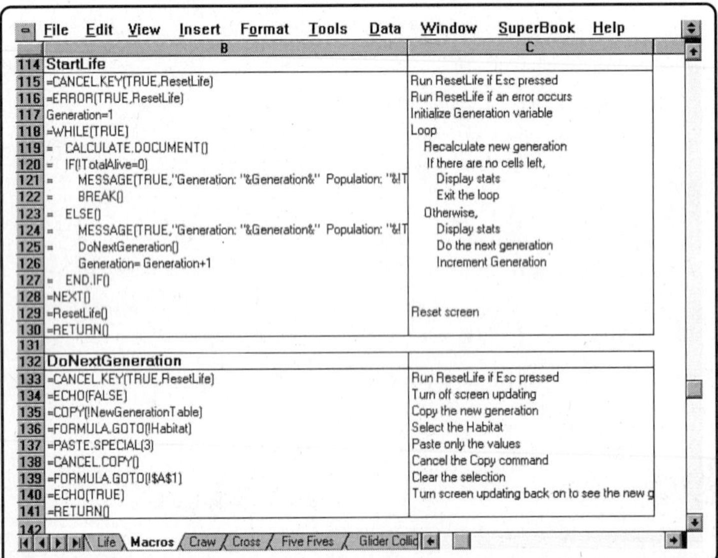

FIGURE 74.11.
The ResetLife macro.

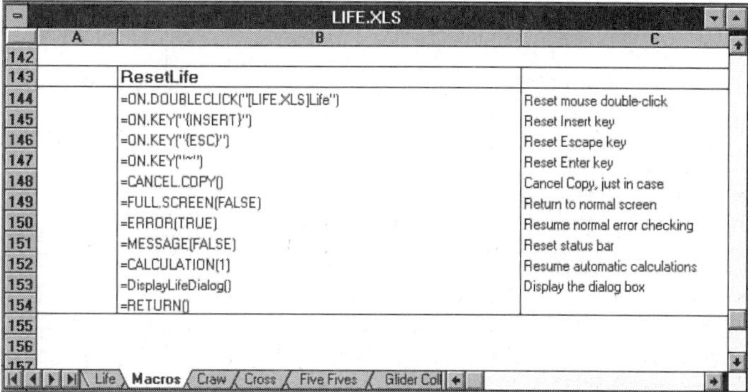

	A	B	C
142			
143		ResetLife	
144		=ON.DOUBLECLICK("[LIFE.XLS]Life")	Reset mouse double-click
145		=ON.KEY("{INSERT}")	Reset Insert key
146		=ON.KEY("{ESC}")	Reset Escape key
147		=ON.KEY("~")	Reset Enter key
148		=CANCEL.COPY()	Cancel Copy, just in case
149		=FULL.SCREEN(FALSE)	Return to normal screen
150		=ERROR(TRUE)	Resume normal error checking
151		=MESSAGE(FALSE)	Reset status bar
152		=CALCULATION(1)	Resume automatic calculations
153		=DisplayLifeDialog()	Display the dialog box
154		=RETURN()	
155			
156			

A `WHILE()` loop is set up to run the game. This loop essentially does two things:

- It calculates the Life worksheet (cell B119). This computes the results of the formulas in the Neighbor Table and the Next Generation Table.
- It checks the current population (using the named formula `TotalAlive`; this formula uses `=SUM(IF(Habitat=9,1))` to add up all the live cells in the Habitat). If the population is zero, the loop is broken and the game ends; if it's not zero, the DoNextGeneration macro is called to process the next generation.

The DoNextGeneration macro copies the New Generation Table and pastes it onto the Habitat. The `PASTE.SPECIAL(3)` function (cell B137) pastes only values because you don't want the table's formulas in the Habitat cells.

The Macro Commands That Clear the Habitat

The Life dialog box's **C**lear Habitat button is the fifth line in the dialog box definition table, so the DisplayLifeDialog macro checks for a dialog result of 5 to process this button (see cell B38 in Figure 74.7). To clear the Habitat, the macro uses a `FORMULA.FILL()` function to fill the range with 0s (cell B39). Then screen echoing is turned on so you can see the cleared area (B40), and a `CALCULATE.DOCUMENT()` function (B41) recalculates the new Habitat configuration.

The Macros That Enable You to Populate the Habitat Manually

To populate the Habitat manually, the DisplayLifeDialog macro sets up a few automatic macros for toggling live and dead cells, canceling the operation, and starting the game. Here's the macro code (cells B43:B51) that accomplishes this:

```
=ELSE.IF(LifeSelection=6)
=     ON.DOUBLECLICK("[LIFE.XLS]Life",ToggleCell)
=     ON.KEY("{INSERT}",ToggleCell)
=     ON.KEY("{ESC}",ResetLife)
```

```
=     ON.KEY("~",NewLife)
=     CALCULATION(3)
=     SetUpScreen()
=     MESSAGE(Status bar instructions)
=     HALT()
```

The first two lines after the `ELSE.IF()` set up double-clicks and the Insert key for entering the population. They both run a macro called `ToggleCell`. Then the Esc key is set up to cancel the operation if you decide not to continue. It does this by running the `ResetLife` macro shown earlier. (Now you know why ResetLife has to reset double-clicks and the Insert, Esc, and Enter keys.) The final automatic macro sets up the Enter key to start the game by running a macro named `NewLife`.

The `CALCULATION(3)` function turns off automatic recalculation to prevent Life from recalculating while you're entering the population. Then the `SetUpScreen` macro is run, a `MESSAGE()` function displays instructions in the status bar, and all macros are halted.

Figure 74.12 shows the ToggleCell and NewLife macros. ToggleCell begins by storing the contents of the active cell in the variable `CurrentLife` (cell B82). Then an `IF()` function tests `CurrentLife`: if it's a 0, the cell is currently dead, and a `9` is entered (cell B84); otherwise, it's alive, and a `0` is entered (B86).

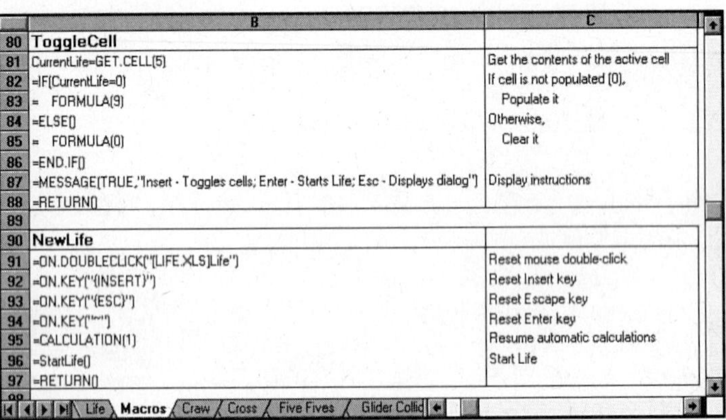

	B	C
80	**ToggleCell**	
81	CurrentLife=GET.CELL(5)	Get the contents of the active cell
82	=IF(CurrentLife=0)	If cell is not populated (0),
83	= FORMULA(9)	Populate it
84	=ELSE()	Otherwise,
85	= FORMULA(0)	Clear it
86	=END.IF()	
87	=MESSAGE(TRUE,"Insert - Toggles cells; Enter - Starts Life; Esc - Displays dialog")	Display instructions
88	=RETURN()	
89		
90	**NewLife**	
91	=ON.DOUBLECLICK("[LIFE.XLS]Life")	Reset mouse double-click
92	=ON.KEY("{INSERT}")	Reset Insert key
93	=ON.KEY("{ESC}")	Reset Escape key
94	=ON.KEY("~")	Reset Enter key
95	=CALCULATION(1)	Resume automatic calculations
96	=StartLife()	Start Life
97	=RETURN()	

Life | Macros | Craw | Cross | Five Fives | Glider Collid

FIGURE 74.12.
The ToggleCell and NewLife macros.

NewLife is straightforward: it resets double-clicks and the Insert, Esc, and Enter keys, turns automatic calculation back on, and then runs the `StartLife` macro.

Appendix

A

Notes for Lotus 1-2-3 Users Switching to Excel

Microsoft recognized early on that many people using Excel would not be first-time spreadsheet users, but instead would be users of other spreadsheet programs who decided to switch to Excel. Because Lotus 1-2-3 is the dominant spreadsheet in the DOS market, it was reasonable to assume that most people making the switch would be former 1-2-3 users.

With this in mind, Microsoft has included a fistful of features to make the transition from 1-2-3 to Excel as smooth and untroubled as possible. Here are a few of these features:

- Excel's Help system includes not only a tutorial designed specifically for former 1-2-3 users, but also a feature that enables you to enter 1-2-3 keystrokes and commands and then see how to do the same thing in Excel.
- You can set up Excel to accept 1-2-3-style formulas and navigation keys.
- Excel will read 1-2-3's .FMT files so that your careful formatting will be preserved when you load a file into Excel.
- Excel has a macro translator that enables you to run most of your 1-2-3 macros in Excel without modification.

This appendix covers just the features you need to know to get started using Excel. To learn more about working with 1-2-3 files, see Chapter 64, "Exchanging Data with Other Applications."

The Basic Differences Between Excel and 1-2-3

If you're switching to Excel from one of the DOS versions of 1-2-3, the most obvious differences you'll see are those related to the Windows environment: being able to open multiple worksheets and display each one in its own movable and sizable window; navigating a sheet using scroll bars; using pull-down menus to select commands.

Probably the biggest difference between Excel and 1-2-3 for DOS is the basic procedure you use to implement most commands. In 1-2-3, first you select a command and then you select the cell or range to use with the command. In Excel, this procedure is reversed: first you select the range and then you select the command. This procedure might seem strange at first, but it has one big advantage: when the command finishes, the range is still selected. Therefore, you can immediately apply another command to the same group of cells.

You'll find that Excel uses slightly different terminology for many commands and features. Table A.1 lists a few common Lotus terms and their Excel equivalents.

Table A.1. Excel equivalents for common 1-2-3 terminology.

1-2-3 Term	*Excel Equivalent*
@function	Function
Address	Reference
Border	Row and column headings
Cell pointer	Active cell
Control panel	Menu bar, formula bar
Cursor	Insertion point
Data range	Data series
Data table 1	One-input table
Data table 2	Two-input table
Database	List
Formula criteria	Computed criteria
Global	Workspace
Graph	Chart
Highlight	Select
Input range	List range
Label	Text
Label prefix	Alignment
Logical 0	FALSE
Logical 1	TRUE
Output range	Extract range
Print range	Print area
Prompt	Dialog box
Range highlight	Selected range
Target cell	Dependent cell

Navigating Excel

As you'll see later, you can use the Help system to learn Excel while still using 1-2-3 commands and keyboard techniques. If you need to get up to speed quickly, however, you can set up Excel to use a different set of navigation keys that more closely resemble those you're used to working with.

Before doing that, however, you should learn the keys that are the same in Lotus and Excel. Table A.2 lists them.

Table A.2. Compatible 1-2-3 and Excel keys.

Key	*Function*
Right arrow	Moves right one column
Left arrow	Moves left one column
Up arrow	Moves up one row
Down arrow	Moves down one row
Page Up	Moves up one page
Page Down	Moves down one page
F1	Displays Help
F2	Edits the current cell
F4	Toggles the reference format
F5	Go To
F6	Moves to the next pane (or window, in Excel)
F9	Calculates the worksheet

To try out the alternative keys, select the **T**ools | **O**ptions command and, in the Transition tab, activate the Transition Navigation **K**eys check box. Click on OK or press Enter to put this new option into effect. Table A.3 lists the keys that change when you activate this option.

Table A.3. Keys that change when you select the Transition Navigation Keys option.

Key	*Normal Excel Function*	*Alternative Function*
Home	Moves to the first cell in the row	Moves to cell A1
Tab	Moves right one column	Moves right one page
Shift+Tab	Moves left one column	Moves left one page
Ctrl+right arrow	Moves right to next block of data	Moves right one screen
Ctrl+left arrow	Moves left to next block of data	Moves left one screen
"	N/A	Right-aligns the cell text
^	N/A	Centers the cell text
\	N/A	Fills the cell with the characters that follow

SUPER NOTE

You can use 1-2-3's left-align prefix (') regardless of whether the Transition Navigation Keys option is selected.

Entering Formulas

An Excel formula is fundamentally the same as a 1-2-3 formula: it's a series of values or functions separated by operators that calculates a final result. Without modifying Excel, you can enter most formulas exactly as you did in 1-2-3. However, Excel will convert the formula to its native format. Here are the differences to expect:

- Excel formulas begin with an equals sign (=) instead of a plus sign (+). You can start an Excel formula with a plus sign, but Excel will add an equals sign to the beginning of the formula.
- Excel functions don't use the @ prefix. You can still use it if you like, but Excel will strip it when you confirm the formula.
- Excel range references use a colon (:) between two cell addresses instead of the double-dots (..) you used in 1-2-3. Again, you can use the dot notation, but Excel will convert it to a colon.

To make formula entry even more similar to that in 1-2-3, Excel has a Transition Formula Entry feature that changes how Excel uses range names in formulas. Excel automatically selects this option when you open a 1-2-3 spreadsheet, but you can use it with Excel worksheets by selecting the **T**ools | **O**ptions command and then activating the Transition Form**u**la Entry check box in the Transition tab. See Chapter 64, "Exchanging Data with Other Applications," for an explanation of the changes this option provides.

Another feature you can use to make Excel more like 1-2-3 is the Transition Formula Evaluation setting. You activate this option by selecting the **T**ools | **O**ptions command. Then, in the Transition tab, you activate the Transition **F**ormula Evaluation check box. This setting controls aspects of how Excel treats certain worksheet values and functions. Again, see Chapter 64 for a summary.

SUPER CAUTION

If you plan to use Transition Formula Entry and Transition Formula Evaluation in a worksheet, set these options before you enter any data and leave them on. Switching them on and off can throw off the worksheet calculations.

Using the Help System to Learn Excel

One of the biggest hurdles you face when you move to a new application is overcoming your ingrained keyboard habits. What felt natural and smooth in your old program will feel strange and uncomfortable in the new one. Of course, because humans are such adaptable creatures, you'll get used to things fairly quickly and soon will find yourself wondering how you ever could have used that clunky old application.

To ease the transition, Excel's Help system provides a feature that shows you how to perform Lotus 1-2-3 tasks in Excel. You can either see a demonstration of the task in Excel or read a text box created by the Help system that contains instructions.

Demonstrating Excel Commands

To see a demonstration of the Excel equivalent of a 1-2-3 command, follow the steps in Procedure A.1.

PROCEDURE A.1. DEMONSTRATING THE EXCEL EQUIVALENT OF A 1-2-3 TASK.

1. Select the **Help | Lotus 1-2-3** command. Excel displays the Help for Lotus 1-2-3 Users dialog box, shown in Figure A.1.

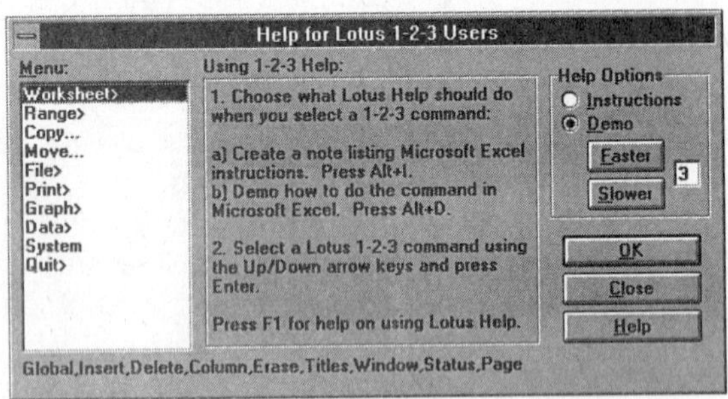

FIGURE A.1.
Use the Help for Lotus 1-2-3 Users dialog box to see a demonstration of the Excel equivalent of a 1-2-3 command.

2. Make sure the **Demo** option is selected in the Help Options group.
3. In the **Menu** list, select the 1-2-3 command you want demonstrated.
4. Click on OK or press Enter.
5. Excel might ask you for more information. Enter the required data and click on OK. Excel performs the demonstration.

SUPER TIP

You can adjust the speed of the demonstration. Display the Help for Lotus 1-2-3 Users dialog box. Before starting the demonstration, click on either the **F**aster or **S**lower button.

Displaying Instructions for Excel Commands

To create a text box containing the instructions for an Excel equivalent of a 1-2-3 command, follow the steps in Procedure A.2.

PROCEDURE A.2. PASTING INSTRUCTIONS FOR AN EXCEL EQUIVALENT OF A 1-2-3 TASK.

1. Select the **H**elp | **L**otus 1-2-3 command. Excel displays the Help for Lotus 1-2-3 Users dialog box (see Figure A.1).
2. Select the **I**nstructions option in the Help Options group.
3. In the **M**enu list, select the 1-2-3 command you want demonstrated.
4. Click on OK or press Enter. Excel creates the text box, as shown in Figure A.2.

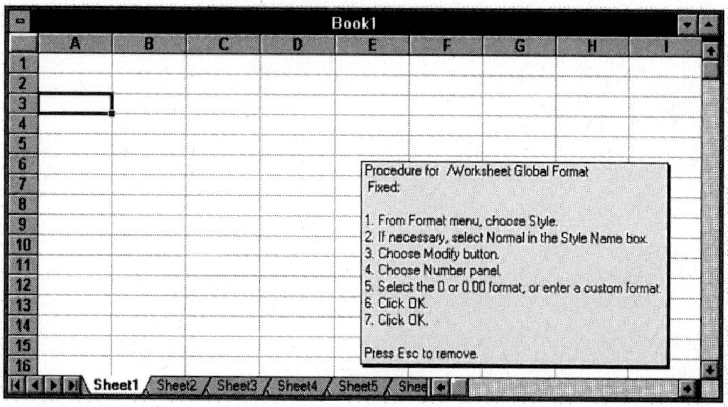

FIGURE A.2.
The Help system can create a text box containing the instructions for an Excel equivalent of a 1-2-3 command.

Appendix

B

The Windows ANSI Character Set

This appendix presents the Windows 3.1 ANSI character set. Table B.1 lists the ANSI numbers from 32 to 255. The first 32 numbers—0 to 31—are reserved for control characters such as ANSI 13, the carriage return. There are three columns for each number:

> **Text:** These are the ANSI characters that correspond to normal text fonts such as Arial (Excel's default font), Courier New, and Times New Roman.
> **Symbol:** These are the ANSI characters for the Symbol font.
> **Wingdings:** These are the ANSI characters for the Wingdings font.

To enter these characters in your worksheets, you can use any of the following four methods:

- For the ANSI numbers 32 to 127, you can either type the character directly using the keyboard or hold down the Alt key and enter the ANSI number using the keyboard's numeric keypad.
- For the ANSI numbers 128 to 255, hold down the Alt key and use the keyboard's numeric keypad to enter the ANSI number, including the leading 0 shown in the table. For example, to enter the registered trademark symbol (ANSI 174), you would press Alt+0174.
- Use the `CHAR(`***`number`***`)` worksheet function, where ***`number`*** is the ANSI number for the character you want to display.
- In a Visual Basic procedure, use the `Chr(`***`charcode`***`)` function, where ***`charcode`*** is the ANSI number for the character.

Table B.1. The Windows ANSI character set.

ANSI	*Text*	*Symbol*	*Wingdings*
32			
33	!	!	✏
34	"	∀	✂
35	#	#	✁
36	$	∃	👓
37	%	%	🔔
38	&	&	📖
39	'	∋	🕯
40	(	(	☎
41	)	)	✆

ANSI	Text	Symbol	Wingdings
42	*	*	
43	+	+	
44	,	,	
45	-	−	
46	.	.	
47	/	/	
48	0	0	
49	1	1	
50	2	2	
51	3	3	
52	4	4	
53	5	5	
54	6	6	
55	7	7	
56	8	8	
57	9	9	
58	:	:	
59	;	;	
60	<	<	
61	=	=	
62	>	>	
63	?	?	
64	@	≅	
65	A	Α	
66	B	Β	
67	C	Χ	
68	D	Δ	
69	E	Ε	
70	F	Φ	
71	G	Γ	
72	H	Η	
73	I	Ι	

continues

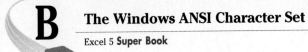

Table B.1. continued

ANSI	*Text*	*Symbol*	*Wingdings*
74	J	ϑ	☺
75	K	Κ	😐
76	L	Λ	☹
77	M	Μ	💣
78	N	Ν	☠
79	O	Ο	🏳
80	P	Π	🏱
81	Q	Θ	✈
82	R	Ρ	☼
83	S	Σ	💧
84	T	Τ	❄
85	U	Υ	🕆
86	V	ς	✞
87	W	Ω	🕈
88	X	Ξ	✠
89	Y	Ψ	✡
90	Z	Ζ	☪
91	[	[	☯
92	\	∴	ॐ
93	]	]	☸
94	^	⊥	♈
95	_	_	♉
96	`	‾	♊
97	a	α	♋
98	b	β	♌
99	c	χ	♍
100	d	δ	♎
101	e	ε	♏
102	f	φ	♐
103	g	γ	♑
104	h	η	♒
105	i	ι	♓

ANSI	*Text*	*Symbol*	*Wingdings*
106	j	φ	er
107	k	κ	&
108	l	λ	●
109	m	μ	❍
110	n	ν	■
111	o	ο	□
112	p	π	◻
113	q	θ	❑
114	r	ρ	❒
115	s	σ	⬧
116	t	τ	⧫
117	u	υ	◆
118	v	ϖ	❖
119	w	ω	⬥
120	x	ξ	⌧
121	y	ψ	⍓
122	z	ζ	⌘
123	{	{	❀
124	|	|	✿
125	}	}	❝
126	~	~	❞
127			▯
0128			⓪
0129			①
0130	‚		②
0131	ƒ		③
0132	„		④
0133	…		⑤
0134	†		⑥
0135	‡		⑦
0136	ˆ		⑧
0137	‰		⑨

continues

Table B.1. continued

ANSI	*Text*	*Symbol*	*Wingdings*
0138	Š		⑩
0139	‹		⓿
0140	Œ		❶
0141			❷
0142			❸
0143			❹
0144			❺
0145	‘		❻
0146	’		❼
0147	“		❽
0148	”		❾
0149	•		❿
0150	–		🙢
0151	—		🙠
0152	˜		🙡
0153	™		🙣
0154	š		🙞
0155	›		🙜
0156	œ		🙝
0157			🙟
0158			·
0159	Ÿ		•
0160			
0161	¡	ϒ	○
0162	¢	′	⭕
0163	£	≤	🔴
0164	¤	⁄	◉
0165	¥	∞	◎
0166	¦	ƒ	❍
0167	§	♣	▪
0168	¨	♦	□
0169	©	♥	⅄
0170	ª	♠	✦

ANSI	Text	Symbol	Wingdings
0171	«	↔	★
0172	¬	←	✶
0173	-	↑	✷
0174	®	→	✹
0175	¯	↓	✵
0176	°	°	⌖
0177	±	±	⯐
0178	²	″	✧
0179	³	≥	⌑
0180	´	×	⯑
0181	µ	∝	✪
0182	¶	∂	✰
0183	·	•	🕐
0184	¸	÷	🕑
0185	¹	≠	🕒
0186	º	≡	🕓
0187	»	≈	🕔
0188	¼	…	🕕
0189	½	⏐	🕖
0190	¾	⎯	🕗
0191	¿	↵	🕘
0192	À	ℵ	🕙
0193	Á	ℑ	🕚
0194	Â	ℜ	🕛
0195	Ã	℘	⮰
0196	Ä	⊗	⮲
0197	Å	⊕	⮱
0198	Æ	∅	⮳
0199	Ç	∩	⮸
0200	È	∪	⮺
0201	É	⊃	⮹

continues

Table B.1. continued

ANSI	*Text*	*Symbol*	*Wingdings*
0202	Ê	⊇	🙟
0203	Ë	⊄	🙪
0204	Ì	⊂	🙫
0205	Í	⊆	🙠
0206	Î	∈	🙡
0207	Ï	∉	🙢
0208	Ð	∠	🙣
0209	Ñ	∇	🙤
0210	Ò	®	🙥
0211	Ó	©	🙦
0212	Ô	™	🙧
0213	Õ	∏	⌫
0214	Ö	√	⌦
0215	×	⋅	⮘
0216	Ø	¬	⮚
0217	Ù	∧	⮙
0218	Ú	∨	⮛
0219	Û	⇔	⮈
0220	Ü	⇐	⮊
0221	Ý	⇑	⮉
0222	Þ	⇒	⮋
0223	ß	⇓	🡨
0224	à	◊	🡪
0225	á	〈	🡩
0226	â	®	🡫
0227	ã	©	🡬
0228	ä	™	🡭
0229	å	∑	🡯
0230	æ	⎛	🡮
0231	ç	⎜	🡸
0232	è	⎝	🡺
0233	é	⎡	🡹

ANSI	Text	Symbol	Wingdings
0234	ê	⎢	⬇
0235	ë	⎣	⬉
0236	ì	⎧	⬈
0237	í	⎨	⬋
0238	î	⎩	⬊
0239	ï	⎪	⇦
0240	ð		⇨
0241	ñ	〉	⇧
0242	ò	∫	⇩
0243	ó	⌠	⬄
0244	ô	⎮	⇳
0245	õ	⌡	⬁
0246	ö	⎞	⬀
0247	÷	⎟	⬃
0248	ø	⎠	⬂
0249	ù	⎤	▭
0250	ú	⎥	▫
0251	û	⎦	✗
0252	ü	⎫	✓
0253	ý	⎬	☒
0254	þ	⎭	☑
0255	ÿ		⊞

Appendix

C

The Software on the Super Disk

Whenever you see the disk icon (shown to the left of this paragraph), a file on the Super Disk is being discussed. If you haven't already installed the Super Disk, see the installation page for instructions (it's the last page in this book).

The Baarns Utilities

Baarns Consulting Group, Inc.
12807 Borden Ave.
Sylmar, CA 91342
Phone: 1-800-377-XCEL (9235)
Fax: 818-367-9673

The Baarns Utilities are a collection of tools designed to increase your Excel productivity. These utilities not only make your everyday tasks easier, but they also give you power user status, enabling you to accomplish sophisticated tasks with ease.

- AutoSave enables you to determine how and how often your open documents are saved.
- Express Math enables you to change a group of numbers by a constant amount.
- Reminders enables you to set reminders that pop up at specific times.
- Print Special enables you to print specific parts of your document that aren't defined as a print area by Excel.
- Template Wizard enables you to easily create reusable documents.
- Zoom enables you to magnify your documents in three easy ways.

These are just a sample. Install the Super Disk and see for yourself how versatile and powerful a utility can be.

The Baarns Utilities documentation is included in Appendix D. Please refer to it for more information and complete installation instructions.

Projects

Following is a list of project templates contained on the Super Disk:

Chapter	*Template*
67	SUPRBOOK.XLS
68	SUPRBOOK.XLS
69	FINANCES.XLS

Chapter	*Template*
70	FORECAST.XLS
71	TRIPPLAN.XLS
72	CHECKBK.XLS
73	CUSTOMER.XLS
74	LIFE.XLS

These project templates will be installed to a directory named \XL5SB (unless you changed this name during installation). See the appropriate chapter for information on using the templates.

Appendix D

The Baarns Utilities Documentation

Productivity Enhancements for Microsoft Excel 5

Documentation written by

Don Baarns

Baarns Consulting Group, Inc.

Overview of the Baarns Utilities

The Baarns Utilities is a collection of utilities designed to increase your productivity when you are using Microsoft Excel. Our design goals included making your everyday Excel activities easier while creating tools that could give you power user status without the power user learning curve. In some cases, the Utilities aren't available to power users unless they are willing to write in the C or C++ computer programming languages.

Who Should Use the Utilities

These Utilities will appeal to both the novice and the power user. The novice will be able to create custom time saving documents (templates) and handle about a dozen operations that formerly took additional knowledge and/or time spent working through the manuals.

The power user will find that the Utilities possess a simple interface and power tools that both enhance their work, and at the same time demonstrate the depth they expect from a set of tools they use to craft spreadsheets for themselves and others.

How This Manual Is Organized

This manual is arranged alphabetically by feature, except for the Installation section (which is first because the rest of the sections aren't valuable until the utilities have been installed).

Installation

How to install the Baarns Utilities, and hardware and software requirements.

Baarns AutoSave

Automatically saves your documents at specified intervals and/or after you perform a specific number of cell entries. Additionally, it can create and keep up to nine incremental backup copies of your files.

Baarns Clock

Displays a clock in its own window while Excel is running. The clock displays 12-hour or 24-hour (military) times—with or without the date—and can be moved anywhere on your desktop.

Baarns Express Math

Enables you to quickly change a table of numbers by a specific amount. Add, subtract, divide, multiply, or compute a percentage of a table or group of numbers. For example, increase all the prices in a two-page price list by 8.7 percent in one simple operation.

Baarns New

Enables you to open new documents, create or modify templates, and give them enhanced 31-character names.

Baarns Print Cleanser

Removes Print Areas, Print Titles, and/or Page Breaks quickly and easily.

Baarns Print Special

Enables you to print areas other than your currently defined Print Area. This includes all pages, selected pages, or just the current selection. After printing, the specified range your previous Print Area is restored.

Baarns Reminders

Set multiple reminders to pop up at specific times. Reminders can be set to display at specific times (for example, 5:30 P.M. on 1/5/93) or a specific number of minutes/hours from now.

Baarns Save As Icon

Saves the current document and creates an icon in Program Manager that automatically starts Excel and loads the current document. Your new icon can be placed in any current program group or you can create a new one without ever leaving Excel.

Baarns Set Standard Font

Resets the standard font on the current document and, optionally, for all future documents.

Baarns Sticky Notes

Creates post-it type notes on your spreadsheets. Useful for creating annotations for bosses, coworkers, or just to remind yourself of the reasons behind a group of numbers.

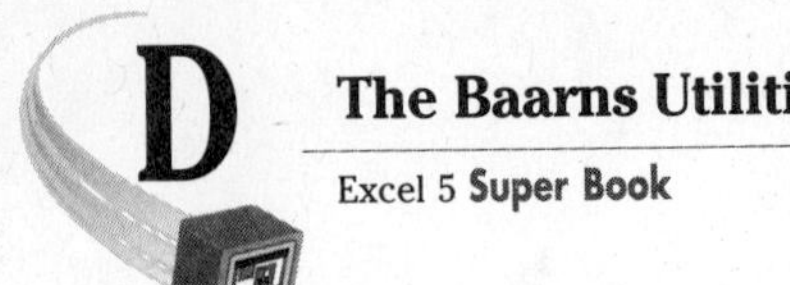

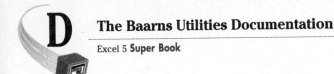

Baarns Template Wizard

Creates templates quickly and easily from both existing and new documents. Enables you to assign longer descriptions (up to 31 characters) to ease the opening of the templates in the future. Makes it easy to replace Excel's standard templates with copies of your own custom versions.

Baarns Timer

Runs a simple timer in the background and finds intervals between events with ease.

Baarns Utilities Options

Enables you to control the Baarns Utilities menu and toolbar displays and control the loading of specific Utilities on startup.

Baarns Zoom

Magnifies or reduces your document quickly and easily. Drag a scroll bar or use one of the built-in presets. Preview your new Zoom level before closing the dialog box.

Getting Started with the Baarns Utilities

The Setup program installs all the Baarns Utilities and configures Excel to recognize them the next time it starts. Additionally, the Setup program enables you to install portions of the Utilities selectively and later install or remove selected portions of the Utilities.

SUPER

NETWORK USERS NOTE

This version of the Baarns Utilities is a single-user product. It will not function correctly with multiple users. A LAN compatible version is available. Please contact the Baarns Consulting Group, Inc. for details concerning the multiuser packs.

Required Software

This special version Baarns Utilities requires the following software:

- Microsoft Windows 3.1
- Microsoft Excel 5

Required Hardware

The Baarns Utilities requires the following hardware:

- All the normal hardware required by Windows and Excel
- Suggested memory: 2.5 megabytes (minimum) or more
- At least one megabyte of free hard disk space

Installation

The files on the distribution disk are compressed and need to be decompressed before they are usable. The Setup program is Windows-based and handles all the details of moving the files to your hard drive. (The Setup program enables you to completely remove all traces of the Utilities *but we would never recommend that!*) Each of the options is explained in the section titled "Installation Options." In order to start the setup process, you'll need to use one of the following methods.

From File Manager

With Windows already running, place the Baarns Utilities disk in your computer's disk drive. Use the Windows File Manager program and change to the A: or B: drive (whichever contains the Utilities disk). Double-click on the file named SETUP.EXE. This starts the Setup program and you'll receive the Baarns Utilities Welcome dialog box. From there, you can follow the prompts.

From Program Manager or File Manager's Run Command

From either Program Manager or File Manager you can choose the File Run... command.

TIP

If you use File Manager, there isn't a Browse button. You'll have to type *A:\SETUP*.

From this command, you can type the line shown in the Command Line edit box or use the browse button on the right to move to the correct floppy drive and select SETUP.EXE.

This starts the Setup program. After about 30 seconds (more or less depending on the speed of your machine), you'll see a welcome message and be given the option to Continue or Exit. Choosing the Continue button will start the installation of the Baarns Utilities.

Installation Options

After the Welcome message, Setup enables you to select the type of installation you would prefer. The two choices follow.

Express Installation

This is the recommended installation option. All the Baarns Utilities files are copied into a new subdirectory (which Setup creates) under the Excel Library directory. The Express Installation also sets up Excel so the Add In Manager is aware of the utilities and they will automatically be loaded when Excel starts.

Custom Installation

If you choose Custom Installation, you'll be presented with the Custom Installation dialog box.

The first three check boxes on the left side of the dialog box enable you to select the options you would like to install. As you select options, the installer recomputes the effect of your choices on your computer's disk drives. Any option you uncheck is removed from your hard disk.

> **SUPER CAUTION**
>
> If you reinstall the Baarns Utilities, be sure to leave the boxes checked for items that are already installed. Removing a check box instructs the Setup program to remove the associated item. Setup won't recopy files that already exist on your machine.

If the Start Utilities When MS Excel Starts box is checked, the installer will write the proper information to your EXCEL5.INI file. Therefore, the Excel Add In manager will be aware of the Baarns Utilities and start them when Excel starts.

Changing the Install Location

If you want to change the directory that the Baarns Utilities installed, choose the Set Location... button and enter a different path. You may set the path to any drive that has enough space and is writeable (in other words, you can't install to a write-protected disk).

> **SUPER NOTE**
>
> If your Install to: directory (at the top of the dialog box) is on the same drive as your Windows directory, you'll only see one set of drive space numbers on the left side. You won't see a Windows Drive set of statistics because the Installation Drive and Windows drive are one and the same.

UnInstall Utilities

To uninstall the Baarns Utilities, uncheck all three boxes shown in Figure D.1. You'll be asked to confirm your uninstall choice, and then the Setup program will remove the Baarns Utilities from your hard disk.

Manually Starting (or Stopping) the Utilities

If you don't want the Setup program to configure Excel to start the Utilities each time Excel starts, you'll need to use one of the following methods for starting the Utilities.

Using the Add In Manager to Load the Utilities

Use the Excel Add In Manager (found with the Options Add Ins... command) and choose the ADD button. You'll need to move to the \EXCEL\LIBRARY\BAARNS directory and add the BAARNSM.XLA file. This automatically loads all the Utilities each time you start Excel. The Setup program does this for you automatically, so leave the box checked that is labeled Start Utilities When MS Excel Starts. You also can run Setup again if you didn't do it the first time, and it can take care of all the details for you.

> **SUPER NOTE**
>
> In some configurations, the Add In manager asks you for a password. Press Esc or choose the Cancel button when the password dialog box appears. If you accidentally choose the OK button, the Add In Manager displays a dialog box that states Incorrect Password and then follows with Macro Error at Cell XXX. Choose the Continue button, and the install will continue successfully.

Loading the Baarns Utilities with File Open

If you just want to use the Utilities during a specific Excel session, and you don't have them automatically loading, you may use the File Open command to load the Utilities. Choose File Open and change directories to the location that the Utilities are stored.

To close the Utilities during a specific session, you can use the Options Baarns Utilities Options... command to temporarily close them. See the "Menus, Toolbar, and Closing the Utilities" section for details.

Baarns AutoSave

Automatically Saving Your Documents

The Baarns AutoSave automatically saves your current documents to minimize the chances of losing your work. AutoSave is found on the File menu or can be started or viewed from the Baarns toolbar.

AutoSave Methods

The Baarns AutoSave enables you to decide how often you want your documents to be saved. You can specify this interval in minutes, number of cells entered, or a combination of both. No matter which method you choose, you will not be bothered by saving any document that hasn't been changed since the last save. Select one of the radio buttons to specify your choice. The AutoSave dialog box is shown in Figure D.1.

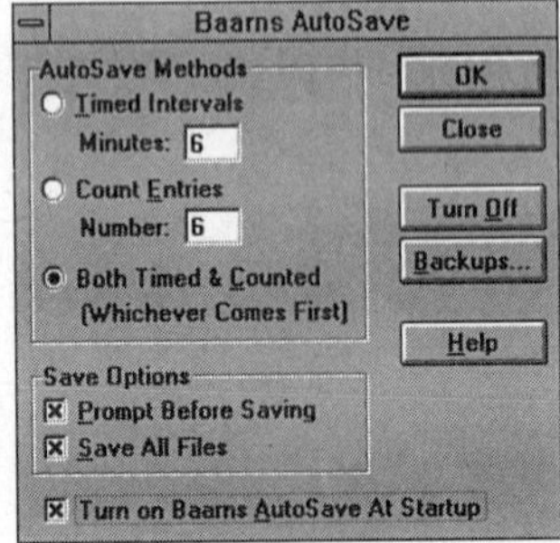

FIGURE D.1. *The AutoSave dialog box.*

Timed Intervals

This enables you to set the number of minutes between saves. The Minutes edit box accepts numbers between 1 and 99. (Recommended settings are between 5 and 15 minutes.) When the specified number of minutes has elapsed, and if no changes have been made, AutoSave resets for the next time interval without bothering you.

Count Entries

AutoSave keeps track of every time you directly edit a formula. This includes entering formulas, text, and numbers into cells. All entries on any open Excel document are counted. When the number of entries reaches the value in the Number box, your document will be saved.

SUPER TIP

Whenever the formula bar becomes active and you press enter, Baarns AutoSave counts that as one entry.

Note that formatting your document, copying, pasting, and some other operations are *not* counted with this setting. Valid entries are between 1 and 300, but we recommend using numbers in the under-twenty range.

Both Timed and Counted

This combines both the Timed Intervals and Count Entries settings, and will save the file when the first of the two settings is reached. This is a favorite setting. It provides maximum protection both when you are entering data and formulas, and when you are formatting your documents. Recommended settings with this choice are 10 minutes or 10 entries, whichever comes first. You'll have to experiment to find the best settings to suit your tastes (and nerves).

Options

The Options are used when the files are actually saved. The options include being asked about every document before it's saved, whether to check only the currently active document, and whether to check all open documents.

Prompt Before Saving

Whenever it's time to save a document (based on the AutoSave Method you choose), you have the option of having the AutoSave ask you before it saves each document. The Prompt dialog box is shown in Figure D.3. For additional information about each of the buttons shown in Figure D.2, see the "Baarns AutoSave Control Buttons" section.

FIGURE D.2.
The AutoSave prompt.

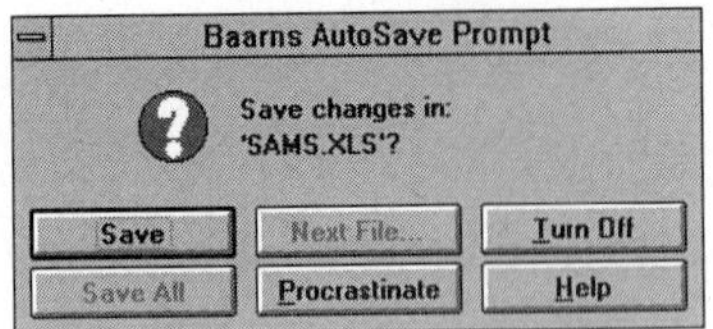

Save All Files

This option specifies that you want to save all the files that have had changes. If you don't select this option, only the active document (the one you are currently working on) will be saved.

Turn on Baarns AutoSave at Startup

A check in this box automatically starts the AutoSave each time the Utilities load. All the settings have been saved from your previous session and are restored.

Baarns AutoSave Control Buttons

After making changes to the settings in the dialog box you will need to inform the AutoSave Deluxe of your intentions. The buttons on the right side of the box determine if your new settings are activated.

OK

Accepts the current settings and sets up the AutoSave to start saving your files.

Close

Closes the dialog and continues with the previous settings. Close also ignores any changes you have made while the dialog box was displayed. If AutoSave was previously running, it continues running with the previous settings. If it was turned off, it is still off.

Turn Off

Stops the AutoSave Deluxe in the current session. All other settings are saved. If you have checked the Turn on Baarns AutoSave At Startup option, the next time you start Excel, it will be running again.

Backups...

Takes you to the Backup Version Control dialog box. This enables you to specify how many (if any) previous copies of your document you would like to save. See the "Backup Version Control" section for additional information.

Baarns AutoSave Prompt

When it's time to save your files and you have the option turned on to Prompt Before Saving, you'll see the dialog box that was shown in Figure D.2.

This enables you to decide what to do with each file that has changed since the last time it was saved. If you've set the option to Save All Files, each file is activated (shown behind the dialog box), and you are asked what you want to do. Following is a list of your available choices and what action is taken for each of the buttons you may select.

Save

Saves the current document. The name of the document is shown in the box, and as a rule the file is displayed behind the dialog box. The exception to the rule (there is one in every crowd) is a hidden file. If you've hidden a file after making changes, the AutoSave Deluxe just displays another file in the background. However, the correct name appears in the prompt dialog. If your settings call for Saving All Files, the next file with changes will be displayed.

Save All

This button will only be available if you have the options set to Save All Files and there's more than one file open. Choosing it will save all changed documents without any additional prompts. If a document has never been saved, you'll be asked to provide a filename.

Next

The Next File... button skips the current file (without saving it) and moves to the next file that has had changes. This button will be unavailable (grayed out) whenever it's inappropriate.

Procrastinate

This button resets the timer and/or counter. The current file won't be saved, and you won't be asked about saving files until the specified number of minutes and/or entries has elapsed again. In other words, it's a "wait a while" button.

Turn Off

Stops the AutoSave from saving your files until you turn it back on. If you have the Turn on Baarns AutoSave at Startup box checked, the AutoSave will be restarted the next time the Utilities are loaded.

Help

Enables you to read through the information you are currently reading.

Backup Version Control

With the Backup Version Control settings you can have AutoSave keep backup copies of your previous versions. You can choose one of the three settings shown in Figure D.3.

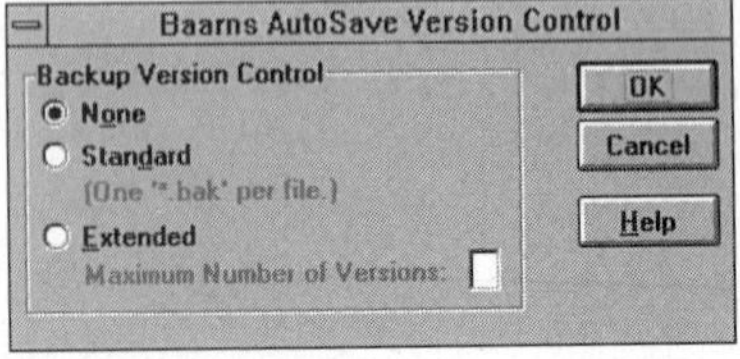

FIGURE D.3.
The AutoSave Version Control dialog box.

None

Doesn't keep any previous versions. The previous version is deleted as each new file is saved. Note that if you manually used Excel's native File Save As Options and checked the box for backup copies, AutoSave will *not* override your settings; you will have backup files created for that specific document.

Standard

When you choose this setting, any document that is saved will also have a single backup file created for it. The backup file will have the extension ".bak." The file(s) will always be set to create the single backup (even if the Utilities aren't running). You can use MS Excel's File Save As Options… command and change the Create Backup File check box to modify this.

Extended

Creates a series of backup files. You specify how many previous versions you would like to keep (up to 9). The file extensions on the PC will be BAK, BK2, BK3, BK4, and so on. Using Excel's File Open command you can change the file filter to *.B* and see all the backup files in a directory.

Baarns Clock

How Late Are We?

The Baarns Clock is a simple, unobtrusive utility that places either the time or the time and date in a separate window on your screen. This window will stay in the same position even if you switch to another application. (This assumes Excel is still loaded.)

Positioning the Clock

The Clock can be moved around the screen by dragging it with the mouse. Being an obedient clock, it will always give focus back to Excel after you stop dragging it around the screen. In other words, when you stop dragging the Clock around, Excel's title bar becomes active again and any cell(s) or object(s) you had selected before moving the Clock are reselected.

When you close Excel, the Clock also closes. If you have the check box set to Show Clock on Startup, the Clock will start every time the Baarns Utilities are loaded. It will also "remember" where you last left the Clock and return to the same position when it opens again. (See Figure D.4.)

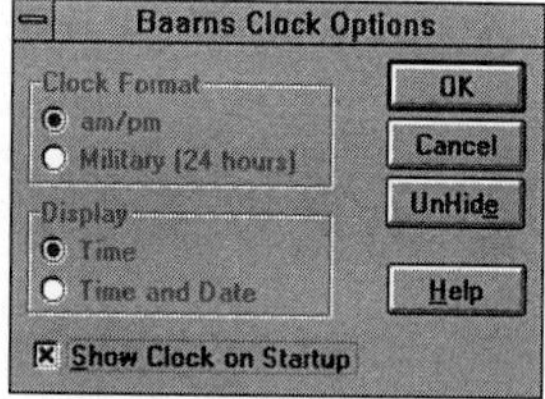

FIGURE D.4.
The Clock Options dialog box.

The Baarns Clock Options

You can change the way the Clock looks by changing the settings in the Clock Options dialog. Here's a rundown of the Options.

Clock Format

Toggles between A.M./P.M. time and Military (also called 24-hour time).

Display

Changes both the information shown on the Clock and the size of the Clock. The Time setting creates a much smaller clock that will almost completely fit in the status bar on the bottom of the screen or the menu bar at the top. Of course, those locations are just "serving suggestions" and you are free to move the Clock anyplace on your desktop.

The Hide/Unhide Button

If your Clock is currently running, you'll see a Hide button. If the Clock isn't currently displayed, you'll find the Unhide button. This button is obviously a toggle between displaying and hiding the Clock and you can change back and forth as you desire. The Clock will retain all your settings and restart where it was last left when it opens again.

Baarns Express Math

Changing Groups of Numbers

Baarns Express Math (see Figure D.5) is designed to enable you to change a group of numbers by a constant amount. For example, if you were Ross Perot, you could have a set of numbers for gas prices in every major city in America. After selecting all the numbers, Express Math could add 50 cents to every price with one command (of course, you would still have to persuade Congress to go along with the idea).

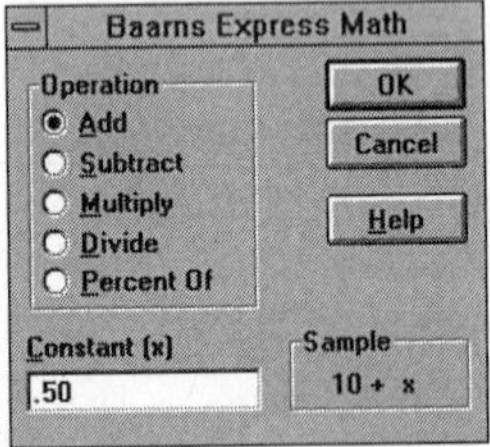

FIGURE D.5.
The Express Math dialog box.

Using Baarns Express Math

Select a group of numbers in your spreadsheet. Then choose the Express Math icon from the Baarns Utilities toolbar (or use the menu command). The Operation selection (radio buttons) enables you to tell Express Math you wish to Add, Subtract, Multiply, Divide or calculate a Percentage Of your original amounts. Compare the before and after for gas prices in Los Angeles in Figure D.6.

Figure D.6 shows prices before Ross.

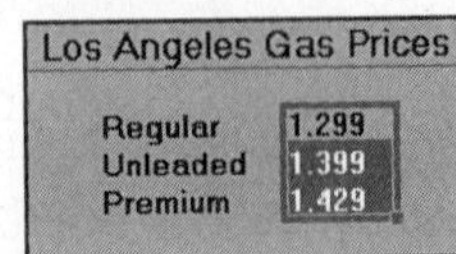

FIGURE D.6.
Before Ross.

Figure D.7 shows prices after Ross (and Baarns Express Math).

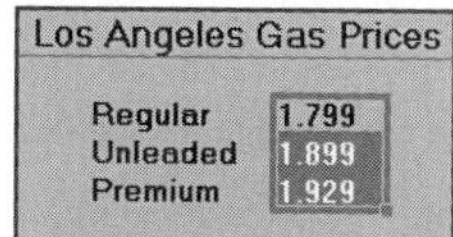

FIGURE D.7.
After Ross.

If you're not Ross Perot, you'll probably find other sets of numbers that need to be increased, decreased, or changed by a constant amount.

SUPER TIP

To add 10 percent to a group of numbers, choose Percent Of and enter 110 in the Constant edit box. Conversely, you can subtract 10 percent by entering 90 in that box.

Undoing Express Math

If there's some reason you don't like the results of Express Math—or if you lose the election—you can undo its results. Be sure to choose the Edit Undo Paste Special command (we know you didn't just use the Paste Special command, but Express Math did when it changed your numbers) before you perform other operations or this option may not be available.

Baarns New

Opening and Creating Templates

Initially, Baarns New works just like Microsoft Excel's File New command: it enables you to open a new, blank document. You may also open templates that you have created and saved in the XLSTART directory on the PC. Additionally, Baarns New enables you to save your custom templates with long (31 character) descriptive names and store them in any directory you choose. You also can remove templates from the list, rename current templates, and create new templates using the Create... button. The Create... button displays the Template Wizard, which enables you to create your own templates from new or existing documents. See the "Baarns Template Wizard" section for additional information.

Opening an Existing Template

Select one of the names in the New list and choose the OK button. Of course, you could also double-click your choice in the list box and a new copy of the template will be opened for you.

Baarns New Control Buttons

The Baarns New dialog box (shown in Figure D.8) has a set of control buttons on the right side of the box. Each of these buttons is explained in the following paragraphs.

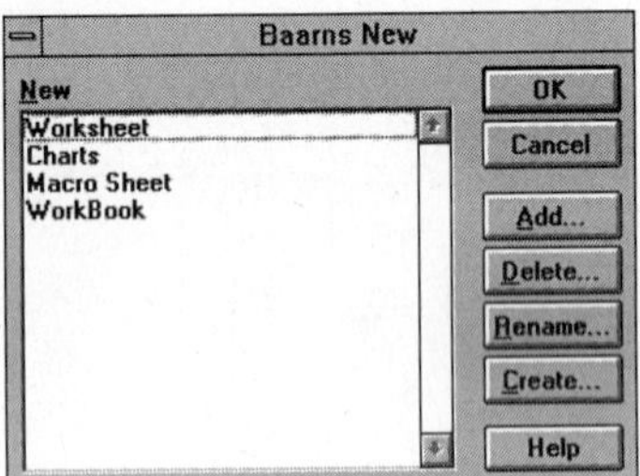

FIGURE D.8.
The New dialog box.

OK

Opens a copy of the template selected in the New list box.

Cancel

Closes the dialog box without opening a template.

Add...

Enables you to add an additional template to the list. The first dialog box (shown in Figure D.9) enables you to move around your hard drive and select the template file you wish to add.

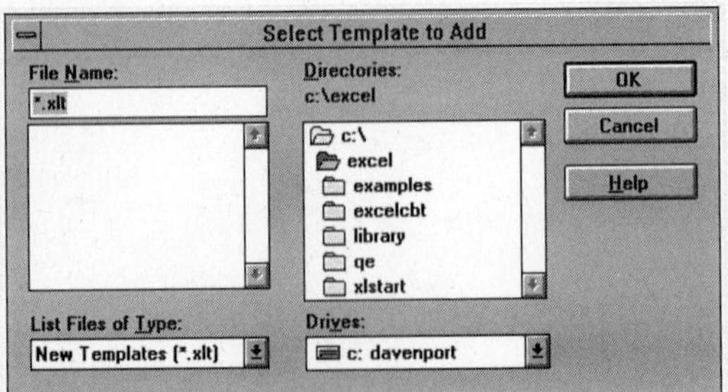

FIGURE D.9.
The Select template to add dialog box.

After selecting your template, choose the OK button and you will be given an opportunity to create a description for your template (see Figure D.10). You can use up to 31 characters.

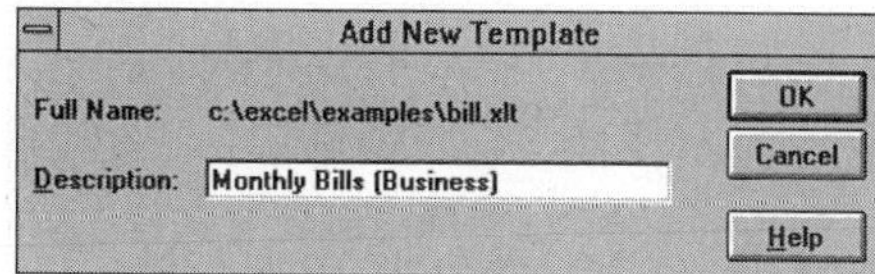

FIGURE D.10.
The Add New Template dialog box.

Choose OK and your new template will be added to your list (as shown in Figure D.11).

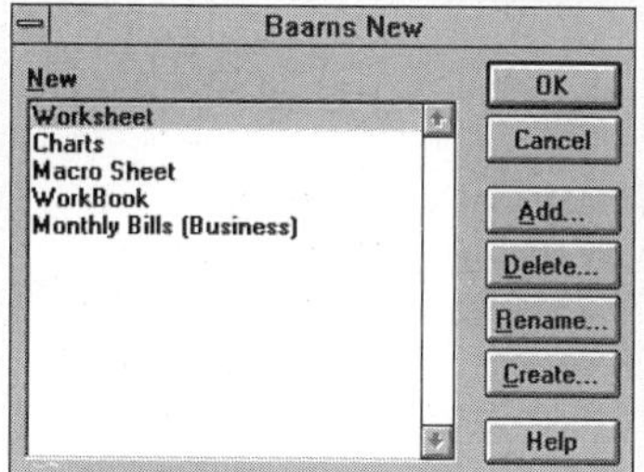

FIGURE D.11.
The new template is added to the list in the New dialog box.

Delete...

Removes the selected template from the list and optionally deletes the template file from your disk. The dialog box shown in Figure D.12 will be displayed to verify your intentions. Your two choices are to Remove the template from the list and delete the template (from your hard disk) OR you may just remove the file from the list and the template will still be available using Excel's File Open command. This assumes the template file is NOT stored in your XLSTART directory. Templates stored in XLSTART have to be deleted (or moved) to remove them from the list.

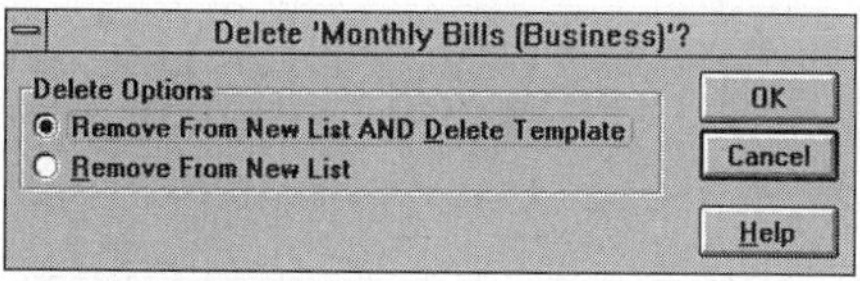

FIGURE D.12.
The Delete verify dialog box.

SUPER NOTE

If the template file you are deleting is stored in your XLSTART directory, you won't be enabled to just remove the item from the list. (Choice number two will be unavailable.) This is because by default, all files in your XLSTART directory show up in File New. The only way to totally remove a file from your XLSTART directory is either to delete the file or move it to another location (subdirectory) on your hard disk. After deleting/moving a file, then use the Delete button to clear the description from the list.

Create...

Starts the Template Wizard. Helps you create a reusable template file. See the "Baarns Template Wizard" section for details on creating template files.

Baarns Print Cleanser

Squeaky Clean Documents without Dishpan Hands

If you've had a "friend" give you a document that contained multiple manual page breaks, and you've spent the time figuring out where they were and removed them one at a time, you deserve a reward. The Print Cleanser isn't magic, but it will remove all the left-over printing setups. Simply check the items you want removed (see Figure D.13), and the Print Cleanser will take care of the rest.

SUPER TIP

Page Breaks that are removed are *manual* page breaks. Automatic page breaks are still retained by Excel.

FIGURE D.13.
The Print Cleanser dialog box.

Print Cleanser Check Boxes

Each box that contains a check will cause the corresponding item to be removed. You can select any combination of the three choices or if you want to remove all three in one step, choose the Remove All button on the right side of the box.

Remove Print Area

Check this box if you wish to have the current Print Area removed.

Remove Print Titles

Removes the Print Titles from your current document.

Remove Page Breaks

Removes all manual Page Breaks from your current document. Excel will still create page breaks automatically when you print. If you still see dotted lines in your document after using the Remove Page Breaks, check Excel's Options Display… command and see if Automatic Page Breaks are selected (checked). If they are, you'll see Excel's automatic page breaks even if the Print Cleanser has removed all the manual page breaks.

More About Automatic and Manual Page Breaks...

Excel visually shows slightly different dashed lines for manual and automatic page breaks. The dashes of the manual page breaks are closer together than those of the automatic page breaks. The difference is very subtle so you may have to experiment with both side-by-side to see it. We use the following dumb memory aid to remind us of the difference in the size of the spaces between the dots: "Autos are big, man is small." (Good thing we aren't in the memory enhancement business….)

Baarns Print Special

For a Quick Print Call...

The Baarns Print Special command will enable you to print parts of your documents that are not currently defined as a Print Area. You can choose to print the current selection, all the pages in the document, or just selected pages. You also can change the page and/or printer setup of your document and preview your printing choices before sending the document off to the printer.

Figure D.14 shows the first Print Special dialog box that is displayed.

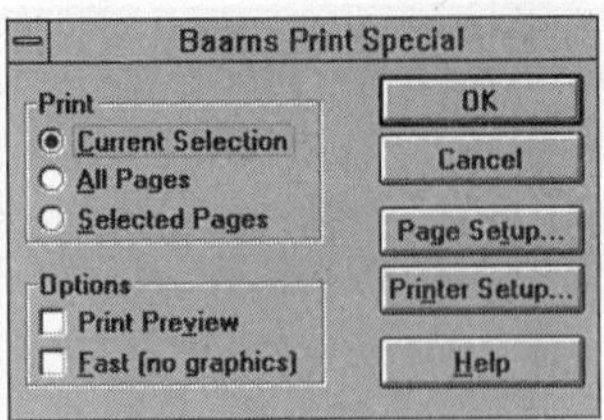

FIGURE D.14.
The Print Special dialog box.

The group of radio buttons at the top left (cleverly labeled "Print") will enable you to choose what you want to print. In all cases those options ignore any previously defined Print Area. (If you just want to print specific pages of the currently defined Print Area, you can use Excel's built-in File Print… command.) After your pages are printed, your original Print Area is restored.

Print Special Options

The Options group will enable you to Print Preview your document before printing. From the Print Preview you can choose either Setup or Margins to further refine the look of your printed document. Of course, if you don't like the look of your document you can always cancel the printing (by choosing the Close button found in Print Preview) before it's sent to the printer.

SUPER TIP

Graphics include text boxes, buttons, charts, pictures, and other items embedded in worksheets.

If you have a check in the Fast (no graphics) box your document will print quickly but none of the graphics in your document will be printed. Uncheck this box if you want to see them on the printout.

What Do You Want to Print?

The Baarns Print Special will enable you to print different parts of your document. You can decide which areas you wish to see on the printouts.

Current Selection

Prints the cells (and objects covering the cells if they're set to print) that are part of the current selection. This is useful for creating a "snapshot" of your current working session. You also can create a multiple selection and each range will be printed on its own page.

SUPER TIP

If you hold down the Shift key while selecting the Print Special command (either from the menu or the toolbar), the current selection will print without first displaying any dialog box. This is great for rough drafts and quickly getting a hard copy of your selected area. All your current print settings are applied to this printout.

All Pages

Prints every page in the document while ignoring any defined Print Area. As with the other two options, your previous Print Area is restored when the printing is finished.

Selected Pages

When you choose this option, the Baarns Utilities will compute the number of pages available to print in the current document. This may take a few seconds, depending on the speed of your machine. After the computing is finished, a list box displays all of the pages (up to 100) available in the document to print (see the dialog box on the next page). You can then select the desired pages and Print Special will print them for you. If you change the Printer Setup or the Page Setup (using the buttons found in the box) the Utilities will recompute the number of pages in your document.

Our recommendation is to change all the Print/Page settings *before* you choose the Selected Pages check box. (See Figure D.15.) This will save you time because your computer won't have to compute the number of available pages twice.

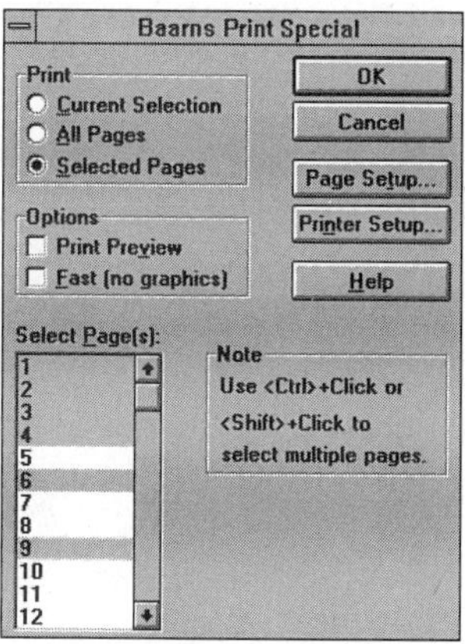

FIGURE D.15.
The Print Special dialog box.

Selecting Multiple Pages to Print

You can select multiple pages by holding down the Ctrl or Shift key while clicking on the pages you wish to print in the Select Page(s) list. There's a subtle difference between the two.

> **SUPER TIP**
>
> Ctrl or Shift + Click also work in Excel's File Open box and in File Manager for selecting groups of files.

Ctrl + Click

Each click acts as a toggle but doesn't change any of the other items already selected. In other words, if the number 2 isn't selected, clicking on it will highlight (select) it. If it's already selected, clicking on it will unselect it. This enables you to select pages 1, 3, 5, and/or any other combination you desire.

Shift + Click

When you want to print a continuous range of pages, select the first page you want to print, hold down the Shift key, and click on the final page you want printed. The pages in between will automatically be selected. For example, if page 3 is selected and then you hold down the Shift key and select page 10, your selection will now include pages 3 through 10.

You also can combine the two methods: for example, select pages 1 thorough 9 with the Shift key and then hold down the Ctrl key and unselect pages 5, 7, and 8. The results would look like the previous dialog box. Techno-babble for this concept is a "discontiguous selection."

> **SUPER NOTE**
>
> Discontiguous selections will not show up in print preview as one document. For example, if you choose pages 1-3 and 6-10 you would preview pages 1-3 as one document, using the Next and Previous buttons to move between the three pages. You can then choose the Print button (to print the document) or Close if you don't wish to print those pages. Then you will preview the next group of pages—in this example, pages 6-10.

Baarns Reminders

Viewing Reminders

Select Reminders… from the Options menu to see the currently set reminders. From this box (see Figure D.16) you can Add, Edit, or Delete reminders. Any reminders that are currently set are shown in the list of Current Reminders.

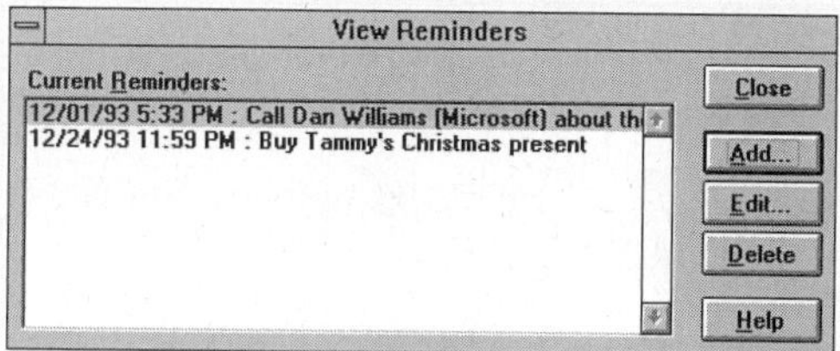

FIGURE D.16.
The View Reminders dialog box.

Adding or Editing Reminders

To Add or Edit Reminders you use the following controls.

Add... or Edit...

These buttons both display the following dialog box. The only difference is that if you are editing a reminder, you'll see the Time, Date, and Reminder Message preset to match your selected reminder settings. (See Figure D.17.) If you are adding a new reminder, the Time and Date default and the Reminder Message will be blank.

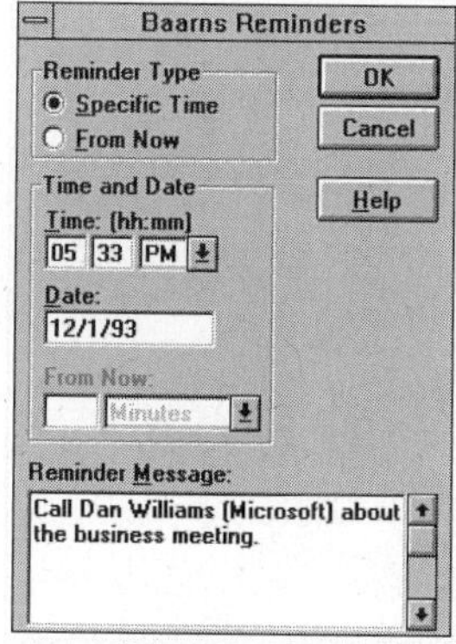

FIGURE D.17.
The Reminders edit dialog box.

The following three steps are used to set or edit a reminder.

1. Choose a Reminder Type.

   Specific Time enables you to set the time to an exact time and date. For example, 5:30 AM or 7:30 PM on 4/10/93. From Now sets the time to X minutes or hours from now. For example, 15 minutes from now or 3 hours from now.
2. Fill in the appropriate Time and Date for the reminder (if you are setting a Specific Time reminder) or change the number of minutes/hours from now you would like to have the reminder displayed.
3. Edit the current message in the Reminder Message box. Your message can be up to 150 characters long.

After you have set your reminder, choose the OK button and your new (or edited) reminder will be added to the list.

When It's Reminder Time

When it's time for a Reminder to be displayed, you'll see the dialog box shown in Figure D.18.

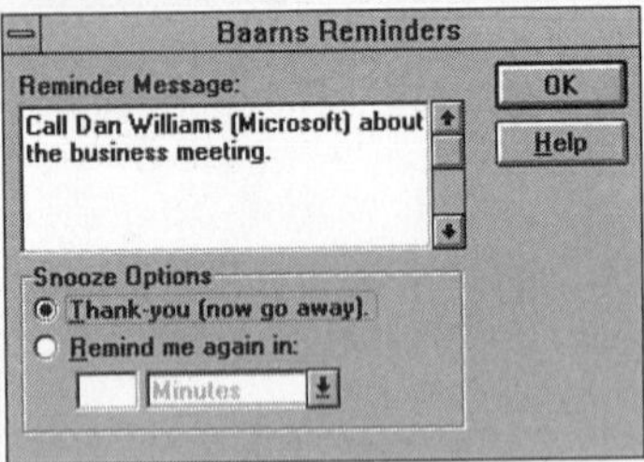

FIGURE D.18.
A displayed reminder.

Snooze Options

When the Reminder is displayed you can either choose the OK button or use the Snooze Options to reset the Reminder for a new time. Your choices are outlined in the following sections.

Thank-you (now go away)

This option is the default. If you simply press OK when the box displays, the message is removed from the View Reminder list and the box disappears.

Remind me again in:

This radio button enables you to reset the Reminder for an additional period of time. When this is selected, you will be able to specify the number of minutes (or hours) from now before the Reminder is redisplayed.

More About Reminders...

You can have up to 12 reminders set at any one time. These reminders can be set for weeks or months in advance. If a Reminder would be displayed but Excel isn't running, the next time you start Excel, the Baarns Utilities will display a list of the Reminders that have passed since your last Excel session. Reminders that haven't yet occurred will be reset and will display at the appropriate time if Excel is running.

Baarns Save As Icon

Icons for Starting Your Documents

The Save As Icon utility will both save your current document and create an icon for it in the Windows Program Manager. (See Figure D.19.) The next time you want to start Excel and use the document, you can simply double-click on the icon in Program Manager. Excel will be started and the current document will be loaded automatically.

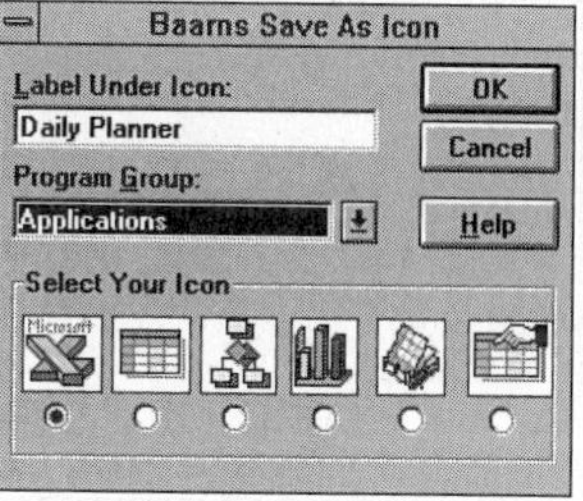

FIGURE D.19.
The Save As Icon dialog box.

Three Steps for Creating Your Icon:

1. Type a label for your icon in the Label Under Icon edit box. This will default to the name of your current document but you can change it to anything you wish.
2. Decide in which Program Group you want your new icon to be placed. If you drop the list box (using the arrow on the right side of the Program Group edit box), you'll see a complete list of the current groups you have in Program Manager. Select the one you want or type a new name if you would like the Baarns Utilities to create a new group for you.

3. Select the Icon you would like to see for your document. You can have anything you want as long as it's one of the six shown. The radio buttons below each icon determine which one is selected.

Baarns Set Standard Font

What is "Normal"?

The Set Standard Font command provides a shortcut for setting the Standard Font in a document and optionally setting the standard font on all future documents. To set the standard font we are really just redefining Excel's Normal Font. This utility replaces a multiple-step process with two steps (and in many cases, just one step).

Microsoft has provided a very powerful feature in Excel's Format Style command. While we recommend you use the Baarns Utilities to handle the details of changing the standard font (see Figure D.20), understanding the broader subject of styles is highly recommended for your own productivity gains. Pages 240 through 246 in the Microsoft Excel Users Guide, Book 1 are dedicated to a thorough discussion of the mechanics of styles.

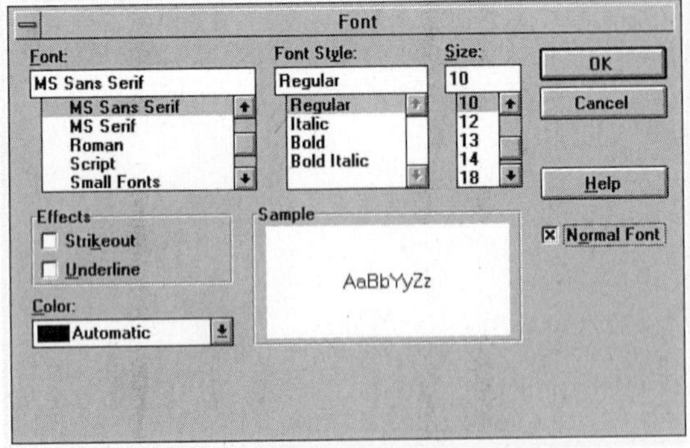

FIGURE D.20.
The Font dialog box.

If you are working with an existing document (as opposed to a fresh Sheet1), just changing the Standard Font may not change the fonts that are already in your document. Any font found in the document that wasn't the old Standard Font will not be changed when you substitute a new Standard Font. The next dialog handles those cases. If you are working with a brand new document, you can just cancel out of this box.

Setting Standard Font Options

You have two primary options after you set the Standard Font for a document, as shown in Figure D.21. Each of the choices is detailed in the following sections.

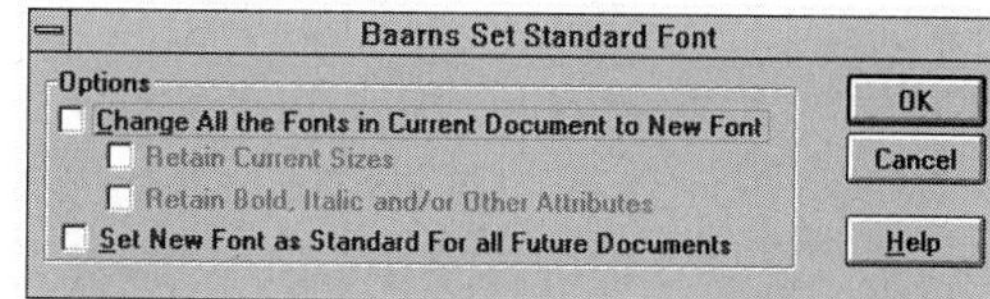

FIGURE D.21.
The Set Standard Font dialog box.

Change All the Fonts in Current Document to New Font

This option will select the complete worksheet and replace all existing fonts in the document with the new Standard Font you selected. Once you select this box, you'll have additional choices to make.

Retain Current Sizes

All Fonts will be changed to the chosen Standard Font but all cells will retain their respective font sizes. If you turn this off, all cells in the spreadsheet will be changed to the size of the new Standard Font.

Retain Bold, Italic, and/or Other Attributes

If this box remains checked (the default), all cells retain their currently assigned attributes (bold, Italic, underlined, and so on) but the font type is changed to the new Standard Font. In other words, MS San Serif Bold could become Times New Roman Bold. If it is unchecked, all cells are changed to match the settings for the new Standard Font you have chosen. This would make every cell in the worksheet the same font, just as they were when the document was new.

Set New Font as Standard for All Future Documents

If this option is selected (checked) the Baarns Utilities will write an entry into your EXCEL5.INI file that will cause all future documents to default to your new Font. New documents created with Excel's built-in Worksheet, Chart, Macro sheet or Workbooks (created with File New) will be affected.

SUPER TIP

If you've customized the built-in templates, this option will not affect documents created with those templates.

> **SUPER NOTE**
>
> This option won't take effect until after Excel has been closed and reopened at least once.

Baarns Sticky Notes

To Post or Not to Post

Well, it's obvious we're not Shakespeare, but our Sticky Notes (see Figure D.22) will create an on-screen note for you that resembles the paper ones found on monitors throughout corporate America.

FIGURE D.22.
The Sticky Notes dialog box.

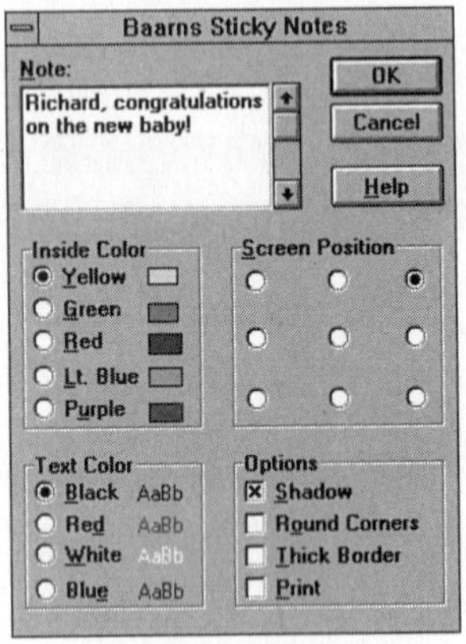

Creating a Sticky Note

The process of creating a Sticky Note is very simple. Type in the text you wish to see in the note, set any additional formatting and starting screen location, and choose OK. Here are some additional details on each of the items you can modify from the box.

Note

Type the note you would like to see in this edit box. This text will be placed in the middle of your Sticky Note. Your note can be up to 255 characters long. Any text you type beyond 255 characters will be truncated (which sounds as if it would hurt if you were an elephant...).

Inside Color

This setting controls the background color of the Note. The default is the "traditional" yellow. (And Post-It brand notes have such a long tradition...)

Text Color

Select one of the colors for your text.

Screen Position

The nine radio buttons in the Screen Position group box loosely represent screen positions. By selecting a radio button, your sticky note will be placed in the corresponding position on your screen. For example, if you select the button in the lower-right corner, your Sticky Note will initially be placed in the lower-right corner of your screen. (You can always move it later if you change your mind about its position.)

You'll find that if you have used the Window Freeze Panes command, the Screen Position works differently. Your Note will always be positioned relative to the pane on the right side, the bottom half or lower right corner (depending on how you split the screen). In other words, the Screen Position is always relative to the UNfrozen part of the window. This will always be the right and/or the bottom pane.

Options

Each of the options is handled with a check box. You can select any or all of the options by checking the appropriate box(es). Here's a rundown of each option.

1. *Shadow:* Will place a shadow behind your Note and create the illusion that your note is floating slightly above the worksheet. The default Note includes a shadow.
2. *Round Corners:* When checked, your Sticky Note will have rounded corners instead of the traditional squared corners. The default is square corners.
3. *Thick Border:* Creates a much bolder border around your Note. The default is a narrow border.
4. *Print:* When checked, your Sticky Note will print when the document is printed. The default setting doesn't print the Note.

SUPER

A NOTE FOR HP LASERJET USERS

At the time of this printing, when most Hewlett Packard LaserJets (II & III model lines) print graphic objects (including Baarns Sticky Notes) on worksheets, the cells below show through. The only known work around at this time is to turn off the gridlines and blank the cells below a graphic object. This may be changed by a future print driver. Please check with HP or Microsoft for print driver updates if this affects you.

For those of you with additional money to throw at problems, you'll be happy to know the HP LaserJet 4 eliminates this issue and gives you another excuse to upgrade the perfectly good printer you already own.

Sizing, Moving, or Deleting Sticky Notes

In order to make changes to a Sticky Note, you'll need to select it so Excel understands you want to manipulate it. When you click on a note you'll find little black squares called "handles" around the edges of the notes. These handles let you know the object is selected. (This is also known as "having focus.") Once selected, use the techniques discussed in the following sections to work with the Sticky Note. Of course, these techniques work with other graphic objects as well. Each of the techniques assumes the Note is already selected.

Sizing Sticky Notes

When you move the mouse pointer over one of the handles you'll see a double-headed arrow. If you drag one of these handles you'll change the size of the Note.

Moving Sticky Notes

Once selected, when you move the mouse pointer over one of the borders (edges) of the Note, you'll see a pointer. When this pointer appears, you can drag the note to any other screen location.

Deleting Sticky Notes

Ctrl+Z is the keyboard shortcut for Edit Undo.

After selecting a note, you simply press the Delete key and your note will disappear. If you really didn't intend to delete the note, immediately choose the Edit Undo command to restore your Sticky Note.

Baarns Template Wizard

Growing Your Own Templates

Templates are just a fancy name for reusable documents. Everyone who's ever started Excel has been faced with the built-in template lovingly known as "Sheet1." While you might agree that this template is rather boring, it does serve as a starting point for all your brilliant spreadsheet ideas. If you've ever said, "But there must be more to life than 'Sheet1,'" you were right. Template Wizard can assist you in building your own reusable documents and even replace the built-in standard templates (like Sheet1) that Excel provides. For example, you might prefer a different font, no gridlines, custom styles, or that your Sheet1 contains a custom header and/or footer. Additionally, when you are finished with Template Wizard you can further customize your template before you close the document.

Three Step Templates

There are three steps the Template Wizard will walk you through in creating your document. The first step in this process is to decide what type of template you would like to create. You then provide names for the document. Lastly, you make any changes you desire and the Template Wizard will handle the rest. Figure D.23 shows the first dialog box presented after you start the Template Wizard.

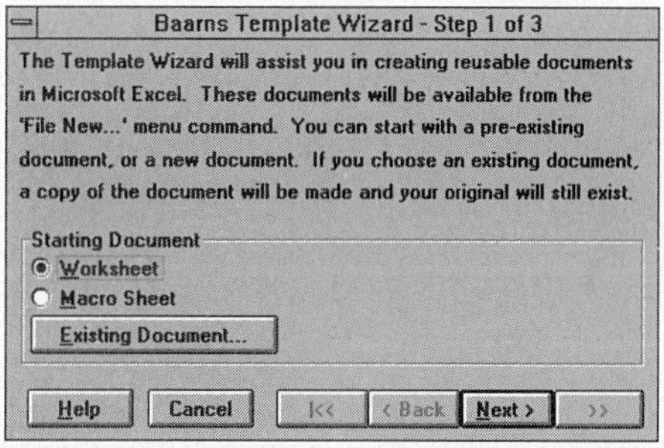

FIGURE D.23.
The first step in creating a template.

Baarns Template Wizard - Step 1 of 3

The Template Wizard will assist you in creating reusable documents in Microsoft Excel. These documents will be available from the 'File New...' menu command. You can start with a pre-existing document, or a new document. If you choose an existing document, a copy of the document will be made and your original will still exist.

Starting Document
Worksheet
Macro Sheet
Existing Document...

Help | Cancel | |<< | < Back | Next > | >>

Template Wizard Step One

Your Starting Document must be one of the following three types:

1. Worksheet

   Opens a file based on the world famous Sheet1 file. Even if you have customized Sheet1 previously, this new file will be based on the original worksheet template provided by Microsoft. You can use the Existing Document button (described in step 3) if you wish to start with your customized Sheet template.

2. Macro Sheet

   Opens the blank Macro1 file as your starting document.

3. Existing Document…

   This button will display the dialog box (shown in Figure D.24) and enable you to open an existing worksheet, macro sheet or chart. This enables you to take advantage of any previous formatting, text, or formulas you have applied to a document.

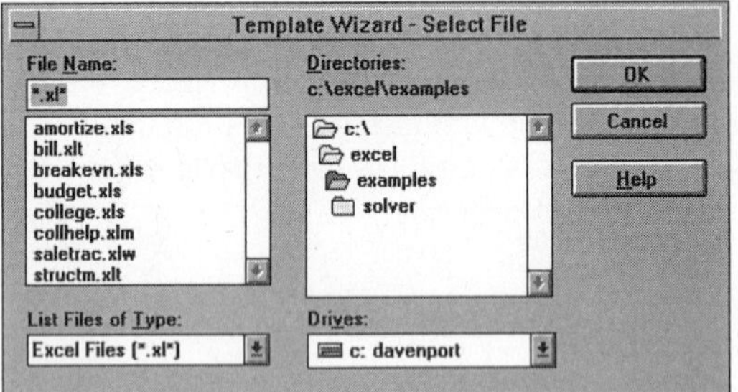

FIGURE D.24.
The Select File dialog box.

Naming Your Template (Step 2)

After selecting your document, you'll be asked to provide a name for the document. Step 2 of the Template Wizard (see Figure D.25) enables you either to name your custom Template or to replace one of Excel's built-in Templates. The following section outlines your two choices in greater detail.

Baarns Template Wizard - Step 2 of 3
Please provide a name for your new Template. The DOS Name can be up to 8 characters (I'll add the ".XLT" extension for you). The Description can be up to 31 characters long and will show up in the 'File New...' dialog box. If you choose to 'Replace Excel's Standard Template', I'll handle the naming.
Template Type
Custom Template
Replace MS Excel's Standard 'Worksheet' Template
Name Your New Template
DOS Name: Monthly
Description: Monthly Bills (Personal)
Help | Cancel | |<< | < Back | Next > | >>

FIGURE D.25.
Step two in creating a template.

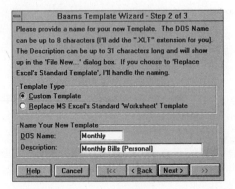

Custom Templates

In most cases this will be your choice. This choice requires you to specify both an eight-character DOS name and a longer Description. The DOS name will be part of the "real" filename used to save the file (along with a .XLT extension). The Description can be up to 31 characters. It will be used by the Baarns File New command and be displayed whenever you select File New from the menu system (or use the icon on the Utilities toolbar).

Replace MS Excel's Standard "XXXXXX" Template

This option is context sensitive. In other words, the XXXXXX will be "Worksheet," "Chart," or "Macro sheet" depending on the type of document you choose in Step 1 of the Template Wizard. If you select this option, Template Wizard will automatically save this document with the proper names required to replace Excel's built-in templates. Then if you select File New you'll receive your custom "Sheet1," "Chart1," or "Macro1" depending on which file you selected (and replaced).

Changing Your New Template (Step 3)

After your file is named, you'll have an opportunity to modify your template. Step 3 will provide the dialog box shown in Figure D.26 (with six buttons in the middle).

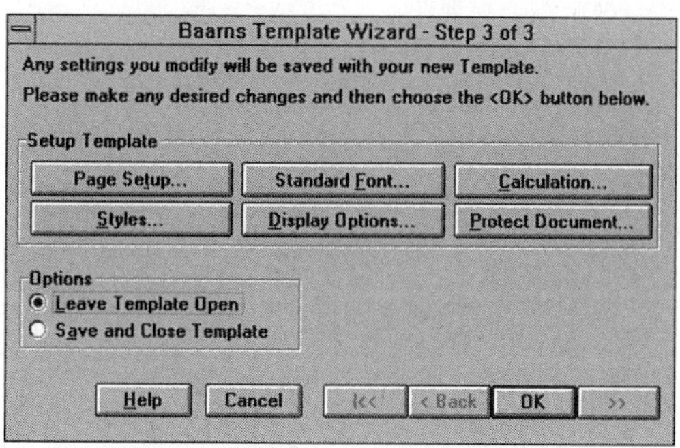

FIGURE D.26.
Step three in making a template.

Or, if your new template is a chart, you'll see the dialog box shown in Figure D.27.

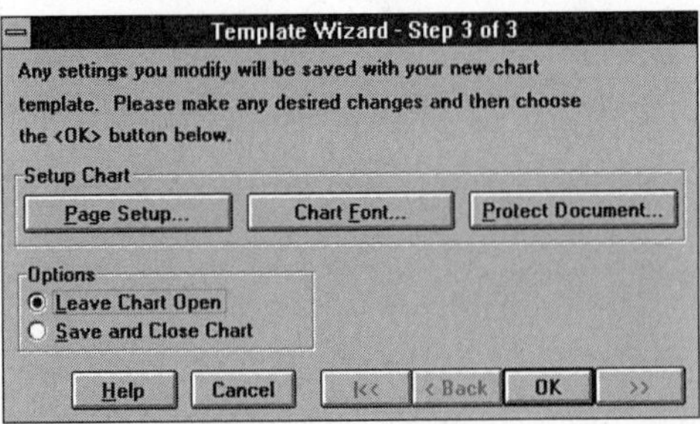

FIGURE D.27.
Step three in making a template (chart).

Each of the buttons in the middle will display another dialog box and provide you with hours of fun (well...maybe just a couple of minutes) to make additional changes to your new template. Before selecting the OK button, be sure to decide if you wish to make additional changes or view your document. Your settings in the Options group will determine whether the Template Wizard leaves your new document on the screen or closes it (after saving changes).

If you don't close the file, you can continue modifying your new template. When you are finished, close the document manually, saving changes (if that's appropriate).

To open your custom template, see the "Baarns New" command.

Baarns Timer

How Long Has It Been Since I Started

The Baarns Timer is a very simple utility. It starts timing immediately after you select the menu option (or press the Timer Start tool) and just runs in the background until you ask to see its display. When started, it places a toolbar in the upper-left corner of your screen. When you press the button on this toolbar you'll see the dialog box shown in Figure D.28.

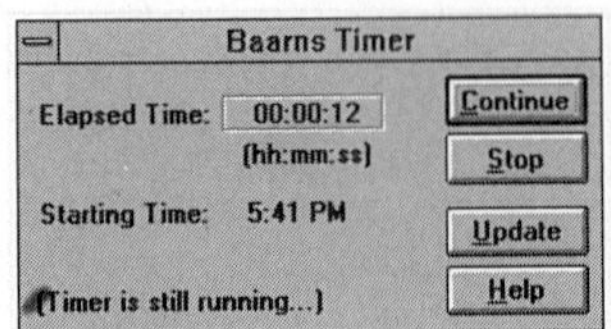

FIGURE D.28.
The Timer dialog box.

The Timer Control Buttons

There are only three buttons you need to know about when using the Timer. (If you're reading this, you don't need the Help button explained.) While this dialog box is being displayed, the current timer is still running in the background, even though the numbers shown in the Elapsed Time box are frozen.

Continue

TIP

Timers stop timing when Excel is closed.

Closes the Timer dialog box and the Timer continues to run uninterrupted in the background. The next time you select the Toolbar icon to display this box, it will reflect the total time since the Timer was originally started. You can display and continue as many times as you would like.

Stop

Closes the dialog box and stops the currently running timer. The Timer is reset to zero and ready for next timer session.

Update

Updates the Elapsed Time in the dialog box. The Timer continues to run in the background, and this button enables you to get the current Elapsed Time whenever you select it.

Baarns Utilities Options

Menus, Toolbar, and Closing the Utilities

The Baarns Utilities Options enables you to control the display of its menus and toolbar, and change other startup settings for specific Utilities. Additionally, it enables you to remove the Baarns Utilities from memory temporarily when you need 100 percent of your machine's available memory and resources for the current Excel session.

The Baarns Utilities Options menu is found on Excel's Options menu. When selected, the dialog box is shown in Figure D.29.

FIGURE D.29.
The Baarns Utilities Options dialog box.

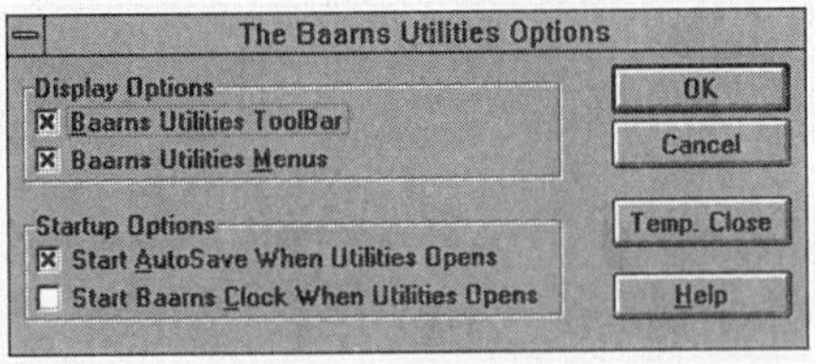

Display Options

Controls the display of both the toolbar and the menus for the Baarns Utilities. If the box is checked, that item will be displayed. The Baarns Utilities Menus option both adds an additional menu (Utilities) and replaces some of the native Excel menus with the enhanced Baarns Utilities versions. If you want to return to Excel's native menus at any time, just uncheck the Baarns Utilities Menus option and Excel's standard menus will be restored.

Startup Options

As the Baarns Utilities starts, it looks at your previous settings for the AutoSave and Clock Utilities and starts them automatically unless you have turned these features off. These settings are also changeable from the individual features. You'll see a similar check box in the Baarns AutoSave and the Baarns Clock Options dialog box. You may change the settings in either place and your wishes will be honored (well, at least the features will respond appropriately).

The Temp. Close Button

Most of you will never use this button. It's provided to enable you to regain 100 percent of your machine's memory and resources for those extra large projects you may be working on. If you ever receive a "Not enough system resources to display completely" error message from Excel, or you're working on huge spreadsheets, you could use this button to remove the Utilities for the current session.

This will remove the Baarns Utilities menus (all except one) and close the Utilities. When the coast is clear (meaning you're finished with that huge project), you can reload the Baarns Utilities by simply choosing one of its toolbar icons or selecting the Options Baarns Utilities Options command. Either way, the Utilities will be reloaded and your previous settings restored.

Hiding/Displaying the Baarns Utilities Toolbar

While you can hide or show the Baarns Utilities toolbar using the Options Baarns Utilities Options command, you also can use Excel's built-in tools to display/hide or modify the toolbar. From the menu you can use the Options Toolbars… command to display, hide or even delete the Baarns Utilities toolbar. It's recommended that you HIDE the Utilities toolbar if you don't want to see it because everytime the Utilities open they rebuild (and display) their toolbar if it's not found. If it's hidden, the Utilities will not rebuild (or display) it.

Using the mouse, you can right-click on any toolbar and you'll find a list (known as the "toolbar shortcut menu") of available toolbars. All visible toolbars have a check mark next to them. If you click on one of the toolbars in the list, it acts as a toggle: hidden toolbars are displayed, visible toolbars are hidden. In other words, click on the Baarns Utilities in the list of toolbars to hide/display the Utilities toolbar. This same concept can be applied to any toolbar you are using.

Customizing the Baarns Utilities Toolbar

You can add, delete, or rearrange the tools found on the Baarns Utilities toolbar or move them to another toolbar.

Adding Tools

1. From the toolbar shortcut menu (right-click on any toolbar), choose Customize.

   You could also use the Options Toolbar command and then choose the Customize command.
2. This will display the Customize dialog box. While this box is displayed, select the category of tools from which you want to add.
3. Drag the tool from the Tools box and drop it on the Baarns Utilities toolbar.

   Microsoft Excel will resize the toolbar to accommodate the additional tool.

You also can drag tools around to different locations if you would like to see them in a different arrangement. As long as the Customize box is displayed, you can continue adding or moving tools to create your own customized Baarns Utilities toolbar.

Removing Tools

1. From the toolbar shortcut menu (right-click on any toolbar), choose Customize.
2. While the Customize dialog box is displayed, simply drag a tool off one of the existing toolbars to any location where there is no existing toolbar.

You also can drag tools between toolbars, or copy tools (so they show up on more than one toolbar) by holding the Ctrl key while dragging between toolbars.

A complete discussion of all the options for customizing toolbars can be found on pages 154—164 in the *Microsoft Excel Users Guide, Book 2.*

Rebuilding the Baarns Utilities Toolbar

If you would like to return the Baarns Utilities toolbar to its original configuration, you can use one of the following methods:

1. Hold down the Ctrl key while the Utilities are opening. The Baarns Utilities will rebuild your toolbar to factory fresh specifications (like the original setup).
2. Delete the Baarns Utilities toolbar. Choose the Options Toolbar command and select The Baarns Utilities from the list of toolbars. Then choose the Delete button.

The next time the Utilities are opened, your Utilities toolbar will be rebuilt. See "The Temp. Close Button" section for a discussion of how to remove the Utilities from memory and then reopen them by choosing the Options Baarns Utilities Options menu again. This will reopen the Utilities and when it finds its toolbar has disappeared (you sneaky person...) it will rebuild it for you.

Baarns Zoom

Quickly Change Your View

Zooming Your Window

The Zoom tool (see Figure D.30) enables you to change the magnification (a fancy word for relative sizing) of your document. There are three methods for changing your current settings. You also can preview a new setting and fine tune the results before you close the dialog box.

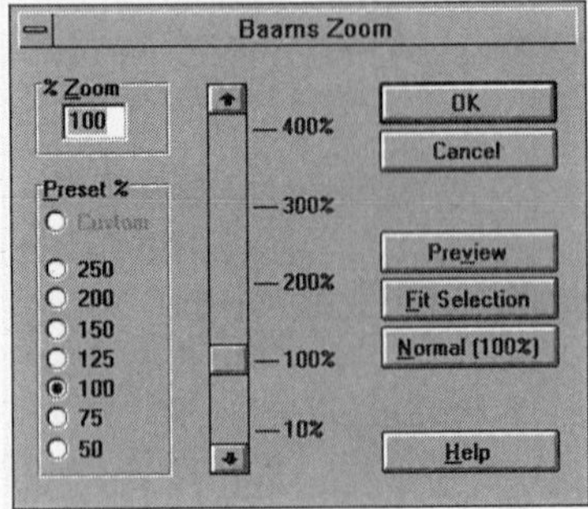

FIGURE D.30.
The Zoom dialog box.

Three Ways to change the Zoom:

1. Directly edit the % Zoom edit box. When the numbers are highlighted, type your desired settings. Notice the scroll bar and the Preset % radio buttons will change to match your settings.
2. Move the Scroll Bar. You can either drag the scroll bar to the desired setting with the mouse or use the tab key to change the focus to the scroll bar. Then you may use the up/down arrow keys and/or the page up/down keys to adjust the percentage of zoom. While the bar is moving, you can watch the % Zoom edit box to see exactly what percentage you are setting.
3. Select one of the Preset % radio buttons. This will also change the scroll bar and the % Zoom edit box to reflect your selection.

SUPER NOTE

The Preset % group includes a radio button labeled Custom. This button can never be directly chosen. It will be automatically selected whenever you edit the % Zoom box or move the scroll bar to a number that is not one of the available presets. In other words, its purpose is to indicate that your current % Zoom isn't one of the available Presets.

The Zoom Control Buttons

The Baarns Zoom has a set of control buttons on the right side of the dialog box that controls how your settings affect the active document. Here's a rundown of the options:

OK

Closes the dialog box and changes the active document's magnification to match the value in the % Zoom edit box.

Cancel

Closes the dialog and returns the active document to the magnification with which it started before you selected the Baarns Zoom.

Preview

Doesn't close the dialog but changes the active document in the background to the percentage found in the % Zoom edit box. You can Preview multiple times (you might consider changing the % before doing it again...) until you are satisfied with the % Zoom. Then choose either the OK or Cancel buttons to retain your current settings or revert to the original settings, respectively.

Fit Selection

Closes the dialog box and expands the currently selected cells to fill the screen (generally speaking). This concept works differently depending on your selection. It will rarely fill your screen. The aspect ratio is maintained and either the width or the height will be expanded to fill the screen or expanded until the maximum zoom of 400 percent is reached. In other words, a rectangle will still look like a rectangle after it is zoomed.

Normal

Return your document to its 100 percent setting.

> **SUPER TIP**
>
> If you hold down the Shift key while selecting either the Baarns Zoom icon or the Window Zoom... (when the Utilities menus are showing), the dialog box won't display, and your document will be reutrned to Normal (100 percent).

Help

Displays the help file for this dialog box.

Messages

What Do You Mean I Can't Do That?!

Most people can totally ignore this section. It's a reference guide to the messages that could be encountered and our comments about the possible causes and/or solutions available to change the issue. Some messages are self-explanatory; therefore, we haven't included any additional comment. The notes are also displayed by the Help button on the box that displays these messages.

I can't add a note when objects are protected.

The current document has the objects protected. Select Options UnProtect Document... and then I can create your note.

I can't add a note to a minimized document.

When a document is minimized, I can't figure out where to place the note. Please restore or maximize the document and then I can create your note.

I can't add a note to a Workbook Contents Page.

Notes (and other graphic objects) are not enabled on Workbook Contents pages. Please select a different document.

I can't add notes to charts (unless they are embedded...).

Charts that are in their own Chart Window do not enable notes (or other graphic objects) to be placed on them. If the chart were embedded in a document, then I could place a note on the worksheet. See the appropriate section of the *Microsoft Excel User's Guide, Book 1* to learn the differences between the two and how to create each type.

I can't add a note when the Info Window is active.

The Info window doesn't enable any notes (or graphic objects) to be placed on it. Please change to a Worksheet or Macro Sheet before using this command.

Your current Options Display settings have objects hidden....

Your current settings will enable me to create a note but it would be hidden. (I doubt you really want an invisible note.) If you select the OK button, I'll change your settings in Options Display and then create the note for you. Cancel if you want me to stop creating the note.

I can only perform that operation on open documents....

This operation requires an open document. Please use the File Open or File New command before using this command.

This is not a valid document for this command.

This command works on both Worksheets and Macro sheets. I can't perform this operation on any other documents. Please select a Worksheet or Macro sheet before using this command.

Express Math doesn't work on locked cells....

Please unprotect the document using the Options UnProtect Document command before using Baarns Express Math.

I can't create an icon unless you have a document open.

The real problem is I need to attach a document to the icon and there isn't a document open. Please use the File New or File Open command. I think you were just testing me to see how smart I am....

Sorry—there's been an error and I couldn't create the icon for you....

I'm not 100 percent sure why, but I suspect either memory or resources are very low. Another possibility is that your version of Program Manager doesn't enable items to be added or changed. If you are running on a network, please ask your network administrator if there are restrictions in your PROGMAN.INI file.

Sorry—your shell program (Windows Program Manager replacement) ....

I can only create Icons in Microsoft's Program Manager. Future versions of the Baarns Utilities may support additional shells. Please let us know about any shells you would like to see us directly support.

There's already an icon in that group with the same name....

Sometime in the past an icon with the exact same name was created. It is legal to have multiple items with the same name; this was just a warning in case you had forgotten the earlier one.

Sorry—this command doesn't work in Group Edit mode.

Because I can't do that to all the sheets in your current group (while in this mode), I can't complete this operation. I could do each sheet individually, so please try again when you only have single sheets.

Sorry—you can't rename built-in templates.

Built-in templates are the standard Worksheet, Chart, Macro sheet, and Workbook that ship with Excel. These cannot be renamed.

Sorry—you can't remove built-in templates.

They are not removable, but you can use the Create... button to create your own customized versions of these documents.

Are you sure you want to remove...?

I just wanted to be sure. Choose OK to remove the document.

Are you sure you want to delete...?

I just wanted to be sure. Choose OK and I'll remove the Reminder from the list.

Template type invalid or EXCEL5.INI is corrupted.

You should never see this error under normal conditions. About the only way to create this error is to hand edit the EXCEL5.INI file. Please use the Temp. Close button on the Options Baarns Utilities Options command and then reload the Baarns Utilities by selecting the same command (Options Baarns Utilities Options). This will solve the issue in 99 percent of the cases.

Template not found. Would you like to help me find it?

Either this template file is missing or the path has been changed when I wasn't looking. If you choose OK, we can find the file and I'll update my listing of files so we won't have to do this again. If you Cancel, I'll just leave the Description alone until you attempt to open the template again.

Selection too big. Continue without undo?

This can't be undone so I thought I'd just let you know BEFORE I've finished the operation. Choose OK to complete the operation or Cancel if you want me to wait.

Sorry—this command works with worksheets....

The current document isn't a Worksheet or Macro sheet and this operation doesn't work with other documents (like Charts or Workbook tables of contents...).

Sorry—... can't be used on a protected document.

Protected documents don't enable this operation. Please use the Options Unprotect Document... command and then try this operation again.

Sorry—this command only works when cells....

You have a graphic object selected and that confuses me. Please select a cell or range of cells before using this command.

Sorry—the document you opened isn't a valid ....

Valid files for templates are Worksheets, Charts, and Macro sheets. All other types are invalid.

This operation doesn't work on locked cells....

Use the Options Unprotect Document command and then try this operation again.

...worksheet is protected or in Group Edit mode.

Use the Options Unprotect Document command (to remove the protection) or wait until you have finished Group Editing before choosing this command again.

...you want to throw away your new template?

If you Cancel now, the Template you were in the process of creating will be thrown away. Choose OK to throw this document away.

Are you sure you want to delete [FileName] ?

I'm just checking before I delete this file for you. If you select OK this file will be deleted.

Sorry—there's been an error starting the Baarns Utilities Clock....

You need to reinstall the Baarns Utilities to correct this problem. Please run Setup from your original disks.

One of The Baarns Utilities support files is damaged or missing....

I can't find the support files I need and I can't continue to load without having major problems. Please rerun the Setup program found on your original disks.

Sorry—I can't zoom this document.

Either the current document isn't a Worksheet or a Macro sheet, or I'm currently not able to zoom the document.

... the Baarns Utilities to be temporarily removed from memory?

If you choose OK, I'll close the Baarns Utilities for this session. The Utilities menus will be removed (except one) but the toolbar will remain (assuming both were being displayed).

When you want to reopen the Utilities, choose the Options Baarns Utilities Options command or click on one of the Baarns Utilities icons. I'll be reloaded from disk at that time.

File NOT Saved! Either your filename isn't valid....

This message occurs when I can't save a document (and unfortunately, I can't tell you exactly why). Either the file name isn't valid, your disk is full, write protected (locked) or if it's a floppy, it's possible there's no disk in the drive or the door is open. It's also possible to receive this message if your disk drive has a hardware problem.

> **SUPER CAUTION**
>
> If you ran out of disk space after Excel started saving your file, any previous version also may have been deleted. This is because Excel deletes the previous version of a document before saving your current document.

You can use Alt+Tab to switch to File Manager to check your disk space. Resave your document after the issues have been resolved.

Do you want to replace [Description]?

If you choose OK, your current file with the same description will be replaced with your new file. If you're not sure, select Cancel and use the Rename... button to view details of the template file that uses the same description.

Sorry—the single user version of the Baarns....

The single-user version of the Baarns Utilities will not work correctly if it's opened as read-only. Please open the file as read-write. If you need a read-only version for network use, please contact the Baarns Consulting Group, Inc. for multi-user packs.

Your new Standard Font won't take effect....

To change the Standard font for all future documents, the Baarns Utilities writes an entry in your EXCEL5.INI file. Excel only reads this file when it starts. Once Excel has closed one time, it will pay attention to the new font for all future sessions.

Glossary of Terms

EXCEL5.INI

A special file stored in your Windows directory that Excel uses to store information from session to session. This file is created by the Excel Setup program. The Baarns Utilities uses this file (along with many other Excel add-ins) to store preferences and settings when Excel is closed. For more information on the EXCEL5.INI file read the file titled EXCELINI.TXT found in your Excel directory.

File filter

A set of characters that enables you to see a subset of the available files in a directory. Excel's default filter is "*.XL*." Using this filter, you only see files that have an extension that starts with "x." The asterisks are called wildcards, and they are placeholders for any character or group of characters. By changing the filter to "*.B*," you would see all files in a directory that have a "b" as the first letter of their extension.

Focus

In Windows, one application always has the focus. That application will accept keyboard or mouse input. In other words, focus is given to the active application. When a dialog box is displayed, only one item (also known as a control) has the focus. For example, an edit field or a list box could have the focus, but never would both have focus at once. You can watch the focus change by displaying the Baarns Zoom (or any other dialog box) and pressing the tab key. This will move the focus from one control to the next. The control that has the focus accepts keyboard input if it's appropriate. To change focus with the mouse, you simply click on the item you want to have focus.

Memory: 2.5 Megs (Minimum)

While Excel and Windows can perform with low memory, Excel is significantly faster when you reach the 3-4 megabyte mark. In memory, as in some other things, more is much better than less.

Multiple Selection

Excel also refers to this term as "nonadjacent selection." This includes cells or ranges that are not touching each other but are all highlighted (selected). With the mouse these Multiple Selections are made by holding down the Ctrl key and selecting more than one range with the mouse. See the *Microsoft Excel User's Guide, Book 1* for examples of multiple selections and explanation the keyboard method for creating one.

Print Area

A special name that Excel can assign to a range that will be printed when you select Print from the File menu. To set a Print Area, first select the range you want to print. Then select the Options Set Print Area command. If you look in the Formula Define Name command at the name called "Print_Area" you'll find it defined as the range you had selected. If you don't explicitly set a Print Area, Excel defaults to printing complete pages. Additional information concerning Printing and Print Areas is found in the *Microsoft Excel User's Guide, Book 1* (and/or Excel's on-line help).

Acknowledgments

The Baarns Consulting Group, Inc. is comprised of some highly intelligent individuals (not including the founder, who is at least smart enough to work with others who are brilliant), and we are also famous for "borrowing" ideas from some of the best Excel minds in the business. While it's impossible to thank directly all the individuals who made this product possible, here's the short list of major contributors:

Primary Design, Development, and Implementation:

Donald M. Baarns
Murray A. Ruggiero

Utility Ideas, Contributions, and Developer Prodding:

Lisa A. Baarns
Leonard Mehrabian
Dan Williams
Frank Reidelberger
Will Tomkins
Dale Arndt
Michael Sessions
Jeff McBride
Arnold Dubin
David Darrow (icons/artwork)
Hundreds of CompuServe users in the MSEXCEL forum

Quality Control (Exterminators):

The testing group for the Baarns Utilities was rather large, and we wish to thank all of you who spent your time helping us find and squash those "nasty bugs" and documention errors that seem to be a part of all software development. The following individuals went above and beyond the call of duty. They helped us find those subtle bugs hiding in the very dark corners.

D. Anthony Hardin
Mike Hoefgen
Carolyn Ward (editor to the stars)
Pete Thompson

Index

Symbols

A

Index

Index

D

H

I

J

K

N

Q

R

S

T

W

X-Y-Z

THE BAARNS UTILITIES™

Productivity Enhancements for Microsoft© Excel

Productivity is everything in today's business environment. The Baarns Utilities make your everyday Microsoft Excel activities easier and give you power user status without the power user learning curve. Included with this book is version 1 of The Baarns Utilities. Version 1 of the Utilities was written for Excel 4.0. To help you be more productive and organized, we have added even more tools to version 5 of The Baarns Utilities, which take advantage of the features in the new Excel 5.0. Upgrade to version 5 for just $19.95*.

Upgrade for just $19.95!

Here's what the experts say...

I found Baarns Utilities to be rock solid, providing fine error handling. The 13 tools are so tightly integrated into Excel that you might think you were actually using new features in Excel.

INFO WORLD

Excel is as loaded with features as Windows spreadsheets get, but The Baarns Utilities takes Excel to even greater heights. It's a must-have collection of Excel tools...this collection of utilities is a number cruncher's dream.

PC Computing

If you spend a lot of time working in Excel, you'll appreciate the nifty set of shortcut tools and gizmos provided by The Baarns Utilities.

PC WORLD

Version 5 Features include:

Baarns File Express allows you to create a file group and then add existing files to that group. These files can be found all over your hard drive or multiple drives, including network drives.

Baarns Path Manager will let you assign long names to custom "paths" for finding or saving files. Now FILE OPEN and FILE · SAVE can consistently and easily be directed to your desired destination.

Baarns Save Now works in conjunction with Baarns AutoSave, allowing you to have a tool to activate the AutoSave at any time you choose. Also, it will access your backup setting of the AutoSave even if AutoSave itself is turned off.

Baarns Case Master quickly and easily changes the text case on selected cells to UPPER, lower or Proper text in one easy step.

Baarns Paste Date & Time inserts the date and/or time into your Microsoft Excel document.

Baarns Text-O-Matic will help you add or delete text to the front or back of selected cells.

Baarns Startup will start Microsoft Excel the way you want to see it. Control how your first document is displayed and its size when opened.

Baarns Open allows you to open your files based on your starting document size preferences in Baarns Startup.

Baarns Phone Dialer will dial your phone for you when connected to your computer if you have a modem.

Hundreds of upgrades to the original thirteen utilities along with completely new on-line help.

Upgrade to version 5 for just $19.95 to experience the ultimate worksheet workout!

About **Don Baarns** and **Baarns Consulting Group, Inc.**

Don Baarns has been a guest speaker at the MS Excel Developers Conference, the Windows & OS/2 Conference, the Microsoft Corporate Developer Tools Conference & Exposition, and many other industry events.

Mr. Baarns has taught the three-hour Advanced Macros training session at the Microsoft Developers' Tools Conference and has lectured on several Advanced Microsoft Excel subjects at the Microsoft Tech-Ed conferences. In addition, he teaches classes on advanced techniques for using Excel as a front-end to SQL Server and serves on a number of panels addressing advanced development issues.

Don Baarns has contributed to the advanced macro content in Ron Person's book, *Excel Tips, Tricks and Traps* (Que Corp., 1989), and has been quoted in *PC Magazine*, *PC Week*, *INFO World*, *Computer Network Reseller,* and featured on the television series "Computer Chronicles."

The Baarns Consulting Group develops worldwide and has extensive experience in LAN development projects using Microsoft Excel, Microsoft Word for Windows and Microsoft Visual Basic as front ends to SQL Server and other DBMs.

Book ISBN 0-672-30385-X

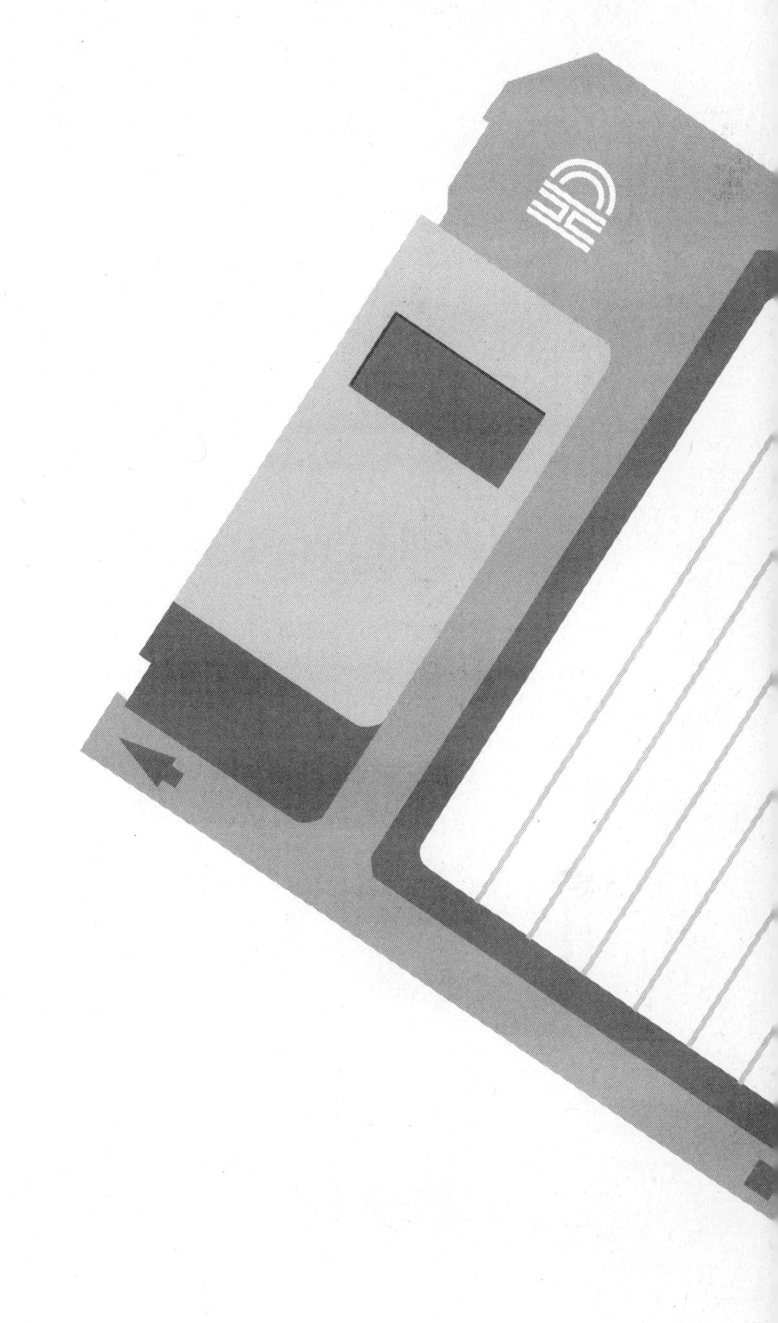

What's on the Super Disk

The disk contains the Baarns Utilities, which, according to *PC Computing,* is "...a must-have collection of Excel tools." These popular utilities enable you to effortlessly become an Excel power user. The disk also contains all project templates and support files used in this book.

Installing the Super Disk

The software included with this book is stored in a compressed form. You can't use the software without first installing it to your hard drive. To install all the files and utilities, you'll need at least 1.5M of free space on your hard drive.

1. From the Windows File Manager or Program Manager, select the **F**ile | **R**un command.
2. Type `<drive>\PROJECTS\INSTALL` and press Enter. `<drive>` is the letter of the drive that contains the installation disk. For example, if the disk is in drive B:, type `B:PROJECTS\INSTALL\` and press Enter.

Follow the installation program's on-screen instructions. The project templates will be installed in a directory named \XL5SB.

When the installation is complete, a text file will be displayed. It contains information on the files and programs that were installed.

SUPER NOTE

To install the Baarns Utilities, you need to run a separate installation program. See Appendix D, "The Baarns Utilities Documentation," for more information.